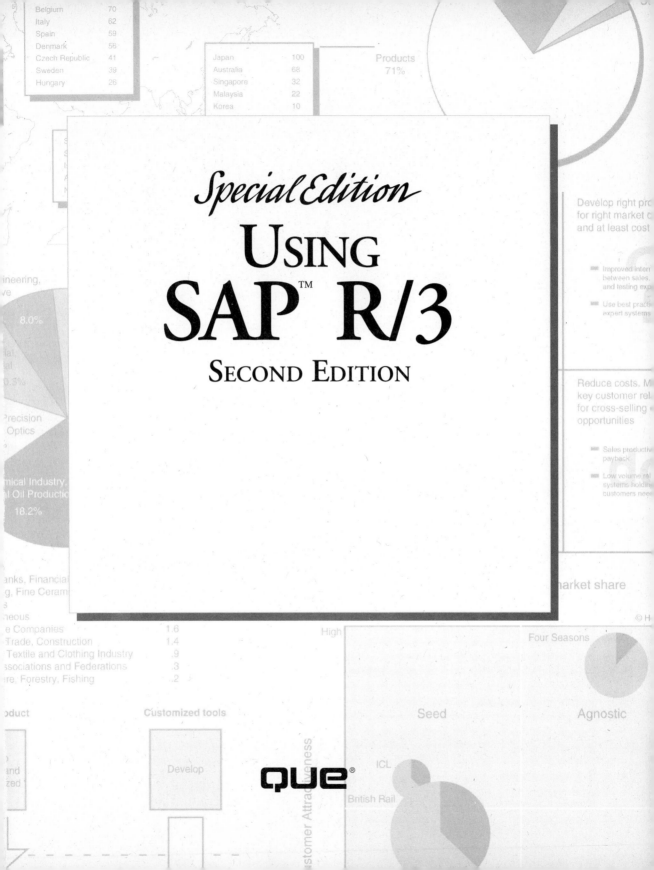

Special Edition

USING
SAP™ R/3

SECOND EDITION

que®

Special Edition

USING
SAP™ R/3

SECOND EDITION

Written by

ASAP World Consultancy
and
Jonathan Blain

with

Mark Denning	*Jonathan Lingard*
Bernard Dodd	*Eric Matthews*
Gray Elkington	*Max Nyiri*
Wendy Hewson	*Jonathan R. Tate*
Kate Hill	*Philippa Worth*

Contributions by
Christian Dannemann, Ian Henderson, Steve Walsh

Special Edition Using SAP R/3, 2E

Library of Congress Catalog No.: 97-68103

ISBN: 0-7897-1351-9

99 98 97   6 5 4 3 2 1

Interpretation of the printing code: the rightmost double-digit number is the year of the book's printing; the rightmost single-digit number, the number of the book's printing. For example, a printing code of 97-1 shows that the first printing of the book occurred in 1997.

Screen reproductions in this book were created by using Collage Plus from Inner Media, Inc., Hollis, NH.

Composed in *Stone Serif* and *MCPdigital* by Que Corporation.

Contents at a Glance

Contents

4 Architecture 65

6 Tool-Supported Optimization with the R/3 Analyzer   115

7 R/3 Customizing   143

III Complex System Management   149

8 Continuous Business Development   151

9 Worldwide Business Computing Systems   163

10 The Open Information Warehouse and Enterprise Data Models   173

13 Understanding the CO-Controlling Module   273

14 Understanding the Enterprise Controlling Module 323

15 Understanding the TR-Treasury Management Module 337

16 Understanding the PS-Project System Module   343

V Manufacturing Applications   355

17 Understanding the PP-Production Planning and Control Module   357

VI Applications in Support   437

20 Understanding the SD-Sales and Distribution Module   439

21 Understanding the Possibilities of Electronic Commerce with R/3 — 471

23 Understanding the MM-Materials Management Module

VII Specialized Configurations   595

24 Understanding the Vertical Market Initiative   597

30 R/3 Business Workflow Management   667

IX Implementation Issues   683

31 Overview of SAP Implementations   685

36 The Human Issues of SAP Implementation   831

X SAP Employment Market   855

37 Overview of the SAP Employment Market   857

38 Globalization of the SAP Employment Market   863

43 Managing the Change in Organization and Job Functions 951

Appendixes 967

A SAP Offices Around the World 969

B SAP Business Partners 977

C Sample SAP-Related Job Descriptions 1021

D Example Request for Quotation of SAP Services 1053

Credits

President
Roland Elgey

Senior Vice President/Publishing
Don Fowley

Publisher
Stacy Hiquet

Senior Title Manager
Bryan Gambrel

General Manager
Joe Muldoon

Director of Editorial Services
Carla Hall

Managing Editor
Caroline D. Roop

Director of Acquisitions
Cheryl Willoughby

Acquisitions Editor
Tracy Dunkelberger

Senior Editor
Mike La Bonne

Editor
Aaron Gordon

Editorial Resources Coordinator
Maureen McDaniel

Product Marketing Manager
Kourtnaye Sturgeon

Assistant Product Marketing Manager
Gretchen Schlesinger

Technical Editors
Brian Bokanyi
Nam Huynh, senior consultants with
CAP Gemini

Software Specialist
Brandon K. Penticuff

Software Coordinator
Andrea Duvall

Acquisitions Coordinator
Carmen Krikorian

Software Relations Coordinator
Susan D. Gallagher

Editorial Assistants
Travis Bartlett
Jennifer L. Chisolm

Book Designer
Ruth Harvey

Cover Designer
Dan Armstrong

Production Team
Maribeth Echard
Trey Frank
Christy M. Lemasters
Sossity Smith
Paul Wilson
Donna Wright

Indexer
Tim Tate

I dedicate this book to my dear wife, Jennifer, and our beautiful daughter, Kezia, who was born Oct. 3rd, 1996, and to my parents, David & Neva Blain, who have been so supportive.

Jonathan Blain

About the Authors

ASAP World Consultancy is an international SAP consulting company. It is in the business of selling high-quality products and services relating to SAP and other enterprise applications, computing systems, and implementations. ASAP World Consultancy is part of the ASAP group of companies whose activities include the following:

- SAP Documentation Consultancy
- SAP Recruitment
- SAP Training
- SAP Access and Security Consultancy
- SAP Internal & External Communications Consultancy
- SAP System Testing Consultancy & Resourcing
- SAP Human Issues Consultancy
- SAP Resource Planning Consultancy
- Business Process Re-engineering and Change Management Consultancy
- Hardware and Installation Consultancy
- SAP Implementation Consultancy
- Introductory SAP Courses for corporate clients and individuals: USA, UK, Singapore & Other Countries—inquire for course dates
- SAP Skills Transfer to Your Employees
- Development of SAP Complementary Solutions
- SAP Market Research
- SAP Acquisitions, Mergers, and Joint Ventures
- SAP Procurement Consultancy

ASAP World Consultancy's headquarters are located in Henley on Thames in the United Kingdom but operate all over the world.

The company prides itself on the quality of its people. It uses a combination of its own employees and associates, who bring a wealth of experience and skills to meet the needs of its customers.

ASAP has a commitment to quality and is focused on meeting the business objectives of its clients through a number of highly specialized divisions and companies.

ASAP World Consultancy can be contacted at the following address:

ASAP World Consultancy
ASAP House
P.O. Box 4463
Henley on Thames
Oxfordshire
RG9 6YN
UK
Tel: +44 (0)1491 414411
Fax: +44 (0)1491 414412
e-mail: **enquiry@asap-consultancy.co.uk**
Author Comments: **info@asap-consultancy.co.uk**
Web site: **http://www.asap-consultancy.co.uk/index.htm**
ASAP - 24 Hour - Virtual Office - New York, USA
Voice Mail: (212) 253-4180; Fax: (212) 253-4180

See the advertisements at the back of this book for more details.

Jonathan Blain is the founder of the ASAP group of companies. He has been working with SAP products since 1991. He has a strong business background, having spent 10 years in the oil industry working in a variety of different roles in the downstream sector for the Mobil Corporation. In his last roles with Mobil, he worked as an analyst on a large international SAP project and later as a senior implementation analyst on Mobil's UK implementation. He has specialist knowledge of large-scale SAP implementations, project management, human issues, planning, communications, security, training, documentation, and SAP recruitment. He has benefited from professional business training with the Henley Management College and other institutions.

As a management consultant, he has specialized in matching corporate business strategies to IT strategies. He has a special interest in business engineering and the effective management of change when implementing large-scale IT systems.

Coming from a business rather than systems background, he is focused on providing business solutions. He believes that the implementation of SAP can improve the way that companies do business and that, provided common sense and logical thinking are applied, SAP implementations need not be daunting.

Jonathan is a keen yachtsman and is the vice chairman of the Yacht Owners Association in the UK. He has been instrumental in the development of the "Hy Tech Sprint" yacht, a revolutionary 43-foot light displacement, water-ballasted ocean cruiser.

Mark Denning After graduating from Liverpool University in mathematics with management, Mark worked in line management before becoming a management consultant. During his time as a consultant he has focused on the IT sector, including projects for clients such as ICL and Apple. He has also developed a specialty in analytical tools, including the development of an outlet analysis tool for retail chains and an in-depth study into the potential market for analytical marketing applications. This has left him with an in-depth strategic understanding of IT systems and their impact on businesses as a whole.

Bernard Dodd After graduating in psychology at Aberdeen University, Bernard built and directed an industrial training research unit over a period of nine years at the Department of Psychology, University of Sheffield. Two years with an international business consultancy led to an open competition direct entry to the specialist Civil Service where he served the Royal Navy for 17 years to become the senior psychological advisor to the Second Sea Lord.

Since 1990, he has specialized in technical interviewing of experts and the writing of system documentation and user handbooks for the computer-intensive industries.

Gray Elkington is managing director of Hambleden Consulting, a firm that helps its clients to develop the customer-focused culture they need to become market leaders. From their base near Henley on Thames in England, Gray and his colleagues work in multidisciplinary teams on key performance issues, always placing the client's company's internal relationships firmly at the top of the development agenda.

Having worked for some years on the people issues involved with the re-engineering of both business and management processes, Elkington has been able to contribute valuable guidance to those tasked with implementing SAP, especially to those concerned with how the changes may affect employees and customers.

Wendy Hewson is a chartered accountant. Before becoming a teacher fellow at Cranfield School of Management, she was a management consultant with Arthur Andersen and vice president with Merrill Lynch. Wendy is a visiting lecturer at City University Business School and is an expert in business planning and lifetime values in the financial services sector.

Wendy is a partner in the Hewson Consulting Group, which was established in 1989, and has specialized in application of information technology to sales and marketing operations. The group is well-known for its research reports and involvement in large systems implementations. Hewson Consulting Group also manages Mercatus—the Association for the Use of Information Technology in Sales and Marketing.

Kate Hill is a director of McHugh Hill Associates, an SAP consultancy company specializing in training and project management. She has spent the last six years working in the SAP training arena. Her work has covered R/2 and R/3 both as a training team manager and "hands-on" trainer. Kate has designed and run courses across a broad spectrum of SAP modules—sales and distribution, materials management, finance and controlling—for organizations such as Arjo Wiggins Fine Papers, Mobil, Tate and Lyle, IBM, and Siemens Nixdorf. Kate co-chaired the SAP UK User Groups' Training Special Interest Group in 1994-1995.

Jonathan Lingard is a freelance SAP consultant and manager. He has spent four years working on SAP implementation projects in Europe and the USA. His clients have been Blue Chip multinational companies using SAP as part of business restructuring projects. His responsibilities have included the coordination, evaluation, and execution of SAP ABAP customization requests, the management of SAP authorization profiles, and the delivery of business process-oriented training. He has also been responsible for business and system process design structures. He received a B.A. in economics and philosophy from the University of Oxford in England in 1990.

Eric Matthews has been involved in the IT industry since 1970, originally with UNIVAC mainframe computer systems, in the UK and Southeast Asia, performing sales, marketing, and branch management roles, before becoming a country general manager. He has since operated as an independent consultant in the IT industry, advising on and performing international recruitment, systems implementations, management, marketing, acquisition, and venture capital-raising projects. He has of recent years been heavily involved in managing market research and has written many published reports as well as managing single-client research. Eric's work has taken him to five continents from his home base in the UK's Thames Valley.

Max Nyiri, Ph.D. psychology, Ph.D. computer science (Germany) is an IT Business Strategist, who has developed extensive experience in the determination and evaluation of Enterprise Application—Management Information Requirements, and the recommendation and implementation of IT solutions for business. He uses project management and strategy implementation experience to ensure strategic alignment of information technology with business requirements. Max was a senior executive consultant to various multinational companies. He worked for the IT Strategy division of Coopers & Lybrand Consulting. His success was marked by being the youngest IT senior executive worldwide for Volkswagen. Currently, he is consulting for the Business Information Technology division of Arthur Andersen Business Consulting as a senior executive.

Jonathan R. Tate is a senior manager at Price Waterhouse, London, responsible for the firm's SAP Control and Security Practice. Before this, he worked for five years in Mobil Corporation as the manager of the SAP Controls Group, providing controls advice to SAP installations worldwide.

In 1995, Jonathan established SAP Audit and Controls User Group, of which he is still chairman, and he is an executive member of the SAP (UK) User Group. He has spoken at numerous conferences on the subject of SAP Controls and contributed regularly to SAP publications.

He graduated from London University with a degree in economics, is an Associate of the Chartered Institute of Management Accountants, and has previously worked for Coopers & Lybrand and for Shell, performing a range of accounting, systems, and consultancy roles.

Philippa Worth A graduate of Sussex University and fluent in French, Philippa has lived and worked in France and Denmark. Her career has encompassed most of the principal elements of the marketing mix, and she has experience in corporate management.

Philippa is a consultant in the UK. Her practice provides marketing and corporate communications services to small-to-medium-sized enterprises, and contributes to regional economic development initiatives in the UK and France. Her client base is drawn from both public and private sectors.

Philippa's skills include corporate publications and law, marketing support material, employee communications, and business development, and inward investment.

Contributions by:

Christian Dannemann is a specialist in client/server technology.

Ian Henderson has been working with enterprise applications for 20 years and has worked in senior roles on many prestigious SAP implementations.

Steve Walsh is a specialist in C and C++.

Acknowledgments

In writing this book we have benefited from the help and support of hundreds of people. There would not be space here to acknowledge everyone. They have each given their time and effort freely to make this book thorough, accurate, and useful to the readers. Equally, there are many companies who have given us much of their valuable time and shared their thoughts and opinions.

Our heartfelt thanks go to everyone who has helped. The writing of this book has been a team effort, and just praise should go to each and every team member.

We'd Like to Hear from You!

As part of our continuing effort to produce books of the highest possible quality, Que would like to hear your comments. To stay competitive, we *really* want you to let us know what you like or dislike most about this book or other Que products.

Please send your comments, ideas, and suggestions for improvement to:

The Expert User Team

E-mail: **euteam@que.mcp.com**

CompuServe: **105527,745**

Fax: (317) 581-4663

Our mailing address is:

Expert User Team
Que Corporation
201 West 103rd Street
Indianapolis, IN 46290-1097

You can also visit our Team's home page on the World Wide Web at:

http://www.mcp.com/que/developer_expert

Thank you in advance. Your comments will help us to continue publishing the best books available in today's market.

Thank you,

The Expert User Team

Introduction

This book is about the products of one manufacturer: SAP AG, or SAP Aktiengesellschaft. The translation of SAP AG is Systems, Applications, Products in Data Processing.

This chapter introduces the book by setting out its scope and its intended readership.

- **How SAP products are identified**

  SAP products require a "Basis" system which is R/2 or R/3, and the application modules are given a letter code and title, such as SD-Sales and Distribution.

- **How this book is arranged in parts**

  There are parts which cover the technical aspects of R/3 and its application modules followed by parts, which set out what is required to implement a SAP installation.

- **How chapters are arranged**

  Most parts contain several chapters. Each chapter begins with a roadmap to its contents (similar to this one) and ends with suggestions for chapters to read next.

- **The intended readership of this book**

  The book is written for managers close to installing a business data processing system and the specialists who will have to understand the relevant SAP products.

- **What can SAP do for my company?**

  SAP can rapidly reengineer your business processes so that you can operate at a higher level of performance.

■ **How can I make use of the SAP expertise?**

The best parts are built into the system and the implementation tools that come with it. There are SAP consultant partners available.

■ **What is the most sensible manner in which to approach this complex technical subject?**

Assume there is a good reason for everything and always read the help texts and brochures.

■ **Is there something special about SAP software that I should know?**

It is very well designed and supported. Whatever you want to do with it has probably been done before, and it has been documented in this book.

System Identification Codes

There are two SAP system identification codes; system identification; designated R/2 and R/3. R/2 was developed as a mainframe system; R/3 intended for the multi-level client/ server environment. A SAP installation may include both R/2 and R/3 systems configured, for example, as central host and satellites.

Each R/2 and R/3 system comprises a Basis module to which is added application modules. A module may comprise several components, and a component may include several functions. Although a module may be installed, it is not necessary for all of its components to be configured to be active. Similarly, a component need not have all its functions available to the user.

This book concentrates on the R/3 system and its applications. The function list used for reference is R/3 Release 3.0 Version 6.1. This can be abbreviated as R/3 Rel.3.0 (V6.1). Developments and enhancements to R/3 Release 3.0, which are discussed in this volume, are available as R/3 Release 3.1, which is fully compatible with Release 3.0. Where mention is made of the R/2 system, the reference is to R/2 Release 5.0.

The Scope of This Book

The intention of the authors is to bridge the gap between hearsay and expertise. Many people are aware of the dominant market position of the SAP enterprise, and they have usually understood that a considerable expertise has been invested in the products and the way they are implemented. They have not been mislead. The SAP systems are indeed complex and sophisticated. And this second edition of the book records additions to the complexity of the SAP range of products in terms of the business processes that can be carried by these systems. Much of the sophistication of the additions is directed at making the business operations easier to implement and as resistant to human errors as possible. The most important developments may turn out to be the new programs to facilitate intranet and Internet communications. These programs enable enterprise-wide business processes and make them open for controlled use via the internet to almost any terminal device capable of responding to Java applets.

However, the process of implementing a SAP R/3 system is conducted by many people who are not computer experts in each of the thousands of specialties—nor need they be. The systems come complete with the most advanced computer-assisted tools for guiding you through the implementation process from first analysis through customizing to performance evaluation of the working installation.

Sections in This Book

This book is partly technical, partly persuasive. The technical parts are intended to convince those who are interested in business process development and reengineering that the SAP standard software library is comprehensive in its use of new technologies and in its coverage of modern business activities in all sectors of industry and commerce, in private companies, and public services.

The Parts in this book are as follows:

- ■ "An Introduction to SAP," which introduces the company and gives an indication of how the user will react with the modules

- ■ "Technical Background," which explains how the R/3 modules achieve their results

- ■ "Complex System Management," which shows how the multi-level client/server R/3 system can serve a global company

- ■ "Steering the Corporation," which describes the financial and planning modules

- ■ "Manufacturing Applications," which details the modules designed for manufacturing and plant maintenance

- ■ "Applications in Support," which describes the modules for sales and distribution, human resources, and materials management, all of which can be accessed from the Internet

- ■ "Specialized Configurations," which introduces some of the enhanced R/3 installations designed for specific industries

- ■ "Maintaining and Enhancing the Implementation," which considers troubleshooting skills, online service and the improvement of business efficiency through workflow management, and the development of company-specific programs

- ■ "Implemention Issues," which surveys the methods of implementation and the management of the changes that new systems require

- ■ "SAP Employment Market," which reviews the methods and the prospects of obtaining employment as a consultant in the context of SAP and its global organization

- ■ "Appendixes," which provide reference information, a glossary, and information on the migration of systems from R/2 to R/3

> **Note**
>
> This is not a user handbook. It is not a glossy demonstration of how easy the system is to use. There is very little of the specific information that will be readily provided by the vendors and the implementers.
>
> Although the authors are arguably the least reliable judges of its quality, this volume does attempt to distill the experience, both good and bad, gathered by its authors in their collective years of toil at the task of applying methods to what people do in order to make things better.
>
> Some of this wisdom is quite definitely peculiar to the business computing realm. Some, equally peculiar, comes from older technologies that enjoyed the titles of "training," "mechanization," and even "automation." One of our excuses for including this know-how is based on the fact that the progress of human evolution has virtually stopped, partly as a result of the very rapid evolution of machinery, especially of the information-manipulating kind. Our observations of the human components yield a more copious flow of error data than our inspections of the error logs of the hardware and software assemblies. Of course an ideal system would prevent human error!

What Will Be Gained from This Book

This book is not intended to be skimmed quickly. Apply a focused search to this book and you will find a pointer to what you are looking for, if not the complete information.

Our most satisfied readers will find that they have acquired the concepts and the language with which to ask questions, of the SAP specialists.

A thoughtful reader may expect to gain a thorough understanding of the changes that will need to take place in each department to implement its module. The book provides the explanations of why the changes have to take place and the benefits to be gained by having them done well.

It would not be an unreasonable outcome if a serious reader saved the cost of the volume by deciding that the SAP system was not what his particular company should have at the top of its shopping list.

If one of our diligent and satisfied readers was in the happy position of being a project sponsor, we should like to think that he or she had developed an eye for this subject: What to look at and what to look for; when to exercise firm control, and on what issues.

Intended Readers

The authors have three groups of readers in mind:

- Those close to a SAP system
- Those who are thinking about a SAP system
- Those who would like to inform themselves on what is entailed in running a modern, comprehensive business data processing system

There are two aspects to the installation of any system which deserve equal attention: The technical details of the system and the effects it is likely to have on the staff and their conduct of your business. This book reflects these two concerns by having both technical and implementation sections.

Consultants and Advisory Staff

The intended readers close to a SAP system are consultants, programmers, launchers and managers, and emergency service providers in the data and personnel categories. They are likely to be:

- People involved in a SAP implementation
- People interested in implementing a SAP system
- People interested in working with SAP

One of the tasks that could fall upon anyone close to a SAP system is to explain why the programs are arranged as they are and why the users have to interact with a standard interface. Such explanations will be required at all levels: To the chief executive officer and to the input clerk. The content for such explanations is available in this book.

Similarly, the technical specialists in a company will want to know why their current methods are not going to be replicated exactly in the new SAP system.

Managers at all levels will find that this book is able to go into considerable detail about the data processing functions provided by the SAP programs so that they can recognize aspects of their own work that could be facilitated by having the system at their command. On the other hand, they will see that a complex system does require a disciplined approach to, for instance, the maintenance of uniform data records in standard formats.

Consultants will see that the designers of the SAP systems have made provisions for them to build for their client a system that is unique, yet assembled from standard business programs that have been thoroughly tested and refined. This book will prepare the consultant to ask the client the right questions and to make proper allowance for the work involved in customizing a system to fit the specific circumstances and requirements of the client.

Those who would like to become a SAP consultant will see that there is an extensive body of technical expertise built into the SAP programs because they have been developed in partnerships with specific industries. The would-be consultant will also recognize that the computer technology of the SAP systems is in continuous development so as to maintain a position in the forefront. Experienced consultants will have come to grips with the necessity of maintaining a continuous schedule of self-education so as to be in position for the next technical and perhaps geo-political development.

Prospective SAP Users

If you are thinking about installing a SAP system, or an extension to an existing SAP system, then this book will be of interest because it maps out the various possibilities. You will see what is available and what it can achieve; and you will see what will have to be done if these kinds of results are to be realized in your own situation. You will not find the costs of SAP programs in this volume, but you will get a good idea of the magnitude of the work and expense entailed if you should go ahead with an installation.

As a person seriously thinking about a SAP installation, you may well find that this book will draw your attention to the possibilities of achieving results that were not at the top of your list of priorities but which nevertheless would be well worthwhile in themselves and as investments in expertise for the future.

If you are a potential decision-maker in the matter of choosing a new computer installation, you should be careful about setting out the standards and parameters on which your decision will be made. You will not want to put your entire business in the hands of a system that is unreliable and inflexible. Yet you will not want to specify a system that is grossly over-elaborate for the job you want it to do. This book will tell you what the SAP R/3 system and its applications can do. It may become the standard against which you judge competitors' proposals.

General Readers

You may consider yourself to be a general reader of this book if you are neither a consultant nor a manager about to purchase a computer system.

Perhaps you are familiar with computing but not with industry and business. You will find that this book will give you the key concepts used by the various departments of business, whether or not a computer is involved. The net result could be that you develop a way of thinking about computing in the context of business applications. This book will point you toward the business concepts that should be given the highest priority.

On the other hand, you may be a general reader who is familiar with one or more sectors of industry and yet not fully conversant with the way business computing is developing. In this book, you will recognize many business ideas. What may intrigue you is the way they are supported by standard business functions and a system of master data records, for example. It is often the case that the best way of processing and storing business data is quite different from the way these operations are carried out in a people-and-paper system where the main retrieval mechanism is in the mind of the person who put the data into storage.

Whether you are a general reader who has neither business experience nor computer experience, this book will give you a comprehensive road map of the territory.

Intended Outcomes of Publishing

There will be a significant increase in the number of successful SAP implementations. In particular, this book is intended to increase the productivity and the reputation of the following groups of people:

- the implementation team for delivering an effective system on time, within budget, and with good omens for successful operations

- the project research team for preparing the decisions

■ the sponsor for making the decision

■ SAP AG for making available efficient tools to do the job

The first edition is being used by those involved with SAP R/3 as a means of filling in gaps in their awareness of the various applications and modules available. It enables them to seek out more detailed information when they need it by looking under the appropriate module titles. The other use of the first edition has been on training courses for those who are preparing for a career as an SAP implementation specialist.

The Business Territory

A good businessperson usually possesses a very good knowledge of the geographical and technical territory in which the business operates. Much is known about who buys what and how these purchases can be obtained or manufactured at a good price. The needs of individual customers are appreciated. The operating problems of the warehouses and manufacturing plants are taken into account when making plans. All this is the business territory.

The territory of a SAP consultant and a manager who might wish to employ one is business process reengineering: Installing new hardware and software, or going over from manual to mechanized business processing in some or all of the work of the company.

SAP software can be set up to assist in any business process in any sector of commerce and industry. Therefore, there are two complex decisions to be made:

What aspects of the business shall be reengineered?

Will the SAP software be the best choice?

Because SAP can handle any type of business structure, decisions have to be made as to how the company should be analyzed so as to yield the best structure for designing the application software that will drive the SAP standard software modules. For example, a simple manufacturing business can be seen as two components: One looks after the product, the other looks after the money. Yet this model has a serious flaw in it. Who looks after the customers?

Mechanization of business processes has been controlled, to a large extent, by the equipment available: its cost and its capability. As capabilities have increased, so the cost of programming the equipment has become an ever-larger proportion of the total cost of reengineering. Complexity can be costly.

The decision-maker has to set out the pros and cons of providing office automation and communications to assist in each element of the business. To reengineer everything might be costly yet fruitful, although the time to achieve this may entail an unacceptable risk that the market will have changed too much in the interim. What is needed is a software tool that will allow the chosen design to be up and running quickly, yet which will be easy to tune to new circumstances as they arise.

Making a complex decision is not easy, and there are several errors to which some decision-makers may be prone.

Some Procedures for Using This Book

You could begin at the end, or, if you must, at the beginning. Although this is perhaps what you do when you first lay your hands on a book, this volume has provided some additional suggestions for sampling its contents. Each chapter begins with a brief intro- duction followed by a road map, or list section, which will give you some idea of the type of information you may expect to find in the chapter. At the end of each chapter, the authors have suggested some other chapters that you might find interesting, either because they are related to what you have been reading about, or because they provide a contrast.

If you are a consultant, you will know a large number of technical terms which you ex- pect to appear in a book of this type. The list of contents will perhaps be a good place to start your reading.

Some readers prefer to see some illustrations before they begin studying the text. Many readers will flip through for some pictures before doing anything else. However, this book is not a picture book, and there is no information in the illustrations which is not also in the text.

A sensible approach to intensive study is to first make up your mind about what you want to find and then keep on looking until you find it. If you have a particular type of business in mind, your own or one you would like to be a part of, then you may find it interesting to cull the volume for information that is directly relevant to your business and deliberately skip anything that does not seem relevant at this stage.

The world of computing is paved with clusters of capital letters that mean something to those who use them as technical terms. If you know what the letters of the acronym stand for, then you may be able to work out what the whole term refers to. A good way of sampling this book is to think of an acronym and see if this book mentions it.

If you already know how computers and other things go wrong, then you will perhaps want to see if SAP and the authors know this as well.

Delegation is a possibility. You could place a sticky note in each part that seems difficult and ask a junior colleague to give you a report by the end of the work week.

Errors in Decision-Making

You may be under pressure to make a choice between making a high-quality decision or a fast one. More information may give extra accuracy and confidence. But the response will be delayed if more input is required. There is a right moment for most decisions. It may be when costs are low; or it may be a matter of cornering the market by spending now to profit later. The right moment may be when you know you can lay your hands on the expertise to get it right.

Reluctance is resistance to change. Timidity may be passed off as prudence but it may also allow the best moment for a decision to pass by. The research team should not be allowed to go on looking indefinitely. Lack of data is not necessarily an excuse for avoiding a decision. If analysis takes too long, a slow movement in the problem may have taken place which renders the solution invalid.

Hunches may have to be the basis for impossible decisions. There may be no rational means of arriving at a choice in the circumstances. In diagnosis, there may not be enough information to come to a single conclusion. A decision may have to be based on a hunch, an unsupported prediction of what might be in the future. With luck, there will be at least one course of action that can be adapted to circumstances if they should change as implementation proceeds. SAP is an example.

Extra information may be sought by decision-makers beyond that necessary for logical choice, particularly if a choice of option has been made and declared already. This is not the same as finding out more about the option chosen in order to make better use of it. Comforting it may be, but redundant verification of a decision already taken can be costly in time and resources.

Tunnel vision or rigid thinking can afflict decision-makers. If no options or alternatives are presented, or if the variety of choice is too narrow, the risk of a bad decision can be high. And it is not good enough for the researchers to dig out some options that are clearly out of the question. Genuine alternatives have to be considered before making a choice. In spite of what may be said about timidity, doing nothing should always be an option to be considered carefully.

A bad decision may occur if the dominant attribute is used without evidence to justify the choice. The sales force for a certain product may seem very knowledgeable because they are always displaying their knowledge. This knowledge may be erroneous and the product may not be suitable for the job in mind.

Looking at the Business

One of the ways of avoiding some bad decisions is to deliberately look at the business of the company from more than one point-of-view. Some politicians are renowned for declaring that growth will come from the service industries rather than the manufacturing. But every manufacturer knows that his customers will judge him on the quality of his service as well as the quality of his product.

These are examples of points of view and worth considering. Should business process reengineering adjust the emphasis within the company between manufacturing and service, between customer relations and supplier relations, between collecting debts and internal economies?

The modules of the SAP software can be used in an infinite variety of ways so that the finished system reflects and serves whatever business structure is appropriate.

Model 1—Material and Finance

The model, in your mind or on paper, you have of your business represents how you think of it. It could be like a tunnel: Things and effort go in; profit and fatigue come out.

Perhaps you have an accounting view of your business. There is valuable material hang-ing about which needs to be managed lest it get misused or wasted. And there has to be someone in charge of the treasury, or else there will not be enough cash to pay the wages and the bills. If that is the first image that comes to mind when you think about model-ing your business, then why not draw it out on very large paper so that you will have room to add pieces and elaborate on your concept.

There will be some more elements to be added to your model if every person and job in your company is going to find a place in the scheme of things. For example, there are probably several departments, or at least work sections, not yet represented:

Accounts Payable

General Ledger

Management Accounting

Accounts Receivable

Transport

The difficulty with this modeling is that not all the elements are of the same type (see Figure I.1). Who put in the Transport Section next to Accounts Receivable?

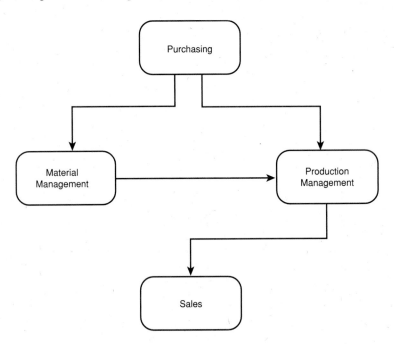

FIG. I.1   A simple business may seem to revolve around material and finance.

Model 2—Customers, Suppliers, and Internal Management
As you add elements to the model of your company, sooner or later you will find that outsiders are getting included—like suppliers and customers (see Figure I.2).

If you have not already guessed, the purpose of this very elementary introduction to business modeling is to convince you that the SAP R/3 system not only provides a wealth of tested and working business software, it also includes the means by which you can build a model of your existing business under the guidance and support of the R/3 system. And you can also use the system support modules to modify this model of the existing situation until it represents how you would like the business of the company to be conducted in the future. You will thus be guided into elaborating a target concept.

The SAP organization is not just providing the means by which you can draw more elaborate models; there is more to it than that. If you take the trouble to describe your existing situation in the way suggested by the R/3 system, you will find that it is but a relatively small and not too difficult step to achieve a specification of exactly which modules of the SAP standard business software would be necessary to have your target concept running as a model in simulation mode followed very rapidly by the same system going live as the basis for the data processing of your business and its management.

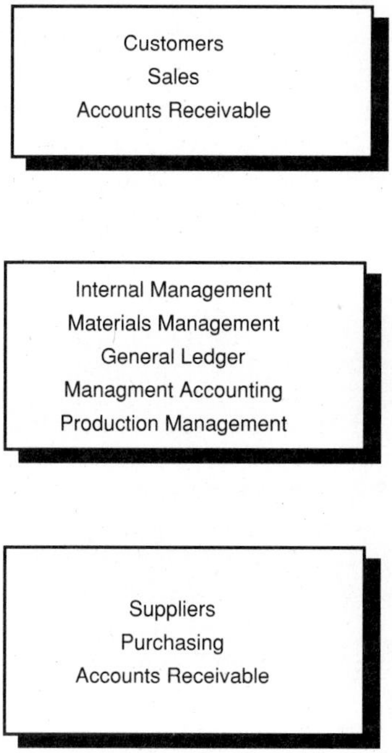

```
        Customers
          Sales
     Accounts Receivable
```

```
     Internal Management
     Materials Management
        General Ledger
     Managment Accounting
    Production Management
```

```
         Suppliers
         Purchasing
     Accounts Receivable
```

FIG. I.2 Customers, suppliers, and internal management may appear to live in separate domains.

The Orientation of the SAP R/3 System

The designers of the SAP R/3 system have worked with thousands of companies effecting the transition from legacy data processing methods based on mechanization of traditional manual procedures. They have seen how difficult a process it can be if you start with the existing procedures and try to stitch on a computer.

So the SAP designers have started at the other end. They have built and tested all the standard business programs that are needed to put together a modern system for just about every type and structure of business, whether the throughput is mainly material objects or mainly information, or even if the throughput is people in hospitals, for instance.

Each one of these standard programs has been specialized so as to perform to the highest possible level in the work it is designed for. There are no compromises.

Now because these standard programs are so highly polished, the user is not allowed to alter them in any way at all. They are sacrosanct.

These highly efficient programs are amenable to only one form of control. They are designed to consult tables. And into these tables, you are allowed to place the words and numbers which will make each program your own. You can tell it what to do without tinkering with its internal mechanisms. The process is called "Customizing" because it tailors the programs to suit the customer.

The Enterprise Data Model
Inside the R/3 system is a complete description of the programs available. You can inspect this description from various viewpoints. And when you find a part that looks like something in your existing company, or in your target concept of how you would like your company to be, then you can have the system save a copy of that part and build it into your model of your enterprise.

If you have a piece of your enterprise modeled in this way, you can command the system to show you just which standard business functions would be needed to implement it. There can be a seamless transition from modeling to designing the implementation.

Business Process Orientation
Once upon a time, businesses, like military armies, were described in terms of the numbers of people at each rank in the hierarchy. You modeled the business like a stack of bricks.

A more modern and fruitful approach is to think, and therefore, to model, in terms of processes. In particular, the logistics processes are modeled as value-adding chains of subprocess rather than according to the division of labor. It is but a small step to conceive of the entire corporation as the subject to which should be applied the event-driven process chain method as part of business workflow management. Watch for this kind of language to acquire the status of technical terminology.

Try "system-controlled industry-specific and company-specific modification procedures applied to standard software components" as a working definition of what the SAP implementation activity entails.

Because quantities and values are invariably posted simultaneously, synchronized logistics management and financial accounting is normal and results in improved quality through efficient logistics.

With the rapidly widening possibilities afforded by improved communications, including the Internet, the business model for the immediate future will take for granted an efficient logistics system and a closely coupled manufacturing organization. The SAP model looks towards customer-driven enterprises that take orders for, and deliver, goods and services on a worldwide basis.

From Here...

The extensive array of SAP products includes many different examples of standard business programs which can be configured and customized to suit individual user corporations.

- How is SAP R/3 developing?

  SAP R/3 has become easier to install, it has established links with all Microsoft systems, and it can reach out to other third-party products. It provides reliable and secure components to conduct business worldwide through the Internet.

- The *methods* are what I am interested in right now.

  Part II, "Technical Background," begins with Chapter 3, "System Architecture and Distributed Applications."

- Where are the specific functions and modules described in detail?

  Chapter 4, "Architecture," includes a list of the main modules which are described in Part IV, "Steering the Corporation," and subsequently in Part V, "Manufacturing Applications."

- How is SAP implemented in practice?

  Chapter 31, "Overview of SAP Implementations," begins Part IX, "Implementation Issues."

- Do I have to learn a new language?

  No. But you may have to be rather precise about how you make use of some familiar words and phrases. Appendix E is a glossary.

Part I

An Introduction to SAP

Belgium	70
Italy	62
Spain	59
Denmark	56
Czech Republic	41
Sweden	39
Hungary	26

479	
54	
24	
16	
14	

Japan	100
Australia	68
Singapore	32
Malaysia	22
Korea	10
Hong Kong	7
Thailand	7

South Africa	69
Saudi Arabia	9
Israel	3
Arabic Emirates	2
Nambia	2

Products
71%

High

Build large market share as fast as possible – at reasonable cost

- Identify effective sales and marketing campaigns – quick feedback on results
- Build sales capacity quickly using standardized multimedia product presentations
- Erect entry barriers to keep out competition – customer database used for attractive after-sales service and support

Develop ri for right m and at lea

- Impro betwee and te
- Use bi expert

Reduce sales and marketing costs while maintaining market share

- Service low value customers using low cost channels eg. telesales, direct mail
- Contact database to help retain key, high value customers
- Link purchase patterns to SOP to prompt for automatic reordering

Reduce c key custo for cross-s opportuni

- Sales payb
- Low v syste custo

Rate of market growth

Low

High

Relative market shar

Steel,
cal Engineering,
utomative

Food and Tobacco Industry

Office & EDP Equipment

Mining, Utilities, Transportation

Trade, Retail and Wholesale

Traffic and News Communication

Metal Products and Primary Metal

Universities and Technical Colleges

Wood, Paper and Printing Industry

- 8.0%
- 7.3%
- 6.6%
- 4.6%
- 4.5%
- 3.9%
- 3.8%
- 3.6%
- 2.9%

mmercial,
nd Social
10.3%

onics, Precision
hanics, Optics
14.5%

Chemical Industry,
Mineral Oil Production
18.2%

Others
(see chart below)
11.6%

Others

redit Banks, Financial Services	1.9
Quarrying, Fine Ceramics, Glass	1.9
Hospitals	1.7
Miscellaneous	1.7
surance Companies	1.6
uilding Trade, Construction	1.4
eather, Textile and Clothing Industry	.9
rade Associations and Federations	.3
griculture, Forestry, Fishing	.2

ble product

Customized tools

Develop
mplete and
customized

Develop

Deliver

High

Four Seasons

Seed

Agnosti

ICL

British Rail

ustomer Attractiveness

Chapter 1

The SAP Corporation

Introducing SAP

SAP was founded in 1972 and has grown to become the world's fifth largest software company.

SAP is both the name of the company and the computer system. The SAP system comprises a number of fully integrated modules, which cover virtually every aspect of business management. The system has been developed to meet the increasing needs of commercial and other organizations that are striving for greater efficiency and effectiveness. Information technology is now at the very core of major organizations around the world and its importance is beyond question. Market forces and customer expectations are putting continual pressures on organizations to improve the performance of their systems. While many software companies have looked at areas of business and developed systems to support those areas, SAP has looked toward the whole business. They offer a unique system that supports nearly all areas of business on a global scale. SAP provides the opportunity to replace large numbers of independent systems that have been developed and implemented in established organizations with one single modular system. Each module performs a different function, but is designed to work other modules. It is fully integrated, offering true compatibility across business functions.

SAP is a German company but operates all over the world, with 28 subsidiaries and affiliates and 6 partner companies maintaining offices in 40 countries. The following is a partial list of countries with SAP installations.

Americas:

Argentina	Brazil	Canada
Mexico	U.S.A.	

Europe:

Austria	Belgium	Czech Republic
Denmark	France	Germany
Greece	Hungary	Italy
Netherlands	Norway	Poland
Portugal	Russia	Slovak Republic
Spain	Sweden	Switzerland
United Kingdom		

Pacific Rim:

Australia	China	Hong Kong
India	Indonesia	Japan
Korea	Malaysia	New Zealand
Philippines	Singapore	Thailand

Africa/Middle East:

Israel	Turkey	South Africa

The Executive Board

1. Dietmar Hopp, Chairman SAP AG
   Sales & Consulting, Administration
   Germany, Middle East

2. Prof. Dr. H. C. Hasso Plattner, Vice Chairman, SAP AG
   and Chairman, SAP America Inc.
   Basis Development, Technology & Marketing
   North and South America, South Africa, Australia, Japan

3. Dr. H.C. Klaus Tschira
   Human Resources and Development

4. Prof. Henning Kagermann
   Accounting and Controlling Development
   Europe

5. Dr. Peter Zencke
   Logistics Development
   Asia Pacific Area

The Name

SAP's name has been derived from:

> Systems, Applications, Products in Data Processing

Corporate Headquarters

SAP Aktiengesellschaft
SAP AG
Neurottstraße 16
D-6909 Walldorf
Germany
06227 34-0

Worldwide SAP addresses are listed in Appendix A, "SAP Offices Around the World."

Corporate Goals

SAP has defined its corporate goals as follows:

- Customer satisfaction

- Profitability

- Growth

- Employee satisfaction

History

SAP was founded in 1972 by five people: Wellenreuther, Hopp, Hector, Plattner, and Tschira. Wellenreuther had, while employed by IBM, developed a financial accounting package running in batch for an IBM customer (Naturin). SAP bought the rights from Naturin and started to design and implement the real-time finance system as a standard package based on Wellenreuther's experience in the application. They sold the first copy of the standard system to ICI for the same price as later customers. Simultaneously, they developed a materials management system as a bespoke software for ICI, but reserving all property rights for SAP. From the cash flow of the MM system, they financed the development of the FI system. The MM system was later converted to a standard package, which in turn was financed by revenue from the FI Package. Both were the first modules of what was called System R, and only later, posthumously, was renamed R/1 to better distinguish it from its successors R/2 and R/3.

SAP's Markets

SAP markets its products all over the world to almost every industry imaginable, as well as government and educational institutions and hospitals.

The following is an incomplete list of industries served by SAP.

- Raw Materials, Mining, and Agriculture
- Oil and Gas
- Chemical
- Pharmaceutical
- Building Materials, Clay, and Glass
- Building and Heavy Construction
- Primary Metal, Metal Products, Steel
- Industrial and Commercial Machinery
- Automotive
- Ship, Aerospace, and Train Construction
- Transportation Services and Tourism
- Electronic/Optic and Communication Equipment
- Wood and Paper
- Furniture
- Consumer Packaged Goods—Food
- Consumer Packaged Goods—Nonfood
- Clothing and Textiles
- Retail and Wholesale
- Communication Services and Media
- Storage, Distribution, and Shipping
- Utilities
- Financial Services, Banks, and Insurance
- Government, Public Administration, and Services
- Museums and Associations
- Health Care and Hospitals
- Education Institutions and Research
- Consulting and Software
- Services

The following is an incomplete list of SAP R/2 customers.

ABB	Eastman Kodak	Mobil
Adidas	Esso	Motorola
AEG	Exxon	Nissan Europe
AGIP	Fuji	Polygram
Allianz	General Electric	Schindler Elevator
Aral	Goodyear	SEAT
Coca-Cola	Hapag-Lloyd	Swissair
Compaq	Krupp-Hoesch	Tchibo
Danone	Lufthansa German Airlines	Texaco
Deutsche Bahn	Marriott	Toyota
Deutsche Bank	Miele	ZDF
Dow Chemical	Milupa	

The following is an incomplete list of SAP R/3 customers.

Airbus Industrie	DuPont	MIT
Akzo	Frankfurt Airport	Nestlé
Alcatel	Henkel	Petrofina
American Airlines	Hercules	Philips
Apple	Hewlett-Packard	Philip Morris
Autodesk	Hitachi	Pirelli
BASF	Hoechst	Procter & Gamble
Bayer	Hoffman-La Roche	Rhone Poulenc
Bertelsmann	IBM	Rolex
BMW	ICI	Rothmans
Bosch	Lego	Royal LePage
British Rail	Mannesmann	RTL
Carlsberg	Mercedes Benz	Sandoz
Chevron	Merck	SAT 1
Ciba Geigy	Metro International	Schlumberger
Digital Equipment	Micrografx	Shell

Siemens	Total Oil	Varta
Solvoy	Unilever	Vattenfall
Thyssen Stahl	University of Oxford	Wuerth

Figure 1.1 shows the makeup of SAP's group sales. SAP's primary business activity remains the sale of its software systems.

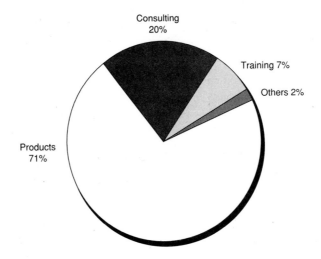

Fig. 1.1   SAP AG's primary sales activity remains software sales.

From Here...

In this chapter, we have looked at the history of the SAP corporation and how it has become the world's fifth largest software company. We have looked at details of the SAP corporation today, its global organization, the industries it serves, and some of its customers.

- Chapter 3, "System Architecture and Distributed Applications"
- Chapter 39, "SAP Workplaces"
- Appendix A, "SAP Offices Around the World"

Chapter 2

User Interaction with the SAP Systems

The principles of the user interface with the SAP systems are concerned to implement the best ergonomic practice, not only in the sense of presenting the user with attractive and informative displays, but also in the sense of asking the user to do things in ways which come easily and seem natural. There should be a provision to streamline repetitive tasks if they cannot be automated altogether.

The Interface Between System and User

The concept of user interface is taken from the usage in communications, where one system has to transfer data to and from another. The design of the screens and the logic underlying their reactions to the entries of the user are consistent across applications and hardware. In the network of client/servers, the presentation servers are assigned considerable computing resources.

Sessions or Modes

When you press keys or click a mouse on a screen, you will probably begin a session. If you have chosen wrongly, the session will begin with an error dialog, which will continue until you have made a valid entry. If the entry was recognized as a command for the system to do something, the screen will change so as to let you know that something is happening. If that something is going on too long for you to wait, you can open another session at the same time. The screen will show you a fresh window for your other session. You now have two modes running at the same time. You could have up to nine, each in its own window.

When any of your modes is ready for you to do something, its window will let you know. By using several modes, you can get more work done in the same amount of time.

In this chapter, you learn:

- How a user learns what to do.

- What happens if the user makes a mistake.

- How much scope you have for setting out the screen in the way that you prefer.

Defining User Profiles

A user is a person who has permission to use the system and has an identification code that tells the system which password to expect if the person logging on is indeed an authorized user.

The user profile is established by the system supervisor and gives permission for the user to use certain functions. For example, a user who has learned only to enter purchase orders will not be allowed to send them off to suppliers without checking and authorization by a supervisor. Another job of the profile is to tell the system which language the user will be expecting and which department they belong to for administrative purposes. Automatically displaying a certain part of the system for a user who has just logged on is a helpful thing for the system to do under the control of the user profile. It may set up more than one mode for you, depending on your profile and what you were doing last time you were at work on the system.

The Role of Tables in SAP

A table is a collection of data fields arranged in rows and columns, not all of which need be visible on the screen at the same time. Because each data field will have a specified length expressed as the number of characters it will hold, the length of a row in a table will equal the sum of the number of characters in each field in the row. Each field in a column will have the same number of character spaces.

However, a screen field may not be as large as the data field. If you are typing into a screen field, the characters will move to the left when you get near the end of the field. You can continue entering characters until the underlying data field is full.

Tables are used throughout the SAP systems to present data that fits into a rectangular pattern of rows and columns. A list of part numbers, their names, and their prices would fit nicely in a table of three columns' width, and it could have as many rows as there were different parts.

You could ask for the table to be sorted so that the most expensive parts come first, or you can have the list arranged in order of the part number. Your screen will seldom be big enough to let you see the whole table, so you have to have some way of selecting which items to look at.

Almost everything you do in a business system will be based on tables, even if you ask for the graphical presentation system to convert the table to a picture for you. Some tables contain data, like the parts list; others contain control data that tell the system how things should be done. For example, there will be a list of screens in a table, so that when you have finished with one, the next one will be presented.

Environments

An environment is a place where something happens. In the business computing world, an environment is a set of events waiting to happen if the right conditions arise. One of these events might be to display today's date in the field you have pointed out with your cursor. This event will not happen unless you do something else besides point: You may have to click, or press a special function key. A different environment might not have a write-the-date event waiting to happen. In very old computer systems, you would probably have had to type in the date for yourself. This is a very simple example!

SAP systems can usually present two or three environments. One is a testing environment, where the system is not allowed to make any changes to the real database. Another is the production environment, where everything you do will be noticed by the system and the appropriate action will take place for real. The third type of environment is usually for training purposes, where the system is primed with data and imaginary customers, so you can carry out training exercises that feel like the real thing although they are just in simulation.

The Transaction Concept

A business transaction is an exchange between one part of a system and another. The production plant, for example, will take delivery of some material from a warehouse in exchange for a delivery receipt. The warehouse will be able to use the delivery receipt to reconcile the stock of material on the inventory. Meanwhile, the accounting department will have noted that the valuable material has passed from the warehouse to the production plant. It will post some financial transactions to record this exchange of value for material.

When a user is working at a terminal, a transaction with the system is not finished until the system is satisfied that the entry of information has been correct. The system will record the transaction automatically as a document that will remain in the system as . proof of who entered the information and when exactly this occurred.

If the transaction concerned a purchase order, for example, the details of that order will have been written on the document by the system wherever possible. The user will have selected a supplier already on the database, so the details can be entered by the system, and so on.

The operation of dynamic programs—dynpros—to manage the interaction of a user with the SAP R/3 system is discussed further in Chapter 4, "Architecture."

Manual Invoice Entry. If you have to enter manually an invoice that has not been posted automatically, SAP R/3 will provide all possible help. You can enter and post a check received and match the payment to specific open items in the customer account, all in one operation.

The successful posting of a transaction does not occur until the necessary data is recorded as a SAP Document and is complete and error-free. You can set aside a transaction document before it is ready for posting, in which case the system will validate any information you have already entered and report to you any discrepancies.

The SAP Document has to end up with a document header showing posting date, document date, document reference number, and currency key. The body of the document will contain one or more line items which will show the amount and identify the product and the terms of payment. The system will generate certain line items such as tax entries, cash discount, and exchange rate differences, as applicable.

You can set up helping routines and use standard data entry functions such as the following:

> Recalling a previous screen for copying and editing
>
> Retaining data for individual users for several transactions
>
> Adapting a copy of a data-entry screen so that it is better suited to a set of transactions that you are expecting
>
> Searching for an account number by using matchcodes to narrow the search

A SAP Document that records a previous transaction can be copied to act as a sample or model to be edited. This sample can be a regular document that has been set aside, perhaps as an incomplete transaction document. The posting date and new values may have to be entered, by you or by the system, before posting.

Recurring Entries. If you are expecting to have to make a series of entries where the amounts are always the same, you can set up a recurring entry. Monthly service fees would be an example.

A recurring entry is a set of data that will not be used until the due dates. Until then, the entries will not update account balances.

You will have to specify the first and last dates and the frequency or time interval between. The system will automatically post the required transaction on each of the due dates.

The Document Principle

A transaction of posting to any account will not succeed unless debits equal credits. The entries for such a posting will not be accepted unless they pass the validation tests applied in the dynpro step of the dialog routine running at the point of data entry.

This successful posting to an account as a result of the transaction is regarded by SAP as a self-contained and coherent unit of data. It constitutes a meaningful business act. Information has to be given to the SAP system, and the system will have checked for all the errors that could be detected at this stage of the business process. It makes sense to mark this off as a task element—and the Generally Accepted Accounting Principles (GAAP) commend the practice of leaving evidence of every accounting task element.

The unit is defined as a SAP Document because evidence of this posting event and the details of the transaction can be displayed in a standard document format. No posting can take place without leaving a SAP Document ready to be used in the audit and in any processing or posting to control or analysis accounts.

A transaction of entry, checking, and posting data can take place directly with the FI-Financial Accounting system, where the results will include posting to the GL-General Ledger and its subledgers. A transaction can also direct data to other SAP applications. An example would be to enter data from original documents such as goods receipt notes and packing lists.

Every SAP application operates the method of transactions that create SAP Documents. For example, the FI-FA Fixed Assets Management component could accept a transaction which recorded an investment in a fixed asset, and, at the same time, the transaction could post the invoice for the investment. This would automatically record the transaction in the following accounts:

- Fixed Assets
- This vendor's account
- General Ledger, Accounts Payable subledger
- Cost Accounting
  - by order
  - by project
  - by fixed asset group or type

The requirements of GAAP are derived from the essence of a reliable accounting system: Any number in the system can be traced through the accounting procedures to the point of origin—either a calculation or an entry from outside the accounting system. The design of a SAP Document includes and is in excess of the requirements of GAAP.

Before a transaction can be successfully completed, the mandatory SAP Document has to be created. This will occur only after strict validation of the entries. Uniform data structures have to be used. The transaction has to obey clear-cut rules about posting. The SAP Document will identify the rules in use for each line item.

A data object is a cluster of data items recorded as fields. Each field is allowed a maximum size and type of content according to the defined data domain that has been assigned to it. A field will not be allowed to accept any value or other content unless it is in accord with this domain definition.

A SAP Document is a data object, and must obey the rules of SAP objects.

SAP Document Header Fields
A SAP Document will be displayed first in overview format and then in more detail, depending on which line item has been selected.

The header of a SAP Document overview will always include organizational data and full identification of the document, as follows:

- Document number
- Company code

- Fiscal year

- Document date

- Intercompany number

- Reference document

- Debit/credit total

- Currency

SAP Document Line Item Detail Fields

The body of a SAP Document will be displayed in overview with one line of column titles and one or more line items to carry summary details of the entries.

Further details of each line item can be accessed using overlay windows at the display terminal, as follows:

- General Ledger account

- Company code

- Intercompany number

- Currency

- Transaction amount

- Debit/credit

- Tax amount

- Tax code

- Business area

- Cost center

- Order identification

- Project identification

- Asset identification

- Material code

- Personnel number

- Allocation code

- Reference document identification

- Document header text

- Document type (transaction type, journal type)

- Posting key (debit or credit, what type of account this line item is allowed to be posted to)

Flexible SAP Document Numbering

Document Number is a mandatory field on a SAP Document header and on each of the detail displays for the line item. SAP R/3 offers a choice of manual or automatic assignment.

Various methods can be specified for automatic SAP Document numbering. It can be quite useful, for instance, to allocate ranges of code numbers, which can include letters, according to the type of transaction. This would have the effect of organizing the listing of journal entries by type of document, such as the following:

- Customer invoices
- Customer payments
- Down payments
- Credit memos

Optional Details in SAP Documents

The line items on a SAP Document display will have to point to fields that contain the information required under GAAP to maintain a reliable accounting system, but each SAP client company will want to use the flexibility of the system to set up not only a chart of accounts to meet the mandatory requirements of company law regarding external accounting, but also additional accounts for the analysis, planning, and control of the business.

The customer may want to define a sort code that can be used for allocation and analysis. He or she may need to customize the system to allow and validate entries that flag such items as special payment terms.

Whatever data is required or allowed in a particular transaction entry will be recorded in the SAP Document. Therefore, this information will be available for subsequent processing, as well as being the content for online accounting by SAP R/3.

The Set Concept. The logical concept of a set is used in the FI-GLX Extended General Ledger for reporting, planning, and ledger processing. A set refers to a data structure and its relationships with other data structures.

A set of numbers can be defined, where the numbers are the identification codes of bank accounts, for example.

A list of cost centers can specify a set.

The actual members of a set may not be known until the set definition is called into use. The "top three operating divisions for gaining new customers in the current month" is a set definition of this kind.

The definition of a set can include relationships between specific firms or companies in a group, not necessarily at the same level. They can be specified by their individual company codes.

A set can comprise any collection of data objects that meet the logical criteria forming the definition for membership of that set.

Specific business functions can call on a set definition stored for use later. Assessment and distribution often take place under the control of sets.

The SAP Style Guide to Screen Design

SAPGUI is the Graphical User Interface common to all SAP modules in presentation style and general manner of use. Specific uses of the special function keys may apply in some components.

The SAP Style Guide sets out the graphical appearance and manner of use of the principal elements of the screen displays, as follows:

- Online help accesses the online documentation via hypertext references, which permits navigation between blocks of text and illustrative material. Terminals running under Windows will present the help within the scope of Microsoft WinHelp and any associated desktop applications.

- Control elements include check boxes, list boxes, pushbuttons, radio buttons. Where necessary, scroll bars are provided to access material that will not fit in one screen or box.

- All SAP R/3 application functions can be accessed via menus, which are consistent in construction throughout the system. Menus can be constructed for specific groups of users.

- Toolbars are provided where necessary to supplement the standard toolbar, which carries the most frequently used navigation commands and the tools for accessing online help.

- The interpretations of the function keys according to the most important functions of the application are indicated by a function key bar.

- Entry values for fields that have designated value domains can be displayed to use as selection options. Where the valid entries can be limited by other methods, the set of options is also displayed for selection.

Office Communications Interface

The SAP R/3 system makes use of temporary sequential object files (TEMSE) to manage texts that are sent or received over the office communications interface of the system.

The central communications interface can send any texts generated within or received by the SAP R/3 system to any of the following destinations:

- Any user of the same SAP R/3 system

- Any user of another SAP R/3 system

- Any user of a non-SAP office communication system

- Users of telex, fax, or teletex services

- X.400 e-mail subscribers

- A printer

The SAPcomm-API is an Application Programming Interface that enables the connection of third-party communications products that set up links to external standard communications services.

Remote Function Call (RFC) techniques are used to implement a gateway to UNIX mail.

Messaging Application Programming Interface (MAPI), which is a component of the Microsoft Windows Open Service Architecture (WOSA), is accessible via the SAPmail electronic mail component. This makes SAP R/3 services available to Microsoft Mail (MS-Mail) as a server. By this means, SAP R/3 is also able to act as a client for MS-Mail services.

From Here...

- How can the system help me find out what I need?

  By having you work on the R/3 Analyzer, which is discussed in Chapter 6, "Tool-Supported Optimization with the R/3 Analyzer." It calls on the SAP R/3 Reference Model described in Chapter 5, "The R/3 Reference Model."

- I would like to look at a straightforward function in some detail. Which do you recommend?

  Look at the Sales and Distribution module described in Chapter 20, "Understanding the SD-Sales and Distribution Module."

- How is system and hardware servicing managed?

  By the Online Service System described in Chapter 27, "Understanding the OSS-Online Service System."

Part II

Technical Background

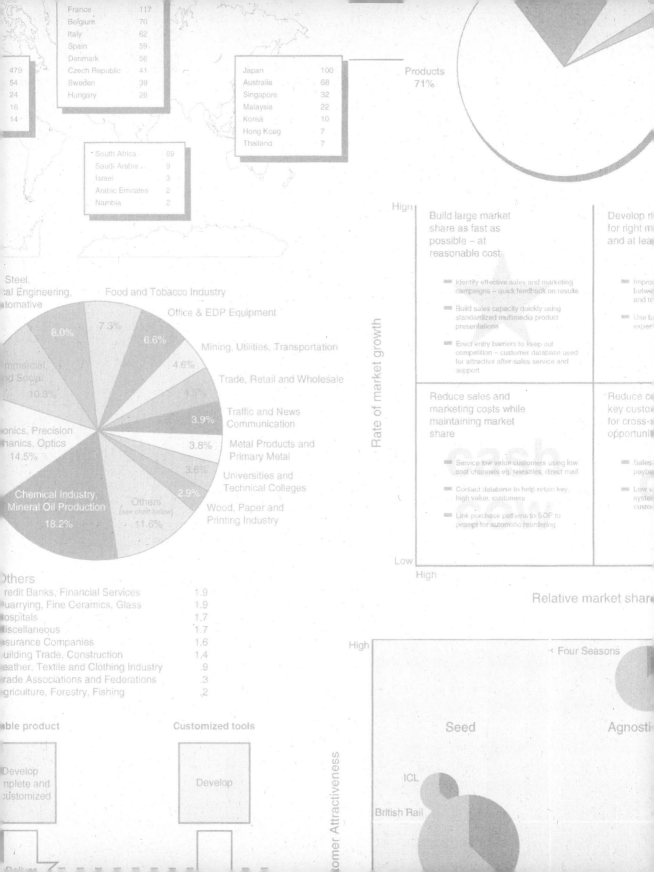

France	117
Belgium	70
Italy	62
Spain	59
Denmark	56
Czech Republic	41
Sweden	39
Hungary	26

479
54
24
16
14

Japan	100
Australia	68
Singapore	32
Malaysia	22
Korea	10
Hong Kong	7
Thailand	7

South Africa	69
Saudi Arabia	9
Israel	3
Arabic Emirates	2
Namibia	2

Products
71%

Steel,
cal Engineering,
tomative

Food and Tobacco Industry

Office & EDP Equipment

Mining, Utilities, Transportation

Trade, Retail and Wholesale

Traffic and News
Communication

Metal Products and
Primary Metal

Universities and
Technical Colleges

Wood, Paper and
Printing Industry

8.0%
7.3%
6.6%
4.6%
4.5%
3.9%
3.8%
3.6%
2.9%

mmercial,
d Social
10.3%

onics, Precision
hanics, Optics
14.5%

Chemical Industry,
Mineral Oil Production
18.2%

Others
(see chart below)
11.6%

Rate of market growth

High

Build large market share as fast as possible – at reasonable cost
- Identify effective sales and marketing campaigns – quick feedback on results
- Build sales capacity quickly using standardized multimedia product presentations
- Erect entry barriers to keep out competition – customer database used for attractive after-sales service and support

Develop ri for right m and at lea
- Impro betwe and t
- Use b experi

Reduce sales and marketing costs while maintaining market share
- Service low value customers using low cost channels eg. telesales, direct mail
- Contact database to help retain key, high value, customers
- Link purchase patterns to SOP to prompt for automatic reordering

Reduce ce key custo for cross-s opportuni
- Sales payba
- Low v syste custo

Low

High

Relative market share

Others

redit Banks, Financial Services	1.9
uarrying, Fine Ceramics, Glass	1.9
ospitals	1.7
iscellaneous	1.7
surance Companies	1.6
uilding Trade, Construction	1.4
eather, Textile and Clothing Industry	.9
rade Associations and Federations	.3
griculture, Forestry, Fishing	.2

ble product

Customized tools

Develop
nplete and
ustomized

Develop

Customer Attractiveness

High

Seed

Four Seasons

Agnosti

ICL

British Rail

Chapter 3

System Architecture and Distributed Applications

The SAP system comprises a Basis system to which applications may be added. Each application has several components which may be installed as required. A component will include a range of functions which may be mandatory or optional.

All of the functions, at whatever level, can be directed to perform in a variety of ways by parameters that are amenable to adjustment by the user during the customizing process which precedes going live.

Basic Principles of R/3 Software

The standard business functions of the SAP R/3 system are able to execute the full range of business system processes used in almost every type of business enterprise. The scope of these functions extends from the conduct of controlled dialog with a user, through the processes required to maintain an integrated data system, up to the higher order statistical and control functions expected in an enterprise-controlling system.

The system extends not only in scope across the full range of data processing required by a complex corporate organization, but also through the implementation process by which the existing business system is described and developed into the target concept of what will be a new business supported by the SAP system.

The transactions with the system can range from data exchange to decision making, from software development to display design, from automatic processing to extensive financial and other reporting.

Multi-Tier Client Server Architecture

The R/3 system operates by using the client/server principle applied across several levels. It is highly modular and the principle is applied primarily through software so that the modes of interaction between the various clients and servers may be controlled.

This chapter looks into the following topics:

■ The distinctive features of SAP software.

■ How R/3 can handle many users and many types of work.

■ How a manager makes best use of system resources.

■ How systems can talk to each other.

■ How difficult it is to join a modern R/3 installation to whatever went before.

II

Technical Background

Dedicated servers may be linked by communication networks and perform certain tasks without impugning the integrity of the data and processes of the central system network.

Open System Principles

An open system allows the interplay and portability of applications, data, and user interfaces by adhering to international standards for these elements.

This definition of an open system is based on the work of the POSIX 1003.0 Committee of the IEEE (Institute of Electrical and Electronics Engineers), which is devoted to POSIX, the Portable Operating System Interface for UNIX.

International Open Interface Standards. The following international standards have been embodied in the R/3 system:

- **TCP/IP**, for the network communications protocol and for other secure protocols

- **RPC**, which is implemented in ABAP/4 as **RFC** Remote Function Call to enable other systems to call R/3 functions and constitutes the R/3 open programming interface

- **CPI-C**, Common Programming Interface-Communication, for program-to-program communications across multiple systems

- **SQL**, Structured Query Language, and **ODBC**, Open Data Base Connectivity, are the standards used for open data access to R/3 business data stored in relational databases

- **OLE/DDE**, Object Linking and Embedding, is the primary standard for integrating PC applications with R/3

- **X.400/X.500, MAPI**, Messaging Application Programming Interface, and **EDI**, Electronic Data Interchange, are the standards for external communications

- Open interfaces are also established to provide access to specialized applications

The following specialized applications entail open interface communications with R/3:

- CAD, Computer-Aided Design

- Optical archiving

- Production-related technical subsystems such as DASS for plant data collection

Production technical systems are discussed in Chapter 18, "Understanding the PP-PI Production Planning for Process Industries Modules."

Portability Across Operating Systems

In addition to running under all major UNIX operating systems, the R/3 system can also run under the following operating systems:

- OpenVMS

- MPE/iX

- Windows NT

Portability Across Databases

The R/3 system is compatible with the database systems marketed by a variety of companies including:

- Informix

- Oracle

- Software AG

- Sybase

Portability Across Presentation Front Ends

The SAP-GUI Graphical User Interface is able to display, in list or graphical formats, all outputs from the R/3 standard functions on most front-end presentation systems, including the following:

- Windows

- OSF/Motif

- OS/2PM

- Macintosh

Integration with Distributed Applications

In many companies, application systems have been developed without online links to a central system. Even when an integrated system was designed from the beginning, there may be technical or economic reasons why some application systems have to be uncoupled so that they can be utilized on their own. Their databases may have to be isolated from the other systems.

Yet the SAP system depends on manipulating complex data objects which may have their constituent data elements located in a variety of databases, including some that are at least occasionally uncoupled.

ALE, Application Link Enabling, is the technology of integrating asynchronously coupled clusters of applications using a method of message-based integration. It allows R/2 and R/3 systems to cooperate with each other and with third-party systems so that both data and business functions are consistent throughout the cluster. It is discussed in Chapter 8, "Continuous Business Development."

Uncoupling Applications, Front Ends, and Databases

Each component of an application, the software, the front-end system, and the database, is likely to be developed independently of the others. For instance, front-end presentation and user interaction systems have changed from simple keyboards, to slave terminals, to intelligent PC-based user interface systems. Similarly, database hardware and software tends to be developed in cycles which are not attuned to the developments in specific business software, nor are they in synchrony with user interface improvement.

Because the SAP modular system of standard business software has always been designed with this diversity of hardware recognized as a salient feature of the business environment, there is no particular difficulty in uncoupling the application logic from the presentation system and the database configuration.

Dedicated Database Servers. The central database can be serviced in a single processor, a multi-processor, or a cluster of processors. The configuration of the database complex can be adjusted to suit the volume of data and the traffic on the system.

Dedicated Application Logic Servers. The advantage of having one or more applications running on dedicated servers is that purely local business may be conducted with the systems uncoupled. Updates to the central facility can then take place at the most convenient time and by the most efficient channels.

As in the case of the dedicated database installation, a computer system assigned to one or more applications can be reconfigured to utilize different numbers and types of processors and interfaces according to the traffic demand and the complexity of the data items being processed.

Scaling the processor capacity does not affect the application logic.

Special Task Servers. The following tasks illustrate the variety of specialized computer systems that can be integrated with the R/3 system:

■ Optical archiving

■ Sending X.400 messages

■ Telex and fax

■ Background processing of transaction data

■ Control systems for complex production plant

Presentation Servers. In accord with the technical evolutionary principle, the range and variety of presentation devices are likely to increase as the manufacturers seek cheaper production methods and specialized niche markets in which their particular products will flourish. For instance, because of the wide market for personal computers, these devices have become viable alternatives to dedicated and custom-built user interface equipment.

The SAP R/3 system supports the following types of presentation device:

■ Windows, based on the Windows Style Guide, and directed by a dispatcher to control the different forms of communication

■ OS/2 PCs

- Apple Macintosh
- OSF/Motif for X terminals
- OSF/Motif for workstations

The R/3 system will tend to adopt the style and local functionality of the presentation platform so that the user will not have to get used to a different look or operating key repertoire.

The interface between the user and an application is discussed in Chapter 2, "User Interaction with the SAP Systems."

Provision for Continuous Business Development

Business processes have always undergone change. New methods are invented to cope with new products or new customer requirements. Old methods are adjusted to suit the new circumstances. New people are recruited to replace those who are used to the old system of working.

Some of these changes are beneficial, some are not. For example, new people may be ready to learn the new ways; but they will lack experience with the customers, the suppliers, and the products. Such wisdom may be needed, even under the new regime.

The SAP system expects a business to change. And the first big change to be expected is the installation of the SAP system itself.

In summary, what is needed is help in describing how things are done now, and help in arranging the system so that it will work well in the future. The last thing an implementer wants is a host of problems with computer code. The last thing a managing director wants is a wonderful system that does not do what is necessary to support the business.

Two methods and the tools to apply them are built into the SAP systems:

- Enterprise data modeling;
- Customizing.

The first helps you plot out where you are now and where you are going: The second allows you to adjust the standard business software so that it fits exactly your future way of doing business, and this is effected without modifying any source code.

Enterprise Data Models

"Input is processed to become output." This is a verbal model of a company. It is an information model, even if not very informative.

"Head office manages a purchasing department, and a sales department." This is slightly more informative; but not really useful.

But suppose you were to name all the work units, the activity centers in your company, and then write down what each one did, then you would be on the way to assembling a useful information model of your enterprise.

Chapter 5, "The R/3 Reference Model," discusses how the system contains a complete information model of itself which you can inspect in list format or explore in graphical presentation. You can see how your model of your existing company's business processes compares with the model in the system.

Chapter 6, "Tool-Supported Optimization with the R/3 Analyzer," shows how this tool is able to guide you through the process of designing a new system for your company which will work first time because all the standard business functions you will need to get started have be predefined and programmed so that they integrate with each other.

Tools for Adapting Software

Another tool which is a fundamental part of the SAP concept and the R/3 system is the customizing system. When you look at part of the R/3 Reference Model, you will be able to recognize many business functions that you already have in your operating departments such as Sales and Production.

With the advice and the support of the R/3 Analyzer, you will have been able to select the functions of interest from the R/3 Reference Model and start to build a system that fits your own situation, and your target concept of how you would like things to be. This first edition of the target system could be run as it stands because it is made up of predefined standard business functions that are all fully working and properly integrated with each other.

But this system will not feel like your own tailor-made system. If you call for a list of your company's products, you will not see your specific products because the system knows nothing about them. If you have one production plant and two warehouses, the R/3 Reference Model will show the plant as the owner of a warehouse: but it will not know you have two warehouses until you tell it so.

The process of adjusting and particularizing your model system without altering any source code is discussed in Chapter 7, "R/3 Customizing."

Client/Server Multi-Tier Architecture

SAP systems are designed for the medium to large corporate business entity with many worldwide locations and many data processing facilities.

The size and complexity of such companies, and the increasing ability of computer systems to rapidly process large quantities of data, have combined to encourage the concept and physical construction of networks of servers providing support to a number of clients or users.

Most business systems have to provide three main functions:

- Database services to retain information, for example, on materials and methods used in manufacture and packaging

- Application data processing, for example, to ensure that materials required for production are delivered to the right place at the correct time and that the stock is replenished

- Presentation services, for example, to report the progress of production and the state of the inventory

The SAP R/3 software system provides the functionality to support all such businesses. It also allows the target system to be fine tuned so as to reach peak performance quickly and adapt rapidly and effectively to changes in circumstances.

Individual Configurations

Your SAP system can be configured to suit your size by allocating different processing systems to the three essential services of Database Management, Application Processing, and Presentation Services.

Central System Alone. A central system by itself can provide Database, Application Processing, and Presentation Services.

Decentralized Presentation. The central system can encompass the Database and the R/3 Application software; but the presentation system is a decentralized network of user interfaces.

Client with Server to Database. The central host system may carry the R/3 Basis and one or more applications. The database then has to be a separate system accessed via a server.

3-Level Client/Server Configuration. The most versatile configuration employs three levels of client/server distributed processing.

In the core of the system is a high-speed network of R/3 database servers. The R/3 applications are networked around the database cluster and have independent access to it. The R/3 applications are fully integrated with each other.

User access to any of the applications, and hence to any of the database servers, is mediated by an outer network of presentation servers which form the R/3 front end systems where they may be integrated with PC tools and subsystems. Figure 3.1 suggests a triple-level client server configuration. There is not a strict interpretation of "level" in this context which could be referred to as "multilevel" client server configuration.

Even Loads. Any user can be in touch with several application servers at the same time. In some areas there may be a need to balance the load by installing specialized application servers. The following areas, in particular, are often served by systems optimized for their differing requirements:

- SD-Sales and Distribution

- FI-Financial Accounting

- HR-Human Resources Management

II

Technical Background

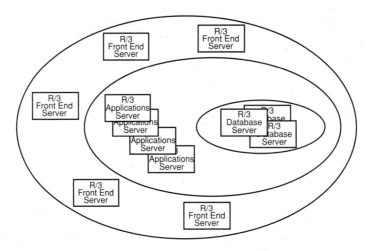

Fig. 3.1   Triple client server configuration.

Front-end and back-end computer systems are subject to different cost structures. The client server architecture allows an economical deployment of computing resources by separating the three levels of server.

The advantage is experienced by the user in the form of generous computing resources for the display and prompting services that make the work easier and more effective. This can be seen in contrast to older systems which had to compromise between the costs of presentation support systems and the cost of providing adequate central system resources.

From the corporate point of view, the economy of providing specialized database servers allows a generous allocation of storage and processing resources for the purpose of maintaining extensive reference data and full historical information down to the business transaction detail level.

Heterogeneous Platforms. The SAP system has been designed to cope with change, not least in the hardware and operating systems. Therefore, the new SAP implementation must expect to integrate with the legacy of database and presentation platforms and operating system which has been serving the company prior to the business process reengineering.

For example, an R/3 installation can consist of the following assembly of heterogeneous platforms, in any combination:

- Presentation by Windows 3.1, UNIX, Windows NT, OS/2, and Windows 95

- Application by Windows NT, UNIX, Open VMS, MPE/iX

- Database by Windows NT, UNIX, Open VMS, MPE/iX

Client/Server Communications

The architecture of R/3 allows various protocols for communication between the elements of the configuration. TCP/IP and OSI are examples.

The standard network protocol for open systems has become the TCP/IP, Transmission Control Protocol/Internet Protocol. It is supported by all of the operating systems that are relevant to R/3 systems.

Transfer Protocols

In accord with the SAP philosophy of choosing the most appropriate method for the task, different protocols have been adopted for each type of communication between the components of a multi-tiered client/server system.

TCP/IP. The TCP/IP, Transmission Control Protocol/Internet Protocol, is used for handling communications within the client/server configurations of the R/3 system.

LU6.2. The IBM network protocol, LU6.2, is used for communication between the R/3 system and the mainframe host.

SAP Presentation Protocol. Whatever transfer protocol is used, the interchange at the user interface is under the SAP Presentation Protocol.

Remote SQL. Data is transferred between an application and a database server using the SQL, Structured Query Language, the fourth generation language for manipulating data which is defined by ANSI, American National Standards Institute.

Data Transfer by WAN and LAN Linkage

The SAP presentation protocol is optimized for linking presentation servers directly to the R/3 system, and via WAN, Wide Area Networks.

When a large volume of data has to be transferred, a LAN, Local Area Network is needed: for example, between database servers and applications.

Program to Program Communications

Basic services for program-to-program communication at the ABAP/4 programming level are implemented using functions from the CPI-C, Common Programming Interface-Communication standard, the start set of which has been integrated into the ABAP/4 language.

When one program has to communicate with another program, an internal gateway is used to convert the CPI-C commands to the protocol used for external transfer, such as TCP/IP or LU6.2, according to whether the transfer is between applications or with a mainframe host.

Synchronous CPI-C. The transfer of the CPI-C commands and the management of transmission between applications or to a mainframe host takes place in a mutually dependent mode in a fixed time relationship. It is said to be synchronous communication.

If it is not possible to employ synchronous communication, the alternative is asynchronous communication which may be necessary under the following types of situations:

- The starting of a process on a target system has to be carried out manually, for example, because particular media have to be loaded manually.

- The target computer is temporarily unable to accept data or provide data.

Asynchronous Q-API. The R/3 system is able to maintain data in buffers which are queued awaiting a suitable moment to be transferred to the receiving computer. This moment may be defined by a schedule or be determined by the availability of the receiving computer. These queues can be freely integrated into any of the SAP application programs. The mechanism of choice is Q-API, Queue Application Programming Interface.

Two types of data format are supported under Q-API:

- The batch input format defined for accepting external data records into the R/3 system, which is directly recognized and entered into normal interactive transactions.

- Data in a format that has been defined for the receiving program to suit the specific situation.

RFC and RPC Protocols. The standard business functions of the R/3 system can be called and accessed freely without any special provision by the user apart from the normal business authorization procedures which may limit access of certain users to specific functions. However, your implementation may include some functions that were specially written in the ABAP/4 programming language to perform functions unique to your organization. The discussion in Chapter 28, "ABAP/4 Program Development with the R/3 Workbench," outlines the method of building these special function modules.

RFC, Remote Function Call, is the SAP ABAP/4 programming language implementation of the RFC, Remote Procedure Call protocol which is the standard adopted for accessing special function modules.

The following types of special function can be accessed using the RFC protocol:

- Functions residing in the R/3 system special function library

- External programs called from within ABAP/4 applications

- Function modules that reside in other computers

RFC may be used by an R/3 application to communicate, in both directions, with other R/3 applications, with R/2 programs, and with external applications running on other systems.

The R/3 runtime system controls any communications with other computers initiated by Remote Function Call procedures. Environments in the C language typically use RFC methods.

Asynchronous RFC Features. The syntax and usage for calling normal function modules in the R/3 system is recognized by RFC. The user need not be aware that the function is employing a remote computing resource. Calls can be dynamic and do not entail setting up static communication modules or stubs. A system table is used to recognize the "Destination Name" of a remote call and cause the setting up of a suitable type of connection with the partner. When the R/3 system is installed, the partners can be configured as logical target systems which the system will later specify in detail.

The RFC protocol is available in the TCP/IP Internet Protocol and in the SNA LU6.2 network protocol.

An API, Application Programming Interface, for an external C language program can be set up by using an RFC. R/3 function modules can be called by external programs by the same mechanism. Error handling is by a standard exception mechanism which allows remote debugging and trouble-shooting across system boundaries.

The RFC protocol supports all ABAP/4 data types, such as single fields, data structures made from data objects, tables. The protocol is fully integrated into the ABAP/4 R/3 Program Development Workbench. A Software Development Kit, RFC-SDK, is available to support the creation of non-SAP programs which will recognize remote function calls.

The Delta Management Functions of RFC. The overhead costs of communications between programs can be reduced by the Delta functions of RFC. The Delta functions are so named because they concentrate on detecting and responding to small changes. A function typically needs to transfer a table of data as one of its parameters. The Delta method allows a first full transfer and then subsequently only transfers data elements that have changed. These changes are communicated by a transfer of log tables that carry details of the changes made by the transactions.

The RFC Delta Management functions offer the following benefits:

- The target system will execute the RFC calls in the same order and within the same program context as in the calling system.

- Each RFC is executed only once.

- The status of an RFC call can be queried at any time to access the data in the log tables and ascertain the progress of the transaction.

- A "callback" function can be activated to invoke further activities in the calling system.

Application Methodology

Between the network of database servers and the front-end or presentation servers of a SAP R/3 multi-tier client/server system is the network of business applications which control the logic of the business transactions. The extensive range of applications is illustrated by the list in Chapter 4, "Architecture." The programs of these business applications are interpreted by an R/3 runtime system that is installed on every application server.

Business Transactions

A business transaction is a unit of work that makes sense to those concerned in the activities of the business. The business transaction has to be carried on a computer system. The combined business requirements and computer constraints dictate the logical functions of a transaction.

Data Consistency. A business transaction must not corrupt data. For example, a value that was entered in one type of unit must not be interpreted as if it were something different unless the system is able to operate a conversion procedure from one to another, and back again, if necessary. The address of a supplier must not appear in different forms if it refers to the same location: The delivery service may be able to recognize their equivalence; but the computer system will tend to regard two differing addresses as references to separate locations.

While a transaction is taking place, a data object which is undergoing an update should be reserved exclusively to the user controlling the transaction. Until that transaction is complete, no other user should be allowed access to the critical data object. Furthermore, until the transaction is complete, it should be possible for the user to backtrack through all the steps and undo any of the data entries or changes that he has effected. The database should be capable of being returned to how it was before the transaction began.

Business Requirements. A computerized business transaction should be at least as subtle as the manual procedure that it replaces. If you are creating an order for manufacturing, you would be advised to reserve the materials required at the same time. If you are posting items in financial accounting, it makes sense to post credit and debit items together.

Dynpros for Dialog Steps. The SAP mechanism for controlling the steps of a business transaction is the dynamic program or dynpro. Its functions are to present the user with screens that make sense from the point of view of the work being progressed and to make sure that the logical data requirements of the business application are correctly met.

SAP Logical Units of Work

Modern database systems are fast. They cannot wait for a user to complete data entry. A database step has to be completed as a single operation so that the database can go on to process the next item, probably on behalf of a different user.

By contrast, the LUW, logical unit of work, of a typical SAP application will involve many database operations as well as a host of interactions with the user and perhaps other systems.

A SAP-LUW is executed entirely or not at all: There is no interim stage. A SAP business transaction may comprise one or more logical units of work. A SAP-LUW may span several dialog steps, each step corresponding to a database transaction, a database LUW, which is the only way a database can be updated.

The end of a SAP-LUW is marked by a COMMIT WORK instruction or by the completion of the corresponding database update.

Runtime Environment

The R/3 runtime system is written in the ANSI-C language: and the R/3 application programs are written in ABAP/4.

The dynpro dynamic programs are interpreted, not compiled.

The runtime environment for R/3 applications is made up of the two processors necessary to interpret the dynpros.

User Session Modes

A user logs on, calls upon a series of transactions, and then logs off again. During this session, you can perform more than one sequence of actions by opening additional modes, which will appear in separate windows in the user interface screen. Within each mode, you can perform the actions in any suitable order, and suspend and later resume processing.

This multiple-mode arrangement allows the user to work on other activities if it becomes necessary to wait for processing resource or data.

The Application Dispatcher

The R/3 runtime system appears to the operating system as an aggregate of parallel processes. Each application includes a central dispatcher which is allocating work processes to a number of work processes. A work process may comprise one or more task handlers. Figure 3.2 illustrates this concept.

There are special work processes for the following types of activity:

- Interactive dialog processing

- Updating the database in response to change documents

- Background batch processing

- Spooling

- Management of locks

A work process can link directly to a database, which may be in another computer, and may entail routing via shared communications services. All other data traffic, such as communications to the SAP-GUI Graphical User Interface, and to other programs, is routed through the dispatcher.

Advanced Program-to-Program Communications. Into the dispatcher is built an APPC, Advanced Program-to-Program Communications, server which can recognize and respond to communication requests submitted by the work processes. It relays these to the SAP gateway which is also integrated into the dispatcher to serve as the R/3 system interface for the supported interface protocols such as TCP/IP and LU6.2, in which role it resembles a transaction monitor.

II

Technical Background

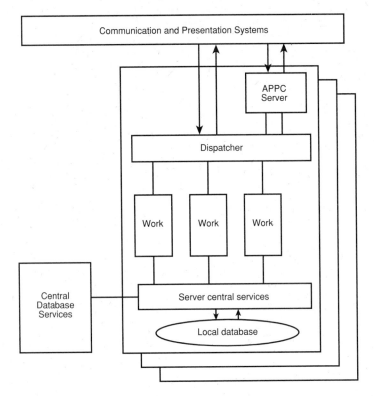

Fig. 3.2 Each R/3 Application has a dispatcher for its work processes.

Figure 3.3 summarizes these possibilities.

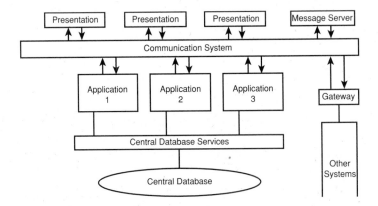

Fig. 3.3 Communications and central database services.

When a user interaction with a dynpro needs to be processed, the dispatcher places it in a queue for the next available interactive work process. When one is available, it will execute exactly one dialog step and then make itself available to process the next item in the queue. The processing of this one dialog step will generate output messages which will include a response screen to be sent back to the mode from which the user input originated. The user may be working with several modes in their separate windows (see Figure 3.4).

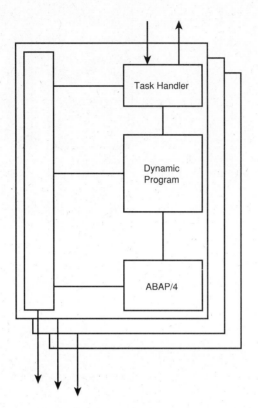

Fig. 3.4 One or more batch work processes support the dynpros.

A work process may conduct more than one activity. Each activity within the work process will be coordinated by a task handler which will activate the dynpro processor or the ABAP/4 processor as necessary to service the request for application logic processing such as dialogs, database updates and background processes (see Figure 3.5).

The number of work process resources in use at any moment will be a function of the workload anticipated by the system controller. The use of multiple modes by the user allows work to progress. Even if delays are experienced in any activity being conducted on behalf of one mode, the user may set up or reactivate another.

Figure 3.6 illustrates that one work process is devoted to controlling the security of individual processes through the R/3 enqueue services which provide a comprehensive lock management facility. This is discussed in a later section of this chapter.

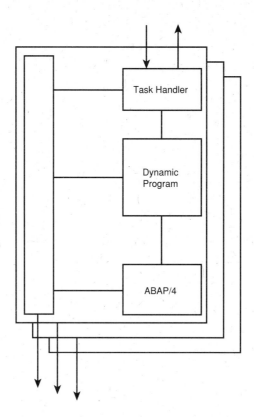

Fig. 3.5 One or more work processes supervise dialogs.

Other work processes are allocated to the management of print spooling functions. See Figure 3.7.

The ABAP/4 Data Dictionary

The R/3 runtime environment is based on two processors, one for ABAP/4, one for the dynpros. Both of them continually refer to the ABAP/4 Data Dictionary wherein are stored all the definitions of all R/3 data structures. Semantic and technical information stored in the dictionary constitutes the universe of data used by the R/3 system.

Figure 3.8 indicates that work processes have to be assigned the tasks of updating the data base on which the ABAP/4 programs depend.

Database Updates from the Transaction Log Records. A dialog program may supervise many dialog steps. Each step generates a log record which is not processed until after the dialog part has been completed. Therefore any database changes resulting from the dialog part of the transaction will not be physically realized until the associated log records are processed. If the user interrupts a transaction during the dialog phase, or if the transaction should fail for any other reason, there will be no database changes to reverse because none were made.

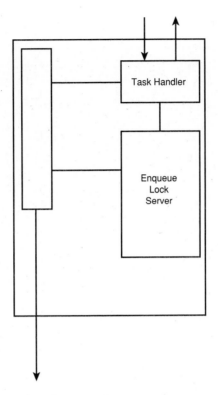

Fig. 3.6 One work process handles the enqueue lock management.

Synchronous Updating. If the updating process is in synchrony with the dialog, the user has to wait for each update to be completed before committing the next. High throughput rates are possible if the system resources can be made available.

If it is required to have fast interaction with the users under conditions of heavy processing load, then the dialogs should be uncoupled from database updates so as to institute asynchronous updating.

Multiple Component Updating

If the decision is to employ asynchronous updating, the dialog elements of transactions are separated from the actual updating of the database. The effect is to allow dialogs to proceed quickly, regardless of what has to happen in relation to the database. The accelerative effect is most noticeable when entering large volumes of data.

The work destined to be performed in updating the database is taken from the log of the transactions. Each log entry record carries all the data needed to perform the changes together with the names of the update routines that will have to be invoked. These entries are complete work elements in themselves. They are referred to as update components. Each is treated as a separate data object and assigned individually by the dispatcher to an update work process.

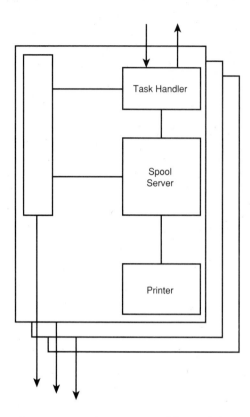

Fig. 3.7   One or more work processes; each serves a spool for a printer.

Primary Update Components (U1). If a data element is declared as a U1 primary up-date component, it will always be assigned by the dispatcher to a primary work process where it will be given high priority. Primary components take preference over secondary components.

Primary update components are usually time-critical control data elements which must be recorded in the database as soon as possible. Seat reservations and changes to the records of material available for immediate production are examples.

The primary components of different log records may be assigned to different update processes and be updated concurrently.

Secondary Update Components (U2). The secondary components in a log record of a transaction have to wait until all the primary components have been processed. The secondary components can then be dealt with in any order, if necessary by different update processes, perhaps running on different computers.

U2 secondary components will carry the data for results and statistical returns which do not need to be updated immediately. The dispatcher will assign them in work packets for the work processes as these resources become available.

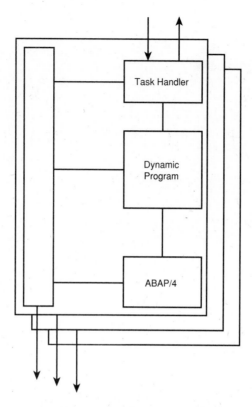

Fig. 3.8 One or more work processes specialize in updating the database.

Error States During Updating. The dialog process under control of the dynamic programs will have caught errors such as values outside the permitted range before the transaction is accepted from the user. Problems in the updating process are more likely to occur for technical reasons such as the overflow of a file or database buffer. These error conditions have to be dealt with by the system administrator to whom they will be routed automatically.

Data Consistency. If a technical error should occur during database updating, it cannot be corrected by the user. Any changes that have already been proposed by the update component will be rejected and the entire update component will be refused.

If the component refused is a U1 primary component, then all the associated primary components in the same log record will be reversed and the whole of the log record will be excluded from the update process.

By contrast, if a U2 secondary update component is found to be unacceptable, only that component is blocked.

Notification of Rejected Database Updates. A rejected update component will be assigned an identifier which will generate a standard message for automatic transmission to the user whose dialog gave rise to the faulty log or whose update was rejected for some other reason.

This message will be processed by the SAPmail component of SAPoffice and can be sent to any user of a SAP application that has the mail facility enabled.

Multiprocessor Environments

The inherent client/server design of the R/3 system lends itself to the employment of multiprocessors. Different work processes are able to be run on separate processors, and on processors of different types. The development of hardware and operating systems can provide enhancements to the operation of the R/3 system without the need for re-programming or extensive reconfiguring.

System Management

If the backbone and nerve center of your organization is an R/3 application, then you will need and expect continuous operation, perhaps over a wide geographical complex working 24 hours a day. The CCMS-Computing Center Management System is discussed in Chapter 11.

In particular, you will expect the system to do much of its work in the form of background processes from which you can demand reports at any time and in any convenient format. There are several different types of work to be done in the background, and each has been given a system designed to optimize the activities.

Dialog-Free Background Processing

With a user in the loop, the R/3 system will be using the online dialog programs to call for input and check its validity before submitting it for further processing. Background processes frequently make use of the same programs that control the dialogs. Any number of background processes can be executed in parallel with the online dialogs.

Spooling Control

The scope of spooling techniques includes all forms of buffered relay of information to media such as printers and fax devices. Many computers may be involved.

It is usual to designate one computer as the spool server through which all spooling jobs should be routed to and from the spooling systems of the individual computers. If a new device is added to the network, it has to be defined only once to the server.

A central file is designated TEMSE, Temporary Sequential file, to buffer the information to be output to the spooling mechanism. For each TEMSE data set, a separate order contains detailed instructions which include the logical name of the destination printer or other device.

Enqueue Central Lock Management

The locking mechanisms of many relational database systems are not adequate to control complex business data objects. To meet this need for controlling access from many users and applications to a complex data object, the parts of which may be distributed among any number of relational tables, the R/3 system uses an internal central lock manager installed on one of the database servers or on one of the application servers.

When a transaction is made up of several dialog steps, the dispatcher may assign them to different work processes. It is essential that no changes are made to any data object which has been locked until all the dialog steps have been completed. The locks assigned have to be transferred when work processes are changed.

If a database operation is to be uncoupled from a dialog process, it is also essential that certain data elements are not changed by any other application in the interim period between the dialog operations and the consequent database updates. For example, an order accepted on the basis of material in stock will rely on that material still being available when the database is subsequently updated to mark it as reserved for the specific order. Some other ordering system cannot be allowed to reserve the same material in the interim.

What the R/3 system does is alert the user if there is going to be a potential competition for access to the same record. The second request is refused until the first is satisfied.

When the log record generated by the dialog has been used to update the database, the update program automatically removes all the locks that have been put in place during the transaction.

Memory Management

Two types of main memory are distinguished:

- Reserved main memory areas exclusively at the disposal of a particular work process

- Shared main memory areas used jointly by all work processes

The reserved areas are used to store mode-specific data that needs to be retained for longer than a single work step. Prior to R/3 Release 3.0, two areas are distinguished by the use to which they are put: roll and paging.

Roll Area of Reserved Memory. Data that has to be made available to a work process automatically at the beginning of a dialog step is rolled into a reserved area of memory. At the end of the dialog step this data is rolled out to be returned to the database if necessary. The memory released is then available for other processes.

The following types of information illustrate the use of the roll area of memory reserved for the exclusive use of a specific work process while it is active:

- Data specific to the particular user including access privileges and identification

- Entry data previously collected by steps of the dialog that have already been completed

- Management information that will be required by the two processors for ABAP/4 and dynpro activities

Paging Area of Reserved Memory. The paging areas of reserved memory can be used by applications to store extensive collections of data which may vary greatly in length. The paging areas are accordingly organized into segments which are assigned to a work process when they are needed and withdrawn when they are needed elsewhere.

Managing the Roll and Page Memories. When each processing step is complete, the contents of the reserved roll and paging areas are buffered in two shared memory pools.

The shared memory areas are used as buffers for database, program, and table operations.

Both pools are within the system's virtual address space, and the memory manager can coordinate external paging through the operating system and internal paging through the dispatcher.

Extended Memory Management and R/3 User Session Contexts

R/3 Release 3.0 introduced an extended memory capability which permits a more intensive use of virtual memory. Reservations for roll and paging areas are no longer necessary and are replaced by the R/3 User Session Context system.

User Context Switching. When a work process is conducting activities as part of a step in a user dialog, it needs ready access to a set of data elements. These elements are the user session context.

If another work process is assigned to the next step in the dialog, the information now in some or all of the data elements of the first user session context will have to be made available to the second work process. The second user session context may also require additional information.

Prior to Release 3.0, the transfer of user session context information was effected by the roll-in, roll-out method of copying information. This occupied time and system resources to a considerable degree.

From Release 3.0, the data needed by subsequent user session contexts is accessed, not by copying, but by mapping. The information transferred to the subsequent step of a dialog is not the actual data, but a set of pointers which indicate where that data can be found. Thus a very complex data structure can be addressed or mapped for use by a work process by the transfer of a simple mapping pointer message.

Where data swapping is required, it is handled by the operating system.

The effects of the change from copying to mapping in this context are expected to be a much faster response time and, in certain installations, the possibility of handling larger loads without adding additional application servers.

Developments in virtual memory made possible by 64-bit architecture are expected to extend the benefits of the mapping concept.

Open Interfaces to Third-Party Products

Three types of interface have been differentiated:

- Collectors of data about the operating system performance, the database, and the network

- Service interfaces to supervise backup, recovery, spooling, and security

- Management interfaces for handling messages and events to do with application monitoring and control

These systems are discussed in Chapter 27, "Understanding the OSS-Online Service System."

Database Services

The design philosophy of R/3 is based on the open system concept which stipulates that communications to and from an open system should be restricted only by the demands of the standards in force.

The standard adopted language for the definition of data and for its manipulation is the SQL, Structured Query Language.

Any database that can interface according to this standard can be utilized by the R/3 system without the user needing to be aware of the detailed mechanisms of the database server. New products can be utilized as they become available without discarding the old and reprogramming the system.

However, not all database manufacturers offer the same range of SQL functions. The ABAP/4 Development Workbench, which is used to write all SAP R/3 business programs, has adopted two SQL standards: Open and Native.

Open SQL
ABAP/4 Open SQL is an extension of the ABAP/4 language which ensures the success of any application which accesses a database using only the functions of the Open SQL. Any database which supports this set of functions can be used by an R/3 system.

Native SQL
Many vendors of database systems have enhanced their products by the addition of functions that are outside the set specified by the Open SQL standard. These improved functions cannot be utilized by a system limited to the Open SQL standard.

ABAP/4 Native SQL can call the enhanced functions of a specific database system if all calls are encapsulated in a module specific to that database system. The module must also recognize the calls made in ABAP/4 Native SQL and respond to them by initiating the database commands specific to the particular system which will initiate the enhanced functions.

New database systems can be utilized by R/3 if the calling modules use ABAP/4 Native SQL and if the specific database system includes the special module to interpret the Native SQL commands.

SQL Set Operations
One of the most useful facilities of the Structured Query Language is its ability to recognize logical set operations and use them to manipulate sets of records such as arrays. This ability has a considerable effect in accelerating network communications in client/server architectures.

Optimized SQL Instructions

If you are seeking a very small number of records from a database, it may take more effort to prepare an optimum search strategy than to seek the result directly. However, if the data volumes are large and diverse, then there may be an advantage in using optimized SQL instructions.

Database vendors offer a range from optimized instructions in fixed agendas to dynamic buffering of optimized instructions.

The R/3 approach is to encapsulate database-specific functions in a system interface that obviates the need for applications programmers to construct their own for each database.

Multiple Database Access

Database vendors usually offer a range of gateways and transparent distribution mechanisms which can be used by R/3 to access these sources.

Open Data

The concept of an open database includes the notion that all data is stored in tables which are apparently ready to be instantly inspected and used without any need for complex data retrieval instructions in a specific language peculiar to the one vendor.

There are at least two routes to achieving this facility: building a specific interface; using a standardized interface such as the ODBC, Open Database Communication interface.

However, it is not enough for a system to be able to locate a specific data element in different types of database. It is also necessary for the user to be able to work out what that data means.

Semantic openness refers to the notion that users can locate the data tables and elements that hold the information they need: data that will have the proper meaning when it is placed in the context of interest.

The SAP Enterprise Data Model

The intention of the Enterprise Data Model is to enable the user of a database network to assemble the data relevant to that enterprise and to attach the correct interpretation to it.

This topic is discussed in Chapter 10, "The Open Information Warehouse and Enterprise Data Models."

Client Caching

The purpose of using client caches to buffer communications with databases is to optimize client/server operations. Every application server has an installed database service as part of the R/3 runtime environment. Client caches are located in main memory and hold the data most frequently used by that application. This has the effect of reducing network traffic and the load on the database server. Typical contents of a client cache include such information as:

- ABAP/4 programs

- Dynpros

- Information from the ABAP/4 data dictionary

- Business parameters which usually remain unchanged in a running system

Cache Content. The exact furnish of a client cache is decided on the basis of the client company usage profile. The cache is managed by the R/3 runtime system database services and therefore individual applications need only read from the cache buffers, they do not have to be concerned with their management. When a change is made to any data element in the client cache, the message servers will respond immediately by promulgating the update to the buffers of all the other applications.

Dynamic Management of Client Caches. When a client/server network is first installed and configured, it is not necessary to specify which application functions should be installed on which application servers. The first time a transaction is called, the corresponding module pool of programs is dynamically loaded from the database into the cache buffer of the next available application server, and so this module pool is available to all users of this server.

The cache is maintained under the control of a "least recently used" LRU condition which ensures that the memory is used to best effect.

Distributed Applications

It is inevitable in a client/server environment that can call upon a very large library of standard business functions and a correspondingly-extensive system of databases, that large amounts of data will transfer between the distributed applications and their supporting servers. Efficient mechanisms have been developed to do this: and they have to operate without the personal intervention of any user.

Dialog-Free Data Input to R/3

Probably the first large parcel of information to be input to your R/3 system without the intervention of a dialog with the user will be the legacy records of your business as it was before the R/3 system went live.

Although a user need not be involved, the R/3 system will accept mass imports of data as if they were generated by a series of transactions. Therefore the system will perform all the checks and updates it needs in order to ensure that the data is consistent and properly stored in the efficient data structures of the R/3 records. Exactly the same ABAP/4 programs will be active as when the data is entered by a user.

BDC, Batch Data Communications, or batch input, is a standard system that works along the same lines. The effect is to simulate a normal user dialog. The system automatically supplies the data for what would be user display screens from a special dataset and any error situations occurring during the BDC session are logged.

The BDC dataset is created by a specific program written, perhaps in a language such as C, to accept the incoming data and store it in appropriate data formats selected from the standard data structures which have been declared in the ABAP/4 Data Dictionary. This ensures that the new data will be recognized by all the R/3 applications and can be used by them when needed.

The preferred method of conditioning incoming data is to use a special ABAP/4 database interface which makes use of ABAP/4 Native SQL to access the legacy database.

Electronic Data Interchange Methods

When your company needs to exchange data with a business partner who is not fully integrated in your R/3 system, and who may be using hardware and software which is not directly compatible with it, the R/3 open EDI interface can be used to exchange normal business documents and messages with specialized EDI subsystems from a variety of vendors.

R/3 offers two methods for handling EDI:

- Direct interface with the relevant R/3 application
- Messages passed for manual handling

IDOC Intermediate EDI Documents. The international standards EDIFACT and ANSI X12 are used to create fields for application data in IDOC Intermediate Documents which also provide encoded fields using ISO codes for data such as units of measurement.

Users can define how they want EDI to be applied. For instance, a user can be informed by e-mail, and certain situations can be monitored so that manual intervention can be mandated under specified conditions.

ALE Application Link Enabling. The IDO intermediate document method is exercised in the ALE concept which is designed to allow an R/3 system to grow by interacting with other systems through asynchronous links which exchange documents that carry messages and application data set out according to predefined business rules.

The ALE architecture is discussed in Chapter 8, "Continuous Business Development."

Relationships with Production Technical Subsystems

Two elements are required to link R/3 with a production-related technical subsystem:

- A component of R/3
- A SAP component installed in the technical subsystem to perform the functions of "transceiver," which entails interpreting the output of a control or monitoring device and transmitting to it a signal to initiate some action, such as to reset a recording instrument or open a valve

The two components are linked by standard communications channels which are predefined in the R/3 element. Conversations with technical subsystems are always controlled by R/3 which initiates and uncouples the linkage when it is no longer active. It ensures that the data read from the R/3 database and written to the technical subsystem interface is error-free and complete.

TCP/IP can be used to establish a link through other computers using the Internet Protocol. The flow of data can also be effected using CPI-C.

Distributed Satellite Systems

The principle of establishing satellite systems that can operate locally and also integrate fully with a central R/2 or R/3 system offers the following advantages:

- The individual local systems can be implemented so as to make best use of the equipment and other resources available.

- The local system may be able to take advantage of low-cost computing power.

- By using SAP standard interfaces, the satellites do not have to be SAP systems or R/3 applications; they may be legacy systems already fully operational and responsible for storing specialized data.

- The local system can run without continuous reference to the central host system which is thereby relieved of some workload which can be scheduled for more convenient times.

Applications as Satellites

The following applications illustrate the type of system that has been successfully operated in the satellite manner:

- DASS production control station

- EIS-Executive Information System

- Treasury Workstation

- Components of the HR-Human Resources Management System

- LVS-Warehouse Management System

The international operation of distributed applications is discussed in Chapter 9, "Worldwide Business Computing Systems."

Reliability and Security

An R/3 implementation will be in a critical role at the center of the management focus of your company. The applications integrated with the R/3 system must be available to the users and must be reliable. The functions in all the applications must work correctly. The data needed must be available when required.

In addition, the integrity of the data must be absolute.

The confidentiality of the data and the applications must be strictly maintained by a structure of authorizations. No data or software code must be altered or corrupted, either intentionally or by accident.

Functionality of the Software

The first consideration when assessing the ability of a piece of software to do the job intended, completely and exclusively, must be the methods used to design and build it.

However extensive the testing of software, it is unlikely that all problem situations will be encountered, and so there must be a degree of doubt as to the absolute reliability of the package. This degree of uncertainty can be made as small as desired by extending the scope of the prerelease testing. Many legacy computer programs have generated maintenance expenses many times their development cost because they were not fully specified in the first instance and not thoroughly elaborated at the design stage. Several chapters of this volume are devoted to the SAP tools for designing and developing reliable and efficient programs.

Security Levels and Confidentiality

The network of R/3 system and applications can be seen to comprise several levels or aspects at which the security of the data and the software must be addressed:

- Desktop presentation system level

- Application level

- Database level

- Operating system level

- Network level

The SAP approach to managing the security of a complex system across all these levels is to establish a set of internal and external security services:

- R/3 internal security services, which concern the desktop systems, application servers, database servers, and network communications at the application level

- Database security services, which are provided by database computer

- System security services, which are assisted by the ease with which the R/3 system can be reconfigured without loss of services, should any subsystem have to come offline

- Network security services

Reliability and Availability Through Support

The CCMS-Computing Center Management System, which is described in Chapter 11, operates a procedure of monitoring, controlling, and checking which covers the applications level R/3 activities, the database activities, the operating systems, and the network.

The SAPGUI-Graphical User Interface maintains a system log at the desktop level. There is remote support at this level by the OSS-Online Service System which is discussed in Chapter 27. Support is available online separately at each of these levels:

- Applications level
- Database level
- Operating system level
- Network level

From Here...

This chapter has noted the technical system components from which SAP systems may be built and in particular the ways in which such systems can be extended, not only toward existing systems which provide valuable data and services, but also toward systems which may become available in the future.

- The names of the modules are in Chapter 4, "Architecture."

- Selecting SAP programs is discussed in Chapter 5, "The R/3 Reference Model."

- Chapter 6, "Tool-Supported Optimization with the R/3 Analyzer," introduces SAP system design.

- Chapter 7, "R/3 Customizing," discusses the process of applying a suite of SAP tools to tailor R/3 to your company precisely.

- Business Process Reengineering is what companies have to do to stay alive. Chapter 8, "Continuous Business Development," tells more.

- System Management is discussed in Chapter 11, "A Computing Center Management System," and in Chapter 27, "Understanding the OSS-Online Service System."

- Chapter 28, "ABAP/4 Program Development with the R/3 Workbench," describes how new programs are built.

- R/3 Workflow Management is described in Chapter 30, "R/3 Business Workflow Management." It is a tool and a concept for making best use of the resources you have.

II

Technical Background

Chapter 4

Architecture

To ensure the success and efficient implementation of SAP systems, a comprehensive suite of mature standard business applications is available for introduction and customizing. Under the guidance of sophisticated tools, a procedure is provided for establishing an accurate model of the existing system and elaborating the target concept system. There are tools to support an efficient process of design to effect the transition.

In cases where a standard business function has not been developed, a sophisticated programming language is available to create bespoke programs that can be fully integrated with the standard SAP systems.

It is the intention of the SAP organization to maintain and enhance the reputation of the R/2 and R/3 systems with respect to the following objectives:

■ Provide a complete infrastructure for corporate information processing

■ Maintain a comprehensive repertoire of standard business functions that can be combined to model a wide range of business processes

■ Ensure that all SAP systems are usable worldwide

■ Retain a thoroughgoing open policy with respect to data access and functionality

■ Support distributed applications and interfaces to non-SAP systems.

A Method and a Means to Implement It

The extensive range of SAP standard software modules allows any model of business flow to be engineered. The precise details of each customized installation will be set up as the application programs are installed, configured, and customized.

This chapter explores the underlying software architecture that is needed to meet the requirement for efficient programming without compromising the speed and efficiency of implementation:

■ What the essential advantages are of the SAP concept as it has been elaborated in the R/3 system.

■ How computer programs can be written before the software developers have seen my business.

■ My business is special. Nobody will have written a program for it.

The SAP R/3 Applications

All R/3 installations include a set of components that form the core of the system. This set is referred to as the R/3 BASIS or the R/3 standard system. R/3 BASIS provides you with the tools to build a suite of integrated programs that can be fitted exactly to the requirements of your company and changed as your company develops.

A SAP R/3 application or module is a set of programs that has been designed for a specific type of business data processing. Each application is fully integrated with the R/3 BASIS. This allows each application to communicate with any other application.

Some application modules depend on other applications. For example, the CO-Controlling module depends on the FI-Financial Accounting module. Some of the components of a module may be optional. Some of the functions within a component may be optional. As a result of this flexibility, each R/3 installation may be built to fit exactly the unique requirements of the client company.

An installation must include the R/3 Basis and will usually include one of the applications of which the FI-Financial Accounting module is the obvious choice.

The SAP system of standard business programs is being developed in a number of directions. A function within a component may be elaborated so as to become a complex module. For example, the requirements of enterprise controlling can be met by the components of the CO-Controlling module. The EC-Enterprise Controlling product is available as a separate module and includes functions not available in the CO-Controlling module.

Another direction of development is to provide extra integrating functions that interact with a group of application modules. For example, the LO-Logistics General module is designed to provide integrating functions for the following applications:

- SD-Sales and Distribution
- PP-Production Planning
- MM-Materials Management
- PM-Plant Maintenance
- QM-Quality Management

A further direction of development of the SAP product range has occurred where there are many companies in a particular sector of business that share a specialized requirement. In such circumstances, a SAP partner company may develop a specialized enhancement of the R/3 system that may be marketed as an "Industry Solution."

As a result of these types of evolution, the title of an application or a component may be changed so as to reflect the change of focus.

The following application modules are discussed in separate chapters:

- FI-Financial Accounting

- CO-Controlling

- EC-Enterprise Controlling

- TR-Treasury Management

- PS-Project System

- PP-Production Planning

- PP-PI Production Planning for the Process Industries

- PM-Plant Maintenance

- SD-Sales and Distribution

- HR-Human Resources

- MM-Materials Management

Each application addresses a main sector of business activity, ranging from financial accounting to human resources. Under each application are grouped the modules most likely to be associated with the title of the application. However, the fully integrated design of all SAP standard business programs allows great flexibility in the assembly of modules to form a specific implementation. For example: If you are installing the SD and FI modules and you wish to pay your salespeople bonuses through the R/3 system, you may be required to implement portions of HR as well.

Every implementation will need a SAP R/3 Basis module that provides the elements of the SAP R/3 runtime system. It includes the fundamental tools and functions of the R/3 Data Dictionary, the SAP R/3 Reference Model, the ABAP/4 Development Workbench, and R/3 Customizing component.

When designing an implementation, the R/3 Reference Model is used to select which module components will be needed in the target system. This process is described in Chapter 5, "The R/3 Reference Model," Chapter 6, "Tool-Supported Optimization with the R/3 Analyzer," and Chapter 7, "R/3 Customizing." Chapter 7 discusses the customizing process, which completes the installation process by making the integrated system exactly fit the host company.

Customizing Standard Software. SAP offers standard software that may not be altered by the business user. What can, and usually must, be customized to suit the individual company is the type of data held in the computer system and type of processing to which it is subjected. It is also necessary to arrange for the flow of data processing to match the needs of the particular company procedures.

Application Integration. SAP software is available in a range of integrated application systems that allow the software to match the needs of the user community. For example, the Real Time Systems SAP R/2 and SAP R/3 are available with individual applications integrated so as to link the areas of company activity that are organizationally related, as follows:

- Production planning and control is integrated with technical data processing to offer controlled inventory management.

- Material requirements planning and procurement logistics are related to yield just-in-time supply.

- Sales information and operating results analysis come together in marketing planning.

System Identification

A SAP product is a suite of standard software made up of individual programs that have been written to carry out computing tasks in the most efficient manner possible. None of these programs can be altered in any fundamental way by the user without the approval of SAP. The OSS-Online Service System will issue a code module for any modification that may be required to accommodate errors remaining in the released version of a program.

SAP R/2 is a system for mainframes. The SAP R/3 System for open system architecture has allowed medium-sized companies and affiliates of corporations to take advantage of the highly integrated SAP software. It applies the client/server concept across multiple levels.

Release and Version Identification

The system identification of R/2 or R/3 is supplemented by the identification of the Release and Version, followed in some instances by an identification of the latest correction set. For example, R/2 4.3B signifies the R/2 System Release 4 at Development Level 3 that has been updated with corrections set B. The discussions in this volume are based on the provisional function list for System R/3 Release 3.0 Version 6.1.

Customizing

These standard programs are designed to be totally reliable and to work together as a coordinated suite of modules.

By itself, a SAP program will not be very friendly to an individual user. It will not know what sort of business is to be conducted or exactly how the user company wants to invoice and conduct other interactions with its customers. If a SAP implementation is to look and behave as if it really understands the company it is working for, it will have to be configured and customized.

Naturally, the SAP software expects to be told how to behave in a specific company and has standard routines which help the company experts to set out what has to be done in a format that SAP can accept. The experts who do this are referred to as Applications Programmers or Applications Developers.

For example, your company may customize a SAP application so that it will insist that Sales Contacts will be recorded as named individuals, with a title and preferred salutation, a job title, an informal first name, and then all the communications and address information divided into fields of characters. If a potential sales prospect telephones your company, the SAP application will be able to fetch a screen that prompts the user to enter this information.

When the user signifies to the system the type of transaction that is to be conducted, a sales inquiry for instance, there may be certain information that is essential, some that is displayed to prompt the user, and some information that is required by the system but need not be shown on the screen. The inquiry number and department are examples of information that the system can generate if it has been configured to do so. You can decide during customizing how much to display on the screen, but the system will insist on the mandatory information being entered before the transaction can be processed.

There is a standard program in SAP for every conceivable business operation. The art and skill of the application programmer is to make the work of the future users as easy and error-free as possible by giving the right operating instructions to these standard programs.

The ABAP/4 Data Dictionary

The Data Dictionary is a collection of data objects such as tables, domain definitions, field specifications, screen formats, and report specifications, which are used in the standard business programs written in the ABAP/4 programming language.

The purpose of the data dictionary is to ensure that SAP standard software always gets the data in a format it is designed to process. All communications to and from a SAP system will utilize the standard formats set out in the data dictionary.

The SAP Data Dictionary specifies over 7,000 domains which are associated with over 80,000 fields and arranged in over 4,000 tables.

Data Storage Structures

Data organization is of vital importance to a system that is specialized to process it, and a SAP program is no exception. There is a consistent data storage policy and terminology throughout the SAP products.

Fields. A field is a string of characters. A character is a letter, numeral, or symbol that can be generated by the keyboard and recognized by the computer operating system. The space character is included.

A text object is a string of characters that usually stay together, such as a ZIP code or fax number.

A single character, a text object, and a field are examples of data elements. Information is recorded in a character field from which the user display element is derived. A field may comprise just a single character, or it may hold more characters than the space on the screen would suggest. Characters previously entered may scroll off to make room for new. The application developer can specify how many characters of a field are to be displayed.

Domains. In order to reduce the possibility of data error, a field used in a SAP program will usually be subject to rules that constrain the scope of its contents. A date field has to be given characters that can be interpreted as a valid calendar date. A Yes/No field will admit only one of the set of entries that follows:

{Y, N, y, n, Yes, No, YES, NO, blank}

A field designated for the identification code of a permitted user will refuse to accept anything that is not on the list of permitted user codes.

The set of permissible entries for a particular field is described as the *domain* of that field. Several fields may have the same domain if they are all allowed to have the same set of attributes, entries, or values.

A domain can identify one value as the default which is to be offered to the user for confirmation or amendment. The default value can be the one previously chosen by this user.

If an operator attempts to enter data into a field that is not acceptable to its domain, the entry will be refused and a specific error message offered by way of explanation.

The operator may be able to ask for help in the form of a list of the values permitted in a domain. One of these can be selected, and the system will enter it in the field and show it on the display. It will be a member of the permitted entries defined by the domain— but it can be rejected as a valid entry for some other reason.

Data Elements of Data Objects. Fields can be grouped together as data elements and handled as a unitary data object. For example, a customer name, address, and phone number are data elements in a data object that represents this customer in the system.

The user can choose which data elements are to be displayed when a particular data object has been selected.

Records. A record is a set of fields. In most cases, the record is a set of data objects that can be accessed by their identification codes. The record can usually be selected by specifying one or more of its constituent data objects. For example, you can select the records of all customers and group them by ZIP code.

Tables. A table is a named set of fields that can be displayed in the rectangular format of rows and columns. There may be only one row or one column. Where a table may have any number of rows, each row can also be referred to as a record. The names of the columns may correspond to fields of the records.

File names, text objects, and system parameters are examples of data stored in SAP tables. Each table comprises one or more fields. A simple example is a list of codes, each with a brief description of what the code signifies. In this case, a line of the table, a record, comprises two fields, one with a domain of, say, three alphanumeric characters, the other with, say, thirty characters for descriptive or explanatory matter.

Such a record can be used like this: The screen can be set to display the description as confirmation when the user selects or enters a valid code. The user may realize that the wrong code has been entered when the description is displayed. If the table does not contain the code entered, an error message will be displayed and the system will wait for a correction.

Files. A file is a named set of records. It can be of unspecified length. It can also be free of any formatting constraints so that it will accept any input. In such instances, however, there will have to be some method of deciding how the entries in the file are to be interpreted when the time comes to attribute meaning to the data.

Master Data and Transaction Data. There are two types of data, which can be differentiated by their functional purpose:

- **Master data** that seldom changes, such as customer or vendor details and material technical records or part numbers
- **Transaction data** that the system uses during data processing, such as when receiving goods or when changing something in a master data record

Both types of data must conform to the specifications of the data dictionary.

Online Transaction Processing. A transaction is being processed online when the system will wait for the user or operator to enter the next data object required.

Batch Transaction Processing. Batch transaction processing can take place when all the information required has been previously arranged on a file so that the system does not have to wait for the operator to enter each data element. A batch processing job can be scheduled to take place in the background as and when computing capacity is available, or it can be scheduled for a date and time. This time can be when spare capacity is likely to be available, or it can be at regular intervals so that transactions are not kept waiting. Backing up part of the database can be a timed batch job.

Creating New Data Objects

Files and text objects can be created by an application programmer or by a user, provided they conform to the SAP Data Dictionary. For example, new customer files must replicate the structure and domains of the existing customer files. The normal result of creating a new file will include adding a record to a table that lists similar files.

Database

A database is a collection of files shared by multiple applications. A SAP system can operate on more than one database. The collection of files can be managed by a database system on another computer. The Database system refers to the management of any elements of online or batch transactions that entail making changes to the database. This can include directing the database management system to conduct a search and report its findings. Certainly, such applications as MM-Materials Management, PP-Production Planning, and FI-Financial Accounting will demand changes to the database.

The BASIS System

The SAP software provides methods for controlling the widest range of hardware. Each item of equipment will have an operating system, which may be as simple as an On/Off signal or as complicated as a multitasking computer operating system.

The SAP BASIS System exercises control over whatever hardware configuration is in use. In particular, it is responsible for the SAP R/3 Runtime System. Chapter 3, "System Architecture and Distributed Applications," is a source for more information on the BASIS system.

Dynpros

A mask is a screen used to enter or view data. An entry field is a space on a mask into which the user can enter data. A series of such screen masks, together with the associated processing logic, can be treated as a unit. The SAP name for such a unit is "dynamic program" or "dynpro." A dialog program is a series of transaction steps, each of which is controlled by a dynpro, which can be used to validate data being entered by a user or by a communication channel, in which case the error messages are stored on file rather than shown to the user.

System Parameters

A system parameter is a value in a field in a table that can be used to control how a standard SAP program is to operate for a specific application. The system parameter may control the type of processing or the flow of process or both. There is no other way of changing or customizing the behavior of a SAP standard program; it must be done by changing the value in one or more system parameter fields.

System parameters can be altered by an application programmer or by a user only within the constraints allowed by the SAP system version and release in use.

The Condition Technique

The SAP R/3 condition technique gets its name from the discipline of formal logic—in particular, from the conditional proposition form that can be expressed as follows:

> If {a certain set of conditions is in fact true}
>
> Then {certain other conditions will be true}

The logical if-then condition technique is used extensively in the SAP R/3 system to enable the computer to carry out specified actions automatically, if, and only if, the proper conditions have been satisfied by the necessary data.

Data Principles

The user of a business computer must expect to be presented with a combination of menus and data forms. The spaces on data forms may be awaiting entries from the operator, or they may have been filled by the system.

One of the keys to effective application design is a respect for data, as follows:

- Data that is obviously wrong should be corrected as soon as the error can be detected.

- Data that is apparently correct should be held in one place only, so that if changes have to be made they can be effective immediately wherever this information is used.

- If the data to be entered can be anticipated or has been gathered previously, the user should be shown the data and invited to confirm the entry rather than type it in again.

Review of SAP R/3 Software Architecture Advantages

The SAP architecture embraces a complete infrastructure of information processing from the finest detail of a business transaction up to the corporate level of enterprise controlling. The SAP R/3 system is based on a system of layers, each operating in a client/server manner, with interfaces as necessary to SAP R/2 systems and non-SAP systems. The international standards for open system interfaces are recognized. The SAP R/3 system is extremely portable across operating systems, databases, and presentation systems. Synchronous and asynchronous coupling between applications is supported.

Enterprise modeling is effected, with provision for rapid response to the changing needs of evolving organizations.

The combined effects of these various software and hardware provisions add up to a powerful system that provides for the future.

Scalability in Response to Demand

The multi-tier architecture based on the client/server paradigm allows fresh equipment to be installed at any level to follow the load profiles and the requirement for additional processing created by adding applications.

Portable Software

Software usually remains in use longer than hardware. SAP software is exceptionally portable across hardware and operating systems, and across database systems.

Interoperability with PC Applications

Object Linking and Embedding (OLE) interfaces are provided, and Remote Function Call (RFC) procedures allow the SAP systems to integrate both the data and the functions of the SAP R/3 system with those of PC applications and data sources.

Simple Customizing Without Programming

Not only do the SAP systems allow themselves to be readily adjusted to fit exactly into the business requirement, they are provided with customizing tools to ensure that this adaptation is carried out as easily and as accurately as possible without broaching the protected standard business software functions, which remain intact and efficiently integrated with the rest of the SAP systems.

New Software Development Is Integrated
The ABAP/4 business programming language is used for all SAP R/3 software. New functions can be developed in this language under the guidance of the ABAP/4 R/3 Workbench tool, which ensures that the resulting code is properly articulated with the rest of the standard software.

Ergonomic User Interface in Windows Format
The SAP Graphical User Interface has adopted the Windows conventions to make it readily operable by new users. Presentations of complex information and relationships are available in tabular list formats and graphical displays at the choice of the user, who can switch readily between formats. It is also standard for the user to be able to "drill down" to underlying data by selecting the graphical symbol of interest or its tabular list representation, and call for even more detailed displays by using the special function keys. There is immediate transfer of skills from previous Windows applications.

Components of the Main SAP R/3 Applications
The applications and their components are discussed in their appropriate chapters. The titles used in the provisional function list for System R/3 Release 3.0 Version 6.1 are presented here to illustrate the type and scope of the SAP R/3 system of integrated standard business software.

CA-Cross Application
The R/3 Cross Application area comprises a set of modules that can be used throughout the R/3 system.

- CA-BPT Business Process Technology
- CA-DM Document Management
- CA-CL Classification
- CA-CAD CAD Integration

R/3 Release 3.0 includes cross application components available in earlier releases and additional integrative modules that are coded without the "CA" prefix:

- SAF Office
- SAP Business Workflow
- R/3 Business Engineering Workbench, which includes the R/3 Reference Model and the R/3 Implementation Model
- R/3 Business Navigator, which includes the R/3 Process Model, the R/3 Data Model, and the R/3 Customizing system

- R/3 Analyzer, which is available online with the R/3 system or as a stand-alone PC-based system and is used to access the R/3 Reference Model

Two additional SAP products should be mentioned in the context of cross-application modules:

- OSS-Online Service System
- CCMS-Computing Center Management System

FI-Financial Accounting

- FI-GL General Ledger
- FI-AR Accounts Receivable
- FI-AP Accounts Payable
- FI-LC Legal Consolidation
- FI-SL Special Purpose Ledger

CO-Controlling

- CO-OM Overhead Cost Control
- CO-PC Product Cost Controlling
- CO-ABC Activity-Based Costing
- CO-PA Sales and Profitability Analysis
- CO-PRO Project Control

IM-Capital Investment Management

- IM-FA Tangible Fixed Assets
- IM-FI Financial Investments

EC-Enterprise Controlling

- EC-EIS Executive Information System
- EC-BP Business Planning
- EC-MC Management Consolidation
- EC-PCA Profit Center Accounting

TR-Treasury

- TR-TM Treasury Management
- TR-FM Funds Management
- TR-CM Cash Management

PS-Project System

- PS-BD Basic Data

- PS-OS Operational Structures

- PS-PLN Project Planning

- PS-APP Approval

- PS-EXE Project Execution/Integration

- PS-IS Information System

LO-Logistics General

- LO-LIS Logistics Information System

- LO-MD Master Data

- LO-PR Forecast

- LO-VC Variant Configuration

- LO-ECH Engineering Change Management

HR-Human Resources

The HR-Human Resources application has been developed to provide an integrated human resource management system by facilitating the use of the components of the PD-Personal Planning and Development module and the PA-Personnel Administration module.

- HR-PD Personal Planning and Development

  - PD-OM Organizational Management

  - PD-SCM Seminar and Convention Management

  - PD-PD Personnel Development

  - PD-WFP Workforce Planning

  - PD-RPL Room Reservations Planning

- HR-PA Personnel Administration

  - PA-EMP Employee Management

  - PA-BEN Benefits

  - PA-COM Compensation Administration

  - PA-APP Applicant Management

  - PA-TIM Time Management

  - PA-INW Incentive Wages

- PA-TRV Travel Expenses
- PA-PAY Payroll

PP-Production Planning

- PP-BD Basic Data
- PP-SOP Sales and Operations Planning
- PP-MP Master Planning
- PP-CRP Capacity Requirements Planning
- PP-MRP Material Requirements Planning
- PP-SFC Production Orders
- PP-PC Product Costing (which is CO-PC Product Cost Accounting)
- PP-KAB Kanban/Just-in-Time Production
- PP-REM Repetitive Manufacturing
- PP-ATO Assembly Orders
- PP-PI Production Planning for Process Industries
- PP-PDC Plant Data Collection
- PP-IS Information System

MM-Materials Management

- MM-MRP Material Requirements Planning
- MM-PUR Purchasing
- MM-IM Inventory Management
- MM-WM Warehouse Management
- MM-IV Invoice Verification
- MM-IS Information System
- MM-EDI Electronic Data Interchange

PM-Plant Maintenance

- PM-EQM Equipment and Technical Objects
- PM-PRM Preventive Maintenance
- PM-WOC Maintenance Order Management
- PM-PRO Maintenance Projects
- PM-SMA Service Management
- PM-IS Plant Maintenance Information System

Technical Background

II

QM-Quality Management

Although the quality management functions originated in the PP-Production Planning application, they are available as a separate module that can be integrated with any of the applications.

- QM-PT Planning Tools
- QM-IM Inspection Processing
- QM-QC Quality Control
- QM-CA Quality Certificates
- QM-QN Quality Notifications

SD-Sales and Distribution

- SD-MD Master Data
- SD-GF Basic Functions
- SD-SLS Sales
- SD-SHP Shipping
- SD-BIL Billing
- SD-CAS Sales Support
- SD-IS Information System
- SD-EDI Electronic Data Interchange

INT-International Development

- IN-APA Asian and Pacific Area
- IN-EUR Europe
- IN-NAM North America
- IN-AFM Africa/Middle East
- IN-SAM South America

IS-Industry Solutions

An IS-Industry Solution is an enhancement of the standard R/3 system that may include some or all of the components of any of the R/3 applications, according to the sector of industry for which it has been designed. The following are examples of Industry Solutions:

- IS-PS Public Sector
- IS-H Hospitals
- IS-B Banks
- IS-IS Real Estate Management

Future Developments in SAP Software

The SAP organization has always had a policy of continuous business development. The driving forces are the need for keeping up with the marketplace in product and requirement details and also with respect to the evolving legal obligations placed on companies with food or dangerous products in their inventories.

The need to prepare for natural human error and pernicious manipulations is no less urgent than in former times. Profit and business survival remain of interest. The software developments may be expected to follow the leads of the Industry Solution products, where some examples are given of specialized assemblies of modules targeted at a relatively narrow sector of industry.

The Internet as a news medium and presentation arena for SAP products can be accessed at the following address:

http://www.sap.com

The Internet as a medium for communications between business partners, customers, and suppliers is likely to develop on the basis of the EDI-Electronic Data Interchange components that are available in many of the current R/3 modules.

The EDI interface methodology uses a range of IDOC intermediate document types to exchange business documents between the SAP system and the EDI subsystem. These IDOC data objects can be developed by SAP or by the user organization, perhaps by adding a segment to a standard SAP IDOC type.

From Here...

This chapter has included discussions of some of the details of software architecture with an indication of how the range of SAP products has developed from modules serving individual business functions, such as sales and accounting, towards the concept of an integrated business data processing system that can provide computer support across a very wide spectrum of activities.

- How will I know whether my company needs to develop new software?

  The SAP R/3 Basis system includes the SAP R/3 Reference Model, which is a detailed specification of the standard business programs available. You can consult this model by using the SAP R/3 Analyzer described in Chapter 6, "Tool-Supported Optimization with the R/3 Analyzer."

- SAP Business Workflow Management—what is that?

  Workflow is a way to control how your work is directed through the resources at your disposal. SAP provides a powerful tool to set this up and run it for the benefit of your company.

- Hardware matters are introduced in Chapter 3, "System Architecture and Distributed Applications."

Technical Background

- Business process reengineering is discussed in Chapter 8, "Continuous Business Development."

- To manage a software development project using a SAP tool designed for this purpose, consult Chapter 16, "Understanding the PS-Project System Module."

Chapter 5

The R/3 Reference Model

The reference model is a data structure that contains a complete description of the R/3 system and the business functions therein. The model can be accessed in various ways and for various purposes. In particular, it can be used to simulate your business as it could be carried on if the SAP R/3 system were to be installed and configured to suit your particular circumstances. How the model is used to develop your business in an efficient manner is described in the chapter on Business Process Reengineering with the R/3 Analyzer. This chapter concentrates on the R/3 Reference Model, which is the basis of the R/3 Analyzer.

This chapter describes the model of the R/3 system, which is provided so that you may select the most appropriate SAP standard business functions in order to reengineer your business processes.

The Data Object Structure of the R/3 System

R/3 is object-oriented. The units that the SAP standard business functions are designed to handle are data objects that can be of any complexity. For example, a data object may comprise only an identification code number for the object and one field that contains the information of interest, a part number, for instance.

Such an object is likely to be much more useful if it is permanently associated with other objects, in this instance, the name of the part in each of the SAP supported languages, for example. The bundle of data elements comprising the part number, part name, and any other information needed about this part, is handled as a single object by the R/3 system. If you ask for this part by name or by number, the system will have available the rest of the information that goes to make up the data object. The user has control over which of the data elements shall appear on the display, but they are all there ready for immediate access.

In this chapter, you learn:

- How to actually use the R/3 Reference Model.

- How the model relates to the Software Architecture.

- What the difference is between a standard business function and one built for my company.

- About an EPC.

- About an event.

II

Technical Background

There is no limit to the complexity of a data object because the data elements may themselves be complex objects.

A purchase order is a data object. It will include many data elements in the header, and each of the order items will represent a complex data object. When the purchase order is entered, it becomes a document that will be posted to various processes that will examine it to see if it is carrying the information which will be recognized as an event to be taken as the trigger or signal for specific processing.

Every item of information that is processed by the R/3 system is treated as an object. A project plan is an object. A user password is an object. An arrow on a graph is an object.

An Enterprise Model for Reference

One class of data objects that is recognized by R/3 is the enterprise model. The enterprise may be a department or the entire company, and the enterprise model is a way of specifying how the information and material moves within the organization as it does business.

In order to help you specify the material and information flows of your company in a standard manner that can be used to develop the efficiency of your business, the SAP R/3 Reference Model is provided as part of the system. It is an information model that is stored in graphical form that can be displayed using a standard symbology.

The R/3 Reference Model contains all the common business process structures, linked in a totally integrated fashion that can be set to work without further adjustment. However, the standard R/3 Reference Model will probably include many functions and data structures that are not relevant to your organization. The process of Customizing is provided in the R/3 system to enable the system implementers to adjust the R/3 Reference Model until it exactly fits the needs and structure of the specific client organization.

When this match is complete, the model is referred to as an Enterprise Data Model.

This topic is also discussed in Chapter 10, "The Open Information Warehouse and Enterprise Data Models."

The Concept of an Event-Driven Process Chain

The components of the R/3 Reference Model, and any Enterprise Data Models derived from it, are event-driven process chains. The graphical representation of these models is designed to show which events lead to which activities.

The designers of the SAP R/3 system found that no other method of specifying the requirements of a standard business software system was as fruitful and as easy to comprehend as the event-driven process chain. Where did the event-driven process chain come from? Why is it so useful?

Three Basic Design Principles

If you are trying to write down what goes on in a workplace, or what has to be done to get a certain result, then you will ask yourself three types of questions. You may not think about these issues at the right time, but if you omit any of them, you will discover that the work is not going as well as you expected, and that there is something missing from your job descriptions for the people involved.

What Should Be Done? Perhaps it is obvious. Surely everyone knows that you should not be working at something if you do not know what has to be done. Yet there are people busy at work who have not stopped to think about the task they are tackling or the function they are supposed to be performing.

If you show someone performing the actions of a job without paying attention to what the purpose of the task is, then you may well raise a laugh. They are just going through the motions, without understanding.

Who Should Do Something? If you are looking at a team of people, a department, or company, perhaps, then the second question is also an obvious one. Which member of the team should be the one to begin the task. Who is on the lookout for an occasion to set the team to work? Who is ready to notice an event of importance to the team if one should occur?

Even if you are working by yourself, the question must still be answered. Is this a job for me, or should I do nothing and let somebody else do something?

In the representation of your enterprise, it is clearly a matter of some importance to identify which organizational unit is responsible for action in response to the significant events. And this responsibility is not just a matter of having someone to blame if something goes wrong. The organizational unit that is responsible for an activity will need to be provided with the tools, time, and energy resources to do it.

What Information Is Needed? In order to perform a function, the responsible organizational unit needs to know what the task is. How to carry out this task will be a question of certain knowledge or skill that can be called upon in the organizational unit. The necessary information for a task can be defined as an information object, a set of instructions together with the essential data, or an indication of where it can be found.

Some tasks are only performed by virtue of a human skill, which is not generally available. In such cases, the critical information must include a specification of who in the company could be called upon to provide this skill or enlist the aid of an outside provider.

The Historical Sequence of Information Models

Perhaps the oldest information model is the family tree. It shows who the parents are and, therefore, who is most likely to have most power and experience. This information model is not necessarily accurate. A child may be more capable than a parent or a grandparent.

The family tree may suggest how the people are grouped into families and thus into organizational units. A structure diagram that has a specified directionality, has arrows rather than plain lines, or has a definite up or down, before or after, which is in some way ordered. Such a structure may be drawn as a digraph, a directed graph.

The standard organization diagram is a digraph in which the ordering is from chief executive at the top to most junior worker at the bottom. Some companies may have a dozen layers of seniority; some have only two or three.

The organizational digraph may indicate who is responsible to whom. What it does not show is who does what or how it is done.

Models of Units in an Organization. The family tree digraph leads to the organizational chart in easy stages. Groups of work people are associated as departments and represented as boxes or nodes on the digraph. Head Office is responsible for Purchasing and Sales.

The trouble with a simple organizational unit model is that it shows, by the arcs or arrows, who is in charge, but not what anyone does. In particular, there is no indication of, for example, how a sales order may cause the generation of a purchase order to replace the stock or commission work for the sales order. There is no flow of material shown, and no indication of how information might flow. From looking at the organization chart, you could be led to believe that all information exchanges between Purchasing and Sales must be routed via Head Office. This is almost never the situation.

Task Models. A simple task model is a cooking recipe. Take the ingredients and carry out the cooking processes. If you see this in graphical form, it would have an input block and an output block, with an arrow from input to output. One worker may perform the function of converting the input to the output. All the skill of the cook, or the expertise of the production worker, is concealed by the arrow that links the input raw materials to the finished products.

Task models can get very complicated if there are many inputs and many outputs, including the finished product, some by-products and some wastes, for example. But these task models do not usually portray the fact that a great deal of knowledge and skill is needed for the inputs to be correctly and efficiently transformed into the outputs.

Information Models. The third type of formal model to be developed has to be a supplement to the others. It concentrates on the information needed to carry out a function.

How does the worker know which materials and tools to select? Where did he acquire the skills? What is he looking at, and what is he looking for, when he is monitoring the quality of his work?

Information is a difficult concept to define. If you know that a coin has two faces, and you know that it has fallen heads up, then you have acquired one bit of information, which your computer could record as one binary digit.

The menu is the troublesome part. How can you possibly choose what to order for dinner until you know what the menu offers? If there are eight possibilities, and you choose one, then the chef will have acquired three binary digits of information from you which will be valuable to him because it means that he need not cook seven of the dishes on the menu, at least not for you.

If your R/3 system can tell whether the document is a sales order or a purchase order, then this will be information that can be used to narrow down the possibilities for subsequent action.

The concept of information is not relevant unless you know the menu. The R/3 system can recognize only a large but limited number of document types. You can add to this list during customizing if you are prepared to tell the system how a new type of document is to be recognized, and what actions are to be taken when one is encountered.

A gardener may know the names of hundreds of plants: She may also be able to recognize them. She could carry out the task of walking through a garden and speaking aloud the names of most of the plants. She has a considerable amount of information. However, this does not mean she is a gardener capable of cultivating any of these plants.

The information model is good at specifying the size of the menu from which the skilled person can make a choice. The larger the possible menu of events that could occur, the greater the amount of information necessary to allocate the correct names.

Naming the parts is a good way to begin to acquire a skill, but it does not necessarily help you to do the right thing every time.

Event-Driven Process Chain Objects

If we are looking for some sort of analytical object as a standard building block for showing how a company does business, then the event-driven process chain is the prime candidate. One process may lead to another and so on down a chain which is complete only when the result is achieved. But a set of process chains that do not have precisely specified events that are their exclusive triggers are of no use. Each process chain must begin only when the specified event occurs. And, if that event does occur, then there must be no question as to whether the assigned process chain will begin or not. When the certain data elements in certain data objects are found to match the conditions laid down when defining the event that shall drive a chain, then that chain and only that chain will be initiated.

There is no limit to the complexity of an event-driven process chain because each of the processes in the chain may itself give rise to a complex data object that is able to take part in the initiation of other event-driven process chains.

The Relationship Between Stimulus Response Theory and Event-Driven Process Chain Methods

If you are teaching a person or an animal to do something that does not come naturally to them, something that is not in their instinctual repertoire or in the knowledge and skills they have learned previously, then you have to attend very carefully to the stimulus and the response.

Suppose you want the user to press key F1. You could get this to happen in several different ways:

> Take the user's finger and push it on the F1 key.
>
> Say to the user, "Press the F1 key."
>
> Say to the user, "Select PF1."

Have you taught the user anything useful? Perhaps the system will respond with a helpful message and the user will guess that the PF1 key may be the key to use if you need help. But not necessarily. The user may not associate what the system did with which key was pressed.

Try a different lesson. Say to the student user of the system something like this: "If you need help, and the screen is showing you a picture or other sign labeled HELP, then try pressing the key marked F1 to call the special programmed function labeled PF1."

This is not a very exciting lesson, but it does illustrate that we learn to do things, such as pressing a Help key, and we learn when this action is likely to be needed or appropriate.

For example, we could all press key F6 without difficulty: But would we all know whether that would be a good idea and would help us do what we are trying to do? The response of pressing a particular key is not much use to us if we have no idea when it should be carried out.

In the language of the psychologists, we have to associate a useful response with the stimulus for that response. If we have managed to do this on a reliable basis, we are said to have acquired an operant, a stimulus-response pair.

This may not seem very momentous, one stimulus triggering one response.

The clever part comes when we can tell the difference between stimuli that might otherwise be confused. We may have names or labels for many of the significant stimuli in our private world. Fire is a name that carries a warning. System Error 1492 is a name for something that seems to be important for the computer. What we can do if we see this on our screen is to ask somebody what to do about it. That, at least, is an appropriate response. One day we might learn a better one.

Many of the errors made by people and machines occur because the response was not quite right for the stimulus situation at the time. There could be two types of fault here:

The stimulus triggered the correct response, which was then executed badly—right but sloppy.

The response was executed perfectly, but there was a subtle difference in the stimulus situation that should have triggered quite a different response—beautiful but inappropriate.

S-R Chains

The stimulus-response model of the operant as a useful way of thinking about how people and machines carry out tasks can be extended to describe a sequence of actions.

The first stimulus is the signal to begin the task with the first response. As this response is carried out, it should create the stimulus situation that will trigger the next operant in the chain.

If the learning has been perfect, there will be no point where the person doing the task asks, "What do I do next?" Every action will serve as the trigger for the next. And with copious practice, the sequence will speed up and the task performer will be looking ahead and getting prepared for the steps ahead. With even more practice, the whole chain may rattle along without the performer paying it any conscious attention. We might say it had become instinctual. As soon as it had been given the go-ahead, the next conscious event would be the delivery of the finished result.

EPCs as Responses by the System to Events

The event driven process chain can be regarded as a sequence of actions that has been developed to provide a stable and appropriate response to the event which is its trigger. There is a simple idea here, but one that can be used to build reliable software.

The Data Attributes of an Event

In the language of SAP system design, the data object recognized as an event is able to store an unlimited amount of data. However, this data cannot be readily accessed unless it is recorded in a systematic manner and uniformly across all events.

The data fields of an event master record are clustered as Attributes. And each attribute cluster is assigned a set of standard data field titles, which can be extended and developed during customizing, if necessary.

Event Attribute One

The following fields are located in Attribute (1):

Name of the event

Identifier code

Synonymous names for this event, aliases

Full designation of the event that places it in the software context

Description or definition of the event

Author of the event specification

Origin of the event

Event Origin. The following data fields are available in the event master to indicate the originating source of the control and substantive information associated with the event:

Outside of company

In-house

Outside of system

Within system

System-interdependent

Event Attribute Two

Additional characteristics of the event are stored in Attribute (2) to specify the type of the event, the classification of the event in terms of its logical function, and the function of the event in the context of an event driven process chain.

Type of Event. The assembly of critical information that constitutes an event can be generated in one of three ways that serve to define the type of the event as follows:

Interactively generated event

Automatically generated event

Manually generated event

Classification of an Event. The status of an event as part of an event driven process chain is used to classify it:

Trigger, which specifies that the event is able to initiate an event driven process chain at any time if the specified data becomes critical

Secondary Condition, which indicates that this event is not itself a trigger but an intermediate or secondary criterion cluster of data that may have to be satisfied or consulted for an event driven process chain to reach its conclusion

State, which indicates that the event serves the purpose of holding the result of other processes that may then be used as required, perhaps by many other event driven process chains

Functional Purpose of an Event. In the context of an event driven process chain, the beginning and end items are clearly of especial importance because they constitute the occasions for input information and output results to be available to the rest of the system. Events are therefore categorized according to their function as follows:

Start event

Finish event

Start or finish event

Internal process event that may be subject to monitoring for special purposes, but that will not normally be apparent to the user of the system

Event Attribute Three

The third attribute cluster of an event carries the data concerned with time. It will be consulted by the system on a routine basis to determine whether the event has to be set to trigger the associated event driven process chain.

Time of Occurrence. The system will need to identify which events have been scheduled for a fixed time or a schedule of times. This attribute value can be Known or Unknown.

Frequency of Event. If the event is scheduled to recur, then the details will be recorded as follows:

Times per year

Times per month

Times per week

Times per day

The Data Attributes of a Function

The standard structure of the data associated with a function is to cluster the data elements as three attributes.

Function Attribute One

The following fields are located in Function Attribute One:

Name of the function

Identifier code

Synonymous names for this function, aliases

Full designation of the function that places it in the software context

Description or definition of the function

Author of the function specification

Source information

System attributes including the transaction code and the release level

Function Attribute Two

The way the function is used and its classification as a standard business program or a function written specifically for the customer is recorded in Function Attribute Two.

Functional Assignment. The assignment of a function in terms of its functional use is categorized as follows:

  Outside of company

  In-house

  Outside of system

  Within system

  Optional function

  Mandatory function

Classification of the Function. The system recognizes the following types of function by a code in the function master record:

  Standard system function

  Customer-specific additional system function

  External system function

Function Attribute Three

The third function attribute cluster is devoted to data concerning the processing type and frequency. There is also a record maintained in the function master of the time needed for the function to acquire the data needed to specify the task to be performed and the time needed to actually process the data to complete it. The system costs of processing are accumulated in this attribute.

Processing Type of the Function. The type of processing entailed by the function will determine the system resources to which it is assigned. The processing types are specified as follows:

  Interactive

  Automatic

  Manual

  Central

  Local

Frequency of Processing. The actual times of processing may be used to accumulate frequency data as follows:

  Times per year

  Times per month

  Times per week

  Times per day

Duration of Processing. The learning time is recorded as a moving average to indicate the time taken for the function to acquire all the data sources and documents that will be needed to perform the function.

The actual processing time is also recorded as a moving average of the time taken to process the data after it has been assembled from its sources.

Costs of processing. The costs of calling this function can be accumulated on a moving average basis and evaluated in financial terms or on the basis of system processing costs expressed in resource usage units.

The Data Attributes of a Process

A process taking part in an event driven process chain can be assigned a very large number of data elements. They are clustered into two attributes.

Process Attribute One

The following fields are located in Process Attribute One:

Name of the process

Identifier code

Synonymous names for this process, aliases

Full designation of the process that places it in the software context

Description or definition of the process

Author of the process specification

Process Assignment. A process can be assigned to a single organizational unit or to an entire system. The details are stored under the following headings:

Organizational unit

System assignment to application, module, transaction

Required input information

Generated output information

Start event identification

End event identification

Process links

Processing Changes. There will be changes in the organization in which a process is carried on. The details of these processing changes are recorded in the process master record under the following headings:

Organizations involved in the changes

Frequency with which the organization is changed

Systems and media affected by the changes

Frequency with which the system or medium is changed

Information Statistics. The information storage requirements generated by the operation of a process can be a source of major costs. These requirements are recorded on the process master in terms of the following groups:

Information storage within the system

Information storage outside the system

Information storage requirements that are not supported by information technology methods and equipment

Process Attribute Two

Additional information about the process is stored in the master in Attribute Cluster Two. The theme is processing statistics.

Duration of the Process. The following data objects are stored in the process master:

Learning time

Processing time

Transmission time

Wait time

Entry time

Output time

Process Quantity Structures. The process master stores data structures to record the quantities of material or information processed, and also the quantities transmitted.

Process Costs. The following process costs are cumulated:

Overall costs

Personnel costs

Machine costs

Material costs

Data Transmission. Statistics are recorded for the following classes of data transmission entailed by the process:

IT-supported, online

IT-supported, batch

Manual

Transmission Medium. The distribution of data transmission across the following media and methods is recorded for the process:

Network

Data processing list

Written documents and forms

Card file

Oral data transmission

Views of an Information Model

It is apparent from the complexity of the data attribute structures that there are very many data elements to be stored in the system. Consistency of data structure and usage is ensured by using, as a standard reference, a suite of data structures that are stored centrally in the SAP meta-database and retrieved by the SAP R/3 Analyzer.

From the point of view of the user, the system contains all the information that is available. What is more difficult to appreciate is the extent and variety of this information, and the infinite flexibility of the systems available to retrieve it.

The SAP approach is to offer the user five avenues by which the extensive SAP database may be approached. Each avenue of approach affords a different view of the data structures and their contents. The standard SAP object orientation is maintained throughout: It is essential to efficient internal program logic.

Because they all originate in the same database, these five views are dovetailed. They are overlapping partial views, each of which is logically consistent because of the shared basis and consistent use of data structures and processing disciplines.

Five Views of the R/3 Reference Model

The **Process View** interprets the R/3 Reference Model as an integrated network of event driven process chains and thus relates directly to the operation of your R/3 system.

The **Data View** sees the R/3 Reference Model as clusters of aggregated data structures that can be represented through the SAP R/3 Analyzer as data objects using their names and "header" data to navigate with the aid of graphical displays. These same data structures can also be viewed down to the detailed level that is required for in-house programming developments using the ABAP/4 programming language.

The **Information Flow** view concentrates on the necessary flow of information between event driven process chains. It can be used in the early stage of system design when the details of the functions have yet to be specified. In the information flow view, it is not necessary to say how or when the information is captured and transmitted.

The **Function View** provides a summary display or listing of the complete array of functions that are active in a specific implementation of the R/3 system.

II

Technical Background

The **Organization View** is used to show the semantic relationships between the various organizational units that you have chosen to represent your company as a functioning enterprise supported by the R/3 system. A master organization view is held in the R/3 system that depicts the organizational structure of the system itself so that you can compare your specific organizational structure with the master to check that the hierarchical relationships correspond. Should you wish to establish an organizational structure that cannot be modeled using the standard R/3 Reference Model components, there is provision to add to these modeling components during customizing.

These views are discussed in more detail in subsequent sections, beginning with the process view because of its emphasis on event driven process chain logic. But first, it is necessary to explicate the graphical symbology that is used for all SAP displays and views of the R/3 Reference Model.

The Formal Components of EPC Modeling

The aim of the Reference Model is to be precise about the events to which the R/3 system can and will respond, and about the actions that will take place as a consequence. To express this model entirely in the form of a spoken language would run the risk of losing much of this precision, not only in the process of translating the model for use in different countries of the world, but also in the interpretation by those who speak the language in which it is expressed. Each reader has a particular educational background that enables him or her to understand his or her native tongue by recognizing symbols that can be combined to become words or concept icons that can then be combined in groups to expressed actions, relationships, and ideas.

The computer will not take this vagueness. It must be told when a number is to be treated as an amount and also be told which currency is to be used, and so on. If the system is to issue a warning if a customer order will exceed the amount of credit allowed, then the system will have to know what this amount is, and which items in the order must be used to compute it.

So the system must work from defined events that it can recognize, and it must have the ability to carry out a series of processes, each of which may be a sequence which will be triggered or not according to precise conditions detected when specific events occur.

And to enable programmers and system managers, consultants, and heads of departments to communicate with precision, across national language barriers when necessary, there has to be a logically formal system of symbols and relationships for this purpose.

A convenient way of sharing ideas about this formal system of symbology is to present it in graphical format.

The exact format or style of the symbols is obviously not the critical factor, but the way they are used and interpreted do have to conform to the defined logic.

Event

The R/3 system defines an event as a set of values for which it has a predefined action that it will initiate if this set of values occurs. The location of these values in the records of the system is part of the definition of the event, and so are the specific amounts or other data elements that will be treated as significant if they occur in these defined locations.

For example, if the total amount on the sales order document that is being processed is going to be the cause of a warning message being sent to the operator, then the system must know that the credit limit for this customer is recorded in a specific field in the master data records for this customer. The system has been set to check all sales orders against available credit.

In logical language, this example situation can be expressed as follows:

> IF the current document is a sales order,
>
> AND IF this current customer has a credit limit,
>
> AND IF the value of the sales order total is greater than the value of the customer's credit limit,
>
> THEN issue a warning to the user who is entering the sales order.

The warning is an action that happens when the system recognizes a significant event. In this example, the event is made up of three components:

> The document being entered has to be a sales order.
>
> The customer has to be one subject to a credit limit.
>
> There has to be an arithmetic relationship between two numbers, namely the order total and the customer's credit limit.

The warning is an action that takes place because the appropriate triggering conditions have occurred and because the system has been provided with a warning function. This warning function will have several constituent processes that will probably include at least the following actions:

> The system will log the event and time stamp it to record the fact that this customer placed an order that exceeded his credit limit.
>
> The system will display a standard text that will include fields to receive the actual values, in this case, of the credit limit and the amount of the excess.
>
> There will be a suggestion or proposal to the operator concerning what should be done, if anything, to get authorization for the extra credit or block the order pending further investigation.

Although this is a very simple example, there are clearly many elements in the process chain that are driven by the event of a customer about to exceed his credit limit.

The Standard Symbol for an Event. The trigger for an event driven process chain is defined in terms of a set of specific data elements and the critical values or ranges of values that will generate consequent activities on the part of the system. Figure 5.1 shows the shape that is used to depict an event on charts of event driven process chains.

Fig. 5.1 Graphical symbol for an event.

Generated Event. Each of the activities in an event driven process chain will bring into being a set of logical conditions that may include the set of values that constitute the critical triggering event for another event driven process chain. This subsequent event is referred to as a generated event.

In our example, the logging of the over-credit event is triggered by a generated event that includes the result of the arithmetic comparison. If the difference is one way, the warning function is triggered; if it is in the other direction, the warning function is not triggered.

Function

In mathematical or logical terms, a function brings about a transformation from an initial state to a target state. For example, an inverse function could be defined as that which changes a plus sign (+) into a minus sign (–). It would also be expected to transform a minus sign (–) into a plus sign (+). Another example would be a currency conversion function.

The transformation effected by a function can be expressed in the conditional form. For example, the inverse function can be specified as follows:

If the sign is (+), then substitute the sign (–).

If the sign is (–), then substitute the sign (+).

In this example, the inverse function would be followed by a chain of other processes if it were called in an accounting situation. And it would be called only if one of certain events occurred that met the conditions for triggering it.

The purpose of a function is to do something. It is activated by one of a set of events, and it can operate on information gathered from any sources. Which items of data are processed can be determined by the function itself. Alternatively, the objects on which the function is going to work can be indicated or passed to it in the function call, which is triggered by the significant event.

The Standard Symbol for a Function. The symbol for a function is rectangular with rounded corners and may be connected by flow lines emanating from any convenient part of it. Figure 5.2 illustrates this symbol:

Fig. 5.2   Graphical symbol for a function.

Logical Operators

There has to be a convention for representing the fact that a process chain may only be driven by a particular set of circumstances. Three logical operators suffice: AND, XOR, and OR.

AND. The conjunction of events is shown by the AND symbol, which is a circle containing an inverted V shape. It is interpreted as meaning that all the inputs to the symbol have to be TRUE for the output to occur. Figure 5.3 shows the symbol for AND (Conjunction).

Fig 5.3   Graphical symbol for AND (Conjunction).

Exclusive OR (XOR). The exclusive OR (XOR) is interpreted as requiring one but not both of its inputs to be TRUE for the output to occur. Figure 5.4 shows the XOR symbol.

Fig. 5.4   Graphical symbol for Exclusive OR.

Either or Both (Don't Care). The Don't Care circled V symbol represents the situation where either of the inputs will suffice on its own, or both may be TRUE, to allow an output (see Figure 5.5).

Fig. 5.5   Graphical symbol for Either or Both (Don't Care).

II

Technical Background

Control Flow

Control flow may be a matter of time or sequence ordering. The dotted line with an arrowhead shows how one event depends on a function, or one function depends on an event (see Figure 5.6).

Fig. 5.6 Graphical symbol for control flow.

The dotted arrow is not used to represent the flow of information such as the details of a purchase order. The control arrow merely indicates that two elements of a graphical model are necessarily joined by a control connection that is able to carry one binary digit that can be interpreted as TRUE or FALSE, YES or NO.

This signal may, in fact, pass along a communication link that also carries large quantities of information. If so, this channel may appear on the enterprise model using the full line arrow symbol.

Process Pointer

The purpose of the process pointer is to show where the next process in a chain is to be found. Figure 5.7 shows a process pointer symbol.

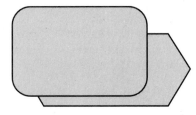

Fig. 5.7 Graphical symbol for a process pointer.

Organizational Unit

The ellipse is used for an organizational unit. It represents the element used in the company organizational structure. It may be a department or a section or a person. You may also define organizational units in terms of the material groups they process or the markets they serve. Figure 5.8 shows the symbol for an organizational unit.

Fig. 5.8 Graphical symbol for an organizational unit.

Information or Material or Resource Object

The real-world objects such as information packages, materials, and resource objects such as energy or services may have to be represented in the event driven process chain model. A plain rectangle with sharp corners is the standard symbol. See Figure 5.9 for the symbol for an object.

Fig. 5.9 Graphical symbol for information or material or resource object.

Information or Material Flow

The flow of information is usually to read, change, or write data. This arrow symbol may also be used to show the movement of material. Figure 5.10 depicts the type of arrows used for the flow of information or material.

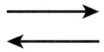

Fig. 5.10 Graphical symbols for information or material flow.

Resource or Organizational Unit Assignment

A continuous line without arrowheads is used to indicate which unit or staff resource is processed by a function. Figure 5.11 illustrates how a plain line may have to make several right-angled turns to depict how a function is associated with a resource including personnel.

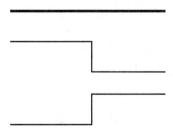

Fig. 5.11 Graphical symbols for resource or organizational unit assignment or attachment.

Combining Events and Functions

In order to draw a true and useful picture of how your company carries out its business operations, the graphical symbols have to be combined. An event is a combination of logic and data that has been defined as the trigger for the initiation of one or more functions. You can build a model of any complexity by combining a fairly small number of symbols in various ways, which are illustrated in the next few sections.

Two Events May Trigger a Function

A programmed business function may be designed to handle many different kinds of events. Some of these events may be exclusive, others may occur in conjunction with each other. These differences in the logic of the event driven process chain are shown in the diagrams by the way the various symbols are arranged.

Either of Two Events May Trigger the Function. Figure 5.12 shows the situation where either one or the other of two events is sufficient to trigger the function. In this illustration, there is no possibility that both of the events could occur together.

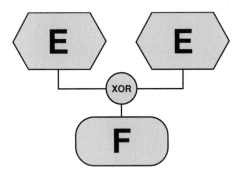

Fig. 5.12   Either of two events may trigger a function, but not both.

Both Events Are Needed to Trigger the Function. If a particular functions needs several events to occur before it can start to run, there are two ways of setting it out in the graphical model:

- Define an event so as to include all the conditions and critical values of the data, which are necessary for the function to be triggered.

- Define the trigger to be a combination of events that have already been defined for other purposes.

Figure 5.13 shows the situation where there are two essential events that have to occur in conjunction for the function to be initiated.

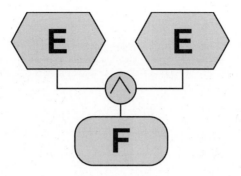

Fig. 5.13 Both events must occur to trigger the function.

One or More of the Events Is Needed to Trigger the Function. If a function has been designed to cope with several events, in any combination, the trigger can be defined as one or more events from a list or set of possibilities. The function will run if any event in the set occurs, regardless of how many others may also occur. See Figure 5.14 for a simple illustration of this situation.

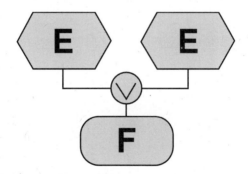

Fig. 5.14 At least one of the events must occur to trigger the function.

A Function May Generate Two Events

It will be very rare for the operation of a function to generate just a single event. At the very least, there will be one event if the function operates successfully and another if a problem is encountered. However, an EPC has to be shown at a selected level of detail. The user will be able to instruct the system to leave out details or include them so as to make the graphical display as helpful as possible.

Figure 5.15 shows part of a model where the function is depicted as being the generator of one or the other of two events, but not both. Figure 5.16 shows a function that generates both of two events every time it runs. Figure 5.17 depicts a function that will generate one or more events according to the results of the computation that goes on as part of the function.

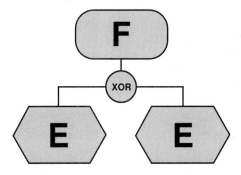

Fig. 5.15 The function generates either of two events, but not both.

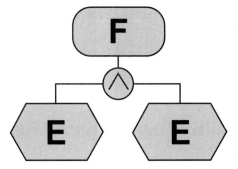

Fig. 5.16 The function generates both events.

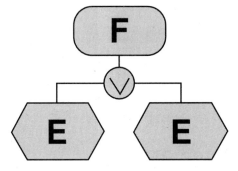

Fig. 5.17 The function generates one or more of the events.

An Event May Trigger More than One Function

The interpretation of data according to predefined criteria is what goes to define an event in a SAP model of your company. When the computer has decided that a particular combination of data has become a critical event, several different functions may be called into action automatically.

An Event May Not Be Ambiguous. The SAP definition of an event is as the reliable trigger for one or more events. There cannot be any doubt as to which event is triggered. Therefore, the diagram in Figure 5.18 that uses the XOR symbol is not allowed because it does not show how each function has a distinct triggering event or combination of events. An EPC diagram cannot include a symbol to show that either one or both events will occur because this would be equivalent to saying that the event is ambiguous about which function to trigger.

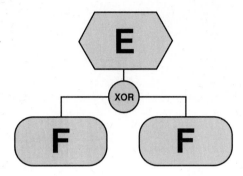

Fig. 5.18   An event may not trigger either of two or more events.

An Event May Trigger Two or More Functions. If your model needs to show that an event will cause the running of two or more functions, the AND symbol is used as illustrated in Figure 5.19.

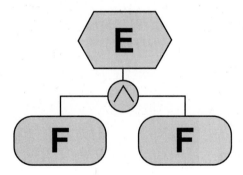

Fig. 5.19   An event can initiate more than one function.

An Event May Not Be Indecisive. The diagram in Figure 5.20 is not allowed because it would suggest that either of the two functions could be triggered. An event is defined as the necessary and sufficient collection of data for the triggering of a specific function. If there are several functions that occur in response to an event, then they must all occur. An event may not be indecisive in identifying which business functions shall perform.

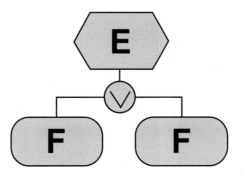

Fig. 5.20 An event must select reliably which function to trigger.

Two Functions May Generate the Same Event

A critical arrangement of data can arise from more than one situation. There are three logical possibilities, all of which are legal in EPC modeling.

One, and Only One, of the Functions Generates the Event. It may be the case that an event that is critical for something else can be caused by a variety of functions. The first of the two functions to operate will generate this event in the situation shown in Figure 5.21.

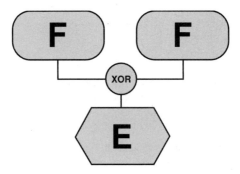

Fig. 5.21 Either of two functions may generate the event, but not both.

All Functions Must Operate to Generate the Event. One of the uses of an event is to register the moment when a certain set of functions have all operated successfully. Figure 5.22 shows the situation where two functions have to have finished before the event is generated.

Either Alone or Both Functions Together Will Generate the Event. If any one or more than one of a group of functions will suffice to generate an event, you can depict the logic as in Figure 5.23.

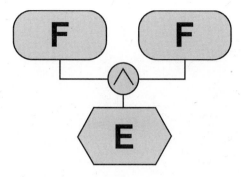

Fig. 5.22 Both functions have to operate in order to generate the event.

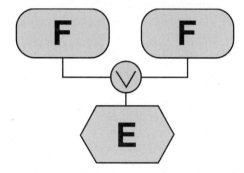

Fig. 5.23 One or more functions have to operate in order to generate the event.

Process View

The dynamics of an information system are best seen from the process view because the objects of scrutiny are the significant occasions, defined in terms of events, which will inevitably prompt the R/3 system into action in the form of one or more event driven process chains.

Lean Event-Driven Process Chains

There are too many events and processes associated with the typical user transaction to make a useful presentation to the user or the system developer. The ABAP/4 programmer will know how to get down to the level of detail he or she needs, but for many purposes, a summary format is more useful. This is provided as a system of lean or sparse displays of event-driven process chains that show the essential relationships in each of the five views and can offer a display of reasonable size and complexity to the user. Drilling down for extra detail is always possible by selecting the item of interest on the display and using the special function keys.

An Example of an Event-Driven Process Chain

To illustrate the semantics of event driven process chain methods of specifying how business is recorded in order to be transferred to a computer support system, a simple scenario is described in text and in graphical terms.

Text Process Description. Goods arrive and are checked. If they are satisfactory, then they are passed to production. If they are not, then they are either rejected or blocked pending further inspection.

Graphical Process Description. Each event driven process chain has to begin with at least one event and be completed by at least one final or finish event. The main constituents of an event driven process chain are passive components, which are events, and active components, which are the functions that do something. The control flow connections between these events and functions are shown as dotted arrows, which may be branched at logical operators shown as circles bearing the appropriate logical symbol to signify AND, Exclusive OR, or Don't Care.

Plain continuous lines without arrows indicate associated organizational elements, such as the department or work center responsible for the function. Continuous line arrows show the flow of information, documents, or material. Figure 5.24 shows part of an event driven process chain seen in the form of a lean EPC that depicts only the main events and functions and their essential relationships.

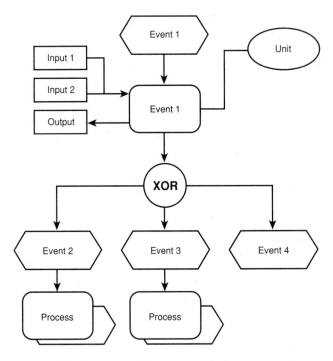

Fig. 5.24 Example model of a lean event driven process chain.

The example is a lean event driven process chain because there are many finer details hidden in order to make the overall structure of the business function clear.

If you place your cursor on an element in an event driven process chain (see Figure 5.25), and call for help using a special function key, then there will be displayed a window pointing to the element and containing the detailed reference document that may be scrolled and bookmarked as required. The reference document may be a more detailed view of the chart or a textual document of notes and procedural instructions. These documents will be developed and annotated as the system implementation proceeds. The whole process of converting parts of the R/3 Reference Model to an enterprise data model (EDM) of your particular company is discussed in Chapter 7, "R/3 Customizing."

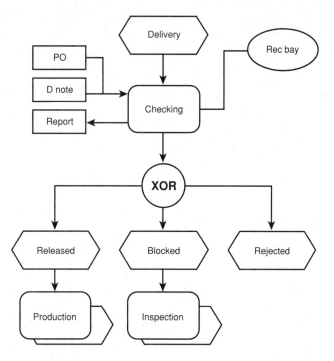

Fig. 5.25 A specific event-driven process chain.

When the particular functions are identified by the graphical element labels, the generalized form of the event-driven process chain becomes particular and will be stored by the system as a unique graphical object. This will gradually build up to the EDM enterprise data model of your company. Figure 5.26 illustrates how a fragment of this model might look when it takes account of the specific work centers and process flows in a target company.

Choosing Key Events

The formal method of depicting the processes of business in terms of event-driven process chains that can be supported by software depends very much on the ability of the implementers to choose the right significant events to become the triggers for the key functions. In the above fragment of an event driven process chain, there are two significant events that initiate production, but only if they occur in conjunction:

Goods released for production

The date for production has been reached

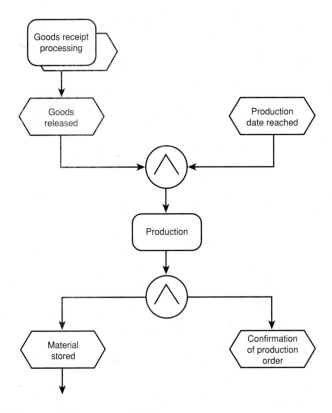

Fig. 5.26   Part of an event-driven process chain.

In the same example, there are two significant events that mark the end of the production function: Material is stored after production processing, and the financial system is informed by a confirmation of the production order. Both of these events should be depicted in the chart of the business process because they will each be needed for subsequent activities.

If the event-driven process chain is not initiated by a carefully chosen event set, or if it does not terminate with events that will take part in other event-driven process chains, then the power of the method will not be fully realized.

Information Flow View

Every event-driven process chain depends on information being input to the function through the data objects of the triggering events. There will be additional inputs of information if the chain is a complex one made up of a structure of event-driven process chains, each with its own data held in the critical events.

And because the purposes of the function will include the generation of events that carry items of information that will cause other event-driven process chains to activate, then every function can be seen to generate output information.

If you had the full details of an event-driven process chain, then you could work out the effective input and output information flow across the function. However, at the early stage in business system implementation, the exact details of the component event-driven process chains may not be known. In such cases, it may be helpful to plot the structure of the business in terms of information flows, knowing that the SAP R/3 system will be able to provide the precise standard business software when the time comes to develop and elaborate the implementation.

The R/3 Reference Model provides a powerful facility to portray automatically the existing and necessary information flows between the standard business functions at the application and functional area levels. Figure 5.27 depicts the information flows that are to be expected between the functions and for which R/3 standard business programs have been developed.

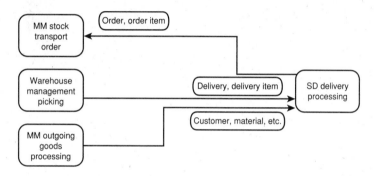

Fig. 5.27   The R/3 Reference Model suggests the necessary information flows.

Data View

Although the operation of event-driven process chains creates and changes the information stored in the individual data objects of the system as a result of the functions initiated, there are also certain relationships that exist between data objects, independently of any processing that may occur.

For example, a plant may "own" a production capacity because it is responsible for the machinery and personnel that can provide it. A warehouse, which is treated as a plant, can be assigned certain materials, quite independently of any functional relationships that may exist when this material is used for production or sales.

These operational relationships between the data objects of the system are stored in the form of information objects that may be seen by calling for the data cluster view of the R/3 Reference Model. Figure 5.28 shows how the necessary data objects are clustered together to form the data structure which, in this illustration, represents a type of material located in a specific plant in your company.

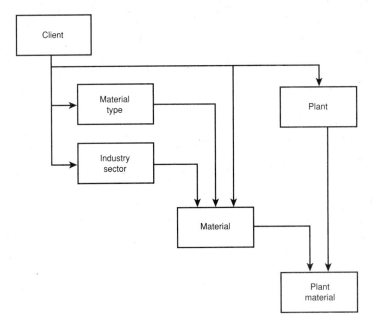

Fig. 5.28   Relationships between data clusters are shown in the data view.

In this fragment of a data cluster view, the Client owns the Plant that is the responsible owner of the Plant Material. The Client is also the owner of data objects representing the types of material used in the company and the definition of Industry Sector that is specific to the industry or perhaps defined purely for the convenience of this company.

The Material data object has to be related to the Client, to the Material Type, and be placed in the appropriate Industry Sector.

The Client may own several plants, each of which may hold stocks of the same material. Therefore, there has to be a data cluster of records in the database which represent the conjunction of plant and material to be labeled in this example as Plant Material. An item of material from one plant is not necessarily treated as identical to the same item from another.

There will, of course, be many other data input relationships for each of the information blocks shown on this data cluster view. And there will also be many additional outgoing relationships to data structures that need the information represented, in this example, by the blocks labeled Material Type, Industry Sector, Material, Plant, and Plant Material.

The Data Cluster Concept

For the purposes of program development, the fine details of data objects have to be made available from the R/3 Reference Model. However, for the purposes of customizing and analyzing your business with the aid of the R/3 Reference Model and the SAP R/3 Analyzer, the data level that is most appropriate will usually be an aggregated data structure in which the objects are displayed at the summary level, which is referred to as the data cluster.

A continuous range of data cluster levels is available from level 0, Entry Level, down to the level of the finest detail as required for software development. These levels correspond to the function view levels discussed in the next section.

At any stage, it is possible to point to a charted element and use the special function keys to drill down for more detailed information.

Function View

The function view of the R/3 Reference Model is able to show how the functions are subordinated to each other in the form of a function tree. The following levels have been found to be the most useful:

> Level 0, which describes an application such as Sales and Distribution as a single entity of which the corporate enterprise will usually have several in the form of an integrated business system.

> Level 1, which shows the functional areas covered by each application as the blocks on the organization chart.

> Level 2, which portrays the principal functions that are needed to support each functional area, such as the preparation of quotations in the Sales area.

> Level 3, which displays the variations within each function that will be recognized by the user as needing a slightly different method of processing in the way that third party order processing is different from standard order processing, for instance.

> Level 4, and the levels below are not usually regarded as part of the functional view because they are the province of the system development teams rather than of concern to the user or the implementer of a standard business software system.

Organization View

The R/3 Reference Model contains a model of the organizational system on which it is based. Although there are many variations of company organization that can be replicated using the components and relationships provided as standard in the R/3 system, it is also possible to design custom-built organizational structures if the standard elements are not sufficient.

Figure 5.29 shows part of the R/3 Reference Model. This model can be used to form the basis for the elaboration of your company organization view of the reference model by replicating the entities or "blocks" at each level until the model corresponds to the organizational structure of your company.

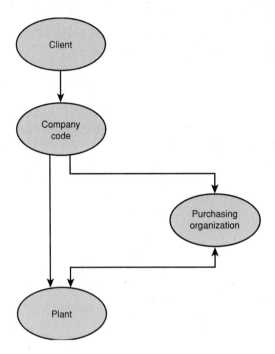

Fig. 5.29 The structure of the R/3 Reference Model can be used as a pattern.

The graphical displays of the model are amenable to a wide variety of presentation style and annotation possibilities. Figure 5.30 shows the standard graphical presentation of part of the reference model as it is being elaborated by copying and editing graphical structures so as to build an EDM enterprise data model of your company as it is now, or as you would like it to be when you have completed the process of business process reengineering.

The main tool for using the R/3 Reference Model in the implementation of your company's business software support is the SAP R/3 Analyzer, which is described in Chapter 6, "Tool-Supported Optimization with the R/3 Analyzer."

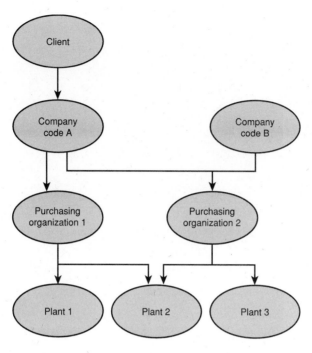

Fig. 5.30 The organizational structure of your company will be in accord with the R/3 model.

From Here...

This chapter has illustrated how the R/3 system contains a model of itself that can be used to find out what standard business functions are available in the R/3 Basis and the R/3 Applications. There are several directions for you to take from here: technical detail, computer management, and business detail, for example.

- How the data is stored and managed.

    The system of data objects is discussed in Chapter 4, "Architecture."

- Computer System Management and Service.

    See Chapter 11, "A Computing Center Management System," or Chapter 27, "Understanding the OSS-Online Service System."

- Business application modules.

    See Chapter 12, "Understanding the FI-Financial Management Module."

Chapter 6

Tool-Supported Optimization with the R/3 Analyzer

All businesses should be in the process of continuous development. They should be seeking ways of adjusting to changing conditions, and they should develop new perspectives on the long-term future.

Optimization is the process of making things work better, not regardless of cost and other relevant factors, but in relation to these factors. The time available to effect a change is often an important factor. The skill of the people who are making the changes and those who will have to live and work with them must also be considered.

Usually, there will be several things that ought to be changed to improve the situation. Which to tackle first and with how much effort are just two of the importance decisions. Optimization is much more than just trying to effect changes piecemeal and without a method.

Some businesses require such radical surgery that the trauma of change is titled "business process reengineering." The intention of the designers of the R/3 Analyzer is to reduce the possible negative effects of this trauma without lessening the benefits of making sensible changes.

The purpose of the R/3 Analyzer is to provide a set of tools for selecting from the R/3 system of predefined software—just those standard business programs that will best serve your company. All the programs in the R/3 system and its applications are fully integrated with one another. Whatever selections you make, the resulting system will be automatically integrated.

Your company may be a good fit for the predefined R/3 standard business functions as they stand. But if some modifications would improve the fit and make the system easier to use by your workforce, then the customizing process (itself thoroughly supported by R/3 tools) will be able to make the necessary adjustments without interfering with the highly-developed and efficient standard software of the Basis system and the associated applications. The objective is tool-supported optimization of business processes across all applications.

In this chapter, you learn:

- The SAP R/3 Analyzer will support you in a focused learning and system drafting program which will guide you through the very sensible and prudent process of specifying the system you want before you begin to build it.

- You do not have to know about the R/3 Reference Model before you start to use the R/3 Analyzer because you will be prompted.

- Customizing is a SAP process, built into the R/3 system, that prompts you to select only those predefined standard programs needed by your implementation.

The R/3 Analyzer includes the following facilities:

- R/3 Reference Model
- SAP Introductory Method
- ARIS Toolset Navigation Component

The full ARIS Toolset Basis Component is additional to the R/3 Analyzer module. It is required if the components of the R/3 Reference Model need to be copied, modified, or supplemented in order to create a nonstandard R/3 Reference Model for specific corporate modeling.

The R/3 Analyzer draws on the R/3 Reference Model as its knowledge base to provide the details of the standard business functions that are available in the R/3 system. Chapter 5, "The R/3 Reference Model," discusses this R/3 Reference Model and the five views it provides:

- Process view
- Function view
- Information flow view
- Data view
- Organization view

The current chapter gives an introduction to the work of the R/3 Analyzer and shows how to use it by selecting from the R/3 Reference Model the components needed for the target concept for your new system.

The Two Uses of the R/3 Analyzer

There are two distinct types of work for which the R/3 Analyzer is optimized: research and implementation. The results of the first will be available to facilitate the second. In particular, the investigation should result in a "Technical Concept" which is the SAP term for an elaborated scheme of standard business functions that will run as an integrated R/3 system and fit exactly the requirements of your company.

Research Studies with the R/3 Analyzer

Your initial contact with the R/3 system will entail a period of familiarization in order to learn what is available and how it may be accessed. This can be conducted under guidance of the R/3 Analyzer which supports the SAP Introductory Method of implementing R/3 for the first time in a client company.

There are four essential stages to a research study:

- Description of the current situation
- Identification of weaknesses and opportunities for improvement

- Identification of possible SAP R/3 functions of interest

- Explication of possible alternative means to optimize the business processes of the company

It is upon the results of the research study that a management decision should be based concerning whether a SAP implementation exercise should proceed to the next stage of elaborating the details of the standard business functions that would be needed.

The Present Situation

One method of describing how things are done at present is demonstrated by the current procedure documents and operational desk manuals. Another method is to ask the opinions of the people doing the work. Yet another source is the training staff who teach newcomers.

The current organizational chart of the company may give a picture of how the responsibilities are delegated. And the troubleshooting specialists in the company will have a fund of information on how things could be improved.

Perhaps the most promising method of describing how things are done now is to set out the structures and the flows in the graphical and logical conventions of the R/3 Reference Model itself.

Five Views of How Things Are Done Now. The **Process View** gives you an integrated network of event-driven process chains and thus relates directly to the operation of your proposed R/3 system.

The **Data View** requires you to be specific about the clusters of aggregated data structures which exist in order for your company to do business.

The **Information Flow** view concentrates on the necessary flows of information between event-driven process chains. It can be used in the early stage of system design when the details of the functions have yet to be specified.

The **Function View** may be developed to yield a summary display or listing of the complete array of functions carried out at present and which would have to be active in a future implementation of the R/3 system.

The **Organization View** shows the relationships between the various organizational units that you have chosen to represent your company as a functioning enterprise.

What to Look for in the Present Situation

The R/3 Analyzer has been developed as the result of extensive experience in implementing business software. It has been designed to apply this experience in the preparation for new installations. It supports a range of techniques for mapping the present situation on to a set of data elements that can be manipulated by the Analyzer. For example, business entities, such as work centers, with relationships between them, such as sequence in a production line, can be displayed graphically.

Shared, Divided, and Confused Lines of Responsibility. The flow of significant information should be directly related to the lines of responsibility. If two departments are responsible for the same activity, then there is a very real possibility that neither of them will admit any fault. Nothing will get done. There is also a difficulty if the group or person who is closest to the customer, who knows what is wanted and what is lacking in your service, is unable to do anything about it. If the one who notices a blemish can put it right immediately and forever thereafter, then there will be more job satisfaction in the work and less complaint from the customers.

Does your organization separate too much the detection of a significant event from the execution of the proper chain of responsive processes? Where are the event-driven process chains in the present situation? Do they cross and re-cross unnecessarily the departmental boundaries?

Some organizations are finding that they can do without several layers of management hierarchy. Even departments may lose their reason for existence if their functions are better performed elsewhere, perhaps automatically by the system, perhaps by a person who enjoys an extended scope and range of work because the technical know-how is so readily available from up-to-date sources.

Disjointed Information Technological Support. Information technology should be focused so as to simplify tasks wherever possible. At a simple level, does the desk manual really tell you how to get the best out of your terminal? Does it help you to use the help system? At a more complicated level, do you have to keep on typing the same phrases, or worse, the same part numbers and customer addresses?

Does your company include any places where data has to be read from a source document and written elsewhere? Are there any checks of its validity? Is anybody else doing the same thing for the same data in another part of the organization?

You may find that the data is presented on a computer screen. The viewer may have to highlight the relevant parts and pick them up for transfer to a form or other document. Could you not have the system do this transfer in a fragment of the time it takes the operator, and with no errors?

If you are studying a work activity with the intention of implementing a SAP module, you will find that the standard business software has been designed so as to give the user all possible support. It would be a mistake to try to copy your existing procedures exactly if they contained operations that would be performed automatically by the R/3 system.

The integrated document concept is a standard feature of SAP systems. Each business transaction causes the generation of at least one standard document. And on to this document are transferred all the data elements that will be needed at the next stage of the event-driven process chain. The user of the system can intervene in this automatic transfer process because there will often be a stage where the system presents for approval the best proposal that can be assembled on the basis of the data available. For example, if one of your customers is speaking to you about a recent order, the system will be able to show you the recent orders from this customer so that you can quickly determine which one is the subject of interest. When you have found it, the system will also have ready all the supporting information that you could possibly require in order to discuss the topic in depth with the customer. And you can also have at hand the latest information from your company concerning the business area and the products likely to be of interest to your contact.

When you are describing the present situation, you must be careful to specify where the information comes from. How much depends on the knowledge in the head of the person doing the work? The information flow view of the R/3 Reference Model is very useful here because it will suggest the information channels that are present in a well-tailored business. You may not find all of them in your own organization as it stands at present.

If you use the R/3 Reference Model as the standard against which to judge the integrity and logical rigor of your present system, you will be well on the way to developing the judgment needed to make best use of the R/3 Analyzer.

Matching Requirements with SAP Functions

If there is a functional module of the R/3 system which covers all you require for a certain aspect of your company's business, then it can easily be pruned to remove the elements which are not needed. There is no reason why your users should see menus and lists of possibilities that contain items they will never need.

The R/3 Analyzer will guide you through the process of picking out from the R/3 Reference Model only those standard business programs that are necessary to support the processes and functions you intend to reengineer. As this identification proceeds, the R/3 Analyzer will store the results and be ready to present them to you in graphical or list form at any stage for you to review the developing design and make amendments.

When you have finished the initial stage of sketching a rough model of the current state of your business, you will be ready to use the more powerful facilities of the R/3 Analyzer to firm up on a design.

Alternative Solutions

Within the SAP system there are sometimes several ways of achieving the same result. There are functions to carry out the standard business processes expected in a wide range of industrial and commercial sectors. However, some modules have been designed with a particular range of client organizations in mind. They may go into much more detail than you require. For example, SD Sales and Distribution is an application which offers a wide scope of functionality in the sales area of work and in the arrangements for making deliveries and processing invoices. If you have few suppliers and few customers, all of whom use a constant system of delivery, you may not need the same delivery management functions as a company supplying thousands of customers. On the other hand, inventory management may be important if your products have to be tracked in dated batches and stored in particular types of storage facilities. You may have a choice of modules.

One of the alternatives a good consultant should always consider is to minimize the automation and computer support used for a business. What would be the consequences of doing everything manually? It may well be that certain functions could be done very much more cheaply and flexibly if there were no requirement to go through a computerized intermediary.

The deliberate attempt to draft a manual system may be a quick route to specifying a very effective computer support system.

Using the R/3 Analyzer Introductory Method to Implement R/3

The idea is to choose from the alternative business processes offered by R/3 and modify them. You have to select from and add to the R/3 Reference Model paradigm functional structures. Then, the results have to be passed to the Customizing module for fine tuning of the system components.

Finally, you will want to go live with your system under the control of the SAP Business Workflow Management system.

The R/3 Analyzer is a tool for carrying out the preparatory work in the most efficient manner possible. It will prompt the user to carry out the necessary steps in the proper order, and it will keep track of the work done and the decisions made.

The Process Matrix

The current situation has to be captured in a formal system that can be processed and take advantage of previous work in order to elaborate the "System Concept" for your company. Three documents are required, and they may be very extensive:

- A chart of the information inputs and outputs throughout the company

- An organization chart of the enterprise

- A process matrix

The procedure for describing the current situation can itself be described by the methods used by the Analyzer. Figure 6.1 shows the first part of a chart of this process.

The process matrix is essentially a table which records the component processes that take place in your enterprise. They are displayed with the names and identification of the R/3 Reference Model.

The chart or matrix is provided by the R/3 Analyzer as a display of the R/3 processes that have been preprogrammed in the form of standard business software using the ABAP/4 language. Against each item, you signify whether the particular function is required in your target system concept. For example, you may have to process requests for quotation documents. There is a standard business function for this. Will you need this only as part of standard order processing, or will you also require it in the context of contracts?

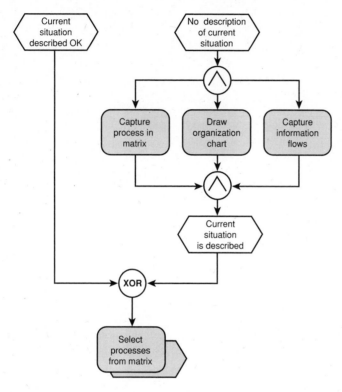

Fig. 6.1 Describing the current situation.

Collecting Trial Data

There may have to be a stage of trial operation, in part of a real plant, or in simulation, to ascertain the statistical information needed to make choices between various possible enactments of your target system concept. You may have to accrue data on the electronic storage and communication demands, for example. It may be wise to see what happens in the worst-case scenarios which represent extremes, for instance, between many simple transactions and a few very elaborate processes. How do these extremes affect the running health of the system?

SAP functions are able to keep track of their processing costs so that you can build up reasonable data on the basis of simulations and limited experimental trials.

Perhaps your company already has the information, but it will be as well for you to confirm estimates of how often various business functions are likely to be performed in the future. A frequently-performed operation should always be designed to be as fast and as economical in system resources as possible. Rare operations may be allowed more time and may be scheduled for off-peak hours perhaps.

Anticipating the Unexpected

An emergency is usually an occasion where the system must respond quickly. But do you know what types of emergency could occur? Do you know their costs and the likelihood of their breeding complications? Who shall do what when something rare happens should be part of the system design. Nothing should be totally unexpected: There should be no gaps in emergency provision. It does not necessarily cost a lot of money to get people to think the unthinkable: But it may be expensive to prepare a reasonable action plan on the day when something goes wrong. These contingency plans may have to be set up for automatic initiation, much in the manner of an emergency power generator that has been programmed to start itself if the normal source goes offline.

On the other hand, experience with disasters and catastrophes has demonstrated that some designs of system and some distributions of knowledge are more prudent than others. The Internet is an example of a system designed to carry on working, even if a considerable amount of damage has been done to its components. The knowledge of how to run the system resides in many places, and there are many pathways along which this information can flow. An alternative approach is to consolidate the knowledge in a central location and defend it robustly.

Another example of a distributable system is medical knowledge. It may be a better strategy to have many people who can do simple medical procedures rather than rely solely on a few who can perform any procedure. The latter approach depends on being able to move the patient to the medical experts when necessary.

The target concept should include what has to be done in the normal course of business and a recognition at least of the types of emergencies that could arise.

Computing the Extent of Change

Change is costly. Paint the walls and people spend time discussing the effect. Changing a procedure bit by bit, by the evolutionary method, is a common practice in all walks of life and places of work. Traumatic or at least discontinuous changes in the form of revolutionary workplace upheaval may have to be a consequence if you decide to go for a target system concept which is quite unlike anything current. The benefits of large scale change must outweigh the inherent costs.

Changing the SAP standard business programs so as to make them better suited to what you want to do is much easier than it sounds because the system has a myriad of supporting functions to help you see how things are progressing and to propose sensible additions and refinements to help you get everything right the first time.

But you do have to arrive at a firm specification of where you are going and where you are starting from.

Selecting Functions from the R/3 Reference Model

As you work down the process matrix which shows what you are going to need in the way of programmed functions, the R/3 Reference Model will be able to present you with scenarios that you will recognize: sales order processing, physical inventory taking, personnel recruiting, and so on. Figure 6.2 illustrates the top level of the process selection matrix. By selecting any item on the display and using the special function keys, the user can see any level of detail about the item of interest. This is referred to as "drilling down."

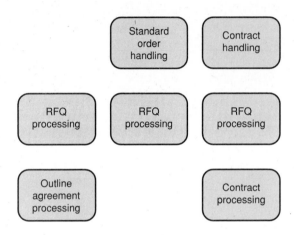

Fig. 6.2   The process selection matrix shows what is in the R/3 Reference Model.

The R/3 Analyzer Determines Processes

As the target concept for the system to support your new enterprise is refined, it can be approved, stage by stage. After the design of a component has been approved, the R/3 Analyzer will automatically select the relevant underlying R/3 processes.

If it should happen that there remain some aspects of your target concept that are not available in a standard business function in the R/3 Reference Model, then you must initiate the process of developing enterprise-specific scenarios from which the programmers can create enterprise-specific processes to be added to your company's version of the standard R/3 Reference Model.

Assigning Responsible Organizational Units to Functions

The first stage of allocating functions to organizational units will probably be targeted on the names and structure of departments and work sections that exist already or are anticipated for the new organization. You will probably wish to assign jobs to the traditional teams that are best able to do them.

However, as you go about this procedure, it may become obvious from the R/3 Analyzer that there could be a different organizational structure based on the way the standard business functions of the R/3 Reference Model interact with one another and with the activities you have identified from your study of the current situation.

II

Technical Background

For example, the R/3 Reference Model will not expect there to be any gaps in the communication channels between departments, nor will it welcome any manual entry of data onto documents that the standard R/3 system will normally complete automatically, as far as possible.

In particular, you may be prompted into recommending that one or more layers of supervisory staff and management be ablated from your organizational chart.

And as you rationalize the structure of your target organization, so the information flows between the new units will fall into place in a better scheme of doing business. Indeed, it may be the recognition that you have suggested unnecessary information channels that prompt you into revamping your structure.

Under the guidance of the R/3 Analyzer, the continuous business process re-engineering cycle is just about inevitable. The following steps will be suggested:

- Describe the present situation.
- Model it from the R/3 Reference Model.
- Study the five views of the model.
- Make needed changes.
- See the new description displayed by the R/3 Analyzer system.
- Repeat the cycle, if necessary.

The Target Enterprise Model

Eventually, adjustments will be stopped and you will be left with the target model of the enterprise you wish to create. It is an integrated model because you have built it by selecting standard business functions from the R/3 Reference Model. It should be close to what you want because you started with a description of the current situation and followed the advice of the R/3 Analyzer. Then, you accepted the information flows that it suggested as essential if the system is to remain a viable and integrated one.

There could be two types of discrepancies between your target enterprise model and the ideal:

- The R/3 Reference Model does not include a function that your particular business requires.
- The selection you have made from the R/3 standard business software covers the processes you need but the ensuing system does not seem to be an exact fit to your requirements and the user interface does not bear the unmistakable imprint of your business and your corporation.

The first discrepancy is a signal to look in the R/3 Reference Model again more carefully. If there is still something missing, then this will have to be defined as a new program development project for work with the ABAP/4 programming language supported by the

ABAP/4 Development Workbench, which is discussed in Chapter 28, "ABAP/4 Program Development with the R/3 Workbench." Meanwhile, your target enterprise model will have to be content with a definition of the information flows and functional specification for the new component until it has been developed and tested.

The second discrepancy between the target enterprise model and what you really want is a matter for customizing.

The R/3 Analyzer Selects Predefined Customizing Activities

The SAP R/3 standard software is designed on the assumption that the client company will want to alter it. Yet the client company does not want to have the software rebuilt in its entirety. And at no stage in the modification process does the client want to have the system fail because of a programming error.

The SAP approach to customizing is to have all the software refer to parameters that are stored in tables in standard formats. The customizing module gives the implementing company access to these tables but not to the underlying software. Therefore, the client cannot do anything that will crash the R/3 system.

For example, a standard business program to conduct warehouse management will refer to a table of the types of storage facilities that might be found in a warehouse. All the common types of bins and pallets, racks and marked floor space, and so on, will be in the table. If your company needs something different, it can be added to the table and you will be prompted to supply the details of how it is to be handled, its size and capacity, for instance. If there are items in the table that you will never need, they can be deleted from it.

With a minimum of manual effort, you can complete the customizing process because the system will propose all the customizing activities that are needed according to the functions you have specified in your target enterprise model.

Rough Survey Procedure

Although the procedure is referred to as "rough," the method entails a precise formal process of capturing the system relationships of the current situation in a format that can readily be adjusted to correspond with the R/3 Reference Model. By so doing, the opportunities for improvement of the current situation will become apparent, and the means to effect the necessary changes will be identified in the suite of standard business programs of the R/3 system.

The procedure for conducting a rough survey of the present situation begins with the identification and recording of the objectives of the organization and the units in the company at present responsible for these activities.

Objectives and the Organizational Units Responsible

By mapping the objectives of the company and the departmental units responsible, it is possible to discern the following types of imperfections in business system design:

- Functions that are specific to the company, not because they are unique in the industry, but because they have developed piecemeal as the company found it necessary to elaborate its procedures to cope with new circumstances

- Functions performed redundantly by two or more work units, or without purpose by one

- Functions that lack information technological support and which could be improved if it were to be provided

- Discontinuities in the flow of information or control caused by unnecessarily strict demarcation between unit responsibilities

- Data held in more than one place

- Information captured or entered manually when it is already available in the system

- Data transcribed from one medium to another

Figure 6.3 suggests that each objective depends on the successful performance of certain functional areas. Similar objectives diagrams can be created at any level of detail.

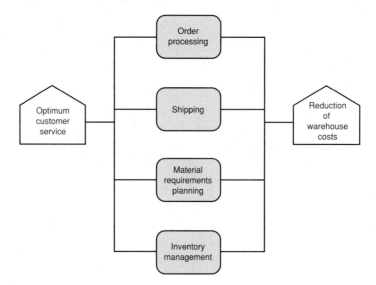

Fig. 6.3   The objectives diagram shows the functional areas responsible.

Existing Organizational Structure

The traditional organization chart can be used in the SAP R/3 system to depict the management relationships between the existing departments and work sections. Figure 6.4 is part of such a chart.

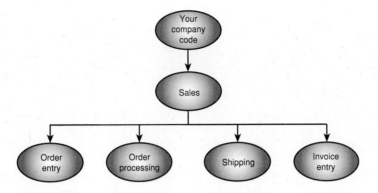

Fig. 6.4   Example of a current organization chart.

The R/3 Reference Model includes typical chart sections which can be edited and articulated to create a graphical model of the current situation.

Function Trees

The complexity of business processes makes it necessary to use some form of hierarchical structure to depict the fact that each process is made up of a series of subprocesses in the form of event-driven process chains, each of which can entail lower levels of event-driven process chains.

The most informative way of describing the current processing structure of your company is in the form of function trees, using the format and models of the R/3 Reference Model and adapting the elements until they accurately represent how you do business at present. Figure 6.5 illustrates part of a function tree.

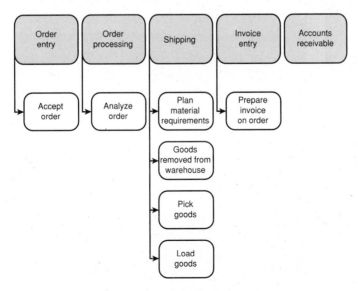

Fig. 6.5   The function tree should define the scope of the organizational unit.

II

Technical Background

Your first edition of the function tree for a department may well use the terms and labels your company is familiar with. On the other hand, you may well find that the R/3 Reference Model will suggest the names of functions that are somewhat different. In particular, you may find that the scope of functionality that you have subsumed under a single function title is defined by the R/3 Reference Model in terms of several subfunctions that appear to increase the complexity of the work of the department. In Figure 6.5, for instance, Order Entry subsumes Accept Order; and Order Processing subsumes Analyze Order. The differences include a recognition that the entry of an order from a customer should concentrate on efficiently capturing an accurate picture of exactly what it is that the customer wants; whereas the analysis of this order is beginning to take account of how the customer requirements are to be met. The same person may do both: But there are two points of view, two sets of priorities.

The R/3 Reference Model may offer a simplification of your existing procedures. Your target concept of how the R/3 will be used to run your new business design may have fewer elements than your model of the current situation. This can happen because the R/3 design will take it for granted that the computer system will have access to a comprehensive database and sufficient speed of retrieval to make good use of it. As soon as you know what the customer wants, the system can tell you how to arrange for it to be provided. The same person can carry out several steps of the process with the support of the technology.

Information Flow Mapping

In the process of capturing an accurate picture of how business is carried on at present, your "rough" model should be supplemented and informed by a view of your company as a series of information flows between organizational units or other entities such as database records. A SAP document is a carrier of data and therefore a collector of data. Figure 6.6 is part of an information flow map and suggests this dual role of the SAP document.

The definition of a SAP document allows for any form of data element to be handled as a document with a header of its own or as a document item in a larger document. There is no limit to the size or complexity of a data structure that can be handled as a SAP document. Therefore, the information flows in a model of your existing company will be treated as documents or document items in any SAP R/3 system you may implement.

During the rough modeling of your existing system, you may find it useful to develop very detailed charts of the information flows necessary to get business done efficiently. There are two techniques that should not be overlooked: Stimulus Discrimination and Response Differentiation.

Stimulus Discrimination. What are the different things and situations that trigger actions in your company? There should be a long list of events to which your company is sensitive.

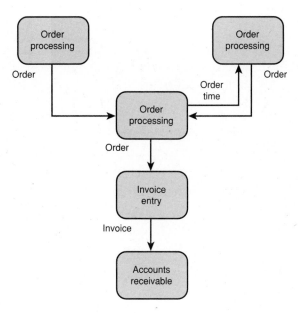

Fig. 6.6   Information flows will contribute to SAP documents.

Your sales departments will be sensitive to opportunities to detect potential customers and determine their requirements. Your marketing people will want to notice changes in the target groups who might be responsive to your approaches. Your manufacturing facilities will need to be monitored to see that they are working well and that new inventions and developments are considered to update the plant. These are examples of the gross stimulus types that your business procedures must be prepared to accommodate.

At a finer grain level, your sales department, for example, will probably have different procedures for regular customers and one-time customers. So the detailed procedures have to include a data capture operation that determines which type of customer is being processed. The data capture may be a simple matter of identifying an inquirer as a previous customer, and confirming that no details have changed. Or a one-time new customer may have to be subjected to inquiry techniques to establish the name and address information, and so on.

These trivial examples illustrate the technique of compiling a list of all the stimulus situations of importance:

- Previous customer

- Regular customer

- New customer or prospect

- One-time customer, and so on

The outcome of this stimulus discrimination should be a set of elements which represent the occasions when a collection of data from outside the system is essential. The information required will be that which is sufficient to determine precisely which stimulus of interest has occurred. Such an occasion will be defined in the SAP system as an event. However, at the rough stage of system description, information flow models may suffice with the graphical elements labeled with the stimulus of interest.

The method of information flow mapping should show how each stimulus of interest leads to a different response. There may be a certain amount of grouping of stimuli, where several different events in the outside world are treated as equivalent by the system, although it is usually the case that the variants of a stimulus class retain their individual identity because of one or more data elements that are carried through the processing sequences.

Response Differentiation. In parallel with the compilation of a list of the stimuli of interest, it is worth compiling a list of the varieties of response that are in evidence in your company. For example, it may be the case that different customers enjoy different terms and conditions of payment. Why is this? How does the system user know which terms should apply? How are new customers assigned to the more favorable terms?

If you know that your company has, say, eleven different sets of credit conditions, then you will be prepared to find eleven sets of stimulus conditions that are necessary and sufficient to mandate the assignment of any fresh customer to the appropriate condition.

You may be unlucky. You may find that your company responds differently to different customers for no reason that you can discern. You have discovered an information gap where there should be an information flow.

Back-to-Front Information Mapping. When your auditor comes to inspect your annual accounts, he or she is entitled to select a value on the financial documents and demand to see how it was computed. Which pieces of data were processed to arrive at this figure?

When your SAP system is fully implemented, you will be able to select any figure in the accounts and use the special function keys to trace back to the primary documents and the information they carry to see for yourself how the final total was compiled. You can drill down the value of the inventory, for example, until you are looking at the subtotals for each warehouse, and for each warehouse you can drill down on the total for a material and so on until you are looking at the valuation given to each batch or each inventoried item of stock.

The back-to-front method of analyzing your current business system follows the same logic as your auditor. You list all the outputs from your company and keep asking to see how they were produced until you have traced their history back to the input of the information and materials which took part in their production.

Of course, if you have already compiled a comprehensive list of the different responsive actions that constitute the repertoire of your business, and if you have also compiled a list of all the situations and events that will trigger an action from at least one part of your organization, then you will have to hand over much of the information needed to conduct a back-to-front scrutiny of how your company's outputs came into being.

The way that the SAP systems describe stimuli and responses is designed to sit comfortably on the logic and mechanisms of computer programming. By and large, the systems do one thing at a time. Complicated things are done by processes chained together and triggered by a specific event.

Process Chains

Each process of your existing business system requires an input, such as a document, a person, or device to recognize that it is significant and deserves a response, and a further inflow of information and perhaps material as the process carries out its activities. Figure 6.7 illustrates part of the complex of process chains associated with order handling.

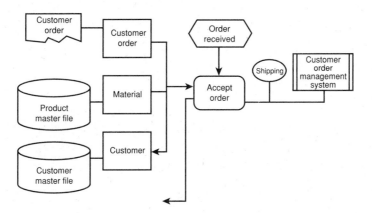

Fig. 6.7 Customer order handling is a process chain.

When the function of the first process has run its course, the next process in the chain is initiated by the passing on of information in the form of a document, and perhaps material.

The more precise your knowledge of the process chains in your business, the better will be your models of the current and future systems.

Reviewing the Rough Survey

The rough survey of the existing situation in your company entails specifying the following:

- Objectives

- Organizational chart with responsibilities assigned

- Function tree

- Information flow diagram
- Event-driven process chains

To achieve this, you may call upon the R/3 Reference Model to show models of typical structures which you can copy and modify to reflect how you do business. You may wish to call for lists of the significant stimulus events to which your company must respond; and you will need to identify all the different forms these responses can take. You may even check the validity of your data by the back-to-front method of tracing how and why things are done as they are.

The next step is to convert your rough survey of the existing situation into the target concept, the enterprise model which will be the design for your future business system. The tool for achieving this is the R/3 Analyzer.

Technical Elaboration of a Target Concept

Technical elaboration is the process of specifying exactly which SAP standard business programs are to be used to run your target business. You also have to make arrangements for these standard programs to interact so as to achieve exactly the result you require.

In the beginning is the process selection matrix.

The Process Selection Matrix

Each application has a comprehensive process selection matrix which you can use to identify the standard business functions that you require in your target concept system. Beneath each item in the matrix is another process diagram at a more detailed modeling level. Figure 6.8 begins to suggest how the process selection matrix can handle the complexity of an integrated business application.

At any stage in a process diagram, the chart may indicate a process pointer symbol to indicate that the process chain may continue through another series of event-driven process chains that may constitute another module or application that cannot be shown directly connected with the chart currently on display.

Company-Specific Functions. If you should find that the R/3 Reference Model does not contain a standard business function that can be adapted to serve one or more of the functions in your chart of the current situation, you may decide to inscribe this function on a new function symbol and add it to your model. The system will be aware that you have created your own version of the R/3 Reference Model, and the whole process will be treated as an Engineering Change Management activity. The original R/3 Reference Model itself will not be modified.

The unique new function will have to be subjected to program development work to establish the program to execute the new functions you require.

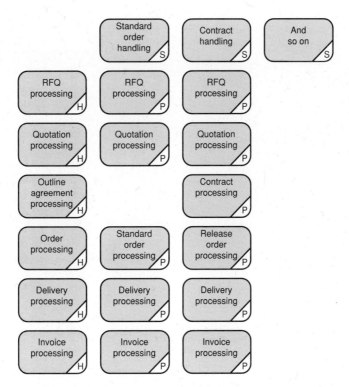

Fig. 6.8 The SD-Sales and Distribution application has a comprehensive process selection matrix.

The R/3 Analyzer includes the navigation component of the ARIS Toolset to which the other components may be added if extensive program development work is intended.

Deleting Functions. As you proceed through the selection process, you may come upon functions that are not required. If you check the "functional use" attribute of one of these functions, you will discover whether it is optional or mandatory. If a function is marked as mandatory, then it may not be deleted from the process selection matrix because it includes processing upon which other functions depend. If a function is optional, you can delete it from the matrix and it will form no part of your target concept.

Additional Standard Functionality. The process selection matrix may indicate that there are certain functions in the system which you do not require in your target concept. These additional functions are of two categories:

- Functions that are almost certainly of no benefit to the target concept system

- Functions that were not specified in the description of the current situation, and which were not necessarily envisaged as part of the new enterprise, but which would indeed be very useful if they were included in the target concept

If a function is of no benefit and it is an optional function, then you may delete it. Mandatory functions cannot be deleted: Potentially useful functions should be retained, even if they are optional.

Input and Output Information Objects

Many functions need data. This they must get from an information item. All functions create information items when they are activated, even if it is only the date and time when they were called. Standard SAP functions accessed from the R/3 Reference Model will show which information items they need and which they will create. Figure 6.9 shows how information inputs and outputs are mapped in the Analyzer.

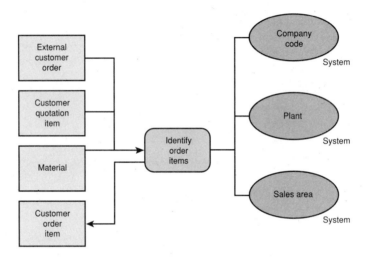

Fig. 6.9 A function requires information input and creates output.

It may be the case that your model of the existing situation necessarily includes information items that are not mentioned in the R/3 Reference Model standard version of the function you are considering. For example, you may have some data on a storage medium used in a system which will be rendered obsolete by your new implementation. The legacy data objects necessary to the functioning of your target system can be so identified in the target model. And the SAP support system will be able to provide the data transfer mechanisms to integrate the legacy records with your target system.

Revisions of Organizational Structure

Client, Company Code, Plant, and Activity Center are all examples of R/3 organizational units that can be associated with particular functions. If you examine the structure of the R/3 functions, you will see that the standard system of R/3 organizational units is applied. You will be able to determine, for instance, whether a particular function is normally executed at the Company Code level or at the Activity Center level.

If you adopt the standard R/3 Organizational Structure for your target concept, you will find that the integration of the various programs is automatically affected and authorization structures can be applied without difficulty.

There can be a reduction in the number of organizational units needed if the standard functions already include the processes carried out in some of the units. Figure 6.10 illustrates such a reduction.

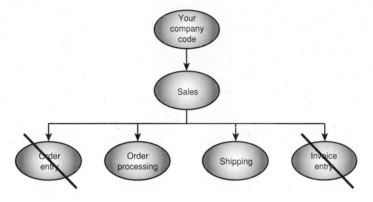

Fig. 6.10   The target organization has fewer units than the current.

Attributes for the Analysis of Models

Each data object in the SAP R/3 system is made up of a set of data elements arranged in a structure. Into these data elements can be placed values or parameters which control the way the data object is used. If the data object represents a standard function, then some of the data elements will be used to control the operation of this function: If the data element is changed, then the function operates in a different manner.

The symbols on a chart used to model the existing situation in your company, and the symbols in a chart of your target concept, are data objects. Some of the data elements control the visual display of the symbol when it appears in a chart. Some of the data elements contain information which can be used to carry out quantitative and qualitative comparisons of different models of your existing or target system.

Modeling Objects

The following data objects are used to depict event-driven process chains:

- Events, hexagonal blocks
- Functions, blocks with rounded corners
- Control flows, dotted arrows
- Logical operators, circles
- Information objects or materials, rectangles
- Organizational units, ellipses

Each object has a unique identification number for each example of its use. Your actual model symbols will have a different set of identification numbers to the objects depicted in the model of your target concept.

Types of Comparison Between Models. The following comparisons illustrate the type of results that can be achieved by using the data elements of the data objects that are used to assemble the models:

- Comparing different variants of a target process

- Comparing a target process with the original R/3 Reference Model process

- Comparing the actual process currently in operation with the corresponding target process

- Comparing the actual process with the corresponding process in the R/3 Reference Model

Dimensions of Model Comparison. The data attributes of the elements used to model business processes in the R/3 Reference Model, in your target concept, and in your model of the existing situation, where you have used the corresponding processes, can be subjected to the following types of analysis:

- Quantity of data and frequency of use statistics

- Time data to be used to compute throughput times, delay times, processing times, transmission times within the process

- Statistics and time data aggregated to higher order processes

- Cost data assigned to various cost types to be used to derive indices which reflect the processing costs

Manner of Use Data. The functions include data elements to indicate how the function is performed according to the following categories:

- Online, interactively with the user

- In batch mode, without interacting with the user

- Automatically, without interacting with the user

- Manually, by the user without system support

The Quality of a Function. The data structure of a modeling element includes a provision to store the degree of user satisfaction with the function. This will depend on the scope and content of the function. For example, a function performed online using interaction with the user may not offer all the choices required. The quality of satisfaction is expressed as "good," "satisfactory," or "poor."

Future Information Flows

When the target model of your business has been created under control of the R/3 Analyzer, the standard business functions that have been identified from the R/3 Reference Model will have been transferred automatically to your model. If you call for an information flow view of this model, you will see that the information flows between functional elements have been depicted. Figure 6.11 suggests how the data flowing between functional elements is transcribed onto standard SAP documents as specific document items, or updates to the header information.

You may adopt the standard titles for the documents or use your own. From your survey of the existing situation, you will be able to see how the information pathways suggested by the R/3 Reference Model relate to the information flows you have identified.

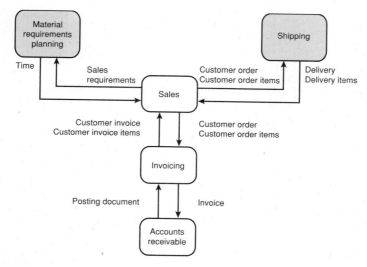

Fig. 6.11 Information flows become SAP document items.

In particular, the R/3 Reference Model will indicate that the receipt of each document at a function will be the occasion for a transmission back to the sending element of a document, which serves to confirm the receipt of the first transmission and to provide a report on the current status of the process.

For example, a customer order document, with details of the customer order items, will be sent to Shipping from Sales. When the shipping process has been completed, the delivery document, with details of the delivery items, will be sent from Shipping to Sales as confirmation that the shipping processes have done what they are supposed to do. If, for any reason, the delivery is incomplete, then the details will immediately become apparent to the Sales department, who will be prepared to discuss the facts of the delivery with the customer should a query arise.

A manual system may not be able to carry out this type of routine confirmation in detail for every function: Under the SAP discipline, it is standard practice.

The integrated functions of the R/3 system are predefined with the necessary information flows established through the system of SAP documents, which ensures that the detailed functioning of the system is logged in the form of electronic documents stored under the master record headings of the functions involved in the communications. The Sales department will be able to look at the stored documents that record the activities of the Shipping section in connection with their customer orders. The materials requirements planners will be able to see how they were kept informed of the sales requirements, and how they transmitted their schedules back to the Sales department.

When you see how the R/3 system can be arranged to carry out all the business functions you will need in the enterprise model of your future organization, and when you look at the information flow views of it, or the process chains, or the responsibilities, then you may get some ideas about changing the organizational structure of your company to make better use of your new system.

If your company is prepared to adjust to future changes, as indeed it must, then you will want to ensure that the information flows to and within your company are aligned to this objective. For example, you will want to check that there is a flow of information from Production to Purchasing to report on the suitability of the materials being delivered from the various suppliers. This flow ought to include all the factors which might impact on current production and any indicators of how things might change in the future.

Future Organizational Structure

Passing a piece of work from one person to another is disruptive and inevitably takes time which may not result in significant added value to the product being handled. It is the same with information processing work: The fewer changes of staff, the better. It is most important to minimize the number of transitions from one department to another. Your organization should be arranged so that the work flow crosses departmental boundaries only with good reason.

In the example fragment of an enterprise model, the existing situation portrayed a work section devoted to data capture for the purpose of order entry. Another set of people was employed to enter the data needed to create invoices. Both sections may have been in the habit of typing the name and address of the customer. Why not combine the sections and have the computer type the details from existing records wherever possible? Figure 6.10 shows this example.

Modeling Organizational Structure

The standard SAP organizational structure is used in the R/3 Reference Model to arrange the levels in the display of the organization and the associated functions. All the elements are assigned identification numbers that also echo this structure.

In the R/3 applications, the standard organizational structure is replicated and also used to shape the display of the elements. Figure 6.12 shows part of the R/3 Reference Model. It contains only one definitive reference model for each element. Your model can freely replicate and rename these reference items.

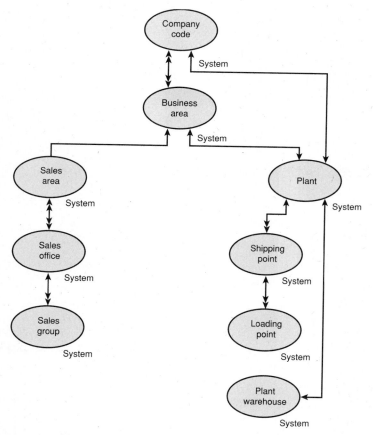

Fig. 6.12 The R/3 Reference Model has the basic elements.

When you take over a copy of the R/3 Reference Model to use as the basis for your target enterprise model, you can insert the elliptical symbols to represent the organizational units of your target company structure. Each unit can be assigned the title currently in use, or the system can be left to assign names based on the R/3 Reference Model. Figure 6.13 depicts part of a target enterprise model.

The elliptical symbols are attached by simple lines to depict the fact that certain functions in the model are the responsibility of specific named units in your company.

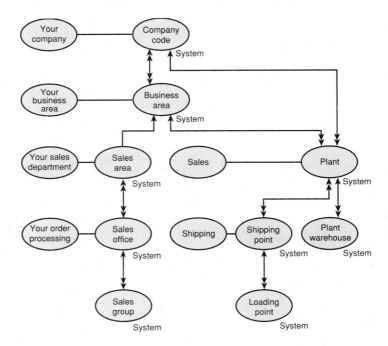

Fig. 6.13 The target concept organization adds to the R/3 Reference Model.

Because the system underlying the R/3 Reference Model is structured according to the standard SAP system of organizational structure using the Client, Company Code, Business Area, and Plant series of levels, the relationship between the organizational units of your target enterprise must necessarily follow the same hierarchical pattern. You may have to take this into consideration in order to harmonize your new structure with your new business support system.

Review of the Required Organizational Changes

You will have been on the alert for signs of blemishes in the existing system which you want to avoid in the design of your new system. Organizational breaks, missing information technology, and discontinuities in the use of information media are the main snags.

If major changes need to be made, then you will have to present a case for these changes based on the details of the defects discovered and the possible consequences of leaving them untreated. On the benefits side of the account, you will want to draw attention to the time saved by having the system provide data and work procedure suggestions wherever it is possible to do so. The improved service to the customer and better use of supplier resources will be noted as consequences of having fewer transfers of business across departmental boundaries.

Transfer of Results for Customizing

The Customizing module recognizes that over 4,000 different types of activity may take place to effect improvements to the target model of an enterprise before it reaches the peak of its potential performance.

The nature of these fine-tuning adjustments ranges from a subtle choice of batch sampling statistical techniques to the presentation of the date and time in the format customary in the user organization. The aim is to make sure that the steps of the event-driven process chains are carried out correctly and in the most efficient manner. This process is discussed in Chapter 7, "R/3 Customizing."

The work of customizing does not normally proceed until the target concept has been fully elaborated under the R/3 Analyzer using the R/3 Reference Model as its database. When the target concept has been submitted and approved, your selection of functions from the R/3 Reference Model, which is the embodiment of your target concept, will be the object upon which the customizing module will work in order to complete the fine-tuning of the system functions before the system goes live.

Summary of SAP R/3 Implementation Procedure

The R/3 Analyzer provides powerful tools to model business processes transparently. You can see what processes and information flows are entailed in what you do now and in what you might want to do in some future enterprise.

There is a powerful form of documentation in the R/3 Reference Model itself because it can be used to display an actual or target model from any of five viewpoints. There is also a related system of online documentation in the form of supporting texts and demonstrations of concepts. Chapter 26, "R/3 Online Documentation," discusses this.

There is a comprehensive system of SAP training courses.

When it comes to implementing a specific system, there is a standard procedure whereby a suite of central application modules can be controlled by adjusting tables of parameters that govern how the various event-driven process chains are to be used.

The user implementation teams can manipulate the parameters of the standard functions without affecting the way they interact with one another and without impairing their fundamental efficiency that is determined at the level of the ABAP/4 programming language in which the standard functions are written.

The user client does not have access to the code of the standard business functions.

Unique customer-specific functions can be developed in the ABAP/4 language and integrated in the target system. Client companies may also add functions to form their own version of the standard R/3 Reference Model using the ARIS Toolset.

Future changes and adjustments to the target concept system can be modeled and simulated by the R/3 Reference Model in advance of implementation.

From Here...

- How is the data stored?

    The system of data objects is discussed in Chapter 4, "Architecture."

- How do you find out what SAP standard business functions are likely to be needed for your company?

    See Chapter 5, "The R/3 Reference Model."

- I need to find details about a specific application.

    See Chapter 9, "Worldwide Business Computing Systems," for an introduction to the SAP modules.

- My interest is in an overview of running the whole complex of standard business software in practice.

    See Chapter 11, "A Computing Center Management System," and Chapter 27, "Understanding the OSS-Online Service System." Chapter 30, "R/3 Business Workflow Management," may also be of interest.

Chapter 7

R/3 Customizing

The SAP R/3 system contains a model of itself in the form of the SAP R/3 Reference Model, which records all the standard business functions available in the system. They are shown in a neutral or paradigm form which is subsequently converted into an enterprise-specific organizational structure. The process of achieving this transition begins with analyzing your business, continues with a selection from the standard components, and ends with the fine-tuning of the whole system, which is termed "customizing."

This chapter will show how the Customizing elements of the SAP R/3 system components combine to support the adaptation of the standard functions of the SAP R/3 Reference Model to the business process systems that your company requires.

An Overview of Customizing

Customizing is a fine-tuning activity carried out on a system that is already running in prototype form. Its design has already been through many processes, each of them guided and supported by a specialized SAP tool that is able to pass on its output to the next tool in the process.

Analysis of the Existing Situation and the Target Concept

The SAP R/3 Reference Model is a data structure which can be consulted to determine just which standard business functions are available in the SAP R/3 system as predefined integrated programs. The best way to consult it is by using the SAP R/3 Analyzer, which is discussed in Chapter 6, "Tool-Supported Optimization with the R/3 Analyzer." The Analyzer will guide you through the process of describing your current system and the target concept of your business that you are aiming for. The Analyzer will help you look at your two companies, existing and target, from the following points of view:

- The process view depicts a company as a structure of event-driven process chains that carry out the necessary work when the right event conditions are in place.

In this chapter, you learn:

- Who performs customizing.

- What you need to know about ABAP/4 programming to use the Customizing system.

- What to do if you make a mistake.

Technical Background

■ The information flow view allows you to see how each activity gets the information it needs, and who is responsible for sending it and keeping it up to date.

■ The data cluster view sets out all the items of information that have to be captured and stored in a systematic manner so that they can be found again when they are wanted.

■ The function view shows how your company has high-level functions that depend on lower-level functions, and so on, down to the functions responsible for handling the information and materials passing through the company.

By looking at all these views of your present situation and of the situation when your target concept has been implemented, you can progressively refine your target to make proper provision for the market and manufacturing or purchasing conditions your company will have to confront during the long lifetime of the software you are designing for your target concept.

Selecting Functions for the Target Concept

Having drawn up various views of your target concept after inspecting similar views of the existing situation and consulting the long-term plans of your company, you will be faced with the task of selecting functions from the many that are available in the SAP R/3 system. You will want to do this carefully because you may decide that the SAP R/3 Reference Model does not include all the specialized functions that your target concept will entail.

Company-Specific Functions. Before you express a need to develop new software, you should use the SAP R/3 Analyzer to explore the possibilities of setting the control parameters of existing functions to achieve the results you seek. If you are still unsatisfied, you should look at the most promising functions and see if you could add what is called a "customer exit." This is an interface, normally quiescent in the function, which can be activated as a way of launching out of the function in a controlled manner in order to execute a piece of program that you have developed to do that extra piece of work that is not part of the function's everyday repertoire.

If you cannot get a simulation of your target concept to perform as you want it to, even with extra customer exits, you have to go over to the ABAP/4 Development Workbench, where you will find the tools necessary to carry out major surgery on copies of existing functions in order to build the functionality you desire.

When you have selected from a standard SAP R/3 Reference Model the functions you need, and when you have built any extra programs, you have to get the whole system customized. All the necessary routines are already in the SAP R/3 system and its applications.

The Beginnings of Customizing

Fine-tuning of your system begins with the approval for your target concept. You will have already gone through the meticulous discipline in which the process selection matrices have been used to select just those functions that are directly needed for your enterprise, together with certain others that will be suggested by the system because they are mandatory stepping-stones to the results you are seeking.

As the system becomes aware of the details of your target concept during the process of identifying functions from the process selection matrix, it can select for itself those Customizing activities that it knows will have to be performed before the new system can go live and work properly from the start. There are some five thousand Customizing activities to choose from.

Objectives

Customizing has to achieve three objectives—economically in terms of cost and manpower, but reliably in terms of building a system that will stand up to battering by real and sometimes erroneous data and real and sometimes careless users. SAP R/3 Customizing has three jobs to do, as follows:

- Introducing and extending SAP R/3 system applications, smoothly and transparently

- Adapting the neutral reference functions to the company's target concept in detail

- Controlling and documenting the process of introducing the system

Milestones in the Delivery of a System

It is always possible to look back on a complex project and divide it into milestone stages identifying the significant events. What is much more difficult, and much more productive if done well, is to set out these stages beforehand.

There follows a summary of the procedural model recommended in the SAP IMG-implementation guide, which is written and structured using hypertext techniques that enable the online reader to move quickly to information relevant to the task in hand.

The implementation guide in its computer-assisted manifestation is at the core of Customizing. It will remind you of what must be done and keep track of what has been done. And it will be tailored to your target as soon as you have decided which applications you are going to be using.

Concept and Plan

To arrive at a definition of the target concept and a plan of how to get there entails both requirements analysis and conceptual design. The organization of the development project itself has to take place alongside the work on the target.

Requirements and Project. Somebody has to gather together all the requirements from all the responsible departments concerning the new system and its purposes. Then there has to be an organizational plan of the project activities and a declaration of the standards to be achieved and the tests to be applied to the work to prove the quality.

System and Training. The installation of the SAP R/3 system has to come early in a project because the tools will need it, although you can get a long way along the line by using the PC versions of the SAP R/3 Analyzer and the R/3 Reference Model. Training will have to take place on the tools and the system. Everyone in the project will have to learn the SAP concepts and methods.

Project Functions, Interfaces, and System Infrastructure. The functions, procedures, and responsibilities have to be set out for the project team. Then work has to start on designing the interfaces required by the target system and the infrastructure it will need in terms of all the physical facilities and resources that will have to be in place in addition to the software.

Documented Prototype

The plan arrived at by the foregoing procedures must be checked for quality before work begins on the prototype. To realize it, detailed design has to be completed and implemented for at least the interfaces and the most frequently called procedures. Organizational structures and basic data must be determined during this stage.

Printed forms, reporting, and authorization need attention next before the prototype can be subjected to proper quality checking.

Productive System Ready

With the prototype working and approved, the productive system enters its final planning phases. User documentation should have been written by your implementation team by now.

The productive environment, peopled with trained users who can call on a competent system administration, is essential. The new organization should be in place and archiving should be well under way.

Before the productive system can be given a quality check, there will have to be an analysis of the likely loading on the system. The integration of the system components should be tested and the final manual entry of master data completed.

Optimization

With the system operational, the two tasks are to optimize both the technical operations and the organizational. Tools are available for measuring system component performance. The Computer-Aided Testing System (CATT) is an example.

Two Model Companies

The SAP R/3 system is delivered complete with Client 000, which represents a neutral test company with the following attributes:

- A simple organizational structure
- Consistent parameters for all applications

- Country-specific accounting schemes

- Standard settings for account determination

- Configurations for control of standard transactions

- Example profiles

The example profiles included in Client 000 are as follows:

- Dunning and Payment

- Material requirements planning and forecasting

- Pricing

- Message control

- Printout and form layouts

- Authorization structure

The test client 000 can be used to explore the integration of the various system components and the way they are controlled by the SAPGUI-Graphical User Interface. According to the type of business conducted by your company, you can set up a working model which uses the functions supplied to demonstrate how your target system might be developed.

It is of course important for the implementers to engage the interest of many people in the organization because it will be necessary to use their experience to improve on whatever system is operating at the time. The test client 000 can provide this demonstration and invitation to cooperate.

Client 001 is reserved for production-related preparatory activities. It lacks master data and movement data. No company-specific parameters have been defined. Standard settings are available for some functions. If your company uses workshop data collecting devices, for example, the client 001 can be used to check that they can be properly linked through the standard R/3 interfaces.

The Procedure of the Customizing Menu

Each SAP application contributes a Customizing menu as an alternative to the IMG-implementation guide. The following information types—infotypes—are addressed in both the system-aided guides and the Customizing menus:

- Concept information

- Dependencies

- Standard settings

- Recommendations

- Activities

- Status management

- Documentation

The intention of using a standard set of infotypes is to ensure that all applications and their users can interpret the data stored in any of the databases. The infotype signals how the data is to be decoded and how it is used in business programs. There may be several thousand infotypes in use in an implementation.

Transactions for Setting Parameters

The user is guided on the basis of business criteria and objects to conduct the essential setting transactions. It is not necessary to know the names of any tables, table relationships, or transaction codes.

The IMG-implementation guide itself provides a plan of activities. Information can be stored on deadlines, resources, and status management. The IMG acts as a dedicated project manager system. Project-specific documentation can be assigned to every element of the guide so that it becomes an effective record of how the Customizing took place.

Entire organizational units can be copied, deleted, and provided with new parameters.

From Here...

- What are the detailed methods for interfacing?

  Chapter 3, "System Architecture and Distributed Applications," outlines the system architecture including interfacing.

- I am ready to begin a new project.

  The SAP R/3 Analyzer is discussed in Chapter 6, "Tool-Supported Optimization with the R/3 Analyzer."

- Where is Customizing most extensively used?

  All applications use it. Materials Management, described in Chapter 23, "Understanding the MM-Materials Management Module," entails very detailed data modeling.

- What comes next after Customizing?

  Either your system goes live, or you have a project on the ABAP/4 Development Workbench, which is described in Chapter 28, "ABAP/4 Program Development with the R/3 Workbench."

Part III

Complex System Management

Italy	62
Spain	59
Denmark	56
Czech Republic	41
Sweden	39
Hungary	26

| 479 |
| 54 |
| 24 |
| 16 |
| a 14 |

Japan	100
Australia	68
Singapore	32
Malaysia	22
Korea	10
Hong Kong	7
Thailand	7

South Africa	69
Saudi Arabia	9
Israel	3
Arabic Emirates	2
Namibia	2

Products
71%

Steel,
ical Engineering,
utomative

Food and Tobacco Industry

Office & EDP Equipment

8.0%

7.3%

6.6%

Mining, Utilities, Transportation

4.6%

ommercial,
and Social
10.3%

4.5%

Trade, Retail and Wholesale

3.9%

Traffic and News
Communication

tronics, Precision
chanics, Optics
14.5%

3.8%

Metal Products and
Primary Metal

3.6%

Universities and
Technical Colleges

Chemical Industry,
Mineral Oil Production
18.2%

Others
(see chart below)
11.6%

2.9%

Wood, Paper and
Printing Industry

Others

Credit Banks, Financial Services	1.9
Quarrying, Fine Ceramics, Glass	1.9
Hospitals	1.7
Miscellaneous	1.7
Insurance Companies	1.6
Building Trade, Construction	1.4
Leather, Textile and Clothing Industry	.9
Trade Associations and Federations	.3
Agriculture, Forestry, Fishing	.2

eable product

Develop
omplete and
ncustomized

Customized tools

Develop

Deliver

Rate of market growth

High

Build large market
share as fast as
possible – at
reasonable cost

- Identify effective sales and marketing
  campaigns – quick feedback on results

- Build sales capacity quickly using
  standardized multimedia product
  presentations

- Erect entry barriers to keep out
  competition – customer database used
  for attractive after-sales service and
  support

Develop
for right
and at le

- Imp
  bet
  and

- Use
  exp

Reduce sales and
marketing costs while
maintaining market
share

- Service low value customers using low
  cost channels eg. telesales, direct mail

- Contact database to help retain key,
  high value, customers

- Link purchase patterns to SOP to
  prompt for automatic reordering

Reduce
key cus
for cross
opportu

- Sal
  pay

- Lo
  sys
  cus

Low
High

Relative market sha

Customer Attractiveness

High

Four Seasons

Seed

Agnos

ICL

British Rail

Chapter 8

Continuous Business Development

The context into which a SAP system will be introduced will seldom be a green-field site for a business that is unique because nothing like it has ever been seen before.

The system will be part of a continuous business development. And as the analysis proceeds, it will become more clear just where the business could, with advantage, be developed. As the first modules of the system go live, there will be a further flood of information on how the business can be improved.

Should you be in the advantageous position of being able to direct the analysis of the data that will inevitably be stored by the system, you will be able to prepare reports to show the best ways of continuing the development process. The SAP modules are designed to facilitate continuous development, not for the sake of running a more elaborate system, but for the purpose of making your business more effective and efficient.

Whether you are looking at an existing computer-supported business, a manual system, or a recent implementation of a SAP-integrated suite of applications, there are certain issues that you ought to address before you take any further steps to develop your business processes.

Contemplating a Transition from Traditional Accounting

Auditors who are used to inspecting the financial documents of a company are sometimes very street-wise. They have seen it all before. They can teach the computer people a thing or two.

Comments on Data Recording

In the days of the handwritten ledgers, there was always a chance that the chief accountant would let you write a marginal note to explain an entry in the ledger. But a computer system will encapsulate the entry with the original annotations, never to be altered. The lesson to be learned from this is that the

In this chapter, you learn:

- The lessons to be learned from the pre-computer world of accounting.

- What SAP says about system design procedure.

- How you recognize the need and prepare for business change.

- What the business reengineering project manager should define as the aim of the first phase of the project.

III

Complex Management

modern system must be very strict about enforcing a consistent input convention, a policy, a habit, a set of rules that are obeyed by everyone and can be interpreted and be informative to a stranger, an auditor for example, some months after entry. All users have to be as accurate in memorandum fields as they are in the fields that will be checked by the accounting procedures.

A Design Checklist

The SAP Design Checklist points to issues that have to be taken into account before beginning implementation or at an early stage. Product IMG—Implementation Management Guide, is a detailed support system for implementation.

The SAP R/3 Analyzer provides tools and prompts for eliciting the necessary preliminary information, but the customer management team will have to arrive at suitable conclusions and decisions.

The task of technical interviewing to determine how work is currently progressed is an art form requiring talent and patience, not to mention an efficient and flexible recording method for which the usual surrogate is a secretary. The modern methods are described in Chapter 6, "Tool-Supported Optimization with the R/3 Analyzer."

How Are Things Done Now?

One of the obvious starting points for business process reengineering is a description of the current mechanisms, be they mediated by people or by machines. There are three possible sources for this invaluable information, and usually they will not correspond on all or even any points of detail.

These sources of a view on how things are done now are the management, the documentation, and the people who do the work.

Management's View of the Current System

Obviously there are some aspects of a business that are known to some managers but not to the workforce and which are not documented.

Then there are some aspects of the business that the management has initiated but not followed up in close enough detail to determine whether their intentions have been put into practice in the way they instructed.

Finally, there are aspects of the business that have developed through local initiatives, for good or for ill, and have not come to the notice of management. Operational doctrine has been recognized as what happens as a matter of custom and practice in addition to or in spite of what instructions have been received from management or what is written in the documentation. Operational doctrine is not necessarily better or worse than the doctrine set out in the book. It is a neutral term.

Documentation on the Current System

It is rare that the current system is fully documented to the extent that a suitable person could do any job, albeit slowly, by following exactly the instructions in the book.

What may be available is the specification drawn up when the system was being put out to tender or when the contractor confirmed what was being implemented. However, the chances are that the system developers and programmers were too busy designing and programming to find time to document everything. And any aspects of the business that were not captured by the software or paper system forms are not likely to be available for inspection by anyone seeking to reengineer the business process some time later.

Embarrassing though it may be to read, one of the most valuable documents pertaining to the current system would be a log of the complaints and snags encountered by its users, including the customers and suppliers—who must be counted as prime users of any business system, even if they press none of its keys.

The user training staff members are a good source of information on the current system. They will perforce know their specialty well through having had to explain it many times and coach many beginners in its subtle ways.

Trainers will also have a hidden agenda of ideas that they promote on top of or in spite of the official doctrine. They will know ways of using the current system to navigate around problems that were not anticipated by the designers or not thought serious enough to warrant additional software or hardware investment. In the craft trades, there are always to be found some tools that have been constructed or reshaped by the users to make them more effective.

Operational Doctrine

Operational doctrine is what you pass on unofficially to your fellow workers in order to make their tasks more successful. It may be a habit of taking a break even if the phone is ringing, or it may be the infamous device of the absent principal. "I am terribly sorry, but my boss has instructed me not to allow anyone a discount." You may pass on operational doctrine in a formal lecture to every newcomer, or you may not even realize that you are a role model for how to survive in the workplace.

There may be an unofficial practice of entering data that is known to be faulty so the difficult work item may land up on the supervisor's screen and, with luck, be dealt with by someone on the next shift.

Not all operational doctrine is bad for business. The implementers of a SAP system have tremendous scope for building into the new system all the best elements of the operational doctrine that have evolved through experience with its ancestor, whether this was a computer system or a paper-and-people system.

Wisdom from operational doctrine does not come without effort. It is amazing how many experts on all subjects pronounce on what is happening, or what has happened, or what is there, without ever having visited the place.

A token visit to the site is better than no visit at all, but the more time spent with the people closest to the work, the better. In skills analysis work, it used to be considered only right and proper that the analyst should have a try at performing the skill. An expert would be on hand to give help and guidance, and if he were really kind, he would

III

Complex Management

set up the job so that the poor old analyst would have a reasonable chance of not making too much of a fool of him- or herself, or worse.

There are two reasons to justify trying the job for oneself. It might become apparent just what sort of job it is for the person doing it on a daily basis, and it might demonstrate to the expert that you think this job important enough to spend a little time looking at it. If you are really lucky you will be able to spend enough time on the spot to allow a little discourse on what really matters and what the challenging aspects are.

Listen very carefully to what is said when you have been on site for some time. So often the most valuable information does not come to light until the contact has matured to the extent that jokes may be exchanged. Listen with utmost care to the last few moments of your contact with the person who knows most about the job and the system.

Layers of Decision

As more and more business processes are mechanized and automated, and as more and more communication channels converge on each individual, it is clear that the responsibility for taking decisions has moved down the management chain.

The telephone operator in touch with a client does not have to transfer the call to someone else for a decision, because the information and the logical basis for a decision are on the screen as soon as the needs of the client can be identified. Indeed, there may well be no telephone operator as such in a telesales organization.

Because the system can take decisions on the basis of prearranged logical rules applied to the individual case, there is no need for a wise supervisor to take part in the interaction with the client. One layer of decision-making has been let go.

The SAP implementers have to be very careful to check out who makes what decision in practice, whatever the books may say. If the business process reengineering fails to make use of the speed and data access of the new systems, it will fall into the trap of simply copying the existing mechanisms, rather than creating new methods based on experience of the old, coupled with the benefits of the new technologies. Will it still be necessary to do things in the old way when the new systems are in place?

The most significant of the benefits of the new systems is the ability to take decisions rapidly and reliably.

All Good Ideas Have Already Been Suggested

People at work think a lot. They have ideas. They may not tell just anyone about these ideas for fear of ridicule. They may not allow them to appear in written reports.

Essential reading for the SAP research team are the reports on the current system and the business conducted on it. Essential listening is what anyone says about the current practices, whether it is good or bad, whether said in earnest or in jest.

Reading and listening are like brainstorming: much is useless; but you cannot tell which is which until afterwards. And a really good idea may be mentioned only once. With all this flow of written material and site visit anecdotes, the SAP researcher needs to be disciplined to look out for the soft spots, the opportunities for improvement.

Researching the Decision to Reengineer Business Processes

The cost and importance of this decision call for the most careful research and preparation, so that the decision is taken on the basis of what really matters and with each of the options given proper consideration. These research resources allocated to prepare the decision may go to waste; the actual benefits may differ in magnitude and direction and may pop up in unexpected places. Nevertheless, the decision to reengineer should be given the best possible chances of being the correct one.

Why Projects Fail

Although there are many reasons why reengineering projects fail, there are some obvious ones that should be considered by all concerned. Preparation may be ill-informed or totally absent; inadequate software or hardware may have been installed; application implementation may be incompetent and poorly resourced. Under each of these headings there are a number of factors that are worth taking care of.

Using a Project Research Team

To prepare for the important decisions, a research team seems an obvious necessity. Yet it is not uncommon for this team to be built from a variety of experts who are so knowledgeable in their own specialties that they cannot be spared to devote any attention to the project. The team does need time to do its work. It also needs discretion, insulation from the possibility of traumatic job turbulence, as well as expertise out of the ordinary.

Who should be in the team? The contractor may have to mix with the in-house research and development people. Expertise, fresh eyes, familiarity with the vendors, products, customers, competitors, and the marketplace as a whole: these are the qualities to be on the lookout for.

Tasking the Project Research Team

The purpose of establishing a project research team is to set up a good decision structure in which each option is supported by the relevant information. The team members will need to know the scope of this decision structure: how wide or how narrow is their brief? Should they consider any relevant issue, whether it be related to business, personnel, hardware, or software in content?

There are certain issues to be raised before deciding to implement SAP: consistency between modules, terminology, programmed function keys, conventions in screen layouts, languages, currencies, legal requirements, pricing data on invoices, health and safety, reporting, tax management, and rounding.

III

Complex Management

It is indeed providential that the SAP designers have built a tool to monitor and prompt all these decisions before the system goes live. It is described in Chapter 7, "R/3 Customizing."

The ABAP/4 Development Organizer

The ABAP/4 Development Organizer is a component of the ABAP/4 Development Workbench. The Organizer is a support tool for the development and maintenance of large software systems developed in SAP R/3. The target users are teams of developers and individuals: centralized efforts and local. Members of a project group may work on one or several computers.

Development projects are best divided up into various jobs, each of which is the responsibility of an individual or the leader of a project group. Any development object that is changed by a person or group assigned to a job will be automatically logged and then reserved exclusively for that specific job. No other developer may alter that object until it has been released by the job team that first changed it. Others can look at it, run it, copy it under a different identification, but only the developer who "owns" it for the time being can make any alterations.

By adopting this principle of a developer owning an object until it is finished, individual jobs can be released independently of one another. Changes are managed.

In addition to being assigned a responsible developer, each object under development is associated with a development class that designates the application area of the object. This allows the object to be found and the knowledgeable people to be identified.

When the development of an object has reached a satisfactory stage, it is released. Current versions of this object are then stored automatically, and the newly released version becomes immediately available to all applications that use it.

Developmental changes are usually first confined to a family of separate test systems, where their effects can be evaluated before being combined and transferred to productive systems.

Each transfer of a changed object from a test system is automatically logged, so that any problems arising may be attributed to the specific transfer responsible. It is usual to perform a simulation using the changed objects before allowing them to be transferred to the target system.

Part of each development job is to arrange hierarchically organized documentation that covers the aims of the project, its status, and any special aspects. The result is that any changes can be tracked and related to the stored versions they have superseded.

Software Engineering

The SAP approach to software development seeks to establish for each development project a structure of self-contained partial functions. They are self-contained in that an individual developer or a team may work on one of them knowing that their efforts will lead to a programming component that will integrate with SAP R/3 and the work of other developers. A partial function is a method and a computerized mechanism that will work effectively within the scope defined for it, not necessarily a complete function that an end user might invoke.

Because the work units are self-contained, they can be tested and adjusted before being built into larger sequences.

Whatever the size and scope of a software engineering development, whether it be a partial function or a complete application module, there are four distinct phases that should be resourced and documented for what they are.

Conceptual Design Phase. The first phase of a development project should reach its conclusion with the production of a conceptual design for the new business program. Conceptual design will seldom proceed in an orderly sequence; but there are four elements which should be recognized and documented: preliminary study, analysis, design, and presentation.

Preliminary Study of Value Adding Pathways. The preliminary study is focused by an overall aim. In general terms, this aim is to optimize performance and cost all along the pathways within the company where value is added, including the process of business process reengineering itself. The preliminary study should make a business case to justify the selection of business functions for development.

Analysis of the R/3 Reference Model. The R/3 Reference Model is discussed in Chapter 5. It is a part of the R/3 Basis system which can be used to determine which of the standard R/3 applications and functions should be selected and customized to suit your company's requirements.

Design from the EDM-Enterprise Data Model. Design is the explication of the right system concept in detail sufficient for its worth to be judged.

The EDM-Enterprise Data Model is derived from the R/3 Reference Model. It provides the business processes of your company as you would like them to be when the new development is completed: process, function, information flow, data, and organization. These views are discussed in Chapter 10, "The Open Information Warehouse and Enterprise Data Models."

Presentation of the Preliminary Study. Presentation is the process of building consensus up to the highest management level for the direction and cost of the development. There will have been a considerable amount of interchange between those who have clear ideas about how the business processes should be developed, and those who know what is achievable with the resources available in the existing system and within the existing staff. Additions to either of these and the allocation of funds for this purpose have to be approved on the basis of the presentation of the results of the preliminary study.

Defining the Application Structure. The second phase of a development project is entered when a budget has been allocated on the basis of the preliminary study for the purpose of elaborating the conceptual design so as to match the structure of the R/3 functions in detail. The main task will be to define the data architecture, the database organization, and to create a prototype of the intended system component. There should be iterative early prototyping of components with end users.

Realization and Implementation. The third phase of a development project begins when the data object management policies begin to be implemented.

For example, any data that will be accessed by the new business function being developed will have to be made available to it. If it is data that is already in a SAP application, then it will be in a format that is already compatible. If it is held in a legacy system for which there is a standard SAP interface, then the data can be accessed online or transferred in a single operation before the new function goes online. Should it be the case that the data in the legacy system is not in a format for which there exists a standard SAP interface, then arrangements will have to be made to have an ABAP/4 interface program written or for the data to be converted by an agency.

The development team has to ensure that all the fields specified in the Enterprise Data Model have been checked to confirm that they contain the proper data or will be able to access it when it is needed.

Final Test and Installation. The fourth phase of a development project has to include user training followed by a final test in which the new function is subjected to the demands it will meet when operational.

A new piece of program is an extension of the EDM enterprise data model and must be tested to ensure that it integrates properly. This entails an additional test which is carried out when the new components and the existing EDM are merged. A mass test and runtime analysis are needed to measure the effects of heavy system loads and prove that the resource allocation provisions are working and can meet the demand. At this stage it is normally necessary for the new function to be authorized for release which will allow it to be called by authorized users.

Making the Decision to Reengineer Business Processes

When all the research has been done and the information presented, there will come a series of decision stages that entail weighing intangibles and estimating probabilities. There are some well-known phenomena that may appear under these conditions. Human beings are not always very clever when it comes to picking winners. It is best to be aware of how good intentions can be led astray when dealing with intangibles and uncertainties.

Let's Face It

Office automation following on mechanization means the end of work for many people. If the human resources philosophy is really applied thoroughly, there can be a minimization of disturbance to those who find themselves without work. Fortunate are the personnel managers who have a means to relocate their staff in new jobs.

There Are Pitfalls

Input errors can give a lot of trouble if they are not detected at the time. Stress and anxiety can move a decimal point without being noticed, the person on the phone may not be the one you were expecting, and you may have called up the wrong screen. Modern business systems try to reduce the opportunities for input error by narrowing down the possibilities and having the operator choose from a list rather than enter the identifier, although there may be speed advantages in allowing people who know what they are doing to anticipate and type ahead.

Misunderstanding what is being said may occur through language and technical communication difficulties. Having the operator paraphrase what was thought to be the requirement may help; and the system can suggest what might be a standard wording. These are techniques that some operators have evolved for themselves and which can easily be supported by SAP and made available to all.

Misinterpretations of incidents and situations may give rise to operational problems. One tactic is to have the operator complete a checklist which is adjusted online so as to avoid asking for any information that is already known from the records or which can be inferred by answers to previous questions. For example, staff at a bank that accepts telephone transactions used to ask how they might help; now they begin by asking for your ZIP code, name, and initials. This allows their system to offer your last known address, which they recite for you to confirm before they move on down their list of questions. It is a quick procedure, and seems friendly.

Misreading of trends has caught many a businessperson. Something that changes only slowly or in subtle ways that are not thought important at the time can cause trouble. If one is reengineering a business process with a SAP system, there is no difficulty at all in having data analyzed to reveal any trends, however gradual. But what is not possible is for SAP to infer a trend when no data have been collected that could bear upon it.

Are customers buying mobile phones because they are fashionable, because they save time or money, or because they might come in handy in the event of a breakdown or threatening event? In the absence of any pertinent data, the SAP system may be able to provide an analysis of customers over several parameters, one of which might suggest a possible explanation. Further data must come from talking to customers, and so the SAP screen will have to be used to record free-text notes or perhaps a choice of key words or an entry in an analysis field based upon answers to some questions.

This example illustrates the use of modern technology to collect current data on what relevant people are thinking: what customers say; what suppliers say; what inquirers are asking about. And the facilities of SAP support such research studies from the exploratory stages right through to the stage where hard data can be collected.

The system will be ready to discern trends in the data as soon as any basis for the analysis can be specified.

Waste has always been a soft spot, whether in time, material, energy, or personnel. Business process reengineering can be the opportunity to set up methods for monitoring the consumption of these resources and for comparing one situation with another, one accounting period with another.

Profit and loss have always been part of business monitoring. Nowadays there are few work people who are totally out of contact with the computer, so there is the possibility of online assessment, in profit and loss terms, of the performance of managers, supervisors, operators, contractors, even advisors.

One might argue that the sort of monitoring of performance that can be carried out by the system is rather trivial: hours worked, calls made, expenses, sales, profits, staff turnover—a mixed bag indeed, some items more important than others, depending on the company and the person being monitored.

Monitoring the New Business

Is it too outrageous to claim that to reengineer a business by applying the SAP concept is to make it a new business?

If it is indeed a new business, it is right and proper to consider how and in what ways it is to be monitored. On what basis shall it be declared a success?

There are some favorite indices of success that are not unimportant, such as profit. Nowadays the success of a business will be judged in part on the basis of its effect on the environment. The employees will have their own dimensions for judging company performance.

However, a project to reengineer some business processes should not get very far before setting out some criteria by which it can be judged. What are to be the indicators of project progress, success, and failure? Where are the critical places to look for telltale signs of whether a project is going well or badly? Which numbers or other indicators should be scrutinized? Where are the pressure points to stop bleeding? Is there anywhere that the stick could be applied?

These queries that have to be answered in the context of a business process reengineering project if it is to be cost-effective are not peculiar to the computer industry. They are matters to which leaders of all work teams should give high priority. They apply with no less force to work teams of one, where the leader and the worker are the same person. You have to know where you are going in order to tell if you are progressing in the right direction.

From Here ...

- Quality management is the name of the game.

  The SAP concept of quality management is integral in all the applications and development tools. Consult Chapter 17, "Understanding the PP-Production Planning and Control Module."

- The problem is getting the right staff.

  There is an interesting collection of components associated with the Human Resources application explicated in Chapter 22, "Understanding the HR-Human Resources Module."

- Our company is not ready to take the plunge.

  You will find some good ideas and not a few powerful techniques set out in Chapter 30, "R/3 Business Workflow Management." Apply this method of serious business workflow control, and you will soon see how to further elevate your chances of business survival.

Chapter 9

Worldwide Business Computing Systems

You may have a world wide business that you run on the back of an envelope; or you may have a worldwide computing system that does hardly any business at all.

Multinational Accounting

Three groups of factors are important to centralized multinational companies—language, currency, and legal business practices, as follows:

- Operating screens and reports must be available in the language of the users.

- Amounts must appear in the local currency.

- The taxes, legal financial reports, and payment methods must be those acceptable to the host nation.

If the corporation has subsidiary companies trading in more than one nation, there may have to be an additional language and currency for use by head office, plus methods of making adjustments for any differences between accounting or other business practices in the overseas host nations.

The SAP system makes copious provisions for all three groups of factors.

Language

SAP supports an increasing number of languages. Each language is designated by a code that is entered during the logon process or defaults to the language defined in the user profile. Screens and online reports will appear in the language of the logon.

Operational Currencies

The following currencies have been defined for operational purposes; Their codes are assigned to each function by default, which you may alter:

- Local currency—is also the reporting currency for the company code

- Document currency—the one specified for entry on SAP Documents

In this chapter, you learn:

- The enhancements of the SAP R/3 system designed to make productive worldwide business processing an everyday affair.

- About the many regulations!

- About some departments where you can hear almost any language under the sun being spoken.

- Why the legal department keeps itself very busy with the regulations of other countries.

- Group currency—an alternative to document currency for group reporting
- Updating currency—defined for posting debits and credits to the GI-General Ledger in parallel with the local currency
- Credit limit currency—the currency chosen to maintain the credit limit
- Ledger currency—an alternative to the updating currency for that ledger

Additional currency assignments are available in the SAP Foreign Exchange Management component, which is part of TR-TM Treasury Management.

Currencies in Transactions

Each company code has a local currency for reporting. The system records amounts in this local currency and also in a currency that has been specified as the document currency, which will be used on all documents in addition to the local currency.

You can enter documents in any currency.

You have the following two options for converting currencies:

1. Enter an exchange rate when you enter the transaction document.
2. The system translates between document and local currencies by referring to a table of daily exchange rates.

The system can be customized in a couple of ways:

1. A specific user is obliged to enter amounts in a particular currency, which can be the local currency or the document currency.
2. A specific user may be permitted to enter amounts in either local or document currency.

Whatever the customizing arrangements, the system will display amounts in both local and document currencies. It will round off minor differences using rules established for this purpose. These differences can occur when several line items are converted and then added in both currencies.

Customer monthly debits and credits are kept by the system only in local currency. The reconciliation account for the Accounts Receivable subledger is kept in local currency and in all the other currencies that have been posted.

Currency Exchange Differences

A line item may be expressed in a currency other than the local or document currency. You can enter payments to clear such foreign currency line items using either local or document currency.

The payment expressed in the system document currency will have been converted from the local currency at an exchange rate adopted by the system according to the rules laid down for assigning the daily exchange rate. If this rate has changed from the rate prevailing when the invoice was written, the payment amount may not match the open item amount. In such cases, the system will automatically calculate and post an exchange difference entry to a separate account established for this purpose.

Currency Translation in Consolidation

There are three basic currency conversion methods used in the consolidation of group accounts:

- Reporting date method
- Modified reporting date method
- Temporal method

Groups of items in the balance sheet and profit and loss statement are converted at one of the three following exchange rates:

- Reporting date rate
- Average rate
- Historical rate

FI-LC Consolidation can translate any items at any rates and use any of the methods for any of the individual companies. There are several problems for which this program provides solutions:

- Exchange differences between the date of the transaction and the date of the currency conversion
- Rounding differences
- The assets history sheet using rates current on the reporting date
- If a transaction difference is posted, the previous translation differences will have to be reversed.

The international law requires that all intercompany balances be eliminated before presenting the balance sheet and profit and loss statement. All possible pairs of individual companies must be investigated for evidence that they have been trading with each other.

If the individual companies have installed and configured SAP accounting applications, there will have been automatic dual currency accounting in which every transaction is documented at the time in both the local currency and the currency designated for all transactions in the group. The FI-LC component will allow you to trace any currency translation differences between the local currency at the prevailing rate of exchange and the transaction currency. An exchange rate difference correction can then be posted in the balance sheet account designated for currency translation gains and losses and thus brought into the consolidated financial statement.

III

Complex Management

Foreign Currency Valuations

At the end of each posting period and at the end of the year, you may have to value open items that are expressed in foreign currency. You may need to value by a method for local tax purposes different from the method that stockholders in the parent company will want to see in the balance sheet and the profit and loss statement. The SAP method is to define two parallel valuation areas, each of which may value open items by a different method.

When the time comes to post a foreign currency payment, the system will clear any currency translation gain or loss that has already been recorded. The posting destination account may depend on the currency and the type of transaction. In any event, the system records on each open item the accumulated translation difference.

There is then a choice of displaying in your local currency either the historical original value of each open item or the current value.

When you clear an item such as this, the system automatically reverses this translation gain or loss. You thus have the capability to monitor the situation at any time, not only at period end.

SAP Foreign Exchange Management System

The purpose of the Foreign Exchange Management system is to record, monitor, and settle foreign exchange contracts. Unlike most other foreign exchange systems, the SAP Foreign Exchange Management system is not targeted at banks. It is directly integrated with TR-CM Treasury, Cash Management and automatically posts entries to FI-Financial Accounting.

The system has international functionality and supports the international communication standards. Its distinctive feature is that it links foreign exchange contracts to the specific open items that are being hedged.

The instruments of foreign exchange are constantly being developed and supplemented by new instruments. You can easily incorporate new means of foreign exchange trading. The instruments currently recognized include the following:

- Various forward exchange transaction types
- Combination of hedging and use
- Global and individual hedging

The standard business functions of SAP R/3 are available to the Foreign Exchange Management system and integrate with it as follows:

- Cash management
- Automatic posting

- Automatic correspondence

- Document history

- Links to contracts, purchase orders, invoices

- Control by internal checking

- Centralized foreign exchange management

- Introduction of new instruments such as options and futures

- Flexible reporting

- Word processing and graphical presentation of reports

Foreign Exchange Business Types

A business type defines the business transaction as a program object and controls the processing logic in the system, including the data recorded by the system and how they are obtained.

The business type can determine the following operational details:

- Sequence of screens for data entry

- Data fields to be mandatory, optional or suppressed

- Manner in which TR-CM Cash Management and FI-Financial Accounting applications are updated by the Foreign Exchange Management System

The controlling functionality of business types can be adjusted online.

The system is provided with definitions for the most common business types covering the foreign exchange market instruments. You can define an internal business type and assign it to transactions by entering its code. The codes can be used to sort your business into the appropriate journals. Such internal business types can be used to control foreign exchange trading within a group of companies and support the concept of a centralized treasury department. There is an extensive range of SAP TM-Treasury Management components.

You can define a statistical business type for a special task. It will not update the TR-CM Cash Management system or any FI-GL, General Ledger balances, and in this respect is analogous to planning data.

Foreign Exchange Management Function Types

A function type defines the stage or milestone that a foreign exchange contract has reached in its life cycle when you post the transaction. You can decide which steps are relevant for your company. The following is an example:

- Initiating a transaction

- Modifying

- Prolonging

- Settling

Each transaction will generate a document on which will be recorded the business type and the function type, and hence the stage reached by a foreign exchange contract.

The business type and the function type together control the data entry and processing. The specific function type will determine the following:

- What appears on the data entry screen and which fields are suppressed

- Which fields require data and which are optional

- The control and release function

- The confirmation printout

- The integration of data into account

The system will automatically record all changes to a foreign exchange contract in the form of documents that log the changes of function type from initiation to settlement and archiving.

The INT-International Development Application

There is an established range of enhancements to the SAP R/3 system that are designed to customize a worldwide system according to the international trading communities in which it operates. These are presented as modules of the INT-International Development Application as follows:

- IN-APA Asian and Pacific Area

- IN-EUR Europe

- IN-NAM North America

- IN-AFM Africa and Middle East

- IN-SAM South America

Foreign Trade

The SD-Sales and Distribution application includes a module that is specialized in the regulations governing foreign trade.

SD-FT Foreign Trade

The following functions are available in the SD-FT Foreign Trade module:

- FT-Processing

- FT-Declarations to Authorities

- FT-Export Control

- FT-Preference Agreements

- FT-Control

Export Data Records

Where your company is operating in a business zone in which local export and import rules are in force, the SAP applications can be configured with the appropriate processing logic. For example, the European Community has imposed special rules on international business transactions since January 1993. The INTRASTAT procedure requires that reports be submitted periodically to the appropriate national authority for all export transactions within the community. The following export data items are relevant to INTRASTAT reporting, and are managed automatically by the SD-Sales and Distribution system and quoted in the delivery and billing documents:

- Community code, country and region of origin of the product are stored in the master record

- The route planned for delivery, which will determine the customs office and the mode of transport

- The business transaction type and the export procedure

The customer master records will include the value added tax VAT REG NO field in which the company's VAT registration number is stored. It applies at the company code level of organization structure, and therefore to all structural elements below it.

Country-Specific Regulations

The business practices and legal requirements of specific countries extend over the following kinds of issue:

- Legal Reporting

- Valuations

- Taxes

- Payment Processing

The following examples illustrate the differences in national codes of practice that can be installed as integral components of a specific SAP R/3 system:

- Federal Republic of Germany—Check/Bill of Exchange

- Switzerland—POR Procedure

- France—LCR and LCC

- Italy—Ricevuta Bancaria

Special National Human Resources Features

A substantial part of the HR-Human Resources application is already defined to accept international operations as a normal part of business. However, there are some aspects that require the integration of supplements programmed to recognize differences in the legal requirements and business practices of different nations and different business communities.

HR-Human Resources National Supplements

The national supplements provide dynpros and the associated screen designs, which can take advantage of different language pools, to conduct the human resources business functions according to the customs, terminology, and legal requirements of the country concerned. With globalized enterprises, the personnel administration need not be for the country where the functions are being utilized.

Multilingual Capabilities

Applications and modules within applications can be presented in any of the supported languages. Alternatively, the application can be maintained in the language of the host installation and then any of its constituent functions can be assigned a different language according to the user profile of the person logging on to operate it.

Language Text Pools for ABAP/4 Programs. When the code in an ABAP/4 program requires a text element to be displayed on a screen, it specifies the number of the text element to be used. The code does not have to be changed in order to access another element if the language of the user is changed. The language in which the text element is presented is determined by the language selected by the user profile.

Language Text Pools are used for screen layouts, online help, and online documentation.

Pictographic Languages. The DBCS is a double-byte character set system that can support the pictographic languages that have a large number of characters—Japanese and Chinese, for instance.

Wide Character String Handling. The ABAP/4 language has been extended to recognize data type W, for wide character fields, and some other functions that permit double-byte characters to be mixed with normal single-byte characters in the same field.

From Here ...

■ The technical problems of worldwide computing seem insurmountable.

  You might feel that, but the SAP standard business software has been there before and already sorted out all the technical problems. See Chapter 3, "System Architecture and Distributed Applications."

■ Where is it possible to find out exactly which function is in each module?

  You will find a method of locating functions described in Chapter 5, "The R/3 Reference Model." See Chapter 6, "Tool-Supported Optimization with the R/3 Analyzer," for a discussion of business process optimization using the R/3 Analyzer.

■ What is an Enterprise Data Model?

A good one will show you what makes your company tick. Try Chapter 10, "The Open Information Warehouse and Enterprise Data Models."

■ What about head office functions?

There are two possibilities: Chapter 14, "Understanding the Enterprise Controlling Module," and Chapter 15, "Understanding the TR-Treasury Module." Or you might prefer Chapter 12, "Understanding the FI-Financial Management Module."

■ Where can I find more information on the topics covered in this chapter?

See Chapter 22, "Understanding the HR-Human Resources Module," and Chapter 20, "Understanding the SD-Sales and Distribution Module."

III

Complex Management

Chapter 10

The Open Information Warehouse and Enterprise Data Models

The purpose of an information warehouse is to provide technical, business, and statistical data for any part of the corporation that might need it. The purpose of an enterprise data model is to provide a structure into which data can be fitted so as to make sense to those who contemplate it.

The warehouse provides the information; the enterprise model gives it business meaning.

The Open Information Warehouse Concept

The concept of an open database includes the notion that all data is stored in tables apparently ready to be instantly inspected and used without any need for complex data retrieval instructions in a specific language peculiar to the one vendor.

An open information warehouse suggests that all the information is readily available in a form ready for use without the need for special access operations. There is also the implication that the inventory of the warehouse is comprehensive and up-to-date.

Data Sources

SAP information systems are available for all the main applications and are an integral part of their operation. They are an obvious source of data concerning their specific areas of business activity. And they already cooperate with one another so as to share master data such as supplier details and materials master data. They are also integrated with the financial accounting modules.

If the open information warehouse is to be developed in support of the EIS-Executive Information System, then there will be a demand for information from the TM-Treasury Management module, which could include online information links to the financial and materials market information systems provided by non-SAP vendors.

This chapter begins by identifying the sources of business data and then goes on to relate it to models of the enterprise:

- What the difference is between a data model and a reference model.

- What a data dictionary is.

- The difference between "data" and "information."

- How you find your way in the information warehouse.

The following SAP sources contribute to the open information warehouse:

Financial Information System (FIS), see Chapter 12, "Understanding the FI-Financial Management Module"

Controlling Information System (CIS), see Chapter 13, "Understanding the CO-Controlling Module"

Shop Floor Information System (SFIS), see Chapter 17, "Understanding the PP-Production Planning and Control Module"

Production Information System (PPIS), see Chapter 18, "Understanding the PP-PI Production Planning for Process Industries and Modules"

Plant Maintenance Information System (PMIS), see Chapter 19, "Understanding the PM-Plant Maintenance Module"

Purchasing Information System (PURCHIS), and Sales Information System (SIS), see Chapter 20, "Understanding the SD-Sales and Distribution Module"

Human Resources Information System (HIS), see Chapter 22, "Understanding the HR-Human Resources Module"

Materials Management Information System (MMIS), see Chapter 23, "Understanding the MM-Materials Management Module"

The DMS—Document Management System

The resources of the DMS-Document Management System will be at your disposal to help you find what you require in the open information warehouse. The R/3 Classification System comprises many functions designed to help you locate information held in document form. You may search on the basis of subject matter, and you may search for an item because you know it is linked with a data object such as:

- Another document
- A material identified by its material number or by its name, or part of its name
- An item of equipment where you have given its name or only the identification of the activity where it is used
- A project identified by its number, the person responsible, the purpose, and so on
- A quotation
- A sales order
- A customer or a vendor identified by an attribute in the master records

EDM—Enterprise Data Model

The purpose of an enterprise data model is to make sense of and take account of how the business uses the data structures defined in the active ABAP/4 data dictionary.

The enterprise data model is built from entity-relationship elements that portray the relevant information objects and their relationships from a business standpoint.

For example, the following relationship is between data structures seen from a data processing standpoint:

```
Value S = Value C + Value P
```

The same relationship may admit a different interpretation when seen from a business perspective:

> Profit **is** Sales Revenue **less** Costs

One view is a model for the computer to specify the calculation procedures; the other is a model of how the business can survive and flourish if the management can manipulate the values in a certain way. These examples are obviously a little sparse. Part of a slightly more developed model is shown in Figure 10.1.

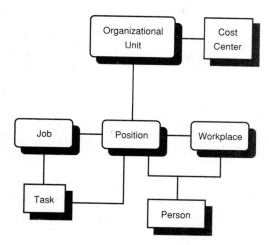

Fig. 10.1   Part of an Enterprise Data Model.

Object Types in an Enterprise Data Model

The following object types appear in the example model fragment:

- **Organizational Unit**, which is part of the R/3 Reference Model and will be assigned the name of the operating company or department that the enterprise data model is being used to represent

- **Position**, which is modeled from the R/3 Reference Model and named to suit the specific company with a title such as Sales Representative

- **Workplace**, of which there may be several assigned the same position, each able to accommodate one person

- **Job**, which is a set of tasks based on a specific workplace but not necessarily the only set of tasks performed there

- **Task**, which is a component of a job and usually comprises a fairly well-defined set of work input materials or messages for which there are appropriate work procedures

Two other object types, not part of the Human Resources Organization and Planning component, are necessarily addressed by relationships in this arena. They serve to particularize any instance of the model by naming a person who is assigned to perform a job and therefore is attached to a workplace which carries the responsibilities of a position, and a **Cost Center** such as a specific plant or department.

Relationships in an Enterprise Data Model

The data model fragment in Figure 10.1 implies the following relationships:

- A named person **holds both** a Workplace and a Position.

- The Workplace **is part of** the Position.

- The Position **is part of** an Organizational Unit.

- The Organizational Unit **is allocated to** a particular Cost Center.

- The Position **describes** a Job.

- The Job **describes** one or more Tasks.

- A Task **describes** a special case of a Position.

There is a system of graphical symbols used by the R/3 system to display different views of the Enterprise Data Model so as to emphasize the relationships between the objects of the model.

Organizational Structure in an Enterprise Data Model

The SAP R/3 general organizational units relevant to all applications are taken from the standard reference that is the R/3 Enterprise Data Model:

- **Client** is the highest level in R/3. The data of one client may not be accessed by another client. There is often a training client and a testing client, in addition to the client code that represents your group or corporate identity and under which the SAP system runs normal business. Some data is managed at the Client level because everyone in the corporate group of companies will want to refer to exactly the same information and be certain that it has been maintained up-to-date and correctly. Vendor addresses would be an example of data managed at the client level.

- **Company Code** signifies a legal unit under the client that produces its own financial documents, the balance sheet, and the profit and loss statement, and may well maintain them continuously reconciled.

■ **Plant** is an organizational unit that is seen as central to the production planning concept. A plant can be a production site, or it can be a group of storage locations that share materials. Plant is the unit for which MRP prepares plans and maintains the inventory. It is the focus of MM-Materials Management. Each plant will have been given planning and control elements such as material, inventory, operations, work centers, and so on.

The lower levels of organizational structure will tend to be specific to the application. For example, the lower levels of a warehouse data structure will reference warehouse areas and perhaps bin types and bin numbers, whereas the lowest level in a human resource personnel data structure will be an individual person.

SAP R/3 Business Objects

An object in the language of Object-Oriented programming is an entity that carries a data element that signifies the state it is in, such as OFF or ON, and some method by which this state can be changed. There may be more than one method of changing an object's state, and it may have more than two states. What matters to the user is what else happens, or could happen, if an object was made to change its state. For example, an object that had the function of recognizing when a purchase order had arrived could also have been given the functions of initiating such other actions as checking the stock availability and the customer's credit status.

You could imagine a more complicated business object that had the function of finding not only the best supplier for the goods required but also other potential customers for these goods. Such a business object might behave very much like a free marketeer. It could be allowed to search widely for both customers and suppliers. You may wish to endow it with rules for choosing the best buy in the context of the pool of customers available. You may also wish it to use the profitability of each potential trading activity as one of the factors to be taken into account when deciding on the best course of action. It might be prudent to set limits to the scope of this free marketeer business object and have a human assessor be called into the functionality when these limits are approached.

This example would not be too creative in many industrial contexts. More and more companies are adopting a flexible structure. There will be purchasing staff, marketing staff, and sales staff carrying out elements of this complex function. A standard business object would add the routine widening of search horizons because the information-gathering process will not entail extra human time.

Now suppose the suppliers identified by our marketeer business object were themselves alerted that a requirement for their type of product was put out to competitive tender. They might well have a similar type of business object that could find the best way of meeting the requirement. And so the marketeer business object could find itself being used over and over again; each reincarnation using different particular details, but each utilizing the standard business process that had been programmed to work as efficiently as possible as a business object.

The SAP R/3 Business Object Repository

The BOR, Business Object Repository, is a database that holds reusable standard business processes that can be called upon to build a specific implementation quickly. This is but an extension of the SAP process of building standard business software elements that can be customized to suit their circumstances; but only within limits that are set so that the functional integrity of the program is not compromised. In particular, a SAP R/3 Business Object cannot be altered in such a way that it is no longer compatible with the rest of any R/3 implementation. It will always remain a fully integrated component.

Patterns of Events

One of the keys to designing useful business objects is the existence of recurring patterns that could be recognized by a system and that would be of business significance. The arrival of a purchase order is an event that can be detected in any of several different ways and checked for validity. Your business will expect other purchase orders. Therefore, investment in business objects to cope with them may be worthwhile. There is a pattern to such events: Purchase orders can be recognized.

If you are looking at a set of events that do not share any common features, you could be said to be a problem solver. You may have to create a new and unique procedure to deal with each event. But you may still find it convenient to make use of a database that contains business objects. If you are repairing a system and decide that a particular part needs replacing, it might be convenient to call up the maintenance object for that system and have it run not only system checks directly, or via keyed-in data, but also the stock control module to determine the best way of acquiring the part you need, its cost and delivery information.

Updating Business Objects

We have been illustrating the concept of business objects with examples of wide-ranging online functionality. An intermediate procedure is to have your data held as business objects that carry information that is static in between formal updates. A price list or book of telephone numbers could be said to be business objects. But if you never make any updates when new information is available, your business objects are not as useful as ones that are updated according to the rules that have been programmed into them, whether or not you decide to update them manually.

The Master Data Object Principle

It has always been fundamental to SAP standard business program design that each data object should reside in only one location where it is known to be the master data object. It may be copied but not altered without leaving a record of who altered it and when. Once a master object is updated, all subsequent calls to that object should encounter the new information.

The standard date functions in SAP have always been business objects that carried information, such as the system date and time, and processes that could transform this value to express the date and time in various time zones and in appropriate languages and formats. If you try to enter a date that is not in one of the acceptable formats, a SAP system will do its best to convert it. It will not let you enter the time or date in a format of your own invention because this may not be understood by other users and the business processes they are running.

Data Mining

The basic purpose of data mining is to look for patterns in data. The simplest pattern is one that satisfies a search query, such as all customers who have placed an order in the current financial year and who live with a specific marketing region. This type of convergent search will terminate when all examples that match the pattern are found, if there are any in the database.

Data mining usually refers to more intelligent searching, which falls into the categories of supervised and unsupervised machine learning. In each case, the machine is seeking to find which records in the database go together in some way because some aspects of their data can be related.

Supervision entails setting off the search by declaring some relationships in the data that have to be considered, at least to begin with. For example, records may only be examined further if they already reveal that the customer referred to has spent more than a certain amount in the period under consideration. Given this baseline, the supervised search can be told to look for patterns, for example, only in the type of goods purchased. You may then ask to find the purchasing patterns associated with the purchase of a particular item.

These data mining operations can only tell you which data values are associated: They can say nothing about the reasons. On the other hand, you may reasonably infer that your chances of making a sale to a prospect who has already bought a product associated with your product will be higher than if there is no discernible relationship.

Where the intelligent data mining engine has discerned a strong association may be the area in which to seek your objective, even if you cannot work out why some of the data values should appear as part of the significant pattern. For example, it was said that prospective air combat pilots who could list a large number of items of sporting equipment were more likely to become successful flyers than those who could name only a few. The explanations for this could be diverse. Sportsmen have better hand-eye coordination; team players are used to doing what they are told and putting up with discomfort.

If you use a pattern discerned by data mining to guide your future activities, you must expect some disappointments. Sometimes the prediction will turn out to be false for individual cases: Some of the rejected candidates would have been successful. This fallibility can be demonstrated by carrying out your pattern recognition and then paying no attention to it until a large sample of data has been accumulated.

How good does your prediction look now? How many successes would you have lost if you had followed the policy suggested by the pattern mined from the data?

Your accountant will be able to tell you how much money you might have saved by applying the policy compared to what you actually spent by ignoring it.

For example, an unselective advertising campaign may reach some unexpected customers. And their unusual data can then be used to help discern yet more significant patterns.

Some data-mining products are set up to develop a range of data models that are then applied to fresh data in a competitive manner to see which variation is the best predictor. By this means it is possible to determine the relative worth of each element in the model. This may be important if the cost of obtaining the data object is high.

Having to conduct an interview, for example, may entail a very high cost, which may or may not be worthwhile in terms of the consequences of making a false positive prediction and the consequences of making a negative or rejection decision when this would not have been justified. More subtle computations of probabilities can be used to steer the data-mining engine in the direction most likely to be fruitful.

SAP R/3 Business Object Repository

The concept of a business object is central to the design philosophy of SAP software. Each SAP standard business process is programmed in ABAP/4 code. These highly reliable software components are not open to alteration by the user organization. However, the actions they take can be controlled by the information stored, perhaps dynamically, in the tables associated with them.

Because the code of a business object is alterable only by the SAP authorized programmers, the system of business objects works reliably together. What the implementation engineers have to do is to charge the control tables with the data required to service the client organization. Now these control tables are themselves made according to master data specifications which are business objects in their own right, because they are able to prevent unsuitable data from getting into their storage locations.

Thus, the total collection of business objects, whether single data records or complex modules of data and procedures, constitutes the SAP R/3 system. If you examine any one of these objects, you will be made aware of the functions it performs and the controls that will be exercised over the information it will accept. The set of business objects is therefore a dynamic system documentation. Whatever you need to know is always available as part of the business object itself.

The way to access this documentation is by means of an API, Application Programming Interface. For example, you could invoke an API that will present the application documentation on your GUI, Graphical User Interface. If you are working with Release 3.1 or 4.0, this GUI could be presented to you across the Internet and displayed on your portable PC or whatever terminal device could operate as a Virtual Machine for Java Applets. If you had a business process modeling tool with a suitable API to your R/3 application, then you could see the system documentation in the form of graphical and other displays according to how you had configured your modeling tool. Should you be operating with a SAP or third-party Business Process Re-engineering tool, then you will probably find a suitable API to look at the structure of your SAP R/3 Application.

Structure of the Object Repository

So that you may access the contents of the R/3 Repository in an orderly and efficient manner, its contents are identified by their purpose.

API Application Programming Interfaces

- Process Models
- Function Models
- Data Models
- Sap Business Objects
- Object Models With Data And Connections

Other Repository Contents

- Data Object Definitions
- Screen Specifications
- Program Objects Needed For Developments to R/3 Basis
- BOR, SAP Business Object Repository

The BOR, Business Object Repository, was introduced in SAP R/3 Release 3.0 to manage the data, transactions, and events in an R/3 implementation as an integrated set of SAP Business Objects. Each of these objects gives access to processes and data that is structured according to specific data models, which themselves are part of the enterprise data model. Thus, by design, a SAP Business Object will only deal with data that conforms to the correct structure as defined by the EDM, Enterprise Data Model. Therefore, any other application or external system that has to interact with this object will be able to interpret data and condition it so as to be acceptable to the model.

The SAP Business Object is a component that is built to integrate seamlessly with the rest of an R/3 implementation.

At runtime, the coding and location of the business object are identified by the registration element, which is defined as part of the definition of object types in the Business Object Repository. The client never knows the registered location of the object. The client may be accessing the business object via a distributed system, perhaps using the Internet. But the business object merely receives a request via the BOR and reports the results back to the client along the same route.

Another opportunity afforded by the inclusion of the Business Object Repository is the facility to allow an individual client to create a Company-specific business object, which is created as a subtype of a standard SAP Business Object. It therefore inherits all the attributes, methods, and events that are essential if the object is to integrate with the rest

III

Complex Management

of the R/3 implementation. The client can then edit the data definitions and store the company-specific business object under its own name. The runtime component of the Business Object Repository is then simply instructed to use the new business object in place of the master that is supplied with the system.

The Business Object Repository is equipped to respond to SAP-RFC, Remote Function Calls, from outside R/3; perhaps from an R/2 or third-party system, for example. There are interfaces currently available to comply with standards such as OMG's CORBA and Microsoft's COM/DCOM.

Release 3.0 contained 170 SAP Business Objects in the Business Object Repository. Release 3.1 includes almost 1,000 different business objects designed to the high SAP standards. Release 4.0 will contain many more.

From Here...

The open information warehouse is a concept that is able to be realized in practice because all the integrated SAP system components can be called upon to supply data that is structured in accord with the Enterprise Data Model that has been established for your company. Particular details are discussed in the following chapters concerning the R/3 application module to which the data of interest belongs.

- How is the data stored?

   The system of data objects is discussed in Chapter 4, "Architecture."

- How do you find out what SAP standard business functions are likely to be needed for your company?

   See Chapter 5, "The R/3 Reference Model."

- How are the materials master records managed in the continuous processing industries?

   See Chapter 18, "Understanding PP-PI Production Planning for Process Industries Modules."

Chapter 11

A Computing Center Management System

The purpose of the Computing Center Management System (CCMS) is to provide an efficient and flexible system for monitoring and controlling the SAP system and its application modules. It is required to manage the routine tasks of monitoring and controlling background processing and database backups. The intention of the design of the CCMS-Computing Center Management System is to build into it the best methods of discovering problems as early as possible.

The complexity of modern worldwide business systems raises certain questions which have to be answered by being able to point to reliable and tested software and hardware that has been proved to be able to cope with this complexity. The following are some of these questions:

■ Can the CCMS-Computing Center Management System manage very large networks and global companies?

The CCMS combines with the various host and application system platforms to build an integrated large network manager.

■ Is the CCMS-Computing Center Management System an open system?

SAP extensions of the SNMP-Simple Network Management Protocol have been developed to provide various MIB-Management Information Bases. These are designed to interface with all types of systems and system platforms.

■ What happens if a component of a distant system breaks down?

A global alert monitor function will display this fact in the CCMS-Computing Center Management System.

■ In a global system, where are the computing loads managed?

The CCMS-Computing Center Management System is able to assign users to sufficient free capacity and oversee the time controlled distribution of system resources.

This chapter covers the following areas:

■ System performance monitoring and watching for early signs that might presage problems.

■ Tools for controlling and managing the workloads over a distributed and complex system.

■ Methods of arranging open interfaces in large R/3 installations and heterogeneous system platforms, so as to integrate with a diversity of network services and third-party applications.

■ Security, reliability, confidentiality, and integrity.

III

Complex Management

■ How is the management of backing up data arranged in a global system?

The backup and recovery of data can be supervised through the CCMS-Computing Center Management System, together with the associated security and authorization.

CCMS Components

The components of the CCMS-Computing Center Management System are included in the standard R/3 system.

The SAP-GUI Graphical User Interface is provided with functions and control options that are easy to interpret by virtue of the extensive use of graphics, and easy to use by selecting items on the screen and applying the special function keys. Beginning with R/3 Release 3.0, the CCMS functions are supported by the SM-Service Management component which is designed to enhance computer center management.

The CCMS receives notification of service requirements which it can relate to its model of the equipment in the system. This model represents the hardware, software, network addresses, cables, and other items from which the network is built. Furthermore each component, such as a local network server, is represented with all its dependent software and hardware, and the object networks such as LAN (Local Area Networks), and WAN (Wide Area Networks).

Each item has been assigned standard partner activities so that appropriate service contractors can be identified if a fault arises. The accounting and pricing arrangements are also set up for each activity so that the administration of the service contracts may proceed efficiently and largely automatically.

The SM-Service Management component also responds to change notices so as to maintain the network models.

CCMS Integration

The SAP R/3 CCMS-Computing Center Management System is integrated with the facilities of the various host platforms and operating environments. For the R/3 system to qualify as an open system, it must support the interaction of any of its applications with any other to the extent that any of the user interfaces should be able to access any of the applications, which should be able to exchange data with each other. The interplay of applications depends on a shared system of international standards for interfaces, services, and data formats.

The following international standards are supported by R/3:

■ **TCP/IP**, Transmission Control Protocol/Internet Protocol, is the standard network protocol for open systems and is supported by all R/3 applications.

■ **RFC,** Remote Function Call, is the SAP ABAP/4 programming language adaptation of Remote Procedure Call, which permits other systems to call R/3 applications.

- **CPI-C,** Common Programming Interface-Communication, is a set of standardized definitions for program-to-program communication across systems.

- **SQL,** Structured Query Language, is the ANSI, American National Standards Institute, fourth generation language for manipulating data.

- **ODBC,** Open Data Base Connectivity, is a Microsoft standard for table-oriented data access based on SQL definitions.

- **OLE,** Object Linking and Embedding, is a Microsoft technology that permits objects to be connected and incorporated across multiple files and programs.

- **X.400** is a series of recommendations for message handling systems with extensive security options. These originate from the ITU, International Telecommunications Union through its agency, CCITT, International Telephone and Telegraph Consultative Committee.

- **X.500** is a series of standards for directory services, also issued as ISO 9594, drawn up by the CCITT. These standards require the use of directory user agents to control access to a directory information base.

- **MAPI,** Messaging Application Programming Interface, is part of the Microsoft WOSA, Windows Open Service Architecture.

- **EDI,** Electronic Data Interchange, is a standardized scheme for exchanging business data between different systems by means of defined business documents such as invoices and orders.

- **CAD,** Computer Assisted Design, is supported by a series of standards for the transmission and storage of technical documents, including drawings and textual materials.

- **COLD**, Computer Output on Laser Disc, is a method of writing image data for optical archiving which is used by the SAP ArchiveLink to store digitized bit-mapped pixel data which is directly linked to documents and data that are coded and which therefore can be used to retrieve the stored image.

- **Technical Subsystems** are company-specific devices to interact with plant controls and instruments through interfaces adapted for this purpose.

Open Network Management Platforms

The overall manager system for an association of large, heterogeneous networks from a variety of vendors may be considered to be a manager of the more local network managers of the constituents of the network. The difficulty is to create a system which allows the components sufficient flexibility to interact with each other without losing the advantages of control by a "super-manager." The central controller has to have intimate knowledge of the details of all the elements.

By contrast, an open network management platform is a product which allows all user direct management of the network technologies. Under these conditions, there is no need for each component network to have its own separate network manager.

III

Complex Management

This concept is also referred to as "Enterprise Management" and is discussed in Chapter 14, "Understanding the Enterprise Controlling Module."

Open Network Management Protocols and Application Interfaces. Although various management protocols have been developed, the formative standard for open management platforms has been SNMP, Simple Network Management Protocol.

The success of an open network management platform depends, not only on a shared management protocol, but also on the availability of an application programming interface (API) for each of the applications in the network. An API should be a well-defined and thoroughly-documented method of exchanging data and commands with the application, no matter which platform it is running on, or which vendor provided it.

A SAP Management Information Base is the data interface between the R/3 system and additional services, not necessarily on SAP system platforms. The open systems philosophy is designed to effect seamless integration with all systems, whatever their origin and configuration.

The following products are examples of open network management platforms that have been accepted by a significant number of user organizations:

- SunConnect SunNet Manager
- Hewlett Packard OpenView
- IBM NewView/6000

These products extend the CCMS facilities to the large network environment with the additional functionality needed to manage the network nodes and the operations centers.

From the R/3 CCMS you can query the current configuration and status information of all internal and external systems. The status information from the integrated R/3 applications can be combined with alarms from other networks, other systems, and from specific specialized applications. You are then in a position to use your central display to present the total system information that is necessary for global problem solving.

The way to global control of automated systems is opened up by this approach. The open network management product can be tailored to the requirements of your global integrated systems by means of a central specification of operator profiles and an integrated set of customizing specifications that can be extended to include all the significant system components.

The essential functions can be controlled through any combination of these systems in order to provide the following services:

Event control

Messaging

Problem handling

System Monitoring

The elements of system monitoring fall into two sections: alarm services and system performance monitoring.

The focus of these activities is the global alert monitor function, which is supplemented with various other monitors for detailed analysis and record-keeping.

Alarm Services

The status of each system component is tested and logged at frequent intervals, together with information on the queues waiting for service and, if there are any, the error messages generated by the local controlling systems.

Global Alert Monitor. The purpose of the global alert monitor function is to assemble in one integrated display system all the alarms and warning messages that have been generated by the peripheral systems and their communications. This information can be displayed under the standard SAP-GUI, Graphical User Interface, which allows the user to select any item and drill down to see the documents which contributed to its calculation: the data and the calculation formulas and conditions.

Database Monitor. The automatic function of the database monitor is to keep track of the free space available and the volume of traffic to and from each database. The systems will also be logging the date and time of each transaction, so that the database monitor can derive performance measures to assess all the significant dimensions of the operation of the database complexes.

Operating System Monitor. The operating system monitor will be tracking the availability of main memory and disk space in order to be able to assign processing workloads to those parts of the global system that can best handle them.

Again, the performance of the system under scrutiny will be measured, for example, in terms of central processing unit task times and throughput capacity.

Network Monitor. The visual display of the network monitor is supplemented by listing displays to show the integrity of the network and the loads on it at all times. These utilization statistics are continuously logged and may be analyzed online.

Job Scheduling Monitor. For the processing of background jobs and the allocation of system resources, the job scheduling monitor concentrates on the incoming requests and the reports of the status of the systems needed and available to meet them.

Applications Monitoring. The application server statistics compiled by the computer center are an important source of information needed for strategic and tactical planning at the global level. In addition, lists can be compiled for any data of interest, and then subjected to whatever statistical analysis will best reveal their significance.

Performance Measurement

There are two main reasons why the performance of an integrated system should be measured. The first is to determine the data which can be used in the future to balance

III

Complex Management

the work loads and prevent bottlenecks. The second is to identify those functions that are most frequently called so that they may be considered for technical improvement to increase their efficiency.

The CCMS module includes tools to monitor the runtime performance of R/3 applications in, for example, the following respects:

- Response time of dialogs
- Number of dialog steps per hour
- Central processing unit utilization and load factor

System Control

The essence of computer network system control is to plan what data processing and storage requirements will be met by the system resources that will be available at the time. It is necessary to know which resources are available and what work loads have already been assigned to them. The endeavor is much like any process controlling: perhaps quicker, and certainly demanding in expertise and rapid decision-making.

Optimizing the Load Distribution in the Client/Server Environment

The optimizing function is a development of resource planning, which has always been a combination of predicting the future requirements and applying historical data about how operations consume resources.

The database has to include measurements of the performance of the system components. And there must also be estimates of the loads which the planned requirements will place on them.

Over and above the assigning of work loads to resources that will be available to handle them, there has always had to be an element of safety planning: keeping capacity in reserve in case a critical resource breaks down.

As a result, there has developed a culture and discipline of safety stocks and reserves, which becomes manifest in guidelines for the utilization of capacities. Work loads are shared so that no resource is overstretched while an equivalent capacity is underutilized.

In the context of a computer-based production system, there is an indispensable requirement for fast and accurate displays of the status of all the production resources and planned requirements. When the production resources are the computers and networks themselves, the same requirement exists. Processing loads and computing capacities have to be integrated with the database operating and capacity factors.

Assigning Users to Sufficient Free Capacity. Having a network with a central global planning and control capability can make it possible for the total productivity of the system to be much increased, since the CCMS will be aware of the requirements for data processing and the planned availability of the resources. The users can be assigned to the capacities that will be best able to cope.

The system functions for distributing loads can provide a load-balancing service for groups of users who share the same set of dialogs. When you sign on to work in a particular area, such as SD Order Entry, or Accounts Payable in financial accounting, you will be assigned automatically to a server that is for the moment handling the smallest load.

Time Controlled Distribution of System Resources

When there is a choice between background and online processing, there are obviously more degrees of freedom for the system resource planners. If the network spans time zones, the daily load patterns may be used to plan a timetable of resource allocations.

The following operating modes are pre-defined:

- Online operations where most work processes are defined as dialog processes

- Nighttime operation where most work processes are defined as background processes

- Maintenance operations which are restricted to certain authorized users

Processing control for the operator-less nighttime mode is based on the following types of function:

- Recognition of different classes of job

- Responses to external events

- Starting and controlling external programs by means of RFC remote function calls

- Reservation of processing resources according to the priority of background jobs

The Computing Center Management System also operates its own system of priorities to ensure the scheduling and monitoring of data backup and recover tasks in conjunction with the application processing workloads.

System Services

The system services emanating from the CCMS in addition to the global alert monitoring function are essentially those entailed in looking after background processing and the safety functions of backup, recovery, and security.

Background Processing

The planning of system resources will seek to make best use of background processing whenever there is no absolute requirement for online immediate response. There are several methods of anticipating the online requirements so that the background processing can provide support in the form of data that has been selected and processed on the basis of the likely needs of the online user.

For example, the user who habitually works with material masters of certain types will appreciate it if the central management system has already updated these masters before his daily work schedule begins.

Backup Management

One of the key benefits of being linked to a system with a formal backup management system is the security of being able to recover much of earlier work in the event of a local system failure.

Yet the costs of comprehensive and frequent backup can be considerable. A policy for backup management has to be in place, and the ideal owner of this policy is the CCMS which can also ensure that it is obeyed.

The HP OmniBack II system is an example of a backup system. It can reach 20 gigabytes per hour.

While this type of system is in operation, it is essential that access to certain records is blocked so that they are available for backup. This is implemented in the R/3 system during the transaction processing.

Online Data Backup. As the speed of available backup equipment increases, it becomes increasingly feasible to adopt a regime of online backup where the records are copied very frequently indeed.

The faster the rate of transactions in a system, the shorter should be the interval between backups so as to minimize the loss of data if any part of the system should go offline. The method of disk mirroring effectively maintains the backup continuously as a faithful replica of the operational storage medium.

Recovery

Recovery from a disruption and the restoration of records that have been backed up are subject to the same developments as the backup operation itself. The frequency of the operation and the resolution of possible conflicts between the old records and the new are matters of the utmost importance that have to be controlled by rigid rules programmed into the system.

Security

The measures that are taken for backing up data and restoring it under controlled conditions after a disruption are clearly central to the maintenance of data security.

The invasion of a system by unauthorized users and unregistered programs has to be prevented at all levels. If the CCMS can indeed monitor the status and performance of all the components in the global system, there will be the opportunity to alert the peripheral units of any unexplained irregularities, and to measure the extent of the impairment.

A suite of authorization policies and security procedures is obviously essential. It is provided as an integral part of the R/3 system and therefore extends to all SAP applications that are integrated with it. However, the security, reliability, confidentiality, and integrity of data and programs held in non-SAP satellite systems have to be ensured by attention to the details of these specific components.

Simple Network Management Protocol Applications

The R/3 system can be used to report the configuration and status of any system component integrated with it by using the SAP Management Information Base system which is based on the Simple Network Management Protocol.

Data Collector Interfaces

The data collector interface currently monitors information from the following systems provided by the Remote Network Monitoring Management Information Bases (RMON-MIBs) maintained by special network analyzers:

- Ethernet

- Token Ring

- FDDI

- ATM

These sources provide network information about, for example, the current segment loads and collision rates.

EarlyWatch

The purpose of the EarlyWatch system is to monitor a system and detect the possibility of operating problems before they have had time to disrupt production. A team of experts is available to interpret the information gathered through the SAP Management Information Base system using the Simple Network Management Protocol.

Chapter 27, "Understanding the OSS-Online Service System," discusses this further.

From Here...

- What is the central manufacturing management equivalent of the CCMS?

  Manufacturing can be controlled from the CCMS-Computing Center Management System. The LO-LIS Logistics Information System, described in Chapter 14, "Understanding the Enterprise Controlling Module," includes components that collate information from each of the R/3 applications that are installed, such as SD-Sales and Distribution, PP-Production Planning, MM-Materials Management, PM-Plant Maintenance, and QM-Quality Management.

- How is a global organization controlled?

  See Chapter 14, "Understanding the Enterprise Controlling Module."

- Can I arrange continuous monitoring and consulting?

  Chapter 27, "Understanding the OSS-Online Service System," describes an extensive monitoring and consulting facility to which you can subscribe.

III

Complex Management

Part IV

Steering the Corporation

France 117
Belgium 70
Italy 62
Spain 59
Denmark 56
Czech Republic 41
Sweden 39
Hungary 26

479
54
24
16
14

Japan 100
Australia 68
Singapore 32
Malaysia 22
Korea 10
Hong Kong 7
Thailand 7

South Africa 69
Saudi Arabia 9
Israel 3
Arabic Emirates 2
Nambia 2

Products 71%

Steel,
al Engineering,
tomative

Food and Tobacco Industry

Office & EDP Equipment

8.0% 7.3%

6.6%

Mining, Utilities, Transportation

4.6%

mmercial
d Social
10.3%

4.5%

Trade, Retail and Wholesale

3.9%

Traffic and News Communication

3.8%

Metal Products and Primary Metal

nics, Precision
anics, Optics
14.5%

3.6%

Universities and Technical Colleges

Chemical Industry,
Mineral Oil Production
18.2%

Others
(see chart below)
11.6%

2.9%

Wood, Paper and Printing Industry

thers
edit Banks, Financial Services 1.9
uarrying, Fine Ceramics, Glass 1.9
ospitals 1.7
scellaneous 1.7
surance Companies 1.6
ilding Trade, Construction 1.4
ather, Textile and Clothing Industry .9
ade Associations and Federations .3
riculture, Forestry, Fishing .2

ole product

evelop
plete and
ustomized

Customized tools

Develop

Deliver

Rate of market growth

High

Build large market
share as fast as
possible – at
reasonable cost

- Identify effective sales and marketing campaigns – quick feedback on results
- Build sales capacity quickly using standardized multimedia product presentations
- Erect entry barriers to keep out competition – customer database used for attractive after-sales service and support

Develop
for right n
and at lea

- Impr
betw
and t
- Use
expe

Reduce sales and
marketing costs while
maintaining market
share

- Service low value customers using low cost channels eg. telesales, direct mail
- Contact database to help retain key high value customers
- Link purchase patterns to SOP to prompt for automatic reordering

Reduce c
key custo
for cross-
opportuni

- Sales
payb
- Low
syste
custo

Low

High

Relative market shar

tomer Attractiveness

High

Four Seasons

Seed

Agnosti

ICL

British Rail

Chapter 12

Understanding the FI-Financial Management Module

The SAP product module FI-Financial Accounting comprises a number of components. They may be installed and configured in various combinations to suit the individual implementation.

This chapter will remind you of the basics of double entry bookkeeping and how they are enacted in a modern integrated management system.

The SAP R/3 FI-Financial Accounting Programs

The SAP FI-Financial Accounting components are discussed in the following sequence, together with some topics which are relevant to them all.

FI-GL	General Ledger
FI-AR	Accounts Receivable
FI-AP	Accounts Payable
FI-AA	Asset Accounting
FI-LC	Consolidation

Accounting is a source of support for the people who do things. At its best it sheds light on the value of what they are doing and the value of the materials they use and those they throw away. It should help them waste less and add more value by using information and skill. Those who have invested in the company will also want to see how things are going. They will want to look at the annual accounts, for a start. At its worst, accounting is the painful process of collecting a confusing blanket of numbers to throw over an enterprise that is really a waste of time and resources. There is a legal requirement to publish the financial documents: But it may take an expert to discern just which elements of the business are contributing to the value of the material and information passing through the company, and which are not.

Some of the main topics in this chapter are:

- The General Ledger is where the information is accumulated for the balance sheet and profit and loss statement.

- What are the Personal Accounts in the General Ledger.

  Accounts Receivable and accounts Payable.

- What is Financial Controlling.

  It is the process of planning the value flows in an organization and then recording the actual values for comparison with the plan.

The possibility—indeed, the necessity, for all but the tiniest of firms—of managing the accounts on a computer opens the opportunity to make one of two mistakes at the design and implementation stage.

The first mistake is to overlook the many ways in which the computer can add value to the information and material work items passing through the company. For example, the computer can make sure that the customer is provided with exactly what he needs and is properly billed so that he pays for it. Manual systems can be used to serve this purpose if the person in charge of them is diligent and energetic. By contrast, the computer can be diligent and energetic in business where everything is going according to plan, and can also detect slow responses on both sides, and call attention to this imperfection—not simply by ringing an alarm bell, but by gathering together the pertinent information and presenting it to a suitable person to make a decision.

The second mistake in conceiving a computer-assisted accounting system is to assume that it is simply a matter of mechanized books.

The computer can be made to be good at what it does only if it is endowed with impeccable behavior. As far as possible, it must be incorruptible. Entry errors may occur which are not detected at the time. In such instances, it must be possible to trace the origin of the error, make corrections to the accounting, and perhaps take steps to make this type of error less likely in the future, or at least have it detected at the time. The SAP system takes this moral stand very seriously. Each time a transaction takes place between SAP and the outside world, a SAP Document is created and stamped with the date and time. The terminal device signs the document, and the user is obliged to leave his or her identification there too. From this moment of formal entry launching the transaction, there is no further opportunity to annotate or adjust anything illegal. The time-stamped SAP Document recording the entry event will be locked. Therefore it is best if it is checked before it is launched, and it would be very helpful to append any annotations or explanatory remarks at this stage. There will usually be a choice of standard annotations to cope with most eventualities, plus the possibility of entering free text by way of explanation.

If the transaction is legal but in error, then a correcting transaction must be enacted. This too will leave its mark on the audit trail by generating a SAP Document.

Accruals are an essential part of modern online accounting. Costs and charges, possibly profits as well, are linked to the time period and cost or profit center to which they belong, rather than to any general fund. The aim is to reveal the true value to the company of whatever activity is using its resources.

Checking the Data

Checks are made at every stage where an automatic assessment can be made as to whether the information coming in is reasonable. Do the figures balance? Is this transaction legal? Has this decision-maker been authorized to make this choice?

SAP standard business software is built around the aim of providing continuous measurement of the profitability of everything that is going on. Each business function will be recording how often it is used and how long it takes to do its work. And this kind of performance information will be available to illuminate any scrutiny of how resources are being utilized.

This sophistication in accounting performance measurement, provided as standard in the SAP systems, is additional to the Generally Accepted Accounting Principles (GAAP); but it may well make a very significant difference to the figures on the profit and loss account.

The ideal accounting system will be able to recreate an unbroken audit trail from each and every transaction to the balance sheet and profit and loss account of the company. The auditor should be able to point to any number on the financial documents of the company and ask to see how it was computed, right back to the documents that came from the outside world to carry the information that found its way into the computer.

SAP FI-Financial Accounting can always deliver an unbroken audit trail, because every external and internal transaction creates a record in the form of a SAP document, which can be called to substantiate the audit and prove the credentials of the company's accounts.

And upon this foundation it is possible to demonstrate just how the system is complying with the GAAP tenets as applied to computerized accounting systems. The GAAP requirements arise from a set of statutory regulations, decrees and ordinances that embody the experience of the accounting professions and serve as the basis upon which each nation may develop additional accounting traditions and requirements.

Worldwide Accounting

SAP International Development is a set of models, one for each geographical area of the world, to enable the SAP system to take account of the rules and practices of the major trading communities.

INT-International Development module includes the following components:

IN-APA	Asian and Pacific area
IN-EUR	Europe
IN-NAM	North America
IN-AFM	Africa and Middle East
IN-SAM	South America

These modules are fully integrated into the R/3 system during implementation. They are additional to the standard R/3 provision for translating screen text and currency values to suit the local language, local currency, and reference languages of the group head office system.

FI-AP Accounts Payable and FI-AR Accounts Receivable are sub-ledgers of the FI-GL General Ledger and are completely integrated with it. They are sometimes referred to as the Personal Sub-ledgers because they contain information that is associated with customers and vendors and might be subject to rules or customs of privacy and nondisclosure.

The balance sheet has a Receivables Account in which line items in customer accounts are subtotaled or totaled. The Payables Account in the General Ledger subtotals or totals the line items from the vendor accounts.

Each customer transaction updates the balance of the Receivables Account in the General Ledger and each vendor transaction updates the balance of the Payables Account in the General Ledger.

TR-CM Cash Management is concerned with bank balances and cash, usually on a daily basis. The associated sub-ledgers will have accounts in the General Ledger and will therefore be integrated with it. The transactions of the various types of Cash Management will include the following functions:

Reconciling and sorting bank accounts

Planning short- to medium-term cash requirements and cash investments

Buying, managing, and selling securities, loans, and time deposits

Managing foreign exchange

PA-PYY Payroll, FI-AA Asset Accounting and MM-Materials Management also have sub-ledgers and balance sheet accounts which enable them to integrate with the General Ledger in the same way as Payables and Receivables.

For each of these transactions in the sub-ledgers and the FI-General Ledger, a SAP Document is created, which can be used to keep track of any element of the transaction details recorded in it. Material code number, asset number, personnel number of the entry clerk—these are all examples of transaction details that can be used to retrieve transactions for analysis.

The FI-General Ledger module also offers some of the facilities of an extended general ledger, even if the SAP Extended General Ledger system has not been installed. The extended facilities allow you to enter cost data such as cost center, cost unit, and project identification with each transaction.

After each transaction, because the General Ledger will have been updated, you can display or print lists of updates to the balance sheet and profit and loss statement. You can also print or display balance sheet reports and any other report of the financial system.

Configuring and Customizing FI-Financial Accounting

The SAP R/3 system with the FI-Financial Accounting Application installed will have been configured for a particular country. The features specific to the accounting laws and customs will have been configured to operate correctly.

The system will also have been configured to comply with GAAP, the Generally Accepted Accounting Principles.

A typical national chart of accounts will be in place (see Figure 12.1). If you have a multinational installation, the necessary additional charts of accounts will be installed.

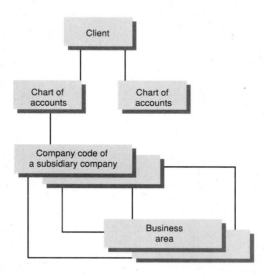

Fig. 12.1   The Client is the unique pinnacle of the enterprise.

If you install another SAP application, the system will generate the FI-General Ledger accounts required automatically.

The parameter settings for specific countries will have been adjusted to suit a particular delivery client for your first installation. This is usually treated as your standard SAP Client. It will be assigned a client code which will ensure that all data and documents are identified as belonging to this client. Client 000 may be used for training purposes and Client 001 for testing. If you install an application additional to the R/3 system, you can allow the specific parameter settings to be installed in your standard client account; or you may prefer to create a set of separate client codes, one for each of your individual companies if you have a multinational group.

FI-GL General Ledger

The internal accounting system of a company is designed to control costs. Investors in the company will want to know how the capital of the company has been assigned in the external accounting system that comprises the general ledger.

For convenience, the general ledger will be supported by a set of sub-ledgers including accounts receivable, accounts payable, fixed assets, human resources, and materials (see Figure 12.2).

The external accounting system should show what the company is worth.

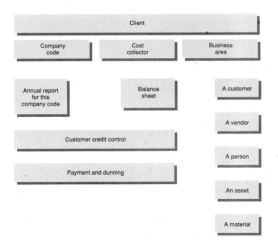

Fig. 12.2   The Enterprise Data Model can represent all the business objects and processes, and their interrelationships.

A Chart of Accounts in Common

Following the principle that any number that appears on the external account documents should be amenable to analysis into its constituents, the cost accounting system should have been supplied with all the expense and revenue entries. Costing data allocated to period or product line will also be posted to the general ledger via a common chart of accounts which is shared by both the financial (external) accounting system and the cost (internal) accounting system.

The general ledger is a series of account balances. Modern online accounting maintains the general ledger balances continuously. Data that have been entered and posted will be posted immediately to the general ledger and also to the CO-Controlling system if it has been installed. The balance sheet and the profit and loss account are based on the general ledger.

The accounts that are named in the general ledger are called general ledger accounts. One or more general ledger account balances can be derived from a corresponding subledger specified in the chart of accounts.

An extended general ledger uses accounts that are based on a range of sub-ledgers that allow analyses from different points of view. For example, accounts may focus on cost centers, product costs, or activities. These options are provided by using the CO-Controlling system as an internal accounting system. Entered data posted to the general ledger will be posted to the CO system and its components as part of the extended general ledger.

Integration of Accounting Through the General Ledger

The general ledger is the source from which are built the external accounting documents, the balance sheet, and the profit and loss statement.

Because this information is to be audited, it will have to be supported by audit trails that show how each summary total has been computed.

If there exists a complete audit trail, there also exists the possibility of using the information therein to make some decisions before the end-of-year results are derived.

Making interim decisions on the basis of accounting information is the province of business controlling, for which the SAP CO-Controlling module has been developed. This will be examined at length in Chapter 13, "Understanding the CO-Controlling Module."

Controlling depends on detailed record-keeping in which the individual transactions retain their identity, their date, their sources, and the identification of the users who worked on them. Only if the accounting information is retained in this fine detail can the controlling functions assemble it and manipulate it to discern what is happening in the business. If the decision-makers cannot establish what is happening, they will be prone to take no action when they should, take action when they should not, or take with enthusiasm completely the wrong action.

The work units of a business controller will probably be the line items of the business transactions and the statements from the journal, the accounts, the trial balance, and the final statements. These will provide fundamental monitoring of business direction in terms of movement and progress, strategic goals, and operating tactics. These are the primary results achieved as a result of investing human and financial capital in the company.

The copious and comprehensive data arising from the SAP standard procedure of capturing all transaction information in the form of SAP Documents can be subsequently analyzed. For example, there can be valuable additions to primary results in the form of interpretations of the data that picture the company from various points of view. A look at profit and loss for each activity over each operating period might be illuminating, for example.

These additional analyses of the accounting data may serve to prompt and direct an interim change of direction or emphasis: but they may also form the essential inputs to business planning.

Profit centers may focus the analysis. Geographical business areas may be of interest. Product groups will often be worth assessing in terms of profit contributions.

Clearly the data should be held centrally if you are seeking widespread analyses; and if you want the information to be up-to-date, then records of every transaction must be available to contribute to the analysis if required. The General Ledger and its Sub-ledgers in the SAP online accounting system provide this central source.

From this source in the General Ledger can be extracted comprehensive analyses of important ratios such as cash flow proportions and workload per person.

Liquidity must be watched. With general ledger accounting, it can be forecast by taking cognizance of projected cash disbursements and receipts in the short and medium term.

If a business plan has been created in the SAP system and efficient tools are available to assist, then the actual results can be compared to planned ones in whatever dimensions and ratios are of interest.

Planning that is integrated across an entire company will have to include plans for the balance sheet and for the profit and loss (P&L) statements. Cash plans will be required which include project receipts and payments.

Controls over the ongoing activities of the company will begin by comparing the balance sheet and the P&L statements, year on year. Short-term cash management using projected cash payments and receipts and a daily financial statement may well be essential. Control of ongoing business can also make good use of financial analyses, comparisons, and ratios based on the organization's structure in terms of business areas or units.

Sub-ledgers can be the means by which control is exercised over the entities they represent. Receivables and Payables can be managed by inspecting analyses of due dates, amounts, selected customers, regions, and so on. Assets may attract the attention of controllers because of automatic reports of their ratios, depreciation, capitalized cost, and net book value. Inventory transactions, invoices, and personnel expenses are other examples of aspects of a business that can be made available to controllers, because the SAP system has the unbreakable habit of capturing all transactions from all system components in the form of SAP Documents that can be collated and analyzed into whatever informative structure is logically feasible.

The logical qualification is an obvious reminder that data that have not been entered into the SAP system at some stage or other cannot take part in subsequent analyses.

If, however, the necessary primary data are in the system, then automatic profit and loss information can be computed. Overheads can be monitored and attributed to such headings as cost center and order settlement. Product cost accounting can shed light on the costs of ongoing jobs. Technical and commercial projects can be monitored, controlled, and brought into the plans. Profitability analysis will be possible on the basis of cost of sales and period accounting.

At any time it is possible to clear individual line items in business transactions and effect a reconciliation of separate controlling units with the General Ledger.

General Ledger Accounting Routine

Each business transaction creates a record in the format of a SAP document. The transaction may be part of a batch input, or it may be the result of a dialogue transaction at a terminal. The transaction will be checked and validated as far as possible and returned for correction if necessary.

When the transaction is posted, it is stored on the record log as a SAP document. The system updates the daily journal file and posts the transaction to the appropriate reconciliation account of the General Ledger. At that moment, the related account balances, trial balances, balance sheet, and P&L statement reports will be accessible on the screen.

Special document types and posting keys provide access to particular types of transactions:

- Customer or vendor invoices
- Cash receipts and disbursements
- Inventory transactions
- Allocations or distributions for cost accounting
- Transactions involving two or more profit centers
- Transactions involving two or more company codes
- Statistical postings (noted items, guarantees, and so on)
- Special business transactions (down payments, bills of exchange, and so on)

Entering and posting a transaction document immediately updates both financial accounting and cost accounting. The General Ledger and its Sub-ledgers use the information, and so do the cost analyses that are elaborated from the data.

The transaction log is available to feed the General Ledger and the subsystems managing asset accounting, inventory accounting, cost accounting, order and project accounting, product costing, profitability analysis, as well as the sub-ledgers of accounts receivable and payable.

And from any or all of this the finance and controlling information system can extract and present whatever primary or derived information is required.

Integrated real-time bookkeeping ensures that verified data are available for processing in all areas at once by automatically clearing cost accounting transactions in the general ledger and its sub-ledgers.

The financial and cost accounting systems are constantly reconciled at the level of the individual general ledger accounts. These accounts are named in the common chart of accounts.

The Chart of Accounts

The chart of accounts is used to configure any account in the general ledger so that it will serve two purposes:

- Permit entry of transaction details required by the business
- Provide for any balance sheet or profit and loss statement required by law.

The business will want to plan and operate some logistic processes—and exercise financial control. The law demands proper external accounting practice so that shareholders can value their holdings and see that taxes are paid.

The processes of the business can be classified broadly according to the focus of the activities and their managers.

The first group of General Ledger accounts monitors activities that are concerned with building the productive resources of the company:

- Procurement of investment items such as fixed assets, current assets, and financial assets
- Extraordinary expense or revenue

The next group of accounts deals with how the day-to-day production and processing activities affect the value of the company:

- Procurement of materials
- Consumption of company resources
- Valuation of finished or semi-finished products

The third group is of activities with their own accounts in the General Ledger to show how sales of products are set against costs to yield the financial statements:

- Sales revenue or sales deductions
- Closing to balance sheet and profit and loss statement

Account Classes

External accounting balances are classified into account classes using the chart of accounts. For example:

- Fixed assets and long-term capital
- Finances, current assets, short-term capital
- Non-operating expense and revenue
- Materials or stock
- Primary cost elements
- Secondary cost elements
- Job order cost elements
- Stock of finished and semi-finished products
- Yield or changes to stock or capitalized internal activity
- Closing balances

Internal Controlling Account Classes

Controlling balances arrived at by internal accounting fall into four categories according to their purpose. Project cost settlement or job order costing allow for the fact that purchases and allocations of resources may have to be made in order to carry out projects and complete specific job orders that may not yield any financial return during the current accounting period. These costs are therefore treated as investment.

Cost center accounting is used to gather specified types of cost under the heading, which is most useful for business purposes. These cost centers may correspond to departments or they may be used to associate costs with, for example, a specific plant or item of equipment that is considered as a focus for understanding and managing the enterprise.

Job order or product costing is the traditional process of associating costs with specific orders from customers or for internal production work, of which the manufacture of goods for inventory would be a common example.

Profitability analysis is the process of relating the financial yield of part of the enterprise to the costs of owning and running it. There are no restrictions on how the parts to be analyzed are defined. The profitability of a work unit may be of interest: or the value of carrying out a change of procedure may be the target. The wisdom of all business decisions may have to be assessed in relation to the short- and long-term profitability of the consequences.

Integration of accounting can be demonstrated by the fact that the common chart of accounts can both record all the costs and revenues and also provide all the factors needed for financial control via internal accounting.

The chart of accounts installed in a specific implementation must comply with statutory requirements under company law as it is practiced in the host country. It must also embody the essential elements of GAAP, the accounting principles that set the standard for a reliable accounting system.

The Two Primary Functions of the General Ledger

The FI-GL General Ledger component recognizes that there are two main reasons for asking for reports from a general ledger.

Monitoring Financial Health. Shareholders may be very interested in the financial statements required by law: the balance sheet and the profit and loss statement. These two financial documents are the basis of external accounting, because they reveal the financial health of a company.

The profit and loss computations depend on closing the accounts in the general ledger at the end of the financial year. One of the primary functions of the general ledger is to allow this year-end closing to take place in an orderly manner.

Reviewing the Results for the Year. The other primary function of the general ledger is financial accounting for the current fiscal year.

The function of collecting and recording data from transactions is one part of financial accounting. Posting data and effecting reconciliation on a continuous basis make up the other part.

The SAP system creates a document for each transaction that can be used for a flexible reporting and analysis system, with the ability to establish a valid audit trail using these recorded transaction documents.

Reconciliation is effected at the transaction level before an entry is posted, but there has to be a closing of the reconciliation accounts at the end of the month and then at the end of the year. A facility exists in R/3 to call up daily or monthly reports at any time.

Special General Ledger Transactions

The accounts in the special general ledger are reconciliation accounts for special sub-ledger transactions that do not directly involve sales or purchases and may not be balanced with the Receivables and Payables. The special general ledger indicator is a single character code to distinguish these transactions from sales to customers or purchases from vendors. The following transaction types are examples of special general ledger transactions:

- Acquisitions
- Dispositions
- Depreciation
- Transfers
- Down payments
- Bills of exchange
- Monthly payroll
- Period closing entries

Year-End Closing

The law for closing a fiscal year requires entries to closing accounts for the balance sheet and profit and loss statement. The SAP FI System ensures that year-end closing entries are transferred from sub-ledgers such as:

- Accounts Receivable
- Accounts Payable
- Fixed assets

Provision is also made for closing entries manually and individually. You can close a fiscal year at any time. The flexible online reporting system will offer separate formats of the financial documents for tax authorities, stockholders, legal consolidation of associated companies, and so on.

Complex Organizations and the Chart of Accounts

The chart of accounts has to include all the general ledger accounts in an accounting system. You can specify what transaction data goes where, so that each account will contain all the required details for closing. Internal accounting will usually require that certain types of data be sent to each of the accounts that are used in the controlling functions.

There are two possibilities for using a common chart of accounts in a complex organization:

- You may have a centralized organization in which there is the maximum number of accounts at group level in a uniform chart of accounts that will apply to all company codes in the group.

- You may be a decentralized organization in which each company code has its own chart of accounts.

In either case it is possible to use sample accounts taken from the reference system with transfer rules for individual company codes. This allows each company to have some flexibility while operating to a common chart of accounts.

International Taxation

The SAP system is international. The taxation functions commonly needed have been programmed as standard business functions with tables of parameters available for customization to the organization and to the specific operational features required.

When you use the SAP system, you will have signified the country where your company is located, and if prompted, the country where your vendor or customer is located. The system will adopt the taxation regimes appropriate to each of these countries.

The system calculates tax or adjusts it automatically. When you enter the transaction you cause the system to create the SAP document containing all the details. Then it immediately posts the taxes as it updates the accounts. The required tax reports are generated automatically.

Standard Taxation Functions

The FI-Financial Accounting module includes the following standard international taxation functions:

- Taxes on sales and purchases

- Bills of exchange tax

- Tax base for tax calculation

- Definitions of all required tax rates

- Methods for the determination of due dates for tax payment

- Tax calculation procedures

- Tax base for cash discount
- Dependent taxes as surcharges or deductions
- European Community acquisition tax
- Division into deductible and nondeductible taxes

Withholding tax can be programmed to suit your requirements. The process makes use of the following functions:

- Tax base
- Definition of all required tax rates
- Flagging of all vendors affected
- Determination of due dates for tax payments

The system verifies withholding tax when you enter a vendor invoice and payment. You do not have to check the tax entries later. The necessary reports are prepared automatically.

Although the system will adopt the appropriate standard tax regime as soon as you have indicated the country, you can adjust parameters to meet your specific tax requirements. For instance, you may have to make adjustments to the standard procedure because of a change in the national taxation regulations, or because you are working in a country that does not exactly follow any of the standard tax regimes programmed into the system.

Country-specific tax requirements are notified in the SAP INT International component, and may have been used to customize your particular implementation.

Examples of Country-Specific Taxation Requirements

Specific taxation rules for charging, disclosing, and paying tax are accommodated by customizing each company code operating in that country. Specific forms of payment and common payment media are prepared for each country.

The following examples illustrate the range of differences that can be handled by the system:

- German-speaking countries in Europe require a tax adjustment if the payment for an invoice is net of cash discount. Other countries calculate tax liability on the invoiced amount.
- Different countries have their own arrangements for tax exemptions and delay of liability.
- Withholding tax is subject to wide differences in scope and method.

Intercompany Accounting

A group comprising two or more individual companies will have an organizational structure designed to facilitate day-to-day operations. For example, each company may buy

4444r

---

material and manage a warehouse. Each may run a sales and distribution division. To increase the complexity of the organization somewhat, suppose there is also a head office, which functions as a separate company.

The head office, as a company, may have oversight of two other companies. Each of these business units will incur expenses and probably enjoy revenue.

For the sake of business convenience, it may well happen that two or even three of these units will combine to make a purchase, perhaps at a discount because of the size of the order. One payment to the vendor will be made against one invoice.

Again for good business reasons, the units may join forces to provide a service to a customer. For example, Purchasing may provide the material goods, and Distribution may look after their delivery. Again, one payment from the customer will be made against one invoice.

If each of these business units is managed as an individual company, all intercompany transactions within the group and with customers and vendors must obey the rules of intercompany accounting. In particular, transactions must leave records that will allow intercompany business to be legally audited so as to give a true picture of the group as a whole and of the individual companies when it comes to drawing up the financial documents.

With modern online computerized accounting systems, the balance sheets and the profit and loss statements of the group and each individual company will be readily available at any time.

The principles of intercompany accounting are applied when your company is part of a group; they also apply when your customer or your vendor is part of another group.

The SAP accounting system uses methods that support intercompany transactions and complies with GAAP.

Intercompany Expense and Revenue Postings

Two divisions of a group, each with a separate company code, may jointly make a purchase or issue goods. (The same principles apply if more than two company codes are involved.)

You have to enter and post the expense item in both company codes, but you post only one vendor account in one of the company codes. It does not matter which one.

The system will automatically calculate and post the Receivables and Payables between company codes, just as if you were entering a regular transaction in one company code.

The system will create line items for Receivables and Payables between company codes. It will also generate a SAP document in each company code. As it does so, it will assign a unique intercompany transaction number, which will appear on all documents and vouchers.

The debits do not have to equal the credits in each company code; only within the entire intercompany transaction do they have to balance.

Paying for Intercompany Purchases

Several companies in a group may purchase from the same vendor. You can pay for the purchase by making a single payment, with the vendor account number being the same in the vendor master record in each company in the group. One company has to keep a central bank account to be used to pay on behalf of the other companies.

Cash Receipt for Two or More Company Codes

Some of the companies in a group may have customers in common. If one of these customers offers payment for two or more company codes in the group, you can use this procedure:

- Match open items to the amount of the payment.

- Process the selected items, sharing the payments flexibly if necessary.

- Apply cash discount calculations in each company.

- Clear documents for each of the companies.

The system will automatically post the required clearing account in each company.

Head Office—Branch Accounts

Your supplier may be a branch with its own account, but its head office may wish to receive your payment. In this case you can enter its head office account number in the master record for the branch vendor. When you enter a transaction to the branch account, the system will post the transaction to the head office account, leaving a cleared entry on the branch account to show who supplied the goods or service.

The master will include data about the branch and a reference to another master to give details of the head office. By this means, dunning letters can be sent to the head office, the branch, or both for overdue refunds, for example.

Vendor Payments to an Alternative Recipient

Your supplier may not have to deal with its payments due. For example, it may have a head office that will receive payment. You can record in its master data the account number of this alternative recipient. The system will then process return transfers and other vendor payment business through the banks to the alternative recipient.

If you do post vendor invoices to an affiliate, you have to record in the master data of the branch vendor a group-wide company account number that will be used during consolidation to eliminate the invoices that would otherwise appear twice in the company accounts. The system will be able to look at the transaction documents bearing this group-wide company account number and identify any entries that are replicated because the payment was made to an affiliate that was not the original vendor.

Intercompany Payments

One vendor may have supplied several company codes in the same group. The payment system can make one payment and then settle the intercompany accounts by calculating and posting Receivables and Payables between company codes.

The transaction needs you to define one of the company codes and enter it as a normal paying company. The system will assign the document a unique intercompany identification number which will be used to ensure that the other members of the company code group will pay their shares.

Eliminating Intercompany Payables and Receivables

FI-Financial Accounting will eliminate intercompany balances by open item only if each trading partner has been marked in the vendor master record. You must also ensure that the reporting procedures inform the consolidating department of the numbers of these trading partners, at least on the items relating to intercompany Payables and Receivables, revenues and expenses.

The law requires that all intercompany balances be eliminated before presenting the balance sheet and profit and loss statement. All possible pairs of individual companies must be investigated for evidence that they have been trading with each other.

In practice, significant differences between the way individual companies keep their records may make complete elimination impractical. The most frequent causes of discrepancies in elimination are as follows:

- Currency translation differences

- Differences in the timing of entries for goods in transit between individual companies

- Specific reserves set aside for doubtful accounts

- Liabilities that are not acknowledged in the records

The cause that is most difficult to handle is currency translation; the others can usually be resolved by applying corporate policies in a thoroughgoing manner.

If the individual companies have installed and configured SAP accounting applications, there will be automatic dual currency accounting in which every transaction is documented, at the time it occurs, in both the local currency and the currency designated for all transactions in the group.

If the FI-LC Consolidation component has been installed and configured in your company, it will allow you to trace any currency translation differences between the local currency, at the prevailing rate of exchange, and the transaction currency. An exchange rate difference correction will then be posted automatically in the balance sheet account designated for this purpose, and thus brought into the consolidated financial statement.

Language Differences

R/3 is an international system. The names of all general ledger accounts can be translated if the language key is entered together with the name of the account in the target language. This process can be repeated for all languages in the group. By this means you might add or modify general ledger account names in the language of the holding company, and later log in and call for the account balances in the language of your log-in profile.

In a listing of the charts of accounts, each chart will be annotated to show the main language and all the alternatives available.

Currency

The following operational currencies have been defined and their codes are assigned to each function by default (you can alter the default settings):

- Local currency is also the reporting currency for the company code.
- Document currency is that specified for entry on SAP documents.
- Group currency is an alternative to document currency for group reporting.
- Updating currency is defined for posting debits and credits to the general ledger in parallel with the local currency.
- Credit limit currency is that which has been chosen to maintain the credit limit.
- Ledger currency is an alternative to the updating currency for that ledger.

Additional currency assignments are available in the SAP Foreign Exchange Management component.

Currencies in Transactions

Each company code has a local currency for reporting. The system records amounts in this local currency and also in a currency that has been specified as the document currency, which will be used on all documents in addition to the local currency.

You can enter documents in any currency.

You have two options for converting currencies:

- Enter an exchange rate when you enter the transaction document.
- The system translates between document and local currencies by referring to a table of daily exchange rates which is either updated manually or maintained automatically by a link to a separate database.

The system can be customized in various ways, which include:

- A specific user is obliged to enter amounts in a particular currency, which can be the local currency or the document currency.
- A specific user can be permitted to enter amounts in either local or document currency.

Whatever the customizing arrangements, the system will display amounts in both local and document currencies. It will round off minor differences, using rules established for this purpose. These differences can occur when several line items are converted and then added in both currencies.

Customer monthly debits and credits are kept by the system only in local currency. The reconciliation account for the Accounts Receivable sub-ledger is kept in local currency and in all the other currencies that have been posted.

Currency Exchange Differences

A line item can be expressed in a currency other than the local or document currency. You can enter payments to clear such foreign currency line items using either local or document currency.

The payment expressed in the document currency will have been converted from the local currency at an exchange rate adopted by the system according to the rules laid down for assigning the daily exchange rate. If this rate has changed from the rate prevailing when the invoice was written, the payment amount may not match the open item amount. In such cases, the system will automatically calculate and post an exchange difference entry to a separate account established for this purpose.

General Ledger Master Data

General ledger master data are comprised of the following.

General data about each account:

- Account number
- Account name
- Type of general ledger account

Data for each company code:

- Currency
- Whether managed on an open item basis or not
- Sort basis when line items are displayed

You can enter this master data through the FI system for each account separately or by groups of accounts. Your installation may have a configured SAP data interface to allow direct input of master data under certain conditions.

Maintaining General Ledger Master Data

Accounts can be added to the general ledger, and certain parameters can be modified. You can block and delete accounts during the fiscal year. As in all SAP R/3 directories, matchcodes set up by the individual user can be used to find specific accounts by entering an easily-remembered name or title.

Your activities with general ledger accounts will be logged, as are all transactions, so that all modifications can be traced.

Instructions on Administering General Ledger Accounts

An open item is one can that can be partially settled; it remains open until the item has been fully cleared. If an item is not to be managed on an open item basis, the settlement has to be in full or not at all. Rules can be established—for example, in the partial payment of accounts outstanding, to determine that the largest items should be settled first, or perhaps those that have been open longest.

Such manipulations may not be permitted in some general ledger accounts, because that would destroy their informative nature.

By and large, if you have authority to manipulate the general ledger accounts, you will not have any restrictions—only obligations.

Some accounts are allowed to display to anyone the line items upon which they are based. Payroll is not usually one of them.

Another example of instructions attaching to a data object representing a general ledger account will be how the line items are to be displayed: their sort order, and perhaps any masks applied to conceal certain values.

Daily Journals and Interim Statements

When it is time for year-end closing, there are SAP programs to help you prepare your system to be closed at the end of the year. But for daily and monthly closings there are no special requirements and no extra entries to make, because the account balances are maintained all the time.

At the end of each day you can see a report of the exact closing balances for the day. These will be based on the line items and the total debits and credits entered.

For periods of a day or more, it is easy to ask for reports of data that have been posted over the period, sorted by date or by any of the fields that appear in the relevant SAP documents that were created for the transactions.

The practice of calling daily or short-period journals can be helpful. You can validate data entry soon after it occurs, and so you can control it.

These journals can help you decide how to close posting periods and account for accruals. You may wish to define two accounting periods that are open for this purpose.

Year-End Closing

Monthly and interim closings entail no technical requirements. Year-end closing, however, has to be anticipated by running a series of SAP programs.

The operation of these year-end programs is automatic to a large extent.

Two main purposes are served by these year-end programs: They reorganize SAP Documents into more convenient groupings, and they reconcile summary records with the individual documents upon which they are based.

Year-End Closing Tasks. The year-end closing sequence has to include the following steps:

- Close posting periods.
- Revalue all line items and general ledger account balances to adjust for foreign currencies.
- Sort open and closed Receivables by their due dates.
- Sort open and closed Payables by their due dates.
- Identify and adjust vendor accounts with debit.
- Identify and adjust customer accounts with credit balances.
- Post reevaluations.
- Post adjustments.
- Post accruals.
- Print the balance sheet with the profit and loss statement.

Automatic Closing. Automatic closing programs compile a series of reports that will support you by preparing what you will need to close the year.

These supporting reports include:

- Reconciliations of documents with monthly debits and credits
- Posting totals
- Accumulated balance trail
- Balances carried forward from the balance sheet of the previous year

General Ledger Online Reports

The main reports in the General Ledger are available online with a range of sorting and presentation options to help in year-end closing and final reporting:

- Account Statements
- Document Journal
- Balance Sheet with Profit and Loss Statement
- Balance Sheet Adjustments
- Reconciliation of Documents with Monthly Debits and Credits

- Posting Totals

- Customer Open Items

- Overdue Receivables

- Customer Open Items by General Ledger Indicator Code

- Line Item Journal

- General Ledger

- Accumulated Balance Audit Trial

- Vendor Open Items

- Accounts Payable in Local Currency

- Open Checks

- Chart of Accounts

- Bill of Exchange Register

Financial Statement Report Formats

The Balance Sheet is always printed with the Profit and Loss Statement; together they satisfy the legal requirement for a company to publish an annual financial statement.

The essential components of the company financial statement are:

- Fixed Assets

- Current Assets

- Equity

- Debt

- Profit and Loss Statement

These essential requirements relate to the basic elements of the Chart of Accounts from which the Financial Statement is constructed.

A complex company is required by law to present a financial statement for each of its components separately and a consolidated statement for the group or company as a whole.

There may be a different chart of accounts for each company in a group. SAP FI-GL General Ledger allows all these variations of organizational structure to be accommodated when preparing the Financial Statement.

The process of designing or customizing the format of the Balance Sheet and the Profit and Loss Statement entails specifying the following details for each account:

- Levels of account detail

- Headings and subheadings

- Text

- Subtotaling and totaling

Separate formats can be designed according to the target readership of the financial documents:

- Stockholders and tax authorities

- Group requirements

- Profit centers

Balances on all accounts are always current. Therefore a profit and loss statement can be prepared at any time, as can a balance sheet.

Extra facilities have been provided as extensions to the functions that allow financial statements to be drafted in a wide range of formats to suit all types of company organization. These facilities have been integrated and placed under the control of a sophisticated user interface.

The EC-EIS Enterprise Controlling-Executive Information System is a SAP tool that is under continual development and improvement, so as to make available to the SAP R/3 user a comprehensive, integrated, online reporting system that offers all the functions that can be exercised on the accounting system.

FI-GLX Extended General Ledger

For historical and legal reasons, the general ledger has been the primary means by which an auditor or an investor might see how well or badly a company has been managed. The results of this management are extracted to form the balance sheet, showing the end-of-year value of the company's assets, and the trading report or profit and loss statement, revealing how the assets have been set to work for profit or have diminished through losses.

The general ledger is thus the basis for External Accounting, but it will not show all the useful information that has been collected in the course of the trading year, such as who bought what.

The manager has to submit to the procedures of Internal Accounting to see more closely how resources might be better applied. Perhaps it is informative if the financial summaries contain breakdowns of activities by geographical business areas, and by type of business, and by product, and so on.

These other ways of collating business information for the benefit of exercising better control of a company have been provided with standard business functions and collected as the CO-Controlling module.

The FI-Financial module primarily serves the requirements of External Accounting. The CO-Controlling module serves Internal Accounting. They both serve the same company by sharing a common chart of accounts that includes accounts that are not necessary to meet the legal requirements of the Financial Statement—those requirements that are met by the general ledger, from which the balance sheet and the profit and loss statement are derived.

These extra accounts are there to improve the usefulness of the financial system in the matter of controlling the company.

The FI-GL General Ledger accounts plus these extra accounts and account subtotals comprise the FI-GLX Extended General Ledger.

The General Ledger is extended by being integrated with the common chart of accounts in order to take advantage of the facilities offered by the CO-Controlling modules.

Although the Controlling system is specialized for internal accounting procedures, its effect is to maximize the favorable values and minimize the unfavorable values that are summarized in the formal legal documents of External Accounting, namely, the balance sheet and the profit and loss statement. After all, the purpose of the company is to realize profit from its activities and its use of the capital invested in it. The CO-Controlling module represents a comprehensive application of the SAP system to all the elements of a company's business.

GLX Stand-Alone Extended General Ledger

The Extended General Ledger is a SAP product that can stand alone and accept data from external systems using software from other suppliers. It can also be installed to integrate with the SAP R/3 system and interact with components of the FI-Financial module and the CO-Controlling module. Either directly, or via the CO-Controlling module, the Extended General Ledger module can link up with any of the SAP R/3 components.

The bridge between other applications and the Extended General Ledger will comprise one or more ledgers. Not all of the transaction data from other applications will find a corresponding account in the Extended General Ledger. The system ensures that updates from another application correspond with at least one ledger. A standard program is supplied with the Extended General Ledger to check that this reconciliation is in fact taking place.

You can reconcile the Extended General Ledger with the transaction data at any time.

Planning in the FI-GLX Extended General Ledger

The plan comprises three operations and a reporting stage which can occur at any time and be repeated as often as required.

Specifying Planning Objects. The first step is to set out the planning cost objects or levels at which planning is to take place, such as:

- Business area
- Cost centers

- General ledger accounts

- Months or other posting periods

Assigning Values. Entering target values and budgets to be assigned to the planning cost objects can be done manually or with assistance from automatic distribution functions.

Collating Data. Collecting transaction data and collating them to match planning levels and objects is the most intensive operation in terms of information flow.

Reporting. The standard SAP R/3 flexible reporting functions will show you, for any combinations of planning cost objects that you require, how actual values stood up against plans and targets.

Any or all of these procedures may be automated by setting parameters under control of the Extended General Ledger component.

Functionalities Enabled by the Extended General Ledger

The following actions may be carried out through the Extended General Ledger program:

- Specify General Ledger account subtotals to collect data on chosen periods or another focus of interest.

- Name the account subtotals.

- Specify the criteria for posting entries to each subtotal.

- Record and update account subtotals from the transaction information entered in SAP Documents.

- Accept data from other SAP applications.

- Accept data from systems that do not use SAP software.

- Enter financial plans in the form of planned values for each relevant account and account subtotal of the Extended General Ledger.

- Report on the planned and actual account totals and subtotals for the period or other focus of interest.

- Design reports based on flexible fiscal years.

- Provide parallel reports in up to three currencies.

Specifying Inflow of Data to the Extended General Ledger

Data reaching the Extended General Ledger system will have arisen mainly by transactions in other systems, other SAP applications, or systems provided by other suppliers.

SAP provides a comprehensive suite of standard interfaces.

The flow can take place immediately after a transaction is posted, at regular intervals, or via batch transfers. Validation can take place to ensure that the incoming data comply with the conditions imposed by the Extended General Ledger; and substitution of transaction data can take place so that what is retained is amenable to further processing by the client systems using the facilities provided by the Extended General Ledger module.

Checking for consistency has to occur. For example, master data in the Extended General Ledger must have elements to name and specify all the data objects that will be needed and that will be used to store data incoming from the associated applications. Account identification, cost center, product identification, and any other attribute of interest will have to find a place in the Extended General Ledger from which it can be retrieved and identified, even though, in the case of nonSAP systems, it may no longer be easily traced in the system which first created it.

One solution is to have the Extended General Ledger acquire master data from the transferring system. This imposes the requirement that transactions in the transferring system shall include all the information of interest as either optional or required entries. Obviously, information that has not been collected by the transferring system cannot subsequently be accessed from the Extended General Ledger.

A set of master data shared by all applications will ensure consistency of data across all systems using the Extended General Ledger.

From other SAP R/3 applications the preliminaries to data transfer include establishing the following specifications:

- Which transactions will update the Extended General Ledger. Sources might include financial accounting, material management, or job order accounting.

- Which particular ledger is to be updated, and how

- Whether each ledger is to be updated immediately or at regular intervals

SAP R/3 provides guidance and prompting to enable you to set up the validation rules in each case, based on rules and combinations of fields that you can define. The system will then validate transaction data, subtotals, or totals in the ledgers specified.

It is usual to have other SAP applications automatically transfer the data for the Extended General Ledger. A direct data entry function is also provided to allow the entry of notes or consolidation entries, for instance. As is normal practice, these entries create SAP Documents. These SAP Documents can be flagged to show they are records of direct entries to the Extended General Ledger and, if necessary, they may be displayed separately.

Assessment in the Extended General Ledger

In this context assessment refers to the process of gathering cost information from a number of sources. Consider freight charges across all warehouses for all products in a particular group, or on a particular list of products. Assessment is the process of seeking out the details and calculating the total of these charges.

This task is in the province of the Extended General Ledger. Needless to say, it will not succeed if the master data of the Extended General Ledger makes no mention of freight charges, nor any data field that could be used to make a proper substitution—delivery charges, for example.

Distribution in the Extended General Ledger

Distribution is sharing. For example, the total of freight charges across the group may be distributed by sharing it as some kind of overhead charge imposed by the accounting system. Who should share this burden may be hotly debated, but in the end the Extended General Ledger will have to be told to divide this cost between various accounts.

There are two types of distribution:

- Single-dimension
- More than one dimension or level of detail

Single-dimension distribution takes place when a value is credited to the sender and debited to a single receiving account. For example, a cost center can be created in order to allow certain costs to be reported under the name of that center. Administration Costs might be the name of a cost center. Freight Costs might be another.

Distribution can also be directed at more than one receiving entity. The set of recipients might include all production departments. The costs can be distributed across specific products in a product group, for example.

Whether the distribution is to a single receiver, such as a cost center, or to a set of receivers, there are three methods of computing how much is attributed to each:

- **Fixed amount method**—You decide how much to charge each individual recipient. A fixed amount is debited to each, and the sender is credited with the total.

- **Fixed share method**—You decide what percentage share of the amount to be distributed shall be charged to each recipient. Each recipient is debited with the fixed share, and the sender is credited with the total of these shares, which need not equal one hundred percent of the assessed charge. The sender may retain a share.

- **Dynamic method**—The amount to be distributed is automatically calculated by the system on the basis of the subtotals already recorded in the Extended General Ledger.

The Set Concept

The logical concept of a set is used in the Extended General Ledger for reporting, planning and ledger processing. A set refers to a data structure and its relationships with other data structures.

A set of numbers may be defined, where the numbers are the identification codes of bank accounts, for example.

A list of cost centers may constitute a set.

The actual members of a set may not be known until the set definition is called into use. "The top three operating divisions for gaining new customers in the current month" is a set definition of this kind.

The definition of a set may include relationships between specific firms or companies in a group, not necessarily at the same level.

A set may comprise any collection of data objects that meet the logical criteria forming the definition for membership of that set.

Specific business functions may call on a set definition which has been stored for use later. Assessment and distribution often take place under the control of sets.

Planned Amounts in the Extended General Ledger

The basic concept is to set target values for account totals or subtotals for one or more periods. Actual values totaled from the transaction data are then compared with these planned targets.

The method is to enter a planned total, and then have it allocated to periods by various standard functions. Flexible planning and controlling facilities are provided through special functions and tools in the Extended General Ledger.

In practice, the planning usually requires several iterations in which suggested budgets and target values are distributed in various ways until a proper distribution system is determined.

The starting point for a plan is a set of plan parameters:

- Basic data and targets to be entered
- Planned currency for transactions, and the local and group currencies
- Planned types of main and additional quantities
- Standard period allocation keys
- Input units (hundreds, thousands, millions)
- Planned number of decimal places
- Plan version identification
- Data objects to be used

The plan parameters are dependent on the authorization profiles of the users. Not all users are allowed to alter certain parameters.

You can specify for display at any time sets of plan parameters that will be used as the basis for planning and for suggesting more appropriate amounts to be set as targets.

Planning Perspectives

Centralized planning entails planning cost elements, for example, for all cost centers. Decentralized planning would plan for each cost center individually.

The Extended General Ledger allows both perspectives, and you can switch between perspectives online.

The technique of setting up plan parameters allows the planning process to begin with a complete plan that can be used without altering anything. On the other hand, any of the parameter values can be changed, if the user is so authorized.

The distribution functions can be changed, as can the sets of account totals and subtotals upon which they act. Individual amounts may be overwritten.

Each version of a plan may be stored for later comparison.

There are many standard ways of distributing planned amounts. Annual or quarterly input values are usually distributed to planning periods by using one or more distribution keys.

A distribution key is a tag or code which may be used simply as a label, or it may refer to a complex data object that serves as a distribution formula. There is a standard distribution key for distributing an amount equally to every working day in the current month, for example. SAP R/3 offers a wide variety of standard distribution keys, and the user may define unique keys that are available for use with other planning periods or other versions of the plan.

There are distribution keys for use with various planning objects such as sales, personnel expenses, and so on. There are standard keys for product groups and for product types such as "semi-finished products." Such keys can be used to plan for production cost centers so that, in this example, the value of semi-finished products will appear in the Extended General Ledger reports under that heading and will also attract a designated share of the cost of warehousing or other assessments.

This system of distribution keys can be used with the suite of distribution functions and the logical concept of sets to arrange for a flexible and focused planning system that can be adjusted to suit changing business conditions.

Reporting Dimensions

The reporting system of the Extended General Ledger is particularly flexible. You can use it to report by any field that is already defined for accumulating subtotals.

Installations of SAP R/3 differ according to the needs of the customer, but there may be account subtotals for planned data and actual data, for product groups and business areas, for individual products, and cost centers. There are many permutations that could make business sense for a particular user. Even the choice of time period may be an important matter for individual purposes. SAP R/3 can work with up to 365 time periods a year.

There are standard reports for the main tasks:

- Reconciling and controlling account subtotals
- Providing an audit trail for internal and external auditors

There is a menu-driven report writer to design and produce your own reports.

Report Design. The design of a report takes place with the aid of a menu-driven system that will apply predefined system standards.

You can accept the details suggested by the system by copying from another report and changing some of the details individually on-screen. You can specify the content and layout in advance by changing the parameters of an existing customized report, or modify a standard report within the permitted domains.

The following factors may be specified or adjusted to design a customized report:

- Report layout
- Sources of data
- Fields to appear in each row
- Level of detail—how data are to be subtotaled and totaled
- Which amounts will appear in the columns (actual, plan, day, month, quarter, total year)
- Which data are to be selected
- Whether and which ratios are to be calculated and their formulas
- Text to appear in the report

Report Output Media. Reports can be produced online or in batches. They can be stored for later analysis or printing, possibly by other users.

The range of output routes available for reporting includes the following:

- Online screen listing with user control of format and content
- Printing in accord with ad hoc designs to replicate screen reports
- Printing to standard report formats
- Printing to customized report formats and selected destination printers
- Printing to sequential files in the system for subsequent processing or printing
- Printing to local PC files available to selected network users
- Sending graphic reports to screen or printers with SAP Business Graphics

Facilities of the Online Reporting System. The SAP system of using a table of parameters to specify report design allows you to make the following changes online:

- Change the level of detailing.
- Change the subtotaling.

- Change the content of the columns.

- Output all or parts of the report to file or to printer.

Display controls enable you to change what you see:

- Switch to another report with another perspective.

- Select a row in the report and see the whole of the SAP Document upon which it is based.

- Select an area of the report—a group of row items and some of the columns—and call on SAP Business Graphics to present the data in one of a range of graphical styles that you can subsequently adjust and annotate before storing it or consigning it to one or more of the output routes.

The reporting system of the Extended General Ledger gives you the ability to extract pertinent data and process them so you can present them in ways which will best serve the cause of effective decision-making.

FI-AR Accounts Receivable

Accounts Receivable is a sub-ledger of the FI-GL General Ledger and completely integrated with it at the following levels:

- Master Data

- Transaction Data

- Reporting System

The General Ledger and its sub-ledgers share the common chart of accounts with all applications, and also share all the details of master records. Reporting can draw from the General Ledger and the Accounts Receivable sub-ledger.

The purpose of the Accounts Receivable sub-ledger is to keep track of customers and the transactions that involve them. Its job is to collect money: To process cash receipts and dun customers who are late in paying. It shares the same accounting needs as the SD-Sales and Distribution module.

Transaction data are stored centrally in the document database, and the corresponding line items and details are stored in the sub-ledgers as appropriate. The system automatically updates a subtotal of a balance sheet account for every business transaction, and reconciles the account subtotals and the line items to ensure that the financial information is always correct and always current.

Account balances by debits and credits for up to sixteen posting periods are maintained by the system.

Every transaction creates a SAP Document, and the data are immediately posted to the General Ledger. Hence every business transaction recorded in this way automatically updates the balance sheet or the profit and loss statement.

This is the defining characteristic of an up-to-date, networked, accounting and controlling system.

Master Records

The sales organization need not have the same organizational structure as the legal structure of the company. One sales department may handle products from two or more associated companies. The system of master records makes provision for this.

Master data are organized into three parts: general data, data applicable only for specific company codes, and sales data.

General data are the information of a general kind needed by all or some departments about each customer:

- Name, address, telephone, fax, modem number
- Customer registration number
- Line of business, business group
- Bank account data

For each separate company using the sales organization there may be different entries against each company code to reflect their different methods of doing business with the customer:

- Standard payment terms
- Data for dunning overdue accounts
- Data for direct debit
- Data for correspondence such as the account number and name and salutation or title of the clerk responsible for purchasing

You may also have to specify a particular General Ledger reconciliation account for each company contributing products to the sales organization.

Processing Master Data Records

Access to customer master data records has to be controlled by limiting the staff who are allowed to modify certain data fields. The method is to use the system of authorizations to restrict the use of certain functions which can affect the critical fields of the customer master records.

These restrictions can then be applied to accounting data, sales data, or both.

When a new or prospective customer is identified, a new master record is created and assigned to an account group.

The account group determines whether you may assign account numbers within specified ranges, or whether this will be done automatically by the system.

You will not be allowed to assign the same account number more than once: but you can have both customers and vendors within the same range of numbers.

The account group also controls which fields will be active in this master record. The fields offered by the account group may be picked and assigned to one of three categories:

- Fields into which the user must make a valid entry

- Fields the user can either leave blank or make an entry into

- Fields that will be suppressed so they will not appear on the screen at all. A whole screen of fields may be suppressed if they are not needed for a particular master record.

The FI-AR Accounts Receivable system will make it easy to create master records by offering various options:

- You can copy a master record from a reference record that has been established for the purpose. You have to make at least one alteration to it before you post it to become a new master record.

- You may copy the master record of an existing customer and edit the unwanted details to make it into a new master record.

- You may create the new customer master record by entering all the necessary details.

Once you have entered and stored a customer master record, you can call it back again and change almost any of the fields. There will be a choice of whether to go through all the fields or work on only one set of fields, for instance, the payment details.

Master records can be selectively displayed so that you need see only those fields that are of interest to you according to the task you have at hand.

One-Time Accounts

If you think a customer is probably not going to become a regular purchaser, you can set up a one-time account by selecting a special function. This will create a master record that contains only the essential control data, such as the number of the reconciliation account to which this sale will be posted. You can supply the address and the bank account data when you enter an invoice. This information will then arrive in the one-time account master record, where the dunning and payment programs can find it when they need it.

Head Office—Branch Accounts

Your customer may be a branch with its own account, but the head office may foot the bill. In this case you can enter the head office account number in the master record for the branch customer. When you enter a transaction to the branch account, the system will post the transaction to the head office account, leaving a cleared entry on the branch account to show who received the goods or service.

The master will include data about the branch and a reference to another master to give details of the head office. By this means, dunning letters can be sent to the head office, the branch or both.

Payments from an Alternative Payer

Your customer may not have to deal with his own payments. You can record in his master data the account number of the alternative payer, and the system will then process direct debits, return transfers and other customer payment business through the banks for the other payer.

If you do post customer invoices to an affiliate, you have to record in the master data of the branch customer a group-wide company account number that will be used during consolidation to eliminate the invoices that would otherwise appear twice in the company accounts. The system will be able to look at the transaction documents bearing this group-wide company account number and identify any entries that are replicated because the payment was made by an affiliate who was not the original customer.

Customer Transactions in Accounts Receivable

As soon as the master data have been stored for a customer, a customer transaction can occur. If the master is for a one-time account, the data will be sparse.

If you have installed and configured SAP SD-Sales and Distribution with the SAP FI-Financial system, invoices entered in the SD system will be automatically posted to General Ledger accounts in FI.

If you have another invoicing system, the route to the FI-GL General Ledger accounts is through a SAP open interface, which will transfer and post invoice data to General Ledger accounts automatically.

If you have to enter manually an invoice that has not been posted automatically, SAP R/3 will provide all possible help. You can enter and post a check received and match the payment to specific open items in the customer account, all in one operation.

The successful posting of a transaction does not occur until the necessary data are recorded as a SAP Document and are complete and error-free. You can set aside a transaction document before it is ready for posting, in which case the system will validate any information you have already entered and report to you any discrepancies.

The SAP Document has to end up with a document header showing posting date, document date, document reference number, and currency key. The body of the document will contain one or more line items which will show the amount and identify the product and the terms of payment. The system will generate certain line items, such as tax entries, cash discount, and exchange rate differences, as applicable.

You can set up helping routines and use standard data entry functions such as:

- Default values that you may edit at the time of entry
- Recalling for copying and editing a previous screen

- Retaining data for individual users for several transactions

- Adapting a copy of a data-entry screen so that it is better suited to a set of transactions that you are expecting

- Searching for an account number by using matchcodes to narrow the search

A SAP Document that records a previous transaction can be copied to act as a sample or model to be edited. This sample can be a regular document that has been set aside, perhaps as an incomplete transaction document. The posting date and new values may have to be changed before posting.

Recurring Entries

If you are expecting to make a series of entries where the amounts are always the same, you can set up a recurring entry. Monthly service fees would be an example.

A recurring entry is a set of data that will not be used until the due dates. Until then, the entries will not update account balances.

You will have to specify the first and last dates and the frequency or time interval. The system will automatically post the required transaction on each of the due dates.

Special Transactions in the FI-AR Accounts Receivable Sub-Ledger

The standard general-purpose data-entry function can be called from FI-AR Accounts Receivable in order to make special entries such as credit memos and adjustments. Down payments, bills of exchange, and security deposits are examples of special General Ledger transactions. Separate account balances are maintained for them.

Currencies

Each company code has a local currency for reporting. The system records amounts in this local currency and also in a currency that has been specified as the document currency and that will be used on all documents in addition to the local currency.

You can enter documents in any currency.

You have two options for converting currencies:

- Enter an exchange rate when you enter the transaction document.

- The system translates between document and local currencies by referring to a table of daily exchange rates.

The system can be customized in various ways, which include the following:

- A specific user is obliged to enter amounts in a particular currency, which can be the local currency or the system document currency.

- A specific user can be permitted to enter amounts in either local or document currency.

Whatever the customizing arrangements, the system will display amounts in both local and document currencies. It will round off minor differences, using rules established for these purposes. These differences can occur when several line items are converted and then added in both currencies.

Customer monthly debits and credits are kept by the system only in local currency. The reconciliation account for the Accounts Receivable sub-ledger is kept in local currency and in all the other currencies that have been posted.

Cash Receipts
When a customer is paying in the traditional manner, it is usual to find references to invoices or other documents with the check or other form of payment. You may find a document number written on the check, on a payment list, or in a payment advice note.

You have to enter four essential items of data:

- Account number for the bank
- Amount paid
- Bank fees
- Document numbers of the invoices being paid

The system has to total the open items for this customer and compare this total with the amount being paid, making allowance for any cash discount due for early payment or other reason. If the total due equals the total paid, the system posts the payment and marks all the line items as cleared.

The action of marking a line item as cleared includes recording for each line the clearing date and the identification number of the SAP Document that is the stored evidence of the transaction—in this case, the payment document.

The audit trail may need to trace any amount to the point where it first appeared in the system.

Searching for Open Items
If the customer has not told you which invoices are being paid by writing their numbers on the check or by including an advice note, you will have to find out by using the system.

For example, you can call for a search for open items for this customer. There may be too many to decide which are being settled by this payment, so you can narrow the search by giving exact values or ranges of values for almost any of the header fields and line item fields that could appear on a transaction document.

It is recommended that you use no more than a handful of search fields. The most useful fields for narrowing a search for open items for a customer are the following:

- Document Reference Number
- Posting Date

- Invoice Amount

- Posting Key

For any of your searching criteria you can accept a range of values: any document number between two given numbers; any posting date over a specified interval; any invoice amount greater than or less than a given amount; any posting key out of a short list that you specify.

The system's first response to a search command is to display a summary screen showing the items it has found.

The summary will total the amounts. If this equals your customer's payment, your search is over. If not, you must refine the search.

You might select a few items from the summary screen, and look at their details in order to find some better entries for a more focused search.

The summary screen layout may be more useful to you if you change its display format by moving or replacing some of the columns until you are looking at only the details that interest you.

At any time you can switch the display between showing the details of a line item, and showing the entire document. This will include the entry offsetting this customer line item, if there is one.

If your search for open items is successful, you will arrive at a list of invoices that add up to the same amount as is being offered as payment by the customer. Allowances for cash discounts will have been calculated by the system, and you will be able to see this from the display. There may also be differences arising because of the conversions between currencies.

When your system is being customized, you can specify the limits within which the system will post minor payment differences automatically. You can also establish special rules for each user, so that any differences larger than a certain amount have to be referred to a user with authorization to deal with them.

When the selected open items balance the payment, you can post the document.

Partial Payments

If the open items do not balance the payment after cash discounts have been allowed, there are three options:

- You can post a payment on account.

- You can clear an open item and post a residual item.

- You can enter a partial payment with a reference to the open item that remains open.

If you cannot find any amounts at all to match with the payment, the only option is to post the payment on account.

If you cannot completely match the payment to the open items, the best option again is to post the payment on account.

If you know the open item concerned, and the payment is only partial, you can clear the full amount of the open item; but open a residual item to cover the difference still unpaid. Alternatively, you can enter the payment with a note to refer to the open item of which it is but a partial settlement.

If there are many possible open items, the system can be given the task of picking open items without defining any search criteria. The system will try various combinations of open items in the attempt to match the amount paid. It will suggest a set of items that together add up to an amount as close as possible to the amount paid.

Bank Fees

If a bank charge is associated with a cash receipt, you can enter it at the same time. The system will automatically generate and display a line item for the bank fee.

Currency Exchange Differences

A line item may be expressed in a currency other than the local or document currency. You can enter payments to clear such foreign currency line items using either local or document currency.

The payment expressed in the document currency will have been converted from the local currency at an exchange rate adopted by the system according to the rules laid down for assigning the daily exchange rate. If this rate has changed from the rate prevailing when the invoice was written, the payment amount may not match the open item amount. In such cases the system will automatically calculate and post an exchange difference entry to a separate account established for this purpose.

Down Payment Entries

A payment which is the first of a series of partial payments can be identified as a down payment and will be recorded as such. The item will remain open, and the amount will be posted to an account established for the purpose of accumulating such payments until the full payment has been received. Only then will the item be cleared, and the holding account will be cleared by the same amount.

Vendor Open Items

Because the FI-GL General Ledger accounts are fully integrated, vendor open items may be cleared at the same time as customer payments.

Open Items for Different Customers

The integrated FI-AR Accounts Receivable component will accept each item as an independent task, because each item will have access to the complete set of data objects needed to process it.

Therefore, open items may be found for several customers and cleared by the appropriate payments in the same session.

Open Items with Different Company Codes

Open items bearing different company codes can be cleared at the same time. The system will record a clearing document in each company code.

Automatic Clearing in Accounts Receivable

If your customer has allowed you to collect by direct debit, the FI-AR component will offer you a payment program, which will collect all invoices when due.

Reimbursing customers with checks or by bank transfers follows the FI-AP Accounts Payable procedures for automatic payment.

If the FI-CM Cash Management component has been installed, you will be able to clear automatically. Your bank statement can be provided by file transfer, and the system will automatically post the entries to the FI-GL General Ledger and also clear the matching open items in the customer accounts. Only if the data from the transfer are incomplete will you have to intervene.

Payment Procedures for Particular Countries

There are variations in the legal payment procedures for different countries. These have been encapsulated in the standard business procedures of the FI-AR Accounts Receivable component.

National payment procedures may be specified for your implementation during the customizing process.

Dunning Accounts Receivable

Each customer's master data include a field to indicate what is to be done about overdue invoices. This dunning code identifies an established dunning procedure.

A dunning procedure is independent of company codes. It records the grace period, the dunning intervals and the number of dunning levels.

The SAPscript word processing program is available to you to design and change the format of dunning letters. You will have been provided with some model letters at each dunning level during customization. You can change and edit the text of the letter and also the company logo, position of the address window, and footers. Open items referred to in the letter may be given a special format and content for this purpose.

A dunning proposal is a set of suggestions assembled by the system, which you can accept as it stands or alter in various ways. The system will start creating a dunning proposal by using due dates and some method of selecting which accounts are to be dunned. You may have defined these previously.

You then process the dunning proposal online. You can target the dunning letters at particular clerks; or you may decide to assign particular dunning letters to the dunning levels, and then designate a level to each of the individual open items. The dunning level of the whole account will be changed automatically to the highest dunning level of any open item. You can release specific open items and accounts to be referenced in the dunning letters. The system records all changes to open items that are to be dunned.

Customizing Dunning Letters. The same letter forms can be used throughout the group, or you can use different forms for each company code. Certain text may appear only for particular company codes. You can decide for each company code whether an individual dunning letter is to be prepared for each dunning level. If this is to be the case, only the items with that dunning level will appear on the dunning letter.

Individual accounts can have their own dunning letters. Customer items can be assigned to different dunning areas, each of which is given a separate dunning letter.

If the SD-Sales and Distribution system has been installed and configured, the dunning areas can be made to correspond to the areas of the sales organization, the distribution channel, or the division.

Refunds overdue from a vendor can be dunned; and you can have the dunning program subtract vendor items from customer items where they concern the same company, if the master records specify that this is permitted.

Selecting the Route for Dunning Letters. The dunning program can direct dunning letters to the EDI-Electronic Document Interchange system on the basis of individual customer or vendor accounts, or in accord with a group or dunning area policy.

You can also use the office system to send the letters by telex, messenger or postal delivery.

Reports on Dunning. The system always prepares a standard processing log. It can also offer the following reports pertaining to dunning:

- List of blocked items
- List of blocked accounts
- Lists of items with special dunning keys
- Dunning statistics

Special General Ledger Transactions

Transactions that are posted to a customer's account will automatically update the FI-AR General Ledger Accounts Receivable, which is a reconciliation account, if they are invoices, credit memos, or payments.

Some transactions posted to the customer account may update FI-GL General Ledger accounts other than FI-AR Accounts Receivable.

These accounts are a type of Special General Ledger Account. They are reconciliation accounts recording business that is neither a sale to a customer nor a purchase from a vendor.

Special General Ledger Transactions include:

- Down Payments
- Bills of Exchange
- Security deposits
- Guarantees

Down Payments. A down payment is a payment for a product or service not yet supplied or performed. They have to be reported in the balance sheet separately from other Receivables or Payables.

Down payments made are reported as assets: down payments received are reported as liabilities.

A down payment request can be recorded as a note to the files which will be displayed with other open items for each customer. As a note, it will not update account balances. However, like any other open item, you can dun the request for a down payment with the dunning program, and collect the down payment by direct debit with the payment program.

You can enter and post a customer down payment gross; the tax is included in the down payment and offset in a tax clearing account. Or you can post the down payment net. The balance sheet will report it correctly either way.

When you post the final invoice, you can display all the down payments and apply them to the customer invoice. They may match the invoice in full or in part, but you cannot clear the invoice until you receive payment from the customer.

Bills of Exchange Receivable. A bill of exchange is a document on which is written a promise to pay a certain amount on a certain date in exchange for a specific business transaction that has taken place. A Bill of Exchange Receivable is a promise that payment can be collected from a customer on the expiration date record on the bill. It is a form of IOU ("I owe you") with a date set for payment.

When a customer submits a bill of exchange, you can use the search facilities to find open items to match it if there is any doubt regarding the invoice it belongs to.

A Bill of Exchange Receivable is an open item until the bill itself has been deposited at the bank and discounted there against your account. Alternatively, your customer could pay cash to the amount of a bill of exchange. Either method of concluding the payment would permit you to close the open invoice item.

Because the bill of exchange receivable is a promise and not a payment, it is posted to a special General Ledger account set up for this purpose and named the Bills of Exchange Receivables account.

If the customer offers you a cash or check payment before the bill of exchange receivable has expired, you can reverse the deposit in the Bills of Exchange Receivable account and post the cash against the open item in the normal way.

Bills of Exchange Discount Ledger. Discounting is the process of depositing bills of exchange that are not yet due. The system can prepare a deposit slip for bills of exchange.

Discounting also refers to the process of depositing a post-dated check and deducting interest on the amount (the discount) until the due date.

Commission or collection fees can be charged on both bills of exchange and checks.

The system can prepare the discount ledger. This ledger is a journal in which all bills of exchange are entered. The following data fields are mandatory:

- Due date
- Amount
- Name and address of the drawer
- Name and address of the previous holder
- Place of payment
- Name and address of the drawee
- Discount

You can specify default values for each company code for the following:

- Discount percentage
- Collection fees
- Bill of exchange tax

These charges have to be posted to separate accounts in the General Ledger. The system can prepare a bill for the customer that details these charges.

Bills of exchange deposits can be recorded and annotated as follows:

- Discounted before the due date
- Collected on the due date
- Factored—an exporter gets cash immediately from a bank or other financial institution which takes responsibility for collecting the receivable amounts or the amounts due on the bills of exchange

Security Deposit

A security deposit is a payment made in advance against the possibility of poor performance by one of the parties to a transaction; for example, the payment by the buyer or the performance of the seller.

Security deposits are reported as noted items in the financial statements.

Guarantee

A guarantee is a contract entered into by a third party to pay up to a specified limit if one of the parties to a transaction fails to deliver the contracted materials or service, on the one hand, or fails to pay the amount due, on the other.

Guarantees are reported as noted items in the financial statements.

Reporting in the Accounts Receivable Component

The online reporting facilities of the Accounts Receivable program can be supplemented by printed outputs in single or batch modes. These reports can be sent to file or to a printer.

There are three main classes of report:

- Master record reports
- Customer account statements and open item reports
- Balance audit trail reports

Customers can be selected by various criteria, singly or in the form of logical expressions that will isolate customers on the basis of one or more attributes of their master records combined with attributes computed from their accounts—for example, customers with a post-code beginning 462 who have not ordered in the previous six months.

The content of a report is under your control. You can mix master data and account data, subject to authorization.

If the items are still in the system, you can call for reports of customer open items which sort the items by ranges of due dates or by values according to the report specification that you build or copy from a previous design.

Audit Trail Reporting

A legally valid financial accounting system has to have a method of demonstrating all the transactions that contributed to each of the balances on the balance sheet. It has to show the balance at the beginning of the accounting period and all the debits and credits that were applied to the account to reach the balance at the close of the period.

Every computer system has limits to the amount of storage space that it can make available for any particular purpose. The SAP approach to the management of storage space is to archive all the line items in a balance audit trail separately from the document data that recorded the transactions.

When a balance audit trail is required, usually at the end of the accounting period, the line item archive can be scanned without also having to read all the document data.

The balance audit trail report contains a list of customer line items and a control total for each customer account. Reconciliation account totals will also be shown, so the accounts can be matched with accounts in other parts of your accounting system.

The customer line items for accounts that are not managed on an open item basis can be sorted in chronological order to assist in tracking them.

When open item accounting is in practice, the balance audit trail will sort the cleared (paid) line items to the beginning of each account, arranged in clearing date order and then by clearing document number. This helps you trace how and when an item was cleared. The uncleared open items will be at the end of each account listing.

FI-AP Accounts Payable

Accounts Payable is a sub-ledger of the General Ledger and completely integrated with it at the following levels:

- Master Data
- Transaction Data
- Reporting System

The purpose of the Accounts Payable sub-ledger is to keep track of the vendors of goods, materials and services. Its job is to pay for them. It is an integral part of the purchasing system.

Master data entered or modified in one application will be available to all the others. Transaction data will be accessible to all. Reporting can draw from the General Ledger and the Accounts Payable sub-ledger.

Transaction data are stored centrally in the document database, and the corresponding line items and details are stored in the sub-ledgers as appropriate. The system automatically updates a subtotal of a balance sheet account for every business transaction, and reconciles the account subtotals and the line items to ensure that the financial information is always correct and current.

Every transaction creates a SAP Document, and the data are immediately posted to the General Ledger. Hence every business transaction recorded in this way automatically updates the balance sheet or the profit and loss statement.

This is the defining characteristic of an up-to-date networked accounting and controlling system.

The Business Functions of Accounts Payable

Accounts Payable includes a program that records orders, deliveries and invoices for each vendor. Operating transactions automatically update accounts in the FI-General Ledger system. When you post a vendor transaction, the system will immediately update the Accounts Payable account.

Accounts Payable is directly integrated with Cash Management, which supports cash planning and dunning.

An automatic payment program can be called from Accounts Payable.

SAP Purchasing is a group of components from MM-Materials Management that can be installed and configured to integrate with Accounts Payable. The Purchasing functions are discussed in the Chapter 23, "Understanding the MM-Materials Management Module."

Reporting on matters concerned with FI-AP Accounts Payable will follow the SAP standard business functions to yield the following reports, for example:

- List of due dates for accounts payable
- Currency lists
- Hit list

Correspondence concerning Accounts Payable can be set to provide automatic letters and messages for such purposes as:

- Balance confirmation
- Information
- Interest calculation

Compliance with GAAP

The methods used by SAP FI-AP Accounts Payable to adhere to GAAP (the Generally Accepted Accounting Principles) are the methods used throughout the SAP system.

Vendor information is stored in vendor master data records which are the only source of this information, and which are kept up-to-date by all users and applications that have reason to interact with them. The master data are entered once, and stays in one place only. Everyone knows where to find it and can discover when it was last updated.

Transactions concerning vendors automatically create SAP Documents that can be used to keep track of the transactions and the actions that arise from them. These SAP Documents can be used to compile a legal audit trail for each balance amount in the balance sheet. They can also be used to record other information that will be used by controlling systems with interests in vendor transactions.

SAP Documents have to comply with GAAP in the matter of capturing the information essential to the proper and legal analysis and control of business. These documents, automatically created during vendor transactions under the Accounts Payable system, can be displayed and altered, in a controlled manner, using the SAP standard business functions for manipulating SAP Documents.

The vendor accounts and others involved with the Accounts Payable system are updated in accord with GAAP recommendations, and the proper record must be created whenever any changes are made to the account balances or the SAP Documents that record such activities.

Vendor Master Records

In accordance with the SAP principle of redundancy-free data storage, the standard practice is to use master records for the control of basic data that are seldom changed. At the master record design stage, you have to ensure that a vendor master data object has a data field for every item of information needed to record and post business transactions with vendors.

If the information you require could have been supplied by the system, you should not have to enter it by hand every time you attempt to carry out a vendor transaction.

Information in a master record is not necessarily available to anyone who is interested in it. Certain data objects may be closed to a user who does not have the authorization to access them. The vendor's bank balance would be an example of data that are not available for scrutiny by just anyone.

The SAP MM-Materials Management, Purchasing components have to have been installed and configured in order to make use of information directed at a purchasing department.

If the Purchasing components have been installed, both the purchasing department and the accounting department will use the vendor master record from time to time. There have to be data fields to suit them both, as follows:

- General data concerning the vendor that everyone will need (address, telephone number, telex and modem codes, and so on).

- Data about the vendor that might be of interest to any of the various company codes representing the different legal entities into which the purchasing company may be divided. Accounting data would be an example.

- Data about the vendor that might be important to any of the purchasing organizations that might buy from this vendor. These may not correspond to the divisions differentiated by the company codes.

The company code divides the company into legal divisions for accounting purposes. Master data for each company code will include:

- Payment terms
- Customer account number under that company code
- Reconciliation account number
- Payment methods
- How the vendor line items are to be sorted on displays under each company code

Creating and Maintaining Vendor Master Records

When a new or prospective vendor is identified, a new master record is created. It must be assigned to an account group.

The account group determines whether you can assign account numbers within specified ranges, or whether this will be done automatically by the system.

You will not be allowed to assign the same account number more than once, but you can have both customers and vendors within the same range of numbers.

The account group also controls which fields will be active in this master record. The fields offered by the account group can be picked and assigned to one of three categories:

- Fields into which the user must make a valid entry

- Fields the user can either leave blank or make an entry into

- Fields that will be suppressed so they will not appear on the screen at all. A whole screen of fields may be suppressed if they are not needed for a particular master record.

The FI-AP Accounts Payable system will make it easy to create vendor master records by offering various options:

- You can copy a master record from a reference record that has been established for the purpose. You have to make at least one alteration to it before you post it to become a new vendor master record.

- You can copy the master record of an existing vendor and edit the unwanted details to make it into a new master record.

- You can create the new vendor master record by entering all the necessary details.

Once you have entered and stored a vendor master record, you can call it back again and change almost any of the fields. There will be a choice of whether to go through all the fields or work on only one set of fields; for instance, the product or service details.

Master vendor records can be selectively displayed so that you need see only those fields that are of interest to you according to the task you have at hand.

One-Time Accounts

If you think a vendor is probably not going to become a regular supplier, you can set up a one-time account by selecting a special function. This will create a master record that contains only the essential control data, such as the number of the reconciliation account to which this purchase will be posted. You can supply the address and the bank account data when you enter an invoice received. This information will then arrive in the one-time account master record, where the dunning and payment programs can find it when they need it.

Head Office—Branch Accounts

Your supplier may be a branch with its own account, but the head office may wish to receive your payment. In this case, you can enter the head office account number in the master record for the branch vendor. When you enter a transaction to the branch account, the system will post the transaction to the head office account, leaving a cleared entry on the branch account to show who supplied the goods or service.

The master will include data about the branch and a reference to another master to give details of the head office. By this means, dunning letters may be sent to the head office, the branch or both for overdue refunds, for example.

Vendor Payments to an Alternative Recipient

Your supplier may not have to deal with his payments due. You can record in his master data the account number of the alternative recipient. The system will then process return transfers and other vendor payment business through the banks to the alternative recipient.

If you do post vendor invoices to an affiliate, you have to record in the master data of the branch vendor a group-wide company account number that will be used during consolidation to eliminate the invoices that would otherwise appear twice in the company accounts. The system will be able to look at the transaction documents bearing this group-wide company account number and identify any entries that are replicated because the payment was made to an affiliate who was not the original vendor.

Transactions in Accounts Payable

When you post a transaction to a vendor account, the reconciliation account for Accounts Payable is updated immediately in the General Ledger.

The system updates a separate account for each type of vendor transaction:

- Purchases
- Down payments
- Bills of exchange payable
- Guarantees

Orders to and invoices from vendors also update financial planning and cash management data.

Vendor Invoices

The SAP FI-Financial Accounting system is integrated with the MM-Materials Management system. An invoice with an order and delivery data can be entered and validated in MM-Materials Management. Validated invoices will be posted automatically to the General Ledger accounts in the FI-Financial Accounting system, if the two systems are suitably configured.

Electronic Data Exchange

Vendor invoices can be received by Electronic Data Exchange (EDI). Data entry starts automatically, and the system converts it from the EDI format to the online entry format for line items.

You will be asked to correct and complete any erroneous or incomplete transactions. These will have been automatically saved for you during the EDI.

Manual Invoice Entry

If you have to enter manually an invoice that has not been posted automatically, then SAP R/3 will provide all possible help.

The successful posting of a transaction does not occur until the necessary data are recorded as a SAP Document and are complete and error-free. You can set aside a transaction document before it is ready for posting, in which case the system will validate any information you have already entered and report to you any discrepancies.

The SAP Document has to end up with a document header showing posting date, document date, document reference number and currency key. The body of the document will contain one or more line items showing the amount and identifying the product and terms of payment. The system will generate certain line items such as tax entries, cash discount, and exchange rate differences as applicable.

You can set up helping routines and use standard data entry functions such as:

- Default values that you can edit at the time of entry

- Recalling for copying and editing a previous screen

- Retaining data for individual users for several transactions

- Adapting a copy of a data-entry screen so that it is better suited to a set of transactions that you are expecting

- Searching for an account number by using matchcodes to narrow the search

A SAP Document that records a previous transaction can be copied to act as a sample or model to be edited. This sample can be a regular document that has been set aside, perhaps as an incomplete transaction document. The posting date and new values may have to be changed before posting.

Recurring Entries

If you are expecting to make a series of entries where the amounts are always the same, you can set up a recurring entry. Monthly service charges under contract would be an example.

A recurring entry is a set of data that will not be used until the due dates. Until then, the entries will not update account balances.

You will have to specify the first and last dates and the frequency or time interval. The system will automatically post the required transaction on each of the due dates.

Special Transactions in the Accounts Payable Sub-Ledger

The standard general-purpose data-entry function can be called from Accounts Payable in order to make special general ledger entries such as credit memos and adjustments. Down payments, bills of exchange and security deposits are examples of special general ledger transactions. Separate account balances are maintained for them.

Entering Net Vendor Invoices. A net vendor invoice records the liability to the vendor after the cash discount has been discounted.

When you process a net vendor invoice, you have to enter the gross amount. The system will calculate the net amount on a line-by-line basis.

When this type of invoice is posted, the General Ledger entries in the Accounts Payable sub-ledger will include the offsetting amounts net of the cash discount. The amount of the cash discount will be automatically posted to a discount clearing account. There it will remain until you pay the invoice, when it will be released.

The purchase of a fixed asset can be recorded as a net vendor invoice. By this means, the amount representing the value of the fixed asset will be net of the cash discount, and can be depreciated in the normal way. The discount clearing account will carry the amount of the cash discount, but it does not have to be cleared later, because it will have been released when payment is made for the fixed asset.

Requests for Down Payments. If you enter a request to the payment program to generate automatically a down payment to a vendor, the system will make the payment and store the request without updating any account balances.

You will have to support the request with all the necessary payment data and the due date for payment to be completed. You can call for a display of all requests for down payment. You have the option to display down payments gross (including tax) or net (excluding tax). The net amount will be reported in the balance sheet, and the tax will appear in the tax account.

When the payment program has carried out all the down payments and you have received the final invoice from the vendor, you can enter it. The system will display all the down payments made on this invoice, and you can apply them to offset the invoice in whole or in part. The payment program will then pay any amount outstanding to the vendor.

Automatic Payment Functions

Manual entering of payments is necessary, for example, if a vendor is to collect from you by direct debits. But the most effective time-saver in Accounts Payable is the automatic payment program.

The payment program proceeds in two stages:

- Generating and presenting for editing a payment proposal
- Executing the approved payment proposal

You can also execute a payment without considering a payment proposal.

Generating a Payment Proposal. The purpose of a payment proposal is to maximize cash discount within the constraints set by certain data in the vendor master records and by the way the payment program has been set up.

Displaying vendor open items will show you who is yet unpaid: you must decide who to choose for payment.

There are various ways to select who to pay on—the basis of due dates, or amounts in order of magnitude and so on.

The system will check the due dates of vendor open items, and propose a method of payment for each depending on the master data and the requirement to maximize cash discount.

The system will also choose one of your banks to provide the funds for each payment.

The system can generate a form for a check or automatic payment medium such as diskette or an online electronic transfer. You will have to assign a medium of this kind for each payment, either individually or on the basis of the default values suggested by the system on the basis of data in the vendor master records. You may have directly specified the choice of medium in advance of a batch of payment proposals.

Editing a Payment Proposal. You may be allowed several options regarding the payment proposal. For example, you may have the authorization allowing you to:

- Change the proposed method of payment for an open item.
- Change the proposed bank.
- Block an open item to stop it being paid.
- Add another open item to the payment proposal.
- Change the cash discount level of an open item to be paid.

Executing the Edited Payment Proposal. Execution of a valid payment proposal is largely automatic.

The payment program will generate SAP payment documents and post payments to the appropriate General Ledger accounts.

The vendor items in the payment proposal will be marked as cleared and given a reference number which will link them to the SAP payment document.

For each country and payment method combination, there is a specific program to print the checks or payment forms in the language and style for that country, and, if a diskette or other electronic payment notification channel is used, in the format for that medium.

The system will compile a log of each payment run and all payment methods applied, so that you can see the effects and exercise control.

Maximizing Cash Discount

Each vendor open item carries a base amount which is the payment due before applying cash discounts. Each vendor master record contains information about the payment terms which that vendor has agreed with the purchasing company. In the purchasing group there may be different payment terms negotiated with each business entity defined by the company codes.

The payment terms for each company code purchasing from a vendor will each include at least one cash discount term, expressed as a percentage discount, and a cash discount date related to the date of the invoice. For example, the following are cash discount payment terms:

> 3% if paid within 14 days of the date of the invoice

> 2.5% if paid on or before the 15th of the month following the date of the invoice

For each open item, you can enter one or two payment terms and a date for net payment. The system can calculate the due discount date by referring to the payment terms and the invoice date. You may wish to enter a date for net payment within a discount period on a date that suits your requirements.

You may find national differences in the practice of settling accounts. In France, for instance, it is customary to pay an invoice with a bill of exchange immediately, so that the due dates of the bill of exchange and the invoice are the same.

The SAP payment program can be set to pay, by bill of exchange, all invoices due within a specific time period. There are many different payment methods available in the system.

The payment program can also be used to make payments by check, by bank transfer, by postal check and by other methods which are specific to particular countries or trading areas.

Multinational accounting is supported by the SAP INT-International Development module:

IN-APA	Asian and Pacific Area
IN-EUR	Europe
IN-NAM	North America
IN-AFM	Africa and Middle East
IN-SAM	South America

Payment Methods

There are no limits to the number of different payment methods you can use for each country. Many of the forms are supplied via a SAP script which is then used to control the printing in the language of the destination country.

You can edit the forms that are supplied so that they precisely suit your payment format.

You can ask the system to select the payment method from a list of up to ten methods that have been nominated in the vendor master record. The automatic selection of payment method can be governed by such factors as:

- Amount to be paid

- Number of open items paid

■ Currency of the receiver

■ Location of the vendor

■ Amount available in the bank account

Open items can be grouped for payment and individual items can be marked to be paid separately. You can nominate a specific open item to be paid in a particular way.

Your system may have been set up to choose one of the vendor's banks on the basis of the suitability of the bank to pay, for example, by bills of exchange.

The choice may rest on the ability of your bank to make a direct transfer to the vendor's bank. Banks are given group codes to indicate who can transfer to whom.

The payment system can be asked to choose one of your banks from which to make a payment. You can rank-order your banks, and have the system work down the list looking for sufficient cash together with the appropriate means of paying. You may have the system choose one of your banks because it has a branch near the vendor. You can also override the automatic selection by commanding it through an entry in the open line item, or by changing the vendor master data.

Alternative Payment Recipient. If payment has to go to a recipient other than the vendor, you can arrange it in various ways:

All payments in all company codes can be redirected by entering the new account number in the general data of the vendor master record.

All payments in a specific company code can be redirected by entering the new account number in the company code section of the vendor master record.

Payments for specific open items can be redirected by marking each open item by a code, but only if this is expressly permitted by an entry in the vendor master record specifying the alternative account number.

Intercompany Payments

One vendor may have supplied several company codes in the same group. The payment system can make one payment and then settle the intercompany accounts by calculating and posting Receivables and Payables between company codes.

The transaction needs you to define one of the company codes and enter it as a normal paying company. The system will assign the document a unique intercompany identification number which will be used to ensure that the other members of the company code group will pay their shares.

Clearing Sales Contra Purchases

If a vendor is also a customer, you can clear vendor and customer open items against each other via a Contra account. The vendor and customer master records must be able identify each other by holding the respective account numbers in the company code areas. And this sort of dealing must be explicitly permitted by the appropriate master data items.

Credit and Debit Memos

A transaction that reduces amounts receivable from a customer—for example, if the customer returns damaged goods—is a credit memo.

A debit memo is a transaction that reduces amounts payable to a vendor because, for example, you send damaged goods back to your vendor.

When you post credit memos, the payment program will immediately process them. If you post a debit memo to a vendor who is to reimburse the amount, then you can apply a multilevel dunning program.

A credit memo can be offset with specific invoices. The payment program will subtract the credit memo amount from the amount due for the vendor open items.

Reverse Documents

Should you mistakenly post a transaction to the wrong vendor, you can reverse this transaction and the associated SAP Document. The system will automatically generate a reversing entry for each item wrongly posted.

FI-FC Financial Controlling

Under the heading of Financial Controlling it is convenient to place Cash Management, Financial Planning, Public Accounting, and Funds Management.

There are SAP standard business functions to support each of these areas, and they can be installed and implemented in various combinations.

FI-CM Cash Management

The purpose of Cash Management is to plan, control, and monitor the liquidity of the business and contribute to its profitability if possible.

The key accounting distinction to be made is between:

- Cash accounts that record actual available liquid assets
- Clearing accounts that represent payments in transit

The operational concept is to:

- Plan all transactions that have payment advices.
- Control cash.
- Invest cash.

The method entails utilizing the SAP fully automatic payment routines to:

- Optimize short-term interest revenue.
- Optimize money market transactions.

The computer context is a closely integrated system comprising SAP Cash Management, the payment program and FI-AP Accounts Payable.

FI-CM Cash Management Procedure. The main steps needed to manage cash efficiently are as follows:

- Store information in the form of payment advices until you receive the payments

- Prepare to clear open items using the information held as payment advices

- Process partial payments, either by open items or by account

- Receive bank statements by file transfer if available

- Clear open items by referring to bank statements or payment advice notes

- Update expected cash receipts

- Use the payment advices to plan cash flow in the short term—up to five days, for example

Managing Cash Accounts and Clearing Accounts. Cash accounts record actual available liquidity; clearing accounts represent payments in transit.

For each cash or clearing account, you can specify individually how it is to be managed. The SAP standard business functions ensure that all the items in these accounts will be consistent with the balance sheet at all times.

You have five options for managing an account:

- Account to be managed on an open item basis

- Account to be kept by value dates

- Account to be kept with various currencies in parallel

- Account to be posted automatically by the payment program

- Account to be cleared automatically by using an electronic banking function

Cash Management Objects. The SAP system operates on objects which are either program objects designed to carry out a business process, or data objects providing information when it is needed by the programmed business processes.

Cash management and short-term cash position forecasting depend on transaction information being made available to the various processes that will prepare data objects such as a daily cash report or plans to control the allocation of cash.

FI-CM Cash Management must be assigned transaction information from the following sources:

FI-GL	General Ledger
FI-AR	Accounts Receivable
FI-AP	Accounts Payable

If there is a schedule of funds to be made available, FI-CM Cash Management must be notified in order to use this information in the forecasting.

If any of the ledgers has recurring entries, then the Cash Management function should know about it.

Many of these relationships between the parts of the SAP system will already be in place by virtue of the integrated design of the various modules. However, the precise details may have to be configured and customized to make the best use of them in an individual implementation, depending on which components are installed and the interfaces to outside systems that are to be active.

Transactions for Processing Payments. The payment program will make available a wide range of options for payment of individual accounts and groupings of sets of accounts. The possibilities include the following functions:

- Enter bank statements quickly
- Optionally clear open items automatically subject to specified controls, such as the availability of cash
- Record payment advices and list them for display
- Delete payment advices
- Provide preliminary information about payment orders, checks received, bank statements, and discounted bills of exchange
- Prepare check deposit slips using default posting instructions
- Manage checks outstanding
- Control checks deposited
- Manage bills of exchange receivable and payable
- Calculate interest automatically

Throughout all these transactions, the integrity of the FI-GL General Ledger is maintained by the automatic functions of FI-CM Cash Management, FI-AR Accounts Receivable, and FI-AP Accounts Payable.

Electronic Banking Facilities

The purpose of electronic banking is to reduce the time needed for entering data and to support the aim of timely cash management.

The methods use data transfer by portable storage media such as tape or by direct communication line transfer of files. These files can contain general data or transaction data in the form of bank statements or transaction documents in the SAP Document format or in formats provided by other systems.

The effects of rapid file transfer include the following contributions to the goal of more secure, quicker and more efficient processing and clearing of payments:

- Bank statements can be posted automatically.

- Bank statements can be transferred and clearing accounts processed automatically.

- Data can be transferred to FI-AR Accounts Receivable and cash receipts can be processed automatically.

- Bank charges can be posted automatically.

- Exchange rate differences can be posted automatically and foreign currency accounts managed more effectively.

Automatic Bank Account Clearing

The result of Automatic Bank Account Clearing is an improvement in your control of cash, because you can process payment advices and clear bank statements on a daily basis. The effects will be to optimize liquidity reserves and interest income.

You will retain the option of intervening in the automatic processes and making manual corrections. The FI-CM Cash Management position display, for example, can be arranged to separate specific accounts or groups of accounts; and it can split the display to differentiate checks, bank transfers, payment advices and so on. Amounts and dates can be used to rank-order or divide into sets the items to be displayed.

Intercompany transactions and the separation into multiple levels of accounts will be facilitated.

You will have control over the processing of different payment methods and the minimum balance to be maintained in each bank account.

The system can be primed to create all the necessary correspondence automatically.

Medium-Term Cash Management and Forecasting

The purpose of a cash management and financial controlling system is to maintain liquidity in order to fulfill payment obligations.

Short-term management consists of looking at the current liquidity position and what the situation might be in a few days, typically one working week. Medium-term cash management and forecasting has a horizon that extends to a year.

One product of medium-term financial planning is the annual cash plan. This plan must show how liquidity is to be secured over the period by exercising financial control.

The annual plan can be set out at any level of detail and for any arrangement of the organizational structure that the data will support.

Financial Planning Annual Cash Flow Plan

With modern accounting systems, the financial planning period can be of any duration, since the information to be reported will be assembled online when the design of the report is used to generate the presentation of the information.

SAP FI-Financial Accounting supports planning in a comprehensive way:

- The fiscal year can be flexible and can comprise any number of periods.

- The multilevel dependencies between totals and subtotals, departments and sub-departments, and so on, are automatically taken into account when assessing and distributing planning data.

- Data transfer from and to other systems occurs through clearly defined data interfaces, which can serve the aims of financial planning in addition to their other traffic.

The information sources of most interest to the financial planner will be as follows:

- Accounts receivable and payable

- Planned cash expenditures and receipts

- Open orders from customers

- Purchase orders to vendors

The financial planning report will have to address the following issues for each period of the plan for each of the groups within the company that are to be part of the plan:

- Overall liquidity

- Committed funds

- Types of risk

Financial Controlling

The control process comes into prominence when values set out in the financial plan are compared with the actual values achieved by the business. A quick reaction demands a short planning and accounting period, so that actual and planned or budgeted amounts can be compared in time to make a correction. The SAP FI-Financial Controlling module can provide for cycles of monitoring and control that range upwards from one day.

Decentralized Funds Management

Public accounting is a form of financial controlling which is focused on a budget that is made available to cover expenses over the fiscal year or a shorter accounting period. Recent changes to the methods of financial controlling have made the concept of public accounting equivalent to funds accounting.

There are two tasks for which the SAP FI-Financial Accounting system provides comprehensive support:

- Preparing a budget

- Monitoring the budget by tracking the achievement of targets in each of the divisions of the budget

Preparing a budget will entail estimating or assigning target values for the following:

- Cash requirements for operations
- Cash requirements for capital investment projects
- Planned cash receipts

You can assign responsibility for providing, managing, and accounting for funds for each of these items separately, and then combine them in a total budget. Under this total, you can then prepare individual plans which can make a division into administrative and capital budgets.

A budget can be stored with a version number and the process repeated using some or all of the parameters as a model from which a new version is created.

If the proposed applications of funds exceed the funds available, you can identify the funding required to balance the budget.

Target Data. When a budget is translated into planned target amounts for each of the account subtotals that make up the structure of the budget, each of these targets represents the best estimate of the costs or revenues that will or should be realized.

As the period passes, fresh targets can well arise as a result of operating costs, investments and cash receipts which were not anticipated exactly in the plan. Targets may have to alter if the budget is not to be exceeded or underspent. And the data for these adjustments may arise from any of the following causes:

- Funds released and allocated to operating areas additional to the original budget
- Amendments to the budget either in total or in allocation to subdivisions
- Internal transfers
- Commitment authorizations which can be anticipated to exceed the budget
- Unexpended balances
- Anticipated expenditures

Checking that Funds Are Available. The funds committed are revealed by the purchase orders. The system checks that they do not exceed the funds available.

The cash available is checked, and the vendor invoices may have to be reviewed by persons responsible for the budget.

Payment from Funds. When you post an invoice, the system will update the "actual" data. Cash payment orders will be printed by the system to be signed and passed to the controller. The system can be set up to maintain a cash journal that records all cash transactions by date.

Liquidity

Reports from the system will allow you to plan liquidity, because you can analyze payment dates and methods for both commitments and invoices.

Reports online will enable you to compare targets, expenses and receipts in accordance with the budget system. Down payments, invoice amounts, and final payments can be gathered into supplementary reports. An individual line item can be scrutinized; and the history of a commitment can be inspected in the form of the related transaction documents.

Funds Controlling

Public accounting and funds controlling activities tend to emphasize monitoring receipts and expenditures: the sources of funds and their applications. Public sector accounting is centered on monitoring payments.

The main aim is to have actual expenses equal the budget.

In organizations that seek a return on investment in financial terms, the orientation is on budgeting for expenses. The cash flow statement is prepared in order to safeguard liquidity, to monitor financing, and to analyze investments.

Aspects of Funds Controlling. The budget uses a plan to allocate funds to each function and organization unit over a period or succession of periods.

The source of funds is an organizational unit, such as Area, Division, Department, or Individual.

Each source can manage the application of part of the budget to activities that are intended to add value to the information or work items passing through the company. The funds can be applied to:

- Investments, such as stocks of materials, energy, or partially completed work
- Output-related expenses, such as raw materials, supplies, or maintenance
- Serviceability costs, such as depreciation, repairs, or capital investments that affect the value of the plant

The progress of the funds through the budget period is monitored by using the ongoing business transactions. Separate records are made of the details of receipts and expenditure, using the budget structure to allocate them to fund sources (fund-holders) so that reports can be written showing how the funds were used in relation to the budgeted targets.

Because the structure of the budget need not coincide with the commercial or production structure of the company, the funds controlling system is able to provide a sophisticated monitoring and control mechanism which can be aligned to whatever decision-making activities will best serve the company.

Liquidity Analyses (Available)

Cash is money that is available. It will usually be in currency or as a credit balance in a bank. It is available to make payments immediately, in contrast to investments and fixed assets, which are not available to pay debts until they are converted to liquid assets.

Liquidity (available) represents the estimated ability of a customer or vendor to settle outstanding debts promptly. Computing it entails two analytical tasks to build up credit and liquidity information about customers:

- Analyzing customer accounts, their credit limits, and payment history up to their current account balance, their dunning program

- Analyzing open items, both Receivables and Payables

Credit Limit Control Areas

A credit control area is a set of one or more company codes and a currency for credit controlling that is to apply to all company codes in that area. This currency need not be the same as the currency of any of the company codes in the credit control area.

You can set a total amount as the credit limit for a group and a limit for each company in a credit control area. There may be several credit control areas under one group.

Different customers may be assigned a credit limit account which they share. Any order or invoice posted to any of these joint holders of a credit limit account will cause the system to check whether the joint credit account limit has been exceeded. For example, different branches that are treated as separate customers may share a credit limit account held by the head office.

You can decide which types of transaction will affect a credit limit account balance. Bills of exchange receivable, for example, are often posted to the credit limit account.

If your installation includes the SAP SD-Sales and Distribution application, there will be an automatic check on the credit limit when you enter an order.

Online customer credit control is essential if you record payments and offset paid items promptly. You can review the credit situation and the liquidity (available) of any customer at any time in terms of the following elements:

- Customer credit limit and current account balance

- Payments due

- Dunning program and dunning level in force

- Payment history

Payment History

Under your direction, the system can automatically record a payment history for any or all customers for each month, going back sixteen months, using the following factors:

- Number of payment transactions

- Payment amounts

- Average days in arrears for each of the sixteen months

For the most recent period, the data are sorted by net payment and payment under each specific cash discount arrangement.

Merely as a simulation or what-if exercise, you can ask to see how the payment history would change if this customer paid immediately all the items open on a particular date that you specify. By this means you can simulate the payment history report, including the current open and overdue items.

The system also contributes to the payment history of a customer by recording totals of authorized and unauthorized deductions. The average discount rate is calculated, as is the interest amount based on the items paid after the due dates, including items still unpaid on the date you chose for making the calculation. A fictitious or nominal interest rate is used for these calculations which you can set so as to give you a fair picture of how much interest has been lost to your company because of the late payments of this customer.

You can total the amounts outstanding on open items and also on items paid in arrears. These will be sorted by number of days in arrears of the due dates for net payment or days in excess of the time limits for payments to attract cash discount.

Tracking Open Items. The financial control system relies on tracking uncleared items. You can identify one or more customers or vendors, and sort their open items in whatever way is most informative for you.

Similarly, you can say how you want the columns of the report and what periods you are interested in. You can have the system choose open items that fall due within any range of dates.

When you have found an individual account that needs your attention, you can display all the open items for that account and use the flexible line item search facilities to focus on just those lines that you require.

FI-FA Financial Assets Management

Financial Assets Management is the process of valuing and controlling financial assets and liabilities with a view to securing the liquidity of the company and managing it. The main financial assets of a company will include:

- Securities
- Time deposits
- Loans granted, for example, from the company to employees

Liabilities are loans to the company.

The FI-FA Financial Assets Management component is integrated with FI-Financial Accounting and Cash Management and closely linked to the SAP FI-FEM Foreign Exchange Management System so that you can hedge your business risks by investments in foreign currency. There is also an option to update FI-CM Cash Management and FI-Financial Accounting according to the results of foreign exchange contracts.

To manage effectively the full range of financial assets, it is necessary to pay proper attention to the following tasks:

- Record keeping

- Liquidity planning

- Financial asset analysis

The SAP system provides the programs to achieve good results in each of these. The FI-CM Cash Management system provides the means to effect liquidity planning, whereas FI-AR Accounts Receivable is specialized in managing customer open items that are overdue; all SAP systems automatically generate the transaction documents from which are drawn all the items of information used in subsequent accounting and analysis for planning and control.

The FI-FA Financial Assets Management system can be used by companies in all types of commerce and industry. There are additional applications for industries, like insurance, for example, that have special relationships between financial assets at different levels and between different classes of business as well as complex interrelationships with other financial institutions.

Business Associate Master Data

A business associate is a company or institution which, in some way, is sharing the financial risks of your business by acting in one or more of the following roles:

- Borrower that owes you money

- Lender that expects money from you

- Banks that may hold some of your money like a borrower

- Banks that may have allowed you an overdraft or loan of some kind and are in the role of lender

- Issuers of financial instruments

The SAP system provides master data records on which you can hold centrally the details of your associations with each of your associates. You can record electronic notes, to whatever length you need, about telephone conversations and any other interchange that is not readily discerned from the operational business documents and transaction records stored automatically by the system. These records can extend back any number of years.

The following fields are standard in the business associate master records:

- Company name, address, and type of business

- Contact people by name, title, position, and department

- Validity checks set up for this business associate

- Links to other SAP and outside systems that concern this business associate

- Total current balance or exposure

- Financial ratios for the reviewing of credit-worthiness

Asset Types

SAP FI-FA Financial Assets Management will expect you to divide your financial assets into asset types, which you will use to differentiate how you conduct transactions. Here are some examples of standard asset types that are recognized by the system:

- Loans

- Securities

- Time Deposits in the money market

The system is customized to suit the range of financial assets likely to be held by each company.

Types of Investments. Each type of asset will include a range of investment types, each of which can be provided with a customized transaction procedure that is adapted from the standard procedures supplied with the system. Bonds which are fixed income securities, variable income securities, zero-coupon bonds, and equities are examples of investment types which have standard procedures. The different types of investment are differentiated in this way because they can affect the liquidity and profitability of the company in different ways. Financial asset transactions can be tracked by calling for reports which are sorted by status, such as offer, reservation, agreement; or by type of business transaction, such as purchase of securities or prolongation of time deposits.

Loan Administration. The asset type "loans" is further differentiated by type of investment to make for more effective processing. The list of loan types will include the following:

- Loans receivable

- Loans payable

- Installment loans

- Annuity loans

Loans can benefit from the flexible business functions of the SAP system because their administration is conducted by the FI-FA Financial Assets Management component which uses the basic system together with any other applications that are installed and configured to interact with it, such as FI-CM Cash Management. The main business functions and data objects that take part in the administration of loans are as follows:

- Basic contract

- Discount management

- Interest plan and the amortization of principal

- Flexible value dates
- Automatic postings
- Cash management forecast
- Reporting
- Word processing and automatic correspondence

Planning Interest and the Amortization of Principal

Standard conditions of interest and amortization are made available by the system. You can call on them to be applied to a particular loan or group of loans for which you have established the amounts and the payment regime.

This loan plan can be printed automatically as a letter.

The plan of interest and amortization of principal will set out the following amounts and other features in a legal format acceptable in the country to which it will apply:

- Fixed or variable interest rate
- Prepayment or additional payment
- Term of loan
- Calculation of effective date of interest based on the payments according to the loan pricing regulations, or other procedures in cases of international securities trading
- Calculation of annuities or principal amounts
- Commission due for origination of the transaction
- Currency arrangements

When a plan of interest and amortization of principal has been approved and the details are established in the SAP system, there are several possibilities. The loan administrator can set up commands for automatic execution, or initiate online any of the following activities which can add value to the loan investment:

- Accrue interest to particular periods or other accounting subheading
- Post interest automatically
- Plan amounts by posting them to the appropriate control accounts in the Extended General Ledger
- Revalue loans in one or more foreign currencies
- Report balances using a flexible formatting system
- Update the cash flow plan for interest and amortization of principal
- Print account statements

If you have installed and configured the Cash Management system, your forecast of liquidity can include and display all the planned flows of payments of interest, repayments of principal, and payments on expenditures.

When a change of your liquidity occurs, such as when a balloon payment or a payment of interest is received, the system will update the cash flow plan, and the Cash Management data when you post the transaction.

Securities Administration

Securities are bought by a purchase order and sold, fully or in part, by a sales order. These orders always refer to the securities master data records for the details, so that data integrity can be maintained.

The master data records for securities can be updated from external data via a SAP standard interface. They can also be created and updated online or in batches.

The master record of a security will contain information of the following kinds:

- Name of the issuer and a description of its business
- Conditions attaching to this security, such as interest rate and arrangements for the amortization of principal
- Classification of this security in terms of the types and groupings use by your company
- Technical characteristics of this security, for example, whether it is tax-free

The interest rate can be variable and linked to a key rate which will be specified during Customizing.

In your company, the asset type "securities" can be divided into the following investment types:

- Bonds that are fixed income securities
- Variable income or floating-rate securities
- Zero-coupon bonds
- Equities

You can be authorized to add investment types to this list of Security Assets.

Securities Purchase Orders. From the securities master record, enter the relevant order data and the amount. Any currency can be selected to denominate securities; the fees, interest, and repayment of principal can also be expressed in any currency.

The system automatically calculates any partial-period interest and fees incurred in the form of commission, foreign exchange, or other charges.

When you purchase a security, the system will take up the plan for interest and amortization of principal, and make the data available to Cash Management, where it will be part of liquidity planning.

You can immediately view calculations of the effective yield and rate of return. The SAP system supports calculations by any of the common methods:

- AIBD
- Braess/Fangmeyer
- Moosmüller

Securities Sales Orders. From the securities master record, enter the relevant order data and the amount. Securities can be denominated in any currency. The fees, interest, and repayment of principal can also be expressed in any currency.

The system automatically calculates any partial-period interest and fees incurred in the form of commission, foreign exchange, or other charges. Immediately, the gain or loss is computed.

When you sell a security denominated in a foreign currency, the system can calculate the gain or loss separately from the gain or loss resulting from the currency exchange. The system will post the currency exchange gains or losses to a profit and loss account designated specifically for that purpose.

You have the option to select individual valuation instead of total valuation. If you choose this option, you must match exactly sales to purchases. Gains and losses will then be reported on the transactions individually.

Valuations

A separate price table is maintained for valuing securities. This table contains the so-called "book value" of each security. It can be updated from external sources.

There are two moments for valuing securities—before you print a balance sheet, and when you sell.

If you value your securities before you sell, the balance sheet will not take into account the unrealized profits and losses. You must define the valuation rules for each balance sheet account in the general ledger. You can have the valuation rules applied to each security, controlling this by parameters which you set. Or you can ask for the valuation of an individual security or for your entire portfolio. Capitalized fees are maintained as a separate item and can be released against subsequent trading.

Managing Money Market Transactions

Transactions on the money market are usually either time deposits or demand deposits. FI-FA Financial Assets Management distinguishes between these two types. The system is directly integrated with FI-CM Cash Management.

You can establish different procedures for each type of money market transaction. The status of a transaction and the approval procedures will control what happens at each stage.

You can determine which staff are restricted to transactions in a particular currency and the fixed maximum amount they can post.

Confirmation letters will be printed automatically upon recording transactions.

The flow of a money market transaction entails the following processes:

- The bank publishes money market data that are transferred to your system and join the basic data you hold on your business associates and customers.

- When a transaction is initiated, the basic data pertinent to the business associate and the money market product are accessed, and the decision on the amount to be bought or sold is recorded on the transaction document.

- The transaction document is passed through the control procedure for approval.

- When it is released from control, there is an exchange with the bank to confirm the details of the transaction.

- The sale or purchase is then fulfilled by an exchange of documents.

- Posting the transaction generates internal documentation which can be revised internally.

Standing Instructions Regarding Time Deposits and Demand Deposits

The SAP FI-FA Financial Assets Management system supports the common methods of paying interest. The financial data to complete the transaction are provided to the Cash Management system when the cash is available.

If you wish to prolong the period of a time deposit, the system offers a function to record the prolongation with all the data, including the amount invested and the terms.

Arrangements to make regular automatic accruals of the interest are straightforward. It is standard practice to set up regular foreign currency valuations of investments in the money market and use the hedging system to cover business risks in foreign currency.

The value of demand deposits can be tracked by setting up a current account, one for each deposit if necessary, into which you have the system enter the new interest rates daily. Sales or purchase orders for these demand deposits are posted to this account, and the system prints confirmation letters automatically.

Controlling Transactions in Financial Assets Management

Transactions in FI-FA Financial Assets Management are identified by the nature of the business transaction and by the status or milestone reached in its progress.

For example, a transaction can have been selected from a list because it concerns the purchase of securities. Another transaction might be a matter of prolonging a time deposit.

The status of a financial asset transaction can be expressed in different ways for different types of asset. A typical arrangement is to define status as one of a set of codes that signify some or all of the following logical and business milestones:

- New investment

- Inquiry

- Offer

- Reservation

- Agreement, conclusion of negotiations leading to a contract, and scheduling arrangement

- Partial payment

- Full payment

- Planned interest and amortization of capital

- Contract prolonged

- Contract ended

Each new form of investment may entail designing or adapting a sequence of data entry screens. You may need to change some of the parameters that control what appears on the screens and how the entries are to be processed.

The SAP system offers a suite of business programs that support an investment transaction from beginning to end. The processing routines are grouped as follows:

- Initiation, which includes inquiry and offer procedures, with internal controls as required

- Concluding establishment of the contract by reaching agreement with the associate and scheduling payments under internal control

- Payment control

- Planning interest and amortization of principal

- Ending a contract or prolonging it

Internal Control and the Separation of Duties

You have the option to define your own methods of internal control over financial asset transactions. You can specify that an investment is reviewed by a minimum of two or even three persons, each of whom must carry, in his or her personal master data file, the authorization necessary to perform the role that has been designated for this type of investment approval.

Limits for each employee who might use the system and each currency will be important components of the automatic control procedures applied by the system.

And you will probably want to prevent processing of an investment transaction from one status to another until the details have been scrutinized and the transaction marked for release to the next status and hence to the subsequent activities.

Interaction with the Cash Management System

When you are setting up a new transaction in FI-FA Financial Assets Management, you can record the planned data in the FI-CM Cash Management system. For example, if you are granting a loan to an employee, you can have the amounts planned and the anticipated dates automatically transferred to the FI-Financial Accounting system and posted to the FI-GLX Extended General Ledger. In the case of granting a loan, for instance, the stages of the entire transaction could be posted automatically:

- Disbursement
- Minimum deposit
- Amortization of principal
- Interest income

Automatic Correspondence

The standard business functions of the SAP system will be available to generate correspondence on behalf of the FI-FA Financial Assets Management system in such matters as the following:

- Cover letters
- Balance confirmations
- Account statements
- Interest payment plans

You can also automatically conduct correspondence by fax or telex. You may wish to use SAPscript to customize your correspondence with individual business associates or groups of addressees.

The functionality of SAPmail will be on call to keep track of key dates and to monitor your investments.

FI-LC Consolidation

This SAP component is also referred to as FI-LC Legal Consolidation.

Legal consolidation is the process of combining the financial statements of two or more individual companies to produce a consolidated financial statement that complies with legal requirements.

The legal consolidated financial statement can also be supplemented and used for internal information purposes.

Consolidated financial statements are often required promptly, yet they often have to be assembled from incompatible data communication protocols in a software environment which is, to say the least, heterogeneous. Extra details can be required, and there can be a need to validate the data.

The purpose of the SAP FI-LC Consolidation module is to optimize and automate the consolidation process. The following additional functionality is offered by the module:

- Integration with the accounting software used by individual companies
- Automatic and reliable transfer of data from the individual financial statements
- Integration of internal and external group reporting
- Multinational accounting functions
- Standards for processing representations of organizational structures

The method of FI-LC Consolidation is first to prepare the financial data in each of the individual companies, and then to effect computer integration.

The Tasks of Consolidating

Preparation entails the following operations:

- Matching the individual company chart of accounts to the group chart of accounts
- Eliminating intercompany Payables and Receivables, revenue and expenses, which arise because individual companies in a group enjoy a variety of sender-recipient relationships
- Recording acquisition years for historical currency conversion
- Consolidation of investments

Computer integration is relatively straightforward if every individual company has installed and configured only SAP applications. In this case they will share a common environment of standard documents and data objects controlled by SAP standard business process software.

If one or more of the individual companies uses a software system which can communicate with one of the interfaces supported by SAP, there are programs to facilitate the transfer of financial data.

If one or more of the individual companies has been in the habit of using only paper forms and ledgers for accounting, there obviously has to be a stage of data input to at least a personal computer with a means to convert the data to a medium suitable for transfer to the SAP FI-LC Consolidation system. The alternative of last resort is probably a conventional mailing of the data to the head office of the host company, where a SAP R/3 workstation can be used to reenter the data.

Standardizing Entries

If the accounting practices of an individual company do not accord completely with the basis chosen for presenting the consolidated financial statements, it is possible to account for the differences in amounts by making a standardizing entry which is posted to a head office account designated for this purpose. These entries are stored in a separate file.

Currency Translation in Consolidation

There are three basic methods used in the consolidation of group accounts:

- Reporting date method
- Modified reporting date method
- Temporal method

Groups of items in the balance sheet and profit and loss statement are converted at one of three exchange rates:

- Reporting date rate
- Average rate
- Historical rate

FI-LC Consolidation can translate any items at any rates and use any of the methods for any of the individual companies. There are several problems for which this program provides solutions:

- Exchange differences between the date of the transaction and the date of the currency conversion
- Rounding differences
- The assets history sheet will be using rates current on the reporting date.
- If a transaction difference is posted, the previous translation differences will have to be reversed.

Eliminating Intercompany Payables and Receivables

FI-Financial Accounting will eliminate intercompany balances by open item only if each trading partner has been marked in the vendor master record. You must also ensure that the reporting procedures inform the consolidating department of the numbers of these trading partners, at least on the items which relate to intercompany Payables and Receivables, revenues and expenses.

The law requires that all intercompany balances be eliminated before presenting the balance sheet and profit and loss statement. All possible pairs of individual companies must be investigated for evidence that they have been trading with each other.

In practice, significant differences between the way individual companies keep their records can make complete elimination impractical. The most frequent causes of discrepancies in elimination are as follows:

- Currency translation differences

- Differences in the timing of entries for goods in transit between individual companies

- Specific reserves set aside for doubtful accounts

- Liabilities that are not acknowledged in the records

The cause that is most difficult to handle is currency translation; the others can usually be resolved by applying corporate policies in a thoroughgoing manner.

If the individual companies have installed and configured SAP accounting applications, there will have been automatic dual currency accounting, in which every transaction is documented at the time in both the local currency and the currency designated for all transactions in the group. The FI-LC component will allow you to trace any currency translation differences between the local currency at the prevailing rate of exchange and the transaction currency. An exchange rate difference correction can then be posted in the balance sheet account designated for this purpose and thus brought into the consolidated financial statement.

Consolidation of Investments

When you are using FI-LC Consolidation, you can say which consolidation methods are to be used for subgroups of individual companies.

For example, step consolidation first consolidates each accounting unit within every subgroup separately. Subgroups at the same level of the organization are then consolidated with each other, and so on until the final consolidation yields the financial information for the group as a whole—the top level, as it were.

Simultaneous consolidation treats all accounting units as equals under the head office, and performs the whole consolidation in one step.

You can say what should happen if different methods yield differing results. Or you can use these methods and options in parallel.

The system will carry out simultaneous consolidation using each of the methods chosen, applied to calculated equity shares which represent the values of the individual holdings. This is known as the matrix method.

Investment Consolidation Procedures

FI-LC will take account of any minority interests in investments and any hidden reserves as it performs any of the following procedures, in most instances automatically:

- First consolidation

- Subsequent consolidation

- Step acquisition and indirect changes in ownership

- Increase and decrease in capital

- Write-down of investment

- Complete divestiture or partial disposal

- Transfer of investment to a new owner

The balance sheet and the profit and loss accounts are corrected in parallel by the system. Goodwill and hidden reserves are amortized. Auxiliary records are updated.

Every elimination entry is explained clearly, concisely or in detail, at your command.

The system meets the legal requirements for an asset history sheet and the special situation of equity consolidations.

What-If Versions and Forecast Simulations of Consolidation
The system allows you to copy the consolidation data to a new version of the consolidated financial statement. You can then edit certain control tables for the new version, so that a different method of consolidation is used. For example, you may wish to see what would happen if valuation were done differently, or if exchange rate differences were handled in another way.

You can also create a simulation of the consolidation process by using forecast data in place of actual financial statements data. All the same manipulations can be carried out on plan data as on actual.

Annual Reporting Requirements of Complex Companies
The SAP FI-LC Consolidation component is the application of choice for analyzing and reporting for large and complex groups. The following types of reports will usually be required, at least annually, but often on an ad hoc basis at any time:

- Asset history sheet, reserves and special items

- Summaries of Payables and Receivables

- Detailed information on selected items

- Group or parent company comparisons

- Sales by region or product line

SAP standard product FI-LC Consolidation includes predefined report specifications that will serve most of these reporting needs.

Special Report Design. Small-volume reports can be generated to view online, to print or to store using the standard display control and item selection functions of the R/3 Basis component. This flexible type of interactive reporting is a specific SAP technique.

Extensive consolidation reports and audit trails can be sent to a printer or a transfer medium. For example, pre-consolidated financial statement data for a subgroup can be sent by online electronic means or transferred to tape or diskette for passing to the next higher level in the group.

In addition, consolidated financial statement information can be directed to word processing and spreadsheet facilities, where it can be attached to letters and prepared for presentation.

Interactive Reporting. The process of interactive reporting starts with a display of data that has arrived on your screen as part of a warning or advisory message from some other part of the system, or because you specifically asked for it by calling for a search based on a range of parameters that you entered to narrow the possibilities. You might ask for items over a certain amount, for instance.

When you see a data object on the screen that interests you, it is possible to find out more if you place the cursor on it and use one of the function keys to show you what you want to know. You might want to perform a what-if analysis using a value or other parameter of your choice in place of the actual value used to compute the item on your screen.

The following types of query can be readily initiated:

- Details of specific items, going to ever-finer detail as you repeat your query action
- Comparisons
- Investments in companies
- Transaction types
- Standardizing and consolidating entries
- Graphical presentations of selected data

If your system is integrated with other SAP application modules, you can gain access to the data recorded by them. For example, you will be able to inspect account balances and documents in the SAP FI-Financial Accounting system if your FI-LC Consolidation component is integrated with it. If your installation uses the SAP AM-Fixed Assets Management system, you will be able to see, and use in reports, the information in the acquisition and retirement records.

Your finished report can be readily drafted to show whatever combination of detail and summary information best serves your purpose.

Ratio Analysis. One of the important benefits of having an up-to-date accounting system with a flexible reporting facility on a powerful computer is the speed with which complex business calculations can be provided with the information necessary to ensure that they are valid.

A frequently used outcome of business calculation is the ratio: a comparison between two numerical values obtained by dividing one by the other.

A ratio that compares one production period with another can be a useful indicator to guide internal management. The financial position of the company can be compared with that of a rival by means of one or more ratios. Ratios between individual company performance and consolidated financial statement amounts can be used to explain or amplify the annual report.

The FI-LC facilities allow you to define the same mathematical procedure for all these ratio calculations, but the actual variables and data will depend on the purpose and the version number of the ratio calculation that you specify when you call for the result.

Suppose you define your ratio calculation in two stages:

- Specify where the information is to come from
- Specify how it is to take part in the calculation

Suppose, for example you are interested in calculating the equity ratio, which you have agreed to define as the ratio of equity to total assets. The information could be gathered from three sources, but only one will give you exactly what you want:

- Equity(1) = Paid-in Capital + Reserves + Retained Earnings
- Equity(2) = Paid-in Capital + Required Adjustments + Pension Reserves
- Equity(3) = Total Assets − Total Liabilities
- Equity(1) is in the language of a business report.
- Equity(2) will appear by law on the balance sheet.
- Equity(3) is expressed in the terms used in cost accounting.

Your definition of the ratio you want corresponds to Equity(3). This is what the system will use to calculate the ratio for whatever time periods or organizational units you are interested in.

If you select an element on your display, the system will show you how it computed this element; it will display the individual values that took part in the calculation on a split screen.

And you can call for a 3D display of the information you have isolated for your calculations.

Periodic Financial Statements

Unlike the annual consolidated financial statement, interim periodic financial statements can be selective in the information they report.

You can flag each individual company to indicate its reporting category, and you can adopt the suggestions of the system based on ratio thresholds:

- Individual company information required
- Data will be derived from prior periods (as plan data)
- This company will be omitted from the periodic report

Consolidation intervals have to be defined for each subgroup of companies:

- Yearly
- Half-yearly
- Quarterly
- Monthly

Different companies tend to post entries to accounts at different times of the accounting period. The system eliminates intercompany Payables and Receivables, which balances the unavoidable timing differences.

Intercompany profits and losses can be eliminated by using information from the previous year's financial statements.

The system automatically posts depreciation accrued during the periods of the periodic consolidated financial statement.

Options for Consolidation

In the format for any account balance, external or internal, there are two fields which can be used to eliminate intercompany balances. You can extend this format and use it to eliminate transactions between companies and business areas with sender-recipient relationships. It can also be used for detailed internal group reporting.

Because the SAP system uses central data administration, simple validation will ensure that external and internal reports use the same data.

From Here...

- The FI-GL General Ledger and the FI-GLX Extended General Ledger systems must be at the center of any management system. There are many spokes radiating out from this hub: and the most important of these is CO-Controlling, because it oversees the collection of operating data and the planning of value flows in the company. See Chapter 13, "Understanding the CO-Controlling Module."

- If you are ready to plan the implementation of a SAP integrated business system, then the various Cross Application modules should receive your attention. Chapter 30, "R/3 Business Workflow Management," and Chapter 28, "ABAP/4 Program Development with the R/3 Workbench," are recommended.

■ If the detailed planning of a project, in whatever sphere, is uppermost in your mind, then Chapter 16, "Understanding the PS-Project System Module," must be viewed with close attention.

■ To see how the SAP methodology would work out in a particular industry, you should look at either Chapter 18, "Understanding the PP-PI Production Planning for Process Industries Modules," or Chapter 23, "Understanding the MM-Materials Management Module."

■ No doubt you have appreciated the importance of the human factors in business. Chapter 22, "Understanding the HR-Human Resources Module," should be given close attention by all.

Chapter 13

Understanding the CO-Controlling Module

The SAP R/3 system includes the CO-Controlling system as an integral part. The concept of business controlling includes the planning of values such as costs and revenues which will appear in the financial documents. The performance of the company has to be monitored and reported in relation to these planned values. Advice and information to management should be the outcomes.

The implementation of the CO-Controlling system will entail specifying the details of which quantities and values are to be subject to planning and therefore to the subsequent monitoring and reporting functions.

CO-Components

The following components comprise the SAP CO-Controlling module, which is an integrated system for overhead cost controlling:

- CO-CCA   Cost Center Accounting

- CO-ABC   Activity-Based Cost Accounting

- CO-OPA   Order and Project Accounting

- CO-PA   Profitability Analysis

- CO-PCA   Profit Center Accounting

The FI-GLX Extended General Ledger uses accounts that are based on a range of subledgers that allow overhead cost analyses from different points of view. For example, accounts may focus on cost centers, product costs or activities. These facilities are provided by using the SAP CO-Controlling system as an internal accounting system.

The implementation of a controlling function in an organization is carried out in a SAP R/3 system in the following phases:

- Defining the structure of the organization in terms of units that can be controlled

This section will show you how to:

- Make use of the integrated systems for costing, production, and materials management and human resources to support planning, costing, and control.

- Use the CO-CCA Cost Center Accounting component to set up the most important parts of your company as cost centers which will keep track of their own costs and revenues for business planning and control.

- Setting up information flows that can monitor the performance of the controllable units

- Running the controlling system through cycles of the controlling tasks, which are repeated at a frequency suited to the type of business process

The R/3 system integrates all these phases by offering standard business programs that are fully integrated with each other. If you install the system in your company, the SAP Customizing procedures will prompt you into selecting the functions that match your requirements. You will also be invited to provide such details as the specific terms and names of work units so that the system as implemented will be an accurate representation of your company.

The structure of a business organization can be seen from different points of view. One company will see itself as a group of complete and self-sufficient units reporting to head office; another will think of the main functional areas, such as procurement, production, sales and marketing.

In order to make use of a fully integrated system and exploit the value-adding functionalities available in a modern, computer-based installation, it is necessary to define an organization in terms of a detailed structure of cost centers with specified relationships between them.

The SAP R/3 system with the CO-Controlling component gives you the functionality you need to capture the structure of your company in the form of a comprehensive cost center plan that clearly defines the responsibility structure of your company. When you have such a structure, the system will use it to run all the controlling functions.

This structure has to be rich enough in features to capture any type of organization and express it in a form that can be used by the computer system to carry out automatically as many of the necessary operations as possible. And where automatic operation is not possible or not required, the system should be able to provide as much support and guidance as possible and make the work as efficient and effective as circumstances allow.

Business Planning and Control

In accord with the basic divide-and-measure approach to business control, it is useful to differentiate the operational controlling systems from the functional controlling systems.

The operational controlling systems are provided with SAP R/3 components to support the four operational tasks:

- Capital investment controlling, which transfers activities to be capitalized and used to calculate depreciation and operating profits

- Financial controlling, which monitors and plans scheduled payments from projects and orders

IV

Steering

- Funds controlling, which sees to the procurement, use, and creation of funds in all areas
- Cost and profit controlling, which monitors the costs of all company activities

The SAP Approach to Alternative Cost Accounting Methods

The SAP R/3 standard business functions provide all the functionality needed to support most modern cost accounting systems.

The main differences between costing concepts arise in connection with the scope of the costs they include and the structure of these costs with respect to the organization structure. There are variations in the use of standard versus actual costs, and in the allocation of costs directly to the products or services, in contrast to allocating them to overhead. Methods may also differ in the relationships between cost center activities, such as in the use of primary costs, cost components and secondary cost breakdown.

The following cost accounting methods can be accommodated in the SAP R/3 system:

- Actual costing
- Static and flexible normal costing
- Static and flexible standard costing
- Variable direct costing
- Activities and services costing
- Functional costing

You may wish to take a step-by-step approach to the implementation of cost control by, for example, using actual costing and collecting the primary expenses in the cost centers by allocation and perhaps later, automatically by direct posting.

Progressive Implementation of Cost and Profit Controlling

The modular structure of SAP R/3 applications is designed to allow you to move progressively according to the developments and requirements of your company. The application modules are discussed in a sequence which is in accord with this concept of progressive implementation.

Cost element accounting is a standard approach which is integral to the R/3 system. Functions are predefined to create and maintain cost element master data and calculate imputed cost elements. The R/3 system can mediate the importing and incorporation of posting data from external systems. There is full reporting on cost elements. Individual business transactions are structured, recorded, assigned and reported using the FI-GL General Ledger profit and loss account structure.

CO-CCA Cost Center Accounting has to plan, monitor, control and settle all business activities and responsibilities. It has functions to create and maintain cost center master data and to accept or modify definitions of statistical ratios. Cost center postings and transfers have their specialized functions, as have distribution, assessment and allocation between cost centers. Primary cost elements can be used in the planning functions for cost centers. The user can define the screen and printed report layout formats from the cost center reporting system. Planning functional dependencies and the detailed planning of cost centers are supported by the CO-CCA Cost Center Accounting component.

CO-ABC Activity Based Cost Accounting is used to cost the internal flow of activities with functions to plan, evaluate and allocate.

CO-OPA Order and Project Accounting is specialized in the tasks of planning, monitoring and settling the activities, services and processes that take place as the result of internal orders and projects.

CO-PA Profitability Analysis is required in order to report on complex sales organizations and complex product hierarchies. In SAP R/3, results analysis is conducted using the cost-of-sales approach or by period accounting.

The Controlling Area Concept

The starting point and method of navigating through the details of a controlling system form a structure made up of units and links. This structure is stored in the SAP R/3 system, and can be inspected in various ways, including a graphical representation. The structure may be the same topological network as the management structure, each level of managers being responsible to more senior managers on the level above. Traditional organizations in business tend to have a pyramid structure rising to the owner on the pinnacle. Government and military organizations are notorious for having very tall pyramids. Modern, small companies in the high-tech domain are notorious for having very flat structures, very few layers of management and a boss who is ready to speak to anyone at almost any time.

The logical justification for any type of structure is based on the demands placed on it by external circumstances and by the need for the owner to exert some control over it.

The controlling area of the owner is perhaps the managing director or the chief executive officer. This person has a controlling area of the whole company. The department heads have controlling areas defined by the territory of their departments; or perhaps their controlling areas are better specified by the activities for which they are responsible.

The SAP R/3 module CO-Controlling holds master data on the controlling areas that you have decided to establish for your company. These may correspond exactly with the departments that exist already, but if you are looking for a method of adding value to information and material as they pass through your company, it would be prudent at least to consider other ways of setting up controlling areas.

What you will be looking for are profit centers that can be controlled on the basis of the measured profit they contribute to the company. One or more of these profit centers will constitute an area of responsibility that will be a proper subject for the application of controlling area discipline.

The conceptual tools of area controlling include the following:

- Cost center—this is defined as a place in which costs are incurred. It may be a unit within a company, distinguished by area of responsibility, location, or accounting method.

- Order—an order is an instrument for planning and controlling costs. In a business environment it will be a document. In the SAP environment it will be a SAP Document, which has a standard set of constituent parts and is subjected to strict internal control by the computer system so that it can take part in the legal requirements of an audit trail.

- Project—the defining characteristic of a project is the fact that it has to achieve a certain result in a specified time without exceeding the budget allocated to it. There are many types of projects: capital-spending, research and development, engineer-to-order manufacturing, investment program, data processing and customer project, for example.

- Cost object—whatever work is undertaken, whether planning, controlling, informing and so on, there are features that can be used to focus the computation of costs. The cost object need not be a real object, and it needn't really engage in any activity that would consume resources or generate revenue. The cost object is a convenient conceptual destination that can appear in the accounts with accrued costs or revenues.

- Market or business segment structure—the control of a business may be improved if information is collected about part of it; for example, the sale of certain products, in a specified market area, over a range of accounting periods. Another example of a segment would be the value of the raw materials in each of the possible locations where the capacity for additional production could take place.

In logical terms, a controlling area is defined as a set of accounting units within an organization that all use the same cost accounting configuration. Normally the controlling area is coextensive with the company code, which usually stands for an individual company in a corporate structure. For cross-company cost accounting, one controlling area may be assigned to cover the areas of responsibility of more than one company code.

These conceptual tools have been efficiently programmed into the SAP standard business processes in the most useful of forms, the generic form, which you can customize to fit your particular circumstance. For example, you can record in the master data how you want to define the business segments and how you want to select which cost objects to monitor. And you can say how orders and projects will be assigned to cost centers.

The CO-Controlling module will accept your requirements and deliver a flexible controlling system that fits your company.

Connecting Financial Accounting with Controlling

At the heart of every accounting system must be the general ledger, and the SAP system is no exception. The FI-Financial Accounting module serves the FI-GL General Ledger.

The common chart of accounts contains all the accounts available to a company. Every company, and therefore every unit identified by a company code, must be assigned to the common chart of accounts.

The concept of the controlling area is integral to the internal controlling functions. Each controlling area is assigned to the common chart of accounts. This ensures that every transaction in each area is posted to an account in the common chart of accounts, and will, therefore, be reconciled and thus take part in the financial accounting that provides the balance sheet and profit and loss accounts required by law.

The CO-Controlling system uses the FI-GL General Ledger accounts directly. In particular, it uses the FI-GL General Ledger profit and loss accounts as primary cost and revenue elements.

With certain exceptions, the CO-Controlling system needs no separate reconciliation with the FI-GL General Ledger and its subledger accounting systems. The exceptions arise if you use the special feature of CO-Controlling which manages imputed costs or accruals. CO-Controlling allows you to create imputed costs at a level of detail other than that used in financial accounting: you can record costs which have no equivalent, or have an equivalent with a different value, in the accounts of financial accounting. These intentional differences can be reconciled and cleared by using the CO-Controlling functions provided for this purpose.

Secondary cost elements are maintained by CO-Controlling in addition to the primary accounts of the FI-GL General Ledger. This constitutes a two-level system of accounts: each level records accounting data using a different degree of detail.

However, the extra details maintained by CO-Controlling in the secondary cost elements are integrated with the FI-GL General Ledger accounts by means of the controlling areas, which are represented in the common chart of accounts. In accordance with GAAP (Generally Accepted Accounting Principles), it is possible to trace any transaction posted on the general ledger down through the controlling area and thence to the cost center, which will be holding all the details of the cost elements which were used to compute it.

The value flow in the subledgers of the FI-GL General Ledger is always reconciled via special reconciliation accounts. You can always analyze data into summaries using these accounts, which will give you such reports as monthly debits and credits, account balances and so on, and you can inspect individual business transactions. With this kind of functionality, you can substantiate any of the values shown in your trial balance.

If you have installed and configured a SAP application such as CO-Controlling, you will have an additional and parallel way of looking at the value flows in your organization.

But because the system is fully integrated, you will know that the values and value flows revealed by the external accounting documents, the balance sheet and the profit and loss statement are fully reconciled with the value flows that are uncovered by your parallel internal accounting system, implemented using the standard business functions of the SAP CO-Controlling module.

You will have a fresh way of looking at how the values change by doing business.

The Value-Adding Process and the Role of Cost Objects

In simple terms, a cost object is something that incurs costs: two of them cost twice as much; ten of them cost ten times as much.

A particular cost object can be declared to be in a market segment by entering it in the master record of that segment.

This cost object could also be identified in the processes of inventory accounting.

A cost center will be charged overhead, because that is where the costs originated. Overhead posted to that cost center will then be transferred to the cost objects that are the responsibility of that cost center. The proportion of the overhead allocated will be according to the quantities of cost objects, or by some other rule. In this way the cost object has to bear a share of the overhead.

Revenues and sales deductions are reported in the relevant market segments and profit centers.

You can use period accounting at profit center level, incorporating changes to the inventory in the period. You can also use cost-of-sales accounting at the market segment level.

The cost object method enables an accurate system of accounting that will help you control the value-adding business processes of your company.

Integrated Planning and Decision Support

One of the important decisions to be made is often the product mix. You want to make sure that you optimize the contribution of each product line to the profit margin. Your methods will include tentative variations in the planned production costs, which the system will develop through the work flows of your organization to arrive at the planned values in each of the areas of interest. You can display any combination of planned values for any cost object or set of objects, right up to the planned figures for the entire company.

This is integrated planning, and it depends on the following functions which are programmed in the CO-Controlling system:

- Planned assessment, distribution and accruals of imputed costs

- Planned allocation of internal activities

- Planned assessment of costs on orders and projects

These functions cannot succeed unless you have provided the data or told the system how to find them. The system will support you in this preparation by guiding you through these essential tasks and performing the necessary calculations automatically wherever possible:

- Planning of cost centers

- Planning of internal orders and projects

- Determining standard costs of products for stock production and for unit costing of customer orders

- Planning contribution margins and profits in sales management

Again, the system needs information to help you in the development of your plans, and CO-Controlling will provide the programs to support the following preliminaries:

- Creating the activity plan using the activities for each work center and cost center

- Integrating detailed planned sales quantities for the individual reference objects, including assigned costs and revenue

- Developing automatic standard cost estimates based on bills of materials and routings

Reporting in CO-Controlling

The SAP EIS Executive Information System and the reporting facilities of CO-Controlling are fully integrated. Within the SAP R/3 computer system, the reporting facilities are highly flexible. Reports are easy to define for ad hoc purposes and to maintain as needs change. The content and format are virtually unlimited, and can be differentiated by user groups.

Reports can be stored, recalled and processed by the SAP graphics presentation component.

Online navigation facilities make it easy for you to switch between report formats without losing the focus of your inquiry. For example, you can select an item on a list and use the function keys to call up a more detailed report on the item selected.

Reports designed in the CO-Controlling module are applicable to all its components.

Standard predefined reports are available for the following purposes:

- Comparing actual values with the planned entries

- Comparing the performance of different cost objects, such as cost centers, orders and projects

- Assembling balance lists and balances of activities

- Inspecting individual line items

You can select a cost center and call up all the settlement objects linked to it. You can also trace the costs on each object back to the individual business transactions which caused them.

Integration of CO-Controlling with R/3 Applications

All the information in all the R/3 applications which have been installed and configured is available directly. Any of the information outputs of the system, from the annual sales and production plan to the individual planning steps and down to the planning and processing details of individual orders, may be called upon by the CO-Controlling system.

For example, standard business functions are available for the following tasks:

- Using bills of material and routings to prepare cost estimates for products and orders

- Updating a costing as production progresses by transferring times and material valuations automatically as they become available

- Evaluating quantities used of supplies and raw materials

- Evaluating semi-finished and finished products in stock

- Using cost-of-sales accounting to provide an ongoing analysis of profitability based on invoiced sales quantities

The success of a controlling function depends on the integration of planned and actual data at all stages and levels of the production process.

Integration with HR-Human Resources Management

Cost centers can be given time factors for each of their activities by applying the methods of activity-based cost accounting. The SAP HR-Human Resources Management system can transfer the planned personnel costs to the FI-Financial Accounting and CO-Controlling modules. The actual, confirmed, monthly personnel costs are updated simultaneously in both FI-Financial Accounting and the cost accounting components in CO-Controlling.

The personnel data used for salaries and wage payments are the same as the data used to allocate personnel costs to orders and projects: HR-Human Resources provides both.

Cost Element Accounting Principles

A cost element is a classification code. It is a mandatory data field on transactions which involve costs arising in a company code. It is used to label and differentiate the following types of cost:

- Direct cost elements for goods and services procured externally
- Indirect (internal activity) cost elements

There may be several cost element types, based on a classification of cost elements by uses or origin, for example:

- Material cost element
- Settlement cost elements for orders
- Cost elements for internal cost allocations

A cost element is also used to maintain a collection of information, in particular, the transaction documents that bear the code of the cost element and that have been selected, for example, for a specific accounting period.

Direct cost elements are maintained in the FI-GL General Ledger master records. Indirect cost elements have no counterpart in the financial accounts, and are maintained exclusively in cost accounting.

The cost element concept ensures that each business transaction posted under a particular cost element in the CO-Controlling system is properly assigned to the relevant cost centers, orders, projects, cost objects and so on.

Each material issue in MM-Materials Management, each invoice recorded in SD-Sales and Distribution, each external invoice in SD-IV Invoice Verification; each of these flows via the FI-GL General Ledger account to the appropriate cost or profit object.

The expense accounts of the FI-GL General Ledger chart of accounts are automatically adopted by the CO-Controlling system as primary cost elements. Additional primary cost elements have to be added to the financial chart of accounts to accommodate accruals and imputed costs. The aim is to ensure that all the costs incurred in a particular accounting period and documented in the CO-Controlling system are properly reconciled with the general ledger. The method of establishing a default coding block cost element is also used to support this aim.

Secondary cost elements are created and managed only in CO-Controlling. They represent value flows such as:

- Internal cost allocation
- Surcharge allocation
- Settlement transactions

Cost Element Parameters

The CO-Controlling system carries an extensive set of standard cost elements which you can adopt and edit for your own installation. There is a matchcode search facility to locate the one you want on the basis of a specific name or label that you have assigned. The matchcode search may also include values such as order number ranges and dates that you define so as to narrow the field of your search. You can block out those you are unlikely to need.

The standard cost elements will begin with certain parameters established, for example:

- Default coding block element assignment to the balance sheet accounts
- Whether quantities are recorded
- How costs are displayed in reports

The system will log any changes you make to the cost element masters.

A cost element group is a technical term for a set of cost elements used in conjunction with select records and to define lines and columns in reports. They can be used for planning purposes. There are no constraints on how you combine and arrange cost elements into cost element groups. You can display the cost element groups in the form of a tree diagram.

Accruals

The accounting period most useful when controlling a business is seldom the same period used for financial accounting. To effect a reconciliation, it is necessary to use accruals which assign imputed costs to the financial accounting periods and under an account heading that indicates their cause. There are three methods:

- This is the percentage method. If the cost elements are known, you can build up a database from which to calculate the imputed costs for each financial period by allocating a percentage to each period. And you can do this for both planned data and actual costs, by period and by cause.

- This is the plan/actual method. If no relevant historical values or quantities are available to enter into your base cost elements, you can make a plan or estimate of them across the relevant time periods and by cause. Then you can have the system post the planned values as imputed costs and later make an adjustment when the actual cost data become available.

- This is the target/actual method. If you expect your costs to be directly related to the operating output, then you can use the techniques of activity-based cost accounting to arrive at target values, which the system will post as imputed costs to the relevant financial accounting periods and causes. Again, you must have the system make an adjustment when the actual values can be obtained.

There are other ways of accounting for imputed costs that entail simultaneous posting of accrued costs to both FI-Financial Accounting and CO-Controlling. Alternatively, you can establish imputed cost objects, which can be reconciliation cost centers or reconciliation orders.

Price Variances

The CO-Controlling system can calculate the influence of price fluctuations for each posting transaction. The difference will be displayed as a variance in the SAP Document recording the transaction.

The SAP MM-Materials Management application can provide the difference between the standard price of a material and the moving average price.

Differences can also be computed between the actual cost to the cost center, and the value posted to it from FI-Financial Accounting as a percentage share of the actual value distributed across a number of cost centers.

Reporting in Cost Element Accounting

The flexible SAP R/3 reporting system allows you to analyze cost elements from any point of view:

- By individual cost elements, cost element groups or subgroups

- By other cost objects, such as cost centers, orders and projects

CO-CCA Cost Center Accounting

A cost center is a place in which costs are incurred because at least one activity originates there. It need not correspond to a real place in the geographical sense: it may be a functional unit that makes business sense. If one person does two different types of work, you might find it helpful to place one type in one cost center and the rest in another. The cost center is a unit within a company distinguished by area of responsibility, location or special accounting method, and by activity-related aspects.

All cost centers have to belong to a controlling area. If there is more than one FI-Financial Accounting company in the area, then you also have to say which cost center belongs to which company by assigning a company code to the master record for each cost center.

Each cost center has a defined validity period, and all changes to the master record will be related to this validity period. You decide when cost center changes are to take effect.

The cost center master record will indicate by parameters which functions can be active:

- Will the cost center master record accept planning data?

- Is posting allowed to this cost center?

- Will the cost center maintain open items?

- Can quantities be entered on the cost center master record?

- What blocking logic applies?

- What is the type of this cost center?

- What is the cost center currency? This defaults to the area currency, but can be changed.

The cost center concept allows transaction data to be validated against cost center masters as soon as they are established, even if CO-CCA Cost Center Accounting is still being implemented.

Cost centers may be grouped in alternative configurations which may be changed at any time. The transaction data itself is always assigned to the relevant cost center. Alternative cost center groups may correspond to organizational or functional distinctions related to decision-making, departmental or controlling requirements.

Actual Costing

When primary costs are entered, you specify a cost center as the destination in the cost accounting system. SAP R/3 will automatically create a SAP Document to record the transaction and post it to the appropriate subledger of the FI-GL General Ledger. At the same time, CO-Controlling will cause a second copy to be made for itself. Thus CO-Controlling can be self-contained, yet the audit trail is still intact.

The following SAP applications are fully integrated with CO-CCA Cost Center Accounting, and may act as feeder systems sending actual cost data to it:

- FI - Financial Accounting
- FI-AM Asset Management
- MM - Materials Management
- PP - Production Planning
- HR - Human Resources Management
- SD - Sales and Distribution

The data from these feeder systems can be used in calculating statistical ratios for the purpose of internal cost allocation and ratio analysis. The data can be formed into groups and used in the same way as cost elements and cost centers.

External data from non-SAP systems may be automatically transferred through SAP standard interfaces, and there is a flexible and supportive interface for the manual input of data. Every transaction is recorded in the standard form of a CO document which is additional to the standard SAP Document created by every transaction.

Costs are transferred between cost centers, but the original cost element data remain unchanged. CO-CCA Cost Center Accounting sponsors two types of distribution of costs:

- Periodic transfer of primary cost totals from FI-Financial Accounting to a temporary clearing cost center in CO-Controlling
- Distribution of primary and secondary costs within CO-Controlling

Cost Distribution Within CO-CCA Cost Center Accounting

The distribution method of CO-CCA Cost Center Accounting is totally flexible and under your control.

The sender is a cost center that has access to rules for distributing the cost elements to the receivers, which are also cost centers. You have control over the allocation structures, so distribution is made to suit the needs of your company. The identity of the sender is preserved in all distribution postings, and the system keeps a log of all the relevant data.

You can simulate distribution to test out the effects of the rules before you post the values. The variety of available distribution rules is illustrated by the following examples:

- Fixed specific amounts, or values calculated at the time and based on shared portions or percentages

- Actual data or planned data

- Allocation across a pattern of cost centers which is determined at the time by the system

Generally, it is advisable to group sender and receiver cost centers in the same controlling area so as to give them identical distribution rules, because you can then combine distribution rules. For example, you could allocate, say, 70 percent of a cost arising from sales evenly to the cost centers for individual sales representatives and split 20 percent between the central sales organizations in proportion to the number of sales representatives working to them. This example illustrates that you do not have to distribute all the costs: the sender cost center still has 10 percent.

The effects of a distribution can be seen immediately by calling for a standard online report available through the special functions keys. And you can repeat the distribution procedures at any time.

Assessment

The processing logic is similar for assessment and distribution. The cost center sending cost data is credited with the total of the accounts that have been assigned to it, and the receiver cost center is debited using special cost elements that signify that the transaction is part of an assessment procedure.

By looking at the appropriate secondary cost elements, you can analyze the results of the assessment.

Surcharge Calculation

A cost allocation method that is additional to assessment and that is available in CO-Controlling is to use the surcharge calculation function. This calculates a supplement, usually as percentage, which is used to apply overhead in absorption costing, for example, as when a service receiver is charged for overhead incurred by the service provider on an individual business transaction basis.

You can call on CO-CCA Cost Center Accounting to calculate a surcharge at a percentage rate based on one or more cost elements. The system will simultaneously credit and debit the relevant cost centers with the calculated surcharge, which will be posted under a predefined surcharge cost element.

Cost Center Planning Procedures

The purpose of cost center planning is to anticipate the volume of costs for a particular period at each of the cost centers you have identified in your company. You can plan for one fiscal year ahead, or for several. You can have the year divided into parts, up to 365 in number, or you can use a rolling system of planning.

Within your overall period of choice, the fiscal year perhaps, the system will reallocate any planned values according to your selection from the predefined distribution keys, to which you may add your own.

One of the things you have to decide is the planning level. The planning level defines the cost center where you set out your plan. If the plan is to be applied across the entire enterprise, then the planning level will be the SAP Client which will subsume all subordinate companies. If the plan is for a single subsidiary, then the level will be Company Code and this code will appear on all master records associated with this plan.

The plan will specify details such as:

- Quantity-based activities

- Value-based primary and secondary cost elements

- Statistical ratios

When you have settled on the planning level, the system will provide you with detailed planning support in the form of standard texts for documenting the plan and formulas for calculating all the standard statistical ratios. The SAP product costing system will be able to supply information to your plan in the form of quantity and value details of particular cost elements.

Although you can change and correct the cost center plan at any time by repeating individual sections of the overall planning sequence, you can also block your plan, version by version, to prevent any changes. You can also use the standard R/3 authorization functions to control changes to your plan.

It may be the case that your cost center plan contains a planned value for a particular cost element that should really be subjected to more detailed attention. The system allows you to define individual items to separate what you regard as the important factors that should be subjected to detailed planning. The following influencing factors illustrate the concept:

- A material may be subject to wide fluctuations in cost due to an unstable market. Your plan could specify the code number of this material, and the SAP MM-Materials Management application would keep your plan up to date by posting the current price of this material to your plan.

- Some cost centers in your plan may be sensitive to employee-related wages and salaries. You could have this influencing factor evaluated using price tables and cost rates, by employee group or by individual employee, if necessary.

- Some cost centers may be sensitive to the costs associated with individual activities and external services. You might well highlight these as influencing factors to be actively and automatically taken into your plan.

There may be risks or overheads that ought to attract surcharges at some cost centers. These can be factored into your plan.

SAP standard business functions are also available to support the concept of having cost centers working to a cost center budget.

CO-ABC Activity-Based Cost Accounting

In cost accounting terms, an activity is a process that can be counted and which attracts costs. In business terms, a production process is achieved by a network of activities. If you want to find out the cost of a process, you have to know the activities and the quantities of work done by each.

The purpose of the CO-ABC Activity-Based Cost Accounting component of the SAP R/3 CO-Controlling module is to help you plan, monitor and settle activity types in the accounts of cost centers.

Activity types serve as allocation bases and are used as cost drivers to determine and send incurred costs to receivers.

The CO-ABC Activity-Based Cost Accounting system allows you to develop fully integrated activity costing in a controlled, step-by-step fashion. There is an inevitable logical sequence:

1. Define the activity types that are of interest to your company because they add value, attract costs or both.

2. Specify how each activity type will be measured and the units to be used.

3. Create a plan using your activity types and their quantities.

4. Extend the plan to include the costs that are dependent on activities and the rates to be applied.

5. Allocate, or set up rules to allocate, activity costs for both planned and actual data.

6. Predistribute the fixed costs and attach a value to each of the activity types that are not amenable to measurement.

7. Determine the variances over the period and allocate them to activities or cost centers.

Activity Types and Allocation Bases

The measurement of productivity has to start with a measurement, or at least a quantitative assessment of activity. In a production cost center, there will be measurements of time required, number, weight or volume of each product, units finished and semi-finished. The service cost centers will have records of jobs, hours worked by each skilled trade, energy and materials used.

Sales and administrative tasks are also becoming subject to measurement of a nominal kind, where something that can be counted, such as the number of calls made, is used as an index of activity: each call entails an amount of work that can be assessed and evaluated, at least in average terms. Data on an activity will typically, depending on the type, include information on the planned activity quantity, the capacity and the output quantity. Activities may be assigned to activity groups, so you can carry out some operations on all the members of the group simultaneously. This might be useful as you change your controlling task from planning to allocation, to determination of cost rates, and so on. There is no limit in CO-Controlling to the number and scope of the activity groups you use.

The master record of an activity group will contain parameters that you can use to define how the group is handled. There are parameters to define settlement cost elements to be used in the direct allocation of planned and actual values. You can flag particular activities as statistical, which will ensure that the system adopts a standard procedure for calculations according to the needs of the moment, including assessment, distribution and computing ratios for use in reporting.

Activity Planning and the Flow of Activities

For each cost center, you have to arrive at a planned value for each activity. And you must reconcile this amount of activity with the amount of activity planned in the Logistics system. The system will assist you with this.

The CO-ABC Activity-Based Cost Accounting module differentiates three types of planning:

- Planning statistical ratios

- Planning activity quantities

- Planning primary and secondary cost elements

A statistical ratio in planning can be simply a number for each posting period, or it can be a cumulative number computed for each period on the basis of data. If the cost center produces activities that are quantified, the planned or actual quantity of output can be the basis for planning the primary and secondary cost elements, because the output quantity of the cost center can be converted to values.

Given the input of primary and secondary costs to a cost center and the output in terms of evaluated quantities of activities, you can have the system compute the efficiency of the cost center in each of its activities.

The same method is used to plan the activities to be produced and consumed in the flow of internal activities.

You then have the basis for planning secondary costs.

Simulation and the Reconciliation of Activities

The logistics plan and the controlling plan may be inconsistent. Bottlenecks and idle production capacity may be foreseen.

Interactive activity analysis allows you to look at several activities at once to see which will have spare capacity and which are destined to be subjected to demands that are beyond their capacity. You may be able to effect a displacement of work or resources, or replace one activity by another. The system will immediately simulate the cost effects of your tentative change of plan, which you can confirm when you are satisfied, or store as a separate version of the plan.

Starting at any cost center, you can command a display of the activity types received from or sent to an adjacent cost center level. This allows you to trace the functional dependencies between individual activity types.

Activity-Based Cost Planning

Each activity type and each cost center can be given as many cost elements as necessary. You can enter the planned cost elements as values, or as values to be computed at the time on the basis of quantities and the rates prevailing. The cost element can be given a planned overall value or a planned quantity.

Both procedures can be carried out as full or marginal costs and can direct a split into fixed and variable components. The system provides formulas, formal specifications, texts and report characteristics.

The CO-Controlling system distributes the planned values for the variable primary cost elements for the year. You can see the effects on costs of any fluctuations in planned activity levels. You can call for the fixed costs to be distributed using standard rules or your own rules.

The internal exchange of activities also causes secondary costs to be incurred. These are computed by taking the amounts of the allocated activity quantities and valuing them at the appropriate standard rates defined in the sender cost centers. The receivers of internal activity costs will include:

- Cost centers
- Orders for cost centers which are overhead cost orders
- Production orders for semi-finished and finished products
- Capital spending orders for fixed assets
- Sales orders or sales cost objects

Having planned values for internal orders, you may wish to allocate the planned costs to the receiver cost centers. The original producing cost centers will retain the information.

Political Prices

Standard prices and standard rates at which cost centers activities should be charged are among the important results to come out of any planning exercise. The total cost is divided by the total quantity in each case.

You may be in a business that prefers not to use the actual or historical standard price computed as an average based on total cost and total quantity.

You may have to set rates which are determined by political factors rather than by computation.

You have to enter political rates manually. You can then use them to evaluate planned and actual quantities. The system thus retains an accurate representation of internal activity cost flows and cost allocations, even if the rates are not the strictly determined product of formal business planning.

Indirect Allocation of Costs to Non-Measurable Activities

The system has indirect cost allocation functions that you can use to allocate costs accurately to the objects which caused them. You may be able to apply standard methods if you can derive an index of activity that can serve as a quantity to which you can apply a rate. But the indirect allocation functions are available for when the most reasonable method is to assess costs and allocate them to their causes.

Cost Center Variances

Variance analysis is a method of monitoring business activity.

A variance is defined as the computed difference between actual costs and planned costs, using the following formula:

Actual Cost = Planned Cost +/–Variance

Variances can be calculated at any level:

Cost center

Cost element

Activity type

There are four variance factors that explain why actual costs can differ from planned costs:

- Price variance, caused by differences between the actual and the planned prices of the goods and services used

- Usage variance, arising from uneconomical working practices in the production process

- Volume variance, which occurs when the planned volume is not reached or if it is exceeded, giving rise to the fixed costs being under- or over-absorbed by the actual volume of product

- Cost center over- or under-absorption of fixed costs as a result of using different standard rates in the plan from those applied in the posting of actual activities, the so-called political rates. The same effects may occur if the cost center plans have not been reconciled.

The total of these variances for all cost elements and activity types within a cost center provides the overall variance for that cost center.

For each combination of cost element and activity type on each cost center, the CO-ABC Activity-Based Cost Accounting system maintains a value structure for controlling. Each of these values is split into fixed part and variable part:

- Planned costs

- Target costs

- Variance types

- Actual costs

- Planned/actual usage

You can have the variances calculated and included as part of the cost components. The formulas follow:

- Actual Cost = Planned Cost +/–Cost Variance

- Actual Price = Planned Price +/–Price Variance

- Target Costs = Actual Volume × Planned Rates

- Usage Variance = Actual Costs–Target Costs–Price Variance

- Volume Variance = Target Costs–Actual Activity × Planned Price

- Over-/Under-absorption = Target Costs–Allocated Costs–Volume Variance

Charging Variances

The CO-Controlling system evaluates each activity by applying the planned rate to the activity quantity. If you have the historical variances, or your system can get them for you, there is the possibility of using them in a fresh version of your plan. Similarly, if you have some way of anticipating future variances, or if you want to conduct a what-if simulation exercise, then again, you can create a fresh plan version.

You may want to use anticipated variances in the cost allocation process. In order to represent accurately the value flow in your company, it is essential to allocate cost center variances periodically. You can specify whether to use historical, standard or anticipated variances for the subsequent charging process, and in this way, transfer all variances directly to your profitability analysis system.

An alternative approach is to pass on usage variances to the receivers but keep as a charge on the producing cost center the variances resulting from too little output. They will go to the profitability analysis system from there.

You can charge variances periodically to the following types of receiver:

- Individual cost centers

- Internal orders or projects

- Production orders, and thence to the finished and semi-finished product inventory

- Cost objects in profitability analysis
- Fixed assets

If you arrange for actual variances to be charged to cost objects in CO-PA Profitability Analysis, you will be on the way toward the creation of the detailed cost structures that are necessary to a system of contribution margin accounting.

Variances are posted under the CO-ABC Activity-Based Cost Accounting system using the rules and procedures of direct cost allocation. The system specifies the allocation cost element by its identification code and by whether the value is fixed or variable on either sender or receiver object. It also ensures that identical variance types are in use.

The effect of all these procedures is to accurately allocate all actual costs to the precise area of the company where they were caused. This serves both the legal requirement of external accounting, and the need for comprehensive internal reporting as a basis for controlling the company.

Alternative Activity Rates in Parallel

The method described above can be regarded as an imputed allocation approach: cost centers accrue costs because of the activities they undertake and the overheads they enjoy.

The CO-Controlling system will also operate a system of parallel activity rates that can provide a family of alternative evaluations relevant to various accounting purposes.

At the cost element level, you can put together a portfolio of costs to be included in an alternative activity rate for each cost element. If these rates are used when calculating internal activity flows, you will be able to produce cost estimates conforming to all legal and tax regulations for which your portfolio is correct.

These calculations lead to the derivation of the balance sheet and profitability analysis. You can compare costs of sales and total costs of production, both estimated and as they appear in the external financial documents—the balance sheet and profit and loss statement.

Activities and Services Costing

By looking more and more closely at the way they produce their goods and services, companies have been able to make extensive improvements. The need is for a system of structured overhead costing.

The first thing to do is to identify and define the cost drivers—the allocation bases that influence how activity costs are allocated to the cost centers that generate them.

The cost driver is a subprocess that can be measured for individual cost center activities; for example:

- Number of purchase order items successfully processed
- Number of quotation items

- Delivery items in sales

- Dunning operations and payment differences handled

Subprocesses are grouped together into primary processes that can be addressed by the product costing system to determine the costs of administrative and service activities.

You will discover what each subprocess costs. You are on the way to an activity-based profitability analysis.

Planning and Simulating the Subprocesses

The basic disciplines of activity-based accounting have to be applied to ensure that the activities at a cost center are integrated with the accounting and controlling systems. However, there is a further level of detail to be considered if activities are to be analyzed into their constituent subprocesses.

A business process can be represented by a chain of activities and products or a network of such chains. In the SAP R/3 system, this chain or network is managed by a process sequence structure, which may be of any complexity.

The process sequence structure can be used to simulate the flow of material through a sequence of activities that create perhaps a series of semifinished products and that terminate with the finished product.

The SAP PP-Production Planning module is specialized in this work.

For the purpose of analyzing overhead activities and services, the CO-ABC Activity-Based Cost Accounting module provides full supporting functions.

The system of costing based on a process sequence structure requires that all the processes and subprocesses be quantified in terms of quantity and value flow, so that analysis and reporting can occur to a level of detail that will yield a balance of activities to document the ways in which the activity level of the parent cost center exerts influence on the costs of the primary processes and their subprocesses. How do support costs alter when business gets better or worse?

Using Process Cost Rates

The purpose of applying the methods of activity-based costing to the detailed processes and subprocesses of a production company is to compute process cost rates. How much does it cost to put one invoice item through the office? How much to move one pallet from production to warehouse?

If you have process cost rates at this level of detail, you can take a standard costing based on a bill of materials and routings, for example, and cost each of the processes entailed. Or you can have the SAP system do it for you.

If you have these process cost rates for all the subprocesses in each activity type, you can transfer the process costs from CO-CCA Cost Center Accounting directly to CO-PA Profitability Analysis.

Because you have the process costs associated with each activity embraced by CO-CCA Cost Center Accounting, you can have these process costs included in the value flow patterns that are identified by both Product Costing and Period Costing.

CO-OPA Order and Project Accounting

The purpose of the CO-OPA Order and Project Accounting module is to analyze and settle the costs arising from internal orders and projects.

The purpose of internal orders is to monitor costs to assist in decision making and to manage the allocation and settlement of activity costs to target objects, including FI-GL General Ledger accounts. Projects may also be used for these purposes. Complex projects are more properly the province of the SAP R/3 PS-Project System, which is discussed elsewhere in this volume.

Internal orders are usually defined for a particular task, event or internal change measure that has to be planned, monitored and settled in great detail. These orders are distinguished by their origin and by the time allocated for their completion. They vary in their settlement arrangements and in how they appear in the reporting functions.

SAP R/3 classifies internal orders as follows:

- Production-related orders used in Logistics

- Sales orders used in SD-Sales and Distribution

- Internal orders used in CO-Controlling

Although the internal orders of the Logistics modules and the SD-Sales and Distribution component serve mainly to monitor resources used and sales achieved, they also document estimated costs, actual costs, and revenues. In the PP-Production Planning and Control modules, the order has the job of annexing information on the latest estimate of costs until the actual costs replace them when the order is complete.

Sales orders that document costs and revenues are accessed by the CO-PA Profitability Analysis system. They also carry the information needed by CO-Controlling and PP-Production Planning and Control, for example. The orders for processing and settling internal costs usually support the integration of different business systems with the ways the particular company likes to do business and settle the costs.

Internal orders in CO-Controlling are differentiated by the following characteristics:

- Whether logistical, controlling, or settlement in main function

- Content of the order, such as product or project

- Whether an individual order or a standing order

- The significance of the values on the order, such as plan costs, actual costs or variances

- Settlement receiver for the order, such as fixed asset account, cost center, cost object, project, stock, business segment, sales order, or FI-GL General Ledger account

It is an important feature of the CO-OPA Order and Project Accounting component that you can assign the relevant costs on each of the orders and projects to the various receivers, split by period and allocated accurately by cause. They can be used for both overhead cost controlling and production controlling.

If you wish to have an internal exercise that is a simple single-level project, used only in the CO-Controlling system, you will be invited to specify how you want to monitor it and settle the costs incurred.

Order Data Formats
The master data record for an order comprises the order number and the parameters for controlling the business and technical system functions that will deal with it. You will have been authorized to use a certain range of order numbers, otherwise, the system will assign the number.

The order master will bear control data to signify the transaction groups in which it can take part. For example, an order type Planning will allow the entry for planning purposes only of information such as primary costs and overhead costs.

The order master will also include parameter fields to organize overhead components and to control the settlement functions. Some orders will have the function of monitoring all open purchase orders, for example; others are intended for the detailed settlement of individual cost items.

This system of order parameters set into the master records enables you to establish a suite of order types that can be used to nominate the manner in which each order will direct the value flow in your company along the lines already defined by your organizational structure and the way in which your company has chosen to group its business functions.

Status Management of Orders
The status of an order is the stage it has reached in its life cycle. The SAP CO-OPA Order and Project Accounting system is particularly flexible in the way that it allows you to decide what should happen at each stage and, indeed, through which stages a particular type of order should proceed on its way to completion. For example, you can choose where to have the system plan primary or secondary costs for each order.

The typical status sequence for an order will encounter the following stages:

- Order opened, basic data identified
- Planning primary and secondary costs
- Released for posting
- Execution
- Technical completion
- Accounting completion

Some of these business functions can be allowed to operate across more than one status. Planning information can be allowed to be added to an order while it is being executed, for example.

Order Classification by Content

Because they are treated differently, orders are classified by their content and controlling objectives into various types.

Job orders collect and analyze the planned and actual costs for a commodity or operational event that is not going to be capitalized, such as minor repairs or staff training. These orders will be settled on the objects that caused them, by means of the periodic cost center accounting procedures.

Capital spending orders on the fixed assets produced in-house and on maintenance costs serve to manage the planning and allocation of costs over the lifetime of the order, which can be an open order.

Production orders are used to set up costing sheets by gathering primary costs from FI-Financial Accounting and secondary costs from overhead assessment. Activity costs come from internal allocation. Issues of raw materials and semi-finished materials are notified from MM-Materials Management. Production orders in Logistics use bills of materials, routings and cost centers. They are fully integrated into the overall capacity planning and monitoring functions.

Sales orders can have posted to them any type of cost and revenue item taken directly from SD-Sales and Distribution. These can be transferred directly to the appropriate business segments in CO-PA Profitability Analysis.

An individual order is typically unique and of long duration. The quantity structures are seldom fully known at the start, so planning is carried out in stages. Where an individual order entails multilevel production processing and a complex web of activities, partial orders may be created. The SAP R/3 Project System is specialized for this kind of work in make-to-order production.

Standing orders are used when cost centers have to be split into smaller activity units, such as small repairs, minor maintenance or individual vehicles in a company fleet.

Statistical orders are used to receive additional account assignments for the purpose of summarizing, sorting and displaying cost objects according to specific criteria. The amount posted appears under the original cost element heading on the appropriate account, and again on the statistical order. Revenues can also be collated by a statistical order.

Order Planning

You can plan the overall value of an order. You can also plan according to the cost elements and activity types, either on the specific order, or by transferring the values from a unit you have already costed. The following cost elements and activity types are amenable to planning on orders:

■ Primary costs by cost element or cost element group, in values or in quantities to which the system will apply cost rates at the time

■ Cost center activities as the secondary costs, planned down to the level of individual operations if necessary

■ Overhead, planned using the overhead application functions

■ Statistical ratios, to be used to form business ratios when reporting

Distribution keys provide a choice between planning orders on a yearly basis with a standard distribution across months, and planning for each month separately. Order groups may be assembled for overhead calculation, planning and reporting.

The functionality and screens used in CO-CCA Cost Center Accounting are available to give planning views of your flexible combinations of planning objects and planning content. For example, you may call for planning views on all or any of the following situations:

■ Many cost elements on a single order

■ Many cost element groups on a single order

■ Many cost elements on an order group

■ Many cost element groups on an order group

Whatever planning steps you take, you can store in the system a choice of standard explanatory texts with additional information to document your decisions.

If the order takes a long time to execute, the assumptions on which the plan was built may become out of date. Each plan is noted as a new version whenever you change something, so that subsequent analysis will arrive at an accurate picture.

If a plan has already been released and changes have to be made, you can have the system document the entry of the modified order plan and the changes made to it, in the form of a copy of the plan line items which have been altered.

Unit Costing

You may have a cost element plan that is too global for certain requirements—perhaps you want to assign only some of the costs, for example, to an order. You can create the order using cost elements and have the system make out a unit cost plan later, when the actual values or quantities are transferred to the order.

Open Items

If you want to place a reservation on a certain quantity of material, or if you still have a commitment to pay for an external service on a specific order, then you enter an open item. In the display, open items will appear as values and quantities under the appropriate cost element heading in the correct fiscal year and in the period that includes the planned supply date.

Open items can arise through purchasing in the MM-Materials Management system. If the invoice has been received, the open item can be evaluated from the actual prices; if not, the anticipated price has to be used. Delivery costs are displayed separately so they can be evaluated in the appropriate currency for the place where each cost element was incurred.

Material reservation in MM-IM Materials Management, Inventory Management will create an open item which will be evaluated at the carrying price.

You can also generate an open item manually in the form of a funds reservation.

As you reduce an open item, the system will help you manage it using the original currency. Analysis and posting can take place under the system rules for foreign currency and its exchange.

The aim is to replace each open item on an order with the corresponding actual costs. If an open item concerns external services, the system will reduce the purchase order by value, using the invoiced amount whether full or partial. The system will identify any price differences by account and by order.

If an open item is a goods purchase order, as soon as the goods are received, the system will automatically reduce the quantity and the value for the open purchase item. If the invoice is received before the goods, the system will adjust the open purchase order by adopting the invoice value in place of the purchase order value. Should any amounts on the invoice or on the services received remain unsettled, the order will stay open until they are finally cleared completely.

The order number and the posting details are retained when an order progresses from one business transaction to the next. The system can thus document the purchase order history, which enables you to trace a partial delivery or a partial invoice to the purchase order and then back to the original purchase requisition.

Open item management illustrates the close integration of Logistics and Accounting in the SAP system.

Actual Cost Accounting Transactions

Every SAP transaction generates a SAP Document. If the document contains a posting to an order number, the CO-OPA Order and Project Accounting system will charge the amount to the order under the relevant cost element heading and with that order number. You can trace the history of origin of each line item throughout the lifetime of the order.

Activities must take place so that production orders, maintenance orders and job orders may be fulfilled. These activities will be the responsibility of one or more cost centers. And for each of these activities, the responsible cost center will demand payment in the form of an internal cost allocation.

The CO-Controlling system will evaluate the activity quantity at the appropriate rate. At the same time, there will be line items created to document the flow of value from the producing sender objects to the receiving objects. These will take the form of a credit to the sending cost center and a debit to the receiving order. This is the process of direct internal cost allocation.

If the activity is not amenable to quantification—if you cannot say exactly how much of the item is needed for the order—you have to use indirect cost allocation, in which a periodic total is shared in some way between the receiving cost centers or orders.

Overhead is a charge that should be allocated as accurately as possible to the items that have to share its burden. This distribution is discussed in the section on CO-CCA Cost Center Accounting.

Settlement of Orders

Order settlement is the process of passing costs from the originating order to other cost objects. There are two groups of these target objects: internal postings within CO-Controlling, and external postings to the accounts managed by FI-Financial Accounting and other applications.

Internal postings settle orders automatically using CO-CEA Cost Element Accounting. This component creates the necessary credit and debit line items, to any of the following objects:

- Cost centers
- Internal orders
- Projects
- Business segments
- Sales orders

Orders may be settled by postings to external objects using the following functions:

- FI-AA Asset Accounting, for assets under construction or capitalized assets
- MM-Materials Management, which settles any product manufactured in-house to inventory under the material number for a warehouse
- FI-Financial Accounting can settle orders to the appropriate FI-GL General Ledger account

Settlement Rules. Each order master includes a data element that determines the settlement rule to be applied to that order. The rule includes the following control parameters:

- Period of validity for the settlement rule
- Target object or objects to which the costs are to be sent—for example, if part of the costs of the order will be capitalized and the rest distributed between certain cost centers

- The cost element or elements under which the order value is to be credited—using cost element groups results in a debit to the receiver under each element

- Settlement of costs to a cost element within the CO-Controlling system

The settlement rule may be a defined debit to the receiver. Several receivers may be targeted in proportions calculated from equivalence numbers or percentages. Absolute amounts may be settled, or costs may be based on quantity and the system will use the rate current when the settlement is performed.

If the order includes information on a suitable target object for settlement, such as a responsible cost center or related project identification, the system will operate a default distribution rule generated on the basis of this information.

Orders that allocate costs to cost centers tend to be settled periodically; capital spending orders will be settled at period-end after the project has been completed.

Orders to be settled can be grouped according to the following criteria:

- Order type

- Date when settlement is to be performed

- Receiver of the settlement

- Corporate or company code

- Settlement to internal or external accounting system

You can create a settlement simulation list in the CO-OPA Order and Project Accounting system using the allocation groups to check that the orders are both correct and complete. When the simulation is correct you can use the list to execute the settlement. You can reverse a settlement made previously, and repeat it at any time.

The system calculates the total settlement and the individual amounts debited to each receiver in the controlling area currency, from which you can convert if necessary. The settlement function differentiates debiting an order with full costs and debiting only direct costs. You may have previously distributed fixed costs in CO-CCA Cost Center Accounting, in which case this is allowed for in the value flow.

The order reporting system will show you the settlement history, which comprises the dates and details of the amounts already settled, any reversals performed and the balance remaining on the order.

Order Summary Evaluations

If you want to compare two or more orders in detail, you may find it helpful to have the system classify orders using a hierarchy. The CO-Controlling system will allow you to put any criterion at the top of your hierarchy and any other criteria at each level below. You might ask these sorts of question:

- How do the various companies in this group compare across these functions: repairs, advertising special campaigns, and so on?

- How do the various companies in this group compare, for all departments, all production orders?

These criteria together create a hierarchy over which the system can collate the data, in this example for all production orders. The SAP R/3 flexible reporting functions allow you to view this data at any of these levels of your hierarchy, and to switch readily from one viewpoint to another.

In fact, the system offers a complete system of order reporting from line item up to order, cost center, controlling area and company. The online reporting techniques allow you to take any summary and "drill down" to the details of the order items that contribute to it.

Capital Spending Orders

The main objective of a capital spending order is to monitor the costs of producing assets and commodities in-house.

Maintenance projects can be controlled and accounted in the same way.

The distinguishing feature of the SAP module CO-OPA Order and Project Accounting is its ability to settle in detail the actual costs according to rules individual to each item. The following must be specified:

- The target object(s) defined as one or more fixed assets in FI-AA Asset Management

- The date of the settlement

- The scope of the costs to be settled

- The settlement cost element heading

- The supplementary information

In addition to this ability to settle capital spending orders in precise detail, the system has the following important capabilities:

- Planning is available for all resources and costs required, in quantity and value.

- Charges can be computed from prices at the time, with imputed allocations of overhead and actual costs.

- Open items for purchase requisitions, purchase orders, and material reservations are closely monitored.

- Display is possible of all cash-related procedures, such as down payment requests and down payments.

- Concurrent evaluation and analysis of order reports can be performed.

Integration of CO-OPA Order and Project Accounting with FI-AA Asset Accounting

If you are managing fixed assets such as buildings and machines, the settlement of capital spending orders is of crucial importance. The SAP R/3 system offers detailed settlement rules and a close integration with the FI-AA Asset Accounting component to yield the following advantages:

- Settlement of costs to the appropriate balance sheet accounts under the heading of Assets Under Construction while the capital spending order is ongoing

- Order-based display of special depreciations for Assets Under Construction

- Recognition of subsidies, grants and downpayments

- Settlement of partial orders over a hierarchy of orders

Because all costs are based on unified posting and settlement rules in the SAP R/3 system, you can allocate costs from orders and projects to the various target objects using the same rules or rules you have specified separately. You can keep track of complex overhead costs with maintenance and capital spending orders—the chance to take effective action in good time will be yours.

Planned Cost Schedules

Costs and deadlines on orders and projects that take a long time to complete have to recognize the financial facts of life. Money is not always available when you need it. Financial and liquidity planning needs to know what costs are expected on the orders and projects. It helps to have some idea of how the costs are likely to be incurred in detail over the first few accounting periods and in broader terms up to the date of completion.

A cost schedule is a plan extending the length of an order or project showing the values expected to be allocated to costs. The schedule has a key date. Until this date is known and entered on the plan, the forecast of costs has to be moved ahead to the best estimated date.

The SAP R/3 system provides support in the following ways:

- The system will automatically determine the tasks from the planned start and finish dates for the order.

- Cost distribution across the schedule can be suited to the specific order.

- Graphical representations of the data model are readily available online and in print.

The following manipulations of the cost schedules and the task plans are automatically available:

- Shifting the start date, retaining the duration

- Compressing the duration, retaining the finish date

- Expanding the duration

If you have carried out cost element planning or created a unit costing for the order, the system can use this information to develop a cost schedule.

Product Cost Accounting

The purpose of product cost accounting is to determine the unit cost of whatever product units your company does business in. These units are referred to as cost objects, with one cost object for each product or each distribution package for each product.

The context is a technical production system that is customized to a particular company; the outcome is a company-specific costing system that integrates the flow of cost information from its origins.

There is a core technical discipline based on the principle that costs should be accurately allocated to the processes that incur them. And there are several costing systems that embody this principle in the particular circumstances of a certain type of business.

Product cost accounting addresses two types of costing:

- Production Order Costing

- Inventory Costing

Four types of cost object controlling are differentiated, because they offer different benefits according to the type of business they are located in:

- Make-to-Stock Production

- Process Manufacturing

- Make-to-Order Production

- Plant Construction

All of these types of product cost accounting are supported by the CO-Controlling module by the flexible use of cost objects.

Costing Requirements of Different Types of Companies

Modern controlling methods have developed to support technical manufacturing processes and service industries. The methods have to match the needs of the individual company. The SAP approach is to establish a core of standard business functions that can be controlled by the implementer through the medium of parameters, so as to yield a customized system finely tuned to the requirements of the different classes of user in the specific company.

Manufacturers require a costing system that shows where and by how much their manufacturing processes add value to their raw materials. They differ in their style of manufacturing according to whether they make to a production order, or make to replace stock on their inventory. Their processes differ over a range, from discrete one-off production, to repetitive production, to continuous flow production.

Trading companies need a method of costing to enable them to apply overhead and surcharges to the cost prices of their goods, which they often have to keep to set or agreed final selling prices.

Service companies are tending to adopt the principles of process costing, which revolves around the concept of cost drivers—in this case, service activities. They need to be able to define, measure, plan and pass on costs incurred by their cost drivers, service calls and other activities.

Make-to-Order, Make-to-Stock, Continuous Flow. The manufacturing industry has a polished costing method based on routings taken by work units and bills of materials. They need to know what processes the product has to undergo, the costs of materials and resources and the quantities. This is referred to as the quantity structure for this product. If you have this information, you can begin to cost the product by assembling the costing components.

In the make-to-order company, the customer order sets off costing. As each order is unique, there may be a shortage of routings and bills of materials that can be applied without editing. Yet it is of the utmost importance to be able to arrive quickly at a cost prediction for this one-off product, so as to be able to issue a quotation and take part in competitive tendering for the work. An effective costing system for this sort of company would have to give this approach to one-off tendering a high priority, for on its speed and accuracy all future business may depend.

Those manufacturers who make to stock will apply standard bills of materials and routings about which they may well have copious actual data. Products and orders can be costed from this database.

Where the manufacturing process is continuous, it is probably not amenable to much in the way of variation. It will probably only work at its best if the rate of flow is within narrow limits. Nevertheless, the contribution of the various cost components to the cost of the finished product will not be without interest for the management and shareholders. It will be important to understand how and why costs vary if the flow rate and quality are allowed to move out of the normal operating ranges. This might happen because of variations in the raw materials or in the environmental conditions at the manufacturing plant.

Product Costing Techniques. A costing system uses a set of costing objects, which are the different products, production and other orders, resources and so on. The only qualification for a costing object is that it can be allocated costs that mean something when they are totaled under that costing object. The costing objects can be conceptual or tangible, organizational or geographical.

The pivotal concept in costing is the structure of cost drivers—cost objects onto which the actual costs are settled according to how they were incurred. SAP R/3 CO-Controlling provides a range of model structures on which you can base a structure specific to the needs of your company.

There are three types of costing values that might be settled on a cost structure:

- Planned values
- Target values
- Actual costs

There are two ways of applying cost data to arrive at a specific costing:

- Allocate the full costing to the cost objects.
- Allocate only the variable costs to the cost objects, and apply overhead or surcharge.

An integrated costing system has to have at least the following abilities:

- Calculate alternative cost plans using different versions and timings.
- Control the activities and the value added by each operation.
- Settle actual costs, according to how they occurred, on a specific cost structure.

Unit Costing. If your company makes unique products only to customer orders, you will need unit costing. You have very little choice but to cost each individual order by deciding which unitary components you will have to put together; and you will have to find out what other costs will be incurred as you do so.

The relevant database is a set of reference unit cost estimates. CO-PC Product Cost Accounting will help you locate which elements you need, and you can transfer them in blocks to the relevant quotes and sales order items or to the cost accounting objects which will be orders and projects.

This will build the planned costs of the quote, which can be compared to the actual costs as the order proceeds towards completion. Materials will be consumed, and these materials will all have their quantities or values assigned to the accounts under the correct cost element headings as data are collected on the activities that consume them. Overhead will be applied, and charges for external activities will add to the cost.

The sales order will be documented with a continuous comparison between planned and actual costs for the whole of its life. From this data a simultaneous calculation of contribution margin can be carried out and the results recorded on the sales order document.

Order Costing. In make-to-stock production, it is useful to combine order and unit costing methods, because order lots and batches of product are usually produced in response to production orders.

Different cost estimates are prepared as alternative versions that take part in simultaneous costing, so as to ensure exact control of the actual costs incurred by the relevant cost elements, sender cost centers and their activities, materials used and so on.

Settlement of some or all of the costs to stock and automatic calculation to support inventory control over finished and semi-finished products are supported by the system. The value of stocks of unfinished goods and work in process can be calculated automatically.

Process manufacturing includes production processes that have a step-by-step structure and those that entail a cyclic input of materials.

Continuous flow production is characterized by long processing runs of a single basic material.

The control document for continuous flow processing is the period production order. Comparisons are made between target and actual costs, planned output for a period and actual output, including cost usages from backflushing surplus material or summarized confirmations of production. The costs are charged to individual cost elements of the production structure in relation to the quantities produced.

Backflushing occurs in the chemical industry, for instance, where some of the output can be returned to the process as semi-finished product. There may be by-products and co-products with alternative uses to the main product, and some product may bypass some of the production stages in the process cycle. The production order will document these variations.

Trading companies need a costing system that can provide accurate valuations of the costs and the prices, taking into account the individual costing and pricing structures that prevail in the type of business and under the market conditions at the time. The basic method is to apply overhead to cost prices. Costing the overhead allows you to apply the overhead according to cost elements, or indeed, in relation to overhead you have already calculated. The system will allow you to use different levels of sales prices, such as net sales price or gross sales price, to compute additional overhead or surcharge, such as discounts or cash discounts. These factors differ in wholesaling and retailing.

Service companies use the functions and elements of process costing. The service operations have to be defined in terms of individual activities that can be measured. If these activities can each be measured, then they can be subject to planning. When the work is done, the actual amount of each activity component can be entered in quantitative terms; the measured activity is the cost driver. This allows the valuation process to cost each activity using predetermined rates, and thus allocate the costs to the service cost structure under the appropriate cost element headings. From this point on, the flexible reporting system of SAP R/3 can be used to collate the information and present it for the benefit of the decision makers in your company.

The SAP R/3 Cost Object as an Account Assignment Device

A cost object exists for SAP R/3 if there is a master record for it. The function of a cost object is to control the allocation, analysis and settlement of costs that are related to the object it represents. It may relate directly to a production unit; it may be an organizational structure component that is useful in reporting value flows. In essence, a cost object is an identification number and a set of master record data fields that can be accessed in connection with that number.

Unit costs of all cost objects are the basis for arriving at all costing values.

The cost object could be an entity which is quite independent of any particular SAP application—a convenient peg on which to hang information relevant to the specific costing procedures of your company.

A cost object may collect the costs of two or more other cost objects. This constitutes a cost object hierarchy, which can branch down any number of layers and extend to any number of cost objects on each level. Most cost structures will be in the form of cost object hierarchies of this inverted tree shape if plotted, for instance, through the SAP R/3 online reporting system using the graphical interface.

If you run projects or production lines, you might find it informative to have certain cost information gathered by cost objects, in parallel to the normal product costing. One way of achieving this is to define unique cost objects for each project or production line of interest.

Should your installation have other SAP modules installed and configured, you will find it convenient to make use of the cost objects from these applications to define your own unique cost objects by copying some or all of the data structures from these predefined SAP cost objects. For example, these cost object types are used in the following application modules:

- PS-Project System network, project item
- CO-Controlling internal order
- SD-Sales and Distribution sales order
- MM-Materials Management material number
- PP-Production Planning production order, routing
- PM-Plant Maintenance maintenance order

If you have the unit costs for all your cost objects, you can display inventory costings and call for profitability analyses using the full set of fixed and variable costs. You can make use of any combination of the costing systems current in your company.

The SAP R/3 system carries the definitions, in the form of master data, for all the cost object controlling functions of the SAP integrated system. Any transaction that bears data relevant to costing will be processed according to these definitions.

Results from Costing a Cost Object. Costing results are stored by version so that different methods and different periods may be compared. Each assembly is itemized in a costing created from a cost object. The data used can be planned or actual, and can be as valuations or as quantities to which standard rates can be applied by the system at the time. The results of a costing comprise information on each of forty cost components for each cost object, itemized for each assembly, and the whole is replicated for each version of the costing structure, if required.

Legal analysis demands that the origins of cost estimates be identifiable. This, in turn, requires that details must be kept for the cost origins of all the contributors to the values recorded as the cost object components. A cost origin has to be a document which identifies a transaction by such means as:

- The vendor number for external procurement and the provision of external activities
- The operation number, the identification of the sender cost center, and the activity type for each internal activity
- The material number or material group code if there were stock movements or the consumption of goods
- The cost center for charging overhead

The SAP R/3 system running CO-PC Product Cost Accounting can carry out the following procedures using cost origins to associate posted movements with cost elements:

- Conduct valuation using individual cost structures or cost rates.
- Assign costs to standard cost elements.
- Establish the costing basis for overhead.
- Accept planning and account assignment directives at any level of the costing structures.
- Prepare reports at any analysis level to display planned or actual resource-usage variances.

Valuation Methods

The following costing systems are available in the CO-Controlling module of the SAP R/3 system and may be used in any combination:

- Unit costing
- Product costing

- Production order costing

- Cost object controlling for make-to-stock production

- Cost object controlling for process manufacturing

- Cost object controlling for make-to-order production

- Cost object controlling for plant construction

The valuation of input factors and the presentation of this data for costing analysis are carried out by a uniform valuation method across all costing systems. The source of the data differentiates the methods, insofar as there have to be different methods for costing when technical quantities are involved, such as when using bills of materials and routings. Variations also occur when existing cost estimates have to be copied or referenced. Manual entry of cost estimates is supported, and the R/3 system will offer suggested default values wherever possible for editing as necessary.

The valuation process extends to the following calculations:

- Planned input quantities with planned allocation rates and planned prices

- Actual input quantities with standard prices and standard activity prices

- Actual input quantities with actual prices and actual activity prices

- Partial or total output quantities

- Scrap quantities

- Order-specific cost settlement according to the quantities delivered

- Calculation of all types of variance

- Profitability analyses to different layout formats

Input quantities can be evaluated by any of a range of methods. The method chosen is recorded as the valuation variant. These variants are listed below:

- Standard prices, current prices, future or previous

- Moving average prices

- Tax-based and commercial or "political" prices

- Standard activity prices

- Actual activity prices

- Applying variances on standard or actual prices adjusted to match changes in planning or historical amounts

In the service sector it is possible to have the system split the costs into fixed and variable components, which allows you to carry out marginal and absorption costing in parallel. Any point of view of output may be taken for the purpose of evaluating services rendered.

By having the required functionality available online, the system is able to offer a modern control system covering products and the analysis of results. The following outcomes are supported:

- The cost of goods manufactured and the cost of goods sold are displayed on efficient and informative cost structures that are understandable from a business point of view and accurate from a product cost accounting perspective.

- The company can see the effects on the financial accounts and year-end closing of using different valuation techniques, so choices can be made on the basis of correct information.

- Not all the divisions of a corporate group have to use the same valuation methods, but can use the ones most suitable for them.

- Detailed costing records can be made available for each alternative or parallel valuation of variances between planned and actual costs for each business segment.

- The costing methods throughout the group are not necessarily dependent on the costing documentation requirements of the logistics operations.

The Role of Flexible Analysis and Reporting in Product Cost Accounting

The structure of a report can be made to suit your requirements. The standard system contains many predefined standard reports which you can modify and extend, often in the online mode. Both the format and the data are under your control.

Orders can be grouped by order type, for instance, and then line items selected on the basis of their connection to a specific cost object. Summaries and graphical representations are available at all stages of analysis and reporting.

Cost objects may be compared and the variances computed using any dimensions for comparison: between orders, between periods, between similar cost objects, between cost objects of quite different kinds.

Planning and Simulation from Unit Costing

You can apply unit costing irrespective of the status of an order, because it is based on a quantity structure that you have defined manually. These are some of the uses of a comprehensive system of unit costing:

- Price determination

- Costing to make quotes and tenders

- Costing to support the processing of orders

- Planning of costs and resources to prepare order and project cost estimates

- Making sample cost estimates for new or existing products using an existing estimate as a reference model to be edited and updated

- Defining sales prices for sales orders

- Preparing, planning, controlling and settling investments by means of orders and projects

- Preparing cost estimates for base planning objects, which can range from a single-level assembly to a multilevel structure that includes other base planning objects. A base planning object may also be an instrument for integrating information from other, non-SAP, applications.

You can display the costing information before, during and after production or project activities and before, during and after sales activities.

In the activities of sales and distribution, you can use unit costing to good advantage in a couple of ways:

- To transfer unit cost estimates at any time to reference objects such as orders, projects and sales orders

- To cost and check quickly the feasibility of extra sales orders, or alternative or modified product components or characteristics, and any changes in the activities involved

CO-PA Profitability Analysis

CO-PCA Profit Center Accounting is closely associated with CO-PA Profitability Analysis. Both are discussed in this section.

There is an important distinction to be made between the following aspects of profitability analysis:

- Profitability Analysis is the periodic analysis of the profit and loss made by the strategic units or by the entire company.

- Cost of Sales Accounting is also a form of profitability analysis. It is used in the management of market-oriented activities.

They both call on the same costing information, but treat it in different ways. Sales managers need to be able to estimate profits in the short term by using interim reports—based on standard values and imputed costs derived from standard manufacturing costs with cash discounts and rebates—because the actual data are not available at the time the billing document has to be issued. Periodic profitability analysis can wait for the actual values to be collated.

The SAP R/3 CO-PA Profitability Analysis component is designed to make available the full range of analyses covering the following requirements:

- Current sales data valued with standard costs and prices at the level of the individual product and for individual customers

- Calculation of actual cost variances for summarized business segments on a periodic basis

- Proportional assignment of fixed costs in order to measure net profit at the divisional level

- Application of period profit center accounting in situations where there are large fluctuations in stock levels

Both the periodic profit and loss statement and the interim sales report have to be able to provide the answers to similar questions, even though their answers may take different forms:

- What is the relationship between gross sales and net sales revenue?

- How were the sales deductions calculated for each market segment?

- What was the profit on this specific order?

- Which products or market segments are showing the greatest increases in sales revenue?

- Which products or market segments are making the highest contribution margin?

- What are the shifts, if any, between the main business segments?

- What are the planned contribution margins for each product?

The Cost of Sales Accounting method uses standard costs to produce interim reports, allowing you to look at any market segment immediately, without waiting for the actual data to arrive.

Cost of Sales Accounting Using Standard Costs (Interim Reports)

The market-driven needs of sales management dictate the requirement to be able to estimate profits in the short term by using interim reports based on standard values and imputed costs. These interim values are derived from standard manufacturing costs with cash discounts and rebates because the actual data are not available at the time the billing document has to be issued.

When the actual data arrive, the interim reports are usually reconciled with them on a period basis to yield the Cost of Sales Accounting Using Actual Costs (reconciled reports). Because of the lag in time, these reports are not so useful for managing the sales activities; their function is more to document and summarize.

Fixed Cost Absorption Accounting

Profitability accounting requires that profit and loss be calculated on the basis of both full costs and marginal costs using contribution margin accounting.

The actual costs can be assigned to the business segments en bloc or in proportion to sales. Therefore the fixed costs can be absorbed across several levels of the organization for each period.

When costs are assigned to user-defined business segments, they have usually been gathered from one or more cost centers. However, costs may have been assigned to orders so that they can be collected from the customers; these costs can also be taken into account. Direct costs can be assigned to any level of a business segment.

The SAP R/3 Organizational Structure

The structure of an organization from an accounting point of view has to be formally defined if it is to be used by a computing system. SAP R/3 defines a multilevel structure in terms of nested classifications, which are known collectively as the EDM Enterprise Data Model. The model is outlined below:

- **Client** is a name attached to a data set that cannot overlap any other client data set. For example, TEST and MYCOMPANY, could be clients with separate data sets. SAP R/3 will work with only one client at a time.

- **Company Code** is the identification number of an independent accounting unit that can generate its own financial statements. It is a legal requirement that a group that operates in several countries must establish a separate company code unit for each country.

- **Business Area** is a subdivision of a company code that further subdivides the figures posted to the general ledger of the parent company code, but has to be reconciled with it. The business area is not an independent business unit, although it will manage the transaction information and the financial results shown in the company code balance sheet and the profit and loss statement, insofar as they concern its own business area.

- **Controlling Area** takes into cost accounting both the accounting units, such as company codes and business areas, and the logistics units, such as plant and sales organization. A controlling area may embrace several company codes, providing they all share a common chart of accounts.

- **Operating Concern** is a unit used in CO-PA Profitability Analysis to focus on the market and sales of a business, in order to set off costs against revenue. An operating concern can embrace several controlling areas, provided they all use the same chart of accounts. The operating concern can also be selective in its zone of interest by defining specific segments of the market—in terms, for example, of a product range for a certain customer group in a sales area.

- **Profit Center** is a subsection of the business that is responsible for its own profit or loss. It must be assigned to only one controlling area.

Under the CO-Controlling system, any profit-related activity, such as sales or the internal exchange of goods and services, will be documented in at least one of the controlling cost objects, such as orders, materials, assets and cost centers. Each of these cost objects must be assigned to the corresponding profit center.

In order to calculate a result from profitability analysis, all profit-related activities are copied to CO-PCA Profit Center Accounting, where they can be associated with their profit centers.

The Routes of Control Data Flow

CO-Controlling uses transaction data from the FI-GL General Ledger accounts to maintain its own set of records. Overhead costs are posted to one of the cost centers according to their source of origin. The CO-Controlling system uses additional postings to assign the direct costs to other cost objects, such as orders, processes, other cost objects and business segments.

The overhead costs that have been posted to the cost centers according to their origins are also reassigned by allocation rules to the other assignment objects, according to their usage of the overhead.

CO-Controlling shares out both direct costs and overhead costs among the assignment objects according to their usage, and also allocates the values to other cost objects for the purpose of control and analysis.

Revenue and sales deductions are posted directly to the relevant business segment or profit center. The cost objects either remain in inventory or are posted through to profitability analysis.

You can thus carry out period accounting at profit center level, taking into account changes in inventory. And you can call for cost of sales accounting in each business segment.

CO-Controlling operates a system which is parallel to the FI-Financial Accounting system, but separate from it. You can display a business-oriented profit and loss analysis, because all the data objects that have a bearing on the computation of value added are represented in the analysis and can therefore be scrutinized down to the details of the individual transactions from which the data are drawn. The cost data are allocated according to rules which are under your control—there need be no obscurity in how to interpret the analysis reports.

Customer quotations and sales orders give rise to the information which CO-PA Profitability Analysis needs:

- Billing documents
- Sales quantities
- Revenues
- Sales deductions

Goods that are issued, received or manufactured give rise to the information that goes, for example, into the calculation of:

- Manufacturing costs
- Standard costs
- Moving average price
- Transfer prices

External activities carried out by contractors, for example, are either posted directly to CO-PA Profitability Analysis from FI-Financial Accounting, or they are settled from the orders and projects, which also input to CO-PA Profitability Analysis.

Analysis for separate business segments can be affected, because cost and revenue data can be posted directly to a business segment, just as they can be posted to any cost center. Any of the following systems can carry out direct postings automatically:

- FI-Financial Accounting
- CO-Controlling
- SD-Sales and Distribution

By contrast, a profit center is not a separate account assignment object. The values held by it are derived from the master data assignments of the cost objects in the CO-Controlling system. Posting these values to a profit center occurs automatically in the background under the supervision of the CO-PCA Profit Center Accounting standard business functions.

Revenue Element Accounting

Generally Accepted Accounting Principles (GAAP) require that the values recorded in the accounts of a company shall be in a permanent state of reconciliation. In order to comply with this requirement, an online accounting system has to maintain a journal, a set of account balances and all the documents to support them. SAP R/3 meets these conditions and, in some respects, exceeds them.

In particular, revenue data transferred to CO-PA Profitability Analysis can be reconciled with the posted revenue in FI-Financial Accounting.

The SD-Sales and Distribution system posts revenue data originating in the invoiced sales orders to the relevant FI-GL General Ledger accounts for revenue accounting. These accounts have to be specified in the common chart of accounts belonging to the company code. This chart will define the usual revenue accounts that have been structured to suit the company code, and there will be accounts that contain sales deductions, return deliveries, rebates, credit memos and any other noted financial instruments used by that company code.

To allow reconciliation between the two systems, the revenue elements defined in FI-Financial Accounting must be in accord with the revenue elements used by the CO-PA Profitability Analysis system. This shared set of revenue elements must reflect not only the financial accounting structure of the chart of accounts, but also the structures that have been developed in order to facilitate a sensitive and timely mechanism for cost controlling and profitability analysis.

The billing data from the SD-Sales and Distribution system, or from an individual user interface, have to be directed simultaneously toward two accounting processes:

- FI-Financial Accounting has to identify the destination in terms of the revenue accounts of the chart of accounts.

- CO-PA Profitability Analysis has to identify the destination in terms of the revenue elements of that system, which are usually derived from the revenue account structure that appears in the chart of accounts.

In company codes where the sources of revenue are not readily matched to the revenue elements of the CO-PA Profitability Analysis system, it is usual to use the facilities of the FI-GLX Extended General Ledger to associate the revenue sources with the appropriate items chosen from the lists of origins that are recognized by this component. The additional subdivisions of revenue accounts supported by the FI-GLX Extended General Ledger remain reconciled with the FI-GL General Ledger revenue accounts. The advantage of calling on the extra analysis information available through the FI-GLX Extended General Ledger is that it enables accurate reconciliation with the revenue elements of the CO-PA Profitability Analysis component.

Estimate Revenue Elements

It may well happen that the billing data transferred to CO-PA Profitability Analysis is not accurate. Revenue elements may have to be estimated. For example, a sales deduction could be estimated as, say, 10 percent of domestic sales revenue on the grounds that previous analysis would support this as a reasonable prediction.

The benefit is that the CO-PA Profitability Analysis system can provide a complete and up-to-date estimate of gross and net revenues as soon as the billing takes place.

Such estimated sales deductions are usually posted and transferred to FI-Financial Accounting, where they can be balanced with the actual sales deductions when they become available. If necessary, the CO-PA Profitability Analysis system will then adjust the calculation for future estimates.

A typical report structure for an estimated revenue element would include the following display fields:

- Gross revenue

- Freight and packing

- Discount

- Estimate rebate or cash discount

- Estimate warranty

- Net revenue

Calculating Profitability

Profitability is calculated for a business segment. The SAP R/3 system is supplied with a set of criteria from which the definition of a business segment can be assembled. The most commonly used criteria are provided as lists of proposals which may be adopted or ignored when you set up your own CO-PA Profitability Analysis system. You can define unique criteria to suit your own circumstances.

These are some of the ways you can specify how you want to define the business segments to be used in your company code:

■ From the customer masters, define some customer groups on the basis of their shared location, line of business, value of past transactions and so on.

■ From the material masters, define a range of products that will comprise a business segment.

■ From the required business classification code that you have defined for entry on each sales order, select certain values to comprise a business segment.

Data that will be used to specify criteria can be taken from any of the integrated SAP applications. Complex criteria can be built up using the objects that appear only in the CO-Controlling module or only in the CO-PA Profitability Analysis system itself.

Criteria may be combined across dimensions and levels to make a business segment specification that will give you the profitability analysis for exactly what it is that you want to take a look at. For example:

Segment A is defined as any transaction that involves any member of Customer Group CG1 that is in Industry I6 and deals with any product in Product Group P4 and has been authorized by Sales Consultant SC26. And it might be that Sales Consultant SC26 is defined as any member of Department G who has been temporarily assigned to Department S and is working from Office O7.

In summary, a business segment is a portion of your business that you have defined in terms of products, customers, activities and organization, combined in any way you want.

Unlike cost centers and order data structures, for example, the business segments do not have to exist in the form of master records. When a segment is needed, the transaction data is assembled according to the definition of the segment. When a document is automatically transferred from another integrated application, SD-Sales and Distribution, for example, all the information about the customer and the products that is needed to meet the criteria for the business segments is copied from the relevant customer and product master records to the sales order or the billing document. When this data is transferred to the CO-PA Profitability Analysis system, the remaining criteria for building the business segment are applied to determine where the item is posted in the CO-PA Profitability Analysis system.

Manual entry of line items is supported, together with the use of planned values. In these circumstances, the CO-PA Profitability Analysis system will derive the information necessary to place the entries or planning date in the appropriate business segments.

A business segment is an account assignment object to which an entry may be posted, provided all the segment criteria are met by valid data in the entry. This proviso ensures that subsequent analysis will be possible, using different subselections from the business segment criteria if necessary.

Key Figures

The R/3 CO-PA Profitability Analysis system uses the concept of key figures to define the lowest level at which it is possible to display the quantities, revenue, sales deductions and costs when you are carrying out a contribution margin calculation for a business segment. The system will offer lists of commonly used key figures as proposals for you to adopt or supplement by key figures of your own specification.

These key figures can be set at any level of detail. Revenue, for example, could be displayed across a revenue element structure comprising revenue from external customers and from partner companies. Revenue alterations, such as credit memos and rebates, and sales deductions can be displayed as separate revenue elements.

Costs are stored as value fields, the details depending on the specific SAP R/3 applications which have been installed and configured. For example, the following costs could be displayed in the CO-PA Profitability Analysis system:

- From CO-PC Product Cost Accounting, the manufacturing costs from product cost estimates

- From CO-OPA Order and Project Accounting, the manufacturing costs, or the cost of the goods sold as documented on sales orders

- From CO-OPA Order and Project Accounting or from the SAP R/3 PS-Project System, the manufacturing costs or the cost of purchases, as documented by projects

- From CO-OPA Order and Project Accounting, or from the SAP R/3 PS-Project System, the costs of overhead projects or orders

- From PP-Production Planning, the variances from production orders

- From CO-CCA Cost Center Accounting, the fixed costs

- From CO-CCA Cost Center Accounting, the variances

- From FI-Financial Accounting, the direct postings

- From CO-PA Profitability Analysis, the estimated costs

Sales, Revenue, and Profit Planning

The planning of sales quantities, revenue and profit in the context of corporate planning is the exclusive province of the SAP R/3 CO-PA Profitability Analysis system. The business segment is the focus of this planning.

The possibilities of business segment planning include the following:

- Planning the sales quantity for a business segment

- Using the planned sales quantity and the values available to the system for revenue, discounts, rebates and so on to compute the planned gross revenue and planned net revenue

- Transferring the planned costs, such as manufacturing cost and cost center overheads, from the CO-Controlling system, and calculating the planned profit for a business segment

- Planning all fixed cost allocations at different levels of the segment

The CO-PA Profitability Analysis system allows you to plan sales quantity data for any number of business segments, defined as you wish. So there is no need to specify a permanent level at which planned values and quantities will be entered. Each business can operate sales and profit planning in the most informative way. And the SAP R/3 graphical interface is available to assist you.

CO-PCA Profit Center Accounting

A profit center is not an independent account assignment object. It derives its information from existing account assignment objects. The master record of each account assignment object includes a field that identifies the responsible profit center. The profit center is defined by an organizational master record in the system, and can therefore store descriptive information, in particular, the criteria that define which account assignment objects it is responsible for.

Profit centers can be summarized and their results combined on any number of hierarchical levels and across different hierarchies.

The profit center is a way of looking at a particular selection of transaction data assigned to various accounts to see how it affects the operating profit of that portion of the business the profit center represents.

Ledger-Based Period Accounting at the Profit Center Level

Profit centers allow you to collate all profit-related posting information under the divisions of your organizational structure.

Every posting is saved simultaneously as a line item and totals are recorded in the FI-GLX Financial Accounting Extended General Ledger.

As a consequence, CO-PCA Profit Center Accounting is functionally separate from the cost-of-sales accounting used in CO-PA Profitability Analysis.

When you place an original account assignment object in the domain of a profit center, you are setting up separate data flows under control of the posting rules that will be obeyed by the CO-PCA Profit Center Accounting system. Transaction data are transferred in real time. When it comes into existence in the FI-Financial Accounting system, the

CO-Controlling system will set up a copy in parallel, and the CO-PCA Profit Center Accounting system will reflect this copy.

Primary cost information will be reflected from:

- Cost centers
- Orders
- Projects
- Product planning orders

Secondary costs may be reflected in profit centers as a result of:

- Cost allocation
- Cost assessment
- Cost distribution
- Transfer postings
- Order settlement
- Accruals
- Surcharges

Revenues can appear in profit centers as the result of:

- Direct account assignment from FI-Financial Accounting
- Billing documents via the interface with SD-Sales and Distribution

Values attributable to changes in inventory and work in process can also be reflected in profit centers.

The Structure of a Ledger-Based Period Accounting Profitability Report. The line item of a period accounting profitability report represents an FI-GL General Ledger account number and its name. The line items can be selected and organized by hierarchies of profit centers.

There is continuous reconciliation at the company code level between the FI-Financial Accounting system and the CO-PCA Profit Center Accounting system. Thus the inputs to each profit center can be any combination of the following sources of information:

- Customer orders and projects
- Cost objects
- Fixed assets
- Materials management
- Internal orders and projects

- Manufacturing orders

- Cost centers

Transaction data from any external system or SAP application integrated with the R/3 system.

The benefits of this integrated system include the following insights:

- The flow of the value of goods from one profit center to another is displayed, having eliminated internal transactions.

- The profitability report reveals the origins of all profit-relevant data.

From Here...

- The SAP R/3 PS-Project System is a system specialized in the definition and management of complex projects where the planning of cost flows is as complicated as the network of activities that forms the basic instrument of financial analysis.

- Human Resources is one of the valuable and valued elements of corporate endeavor. The SAP R/3 system not only supports the most detailed recording and analysis of personnel costs, it also provides an online system of finding the right people for the job positions, either from the staff in the building at the time, or by looking ahead to the possibilities of bottlenecks, and initiating recruiting if necessary.

- The cost controlling system uses the FI-GLX Extended General Ledger to maintain accounts that are essentially statistical rather than financial. You may like to refresh your understanding of the ways in which a modern integrated system of standard business programs can be organized to yield the all-important profit and loss statement from the balance sheet data. The section on the SAP FI-Financial Accounting module is relevant.

- If the high cost of materials and the complexities of keeping track of them in multifarious manifestations are what you see as the realm where the really big improvements in productivity are to be engendered, then perhaps the MM-Materials Management module will be the next object of your attention.

Chapter 14

Understanding the Enterprise Controlling Module

The essence of enterprise controlling is the translation of management objectives into planned target performances, usually expressed as monetary values, for the parts of the enterprise. These planned values are frequently compared with the actual, and steps taken to adjust the plan for the next period and the resources allocated to achieve it.

The basis of this endeavor has got to be reliable and timely information. The realm of the enterprise controller has to include the business data processing system. In terms of the SAP R/3 system, the data of interest reside, at least conceptually, in the Open Information Warehouse—discussed in Chapter 10, "The Open Information Warehouse and Enterprise Data Models"—along with the EDM-Enterprise Data Model that will help make business sense of the stored information.

The SAP product at the center of Enterprise Controlling is the SAP-EIS Executive Information System.

This chapter will identify some of the constituent functions:

- How big the enterprise is.

- What control means.

- The market forces could control the enterprise.

- This chapter can make you a better enterprise controller.

The SAP-EIS Executive Information System

The purpose of the SAP-EIS Executive Information System is to provide flexible access to the Open Information Warehouse for the purpose of reporting on the following matters of concern to the enterprise controller:

- The financial status of the company

- The results of corporate planning and controlling

- Investment in the resources of the company

- Maintenance of the assets of the company

- Acquisition and development of the company's human resources

- Market factors related to decision-making, including supply markets, market segment performance, competitor performance

■ Structural factors in the business processes, such as production structure, cost structure, financial accounting structure, profitability analysis procedures

The originating sources for the data needed for this type of reporting are necessarily located both within the company and in the external environment. For example, the performance of the various markets and the competitors in them will need subtle data collection if the results are to be meaningful to the enterprise controller.

By design, the data generated by the SAP systems in the company will always be available in a form that can be immediately processed and interpreted in terms of the EDM-Enterprise Data Model of the company and its various views.

Each of the SAP R/3 system applications has a suite of information system functions that can be integrated to provide the necessary flow of data about the internal systems of the company and, to a certain extent, about some of the market factors.

Each of the R/3 applications that has been installed and configured in your installation will be set up to provide information for the SAP-EIS. The enterprise controllers will be able to operate the "drill-down" procedure on any item appearing on their user interface screens. This will allow them to work down the hierarchy of data objects until they have reached the individual item of interest, or until they have called functions to collate the data in summary form.

The SAP-EIS also includes the ability to report on exceptions. This allows the enterprise controller to define just what trends or specific values shall be used as indices of the health of the enterprise. Acceptable ranges of these indicator variables can be defined so that the EIS will report only when the specified indicator is found to be out of the acceptable range. Calculations of any complexity can be undertaken automatically by the system in order to arrive at a value which will be indicative of the enterprise parameter that has been selected as one of the indices for exception reporting to the enterprise controller.

LO-LIS Logistics Information System
The integrated logistics module is essentially focused on managing production from purchasing through to sales and distribution. It will embrace many of the profit-generating activities of your company and therefore be of vital interest to the enterprise controllers.

The LO-LIS Logistics Information System includes components that collate information from each of the applications that are installed in your implementation, such as SD-Sales and Distribution, PP-Production Planning, MM-Materials Management, PM-Plant Maintenance, QM-Quality Management.

FIS-Financial Information System
The scope of the FIS-Financial Information System includes information on customers and vendors, including prospects and alternative suppliers.

HRIS-Human Resources Information System

The Human Resources Information System is able to maintain detailed information on the skills and qualifications not only of the people currently on the payroll, but also of those who have left and might be considered for re-employment. Furthermore, the system is able to maintain personnel profiles for all the work positions in the company using the same system of classification as is used to record the capabilities of staff.

As training takes place, and work experience accumulates, so the value to the company of its human resource assets is increased, and this is information which is recorded in the Human Resources Information System.

This information is available at any moment to the enterprise controller. If part of the enterprise is being controlled automatically—the assignment of sales representatives to callers, for example—the system can determine which members of staff are available at that moment, and the call can be routed to whichever one of them is best qualified to take it.

The same logical approach to the distribution of enterprise controlling is ready to be applied at many levels and aspects of the business of your company. If the information in the system is complete and accurate, and if there is a good set of rules that can be applied to it to arrive at a valid decision, there may well be a good case for having the system carry out the decision-taking process automatically. Depending on the importance of the decision, you may decide to have the system merely propose a course of action for the approval of a human decision-taker. On the other hand, you may wish to take advantage of the speed and timeliness offered by the system, and rely on an automatic logging of the events and perhaps a scheduled report to keep you aware of what enterprise controlling decisions are being automatically taken on your behalf by the system.

Standard Business Management Programs

Most of the components of the financial and controlling modules needed for enterprise controlling are normally integrated in a SAP R/3 system, and their functionality therefore will be part of the SAP-EIS Executive Information System and available to the EC-Enterprise Controller.

The following standard components are obviously relevant:

- EC-BP   Business Planning
- EC-MC   Management Consolidation
- EC-PCA   Profit Center Accounting

The following components are in the process of being established as extended facilities available to the EC-Enterprise Controller:

- Strategic Planning
- Budget Management
- Function-Oriented Cost Accounting

Additional Components for Enterprise Controlling

The wide variety of enterprises using the SAP R/3 system has demonstrated how versatile it can be. In particular, the relative importance of the different types of business accounting will not be the same for each enterprise. Different combinations of the following components from the CO-Controlling module can be configured in support of the EC-Enterprise Controlling module:

- CO-CCA   Cost Center Accounting
- CO-OPA   Order and Project Accounting
- CO-PC   Product Cost Accounting
- CO-PA   Profitability Analysis

CO-CCA Cost Center Accounting

The distribution method of CO-CCA is totally flexible and under your control. You can simulate distribution to test out the effects of the rules before you post the values; the effects of a distribution can be seen immediately by calling for an online report; and you can repeat the distribution procedures at any time.

CO-OPA Order and Project Accounting

The distinguishing feature of the SAP module CO-OPA Order and Project Accounting is its ability to settle in detail the actual costs according to rules particular to each item. In addition to this ability to settle capital spending orders in precise detail, the system has the following important capabilities:

- Planning is available for all resources and costs required, in quantity and value.

- Charges can be computed from prices at the time, with imputed allocations of overhead and actual costs.

- Open items for purchase requisitions, purchase orders, and material reservations are closely monitored.

- All cash-related procedures such as down payment requests and down payments are displayed.

- Order reports are evaluated and analyzed concurrently.

Integration of Order and Project Accounting with Asset Accounting. If you are managing fixed assets such as buildings and machines, the settlement of capital spending orders is of crucial importance. The system offers detailed settlement rules and a close integration with the FI-AA Asset Accounting system to yield the following advantages:

- Settlement of costs to the appropriate balance sheet accounts under the heading of Assets Under Construction while the capital spending order is ongoing

- Order-based display of special depreciation for Assets Under Construction

- Recognition of subsidies, grants, down payments
- Partial orders can be settled over a hierarchy of orders.

Because all costs are based on unified posting and settlement rules in the SAP R/3 system, you can allocate costs from orders and projects to the various target objects using the same rules or rules that you have specified separately. You can keep track of complex overhead costs with maintenance and capital spending orders—the chance to take effective action in good time will be yours.

Capital Spending Orders. In the context of a company able to produce some assets and commodities in-house, the main objective of a capital spending order is to monitor the costs of doing so. Maintenance projects can be controlled and accounted in the same way.

Planned Cost Schedules. Costs and deadlines on orders, and projects that take a long time to complete, are constrained by the financial facts of life. Money is not always available when you need it. Financial and liquidity planning needs to know what costs are expected on the orders and projects. It helps to have some idea of how the costs are likely to be incurred over the first few accounting periods in detail and in broader terms thereafter up to the date of completion.

A cost schedule is a plan, extending the length of an order or project, showing the values expected to be allocated to costs. The schedule has a key date. Until this date is known and entered on the plan, the forecast of costs has to be moved ahead to the best estimated date.

The SAP R/3 system provides support to the EC-Enterprise Controller in the following ways:

- The system will automatically determine the tasks from the planned start and finish dates for the order.
- Cost distribution across the schedule can be suited to the specific order.
- Graphical representations of the data model are readily available online and in print.

If you have carried out cost element planning or created a unit costing for the order, the system can use this information to develop a cost schedule.

A costing system uses a set of costing objects, which are the different products, production and other orders, resources, and so on. The only qualification for a costing object is that it can be allocated costs that mean something when they are totaled under the heading of that costing object. The costing objects can be conceptual or tangible, organizational or geographical.

The pivotal concept in costing is the structure of cost drivers, or cost objects on to which the actual costs are settled, according to how they were incurred. SAP R/3 CO-Controlling provides a range of model structures on which you can base a structure specific to the needs of your company.

CO-PC Product Cost Accounting

The purpose of the CO-PC Product Cost Accounting module is to determine the unit cost of whatever product units your company does business in. These units are referred to as cost objects, with one cost object for each product or each distribution package for each product.

SAP is an integrated system. The CO-PC Product Cost Accounting module is directly linked to the results from the Logistics modules and passes data to the SD-Sales and Distribution module for sales orders and to the CO-OPA Order and Project Accounting component and the SAP R/3 Project System for internal cost control.

The CO-PC Product Cost Accounting component addresses the following two types of costing:

- Production Order Costing, in which the costs of producing a batch or run from the production line are computed and associated with the production order that initiated this production run

- Inventory Costing, in which the cost is computed of each item on the inventory of stock and part-finished products

These costing procedures are discussed in Chapter 13, "Understanding the CO-Controlling Module."

Four types of cost object controlling are differentiated because they offer different benefits according to the type of business they are located in, as follows:

- Make-to-Stock Production
- Process Manufacturing
- Make-to-Order Production
- Plant Construction

Costing Requirements of Different Types of Company. Modern controlling methods have developed to support technical manufacturing processes and service industries. The methods have to match the needs of the individual company. The SAP approach is to establish an extensive library of standard business functions that can be controlled by the implementers through the medium of parameters to yield a customized system finely tuned to the requirements of the different classes of user in a specific company.

Manufacturers require a costing system that shows where and by how much their manufacturing processes add value to their raw materials. They differ in their style of manufacturing according to whether they make to a production order, or make to replace stock on their inventory. Their processes differ over the range from discrete one-off production to repetitive production to continuous flow production.

Trading companies need a method of costing to enable them to apply overhead and surcharges to the cost prices of their goods, which they often have to keep to set or agreed final selling prices.

Service companies are tending to adopt the principles of process costing, which revolves round the concept of cost drivers, in this case the service activities. They need to be able to define, measure, plan and pass on the costs incurred by their cost drivers, the service calls and other activities.

Make-to-Order, Make-to-Stock, Continuous Flow. The manufacturing industry has a polished costing method based on routings taken by work units and bills of materials. Manufacturing companies need to know what processes the product has to undergo, the costs of materials and resources, and the quantities. This is referred to as the quantity structure for this product. If you have this information, you can begin to cost the product by assembling the costing components.

The customer order sets off costing in the make-to-order company. As each order is unique, there may be a dearth of routings and bills of materials that can be applied without editing. Yet it is of the utmost importance to be able to arrive quickly at a cost prediction for this one-off product, so as to be able to issue a quotation and take part in competitive tendering for the work. An effective costing system for this sort of company would have to give this approach to one-off tendering a high priority, for on its speed and accuracy all future business may depend.

Those manufacturers who make-to-stock will apply standard bills of materials and routings, about which they may well have copious actual data. Products and orders for quantities of them can be costed from this database.

Where the manufacturing process is continuous, it is probably not amenable to much in the way of variation. It will probably work at its best only if the rate of flow is within narrow limits. Nevertheless, the contribution of the various cost components to the cost of the finished product will not be without interest for the management and shareholders. It will be important to understand how and why costs vary if the flow rate and quality are allowed to move out of the normal operating ranges. This might happen because of variations in the raw materials or in the environmental conditions at the manufacturing plant.

The SAP R/3 Cost Object as an Account Assignment Device. A cost object exists for SAP R/3 if there is a master record for it. The function of a cost object is to control the allocation, analysis and settlement of costs related to the object it represents. It may relate directly to a production unit; it may be an organizational structure component that is useful in reporting value flows. In essence, a cost object is an identification number and a set of master record data fields that can be accessed in connection with that number.

Unit costs of each cost object are the basis for arriving at all costing values. If your installation has other SAP modules installed and configured, you will find it convenient to make use of the cost objects from these applications to define your own unique cost objects by copying some or all of the data structures from these predefined SAP cost objects. For example, these cost object types are used in the following application modules:

- PS-Project System—network, project item

- CO-Controlling—internal order

- SD-Sales and Distribution—sales order

- MM-Materials Management—material number

- PP-Production Planning—production order, routing

- PM-Plant Maintenance—maintenance order

If you have the unit costs for all your cost objects, you can display inventory costs and call for profitability analyses using the full set of fixed and variable costs. You can make use of any combination of the costing systems current in your company.

The CO-PC Product Cost Accounting component of the SAP R/3 system carries the definitions, in the form of master data, for all the cost object controlling functions of the SAP integrated system. Any transaction that bears data relevant to costing will be processed according to these definitions.

Valuation Methods in Product Costing. The following costing systems are available in the CO-PC Product Cost Accounting component of the SAP R/3 system and may be used in any combination:

- Unit costing

- Product costing

- Production order costing

- Cost object controlling for make-to-stock production

- Cost object controlling for process manufacturing

- Cost object controlling for make-to-order production

- Cost object controlling for plant construction

The valuation process extends to the following calculations:

- Planned input quantities with planned allocation rates and planned prices

- Actual input quantities with standard prices and standard activity prices

- Actual input quantities with actual prices and actual activity prices

- Partial or total output quantities

- Scrap quantities

- Order-specific cost settlement according to the quantities delivered

- Calculation of all types of variance

- Profitability analyses

The EC-Enterprise Controlling module can reveal the effects on the financial accounts and year-end closing of using different valuation techniques, and choices can be made on the basis of correct information.

CO-PA Profitability Analysis

CO-PCA Profit Center Accounting is closely associated with CO-PA Profitability Analysis. There is an important distinction to be made between the following aspects of profitability analysis:

- Periodic analysis of the profit and loss made by the strategic units, or by the entire company, is usually referred to as Profitability Analysis.

- Cost of Sales Accounting is also a form of profitability analysis, which is used in the management of market-oriented activities.

They both call on the same costing information, but treat it in different ways. Sales managers need to be able to estimate profits in the short term by using interim reports based on standard values and imputed costs derived from standard manufacturing costs with cash discounts and rebates, because the actual data is not available at the time the billing document has to be issued. Periodic profitability analysis can wait for the actual cost values to be collected and collated.

The CO-PA Profitability Analysis component is designed to make available the full range of analyses covering the following requirements:

- Current sales data valued with standard costs and prices at the level of the individual product and for individual customers

- Calculation of actual cost variances for summarized business segments on a periodic basis

- Proportional assignment of fixed costs in order to measure net profit at the divisional level

- Application of period profit center accounting in situations where there are large fluctuations in stock levels

Questions for the Enterprise Controller

What is the relationship between gross sales and net sales revenue?

How were the sales deductions calculated for each market segment?

What was the profit on this specific order?

Which products or market segments are showing the greatest increases in sales revenue?

Which products or market segments are making the highest contribution margin?

What are the shifts, if any, between the main business segments?

What are the planned contribution margins for each product?

Cost of Sales Accounting Using Standard Costs (Interim Reports)

The Cost of Sales Accounting method using standard costs to produce interim reports allows you to look at any market segment immediately, without waiting for the actual data to arrive.

The market-driven needs of sales management dictate the requirement to be able to estimate profits in the short term by using interim reports based on standard values and imputed costs. These interim values are derived from standard manufacturing costs with cash discounts and rebates, because the actual data is not available at the time the billing document has to be issued.

When the actual data arrives, the interim reports are usually reconciled with it on a period basis to yield the Cost of Sales Accounting Using Actual Costs (reconciled reports). Because of the lag in time, these reports are not so useful for managing the sales activities; their function is more to document and summarize.

The Company Organizational Structure

The structure of an organization from an accounting point of view has to be formally defined if it is to be used by a computing system. SAP R/3 defines a multilevel structure in terms of nested classifications which are known collectively as the EDM Enterprise Data Model. The model is outlined as follows:

- **Client**—a name attached to a data set which cannot overlap any other client data set. SAP R/3 will work with only one client at a time.

- **Company Code**—the identification number of an independent accounting unit that can generate its own financial statements. It is a legal requirement that a group that operates in several countries must establish a separate company code unit for each country.

- **Business Area**—a subdivision of a company code that further subdivides the figures posted to the general ledger of the parent company code but has to be reconciled with it. The business area is not an independent business unit, although it will manage the transaction information and the financial results shown in the company code balance sheet and profit and loss statement insofar as they concern its own business area.

- **Controlling Area**—takes into cost accounting both the accounting units, such as company codes and business areas, and the logistics units, such as plant and sales organization. A controlling area may embrace several company codes providing they all share a common chart of accounts.

- **Operating Concern**—a unit used in CO-PA Profitability Analysis to focus on the market and sales of a business so as to be able to set off costs against revenue. An operating concern can embrace several controlling areas, provided they all use the same chart of accounts. The operating concern can also be selective in its zone of interest by defining specific segments of the market, in terms, for example, of a product range, in a sales area, for a certain customer group.

- **Profit Center**—a subsection of the business that is responsible for its own profit or loss. It must be assigned to only one controlling area.

Under the CO-Controlling system, any profit-related activity, such as sales or the internal exchange of goods and services, will be documented in at least one of the controlling cost objects, such as orders, materials, assets, and cost centers. Each of these cost objects must be assigned to the corresponding profit center.

In order to calculate a result from profitability analysis, all profit-related activities are copied to CO-PCA Profit Center Accounting, where they can be associated with their profit centers.

Revenue Element Accounting

The Generally Accepted Accounting Principles (GAAP) require that the values recorded in the accounts of a company shall be in a permanent state of reconciliation. In order to comply with this requirement, an online accounting system has to maintain a journal, a set of account balances and all the documents to support them. The SAP R/3 system meets these conditions and, in some respects, exceeds them.

In particular, revenue data transferred to CO-PA Profitability Analysis can be reconciled with the posted revenue in FI-Financial Accounting.

In company codes where the sources of revenue are not readily matched to the revenue elements of the CO-PA Profitability Analysis system, it is usual to use the facilities of the FI-GLX Extended General Ledger to associate the revenue sources with the appropriate items chosen from the lists of origins that are recognized by this component. The additional subdivisions of revenue accounts that are supported by the FI-GLX Extended General Ledger remain reconciled with the FI-GL General Ledger revenue accounts. The advantage of calling on the extra analysis information available through the FI-GLX Extended General Ledger is that it enables accurate reconciliation with the revenue elements of the CO-PA Profitability Analysis component.

Estimating Revenue Elements

It may well happen that the billing data transferred to CO-PA Profitability Analysis is not accurate. Revenue elements may have to be estimated. For example, a sales deduction could be estimated as, say, 10 percent of domestic sales revenue on the grounds that previous analysis would support this as a reasonable prediction.

The benefit is that the CO-PA Profitability Analysis system can provide a complete and up-to-date estimate of gross and net revenues as soon as the billing takes place.

Such estimated sales deductions are usually posted and transferred to FI-Financial Accounting, where they can be balanced with the actual sales deductions when they become available. If necessary, the CO-PA Profitability Analysis system will then adjust the calculation for future estimates.

Calculating Profitability

Profitability is calculated for a business segment. The SAP R/3 system is supplied with a set of criteria from which the definition of a business segment can be assembled. The most commonly used criteria are provided as lists of proposals which can be adopted or ignored when you set up your own CO-PA Profitability Analysis system. You can define fresh criteria to suit your own circumstances.

Sales, Revenue, and Profit Planning

The planning of sales quantities, revenue, and profit in the context of corporate planning is the exclusive province of the SAP R/3 CO-PA Profitability Analysis system. The business segment is the focus of this planning.

The possibilities of business segment planning include the following:

- Plan the sales quantity for a business segment.

- Use the planned sales quantity and the values available to the system for revenue, discounts, rebates and so on to compute the planned gross revenue and the planned net revenue.

- Transfer the planned costs, such as manufacturing cost and cost center overheads, from the CO-Controlling system, and calculate the planned profit for a business segment.

- Plan all fixed cost allocations at different levels of the segment.

The CO-PA Profitability Analysis system allows you to plan sales quantity data for any number of business segments, defined as you wish. So there is no need to specify a corporate level at which planned values and quantities will be entered. Each business can operate sales and profit planning in the most informative way. And the SAP R/3 graphical interface is available to assist.

EC-PCA Profit Center Accounting

A profit center is not an independent account assignment object. It derives its information from existing account assignment objects. The master record of each account assignment object includes a field which identifies the responsible profit center. The profit center is defined by an organizational master record in the system and therefore can store descriptive information, in particular, the criteria that defines which account assignment objects it is responsible for.

Profit centers can be summarized and their results combined on any number of hierarchical levels and across different hierarchies.

The profit center is a way of looking at a particular selection of transaction data assigned to various accounts to see how they affect the operating profit of that portion of the business the profit center represents.

Ledger-Based Period Accounting at the Profit Center Level

Profit centers allow you to collate all profit-related posting information under the divisions of your organizational structure. Every posting is saved simultaneously as a line item and a totals record in the FI-GLX Extended General Ledger.

As a consequence, CO-PCA Profit Center Accounting is functionally separated from the cost-of-sales accounting used in CO-PA Profitability Analysis.

Revenues can appear in profit centers as the result of the following:

- Direct account assignment from FI-Financial Accounting
- Billing documents via the interface with SD-Sales and Distribution

Values attributable to changes in inventory and work in process can also be reflected in profit centers.

The Structure of a Ledger-Based Period Accounting Profitability Report. The line item of a period accounting profitability report represents an FI-GL General Ledger account number and its name. The line items can be selected and organized by hierarchies of profit centers.

There is continuous reconciliation at the company code level between the FI-Financial Accounting system and the CO-PCA Profit Center Accounting system.

Thus the inputs to each profit center can be any combination of the following sources of information:

- Customer orders and projects
- Cost objects
- Fixed assets
- Materials management
- Internal orders and projects
- Manufacturing orders
- Cost centers
- Transaction data from the FI-Financial Accounting, Logistics and external systems

The benefits of this integrated system include the following:

- The flow of the value of goods from one profit center to another is displayed, having eliminated internal transactions.
- The profitability report reveals the origins of all profit-relevant data.

From Here...

The EC-Enterprise Controlling module serves to integrate the information derived from the various applications installed in your implementation or associated with it in the role of satellite systems. The EC module also includes components to provide more sophisticated analytical and reporting services.

- I need more detail.

  See Chapter 13, "Understanding the CO-Controlling Module."

- My enterprise controller would be more interested in managing financial investments.

  Try turning to Chapter 15, "Understanding the TR-Treasury Management Module."

- It is the people that need to be controlled, not the enterprise.

  You may find it interesting to see how carefully SAP tries to put the right people in the right jobs. Chapter 22, "Understanding the HR-Human Resources Module," is illuminating.

Chapter 15

Understanding the TR-Treasury Management Module

The scope of TR-Treasury includes liquidity, market risk, planning, and portfolio management. The areas of application include all businesses that care about their cash flow and assets. The TR-TM Treasury Management component is shared with the IM-Capital Investment Management module which is also discussed in this chapter.

The Association of TR-Treasury and IM-Capital Investment Management

The Treasury is that part of your organization concerned with medium and long-term financial planning, together with the medium-term management and control of revenues and expenditures. The focus is on the financial state of the company in the future.

These objectives can be met to some degree by using the FI-Financial Accounting module: but the TR-Treasury module provides some enhanced functions additional to FI-IM—Investment Management and FI-AM—Fixed Assets Management.

As of R/3 Release 3.0, the long-term financial management functions are available in two separate but overlapping modules which can be installed independently of each other:

- TR-Treasury

- IM-Capital Investment Management

Individual components from these modules can be installed and configured to integrate with the FI-Financial Accounting module. They are also available in the form of integrated enhancements of the R/3 designed for specific sectors of business and industry and presented with an IS prefix to designate an Industry Solution.

In this chapter, you learn:

- How liquidity is monitored.

  By the TR-CM Cash Management component.

- Whether you can call on the components of the IM-Capital Investment Management module to reduce the element of chance.

- How the Treasury looks after the land and the plant.

IV

Steering

The TR-Treasury Module

The TR-Treasury module comprises the following components:

- TR-CM Cash Management
- TR-FM Funds Management
- TR-TM Treasury Management

The IM-Investment Management module includes the following components:

- IM-FA Tangible Fixed Assets
- IM-FI Financial Investments

The TR and IM modules overlap because the functions of IM-FI Financial Investments are the same as those of TR-TM Treasury Management.

The purpose of the TR-Treasury module is to integrate cash management and cash forecasting with the logistics activities in your company and with financial transactions. For example, TR enables you to apply cash budgeting tools and commitment accounting methods that take into consideration the allocation of responsibilities. These methods also take into consideration the current budget positions and the sources of the relevant funds to allow very subtle monitoring and control.

The TR as of Release 3.0 includes tools to analyze money market, securities, and derivatives. The functions also presented as the SAP Foreign Exchange Management component are included in TR-Treasury to enable the analysis of foreign exchange risk online with electronic banking features to enhance the integration with FI-GL General Ledger and FI-AR Accounts Receivable components.

TR-CM Cash Management

The day-to-day management of short-term and long-term cash flows is integrated with the CO-Controlling module and its planning capabilities to allow you to ensure that fund reservations are not likely to compromise future liquidity.

Electronic banking functions are associated with payment advice note processing to allow you to make provision for automatic adjustment of standard or your own interpretation algorithms for clearing payments. You can also carry out a post-processing transaction to gain access to line items that could not be posted automatically.

TR-FM Funds Management

At the center of the TR-FM Funds Management component is the twin concept of budget objects and budget commitment funds centers. The structured budget data objects can be maintained and assigned to the budget commitment funds centers to provide a flexible system which can display clearly the way in which budgets are allocated to the hierarchy.

The allocation of budgets can be carried out from the bottom up so that subordinate items can be committed, even if the higher-level budgets have not been allocated.

Different versions of budgets can be maintained separately and different sources of funds can be designated for each financial management area.

TR-TM Treasury Management

The treasury management component is designed to support business transactions from the trading stage to the back-office processing and then to their eventual posting in the financial accounting system.

The scope of TR-TM includes the following types of activity:

- Short-term cash management

- Long-term cash management

- Long-term financial budgeting

- Money market dealings

- Foreign exchange dealings, including spot dealing, forward exchange, and swap dealing

- Derivative financial instruments, including hedging transactions, swaps, caps, floors, options, and futures

- Securities management, including buying and selling, maintaining deposits and portfolios, acquiring and exercising conversion, and subscription and option rights

- Loan management, including fixed-term and at-notice deposits and loans, both loans granted and loans obtained

- Collateral security management, including encumbrances on real estate and guarantees

Functionality. The displays and functions provided by the component include the following:

- Up-to-the-minute liquidity, currency, and risk position data for your company and its assets

- Portfolio updatings and valuations

- Option prices

- Cross rates

- Transaction data monitoring

- What-if scenario simulations in association with IS-IS, the SAP Industry Solution for insurance companies

Risk management functions include monitoring of changes in market prices, interest rates, and exchange rates.

Shared Functions and Tools. The central functions and tools which can be accessed from all TR-TM components include the following:

- Partner and address administration
- Investment mathematics
- Flexible instrument generator
- Status-controlled transaction processing
- Correspondence processing
- Limit monitoring
- Real-time reporting

Integration with the SAP Industry Solution for Insurance

This application is integrated with the Industry Solution for Insurance and Real Estate management, IS-IS, through which it is able to support the following functional areas:

- Extended management of loans
- Extended treasury management
- Real estate management
- Premium reserve funds and statutory reporting for insurance companies

Integration with the SAP Industry Solution for Banks

The TR-TM application is also integrated with the Industry Solution for Banks, IS-B, through which it is able to support the following functional areas:

- Back office data pooling
- Single transaction costing
- Bank profitability analysis
- Risk management
- Statutory reporting

IM-FA Tangible Fixed Assets

The purpose of the IM-FA Tangible Fixed Assets component is to perform analysis of capital investments and support their management.

The principal functions of the component are as follows:

- Preinvestment analysis
- Capital investment master data, planning, budgeting, and allocation
- Measurement of capital investment performance and integration with the CO-Controlling module CO-OPA Order and Project Accounting component

- Valuation and settlement

- Depreciation simulation

- Asset controlling

- Information system and connection to the EIS-Executive Information System

This component shares functionality with the FI-AM Asset Management component.

IM-FI Financial Investments

This component carries out the functions of TR-TM Treasury Management.

From Here...

This chapter has demonstrated how individual functions within components can be integrated and enhanced to create higher-level management systems. Treasury and Capital Investments were the two modules that illustrated this development.

- Where can I learn more about the financial functions?

   From Chapter 12, "Understanding the FI-Financial Management Module."

- Manufacturing continuously is what my company does.

   The manufacturing applications are mentioned at some length in Chapter 17, "Understanding the PP-Production Planning and Control Module," and in Chapter 18, "Understanding the PP-PI Production Planning for Process Industries Modules."

- The really critical areas in my company are the costs of materials and the costs of maintaining the building and equipment.

   See Chapter 19, "Understanding the PM-Plant Maintenance Module," and Chapter 23, "Understanding the MM-Materials Management Module."

- What about the skill of the work-people?

   Try Chapter 22, "Understanding the HR-Human Resources Module."

Chapter 16

Understanding the PS-Project System Module

The purpose of the R/3 PS-Project System module is to manage efficiently the stages of a project from planning to completion. The system is fully integrated with all other SAP modules. Four types of projects have contributed to the definition of what functionality is required of a project system that is not to be specific to any one industry or field of business:

- Research and development
- Engineer-to-order development
- Investment programs
- Data processing projects

Each project proceeds along a trajectory, a path of activities that consume resources, until the purpose of the project is achieved and reported. At each stage are SAP R/3 standard business functions organized in support by the R/3 PS Project System.

Setting the Project Trajectory

Although some of the stages of a project may be abbreviated, and some extended, according to the nature and complexity of the endeavor, it is usually possible to discern the following groups of tasks, especially if the R/3 PS Project System is at work:

- Rough-cut planning with times and values set against a work breakdown structure or at least a listing of what has to be done

- Fine planning which may utilize cost element planning or unit costing methods and entail the manual entry of critical dates, detailing of activities, automatic R/3 scheduling and highlighting of critical activities

- Coordination of resources through automatic purchase requisitions and materials reservation plans, inventory management, network planning of people, capacities, materials, operating resources, and services

- Monitoring of materials, capacities, and funds as the project is approved and executed using budget management of approved and released project budgets, funds commitments and assignment to projects, checking availability of funds, materials and capacities with an overrun alarm to the project manager

- Project closing with results analysis and settlement

Understanding the SAP Enterprise Data Model

The R/3 Basis system is provided with a comprehensive suite of data structures on which it is possible to map in detail the structure of your company, no matter what business or industry you operate in and no matter how individual your organizational structure.

To help you become aware of the data architecture of the R/3 system, an information model is provided showing the information objects of all the integrated application software. This is discussed in Chapter 5, "The R/3 Reference Model." This model not only shows you what data objects are available in the R/3 system, it also reveals clearly how these data objects relate to each other. You will see how your specific business can be accurately represented in the R/3 data objects. If you choose to make a decision on which functions are going to be required, the R/3 Basis system will annotate a copy of the reference model so that you may see what you have selected. This copy is then referred to as the EDM-Enterprise Data Model of your implementation and will be the principal instrument for controlling how your system will be built. And when you have identified the processes and business control instruments of your company in the Reference Model, you may be certain that they will be fully integrated when the time comes to run the finished system.

Understanding the R/3 Standard Project System

The PS-Project System is delivered ready to be configured and customized to fit your particular situation. There is an implementation guide (IMG), which introduces the business functions and a customizing menu to access the standard settings and technical recommendations. You can set up the R/3 PS-Project System in the IMG-Implementation Guide itself.

The R/3 PS Project System makes extensive use of the SAP Enterprise Data Model to support you in the definition and management of your projects. For example, the standard organizational structures in the FI-Financial Accounting module have a strict logical form. "Client" in a SAP system refers to the highest level of the organizational structure. The owner of the entire corporation is identified as the Client and assigned a Client code such as 000. Client 001 will probably be a client created for testing purposes. The data associated with one client cannot be transferred to the records of another.

Although the R/3 Reference Model contains only one definitive example of each data structure, a particular company may build any number of replications into its EDM-Enterprise Data Model so as to represent all the working elements that exist.

Logistics organizational structures, for example, follow strict logical definitions. The modules in the logistics group are as follows:

- SD-Sales and Distribution
- PP-Production Planning
- MM-Materials Management
- PM-Plant Maintenance
- QM-Quality Management

Because all applications are integrated with the FI-Financial Accounting module, the logistics structures have to map on to the financial structures. The financial statements have to be prepared up to the client level. In the applications modules, the data structures have to extend to a great depth of detail so as to encompass the operational entities that add value to the business through the activities in which they engage. If managers care about it, then the system will have a place for it.

A client can have any number of:

- Controlling areas
- Business areas

A controlling area can have any number of:

- Profit centers
- Cost centers
- Company codes, which is how subsidiary companies are identified

A company code can have any number of:

- Purchasing organizations
- Plants

A purchasing organization can have any number of:

- Purchasing groups

A plant can have any number of:

- Functional locations or pieces of equipment
- Storage locations
- Work centers

A work center can have any number of:

- Activities
- Machines
- Persons

A project can be concerned with any combination of entities in the company: It may even cover the entire corporation from the client level downward.

Assigning Organizational Structures in the PS-Project System

The project system itself illustrates how the data objects of the R/3 system are used to monitor and control the costs and revenues of the work done in your company. Each element points to the organizational unit that is responsible and which will be represented by a data object. And these data objects can attract not only the costs and revenues information, but also any technical information that is relevant to the operations of the accounting system or the other functions of your company.

This illustration of the relationships between project elements and organizational entities is an example of the application of the SAP Enterprise Data Model and could be a model for part or all of the activities of your company.

The master data records used by the PS-Project System are formally structured. Thus a "project" is represented by a master record that has a predefined structure of data fields. One of these fields contains the unique identification code of the project which is then associated with all the elements attached to this data structure, such as work breakdown structure elements, profit centers, and so on.

A project has:

- One project definition

- One or more work breakdown structure elements

- One or more networks or subnetworks

A project definition has:

- One project identification

- One or more controlling areas

- One or more company codes

- One or more cost centers

A work breakdown structure element has:

- One or more profit centers

- One or more business areas

- One or more cost centers

- One or more plants

- One or more activities

- One or more functional locations or pieces of equipment

A network has:

- One or more profit centers
- One or more business areas
- One or more plants
- One or more activities

An activity has:

- One or more activity types
- One or more material components

An activity type is one of the following:

- An activity processed internally at a specified work center
- An activity processed externally, via a purchasing organization and a purchasing group
- A general costs activity assigned to a company code

A material component has:

- A purchasing organization
- A purchasing group
- A plant
- A storage location

Setting the Project Definition

The project definition is a data object requiring certain fields to contain valid entries, to relate it to the company organization, for instance. It also includes text to describe the project goals or mission. You may also add a reference to the settlement rule that will cover all the objects in the project.

It is not necessary to define any activities or networks in order to establish a project definition: these can be added later.

Assigning the Work Breakdown Structure

The work breakdown structure (WBS) can be used to track costs incurred in an activity network. It comprises a hierarchy of tasks and subtasks to any number of levels and may be represented by a tree diagram.

The individual tasks have to be described by a member of the project team by selecting activity types and entering the details so as to generate valid WBS elements. The level of detail can be increased at any stage of a project. The WBS elements must contain all the data necessary to carry out the work of the project, together with the time and costs.

The WBS elements can also be used to plan dates, costs and budget, before and during a project. Each element will be assigned an operative indicator which will determine its properties for the duration of the project:

■ Planning elements for actual costs

■ Account assignment elements to which you want to post costs

■ Billing elements to which you want to post revenues

WBS structures already in existence may be referenced during data entry, as may portions of the hierarchy from other projects

Defining Networks

In general terms, a network is a connected structure of nodes and of links that signify relationships between the nodes, such as "Must be completed before… ." The nodes in a network may also be networks. A subnetwork is part of a network. In the R/3 system, a network is defined formally as an activity-on-node structure containing instructions on how to carry out activities in a specific way, in a specific order, and in a specific time period.

A complex project will use both a work breakdown structure and an activity network. The R/3 Network Library contains neutral network structures for the commonly used processes that may be copied into your project. The network type distinguishes networks by their usage. The network type controls:

■ Costing variants for plan, target, actual costs

■ Order type

■ Number ranges permitted, for example, for activity numbers

■ Open items into which the user may insert information

■ Status profile

■ Authorizations

Understanding Project Time Planning

The R/3 system recognizes the following calendar types, and they can be used in project planning:

■ Gregorian

■ Factory calendars (any number)

■ Work center specific operating calendars, with shifts if appropriate

The following types of dates will be accepted:

■ Basic dates manually entered for the work breakdown structure valid at the time of entry

- Forecast dates entered manually
- Actual dates to show the progress of the project
- System calculated dates created during network scheduling

Planning dates can be entered on the lists and overviews, in the hierarchy display, or in the Gantt chart. Three methods or forms are available for planning:

- Top-down, beginning with the dates for the highest WBS element in the project hierarchy
- Bottom-up, starting with the subordinate WBS elements
- Free, in which you plan without reference to hierarchical dependencies

It is characteristic of the R/3 PS Project System that all possible checking and automatic updating is carried out automatically.

Understanding Project Cost Planning

At the conceptual and rough-cut planning stage the planning of costs will suggest the costs you expect the project to incur. At the approval stage, planning indicates the way ahead for budget allocation. During project execution the role of the planned dates and costs is to monitor variances between planned and actual values.

The system offers the following forms of cost planning:

- Structural planning that is independent of cost elements
- Detailed planning of direct costs by quantity and value
- Detailed planning of secondary costs using planned activity quantity and the standard CO Controlling rate for the sender activity
- Unit costing using data and methods from CO-CEA Cost Element Accounting, and Purchasing in MM Materials Management, if required
- Cost planning in the network in which the network activities are used as cost elements in the unit costing technique

Copying of work breakdown structures and parts of them can be used where projects entail the same processes. Different versions of a project plan can be saved and maintained in parallel, for example, in the best case and the worst case scenarios.

Understanding Capacity Requirement Planning

For internal activities in each work center you define available capacities and specify formulas for calculating them. As you enter the quantity of work to be performed you indicate the required capacity units. This information is used automatically by the system when scheduling capacity requirements.

You plan external activities by referencing a purchasing information record for a contractor which shows the prices and delivery times. The project system will create a purchase requisition automatically from this information, which it will then convert to a purchase order when the activity is released.

Maintaining Documents, Production Resources, and Tools

The project documents may include drawings and technical specifications and other matter from word processing sources. They may be managed along with PRTs, the production resources and tools. Alternatively, documents may be allocated directly to WBS elements from a document management system, even if this is not the one installed in R/3.

The R/3 PS Project System recognizes and maintains three categories of PRTs:

- PRTs with a material master record that are stock items on inventory

- PRTs with a document info record that are part of the R/3 document management system

- PRTs with their own PRT master record that can be allocated in network activities

Document management under R/3 for work breakdown structure elements maintains the following information about each document:

- Storage location of the document such as CAD system, PC file, filing cabinet

- Object status

- Location of the original data

- Person responsible

Availability checks by the R/3 PS Project System cover capacities, materials, production resources, and tools. When you are customizing your R/3 PS Project System, you tell the system whether and how checks are to be made on material availability, and whether scheduled receipts should be scanned or only the on-hand inventory.

A complete workflow for missing parts is provided to manage the shortage through to goods receipt and backorder updating.

The system determines whether each PRT is available according to its status and refers to the PS information system in order to compare the available capacity with the capacity load per work center. It calculates the capacity utilization.

Capacity leveling is available and simulations can be performed to see how the capacity available might be affected by such measures and events as:

- Orders

- Mid-point scheduling

- Rescheduling

- Out-sourcing

- Work center changes

Understanding Project Budgeting

A budget for a project is created when planning has been completed and approval granted. A cost plan is an estimate. A budget is a fixed amount which has to be allocated to the WBS elements, either by adopting the values arrived at by detailed planning, or by distributing the budget manually by entering the values directly into the WBS elements.

Your finance director may not actually release all the funds for your approved budget. The R/3 PS-Project System is being extended to control the release of funds in relation to specific WBS elements.

Changes in a budget can be accommodated by the following instruments, all of which are reversible:

- Supplements that you can process from the top down in the WBS
- Returns of excess funds that you can process from the bottom up in the WBS
- Transfers of funds that you can process from one WBS element with a budget to another, which also has to have a budget although it need not belong to the same project

Developments in Project Budget Management

The following functions are being developed by SAP:

- Logging all budget updates in an approval history
- Copying of a work breakdown structure with its planned values and budgets for the purpose of budgeting a comparable project
- Reassigning individual WBS elements or project branches along with their budget values

Executing a Project

Execution begins with project release. In order for business processes to be assigned to a project, you must signify an account assignment to a network activity or a work breakdown structure element. As the project is executed, funds assignments will arise in the project, appearing in the form of open items and actual values.

Variances will arise between plan and actual values. These require planning updates from you to supply the fresh information that will be used in planning subsequent activities.

Each activity will appear on a completion confirmation slip when it is finished. These will update the capacity load of the work center and record the actual costs. The remaining duration and work to finish the network will also be updated by these confirmations. A confirmation can be canceled.

You will have to enter the following information either manually or automatically into your activity and network completion confirmations:

- Degree of processing
- Work center
- Dates
- Duration
- Forecast values

The network and the work breakdown structure will remain in accord: Changes in one will be reflected in the other.

The system provides for passive funds availability control, which monitors the funds assigned, and active funds availability control, which can stop any funds commitment to prevent it from going into excess. You can influence the configuration of availability control by determining the following:

- Whether funds are checked against the total project budget or the allocation for the current year
- Which activities, such as purchase orders or postings in CO-CEA Cost Element Accounting are to be subject to availability control
- Whether a percentage tolerance and/or an absolute tolerance is to be allowed on an activity
- Which action is to be taken if a tolerance limit for an activity is approached or exceeded, for example, a warning, a message to the project manager, or a rejection of the posting with a "tolerance" error message

Settlement of costs incurred in a project on one or more receivers will be automatically accompanied by corresponding credit postings to the project itself. The costs settled are recorded in the relevant receiver. Debit postings assigned to the project remain on display even after settlement.

The following types of assignment account objects could accept the settlement as receivers:

- Cost center
- Project
- Asset
- General Ledger account
- Business segment

The project or the work breakdown structure element master must include a specification of the settlement rule. This may comprise several distribution rules, each defining the settlement receiver, the distribution of costs, and the settlement type.

The settlement structure determines how the process is controlled. It specifies the settlement cost elements, or the value fields from an operating concern, that are to be assigned to cost elements and cost element groups.

There is a separate structure for use by CO-PA Profitability Analysis, which is known as the PA Settlement Structure.

Differing Project Views

Within an organization, each area will look at a project from a different point of view. Each department needs a different selection of information:

- Sales focuses on the customer order and the sales cycle from inquiry to quotation to sales order, billing, and delivery notes.

- Manufacturing operates with planned orders and production orders in conjunction with bills of materials, plants, work center hierarchies and production schedules.

- Materials Management has to manage vendors and manage inventory.

- Financial Accounting has to ensure cashflow and see that interest is managed properly.

- Cost Accounting will see a project from the point of view of the cost controller.

- Capital Spending depends on planning to be effective, and the project system discipline is central.

- Asset Accounting can be used with capital spending projects to provide accurate forecasting, even before the asset is commissioned.

- Profitability Analysis on a periodic basis is essential for long-term customer projects which need accurate controlling and account balancing.

By virtue of its ability to adopt any or all of these viewpoints, the R/3 PS-Project System is an embodiment of integrated business accounting. Not only can a specific project take advantage of the functions of the separate applications, the PS-Project System itself can also be the main executive controller for the business as a whole.

The PS-IS Information System is an efficient project analysis tool which is undergoing continuous program development in order to increase the depth of its analytical penetration as well as the clarity and pertinence of its presentation methods. The following additional functions are in development to enable you to better assess the progress of a project:

- Portfolio graphics will represent dates and costs of several projects at once.

- Milestone trend analysis will detect and compare schedule deviations and trends.

- Earned value calculation will provide another internal progress check and an activity confirmation for the customer by comparing various methods of measuring earned value during the progress of an activity.

Good business practice is built into the R/3 PS-Project System in a thoroughgoing way.

From Here...

- If your interest is in a software development project, then Chapter 4, "Architecture," will be pertinent.

- The details of project costing are discussed in Chapter 13, "Understanding the CO-Controlling Module."

- The PS-Project System can be applied to investement projects. Chapter 15, "Understanding the TR-Treasury Management Module," points the way to this type of project.

- If you do not expect your requirement to be met by a SAP standard business software component, then Chapter 28, "ABAP/4 Program Development with the R/3 Workbench," may be of interest.

- The R/3 Workflow Management method is an integral part of the SAP integrated business concept. Chapter 30, "R/3 Business Workflow Management," describes this component.

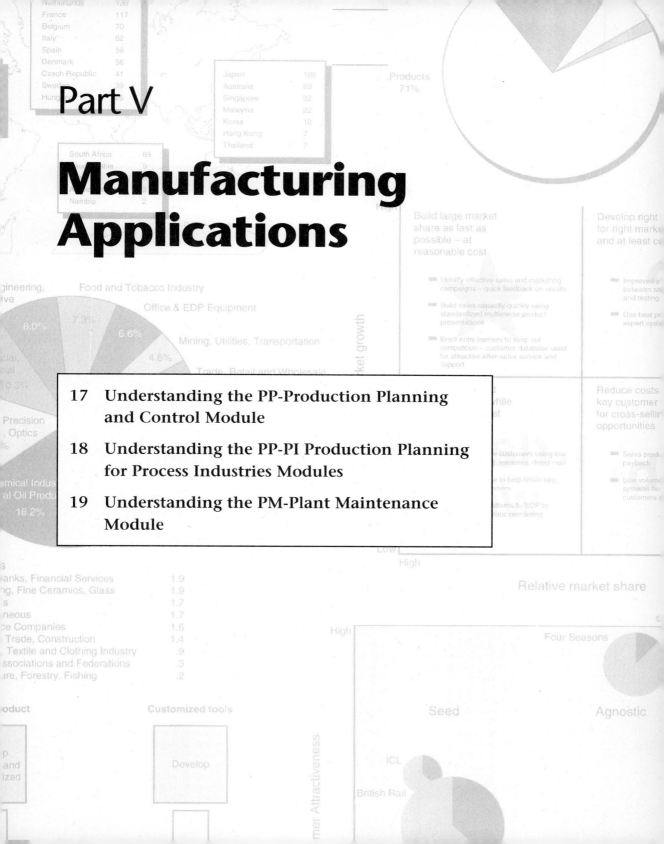

Part V

Manufacturing Applications

Belgium 70
Italy 62
Spain 59
Denmark 56
Czech Republic 41
Sweden 39
Hungary 26

479
54
24
16
14

Japan 100
Australia 68
Singapore 32
Malaysia 22
Korea 10
Hong Kong 7
Thailand 7

South Africa 69
Saudi Arabia 9
Israel 3
Arabic Emirates 2
Nambia 2

Products 71%

Steel,
al Engineering,
tomotive

Food and Tobacco Industry

Office & EDP Equipment

Mining, Utilities, Transportation

Trade, Retail and Wholesale

Traffic and News Communication

Metal Products and Primary Metal

Universities and Technical Colleges

Wood, Paper and Printing Industry

8.0%
7.3%
6.6%
4.6%
4.5%
3.9%
3.8%
3.6%
2.9%

mmercial, nd Social 10.3%

onics, Precision anics, Optics 14.5%

Chemical Industry, Mineral Oil Production 18.2%

Others (see chart below) 11.6%

thers

edit Banks, Financial Services	1.9
uarrying, Fine Ceramics, Glass	1.9
ospitals	1.7
iscellaneous	1.7
surance Companies	1.6
uilding Trade, Construction	1.4
ather, Textile and Clothing Industry	.9
ade Associations and Federations	.3
griculture, Forestry, Fishing	.2

High

Rate of market growth

Build large market share as fast as possible – at reasonable cost

- Identify effective sales and marketing campaigns – quick feedback on results
- Build sales capacity quickly using standardized multimedia product presentations
- Erect entry barriers to keep out competition – customer database used for attractive after-sales service and support

Develop for right and at le

Reduce sales and marketing costs while maintaining market share

- Service low value customers using low cost channels eg. telesales, direct mail
- Contact database to help retain key, high value customers
- Link purchase patterns to SOP to prompt for automatic reordering

Reduce key cust for cross opportun

- Sal pa
- Low sys cus

Low
High

Relative market sha

ble product

Customized tools

Develop plete and ustomized

Develop

Deliver

High

Customer Attractiveness

Four Seasons

Seed

Agnos

ICL

British Rail

Chapter 17

Understanding the PP-Production Planning and Control Module

Scope of the PP-Production Planning Module

Versatility is the distinctive feature of the PP-Production Planning module. It is designed to be used in any sector of industry. The scope of this module includes groups of functions in the following components:

- PP-BD Basic Data for Production
- PP-SOP Sales and Operations Planning
- PP-MP Master Planning
- PP-MRP Material Requirements Planning
- PP-CRP Capacity Requirements Planning
- PP-SFC Production Orders (formerly Shop Floor Control)
- PP-PC Product Costing
- PP-PI Production Planning for the Process Industries. See Chapter 19, "Understanding the PP-PI Production Planning for Process Industries Modules."

Integrated Supply Chain Management

The classical Material Requirements Planning approach (MRP II) takes as its starting point a plan of the operations to be carried out, whether in sales or orders and projects. From this stage, the system offers accepted methods of planning and control of materials through to delivery of the products.

Now that online management of all aspects of business is becoming the norm, and not only in medium-sized and large companies, it has become essential for a company to link the MRP II disciplines to the sales and controlling functions. In the context of the SAP standard business functions and integrated applications, the linking of MRP II and SAP takes place in three stages that are linked seamlessly together:

■ Customer order details are passed automatically to the SD-IS Sales Information System and to the CO-PA Profitability Analysis system.

■ The PP-SOP Sales and Operations Planning system selects the necessary information from the SD-IS Sales Information System and the CO-PA Profitability Analysis component.

■ The sales and operations plan is then passed to the PP-MRP Material Requirements Planning component, which initiates the MRP II Planning Chain that ends with the generation of the necessary order proposals.

When new customer orders arrive, they are offset with the orders previously planned, and the next cycle of the optimized planning run can begin.

The integrated quality control provided by the SAP R/3 QM-Quality Management System is applied to all the operations of the PP-Production Planning and Control module.

PP-BD Basic Data for Production

The objects of interest to production planning are obviously the products and the methods by which they are produced and managed. The SAP R/3 system is designed for medium-sized and large organizations. The same products and production processes might appear in different divisions, therefore the organizational structure must be defined and then referenced in the basic data records for production and production planning.

Organizational Units

The SAP R/3 general organizational units relevant to production planning are taken from the SAP R/3 Enterprise Data Model:

■ **Client** is the highest level in SAP R/3. The data of one client may not interact with another client. There are often a training client and a testing client, in addition to the client code that represents your group or corporate identity and under which the SAP system runs normal business. Some data is managed at the client level because everyone in the corporate group of companies will want to refer to exactly the same information and be certain that it has been maintained as up-to-date and correct. Vendor addresses would be an example of data managed at the client level.

■ **Company Code** signifies a legal unit under the client that produces its own financial documents and the balance sheet and profit and loss statement, and may well maintain them continuously reconciled.

■ **Plant** is an organizational unit that is seen as central to the production planning concept. A plant can be a production site, or it can be a group of storage locations that share materials. Plant is the unit for which MRP prepares plans and maintains the inventory. It is the focus of MM-Materials Management. Each plant will have been given planning and control elements such as material, inventory, operations, work centers, and so on.

Planning can take place across plants. For example, products manufactured in different plants can be combined for planning purposes into a product group. Manufacturing can also take place and be controlled on a cross-plant basis.

The stocks held in individual storage locations within a plant can also be managed separately with respect to inventory, and planned using MRP.

You may have defined other organizational units to suit your own planning and production needs. These user-defined organizational units can be used to focus materials requirements planning:

- **Planning Plant** is the one plant chosen as the central unit when you are engaging in cross-plant material requirements planning.

- **Work Center** is the central planning element to use when you are applying shop floor control and capacity planning. The system will allow you to build work center hierarchies and use them for MRP.

- **Planner Group** is a definition of people who are chosen, not by name necessarily, but by their personnel group, which is assigned by the Human Resources functions. By this means, the members of a planning group can be selected from those who are available on the day they are needed and who have the necessary experience and qualifications. You can define other planning groups. There are three planner groups that are commonly assigned materials, resources and production tools.

- **MRP Controller Group** is an identification for those who are experienced at materials requirements planning.

- **Work Scheduler Group** is an identification of those with experience of the scheduling of work resources including people.

- **Shop Floor Controller Group** is an identification of those who have experience in the detailed management of shop floor personnel and the places where they work.

Material

It is standard throughout the SAP R/3 system to define "material" to include whatever is used in the production process. The following are examples of material in the SAP R/3 system:

- Finished products
- Intermediate assemblies
- Unfinished products
- Raw materials
- Part-processed materials
- Resources such as energy, air, and water

- Packaging
- Services

Materials Data Structure

Two principles apply to the storage of data in the SAP R/3 system:

- Information that is expected to remain constant for a long time is entered in one place only, and any changes to it are logged.

- Information that is local is stored at the level encompassing all the operational units for which it is pertinent but can be made available elsewhere on a flexible basis.

You have the following range of options:

- At the level of the client or the company code, maintain general data valid for the whole organization, for example, material code numbers, multilingual text concerning each material code, and classification rules applicable to material.

- At the plant level, maintain the data for Material Requirements Planning and Production Planning and Control and also valid bills of material and routings.

- Maintain inventories at the level of the individual storage location, of which a plant may have more than one.

- Maintain the sales data at the level of each purchasing organization and distribution channel.

You can define individual access authorizations as create, change, or display only. These can be specific to each user and each organizational level. If you are authorized to create transaction data you can obviously display and change it unless the item is reserved as "read-only." At the intermediate level of authorization comes the permission to alter a record but not generate a new one. For example, a sales representative might be allowed to change the address of a supplier, but not to create new suppliers or delete existing addresses.

Material User Departments

Sections of the information on a material master can be allocated to different user departments, such as the MRP department, the work scheduling department and so on. By doing this, you will be able to give each department access just to the information it needs about a specific material.

Material Types

Material data is maintained centrally. Different views of the master records can be called for by making reference to the material type. For example, you could maintain data for work scheduling in the case of a material of the type "semi-finished goods," but you cannot schedule raw materials.

The material type determines certain other control parameters:

- Which user departments can maintain the data for a material of this type

- Procurement type, which indicates how this material is procured: in-house manufacturing or external procurement

- Type of inventory control to be used, for example, whether by quantity, value, or both

You may create and configure material types to suit your business.

Industry Sectors

If material is used in more than one industry, you may decide to create industry sectors in which the material type is configured in a special way for each sector.

Batches and Special Stock

Batches of a material are managed at the storage location level, but you may wish to differentiate between, for example, special stock and batches:

- A batch is a partial quantity of material. The material in the batch is managed separately on the inventory. It may be a production lot or a delivery lot, for example.

- Special stock may be designated vendor special stock, for example, because it is a consignment from a particular vendor.

- Customer special stock might be the designation of, for example, packaging materials returnable by the customer.

- Activity-related special stock may be identified because it is going to a particular customer on a make-to-order product, for example.

Tools for Processing Materials Data

An existing material master record can be used as a reference when creating a new material master. The data necessary on the user departments of your company can be maintained in the form of user department profiles, which contain no reference to any specific material, but you can reference them when creating a new material master. Each user department can set individual options to control how this data is applied.

Bills of Material

The bill of material (BOM) is an instrument for describing the structure of a product for any of the following types of production:

- Repetitive manufacturing

- Manufacturing products with variants

- Process manufacturing

- Make-to-order production

You can also maintain bills of materials for sales orders, projects, equipment, and documents.

The BOM is used in central planning functions such as materials requirements planning and product costing. Five forms of the basic BOM are supported in PP-Production Planning and Control. They may be created at any time by extending a Simple BOM:

- **Simple BOM**—one rigidly-defined bill of material is associated with one material

- **Variant BOM**—several similar materials are associated with one bill of material

- **Multiple BOM**—a set of bills of materials describing each of several different production processes, constituents or relative quantities of components, all of which produce the same material. There are several ways of making the same thing.

- **One-Time BOM**—a bill of material for a specific sales order that is used in make-to-order production

- **Configurable BOM**—a bill of material that is configured automatically on the basis of logical links. It is used for complex variant structures or process-dependent BOM configuration in continuous flow production.

BOM Data Structure

The BOM has a header and one or more items. The header indicates that the BOM is assigned to one or more plants and specifies its validity period. The header also carries its status indicator, which determines whether the BOM is released for production in its current form.

The BOM items each describe a component of the assembly in terms of the following categories, which you can subdivide as the need arises:

- **Stock items** are components kept in stock.

- **Non-stock items** may have purchasing data that you have maintained and that can be used to link with MM-Purchasing.

- **Variable-size items** must have the quantity to be used calculated automatically from the sizes entered.

- **Document items** include drawings or safety instructions integrated into the BOM.

- **Text items** are available for you to store all types of text in association with the BOM.

By-products and scrap can be represented on the BOM by negative quantities that will be processed in PP-MRP Material Requirements Planning and CO-PC Product Cost Accounting.

Parts of a BOM can be marked for the attention of a particular department, or a separate BOM can be used for each department.

BOM Maintenance

You can update a BOM from the CAD system or directly in PP-Production Planning and Control. Copy and editing functions are available. The standard SAP R/3 Classification System is able to search for suitable materials quickly.

Engineering change management is facilitated by mass changes to bills of material. The integrated engineering change management functions allow you to track the complete history of changes to a bill of material.

BOM Explosion Numbers

A BOM Explosion Number is a method of making extra information available to the users of a BOM in a controlled manner. The BOM is given a master record that indicates whether it applies specifically to one product or to many. The BOM Explosion Number may go through several revision levels, each of which will carry the Fixed Key Date, which is the date on which that particular version of a BOM explosion should come into force. From that date, the content of the BOM Explosion Number has to be taken into account by the production scheduling and routing functions.

The BOM Explosion Number is a reference to a technical document that can serve a range of functions, for example:

- Notifying the details of product liability obligations

- Referencing ISO standards for quality assurance

- Documenting an engineering change made during the production process

- Referencing the relevant technical drawings and pointing out the salient features

- Documenting the technical status according to which a product is manufactured for all BOM levels

- Ensuring that the correct BOM and the corresponding routing are used in orders for spare parts

Work Centers

A work center is both a place where a process is carried on by means of activities and a technical concept in the PP-Production Planning and Control system. The real work center has people, machines, production lines, assembly lines, and all the paraphernalia of industry. The work center in SAP R/3 is a data object.

In the data object of the type "work center" you can specify the data for the scheduling, costing, and capacity planning of operations. Formulas held there can compute execution times, costs, capacity requirements, and so on.

The SAP Customizing module allows you to specify the data at your work centers so as to serve your company's needs. The system will supply default values for a work center to simplify and speed up work scheduling, or you can copy or reference from one source to another. The work center will have standard texts to assist you in maintaining the correct operation descriptions in routings. Any parameter unit held at a work center can be given up to six standard values to speed up complex costing or duration calculations, for example. You just specify by a key the value to be used on each occasion.

Work centers are assigned to a cost center during work center data maintenance. This provides the link to the CO-Controlling system.

Every aspect of activity at a work center can be assigned a capacity value, which will then take part in capacity planning, production control, and the scheduling of routings. Not only can you define capacities for machines and labor, you can set up capacity parameters to define virtually any resource that you might need to improve the value added by each work center. Here are some examples:

- Energy consumption

- Emissions

- Reserve capacities for rush orders

Routings

A routing is the industrial equivalent of a cooking recipe—what you need and the sequence of what has to be done to it, including advice on how you will know when the process has reached a satisfactory conclusion. The SAP R/3 PP-Production Planning and Control system uses a routing to document all aspects of a the production process:

- The individual manufacturing steps or stages

- Material

- Capacities

- Production facilities

- Tools and plant fixtures

- Inspection procedures and quality standards on all aspects of the production processes in the routing

You can portray a routing as a digraph—a directed graph showing activities linked by arrows that show you which activities have to be completed or partially completed before the next activity begins. A complex production process that can cope with a range of products and variants will need a complex digraph to portray it. You can have it displayed in tabular form or in network form. A digraph can have the activities represented by arrows, perhaps to a scale where the length of the arrow is in proportion to the length of time taken by the activity, but SAP R/3 always adopts another convention that represents the activities as nodes, often drawn as rectangular boxes, with the arrows showing the logical relationships between the activities. How long they are or how many changes of direction they take on your diagram is of no significance.

SAP R/3 pathways or network routes are made up of a combination of the following subnetworks:

- **Linear** routings have the form of a chain of activities, each one beginning when, but not until, the previous one has finished.

- **Parallel** routings have sections where two or more linear routing subsections start and end at shared junction points

- **Split** routings contain steps where two or more activities all start and finish.

■ **Overlapped** routings have sections where one activity begins before the previous one has fully completed its work.

The conventional routing shows, in diagram format, the progress of materials or workpieces through the production sequence. If you have some operational sequences that are repeatedly used in a routing, you can assign them to a named reference operation set maintained by the work scheduler. The routing can then simply refer to this reference operation set when the operational sequence is needed as part of the production process.

Routings are maintained separately for each plant, but you can have the same routing applied to the same material at other plants and at other work centers. This is how the SAP R/3 system would represent crossplant manufacturing. Here are some of the options:

■ Allocate one material to one routing.

■ Allow several routings to show different ways of producing the same material.

■ Allocate several materials to the same routing in order, for example, to document the production of very similar variants.

Work Scheduling of Operations and Sequences

The work scheduler provides an overview function that allows you to maintain all the essential information in one step. The work center will contribute default values that you may amend if necessary.

■ Identification of the work center at which the operation will take place is mandatory.

■ The control key must be confirmed or changed, which will enable the work scheduler to determine the following matters:

- Whether the operation is to be costed

- Whether capacity loads are to be computed for it

- Whether and how the operation is to be confirmed

- Whether time tickets are to be printed if this operation is to be used in an order

■ The default description of the operation can be accepted, or a different one entered from the work scheduler in the form a standard text chosen from a list of options. Alternatively, a unique text may be created by using the SAPscript word processing tool.

■ Default standard values for the technical aspects of the operation can be accepted, or fresh standard values can be entered manually. Alternatively, they can be calculated automatically by the CAPP-Computer Aided Process Planning module.

External processing is signaled by operations marked with an external processing control key that ensures integration with MM-Materials Management purchasing functions. For example, if a goods receipt has been given in acknowledgment of external processing of this operation carried out by a vendor, this fact will be confirmed in the order.

You can specify work data in detail down to the level of suboperations, and the standard values in the suboperations will be cumulated automatically in the operation. You might want to do this if, for instance, it is better to have costing and capacity planning done on each of the suboperations, even though scheduling is carried out at the level of the operation. If there are going to be several work centers cooperating in an operation, you might again usefully employ the concept of suboperations. The functions are provided for you to specify what parts of operations are to be carried out by specific manufacturing cells.

The operational sequences of a routing can be used in a variety of ways. For instance, a standard routing sequence that is fully linear may be all you need if there is only one way to do the job—only one production sequence is feasible. Parallel sequences may be created to portray and manage the situation where you have two or more essentially similar production sequences with nothing to choose between them. The third possibility is a set of two or more alternative sequences. In this case, you may have parts of your standard routing sequence which can be carried out using some other operations or, indeed, other work centers. You may want to call into play these alternative sequences if your standard routing is expected to become overloaded for some reason if you do not divert some of the work.

The display functions available to the work scheduler include many standard functions which can be customized for your own company.

Any of the data objects in the SAP R/3 system can be inspected by calling for an intelligent listing. To do this, you specify something that will identify a group of data objects that you expect will include those that interest you the most. You might select on the basis of work centers, orders, or production resources and tools, or on any combination of these search factors. With the list in front of you, the intelligence will become apparent when you select a line item that interests you and press one of the function keys. You will then see the line item displayed in more detail, according to which drilling-down function you chose.

A scheduling overview can be called by nominating routings. A Gantt chart, for example, may be your display of choice. It will give you a quick overview of the durations of overlapped or parallel sequences of production processes, and the information you need to get to the required controlling functions. You also have the option of going deeper into the information available on any data object on your screen.

Yet another source of information is the Where-Used listing, which will focus on a particular tool or other production resource, and show you every operation in which it takes part. By this means you can ordain a mass change—for example, to replace one tool by another wherever it is used.

The PRT maintenance component is provided as a source of information on all the production resources and tools (PRTs) that are used throughout the company. The PRTs are classified so that you can rapidly find a tool for whatever job you have in mind, or you can find all the jobs for which a certain tool or other resource has been used in the past. Master records of relevance to production planning are of three types:

■ Material master records are used if purchasing and inventory functions are needed in relation to a PRT.

■ PRT master records carry the minimal information needed simply to document that a specific production resource is needed in a routing.

■ Document master records are used if the resource needed for production has the status of a document, such as a drawing or a program for a numerically controlled machine.

The resources of the SAP R/3 DMS-Document Management System and the CAD system will be at your disposal.

The SAP R/3 Classification System

No matter where you are working in the various application modules, the SAP R/3 Classification System can be accessed. It comprises many functions designed to help you locate information held in document form. You can search on the basis of subject matter or for an item that is linked with a data object such as:

■ Another document

■ A routing

■ A material identified by its material number, its name or part of its name

■ A material because it is similar to one you have already identified that may be out of stock, for instance

■ An item of equipment for which you have given its name or only the identification of the activity where it is used

■ A project identified by its number, the person responsible, the purpose and so on

■ A quotation

■ A sales order

■ A customer or a vendor identified by an attribute in the master records

The SAP R/3 Classification System allows you to give classes, of products, for instance, catchwords or local names that help the user locate what is wanted. Each class of objects in the system will have a set of characteristics, some unique to that object, some shared by other objects—variants, for example. If you establish a class hierarchy with classes, subclasses and so on, the characteristics of the class will be passed on to members of the subclasses lower down the hierarchy. When you are entering the data for an individual item, you do not have to repeat all the data, which will be inherited from the parent class, the grandparent class and so on. If you have to generate a master record for a new object—a new routing, for instance—the system will prompt you to supply the data required, depending on the level at which you are creating something new. In this example, the standard characteristics of a routing will be offered as defaults, and you will be prompted to carry on from there.

Searching with the SAP R/3 Classification System proceeds in two stages:

- Find the class that contains the object of your search by means of its name, by catchwords you have assigned to your classes, by viewing a graphical display of the class hierarchy and stepping through it until you find what you want, or by searching with a matchcode;

- Use object characteristics to narrow down the search until you have the object you require. Characteristics may be identified by constant values or value ranges.

You may wish to define different lists of characteristics for each of the departments in your company. Then you can be sure that the objects you find will be only those that are relevant to the area you are working in. Because of the hierarchical structure of the classes of objects in the classification system, you can find anything you are looking for rapidly and with the specification of only the minimum of search data.

The User's Interface to the CAD System

Many production environments are developing with this fact of life at the forefront of their design philosophy: Very few products remain the same for very long. No step in the production cycle can afford to stand still in the search for speed and relevance when it comes to making changes. Computer Assisted Design (CAD) and Engineering Databases (EDBs) have to be integrated with the PP-Production Planning and Control system.

The SAP CAD user interface with the SAP R/3 system offers the design engineer the following functionality

- The SAP R/3 Classification System can be used to search for suitable parts and avoid duplication of design work.

- The SAP R/3 DMS-Document Management System is available to manage documents and drawings and to integrate information from Engineering Databases (EDB).

- All the basic data held in materials masters, bills of materials and documents in the PP-Production Planning and Control system will be accessible.

- An assembly drawing created in the CAD system and containing the basic design and engineering data can be designated a Bill of Material in the PP-Production Planning and Control system, which will maintain it during work scheduling.

- From the CAD system, the functional locations and the equipment data objects used by the PM-Plant Maintenance system can be maintained.

- The CAD user interface has access to a library of functions containing subroutines that enable data exchange with any CAD systems, EDBs, Technical Information systems or nonSAP applications, and any workstation, PC, or host system on which they may reside.

Resources for Production

When you or the SAP R/3 system and its applications have assigned a work center for a particular task, the capacity of this work center to carry out the required activities will already be known, and the calculation can proceed to ensure that sufficient capacity will be available when it is needed. However, the materials, the work-pieces and the resources needed for production, including the tools, jigs, and fixtures, have to be allocated to the work center.

The work scheduler will look for the specifications of the materials in the bill of materials and select what is needed. If there is no bill of materials or if it lacks some of the necessary information, the scheduler has to seek this information from the unit responsible for maintaining bills of materials.

Engineering Change Management

Change numbers are standard practice throughout SAP R/3 and its applications. If a bill of materials or a routing is to be changed, the engineering change management system in your company will have signaled this change by publishing a change number and a date when it will be released. Alterations in the work scheduling have to take this into account and ensure that the new routings, for example, take effect from that date and have been anticipated in the planning processes.

Each engineering change master document is given a unique change number using a system determined by the user organization. It is dated and contains a note explaining the reason for the change. You can define its status so as to block it and prevent it from being released until, for example, all the items to be changed have been specified. The change master will also carry a valid-from date.

The object list in the change master records will identify all the data objects to be affected, such as:

- Materials
- Bills of material
- Task lists, such as routings
- Documents

Any number of objects may be included in the same change number master.

All changes are stored according to date and the reason for making the change. The following change history information is stored in the list of changes:

- Old and new status of the changed data
- Change date
- Person who made the change
- Date from which the change is valid
- Type of change or reason, such as "item deleted" or "new item"
- Old and new values for what was changed

QM-Quality Management

The standard business functions that support the SAP system of quality management are an integral part of the PP-Production Planning application. They are also available as a separate module, QM-Quality Management, which may be installed and configured when the PP-Production Planning module is not part of your R/3 system.

Quality Inspection

It has become standard business practice to address the issue of quality at every level. The bill of materials and the routings describe what has to be done, and so they have to include the operation of inspection. The task of quality inspection takes time and resources, which means that it has to take its place in the marketplace for time and other resources under the aegis of the PP-Production Planning and Control system.

Unspecific inspection has its place, but where there are known possibilities of variations in material, processing operations, and personal skills, the inspection has to be given very clear direction in terms of the following factors:

- At which stages in the sequence of production processes will inspections take place?

- Will the work flow be sampled or inspected in its entirety?

- Who will be responsible for each inspection?

- What processing has to take place to prepare the product for inspection?

- At which parts or attributes will the inspector look, measure or test with a gauge, or send off a sample for analysis by the laboratory at each inspection stage?

- What will the inspector see if everything is fine, if further testing is needed or if one of the known faults is present in the piece of work?

In summary, the inspector has to be told formally by the production documentation what to look at, what to look for, and what action to take in every case. And a fresh pair of eyes available to look at the quality of work is not a bad idea.

In accord with the master data philosophy of the SAP R/3 system, data that are used frequently are written in one place where they can be updated and used in exactly the same form by everybody who needs them. This principle applies to production data. The quantitative and qualitative aspects of inspection, the sampling parameters, target values, and tolerances, all these are created as independent basic data elements. The components of a specification that will be used to inspect and test quality are all data elements that can be used in other inspection specifications, and they will also be used in production and can be printed on the order to show what standards are in force.

Standardized Inspection Plans

Overall, modern quality management requires inspection at every operation. The routing is a plan of operations. The inspection planner can use the same functions as the routings. And the inspections can be integrated with the production routings. If the inspection has to take place outside production, as in the case of goods received or goods to be issued, the inspection planner can use the inspection criteria to create a special inspection plan. Better than that, the inspector can call upon predefined reference operation sets and master inspection characteristics as the starting point from which a customized plan can be created.

Inspection plans fall into a logical grouping:

- Material inspection plans concentrate on what might be, in some cases, a very specialized method of inspection specific to that one material.

- Individual inspection plans are usually intended to be used for a material in relation to a specific customer or vendor, for instance.

- Family inspection plans circumscribe the inspection scope of a family of parts. This family can be defined in terms of the materials, the sources or the destinations, or it can be defined in terms of a combination of certain materials from certain vendors, and so on.

When the inspection planner assigns a material to a plan, it is usual to define at the same time the target values and tolerances to be applied across the scope of the plan.

The scope and details of an inspection plan can be reassigned at any time. Dynamic modification refers to the process of adjusting the inspection plan according to the most recent inspection results.

CAPP-Computer Aided Process Planning

The SAP R/3 Configurator database interface provides a wide range of functions for the automatic generation of routings from a knowledge base. The CAPP-Computer Aided Process Planning automatically calculates standard values, such as setup times and machine times, and applies them to the routings generated by the SAP R/3 Configurator to provide the following facilities:

- Generation of operation sequences

- Selection of work centers

- Selection and allocation of production resources and tools

- Allocation of material components to operations

A knowledge base is required to be set up in the form of tables and formulas that must include, for example, the following types of information for all operations:

- Calculation rules for standard work center operating values as stipulated in a labor union contract

- Company-specific tables of planned times for operations

- Materials

- Weights

- Tolerances

- Feeds and so on

SAP R/3 provides functions to check this knowledge base for consistency and for maintenance of the data.

The knowledge base must also contain methods. A method is a description of how particular tables and formulas are to be linked to arrive at a result—for example, a calculated setup time for a particular process. The calculation of a standard value can be split into subcalculations—for each step in an operation, for example. Existing data can be used to reduce the amount of fresh calculation entailed.

The methods have to be combined in sequence into the sets of calculations that provide all the results needed to plan each particular process. The process has to be assigned to a work center.

When you come to creating or changing a routing, you might find that several alternative processes could occur at a certain point in the routing. You have to select the one to be used. Then you must look to the methods to be used in the process you have selected; there may be several options. Again, you have to select which methods are to form the basis of the process.

When you have selected the methods to be used in a process at a work center, the PP-Production Planning and Control system will calculate the standard values.

Output Control in PP-Production Planning and Control

Corporate financial viability may well depend on the accuracy and timeliness of the information flows in your company. The SAP R/3 output control functions offer flexible management of workflow across all SAP applications.

The following examples of user-defined events illustrate the variety of services offered:

- Delivery notes generated and sent automatically to the ship-to party via a medium of your choice

- Invoices sent at a time you specify

- Automatic mail to the work scheduler if a bill of material is changed

- Formulation of production output proposals and their conditions

- Generation of an output proposal during transaction processing

- Generation of an output document

- Editing of outputs

- Sending outputs at a time you specify

- Status reports generated automatically on the processing stage of an output

- Output proposals generated when a specified set of conditions (a data constellation) is detected

When you are offered an output proposal, it will include details as follows:

- Time when the output is to be sent

- The recipient of the output

- The medium to be used for sending, such as printout, Telex, R/Mail, Teletex, Telefax, and Electronic Data Interchange

You can accept the output proposal or edit any of the details.

PP-SOP Sales and Operations Planning

If you want to set targets for long- and medium-term sales quantities and to plan roughly the production activities that are necessary to achieve these targets, you should use the PP-SOP Sales and Operations Planning system.

At a later stage, the detailed planning through BOM explosion and scheduling via the routing will take place under the direction of the SAP PP-MP Master Planning standard programs.

The PP-SOP Sales and Operations Planning Sequence

The broad-brush planning mediated by PP-SOP Sales and Operations Planning can be carried out at the level of the finished product or at the product group level. Any combination of materials and products can be designed at product group and planned together as a unit. This is the method of choice if there are too many products to justify planning at an individual level.

When you have decided on the level of planning, products or product groups, you must set up the sales quantities for each of the future periods you are planning. There are various ways of arriving at these values or quantities of the products or product groups:

- Manually enter sales quantities or values for each period.

- Have the system use historical values to forecast automatically.

- Copy the values from CO-PA Profitability Analysis.

- Copy the sales quantities from the SD-IS Sales Information System.

- Copy the sales quantities from a nonSAP system.

From the sales forecast, you must next generate production plans that are capable of meeting your planned sales. The system will help you ensure that you make best use of your existing resources as you put together your production plan.

The last stage of this rough planning process is referred to as disaggregation, because it entails the taking apart of any product groups you may have aggregated for rough planning purposes. In the end, you must pass on to PP-MP Master Planning only individual product plans.

Product Groups

The purpose of establishing a product group is to be able to conduct in one operation the sales and operations planning for many individual products. A product group may be made up of any materials or product groups arranged in product group hierarchies. Thus, for example, Product Group A may be defined by listing any combination of products or product types.

A material can be assigned to several product groups—you can have alternative product hierarchies. You can also define and plan product groups that span some or all of your plants.

The product group hierarchy concept illustrates the general principle, used throughout SAP R/3, of data objects inheriting the characteristics of their parents in the hierarchy. In this case, the inheritance consists of the planning data assigned by the processing conducted by PP-SOP Sales and Operations Planning.

It may happen that the units of measurement are different at different levels of a product group structure. There may be a simple arithmetic calculation to be carried out to effect the conversion; or it may be a matter of converting a rough plan forecast of weight or bulk into a target in terms of individual work-pieces. If there is more than one product sharing a planned total, you have to specify the proportional factors that will be needed to disaggregate the total into the relative percentage and thence to the planned numbers of each product.

The system can be asked to calculate proportional factors on the basis of historical data, or you can enter them manually.

Forecasts

A graphical display of forecast results is standard across all SAP applications. In the case of PP-Production Planning and Control, the main tasks of the forecast are as follows:

- Forecasting product groups and finished products
- Forecasting material requirements in support of consumption-based planning
- Determining the data used to calculate safety stock and reorder levels

Although any data can be accessed in the SAP R/3 system, a standard interface has been programmed between the PP-Production Planning and Control system and the following SAP applications:

- LIS-Logistics Information System, which includes the SD-IS Sales Information System and the PIS-Purchasing Information System
- MM-Materials Management, for the materials consumption data

The forecasting process takes place in the background for several materials at once until all the objects in the plan have received attention. If you are not satisfied with any of the forecast values or quantities arrived at automatically, you can make any adjustment manually at the online display.

The historical data may conceal trends and patterns that could be used to make better forecasts. You can find out what they are by having the system carry out model analysis on the data. The system will determine which of its model profiles makes the best fit with the historical data, and from then on the system will keep checking that the one chosen is the best. It will change models automatically if you allow it. Alternatively, you may say which model you want to be used. The models currently available for analyzing the historical time series of data for any variables you care to specify are as follows:

- Constant value model—to determine a steady forecast amount or a moving average

- Trend model—to determine an equation to plot the future trend of values

- Seasonal model—to plot a cyclical pattern

- Trend and seasonal models combined—to predict a shifting cyclical pattern

The models are recorded as forecast profiles, which are not tied to any one material. The material master record will contain a reference to the forecast profile with which it has been associated. In this way, data entry is minimized and the forecast can be generated for any material over any time line.

Fine-Tuning the Sales Plan

Sales quantities can be changed at any time in the PP-SOP Sales and Operations Planning system. This gives you a continuous planning horizon.

Your sales forecast will perhaps utilize product groups, in which case the system will automatically accumulate the historical values for all members of the product group.

The forecast is a simulation into which you can inject fresh parameters on a what-if basis. Each run can be stored as an alternative version of your forecast. In this interactive process, you are at liberty to adjust the figures taken from historical values if you think this will improve your forecast.

When you have before you a graphical display of your forecast and plan, you may make permanent adjustments to it simply by moving the graph points with your mouse.

If your installation can give you values from CO-PA Profitability Analysis, your PP-Production Planning and Control module will be able to aggregate the detailed data automatically, ready for you to install it in your sales plan.

In a similar fashion, the SD-IS Sales Information System or any nonSAP system can send you data for your product group or material level sales plan. You can, of course, redistribute it over different production plants in your plan and enter refinements of your forecast data manually.

Production Plan

The starting production plan is usually one that exactly matches your sales plan. The system copies quantities and dates directly from your sales plan to make the production plan.

You can also specify a target in terms of the number of days the stock of each product is expected to last—a measure of the stock in hand related to the expected consumption of this stock. The system will then calculate the production quantities needed to maintain this amount of stock, referred to as the Target Days' Supply.

Using various distribution tools if necessary, you can also manually enter the stock levels required.

Versions of your production plan can be simulated and stored separately.

Disaggregation
When the PP-SOP Sales and Operations Planning system has developed sales and production plans using product groups as the working units, the plan values have to be disaggregated into plan elements that apply to the individual members of the product groups.

There are two methods for automatically disaggregating a product group:

- Group members can be finished products or product groups that are split according to the proportional factors assigned to them.

- Product group members can be distributed over time using a splitting key to choose between calendar months, works time periods, calendar days, and working days.

Integrated Corporate Planning
The detailed actual planning takes place under the control of the PP-MP Master Planning functions. There are two routes for the data to pass to this system from the PP-SOP Sales and Operations Planning system:

- Direct passing of independent requirements for each finished product as indicated in the sales plan or the production plan

- Copy for reference only, in which the data on the independent requirements for finished products may be subject to alteration by the PP-MP Master Planning system

PP-MP Master Planning
The master plan has to settle on master schedule items, the resources they will require, and their start and finish times.

A master schedule item is a finished product or an important assembly that will make a big difference to total turnover or profit or will dominate the production process because of its complexity.

The planning for these important master schedule items has to make the key decisions for your company on how production resources are to be used. Three things have to be done:

- Select the planning and production strategy.

- Determine the requirements quantities and their delivery dates.

- Assemble the master plan for the master schedule items.

Demand Management

There are three functions that demand management has to serve:

- Determine the quantities and dates for the finished products and important assemblies that are being made in anticipation of future orders.

- Specify the strategy to be used for planning and producing or procuring a product.

- Define the planning strategy to be used for order-oriented production and the planning for pre-production of assemblies for future make-to-order production.

There are three production strategies and hence three planning strategies, each of which may admit of several variations:

- Make-to-stock in anticipation of sales, net, or gross.

- Make-to-order using sales orders copied from SD-Sales and Distribution or orders created directly in PP-Production Planning and Control, keeping all requirements and costs information attached to each separate order.

- Make in lots in response to one or more sales orders and internal stock replenishment orders.

There also has to be a decision made as to how planned values are to be offset with sales orders when they occur.

Planning with and Without Final Assembly

Sometimes you cannot afford to wait for sales orders before you start to produce or procure certain assemblies, part-finished products, or raw materials. What you can do is to set up independent requirements that trigger planning and production for stock. When orders arrive, you can by this means offer faster delivery.

You can take the independent requirements to the final assembly level, or you can stop production before this stage so as to carry out the rest of the assembly only when you have an order. This will then create a dependent requirement which you can meet partially from stock, offsetting this against your planned independent requirement.

Applying the Planning Material Concept

When several products begin life looking the same and sharing the same preliminary production processes, you can establish a planning material to represent the product up to the point when it is treated differently to make the distinct products.

A planning material can be treated exactly like any other material and can be subjected to the various planning strategies.

Using Assemblies to Focus Planning

When assemblies are used to produce a large number of variants according to customer requirements, it may be easier to focus the planning on these assemblies. You can plan assembly requirements that are independent of orders, and later offset them when the customer orders inform you which variants are needed and hence which assemblies.

Reference Figures for Maintaining Independent Requirements

There are risks attached to planning and producing products that have not been confirmed as orders. The following reference figures are available to help you if you are in the role of materials requirements planner:

- The sales plan for the product

- A forecast for this product calculated automatically from sales planning information

- A rough-cut production plan for the product from PP-SOP Sales and Operations Planning

- Independent requirements that will have been planned and perhaps already produced for this product and perhaps for specific customers

The MRP controller is warned automatically if any of these reference figures are changed.

The independent requirements can be split across any planning periods: near future in weeks, for example, or far future in months. A complete change history may be mandated for each independent requirement. In common with other planning instruments, an independent requirements plan may be given a version number and therefore exist in alternative versions.

Master Item Production Scheduling

Extra attention is given to planning and scheduling those items that take up critical resources or that can have a big influence on profits. Items marked as master schedule items can be finished products, assemblies, or raw materials.

In a master planning run, only the master schedule items are considered. For each item, a Bill of Materials (BOM) is used to generate the dependent requirements. Further levels of detail below this—the BOM Explosion data—are not processed at this stage. Thus the MRP controller can manipulate the master plan before any extensive processing takes place on the various BOM Explosion detail levels.

You can protect the master plan from automatic changes by using a planning time fence created for each material. This prevents the MRP run from altering any order proposal within the time fence unless authorized.

The master plan can be adjusted online, and simulation can be used to check the results. A series of standard evaluations is available to the MRP controller through a variety of display presentations. Available-to-promise (ATP) quantities can be displayed to show stocks and receipts that have not yet been reserved by planning against any particular sales order.

Master planning across several sites is supported by full information flows and by, for example, distributing production quantities among various sites according to quotas that may also be applied to the procurement of materials from various plants.

Using the Distribution Warehouse Concept

A distribution warehouse may be defined as a plant that is the supplier for several companies, for several countries or for several companies, each in a different country. Such a warehouse is a unit that should be subject to planning.

One advantage of the warehouse concept is that you can use various planning strategies for the same product, depending on the warehouse through which it is to be distributed. One warehouse may use consumption-based planning, another might be better planned using an MRP procedure. Forecasting and evaluation can be carried out with and across the distribution warehouses.

The supply of goods from the production plants to the distribution warehouses is handled by the purchasing and distribution functions in the MM-Materials Management and SD-Sales and Distribution systems.

PP-MRP Material Requirements Planning

The purpose of the PP-MRP Material Requirements Planning component and the MRP II Planning Chain is to propose orders for materials so that they will be in the right place, at the right time, and in the right quantity.

The method is based on the principle of exception reporting. So material requirements planning is generally a matter of planning only those materials whose stock has changed or those that have anticipated demands that have changed since the previous computation.

An MRP net change planning run is a limited exercise that can be repeated at short intervals so you can always be up-to-date. Furthermore, you can limit the planning horizon to match your current priorities. You can re-plan a single item if you want, on a daily basis if necessary.

An MRP run will generate exception messages for the controller under situations such as the following:

- If material is ordered but not delivered on time
- If stock is below safety level

If a planned purchase order or production order is not required, the system automatically creates a proposal to cancel or reschedule the order, whichever makes better sense, rather than have something that is not likely to be needed at the time scheduled.

The controller can call for an MRP list per material, or for an overview per material of the stock or requirements situation that is similar to the MRP list, except that the current situation is portrayed in the form of changes. If you have several MRP controllers, you can allocate certain groups of materials to each.

V

Manufacturing Applications

The controller can display receipts and issues on the time axis in any time period, and can call up more detailed information on any item. From the list, you can make any kind of change to an order. Multilevel pegging enables you to locate the original source of each receipt or issue, so that in the case of a delay, for example, you can identify the requirements that generated the order and that will therefore be affected by the delay. Available-to-promise (ATP) quantities can be displayed by the MRP controller.

The controller has two procedures to use in planning material requirements:

- Consumption-based planning, including reorder point planning and forecast-based planning
- Material requirements planning for each production plant or procurement plant

Consumption-Based Planning

Reorder point planning depends on specifying a safety stock level below which the stock should not be allowed to fall, bearing in mind the possibility of unexpected requirements. The reorder point makes allowance for the fact that stock is predicted to fall while the replacement stock is being delivered. When stock reaches the reorder point, the system generates an order proposal to replenish the stock.

You can enter both the reorder point and the safety stock level, or the system can call upon forecasts to calculate both, depending on the service level and the replenishment lead time. The SAP R/3 regular forecast program ensures that the reorder and safety stock levels are automatically adapted to the current delivery and consumption situation.

Material Requirements Planning

Sales orders and planned independent requirements, together with the dependent requirements arising from BOM explosion, define the material requirements. The availability calculation is precise down to the nearest day. The system can also cope with additional unplanned withdrawals on the basis of previous consumption patterns.

Any material requirement that will greatly influence the overall planning result can be designated as a master schedule item. It will then receive extra planning attention, including a check on resources before BOM explosion is carried out, which might otherwise initiate an automatic change of the complete master plan. Net planning has to have stock levels checked and gross planning does not.

Lot-Sizing

If the net requirements calculation anticipates a shortage on a specific date, the system determines the exact quantity to be procured or produced. There is a choice open to the MRP controller of lot-sizing procedure: static, period, optimum, and user-defined. The controller also specifies the minimum and maximum lot size, and a rounding value to allow the lot size to cover an exact multiple of the order unit. Production or assembly scrap is predefined and also taken into account in the lot size.

Static lot-sizing covers three procedures:

- Lot-for-lot, where the shortage quantity is used as the order quantity
- Fixed lot size is defined in the material master and several orders are generated if necessary to cover the shortage.
- Replenishment up to the maximum stock level specified in the material master

Period lot-sizing takes the requirement quantities for a certain period of time as the lot. The period can be daily, weekly, or monthly, or an individual planning calendar can be maintained for this purpose.

Optimum lot-sizing takes note of the storage costs per unit of material compared with the costs that are independent of lot size. The optimum lot size is when the sum of both cost factors is at a minimum.

The MRP controller has a choice of optimum lot-sizing procedures:

- Least unit cost
- Part period balancing
- Groff reorder procedure
- Dynamic lot-size creation

For materials to be produced in-house, order proposals have to be converted to production orders within user-defined planning horizons. For parts to be purchased, the MRP controller can specify which of the following the system is to create:

- Planned order, which must be converted to a purchase requisition at the appropriate time
- Purchase requisition, which will be converted by the purchasing department to a purchase order, a release order (from stock) or a delivery schedule
- Delivery schedule, which is an agreement that comes into force when the requirements are needed. A valid delivery agreement will have been specified via the material source list.

The relevant BOM explosion has to be initiated for in-house production and also for purchase requisitions and delivery schedules used for subcontracting.

Order Proposal Scheduling in MRP

Backward scheduling applies to material requirements planning and forecast planning, because the requirement date in the future is known in both cases. The start date is found from the replenishment lead time. If the system finds that the material cannot be delivered on time, the controller is informed of the expected delay and the system automatically begins forward scheduling.

Reorder point planning requires that stock replenishment begin as soon as the shortage becomes imminent, that is, not likely to be covered by the normal reordering provision. The system then determines when the stock will be available again. If goods have to go through quality control, an allowance can be made for goods receipt processing time.

PP-CRP Capacity Requirements Planning

The purpose of capacity planning is to provide planners with a flexible system of overviews of the capacity utilization at all the work centers at a plant, and also of the planning instruments that are used to effect capacity leveling.

The capacities available at a work center may be defined in a variety of ways that allow you to create requirements for different types of order and monitor how the capacity is used. Capacity planning deals with the capacity categories at a work center, and the amounts of these capacities available to meet the loads accumulating for them. The following types of capacity illustrate the wide-ranging uses of the concept:

- Labor
- Pooled capacity shared with certain other work centers
- Machine capacity
- Energy consumption
- Wastes from a process
- Reserves set aside for rush orders

Every type of capacity available at a work center can be plotted on the time axis to show how much of it is available at any moment. A graphical display of each availability through time is provided by the system. Work center hierarchies can be subjected to a choice of capacity cumulating calculations.

Shift sequences are defined and maintained centrally in SAP R/3, and can be applied to work centers to have the necessary adjustments made automatically by the system.

Scheduling in Capacity Planning

The scheduling process can be carried out at the rough-cut level, using internal production time per operation, for example, but to control production activities accurately, it may be necessary to establish time elements to cover the details; for example:

- Floats, order floats before and after production, and queue times
- Setup and tear-down times to take account of the time costs of changing from one activity to another
- Inter-operation times where a minimum wait time is required, or a time to move the piece from one place to another

Basic planning data has to be maintained as entered values and as tables or formulas from which the necessary values can be calculated.

Capacity Requirements Calculation

Planned orders are the basis for rough-cut and medium-term planning. The capacity requirements will have been calculated for these planned orders, and a detailed picture will be available of the way the critical work centers will be occupied by the various activities.

Production orders are the instruments for detailed planning and control. The capacity requirements for production orders are the basis of shop floor control of work centers.

Maintenance orders derived from the PM-Plant Maintenance system will include capacity requirements, and so systematic capacity leveling can be carried out in that system or in the PP-Production Planning and Control module.

Networks are used in project management and in the SAP R/3 PS-Project System. Every activity in a network can have its capacity requirements planned.

Quality inspection orders are available in SAP R/3. They will also generate capacity requirements that can be subjected to planning calculations.

An operation can impose more than one type of capacity load on a work center, and it is possible to calculate more complex capacity requirements, as in operations that require more than one machine, for example.

Evaluating the Capacity Load Situation

The capacity load refers to the capacity requirements in relation to the capacity available. However, particular users will want to have this sort of information processed differently according to their interests. Customizing allows you to have a custom-made and pertinent display of the capacity situation and its significance for your work.

For example, the following tools are provided to individualize the presentation of load evaluations in the form of overview lists or graphics:

- **Profiles** define the period under consideration by the planner, the work centers and capacities to be evaluated, and the orders and operations to be analyzed.

- **Groupings** allow evaluations to summarize any set of capacities, no matter from where they are drawn, no matter from which time period.

- **Sortings** allow user-defined data to be arranged according to the most informative scheme.

- **Cumulation** allows capacity load data to be combined using work center hierarchies, selecting by level, and across time periods.

As is standard across SAP R/3, presentations can be used to select data objects on which further information can be released by the touch of a special function key.

Capacity Leveling

Simulation is available to the planner at every level. You can make changes to the available capacity and adjust the lot size. Deadline movements and changes of work center can be tried out in the simulation. Plan versions can be stored until the optimum plan is released for production.

Simple lead time scheduling can result in a loading of infinity for one or more work center capacities—in other words, a bottleneck. On the other hand, capacity scheduling takes into consideration the orders already dispatched when it calculates the operation dates for an order; overloads are thus avoided.

Because the dispatching sequence reflects the priority attached to work items, it is crucial to successful capacity scheduling. Optimization of the production sequence is often combined with capacity leveling. There are programs to conduct sequencing so as to optimize setup time, which can be adjusted automatically according to criteria defined by the user.

Manual capacity leveling is effected by resource planning, which has the aim of dispatching only as many orders to a work center as can be processed there. A graphic planning table is provided on which it is easy to see the orders already dispatched to a work center and the orders or operations waiting to be dispatched. The system supports you with detailed information on the availability of material and capacity, the stage reached by preceding operations, and the dispatching rules offered as guidance to simplify the planning of resources.

Capacity Availability Checking

A bottleneck occurs when the required capacity is not available. Availability checking ensures that it is available. It is possible to check, at every planning phase, that the required capacity will be available at the particular work center when it is required, either for an individual order or for an entire order structure.

If the required capacity is not going to be available, the system will propose a date by which the order can be produced without bottlenecks.

This sort of decision on capacity can also be made on the basis of a simulation of an order structure that you create on behalf of a customer inquiry. You need not then venture delivery dates that could not be realistically met according to the current capacity utilization in your work centers.

At the time of order release, when detailed planning has already taken place, you can again have an availability check carried out to make sure that the capacities you need will actually be available at the work centers.

PP-SFC Production Orders

This PP Production Planning and Control component is also referred to as Shop Floor Control.

The role of the PP-SFC Production Orders component is to convert the planning specifications of the PP-MRP Material Requirements Planning component into actual production orders to be carried out, and then to coordinate all aspects of the production process and the utilization of resources.

The benefits of close control of production activity include minimization of costs and inventory, utilization of the available capacities to best effect, adherence to delivery dates, and elevation of quality standards.

Production Activity Control

Production activity is controlled mainly by means of the production order, which describes all planned and actual elements that are related to production. The production order informs the shop floor controller of the following matters:

- What is to be produced

- The production deadlines to be met

- The resources needed, such as materials, documents, capacities, production resources and tools, and so on

- Which costs are to be incurred

- How the costs are to be settled

The production order passes through four phases, each receiving a slightly different emphasis in the matter of production control:

- Order creation, including the conversion from planned orders, routing selection, scheduling of capacities, job order costing, and the creation of requisitions

- Order processing, including order release, material issues, completion confirmations, and receipt to stock

- Order completion, including technical order completion with the deletion of outstanding capacity loads and reservations

- Order settlement

Order Creation

Although you can always create and enter manually a production order for a rush order or other special order, most production orders are created by converting planned orders that have been generated automatically by the PP-MRP Material Requirements Planning system.

This conversion is carried out automatically by the system. Manual intervention only when a problem is foreseen. For example, if no suitable routing can be found, or there is a choice of alternative routings for which no selection criterion is available to allow it to be made automatically, then the user has to be asked to make a choice. By identifying the relevant opening period, the MRP controller can select the planned orders that are due for conversion into production orders. The conversion process carries out the following tasks in the background:

- Transfer general data from the planned order to the production order.

- Transfer details of the material to be produced.

- Transfer the Bill of Material components.

- Transfer the order quantity.

- Transfer the basic dates.

- Assign to the production order the component requirements created by PP-MRP Material Requirements Planning.

- Create requisitions automatically for BOM components that are not going to be produced in-house, and initiate purchasing action by the MM-Materials Management system.

- Create material reservations automatically for BOM components manufactured in-house.

- Select routings.

- Select bills of material in special cases and carry out BOM explosion.

- Transfer the results, if they are available, of rough-cut planning of planned orders.

- Schedule the production order according to the dates calculated in PP-MRP Material Requirements Planning.

- Calculate capacity loads and dispatch them to the work centers.

- Carry out job order costing on the basis of the planned material consumption, prevailing cost rates for internal labor and costs of external processing, as appropriate.

- Update on the production order the actual costs when completion confirmations and material issues are carried out.

- Delete the planned order if the conversion to a production order has been successful.

Order Processing

The work scheduler has the following functions available in support from the PP-SFC Production Orders component:

- Order release to the shop floor with the printing of shop papers for the specific operations of an order, for an order as a whole or for all the orders released for that period

- Material issues

- Completion confirmations

- Receipt to stock

You also have a Status Management function, which displays an overview of the current status of an order at any given time, using a status sequence that you may define to suit the methods of your company. The details of all orders on hand are available when required.

The following shop papers can be printed:

- Operation control ticket and job tickets
- Pick lists
- Material issue slips
- Lists of production resources and tools
- Time tickets
- Completion confirmation slips

The shop papers may carry bar codes, and you have control over the selection of the information to be printed. They may be formatted in a company-specific layout and directed to the outlets of choice.

Material issues can be carried out for an entire order or against individual reservations. The issue of material components automatically updates the actual costs on the production order. Backflushing of material issues can take place, in which the confirmation of an operation automatically creates a withdrawal posting of the material components allocated to that operation.

Completion confirmations allow you to document the quantities produced, the scrap and the production times for an operation. By this means you can monitor production capacity utilization and the incurred manufacturing costs. The actual quantities, the attendance times and the actual costs will be automatically updated in the order as each completion confirmation is posted at a Plant Data Collection (PDC) station or through the online functions of the PP-Production Planning and Control system. The system will have assigned a completion confirmation number to each operation that can be entered by presenting the bar code on the system-printed confirmation slip.

Various completion confirmation arrangements are available:

- Normal confirmation of each operation individually
- Standard confirmation using target values as actual values to minimize the number of entries required
- Collective confirmation to allow several completion confirmations for different orders to be confirmed against a list
- Milestone confirmation when an operation that has been marked as a milestone is confirmed. This automatically confirms all preceding operations that are not themselves milestones.

Receipts to stock from production orders can occur for partial lots or for the entire production lot. The receipt will be posted, according to the job control, to an individual customer stock or as stock that is not related to an order. The valuation strategy will be specified in the material master so as to use, for example, planned costs, planned price, or standard price.

The work scheduler can call upon reports that will make use of the extensive capacity planning functions. You can select the orders for your report using the following criteria:

- Orders for a particular material

- Orders under a particular MRP controller

- Orders for a particular shop floor controller

- Orders in which particular production resources and tools are used

Integration of Production Activity Control with Technical Subsystems

Because the PP-Production Planning and Control system has been designed as an open system, there is no fundamental reason why it should not be connected to any technical subsystem. The following list illustrates the variety of possibilities:

- **PDC/MDC**—Plant data, machine data, and attendance time data collection can be arranged through this channel to link with the PP-Production Planning and Control system and the HR-Human Resources system.

- **DNC (Digital or Numerical Control)**—This channel transfers information on required production resources and tools to a subordinate DNC or PRT management function.

- **Transfer control**—This channel sends requests to have material moved from one activity to another in the production area.

- **Process visualization**—This channel exchanges master data and movement data with process engineering and process visualization systems.

- **Quality data collection**—This channel transfers information, on the check procedures specified, to automatic measurement data entry systems which return the results to the QM-Quality Management system.

- **Technical optimization**—This channel links scrap minimization and setup time optimization systems at work centers to the PP-Production Planning and Control system.

Order Completion

Technical order completion is signaled by marking an order using the status management function. This causes the deletion of outstanding capacity loads and reservations. Further postings to this order are prohibited.

Order Settlement

When delivery has been completed, an order can be settled. The system calculates the balance between debit postings to the order and credit postings. The order account is then debited or credited accordingly. Only when an order has been technically completed and settled is it archived.

Debit postings to an order may include:

- Material issues

- External labor

- Completion confirmations debited to the order

Credit postings to an order can be caused by receipts to stock.

Production Controlling

The purpose of production controlling is to effect a balance between the following factors:

- Product quality

- Short delivery times

- Highly reliable delivery dates

- Minimum costs

- Low stocks

- High utilization of work center capacities

The LIS-Logistics Information System has a subset of functions that serve the PP-SFC Shop Floor Control and Information System which is being developed into the CAPISCE Computer Architecture for Production Information Systems in a Competitive Environment for the European Community. This is a flexible tool for consolidating, summarizing, and analyzing data gathered from production activity control. It offers two types of analysis:

- **Standard analyses** utilize statistical databases, which are information structures to which important performance measures are written automatically.

- **Flexible analyses** are based on one or more of the SAP database structures and can include data selected using criteria that you have defined.

The data for a standard analysis can be consolidated at levels of your choosing. For example, your report can collate information from the following levels:

- Plant

- Work scheduler group

- MRP controller group

- Work center hierarchy

- Material

With the report on your screen, you can select any value and press a special function key to "drill down" and see the data that was used to compile the value of your choice. Switching between tabular and graphical displays of your data is always an option.

Input and output diagrams can be called for any work centers of interest. They show the incoming and outgoing production orders cumulatively along the time axis. You can display the scheduled activity values for these orders and the capacity available at the work center for them. Operating hours at the work center can also be displayed on a time axis.

If you should require a particular analysis, the data objects and the performance measures you need can be selected on the screen, whereupon the system will devise and present an evaluation report using these measures on these data objects.

Inventory controlling is an integral part of production controlling. It concentrates on the receipt and issue of goods from various points of view, including the following:

- Inventory turnover
- Range of coverage
- Dead stock
- Stock value
- Number of goods receipts and issues

The MM-Materials Management system specializes in the management of inventory.

PP-PC Product Costing

The SAP R/3 system guarantees a detailed costing procedure for all common production types. Cost objects are defined and maintained using data entered manually or via the CO-Controlling and the PP-Production Planning modules.

The link between logistics and managerial accounting is the discipline of cost object controlling, which seeks to determine the planned costs and the target production costs, or costs of sales, of a product or an order.

For each product or order, a value structure determined by internal accounting is applied to evaluate the corresponding quantity structure, and this process is replicated for plan, target, and actual values.

The information units for cost object controlling are the work center and the order, or, if there is no order, the work center and the bill of materials and routing. Unit costing is also possible.

The results of costing in general are used to arrive at the following analyses:

- Price formation and pricing policy
- Valuation
- Control of costs of goods manufactured
- Profitability analysis

Product Costing

Repetitive manufacturing and standard manufacturing from production orders both depend on product costing. Planning and calculating the manufacturing costs are of central importance. In these examples of non-order-related costing, you use the bills of material and routings in order to plan and control manufacturing costs. Here are some examples of costing variants that can be adapted to your situation:

- Standard costing at the beginning of the fiscal year for each cost object
- Monthly modified standard cost estimates
- Current costing
- Inventory costing

Costing results are divided up into a selection from forty standard cost components recognized by the SAP R/3 system. The same classification is used for both standard cost estimates and the cost elements used to control manufacturing costs. Each cost estimate can be stored in itemized form, and you can identify control objects for each estimate.

Bills of material and routings can be fully exploded into their constituents over all stages of production, so that if you wish to define a particular cost split, the results will be automatically rolled up over all levels. Each level will be displayed using the same selection from the forty cost components.

Every costing variant used in product costing can be associated with a corresponding valuation variant or strategy which you may define as a rank-ordered sequence of prices. For example:

- Planned price
- Moving average price
- Price relevant to a specific tax or trade law
- Price determined from standard cost rates

Thus you can establish costing strategies for the following purposes:

- Inventory stock valuation
- Inventory accounting
- Order accounting
- Profitability Analysis

Further details of product costing may be found in the section on CO-PC Product Cost Accounting.

PP Functions for Special Types of Production

The SAP R/3 system provides functions that were developed specifically to serve the following types of manufacturing:

V

Manufacturing Applications

■ Make-to-order manufacturing is particularly well served by the PP-Production Planning and Control system and the SAP R/3 PS-Project System.

■ Make-to-stock repetitive and continuous flow manufacturing types are supported by the PP-Production Planning and Control system, which offers the production controller a versatile and flexible system of assessing the master production schedule from different points of view—for instance, by individual order, by all activities concerning a specified material or set of materials, and so on.

■ Process manufacturing makes good use of the resource management, recipe management and warehouse management functions. The specialized SAP R/3 module is PP-PI Production Planning for Process Industries.

From Here...

■ My staff is not really used to working with computers.

Have a look at Chapter 2, "User Interaction with the SAP Systems," where you will see that the systems all use a very helpful way of interacting with the user that can be used quickly if you are an expert and slowly with copious help if you are not.

■ Does SAP provide a system for managing a complex plant?

Chapter 11, "A Computer Center Management System," describes CCMS.

■ How can one use the SAP R/3 system to determine cost-effectiveness of part of the business?

Chapter 14, "Understanding the CO-Controlling Module," includes a section on profitability analysis that may be of interest.

■ How can a new user find out what is available in the R/3 system?

The R/3 Reference Model is part of the R/3 system and allows the user to see which standard business programs are available and how they might be used in a specific company.

■ How does the Production Planning application work with continuous process industries?

Chapter 19, "Understanding the PP-PI Production Planning for Process Industries Modules," discusses the extensive supplements to the standard SAP R/3 system that have been developed specifically for continuous process manufacturing.

Chapter 18

Understanding the PP-PI Production Planning for Process Industries Modules

The following features mark out a company as a candidate for the application of PP-PI Production Planning for Process Industries modules:

- Noncontinuous forms of manufacturing take place in batches grouped together as production campaigns that are characterized by an unchanging basic recipe throughout the campaign.

- The plant itself can be used in various ways to produce a range of related products.

- Unnecessary clean-out operations and changeovers are to be avoided.

- Process control is active because the quality of the ingredients and the environmental conditions may vary.

- The control of product quality depends on close coordination with a dedicated laboratory.

- The production plant is only partially automated, so some of the process control instructions have to be in natural language and some in a machine-readable language.

- The recipe and the production order must be archived for each batch, together with the actual data on the process.

- All messages, whether in machine or natural language, must be archived for subsequent analysis.

The following industries have been shown to be amenable to effective application of the methods programmed in the PP-PI Production Planning for Process Industries modules:

- Chemical

- Pharmaceutical

- Food

In this chapter, you learn:

- Describing a process in detail is essential.

- Using production plants efficiently depends on process orders being scheduled to the various production work centers.

- When a production campaign is in progress, the results have to be carefully monitored.

- There may have to be an extensive network of communication links between measuring instruments on the plant, the laboratory, and the plant controllers.

V

Manufacturing Apps

- Beverages

- Parts of the electronics industry where process manufacturing is prevalent

Overview of Functions

The following groups of functions are provided in PP-PI Production Planning for Process Industries:

- Materials master data

- Resources master data

- Master recipes

- Process order planning

- Campaign and process capacity planning

- Process management

- Process data documentation and evaluation

- Integration with Laboratory Information Systems (LIS)

- Integration with SAP R/3 QM-Quality Management

- Integration with higher-level systems, SAP R/2, nonSAP, SAP R/3 MM, SAP R/3 MRP

Materials Master Data

The concept of resources subsumes the SAP concept of materials. The MM-Materials Management system has a well-established system of standard business programs to manage the following in a uniform manner as examples of materials that can be identified from the materials master records:

- Raw materials

- Semi-finished products

- Finished products

- Assemblies and component subassemblies

- Batches of products or resources

- Services

Resources Master Data

In addition to the type of resource already identified by the MM-Materials Management system, a class of resources defined by the users has been established in the PP-PI Production Planning for Process Industries module. The following are examples of the types of resources recognized by PP-PI:

- Production plant and equipment

- Production staff

- Waste disposal facilities

- Recycling facilities

- The persons working in waste disposal and recycling facilities

- Energy sources

- Transport

- Storage facilities

The concept of a resource is used as an organizational unit on which to focus not only the control of the production processes, but also the calculations associated with requirement and output planning, capacity planning, and the analysis and evaluation of the utilization of these resources.

Resource Hierarchies and Categories

The user can form resource hierarchies to allow capacity aggregation and the simulation of resource activities, using several different resource structures in parallel, if required.

Resources can be assigned to categories formally defined by the user or selected from the suggestions offered by the PP-PI Production Planning for Process Industries component. The following illustrate the variety of possibilities to employ the resource category concept:

- **Line** is a route through the production plant passing through one or more processing units that may be used in more than one way to produce complete batches of product, recycled materials remaining or disposed wastes. NAMUR and ISA/SP88 are references that include definitions of the concept of line. A line may be regarded as the root of a resource hierarchy that includes one or more processing units. A plant may comprise one or more lines or resource hierarchies.

- **Processing Unit** is defined as the smallest logistic unit at which a batch can be manufactured. It may be a vessel in which several process operations can be performed.

- **Labor** may comprise the resource of a single person or be specified in terms of a group of persons with the same qualifications.

- **Transport** is a resource that can carry material between warehouse and plant lines. Pipes and transporting tanks can be used for this purpose in addition to conventional vehicles.

- **In-Process Storage** refers to the facilities for holding material between production steps.

One of the effects of assigning a resource to a resource category is to have this resource displayed in the format of screens and fields common to all resources of that resource category. A default resource is a user-defined master resource record created during Customizing so as to set up values which can be accessed and edited when creating a new instance of that resource in that plant.

Primary and Secondary Resources

The primary resource, from the point of view of planning and control, is the space and equipment in the plant that must be regarded as occupied or committed exclusively to the operation while it is taking place. All the phases within this operation are scheduled to last for the whole of this time period, because nothing else can happen in this primary resource until they have all finished.

If some resources are needed for only some of the phases of an operation, and if they are the kind of resources that could be used elsewhere if they were free, then these flexible resources are nominated as Secondary Resources. You can specify when they start and finish in relation to the start or the finish time of the primary resource operation or the phase in which they are required. For example, a line operator may be required for only one or two critical phases of an operation.

You may have several resources that can be called upon to do the same thing during an operation. You need not choose which one to use until you are ready to release the process order for that batch. These equivalent resources can be assigned to a resource class, which is identified in the master recipe for that operation. Before the actual selection is made, the system will check that the characteristics of the resource make it suitable for the intended purpose.

Resources have to be aggregated up through their hierarchies in order to carry out rough-cut capacity planning and medium-term planning. You may want to add resources to a hierarchy. The SAP R/3 graphic editor will display and enable you to maintain any resource hierarchy by editing the symbols. The resource records will be updated automatically when you have finished making adjustments.

Resource Networks

Processing units and the other resources that serve them are inevitably constrained by demands of the production processes and by the interrelationships between resources. A material cannot flow from one unit to another unless there is a route or pipeline connecting the two, and that channel has to be free in order to accept the traffic. The picture is best displayed as a network that can change automatically to report the situation and can be changed by the controller to effect an improvement. SAP R/3 provides a graphical convention to express the predecessor-successor relationships as blocks connected by lines. The blocks contain data fields. You can readily navigate about the network.

Links may be shown as lines on a network or they may simply cause a field to display a data object. You can link resources with any of the following objects:

- Cost center
- A named person

- A position defined in the HR-PA Human Resources, Personnel Administration system

- A specific qualification or suitability assessment—the SAP R/3 Classification system will help you identify this

- A profile which specifies a set of qualifications or other personnel requirements, such as experience

Every resource has to be allocated to a cost center. This association is used when the CO-PC Product Cost Accounting or CO-OPA Order and Project Accounting modules are computing costs. The link to a person will tell you who is working at a resource.

Resources and Capacity Categories

Capacity is the availability and capability of a resource to perform a task within a particular period of time. The capacity may remain idle if the people and equipment have no work to do. Resources can be assigned to resource categories, and capacities can be assigned to corresponding capacity categories. If a resource is available, it will automatically be assigned the proper capacity categories.

Process orders are scheduled to capacities. Shop floor control and capacity planning are likewise focused on capacities.

Although a capacity is typically measured and maintained in time units, usually hours, conversion factors can be applied to allow the system to manipulate a capacity in other units, of volume or energy, for example.

A pooled capacity can be provided by, for instance, a clean-out team that can be called to work on several different plant lines.

An exclusive capacity commitment indicates that the resource is unable to make available any spare capacity—for example, when it is processing a part load. A nonexclusive capacity can be committed to several orders or to several operations that take place in the one resource.

If you need to go into finer detail for resource planning, you can subdivide capacities and maintain availability data on each part separately. Similarly, you can divide a resource consisting of a work team into individual persons who may have different qualifications that you may wish to schedule and cost in a particular manner.

Resource Data Functions

Default values can be associated with a resource to simplify the maintenance of operations in recipes. For example, standard texts can be assigned to a resource so that they can be referenced when compiling the operation texts in a recipe that uses this resource. The wage group of employees at the resource may be another useful default that is dependent on the resource master data. Standard values for the time taken and the energy requirements can be referenced in a similar way, with the choice of having them used automatically or only in the form of proposals to be confirmed by an operator or planner.

Formulas assigned to a resource can give you the ability to calculate the execution times and the costs. Every capacity defined for a specific resource can be given a formula to be used when the system is computing the capacity requirements of a particular process order assigned to it.

Where a resource is used in a recipe, standard values for the activity types can be entered. And for each activity type assigned to this resource, you can say how these standard values are to be costed. In-house activities will use the cost rates as defined in the cost center to which each resource has been assigned.

Capacity Load Analysis

Each operation master carries data on the standard values of each of the capacities associated with that operation and the quantities needed. This information comes via the formulas stored for the resources.

During capacity load analysis, the system works out how much of each capacity is required to carry out the operations entailed in completing the process order. This is compared with the quantities available of all the capacities needed.

If you call up the interactive graphic planning table, you can dispatch operations to resources and effect capacity leveling. You can also send the load analysis through the interface to Microsoft Excel or a word processing system.

At any stage of planning, you can ask for the capacity availability to be checked for an order or for an entire order structure. If the system sees a bottleneck ahead, it will propose a date to the planner for a revised schedule for this order to avoid the bottleneck.

These are some of the questions to which the system will give you immediate answers:

- What are my available resources?
- Which cost centers are assigned to these resources?
- What are the capacities at these resources?
- Which resources are currently using this specific capacity?
- What is the hierarchical structure of my resources?
- Which materials are being used at this specific resource?
- Which recipes are using this particular resource?

Master Recipes

A master recipe documents all the specifications of a process and describes in detail how a particular plant is to be used to produce one or more materials in a production run.

The SAP R/3 module PP-PI Production Planning for Process Industries has been designed to conform with the norms and guidelines published by the following institutions:

- Instrument Society of America, ISA Norm SP88

- NAMUR, a multinational norms working committee for measuring and control techniques in the chemical industry

- European Batch Forum, which coordinates ISA and European multinational committees such as NAMUR

- Food and Drug Administration Good Manufacturing Practice guidelines for documenting process specifications

Changes are documented separately by the PP-PI Production Planning for Process Industries system for each recipe and for each data object in it, both material and process. Change numbers may be used to control the time period of validity of a change.

The master recipe is used in PP-MRP Material Requirements Planning and in campaign planning under the PP-PI Production Planning for Process Industries system. Links are maintained with the PP-Production Planning and Control module and the functionality offered by it.

Master Recipe Functions

The steps of the production, the resources and materials to be used, the process instructions and the data necessary for control—these are the constituents of a master recipe. It is much like a routing, an inspection plan or a maintenance task list; all can be usefully represented by a network and handled by the SAP R/3 network library.

The recipe has to show the time sequence of the operations and phases. The operation is defined as an independent part of a recipe which is carried out at a primary processing unit, perhaps in phases, and perhaps with secondary resources allocated to it for some or all of the time it spends at the resource.

A process instruction is a structure stored in the master recipe that serves to transfer data or instructions from process planning to process control, and in particular to the phases of a recipe. Once a process order containing a recipe is released for production, the operations and their phases are combined to form control recipes.

Control Recipes

A control recipe destination is defined in the master recipe. It specifies which operations and phases are to be made into control recipes for that destination.

The destination for a control recipe can be a line operator, or it can be a process control system, in which case you can specify the technical address and whether the data transfer is to be triggered by the SAP R/3 system or by the process controller.

Master Recipe Material List

The bill of materials (BOM) is designed to specify the materials that go to make up a finished product. The master recipe material list used in the PP-PI Production Planning for Process Industries module is designed to specify all the materials that are associated with a process, inputs as well as the products. For example, a catalyst, or indeed, part of the output product can be recycled through the process. There may be more than one output product.

The material list shows the following:

- Planned values for each input material
- Mixing ratios
- Yields of each product
- Substances remaining, which may be considered as by-products or wastes

You have to establish a definition of all of these materials, the finished products, the input materials and the materials remaining in the material master records of the MM-Materials Management system.

Intra Materials

Some processes create substances that are sampled, measured and controlled, but which are then consumed in the process and do not appear as an output material. These are intra materials, and they do not have to be defined in the materials master records of the MM-Materials Management system. The intra material may be simply a charge load that is made up in some preliminary operation before being passed to the main process. However, it may be a material which is substantially different in physical or chemical properties from the input material because it has passed through one or more operations.

These intra materials have to be defined in process orders because they need to be part of the materials requirements calculations and they usually have to be inspected.

Because an intra material may have to be handled during inspections and because the plant carrying it may be subject to failure, the intra material may have to be defined in the substance master records of the PP-SHE Safety, Health and Environment system which is being developed by SAP.

Nonmanufacturing Master Recipes

The manufacturing master recipes control the production of a batch. There are other types of recipes supported by the PP-PI Production Planning for Process Industries system:

- **Clean-out recipes**, which are inserted between two operations if required
- **Changeover recipes**, which specify what has to be done and the resources and substances needed to change from one production campaign to another
- **Equipment-testing recipes**, which specify the process instructions that have to be followed to carry out and document the periodic functional testing of a plant line

Process Order Planning

A process order is a SAP R/3 transaction which describes the actual production of one or several lots or batches giving dates and quantities. Before it can be released for production, a process order has to be built up from the master recipe by adding dates, floats, specific resources and so on.

Planning for these process orders takes up data from PP-MRP Material Requirements Planning or from campaign planning runs, and generates process orders for batches within a plan that coordinates all resources. The process order contains all the planned and actual data related to production. It is therefore the prime control instrument.

The master recipe data provides the information necessary to generate control recipes for all required operations and phases. If you do not select a master recipe, the system will automatically create a process order with one token operation, on which you may later elaborate.

The system will not allow you to release an order unless the material components are available. It will then reserve the materials. The MRP run will have already carried out availability checks based on planned data, but this second check will inform the controllers if any unplanned circumstance has upset the plans.

With the basic order dates from the MRP run and rough-cut capacity plans, if available, the scheduling function can determine the start and finish dates for the order and its operations.

Order release initiates the following actions:

- Material reservations made for available and reserved stock are updated in the corresponding material master record in MM-Materials Management.

- The availability of the material is checked automatically.

- Individual resources can be selected to replace the previous specification. The customer may have requested the alteration or the process controller may have placed restrictions on the allocation of resources.

- The controller can allocate an inspection lot record to receive the inspection results.

- Shop floor papers can be printed.

- Permission is granted for the controller to carry out movements to and from the warehouse for this order.

- Permission is granted for the controller to carry out confirmations for this order.

The following displays illustrate the variety of evaluations and analyses available to the planners and the controllers:

- All process orders for a material—for example, for a particular MRP controller or shop floor controller

- List of missing materials

- List of pegged elements

- Orders in backlog

Outputs from shop floor information systems and comments from the line operators can also be displayed for the planners and controllers. The following are examples of potentially important evaluations:

- Resources
- Materials
- Operations
- Orders
- Material consumption
- Product costs

Cost Object Controlling

Cost objects are used to allocate costs according to how they were incurred—an order, a material, a network of cost centers and so on.

Costing of process orders proceeds from planned material consumption and the charge rates established for in-house production activities on the basis of actual production costs. You can use the following functions on process orders:

- Calculate planned costs
- Calculate actual costs
- Transfer actual costs to other objects in the SAP R/3 system, such as materials or customer orders
- Analyze planned and actual costs

You may use the CO-Controlling system to collate cost element data and focus on your total costs.

It is also possible to determine the costs of process orders yet to be settled, and to transfer the value of work in progress to the FI-Financial Accounting system. Schedule dates are important because the planned costs have to be distributed over the scheduled periods, according to the dates when the operation or phase is actually carried out.

Cost element analyses are displayed by the following suite of screen functions:

- Primary cost elements corresponding to FI-GL General Ledger accounts, such as raw materials and semi-finished goods
- Secondary cost elements derived from the CO-Controlling system, such as internal activity allocation and overhead cost
- Cost itemization using cost element groups and origin groups, or according to costing items previously calculated for individual materials and activities
- Cost component split into individual cost elements defined during Customizing and used in material valuation and profitability analysis

Campaign and Process Capacity Planning

A campaign is an extended run of production that may entail a train or line of processes intended to run continuously or by producing a series of batches to what is essentially the same master recipe.

Campaign planning is rough-cut or long-term planning; process planning is detailed or short-term planning. New functionality for campaign planning is under development.

Production plant planning tends to be initiated by publishing planned requirements in the form of a production plan or a campaign. Waste or recycling plants usually receive inputs from many other production plants in the form of remaining materials that have to be processed. These ingredients and their expected scheduling initiate planning for waste and recycling operations.

Capacity Leveling

The aim of capacity leveling across company-wide process chains is to schedule required resources so as to make the best use of limited capacities available. And by "best use," you probably mean some blend of contradictory goals such as:

- Short lead times
- Low inventory
- Adherence to delivery dates
- Optimum order mix, and so on

Capacity leveling is an art that takes a different form, depending on where you work, but SAP R/3 provides some very powerful tools to assist you.

During Customizing, you can define an overall profile for capacity leveling and several subprofiles for displays and list formation. For example, you may elect to have a planning table display something like the following over a range of time periods:

- Capacity requirements per capacity category
- Capacity requirements listed by planned and process orders
- Capacity requirements per process order and/or operation

You have freedom to set up your displays over a wide range and to have the data selected and filtered to suit your convenience. In particular, you may find it helpful to have a planning window displayed which can be moved forward and backward across the planning schedule, and which shows a few time periods either side of the central time period. You can customize the colors and add extra symbols to make the display more informative.

Objects of direct planning relevance, such as capacities and dates, can be changed on the screen and the consequences simulated before confirming the alterations. Planned and process orders can be dispatched from the planning table, and you can deallocate operations or reschedule them. Phases and secondary resources are amenable to similar manipulations.

Strategies for Planning

There is no one optimum strategy for planning complex work processes so as to make best use of resources and yet have short lead times, for example. But there are several techniques and guidelines that have been developed in the process industries and should be considered by anyone in the position of work scheduler or process planner.

You have to dispatch jobs to resources at the right moment, so you need to know how long they are going to take and what resources to send them to. The system offers the following functionality by using parameters and indicators to build your planning strategy:

- **Planning Direction**—The system will schedule operations forward from the next start date or backward from the required completion date.

- **Dispatch Soonest**—An operation can be marked with this indicator to ensure that it is scheduled as early as possible in the planning period.

- **Insert**—One or more operations can be inserted on a particular date. The system will shift other resource commitments to make room for the insert and will re-schedule them around it, using the planning direction you have specified.

- **Close Gaps**—If you mark an operation with this indicator, it signifies that the system can bring forward other actions if you decide to deallocate the marked operation.

- **Terminate Planning if Error**—This indicator on an order signals that all planning activity is to cease if an error condition is reported by another function—if material is not available, for example.

- **ATP Period Logic**—This indicator takes its name from the Available-to-promise sales concept, which reminds the sales planner that material is available to sell only if it has not already been promised elsewhere. In the process industry, for example, if the plan is for each period to process the same amount, and if the planned production for one period is exceeded by 100 percent, perhaps because it makes no sense to interrupt the process, the next period should contribute no production at all. From the planner's point of view, this will bring the actual production back to the planned. In this example, however, the result of overproduction may leave the stock situation critical and additional rush orders may have to be turned away.

- **Dispatching Sort Key**—You can define a sort key to arrange process orders selected for dispatch in a particular sequence. Alternatively, you can arrange for a tailor-made program written in the SAP ADAP/4 programming language to be called to carry out a sorting to your requirements. Each SAP application is supplied with a range of so-called "User Exits," which can be set up during Customizing to pass data to and from other software programs. If these programs have been installed and configured, their User Exits will appear as options in the relevant menu screens at the user interface.

- **Planning Log**—As a planning run is taking place, the system will generate log messages for the operations according to the functions that have been activated. The messages may signal warnings or errors, or just extract information. You can have these messages analyzed to see if the planning strategy can be improved.

Operations can be dispatched in ways that will influence the data assigned to them and hence how they are executed. For example, if you dispatch an operation that is only part of an order to a vacant float that is not large enough to accommodate the rest of the order, there may be a long delay before suitable capacity becomes available to complete the order.

The following functions can be deactivated if necessary:

- Sorting of operations to be dispatched

- Checking dates—for example, of the order dispatch against the basic order date recorded on the planned order, or against previous or following dates of items from the same order

- Checking material availability on the planned date

- Immediate midpoint scheduling of the order

Capacity requirements can be split across resources, including individual resources such as people.

Resource Selection and the Resource Network

The master recipe is the place where you define how resources are to be selected. These selection criteria are used by the SAP R/3 Classification system when preparing a list of possible resources that could be committed for a particular order, either by manual selection or automatically. If several operations are dispatched automatically, the characteristics of the operations defined in the master recipes are compared with those available, in order to make the appropriate choices.

If a planning strategy is in force, this may constrain the automatic dispatching tactics.

The system will always check that the network of resources includes a link from the preceding resource before dispatching the next operation.

Process Management

The aim of process management is to coordinate process control and quality assurance for each process order.

The process order includes the process instructions in the form of control recipes, which are sent to the people who will control the process or the SAP LIMS-Laboratory Information Management Systems. (Process management, in turn, gets back process messages containing the actual data arising from the execution of the operations, the quantities and the qualities, which it will pass on to various destinations. The details are established during Customizing.)

Process Instructions

The process order defines the phases of an order to which are assigned the process instructions. These instructions are expressed as characteristics such as material number or quantity, and for each characteristic a value will be assigned, such as the code number of the material and the number of quantity units.

These instructions are defined by the user to suit the specific installations on the plant line. You can have instructions in natural language just as the line operators have machine instructions for automatic process control equipment. This list indicates the range of process instruction variables you can specify:

- **Process parameter**—a machine instruction or a text

- **Process data request**—addressed to process control to send actual process data to PP-PI

- **Process message subscription**—a list of the unplanned event types to be reported, such as alarms and the exceeding of limits

- **Process data calculation formula**—specifies the calculation that must be recorded on the Process Instruction sheet and have its value sent to specified destinations using a process message

- **Inspection results request**—commands that one or more of the operations or phases are to be subject to inspections and have the results recorded

- **Dynamic function call**—enables the line operator to call a user-defined function module from within the PI sheet procedure. For example, this function module can conduct a dialogue with the line operator or automatically retrieve data from internal or external applications. The dynamic function call is the line operator's connection with the rest of the SAP R/3 system and its interfaces to SAP and nonSAP applications.

Control Recipe Destinations

The control systems or line operators who need to know the process instructions are defined during Customizing as the control recipe destinations. They are assigned to a process order at the level of the phase of an operation so that the controller of that phase will receive the process instruction, regardless of who or what is getting instructions about the other phases. This assignment can therefore take account of the resource network and its links, and detailed interactions between controllers and processing resources as the operations pass through their respective phases.

The PI Sheet

The process instruction sheet procedure may be mediated by a handwritten sheet, a computer-printed document or a screen available to the line operator. In the electronic format there is the added advantage that the operator can enter information and initiate calls to function modules to send or receive information. The following functions are supported by the online PI sheet procedure:

- Display of control instructions in natural language

- Operator input fields that are immediately validated and sent to the predefined destinations in the form of process messages

- Quantity calculations using entered data and predefined formulas from the control recipe that are sent to predefined destinations as process messages

- Direct connection to the SAP R/3 QM-Quality Management module for the purpose of entering the results of in-process control or inspection tasks

- Direct calls of user-defined functions to conduct dialogues or call data from internal or external applications

Process Messages

Message categories for transferring data to SAP components are predefined. The following types of SAP R/3 objects are predefined SAP message destinations:

- SAP R/3 function modules

- External functions

- Users of SAPoffice mail system

- ABAP/4 tables which are used by company-specific programs written in the SAP ABAP/4 programming language

However, you can define company-specific message categories during Customizing. These may be used, for example, to call nonSAP external functions or to access user-defined ABAP/4 tables in which the contents of a message can be stored for subsequent evaluation.

The following examples of process messages to SAP R/3 modules illustrate their use:

- The process control system sends a process message on the amount of ingredients charged into the process vessel. This is a change of stock that is automatically posted to the inventory control module of MM-Materials Management

- The status of an operation is sent for display on the planning table

- Product quality is reported and transferred to the batch record for archiving

Control Recipe and Process Message Monitors

The control recipe monitor is a display screen showing the current status of each control recipe as it passes from generation to completion. The overview of control recipes can be supplemented by logs containing detailed information of the history of each control recipe, including all changes and malfunctions, all of them time-stamped.

V

Manufacturing Apps

In a similar fashion, the process message monitor displays the status of process messages from the moment they are received by process management until they are sent to their destinations. A message is stored if the destination does not exist or is temporarily not accessible. Incomplete or incorrect process messages can be edited at the monitor and dispatched to their proper destinations.

Integration with SAP R/3 QM-Quality Management

The SAP R/3 QM-Quality Management system is linked to the PP-PI Production Planning for Process Industries system, whether or not there exists an additional link to a SAP LIMS—Laboratory Information Management System.

One of the functions of QM-Quality Management is to maintain the master data necessary to comply with the recommendations of ISO900~0, which includes the complete documentation of all activities and procedures. In particular, it is essential to document the information necessary to measure and assess the quality of any product at any stage in its production, from raw materials to finished product. The inspection operations will require resources which can be preplanned and costed from the beginning of product development only if this kind of information is available.

When an inspection lot is generated from a process order, its first function is to document the fact that an inspection is to be conducted. Several partial production lots may be allocated to an inspection lot. When the inspection results are available, they are stored under the inspection lot number in the QM-Quality Management database. Access to these results has to be via this inspection lot number.

A distinction can be usefully drawn between in-process control or inspection, and post-process control or inspection.

In-Process Control

The attraction of in-process control is that the inspection results can be used as feedback to change the control recipe and thus control the current processing. If a laboratory facility is involved, the production order can include the provision of an inspection lot for the purpose of analysis, together with the specification of the quality standards that must be met.

If batch inspection is the practice, then the MM-Materials Management system will manage the material in stocks of batch size, and the SAP R/3 Classification System will contain a specification of the attributes of a batch of each of the materials to be handled in this way. Each batch will retain its individual identity and quality information.

The capacity of the laboratory to carry out these analyses of inspection lots can be made the subject of capacity planning and scheduling, an important consideration if the laboratory working hours do not extend to cover the production hours.

Communication to a laboratory can be mediated by the QM-IDI Inspection Data Interface.

Integration with Higher-Level Systems

There are various ways of linking the PP-PI Production Planning for Process Industries system with the many and varied material requirements planning (MRP) systems to be found in this industry. The linking is differentiated as vertical or horizontal.

Vertical linking is where the PP-PI system is subordinate to a higher-level MRP system. Horizontal linking refers to a PP-PI system and an MRP system that have a common network serving to link their rough-cut or campaign planning systems and their detailed planning systems. Neither is subordinate to the other. No cross-system linking logic is available at present for this horizontal configuration.

SAP R/3 will provide the functionality to link the MRP level of any higher-level system with the detailed planning system of PP-PI Production Planning for Process Industries.

There are three types of integration:

- Linking one SAP R/3.3 installation to SAP R/3.3 system is possible in both the vertical and the horizontal forms because each system has its own database. This arrangement is not supported for SAP R/3 Release 3.0 because of the limitations imposed on a system with more than one central database.

- A SAP R/2 mainframe system can be linked to a client/server system which uses SAP R/3 Release 3.0. The SAP R/2 system can be vertically integrated with several subordinate SAP R/3 systems. This arrangement is carried out via CPI-C/LU 6.2.

- SAP R/3 linking between an external host system and the SAP R/3 system is supported as a vertical integration by Release 3.0, using file transfer tools. Releases of R/3 from 3.1 onward use other methods.

Vertical Linking in SAP R/3 Release 3.0

The requirements of a logic that will integrate the MRP level of any system with the detailed planning system of PP-PI Production Planning for Process Industries include the following:

- Transfer material master data using file transfer methodology as part of the migration project.

- Transfer material requirements by reading them into the list of external requirements of the PP-PI component. If the higher-level system is a SAP R/2 system, the requirements can be transferred from the production order with quantities and dates; otherwise, the requirements have to be first converted to a UNIX file.

- Transfer inventory records via the batch input interface for goods receipts.

- Allocate requirements to process orders using the copying techniques established during Customizing.

- Confirmation of material consumption for the process order by reading this into a UNIX file after the order has been processed, and returning the file to the SAP R/2 or other higher-level system.

- Confirmation of processed material requirements by posting order confirmations back to the SAP R/2 or other higher-level system.

Process Data Logging and Evaluation

It is becoming increasingly important for manufacturers to maintain detailed records of process data in the form of planned values for recipes and actual values for executed process orders. There may be a legal requirement to hold proof of the correct execution of production runs and a commercial requirement to discern opportunities to improve the efficiency of the plant and its associated activities.

For example, the Federal Drug Administration (FDA) advises that the following information should be documented for each batch produced:

- Process order number, batch number
- Charging and yield information
- Process instruction sheet
- Equipment and resources used
- Laboratory analysis values for quality inspections
- Errors and malfunctions during the batch operations
- Location and identification of the finished products
- Confirmation by the line operator

In accordance with the FDA Good Manufacturing Practice (GMP) guidelines, the electronic batch record contains all the above information, which is written under a time stamp for each item and event from the moment when the order is released until it is located in the warehouse.

The process order is the main focus of the electronic batch record, which is formatted as print lists. The following objects also contribute data in the same format:

- Process instruction sheets with comments and notes listed at the end
- Inspection lot data records
- Process messages from the process message log
- User-defined lists that the user has generated and archived

PP-SHE Safety, Health, and Environment

This module is under development by SAP and will be completely integrated with the PP-PI Production Planning for Process Industries module. The functionality is expected to include the following:

- Substance database with predefined attributes
- Product database with predefined attributes

- Substance database with user-defined attributes

- Product database with user-defined attributes

- Risk and safety phrases catalog with management of translated phrases

- Distribution of substance database over organization structures

- Material safety data sheet for reporting and evaluation

- Accident procedures for reporting and evaluation

PP-SHE will also be completely integrated with the following SAP applications:

- SD-Sales and Distribution

- MM-Materials Management

- WM-Workplace Management

- PM-Plant Maintenance

From Here...

You can find out more information about the PP-PI Production Planning for Process Industries by looking in other chapters of this book. Here are a few mentions:

- Technical matters are further discussed in Chapter 3, "System Architecture and Distributed Applications."

- The accounting side of process planning is handled by the FI-Financial Accounting module which is discussed in Chapter 12, "Understanding the FI-Financial Management Module."

- In all production facilities, staff are of critical importance. The relevant SAP application is HR-Human Resources, described in Chapter 22, "Understanding the HR-Human Resources Module."

- "ABAP/4 Program Development with the R/3 Workbench" is described in Chapter 28.

- PP-PI is a type of Industry Solution which is a development that supplements the SAP R/3 system for a specific industry. Other SAP Complementary Solutions are mentioned in Appendix H, "Complementary Solutions."

Chapter 19

Understanding the PM-Plant Maintenance Module

The increasing application of mechanization and the use of power-assisted tools in modern industry have emphasized the importance of plant maintenance. In addition, automation and the attendant instrumentation and control technologies have continued to extend. Variations in the quality of output and the unscheduled interruption of output flow continue to be of the utmost significance to the profitability of an enterprise.

Plant maintenance is clearly essential, and the cost of doing it badly can be high. In addition to the owners and shareholders in an enterprise, members of the public are rightly concerned that industrial plants should not be allowed to malfunction. There are all too many instances of very serious outcomes arising from lapses in preventive maintenance and inadequate performance in corrective maintenance.

The SAP approach of developing standard business software which is customized to suit a particular installation has been applied to the management of plant maintenance. The system is based on a rigorous specification of data objects and the processing with which they are associated. Flexible user interface systems make the PM-Plant Maintenance module easy to operate, and it is fully integrated with the other SAP R/3 modules that have been installed and configured.

The SAP R/3 PM-Plant Maintenance module comprises standard business programs, grouped into the following components:

- PM-EQM   Equipment and Technical Objects
- PM-PRM   Preventive Maintenance
- PM-WOC   Maintenance Order Management
- PM-PRO   Maintenance Projects
- PM-SMA   Service Management
- PMIS   Plant Maintenance Information System

In this chapter, you learn:

- How the PM-Plant Maintenance module supports and controls the effective maintenance of equipment and buildings.

- How to organize plant maintenance data.

  Each item of equipment to be maintained is assigned a master record.

- How to specify subcomponents in an assembly for maintenance purposes.

  Each component is represented on the complex data structure which represents the piece of equipment.

- How to represent an operational system as a network.

The Organization of Plant Maintenance

The operational units of interest to PM-Plant Maintenance are the production and storage facilities of your company and those of any of your customers for whom you manage plant maintenance. In accordance with the data management philosophy pervading all SAP products, the operational systems of interest have to be defined in terms of a common organizational structure that, if so called upon, can take the smallest item and trace its owners up through the organizational chart to the very top, which in SAP R/3 terms will be the client. In the PM-Plant Maintenance module, there are several layers of organizational structure that have been introduced for the purpose of managing plant maintenance, but they have to be placed in the common organizational hierarchy which will eventually link them to the client.

SAP Organizational Units

The SAP R/3 general organizational units relevant to PM-Plant Maintenance are taken from the SAP R/3 Enterprise Data Model, as follows:

Client—the highest level in SAP R/3. The data of one client may not be accessed by another client. There is often a training client and a testing client, in addition to the client code that represents your group or corporate identity and under which the SAP system runs normal business. Some data is managed at the client level because everyone in the corporate group of companies will want to refer to exactly the same information, and be certain that it has been maintained as up-to-date and correct. Vendor addresses would be an example of data managed at the client level.

Company Code—signifies a legal unit under the client that produces its own financial documents, the balance sheet, and the profit and loss statement, and may well maintain them as continuously reconciled.

Plant—an organizational unit that is clearly central to maintenance management. A plant can be a production site, or it can be a group of storage locations that share materials. Plant is the unit for which MRP-Materials Requirement Planning prepares plans and maintains the inventory. It is the focus of MM-Materials Management. Each plant will have been assigned planning and control elements such as material, inventory, operations, work centers, and so on. Under PM-Plant Maintenance, a plant is the place where operational systems are located and where they have to be maintained.

PM-Plant Maintenance Organizational Units

In extension of the SAP R/3 structure of organizational units, the PM-Plant Maintenance system uses some units that are primarily related to physical locations, and some that are created mainly for the purposes of planning.

The following location-related organizational units are recognized and have their own master records:

■ **Maintenance Plant**—The plant where the operational systems of a company are installed, and hence where their maintenance is most likely to take place

- **Application Area Part**—A part of a production plant that can be designated an application area and assigned to a particular contact person who is responsible for coordination between the production and maintenance departments

- **Piece of Equipment**—The data object which represents the resource used to carry out a maintenance task may be a piece of equipment, a production resource, a tool, a test instrument, and so on. It may be a resource in a production line. It may be a suite of implemented software. A piece of equipment cannot be allocated to more than one plant at a time.

- **Functional Area**—The place where a task is carried out, a functional unit in an operational system. A functional area cannot be allocated to more than one plant at a time.

The following planning-related organizational units are recognized and have their own master records:

- **PM Planning Plant**—Several maintenance plants can be associated for planning purposes, and one of the group will be given the status of the PM Planning Plant. If a plant undertakes its own planning, it will be treated as the PM Planning Plant. Maintenance requirements may arise from the PM Planning Plant to be directed there from other maintenance plants.

- **PM Planner Group**—For a large company there may be a central work scheduling department that constitutes a PM Planner Group. At the workshop level, the planner group may be comprised of just one foreman or perhaps the group of shop floor area supervisors.

- **PM Work Center**—The capacity unit for maintenance work is the work center, usually allocated to the PM Planning Plant. The PM Work Center may be a mobile capacity that can be deployed to other plants or loaned to the PM Planning Plant.

The Description and Structure of Operational Systems

The part of an operational system that appears on the inventory—the inventoried object—is known for maintenance purposes as a piece of equipment. It lives, at least conceptually, in a functional location. It can be dismantled from this functional location and installed in another functional location. An area of a plant that has been designated a functional area for maintenance purposes may contain one or many functional locations, depending on the number of pieces of equipment that are located in it.

The PM-Plant Maintenance system allows an unlimited number of levels in a structure—as many as you need to represent properly the piece of equipment that you are going to maintain. Variable systems structuring is supported: The system allows you to define the depth and type of structure you are going to use for numbering pieces of equipment, and you indicate which numbering structure you are going to use by means of a Structure Indicator.

V

Manufacturing Apps

A piece of equipment may comprise an Individual Technical System, or a technical system may include one or more pieces of equipment.

The piece of equipment may need to be subdivided into materials of type Assembly and of type Spare. The assemblies and spares making up a piece of equipment can be specified in an Equipment or PM-Bill of Materials.

The data structures used by the PM-Plant Maintenance module follow the data object conventions used throughout SAP systems. Any field in a master record can be assigned data, which is used by the application. The field may be assigned the name of a data object, in which case the system is able to access that named object and make use of the data it contains. Indeed, the named object may bear the names of yet other objects which can be accessed in the same way. The structure is hierarchical because the user can drill down the linked data objects to find any item of data that is required. Functional locations, pieces of equipment and assemblies can all be hierarchical structures themselves, and so on without limits to the depth.

Functional Locations

All the processing required by PM-Plant Maintenance can be carried out in relation to functional locations. If additional information about operational systems is required, you can refer to the equipment management data held in these functional locations.

The user can decide how to allocate operational systems to the functional locations used by PM-Plant Maintenance. The structure may correspond to the structure of the manufacturing process, or to the operational function, or to the plant area in which the maintenance work will take place. Indeed, the business may have no physical space that could be recognized as the plant.

Here is an example of a maintenance numbering structure with four levels and no punctuation symbols:

Production Area	1234
System	1234123
Subarea	123412312
Functional unit	1234123121234

This next example of a user-defined systems structure in PM-Plant Maintenance has six levels and uses alphanumeric coding with some punctuation:

System	an	B6
Area	an-n	B6-3
Subarea	an-n-aann	B6-3-SA26
Function	an-n-aanna	B6-3-SA26Z
Subfunction	an-n-aanna/a	B6-3-SA26Z/G
Item	an-n-aanna/a/nnn	B6-3-SA26Z/G/123

Whatever structures your maintenance operations are working with, you can have them displayed in graphical form. By selecting an item on your display and using the special function buttons, you can call up additional information on the item you have selected, and make alterations to it. Alternatively, you can move the display up and down the levels of your hierarchy.

Each of the functional locations has associated master data, which identify its place in the maintenance structure and locate it in the plant. The master data also points to the PM-Plant Maintenance accounting and planning data. The information can be supplemented by references to word processing documents and drawings, and the SAP R/3 Classification system. Multilingual texts and access to the equipment usage information complete the catalog of data associated with a functional location.

Reference Functional Locations

If several individual systems belong to the same category, and will therefore be likely to have data in common, you can set up a reference functional location, which contains all the data except the actual location information. When you create a new instance of this system, all the reference data will be copied to your new master for you to edit if necessary and supplement with the information that is particular to the new system.

Changes to a reference functional location may be allowed to propagate to all the functional locations of the same category.

Pieces of Equipment

These are defined as the tangible objects in a company that are subject to the PM-Plant Maintenance system. They fall into categories, which can be defined during customizing by the user. The following types of serialized objects are likely to be in the list of objects that require maintenance:

- Production equipment

- Production resources and tools

- Test and measurement equipment

- Transport equipment

- Customer equipment maintained under contract

The following guidelines suggest when it is worth creating an equipment master record in the PM-Plant Maintenance system:

- The object will require individual data management

- The object will require maintenance, whether planned, regular or repairs

- Maintenance has to be recorded, for example for insurance, safety, annual checks

- Technical data on the object will have to be collected and evaluated over a long time

- Maintenance costs for the object are to be monitored

- Records are to be kept of the usage time at functional locations

A piece of equipment retains its individual identity through its master data records, no matter where it is being used. It has its usage time segments cumulated from purchase to disposal. By this means, the person responsible for planning is identified and the account assignment data are documented, whether the equipment is being used in production, is in storage, or is on the inventory of a customer.

The equipment master usage time segment also documents the status changes of a piece of equipment according to a status structure, which can be defined by the user, as in the following examples:

- Planned
- Undergoing testing
- In productive use
- Broken down
- Scrapped

The main data attribute clusters of an equipment master are structured as follows:

- Identification, general data, location data
- SD-Sales and Distribution data
- PM-Plant Maintenance data
- Documents and drawings
- Multilingual texts
- Internal remarks and notes
- SAP R/3 Multiple Classification and supplementary technical characteristics
- Equipment usage records

Install and Dismantle Functions

Equipment can be given the installed status by accessing the appropriate master record and applying the install function to assign it to a functional location, having perhaps first dismantled the item it is to replace.

The same result can be achieved by first accessing the functional location master record and then dismantling and installing as required. The usage records are updated automatically by these functions, and a new time segment begins every time there is a change of functional location.

If the equipment is main equipment at the head of an equipment hierarchy, the entire structure below the equipment selected will be given the installed or dismantled status. The equipment master records will have been assigned a numbering system during customizing, which will have been followed when the details of your company's plant are defined for maintenance purposes. At any stage, you can see where an individual piece of equipment is located in relation to the hierarchy: to which higher order equipment it belongs, and which pieces of equipment come below it and will therefore be subjected to the same maintenance planning procedures.

Maintenance Assemblies and PM Bills of Material (BOM)

An assembly, in the engineering context of the PM-Plant Maintenance system, is not an individual object like a piece of equipment; it represents a category that is useful for directing attention to parts or aspects of a piece of equipment. Assemblies in the PM system are managed as material master records. Only the engineering data need to be maintained. They can be used across plants.

However, assemblies that are also used in the MM-Materials Management system for procurement and as stock items for storage will have to be assigned to a plant, because they will have to have comprehensive data maintenance.

A Bill of Material (BOM) for plant maintenance will display the structural elements of a technical object, such as an operational system, as a list of the material items marked as maintenance assemblies. A PM-BOM can be created for an individual piece of equipment or for a functional location. It can also be valid for a list of technical objects.

If all the technical objects assigned to a BOM are identical, they can share the BOM. If only some attributes are in common, the differences can be managed as variants on the common BOM. If you have many identical pieces of equipment, you may find it useful to define a category for them by assigning a category name to a material master and have it adopt the BOM that applies to all present and future examples of that category.

When a technical object such as a functional location or a piece of equipment is considered from the point of view of a higher-level structure of which it is a part, the system will automatically take account of all the details in the BOM. You can keep track of the usage of materials and assemblies, even when you are working at higher levels, by calling up one of the "Where-Used" lists. If you highlight on the user display a material or an assembly, you will be offered a choice of special function keys. If you have selected a material that is used in various places in the plant, then the "Where-Used" function will provide you with a list of these places and the pieces of equipment that are involved. If your display includes a technical maintenance procedure, for example, you can ask for a list of all the situations where this procedure is used in your plant.

The validity of a BOM is specified by means of a starting date from which any changes are valid. An ending date can also be specified. You can use this information to identify which BOM was used on previous maintenance schedules, for example.

The BOM has a header in which the planner has assigned the BOM to one or more plants, specified the validity, and set the status management key to indicate whether the BOM is released for maintenance purposes in its current form.

The object parts itemized in the BOM can be assemblies for engineering maintenance or spares, or documents or drawings. They are differentiated by item category, as follows:

■ **Stock items**—are automatically reserved when used in a PM-Plant Maintenance order

- **Non-stock items**—automatically create a purchase requisition and therefore an order-specific material procurement via SD-Sales and Distribution, Purchasing. A materials master does not necessarily have to be present in MM-Materials Management.

- **Variable-sized items**—can be entered in the size required because the system will automatically convert to the stockable size and quantity to draft the purchase requisition

- **Document items**—include drawings and safety regulations

- **Text items**—free-format text added for user-defined reasons

Engineering Change Management

The SAP R/3 system manages engineering changes as a central basic data function, which is used on the following data objects:

- Materials

- Documents

- Bills of Materials

- Task lists

Each change is dated and assigned a standard reason. Changes can be sorted by number, date, or reason. Any number of basic objects can be changed using one change number.

Network Representations of Operational Systems

The functional locations and pieces of equipment in one operational system can be connected in various ways with other systems. The PM-Plant Maintenance system must take account of these connections when planning and executing maintenance.

The SAP R/3 standard ways of representing operational systems are the work breakdown structure and the network. Both are described in Chapter 30, "R/3 Business Workflow Management."

The essence of a network is the link between objects. In the context of the PM-Plant Maintenance system, the object is often a functional location or a piece of equipment. The link can be in terms of workflow, energy flow, control, and so on. The linked objects can be in different systems.

In the SAP R/3 system, an object link master record will include the following types of information:

- Descriptive information on the type of link

- Whether the link is directional or nondirectional

- The technical, not necessarily tangible, objects at each end of the link

Technical links can be classified and evaluated using specific criteria by the SAP R/3 Classification system.

Through the PM-Plant Maintenance system, the network of links can be used to plan and notify the connected systems of maintenance activities and also to analyze the consequences of any malfunction that may occur.

The SAP R/3 Classification System

The R/3 Classification system is a central function available to all applications. It is particularly relevant to maintenance because of the large numbers of different objects that fall into the scope of a PM-Plant Maintenance system.

There are types of objects, such as the following:

- Pieces of equipment
- Functional locations
- Assemblies
- Spares
- Materials
- Task lists

For each of these object types there may be the need to maintain data on many instances and many variations of class-specific data.

The SAP R/3 Classification System recognizes the following structural elements:

- Classes, each with a catchword assigned to it
- Multilevel class hierarchies
- Classifiable objects
- Characteristics that describe the properties of classifiable objects
- Values that particularize a characteristic and can be expressed in user-defined or standard formats, with value ranges also user-defined or standard

The descriptions of the characteristics and the values that can be assigned to them are available in all of the SAP-supported languages.

When you create a new object using the SAP R/3 Classification system, you can copy data fields from the master records, including the extensive descriptive information that is often stored there.

You can also copy from external storage media any data that has been stored in standard formats such as DIN 4001. This is an example of a data format, which has been used in several plant maintenance record systems. The classes and characteristics of the equipment recorded on a DIN 4001 database will be generated automatically if the data is transferred to the PM-Plant Maintenance application module.

You can also classify a material directly from the CAD system or search there for materials.

To search using the Classification system entails first selecting an object class, then searching within the class using characteristics and their values.

If your search yields a data set rather than a single item, you can call upon an extensive range of standard evaluation functions and perform a systematic analysis of your data set.

Notification of Unplanned Maintenance Requirements

A maintenance notification describes a technical state of exception in a reference object. It may be a malfunction or other exceptional circumstance that requires prompt action which is in addition to the regular activities in maintenance.

If you know the reference object, you can define the functional location and the affected piece of equipment or the malfunctioning assembly. You can document this in the maintenance notification.

However, you may not know exactly what has gone wrong, only the production area or the approximate position within a technical system where the problem lies. This is a situation where the hierarchy data structures of the PM module will assist. You select the name of the area in which you think the problem has arisen. The special function keys will offer you a variety of options for refining your search until you have identified the suspect unit. At any stage in your search, you can call for technical information such as the relevant BOM, which may well help you narrow your focus to identify an appropriate target for a maintenance procedure.

After work is technically complete, the maintenance notification can be used to document the completion confirmation. This technical explanation can result in further maintenance notifications.

The Structure of a Maintenance Notification

A flexible maintenance catalog system based on location-specific or equipment-specific data is used for allocating types and causes of damage and the effects on the objects and the tasks to be performed. Catalogs are structured in the following manner:

- By type—such as damage catalog, tasks catalog, causes catalog

- By code groups—such as vehicles, pumps, instruments

- By code group task codes—such as vehicle brakes tested

The SAP R/3 Classification system can be used to classify maintenance notifications and amplify them with specific data.

When you create a functional location or a piece of equipment master, you can assign the maintenance catalog that would be appropriate in the event of a malfunction or unusual event.

An extra task may be required in addition to carrying out maintenance. For example, it may be necessary to document an incident and collect evidence at the location. Tasks of this kind can be specified in the maintenance notification. Activities to effect the repair can be allocated from the task catalog, which is based on experience. New tasks can be specified and documented through the SAP word processing system.

Maintenance notifications already in the PM-Plant Maintenance system can be selected for processing by using a search criterion. This may entail specifying temporal parameters, organizational parameters such as cost centers, or functional parameters such as downtime or damage description. When you have refined your selection of maintenance notifications, you can assign one or more of them to an order, in which case the data in the notifications will be copied to the order, from which they can eventually be evaluated in the maintenance order history.

The PM notifications can be controlled by a flexible status management system to which you can add status processing steps such as the following:

- Creating a maintenance notification
- Confirming a technical explanation
- Start of processing a maintenance order
- Completion confirmation of a maintenance order
- Completion of notification processing

You can use this status management system to select maintenance notifications for further processing, which may enable them to graduate to the next status. For example, you may call for a piece of equipment to be dismantled far enough to determine whether it has indeed failed in the way that has been suggested from previous maintenance histories of this type of assembly in each location in which it is installed in your plant. This investigation may give you the information you need to decide whether to replace this item or have it repaired.

To withdraw a piece of equipment from production may entail serious consequences for the production schedule until it can be replaced. On the other hand, the interruption may give you the opportunity to schedule other items for maintenance at the same time.

Maintenance Orders

The execution of a maintenance task is initiated and controlled by a maintenance order, which specifies the following details:

- Type of maintenance order
- Scope of the order
- Dates of starting and finishing the whole maintenance order and its stages, if there are any
- Resources to be used to carry out the order

Maintenance orders are of three types, which differ by the extent of previous planning possible, as follows:

- **Regular PM-Plant Maintenance orders**—released by maintenance schedules at due dates with their scope prescribed

- **Planned PM-Plant Maintenance orders**—arising from maintenance notifications, from which they can be directly converted into maintenance orders to ensure that foreseen repair tasks will be carried out

- **Unplanned PM-Plant Maintenance orders**—tend to be rush orders created with a minimum of information in response to an unforeseen machine breakdown or malfunction, or as immediate action after an accident

One of the essentials of a maintenance order is a precise reference to one or more technical objects. The period of validity of a maintenance order is differentiated between individual orders and standing orders, which are valid for a longer period, but which have to be confirmed on each occasion they are scheduled.

On either basis, an order is created for each maintenance task so that the costs of maintenance and the history of maintenance tasks can be documented for each technical object in the order.

A maintenance order can be processed internally through your own maintenance workshops, or externally by service companies if, for example, the cost-effectiveness is superior, the specialized knowledge is unavailable in-house, or temporary bottlenecks would otherwise occur.

Maintenance Order Elements

The structure of a PM order includes the following elements:

- Order header
- PM order object list
- Operations and suboperations that are within the scope of this order
- Material list for the order
- PRT, production resources and tools

In the order header there will be general information and precise data on the following essentials:

- Order type
- The person responsible
- Dates
- Priorities
- The PM order reference object list

A reference object can be specified as a whole system or as a subsystem. The PM-Plant Maintenance module will amplify the reference object by also listing the individual functional locations, pieces of equipment, and maintenance assemblies.

The scope of a maintenance order is expressed in terms of the operations and suboperations that comprise the individual work steps needed to complete the maintenance task. The specification of each operation has to include the following information:

- Description of the operation or suboperation
- The work center that is to perform the operation
- The amount of work required
- The duration of the work
- Whether the operation is to be processed internally or externally by a third party

The numbered order of the list of operations will normally be the sequence in which they are to be performed. SAP is developing a facility to specify a network structure where the maintenance task can benefit from parallel working of some of its suboperations. Major maintenance operations can take advantage of the functionality of the SAP Workflow and the SAP R/3 Project System modules, which are designed to support networked activities.

Materials listed for a maintenance order can be allocated directly to each operation, or they can be assigned by including the relevant PM-Plant Maintenance Bill of Materials. Either way, the material number, quantity and prices have to be documented in each instance.

The material list can include stock and nonstock materials, which may or may not have master records already established. If they do not, you have to enter the details, rather than have them copied from the master records. The stock materials will cause stock reservations to be generated automatically; the others will be passed to MM-Materials Management, Purchasing, under control of purchase requisitions, again generated automatically.

All the resources, such as tools, measuring equipment, and documents or drawings, needed for the maintenance operations are managed in the system as PRT, production resources and tools. They can be assigned to the operations in any quantity. The type of tangible objects, which can be managed as PRT include the following:

- Sets of instructions
- Hand tools
- Portable power tools
- Machine tools established in the plant for maintenance purposes
- Machine tools established in the plant with capacity available for maintenance purposes

- Measuring and calibration equipment

- Programs for numerically-controlled machine tools

- Drawings

- Jigs and fixtures

Processing Maintenance Orders

Regular maintenance entails planning ahead. How far ahead to plan, the call horizon, will depend on the anticipated loads on the equipment and their maintenance requirements. Regular maintenance orders are created by scheduling maintenance plans containing the maintenance strategy and the scheduling parameters. When they are released they are complete and ready to be carried out.

If you are entering a maintenance order directly, or if the order has been converted from a maintenance notification, the details of the order may have to be elaborated as the result of subsequent planning or processing.

When the origin is a maintenance notification, an individual maintenance order will be complete as far as the list of reference objects, the scope and purpose of the task, and the required execution dates. All that remains to be added is the execution data. You may have a bundle of maintenance notifications that are all to be covered by a single maintenance order. In such a case, you can refer to a main object such as a technical system, a subsystem, a piece of equipment, a cost center or a location. When you see the object list that the SAP R/3 system will produce, you can link the individual maintenance notifications with the reference objects to which they should be directed.

A maintenance order is subject to status control, which can be user-defined, as it traverses the main documented steps in the order cycle, for example as follows:

- Order creation

- Order release

- Order printing

- Order confirmation

- Order completion

Each status defines the forms of processing that are permitted and forbidden, and also the automatic documentation that will occur. For example, you cannot have an order printed until its status has reached the "Released" level. When printing has occurred, the status will automatically shift to "Printed" if this is what you decreed should happen when you were customizing your system.

Circumstances may oblige you to interrupt the maintenance order processing. In these instances, the system can document the exceptional status according to its cause. For example, a maintenance order might have to be held up because a wrong component has been delivered. You can also manually interrupt a maintenance task because there is a more urgent demand on the resources allocated to it, and you wish to alter the priority.

This intrusion will be documented automatically, although you will be invited to record an explanation by selecting a reason from a list offered by the PM system, or by entering free text.

Maintenance Order Settlement

The estimated costs for a maintenance order are calculated at the planning stage, and the actual costs are computed when the order completion is able to provide the information necessary in the form of the times of the capacity loads at the internal workshops or the loads on the external services.

All the costs are displayed by cost element, selected as appropriate from the list of forty standard cost elements recognized by the CO-Controlling module. The accounting period is assigned on the basis of the activity dates, and the amounts are debited to the appropriate target account.

Resource Management

The capacity available at a maintenance workshop is defined in terms of work centers. A work center is a data object representing any of the following kinds of resources:

- A group of people, in a maintenance workshop, for instance
- An individual person
- An individual machine or machine tool

The SAP R/3 functions devoted to work center costing have a list of standard formulas that can be assigned to a maintenance work center in order to determine the execution time, costs and capacity requirements of any work that can be sent there. You can supplement and adapt these formulas to suit your own company maintenance methods.

The work center is the focus for maintenance planning. When an order is placed, the system automatically checks that the necessary capacities will be available at the times required and that the spares and reserve parts or operating supplies will be on hand when the order is released for execution. PRT such as special devices and lifting gear may be assigned permanently to reference objects, or they may be available for more general use.

A work center may have been assigned default values which can be copied to any maintenance order allocated to it. There will be a link to a cost center and to an activity type in the CO-Controlling module, so that internal activities can be costed and cleared on the basis of the maintenance activities allocated to the cost center.

Budgets for maintenance projects are monitored using the SAP R/3 Project system.

Maintenance Work Center Capacities

The units for measuring capacity at a maintenance work center can be defined to suit the circumstance, and any amount can be allocated. The capacity available can be defined as a standard available capacity, which is governed by the following factors:

V

Manufacturing Apps

- The capacity rate per unit time of the available people and their machines

- The number of shifts

- The usage time per shift

- The degree of utilization authorized

The available capacity might not be evenly distributed over time; it may have to be defined as a profile or distribution function.

The capacity requirements entailed by the maintenance order are based on the operations, the suboperations, and the time required. The activity capacity requirements may have to be allocated to more than one work center in order to provide the range and quantities of the various capacities necessary. Not every work center is omnipotent: some are specialized; some are too heavily committed elsewhere.

The maintenance planner will call up a capacity load situation display for each work center to see how the capacity requirements allocated to this resource in each planning period match up to the capacities available. If the work center can provide a range of maintenance capabilities, the planner will have the display show how the capacity requirements are loaded on the capacities available in each activity category.

If you are carrying out estimate planning, you may find it useful to build a work center hierarchy specifically for the estimate. You can have this evaluated and analyzed to make your estimate more precise.

Planning and Scheduling Regular Maintenance Tasks

Quality control depends on reliable processing to make sure that the planned adjustments are accurately sustained. An unreliable plant will produce unreliable products. Unreliable production lines can become the target of legal and market reaction because the consumers of the product—and the neighbors of the plant—lose faith in the company.

Worn plant is unreliable; unreliable plant can malfunction catastrophically. Regular maintenance should identify sources of unreliability and accidents waiting to happen. These are not new arguments, but they are becoming salient. Companies are seeking better maintenance management. Prevention costs less than cure.

A maintenance strategy is a data object that represents the scheduling rules for regular maintenance tasks and describes the maintenance packages that specify the maintenance activities prescribed for particular technical systems or categories of systems. The details are established during customizing.

Maintenance scheduling rules fall into various groups, such as the following:

- Calendar scheduling

- Factory calendar scheduling

- Fixed key date scheduling on a monthly or yearly basis

- Activity-based scheduling that arranges maintenance according to the work done by the technical system or functional location to be maintained

A maintenance package is a data object that gathers unneccessary the details required to schedule planned maintenance orders. It includes the following data:

- Package number
- Frequency of package
- Unit of time or activity
- Package hierarchy relationships
- Description of the operations and suboperations
- Package start offset
- Float periods

Maintenance Items

A maintenance item specifies the activities to be carried out on an object and their frequency. The objects can be specified as an object list of unlimited length comprising equipment numbers and functional location numbers, or the uppermost item of a structure of objects in the form of an object hierarchy. General maintenance task lists or equipment-specific task lists are the sources of the activities specified in the maintenance item in the form of short or long texts.

The maintenance item also determines the account assignment data for settling the maintenance task.

Maintenance History

The maintenance history comprises the following components:

- Location history of the piece of equipment installed at functional locations
- Notification history and completion confirmation documentation
- Task history of completed maintenance orders, including the resources used

Parts of the maintenance history are generated automatically in the PM-Plant Maintenance module whenever any of the following types of processing occurs:

- Maintenance of master data
- Creating maintenance notifications
- Processing maintenance notifications
- Scheduling maintenance plans
- Processing maintenance orders

V

Manufacturing Apps

You can use the maintenance history to analyze by object, by function, or by task-specific criteria, in any combination. The variety of questions that can be answered by this means is illustrated by the following examples:

- Where has this particular pump been used over recent years?

- Which pieces of equipment have been installed at this particular functional location over the past few years? Is it possible to discern any differences in the suitability of the equipment supplied by different manufacturers at this functional location over this time?

- Which functional locations have suffered damage over the past few years? Which of them improved once they started using the new material?

Usage History

Usage histories can be compiled for pieces of equipment and for functional locations. When you carry out customizing, you can define the changes of status or other events that are to be used to mark out usage periods. For example, the following changes will initiate a new usage period marker in a usage history:

- Change in the location of the equipment, such as functional location, actual location, area

- Change in the assignment account data for cost center or asset

- Change in planning structure data, for example, the responsible work center is changed

- Status changes, for example, between freely available, undergoing testing, in production, canceled

You can also trace changes under the ECM-Engineering Change Management system.

Notification History

When maintenance notifications are completed, they become historical notifications. These are linked with the maintenance tasks they initiated to form the notification history of the particular technical system or piece of equipment.

Maintenance Task History

A maintenance order subsequently acquires the documentation of all the materials issued and the internal or external services used in the course of its completion, as well as what was done and how much it cost. Upon completion, this information is transferred to the maintenance task history, where it is available for analysis. Archiving of completed maintenance orders can be arranged in addition to the standard provision for storing completed orders only for a limited period.

PMIS-Plant Maintenance Information System

This SAP module is a component of the LIS-Logistics Information System, and therefore, has access to the LIB-Logistics Information Library and a statistical database.

PMIS is able to provide two types of analysis, as follows:

- **Standard Analysis**—the system maintains statistical information structures that are updated automatically from the SAP R/3 application, in this case, the PM-Plant Maintenance application

- **Flexible Analysis**—the user can call on any SAP data structures and perform analyses for the purpose in hand

The PMIS allows you to perform analysis of actual data using the information structures. You can also enter planning data into these structures for the purposes of comparison and simulation.

A PM-Plant Maintenance statistical information structure in the PM Information System includes the following types of information dimension:

- **Objects**—the entities that are to provide the focal points for the consolidation of actual data, such as functional location, piece of equipment, manufacturer, location, maintenance plant

- **Performance Measures**—statistical compilations of data that could be particularly significant for plant maintenance, such as the number of notifications, the number of damage incidents, the length of downtime

- **Time Unit**—day, week, month, posting period

Thus, the PMIS can report the value accumulated in a particular performance measure for a particular object over a specified period.

Standard Information Structures

The PMIS-Plant Maintenance Information System is provided with five standard information structures, which contain the performance measures that are important for the effective analysis and control of a plant maintenance facility. These measures are grouped according to the following theme clusters:

- Location and Planning
- Object Class and Manufacturer
- Damage Analysis
- Object Statistics
- Breakdown Statistics

When you call for an analysis under the PMIS, the system will apply formulas to calculate summary values as necessary; for example, Mean Time to Repair.

Over twenty performance measures are available, based on up-to-date information collected automatically from the PM-Plant Maintenance system.

During customizing, you can create additional information structures to suit the requirements of your plant maintenance enterprise.

Standard analyses are available through the normal SAP R/3 system, which offers numerous standard business programs to perform various types of calculation and statistical summation over the following objects, using a scope which you define using various selection options to focus on the data to be used:

- Object class
- Manufacturer
- Location
- Planner group
- Damage
- Object statistics
- Breakdown

When you have a data object on your display screen, you can select a special function key to perform a drill-down function to inspect the analysis at various levels. You can also apply a predefined analysis path, which is referred to as the standard drill-down sequence.

For each level of analysis, the following types of functions are provided to analyze and display the data in graphical form:

- Cumulative curve
- Correlation
- ABC analysis
- Classification
- Dual classification
- Rankings

Maintenance as a Customer Service

Functions in this sector are undergoing continuous development. The increasing significance of manufacturer liability and the complexity of products are both factors which press for the development of more effective ways of managing and executing maintenance activities as a service to the customer.

The PM-Plant Maintenance system provides most of the functionality needed to support a business of providing maintenance as a customer service. SAP R/3 Release 3.0 will provide some enhancements.

Customer's Equipment

The tangible objects that are to be maintained on behalf of a customer could be categorized by PM-Plant Maintenance in the same way as pieces of equipment. These maintenance objects might include the following categories:

- Equipment and instruments that are standardized to a large extent, such as medical instruments, forklift trucks, photocopiers

- Special machines

- Buildings

- Computer systems, both hardware and software

The master record system of PM-Plant Maintenance is perfectly suited to the task of keeping track of such objects. The enhancements of Release 3.0 will include, in the equipment master records, data fields for the people in the customer company who will be the contacts for executing maintenance tasks, and for mailings and queries. These fields will be titled Customer, End Customer, and Operator.

Your company will probably have internal employees who are assigned to support particular customers. If maintenance service is to be provided, there may have to be more than one person from your company assigned to the customer in support. You can link one or more personnel records to a customer master equipment record for this purpose.

A piece of equipment can be assigned to a customer sales area to assist in managing the maintenance service. The equipment can also be assigned to a customer functional location.

Customer Maintenance Service Contracts

A contract is represented by a data structure that differentiates maintenance contracts on the following bases:

- **Contract Items**—refer to pieces of equipment, functional locations, and their PM-Plant Maintenance assemblies. Several objects can be linked as an object list.

- **Contract Types**—may be leasing or rental, with or without maintenance services.

- **Validity**—refers to the period of validity of the maintenance contract for each item separately and the validity of the contract as a whole

- **Status**—the contract for each item is subject to status maintenance, which can be set to locked, inactive, straightforward, and any user-defined status indicator

- **Deletion**—can occur only through subsequent contract file reorganization in response to the setting of a deletion indicator for the contract or individual contract items

- **Employees**—internal and customer, can be allocated to the contract header in the same way as pieces of equipment

- **Commercial Aspects**—including price, conditions, and payment methods

- **Termination Conditions**—specified from a system-provided list by a key

- **Settlement Procedure**—specified at the contract level, although items which are inactive will not be invoiced

- **Response Times**—the contracted call-out time will depend on the contracted service window, the time the notification was made, the type of damage and the equipment assembly affected

- **Maintenance**—the periodic or activity-dependent service contract can be represented by including planned maintenance items in the contract

- **Services**—usually directed at an object or object category. Continuous services, such as a hot-line, can be included in the service master records.

- **Control**—the control object to which all costs and revenue affecting the maintenance contract can be specified in order to facilitate the monitoring of the cost-effectiveness of the maintenance contract

Malfunction Notification

Speed is of the essence when a customer calls for service in response to a malfunction. The PM procedure can begin with the absolute minimum of manual data entry, as follows:

- Functional location or equipment number

- Damage

- Customer contact

- Repair date required

The system will display the customer number for control purposes, and your customer service representative can check over the telephone the type of contract the customer has. This can affect whether he is entitled to use a hot-line service.

The customer representative may need to use a help system to find relevant information. The PM-Plant Maintenance system can then provide the information normally available for in-house maintenance, as follows:

- Long texts on equipment category-specific damage symptoms

- Access to the equipment history

The response time is monitored by the system, and a warning is issued if the order dates arising from the notification will exceed the response times permitted in the contract.

Varieties of Processing of Customer Service Orders

There can be a wide variation in the type of response to a customer's call for service under contract, as follows:

- There is no planning, the order is entered during or after the service task is performed, the resources used are entered on the customer order, and only brief documentation is entered for the maintenance history. The whole operation, including contract and warranty checking, can take place within SD-Sales and Distribution.

- The customer calls, a maintenance notification is generated and the repair is made at his premises. The service technician records the times and materials, and the billing proceeds after contract and warranty checks.

- Maintenance processing occurs with a quotation, which is referenced in a customer order if it is accepted.

- The maintenance task is extensive and warrants the use of the SAP R/3 PS-Project System.

- The maintenance task is part of a regular maintenance contract.

- The piece of equipment to be maintained is collected and returned after maintenance. A goods receipt has to be posted to the customer's special stock account and balanced by a corresponding goods issue when the repaired item is returned under a delivery note.

- The maintenance entails travel expenses accounted for in the HR-Human Resources module and as one of the resources used, copied to the PM order, and thence to the SD-Sales and Distribution order.

If your company is providing a maintenance service to other companies in your group, or to outside customers, you will want to be able to integrate any or all of the above requirements into a single system. When a call arrives at the customer service representative, there should be no hesitation in calling on the required information and progressing the inquiry or request for maintenance. The PM-Plant Maintenance module can be configured to provide this facility through its seamless integration with the other R/3 modules.

From Here...

The PM-Plant Maintenance module provides a database that can represent every object in your company that could possibly require maintenance. This database is used to support a detailed system for planning and managing regular plant maintenance and for handling unplanned maintenance orders.

You may like to examine one of these related chapters.

- "Maintenance is a matter of careful management of materials and human resources."

  Chapter 22, "Understanding the HR-Human Resources Module," shows how the personnel administration and personal development activities can be integrated with production and maintenance activities. Chapter 23, "Understanding the MM-Materials Management Module," is a discussion of the ways in which your company can add value by close attention to the material resources you use.

■ "Effective plant maintenance is a skill."

The planning of preventive maintenance activities has to be subject to the cost control disciplines that are introduced in Chapter 13, "Understanding the CO-Controlling Module."

■ "Maintenance always gets in the way of production."

This view is not necessarily shared by companies who operate a rational system of workflow management so that time for prudent maintenance is scheduled. Chapter 30, "R/3 Business Workflow Management," is relevant.

Part VI

Applications in Support

France 117
Belgium 70
Italy 62
Spain 59
Denmark 56
Czech Republic 41
Sweden 39
Hungary 26

479
54
24
16
14

Japan 100
Australia 68
Singapore 32
Malaysia 22
Korea 10
Hong Kong 7
Thailand 7

South Africa 69
Saudi Arabia 9
Israel 3
Arabic Emirates 2
Nambia 2

Products
71%

High

Build large market
share as fast as
possible – at
reasonable cost

- Identify effective sales and marketing
  campaigns – quick feedback on results
- Build sales capacity quickly using
  standardized multimedia product
  presentations
- Erect entry barriers to keep out
  competition – customer database used
  for attractive after-sales service and
  support

Develo
for righ
and at

- I
  b
  a
- u
  e

Reduce sales and
marketing costs while
maintaining market
share

- Service low value customers using low
  cost channels eg. telesales, direct mail
- Contact database to help retain key,
  high value, customers
- Link purchase patterns to SOP to
  prompt for automatic reordering

Reduc
key cu
for cro
opport

- S
  p
- L
  s
  c

Rate of market growth

Low

High

Relative market sh

Steel,
cal Engineering,
utomative

Food and Tobacco Industry

Office & EDP Equipment

Mining, Utilities, Transportation

8.0%

7.3%

6.6%

4.6%

Trade, Retail and Wholesale

mmercial
nd Social
10.3%

3.9%

Traffic and News
Communication

ronics, Precision
chanics, Optics
14.5%

3.8%

Metal Products and
Primary Metal

3.6%

Universities and
Technical Colleges

Chemical Industry,
Mineral Oil Production
18.2%

Others
(see chart below)
11.6%

2.9%

Wood, Paper and
Printing Industry

Others
Credit Banks, Financial Services   1.9
Quarrying, Fine Ceramics, Glass   1.9
Hospitals   1.7
Miscellaneous   1.7
Insurance Companies   1.6
Building Trade, Construction   1.4
Leather, Textile and Clothing Industry   .9
Trade Associations and Federations   .3
Agriculture, Forestry, Fishing   .2

able product

Customized tools

Develop
mplete and
icustomized

Develop

High

Four Seasons

Seed

Agno

ICL

ner Attractiveness

British Rail

Chapter 20

Understanding the SD-Sales and Distribution Module

The design of this module puts the emphasis on using a sales strategy that is sensitive to the market. A priority of customizing should be to set up a data structure that can record, analyze, and control the activities that will satisfy your customers and yield adequate profit over the next accounting period and into the future.

The SD-Sales and Distribution system provides a set of master data records and a system of documented business transactions. The standard business programs of the module are organized around the following five functions:

- SD-MD Master Data
- SD-CAS Sales Support
- SD-SLS Sales
- SD-SHP Shipping
- SD-BIL Billing

You will know that these activities represent value-adding processes because your company will lose value, in terms of reputation and in financial terms, if any of them is allowed to perform badly.

Two other functions are available from the R/3 system and are used by the SD-Sales and Distribution module. They are important because they control the flow of information between the parts of a sales and distribution organization and the other SAP applications in the R/3 system. They also provide the links between the system itself and its users, wherever they might be:

- SAP EDI Electronic Data Interchange
- SD-IS Sales and Distribution Information System

Electronic Data Interchange (EDI) refers to the electronic channels of communication that, in modern business practice, have replaced the messenger systems carrying printed documents. The term "document" is used for both an electronic record and a paper one. Similarly, "printing" may in fact refer to the transmission by electronic means of information that could be printed if required. This topic is discussed further under the heading of EDI elsewhere in this volume.

The SD-IS Sales Information System will allow you to gain insight on all matters concerning prospecting, sales, and delivery. This system of displays and analytical processes is provided to access the master records and the transaction data in a flexible manner that allows you to conduct statistical analyses and evaluations in support of decision-making and strategic planning.

Organizational Structures

The SAP R/3 general organizational units relevant to SD-Sales and Distribution are taken from the SAP R/3 Enterprise Data Model (EDM):

- **Client** is the highest level in SAP R/3. The data of one client may not be accessed from another client. There is often a training client and a testing client, in addition to the client code that represents your group or corporate identity and under which the SAP system runs normal business. Some data is managed at the client level, because everyone in the corporate group of companies will want to refer to exactly the same information and be certain that it has been maintained as up-to-date and correct. Vendor addresses would be an example of data managed at the client level.

- **Company Code** signifies a legal unit under the client level that produces its own financial documents, balance sheet, and profit and loss statement, and may well maintain them as continuously reconciled.

- **Plant** can be a production facility or a group of storage locations where stocks are kept. This term is also used in the context of "transportation plant" in the SD-Sales and Distribution system. The vehicle is treated as a temporary storage location. Planning and inventory management take place at the level of the plant, and it is the focus of materials management. It can supply its material stocks to more than one sales organization.

- **Sales Organization** has a legal connotation, in that it represents the unit responsible for selling and, therefore, is responsible for product liability and rights of legal recourse. All business transactions in SD-Sales and Distribution have to be processed financially within a sales organization. A sales organization can draw its materials from more than one plant.

- **Distribution Channel** defines how different materials reach the consumer—directly, or through a materials wholesaler, for example.

- **Sales Division** is a subdivision of a distribution channel. The division may have been assigned only some of the total product range, and there may be customer-specific agreements for each division.

- **Sales Area** defines a combination of not more than one division, distribution channel, and sales organization. Thus, if there are two divisions using the same distribution channel, each division will be considered to belong to a different sales area. An individual customer can be assigned to more than one sales area if there are differing requirements and agreements to be considered. Prices, minimum order, or delivery quantities are the sort of factors that may have to be recognized by creating unique sales areas for them, always in the SAP R/3 structural context of a sales organization and perhaps a sales division and distribution channel as well.

- **Sales Office** is a method of representing the internal organization. It is a division under the client level.

- **Sales Group** is a further internal subdivision of the people in a particular sales office.

- **Salesperson** is the subject of a unique personnel master record.

- **Shipping Point** is a location within a plant where deliveries are processed. Each delivery is assigned to and processed by one, and only one, shipping point.

- **Loading Point** is a part of a shipping point that is able to offer a capacity to handle deliveries. There may be several similar loading points, and there may be different equipment at some loading points that makes them more suitable for particular types of deliveries—forklift trucks for pallets, for example.

The flexibility of the SAP R/3 system to represent complex and company-specific shipping structures depends on the technique of combining the various types of organizational units.

SD-MD Master Data

In a SAP system, information that is needed in several places or at different times is entered only once. It resides in *master records* where it may be kept up-to-date so that all who access it are given the most accurate and recent information available to the system.

Each master data record has a unique number, and you can arrange to confine certain ranges of these numbers to specific sales areas.

The sales department will make use of this master information in its business transactions. Here are some of the uses the sales department will find for the master data record:

- General details about business partners

- Information specific to particular customers

- Materials, including services as well as objects and assemblies

- Texts about materials and sales conditions

- Prices from cost data collected, from standard calculations, from direct entries, and from planning processes

- Surcharges and discounts

- Taxes applied according to local rules

- New product proposals to be offered during the sales processing

It is clearly important to have accurate information available to those who have need of it. It is fundamental to the design of all SAP systems that a database of master records is held and maintained under strict conditions which ensure that any user who calls upon this information can be informed of the date when it was entered or last amended, and of the identification of the person responsible for the change. It is also a principle of design that any automatic function that is operating in support of the user will also use the master records. For example, if a sales representative is compiling an order for a customer, the address of that customer will be accessed from the master record. If the customer changes his address, then the master will be changed—not a local record held by the person who was first informed of the change.

Such a strict system of data maintenance can succeed only if it is also flexible in the ways in which the stored information can be presented to the user and applied to the business processes. The next few sections illustrate the range of options open to the user in relation to the master data records.

Master Data Record Processing

You can copy master records and change them, using a variety of standard functions to do so, but the system will record and time-stamp every change.

In order to find a master record speedily, you can use any part of any data field as a matchcode.

Business Partners

A *business partner* is any person or organization who is involved in some way with a business transaction in SD-Sales and Distribution. For example, the customer, your sales representative, the carrier—each of these is represented by business partner functions in the system.

Customers

The persons or companies who have bought from you in the past or are accorded the status of prospective customer because you have a reasonable expectation of their purchasing from you in the future are each represented by a master record. The *customer master record* stores the following types of data:

- General data about the customer and the contact person

- Sales-specific data about pricing, deliveries, and output documents

- Company code data, which will include banking and posting details or payment data for that part of the customer corporation that is trading with you

If a customer is unlikely to deal with you more than once, you do not need to create a full master record. Such a transaction can be recorded on a one-time customer record or CPD (Contra Pro Diverse) customer record.

Account Groups

Your customer might have a complex organizational structure that prevents you from entering a simple sold-to party record for the requirement. The customer master record can be used to represent any of these account groups:

- Sold-to party

- Ship-to party

- Bill-to party

- Payer

Each of the account groups can be assigned a specific selection from the available transaction data. Their documents will then be automatically tailor-made for them by the system. The SD-Sales and Distribution module is provided with definitions and models for the common types of customer relationships. You can also define your own account groups and specify which elements of transaction data are to be included in documents assigned to these groups.

Contact Person

All the information you need to carry out sales support is held in the contact person records that are part of the customer master.

Carrier and Supplier

A business partner that is also a carrier and supplier would have a master record maintained in the MM-Materials Management module, and also in the FI-Financial Accounting module. If the supplier is also a customer from time to time, you can enter its supplier number in its customer record in the SD-Sales and Distribution system, which will automatically create a link so that the two records always share exactly the same data in all the fields they have in common.

Relationship to the HR-Human Resources Records

If you create a personnel record, for instance, for one of your customer sales representatives, the master will be managed by the HR-Human Resources module. You will therefore be able to refer to a member of your staff by entering his or her personnel master record number. This will make available to you any other details about the person that you have been authorized to see.

Relationship to the MM-Materials Management Masters

The products and services represented and managed by the MM-Materials Management system can also be created and referred to from the SD-Sales and Distribution module. For example, a sales representative might acquire information about a new supplier of a material that is already represented by a materials master record. The details can be posted to the MM-Materials Management system where they will be verified and incorporated into the database. If a prospective customer inquires about a material that he has not previously purchased from your company, the details available in the material masters can be used to provide up-to-date accurate information. If there is no relevant material master, the MM-Materials Management system will record this inquiry and alert the material controller.

Material Type. The material type is assigned during Customizing, and is used to associate a material with an appropriate material master data structure. This will ensure that the data fields that are not relevant to a specific type of material will be suppressed when the record is displayed on the screen.

Industry Sector. The sectors of industry that you find in your business and that should be given differential treatment in one or more aspects of SD-Sales and Distribution can be defined during Customizing. You can then make sure that products for each sector of industry are assigned the corresponding type of master data structures, which will allow the system to maintain particular information and use it to be responsive to the needs of that sector. For example, the difference between one industry sector and another may be in the matter of distribution lot size, or in the way billing takes place. In this instance, you may decide that some of your products will be sold and packaged in two or more different ways: single units for the "Retail" industry sector, and pallets for the "Wholesale" industry sector. Each sector will have a different costing and billing procedure.

There are four attributes that serve to format the material master data into clusters: general data, data specific to a particular sales area, plant-specific data, and storage location and inventory management data. The SAP term for a cluster of associated data elements is an "attribute."

General Data. Any characteristic of a material that is always going to be the same is stored in the general data attribute and will be made available every time the material takes part in a transaction. For example, a specific type of steel will have a unique material number and a particular description or specification.

The units of measurement may be a function of the method of manufacture, such as a roll of spring steel, or they may be decided on the basis of the most economical unit for procuring this material, such as a pallet.

The following are examples of data that may be stored as general data because it is invariant across all sources and uses of this material:

- Material number
- Description
- Units of measure
- Weight
- Volume
- Material division, and so on

Sales Area Specific Data. Each sales area may be supplied from a particular warehouse or manufacturing plant. Even though the material number is the same, the division of the supply between delivery plants will entail a relevant record on the material master.

If, for example, the same material can be obtained from another sales area, if necessary, then the material master records should show this, even though each sales area normally uses a separate source.

The following are examples of data that may be specific to each sales area:

- Delivering plant
- Sales texts
- Units of measure
- Product hierarchy information
- Shipping data

Plant-Specific Data. Whether the supplying plant is a warehouse or a manufacturing unit, the costs of storing a material there, and the Materials Requirements Planning procedures, will need to be known in order to plan and cost and schedule a sales order. This information also finds its place in the appropriate attribute of the materials master from which it can be accessed by the SD-Sales and Distribution module.

The following are examples of data that may be specific to each plant:

- MRP profile
- Production costs
- Export data

Storage Location and Inventory Management Data. A warehouse may have storage locations that are designed specifically for particular materials. If a material has to be stored in such a location, this information is stored in the material master records.

The following examples illustrate the material data that may have to be stored in the storage location and inventory management attribute:

- Temperature conditions
- No other material to be stored in the location reserved for this material
- Storage conditions, such as dust and humidity control, special handling facilities essential

Relationships to the particular sales organizations and distribution channels may affect some or all of the entries. Any particulars that have been determined by the master records of a superior level in the organizational structure will be inherited by a data object in a lower level, unless the record at the lower level carries specific instructions to the contrary. For example, a material that has to be stored in a cooled warehouse will show this requirement in its material master data record. If a particular method of packaging has been determined for a whole class of materials, any material belonging to this class will be packed in this way unless the individual material master record carries contrary instructions.

Bill of Materials

When a product is made up of several components, the details are documented in a bill of materials (BOM). If additional information is required about any of these components, a BOM explosion may be used to call in the extra documentation. If several products differ by only a few components, the technique of BOM variants may be employed. These topics are discussed in Chapter 17, "Understanding the PP-Production Planning and Control Module."

Material Status

You can adopt the standard status indicators of the MM-Materials Management system or define indicators of your own to serve the purpose of exercising control over sales activities. For example, you may want to block the taking of orders for a batch of defective material but permit inquiries about the product in anticipation that a future batch will not be defective.

A discontinued product can be the subject of status control so that future orders will be blocked even though the product is still being shipped to satisfy existing orders.

Stock and Inventory Inquiries

Flexible display facilities permit you to assess the various plant stocks and summarize them in the form of overviews. Special stocks can be identified for different treatments. Special stock destined for only one customer would be an example.

Customer Material Info Records

If a customer needs special sales and delivery requirements which would not be met by the information stored in the customer master or the relevant material masters, you can set up a customer material info record which takes precedence over the rules established elsewhere. The info record contains the following kinds of information:

- Customer, sales organization, and distribution channel

- Your material number and description

- The customer's material number and description

- Shipping data

- Partial delivery arrangements, and so on

The system will use the customer material info record to prepare a sales proposal ready to be placed in the sales order if you approve it.

The SD-Sales and Distribution module will operate material determination and material substitution procedures if they have been established. For example, you can define a set of criteria to select a suitable material automatically. You may also have set up the criteria for a material to be substituted automatically in orders for a particular customer. The material listing and material exclusion rules are valid for a certain period of time and serve the purpose of restricting the choice of options presented by the system when preparing a sales proposal.

The Condition Technique

The SAP R/3 condition technique gets its name from the discipline of formal logic and, in particular, from the conditional proposition form that can be expressed as follows:

```
If {a certain set of conditions are all, in fact, true}
Then {certain actions can be taken}.
```

The logical if-then condition technique is used extensively in the SAP R/3 system to enable the computer to carry out specified actions automatically if, and only if, the proper conditions have been satisfied by the necessary data.

The choice of price information and the imposition of discounts or surcharges are matters that vary from business to business. You can use any data in a document as the condition or trigger for the application of your pricing structure.

Price lists can be standard, based on the material used, customer-specific, and so on. Discounts or surcharges can be allocated by customer, material, price group, material group, and any combinations of such criteria.

Each condition master record has a specified time validity, and can be constrained so as to permit or forbid manual changes during this period.

Conditions can also be used to define the circumstances when the system may be allowed to handle sales taxes as surcharges. The standard SD-Sales and Distribution system is provided with sales tax formulas for most parts of the world, and you can add your own.

Business Transactions

Every business transaction is documented automatically by the SAP R/3 system. The SD-Sales and Distribution module provides for a separate document type to be created for every stage of the sales and distribution chain of processes. Changes to a document, such as revisions of prices or quantities, are stored in the change history associated with each document. Standard business programs are available for executing and displaying the results of all the usual sales and distribution functions, to which you can add your own variants during customizing.

The Many Functions of a Sales and Distribution Document

The SAP business transaction document is a versatile instrument, created automatically and always subject to the rule that changes must be documented and time-stamped. These are some of the day-to-day uses to which the SAP document is put in the SD-Sales and Distribution system:

- Pricing
- Availability checks
- Transfer of requirements
- Sales or distribution document printing medium and formatting

- Management of short standard texts or long texts and drawings

- Delivery management and document printing

- Billing management and document printing

- Provision of data to the SD-IS Sales and Distribution Information System

Sales and Distribution Document Types. Each sales and distribution transaction will generate a document adapted to the business in hand. If some of the many possible functions are not required by a certain type of transaction, the resulting document need not contain any reference to them. Should you or the system have reason to carry out additional functions on the document, the new activities will leave evidence in the usual way.

Document Flow

The typical flow of activities in a sales department is reflected in the flow and development of the corresponding SD-Sales and Distribution documents.

For example:

1. A sales representative makes a series of calls to a potential customer, and information is collected in sales activity documents.

2. If the potential customer makes an inquiry, a quotation can be created and assigned a limited validity period. An Inquiry document can be created for the same purpose. This can subsequently lead to a quotation.

3. If the potential customer accepts the quotation, a sales order has to be delivered by a specified date.

4. In order to do this, the system must check that the material will be available, and this must be confirmed.

5. Scheduling of the necessary transport for the required date has to be arranged.

6. There may have to be a picking control document to collate the parts of the order.

7. When the goods are about to leave the plant, there has to be a series of stock and value adjustments in the MM-Materials Management and FI-Financial Accounting departmental systems. If the relevant delivery document has not been received when goods are issued, then a goods issue document has to be created to initiate the same processes.

8. The billing document may be sent, e-mailed, faxed, or transferred via EDI to the customer, and the event is recorded with a transfer of data to the FI-Financial Accounting department.

At any stage in the document flow, you can find out what is in the previous document, and so on, right back to the first contact between your company and the customer. If the flow you are scrutinizing has been completed, you can inspect the delivery document and the invoice. Whatever your query, the automatically generated process documentation will be readily available to show you what you want to know.

Processing Status. Progress along this document flow and the transaction processing that it represents are documented automatically and can be controlled by a system of status indicators to signal the stage reached in the transaction. You can call for information using the status indicator, which will cause the system to respond with information to answer the following kinds of questions:

- Has the customer accepted all the quotation items, and have they been copied to a sales order?

- Is the sales order complete?

- Which items have not yet been delivered?

- Has this transaction reached the stage of being fully invoiced?

You can issue commands to block the progress of a transaction if, for instance, you see a problem with the quality of the stock that might be assigned to this order.

Locating a Document. A document can always be accessed by entering its document number. The standard SAP R/3 system is applied in SD-Sales and Distribution of using matchcodes to initiate a search that will narrow down the list from which you have to select the document you require. Matchcodes can be customized to meet any requirements. The following matchcodes are standard:

- Sales activities selected by nominating one or more of the short texts that may have been copied to the document

- Sales documents by customer purchase order number

- Credit and debit memos that have been released for further processing

- Deliveries from a specific shipping point according to a range of goods issue dates

- Billing documents that have not yet passed on to the FI-Financial Accounting system

Document Structure and Data Sources

The documents created by the SD-Sales and Distribution system follow the standard SAP R/3 convention of comprising a header plus one or more items.

The system differentiates between SD-CAS Sales Support activities carried on without any specific reference to individual customers, and the activities that entail dealing with sales and distribution to individual customers. It is the sales and distribution activities for specified customers that are being discussed in this section.

Sales and Distribution Document Header Contents. The general data in the header apply to the whole document, unless specifically countermanded by a particular line item. The data will include information and references to standard documents or master records concerning the following matters:

- Sold-to party
- Sales area as defined during customizing
- Terms of payment
- Technical and legal texts
- Purchasing data
- Ship-to party
- Carrier
- Other business partners

Sales Document Items. The items in a sales and distribution document consist of data about the goods and services ordered by the customer. Attached to each document item may be one or more sub-items, each of which will be followed by one or more schedule lines.

The document items and their sub-items will include the following data:

- Material number
- Quantity
- Alternative shipping addresses
- Prices
- Business data, if different from the header information

The schedule lines applicable to document items or their sub-items can each include the following types of data:

- Delivery date
- Quantity
- Shipping data
- Procurement data
- Partial delivery information in the form of an initial delivery schedule line followed by the subsequent and final delivery schedule line.

Item Categories. Your system can be set up to differentiate between item categories by applying rules determined during customizing. For example, you can adopt the following item category scheme:

- Sales order document items
- Delivery and billing document items
- Text document items
- Value document items

In this case, you can establish from the category type:

- Whether an availability check is required
- Whether the item has to be priced
- Whether the item is deliverable

Data Origins and Creation Techniques. In addition to entering data manually, the SD-Sales and Distribution system can make extensive use of copying. You can copy data from master records, and you can usefully copy information from the preceding document in the processing of an order. By these means, you can rapidly and accurately assemble documents. For example, you can copy the details of the sold-to party and of any business partners from the relevant master records. You may be able to reference previous customer material info records or product proposals, and the system will be able to do this for you if suitably pre-armed with the logical conditions to control the copying.

Before you release any stage of document in a sales transaction, you can amend any of the standard or proposal data if you have made a special arrangement with the customer. You can copy the sales order to create a delivery note, for example, and then edit it if the customer requires a different destination for this particular delivery.

If you do decide to use a document as a reference, the system will check that it can be released for this purpose, and you can have it checked to see that it is still valid before you copy from it.

Texts in SD-Sales and Distribution Documents. The SAPscript word processing system is available to you for preparing text. You can store text at the header level, where it will be applicable to all the document items and sub-items, and where it will remain if you create another sales and distribution document using this header. Shipping regulations and terms of payment are examples of the kind of text that might be usefully stored at the header level.

Alternatively, you can store a text at the level of an individual item. In this case, it will apply only to this item, but again, if you decide to use this item elsewhere, your text will be available there also, because it will still be attached to the item. Material short texts and packaging instructions are examples of the kind of written material that can remain with the item.

The SAPscript module can provide these texts in any of the supported languages. The SAPscript component of the R/3 system is provided for generating texts for storage as data elements for reuse and for generating one-off messages to other users and customers or suppliers. It is discussed in Chapter 2, "User Interaction with the SAP Systems."

Types of Business Transactions

The standard version of the SD-Sales and Distribution system is able to recognize and support the most frequently used types of business transactions. You can refine or modify these functions to suit your company and create new business transaction types with the pertinent business functionality.

Inquiries and Quotations. These are standard SAP documents that are created before a sales order is taken and that are limited to a specific period of validity. They should be customized so as to gather information on the reasons for the inquiry and the reasons for rejection if a sales order does not arise.

By accessing one of the overview screens, you can find out whether the materials or services in the inquiry or quotation would be available on the date required. However little information is recorded as the result of an inquiry, you can use it to begin to plan a sales strategy for this potential customer. As you seek further clarification of the customer's requirements, you will be able to build a better relationship and have the results of your prospecting endeavors stored in the documents and customer master records.

Sales Orders. Even if you have not offered a quotation, you can still enter a sales order to check availability and carry out a credit limit check. You will want to carry out pricing at this stage, if you have not already done so. The required delivery date may well affect the price.

Scheduling Agreements and Contracts. This type of business transaction is an outline agreement with a customer to supply goods and services over a specified period of time. The quantities and dates are specified in the scheduling agreement.

A contract is also an outline agreement to supply goods and services in the future, but the delivery date is not specified until later, when it is published in a release order.

Rush Order. You can create a sales order and initiate a delivery at the same time. This is a rush order, which will cause the system to create the delivery for you as soon as you enter the order. It will check availability and carry out scheduling for both the order and the delivery documents at the same time.

Production to Order. If you have elected to enter this type of order, a production requirement is created to produce the material directly as a result of the customer order. When the material has reached the finished product stage, it will be treated as special stock.

The individual customer requirement is passed to material requirements planning, and the availability is checked against the customer special stock. When both the production and the external purchase order processing are completed, the appropriate inward goods movement for the customer special stock is posted. This records the fact that goods have been produced specifically for the individual customer and been assigned to his or her special stock. Delivery takes place from this stock.

Customer Consignment Stock. If you have set aside some goods that one of your customers can call upon at any time, and you have not yet been paid for these goods, they are treated as consignment goods. If you are the vendor, you still own the consignment.

The warehouse holding these consignment goods will notify the vendor if the customer picks up or is issued with any of them. The vendor will charge the customer for them. If any of the consignment goods are not required by the customer, they can be returned to the vendor.

In the SD-Sales and Distribution system, customer consignment stock is managed separately by generating consignment fill-up orders for the customer, consignment issues from the stock, billing documents, and consignment pick-up documents.

Returnable Packaging. The system maintains a separate stock of returnable packaging or transportation material for each customer. This material has to be returned within a specified time period. The vendor still owns it.

The SD-Sales and Distribution system offers functions for dispatch and pickup of returnable packaging, so that you can enter it in deliveries and bill the customer for any not returned within the set time.

Complaints. If a customer complains of damage during transportation or is not satisfied with the goods or services, you can call upon special SAP R/3 functions to process these complaints.

A Return is a transaction that arranges for the faulty goods to be picked up or for replacements to be delivered free of charge.

If you find that you have overcharged or undercharged a customer, you can create a credit or debit memo request document that will set in train the appropriate financial procedure.

Third-Party Deal. If you are the contractor in a third-party deal, you will commission a third-party vendor to deliver the goods directly to the customer or to the destination specified as the customer's ship-to party. In these cases, the SD-Sales and Distribution system automatically creates purchase requisitions for the sales order that specify the delivery dates and quantities. The purchasing department, using the MM-Materials Management system, will process these purchasing requirements and create purchase orders for them. If the vendor notifies the system that the quantities or the dates have to be changed, the system will automatically correct the sales document.

The third-party vendor will send you an invoice as soon as the goods have been delivered to the customer. You can then carry out billing for the third-party deal by having the system copy the quantity delivered from the invoice document to the billing document that goes to the customer.

Stock Transfer Transactions. A requisition for stock to be transferred can be created automatically by PP-MRP Material Requirements Planning. It could also be initiated from a purchase requisition entered manually.

When such a requisition is converted to a purchase order, the plant that is to deliver the material is informed of the stock transfer requirement, and the purchase order will appear in the Delivery Due list on the SD-Sales and Distribution system display.

All the shipping functions can then be applied to the stock transfer. The FI-Financial Accounting system of the delivering plant will get a goods issue posting, and the receiving plant will be posted a goods receipt.

Cross-Company Sales. When one company needs products and services from other parts of the group, the cross-company sales function of the SD-Sales and Distribution system can be invoked. A sales organization can sell for plants in a different company code. Legally, this means that more than one company is involved in the processing of a sales order. It is necessary to apply intercompany invoicing between the company codes to adjust the value flow after the sales order has been completed.

SD-CAS Sales Support

The aims of a sales support function in a business may be listed, although not in order of any particular priority, to:

- Promote business development
- Improve customer service
- Provide a mechanism through which all in-house and external sales personnel can contribute any useful information to a central facility, from which they can also draw freely in order to further their own sales activities
- Support sales promotion by individuals
- Improve communication throughout the sales force
- Provide methods for evaluating competitors and their products

A computer-based sales support function would also be expected to automate as many as possible of the routine tasks of the sales department. Master data and the documented evidence of business transaction processing are the prime sources of direct information of use to sales support. The SD-IS Sales and Distribution Information System is a further source of analyses based on sales summaries and the statistics of sales orders. The sales support activities also provide inputs to the SD-IS Sales and Distribution Information System.

Partners and Personnel

Because they represent your company in the market, each sales and sales support person is given a master record in the SD-Sales and Distribution system.

Sales personnel are defined as people who are documented in the HR-Human Resources system as direct employees of your company, and who also are recognized by the SD-Sales and Distribution module because of the roles they may be called upon to play in the sales and distribution activities.

Sales partners are recognized and documented in the SD-Sales and Distribution system as consultancy partners or sales agents, but they are not direct employees of your company and do not necessarily have personnel records in your HR-Human Resources system.

Customers, Prospects, and Contacts

The management of customers and sales prospects constitutes a major part of the SD-CAS Sales Support software component. The customer master record holds most of the information in the standard SAP format of attributes, which are clusters of thematically related data fields.

A customer master has records for general details as well as:

- Company organizational structure, annual sales, number of employees, status as a customer of your organization, and market areas of goods and services

- Contact persons by name and position

- Contact person details such as first name, form of salutation, birthdate, marital status, buying habits, sales strategy to use, visiting hours, home address, business address, interests, and pastimes

A prospect is handled by the SD-Sales and Distribution module as a customer without a record of past purchases. The records and processing functions are the same.

If you are looking for a particular contact person, you can search for the company by name or number; alternatively, you can search for the person's details, which will enable you to keep track of that person if he or she moves from one of your customers to another. You may have a very large database of potential customers on which you are keeping a watching brief and a diligent data-collecting effort.

There are no restrictions on the definition and number of attributes maintained in your master records for customers, sales prospects, and contact persons.

Competitors and Their Products

New markets and new market segments are often detected by closely observing what your competitors are doing and not doing. You can store this kind of data systematically in the SD-Sales and Distribution system.

Competitor Companies. You can use the system of master records to store data on your competitor companies, using the same structure as you use for customers but with some important additions:

- Industry classifications

- Annual sales

- Employees

- Other information about the competitor stored in a structured format that will allow you to conduct searches and compile statistical summaries

Competitive Products. You need a database that includes all the details that are important for your own products, but if you want to make a comparison, you will also need your competitors' products to be entered on the same set of master attributes. You can also have structured texts to locate critical information in ways that are susceptible to classification and search techniques.

Like your own, competitive products will be assigned to product hierarchies upon which a comparison can be based.

Sales Activities and Promotions

The outcomes of previous sales activities have to be stored in order to become an input to the design of the next sales campaign. The method used by the SD-Sales and Distribution system is to store all interactions with the potential customer population in the data structures referred to as Sales Activities. The following are examples of activities by SD-CAS Sales Support that are documented by recording the outcomes of sales activities in such records:

- Sales calls in person
- Telemarketing calls
- Brochure mailing
- Calls received from potential customers
- Presentations
- Conferences
- Promotions

The standard SD-Sales and Distribution system recognizes three activity types:

- Sales call
- Sales letter
- Telephone call

You may define other sales activity types to add to this list during customizing.

Processing a Sales Activity. The basic information on the SAP Document generated as a result of a sales activity will include the following data elements:

- Customer number
- Contact person at the customer company
- Your sales organization or sales group conducting the sales activity
- Date and time of the sales activity
- Type of sales activity carried out
- The reason for the activity, which can be entered using standard keys
- The outcome of the activity, which can be entered using standard keys and can have additional standard short text or free-form text. For example, "sales order" and "invitation to give a presentation" are standard activity outcomes that the system will offer as options from which you can choose.

Authorization may be required to change or display a sales activity document.

When an authorized salesperson is processing a sales activity, the data from the SD-IS Sales and Distribution Information System can be accessed to show, for example, sales trends for this market segment or for this customer, and so on.

You can amplify the information carried by a sales activity master record by defining a set of standard texts that specify how a set of keys is to be interpreted. For example, you can set up codes for preparation notes, reports, and reactions to sales promotions. If you attach one of these codes to a free-text note or a standard short text phrase, you can store the data in a way that will make them easy to access, classify, and use in the future.

Your sales activities will often have specific follow-up actions that can be predefined and permanently associated with the sales activity. They can be scheduled by elapsed time or given a firm date for completion. When you are planning your sales support work, you can call for a display of the planned sales activities and follow-up actions that are outstanding. The system will also give you complete histories of previous sales activities.

Direct Mailing

The standard SAP R/3 direct mailing function requires you to provide the following data elements:

- Address list for direct mailing
- Content and layout for the correspondence
- Enclosures for each addressee

This information will be stored in a direct mailing master record, so that you can use it again or take it as a reference model when creating a new mailing.

You can use selection variants or search specifications to cull addresses from customers, sales prospects, and contact persons. Editing and all variants of customized texts can be used to make each mailing specific to each company in your group and to each of the units in your customer's company, if necessary.

If you buy address lists, the system will automatically check that the new addresses of potential customers are in accord with the information you already have about them.

The person responsible for each mailing can be identified in the mailing master record.

SD-SLS Sales

The functionality of the SD-SLS Sales component of the SD-Sales and Distribution system is concentrated on the processing of sales transaction data in the wide variety of modes and contexts characteristic of the sales and distribution sector of business. There are many varieties of sales order, and many uses to which the resulting documents can be put.

The variety of business transactions in the sales and distribution departments has been discussed previously. The intention here is to concentrate on some of the unique functional enhancements provided by the SAP R/3 system.

Inquiries and Quotations

The inquiry or quotation will be handled by the system as the beginning of a sales order into which it will be converted if a sale is forthcoming. The quotation will carry a date marking the end of its validity period that you can use to monitor the inquiries and quotations and to determine the order in which they should receive your attention.

You will have identified the material required by the inquirer, perhaps by its material number, or perhaps because you have used a previous quotation or order for this customer. You can also enter the material in text form, which the system will interpret using the SAP R/3 Classification System, then find a material number for you to consider entering at a later date or having the system enter automatically.

There may be several alternative materials that could possibly interest the customer. You can quote for these as well as for the material requested. If the customer places an order, the system will work on the material the customer chose from your quotation.

SD-SLS Sales

The philosophy behind the functionality of the SD-SLS Sales component is to minimize the work you have to do to complete an order. The standard approach is to find what is required and propose it to the user for adjustment and confirmation.

So if you simply enter a list of items, the system will try to find these items in a previous order for this customer. If there are none, then it will look for this item in the master records and offer you the default values it finds there.

For instance, it will suggest business partners to deliver the material if that has happened before. It will propose that you use the lot size and packaging customary for this material, and so on.

Much of the information will be in materials and customer master records:

- Pricing
- Tax determination
- Weight and volume determination
- Delivery scheduling
- Payment methods

The system will offer textual materials to be included in the sales order if this is customary, and it will have proposals in detail for creating the commercial papers.

Should you have to save a sales document before it has been fully serviced with appropriate and valid information, the system will accord it the status of an incomplete document and remind you with a list of the missing items.

When you return to the work, the system can show you all the incomplete documents in your task list, together with the lists of defects for each.

Outline Agreements

There are two types of outline agreements with a customer to supply goods and services over a specified period of time: contracts and scheduling agreements.

A contract is an outline agreement to supply goods and services in the future, but the delivery date and shipping arrangements are not specified until the customer requests delivery of the goods in the contract. At this time, a release order is issued and processed in the same way as a sales order. The quantities and general data of each release order are noted in the contract, and the quantities remaining to be delivered are updated there accordingly.

The quantities and dates are specified from the beginning in a scheduling agreement that is otherwise processed much like a series of contracts, using the dates and quantities specified in the outline schedule.

Updating Backorders

If you call for a list of backorders, you will see the order items that could not be confirmed because something was not available. The availability will be checked again automatically, and you will see the current situation. If some of the orders could now be satisfied, you can use the update functions to have the sales orders confirmed directly.

Pricing

The SD-Sales and Distribution system will carry out pricing automatically using predefined prices, surcharges, and discounts. You can change the data proposed by the system for computing the prices, and you can also change the price for a particular business transaction.

This pricing method is applied to quotations, sales orders, and billing documents. At any time, you can call for pricing analysis so that you can inspect the figures and the procedures used to arrive at the price proposal.

The price to be charged for each particular material is what has to be found. The system looks first for a customer-specific material price and uses that if it finds one. If it does not, then it seeks a price-list price valid for a business segment or some other sector of the market that includes this customer. Only if there is no valid price list will the system use the basic price for the material.

This logical sequence of methods for determining a price for a material is set out in the form of a "condition" that is stored as a condition master record. There is no limit to the complexity of a condition because it has the task of controlling how the system assembles the cost data and other factors that go into the calculation of a price.

For example, a material might have a base price and a price for the duration of a sales promotion. The material may be a member of a price group that specifies that it shall be subject to a certain surcharge or discount. There may be a surcharge if less than a specified minimum quantity is ordered. Some materials have to be priced so as to reflect the changes in the currency exchange rate of its country of origin to its point of sale. A particular customer may be allowed a particular price discount; and the quantity ordered may attract further discounts. If the customer agrees to pay in advance, there may be a rebate to be taken into the price calculation.

Any of these factors that can affect pricing may be computed according to specific formulas and logical conditions that control when and how each of the contributory elements are to be taken into the calculation.

Although the calculation will take place automatically, the user and the customer can be shown the details of the calculation under certain conditions that will appear as data in the relevant condition master.

Sales taxes are handled in a similar manner, using logical conditions and formulas appropriate to the pertinent legal system in force.

When the system has arrived at a price to charge for the specific material, it then looks to see if a discount has been defined for this material, this customer, or this material only if bought by this customer. Thus, the system ends up with a price to charge for each item in the sales order.

A further check is then made to see if the total value or total quantity should attract further surcharges or discounts.

When the system has arrived at an appropriate material price for each item, applied the discounts and surcharges, and reviewed the totals for further surcharges and discounts, only then will it copy the price into the quotation, sales order, or billing document.

These pricing processes are further discussed in Chapter 12, "Understanding the FI-Financial Management Module" and in Chapter 13, "Understanding the CO-Controlling Module."

SD-SHP Shipping

All the data required to arrange a prompt delivery can be determined in the sales order. By having the system display all the orders due for delivery, you can manage the deadlines. Bottlenecks will be foreseen and the remedies will be at hand. These are the main activities empowered by the SD-SHP Shipping functions:

- Monitoring the deadlines of orders due for deliveries
- Creating and processing deliveries
- Monitoring the availability of goods
- Supporting the picking operations
- Supporting packing and loading
- Managing transportation
- Creating shipping output documents and transmitting them

- Managing decentralized shipping

- Posting the goods issue document to FI-Financial Accounting at the time of delivery

The Shipping Work Lists

For every shipping point under the control of the shipping department, there can be a work list of sales orders due for delivery. How frequently these work lists are processed will be a matter to be determined by the management and operating staff—all things being equal, the sooner the better.

A shipping point is a facility that offers a separate shipping capacity. It may be one of several identical loading bays, for example, or it may have a special handling capacity such as a forklift truck that is larger than the other shipping points. The shipping point may owe its individuality to the fact that it is dedicated to the orders for one particular customer.

The appropriate shipping point is either automatically determined by the system, or entered manually during order creation. The criteria for automatic shipping point determination are as follows:

- Shipping conditions specified for the sold-to party—for example, "as soon as possible" or "normal shipping conditions"

- Loading group of the material—for example, "by crane," "by forklift truck," or "by special staff loading team"

- Delivering plant—for example, "road truck," "rail wagon," or "dedicated transporter"

Each order item has to be assigned a route. Which route is chosen will depend on the following criteria:

- The shipping conditions specified for the sold-to party

- The delivery weight of the order item

- The geographical relationship of the destination to the shipping point

Each route will impose certain restrictions in the choice of means of transport and the number and nature of the legs of the journey. If the order item has to change delivery plant en route, there will be extra costs and delays, yet to have the whole route executed in one particular means of transport may be unacceptable for other reasons: It may take too long, the atmospheric pollution by the vehicle may be damaging to the reputation of your company, or the vehicle may have to make the return journey without a payload.

You can call up a list at any time to see which deliveries are scheduled to use a particular route or shipping point over a selected time interval. You may be able to effect an improvement in the planning of loading and transportation activities by a manual change to one or more of the parameters assigned by the system.

Creating and Processing Deliveries

To the SAP R/3 system, a delivery is a document. It has to carry all the data necessary for preparing and delivering the material in the sales order.

Creating a Delivery for a Particular Sales Order. The goods specified by material number and quantity can be copied from the sales order to the delivery document. The shipping point can be selected automatically using the shipping conditions that will be available from the customer master records.

If the shipping conditions have changed, or if there has been no previous specification of the customer shipping conditions, you can correct matters by a manual entry before you post the delivery to have it executed.

Creating All Deliveries Due. From your display of all sales orders due for delivery, you can select, if you so wish, on the basis of a specific shipping point, a particular material, or a single ship-to party, and so on, in any combination that leaves you with the selection of deliveries due that you intend to create. You may also wish to refine your list by imposing other restrictions, such as the maximum gross weight your vehicle can carry, or the maximum overall dimensions.

The list of sales orders due, perhaps refined by your selection procedures, can then be processed simultaneously to become delivery documents. The system will log for your attention any sales order documents that are not correct or that lack a needed data element. You may be able to return to these later and enter the missing data.

Deliveries that Do Not Refer to a Sales Order. It is possible to enter manually all the relevant information needed to create a delivery. You may want to do this if the central system is unable to provide access to the sales order, or if the information you require is not there.

The section following on Decentralized Shipping discusses deliveries in which the relevant data is all entered from a separate source, rather than copied directly at the time from the relevant sales order document.

Automatic Checks in Delivery Creation

The system carries out checks to help ensure that the delivery data is complete and correct. When you see the display of the delivery due list in detail, you may find that you have to change some of the data entered by the PP-MRP Material Requirements Planning function because the situation has changed since that planning operation was performed.

The specifications in the material master records in MM-Materials Management will have provided the data for automatically calculating the weights and volumes of the individual delivery items and the totals for the delivery as a whole. The same MM system will be the source of stock data that the system will use to check that the material intended for the delivery is indeed going to be available for this purpose.

At this moment, just before a delivery is created, the system will take another look at the scheduling specifications in the sales order: the customer's required delivery date, or the standard delivery conditions assigned in the customer's master records. You will get a warning and a proposal if a change in scheduling is called for.

Managing the Delivery Situation of an Item

A delivery situation is the result of taking account of the goods availability position and the agreements in place with the customer or the sold-to party concerning partial deliveries.

If the sold-to party will not accept partial deliveries, you have to see that all the items in the sales order are collected together in one delivery group that then becomes the focus. The availability check and the transfer of requirements have to be adjusted to fit the earliest delivery date possible for the delivery group.

If the sold-to party has agreed to accept partial deliveries, you can, if necessary, create several deliveries from the one sales order. This might suit the availability situation, both of goods and of shipping facilities.

It might make sense to combine several sales orders into one delivery group, if the customer has agreed to such an arrangement.

In all these procedures for effectively managing the delivery situations as and when they arise and planning to smooth their passage before the time comes, the SAP R/3 system can be allowed to act automatically by setting up the appropriate logical conditions and data elements.

Delivery Status Update. The creation of a delivery document, when it is posted and proved to be valid, is the occasion for the system automatically to update the material stocks and the work list of the shipping department, where the display of delivery situation of the sales order will show the updated status key.

Shipping Output Documents. When the delivery has been posted, the system will offer you a proposal to print or send by electronic mail the shipping output documents mandated during customizing.

Shipping Elements. A shipping element is an item of material that is managed separately in the SD-Sales and Distribution system because it is used in shipping and is necessary for the purpose of handling and protecting the goods in transit. It may be on loan to the customer for a specified period, and a charge may be raised if it is not returned within that period. The following items can be managed as shipping elements:

- Boxes
- Cartons
- Pallets
- Trucks
- Trailers
- Supporting travel rigs

In order to protect and handle a particular delivery, it may be necessary to have the item first packed in cartons. A group of cartons, perhaps, are protected by a box, and several boxes loaded into a freight container. All these shipping elements can be treated as a hierarchy of shipping elements that is recognized by the system and specified for use for one or more types of material or one or more customers.

The shipping elements need not be specified as a hierarchical structure; they can be referenced simply as a packing list, which is also recognized by the system as a data object and can be changed under control of the procedures of change management.

Picking

A picking list, or pick list, is a document that makes sure that the goods in the warehouse arrive at the shipping point at the right moment to become part of a delivery. Clearly, only the right goods and the right quantities will do. And it is no use getting the goods to the shipping point just before the transport is due to leave if some work has to be done to prepare the goods and protect them with the specified shipping elements. If the goods need special storage conditions, picking will have to make allowances for this.

The typical sequence is as follows:

- A picking location or loading zone is automatically determined for a delivery, using data on the sales order delivery document that will indicate the shipping point and the storage conditions to be observed.

- A picking list is printed for each delivery when the delivery is created, or later. The picking list can be sent by electronic means.

- When the picking has assembled the available quantities at the picking location, the quantities are confirmed to the system. If they are insufficient but stock is available, picking is carried out again for the shortfall, using the same loading zone. If the quantities required cannot be picked to the picking zone, for whatever reason, then the delivery quantity is reduced. The system will make the appropriate adjustments to the order, shipping, and billing documents.

In some circumstances, you may have to enter the batch specification or the valuation type after picking has been completed, because only at that stage will the necessary data be accurate. For example, some process industries have to expect a variation in the makeup of the finished product, because variability in the input materials and the environmental conditions have an effect on the product.

Links to the MM-WM Warehouse Management System

If you have installed and configured the MM-WM Warehouse Management system, the initiation of picking can take place through this system.

The system maintains materials master data which indicate the fixed storage bin or circumscribed storage area in which the material can be found during picking.

If the warehouse does not use fixed bin storage, it is treated as a random warehouse. The MM-WM Warehouse Management system makes sure that a transfer order is created for each delivery item. When the goods arrive at the picking area, the transfer order is confirmed and the system will enter the picked quantities directly into the delivery items on the delivery document.

The Formalities of Goods Issue

From the point of view of the shipping function, the business transaction is complete when the goods leave your company. In the SD-Sales and Distribution system, this event is represented by the posting of a goods issue corresponding to the delivery.

Stock values are updated in the FI-Financial Accounting module as the stock level of material is reduced by the quantity of the goods issued.

The goods issue brings to an end the delivery processing. The information on the goods issue is stored in the sales order from which the delivery was initiated. The billing due list will now show the details of the delivery, so that it can be invoiced.

Decentralized Shipping

When the SD-Sales and Distribution system has reached the point of being able to specify a delivery, it may be convenient to pass this delivery document to another system. For example, there could be several satellite systems working on a decentralized shipping basis, each receiving a subset of the deliveries due from the central system.

These are some of the advantages recognized by those companies that adopt the decentralized shipping approach:

- Shipping processing can be carried out continuously, even when the main computing system is unavailable.

- The SD-SHP Shipping module can be used on a satellite computer in conjunction with another sales order processing system, for instance, from the SAP R/2 system.

- The system load can be distributed over various computers by relieving the main system of the shipping functions.

The net effect of decentralizing shipping in this manner is to minimize delivery times and improve customer service.

Distribution of Functions under Decentralized Shipping. The sales order is entered on the central host computer system where the stocks are managed. The availability of the order items is checked there, and the scheduling takes place there for the shipping activities of perhaps all the satellite shipping subsystems.

When the due date arrives for a delivery, the satellite initiates the shipping activities and has the delivery data transferred from the host. Data relevant to the materials handled by the satellite will already be held there in the form of copies of the material master records.

A transfer of customer data takes place for every business transaction so that the information is up-to-date.

Picking at the satellite may be linked to a MM-WM Warehouse Management system there or in the host. As the batches and quantities are gathered to the picking location, the specifications are confirmed in the delivery document. You can add packaging and other shipping elements at the same time, together with the weights and volumes for the loading data that will appear on the shipping output documents to be generated locally.

When the delivery is completed, the goods issue for the delivery is automatically confirmed. The data is transferred back to the host, where the status of the sales order is updated.

The satellite system does not post quantities or values to the FI-Financial Accounting system; this is done centrally when the delivery confirmation is returned.

As soon as the delivery has been confirmed, the central host system will release the delivery for billing, and it will appear on the billing due list.

SD-BIL Billing

The task of billing is to create the billing document and transfer the data to FI-Financial Accounting and profitability analysis.

SD-SLS Sales and SD-SHP Shipping are the source systems that provide the information used by SD-BIL Billing in the form of, for example, quantity and price data from the reference documents of the inquiry, quote, or sales order. In their turn, these documents will have called upon, for instance, the MM-Materials Management system to supply materials data.

The functions of SD-BIL Billing are designed to support the following operations:

- Create invoices for deliveries or services rendered.
- Respond to debit memo requests by creating debit memos.
- Respond to credit memo requests by creating credit memos.
- Cancel billing document.
- Transfer posting data to FI-Financial Accounting.

Creating Billing Documents

A billing document can be created for a single delivery or sales order by entering the number of the delivery or sales order.

If there are several deliveries or sales orders awaiting billing, you have to direct your attention to the items on the billing due list.

Processing the Billing Due List. The work list of documents due for billing can be processed as a collective. You may prefer to restrict the selection of items from this billing due list by defining selection criteria, such as the billing date for a particular sold-to party.

As the system collects the details of the documents due for billing, it will compile a log showing the defects of any that are incorrect or incomplete, insofar as the system can check on these matters. You can examine this log and perhaps supply the information needed to correct the defective or incomplete items.

For all the items that are correct in the billing due list or the subset of it that you have defined, the system will automatically generate the billing documents and carry out the posting necessary to the accounts of the FI-Financial Accounting system.

Pricing and Tax. When you are about to create a billing document, you have to decide whether to carry out pricing and tax determination again, using the latest figures, or instead to copy the prices, surcharges, and discounts from the sales order on which the billing document will be based. You can also change the price manually right up until the document is forwarded to the FI-Financial Accounting system by posting the completed billing document.

Canceling Billing Documents

The way to cancel a canceling billing documents is to create a cancellation document that cites the original billing document. When you post a cancellation document, the system will create the necessary reversal documents in FI-Financial Accounting. You can cancel credit memos and invoices.

Billing Methods

The choice of which of the several billing methods to use is determined by looking at the calendar that contains the billing schedule for the particular customer.

There are three main options:

- A separate invoice is created for each delivery.

- All deliveries within a particular user-defined period are combined to form a collective invoice.

- Several invoices are created for different parts of a delivery according to the criteria defined by the customer, such as material pricing group.

Invoice List. If there is one payer responsible for several invoices, they can be combined in an invoice list. This list can be compiled by a collective run, and can include both single and collective invoices.

There may be an advantage to the payer in this, because you can total the invoices on the list and apply discounts on the total value. You may grant factoring commissions, for example.

Either the individual invoices on the invoice list or the total of the list may be posted to FI-Financial Accounting.

Billing Methods Rules. You can define the rules used to decide how to combine deliveries in a collective invoice or invoice list. You also have control over the rules about splitting invoices for each customer or each type of business transaction.

Here are two examples of billing methods rules:

- The sales order has to be completely delivered and the goods issue has to be posted before a delivery can be invoiced.

- Deliveries or invoices may not be combined if there is more than one payer.

Processing Complaints

There are two types of processing complaints: One can give rise to a credit memo, the other to a debit memo.

Returns. If a customer makes a complaint about a delivery concerning the quality or the type of goods, you can pick up the goods free of charge from the customer location and generate a returns order in the sales department, which will lead to a credit memo request and eventually a credit memo posted to the customer's account in FI-Financial Accounting. The returns order will carry information about the complaint in short texts and perhaps free text, both of which can be analyzed later.

Credit Memo Requests. A credit memo request may also arise in the sales department because the customer has complained about a late delivery. This request will be blocked for billing until the amount of the credit has been decided, when the request can be released, and a credit memo created. The credit memo is posted to the customer's account in the FI-Financial Accounting system.

Debit Memo Requests. If a debit memo request is created in the sales department, perhaps because a customer has been undercharged, a similar procedure is followed. This time, the result is a debit memo amount, which is posted to Accounts Receivable in FI-Financial Accounting.

Links to FI-Financial Accounting

The integration of SD-BIL Billing with the FI-Financial Accounting module allows the system to carry out posting automatically when a billing document is created.

Payments from the customer are monitored from the FI-Financial Accounting system, and any dunning of overdue payments will originate from this system. The dunning key that determines the dunning procedure to be applied is first recorded in the sales order, either on the basis of customer master records, or because you have made a manual entry of a dunning key or canceled the default key placed there by the system. This enables you to exclude the dunning of a customer for particular invoices.

Although the procedure is automatic, you can place a posting block on the transfer of invoices and credit or debit memos by an entry on the billing document. The posting will not take place until you release this block.

Your display facilities enable you to list blocked billing documents so that you can easily attend to them.

Revenue Account Selection by the Condition Technique. When you post a billing document to the FI-Financial Accounting system, the appropriate revenue accounts and sales deduction accounts will be determined automatically by the system, using the condition technique.

A condition is a set of criteria used to make a decision. The standard account determination condition is to use defined ranges of values over the following criteria to determine the appropriate accounts for posting:

- The material
- The payer
- The business transaction type
- The condition type of the prices, surcharges, and discounts in the billing document

You have control over the critical values in each criterion, and you may wish to define other criteria and their critical values during customizing.

Revenue Account Determination Analysis. During billing processing, you can call for Revenue Account Determination Analysis, which will show you a listing of the FI-GL General Ledger accounts being used for prices, surcharges, and discounts for the particular business transaction you are working on.

Business Area Processing. The revenue and sales deduction accounts in FI-Financial Accounting may be segmented according to user-defined business areas in order to provide a more structured analysis of profit and loss. When you are posting as a result of billing processing, the system will take the data on the deliveries or sales orders to determine the business area segments of the accounts to which posting should take place.

CO-Controlling Account Determination. Costs and revenues can be distributed between profit centers, business segments, or projects. These values are used for profitability analysis in the CO-Controlling module. This control account determination is specified in the CO system and in the SAP R/3 PS-Project System, both of which make use of the FI-GLX Extended General Ledger.

Cost can also be assigned to the cost centers where they originated, as well as to orders such as production orders. The cost centers are defined and maintained in the CO-Controlling module; see Chapter 13, "Understanding the CO-Controlling Module."

Volume-Based Rebate Processing

After a specified period of time has passed, the sales to a specific customer in that period may qualify for the grant of a volume-based rebates.

The rebate is a payment subsequent to the settlement of all the individual orders, and is arranged in the form of a credit memo posted to the account of the customer to whom it has been granted.

Rebate Conditions. In the SD-Sales and Distribution system, the rules for automatically granting volume-based rebates are set up in the form of logical conditions that have to be met. During customizing, you can define the criteria and the critical values making up the conditions for a rebate agreement.

For example, you may agree to grant a rebate rate based on the overall volume of sales to a specific customer in a certain period. You could offer an additional rebate for sales in a defined product group. And you could offer yet another additional rebate if the volume of sales of certain specific materials reached a predefined value.

Any bill-to party can enjoy a rebate. This facility allows you to use rebate agreements to control the payment of licensing fees or commission payments.

Accruals in FI-Financial Accounting for volume-based rebate processing are created automatically. In every invoice, the rebate rate is recognized as an accruals rate, and the amount is posted to the appropriate account.

Rebate Calculation. Rebate settlement begins with a run to compile a list of credit memo requests. This will be based on the sales and the accruals. You may wish to edit this list manually.

When the credit memo request list has been released, you can create the credit memos. These will reverse the accruals in the FI-Financial Accounting system. You will thus credit the customer for the rebates you have granted.

From Here...

This chapter has shown how the SAP SD-Sales and Distribution Module includes the standard business programs that are needed to support all aspect of sales and distribution for almost every type of business. The emphasis of the design of the module has been on the individual person at a user interface terminal representing his or her company to the prospects and customers from whom future business will come. The module is designed to be easy to use, yet comprehensive in its ability to pull together, rapidly and with clarity of presentation, all the information that the customer needs to make an informed purchase and have it delivered promptly in good condition.

You might like to move on next to one of the following:

- Chapter 6, "Tool-Supported Optimization with the R/3 Analyzer," shows how you can describe and improve your current business system by selecting from the range of SAP standard business software.

- How costs are controlled is introduced in Chapter 13, "Understanding the CO-Controlling Module."

- Chapter 22, "Understanding the HR-Human Resources Module," points out how this module is designed to carry out the very best management of staff.

Chapter 21

Understanding the Possibilities of Electronic Commerce with R/3

This chapter shows that the range of standard business programs offered by the SAP organization has been extended to cover the business processes that have come into use because of developments in communications and data processing.

The implementation of local networks based on mainframe computers and dedicated communications has a relatively long history. Client/server configurations allowed distributed computing whereby the user at a workstation or simple terminal could be connected, not only to databases, but also to additional computing power to process the data. In simple terms, the concept entailed accessing a system through a terminal dedicated to this purpose. The extent and complexity of the system is often not apparent to the individual user, nor need it be in most applications.

However, there are very real limitations on the number of terminals that can be operating at the same time. SAP R/3 and R/2 are able to adjust the allocation of computing resources to the workload on a dynamic basis, and the provision of procedures to cope with equipment and communication channel malfunctions is well understood.

Apart from automated banking terminals, the direct conduct of commercial business by individual users is not yet widespread. But the SAP R/3 range of standard business software is anticipating a change.

The next generation of Internet servers will be running at many times the speed of the current devices, but there will be much more traffic on the net. There are several developments at the research stage that, if adopted as standards, will facilitate the setting up of systems that can accommodate literally millions of users online at the same instant.

In this chapter, you learn the following:

- How customers can see what is available and communicate rapidly their choices or their queries.

- How customers can access potential suppliers on a worldwide basis and make comparisons.

- How suppliers can have access to information about their potential customers.

- How orders and invoices can be transmitted electronically.

- How manufacturing can be synchronized with the details of the demand.

VI

Application Support

SAP R/3 Components for Electronic Commerce

The work unit of SAP systems is the transaction, and so it is for Electronic Commerce. The components available for electronic commerce are software units that can be carried in a range of operating systems and hardware devices. The concept is to make them available for use by any system that has received the SAP certification. Fundamental to R/3 Release 3.1 and 4.0 is the R/3 Internet Architecture, which allows the system to be scaled up to serve very large numbers of users via the SAP Internet Transaction Server, which runs on Window NT 4.0.

BAPI and IAC

BAPI, Business Application Programming Interfaces, are standards that can be used to design ways of controlling how a business application will respond to a transaction. In essence, the application receives a message through a BAPI that sets up the procedures for dealing with the data that also arrives at the BAPI. For example, a BAPI to a Human Resources database server may be configured to recognize a request for a person who has particular qualifications and who is also available to carry out a task, such as process a sales order. The server finds such a person, if possible, and returns the details to the system or person who initiated the request.

An IAC, Internet Application Component, is a standard business interface specifically designed to operate with the Internet or with an intranet. It is a characteristic of SAP R/3 Internet Application Components that they are isolated from the kernel of the R/3 system. They can be seen as separate components which can be developed and adapted without requiring any change in the main R/3 system. In particular, the way an Internet Application Component reacts is determined when the Internet Web page is designed.

Full multimedia facilities can be available, and the very style of the interchange between user and system is to build on the idea that the whole supply chain is responding without delay to the requests and requirements of the user. Both goods and information are handled in the style of a production process in which the customer is the source of the prime information.

Facilities Online

The following titles indicate the range of services that have been rapidly elaborated by using the SAP R/3 Internet Application Components and their supporting Business Application Programming Interfaces. Some of them are available as loosely coupled systems by using the ALE, Application Link Enabling, protocol.

- Product catalog with facilities to service Interactive Requests
- Employment opportunities with reporting to users on their Application Status
- KANBAN stock control logic and reporting from the SAP Available-to-Promise server
- Service notification
- Sales order creation with reporting on Sales Order Status

- Measurement and counter readings from production plant and laboratory systems
- Quality notification and quality certificates
- Consignment stocks status
- Project data confirmation
- Collective release of purchase requisitions and purchase orders
- Who is who staff listing and integrated inbox
- Internal activity allocation and workflow status
- Internal price list, requirement Request, and requirement request status
- Asset management

Electronic Commerce and Security

The variety of processes and the very large numbers of users who will have access to a networked electric commerce system inevitably raise queries about the privacy of personal data and the restriction of commercially sensitive information. Malicious damage to databases and other forms of hacking are real threats.

Firewalls are interfaces that allow only the transmission of information and commands that have been authorized and their sources verified. Encryption is the process of transforming a data stream according to a code that can be used by the recipient to restore the stream to its original structure. The complexity of encryption procedures increases as code-breakers acquire the ability to decode private data.

The SAP R/3 business interfaces and Internet components are designed to be able to implement the SET, Secure Electronic Transaction, standard that is under development by the Internet Engineering Task Force. Transactions, whether by personal or electronic means, will always receive the attention of would-be fraudsters. Yet the enterprise with a single-computer network system will have the advantage of being able to promulgate security measures very rapidly.

SAP R/3 Year 2000 Compliance

All releases of R/3 are Year 2000 compliant. No migration or upgrade is required for R/3 users. All date fields are four bytes, as are all related record layouts, screen layouts, matchcodes (secondary indexes), and data dictionary definitions.

Certification Tests

Year 2000 certification tests have been conducted on fields, transactions, and reports by using hundreds of consultants and developers who entered predefined and arbitrary data to verify software quality. Using the SAP R/3 CATT, Computer-Aided Testing Tool, many of these tests were repeated with various system dates in the range of years from several years before to several years after 2000.

Data Interfaces

Third-party data interfaces may present dates in two-digit format, but the SAP system will automatically convert a two-digit year into the proper four-digit number, so there is no impact. The input of data simulates data entry from a keyboard, so existing programs that process keyboard data entry correctly will interpret and automatically convert two-digit year dates to the proper four-digit number.

Using Electronic Commerce

If a business is to make best use of the possibilities of electronic commerce, it is essential that the workflow through business processes should be amenable to adjustment so as to be in a position to benefit from any change or anticipated change in the market conditions. An installed and configured SAP R/3 implementation must be capable of improvement without disruption.

Continuous Process Improvement Capabilities

The Business Framework architecture includes two types of Business Application Programming Interfaces. The earlier type is used to access SAP and third-party applications from the R/3 Basis core. The most recent type of BAPI resides in the application where it can process instructions that, in effect, reconfigure the complex of business processes.

It is used to enable customer organizations to apply new process-control logic and to change the presentation logic to correspond. This is achieved without disrupting business but, of course, under the strict discipline of change management wherein all adjustments are held in abeyance until the release date when their introduction is recorded in the change management documentation. For example, a production company might adjust its logic from an emphasis on process control to a distribution logic if the production plant became part of a different enterprise.

SAP R/3 Release 3.1 Java User Interface

The Java Virtual Machine can be deployed into virtually any presentation device. The SAP R/3 Java User Interface can then be transmitted to any of these devices, which can then be allowed access to R/3. In particular, this process can take advantage of low-cost devices such as the NC, Network Computer, and the NetPC, Network PC, which will hold very little functionality locally because they are continuously in touch with the parent system over an intranet or the Internet.

The essential feature of the SAP Java BAPIs is that they use standard business objects, and therefore, provide a way of operating with standardized business content and logic without reference to the specific terminal device used for access.

SAP R/3 Unified Modeling Language Repository

The SAP R/3 Reference Model is held in the Business Repository from which each function and data object can be drawn as needed. In order to raise the standards of business programming, cooperative work is in progress to define a UML, Unified Modeling Language that uses high-level modeling to organize and refine the components that can then take part in specific workflow sequences.

Business processes that have been defined to the UML standard can be transferred to any UML-compliant repository. The Microsoft Repository has been populated from SAP R/3 and so the programmers and tool developers who use the Visual Basic language can call upon the SAP standard business processes and use them in their own environments such as Visual C++ and other high-level languages.

SAPoffice

Although the SAPoffice electronic mail system has been available since SAP R/3 Release 3.0, it illustrates the way that a standard SAP system can be related to a variety of third-party systems. R/3 applications use SAPoffice to automatically generate electronic messages that inform users of critical business process events. Electronic messages from SAPoffice can start application processes and are integrated with SAP Business Workflow to provide automatic messaging services for workflow processes.

SAPoffice can send and receive electronic mail messages over the Internet by means of an SMTP interface. There is an interface to X.500 directories and you can send external messages from SAPoffice using SMTP, fax, or X.400 interfaces. SAPoffice can receive, process, and archive incoming faxes. You can upload and download files between SAPoffice and desktop applications such as Microsoft Word, Excel, PowerPoint, Microsoft Project, AmiPro, or WordPerfect.

The Documentum—R/3 Interface

Documentum has built on standard Document Management Systems and ArchiveLink technologies to develop a technology to handle most formats such as images, word processing documents, spreadsheets, HTML Web pages, archives, and CAD drawings. The ability to access both SAP and non-SAP documents is included.

Attraction of Business on the Internet

The development of network software is proceeding rapidly because the mechanisms are available and there are many advantages. The attractions, or at least the potentials, are distributed between consumer-to-business, business-to-business, and within-business applications.

- Easy to use, around the world, at any time

- Selective and easy access to information that is relevant at a pace and complexity under the control of the reader

- Low cost marketing channel with wide market exposure and considerable penetration

- The same familiar interface can access a variety of services in-depth if required

- Inquiries are answered immediately

- Inquirer can be asked intelligent questions because previously collected questions can be taken into consideration, either automatically or by the operator

- Moving images with sound can be under the control of the viewer to demonstrate the product and discover which aspects interest the prospective purchaser

- Increased revenue may arise from a low cost of sales

- The Internet may have become the preferred source of information on all matters for some sectors of the market

- Simple cut and paste can be used to compile e-mail purchase orders and to request other services

Electronic Commerce Partner Applications

SAP has always made use of development partners in order to accelerate the introduction of products that meet the SAP certification standards. Some of the more recent partner applications illustrate the widening range of business applications that has become apparent as the potential market is opened by the introduction of reliable network standards.

SAP R/3 PP-CBP Constraint-Based Planner

If there are two systems linked by reciprocal messaging interfaces, there is the potential for conflict and circular processes in which the demand for action is passed back and forth. The R/3 PP-CBP Constraint-Based Planner carries out planning and scheduling material requirements and capacity requirements in real time. The application includes a real-time Due Date Quoting capability as an option within the ATP, Available-to-Promise, server.

Intelligent planning and scheduling for global supply chain management across both inter-enterprise and intra-enterprise supply chains is embedded in SAP R/3 Release 4.0 to give fast, advance warning of impending constraints in their supply chain plan. These potential trouble spots can be published to the relevant part of the company or network of business partners. The intelligent planner will automatically suggest ways of removing the constraints.

Networked Workflow

Standard Web browsers, Microsoft Exchange, Lotus Notes, and custom applications can use R/3 Workflow Wizards to automate workflow design and thus control the workflow via a network. Workflow status reports are made available in HTML format. The WfMC, Workflow Management Coalition, is an integrated implementation that includes the 52 published Workflow Application Programming Interfaces and provides the following components:

- Session Manager

- Distribution Architect

- Reference Model

- CATT Testing

- Organization Architect

- IMG, Implementation Management Guide

Workflow templates can be executed and may serve as a guide for a company's own development. The individual steps of workflow templates are predefined as standard tasks. They contain a task description, linkage to the application logic through business objects, and prepared linkage to the company organization structure.

The business object repository delivered in R/3 includes predefined key fields, attributes, methods, and the events associated with the business objects Workflow Definitions made from standard tasks can easily be combined and changed at any time using the graphical editor.

Workflow templates have been integrated into the IDES, International Demonstration and Education System. This can "play through" the operational sequences of a sample company. The preconfigured workflow scenarios can be executed and analyzed for learning and planning purposes.

Open Finance

The essence of Open FI is the notion of a network of information sources and business processes that can be called upon in real time to generate the data that is relevant to each decision in the commercial and financial processes. With global business being conducted between complex enterprises, it is not a simple matter to determine credit worthiness, for instance. The fulsome computing resources of SAP R/3 may have to be used.

At each phase of a business process there can be activities in support that can be managed so as to add value to the sequence by applying information to control the process. The SAP components are designed to do this. The following sales sequence illustrates the way the components can be configured.

- Quotation, Marketing Services
- Customer Credit Control, Real Time Scoring
- Order, Monitor Export Credit Insurance
- Invoice, Factoring, Asset Backed Securities
- Dunning notice, Export Credit Insurance Premium Notification, Collection
- Payment, Payment history
- Asset-Backed Securities

An example of the way SAP R/3 FI is being used as a core application is in the enhanced FI-AR Accounts Receivable component available to manage ABS, Asset-Backed Securities. Expected cash flows from orders and revenues are at the heart of short and medium-term budgetary planning. Currency exposure cover, in the form of a micro-hedging transaction, can be effected by allocating forward exchange dealings to the order or billing document from which they originate. The Internet and intranet will change the way Receivables are dealt with.

Business Partner Networking

An example of how the network can be used to improve profitability by enabling early warning information to drive an efficient system of managing Receivables is illustrated by the Dun and Bradstreet "D&B Access" program. Its task is to monitor business partners on a discreet but continuous basis. The important information concerns corporate customers and the business transactions carried out with them and with their affiliated companies.

The source of this information is an integrated online network of external information suppliers such as credit reporting agencies and credit sales insurance firms. The D&B database carries up-to-date information on over 17 million European companies. The information is available in 26 data elements that can be culled selectively from the database.

The following are the Dun and Bradstreet Data Elements:

- Identification, D-U-N-S Number, Balance sheet filing date
- Rating (Risk grading), D&B Rating, Recommended credit limit, Loan recommendation
- Payment history, D&B payment index, Mean payment history
- Size, Capital shares issued, Shareholders' equity
- Revenues, Employees
- Financial analyses (Financial position at a glance)
- Quick Ratio, Current Ratio
- Working Capital, Profit/Loss
- Business activity, SIC 1 (Industry branch), SIC 2, Fields of activity
- Year founded, Ownership structure
- Parent company name, Parent company D-U-N-S number
- Holding company name, Holding company D-U-N-S number
- Negative information, Negative data indicator

From Here...

This chapter has pointed to some of the ways in which an SAP implementation can be enhanced to extend the business network to the consumers and the suppliers.

- How do you know what components are available from SAP?

    Each SAP R/3 contains the Reference model, which is described in Chapter 5, "The R/3 Reference Model."

■ What guidance is available on designing an electronic commerce system?

The R/3 Basis system includes many guidelines and tools to assist design. See Chapter 29, "The Business Engineer."

■ How can a company adjust its manufacturing to keep up with changes in the market?

Chapter 30, "R/3 Business Workflow Management," shows how there is a system of altering the flow of work without disrupting the profitability of the process.

Chapter 22

Understanding the HR-Human Resources Module

The SAP R/3 HR-Human Resources application brings together an extensive family of components that is fully integrated with the SAP R/3 system. These components are divided between two personnel modules:

- PA-Personnel Administration
- PD-Personnel Planning and Development

Integrated HR Management

Most of the components of the HR-Human Resources application can be progressively implemented as required. Some of them can be configured as stand-alone systems, perhaps in a transitional stage in the progress towards a fully integrated SAP installation.

The constituent modules of the HR-Human Resources application are designed to serve two themes, one financial, one concerned with the skill of the workers:

- PA-Personnel Administration has an emphasis on payroll and associated procedures.
- PD-Personal Planning and Development seeks to add value to the personnel resource by career management, beginning at first recruitment and with continuity across extended absences.

The HR-Human Resources system can stand alone or be fully integrated with the following SAP applications:

- FI-AM Asset Management, in order to reference the fixed asset master records—for example, the asset of a specific company car
- FI-Financial Accounting—for example, to relate to payroll accounting and posting
- CO-Controlling, and CO-OM Overhead Cost Control—for example, to analyze wages and salary costs

The scope of this chapter includes the following:

- The efficient and timely management of salary, benefits, and expenses is supported by the components of the HR-PA Personnel Administration module.

- Personnel data has to be maintained and secure from unauthorized access.

- Recruiting and personnel development can be costly activities, yet to perform them efficiently will add value to the work carried out by the beneficiaries.

- PM-Plant Maintenance—for example, to transfer completion confirmations to the plants concerned and subsequently release the employees for other work

- PP-Production Planning and Control—for example, to transfer completion confirmations to the production departments and to assign employees to other activities

The comprehensive system of access protection is applied to all interactions of the HR-Human Resources application with any other SAP or non-SAP application.

Components of the HR-Human Resources Application

The functions of the HR-Human Resources application are allocated to the constituent modules, PA-Personnel Administration, and PD-Personnel Planning and Development. All the functions are fully integrated with each other and with the rest of the R/3 system.

The Components of HR-PA Personnel Administration.

- PA-EMP Employee Management

- PA-BEN Benefits Administration

- PA-COM Compensation Administration

- PA-APP Applicant Management

- PA-TIM Time Management

- PA-INW Incentive Wages

- PA-TRV Travel Expenses

- PA-PAY Payroll

The Components of HR-PD Personnel Planning and Development.

- PD-OM Organizational Management

- PD-SCM Seminar and Convention Management

- PD-PD Personnel Development

- PD-WFP Workforce Planning

- PD-RPL Room Reservations Planning

Fundamental Concepts in the HR-Human Resources Application

There are certain concepts and procedures that are part of the SAP R/3 system and available for all applications integrated with it. However, there are nine operational concepts that have been particularly developed and exploited to good effect by many users of the HR-Human Resources application:

- Real-time operation of personnel functions

- The use of business areas to define the parts of the HR-Human Resources application and direct the user to the functions required

- Infotypes to manage and control access to sensitive areas of personal data

- Personnel events, which are occasions when several infotypes are presented on the same screen, information is entered, and the system is called upon to update the relevant infotypes automatically

- Dynamic events, which are initiated by the system when the user starts to enter the information that indicates what he wants to achieve

- Fast entry screens that allow you to deal with many individual personal records and transactions at once

- Automatic date monitoring, which is continuous for all dates of significance to the personnel functions

- Interactive Voice Response (IVR), which can be used in personnel departments to deal with the typically large volume of routine inquiries

- Automatic sifting of résumé submissions in preparation for a recruiting or job reassignment interview

Real Time Personnel Administration. The SAP R/3 HR-Human Resources application is designed to run in real time and make use of the database in real time. There are many important advantages to this method, of which the following is but a selection:

- Although all processing can be performed online under the control of dialogues, it is also possible to set up batch processing, which is the normal procedure for writing to storage media and for reorganizing the data base.

- If you have installed and configured the CO-CCA Cost Center Accounting component, checks can be made against the cost center master data when an employee is assigned to a cost center. If this installation has not been effected, the HR-Human Resources application will check with its own table of records.

- When fresh data is entered, the system checks it for validity without delay, and there is less risk of making errors.

- Valid data is stored directly, with a time and date stamp, on a uniform database that is available immediately to all authorized users and is automatically subject to change control management that will cause all modifications to be logged.

Business Areas. The particular aspect of human resource management that is being addressed by a specific program is known as a Business Area. The following are examples of HR business areas that are serviced by the PA-Personnel Administration suite of standard business software:

- HR master data maintenance
- Payroll
- Time management
- Applicant administration
- Travel expenses

VI

Application Support

The following are examples of HR business areas that are serviced by the PD-Personnel Planning and Development suite of standard business software:

- Organization and planning
- Workplace and job description
- Qualifications and requirements
- Career planning
- Succession planning
- Personnel costs planning
- Seminar and convention management
- Workforce planning
- Shift planning

HR Infotypes. Personal data is stored in information groups, each of which can be controlled for scope and access authorization. These information groups are referred to as infotypes. Not every personal record need be assigned every infotype. The particular use of infotypes in your implementation will be specified during Customizing.

The SAP R/3 HR-Human Resources application provides over one hundred standard infotypes. The following are examples of standard HR infotypes:

- Organizational assignment—for example, position, organizational unit, job
- Personal data—for example, current name, name at birth
- Payroll status—for example, last payroll, date for recalculation
- Disability—the categories used in this infotype may be subject to specific national regulation
- Leave entitlement—for example, negotiated leave, disability leave, additional leave
- Leave compensation
- Address—for example, permanent residence, temporary residence, home address
- Work Schedule—for example, shift, time recording, work hours
- Contract elements—for example, hourly paid terms, fixed price terms, chargeable expenses
- Base pay—for example, change in classification, pay scale increase, change in pay
- Garnishment of wages—for example, child support or alimony, garnishment of property, cession of wages
- Bank connection—for example, main bank connection, additional bank connection

- External transfer

- Recurring benefits and deductions—for example, commuter's allowance, rent with-held, company housing

- Additional payments—for example, Christmas bonus, service anniversary

Personnel Events. The infotypes used to manage personal data in the HR-Human Resources system can be combined to form data entry screens. Within the scope of your authorization, you can have any infotypes displayed together. When the screen data is entered, the system automatically updates all the relevant infotypes. This sequence is referred to as a "Personnel Event."

Dynamic Events. When you have responded to a personnel event by entering some data, the system will evaluate that data and respond accordingly to generate a dynamic event. For instance, if you take on a new employee, the system will create a new personnel master record. At the same time, it will calculate the end date of the probationary period and create an appointment record. This dynamic event will, in turn, generate another personnel event, because you will have to confirm that you accept the proposed appointment for someone to interview the new employee at the end of the probationary period.

A standard consequence of a personnel event is the generation by the system of a series of electronic mail messages informing all those who should be told what changes have been made as a result of the personnel event.

Fast Entry Screens. If you need to deal with several employees in the same way—the staff of a particular cost center, for example—the system will select the employees for you and display their relevant records on your screen, where you can make individual or group adjustments before you commit the screen for processing.

If you are unfamiliar with any field on any screen, you can point to it and call for online help, which will take the form of first, the name of the field and then, if you require it, a longer explanation of how you can make use of it.

Automatic Date Monitoring. It is characteristic of personnel departments that many events recur on a calendar basis—for example, renewal of work permits and scheduled performance appraisals. The HR-Human Resources system will monitor all such dates and let everybody concerned know the details, and if necessary, the system will update their diaries automatically.

Interactive Voice Response in Personnel Departments. A large part of the time of staff in personnel departments is taken up by answering routine inquiries from employees, such as "How many days can I have for my vacation this year?"

SAP has set up a system of digitized recordings of all the phrases commonly used in answering personnel queries. These phrases are used to guide the caller through an automated telephone response system with a recorded message.

Resumix. The Resumix System, of Resumix Inc., is integrated with the SAP HR-Human Resources application to provide a completely automatic method of handling résumés. Applicants for an advertised position, or people who might be suitable for a job that is expected to become vacant, can be identified through the HR-Human Resources application.

If the job specification has been written using a standard vocabulary of terms which accurately express the attributes needed for the position, and if the applicants have drafted their résumés using the same vocabulary, then a rank ordering of the applicants can be made on the basis of the comparison between job specification and résumé. A more precise matching is possible if an application form is used.

If the suitability of an existing employee is being considered, facilities are available for building up a profile of qualifications on the basis of existing data in the HR-Human Resources application. This will include job history, assessment reports, and textual material written by the employee and the management.

Benefits Administration

The SAP R/3 system of benefits and salary administration is supported by the following components from the PA-Personnel Administration module of the HR-Human Resources system:

- PA-EMP Employee Management
- PA-BEN Benefits
- PA-COM Compensation Administration

The system is driven by a series of tables that you can alter to provide for whatever system of benefits and salary your company uses.

Enrollment for Benefits and Insurance Coverage

A standard screen is provided to manage the enrollment of each employee individually. The PA-BEN Benefits administration component recognizes the following types of benefits and insurance coverage:

- Welfare, including medical, dental, vision, and so on
- Spending and dependent care accounts
- Insurance, including life, AD&D, and dependent life
- Defined benefits and pensions
- Defined contributions, 401K, RRSP, ESOP, and so on

Insurance coverages are specified by a system of tables that allow you to set out the method of calculation of premiums and benefits, and also how the associated costs are to be settled. There are facilities for employees to purchase additional coverage.

A flexible system is provided to enable you to particularize deferred compensation plans as part of a benefits package. The following details can be specified in this process:

- Eligibility requirements

- Contribution levels by employee

- Contribution levels by employer

- Vesting schedules

- Investment options

- Stock purchases and options

Salary Administration

The aim of salary administration is to relate the salary structure of the organization to the aims of providing rewards for good performance identified during the review process and removing any imbalances within the current salary structure.

Facilities are provided by the PA-COM Compensation Administration functions to achieve the following results:

- Apply standard pay changes across organizational units.

- Override the standard pay change for any individual as an exception.

- Analyze the impact of any proposed salary changes upon the organizational units and sub-units.

- Assign future salary records and calculations automatically to the changed structure.

One of the methods used to assign salary changes to employees is to use matrices to compare performance appraisal information and current salary across employees in similar jobs.

National Supplements to the International HR-Human Resources System

The variations in the tax and benefit systems of different nations are accommodated in the SAP R/3 HR-Human Resources system by appending the appropriate National Supplements during Customizing.

Each special national supplement has the effect of adding to the suite of HR infotypes, which can be referenced when configuring the PA-BEN Benefits Administration module.

The following special national supplements are being complemented by new supplements under development.

Austria
- Tax—for example, previous year, current year, subsequent year
- Commuter lump sums
- Social insurance
- Family allowance
- Sick certificates—for example, main person insured, insured spouse, insured child
- Previous employer

Belgium
- Social Insurance—for example, category, registration of substitute employee, Pension number, Social Insurance number
- Tax—for example, spouse, children, other persons in the same household, tax rule indicator
- Personal data—for example, Personal Registration number, Royal Service number, Pension Insurance number, Work Permit number, Social Security number
- Work schedule—for example, RSZ category, RSZ code, RSZ number, work regimen, work rhythm, work regulation, employee type (part-time/full-time), country indicator, work interruption, pay period
- Contract elements—for example, "Paritair Kommitee," Compensation Fund number, meal coupons, CAO/pension data

Canada
- Residence status—for example, citizen/alien, passport data, work permit
- Additional personal data—for example, ethnic origin, military status
- Benefits—for example, employee welfare plans, medical, dental, vision, legal
- Insurance—for example, life, AD&D, dependent
- Deferred compensation and savings plans—for example, ESOP, RRSP, RRP, pension
- Tax—for example, federal, provincial
- Bond purchases—for example, denomination, recipient
- Injury and illness—for example, extended accident or illness tracking, accident data
- Workers' compensation—for example, entitlement, contribution, record-keeping, reporting
- Union—for example, job title, seniority
- Grievance tracking—for example, status, disciplinary action

Denmark

- Tax

- Private pension

- Vacation or statutory holidays—for example, previous year, current year, subsequent year

- ATP pension

France

- Social Insurance—for example, Social Insurance number, fund model

- Capital formation—for example, profit-sharing

- Leave processing

- Maternity protection

Germany

- Tax—for example, previous year, current year, subsequent year

- Social Insurance—for example, obligatory, voluntary, Retirees' Health Insurance

- SI Supplementary Insurance

- Capital formation—for example, Saving Through B&L Association, Saving by Installments, life insurance

- DÜVO—for example, registration, interruption

- RWH/BWP

- BAT benefits

- Company pension plans

- Wage maintenance

- Direct insurance

- Previous employer—for example, tax, Social Insurance

United Kingdom

- Income tax

- National Insurance; employee and employer contributions, arrears

- Court orders, payments, protected earnings, administration fees

- Pensions

- Statutory sick pay

- Statutory maternity pay

VI

Application Support

Netherlands

The following functions are handled by the standard HR functions:

- Maternity protection cutoff dates

- Options for capital formation

- Travel expenses for trips between home and business

The special national features extension offers the following extensions to the general functions included in the international HR-Human Resources system:

- Employee taxes—for example, tax class, Sofi number, tax code indicator, deduction items, OT annual salary

- Social Insurance—for example, person-related data such as the codes WW, ZW, WAO, ABP, VUT, BPF

- Health Insurance funds—for example, private HI funds, compulsory HI funds

- Social funds—for example, application types, decisions, appeals, payment options

- Additional absence data—for example, data for tracking illnesses, dates for multiple treatment appointments, dates for work restrictions

- Accident data—for example, accident status, accident class, type of injury

Spain
- Tax—for example, recipient key, annual gross

- Social Insurance—for example, Social Insurance number, multiple work percentage

- Various payees—for example, payee key, gross amount

- Union—for example, union function, contribution

- Seniority

Switzerland
- Tax—for example, canton, municipality, tax liability

- Social Insurance—for example, AHV number, FAK, ALV

- Pension fund—for example, fund, insurance type, premium

- Residence status—for example, status, expiry date

- Family—for example, Child Allowance

United States of America
- Residence status—for example, citizen/alien, passport data, work permit

- Additional personal data—for example, ethnic origin, military status

- Benefits—for example, medical, dental, vision, legal

- Insurance—for example, life insurance, AD&D, dependent insurance

- Savings plans and deferred compensation—for example, pension, 401(k), ESOP

- Tax—for example, federal, state, local

- Bond purchases—for example, denomination, recipient

- Injury and illness—for example, illness tracking, accident data, OSHA, Workers Compensation data

- Workers' Compensation—for example, entitlement, contribution

- Union—for example, job title, seniority

- Grievances—for example, status, disciplinary action, grievance tracking

- US I-9 compliance

PA-TIM Time Management

The purpose of the PA-TIM Time Management component of the Personnel Administration module is to provide the standard software for recording, assigning values and evaluating all employee data relevant to time management.

Since the topic is often associated with time management, the PA-INW Incentive Wages component is also relevant.

The instrumentation and hardware of time measurement and recording is under continuous development, and SAP is able to update the standard interface modules to provide a comprehensive interface support system.

The Concepts Underpinning Time Management

In order to take advantage of the benefits of an integrated business system, it is necessary to translate many of the concepts and working practices of business into precise yet flexible operational definitions that can, in turn, be represented in a computer program.

Plant Calendar. The calendar that shows the possible working days of a particular plant is the plant calendar. This calendar must show the days of the working week, together with the days observed as general and regional holidays.

Day Program. The way that one day is treated from the point of view of measuring the time at work is referred to as the day program. A series or pattern of day programs can repeat itself over the course of a plant calendar, taking into account only the working days in that calendar.

Time Model. The pattern of day programs that repeats in a plant calendar is called a time model. You can define as many different time models as you require, and they can have any duration you wish.

Shift Scheduling. If you roll a time model over the plant calendar, you get a shift schedule. You can intervene, for example, to allow extra days before and after a planned plant shut-down; but common features, such as reduced working hours before holidays, can be taken into the time model in the form of special day programs that have the shorter working hours.

Work Time. If your company works flexible work times or flexitime, you have to specify the components of a working day in terms of a time frame and core times. Tolerance zones in the working day are usually designated to account for the short periods of irrelevant time before work officially begins and after it officially ends. You may wish to allow a tolerance zone for people coming late to work.

The system allows you to define as many breaks in the day as you like. You can designate them as paid, unpaid or paid at a special rate. Breaks can be defined as fixed, variable or dynamic, in which case the length of the break depends on how long has been worked or how much work has been completed.

You can allocate part of the day for orientation or "warming up," and you can record if people are working extra hours to save up for time off later.

Any decisions you make on the rules attaching to time measurement have to be given a period of validity, and the system will automatically record the time and date of any changes that you make to the tables that store this information. If necessary, the system can be called upon to deliver a history of the changes that have been made to a set of master data records.

Time Recording Variants. There are two common variants and several hybrid forms:

- Negative time recording
- Positive time recording

The base assumption of negative time recording is that everyone is at work all the time unless recorded as absent. You can ignore brief absences of a few minutes, and you will have a range of good reasons for deviating from the official work schedule:

- Absence, such as vacation, work incapacity or stipulated day off
- Special work attendance, such as attending a seminar
- On-call duty
- Overtime
- Work time substitution

The recording methods at your disposal are as follows:

- Enter data on an individual record.
- Enter data for a group of people on a fast entry screen, such as overtime for the whole work center.
- Enter data using a special recording screen, such as an absence calendar.

Positive time recording entails recording the deviations from the work schedule and the actual times of work. This method is becoming more prevalent as a result of the following factors:

- Flexibility of work time is increasing, using formal and informal methods of time management.

- Flexitime using time recording is more widespread.

- Workers more often determine their own work times.

As a consequence, the role of the shift schedule may often be restricted to providing a time frame and serving as the basis for the valuation of absences.

Links to Recording Equipment

The so-called front-end, time recording systems are installed with the purpose of establishing the time facts and collecting the data. They should not be treated as the method of evaluating the time data. This is the province of the HR-TIM Time Management system.

The usual method is for the central system to dispatch to the front end time recording system a record known as a mini-master data record. This carries just enough data to accomplish what is required: to collect the time data for a given individual at a specified work center in relation to the time schedule that has been assigned.

Admittance Control. Some companies combine time recording with admittance control. Depending on the equipment fitted in the workplace, the people admitted to a particular work center may be defined in terms of their assignment to that work center and perhaps also their authorization to enter locations elsewhere in the plant.

Time Data Maintenance

The standard SAP system of infotypes is used to organize the time data of the HR-Human Resources system. The following infotypes are recognized:

- Absences—for example, vacation, illness, temporary layoff

- Special work attendance—for example, different work center, errand, business trip, seminar

- Overtime—for example, overtime compensated by payment, overtime compensated by time off

- Substitutions—for example, shift substitution, workplace substitution

- On-call duty—for example, on-call duty, standby duty

- Absence quotas—for example, sabbatical, time off

- Attendance approvals—for example, overtime approval

- Actual work times—for example, with additional account assignment, differing payment, premium work time

■ Time events—for example, clock-in/clock-out messages, work order confirmations

■ Balance corrections—for example, rebooking overtime to flexitime, paying out time off credits

Time data can be managed directly by the PA-TIM Time Management system, or through the technique of assigning people to time data agents, which can be cost centers, departments, or some other organizational entity that you have created for this purpose. The time data agent is assigned only some of the personal infotypes—just the ones that are needed to manage time on this local basis. In the central system, there will be a second person responsible for unlocking time data collected by the time data agent only when the central "personnel clerk" authorizes its release.

Distributing Work Attendance Times to Cost Objects. The attendance times, however entered, can be subsequently distributed to cost objects such as cost centers, orders or projects. Facilities are provided for you to make manual adjustments to the data before or after distribution to cost objects. If the data has already been posted, only the differences will be transferred.

There is full integration with CO-CCA Cost Accounting and PA-PAY Payroll.

Time Valuation

The PA-TIM Time Management module stores all its control logic in tables which you can adjust so as to yield a precisely tailored system suited to your requirements.

Each day, for each employee the attendance or absence time is analyzed in relation to the preset values of the relevant shift schedule. The first result is a series of time pairs that signal when something began and when it finished—work, absence, and so on. Each of the time pairs is then classified. By referring to the rules for overtime and so on, the system can refine the classification until each unit of time has been identified by its type, which will be used to choose the wage type and eventually to compute the compensation.

All the logical rules for performing this classification and calculation procedure are stored in the form of tables, to which you can have access if you want to change the way the process is to be performed or any of the rates or base values.

If a new type of work time or absence category comes into being, you can set up the logic for identifying it and computing the appropriate compensation.

Automatic Recalculation for Retroactive Changes. All time management data is stored in the form of time pairs and time types. When these are evaluated, it may be discovered that there has been an error in time recording or in the way in which the time types have been generated on the basis of the work schedule and plant calendar.

If you decide to make a change in retrospect, and if you have the authority to do so, you can alter the original data, and the system will recalculate the time data and hence the consequent compensation due.

For example, you may decide that a new scheme should be backdated. As you redefine the dates for the validity of the scheme, the system will recognize that a recalculation is needed and will carry it out automatically.

PA-INW Incentive Wages

It is customary to associate the collection of data for incentive wages with the same organization that manages time data. By integrating the collection of individual incentive wage data with group data, it is possible to achieve the following kinds of results:

- Recording group-relevant incentive wages data

- Determining such evaluation factors as the duration of group membership or the percentage distribution

Premium rates are calculated by reference to tables to which you have access.

Time Tickets. The standard system recognizes the following types of time ticket:

- Premium time tickets in individually computed incentive wages

- Time tickets for work times to be paid on average

- Quantity time tickets for planned times in group incentive wages

- Personnel time tickets for actual times in group incentive wage schemes

- Supervisor time tickets for individual piece-work with relevance to a reference work group

You can readily add other types of time tickets.

Human Resources PD-Personnel Planning and Development

The purpose of personnel planning is to determine who will be required, and when. The purpose of personnel development is make sure that the aspirations of the personnel planners can be realized by selecting suitable applicants and giving them the broad educational qualifications and specific training requirements that will ensure sufficient suitable staff will be available to do the jobs when they are required.

The functionality of the PD-Personnel Planning and Development module is embodied in the follow standard business program components:

- PD-OM Organizational Management

- PD-WFP Workforce Planning

- PD-PD Personnel Development

- PD-RPL Room Reservations Planning

- PD-SCM Seminar and Convention Management

VI

Application Support

The SAP standard business software in the Human Resources domain is under continuous development as this aspect of business grows in complexity and becomes ever more critical as the productivity of individual workers is increased by technological improvements in production and communication methods.

Business Areas

The business areas addressed by the PD-Personnel Planning and Development Module include the following:

- Organization and Planning, the basic component
- Workplace and Job Description
- Applicant Data Administration
- Applicant Screening
- Qualifications and Requirements
- Career and Succession Planning
- Workplace and Job Grading
- External Training Administration
- Education and Training Administration
- Education and Training Planning
- Manpower Planning I (Long-Term)
- Manpower Planning II (Short-Term)
- Cost Planning
- Personnel Assessment and Trend Procedures

Data Model Development for Human Resource Management

It became apparent during the research and development phases that the SAP standard business software approach could be extended to the data manipulation areas associated with human resource management. The most significant technical development requirement was in the matter of handling more complex data structures concerning, for instance, qualifications and job requirements. In particular, it is obviously essential to be able to store information about the positions in a company that its personnel might occupy.

If a person doing a job is to be replaced—by a substitute during the employee's absence, for instance—then the knowledge and skill needed for that job should be specified so that the replacement can be chosen and prepared by training to do that job with the absolute minimum loss of performance due to the changeover.

You might assume that the replacement person knows nothing and has to be trained in everything. If that person is already working in your company or in a similar job, then you would be wrong in your assumption. Furthermore, you would be wasting resources and probably squandering the goodwill of the trainee if you made him or her take a full course of training.

So it is necessary to specify the starting qualifications and experience of anyone about to undergo training or about to take over a job they have not done before. This is true for a fresh applicant from outside your company and for internal applicants.

SAP has adopted an extension of its data model approach to cope with this requirement to record the jobs and skills of the staff. The standard system of information types—infotypes—is still in operation. Over one hundred infotypes have been defined in the SAP R/3 system. The standard models of organizational structure still apply.

But several additional data models have been introduced to cope with the complexities of personnel data. The result is an extensive object-oriented data scheme.

The scheme requires a clear distinction to be recognized between methods of representing structural relationships among planning data objects and other information about them. You can allocate several workplace positions to a cost center, the master records will show this "ownership" as a relation, and your graphical display will be able to draw an arrow to represent it.

The accountants need to know who will pay for work done in a workplace, and they may wish to analyze this in relation to a system of cost centers. But this kind of information does not help the personnel department when it comes to filling positions with people. This is the kind of "other" information that has to be associated with positions and people, and it must be done in a very flexible manner if it is to be of any use.

The standard system of infotypes is used to associate sets of data elements with the attributes of data objects. During Customizing you can define which infotypes are required for each attribute of each type of data object, and how they should be displayed on the user interface screens. Infotypes may be assigned directly to planning objects independently of the object type.

The benefits of this approach stem from the fact that the standard methodology can be used to identify and link objects and to evaluate them. It also means that planning can be installed step by step, because a set of planning objects is no longer defined during system design, but rather during the actual installation and Customizing of the system. The set can be extended later.

The method is used to establish extra data models in HR-Human Resources.

Data Model for the PD-OM Organizational Management Component. The following object types are used:

- Organizational Unit
- Position
- Workplace

■ Job

■ Task

There are two anchor object types accessed by the PD-OM Organizational Management component:

■ Person as defined in the HR-Human Resources, PA-Personnel Administration module

■ Cost center as defined in the CO-CCA Cost Accounting component

These anchor object types are not managed in the PD-OM Organizational Management component. Their data can be accessed via relationships which are master records that record the permanent association of a data element of a record in one database with a data element of a record in another.

A cost center specified in CO-CCA Cost Accounting has allocated to it one or more organizational units, which can be all on the same level in a flat structure, or arranged into hierarchies, parts of which may be flat structures.

A person defined in the HR-Human Resources, PA-Personnel Administration system holds or occupies both a position and a workplace. The position is attached to a particular workplace, and the workplace is defined as having room for only one person. For example, a machine operator is a position. A position may be unoccupied, in which case it takes up no space in the workplace. There may be several positions that could occupy a workplace, each held by different people but not at the same time. They would have to be shift-workers or those engaged in job-sharing. In addition, one person can have positions in more than one workplace, but again, not at the same time.

The position is part of an organizational unit.

A job is a description of what is entailed by a position—what the person holding that position has to achieve. There may be more work than one person can do, in which case there will be more than one position for the same job.

A task is what has to be done to carry out part of a job. There may be several different tasks entailed in one job, or separate tasks may be repetitions of a basic task, perhaps with minor variations from time to time due to variations in the material being processed or in environmental conditions. The distinction between task and job is a matter to be established to suit the individual company.

A position may entail a specific personnel requirement, so may a specific workplace or one or more of the tasks entailed by the job to be performed there. For example, to be a high tower crane driver requires a person who is reliable and patient. This particular workplace could not be occupied by a person who was afraid of heights. The task of controlling the swing of the load on the crane as it is being moved needs to be done by somebody who has both the knowledge and the eyesight to judge the situation. The crane driver also has to have a very special skill with hands and feet to operate the crane precisely and quickly so as to cancel the tendency for the load to swing on past the point where it is required to be placed. Each crane comprises one workplace. A person with the position of crane-driver could be qualified to occupy any of them.

A person appointed to a position may have some of the requirements, but not all, in which case there is a requirement for a training program and, certainly in the case of the crane driver, a period of personal supervision by an experienced operator, perhaps leading to a formal certification of competence. The SAP R/3 system needs the object type "Qualification" to be recognized in order to support the Qualification and Requirements component of the PD-OM Organizational Management module.

Data Model for PA-APP Applicant Management. The PA-APP Applicant Management component adds the data object type "Vacancy" to the objects required to effect the data model for PD-OM Organizational Management.

Data Model for Education and Training Administration. Each element in this data model is supported by standard infotypes. For example, a training course will need a data structure with data elements to represent the start date, the finish data, the location, the account settlement arrangements and so on, all of which can be assigned standard infotypes that can be used to build data entry and display screens using the standard SAP R/3 methodology.

For example, a system of infotypes to contain the data necessary to administer education and training courses has to include the logical relationships and the structure to contain the details of the elements.

A training program is the sequence of course types needed by one person to qualify for a specific position within a stated time period. Each course of the same type is assumed to be equally effective and cover the same content, even though the venue and the teachers may be different.

A course type requires one or more resource types, such as teachers, premises and equipment.

A course type may impart one or more qualifications, which are defined in terms of the positions they are preparation for.

A course type may impart one or more task requirements, which may exceed the skills necessary for qualification, or fall short of this.

A course type is defined by an entry in the catalog of course types. The course type is therefore a very flexible planning entity.

A course is a specific instance of a course type and uses one or more resources of one or more resource types. A course group is a set of courses. A course needs one or more instructors and one or more attendees. An instructor is either a person internal to the company or an external person. An attendee is either an internal person or an external person.

The Catalog of Course Types

The definition of a course type or other training event type is specified in a catalogue of course types maintained by the HR-Human Resources application. The data attributes and elements of this catalogue are as follows:

- Courses or other qualifications that are prerequisites for attendance at this event

- Qualifications provided by this course

- Contents of the training event

- Methods of this training event

- Dates and time patterns of this event

- Planned internal costs of this event, including currency, hours, and persons absent from normal work

- Minimum or maximum critical numbers for this event

- Technical resources of equipment and instructors required

- Course description in text form for use in brochures

Human Resources Planning

An organization is made up of organizational units, such as departments, teams, groups, and projects. It is displayed as an organizational chart.

Organizational units have jobs, and there is one job for each job title in the SAP R/3 Classification. For example, Secretary, Programmer, and Clerk are job titles for jobs. A job may have too much work for one person: there may be several positions for a job. There may be shift-working, which increases the number of positions that have to be filled for the same job, and there may be several equivalent positions for that job in each shift.

The arrangement of positions is represented by an organigram, an organization diagram. It shows the conventional hierarchical organization chart with the added feature that the number of positions at each job is also represented, usually graphically.

The scope of the HR-PD Personnel Planning and Development functions is illustrated by the following structures to which the planning procedures may be applied:

- Multiple reporting paths up and down the company hierarchy from any position selected on a display of an organization chart or organigram

- Organizational structure of any specific project

- Diversified responsibility organizations represented by the matrix methodology

HR Plan Versions and Status Control. When you allocate values to a structure of planning objects, you may be testing or simulating a tentative plan that you do not wish to release for the moment, so you can store it as a plan version and retain control over its status. Changes can be effected only in a planning object with the status of "planned." Every planning object has to pass through the following status stages:

- Active (in use)

- Planned

- Submitted

- Approved or rejected

Rejected data can be returned to the planned status for revision. You can also introduce other status control stages during Customizing.

Job Charts and Staffing Schedules. A job chart, in the context of the SAP R/3 PD-Personnel Planning and Development module, is created on-line by the system in response to the entry of a search specification determining the scope of the items to be included in the chart. They can be tasks, jobs, or positions, and any of the items displayed can be selected as the subject for a "drill down" operation, in which you use the special function keys to direct the system to display particular attributes of the item selected. In this manner you can access and alter any of the job data records, to the extent that you have authority to do so.

A staffing schedule is an attribute of a job or, if the job entails several different positions, of a position. The following types of staffing schedule are recognized and supported by the SAP R/3 PD-Personnel Planning and Development module:

- The position can be held by two or more persons.

- The position can be held by one person or a substitute.

- The position can be held by two people simultaneously for a fixed period.

The first type of staffing schedule represents the situation where a job is planned to exist at a position only if there is work to be done. The position can be vacant because there is no suitable person available. If there is more work than one person can do, there can be more than one identical position planned for the same job. If the work is not enough for the number of positions occupied at the workplace, there can be work-sharing on the basis of percentage of material or by the number of hours worked.

If a person at a position is expected to be absent for a long period, a substitute person can be assigned to that position for the anticipated length of the absence. The substitute does not replace the person who is on long leave of absence.

Having two people occupying the same position may occur when one of them is seconded to the other for training. The trainee may be intended as the successor, or the intention may be to create a second identical position for the same job when the training is completed. This form of simultaneous occupancy is usually of fixed duration, although the end of training may be dependent on the trainee reaching a defined standard for a formal qualification or for an internal award which is recorded as some kind of "authority to operate unsupervised."

The staffing schedule data for the jobs you have selected for display will be generated automatically. The persons allocated to the positions on your display will be identified from the master records, and their personal details, where relevant, will be available from the personnel master records.

If one of the positions on your display is determined to be vacant, you can call for the system to suggest suitable people on the basis of their qualifications and personal profiles. The system will attempt to match the people available with the personal requirements specified for the vacant position. The system will operate with any set of personal attributes that you have defined: formal qualifications, previous experience, geographical location, and so on.

This process is a planning activity and, as such, can take place within any time frame. You can ask for a person to fill a vacancy as soon as possible. For example, you may have an overload in a telephone sales function and be seeking someone who is in the building or on the computer network, and who can be diverted from other work until the overload situation has passed, or at least until an extra position has been created and filled on a permanent basis.

On the other hand, you may be looking at the staffing schedule for a planning period in the future. In such cases, the system will offer you people who are suitable for the position and likely to be available when you plan to use them.

If the system cannot locate any existing personnel who could be assigned to a position that you plan to have filled by some specified date in the future, the HR-Human Resources system will create a vacancy specification based on the information it has about the job. The processes of filling this vacancy from external sources or recruiting activities can then go ahead when this course of action has been submitted for and granted approval.

All this automatic action depends absolutely on your having assembled an accurate job description.

Describing Jobs and Workplaces. The system will accept various conventions regarding the use of the concepts of jobs, tasks and positions. This discussion will not seek to draw any firm distinctions between them.

SAP R/3 has a defined data object type designated as "Task."

A SAP task is made up of any number of tasks and task complexes in any arrangement. The elements of this structure are either task structures themselves or individual tasks. A task structure may comprise a block of tasks with no particular interrelationship except the fact that they may well have to be time-shared by the person holding the position. For example, the receptionist may have to operate the security procedures and the telephone switchboard and the visitors' coffee machine. Only the last would be regarded as a single task rather than a task structure.

For some workplace positions, there may be good reasons why the job description should specify quantities or percentages allocated to the different tasks.

During the elaboration of a system of job descriptions for a newly designed work complex, it may be convenient to begin with a rather general job description which becomes progressively more detailed as the necessary information comes to hand. During this process, it may become apparent where and on what basis one job should be allocated to more than one position. This is a reasonable approach, and the SAP R/3 PD-Personnel Planning and Development module will support it in a very flexible manner.

The task descriptions at the lowest level of detail of a task structure may be merely titles that serve as references to a job procedure manual, or they may be rough descriptions of an element of a job that is going to be taught by an instructor or by someone who is doing the job already. In other cases, it may be legally required that the details of a task element be formally documented. The system will support all varieties of job description.

PD-WP Workforce Planning

This component is available to manage the details in installations where there is a very large volume of processing entailed in job and workplace specification. Where this component has been installed and configured, your displays of job charts and staffing schedules will indicate how you can evaluate the supplementary job information as and when you need it.

The component makes available a wide range of data and evaluative processing which may be initiated in the context of the PD-Personnel Planning and Development module. This area of human resources management is under continuous research and development as the nature of work undergoes evolutionary and sometimes revolutionary changes. Methods of job evaluation have to be elaborate to track these developments.

The sections that follow give an illustrative description of some of the additional functions provided by the PD-WP Workforce Planning component.

Planned Compensation

Pay scale groupings or absolute amounts can be stored, precisely or in form of ranges of values, to be the planned compensation for any of the following job description elements:

- Workplace
- Job
- Position
- Task

Standard evaluations can be called to provide the following results:

- Planned monthly costs for each organizational unit
- Comparison of planned payments with actual costs

Job Description Supplements

Information can be stored on any of the job description elements regarding the following matters:

- Authorizations necessary to perform the task element or to change its specified task description

- Auxiliary elements of the job description not detailed in the main description of the job or task—for example, whether a specific qualification is required by law to do the job, or whether special equipment is used at a workplace

Health Care Data

Medical histories can be entered against particular workplaces where, for instance, follow-up data has been collected on previous incumbents of jobs dealing with hazardous materials or processes.

A workplace can be marked to indicate the requirement for preventive medical examinations at prescribed time intervals.

Restrictions

Some jobs and workplaces require special protective clothing to be worn and may therefore not be suitable for persons who might have difficulty wearing it. The place of work may be inaccessible or difficult to access by persons with certain disabilities. Some positions may be unsuitable for particular persons because of the hours worked or the types of activity performed. If a workplace has difficult emergency exits or hazardous emergency procedures, it may be unsuitable for certain persons. These matters would have to be raised at some stage in the recruitment and appointment process.

Location Data

Although the location of a job in a workplace and the identification of the position or positions held there are matters documented in the central organization master data records, the supplementary records of the Workplace and Job Description component can be used to store additional information of importance, such as:

- Building identification

- Room number

- Telephone number

- Fax number

- Network address

- Complete postal address

This location data is used to compile telephone and organization directories, for example.

Planned Working Hours

The planned working time, to any level of accuracy, can be stored as data attached to an individual workplace or position. If the position is filled, the PD-Personnel Planning and Development system can compare the planned working hours with the contractual working hours of the person appointed. And when positions are summarized up to higher levels of the organizational structure, evaluations can be conducted not only on the basis of positions filled but also on the planned or actual working hours.

Person Grouping

Certain personal indicators can be used to establish person subgroup types into which individuals can be classified. Certain positions or workplaces can be reserved for persons in a specific person subgroup.

Some companies, for instance, reserve certain positions for hourly paid employees and others for those paid on a monthly basis. In some cases, certain positions are reserved for members of a particular trade union, or for persons who are accredited members of a particular professional organization.

Assignment of a person to a person subgroup type can be determined by a SAP R/3 condition which specifies the logical relationships between two or more personal attributes, such as "Within a given age range" and "Chartered member of the XYZ Institute."

Task Structure

The information stored on a task can be in the nature of a comment on the duties involved rather than a description of the steps or technical stages. For example, the task can be characterized in terms of the main function of the person holding the position:

- To plan the work of the section

- To check the work of other people in the section

- To perform the task personally

The overall function of the task can be documented in the task structure record. For example:

- The purpose of this position is to provide a pleasant and efficient welcome to strangers visiting the plant for the first time.

- The function of this position is to make sure that no object or person enters the premises without leaving an adequate record of identity, purpose, and destination.

- The purpose of this position is to ensure that adequate records are kept securely of all materials of interest to the U.S. Customs Service that enter or leave the bonded warehouse.

Personnel Development. If the aim is to provide a comprehensive human resources service to your company and the people in it, the place to start is with a set of clear job descriptions. These descriptions not only portray what is done, they must also show how these results are to be achieved. In some form or other, the necessary knowledge and skills have to be identified. There are two obvious methods:

- Identify people who can do the job and then find out how their knowledge and skills are different from people who have just been recruited.

■ Identify people who can do the job and find out how they came to be in that happy position.

Neither method solves all the problems of getting good people into jobs they do well. The approach of personnel development is to assume that you have recruited at least some good people who will want to stay in your company, and then provide them with a trajectory of jobs that will afford them the opportunities to acquire not only the necessary knowledge and skill, but also the confidence in their own ability that is so essential to good performance.

Requirement and Qualification Profiles. The logic is simple. A person is suitable for a position insofar as their qualifications match up to the requirements of all the jobs that will be their responsibility if they take the appointment.

So a person can be more, or less, suitable. And they can be suitable in some respects and not in others. Put this data on a scale, and you have a suitability profile.

Some of the requirements of the job can be documented, some can be set up in the form of admission tests. Some of the requirements can be described in general terms, such as "resourceful" or "sociable." The difficulty with using this type of word to describe the appropriate response to an unknown future situation is that, by definition, there is no way of knowing whether a specific individual will be able to cope. For some personnel selection assignments, it may be best to concentrate on the negative side. For example, a person who has had no practice at first aid should not be placed in a position where it might be needed. A person who had shown no sign of being friendly to strangers should not be in charge of crowd control in cases of emergency.

Where you can define what is needed in terms of the amount or weighting of each of several characteristics, you can draw a job requirement profile. Some requirements will be absolute and admit of no leniency, some will be desirable but not essential. In some positions, the lack of one good quality can be compensated by an abundance of another. For example, a very good memory can serve as well as intelligence in some circumstances.

If you have a personnel selection procedure, even if it is just an interview, you might arrive at a measurement of the capability of each applicant in each of the dimensions of the job that you have used to build the job requirement profile.

Put this data on a scale, and you have a qualification profile.

If you are bold enough to compare the qualification profile of a person against the job requirement profile, you can derive the data to yield a suitability profile of this applicant for this job.

And if you were to carry out this profile matching for all your applicants for all your vacancies, you would arrive at a list of people in rank order of suitability for each vacancy. This function is available through the PD-WFP Workforce Planning component.

These are the main functions:

- Manage the requirements for jobs, positions, workplaces, and tasks, and set priorities and weightings if required.

- Manage the qualifications of applicants and the quality or level of these qualifications.

- Mediate the substitution of qualifications in relation to job requirements when compiling a short-list of suitable people.

- Create job requirements profiles.

- Create applicant qualifications profiles.

- Carry out matching of requirements and qualifications profiles and produce suitability profiles.

- Maintain a catalogue of model qualifications and requirements.

This catalogue of qualifications and requirements is supplied as standard in the PD-WFP Workforce Planning component. You can attach items from it to both persons and to positions or workplaces, and you can extend or adapt the catalogue to suit the type of work carried out in your company.

The quality of a qualification can be expressed in terms of the level of proficiency attained by the person holding it. If this same qualification is associated with a position, the level will perhaps indicate what is regarded as an acceptable proficiency for that position.

Some qualifications represent knowledge and skills that can deteriorate over time, either by disuse or by becoming out of date. The PD-Personnel Planning and Development module provides the ability to enter a half-life value for a qualification, which is the period of time taken for the skill to deteriorate to half its proficiency if it is not required by the job and if it is not kept up to standard by refresher training. The system will compute the exact degree of deterioration to be assumed for any other period under consideration if you have specified a value for the half-life.

If you are looking at a person who has been in a job that demands the exercise of the skill or other requirement corresponding to the qualifications they possessed on appointment, there is no reason to suppose that their proficiency has deteriorated at all.

Career Models. A career model is an ordered list of the types of opportunity open to a person in your company or a person you would like to recruit. Clearly, each of the steps in the career model will be taken only if the person is suitable and willing to move, and if there is a vacancy in the target position.

The same approach is used for new recruits, selection of suitable successors for existing positions and management of career paths.

The HR-Human Resources, PD-Personnel Planning and Development module provides the following functionality:

- Representation of careers
- Association of the career potential assessments taken from the selection procedure with the steps of potential career models
- Determination and representation of further training needs of individuals embarked on career paths
- Representation of further training programs
- Graphical editing of profiles and profile comparisons

Career Planning. The planning of an individual career begins with a discussion with the person concerned and the identification of one or more positions for which this person wishes to be considered. This data is entered under the organizational structures established in the PD-OM Organizational Management component and the suitability profile of this candidate as computed.

The integrated PD-Personnel Planning and Development module offers a list of all the positions for which the candidate would be suitable and a sub-list of those that are vacancies, or likely to be so on a future date suggested to the system.

The system can be run in simulation mode to analyze any domino effects. If the career candidate elects to accept an offer of a change of position, a vacancy will be created elsewhere, and so on. When the transfer or recruitment actually takes place, the system suggests all of the vacant positions in succession, so that the planner can be sure that the subsequent transfers are processed.

Representation of Human Resource Potentials. The first potentials of a candidate are derived from the assessment procedure, whether it be formal or informal. For every position for which the candidate is likely to be considered, his or her assessed potential is stored.

As time passes and experience is accumulated, these potentials can be adjusted on the basis of the new information coming to light. Alternatively, the assessed potentials can be stored with their original values intact and a set of current potentials maintained separately.

Succession Planning. While career planning is looking from the point of view of the employee, the function of succession planning is to be concerned with who will maintain the work of the company by succeeding to a specific position if and when it becomes vacant.

There may well be several candidates who would be suitable successors. This is a matter which can be illuminated by considering their qualification profiles in relation to the requirements profile of the position. Even so, there may be no real differences in the suitability profiles of several of the candidates. Other factors must be considered, for example:

- Time with the company
- Time served in the present position
- Staff association membership
- Educational background as a potential for further career development

Further Training Needs. It can easily happen that no candidate can match qualifications with requirements for recruitment or career progression, as the case may be.

Your company will have to weigh the costs and other considerations to decide whether to look again, perhaps elsewhere, for a person with the right qualifications, or whether to accept one of the candidates and make up the difference by having them trained.

The system will tell you what qualifications are lacking, and to what level of proficiency they are required by the vacancy. If the training course data base is accurate, the system will also tell you where and by what method the additional qualifications may be obtained.

This functionality enables you to create an education and training plan for an individual by reference to the qualification deficits discovered by the career planning activities. You can also modify these plans before they are released for processing.

The following functions are available through the PD-Personnel Development component:

- Manage internal and external training events.
- Manage and plan all the resources required for internal and external training events, such as rooms, instructors, course materials, and equipment.
- Process all correspondence in connection with training events.
- Check the prerequisite courses or other qualifications of the employees or external people who intend to enroll.
- Automatically update the qualification master records of those who pass the course standards.

The component is also able to manage the booking of internal and external participants with the following facilities:

- Automatic creation of waiting lists
- Automatic sequential processing of waiting lists
- Booking with priorities
- Booking from lists
- Canceling from lists

It is a feature of the component that all training events can be processed without regard to their time dependency, if necessary. For example, it can be asked to create a complete catalogue of all the further training events scheduled throughout the company.

The system ensures that a participant is not booked on the same course twice, and is not destined for two courses that overlap in time. If you have installed the PA-TIM Time Management component, employees identified automatically by the system as suitable to act as instructors on a course will not be assigned to it if, for example, their vacations will make them unavailable.

Events can be linked to specific locations if this is necessary—for instance, if a particular resource is available nowhere else. A specific language for the conduct of a course can be dealt with in a similar fashion.

Different calendars can be invoked to ensure that the courses are not planned for statutory holidays, for instance.

Pre-booking for a general course topic or theme, delimited by a range of dates, can be later confirmed by the release of firm booking for specific training events. Booking priority is covered by the following standard scheme:

- Essential for the good of the company

- Normal, first come, first served

- Waiting list for places not filled by participants with higher priority. The system will propose a redistribution to subsequent courses of those remaining on the waiting list after the event has taken place.

Education and Training Planning. Included in the PD-Personnel Planning and Development, PD-PD Personnel Development component is a suite of functions to carry out quantitative planning of education and training events and make optimum use of time.

Requirement for planning arises in the form of data on the estimated numbers of courses made up from the requirements per subject and per calendar quarter. Alternatively, the requirements can be expressed as pre-bookings for each course type that specifies the subject or theme of interest. There are career and succession planning functions in the PD-OM Organizational Management component which provide a source of pre-bookings. These functions will have identified the needs for further training in connection with career planning and the preparation of successors for those who are moving on.

The education and training requirements are serviced by the following functions:

- Scheduling of numbers of different training events

- Optimizing of event schedules with respect to the resources available

- Scheduling sequences of training events for individuals or groups of participants

Overall scheduling depends on the following factors:

- Preset limits on the number of events each year

- Number and timing of events according to the pre-bookings

- Education and Training budget
- Demands from career and succession planning

Optimized event scheduling has to take account of the resources required and their availability, as follows:

- Suitable rooms according to the PD-RPL Room Reservations Planning component
- Instructors available according to the PA-TIM Time Management component
- Course materials and equipment

Applications for Personnel Recruitment. The PD-Personnel Planning and Development module is used in the recruitment situation in conjunction with the following PA-APP Applicant Management component, which includes applicant screening support functions:

A separate applicant database is maintained in the PA-APP Applicant Management component to which all the functions of the PA-Personnel Administration module may be applied. The data on any applicant who is accepted and hired is automatically transferred to the HR-Human Resources database which is controlled by the PA-EMP Employee Management component.

Applicant Data Administration. The following services are provided by the integrated HR-Human Resources system:

- Management of internal and external applicant data
- Recognition of multiple, repeated, and duplicate applications
- Determining vacancies automatically from the HR planning components
- Triggering job advertisements automatically from the HR planning components, using job description text and a detailed breakdown of media and recruitment instruments in each
- Assigning applicants to advertisements to check cost effectiveness
- Processing correspondence
- Applying the PA-TRV Travel Expenses component to process job interview costs and to reimburse interviewees
- Automatic data transfer to PA-EMP Employee Management

Applicant Screening. A position can be marked as vacant, which allows it to be released for filling. If an unoccupied position is not so marked, it will be ignored. If a position is subject to a long notice period, it can be marked as vacant although still occupied.

The applicant screening process can be used to find all applicants who are suited by their qualifications for any set of positions. You can screen for all positions in the company, for those on a particular set of career paths, or for those marked "Vacant."

The ensuing hit list for each position will contain those applicants whose qualification profiles most closely match the requirement profile for the position. There will be an automatic estimation of the possible training needs of any applicant who does not have each of the requirements to the degree required by the position.

Personnel Cost Planning

One of the functions provided by the PD-WFP Workforce Planning component is to estimate the wage and salary elements for a specified period. Simulations can be conducted that take into account various factors, such as:

- Collective agreements

- Modified tax contributions

- Modified social insurance contributions

- Work schedules that attract special pay rates

The scope of the cost planning functions is as follows:

- Annual preview and budget planning

- User-defined estimation of individual elements from wages and salaries, as direct data entries, by transfer from the CO-CCA Cost Accounting or PA-PAY Payroll modules

- Integration into the planning of facts, such as negotiated pay rates, which have already been dated and which affect the personnel costs

- Support for different simulations

- Graphical editing of the results and the target versus actual comparisons

Evaluation of Jobs and Workplaces

This component is under development. It is intended to determine suitable compensations for individuals holding particular jobs. The values will be designed to reflect the importance of the job to the organization, as indexed by the type and skill needed to do the job, and the responsibility for budget and personnel. Analytic work evaluation and various other schemes of assigning monetary values to different kinds of work are being considered for inclusion in the component.

Manpower Planning I Component

This component is under development. The long-term planning of manpower requirements of the company will include the distribution of planned amounts to each workplace on the basis of guideline figures that you enter, such as:

- Planned turnover per product

- Planned output per product

- Planned turnover per location

The employees and their qualifications will be taken into account, along with the number of employee-hours available in the planning period.

The hours available will first be distributed to take account of shift schedules and overtime planning. A second operation will adjust these hours to take account of the nonproductive hours arising from a range of causes.

Manpower Planning II Component

This component is under development. The purpose of Manpower Planning II is to improve short-term planning by ensuring that business needs are covered by sufficient personnel.

The SAP R/3 Basis System provides full integration of your system so that Logistics data relating to the workplace and time data from PA-TIM Time Management are normally available to PD-Personnel Planning and Development. Your company may elect to keep the PD-Personnel Planning and Development system separate from the integrated logistics application modules which are:

- SD-Sales and Distribution
- PP-Production Planning
- MM Materials Management
- PM-Plant Maintenance
- QM-Quality Management

The manufacturing data transferred from the Logistics modules will be concerned with the following aspects of short-term manpower planning:

- The general amounts of work planned and in progress
- General data from the work plans of your company, including the plant locations in relation to the addresses of the personnel who might be employed there
- The patterns of qualifications, formal and in terms of experience, needed throughout the planning period

It is necessary for the Manpower Planning II component to call on the PA-TIM Time Management component for the following types of information:

- Company time models
- Shift schedules
- Personal calendars of individual employees, which will yield information on employee hours that cannot be planned for normal work activities because they have been already assigned to such activities as vacation, education, training or business trips

VI

Application Support

The PA-TIM Time Management component is also important in this context because it initiates manpower planning, and hence possibly re-deployment or recruitment, if it should happen that the number of suitable employees at a workplace at any time falls below the minimum required or is forecast to do so.

The Manpower Planning II component requires certain PD-Personnel Planning and Development components to be installed and configured, whether or not there is direct transfer from the Logistics modules. PD-OM Organizational Management, and PD-WFP Workforce Planning, are required to provide the data on workplaces, the activities that need to be performed, and the employees assigned to them on specific dates and times throughout the planning period. These components are also needed to supply the job specifications of workplaces and the qualifications held by the employees in these positions, together with their suitability profiles.

The HR-Human Resources, PA-Personnel Administration module will also have to be installed, because it contains the employee master file required to gain access to the personnel data.

Functionality Intended for Manpower Planning II. The emergency role of this component is to enable you to deal effectively and swiftly with unplanned staff shortages. You will want to locate the right people to fill the gaps.

The right person is one with all the requirements of the vacancy and no disadvantages. This is a true statement of the aim but is difficult to realize in practice.

The approach taken by this component will be to assemble and make readily available all the information that might help you cover the staff shortage. For example, you might wish to have records of the following types of information about employees:

- Whether a person is incompatible with another and should not be assigned to work with him or her
- How a particular work team should be made up from a specific mixture of person types and capabilities
- Which persons have registered preferences or requested limitations on the working hours or working days of the week assigned to them

Workplaces should be assigned master records carrying data on factors that could help or hinder your efforts to fill an unplanned vacancy there, such as:

- Minimum number of positions that should be occupied at the workplace
- Maximum number of positions that could be accommodated at the workplace
- The optimum number of people to be located at this workplace
- Preferred staffing arrangements for the different shifts or other working patterns that sometimes or regularly occur at the workplace

The solutions that the Manpower Planning II component will propose to you will have to include the schemes and arrangements your company has discovered or developed over the years, plus any new possibilities that can be conceived now that you have a flexible integrated manpower planning system in operation. The list will probably include such tactics as:

- Assigning a person to be on call in case his or her expertise or work capacity is needed at the workplace suffering a staff shortage
- Assigning standby duty
- Effecting a temporary transfer from another workplace or from another section of the plant
- Engaging outside personnel through a placement agency
- Engaging a person who was previously an employee
- Engaging a freelance worker
- Engaging a seasonal worker directly or via a seasonal worker agency

The component will make extensive use of the standard SAP graphical display facilities to make the operation of the functions easy for inexperienced users.

PA-TRV Travel Expenses

The purpose of the PA-TRV Travel Expenses component is to provide a seamless software system for managing a business-related trip from application, through approval, to update and correction, by means of retroactive accounting. The scope of the component includes domestic and business trips, in the home country and abroad, for individuals and groups.

The approach is standard SAP: maximize the integration between modules and components of the SAP R/3 system and any non-SAP connections; minimize the redundant storing of data.

The component is intended to be integrated with the SAP R/3 system in an open system architecture—UNIX, for example. It can also be used as part of the SAP R/2 systems on mainframe hosts. The PA-TRV Travel Expenses component can also be used as an output interface to external systems.

The following SAP R/3 modules and components will normally be installed and configured before the PA-TRV Travel Expenses component is set to work:

- FI-Financial Accounting
- CO-Controlling, CO-OM Overhead Cost Control
- HR-Human Resources

The Structure of HR-TRV Travel Expenses
The component comprises three groups of functions:

■ Basic version, which provides the transactions, forms, and evaluation tables needed to carry out travel expense accounting in accord with the tax law of the country in which the R/3 system is installed

■ Cost distribution, which allows the component to redistribute travel costs from the employee level to such cost objects as trip, receipt or cost type, or stopover

■ International supplements, which allow variations of the basic evaluation procedure according to the requirements of other nations

The supplements for tax calculations and country-specific payroll calculations are organized according to the divisions of the INT-International Development module:

■ IN-APA: Asian and Pacific Area

■ IN-EUR: Europe

■ IN-NAM: North America

■ IN-AFM: Africa/Middle East

■ IN-SAM; South America

Basic Version Functionality

The functions of the component can be grouped as follows:

■ Lump-sum accounting, where the amounts are taken from standard rates regardless of the expenditure actually incurred

■ Representation of company regulations

■ Procedures and administration

Lump-Sum Accounting. The following functionality addresses the requirements of lump-sum accounting:

■ Lump-sum accounting for accommodations, meals, and commuting costs

■ Itemizing per invoice as accommodations, meals, commuting costs, business entertainment, or incidental costs

■ Trip itemization and lump-sum accounting

■ Reduction of lump sums and maximum amounts by predefined adjustments for active or passive business entertainment events

Representing Company Regulations. The PA-TRV Travel Expenses component affords flexible arrangements to record and automatically apply the rules and customs of the individual company, as follows:

■ Definition of permitted circumstances via table entries

■ Reduction of the daily rate for meals if a trip lasts less than one day

■ Statutory trip types, errands or business trips

- Trips with stopovers

- Round trips

- Special business trips with day excursions to different customer sites

- Company-specific regulations that apply to trips representing the company and which may apply different rates according to the status of the employee and according to the nature of the trip or the territory in which it is made

- Company-internal event trips, such as attending a seminar, attending a course, or customer advisory service trip

- Trip-specific account assignment to company code, plant, cost center, order, or project

- Employee-specific overall proportional cost distribution to company code, plant, or cost center

Trips Worldwide.

- Automatic currency conversion

- Border crossing

- Foreign trips worldwide

Procedures and Administration.

- Application and approval procedures, trip approval notification at the planning stage, approval notification immediately prior to departure, advance of travel expenses, cancellation of a trip

- Internal or external number range assignment for trip number

- Model trip plans which may be edited

- Table-controlled statement per employee

- Interfaces to other SAP applications

- Day-specific accounting

- Special function keys to control fast entry of data

- Short form of travel expense accounting procedures for external services

Interfaces to other SAP applications will be established if the following applications have been installed and configured:

- FI-Financial Accounting

- CO-Controlling, CO-OM Overhead Cost Control

- HR-Human Resources, PA-PAY Payroll

Day-specific accounting is achieved by storing tax-free and company-internal refund rates in tables, which are also accessed to provide determination of additional amounts or income-related expenses.

Cost Distribution Functionality

The source of costs to be distributed can be an individual employee or a trip.

If several employees go together on a trip, the total costs associated with the trip can be distributed, in equal shares for each employee, to the company code, plant, or cost center with which that employee is associated.

Another cost distribution variant available in this component is to allocate to each cost center, project or order the deviation account value representing the difference between planned and actual costs of the trip.

You can also enter a percentage distribution structure for each trip, and have it applied to the following item types in order to distribute the amounts to the appropriate company code, plant, cost center, order, or project:

- Total costs of the trip
- Costs pertaining to individual stopovers
- Individual travel expense receipts

You can also assign an individual expense receipt to a specific cost object and so prevent it from being distributed with the other expenses of the trip.

Each employee master record will include an infotype for cost distribution and an infotype subtype for travel expenses. Therefore, you can call for a display of the proportional overall cost distribution of an individual employee over a range of trips. You can see if he or she tends to spend more money on one thing than another, and how these priorities change over a succession of trips.

It may make sense to allocate a percentage distribution for planning purposes to the overall costs of a trip, which can then be assigned to cost centers, for example. You can also separate the expenses of the individual stopovers and distribute one or more of them according to a percentage scheme.

Individual receipts can be distributed in proportion or in absolute amounts to the cost objects specified in your distribution plan.

Functionality Empowered by International Supplements

International requirements for travel expense accounting may require additional information to be recorded.

Mileage distribution can be recorded for specific dates and the number of passengers, and luggage can be recorded on the basis of distance. Company lump sums can also be attributed on the basis of distance. Vehicle characteristics such as horsepower, engine capacity and price may have to be recorded and taken into the valuations.

Mileage rates by country of destination can be applied. Cumulative miles covered by each employee can be recorded on a flexible time basis. The user can define mileage ranges over which lump-sum payments per mile can be specified.

The INT-International Development module can provide for lump-sum accounting for additional expenditure on meals under the following circumstances:

- Border crossing for inward and outward legs of trips

- Trip duration can be calibrated in calendar days, 24-hour periods or by times of day

- Days on which an employee is traveling for less than 24 hours can be evaluated according to the number of hours in transit or the time of day

- Lump sums and maximum amounts can be reduced on account of lunch coupons given out monthly

Certain trip activities can each attract a fixed lump sum, and all employee-specific travel expense regulations controlling travel privileges can be altered for each trip.

Cash advances are deducted from subsequent payments.

Personal Master Data

The following employee personal data is required by the PA-TRV Travel Expenses component:

- Name of employee

- Organizational assignment—for example, to plant, cost center, or person in charge

- Travel privileges—for example, authorization to run an expense account and the particular internal regulations under which it may be operated

- Banking connection for direct payment

Travel Expenses Procedures

Central data recording can be used or the travel expense procedures can be managed on a decentralized basis. Travel expense data recording without the submission of a prior application occurs in the following sequence:

- Employee submits a travel expense claim form.

- Data on the trip is checked and recorded.

- Trip claim is approved.

- Travel expense accounting action takes place in the PA-TRV Travel Expenses component.

- Data is transferred to the FI-Financial Accounting module and to the CO-Controlling, CCA-Cost Accounting component.

- Marked claim document is returned to employee.

VI

Application Support

Your company may require prior approval of a trip and use this occasion to provide help with booking travel tickets and accommodation. The benefits of advanced travel expense planning may include the following opportunities:

- Coordination of the means of transport for several employees making trips

- Overview of travel and hotel usage patterns

- Discount negotiations on means of travel and hotel bookings

- Advance payments through the FI-Financial Accounting component can be credited to the employee's bank account or paid directly in cash or foreign currency

If the employee has to obtain prior approval, the following sequence is enacted:

- Employee submits a travel expense claim form with a request for an advance.

- Data on the trip is checked and recorded.

- Trip advance payment is approved.

- Travel expense planning action takes place in the PA-TRV Travel Expenses component.

- Data is transferred to the FI-Financial Accounting module and to the CO-Controlling, CO-OM Overhead Cost Control component.

- Trip advance is paid to the employee.

- After the trip, the employee submits a record of the trip and the expenses incurred.

- Data on the trip is checked and the records supplemented and updated.

- Trip claim is approved.

- Travel expense accounting action takes place in the PA-TRV Travel Expenses component.

- Data is transferred to the FI-Financial Accounting module and the CO-Controlling, CO-OM Overhead Cost Control component.

- Marked claim document is returned to employee.

A development of this travel expense procedure is to have the employee enter the data to which the central facility applies the checking and financial actions.

Trip Data Processing

A single trip—from a short-distance errand, to a long-distance business trip, to a complex trip abroad—can be processed for an individual employee.

The following choices are offered if you want to review the documents on previous trips:

- Trip period

- Trip destination

- Customer
- Processing status of the trip

You may use any of these search specifications to locate a previous trip to copy as the basis for a new trip.

Creating a Trip. The system will require your personnel number and a trip schema, unless you opt to copy a previous trip.

A trip schema is an instrument for controlling the sequence of screens. You can create a new trip schema or edit the table containing one of the standard trip schemas.

Data entry is required under the following headings:

- Beginning and ending time and date of trip
- Trip destination
- Number of domestic and foreign miles driven
- Number of passengers for calculating the passenger lump sum
- Lump-sum accounting for meals
- Number of overnight stays with lump-sum accounting
- Cost center for travel expense account posting if this is not to be the master cost center for the employee
- Trip activity types, such as seminar, customer visit, and so on
- Border crossing on return trip

Individual Receipt Entry. Trip receipts relevant to accounting are recorded. Each is assigned an expense type key which determines the FI-GL General Ledger account to which expense receipts are to be posted. The keys and their associated FI-GL General Ledger accounts can be established to suit your company. This will normally take place during Customizing.

These keys may also be used for statistical summaries of the travel expense types, both standard and user-defined.

Foreign currency may be entered on the trip receipt along with the exchange rate. The system can provide a default exchange rate and, if necessary, a default currency identifier based on the trip destination.

Business Entertainment. If an employee is invited to a meal for business reasons, the lump sum payable for meals on that day will be reduced by an amount determined by a predefined table. The maximum travel expense amount will also be reduced.

The default entry for every day will assume that there is to be no deduction of travel expenses for business entertainment received.

Advances. Entries on a trip with the status "Travel Expense Application," and which concern advances, are evaluated by the PA-PAY Payroll program and the FI-Financial Accounting system. If the advance is approved, the employee will receive it in the next payment run.

If an advance is approved for payment in cash, that amount has to be posted to a specific vendor or customer account. This might be a company to be visited by the person making the trip. In this instance, the advance claim will serve as documentation for this posting.

The exchange rate is entered automatically when the currency is identified. The rate may be changed manually at any time, which will leave a change record in the system.

Advances can be refunded in the same manner.

Stopovers. In addition to the main destination, one or more stopovers may be entered, with their exact times of entry and departure.

Maximum amounts for travel expense claims and the lump sum or blanket allowances for meals and accommodation are determined from predefined tables for each country. The 24-hours rule is applied: Standard rates and individual receipts are assigned for each day of a trip according to the last country the person was in before midnight, local time.

Mileage Distribution. Passenger allowance to an employee is payable on the miles actually traveled by the passenger. The function allows this to be recorded in preparation for distribution to the cost objects. Mileage per employee is cumulated in this function.

Trip Text. Text can be assembled from standard text elements or written free-form through the SAPscript word processing facility. It can be used for two-way communication between the travel expenses accounting office and the employee, and as additional documentation for trip activities. The format and printing destination will depend on the purpose of the text.

Trip Status. The trip status maintenance screen offers a choice of status indicators. Which of them are open to alteration will depend on the authorizations of the user and the stage reached in the trip travel expenses transaction sequence. The following menu of possibilities is offered as standard:

- ■ Approval status:
  - Application
  - Application approved
  - Trip occurred
  - Trip approved
- ■ Accounting status
  - Open

- For accounting—to be settled

- Canceled

Function keys control the recording of trip status data. If the Accounting status is "Open," there will be no accounting action, but changes to the documented will be stored.

If the status combination is "Approved" and "For accounting—to be settled," the trip is settled on the next billing run.

Fast Entry. The purpose of fast entry is to allow you to enter several domestic trips for one employee in the same transaction.

Each trip in a multi-trip fast entry is assigned an internal trip schema which controls the trip number allocated and marks the trip as domestic. For a trip lasting more than one day, you must enter the starting and finishing dates and times. All other trip data is entered on the line for the beginning date. The following fields will be filled by the system with default values:

- Area—the area to which the employee is normally assigned

- Errand or business trip—the distance of the destination

- Status—defaults on entry or when a detail is changed to "Trip approved—to be settled" on the assumption that the travel expense claim is being submitted after the trip has taken place

To postpone a trip, you can change the date fields.

A copy function is provided to accelerate entering several one-day trips for the same employee.

The system will print for each employee a list of the trips that have been validated and settled.

Trip Accounting. The accounting period for travel expenses can be defined by the user. The normal choice is between weekly, every two weeks, or monthly.

If an error is detected during a travel expense accounting run, the cause of the error is logged, and corrections have to be made by the user travel accounting department.

Settlement is carried out only if the status of the trip document indicates that the travel expense application is approved and the trip is to be settled or, in the case of a planned trip, the trip is approved and is to be settled, for instance, by paying an advance to the employee.

The settlement action will normally include the following processes:

- Conditions are accessed to determine the calculation procedures to be followed according to the country of destination, the area, the refund class or group, and any deductions to be incurred.

- Lump-sum charges and maximum charges are determined.

- The refund, tax-free, and additional amounts are calculated.

- Adjustments are made to take account of the duration of the first and last days of the trip.

Forms. Two standard forms are provided as suggestions for printing the results of a trip settlement transaction for the benefit of the employee:

- Detailed statement

- Condensed statement

Control of the printing of the standard forms is effected by reference to SAP R/3 tables, to which you have access in order to manipulate the form and content of the printed statements.

Each day for which meals were taken is evaluated separately. The lump-sum accounting for accommodations, meals, and commuting expenses for each main destination or stop-over are displayed first. Then follows the accounting data for the individual receipts.

The condensed statement is particularly useful for external service employees who make the same trip every day, because it allows you to present the accounting results of many standard trips in compact form.

Payment

There are several methods of effecting payment for travel expenses. It may take place along the channels of the SAP R/3 integrated system, or via a standard interface to a non-SAP system.

Payment via the FI-Financial Accounting System. Transfer of trip data to vendors or customer accounts for settlement of the travel expenses of an employee making a trip to their plant, or elsewhere on their behalf, can take place at varying time intervals.

If a trip that has been posted is subsequently changed, the differences are posted. If additional amounts occur, they have to be transferred to PA-PAY Payroll.

Payment via PA-Payroll. All travel expenses relating to trips which have been fully entered and evaluated are paid out on the next payroll run.

Payment via External Non-SAP Financial Accounting or Payroll Accounting Systems. The programs to effect a transfer will have been configured to access the external systems, so that you can directly access the travel expense accounting results database or a predefined sequential data set, depending on the system.

Payment via the DME-Data Medium Exchange. The DME provides a fully configured means of paying from the PA-TRV Travel Expenses component.

Evaluating Trip Data

Three points of view have to be taken into consideration when evaluating trip data:

- The maximum tax-free lump sum and maximum amounts legally refundable by the employer
- The travel expense regulations and practices established in your company
- The amounts to be billed

There are three significant amounts to be billed:

- The amount that can be refunded tax-exempt to the employee under the legal regulations in force at the time
- The amount actually refunded by the company to the employee
- The amount that can be debited to other accounts

An additional amount is defined as an amount that is paid to an employee over and above what is legally refundable free of tax. This additional amount is included in payroll accounting and may attract tax deductions in the normal way.

If the amount refunded is less than the amount that can be refunded tax-exempt, the difference can be taken into account when claiming income-related expenses in the annual wage tax adjustment.

The tables used to evaluate trip expenses contain the dates when regulations come into force. If such a change takes place during a trip, the differences can be computed automatically.

The PA-TRV Travel Expenses component offers the following evaluation variants:

- Lump-sum amounts valid on the first day of a trip are valid throughout the trip.
- The lump-sum amounts valid on the last day of a trip are applied throughout the trip.
- The evaluation refers to the lump-sum amounts valid for each day of the trip.

Representing Company-Specific Regulations

Trip travel expense data can be evaluated by a combination of two standard methods available in the PA-TRV Travel Expenses component:

- Employees are assigned to refund levels valid for all their trips.
- Each trip is assigned to an area, which is an accounting instrument defined to suit the requirements of your company.

For example, employee-specific lump sums and maximum amounts are defined according to the refund level to which the employee has been assigned. The refund class or refund group may define the level at which the accommodations and meals are refunded. Vehicle regulations specific to your company may be specified by the refund class or group.

The area method of representing company-specific regulations can be used to apply differential rates in the following circumstances, for example:

- Additional allowance for trips to capital cities

- Trips between different company sites

- Seminar attendance

If an employee works for several company codes or plants, there will be an indicator in the specification of their travel privileges, so that their travel expenses can be distributed and posted appropriately.

Area and Vehicle Regulations. Tables are used to set up area and vehicle regulations that specify the amounts refundable for different vehicle classes and travel expense areas. The effect is to impose logical conditions, as in the following examples:

- If an employee is entitled to refunds under regulation A, the basic mileage rate is $x, and under regulation B, it is $y.

- The regulation A exception mileage rate for trips to Area 1 is $x + 10%, and for trips to Area 2 it is $x + 5%.

- The regulation B exception mileage rate for trips to Area 1 is $y + 8%, and for trips to Area 2 it is $y + 4%.

Accommodations and Meals. Tables are also used to specify the allowances for accommodations and meals, so as to award different amounts according to the regulation associated with the employee's refund group. Again, there can be any number of exceptions to the basic rates which are to be applied if the trip destination is in an area which attracts different accommodations and meals refund lump sums.

From Here...

The HR-Human Resources application serves to integrate the financial aspects of personnel management with the training and personal development objectives that have to receive high priority in modern business practice. The SAP methods of strict control over data maintenance are used to support the aim of providing the user with rapid and helpful reporting and forecasting in the human resource area. The HR-Human Resource application can be fully integrated with all R/3 system applications so that, for example, capacity planning which entails activities which require the use of qualified personnel can be supported by lists of the people who are likely to be available to meet the requirement at the scheduled time.

The following suggestions for your next point of scrutiny may be of interest:

- My company has very special requirements in the Human Resources area. I do not expect to find a standard business program already written which will be adequate.

  Chapter 5, "The R/3 Reference Model," will show how the standard business programs can be studied with a view to adjusting them during Customizing. If a standard program can be modified or supplemented by extra functions, Chapter 28, "ABAP/4 Program Development with the R/3 Workbench," will describe the methods and tools available.

■ Keeping the production process equipment in good order is essential but often labor-intensive.

Chapter 19, "Understanding the PM-Plant Maintenance Module," describes how the business of maintaining your plant, or the plant of your customers, can be optimized by the R/3 system.

■ Can the HR-Human Resource application find people who could provide technical help in an emergency?

Chapter 27, "Understanding the OSS-Online Service System," includes a discussion of how a query can be directed to the person best qualified to handle it.

■ How work is directed from one team to another can make a big difference in profitability.

Chapter 30, "R/3 Business Workflow Management," describes a suite of programs that support the work scheduler and may carry out many functions automatically.

Chapter 23

Understanding the MM-Materials Management Module

The purpose of the MM-Materials Management Module is to provide detailed support for the day-to-day activities of every type of business that entails the consumption of materials, including energy and services. The word "material" is given the widest connotation.

The module comprises the following components:

MM-MRP	Material Requirements Planning
MM-PUR	Purchasing
MM-IM	Inventory Management
MM-WM	Warehouse Management
MM-IV	Invoice Verification
MM-IS	Information System
MM-EDI	Electronic Data Interchange

Understanding the Organizational Structures

An essential characteristic of the SAP R/3 standard business programs is the strict adherence to a formal structure of data, no matter what the meaning of the data, no matter how complex. In no other way is it possible to build and maintain the very large systems of databases and transactional processing routines that a modern integrated system demands.

The structure of SAP R/3 data is designed to be adaptable to the structure of all the common configurations of head office and subsidiary operating units and work teams that are to be found or imagined in the context of modern business. The standard software is not itself altered when it is implemented in your particular company: Only the tables of parameters that control it so as

In this chapter, you learn:

- How I work out what materials will be needed and when.

- How the system helps, purchase the things we shall need.

- Holding too much stock is costly; holding too little is risky.

- There may be several warehouses holding my materials, and some things are held in more than one warehouse.

- What happens to invoices.

- There may be a great deal of money tied up in materials in the warehouses and in process of being manufactured into the final products.

to make it fit your specific organization and its data processing requirements. There has to be a set of definitions of terms to make sure that everyone understands what the titles of the organizational units stand for.

Defining the Client
The owner of the entire SAP R/3 system is the client, as far as the computer programs are concerned. The client has access to all the data. Some of the data may be stored and maintained for accuracy and timeliness at the client level because other parts of the organization may have need of it. The details of a vendor of a product used by some or all of the departments of a company would be an example of the type of data that should be stored at the client level.

The client is assigned a client code, so that a data record maintained at this level can be recognized by this code prefixing the record number.

The system will have only one genuine client for the purpose of assigning real data needed for the running of the corporate group of companies. A training client can be set up so that staff can carry out exercises on the system, using "for practice" data records prefixed by the training client code, but the training client will not be able to gain access to the data owned by the real client.

Similarly, the implementing team can set up a testing client, which is used to verify that all the standard business programs are producing the results and effects they have been designed to produce. Again, there will be no way of confusing the testing data and the training client data or the real client data because the testing client records will carry the testing client code, which will trigger various protective routines.

Defining the Company Code
When a corporate group is made up of one or more separate companies, each of which is legally allowed to maintain its separate balance sheet and profit and loss statement, the SAP R/3 system requires that the head office be recognized by the client code, and each of the subsidiary companies be assigned a separate company code.

The structured data principle is applied: data not required by an organizational unit belonging to a different part of the corporate organization can be confined to the company that uses it by storing it under its own company code. For example, the information necessary to manage the maintenance of a particular plant that one company uses may be of no interest to another part of the group. Personnel records may have to be stored at the client level, because people may be asked to move from one company code to another.

Naturally, the SAP R/3 system has provided for the situation where a set of records belonging to one company code can be copied for reference to another.

Defining the Purchasing Organization
A purchasing organization must be assigned to only one company code. These are legal requirements that stem from the fact that the purchasing organization is assigned

responsibility for negotiating terms and conditions with vendors of the materials and services needed by this company code, and when a purchasing transaction takes place, this company is responsible for the payments, not its purchasing organization. "Company code" is SAP shorthand for a company that is a subsidiary of the client code enterprise.

Defining the Purchasing Group

Most purchasing organizations have more than one buyer. Even if there is only one person in it, this purchasing organization can be divided, for purchasing accounting convenience, into purchasing groups according to any criteria you may find helpful. Very often, there have to be specialist buyers who are knowledgeable in particular materials, and they may constitute the purchasing groups within the purchasing organization.

Defining the Plant

The SAP R/3 system recognizes a plant as a data object belonging to a specific company code. In fact, the plant need not be a production plant as such. It could be a warehouse or even part of a warehouse. What distinguishes a plant is the fact that it is the site at which value can be added by production activities or at which valuable stock is held in an orderly fashion, as represented by an inventory in which the items are identified along with their bin or other storage location. Their value is enhanced if you know they are there, and if you know how to find them quickly if they are required for a production order or you need to know something about them to respond to a customer's inquiry.

Defining the Storage Location

The storage location is a data object that SAP R/3 treats as a collective label for a set of storage bins or other units in which material is held. A single bin may be a storage location. Any number of bins can be managed together as a single storage location; in which case, the system will not be able to select material from one bin rather than another, unless special steps are taken to tell the system which bin is which. This facility is provided in the MM-WM Warehouse Management component.

Understanding Basic Data Master Records in MM-Materials Management

The information needed to manage materials and services is stored as basic data master records. The fundamental method of entering such data is by using an existing master record as a reference or model to be copied and modified to correspond to the data that has to be stored.

If you change any master record, you can be sure that the system will have logged this event. You can look back over the history of such changes for any record you select.

There are provisions for attaching texts to materials master records for whatever purpose is apposite to your company.

The standard display facilities enable you to select a specific materials master or set of masters by any of a wide range of methods. When you find what you need, you can "drill down" to see all the data associated with the material of interest.

Vendor Records

The main purchasing functions served by the set of vendor master records are as follows:

> Requests for quotations
>
> Processing quotations
>
> Ordering

The main financial accounting activities supported by the vendor masters are as follows:

> Data entry during processing
>
> Verification of invoices from the vendors
>
> Payment of invoices to the vendors

Both of these groups of activities call upon the same common set of vendor masters when processing transactions.

Once-Only Vendors. The system offers a master record upon which can be stored the basic transaction data for all vendors who are not expected to supply your materials or services on a recurring basis.

User Departments. The purchasing department needs the vendor information for ordering and checking deliveries, for example. But the financial department is also interested in the vendors because payments have to be effected. The sales function may also have an interest if the vendors are also to be customers. Each of these different user departments in your company will have a particular set of data fields in the vendor records that they need. These are formally recorded as "views." The system provides for these views by a series of tables in which each user department can specify which data elements of the vendor master records are to be accessed for their particular operations. Not everyone has to look at everything.

The Structure of Vendor Master Records. The level of the organizational structure at which the master records of a vendor are stored will depend on who normally uses that vendor. For example, if your company has, say, two purchasing organizations, Office and Plant, then vendors of office supplies will have their records associated with the Office purchasing organization code, and the materials needed by the manufacturing and storage facilities will be supplied from vendors with their master records stored under the Plant purchasing organization code.

Each vendor master will have the same data structure, which will be adjusted to suit your company during Customizing. The attributes of this data object will include such data clusters as the following:

> General data, such as the address and details of the communication channels to be used for e-mail and fax.
>
> Purchasing data concerning prices and delivery, together with the conditions and agreements made with this particular vendor.

The accounting data, which will include details of the vendor's bank for direct payment and any agreed arrangements for payment; this data will be managed and maintained at the company code level.

The Roles of the Vendor Data Object. When an invoice or a purchasing transaction is being verified, the idea is to check the details of the vendor that are needed on this particular document and any calculations or authorization restrictions.

The vendor company may have a complex structure in which its sales organization is separate from the parent company. The vendor head office may bill you for goods supplied by the sales department, for example. So it may happen that the vendor master record has attributes or clusters of data fields to manage the monthly debits and credits, and an attribute for purchasing data concerning the purchasing organization, such as the currency to be used on orders and the defined trading conditions that specify how intercompany transactions are to be conducted. And there will also be data attributes for the accounting information under the company code, such as control account identification, terms of payment, and bank details.

Account Groups. Vendor accounts are assigned to account groups on the basis of their similarity according to criteria that you define during Customizing. One group is for one-time vendors, about whom you will not wish to store more data than needed to complete the current transaction because you do not expect to use them again. The structure of their master records will be truncated as soon as you identify them as one-time or once-only vendors by assigning them to this account group.

The system will also suggest specific master data structures for account groups confined to banking connections or head office business, and so on. You can adjust the account group master data structures to suit your company.

Account Group Functions. The main effect of assigning a vendor to an account group is to allow the system to filter out data fields that are not required for transactions with members of that group, so they do not appear on your screen when you are doing business with them. For example, if you are building a purchase order, you do not normally need to process the screens that deal with bank data.

Each vendor account group is allocated a specific range of vendor master record numbers. You can tell by looking at the vendor account number which vendor account group you are dealing with. If the company code appears, you will know also that this record is maintained at the company code level.

In general the concept of vendor is used to represent a source from which material can be procured. The nature of this material as a tangible object or in the form of a service, how it is bought and handled—these are matters documented in the material master records.

Materials Masters

To implement an integrated system of production planning and materials management, you must have a central database wherein anyone in your company can find out all there is to know about any material passing through the plant. Everyone must use the same rules and data structures when they enter data about part numbers and descriptions of these parts. All finished products and semi-finished products must be subject to exactly the same information discipline, and so must all raw materials.

The SAP R/3 system will expect you to use a system based on the organizational structure you defined during Customizing, but the system is flexible, and you can construct whatever arrangement best suits your company.

For example, you will probably want to maintain data at the company code level if it is to be used throughout the company. Accuracy and uniformity are ensured by this arrangement, but there is also a very compelling additional benefit: if you wish to change any detail—a change of address of the expert on this material, a change of raw material specification, as examples—you have only to alter the material master at the company code level for the new information to be immediately in place on every screen that needs it.

Material requirements planning data is kept at the plant level, where it is needed on a moment-to-moment basis. Purchasing data will be needed at the plant level to maintain the inventory and anticipate potential shortfalls in the materials used in production. The economical batch size is an example of a purchasing data element that can be used to minimize the costs of production.

Stock data, product details and quantities, quality inspection reports and so on are maintained at the storage location level, because they can be planned into the production process with full cognizance of the inventory, handling and transport implications. These may affect which storage location is chosen as the source.

Thus a typical materials master may have data attributes as follows:

- General data—such as material number, description, units of measure, and technical data

- Plant-specific data—such as material requirements planning type, planned delivery time, purchasing group, and batch indicator

- Evaluation data—such as evaluation price, evaluation procedure, and evaluation quantity

- Warehouse management data—such as unit of measure, palletization instructions, and directions to place in or remove from stock

- Sales-specific data—such as delivering plant and sales texts

Any of these data clusters can be further subdivided. For example, the plant-specific data might be extended to include the following types of data:

- Storage location data—such as the permitted period of storage, the individual stockfield or storage area within a storage location where the material is kept

- Forecast data for this material

- Consumption data for this material

Customizing the MM-Materials Management Module. The R/3 system includes a Customizing component as standard. It allows the implementers of the R/3 system and its applications to select the functions which are relevant to the client company from the full array of SAP standard business programs. The Customizing component requires the implementers to select or enter all the details which will appear when the standard programs are in use. The process is discussed in Chapter 7, "R/3 Customizing."

The format of a materials master record is defined by a template. This is suggested by the system when you have identified your requirements by selections from the materials management sections of the Customizing menu.

At this time you can also specify how long you want your material numbers to be, and the format to be used to separate such data elements as the company code and the purchasing organization identifier.

You will probably prefer to have each user department see only those elements of the material master that it needs, according to the type of transaction it undertakes. The system will prompt you to identify the user departments during Customizing.

Material Type

The type to which you assign each material is a matter that you decide according to the custom and practice in your company. For example, you may establish the following material types:

Raw materials

Semi-finished products

Finished products

Services

Trading goods

Internally owned empty containers or transit rigs

Externally owned containers

The Control Functions of a Material Type. The consequences of assigning one of your materials to a particular material type will include a variety of constraints and restrictions that will make the system easier to use and less likely to generate errors. For example, the material type master record may contain data elements that control the following activities in relation to each of the materials assigned this material type:

■ Which user departments can maintain the material, in the sense of making alterations to the data in the material master records

■ The procurement type of this material

■ How the FI-Financial Accounting module will assign a stock account automatically

■ Whether quantities of the material on inventory are updated, or the financial values, or both

The materials management system will offer you a choice of all the standard material types, to which you can add your own by establishing new material type master records and specifying how you want the system to respond.

Assigning Materials to an Industry Sector. If your company, or one or more of the companies in your group, has to deal with a material that must be treated differently according to some criteria that you specify for your own convenience, the concept of an industry sector can be applied.

In the material master there will be a data element that can hold an industry sector indicator which can then be consulted in order to control how this material is used. For instance, you may wish to differentiate between products sold directly to the public and those going to other manufacturers to be incorporated into their products. The industry sector could be used to identify where the transaction processing methods should be adjusted for the different customers. The same industry sector can be used to identify important differences in how you deal with different types of vendors supplying your company with goods and services. It may be convenient to define some industry sectors purely on the basis of one data element, such as the unit of measure—for example, European pallets, bags, or truck-loads.

Units of Measure. The management of material can take place using the individual piece as the atom or smallest indivisible entity. On the other hand, some materials have to be handled in groups defined by their packaging or their containers to be manipulated by the transport equipment.

If your company has a variety of units of measure for the same material, you can define conversion factors to be applied to the base unit. These factors can work either way. The system can be set to compute the size and weight of a single piece from a pallet that had been weighed and carried a specified number of base units; or the system could use a factor to compute the size of a quantity of base units, assuming that they were to be packed on the standard pallets, and so on. These calculations can be defined for each material individually.

Batches. A batch is a partial stock of material that should be managed separately from other partial stocks of the same material. This partial stock will usually be given a batch number and other documented characteristics, such as the day it was produced and the quality inspection report.

A batch or lot may be distinguished as a production lot because it was all made from the same constituents in the same production campaign. This tracking of lots can be a legal requirement—in the food processing industry, for instance—or it may be a recognition that, although the circumstances of production may not be wholly controllable, the quality of the material can be monitored and this information can be related to the individual batch while it remains in the plant. The weather and the composition of the raw materials are two factors that can affect a production process. Knowing the identity of a batch and the laboratory analysis to which it has been subject can be very important when it is time to use the lot in further production processes or when it is to be sold to a customer.

A batch may also be identified because the quantities of materials in it arrived together from the delivery route. A delivery lot may have been subjected to influences during its transportation which could be important for its users. If one item from a delivery lot is found to be unusual, then the other items from the same delivery may have to be set aside for a quality control inspection.

Special Stocks. A batch or a single item can be assigned as a special stock for a number of reasons that you may wish to redefine during Customizing. The standard special stock definitions fall into the following groups:

- Vendor special stocks—materials that arrive on consignment from a particular vendor, and for which there may be a deferred payment arrangement whereby the user of these special stocks does not pay for them until they are used. Chapter 18, "Understanding the PP-Production Planning for the Process Industries Modules," explains more about this usage.

- Customer special stocks—containers or other transportation equipment that still belong to your company but are temporarily with your customer because they have been used to hold your products. The customer may have to incur a special charge if this packing material is not returned before the due date.

- Event-related stocks—materials that have been ordered specifically because they will be needed for a planned event; for instance, the building of a make-to-order product for which the customer has placed a firm order.

Alterations to Materials Masters. It is a standard feature of the SAP R/3 system and its application modules that every transaction effecting a change in the master data records will be recorded in a log compiling the change management history for this record. The date and reference of the update will be recorded on the master.

Materials masters can be maintained and corrected centrally or in each user department, where the relevant information at hand. The records will still be held under the company code, so other departments may use them.

There are several security levels to protect a master from unauthorized access. You may be prevented from looking at a data object or from changing it. You may also be prevented from creating new data objects by copying a master or generating one from the beginning.

Purchasing Info Records

If you want to find out which vendors have supplied a particular material in the past, or which materials can be obtained from a specific vendor, you should look in the purchasing info records. These are master records containing information on the relationships between vendors and the materials and services they have to offer.

Info Record Types. There are two types of purchasing info record, depending on whether there is a material master record associated with the vendor. If there is a material master record, the relationship established by the purchasing info record is between this material master record and a vendor master record. This vendor can supply this material.

If there is no material master record but there is a vendor master record, the purchasing info master record will carry the information needed to relate the vendor with one or more materials that are members of a material group. The relationship established by the purchasing info record is between a vendor master and a material group master. This vendor can supply some materials of this material group.

The Data Environment of a Purchasing Info Record. If you have located a particular purchasing info record, you can use it to gain access to the rest of the materials data environment. The following types of information will be available to you by pointing to the appropriate parts of the of the screen and using the special function keys:

Current and future prices and purchasing conditions

The identification number of the most recent purchase order that included one of the materials on the purchasing info record, which will help you compare prices and packaging requirement, for example

The number of the most recent purchase order involving the vendor on the purchasing info record

Descriptive text concerning the material that is normally printed on the purchase order

How much of this material has been ordered from this vendor to date

Other ordering statistics regarding this material or this vendor

The price history of this material as ordered or quoted by different vendors

The rating assigned to this vendor by the vendor evaluation system

Central Control Function. The process of creating a purchase order will automatically cause the system to look for purchasing info records that might be relevant. If one is found, the system copies the data into the new purchase order for your approval.

By this means, the important information, such as the price and the vendor details, can be determined centrally and maintained there for use by all who need it. It will appear without error on the purchasing documents.

Info Record Structure. The header of the info record contains general information that will be relevant to all the organizational levels of the purchasing info record. These levels will carry the data applicable to the individual purchasing organizations or plants that will make use of the material when it arrives.

By using this structured level approach, the purchasing info record can show where there are different purchasing conditions for the different purchasing organizations in the company. When the purchaser accesses a material, the purchasing conditions, for example, that are applicable at his or her level of the company will also be accessed, through the medium of the purchasing info record.

The following types of information would be expected to be found in the purchasing info record:

Certificate of inspection data

Texts to be used on purchase orders

Reminders

Unit of measure

Purchasing conditions

Purchase order history

Assignment to stock or consumable material

Any of the data fields on a purchasing info record can be used as a search specification to retrieve all the info records that have the same data field value or a logical or mathematical function of it. For example, you can seek all info records that concern a specific material type or all info records that do not.

Creating Purchasing Info Records . A purchasing info record is created or changed automatically when any of the following events occur:

A quotation is entered.

A purchase order is entered.

A long-term purchasing agreement is created.

It is also possible to create or edit a purchasing info record manually.

Net Price Simulation. The buyers will want to know who is the best supplier. The purchasing info record system can be used to set up simulations, as in the following examples:

- Comparing the prices of various vendors for a material or material group

- Comparing the sales conditions of various vendors for a material or material group

- Showing the vendor's prices for all his materials

- Reviewing the net price of a range of vendors for various order quantities and other order data, such as delivery times and conditions attached to late deliveries

The system can be asked to determine the best source on the basis of the quantity required, the date required, and the vendor net price. And it can do this for any number of plan versions which you have set up to explore the shape of the purchasing decision environment. The flexible display functions will present the results in graphical form should you so wish.

Vendor Net Price. The net price simulation can operate with any order quantities and other order data. It will take into account any incidental costs of delivery. If there is a cash discount for prompt payment, it will factor this into the simulated price. In the same way, the system will recognize if there are any price breaks applicable because of the quantity required or the expected total price of the order, or if part of the order would qualify for such special purchasing conditions.

And because the order information will include the date by which delivery is required, the system can check that the net price has been computed using conditions that will be valid at that time.

Bill of Material (BOM)

Chapter 18, "Understanding the PP-PI Production Planning for Process Industries Modules," is the source of information on bills of materials (BOMs). In essence, the bill of material is a list of the constituents of a composite product. It may be a list of the component subassemblies or a list of the parts to be included in a conglomerate—for example, of products and a set of compact discs and documents on how to assemble these products and set them to work. It is a flexible instrument now that it has made the transition from a list on a piece of paper to a data object in a computerized, integrated business system.

To the bill of material can be attached other data objects, such as technical drawings and reports, which are not themselves components of the product, but which are vital for its well-being while it is being processed or stored in your plant.

Applications of the BOM. The list of components that go to make up a product is obviously an important document. The following areas of activity depend on the BOM:

Production planning and control

Material requirements planning

Costing

Procurement

Inventory management

Warehouse management

The Structure of a BOM. A product is regarded as an assembly in the SAP R/3 system. Each assembly can be made from many parts which are themselves assemblies, and so on. The SAP R/3 system avoids data redundancy by following the convention that an assembly can be represented by any number of components. The fact that some or all of these components are themselves complex assemblies is not taken into account at the top level of the BOM.

If you want to see a list of all the constituent parts that go to make up a BOM, you have to indulge in a BOM explosion.

BOM Explosion. The notion of exploding a BOM is easy to understand if you start to do it. For each part of an assembly, list the constituent parts. For each of these constituent parts, list the constituent parts, and so on until every item on your list is a material which has a master record of its own, rather than a BOM telling you that the item is an assembly made from other parts.

This exploding procedure is precisely what has to be done if you want to calculate the weight of a complex product before it is assembled. This is also what you have to do if you are going to calculate the cost of producing this item. You cannot get away from the task of listing all the separate constituents and finding out what they will cost to purchase and what you will have to pay for the activities that will be needed to put them all together.

The BOM can obviously be a very complicated document. The SAP R/3 approach is to treat it as a hierarchy, in which the product identification code is at the pinnacle and the first-level BOM specifies the components at this level. Each component can have its own BOM, which will extend the hierarchy down one layer, and so on.

Uses of the BOM Explosion. Because the BOM is a list of component parts, it has a wide variety of uses:

When you are creating an order for a subcontract, the mention of a BOM will initiate the opening of all the subassemblies down to the level of materials that have their own material master records and can therefore be regarded as the lowest level of the BOM explosion hierarchy.

If you wish to reserve items from stock against a planned order, the exploded BOM for the ordered product will generate automatic reservation of all the necessary materials.

If you have to issue materials from stock to the production or delivery functions, the exploded BOM will generate a full listing of materials, edited appropriately for the quantities needed.

Classification

The SAP R/3 system supports a general classification system which can be applied to any master data records in the system or in the integrated applications.

If master data records exist, then they can be classified: materials, routings, documents, customers, vendors, batches, plants, storage locations, accounts, passwords, and authorizations.

Should you know the classification of what you are looking for, the system will show you a list of all items that have been assigned that classification. Then you can refine your search specification by going deeper down the classification hierarchy, until you have before you the very master record that you need.

It might happen that the material you need is out of stock. In such a case, the system can tell you which other materials are in the same group according to the classification system. One of them might be suitable.

The classes in the classification can be single-level or multilevel. You can assign matchcodes freely. These are names of your own choosing that represent a particular level in a multilevel classification scheme. A classification scheme managed by the computer purely in terms of class code identifiers can also be understood by the users in terms of more familiar titles, assigned as matchcodes. Here is part of a multilevel classification scheme that might appear in a marine insurance document:

> Vessels include marine vessels, objects being towed by marine vessels.

> Marine vessels include ships, boats, and floating objects.

> Floating objects include flotsam, jetsam, seabirds floating, undersea objects temporarily on the surface, and marine vessels apparently without any means of propulsion or steerage.

Any data object being processed by SAP R/3 which is identified by the classification system can be used to call up a list of the objects with the same classification; you can move up or move down the classification scheme to elicit details of the objects to be found there by selecting the item of interest and using the special function keys to effect the drill-down search operation.

The ways in which objects differ are defined as their characteristics. You can set up a scheme to describe your company's products and the materials used to make them. You need enough characteristics to specify each material and product uniquely. Each characteristic may have a limited range of possible values. For example, color may be assigned one of the following values: Blue or red. You can choose any color as long as it is either blue or red!

Text descriptions or definitions of the characteristics of the classification scheme and their possible values can be maintained in several languages. You can search for classified objects in any of the supported languages.

It may be useful to define one or more fields in a master record as characteristics to be used for classification purposes. If your material masters have data in the DIN 4001 format copied from an external storage system, the SAP R/3 system will automatically generate the required classes and characteristics.

An object can be assigned to more than one class.

Conditions

The SAP R/3 system supports a mechanism for establishing conditions in the form of condition master records. They can refer to any subject-matter domain or any SAP R/3 application. The logical interpretation of a condition is illustrated by the if-then format:

> If X is true, then Y becomes true.

> If the sales quantity is equal to or greater than the first price break, then the order attracts a discount of three percent.

The conditions that are most commonly met in materials management are provided by the system in predefined standard form. You can also add to this list by creating your own conditions.

The Scope of Predefined Conditions. The main use of conditions is in specific price determination based on the following types of considerations:

Discounts

Surcharges by percentage and absolute amounts

Delivery costs

Cash discounts for prompt payment

Taxes

Price Determination. The user can define the sequence in which price determination conditions are applied during the pricing process. The system will propose a set of default values in the purchasing document, which you can amend and supplement with additional charges.

Each purchasing organization in a company can have its own pricing procedure. And each vendor or vendor group can be assigned an individual pricing procedure.

Master Price Determination Conditions. The pricing of purchase orders takes place automatically on the basis of the conditions established in the price determination master records.

The conditions set out in purchase info records are master conditions to be applied to all purchase orders issued to that vendor. If there is a purchasing contract in force with a vendor, the master conditions will be stored in the contract document.

Starting with the master pricing conditions, there are various factors which may have to be taken into account before the final price is determined:

The purchasing organization

Whether the individual vendor is subject to specific pricing conditions or modifications of the master conditions

Whether the invoicing party differs from the actual supplier of the materials or services

Whether certain items are subject to special conditions on the basis of, for example, the material, the material group, the material type, or the plant

Whether there is a contract item involved which attracts special conditions

Validity of Master Pricing Conditions. A set of pricing conditions stored in a master record is given a validity defined by a starting date and a validity period.

If the starting date is in the future, the purchasing conditions will not be applied until that date. When the validity period is reached, the new base prices, discounts, and surcharges will be automatically used in price determination.

Limitations on the Manual Alteration of Default Prices. In the central purchasing conditions master records, the purchasing manager can specify upper and lower limits on the adjustments that are allowed to be made by users at the various levels of authorization. These limits can be defined in percentage terms and as absolute amounts.

Advantages of Central Master Conditions. When a purchasing master conditions record is changed, the alterations are promulgated automatically through all the purchase orders and contracts in which they appear.

By this means, you can quickly check the effects of any changes in a vendor's price strategy.

If a vendor is prepared to offer your company a global discount using a percentage or absolute discount on all purchase orders you have placed, this will affect your prices, as you will see, by making a temporary alteration in the master purchasing conditions for this vendor. The effect can be displayed by viewing, for example, a listing of all your purchase orders for this vendor and comparing the total under the new and the old purchasing conditions.

Materials Requirements Planning

In the context of materials management, the main function of material requirements planning is to monitor stocks at the end of each day and automatically generate purchase order proposals to be forwarded to the purchasing department. Material requirements planning is normally carried out at the plant level, so all the stock available in the plant is recognized by the planning run, whatever its storage location. However, you can also carry out material requirements planning runs at the level of individual storage locations, or at the plant level, with certain storage locations excluded.

Net Change Planning

The material requirements planning run usually applies the net change planning procedure, in which the only materials to be subject to planning are those whose stocks have changed. If the planned requirements have also changed, there will have to be a corresponding alteration in the purchasing proposal.

The material requirements planning run can be further shortened by predefining a planning horizon.

The effect of these procedures is to give the material requirements planner a current view of planning results to which can be appended information about important parts or assemblies and warnings of exceptional situations.

Consumption-Based Planning

There is a simple and easy-to-use planning method used in companies that do not have their own production plant. It works on the assumption that stock that has been promised by a planned order is no longer available to promise (ATP) and should be replaced by initiating a materials planning procedure.

There are two procedures for consumption-based planning:

Reorder point planning

Forecast-based planning

Reorder Point Planning. The reorder point is also known as the reorder level. If the warehouse stock of a material falls below the reorder level, the system automatically creates a purchase order proposal, unless the purchasing department has already created a purchase order for the required quantity.

To replenish stock takes time. Therefore, the reorder point will have to be calculated on some assumption about how the remaining stock might be used while awaiting a delivery. The expected average consumption would be a reasonable value to use in default of anything better.

Previous consumption values over a comparable period under similar trading conditions would be a refinement, and a knowledge of future requirements would complement the picture.

Prudence would counsel you to add a little safety stock in case the delivery is held up for any reason.

These key parameters—the reorder point and the safety stock—can be entered manually, or they can be proposed by the system on the basis of past data and extrapolation rules which you have specified for this purpose.

Inventory Management and Automatic Reorder Point Planning. It will be important for you to keep stock levels low. Having the system operate automatically to reorder stock in the light of evidence it has collected regarding consumption and delivery will enable this.

The inventory management function ensures that every time a material is taken from the warehouse, the stock level is checked to see if it has fallen below the reorder level. If this is the situation, then an entry is made in the material requirements planning file so as to generate a purchase order on the next material requirements planning run.

Forecast-Based Planning

This method uses a forecast value or forecast quantity of stock rather than a stock reorder level as the starting point for the plan to replenish the inventory.

The material requirements planning controller will carry out a material requirements forecast at regular intervals for each material needed over the period. For this purpose, the period can be defined as day, week, month, posting period, or split periods within these. The planning horizon can be set in terms of the number of planning periods to be included in the calculations.

The basis for the forecast calculation will include provision for safety stock and assessment of the historical consumption data.

As material is reserved to be withdrawn from the warehouse in each planning period, the forecast requirement for that period is reduced by the corresponding amount. The remainder of the original forecast requirement for the period is then entered for the material requirements planning run and will be subject to a purchase order. Stock that was planned and has been used will not be reordered because purchase orders for the planned values will have been created already.

Net Requirements Calculation. The calculation of net requirements compares the forecast quantities of each material for each period with the quantities that are expected to be available. Some of this stock may be in the warehouse now, and some of it may be scheduled for delivery in time to meet the requirement.

If a deficit is foreseen, a purchase order proposal is generated.

Lot-Sizing Procedures

When a material requirements shortage is anticipated as the consequence of a planning run, the lot size for reordering is taken from the material master record, where it has been specified by the material requirements planning controller. The way it is determined and used depends on the choice of lot-sizing procedure. The SAP R/3 system supports an extensive set of lot-sizing procedures, to which you can add user-specific procedures as required. There are three basic procedures: Static lot-sizing, periodic lot-sizing, and optimum lot-sizing.

Static Lot-Sizing. The lot size is calculated from the quantity specifications in the material master record. There are three criteria which can be used:

> Lot-for-lot order quantity
>
> Fixed lot size
>
> Replenish up to the maximum stock level

Periodic Lot-Sizing. The size of the lot to be reordered can be determined from the requirement quantities of one or more planning periods added together to form a purchase order proposal. There is a choice of time period over which the requirements are to be totaled:

> Daily lot size
>
> Weekly lot size
>
> Monthly lot size
>
> Lot size based on flexible period lengths within the accounting periods
>
> Freely definable periods according to a planning calendar used to determine lot size

Optimum Lot-Sizing. The cost of a large lot of material may yield a low unit cost, but there will be associated costs independent of lot size, plus storage costs which are usually related to lot size. There are several methods of working out an optimum ratio between the lot size and the independent and storage costs. SAP R/3 supports the following optimization procedures:

Part period balancing

Least unit cost procedure

Dynamic lot-size creation

Groff reorder procedure

Additional Restrictions on Lot Size. The material master records will allow you to impose additional restrictions of the reorder lot size. The following types of restriction are supported:

Minimum lot size—causes the system to round up the quantity reordered to meet the minimum lot size.

Maximum lot size—ensures that the system will not group together period requirements that will generate a quantity larger than the maximum lot size.

Rounding adjustment—specifies that the lot size shall be rounded up or down so as to arrive at an exact multiple of the order unit to obviate the need to split a packaging unit, for example, or to ensure that the delivery transportation vehicle will be used efficiently.

Quota Arrangements. You may take some of your supplies from several vendors, each of which operates its own delivery schedule. You can have the system take this into consideration automatically by specifying quotas across vendors, across schedules, or both. This restriction will be built in automatically at the stage of the material requirements planning run, using the specification you have established.

Material Requirements Planning Result

The output results from a material requirements planning run are summarized in two lists which you can display in various ways. The contents of these lists are as follows:

Material requirements planning list—shows the stock and requirements at the time of the last planning run.

Stock and requirements list—shows the current situation, including goods receipts, goods issues, and any other events relevant to planning the material requirements.

The following display formats are available for the material requirements planning results, and you can readily change from one to another:

Days

Weeks

Months

According to posting period

According to the planning calendar

According to the user-defined flexible period split

Material Requirements Planning Run Exception Reporting. During a material requirements planning run, the system will generate exception messages to alert the controller if any of the following events occur:

Scheduling delay

Rescheduling and cancellations

A material stock level falling below the safety stock level

The controller may decide to group exception messages so that they can be displayed together. This is done by specifying the structure in an exception group master record.

Material Forecast

The material forecast is used to determine requirements and to compute the safety stock and reorder level, for individual materials if necessary, but normally in batch mode. The material forecast depends on historical data, and its validity will therefore depend on the accuracy of this data. The other crucial assumption is that material consumption patterns can be discerned in the data that are likely to continue into the future.

To represent a pattern of material consumption, the system has available a choice of four basic models, from which it will choose automatically if you do not want to impose a choice of your own:

Constant model—finds a single value which best fits the varying consumption values for the material as recorded in the historical data; it represents the average value, slightly refined, if you want, to play down the effects of occasional very high or very low values.

Trend model—finds a steady increase or decrease in the quantity of a material consumed.

Seasonal model—finds a regular pattern which repeats itself every year, with the peaks and troughs occurring at the same time of year and reaching to about the same value each cycle of the pattern.

Seasonal trend model—finds the data that best fits a seasonal pattern imposed on a central value which is steadily increasing or decreasing.

If the system has found which model best fits the historical data, or if you have told the system which model to apply, the chosen model can be used to predict the value or quantity of material likely to be required at any time in the future. The assumption is that the pattern discerned in the data, or mandated by the material requirements planning controller, will continue to be applicable. You have to take it for granted that there will be no discontinuity in the pattern of consumption of this material.

Your assumption that nothing is going to change may be an error!

The only real comfort offered by the system in this matter is its ability to recalculate the parameters of the models at any time, and rebuild its forecasts using the latest data available. Chapter 13, "Understanding the CO-Controlling Module," discusses the subject of planning at greater depth.

MM-PUR Purchasing

The aim of the MM-PUR Purchasing component is to automate the purchasing function of your company as much as possible so as to leave the buyer only the exceptional circumstances to deal with—no routine paperwork.

Almost all the data needed to create a purchase order should be in the system already. It should be copied automatically so as to reduce errors and speed up the task.

A purchase order may start life as a purchase requisition originating in one of the user departments, or it may be created as a result of material requirements planning.

A source of supply of the material or service has to be identified by the system, by the user who needs the material, or by the purchasing department, perhaps after soliciting quotations from a number of potential suppliers.

The most common method of generating a purchase order is by copying one prepared for a previous purchase and updating it as necessary.

The Purchasing Documents

The traditional paper documents associated with purchasing in a large organization have been reengineered to take advantage of the benefits of a fully integrated system in which almost all of the information required to complete them can be found in the master records of the system, where they are kept up to date.

The following documents are used in purchasing:

Purchase requisition

Request for quotation

Quotation

Purchase order

Contract

Delivery scheduling agreement

Purchasing Document Structure

The header of a purchasing document contains the document number and the details of the vendor. The remainder of the document comprises one or more items referring to specific materials or services to be procured and the quantities required.

Each item in a document can refer to one or more supplements. For example, an item in a purchasing document could refer to a supplement which detailed the order history of this item from this supplier.

Purchase Requisition

A requisition is a request for a service to be rendered by another department; in the case of a purchase requisition the request is for the purchasing department to procure a certain quantity of a material or service and have it delivered to the originator by a specified date.

The purchasing organization responds to the requisition by going through a series of steps to determine a source of supply, perhaps after a request for quotation submitted to several potential suppliers. When the purchase requisition has been checked and a supplier chosen, the requisition is released to be converted to a purchase order, which is checked again and released to the vendor for purchasing action, with the obligation to pay for it when the time comes.

Generating a Purchase Requisition. There are two ways to create a purchase requisition:

> Use a reference document as a model and edit a copy of it on behalf of the requesting department.

> Have the purchase requisition generated automatically by the material requirements planning process.

Sources of Supply. If the system is aware of a suitable source of supply, it will use it automatically to create a purchase requisition. The following sources of supply will be recognized and used to generate the purchasing document if they are relevant:

> A fixed vendor as specified in the material master record

> An outline purchase agreement that has a validity period which includes the required delivery date

> A purchasing info record that identifies a possible vendor of the material or service required

Purchase Requisition Release Strategies. Whether or not a purchase requisition is approved for release as a purchase order depends on the conditions imposed by the release strategy, which usually takes the form of a chain of release points. These release points are the individuals or the organizational units assigned the responsibility of approving requisitions once they have been assigned a particular release strategy.

The release strategy is assigned automatically when the purchase requisition is entered. The strategy chosen will depend on such factors as the value of the requisition and the material type of the requested items.

Allocation of Purchase Requisitions. Given a list of the items awaiting purchasing action, the buyers may well generate the purchase requisitions that fall into their areas of responsibility, because they will know where to obtain the particular materials.

If no approved sources can be identified, a list of possible suppliers has to be created in order to be able to distribute a request for quotation document.

Request for Quotation

When a request for quotation to a vendor elicits a quotation, it will be returned in the form of a list of the vendor's prices for the material, together with the purchase conditions and perhaps some additional information. This data is entered on the original request for quotation document, which thereby becomes a store of all the information necessary to make an informed choice between the vendors who have responded to the request for quotation.

When all the quotations have be entered, the buyers can access the price comparison list and use it to have the system conduct a comparative analysis of the quoted prices and conditions, with a view to determining the most favorable quotation.

The analysis data can then be automatically stored in a purchasing info record and the unsuccessful bidders automatically sent rejection letters.

Purchase Order

The aim of the automated purchase order component is to reduce the time taken to process purchase orders and minimize the chances of an error. The method is to use data already in the system as far as possible.

Using References to Minimize Data Entry Work. The buyer can elect to use any of the following methods of finding an existing document to provide the data for a new purchase order:

Select from a list of current requisitions.

Select from a list of previous purchase orders.

Call up an existing longer-term buying contract for this material and create a release order for the required amount of material to be delivered on the date specified, which will cause the texts, prices, and conditions to be copied automatically from the contract to the release order.

Referencing a Purchasing Info Record. The purchasing info record performs some of the functions of a contract, in that it contains details of the vendor's prices and conditions for specific materials. When you create a purchase order, you may initiate the creation of a purchasing info record or the updating of one that exists already.

When you have called up a purchasing info record as a reference for a purchase order, it is only necessary for you to enter the material number, the order quantity, and the delivery date required.

Automatic Generation of Purchasing Documents. The place most often used to begin generating purchasing documents is the purchase order item overview screen, which will display the most important information you will need to create a new purchase order, a request for quotation or a delivery schedule. The information you can identify and copy from this screen is as follows:

Material number

Purchase order quantity

Purchase order price

Plant

Storage location

Creating a Purchase Order. The buyer will be offered a range of options at this stage to progress the creation of the purchasing document:

Vendor known—the preferred choice if the buyer knows perfectly well who will be the supplier.

Vendor unknown—will cause the system to try to find suitable vendors on the basis of the purchase order items that have been entered up to that point in the creation of the purchase order. The buyer may have to allocate particular orders among the proposed vendors if there is more than one suggested by the system.

Allocated purchase requisitions exist—a reminder to the buyer that he can call up a list of all the purchase requisitions that have been placed with sources of supply from the purchasing group to which the buyer belongs. From this historical data the buyer can choose a vendor, if one is suitable, and the system will copy the relevant data to the new purchase order.

Account Assignment. The account to which the amount is to be posted when the goods are delivered has to be determined during the creation of the purchase order. The user has to select the type or name of the account, and the system will carry out an internal check and propose an account number that will be entered on the purchase order if it is accepted.

Several accounts may have to be posted when the goods ordered by a purchase order are delivered. The net order value can be apportioned on a percentage basis or in terms of specified amounts to any number of individual cost objects, such as projects or cost centers. Chapter 13, "Understanding the CO-Controlling Module" provides further information on cost accounting.

The allocation of a net order value to cost objects and the posting of the value to an account in the FI-Financial Accounting system are initiated by data copied automatically from purchase requisitions or contracts and replicated on any other documents that are generated using them as references.

Outline Purchase Agreement

If your company frequently uses the same supplier for one or more materials or services, each subject to specified conditions that are likely to remain essentially the same for a period of time, it may be useful to set out a purchase agreement in outline form. This outline purchase agreement will have a period of validity during which the conditions of the agreement will remain valid, and it will have a limit set to the quantity or value of the goods that can be supplied under this agreement during this period of validity.

The agreement is in outline form because it does not make any reference to the date required or the actual quantity or value of the material or service that is to be delivered. This information has to be supplied by a subsequent issue of a release order or a delivery schedule, which will refer to the outline purchase agreement so as to be able to define the conditions and other details of the contract to supply.

Types of Contract. There are many terms used to refer to an outline purchase agreement. This discussion treats all of these names as equivalent to an outline purchase agreement:

> Blanket order
>
> Blanket contract
>
> Period contract
>
> Bulk contract
>
> Master agreement
>
> Master contract

The contract to which an outline purchase agreement is the preliminary, and which is the source of data for generating documents, may be a value contract or a quantity contract, according to the manner in which the upper limit is defined. The value or quantity specified in the outline purchase agreement will be the limit for the period of validity.

Scheduling Agreements. In many industries, the price of materials may be much affected by the uncertainties of supply and demand. Your company may wish to introduce a degree of stabilization into such a situation by setting up an arrangement for a schedule of material deliveries over a defined period of validity, during which the prices and conditions are to be kept constant.

The scheduling agreement will usually specify a total or target quantity for the period and a particular type of vendor scheduling of the constituent deliveries. Each material or service in the agreement may well have its own vendor schedule. The details of the schedule within the validity period will be regularly updated as the requirements of the purchasing company become known.

Vendor Delivery Schedules. The vendor undertaking to supply according to a schedule does not receive a purchase order or a release order. Once the scheduling agreement validity period has begun, the vendor works to a vendor delivery schedule which is regularly updated.

Each line of the vendor delivery schedule represents an individual delivery shipment consisting of a specified quantity of the particular material, delivered to a precise storage or holding location in your plant on a particular date, and perhaps also at a particular time on that date if you are operating in a just-in-time or KANBAN environment.

The Benefits of Vendor Delivery Scheduling. Where vendor scheduling agreements are in place for all the component parts that go to make up a product assembly, the company can take advantage of a wide range of favorable effects that may add considerable value to its products and give it a competitive edge over rivals.

A vendor delivery schedule can reduce the processing time and the amount of paper or electronic transmissions entailed by the equivalent series of individual purchase orders or release orders.

The production at a plant can take place with the minimum of waiting stock, perhaps none.

The vendor need not hold up shipments in order to amass the quantity needed for a large delivery because the order is dispatched to the schedule. From the vendor's point of view the schedule gives a steadier basis on which to plan production.

Sources of Supply

The buyer needs a list of sources for each of the materials and services of interest to his purchasing group within the purchasing organization. This list is usually maintained manually because there are frequent changes in the details, and sometimes new entries as fresh vendors come into the market and the products of the purchasing company undergo development and thus require new sources of materials.

The source list for a material can also be maintained automatically by the following techniques:

Adopting an existing source list as a first proposal for manual editing

Copying from outline purchase agreements that refer to this material

Copying from purchasing info records that have been used to generate purchase orders in the past

The source list data maintenance functions provide facilities to assign dates and time periods to sources so that they are used only during the periods defined. They are not allowed to supply goods "out of season."

A quota system can be set up by which two or more vendors or internal sources share the requirement. The time-dependent condition can be applied in conjunction with the quota system. This is taken into the calculation when a choice of sources is being evaluated automatically.

Vendor Evaluation

An experienced buyer may be able to make a wise choice of sources from the vendors and any internal production plant or storage location that has material available to meet his requirements. However, it may be difficult to build this experience in a changing market and with a changing labor force made up of people who share many tasks rather than specialize in one. If this scenario is even remotely like parts of your organization, the automatic vendor evaluation function should be given serious attention.

Automatic Vendor Evaluation. Every vendor for a particular material, including internal providers, is awarded a score out of one hundred by the vendor evaluation system. The main criteria used by the system are as follows:

Price

Quality

Delivery

Service

Up to 99 main criteria can be defined by the user, and the contribution of each of them to the total score can be weighted so as to emphasize the factors that your company feels to be most important.

The system provides five sub-criteria for each main criterion. The user can define up to twenty sub-criteria.

The scores for sub-criteria can be calculated in different ways according to the type of data or other input that can be made available, as follows:

Automatic calculation uses data that already exists in the system.

Semi-automatic calculation relies on values entered by the buyers, from which the system then calculates the score for the sub-criterion.

Manual input occurs when a buyer enters a vendor's score for a sub-criterion and cuts out any assessment of other data for this part of the evaluation.

Buyers can be allowed the option of manual entry or one of the varieties of automatic evaluation, according to the importance of the material or the other attributes of the pool of possible suppliers.

If any change is made to the data or the formulas used by the vendor eevaluation system, a log entry is made and the event is recorded.

Displaying Automatic Vendor Evaluations. The system allows a wide flexibility in how the results of vendor evaluations are displayed. You can have a rank ordering of all vendors on the basis of all their scores on the materials they supply, or you can call for a rank ordering of suppliers for a specific material or service.

Reporting

Purchasing managers have to keep track of all their purchase orders and all their purchasing organizations. They must also be continually aware of their vendor population and newcomers to it that they have not yet used.

If there are trends in the requirements of their own company, they must notice them in time to plan their purchasing schedules.

VI

Application Support

Analyses of Purchasing Documents. The following inquiries can be answered by calling for the relevant report:

> Which purchase orders were placed with a certain vendor over a specific period?

> Which purchase orders have been processed as far as delivery?

> Has this vendor delivered all or only part of this purchase order?

> Does this vendor have a good record for delivering on time?

> How many orders from this vendor have been received and found to be invoiced correctly?

> What is the average value of purchase orders handled by this purchasing organization or this buyer group?

> What are the total values of orders placed by each of the purchasing organizations in this company?

Standard Analyses of Purchase Order Values. The standard SAP R/3 analysis functions are available to be applied to the historical data to be found in the purchase orders and the associated purchasing documents, as in the following examples:

> Totals analysis will let you see the number and total value of existing purchase orders.

> ABC analysis shows the distribution of vendors across three groups, defined as (A) vendors that account for the highest value of material purchases, (B) vendors accounting for an average value of purchases, and (C) vendors from which the value of purchases is lowest.

> Analysis in comparison with a reference period is designed to show how a composite value has changed over time or across data objects, such as a comparison between this period last year and the current period for the total value purchased by each of the purchasing organizations in the company.

> Frequency analysis shows which order values occur most often in each purchasing organization and can be used, for example, to negotiate a better discount, based on an immediate discount for large orders rather than an end-of-year volume rebate.

Purchase Document Listing Options. The large volume of purchase documents and master records to be found in most systems running the MM-Materials Management module necessitates a powerful yet flexible suite of functions to display to the user just what is wanted for the immediate purpose, and to leave out what is not wanted. The following search specifications are typical of the needs of the purchasing management departments; many of them are, or could be, initiated by special function keys:

> List all purchase orders issued by this particular purchasing group during this specific time period.

> List the requisitions for this material from any or all of the following group of vendors.

List all archived purchasing info records for this material for this plant.

Display the purchase order history of the selected item.

Inventory Management

The inventory is both a list and a physical collection of material items. Inventory management entails the planning and control of material stocks by quantity and value. It has also come to include the planning, data entry, and documentation of all goods movements to, from, and within the storage locations in the warehouses used by the company.

Managing Material Stocks by Quantity

Any transaction that will cause a change of stock is entered in real time, and the consequent update of the stock situation will take place immediately. The effect is to give the user an overview that is always current of the stock level of any material.

Anyone else in the company who is thinking of placing some kind of reservation on this stock will immediately know whether it is available or not. The material requirements planning file will receive an entry for this material if the reorder level has been reached.

Managing Material Stocks by Value

When you post a movement of goods, the value of this stock is also updated. A chain of consequent postings will occur:

There will be an automatic posting of the value change to the GI-General Ledger account in the FI-Financial Accounting module.

Line items will be created for the account assignments needed in the CO-Controlling module, such as cost centers, orders, projects, and assets.

The system will work out the amounts to be posted using the actual quantity of material to be moved, which you have to enter, and the value of this amount of material, which it computes using the data in the order and the master records for this material.

It is also possible to post goods receipts for which the prices have not been ascertained. The values will be calculated when the invoices are received and entered.

Documentation of Stock Movements. Each movement of material causes the system to create a document recording the amounts and values, as well as the time and date of the movement. This serves as a proof that the goods were dispatched. When they arrive at their destination, the entry of their goods receipt will complete the proof of the movement.

The planning of inventory movements can be effected by using reservations identifying the material which has been allocated to a particular customer or production order, or perhaps assigned to some kind of special stock.

The physical movement of the stock within the warehouse can be controlled by means of printed goods, receipts, and goods issue slips, which can carry the appropriate bar code to speed data entry.

VI

Application Support

There are several standard methods available in the system that will support the comparison of the physical stocks with the book inventory balances:

Periodic inventory

Continuous inventory

Sample-based inventory

These methods can be supplemented by installing and configuring the MM-WM Warehouse Management module which will allow the detailed oversight and control of warehouses with complex systems of storage bins and storage areas. This system is discussed in more detail in Chapter 17, "Understanding the PP-Production Planning and Control Module."

Goods Receipts for Purchase Orders

When goods are delivered that have been ordered by a purchase order, the system will locate this purchase order document and propose default data from it to form the goods receipt documentation. If there has been no over-delivery or under-delivery, the goods receipt is documented on the purchase order, which can then be given an updated status.

The goods receipt data is used to update both the purchase order and the vendor evaluation record.

If the purchase order shows no goods receipt by the required delivery date, the purchasing department can begin the reminder procedure. Because the goods receipt data is recorded on the purchase order, there can be a follow-up of the purchase order history, to judge how reliable the vendor has been with respect to delivery dates and the correctness of the quantities and specification of the goods or services supplied.

When the vendor invoice arrives and is entered, the system again refers to the purchase order to verify that the material and the quantity are in accord with what was ordered.

When the purchase order and the invoice have been shown to be in agreement, the system can value the goods receipt by applying the price to the quantity.

The system will allow you to enter goods receipts for several purchase orders in one transaction.

Contingencies in Goods Receipts for Purchase Orders. If it is the case that a delivery note has arrived with no reference to a purchase order, the user can look up the possible purchase orders under the material code number or the vendor number.

The entry of a purchase order number will cause the system to display a collective entry screen showing all the open purchase order items separately. The scope of this display can be the plant under the user's company code or all plants in the group.

If there is still no reconciliation of the delivery note or goods receipt with an open purchase order, the user can ask to see detailed information about the order item and make notes against the item in the document by selecting a standard short text or by using free-form text from a word processing system.

You may have to enter a goods receipt using a different unit of measure from that given in the purchase order. The system will tolerate this and effect a conversion. The storage location and the quality inspection indicator will default to the values in the purchase order item, and these can be overridden by manual entries. The delivery costs determined by the planning procedures will also be transferred automatically. If there are tolerances allowed for under-delivery or over-delivery, these will be checked automatically.

One purchase order item can be assigned to several storage locations by creating several goods receipt items, one for each of the separate destinations. For example, a partial quantity can be posted to quality inspection and the remainder to goods receipt blocked stock, where it will remain until a favorable quality inspection report allows it to be released for production.

Goods Receipt to Consumption. Some goods are destined for immediate consumption rather than storage. In such cases, the system will pick up the account assignment—to a cost center or order, for example—from the purchase order data. Even if such just-in-time purchases are to be allocated to several control accounts, this can be done by the system when the delivery has occurred and the goods receipt has been entered.

Whoever in the procurement department is dealing with purchase orders that go directly to consumption will be notified of the arrival of the goods by an automatic letter via the SAPmail system.

Reservations

A material that is going to be required in the future will obviously have to be subject to planning. A quantity and therefore a provisional value will be computed for each of the planning periods that stretch away from the current period to the planning horizon. The planning department will have decided, on the basis of past data or orders for products that are already on the books, that a certain requirement for this material will exist for each of the planning periods. A wise purchasing department will have set in train the purchase order, the outline purchasing agreement, or the contract, which will make it very likely that the required material will arrive at the production line on the due date, and perhaps at the due time of day, so as to be ready to be incorporated in the product.

A reservation is an instrument for making sure that this material is moved from stock to consumption at the correct moment. It assumes that the stock will be on inventory to enable this to happen, and it assumes that no other production order or customer order has already been promised this quantity of this material.

Dynamic Availability Checking. The system will automatically check that the material mentioned in a material reservation has not already been assigned elsewhere. If it is free—available to promise (ATP)—the system will show this amount of stock under the heading of reserved stock for this material. The quantity of stock available for other purposes will be reduced by the same amount, so that "double-booking" of the material does not occur.

The following data will be included in the entry to initiate a reservation:

Material number

Batch number if applicable

Planned quantity

Scheduled delivery date

Intended use of the reserved material, such as the production or customer order number for which it is to be reserved

When the reserved material is approved for release to production or another destiny, the actual quantity will be substituted for the planned quantity in the calculation of the costs and values.

Goods Issues

When goods are moved from a warehouse, there has to be a posting of material withdrawal. This will trigger the posting of a reduction in the quantity and value of the warehouse stock of this material.

Every transaction concerning a withdrawal from a warehouse can be treated as a planned withdrawal or an unplanned withdrawal. The consumption statistics will show them separately.

If you begin to create a goods issue for material which has been reserved, the system will assume that you need the quantity stated in the material reservation and that you will want to post the withdrawal to the account assigned in that document also.

Before you can complete the goods issue, the destination of the withdrawn material has to be stated in the ship-to party field. This location will be printed on the withdrawal slip.

If you are running a complex warehouse system under the MM-WM Warehouse Management component, the system can show you all the storage locations holding the type of goods you require. If the materials are shipped and inspected in batches, the batch identification will be part of the reservation procedure. There can be rules for the utilization of batches.

Transfer Postings and Stock Transfers

A simple system is for the goods to be received to a warehouse and then withdrawn to be sold or to be consumed by the production processes. The arrangements are necessarily more complex if there is more than one warehouse and more than one production plant, particularly if some or all of these cost centers belong to different parts of the company and have their own company code, which signifies that they are legally obliged to publish their own separate financial documents—that is, the balance sheet and profit and loss statement.

If some material stock is transferred from one warehouse to another, and if these warehouses belong to different company codes, the financial accounting systems of both company codes have to be coordinated so as to reflect the fact that something of value has moved from one to the other.

One Step and Two Step Stock Transfers. A transfer of stock in one step entails two posting operations in the transaction, as follows:

Withdraw the stock from the warehouse and credit the sender.

Deliver the stock and debit the receiver.

An interim receiver may have to be introduced with the title of transfer stock if the stock is going to spend a long time in transit, as in the following example:

Withdraw the stock from the warehouse and credit the sender.

Assign the stock as transfer stock and debit the transfer stock account.

Transport the stock to the new location.

Release the stock and credit the transfer stock account.

Deliver the stock and debit the receiver.

The important feature of the transfer stock is that it is not unrestricted stock: It cannot be used until it is received in the storage location and in the accounts of the receiving cost object—the production plant, for instance.

Stock Transfer Reservations. The classic example of transfer stock would be the goods in a cargo vessel on the high seas. The stock has value, but it cannot be used until it is delivered. However, quantities of the stock can be reserved for specific orders and also traded on the commodities market, so that value is added or taken away from the stock while it is still in the status of being transfer stock.

Goods Movements for Production Orders

Material components for production are received into the warehouse, and their receipt is posted in inventory management. Any of these components which have been planned for production will have been automatically reserved for consumption by the production process on a specific date. Unforeseen circumstances may arise, necessitating the withdrawal from the warehouse of components that were not part of the reservation because they did not figure in the plan. Nevertheless, if they are used in order to complete a customer order or a production order, they have to be costed along with the planned materials, and documented on the order.

Where the order being completed is a production order using bulk materials, the quantity needed may not be known exactly until the completion confirmation document for the production order has been posted. It is at this stage that the adjustment of inventory will be confirmed by supplying the actual quantities in place of the planned estimates.

Many processes give rise to by-products, co-products, and waste materials. The difference between these types of product is in their cost consequences. Some yield sales revenue; some incur costs of disposal. The quantities and sometimes the values can be planned and recognized in the accounting procedures.

Quality Inspection

The processes of inventory management make provision for the temporary or permanent absence of part of the stock for the purpose of quality inspection. A partial delivery quantity, perhaps a selection of batches or a sample of items taken from them, becomes a transfer batch, which is transferred immediately to stock in quality inspection.

If the quality is acceptable, the remainder of the stock in quality inspection is transferred to unrestricted-use stock, where it can be reserved against future orders or withdrawn to consumption when required.

The quality inspection may also take place after the material has been received into the warehouse and planned for issue. In such cases, it would be transferred to quality inspection stock on its way to the consumption location.

Batch Data

Certain materials have to be permanently associated with the batch identification they received when first manufactured and inspected. Pharmaceutical products and some foodstuffs fall into this category.

Even if the material can be repackaged, it may still have to be managed in conjunction with batch numbers.

The system will maintain a unique batch number master record, on which will be stored the data pertaining to that batch, such as:

Country of origin

Date of goods receipt

Storage location and conditions of storage

Batch quantity, weight, and dimensions

Shelf life expiry date

Status as warehouse stock or quality inspection stock

The use of a material which is managed in batches will be scheduled on a batch number basis so that the material will be selected for withdrawal in order of its date of manufacture, although it is possible to enter a different priority manually or choose batches from a list.

All movements of the material must identify the batches by number.

Special Stock

The essential characteristic of a special stock of a material is that it is owned by a company or a person different from the owner of the storage location in which it is on inventory. For example, your company may be renting storage space in another company. Your stock will be listed on that company's inventory as special stock. Conversely, you may have special stock on your inventory because it is owned outside your organization. The point is that special stock has to be managed separately.

Two types of special stock are recognized by the system and managed separately:

> Vendor special stock
>
> Customer special stock

Vendor Special Stock. There are three types of special stock held on behalf of a vendor:

> Consignment material belonging to the vendor but stored on your premises
>
> Returnable packaging material belonging to the vendor but stored on your premises
>
> Material provided by you to the vendor who is a contractor to you

Customer Special Stock. There are three types of special stock held on behalf of a customer:

> Consignment material that is yours but is still at the customer's location, awaiting your decision as to its disposal
>
> Returnable packaging material of yours that is at the customer's location
>
> Sales order stock that has not been settled and is therefore still owned by you

A data entry for special stock movements has to include the identification of the vendor, the customer, or the sales order.

Special stock is discussed in more detail in Chapter 20, "Understanding the SD-Sales and Distribution Module."

Physical Inventory

It is a legal requirement that every company perform a physical check of the inventory at least once in the course of a business year. SAP R/3 standard business programs are available to carry out the following physical inventory procedures:

> Periodic inventory
>
> Continuous inventory
>
> Inventory sampling

The Scope of Inventory Procedures. The system will take stock of the following types of material:

> Unrestricted-use stock
>
> Stock in quality inspection
>
> Special stock

Inventory Functionality. There are many functions to support the taking of a physical inventory:

> Physical inventory documents can be created.

Warehouse inventory lists can be printed.

A block can be placed on stock movements of materials being inventoried.

Data entry of the results of physically counting the stock is automatically related to the entries on the physical inventory documents.

Differences between the physical inventory and the book inventory are presented in list format.

Differences are posted using the items of the physical inventory documents for reference.

Large differences prompt the creation of documents to support a recount of the discrepant items.

Every physical inventory is recorded for each material and retained indefinitely, so that the history of any stock item can be traced over any number of years for which data has been collected.

Physical Inventory Sampling. When a warehouse contains a very large number of stock management units, it is possible to manage them and conduct a physical inventory of them on the basis of samples. Because the relationship between the sampled items and the rest of the warehouse can be determined automatically, it is possible to infer the full warehouse inventory from the results of physically counting the selected sample.

The goods receipts and issues at the warehouse can be managed by using the same technique.

Material Evaluation

The standard approach of the SAP system is to assign values automatically to materials on an ongoing basis. The data is stored in material master records and can be adjusted manually.

When it is necessary to value materials for balance sheet purposes, the system offers the last-in-first-out (LIFO) evaluation procedure, to which can be applied the lowest value determination procedure.

Evaluation Control Structures

The scope of a evaluation exercise can be controlled by choosing company code or plant to specify the level of the separate evaluation areas.

If the evaluation area is company code, all the stocks in each company code area are evaluated on the same basis, and the results are accumulated over the company code.

If the evaluation area is a plant, each plant in the company will have its stocks evaluated separately.

Evaluation Classes. Materials with similar characteristics can be grouped together to form a evaluation class. The FI-GL General Ledger stock account to which the evaluation will be posted will depend on the evaluation classes assigned to it.

Evaluation Categories. Different sets of material evaluation criteria can be associated with particular evaluation categories. For example, you may wish to use different evaluation criteria because the material may have a net value that is partially dependent on where it has come from, the amount of work that has already been done on it and, perhaps, the taxes or surcharges it has attracted.

The following are examples of evaluation categories:

Procurement

Origin

Status

The evaluation category system can also be used to represent differences in the condition or makeup of a material. A material stock can be split into separate lots for evaluation purposes according to a evaluation category scheme based on such factors as:

Quality

Batch purity

Batch quality control results, such as the variance in the critical dimensions

Batch specification

Batch history

Evaluation Types. Evaluation types are nominal values specified for each evaluation category. You may decide that your stock of a particular material should be evaluated according to the formula specified for each of the evaluation types to which it could be assigned. You can specify a different evaluation formula for each country of origin, for example, according to the following set of evaluation types belonging to the material evaluation category Origin:

Domestic, which may be the country of the plant or the company code

European Community

U.S.A.

Other country

The lists of possible evaluation types and evaluation classes are matters which depend on your company's requirements as established during Customizing.

Price Control and Evaluation. The price control strategy in force will determine how a material stock is to be valued:

Standard price—requires all the stock of a material to be valued at the same standard price, regardless of the costs of any fresh postings to the inventory.

Moving average price—computes the price to be used to value the entire stock of a material by averaging the prices of all postings held in the inventory.

LIFO Evaluation. Each material can be selected individually or on the basis of membership of a material group to be subject to last-in-first-out (LIFO) evaluation. It can also be allocated to a LIFO pool, and valued in this context.

Changes to Stock Values. The transactions that can be expected to alter the material stock quantities and stock values include those posted in connection with the following events:

Goods receipts

Transfer posting

Goods issues

Invoices

Detection of stock differences between book inventory and physical inventory results

Reevaluation of material stocks

The amounts arising from these transactions will depend on the price control strategy in operation for each material involved.

Evaluation Procedures

The basic evaluation procedure entails applying prices to inventory and posting the total to the general ledger. The aim is to have the inventory situation continuously monitored by the system so that reports can be generated at any time. The choice of price control method for a material affects the posting procedure at goods receipt and invoice receipt level.

Price Control. Standard price control technique uses prices derived from historical data, with various adjustments made to arrive at values that can be used throughout the planning period. All inventory postings are carried out using the standard prices for the materials. If there are variances between the standard price and the amounts charged on invoices or goods receipts, these differences are posted to price difference accounts. These differences provide a method of monitoring price changes and comparing them with the moving average prices, which are displayed for each material in order to provide a comparison.

Moving average price control technique requires that all goods receipts are posted with the goods receipt actual values, rather than standard prices. These acquisition prices are used to update the material master records automatically. There are very few circumstances in which a price variance can arise. This might occur if there are stock shortages. Manual changes to the acquisition price can be effected in the material master, but these are seldom necessary.

Posting Procedure. When you post a goods receipt, the system will multiply the net order price by the quantity, and post the resulting value to the goods receipt and invoice receipt clearing account in the FI-GL General Ledger. If the price control technique in use is standard price, the quantity entered is valued at the standard price. If there is a difference between the net order price and the standard price for the order, the difference is posted to the price difference account.

When the corresponding invoice is received and entered, the goods receipt and invoice receipt clearing account is cleared if there is no difference in the prices. Otherwise, the difference is posted to the price difference account, where it should clear the amount previously posted there when the goods were received and found by the system to be priced at a set of rates different from the standard.

If the moving average price control technique is being used, the difference is posted to the stock account, where it will contribute to the average price next time this is computed.

Delivery Costs. The planned delivery costs are entered in the purchase order. The actual delivery costs are included in the goods receipt posting, which will be to a freight or customs clearing account.

If the standard price control is in operation, any difference between the actual delivery costs and the planned delivery costs will be posted to the price difference account.

If the moving average price (MAP) control is being applied, the difference between planned delivery costs of the material and the actual delivery costs will be posted as an offsetting entry to the stock account of the material concerned, where it may affect the moving average acquisition price held on the material master.

Cash Discount. If a cash discount is part of the agreed terms for a purchase order, you can make a net posting for the goods receipt and for the invoice receipt.

The moving average price of materials being priced on this basis will be reduced as a result of the stock posting of the relevant discount amount. An offsetting entry will be made automatically to a cash discount clearing account, where it will remain until cleared at payment.

Split Evaluation. If a material is to be split for evaluation, the different stocks of the same material will be treated independently. Each sub-stock will be valued according to the evaluation category assigned to it.

An evaluation category master record has a header record in which each of the corresponding evaluation types is represented by the quantities of the material of that evaluation type comprising the sub-stock, and their values computed according to the price formula defined for that evaluation type.

Reevaluation. A stock of material is revalued when there is a price change or if there is a credit or debit posting to its stock account.

Changes can be entered manually under the following functions:

> Material price change can be effective immediately or from a specified date.

Material debit or credit posting for a material will only affect the evaluation of the stock if the price control method decrees that the evaluation shall take place on the basis of the moving average price of the stock.

Balance Sheet Evaluation

When it is necessary to value an inventory for the purpose of drawing up a legal balance sheet, there are two standard computing functions available in the SAP R/3 materials management component:

> LIFO evaluation
>
> Lowest value price determination

The results of these evaluations are used to compute evaluation adjustment postings to the FI-GL General Ledger for tax purposes and for commercial reasons concerning financial management.

Last-In-First-Out (LIFO) Evaluation. If the market price of a material is rising due to inflation, the value of the company may appear to be increasing merely because the stock held in inventory is increasing in acquisition price. On the other hand, if it is assumed that the material most recently acquired, which will be at the higher price, is the first material to be taken out of the warehouse into consumption, then the value of the stock remaining will be based on the lower acquisition price of the older stock.

This will be the stock evaluation used for balance sheet purposes under the LIFO régime.

If there is no difference in the important attributes of the old and the new stock, either can be released to consumption. If a limited shelf life is specified, the older stock will be released first. However, for inventory purposes the evaluation will apply the acquisition price of the older stock to the total quantity on inventory.

Similar materials and materials with similar functions can be aggregated into pools which are valued together. The system provides two procedures for LIFO evaluation:

> Quantity LIFO procedure
>
> Index LIFO procedure

Quantity LIFO Procedure. If the stock at the end of a fiscal year is greater than the stock at the end of a previous year, the system creates a layer, which is a data object. The layer contains the following data elements:

> Identification of the fiscal year to which it is assigned
>
> The material number or material pool number to which it refers
>
> The quantity of the material in stock at the end of the year
>
> The quantity of the material in stock at the end of the previous year
>
> The computed difference in stock of this material between the reference year and the previous year

The increase in stock of this material in the year is defined as the layer, and the value of this layer is calculated using the price for this year.

The layer defined by the stock of this material carried over from the previous year will still be on inventory, and will be valued at the price used when the inventory was valued for balance sheet purposes at the end of the previous fiscal year.

When the time comes to value the stock of this material at the end of this financial year, the quantity may be less than the previous year because the quantities issued have exceeded the quantities received. In such cases the balance sheet evaluation procedure has to decide which layer of stock is to be regarded as the source of the stock consumed: should it be the older layer or the newer?

If the LIFO procedure is in operation, evaluation will start valuing the stock consumed as if the most recently acquired layer is the source, regardless of whether goods issue has actually been on the basis of batch production date, delivery batch date, or some other régime. The price of the goods consumed from inventory will be taken from the stock layer for the current year until the quantity in this layer has all been assigned to the consumption account. If yet further quantities of this stock must be considered in order to reach the quantity consumed in the year, the price will be taken from the stock layer for the previous year in accord with the last-in-first-out rule.

Stock Layer Evaluation Methods. The SAP R/3 system provides various methods for valuing a stock layer of a material or material pool:

Evaluation on the basis of the current value of the moving average price maintained in the material master record

Price for the total year—carries out evaluation on the basis of the moving average price for all goods receipts in the reporting year

Price for the partial year—values the stock of each material on the basis of the moving average price for goods receipts in part of the reporting year, specified in terms of the number of months, starting with the first month in the reporting year

Price by quantity—applies the moving average price for each period separately, starting at the beginning of the year, and stopping when the quantity of stock that has been valued is equal to the quantity recorded in the stock layer master

The differences between these methods can be expressed as a difference in the assumptions made about the value of the stock in a layer:

Evaluation of the whole layer at the current moving average price assumes that the value of the stock has kept in step with the moving average price, and therefore, the balance sheet should show what it is worth by applying the moving average price as it is at the time of the report, which may be some months after the end of the fiscal year being reported.

Price for the total year evaluation assigns to the whole layer the moving average price current at the end of the reporting year.

Price for partial year evaluation assumes that the most reasonable price to use for the balance sheet is the moving average taken over the beginning few months of the reporting year.

Price by quantity evaluation assumes that the balance sheet will be best served by valuing a layer at the moving average price determined on a month-by-month basis, whereby it is more closely in tune with the cash flows of the company at the time.

Index LIFO Procedure. The index procedure refers to a price index for the material or material pool, and manages it by value alone. The value of a layer of a material or a material pool at the end of a fiscal year is calculated using a price index and is recorded as the base year value of the layer.

At the end of the year, the value of the pool is recalculated using the price index applied to the base year value of the previous year. If the pool includes various layers from previous years, their separate values using their own base year prices are added together. If the value of the pool is greater than the total of the values of the separate layers, a new layer is created for the reporting year, and valued by the amount of this increase. If the value of the whole pool using the current base price is less than the total of the values of the separate parts, the LIFO rule is applied, and the most recent layer is diminished in value until the pool is valued at the amount calculated on the basis of the price index applied to the base year.

Lowest Value Determination

In the custom and practice of drawing up a balance sheet, the evaluation of the inventory can take place in accord with either of the following principles:

The strict lowest value principle specifies that where the price of a material can be determined by more than one method, the lowest value must be used.

The moderate lowest value principle specifies that where the price of a material can be determined by more than one method, the lowest value can be used.

For example, the value of a stock layer can be calculated on the basis of the acquisition costs of the raw materials or other components, to which you add the production costs. The alternative might be to value the layer at the price quoted on the appropriate commodity exchange or other market price listing.

The SAP R/3 system is able to support a range of procedures for automatically computing the lowest value that could be applied to stocks of material procured externally.

Lowest Value by Market Prices. The value for a material on inventory at the end of the fiscal year can be determined automatically by nominating the following sources of information:

Purchase orders

Contracts

Purchasing info records

Receipts of goods for purchase orders

Lowest Value by Range of Coverage. The range of coverage represents the time that the inventory stock of a material will last according to an estimate of its rate of consumption. The range of coverage can be based on past consumption data or on the values forecast.

The lowest value for a stock layer can be determined according to the range of coverage, calculated in months, and a percentage discount is then applied, depending on the number of months.

Lowest Value by Movement Rate. The movement rate of a material is an index of the relation between goods receipts and goods issues of the material. It is calculated as a percentage.

If a material is classed as slow-moving or nonmoving, a devaluation indicator is set for it that will cause the system to apply a percentage reduction in value according to the calculation rule specified for the devaluation indicator.

Linked Procedures. The system allows you to link evaluation procedures in sequence. For example, you can have the system determine the lowest price of a material according to market prices and then apply a reduction to allow for range of coverage or movement rate.

Results. The outcome of material evaluation using the lowest value determination procedure can be used to update the commercial price field and the tax field in the material master record.

Once this has been accomplished, you can call at any time for a list covering all your materials on inventory, in which the system will offer proposals on how you could effect transfer postings for the purpose of devaluing your individual stock accounts.

Invoice Verification

When an invoice receipt is posted in the MM-Materials Management component, the system verifies it with the data in the purchasing and goods receipt functions, and then transmits the information to the accounting modules:

FI-Financial Accounting

CO-Controlling

FI-AM Assets Management

When the invoice receipt is posted, an open item is generated in the vendor account that will not be cleared until the FI-Financial Accounting component has confirmed that payment has taken place. In order to do this, the invoice receipt must reference a purchase order or goods receipt, so as to be able to have access to the details of the materials and quantities.

The maximum amount each user is permitted to post during invoice verification is determined during MM-Materials Management Customizing.

Entering Invoices with Order Reference

If you are entering an invoice receipt which has a reference to a purchase order, you have only to enter or confirm the order number, and the system will propose the vendor and also the following data:

> Tax rate
>
> Terms of cash discount
>
> Individual quantities and values of each material

When you post this entry, the system will send you system messages to inform you of any variances between the invoice data and the purchase order data. You are allowed to define tolerance limits for the individual invoice items so that you will not be subjected to unimportant system messages. If the lower limit is exceeded, you will be informed that the lower limit should be corrected. If the upper limit is exceeded, the system will allow you to post the invoice receipt document, but it will be blocked for payment.

To release a blocked document for payment by FI-Financial Accounting, you must enter a separate release transaction to document how you have resolved the discrepancy.

Assuming that the system has accepted any variances between the purchase order and the invoice receipt, the act of posting the invoice will create a document to record the event and post the amounts to the relevant accounts, which are determined automatically. At the same time, the price history will be updated if the invoice has referred to a purchase order.

If the material in an invoice item is marked to be valued by the moving average price method, the relevant material master record will be updated at this time with the price and value of the material.

Order Receipt References. If the invoice arrives with a reference to a goods receipt, the accounts payable clerk will enter the document number for the goods receipt or the delivery slip number. The system will locate the required data and propose it for inclusion in the document that will record the receipt of the invoice. Alternatively, the user can enter the purchase order number to elicit the same information.

An individual delivery can be settled by entering the invoice receipt with a reference to the delivery note or goods receipt document.

If you enter a purchase order number during the invoice receipt entry, the system will create an invoice item for each item on the order for each goods receipt. This enables you to relate each particular goods receipt item to the order item to which it belongs.

Entering Invoices Without Order Reference. A bill for expenses—at a hotel, for example—does not necessarily have any reference item in the system from which the details can be retrieved so that the system can propose the details for invoice receipt entry.

In such cases of purchases without purchase orders, you first create a vendor item and then create a document item corresponding to each item on the invoice you have received, so as to record all the details of the material or service for which payment will have to be made.

The resulting document can be posted to a material account, a general ledger account, or a fixed asset account, as appropriate.

Invoice Entry Functions

The wide range of standard SAP R/3 display and data entry functions is available for use in the invoice verification process. Some of the functions are particularly apposite:

Search for a open purchase order—can be initiated after identifying either a vendor or a material.

Search for a group of open purchase orders—used to find all the purchase orders relevant to an invoice that contains items from different orders.

Document editing—allows you to adjust an invoice receipt document as many times as you need before you post it.

Document simulation—lets you see the balance for the document and how the accounts would change if you were to actually post this particular invoice at this moment or at some future date.

Retrieve related information—enables you to access additional information not only on accounting matters, such as purchase order details, order history, or vendor data, but also material data, which could include the technical documents linked to the material master records.

Taxes

The system can be provided with the INT-International module, from which you can obtain automatic access to the valid deductible and nondeductible tax types for your own country and any other countries for which the module has been configured.

As the invoice receipt is entered, the tax record and the tax amount will also be entered, if they are part of the invoice. The system will check the correctness of the invoice amount, the tax record or code, and the tax amount. If there are any variances, the system will inform you via system messages, but you will still be allowed to post the invoice receipt.

If the invoice receipt does not include a tax amount, the tax can be calculated by the system using the local tax module. If the invoice items have different tax records or codes, the tax is calculated for each one separately.

When you post an invoice receipt, the appropriate tax items are created automatically.

Gross and Net Posting

During the process of entering an invoice receipt, you can nominate the terms of payment. The system will propose the conditions from the purchase order or suggest the

VI

Application Support

standard conditions as specified in the vendor master record. The standard terms of payment are expressed in the following manner, for example:

> Three percent cash discount applies if payment is made within 10 days
>
> Two percent cash discount applies if payment is made within 20 days
>
> Net payment is required within 30 days

The cash discount can be cleared as a gross posting or as a net posting, as you specify.

Gross Posting. The effect of specifying clearance by gross posting is to have the system ignore any cash discount amounts until the invoice is cleared for payment, when the discount amount is posted to a separate account assigned for the purpose of recording cash discounts.

The advantage of this procedure is that the balances in the stock account and the cost accounts are not affected by the cash discount.

Net Posting. If the posting is to be cleared net, the cash discount amount is credited directly to the account to which the costs detailed on the invoice receipt are posted. The cost center, for example, will receive only the net amount from the invoice.

Excluding Items from Cash Discount. If an item on an invoice is not going to attract any cash discount for early payment, it can be so marked on the invoice receipt document and thereby excluded from any discount calculations.

Other Functions

In support of the invoice verification functions, the system will conduct a wide range of automatic business processes. They are all fully integrated with the MM-Materials Management Module and therefore with the other modules of the SAP R/3 system

Foreign Currency. It is the practice in SAP R/3 systems that invoices shall be posted only in local currency. If the user wishes to enter the invoice receipts in another currency, the system will convert the amounts to the local currency and record both in the invoice receipt document.

The method of establishing the exchange rate to use in currency conversion can be any of the following:

> A fixed exchange rate is stated on the purchase order.
>
> The exchange rate to be used is stored in the system.
>
> The exchange rate to be used is entered directly during invoice verification.

Account Assignments. Any materials not procured for stock and services must identify the accounts to which the amounts are to be assigned. An amount can be distributed to more than one account on a percentage basis or in terms of fixed amounts.

If an account has been assigned in a purchase order, that account cannot be changed if a goods receipt which has been subjected to evaluation is entered during invoice verification. If the goods receipt has not been valued, the accounts payable clerk can change the account assignment.

Subsequent Debits. If a transaction has already been cleared and additional costs are incurred, it will be necessary to make a subsequent adjustment in the form of a debit. The adjustment is posted directly to the material or cost account, whereupon the system will automatically update the order history with respect to the value, although the quantity will remain the same.

Credit Memos. If it becomes apparent after invoice verification has been completed that a credit has to be posted, the credit memo function can be called from the invoice verification program. If the system encounters a credit memo document referring to a purchase order or a goods receipt, it will be treated as a cancellation of the corresponding invoice receipt document.

Down Payments. A vendor may have agreed conditions that stipulate a down payment for all purchase orders. Alternatively, the terms for a down payment can be agreed with the vendor in a particular purchase order.

The down payment can be agreed for the order as a whole or for individual order items.

If any down payment arrangement has been agreed, you will receive a system message to this effect when the invoice verification function becomes aware that you are about to enter a invoice receipt for that order or for that vendor, if a standing arrangement for a down payment is in force.

The down payment will have to be the subject of a separate transfer posting to a vendor account established for this purpose, where it will remain until the transaction is closed by the final payment.

Correspondence. The standard communication channels for internal mail are available to the invoice verification component, together with the standard interface to external systems. The SAP R/3 word processing system can be used to provide texts for automatic entry into an invoice receipt document or to copy parts of the invoice itself into this document.

Planned Delivery Costs. The delivery costs can be planned and divided into a range of delivery cost types:

> Freight costs
>
> Customs duty
>
> Insurance
>
> Packaging labor, materials, and so on

Each of these types can be related to a method of calculation, for example:

> Fixed costs per delivery
>
> Delivery costs proportional to the quantity

Delivery costs proportional to the number of shipping units or transportation plant units required

Delivery costs to be computed as a fixed percentage of the total value or weight of goods delivered

The planned delivery costs are recorded on the purchase order for each order item, and the relevant amount for planned delivery costs is posted to the material account or to the cost account when the goods receipt is entered.

At the same time, an offsetting entry is posted to a special clearing account, such as a freight clearing account.

When the invoice receipt document is being created, you can list all the delivery costs for a specific purchase order, for a particular vendor or for a delivery note. You can then decide how you want the system to allocate the total delivery costs recorded in the invoice you have received.

When you do so, the planned delivery costs will be updated in the order history to take account of the actual delivery costs.

Unplanned Delivery Costs. The first time you have any information on unplanned delivery costs may be when you catch sight of the invoice. There will have been no previous entry of planned delivery costs.

The unplanned costs have to taken from the invoice during invoice verification and entered in the invoice receipt document. The system will automatically distribute the total delivery costs among the individual items in proportion to their contribution to the value of the entire value invoiced. You can override this proportional distribution by a series of manual entries, for which rapid data entry functions are provided where relevant.

Unplanned delivery costs are posted directly to the material account or to the appropriate cost account.

Blocked Invoices

If you receive a system message to inform you that there is some variance between the planned amounts and the actual amounts, or if you are aware of this anyway, you must write the new values over the proposed quantities and values.

The following causes of variance may exist, perhaps at the same time:

Quantity variance

Quality variance

Price variance

Schedule variance

Project budget overrun

Tolerances. To protect your users from excessive outpourings of system messages, you can define tolerances for individual variances by establishing upper and lower limits within which the system will accept the discrepancy. Outside these limits—above or below—the user sees a message.

You can always post an invoice receipt that includes a variance. However, if the value exceeds the upper limit, the invoice will be blocked for payment.

Releasing Block Invoices. When an invoice item has been found to have a discrepancy that exceeds the upper tolerance limit, the item is marked with a key indicating the reason, and the whole invoice is blocked. An item can be assigned several blocking reasons at the same time.

If you call up a list of all blocked invoices, you can deal with each one in a variety of ways:

> Cancel one or more of the individual item blocking reason keys if further investigation uncovers a good reason for the discrepancy, such as when a price variance is justified, but there is still a discrepancy in the quantity.

> Release the invoice for payment, perhaps after changing the date from when the terms of payment are valid, so that the financial accounting department can pay the invoice without waiting for the outcome of an investigation into the reason for the variance.

Sometimes the reason for blocking an invoice may no longer be valid. Perhaps the shortage in delivery quantity has been made up, or perhaps the critical date in a schedule has passed.

You can release an invoice yourself, or the system will automatically release all blocked invoices for which the reasons are no longer valid.

MM-WM Warehouse Management

The MM-Warehouse Management component is designed to support the efficient and effective processing of logistic requirements within a company. In particular, the following logistics operations are provided with standard business functions:

> Manage complex warehouse structures

> Define and manage storage bins

> Manage storage types

> Create transfer orders

> Monitor stock movements

> Execute stock placement and removal strategies

> Process differences

> Manage hazardous materials

Take inventory at the storage bin level

Use bar codes

Make use of warehouse reports

The MM-WM Warehouse Management system supports the processing of all movements, including goods receipts and goods issues initiated by the inventory management system, and goods issues from the sales and distribution system.

The MM-WM Warehouse Management system provides control over the movements within a warehouse, including stock transfers for replenishment orders.

Transactions in the inventory management system or in the sales and distribution system automatically trigger the Warehouse Management system to generate transfer requirements such as:

Material movements

Staging of materials for production orders

Shipping of goods for sales orders

Warehouse Structure

The representation of the warehouse structure in the SAP R/3 system follows the standard system of hierarchical levels stored in master records, starting with the client code, which is unique, below which there may be one or more company codes, each of which may operate one or more plants and warehouses.

Tables of logical and numerical values are provided so that you can adjust the system in order to make it represent the detailed structure and relationships within your configuration of warehouses and storage locations.

Warehouse Number. The physical warehouse complex is represented as a single number identifying that warehouse, and a warehouse master record on which may be stored a data structure.

Each warehouse will include various types of storage locations.

Storage Type. A storage type can be differentiated by its physical location, its technical characteristics and its place in the organizational structure of operational units and cost centers.

A storage type is divided into sub-areas that may use different storage techniques and serve different functions or parts of the organization.

The sub-areas of a storage type will be divided into storage bins.

Storage Bin. A storage bin is the smallest part of a storage area within a storage type that can be addressed for the purpose of directing material there or withdrawing material from it. All products within a storage bin, or in a space that is treated as a storage bin, are regarded as of exactly the same type. Any one of them can be withdrawn for assignment to an order or transfer; there is no effective difference between them.

Storage Section. A storage section is a grouping of storage bins represented as a section in the system according to criteria defined by the user. They have certain characteristics in common but not necessarily a shared location in a warehouse.

Storage Bin Type. The size of a storage bin is used to assign that bin to a storage bin type. The type is used in storage bin search to build up the quantity of material required for a transfer.

Transfer Requirements

When a movement of stock has been planned in the MM-Materials Management system and needs to be executed by the MM-WM Warehouse Management system, a transfer requirement document has to be created. This can be done manually in the MM-WM Warehouse Management system, or it can be generated automatically in response to a goods movement posting in the MM-Materials Management system.

The transfer requirement can be used to plan for the following operations:

Place goods into stock

Remove goods from stock

Prepare for other goods transfers by moving stock within the warehouse

The transfer requirement does not execute the stock movement. A movement will be executed only if a transfer order has been created and confirmed.

If you want to know what should be moved, and how much, the creation of a transfer requirement will provide the answers. If a movement has already been started by the confirmation of a transfer order and you try to create a transfer requirement for the same goods, you will discover whether the order was created automatically or manually, and whether an amount of the transfer has already been moved.

Transfer Orders

Stock movements are controlled by transfer orders specifying the material number, the quantity, and the storage bins from which the stock is to be removed. A transfer order is also used to release goods from quality inspection, even if no physical movement is entailed.

Transfer Confirmation. Some stock movements may have to be confirmed. The system provides a confirmation function which will execute a confirmation automatically as soon as the physical transfer has taken place. If the planned quantity is not the same as the actual quantity transferred, you can record the difference before confirming the transfer order.

Goods Receipt. A typical delivery of goods to a warehouse entails the following series of tasks:

A delivery vehicle arrives, and the supervisor has the system create a material movement document.

The system generates a transfer requirement and a quantity posting to the goods receipt area.

The goods are unloaded to the goods receipt area.

The system creates a transfer order for the goods to assign them to destination storage bins, which are then reserved for these goods.

The transfer order is printed or electronically displayed to the goods movement section.

The goods are transferred to the storage bins reserved for them.

The quantities in the storage bins are checked and confirmed to the system.

The system prints the confirmation from the storage bin checking operation on the transfer order document, which is then confirmed.

The system updates the inventory so that the goods are available for consumption or further movement.

The transfer order can support the following types of goods receipt:

Goods receipt based on a purchase order

Goods receipt without a reference purchase order

Goods receipt destined for an in-house production order

Goods receipt for a batch reserved for inspection

Goods receipt from a customer who is returning goods that are unwanted for any reason

Goods Issue. The transfer order function can also effect goods issues for the following purposes:

Goods issues to a cost center

Goods issues to a project

Staging of materials for production

Delivery of goods to customers

Picking Goods for a Delivery Note or Transfer Order. If the SAP R/3 SD-Sales and Distribution module has been installed and configured, the MM-WM Warehouse Management system can be automatically tasked to begin the picking of goods as soon as the delivery note has been posted.

If goods are to be picked using the fixed bin picking procedure, the bin to be used will be determined from the material master, updated by goods receipts and withdrawals. If the warehouse is organized on a random basis, a transfer order will be created for each delivery item. When the transfer order is confirmed in the system, each delivery item will be updated by the quantities picked, which may not be the same as the quantities planned. In such instances, a difference is documented.

Posting Changes and Stock Transfers. If a transaction does not entail the physical movement of goods, such as the receipt of goods, their issue or their movement from one storage location to another within the warehouse, the system will be able to offer the following choice of posting changes and stock transfer functions:

Release stock from quality inspection.

Convert stock from consignment stock to company stock.

Effect a posting change from one batch to another.

Change a material number of a quantity of stock.

Accept the return of goods and complete the necessary processing.

Effect a posting change for a stock replenishment warehouse.

Confirmation. If certain stock movements require confirmation, the system will not recognize any change in the relevant storage bins until the confirmation process is completed. You have to inform the system that the processing for the transfer order is finished. If only some of the transfer order items are subject to confirmation, you can register the confirmation on an individual item basis.

Differences. If the processing of a transfer order reveals that some of the goods were damaged during transit, or the quantities in the storage bins were insufficient or of the wrong material or batch specification, the system will have to be informed in the transfer order confirmation. This will automatically generate a difference posting to inventory management.

Setting the Control Parameters for Transfer Order Processing. You have the facility to determine which functions can be executed automatically and which must be held up until a valid manual input has been entered.

The control functions also direct the warehouse documents to the appropriate printer or other output channel.

The output can include bar codes.

Strategies

The method used by the system to find the storage bins to be used for the placement or withdrawal of stock is defined as a strategy. When the system has used a strategy to find a suitable set of storage bins, it will propose these for your approval or for you to change by manual entry.

The advantages of applying predefined search strategies are that the warehouse can be managed in an optimal manner for stock placements, and the system can quickly find the materials specified for stock removals.

This approach can be applied to all types of warehouse configurations and placement regimes.

Storage Type Search. You can specify that a particular material is to be stored in a specific type of storage. You can also assign classes of material to specific storage types—for example, subassemblies to be stored in high rack storage area number 1, finished assemblies in protected area 6.

Storage Section Search. Each material can be assigned to a particular area within the storage type for that material group—for example, fast-moving items in the front area F, slow-moving items in the back area B.

Bin Type Search. Certain bin types can be assigned to specific storage unit types so that the goods placed there can be accommodated in the best possible bin type. For example, bin types can be defined as pallets, wire baskets, or warehouse floor area. Each of the bins of each type will be identified by number and, through the bin master record, by storage type and location. Restrictions on the type of materials to be stored in a bin type may also be established in the bin type master record.

Storage Bin Search. The search for a specific storage bin can be conducted using a similar strategy for both stock placement, which will be looking for unoccupied bins, and stock removal, which will be looking for bins occupied by the material required, subject to other constraints depending on the stock removal strategy being employed.

Stock Placement Strategies. The following stock placement strategies can be specified to enable the system automatically to generate proposals for the placement of any stock arriving at a warehouse:

The material is placed in the next suitable empty bin.

The material is always assigned to the same fixed bin.

The system does not make any proposal for placing the stock, but waits for the user to enter a destination.

The system finds a bin that already contains this material and attempts to place it there, unless this would exceed the capacity of the bin, in which case it automatically begins a search for another suitable bin. If no space can be found in an occupied bin, a suitable empty bin is used.

Block storage is specified for materials that are to be stored in large quantities without taking up too much storage space.

Shelf section storage is used where the storage area is able to take a different number of delivery units, depending on the size of the unit—for example, three European standard pallets can be stored in the space taken by two pallets of the size previously common in that industry.

Stock Removal Strategies. The choice of stock removal strategy is constrained by the placement of the goods in storage bins according to the placement strategies. The system will know where everything is located, down to the bin identification.

There are two main stock removal strategies that can be assigned to a specific material:

FIFO (first-in-first-out)—requires that the materials to be removed first are those that have been in the warehouse longest; they will have the earliest goods receipt date.

LIFO (last-in-first-out)—identifies for first removal those goods with the most recent goods receipt date.

Partial Quantities. If the system finds that a material has been placed in a storage type which includes storage areas that are not all completely full to capacity, it seeks to fulfill the transfer order by selecting a combination of full and partly full storage areas that will exactly match the quantity required. This will tend to optimize the use of storage facilities and the material-handling activities.

Large and Small Quantities. A warehouse may contain two types of storage area for the same material—one for large delivery units containing a large quantity of the material, the other for single assemblies or small deliverable units.

You can define a search strategy parameter instructing the system which removal source to use on the basis of a set quantity of the material required. You can also allow the splitting of large delivery units.

Inventory

The legal requirement for conducting a physical inventory is that every storage bin should be checked at least once each fiscal year for quantity and the identity of the material it contains.

The SAP R/3 system allows you to define the physical inventory procedure individually for each storage type. This facility allows you to take account of any special technical or organizational factors concerning the materials or the storage arrangements that should be documented in conjunction with the inventory. The following inventory procedures are provided as standard programs which can be controlled by parameters established during Customizing:

Annual inventory count

Continuous inventory

Continuous inventory during stock placement

Continuous inventory based on zero stock check

Inventory based on sampling procedure

Inventory Indicator. When a storage bin has been inventoried, the corresponding storage bin master record is updated with an inventory indicator showing the date and which inventory procedure was used on it.

This indicator also serves as legal proof that the physical inventory was carried out.

Differences. If any difference is detected between the recorded inventory and the physical inventory, the details are posted automatically to an interim storage area record for differences. The MM-IM Inventory Management component has access to this interim storage record, and the inventory manager can authorize the clearing of these differences by difference postings to the appropriate stock accounts.

Inventory History. A history log is automatically maintained by the system to document the inventory history of every storage bin over a very long time period. This can be accessed in dialog mode.

System Inventory Record. The task of conducting the annual physical inventory is assisted by the system inventory records that are automatically generated when required, and by their associated functions, as follows:

Printed warehouse inventory list

Entry functions to post the counting results to the corresponding warehouse inventory list items

Initiation of a recount if serious discrepancies are detected

Investigation support to establish the reasons for discrepancies

Clearing of differences with the creation of explanatory documents

Storage Unit Management

The storage unit management function in the MM-WM Warehouse Management component is able to maintain storage unit number records that include indicators of the type of storage unit, such as pallet, wire basket, and so on.

Under this storage unit number it is possible to group material quantities in logical units comprising a homogeneous or a mixed quantity of materials.

The storage unit number master record also stores data about the single material or combination of materials contained in the storage unit, such as:

The material number

The quantity of material

Which operations have been performed on this material

When this storage unit was last subjected to physical inventory

Storage Unit Functions. The following functions can be initiated from the storage unit management component:

Create a transfer order for one or more storage units.

Confirm a stock movement.

Add stock to existing storage units.

Print documents to accompany the storage unit.

One of the uses for a storage unit system is to assemble a set of constituents or component parts that are thereafter documented and marshaled to the production or sales processes as a single composite object.

Decentralized Warehouse Management from the SAP R/2 Host System

An asynchronous program-to-program communication interface can be installed to integrate the SAP R/3 MM-WM Warehouse Management system with the SAP R/2 applications for Materials Management, Sales, and Distribution.

Stock movements in the SAP R/2 Materials Management system initiate quantity postings in the SAP R/3 MM-WM Warehouse Management system as required. Delivery orders are transmitted to a decentralized warehouse unit for shipping. When picking is completed and confirmed, the actual quantities are ready for transmitting to the SAP R/2 host computer. If the host is not available at the time, any differences on the delivery orders and any goods receipts taken from the production department are entered in the terminal of the decentralized SAP R/3 warehouse unit. When the host becomes available again, the SAP R/2 central inventory management system is updated from the SAP R/3 decentralized unit.

Special Functions

The MM-Materials Management module is provided with a range of flexible special functions that can operate in any of the constituent components, such as:

MM-MRP Material Requirements Planning

MM-IM Inventory Management

MM-IV Invoice Verification

The MM-Materials Management special functions comprise the following program elements:

Consignment material

Special stocks of consignment material

Material movements

Subcontracting

Vendor special stocks

Goods receipt from a subcontractor

Physical stock transfers by stock transport orders

Consignment Material

If you buy material from a vendor and pay for it, this material is valued on your balance sheet. However, the vendor may have delivered to your company a stock of material that you do not have to pay for unless and until you need it. Such material is treated as consignment material, and it will not be valued on your balance sheet even though it will be on your inventory.

You may return the consignment material, or part of it, when you no longer expect to need it.

If you do withdraw for consumption a partial quantity of consignment stores, or transfer it to your own stock, the quantity you move will be valued at the vendor's defined selling price, and you will have to pay for it. Settlement of consignment material is usually effected on a monthly or quarterly basis.

Special Stocks of Consignment Material. You can manage consignment material using the normal material number, and you will therefore be able to call on the associated data from the material master records. However, these special stocks of consignment material are managed in separate areas of the storage location, according to vendor. Purchase prices of consignment stocks withdrawn are recorded according to vendor, and a moving average price is maintained on the vendor master records for evaluation purposes.

Material Movements. When a goods receipt is processed for a consignment order item or a consignment scheduling agreement, the value and quantity are posted, according to the special stock indicator, to one of the following stock master record data fields:

Unrestricted-use stock

General goods receipt blocked stock

Stock in quality inspection

The same actions can be carried out on batches of consignment material if the system has been preset to apply the batch status management facility.

Consignment materials can also be withdrawn in a random sample for quality inspection.

All the movements will be posted under the control of the special stock indicator so that the pricing and evaluation procedures will be alerted to the special circumstances.

There may be a contract in force stipulating that consignment stock remaining at the end of the fiscal year is to be transferred to the company's own stock. Such a transfer may be effected at other times as a periodic replenishment of company stock according to consumption or planned requirements.

Reservation of consignment stock can be effected as a method of planning the withdrawal of material to consumption or in replenishment of company stock.

Subcontracting

The subcontract order is a method of outsourcing a business process. The subcontracting function in the MM-Materials Management Module offers support for the following operations:

Placing an outside contract for production activities and services

Providing material components to the subcontractor for the production or assembly processes

Issuing material such as equipment to the subcontractor from the ordering company's own stock of plant

Posting as goods receipts the services performed and the goods produced by the subcontractor

Posting the consumption or usage of the issued material in the same transaction as the services and goods receipts

Vendor Special Stocks. It may be convenient to maintain a stock of your materials at the premises of a subcontractor. These will be represented as vendor special stocks, because they are not available for other purposes, but still belong to your company because you engaged the subcontractor as a vendor.

If the material to be provided to a subcontractor has to be drawn from several batches, the identity of these batches is recorded in the delivery documents in case they are returned from the subcontractor or are subject to reversal because, for example, they are damaged or faulty.

Goods Receipt from a Subcontractor. When goods that have been produced or assembled by a subcontractor are received at the contracting company, the quantities of the materials supplied are valued at their evaluation price taken from the material master records. The quantity and value are posted out of the stock for each material, and the quantities are included in the consumption statistics.

The value of the material received from the subcontractor is computed as the net purchase order value plus the evaluation cost of the material posted out of stock for this subcontract.

If the material is managed in batches, a separate goods issue item is created for each batch from which materials have been provided to the subcontractor.

If some of the material used was already being held by the subcontractor as vendor special stock, this amount will appear as default values in the ratio of goods receipt quantity to purchase order quantity, which can be corrected by the user.

When the invoice is received from the subcontractor, the quantity of each material, which will have been already posted to consumption, can be corrected to account for any differences between the planned usage and the actual.

Physical Stock Transfers by Stock Transport Orders

If there are two or more plants in your company—and a plant can be a warehouse—you can transfer stock by means of a stock transport order. This can make sense if the costs of transporting stock are significant and if the time in transit is considerable.

VI

Application Support

The acquisition price of this material for the receiving plant is computed as the evaluation of it in the issuing plant plus the costs of delivery. If it should happen that the material is subject to moving average price control, the moving average price may change after each delivery.

The receiver plant orders the material from the issuing plant and plans the delivery costs such as packaging, freight, transport insurance, customs duty, unloading, and so on. The planned delivery costs are recorded in the specific item of the order.

The source of the material posts a goods issue referring to the stock transport order. The quantity withdrawn from stock at this issuing plant is listed as stock in transit at the receiving plant.

When the goods arrive at the receiving plant, the system is posted with the goods receipt document referring to the goods transport order. This event has the effect of reducing the quantity and value of the stock in transit account and the value of the total of the purchase orders still open at the receiving plant.

MM-IS Information System

The information systems are clearly central to efficient controlling of materials management. There are particular display functions optimized for the purchasing functions as the PURCHIS-Purchasing Information System, and for the inventory management system under the title of MM-IC Inventory Controlling.

PURCHIS-Purchasing Information System

The aim of an information system is to select only the pertinent information and then to present it in ways that increase the probability of correct decisions being taken by those who view it.

There are two types of error associated with information presented to the user for a decision:

- Error one is to offer the user a choice of items which do not mean anything, or mean something to the viewer which was unintended by the system designer.

- Error two is to omit from the list of options some of the important possibilities, which can include such options as Do Nothing and None Of The Above Is A Sensible Choice.

The PURCHIS Purchasing Information system maintains its own database and can perform several important analysis procedures on it. For example, it can produce an analysis of vendors and of purchasing group activities. It can publish its results in terms of some thirty performance measures, such as the number of purchase orders in the period.

Not only can the PURCHIS present data in a wide variety of list and graphical formats, it can also assemble the data using the widest range of search strategies.

The PURCHIS Purchasing Information System is part of the LO-LIS Logistics Information System and shares many of its routines with the SD-IS Sales and Distribution Information System.

The inventory controlling system, which is also part of the logistics information system, is designed to reduce the information held in the Inventory Management system to a few informative performance measures that show which areas offer opportunities for improvement.

Standard Analyses. The basis of analysis using the PURCHIS methodology is the information structure, which comprises data objects and performance measures associated with a time unit or period. For example, an information structure can be defined for a weekly period, comprising the following data objects:

> Purchasing group
>
> Vendor

The performance measures to be gathered on this information structure may include:

> Invoice value
>
> Net order value
>
> Number of order items
>
> Number of deliveries and so on

Standard Information Structures. The standard PURCHIS component is provided with three information structures containing more than thirty meaningful performance measures for all the analyses relevant to purchasing, grouped in thematic clusters.

You can also define your own information structures by selecting objects and performance measures from lists and using the "pickup" technique to copy them to a display or printing format of your own design.

Update rules are predefined for every field in the information structures, and you can change the rules if you wish. The updating of these statistical files can take place in synchrony with interactive processing or as a separate update processing run.

The standard analyses cover the statistical information that you might need for the following organizational entities:

> Purchasing groups
>
> Vendors
>
> Material groups
>
> Materials

The scope of the data used for these compilations can be restricted interactively by applying selection criteria. Any item of interest in the display of results can be selected and become the focus for the "drill-down" technique, in which you can call for information about the selected object at each layer down the information hierarchy that was used to compile the value in the report you selected in the first instance.

At every level of a drill-down search, you can call for graphical and list displays including the following functions:

ABC analysis

Dual classification

Classification to the SAP R/3 scheme

Ranking lists

Planned versus actual comparisons

Detailed information can be sought at any level from the associated vendor master records, material master records, and purchasing documents.

ABC Analysis. The ABC analysis concept refers to groupings of data objects according to the relative importance of one of the values held in a specified data element of all of these objects.

For example, you can rank-order all vendors in terms of their contribution to the total order value in the period of scrutiny. You can then specify that the A vendors will be those who together account for the first 70 percent of the order value, the B vendors will be those who together contribute the next 20 percent of the total order value, and the C vendors will be the remainder in the rank-ordered list because they have individually contributed least and together contribute only 10 percent of the total order value for the period. The number of vendors in each of the A, B, and C groups will be in itself an interesting result of the ABC analysis.

There are four different strategies of this kind available for structuring ABC analysis, and it can be conducted using planned or actual values of the performance measure in question. The four standard sets of percentage values for the ABC analyses can be modified at Customizing.

R/3 Classification. The classification function which is an integral part of the R/3 system provides a standard method for grouping together several data objects specified by a range of one of their values—for example, all production cost centers with company codes A to D and F. The members of this group are then examined with regard to one or more of the other performance data elements in their records, such as the number of work calendar days lost to production and the total value of output in the period.

Dual classification can be applied to reveal the relationship between the two performance measures and to demonstrate it in graphical or list format, using any of the materials or vendor data fields.

The PURCHIS component can be primed to execute user-defined analyses specified by settings on the following dimensions:

Number of periods to be analyzed

Performance measures to be displayed

The standard structure to be followed when the user calls for a drill-down sequence

The format and layout of the displayed or printed reports

Flexible Analysis and Evaluation Structures. It is characteristic of SAP R/3 standard business programs that the reports can be tailored to suit the needs of the viewers. For example, those who need detail can see it and those who need an overview can get that, both from the same analysis.

The method uses a set of standard evaluation structures, which can be supplemented by the user on the basis of edited copies of the standards, if convenient. A data dictionary has to be identified, on which the evaluation structure will call in order to assemble the data it needs. A system document file containing purchasing documents would be a convenient type of data dictionary for many purposes.

An evaluation structure can be created by using standard performance measures in an appropriate formula.

Planning. It is often helpful to see how the planned values compare to the actual results. The same information structures will accept planned and actual values, with the full facilities of the flexible display functions on hand to make clear the relationships in the data.

In this context, the technique of simulating future possibilities can be enacted using copies of the analyses, each conducted on a different set of hypothetical parameters. The simulation that has the best outcome can then be designated as the official plan.

Inventory Controlling

The essence of inventory controlling is to make a plan that attempts to anticipate the requirements for all the materials for the planning periods out to the extent of the planning horizon, to compare the planned with the actual, and to make effective and timely adjustments to the replenishment arrangements so that no shortages occur. This is a difficult assignment, and there are some rules of thumb about keeping safety stocks on hand in case of unforeseen material requirements or unscheduled late deliveries.

If your company has a large inventory with many different materials, the problem is one of sampling the data. Here the MM-Materials Management system can help a great deal through its MM-IC Inventory Controlling component.

Firstly, it can demonstrate to you which materials and subassemblies ought to be monitored for such reasons as the following:

High capital lock-up while in storage or production

The materials needed are purchased or stored in quantities that are not efficient purchasing or storage units.

Materials are stocked in excess of a reasonable coverage requirement, bearing in mind their expected consumption.

Materials are seldom withdrawn from inventory and might be better purchased only for specific orders.

Optimization. The inventory controller may be authorized to adjust the safety stock levels and may be able to influence the purchasing lot size. The MM-IC Inventory Controlling component will enable you to reduce stock by a specific amount through the automatic distribution of the target savings to the material stocks that are most sensitive on account of their values or the costs of storing and handling them. There can also be some worthwhile lessons to be learned from a study of fluctuations in inventory that could be directed at improving the synchronization of goods issues and receipts.

Meaningful Performance Measures. The MM-Inventory Controlling component has been able to concentrate the most important analysis data into six composite performance measures:

Consumption value using ABC analysis

Stock value

Dead stock

Range of coverage

Slow-moving items

Inventory turnover

The results of these compilations can be studied in two- and three-dimensional graphics and replicated in detailed checklists for closer examination. Any displayed aggregate value can be subjected to the drill-down procedure to reveal the data elements used to compute it.

Objects to Analyze

The standard data structures of the SAP R/3 system are designed to be analyzed at any level. Every materials analysis can be carried out using the data aggregated to any particular level down to the plant level, which is the lowest used for material master records. This means that you can see what is happening at any of the following levels in the organizational hierarchy:

All plants, cumulated in a specified sequence

Sales organization level

Purchasing organization level

Plant by plant

Analysis Types. There are two types of analysis:

> Total analysis

> Ranking list analysis

Total analysis allows a completely flexible definition by the user of the way the data records are to be collated and the measures that are to be computed. How the results are to be related to operational units and to materials are also matters under complete control of the user.

Ranking list analysis prepares the data in the form of rank orderings of the records according to the values specified by the user. They may be grouped, as in ABC analysis, or narrowed by the exclusion of very high and very low values. The scope is flexible with respect to the accounting periods.

From Here...

- There must be a great deal more to this drill-down information function.

  For an overview, see the "Logistics Information System" section of Chapter 2, "User Interaction with the SAP Systems." For how it is achieved, see Chapter 4, "Architecture."

- My interest is in how the R/3 system components are put together.

  See Chapter 3, "System Architecture and Distributed Applications."

- How are the materials managed in the continuous processing industries?

  See Chapter 18, "Understanding the PP-PI Production Planning for the Process Industries Modules."

- I need to know more about material distribution.

  This can be found in Chapter 20, "Understanding the SD-Sales and Distribution Module."

- Show me something completely different from materials management.

  Try the Chapter 22, "Understanding the HR-Human Resources Module," for a treatment of master record technique applied to people.

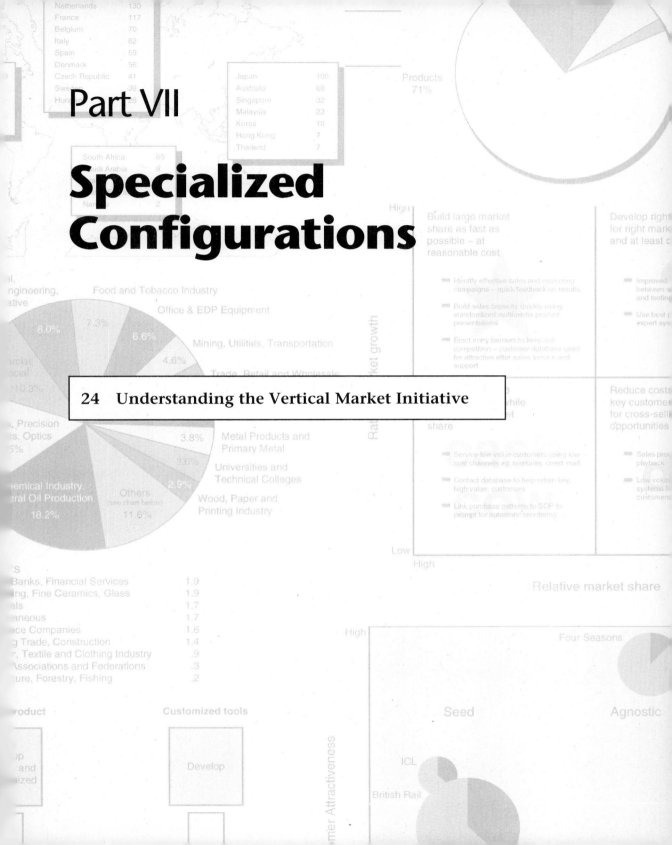

Part VII

Specialized Configurations

24   Understanding the Vertical Market Initiative

Belgium	70
Italy	62
Spain	59
Denmark	56
Czech Republic	41
Sweden	39
Hungary	26

479	
54	
24	
16	
a 14	

Japan	100
Australia	68
Singapore	32
Malaysia	22
Korea	10
Hong Kong	7
Thailand	7

South Africa	69
Saudi Arabia	9
Israel	3
Arabic Emirates	2
Namibia	2

Products
71%

Steel,
cal Engineering,
utomative

Food and Tobacco Industry

Office & EDP Equipment

Mining, Utilities, Transportation

Trade, Retail and Wholesale

Traffic and News
Communication

Metal Products and
Primary Metal

Universities and
Technical Colleges

Wood, Paper and
Printing Industry

8.0%

7.3%

6.6%

4.6%

4.5%

3.9%

3.8%

3.6%

2.9%

ommercial
nd Social
10.2%

ronics, Precision
chanics, Optics
14.5%

Chemical Industry,
Mineral Oil Production
18.2%

Others
(see chart below)
11.6%

Rate of market growth

Build large market
share as fast as
possible – at
reasonable cost

- Identify effective sales and marketing
  campaigns – quick feedback on results
- Build sales capacity quickly using
  standardized multimedia product
  presentations
- Erect entry barriers to keep out
  competition – customer database used
  for attractive after-sales service and
  support

Develop
for right
and at le

- Imp
  bet
  an
- Us
  ex

Reduce sales and
marketing costs while
maintaining market
share

- Service low value customers using low
  cost channels e.g. telesales, direct mail
- Contact database to help retain key,
  high value, customers
- Link purchase patterns to SOP to
  prompt for automatic reordering

Reduce
key cus
for cros
opportu

- Se
  pa
- Lc
  sy
  cu

Low

High

Relative market sh

Others
Credit Banks, Financial Services	1.9
Quarrying, Fine Ceramics, Glass	1.9
Hospitals	1.7
Miscellaneous	1.7
Insurance Companies	1.6
Building Trade, Construction	1.4
Leather, Textile and Clothing Industry	.9
Trade Associations and Federations	.3
Agriculture, Forestry, Fishing	.2

able product

Customized tools

Develop
mplete and
customized

Develop

Deliver

stomer Attractiveness

High

Four Seasons

Seed

Agno

ICL

British Rail

Chapter 24

Understanding the Vertical Market Initiative

The extending range of SAP Industry Solutions are enhancements of the R/3 system, which have been extensively developed to suit the needs of a particular type of industry or a particular type of enterprise. Several of them have evolved from standard applications because the users and the system developers have discerned ways in which the logic and software methodology of the SAP programs could be extended to suit the particular type of business.

Some industry-specific implementations of SAP R/3 are identified by the IS-series of codes. For example, IS-Aviation was developed from the MM-Materials Management module so as to be optimized for the aircraft production and maintenance sectors. Where there was a need for additional integration of pre-configured SAP R/3 modules, as in the case of the aerospace industry, for example, the specialized system would be identified by a title such as *SAP R/3 Aerospace and Defense*.

In essence, to configure to the industry initiative is based on the development of standard business process configuration templates, which can be applied to prepare the R/3 system and its applications to be quickly implemented in any enterprise in the particular industry.

Industry Centers of Expertise

Each industry that receives the special attention of the SAP research teams is able to refer to an ICOE, Industry Center of Expertise, for its particular industry. This is where the collective wisdom of user groups and professional associations can be shared with the group of client companies who are using and extending the Industry Solution.

For example, the banking industry has experienced a change of emphasis from an orientation toward managing money as a service to a particular community. The new emphasis is on income and risk management. The profitability of a banking product in a limited sector of the market has become a common calculation.

In this chapter, you learn the following:

- Learn about Industry Solutions, those extensions and enhancements of the standard R/3 system.

- Learn what industries currently have Industry Solution options. Nearly 20 major industries are involved.

- Learn about the advantages of an SAP Industry Solution—most of the customizing will have been done already and the system will be recognizably close to going live.

To respond to this requirement, the SAP IS-B, Industry Solution for Banks, has been developed as an enhancement of the standard R/3 system, which includes a system for determining market risks quantified on the basis of the money-at-risk calculation. This particular industry solution also provides the reporting structures, which are needed to meet the statutory obligations of the country in which the system is operating. The shared information is collated in the Banking Industry Center of Expertise.

If your industry has not yet been targeted for an industry solution, then the way to accelerate an implementation for your situation is to apply the disciplines of the SAP Business Engineer. This is comprised of a set of tools that plot out what you need and identify how these needs can be met from standard R/3 components. This chapter illustrates how various industries have been able to accelerate implementation of SAP R/3 by adopting a version of R/3 already customized for their type of requirement, and therefore needing only relatively minor adjustments to fine-tune the customizing.

SAP R/3 Aerospace and Defense

Many of the requirements of the aerospace and defense sectors have been met by using the standard SAP R/3 components; and some aspects will be best served by the high-tech industry solution described in the following. The highest quality control and absolute tracking of all objects and documents throughout their production, use, and disposal are features of this sector.

The SAP R/2 mainframe system, IS-Aviation, has been used in the aviation industry for the following purposes:

- Production planning and control

- Materials management

- Maintenance planning and processing

- Sales, dispatch, and invoicing

- Financial accounting

- Assets accounting

- Human resources administration and payroll accounting

- Cost accounting and profitability analysis with order accounting

- Project management and control

The SAP R/3 IS-Aviation industry solution provides a client/server configuration to cover the same areas. It includes the following enhancements:

- Spec2000 communication standard applied to real-time logistics modules

- Serialized parts management

- Manufacturer part number management

SAP R/3 Automotive Industry

It is in this sector that the Customer-Driven Supply Chain has received a great deal of emphasis. The products are constantly under development and there are many variants. Surplus production of an out-of-fashion variant can be very costly.

The following are elements in the SAP Automotive Industry Solution:

- Product features and options can be easily configured and ordered over various communication channels such as the Internet

- Release accounting inbound and outbound with complete EDI, Electronic Data Interchange, to enable JIT, Just In Time, scheduling

- Retrobilling, evaluated receipt settlement, can be used to provide paperless invoicing or third-party consignee functions

- Electronic KANBAN Engineering change management can be accomplished through direct CAD and PDM, Production Document Management

- Integration warranty, service management functions, and equipment maintenance control are standard

In addition, there is complementary software for the automotive industry. The interfaces for CAD, Computer Aided Design, and PDM, Product Data Management, facilitate the integration of R/3 with specialized and legacy data systems where the required SAP certification has been effected.

SAP R/3 Banking

The banking industry is passing through a period of change because customers are prepared to change banks. National boundaries are disappearing to allow cross-border business, but not without introducing another set of regulatory requirements. There are more products and lines of business, and management needs more precise information.

The IS-B Industry Solution for Banks is suitable for various types of financial institutions. It can also be used by companies in commerce and industry. There are additional applications for industries, like insurance, for example, that have special relationships between financial assets such as securities, loans, and real estate. Provisions have been made for complex relationships with other financial institutions.

IS-B is fully compatible with existing R/2 and R/3 installations and all the R/2 and R/3 product ranges.

The following facilities are provided through IS-B, which are in addition to the standard functions of the FI-Financial Accounting and CO-Controlling modules:

- Profitability analysis

- Single transaction costing

- Single security position costing

- Risk analysis by assessment of the risks specific to the banking sector, such as interest rate, currency, stock price, and precious metal prices

- Specific bank reporting functions that may be interfaced to country-specific products

- Premium and benefit payment management for insurance companies and a software package specifically aimed at mortgage banks

For the banking industry, there are SAP R/3 applications for integrated bank controlling and risk management. A global data-pool can be used to create a data warehouse for external regulatory reporting integrated into the R/3 System.

SAP R/3 High-Tech and Electronics

Decreased time-to-market and increased manufacturing productivity have to be reconciled in high technology industries where products become obsolete rapidly. Fewer people have to achieve more. In particular, each person may have to manage the entire business process for the order in hand rather than have it pass from department to department. To do this the relevant information has to be accessed without delay. The technology to do this has to be seen as an asset rather than an expense.

Integrating purchasing, inventory management, sales, and distribution is configured to implement ETO, Engineer to Order, and CTO, Configure to Order, from the sales order stage using ATP, Available to Promise, information on the components. Extremely flexible production facilities can be engineered to support MTO, Make To Order, discrete and repetitive manufacturing along with JIT, Just in Time, and KANBAN reordering logic.

ECM, Engineering Change Management, can be accomplished through direct CAD and PDM, Product Document Management, integration. Coherent quality management across the supply chain is essential to ensure consistent product, service, and process standards.

Customer loyalty may depend on the quality of after-sales service. The SAP Service Management component is available for integrated product support.

SAP R/3 Real Estate

The data objects controlled by this industry solution are real estate, buildings, rental units, and rooms. The target user is a manager of a large property portfolio who manages contractors and tenants. The system is sensitive to the due dates for payments and receipts by virtue of its links with the CO-Controlling module. It also performs the functions of project management for property maintenance in which it may be integrated with components of the PM-Plant Maintenance application. Earlier releases of the real estate software appeared with the code IS-IS.

Developments in the industry include the setting up of premises for specific purposes for a limited period, but with a wide variety of furniture and plant to be managed along with the property.

SAP R/3 Chemical

At the center of this industry solution are the standard SAP R/3 modules to support process manufacturing, quality management, process costing, and batch/lot management. The first customer of SAP was a chemical company and there are over 600 chemical installations worldwide. There is a long-established Chemical Industry Center of Expertise. Customer expectations are high, not only with respect to price and delivery, but also concerning the control of potentially dangerous substances. There are many competing products for each niche and the time-to-market of a new product may well be crucial. Flexible workflow control can adapt the processing to meet requirements and conditions, if necessary, through remote links directed by the Internet.

SAP R/3 Consumer Products

The concept of this industry solution is based on global brand management by integrating control over the extended supply chain from forecasting, via procurement and production, through to delivery to retailers. Brand promotion and marketing or pricing life cycle management are treated to the proven SAP expertise in the production processes to encourage faster product innovation and improved time-to-market. The SAP Business Workflow and R/3 Project System are applied to coordinate product and packaging development activities.

Comprehensive sales and marketing tools are combined with efficient consumer response mechanisms to enable a faster exchange of point-of-sale data between production and retailers. The outcome is real-time information on consumption and consumer preferences.

Standard cost accounting capabilities allow enterprise-wide product and customer profitability analysis, and the integration of R/3 with LIMS, Laboratory Information Management Systems, provides the link between the laboratory and business supply chain processes.

SAP R/3 Education

The SAP R/3 HR-Human Resources application includes modules to manage the selection and booking of students on courses. Several third-party DMS, Document Management Systems, have received SAP certification because they can be seamlessly integrated with R/3 and its applications. And a document can be any unit of text, sound, vision, animation, video, or any product of computer assisted design.

It is expected that further assistance with the design and structure of tuition sequences will be available as the SAP development teams address the process of education with the concepts elaborated in physical manufacturing.

SAP R/3 Healthcare

It is apparent that the healthcare industry is faced with legal requirements, increasing competition, and cost pressures. These factors combine with a demand from the patients for better services, less waiting, and treatment which is as rapid and painless as possible. All activities are increasingly scrutinized because the public is interested. Private and public funds are always less than the requirement and so cost management at all levels of the organization is essential. Financial and asset accounting has to be efficient and provide an up-to-the-minute picture of a hospital's status.

The disciplines of production planning and control in which SAP is so well practiced are clearly relevant. Materials management for efficient purchasing, inventory control, consumption analyses, and preventive maintenance are some of the obvious parallels. Human resource management has to be of the highest priority.

In addition, there is complementary software for the healthcare industry. The R/3 business applications can by extended by integration with clinical subsystems for laboratory, radiology, or surgery scheduling.

IS-H SAP Industry Solution for Hospitals

This SAP Industry Solution has been developed in the context of the type of hospital environment where a nonprofit organization is required by law to carry out modern cost accounting and controlling. At the same time there is a recognition of the benefits of bringing online such supporting facilities as laboratories, patient communications, and staff administration.

The IS-H Hospital Administration application comprises the following components:

- IS-HPM Patient Management
- IS-HPA Patient Accounting
- IS-HCM Communications
- IS-HCO Hospital Controlling

The IS-H Hospital Administration application may be installed as a hospital information system. It will normally be integrated in stages with the following R/3 modules:

- TR-AM Asset Management
- FI-Financial Accounting
- MM-Materials Management
- CO-Controlling

IS-H and SAP R/3 Integration Benefits

The benefits of an integrated combination of standard R/3 applications and the specialized IS-H components are seen by hospital authorities in contrast to the separate stand-alone systems (that have been installed previously). Of particular value is the precise support of professional patient management in the context of strict legal requirements for cost control. The standard R/3 system of access authorizations is important in the hospital environment.

The wide variety of medical databases and technical instrumentation components can be accessed through the R/3 standard interfaces, and the SAPGUI can be used to communicate with medical and administrative staff.

Individual reporting programs can be developed from the models provided in IS-H, and new technical systems can be accommodated by developing ABAP/4 interface programs where necessary. The extension of medical databases and communications between hospitals are considered prime requirements for future developments.

SAP R/3 Metal

The SAP Industry Center of Expertise for the metal industry has been at the heart of research to determine the special software requirements of the aluminum and steel industry, both on the production side in the metal trades. Developments are expected in applications of constraint-based planning technology.

Industry-specific templates have been configured to customize the SAP R/3 standard business modules to be ready to run in the metal industry. The material management functions allow the user company to store data on the particular sizes and shapes, for example, that are in use. The metal industry has many common standards and these can be set up as master records before the system is installed. Similarly, the operations of selecting and handling metal items are common throughout the industry. The configuration template can thus include both material data and many of the operations and tasks that will be required.

SAP R/3 Construction

The construction sector is characterized by shifting production sites and joint undertakings in which several building contractors work together on a project. It is common to order design services, materials, and equipment from internal departments as if they were outside companies. Subcontracting and complex payroll and human resources management are common in construction companies. There are complex warranties, suretyships, security deposits of varying duration, and advance and partial payments. There may be legal constraints on joint ventures that require special documentation.

SAP R/3 Release 3.0 is designed for distributed installation in geographically separate units such as branch offices and subsidiaries. New functionality has been added as ABAP/4 enhancements to carry the specific procedures and terminology of the industry. Equipment control and maintenance at distant sites have received special emphasis.

The R/3 Project System has been customized for the construction industry. Project-based information views are provided. Settlement of all incurred costs and activities and periodic analysis by construction site are examples of project evaluation procedures. Allowance can be made for partial inspections, impending losses, and stock corrections. There is a comprehensive cross-application reporting system for construction companies.

These business applications also form part of a complete enterprise solution for the construction industry available from HOCHTIEF Software GmbH under the brand name of ARISTOTELES.

SAP R/3 Oil

The needs of the oil and gas industry are focused on exploration, transportation, and distribution. It is global and becoming deregulated; eastern markets are opening. But new competitors have appeared, such as the superstore outlets in UK and France. Differentiation is necessary, and the industry must react in different ways to specific markets. The SAP R/3 Industry Solution for the oil and gas industry links the entire value chain from crude supply to commercial and retail customers.

IS-Oil Features

Some of the features of IS-Oil are the following:

- A comprehensive accounting system capable of handling multiple ledgers—legal and regulatory—as well as accounts payable, accounts receivable, sales and expense processing

- Association of cost drivers with business processes which allows decisions based on the most up-to-date operational cost data without having to retrieve information from other systems

- Human Resources System enables control of labor costs and skills availability

- Integration with Plant Maintenance yields accurate labor costs for internal and external workers

- Critical EDI transactions are supported

- SAP Business Workflow allows automation of business processes

The oil and gas industry solution combines the core R/3 system with two industry-specific modules:

- IS-Oil Upstream—The Upstream module was developed specifically for joint venture accounting. It integrates the complex accounting requirements of joint venture accounting while reducing staff overhead and data redundancy.

- IS-Oil Downstream—This module offers an open, scalable, integrated solution that enables oil companies to support the majority of their information processing requirements with one integrated package that provides numerous functions unique to oil and gas marketing and refining.

Exchanges. Exchange transactions are monitored to yield real-time exchange balance information. This component deals with complex fees and differentials.

Order Fulfillment. Streamlining the order process is effected by automating selection of supply location and allowing changes of product volume and temperature throughout the delivery. All types of packages and containers are managed.

Bulk Distribution Requirement Planning. This feature uses data within SAP to automate the entire order process. The system also handles complex international taxation, pricing, and exchange rate issues.

Hydrocarbon Inventory Management. This component amends existing core SAP inventory functionality in order to meet the standards of ASTM, American Society for Testing Material, and API, American Petroleum Institute, with respect to temperature correction, density, and specific gravity calculations. These convert ambient volumes, temperatures, and product densities to standard volumes and weights corrected for temperature so that they can be used in calculations for material movements and measurements.

Retail. This component of IS-Oil provides a comprehensive picture at the service station level by consolidating data from numerous sources into a single, virtual database. This facilitates a variety of functions from distribution planning through profitability analysis.

SAP R/3 Pharmaceuticals

The specialized modules of SAP R/3 are ideally suited to the pharmaceutical industry with its emphasis on tight control over documentation and quality through a wide range of production and distribution processes.

A pharmaceutical customer can place an order against up-to-date inventory and production planning data while retaining close control over the detailed specification. Production will take place exclusively by approved processes under supervision of the production planner and to controlled recipes. Certificates of analysis will be generated and checked against production data and customer specification. Real-time profit analysis will be available.

SAP R/3 Public Sector

Budget administration and fiscal accounting are the themes of this SAP industry solution, which can be fully integrated with other R/3 system applications. It has been developed as an enhancement of the TR-FM Treasury Funds Management component to suit the needs of public sector administration and non-profit organizations. The components provide an efficient workflow-supported facility, which enables you to distribute a budget across the various authorization levels. IS-PS meets requirements for complete accountability to governing bodies and legal authorities who may wish to scrutinize the conduct of business from several different points of view which may not be easy to anticipate. The flexible reporting methods are seen as important in this connection.

SAP R/3 Public Sector manages administrative and budgeting processes commonly performed by agencies and organizations in national and state governments, universities, and non-profit organizations.

SAP R/3 Retail

The R/3 Retail solution includes the retail industry (IS-R) component and supports retailers' core business processes such as sourcing, planning, and tracking merchandise movement along the entire value chain. Over 200 new retail-specific business processes have been formed as templates or models from which a particular retail business can assemble an integrated system. The leading retail point-of-sale systems have received SAP certification.

Online Purchasing and Banking

Supermarket and superstore companies are competing to build customer-driven services that make the best use of information technology. SAP R/3 Retail is being extended to facilitate Internet connections for the purpose of goods and services purchasing, including the provision of banking.

Retail Management Functions

The standard management tasks are represented:

- Assortment Planning
- Price and Promotion Management
- Distribution
- Store Management

Continuous Flow Logistics

ECR, Efficient Consumer Response, represents the notion of linking consumer product companies with retailers and wholesalers to share data on store assortment, replenishment, promotions, and product introductions. Implementation of this concept depends on establishing effective communications for which the Internet may prove to be suitable.

SAP R/3 Transportation

Transportation occupies a special place in the supply chain of many industries and is well served by elements from the various applications. However, it is recognized that some parts of the industry have developed effective solutions to their particular problems. Shipment optimization and shipment tracking have been identified as specialized skills for which it is appropriate to call on the existing solutions via a suitable BAPI, Business Application Programming Interface. Shipment papers and shipment cost calculation also fall into this category.

Bulk transportation has already been addressed in SAP IS-Oil, so the relevant parts of this application have been built in to the transportation system.

The safety and regulatory constraints on the transport of dangerous goods demand the use of specialized equipment and service agencies that have to be brought in to the planning and costing computations.

Future developments will include automatic intelligent planning of routes and handling facilities to enhance the value-added chain, together with the monitoring and control of all aspects of the quality of the transportation processes.

IS-T Telecom

The communications industry was once dominated by regional monopolies, but now there is intense competition. The scope of work can range from the construction of facilities for the company itself and its network, to providing repairs, upgrades, and modifications to the equipment owned by the telecoms customers. Pro-active control of costs is sought by integrating business processes and people. Integrated work management is needed to control the complete work order cycle from a customer request through resource scheduling, execution, and history analysis. Service and control of the installed base of customer equipment and warranties is integrated to comprehensive reporting capabilities to meet regulatory reporting requirements. The IS-T industry solution for the telecommunications industry can be pre-configured to include any of the SAP R/3 applications.

SAP Industry Solution for Utilities

IS-U is focused on the RIVA real-time customer information and billing system developed in the utility and service companies. The industry is characterized by a shift from monopolies in a regulated market to a competition-based energy and service industry. There are restrictions. Security of supply to the customer and the protection of the environment are recognized as onerous. Yet many of the legacy industrial enterprises are not able to meet these kinds of conditions without considerable business process re-engineering. In particular, the necessity is recognized to adapt quickly and efficiently to changing circumstances of whatever nature.

Once the concept of a business process has been applied to the various utilities, it becomes possible to build and operate a composite system that operates between business partners across several sectors.

Business Partner Categories

Some of the business partner categories are as follows:

- Residential
- Non-Residential
- Customer
- Prospect
- Owner
- Bill Recipient

- Installer
- Uninstaller
- Disposal Agent

Utilities Sectors

Some of the utilities sectors are as follows:

- Electricity
- Gas
- Water
- Waste Water
- District Heating
- Home Heating
- Waste Disposal
- Cable TV
- Telephone
- Service Order
- Service Contract
- Goods
- Charges
- Taxes
- Fees and Licenses

From Here...

This chapter has noted the existence of a number of SAP products that are enhancements of the R/3 system. These industry solutions have taken the customizing process a long way towards meeting the requirements of a particular sector of industry. Additional functionality may be included to improve the integration of standard R/3 components with industry-specific components.

- Does SAP plan on adding more industry solutions in the near future?

  Yes. IS-P Publishing is about to be released and a variety of new industry solutions are to be expected in business sectors where there is a trend to distribute tasks by outsourcing and where the lean management philosophy is seeking ways of moving decision making down the organizational structure.

- Are the industry solutions restricted forms of the R/3 system?

  No. They are extensions and enhancements that add features that their target users find beneficial without abandoning any of the benefits of the standard business functions of the R/3 system.

- How do they know what extra functions to include?

  They study the user communities through the Industry Center of Expertise and refer to the R/3 Reference Model discussed in Chapter 5, "The R/3 Reference Model," under the guidance of the R/3 Analyzer discussed in Chapter 6, "Tool-Supported Optimization with the R/3 Analyzer."

- How are SAP industry solutions developed?

  On the ABAP/4 Development Workbench described in Chapter 28, "ABAP/4 Program Development with the R/3 Workbench."

Part VIII

Maintaining and Enhancing the Implementation

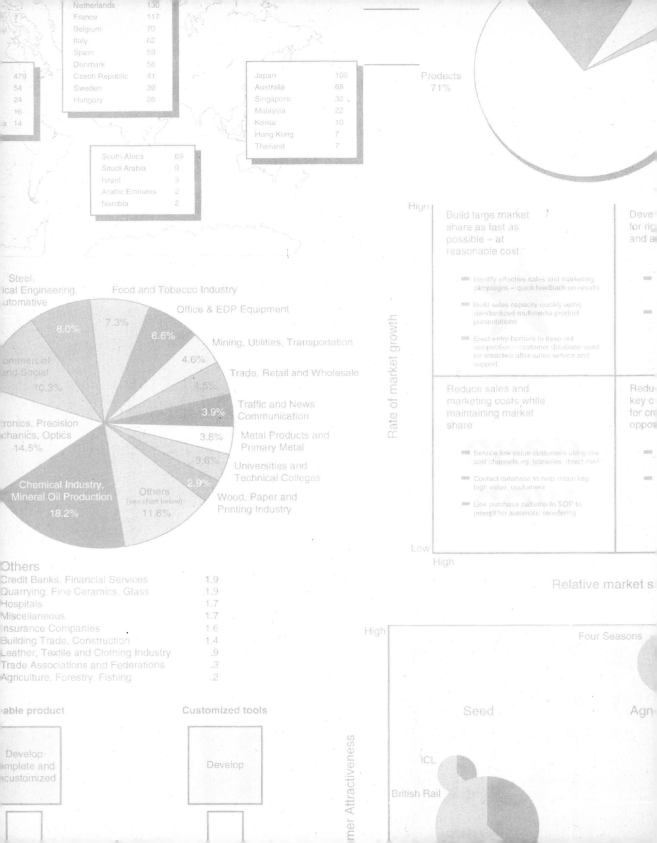

Netherlands	130
France	117
Belgium	70
Italy	62
Spain	59
Denmark	56
Czech Republic	41
Sweden	39
Hungary	26

| 479 |
| 54 |
| 24 |
| 16 |
| a 14 |

Japan	100
Australia	68
Singapore	32
Malaysia	22
Korea	10
Hong Kong	7
Thailand	7

South Africa	69
Saudi Arabia	9
Israel	3
Arabic Emirates	2
Namibia	2

Products
71%

Steel,
ical Engineering,
utomative

Food and Tobacco Industry

Office & EDP Equipment

7.3%

8.0%

6.6%

ommercial
and Social
10.3%

4.6%

Mining, Utilities, Transportation

1.5%

Trade, Retail and Wholesale

3.9%

Traffic and News
Communication

ronics, Precision
chanics, Optics
14.5%

3.8%

Metal Products and
Primary Metal

3.6%

Universities and
Technical Colleges

Chemical Industry,
Mineral Oil Production
18.2%

Others
(see chart below)
11.6%

2.9%

Wood, Paper and
Printing Industry

Others

Credit Banks, Financial Services	1.9
Quarrying, Fine Ceramics, Glass	1.9
Hospitals	1.7
Miscellaneous	1.7
Insurance Companies	1.6
Building Trade, Construction	1.4
Leather, Textile and Clothing Industry	.9
Trade Associations and Federations	.3
Agriculture, Forestry, Fishing	.2

able product

Develop-
mplete and
ncustomized

Customized tools

Develop

Rate of market growth

High

Build large market
share as fast as
possible – at
reasonable cost

- Identify effective sales and marketing
  campaigns – quick feedback on results
- Build sales capacity quickly using
  standardized multimedia product
  presentations
- Erect entry barriers to keep out
  competition – customer database used
  for attractive after-sales service and
  support

Deve
for rig
and a

Reduce sales and
marketing costs while
maintaining market
share

- Service low value customers using low
  cost channels eg. telesales, direct mail
- Contact database to help retain key,
  high value, customers
- Link purchase patterns to SOP to
  prompt for automatic reordering

Redu
key c
for cre
oppo

Low

High

Relative market s

mer Attractiveness

High

Four Seasons

Seed

Agr

ICL

British Rail

Chapter 25

Understanding SAP R/3 Accelerated Implementation Methods

Before a computer installation is delivered, Hewlett-Packard can load, configure, and test an SAP R/3 solution in HP-UX and Microsoft Windows NT environments, or in the HPO-UX(I) mixed environment. This service minimizes on-site time and disruption to normal business and promotes higher uniform standards across processes and vendor technologies.

Integrating R/3 with Existing Business Systems

Although SAP R/3 is a global enterprise system of great versatility and scope, it can take a great deal of time and expensive effort to install and configure. One of the ways of accelerating implementation is to make use of your existing systems and look at systems available from third parties. Some implementation examples follow.

R/3 with HP OpenView OmniBack II

Problems can be centrally monitored and solved from a graphical control station. In addition, data can be restored to multiple disks simultaneously using HP9000 Unix system servers, Windows NT NetServer systems, and HP digital linear-tape libraries.

R/3 for IBM System 390 Mainframe with DB2

The IBM S/390 and OS/390 can support SAP R/3 in the role of DB2 database server. Because System 390 is scalable, many more users can access the database. This is seen as a way of allowing both R/2 and R/3 users to make use of their existing data and production systems in an R/3 enterprise management environment.

In this chapter, you learn:

- How you can implement a complex system quickly.

- How you can integrate SAP R/3 with your existing systems.

- How you can rapidly migrate your data and your business process software from an R/2 mainframe system.

- How you can add to and reconfigure your SAP R/3 system without disrupting business.

R/3 on IBM Advanced System 400

The availability of R/3 on AS/400 systems is seen as important for the mid-sized companies. For example, wholesalers, distribution specialists, and publishers may well find the AS/400 hosting R/3 an attractive configuration, enabling them to integrate the sophisticated R/3 modules with their existing databases and specialized business processes.

MVS Mainframe Version of R/3

There exist very large databases, particularly in the banking and insurance business, which are held on secure mainframes. The MVS mainframe version of SAP R/3 allows the user to run the application portion of R/3 on a UNIX or Windows NT server and access the MVS mainframe where the secure data is held.

Rapid Migration from R/2 to R/3

Versions of a SAP R/2 to R/3 migration package are available with R/2 Releases 4.3, 5.0, and 6.0. These packages are designed to be simple to operate. It is recognized that the migration of data objects has to be reliable and thorough because of the high value of this information to the company. The disciplines of change management are applied so that there is a complete record of what came from where. The newly placed data can then be properly interpreted.

The migration package includes program generators to build customer-specific export and import programs. Archives that must remain available (for legal reasons) in an acceptable alternative form are not migrated. A method for copying data that has been archived in R/2 directly to an R/3 archive has nevertheless been developed. The migration package first processes the data to be migrated with the generated program logic, interprets the field assignments, and then writes the data to the R/3 System database.

Migration objects like material master records, accounting documents, and purchase orders have the physical structure of one or more chains of ABAP/4 data statements that specify field headers. These field headers, as well as all export and import programs, are generated individually in the customer system. This procedure enables a customer's modifications to the record layout (such as added fields, changed field lengths, and changed field types) to be taken into account during migration.

This technique allows substantial time savings to be achieved in comparison with standard R/3 batch input. A data transfer rate of at least 2M/sec is necessary for transfer to a nearby installation. If not, the recommended method for data transport is via 3480/3490 cassettes using the SCSI port. This step includes decompression of the dataset and the necessary code conversion from EBCDIC to ASCII.

The Migration Enterprise IMG

A procedure model guides the customer through all the phases of migration, from the conceptual phase through to productive operation of the R/3 System. It is not expected that external help should be necessary.

The IMG, Implementation Management Guide, for the migration enterprise is presented in HTML, Hypertext Markup Language. It offers the same structure for all migration objects, which are displayed with the ticked icon to be processed in the prescribed order. Double-clicking any icon reveals extra text and help. There is a display of migration sequence reminders and facilities for cross-application migration customizing so that the finished system has a uniform appearance and functionality.

A migration environment is available as a CD-ROM with a comprehensive installation guide for R/2 customers.

Integrating R/2 and R/3 Without Migration

By the year 2000, there will be about 1,000 productive R/2 installations, many of them very large. Releases 4.3 and 4.4 of R/2 will continue to be supported by the SAP Hotline, although they were not maintained after 1996. SAP will continue to support R/2. For example, there is a body of accurate problem descriptions, which allow the OSS, Online Software Service, to access over 40,000 solution notes with fast processing for customer queries. SAP R/2 Release 6.0 includes a number of interface configurations to cooperate with R/3. The Internet components of SAP R/3 Releases 3.1 and 4.0 will be available to the large R/2 installations that have integrated with an R/3 system.

The SAP Business Framework

The Business Framework is designed to allow configurable software modules to collaborate via standard interfaces in an architecture that is open to components from SAP and third parties. Client companies may add elements incrementally. The Business Framework will allow SAP to deliver new capabilities, components, and technology to its customers on a continuous basis, independent of conventional upgrade release cycles.

Business Framework Building Blocks

Some of the business framework building blocks are as follows:

- HR—Human Resources is a multi-industry component with a dedicated database and independent release cycle. Customers will be able to quickly and easily deploy new HR functionality as it is released. The HR component is integrated into R/3 Release 4.0 where it includes workflow, and human resource management enhancements. There are new country-specific versions. Internet and intranet components are shipped with this release.

- PDM—Product Data Management is a component building block that combines its own engineering database with the workflow integration of the R/3 manufacturing and logistics modules.

- TM—Treasury Management is a Business Framework building block for managing financial transactions and portfolios. The integration of this treasury component will enable customers to streamline financial cash flows, liquidity, portfolio, and risk-management operations.

■ ATP—Available To Promise is an advanced global server for order processing and decision support. R/3 users with systems and sources distributed worldwide will be able to perform sophisticated product availability checks across corporate networks or the Internet.

Another Business Framework building block is a dedicated reporting server that yields high-performance, cross-corporate reporting and decision support. It can take data from active R/3 components as well as from SAP's distributed Open Information Warehouse component and third-party database servers through corporate intranets or the Internet.

Collaboration and Open Interfaces

Business components collaborate within the Business Framework through BAPIs. BAPIs provide a stable, standardized method for third-party applications and components to integrate into the Business Framework. These interfaces are being specified as part of SAP's initiative with customers, partners, Microsoft Corporation, and leading standards organizations.

Using Templates to Accelerate Configuration and Customizing

One of the records for a SAP R/3 implementation is at a newspaper. From start to productive running took 88 days. This rapid implementation was facilitated by using an industry-specific template that preconfigured and customized R/3 so that the master data and the associated processing routines were exactly what was required in the newspaper industry. There were preconfigured newspaper business processes to accept copy from the reporters. Sales and Distribution modules were set up to handle advertising and distribution of printed papers to the various transportation facilities. The inquiry section was ready to receive telephone, e-mail, and fax inputs.

A template is able to specify how the whole system will work when the default settings are used. If the defaults are in fact very close to the finished requirement, it is possible to set up training schemes for the users. The users on the day the system is delivered will thus be able to handle routine business; and they will probably be able to take in their stride any changes that are made during the final customizing of the template to make it fit exactly the target company.

There are over 200 templates available for most of the main industry sectors, each of them as comprehensive as it is possible to be without knowing the details of a specific user enterprise.

Simulating R/3 with IntelliCorp Live Model

The Live Model software uses the R/3 Reference Model and the IMG, Implementation Management Guide, to simulate the execution behavior of a proposed R/3 implementation. This allows the system to be checked and configured before acquisition.

The simulation of an intended R/3 system may have an important function in building the confidence of the staff who will have to operate it and live with the consequences if anything should fail to work as intended. But a simulation can also provide benchmark information to show how the system will behave under high-load conditions. It may be wise to have a simulation of a mix of work that is not likely to occur, but which would have serious implications for the company if the system could not cope with it. The Internet has provided examples of service providers reducing their prices only to find their networks swamped with customers who then become disenchanted and leave, never to return.

Versions of R/3 for Particular Language Communities

If you are in a particular language community, then the availability of a version of SAP R/3 in your language could constitute a big advantage in terms of the speed with which you could effect an implementation.

For example, the core modules FI, CO, MM, SD, and PP were available in Finnish with SAP R/3 Release 3.0, and all modules except HR with Release 3.1. Some of the details have been localized for the Finnish market. This Finnish version will include:

- Outgoing and incoming payments
- Bank account number validation
- Intrastat reporting
- Finnish tax calculation procedure, tax codes
- Chart of depreciation
- Finnish calendar
- Chart of accounts

The development of SAP applications for specific language communities is expected to take a number of different directions. In some instances, the visual layout and symbol system of a language community will be related to the conventions of countries already using SAP applications. The standard business software can be translated or converted in such cases.

If the legal system of a target language community is unfamiliar to SAP designers, then a package of processing logic and reference data can be installed and configured by specialists in that culture.

But if the notion of symbolic transactions with a machine is not one with which the target community is comfortable, then a radical approach may be needed. The SAP research teams are looking at a variety of input and output devices which can be served by the Internet and which may be a route to the potential users who are not yet able to use the conventional terminals.

From Here...

This chapter has drawn attention to some of the ways in which a SAP R/3 system can be rapidly installed and configured without sacrificing any of its efficiency or effectiveness.

■ How can I persuade my management to look at SAP?

Chapter 24, "Understanding the Vertical Marketing Initiative," is where many of the SAP R/3 industry solutions are described. They are a very powerful way of introducing SAP R/3 into your industry.

■ How are the SAP programs written?

Chapter 28, "ABAP/4 Program Development with the R/3 Workbench," gives an account of the way most SAP programs are written and how you could have new software developed to empower your particular business processes.

■ Has the SAP organization tried to program the process of installing their programs?

Chapter 29, "The Business Engineer," presents the latest SAP approach to integrating all the implementation and development tools for the purpose of adjusting your business processes to gain the best advantage in a rapidly changing and complex environment.

■ Is there a great deal of organizing to do after the software is installed?

Chapter 30 "R/3 Business Workflow Management," describes a powerful method of accelerating, not the installation of the software, but the assembly of it ready to do the work of your enterprise.

Chapter 26

R/3 Online Documentation

If you require business information when you are online to the R/3 system, then you can access it via the DMS-Document Management System if this component has been installed and configured.

If you require information about your R/3 system itself, then you must refer to the R/3 documentation library, which is available in CD-ROM and may be read from any PC equipped with a CD-ROM drive. The documentation library is also available in book form.

As of Release 2.2, the R/3 documentation library can be accessed online using the Microsoft Windows Help system. This entails installing a CD-ROM on a network server, which will then provide context-sensitive access from R/3 transactions.

The intention of the SAP system designers is to make all relevant information, whether from transactions or from reference sources, easily accessible to the user. It is also their prime objective to make sure that the presentation of this information is focused as much as possible on the immediate needs of the user, and that it is offered in a format that will be directly meaningful in its layout.

The Document Management System (DMS)

The purpose of the DMS-Document Management System is to describe, manage, and display documents of all types, independently of the application from where they may have been generated or from which they are most frequently accessed.

The following types of documents are included:

Drawings

Graphics

In this chapter, you learn:

■ About the methods of accessing business information and R/3 system documentation.

■ The difference between a business document and "documentation."

■ How you find the document you need.

■ How the system helps you if you are not sure what you need.

Contracts

Patents

Business transaction documents

Document Linking

Documents may be linked to objects in other R/3 applications and retrieved from elsewhere. The online message system may be used to control them and manage workflow strategies. A document may be linked to one or more of the following kinds of data objects:

Another document

Materials

Pieces of equipment

Projects

Quotations

Sales orders

Customer master records

Vendor master records

For example, a drawing may be linked to material. This will automatically cause work scheduling and production control to be informed by the online message control system of any changes to that drawing, which can be viewed from production work centers.

Classification of Data Objects

The R/3 Classification System, which is central to the retrieval procedure of the DMS, comprises many functions designed to help you locate information held in records that can be retrieved in document form. You may search on the basis of subject matter and you may search for an item because you know it is linked with a data object such as:

Another document

Material identified by its material number or by its name, or part of its name

An item of equipment where you have given its name or only the identification of the activity where it is used

A project identified by its number, the person responsible, the purpose, and so on

A quotation

A sales order

A customer or a vendor identified by an attribute in the master records

Any document can be located and displayed by using the retrieval functions of the classification system or by searches based on document info records.

Document Info Records

Information about a document can be stored in a document info record, which may include a text in several different languages. It will also store the name and department of the person responsible for the document, the place of the document in the case of hierarchical documents, and the authorization group necessary to view the main document.

Additional details of the document may be inserted in the document info record by means of a wide range of functions that are part of the R/3 Classification System.

Document Change Control

You can establish your own sequence of status conditions to represent the life cycle of a document. The message control system can be tasked to inform certain users when the document changes status.

Document info records may be maintained from the R/3 CAD User Interface.

Changes to a document will be associated with change numbers, which allows them to be integrated with the engineering change management system and therefore with the production system.

Language Text Pools

Language Text Pools are used for screen layouts, online help and online documentation.

When the code in an ABAP/4 program requires a text element to be displayed on a screen, it specifies the number of the text element to be used. The code does not have to be changed in order to access another element if the language of the user is changed. The language in which the text element is presented is determined by the language selected by the user profile.

R/3 System Documentation

The R/3 documentation library is available on CD-ROM, which may be read from any PC equipped with a CD-ROM drive. The documentation library is also available in book form.

As of Release 2.2, the R/3 documentation library can be accessed online using the Microsoft Windows Help system, which will provide context-sensitive access from R/3 transactions.

Context-Sensitive Help

The help system requires the R/3 documentation to be installed as a CD-ROM on a network server. The following options are available during transaction processing from the user interface:

- R/3 Extended Help, which automatically links you to the documentation relevant to the current active transaction

VII

Maintaining

- R/3 Library Manager, which allows you to browse the documentation by selecting graphical icons and hierarchical menus

- Search Dialog Box, which you can use to enter a key word before choosing a topic so that your search is focused

You can copy files from the R/3 Documentation CD-ROM to a hard disk drive for faster access subsequently, for instance, on a laptop computer.

Independent Documentation Servers. A separate Windows Help File is provided for each application. The R/3 online documentation can be arranged selectively on several documentation servers, which are independent of the application servers and which can be configured to provide the optimal response times for a group of users and to conserve system resources.

You may attain even faster retrieval by selectively copying files from the R/3 documentation library to individual machines.

R/3 Documentation from the OSS-Online Service System

If you encounter a problem that cannot be solved by reference to the online documentation, and if your installation is configured to interact with the OSS-Online Service System, then you may take advantage of the advisory services and receive system information directly relevant to your problem.

The OSS-Online Service System provides the follows facilities that are further discussed in Chapter 27, "Understanding the OSS-Online Service System":

- Orders for specific documentation

- An error notes database, which contains information about known problems and the methods for circumventing them

- HotNews, which gives notice of system developments

- HelpDesk, which provides personal advice including suggestions for pertinent documentation

Other Documentation

A wide range of documentation is available directly from SAP and through the online services. The following types of documentation exist:

- SAP consulting services

- Product guidelines

- Marketing information and brochures

- R/3 handbooks

- Upgrade and installation instructions
- Release information
- SAPVisual CD Presentations

Internet Information Sources

The SAP sites on the World Wide Web are at:

http://www.sap.com in Philadelphia

http://www.sap-ag.de in Walldorf

This site gives access to the promotional material freely available to the public and is directly comparable to the CD-ROM and document forms of this information.

From Here...

- Where can I find information on the R/3 Reference Model itself?

  See Chapter 5, "The R/3 Reference Model," for a complete description of the R/3 Reference Model.

- Where can I get help if I am not sure why I have a problem with the R/3?

  You can call on a HelpDesk and various other supporting services. See Chapter 27, "Understanding the OSS-Online Service System," and Chapter 11, "A Computing Center Management System."

VI

Maintaining

Chapter 27

Understanding the OSS-Online Service System

During implementation of the R/3 system, the OSS-Online Service System is used to solve problems found in a test system before they get to production. After the production system is "live," the usual purpose of the OSS is to solve an existing problem thought to be a bug in the software, for which there is a known SAP solution. If you do have any areas of uncertainty, the components of the OSS-Online Service System are available in your installation to help you identify the reason, and to see how to clear up the difficulty. There is also a remote connection to the OSS-Online Service System library of error notes organized so that you can search for a question that corresponds to your query. Further questions may be posed to you to clarify what it is you want to know. When the system is clear about this, it will offer some solution proposals. And as a fallback position, the OSS-Online Service System will facilitate a direct communication link to the SAP service team who will solve your problem.

The OSS-Online Service System also takes a proactive role by alerting the user to any changes in SAP product releases and in providing notices of selected training courses that are likely to be of relevance.

The full OSS-Online Service System can be installed at a client site in the form of the Customer Competence Center, which is designed to specialize in solving the SAP R/3 system problems of a particular company.

Features of the OSS-Online Service System

It is necessary to register individual employees as users of the OSS-Online Service System. Forms are provided with new installations, and an online registration function is predefined so that you can start the OSS directly from your SAP R/3 system.

This chapter will demonstrate the benefits of using the SAP R/3 OSS-Online Service System and shows you how to deal with the following:

VI

Maintaining

- Where to begin if there is a problem.

- Which levels of detail to use when seeking help from the OSS-Online Service System.

- How to know if there is a problem building up before the system stops working.

- If you cannot fix the problem alone, what to do until help arrives.

- The differences between a good troubleshooter and a poor one.

The system operates by processing problem messages entered by the user. By interacting with the user, the OSS determines the nature of the query or other type of message.

Before submitting a problem message, the user searches the error-notes database to see whether the topic has previously been encountered.

The error-notes database can be searched according to any combination of the following characteristics:

- Hardware specification
- Operating system
- Database
- R/3 release number

This search, even if not directly fruitful, may suggest how the problem situation may be presented as a message to the OSS. Problem messages may be indexed so as to optimize the search procedure.

The OSS looks through your logged problem messages and automatically sends you the error-note solutions which might be relevant because of the key words which have been recognized. From this set of notes, you may further select according to any combination of the following characteristics:

- Language of the notes
- SAP release
- Topic
- Application
- Error-note number
- Last change date
- Words or phrases appearing in the text strings of the error notes

If you want to be kept up-to-date on a particular topic, you may set up a periodic error-note search over a specified time span using the same search specification.

If the user logs a message that is not a problem but a request for some other type of inter-action with the OSS, there will be an appropriate exchange of information and perhaps some follow-up action, such as the booking of a training course place.

Problem Messages

The following sequence of activities is typical of a problem-solving interaction between a customer and the OSS:

1. Customer creates a problem message in the OSS.

2. Customer logs the message in the OSS.

3. The OSS automatically indexes the problem message and identifies the keywords in it.

4. The OSS assigns one or more specific category types to each keyword that it has recognized.

5. The customer can see the colored highlights on the keywords to which the OSS will respond, and can revise the message if necessary.

6. The OSS searches the error notes database for any notes that are relevant to each of the keywords in the problem message.

7. The customer calls up a display of the error notes that have been found and classified by the system.

If there are any elements of the problem which have not been solved by the system administrator using the selected error notes, then the customer sends a message directly to the SAP R/3 First Level Customer Service.

Creating a Problem Message. When you log in to the OSS, the following details will be automatically copied into the problem message document header as soon as you have entered your user ID:

- Name of the reporting employee

- Customer installation hardware type and operating system release number

- Customer database type and release number

- SAP R/3 release number installed, for example, R/3 2.2, R/3 3.0, R/3 3.0A, R/3 3.0B

- System status at the time of the logon

A customer data verification function is available to help you to keep this information up-to-date.

The problem message content has to be formed by entering or selecting data elements for the following problem message fields:

- SAP R/3 application (App.), such as MM, HR, FI, PP, SD

- Problem priority (Prio), such as High, Normal

- A description of the problem in free text, using the standard keywords if they are known, and with a system-generated problem number and the default language code

- Short text (STxt), which will be a standard system text such as an error identification code reported by your system

VI

Maintaining

Classifying a Problem Message. When your problem message has been entered and validated, a pop-up menu will invite you to classify it by selecting one of the following message types:

- Error message
- Application consulting
- Technical consulting
- HelpDesk query
- Message for your SAP R/3 consultant or SAP partner
- Message for a SAP employee worldwide who will use the "Reply" function

Automatic Indexing. The system uses its internal indexing function to identify and color-code the keywords by category type if it recognizes any in your message. You will obviously get a better response from the system if you make sure that your message refers to the appropriate keywords, insofar as you can determine what they should be for your problem. The colors will appear on your message as soon as you save it, so you can ensure that it contains a useful range of keywords, used with precision, before you transmit it for processing.

Keyword Category Types. The following category types are used to color-code the keywords in your problem message:

- Object names, such as SAP transaction codes, program names, table names
- System message codes, for example ORA1547, SO999, ERROR 1155
- System-specific terminology, such as tablespace, GUI, administrator, menu

Problem Message Processing

The error notes selected by the system as being possibly relevant to your problem can be viewed by selecting the problem message again. The system allows you to filter out error notes not relevant to your situation, so you can quickly arrive at the best information that can be assembled automatically.

The OSS allows you to download the error notes so that you can print them and direct them electronically to other users.

If the error notes presented on your problem message document are not applicable to your problem, you can submit the document for the attention of the First Level Customer Service. If the staff there cannot find the answer, the SAP development team will continue to work with you until a satisfactory solution has been found.

Problem Message Status. Each time you log in to the OSS, you will see a status display which will show you what has happened to all your problem messages.

The left side of the problem message status screen shows how many messages are in each status at your company and the dates of the most recent status changes:

> **Entered**—shows the number of messages not yet processed

> **For your action**—indicates how many messages are awaiting further data from you or are waiting for you to do something requested by SAP

> **For confirmation**—indicates how many problem messages have been returned from SAP with a set of error notes for you to accept and confirm to complete the problem, or resubmit to First Level Customer Service for additional work

> **Completed**—shows how many problem messages have been returned to your company and confirmed by you as satisfactory solutions to your problem

The right side of the problem message status screen shows how many messages are in each status at SAP and the date of the most recent status change:

> **Received**—indicates how many problem messages have been received by the SAP First Level Customer Service but have not been processed

> **In process**—shows how many problem messages are being processed currently

> **Completed**—shows how many problem messages have been processed to the stage of submitting error notes but have not been confirmed by you as having reached a satisfactory state of resolution by your having solved the problem or passed it to the First Level Customer Service

A Database of Error Notes

The error notes in the database are written by SAP staff as detailed solutions to the problems posed by customers through the OSS and the First Level Customer Service.

Error Note Content. The typical error note will include the following information:

> Problem symptoms to which this note is relevant

> A short description of the cause of the problem

> Detailed information on how to solve the problem

> Corrections to your system that can be made in advance to forestall a problem or the recurrence of your current problem. These may take the form of a set of patch updates that will correct the system bugs concerned in the problem.

The error note will also specify the system platform information needed to identify the configurations to which the error note is applicable. For example:

> SAP R/3 release number

> Applications affected

Operating system

Database

Graphical user interface front ends used

Searching for Specific Error Notes. In addition to the selection of error notes that will be made for you by the staff of the OSS, you can also search for specific error notes on the basis of any of the following search criteria, used in any logical combination of AND and OR:

Language

SAP R/3 release number

Topic or keyword

Application

Error-note number

Last change date

Error-note text strings

Regular Searches for Error Notes. When you have defined a search specification to find the error notes that are likely to be relevant to your particular situation, you can store the profile and have the search carried out on a daily, weekly, or monthly basis over a specified period.

The Error Note Status Overview Display

When you log in to the OSS, you will be shown the Error Note Status Overview Display in which the error notes are displayed under one of two headings:

Notes assigned to you

New information from SAP

A display of the number of notes and date of the most recent change is divided into the following fields:

Notes assigned to you—shows the number of Previous Notes and the number of New Version notes

New info from SAP—divided into HotNews, Release Planning, and Installation and Upgrade

Previous Notes. This part of the problem message overview shows the total number of error notes that have been assigned to you in response to all your previous problem messages.

New Versions. If any of the Previous Notes has been updated since it was first sent to you, it will be counted in the New Versions field, so that you will be alerted to the fact that some of the information you may have applied to the solution of your problem may now be out of date and perhaps overtaken by better information.

HotNews. The latest high-priority information concerning the SAP R/3 system and its error alarm messages will be promulgated in HotNews messages, so that you can prevent problems. These messages are not necessarily relevant to the problems you have previously reported through your problem messages.

The number of HotNews messages will be shown in the New info from SAP section of the display.

Release Planning. Messages in this category will be counted and displayed in the New information from SAP section. They concern new developments in certain operating systems and database environments and the dates when the updated versions will be released.

Installation and Upgrade. If there have been any messages concerning the installation or upgrading of your SAP R/3 system, they will be counted in this section of the display. It is important to read them before upgrading your SAP R/3 system.

HotNews

The characteristic of HotNews is that it is received directly through the OSS. The main category of HotNews is Alarm Alerts, which comprise error descriptions and their solutions which have to be implemented to avoid serious problems with your SAP R/3 system.

Training courses and company-specific events such as the start-up of a production plant under SAP R/3 will be topics to be promulgated via HotNews messages.

When you have signified that you have read a HotNews message, a confirmation is sent automatically to SAP. If the message requires some action on your part, it will generate the appropriate checklists, which will be transmitted back to SAP to confirm that you have seen the information about what you should do.

The following categories of HotNews are under development:

- Special interest topics—will include changes in release strategy and scheduling

- News and recommendations—will suggest ways of improving your SAP R/3 system

SAP R/3 HelpDesk

The OSS will convey a direct message to the SAP R/3 HelpDesk if you have not been able to get the information you require through the problem message procedure or by directly accessing error notes.

VI

Maintaining

When you call or fax a SAP HelpDesk, the staff there enters your problem into the OSS. If the local HelpDesk is not immediately available, your inquiry is passed on to the appropriate contact person in one of the SAP worldwide service centers. You can still use the OSS to monitor how your inquiry is progressing.

SAP Remote Services

The main elements of the SAP remote services are as follows:

> SAP OSS-Online Service System
>
> Customer Competence Center with own OSS updated from the SAP OSS
>
> Local SAP HelpDesk
>
> SAP R/3 HelpDesk
>
> EarlyWatch
>
> Remote Consulting
>
> The HotNews and Upgrade Services
>
> SAP Error Notes database

Technical Requirements of the SAP Remote Services

You must have a network connection to your nearest SAP Service Center, which will establish your official IP network address to allow your system to be accessed worldwide, if necessary.

You will need the SAPGUI Graphical User Interface software, version 2.1J or higher.

Network Connections. A suitable network connection can be established over one of the following links in coordination with your SAP Service Center:

> **X.25**—a system available worldwide through the local telephone companies or via private network providers. It may be wise to refuse it permission to initiate incoming connections so that you have control over access.
>
> **ISDN**—currently being tested and is gaining in acceptance. A gateway is required to enable the connection between the ISDN network and the provider network.
>
> **Frame Relay**—a system of connections offered by telephone companies such as AT&T, MCI, Sprint, WilTel, BT, VIAQ, INTERCOM, Deutsche Telekom, and Info AG.

IP Address. Your company must have at least one unique IP address in order to connect to SAP if you are using the SAProuter software. If you are not using this software, your entire network must have a unique IP address to avoid collisions with other networks.

Data Protection

Any network with an outside line is vulnerable to security breaches. The recommended security measures include the following:

Configure the remote connection so that it cannot be opened by incoming connection requests.

Use routers that can be configured to allow access only to certain business partners and SAP partners.

Use passwords to protect accounts on computers accessible from the outside.

Use access lists to limit the traffic over routers to certain specified software programs.

Install the SAProuter software.

The SAProuter Software. The purpose of the SAProuter Software is to form a "firewall" security stage intermediate between the SAP Gateway and the network, such as Frame Relay, X.25, or ISDN. It imposes a password check to allow access to the network IP addresses. The same system is used again between the network and the customer SAP R/3 system.

The movement of all messages is under the control of route transmission tables and SAP passwords, giving the system administrator an additional means of control over the access allowed to sensitive data or restricted systems.

Only the IP address of your computer is known to the SAProuter, and your network knows only the IP address of the SAP system using the SAProuter. This ensures that unauthorized access is not possible from one network to another.

Using the SAP EarlyWatch System

The purpose of the EarlyWatch system is to provide a proactive method of monitoring customer SAP R/3 systems by conducting regular analyses. Teams of experts at SAP carry out remote diagnosis of customer SAP R/3 installations worldwide.

Scope of Remote Diagnosis

The following elements can fall within the scope of EarlyWatch remote diagnosis:

Network components

Operating system

Database

SAP applications and configurations

Monitoring Technique. The operation of the SAP R/3 system is monitored by evaluating statistical data collected by the individual system components. For example, the current status of the system and its resource utilization are available to EarlyWatch at all times and provide the basis for the regular performance and error analyses that are carried out by experts with a thorough knowledge of the platforms, databases, networks, and applications.

VII

Maintaining

EarlyWatch Support During Implementation

The expertise of the EarlyWatch specialists can best be put to productive use when you are installing a new system or adding a new module. These are the times of greatest change, and it is under these conditions that deep knowledge and experience can be applied to make sure the new configuration performs to its top specification right from the start. The benefits will be seen not only in the rapid improvements in your company's methods of doing business, but also in the reduction of stress on the staff over what is always a difficult period when they are not sure just how much of their previous know-how is going to be useful under the changed circumstances. In some cases, their ingrained habits will not be recognized as such until the new method of working demands that they change.

The teams of experts are available to assist in the planning of master data transfer prior to going live and will advise on the setting up of test runs for the new system. For example, the EarlyWatch team can carry out the following tasks:

Dimensioning the free space of the table spaces

Dimensioning SAP buffers

Transferring the master data

Transferring the transaction data

Monitoring the disk space requirements for live operating

Checking the free space of the table spaces

When the system is approaching live operation, the EarlyWatch team can provide planning support and execution assistance for system testing under near-productive conditions. They will monitor the tests and evaluate the results. It will be their judgment that governs the fine-tuning of the system components to give the best results. And they will advise and set in motion the data backup provisions.

When the system has commenced live operation, EarlyWatch experts will analyze the significant response times and carry out further component tuning, if necessary.

Reporting from the EarlyWatch Service

The focus of the EarlyWatch reporting methods is on the client/server load distribution and any bottlenecks that are foreseeable in the system components.

The findings of the reports are demonstrated using visual methods such as charts, tables, and diagrams, which are also used to give an overview of the effects of any changes recommended by the EarlyWatch team.

Where there are areas of doubt, the reports will describe the implications and suggest methods of collecting additional data, if necessary, and taking other steps to address the uncertainties and to make provisions to control the system should problems develop.

EarlyWatch and Data Security

The standard methods of providing data security when networks are connected will be used in the remote diagnosis operations of EarlyWatch.

Every operation performed by an EarlyWatch specialist can be monitored from the customer's system.

The Technical Requirements of EarlyWatch

The operation of the EarlyWatch system depends on a data link to one of the SAP service centers, where teams of specialists are located. The details of this technical requirement are the same as for the other SAP remote services described above.

An additional requirement for the provision of the EarlyWatch service is that your system must be equipped with a Computing Center Management System that provides the graphics monitors upon which the EarlyWatch system depends.

Remote Consulting

Specific customer problems are analyzed and remedial actions suggested as a result of EarlyWatch reports. If there is a case for developing new functionality to meet the needs of the customer, this is undertaken where appropriate.

If a customer has indicated through the OSS-Online Service System that a consultation with a SAP partner is required, the remote services can be used to establish the background to the request before a consultation takes place. Using any combination of communication media, including online monitoring of the customer's system, the consultation can proceed with all parties sharing the same data, namely, the customer's system and the reports of its performance prepared in advance or called up at the time.

Using the SAP R/3 Information Database

The purpose of the SAP R/3 Information Database is to provide you with the latest information about SAP R/3 products and releases. In particular, the database will carry the following types of data:

SAP R/3 development strategy and product planning

System development and delivery dates

Duration of the maintenance period of new releases

SAP R/3 services and certified SAP partners

Training course enrollment calendar

Available documents and publications in other media

Technical information concerning remote connections and network products

Searching the SAP R/3 Information Database Through OSS

The OSS-Online Service System supports searches over the SAP R/3 Information Database using any of the following types of criteria:

Key attributes, such as the release status of a specific application module

A particular date for new information

Keywords taken from the controlled index used on problem messages

If any of this information changes, the user is alerted upon logging in to the OSS when a key appears on the screen labeled "News on OSS." This key will appear only if the particular user has not already seen the new or changed messages.

Any of the information you receive from the OSS and the SAP R/3 Information Database can be downloaded to your own computer for later reference.

Development Requests Via the Online Service System

It has long been a tradition in the SAP organization that the users will be considered one of the most important contributor communities for the purpose of developing the product range. If you have a suggestion for improving or enhancing the SAP R/3 functionality, a developmental message sent through the OSS is a convenient way to make it known. You will have the advantage of being able to monitor its progress and see what becomes of it.

It is important to classify your message as a problem message if you discover that an existing function in an application does not work properly, and as a development request if you would like an existing function to be improved or a new one added.

Online Service System Alteration Service

The OSS-Online Service System Alteration Service is being developed to support you in reviewing and correcting, if necessary, the data held by SAP about your installation and your use of it.

Verification of Customer Data

The OSS Alteration Service will help you make changes to the list of contact staff who are in charge of your SAP R/3 system by offering you the existing data for editing and confirmation.

Support Prior to Going Live

If the OSS Alteration Service is aware of the dates when you are going to go live with your SAP R/3 system or any of its application modules, you will be able to take advantage of the additional services that are provided. These include intensive support before and just after the critical dates.

Training Course Planning and Registration

The planning, selection of content, and registration of SAP training courses are all supported by the OSS-Online Service System.

The following information systems are provided:

Overviews of selected courses

Assistance in choosing the right courses

Details of prices and dates

Enrollment information and joining instructions

General information about SAP training courses and their methods

Registration for Training Courses

The OSS will allow you to register online for a selected course. You will be able to retrieve an area hotel list and directions to the SAP Training Center.

You can review the information on all training courses for which employees in your organization have been registered, and you can select the format to show individual employees or time periods.

Detailed Information Resources

As part of the OSS-Online Service System, the following products can be ordered:

Service Guidelines, which are descriptions of the SAP R/3 services

Product Guidelines, which are marketing information and brochures

Documentation, which includes SAP R/3 handbooks, upgrade and installation instructions, and release information

Presentations, which include the SAPvisual CD-ROM programs

Registration for Other Services Through OSS

The registration procedure for the following SAP services can be effected through the OSS-Online Service System:

EarlyWatch sessions

Consulting sessions

Customer Data Verification Service

First Customer Shipment of prerelease versions of software

Summary of the Benefits

If you have installed and configured the full range of the OSS-Online Service System and the SAP Remote Services software and communication equipment, there is a comprehensive and powerful support system at your disposal. The characteristic feature of this complex of functions is that you can ask for as much or as little assistance as you require: an automatic fault-location service up to a consulting visit, with information provided selectively and automatically at every level.

The list of benefits for your specific company will depend on your circumstances. However, some of the following may be important:

Continuous problem processing worldwide

Immediate first-level customer service

Direct access to the error-notes database

Problem prevention

Review of the progress and history of a problem solution process

Access to SAP staff and SAP partners

Communication with other SAP R/3 users

Latest information on SAP R/3 products

The Customer Competence Center Product

It may be advantageous to install a Customer Competence Center at your main site to build up the knowledge that is specific to the type of business you conduct. Special SAP training for the staff of the center can be provided.

The OSS can be installed in your competence center and will automatically receive updates from the latest SAP R/3 system information maintained in the central SAP Online Service System.

From Here...

■ I should like to know more about data security.

See Chapter 33, "SAP Control and Security."

■ What types of SAP training courses are available?

See Chapter 35, "Training for SAP."

■ What is a SAP Partner?

See Chapter 40, "Employment Opportunities Working with SAP."

Chapter 28

ABAP/4 Program Development with the R/3 Workbench

The SAP software is written in ABAP/4, which is the SAP fourth-generation Advanced Business Programming Language. The ABAP/4 Development Workbench is a complete environment for creating business applications in this language to run in client/server installations.

This chapter describes the tools and methods available through the Workbench environment and discusses how it can be used to develop new business software that will integrate efficiently with the SAP R/3 system and its applications.

The Realm of the ABAP/4 Development Workbench

A wide range of tools can be used on the Workbench. The workpieces can be absolutely new software for which there is no existing SAP standard business program that can be Customized to suit your company. You can also work on copies of the existing components that you have decided to extend to meet your requirements.

In either case, the strict control disciplines exercised by the ABAP/4 Development Workbench will ensure that the resulting software will run immediately on all types of computer and all database systems supported by SAP. All supported graphical user interfaces will run the products of the Workbench without requiring any changes or modifications.

The developer working in the SAP R/3 environment does not have to be concerned with the complexities of client/server networking. Developed application modules can be run locally or on central host computers and can use any of the existing servers.

The Workbench

SAP software was, and is, designed exclusively using the ABAP/4 Development Workbench. It has a long pedigree and proven performance record.

In this chapter you learn:

- How new programs come online.
- Who uses this Workbench.
- About text already programmed that can be modified.
- About metadata.
- How complex programs are built.

VI

Maintaining

New concepts and products that come under SAP support are built into the support systems of the ABAP/4 Development Workbench as soon as they are released, so the application developer can be assured that the suggestions and advice offered by the Workbench are up-to-date with new technology, and that the detailed proposals will actually work when integrated with the existing SAP R/3 implementation.

Developmental Phases and Levels

Program development has to go through phases and cycles to prove that the software which is going to go live will indeed do what it was intended to do and not do anything which it should not. The ABAP/4 Development Workbench expects the program developer to need help and support throughout this process. It is also assumed that any developed application will itself undergo business development sooner or later. The Workbench is able to store its working materials for later consultation.

Any new system or component added to an existing implementation will have to communicate with the rest of the system and make use of all the hardware and software facilities in an efficient manner. The standard guidelines still apply, as follows:

- Data consistency must be achieved by maintaining it in a unique master record location.

- There should be no breaks in technological communication channels, and no manual copying or pickups if the system could have made an intelligent proposal for the user to confirm.

- Software components should be designed to be transported to new homes as the equipment manufacturers make better devices from which to assemble complex systems.

The application developer using the ABAP/4 Development Workbench will find all the support needed to work at any level of detail, as follows:

- Metadata for the development of applications

- Proposals and standards for interfacing with databases

- Standard interfaces for linking to any of the networks already established—for instance, to communicate with SAP R/2 systems and with database services provided for specific sectors of industry

- Procedures for detailed design of graphical user interfaces to suit both the requirements of the new application and the ergonomic needs of future users

Organization of the Workbench

The reader will not be surprised to find that the ABAP/4 Development Workbench is itself thoroughly organized in a manner consistent with the organization of other SAP R/3 products. Software objects under new construction or development from standard SAP R/3 components are recognized as development objects and are attributed to a data structure which is appropriate.

A version of a software component is maintained as a data object separate from its predecessor or reference model. Strict control is exercised to ensure that software under development does not get tangled with the software of the SAP R/3 system itself, on which the ABAP/4 Development Workbench tool is being presented.

The ABAP/4 Repository

All development objects being handled on the ABAP/4 Development Workbench are stored in the ABAP/4 Repository.

The following types of objects may be under development:

- Dictionary data
- ABAP/4 programs
- Dynpro dynamic programs
- Documentation
- Help texts

The ABAP/4 Data Dictionary is itself lodged in the ABAP/4 Repository.

The ABAP/4 Repository Information System

The contents of the ABAP/4 Repository can be studied and selected by a comprehensive facility to create object lists, menus, and multiple windows for viewing and evaluating the information and objects in the Repository. This helps the application developers and their managers maintain orientation during what can be a complex process.

Data Object Listing. The ABAP/4 Repository Information System can provide lists of data objects available from the Repository, such as the following:

- Programs
- Tables
- Fields
- Data elements
- Field domains

These lists can be selective and can be sorted using attributes of the data objects or, for example, by the date of last amendment, or by the name of the team responsible for amending them.

Investigating Relationships. The developmental programmer working with an existing system needs to know what exists already. It is essential to work out what is related to what.

The ABAP/4 Repository Information System can focus on a table and its fields and report where they are used in existing dynpros and ABAP/4 programs.

VI

Maintaining

There are also report programs to reveal the "foreign key" relationships between different tables.

Navigating the ABAP/4 Repository. In accord with the standard SAP "drill-down" facility, any Repository object selected from a display from the ABAP/4 Repository Information System can be investigated further by using the special function keys. Any semantically meaningful change of direction can be made.

For example, from a list of data elements the information system can be asked to derive a list of all the table fields in which these data elements appear. From this list of table fields, the system can create a list of the places where they are used in programs.

Software Tools
The maintenance of software during its development is supported by a full range of editing and debugging tools, so that the processes of testing and tuning can proceed with alacrity. These tools live in the ABAP/4 Repository.

Predefined Business Function Library
Most good ideas have already been thought of before, and this is no less true in software development. Very often, the best place to start from is not the beginning. The ABAP/4 Development Workbench offers a comprehensive repertoire of predefined standard business programs that are already fully operational and will integrate immediately with the rest of the SAP R/3 system.

The ABAP/4 Data Dictionary, Active and Integrated

When a function is required to execute as part of a program or a dynpro, the SAP R/3 runtime system checks the time and date stamp on the program object code and compares it with the time stamp on the corresponding parts of the Active Data Dictionary. If the Data Dictionary has been updated since the program object was generated, the SAP R/3 runtime system reinterprets the program and uses the latest Data Dictionary to regenerate the program object.

By this means, any changes in the Active Data Dictionary are immediately promulgated to all parts of the SAP R/3 system and its applications. For example, if the domain of a particular field in a data object is increased by the addition of another acceptable option, the new domain list will immediately appear on all screens that refer to this data object, in order to present users with the list of valid alternatives.

There is only one ABAP/4 Data Dictionary. It is actively integrated. However, the application developer can save a version of this dictionary and declare it to be inactive, so that the new items can be added as the new program development proceeds. When everything is working correctly and the new component is ready to go live, the inactive Data Dictionary can be declared active and will replace the old one. You will need high-level authority to release a development object and promote it to the production system. The ABAP/4 Development Workbench is provided with a promotion utility function to manage the transition of a program from a development object to a standard business program that could be called upon by any of the integrated applications whose users have the necessary authorization.

Understanding Metadata

If you think of a program as data, then metadata is information about that program. In particular, an account of what a program does and how it should be used to improve your business would be classified as metadata.

The SAP system is more precise. Metadata consists of descriptions of the data structures used in the programs. Therefore, metadata includes table and field definitions, and the specification of the domain of acceptable values for each field. The relationships between tables are also stored using foreign key tables as metadata in the Active ABAP/4 Data Dictionary.

Internal Program Structure Metadata

The interrelationships between the parts and objects of a program in the context of a complex system are necessarily intricate. For example, program metadata has to include definitions for fields that can only occur in a dynpro and not in a database table. Temporary tables in a dynpro have to be differentiated from tables permanently available to all.

Interfaces between programmed functions are concerned with passing parameters and control data. They have to be specified in the metadata.

Online help and checking services are available for the metadata as well as for data normally residing in a database.

The SAP R/3 system automatically generates metadata definitions for table and view functions for all the supported database systems, so that any use of them by SAP R/3 is assured a consistent and reliable service based on the specifications in the Active ABAP/4 Data Dictionary.

Table Definitions. A table comprises fields. The functions performed by the data stored in these fields depends on the purpose of the table. For example, at least one type of table will be specified so as to be able to hold data received from a database system, which may be on another computer. By contrast, an internal table associated with a dynpro may serve the purpose of exchanging data with an ABAP/4 program.

Every field used in generated database tables, dynpros, and ABAP/4 programs is specified in the Active ABAP/4 Data Dictionary by means of its attributes, which include format, length, and whether or not this field is used in the table's indexing key. Relationships with other tables are also part of the attributes of a table.

A field has a domain which is the specification or listing of the set of values which are accepted as valid entries for this field. The domain also includes the data type and length in terms of characters. How this field should be displayed on a screen is also part of the field domain. Domains exist as data elements, with their own identification code which can be used to refer to them.

A field also has a data element associated with it. The data element of a field describes its business meaning. It can specify keywords which place it in a specific technical or business context. Headings or labels for the field can be included in the data element. A documentation text for use by the online help system will reside in the data element of a field. The domain of the field will be identified by code name in its data element.

The data element associated with a field can also be associated with other fields. It exists as a separate data object with its own identification code. It can be replaced automatically by its equivalent in the language of the user.

Data Structures Embedded in Tables. A field in a table can use an "include" function to represent an embedded data structure. By this means, a data structure of any complexity can be built from a starting table, and this structure can itself be "included" in a larger structure.

If any element in a complex data structure is changed, all the related structures are updated accordingly.

Data Structures for Calculation. If a calculation is required within a program or for transferring data between programs, a calculation data structure can be defined and maintained centrally in the Active ABAP/4 Data Dictionary. The calculation structure can call upon the same domain definitions and explanatory data elements as are used with database structures.

Foreign Keys. If you try to enter impossible data, a SAP dynpro will intervene and point out the nature of your error. Suppose you have said that your corporation consists of a head office, code 01, and two separate company codes, 011 and 012, to represent two independent cost centers, each with a single plant with its own warehouse, codes W1 and W2.

If you try to place some material for company code 012 in warehouse W1, which belongs to the other company code, the system will object, because it has consulted a check table revealing that company code 011 owns warehouse W1 and company code 012 owns warehouse W2.

The table of who owns which warehouse is a foreign key source for checking entries to the materials list.

Because you have defined the foreign key relationships in the Active ABAP/4 Dictionary, the dynpro can validate the entry data before the transaction is posted. Much unnecessary processing is obviated thereby.

Virtual Tables. A data view is an arrangement of data for a particular purpose. An application may require certain data to be gathered from a variety of tables residing, perhaps, in other systems. This will have to be arranged and presented in table form to the application user.

If the application programmer specifies a virtual table that includes the fields needed in the most useful format, the system can be tasked to assemble the necessary data elements by declaring the foreign key tables that will form the stepping stones to the desired data.

At the presentation stage, the fields obtained via the foreign keys can be assigned more appropriate titles if necessary. It is also possible to specify filtering functions that will suppress from view any lines of the virtual table that are not wanted.

Matchcodes. A matchcode is an index pointing to original data. It is linked with a database index or with a view that effectively narrows the target of the search. A matchcode can also appear as a table entry, which is updated in response to certain predefined trigger situations.

The matchcode can hold pointers to fields from more than one table, and criteria can be stipulated to limit the data records targeted.

Automatic Functions for Screen Fields. How a field is displayed on a user's screen is normally determined by the Dictionary tables, which define the length and data type of the screen field, and the text elements, which describe the significance of the content of the field in the Enterprise Data Model of the business.

If your application has to import or output the contents of a field, the system looks in the dictionary for routines to convert between the internal and external representations. Fields for amounts or quantities can be displayed according to the parameters defined for certain reference fields in the Dictionary, which will include the currency or unit of measure appropriate to the installation.

The F1 special function key will always display documentation on the field indicated by the cursor, giving the business description of the field and the technical attributes from the corresponding domain. For certain fields, the F4 key will reveal possible entry values, from which one or more can be selected. This facility will always be active when a matchcode, a check table, or fixed values have been defined for the field.

Entries to a field are automatically checked, at the moment of entry, against the range defined in the Dictionary. If foreign keys have been identified, they will be taken into account and the check table procedure applied.

Generation of Database Definitions. The ABAP/4 Data Dictionary effectively defines a relational database independent of the database systems of individual vendors. The tables in the Dictionary are mapped on the underlying database system to generate catalog definitions and catalog changes for all supported database systems.

The application developer does not need to be aware of the mechanisms of an individual database system. For example, if a system does not have an ALTER TABLE operation, the SAP R/3 system will automatically create programs to unload the data and write them back in the new structure. If the database system does recognize the INSERT FIELD and similar functions to alter a table, SAP R/3 will use them.

The SAP Enterprise Data Model. The table definitions in the ABAP/4 Data Dictionary are designed to optimize data processing. The Enterprise Data Model is there to make business sense of what is going on.

The model is built from entity-relationship units which refer to the real objects in business, such as documents, messages, and materials. Staff are also included in this usage of the concept of "object." The relationships stand for such concepts as ownership and membership. For example, a purchase order, when it is complete, will have a header and one or more documented line items representing the items to be purchased and their prices.

This works as follows:

- Purchase order line is part of a purchase order.

- Purchase order header owns one or more purchase order lines.

If you call for help with key F1 on a purchase order display screen, you will see what the business significance is thought to be of the item your cursor has selected. This is an indirect reference to the Enterprise Data Model (EDM).

The user can choose how to view the Enterprise Data Model. The first selection offered will be based on the application from which the model is called, but you can inspect any section of the model at any level of detail. Figure 28.1 illustrates part of an EDM in list-display format.

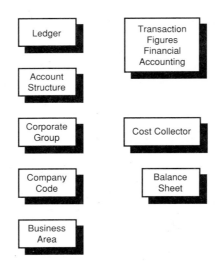

Fig. 28.1   Part of a list display of the Enterprise Data Model.

You can also choose between a list display and a graphical presentation from which you can choose to suppress certain types of entities to make the picture clearer for the purpose you have in mind. Figure 28.2 illustrates part of a graphical display of an EDM.

The elements of most interest to the business user may not all be available in the host application. For this reason, a system of data views is available in which the tables of interest are assembled automatically by accessing other sources of data if necessary, so as to create virtual tables that include the fields of interest.

These views can be used to program at the business level and to display the Enterprise Data Model in the level of detail and with the content most suitable for your purpose.

Since all the data elements used to build views, and virtual tables are defined in the ABAP/4 Data Dictionary, the user is assured of consistency of data and formatting.

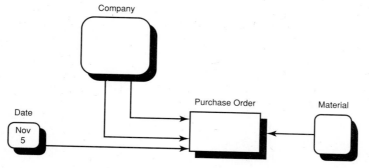

Fig. 28.2 Part of a graphical display of the Enterprise Data Model.

Programming Dialogs with Dynpro Technology

Every background processing procedure and every dialog with a user is controlled by dynpros—dynamic programs—that comprise a screen and its processing logic, including validation procedures for checking entries.

Each dynpro controls exactly one dialog step. Even if there is no user to view them, the appropriate screen displays are available, and any error messages will be sent to file.

The system works with more dialog steps than the user would imagine. Each dialog step comprises a Process Before Output (PBO) and a Process After Input (PAI).

The commands and data of the dynpro have three objectives, as follows:

- Presenting the screen layout that defines the positions of input and output fields, selection fields, graphical controls, texts, and so on

- Defining the attributes of all screen fields, such as their formats, value range checks, justification, leading zeros, and colors

- Specifying what has to happen in the PBO and PAI phases

The dynpro may also have to activate the SAP multilingual capabilities and language-dependent documentation, help texts, error messages and screen formats for large or pictographic character displays.

Dialog Module Pools

Each dynpro is based on exactly one ABAP/4 dialog program which is organized into modules and can therefore be referred to as a module pool. The dialog program handles calls to the constituent modules in its pool.

The dynpros likely to be invoked in the course of a given transaction must share the same common module pool. The only exception is a function module that has its own dynpros. This can be called from within a transaction without sharing the module pool of the rest of the dynpros of that transaction.

Dynpro Chains

The dynpros corresponding to a given module pool, or dialog program, are numbered, and will execute in that order unless an invoked dynpro causes a deviation from this static chain.

Field Attributes and Standard Functions

Two fields with the same name are automatically linked. Thus most of the attributes of the dynpro field are taken from the ABAP/4 Data Dictionary.

The field attributes, and possibly the explanatory data element and the domain of the corresponding dictionary field, are used as the basis for the standard functions a dynpro will perform as part of a dialog.

Standard Functions of a Dynpro. The following activities are standard and performed by the dynpro itself for the one step of a dialog which is its scope:

- Automatic format checks for the screen fields

- Automatic value range checks using the fixed range of the domain or the check table of the dictionary field

- Online help, including searches in the glossary and the presentation of help texts from the data elements of the fields

- Conversion of user entries into internal representations that are made available to the dialog program for which this dynpro is managing a step. The converse process is conducted for output to the user.

- Presentation of default values as directed, or acceptance of values to assign to specific user parameters

- Operation of matchcode search if it has been declared as an attribute for the field concerned

Processing Logic

The two halves of the dynpro processing logic are PBO and PAI—Processing Before Output and After Input, respectively. The syntactic structures of the ABAP/4 language are used in the PBO to initialize the screen in ways that are sensitive to context, and in the PAI to validate entries and invoke appropriate subsequent dialog steps, including the updating of the database.

Error Dialogs

The dynpro is autonomous in its execution of error detection and the presentation of context-sensitive error dialogs. In particular, the dynpro will offer for correction only those fields that are logically related to the error and that might therefore include the erroneous entry.

Re-validation and interchange with the user continues until the dynpro is satisfied that the step has been properly completed.

Advanced Business Application Programming

The ABAP/4 language is distinctive for the following reasons:

- ABAP/4, with the SAP R/3 Repository and the individual development tools, makes an integrated architecture for the development of new programs and the modification of existing SAP R/3 components.

- The developer does not have to be familiar with the technical details of the system environment, such as the operating system, database, network, or client/server communications.

- Structured programming is supported, with all the requirements for modularizing programs.

- The language is portable because the programs are translated into optimal internal representation, which is interpreted at runtime. The data is controlled by the ABAP/4 Data Dictionary, which can be altered independently of the programs because they are regenerated automatically under control of the dictionary.

- The scope of the language is tailored to the context of business information systems.

Prototyping

A preliminary version of the program can be prepared as a prototype which can be run. Because the language is interpreted at runtime, modifications and additions to the prototype can be tested until it becomes the final version and is released for business use.

During prototyping, ABAP/4 programs can access all the SAP R/3 external channels.

ABAP/4 Language Structure

The language in which all SAP R/3 programs are written is interpreted at runtime. It is made up of four types of program elements:

- Declarative elements—specify the structure of the data to be processed in a program such as tables, which will be formed using field definitions specified in the ABAP/4 Data Dictionary

- Operational elements—initiate basic data manipulation such as MOVE and ADD

- Control elements—implement sequence structures such as loops, branches, and subroutines under the control of operators such as DO, IF, CASE, and PERFORM

- Trigger elements—link program parts to events that can occur while a program is being executed, such as TOP-OF-PAGE or AT USER-COMMAND

Multilingual Capabilities

The demands of worldwide system development include requirements to ensure that different language communities can be integrated with a common business system.

Language Text Pools. A text element is a word or phrase which can be associated with any data field. The text element is designed to tell you what the data means in terms of its business significance.

When the code in an ABAP/4 program requires a text element to be displayed on a screen, it specifies the number of the text element to be used. The code does not have to be changed in order to access another element if the language of the user is changed. The language text pool from which the element is drawn is governed by the language selected in the user profile.

Pictographic Languages. The double-byte character set system (DBCS) can support the pictographic languages that have a large number of characters: Japanese and Chinese, for instance.

Wide Character String Handling. The ABAP/4 language has been extended to recognize data type W for wide character fields and some other functions which permit double-byte characters to be mixed with normal single-byte characters in the same field.

Elementary Business Data Types and Operations

In addition to the string processing facilities common to all computer languages, the ABAP/4 functions include some operations that are ubiquitous in business. For example, special data types are defined for dates and times. In mixed expressions, numbers are interpreted as time intervals, depending on context. For instance, a number added to a date produces the result of that date shifted by the number of calendar days. Subtracting two time values yields their difference in seconds. The most-used business functions have been streamlined.

Table Processing and SQL

Tables in SAP systems are the most important data structure. The advanced business language offers many functions for handling them.

In particular, the ABAP/4 Data Dictionary defines logical tables which can be matched to open SQL elements. The SAP R/3 database interface uses a high-performance buffering method which it can use on all supported database systems. The application programmers can declare special work areas for these database exchanges.

Furthermore, the ABAP/4 Editor can directly check the syntax of Open SQL statements embedded in ABAP/4 code.

Internal tables can be used that exist only as long as a program is running. There are many ABAP/4 functions available to operate on them. They also have the advantage that they can be dynamically enlarged. This promotes an efficient use of memory and helps optimize runtime performance.

Modularization

Simple subroutines can become modules, or function modules can be established for this purpose.

Subroutines

Subroutines of ABAP/4 and other programs can be called, and the name of the programs in which they are located can be dynamically determined when the call is made. Parameters can be passed by value or by reference.

Function Modules

Function modules are fundamental to the organization and integration of applications in the SAP R/3 system. They enjoy the following essential characteristics:

- The data interface of a function module can be extended in an upwards-compatible manner, and uses the definitions of the ABAP/4 Data Dictionary.

- Function modules can be validated in their own separate test environment by supplying input data and collecting the results for subsequent analysis by the SAP R/3 system itself through the Computer-Aided Testing Tool (CATT).

- Function modules can be managed in a function library.

- A function module will be able to handle exceptions by itself.

- It can be called across system boundaries by Remote Function Call (RFC).

Customer Exits

The functionality of a standard SAP R/3 system component can be extended by using the customer exit facility without affecting the core logic. This is cheaper than developing a new function.

For example, the following standard customer exit calls are already in the system, but will not have any effect until the customer logic is associated with them:

- CALL CUSTOMER_FUNCTION

- CALL CUSTOMER_SUBSCREEN

All potential customer requirements not already catered for by the existing standard business programs are implemented in the software as predefined interfaces which can be used as needed to insert customer-specific logic. The standard logic has the calls, but they are disabled until explicitly activated.

There is a clear division between SAP logic and customer logic which is maintained by explicitly assigning each customer exit to an individual customer system. When SAP installs a new release of the standard software, the customer logic modules will remain untouched; SAP guarantees that the customer exit calls will still be there in the new release and that there will be no hiatus when it goes live.

Development Tools

The tools of the ABAP/4 Development Workbench are easy to use. They employ dialogs to guide and advise the application developer in creating and combining development objects. One tool manages these objects and provides general functions such as list, display, create, copy, test, and show where used.

If you select an object, the function and the appropriate tool function will be automatically called.

Screen Painter

To create, modify, display, or delete a dynpro, use the screen painter. It has three specialties, as follows:

- Arranging and positioning field designations and templates in the full-screen editor

- Specifying the display attributes of each field in the layout

- Entering processing logic

The screen painter will also accept general specifications for language and record the number of the next dynpro in the series for a static dynpro chain. You can specify the display type as dialog box, selection screen, pop-up menu, and so on.

Support is provided for creating foreign-language versions of a dynpro that already exists.

Dialog Boxes. A secondary or "modal" dialog box can be used to supplement or simplify a dialog being conducted in a primary window. Additional work steps can be carried out there, as well as error-handling routines. It is planned to extend dialog boxes to allow parallel or "amodal" windows in which two related activities can be conducted in tandem. This facility is demonstrated in the ABAP/4 Editor development tool.

Graphics. A graphics editor is provided through Screen Painter in addition to the text editor. It can insert graphical control elements such as the following:

- Pushbutton

- Radio button—offers the user a selection of one of several choices

- Checkbox—allows the selection of more than one of the options

- List box—facilitates work with very long lists

- Frame—can have a built-in header field and serves to encompass several related dynpro fields into a visual unit that accommodates automatically to variable amounts of field data

Any dictionary table can be displayed and used in a cut-and-paste mode to transfer fields to the screen layout. Multiple table fields can be placed using this technique. When a field is selected, all the relevant attributes are also displayed for the developer to inspect.

Menu Painter

In a central window, the application developer can see how the menus and graphical control elements such as pushbuttons are structured. The functions implemented in a program can be assigned to certain menus, function keys, and pushbuttons in a consistent way throughout the application.

The SAP Style Guide is a set of ergonomic standard designs for the visual elements. You can use your own designs or modify the standard assignments, and have the system generate lists of where you have violated the standards of the SAP Style Guide.

The language to be used is stipulated when creating a program. It is the same for text elements, the Screen Painter and the Menu Painter. Other languages can be accommodated at runtime by referencing other language pools for the text elements.

A menu can be copied as a unit. Individual functions in a menu may be disabled, in which case they will appear dimmed. A main menu can consist of up to three nested levels of up to fifteen items each.

ABAP/4 Editor

Programs are entered and modified using the Editor. Standard text operations are available, together with a number of special functions for easy program development, as follows:

- Systemwide navigation and display of development objects
- List of where development objects are used
- Calling of ABAP/4 report programs
- Elimination of programs embedded by an "include" instruction
- Display of syntax rules and permitted keywords
- Syntax checking of programs under development
- Insertion of program sections and routing control logic prepared in advance
- Structuring of source code using the Pretty Printer to reveal the structure of the code to make it easier to inspect
- Comparison of two programs using a split-screen editor

VI

Maintaining

Browser. The browsing functions of the Editor start with object lists, from which a cascading navigation mode is possible, extending over many definition levels, to identify where the focal object is used throughout the system.

The following operations, for example, are possible under the browser:

- Jumping from a subroutine call to the subroutine definition while still in the Editor
- Branching from a table declaration in an ABAP/4 program to the corresponding table definition in the ABAP/4 Data Dictionary
- Branching from a table field in the ABAP/4 Data Dictionary to the corresponding data element and from there to its domain
- From the control logic of a dynpro, jumping directly into the program editor, opening the corresponding ABAP/4 modules

Your route while navigating is tracked, so you can always retrace your steps back to where you started.

Where-Used Lists. A search can be performed at any time on any development object to determined where it is being used at present within the system as a whole. For example, functions, fields or tables can be identified wherever they are referenced throughout the system.

Debugger

Errors in both ABAP/4 programs and dynpros can be detected. The debugger can switch between dynpro and module pool levels.

Interruption of the program by the debugger can occur after every command or at defined breakpoints, after a runtime error or directly from the process monitor. Details of the objects involved in the error are displayed, and changes can be effected before operation is resumed.

Remote debugging across system boundaries can be effected via Remote Function Calls (RFC).

Performance Measurement

The consumption of computing resources can be measured and attributed to causes such as the following:

- Modular units such as subroutines
- Database operations
- Operations involving internal tables in ABAP/4 programs

Performance statistics can be aggregated at various levels and separated into breakdowns for individual consumer processes.

Computer-Aided Testing Tool (CATT)

The CATT is designed to support the description, combination, and automation of recurring business procedures for the purpose of setting up test runs.

It can automatically simulate input dialogs and insert data from a background process. The tests are standardized and systematized, so they can be repeated precisely, and as often, as desired.

Reporting

A report program reads and processes part of a database.

This can be a specialized database system accessed via the vendor's software or a SAP system. The most convenient way is to operate through a logical database.

Logical Databases

A logical database is an ABAP/4 program and the data tables that are generated by it from the source database.

The fields required for a particular question or problem arising from an application can be declared and filled, perhaps by using foreign key relationships, to yield a validated hierarchical data structure amenable to interactive searching and printing.

A similar method is used to assemble virtual tables from diverse sources for immediate use by an application.

As each line of a logical database is transferred from the source, the "running through" process allows that line to be processed by a part of the program selected according to the source table for the data. In this way, the ABAP/4 logic can influence the assembly of the logical database according to the outcome of processing parts of the data being transferred.

There can be an efficiency benefit to this: Each logical database will serve more than one report. The access paths from the source databases need be coded only once, the validity and authorization checks performed only once, as well as the provisions for navigating the data records.

Strategic Indexes

A strategic index—for example, of the company's hundred largest customers—is a type of report that demands a great deal of computing power, but not necessarily on a daily basis. It can be updated at a frequency that is in accord with the expected rate of change of the data. If your company normally sells to the same set of customers who are relatively unchanging in their requirements, the strategic index, of sales, in this example, need not be calculated very often. If you operate in a volatile market, you may have to accept the computing overhead and call for a strategic index at frequent intervals.

VI

Maintaining

Report Starting

ABAP/4 reports are started from a special report menu. Each choice will typically initiate a special dynpro, called a selection screen, which requires the user to define or recall a search specification to limit the scope of the report.

A report can also be called from within other ABAP/4 programs, a capability that is needed to support interactive reporting.

ABAP/4 Query

For users who are not familiar with ABAP/4 programming, the ABAP/4 Query application is able to generate reports automatically if they are not already included in the standard SAP R/3 system.

The sophistication of ABAP/4 Query reports is limited to ranking lists and statistics; but the user is able to select a functional area, go to the pertinent tables, and finally to the fields to be included in the report. The source is usually a subset of a logical database, and the user has choice of report layout and sequence. The application can supply explanatory texts from the ABAP/4 Data Dictionary.

Organization of Development Work

An integral component of the ABAP/4 Development Workbench is the ABAP/4 Development Organizer. It is suitable for projects small and large. In many respects, the Development Organizer performs the functions of the Project System Module which is discussed in Chapter 16, "Understanding the PS-Project System Module." The project system methodology can be applied to software development.

However, particular care has to be taken when the R/3 system is being used to prototype new components, or test new componets prior to their incorporation into the production data processing system of your company. The ABAP/4 Development Organizer is designed to control the software development process through the functions of Change Management which depend on the management of software classes and release versions.

Change Management

A development project typically employs several programmers or programming teams, each working on part of the program. Each job automatically logs every development object that has been a candidate for change. That development object is then reserved exclusively for that programmer or team. Others can inspect, but not alter it, until it has been released by the team that first took on the job of developing it. Another team can then work on it under the same exclusive arrangement. There is no possibility of having two teams working on the same development object at the same time.

Development Classes

Each object under development is assigned to a responsible developer and to a development class which indicates the type of expertise needed to understand it.

Version Management

When a job is released, the current versions of all the involved development objects are automatically stored, and the new objects become current.

The changes are logged so that it is possible to determine or reconstruct the state of affairs prior to the release of the new version. Performance measurement may well ensue.

Revision Security

The developers are responsible for creating hierarchical documentation of their objects, which is referenced in the change management records.

Promotion Utility

Development usually takes place in a system separate from the productive system. A testing client code can be declared so that the development environment does not interfere with business.

The promotion utility is so named because it supervises the promotion of a program from the development environment to the production system. It is responsible for transferring objects, having carried out a simulation if necessary. The objects are locked in the production system to prevent direct changes to the code. Customizing then takes place.

The promotion utility carries out complete documentation of the process, and the SAP R/3 Repository Information System can be consulted to determine which developmental objects still reside there.

From Here...

The ABAP/4 Development Workbench is an advanced software tool which ensures that programs you develop under its control are going to be successfully integrated into the rest of your system.

- What is the connection between the SAP R/3 Analyzer and the ABAP/4 Development Workbench?

  The Analyzer, described in Chapter 6, "Tool-Supported Optimization with the R/3 Analyzer," will help you define your business in a manner which will make it very clear to you which SAP R/3 programs exist already. You may not need to use the ABAP/4 Development Workbench. If you do, your work with the Analyzer will be an excellent starting point.

- I need to take an even closer look at how my company does business.

  Apply the discipline of the SAP R/3 Analyzer, described in Chapter 6, "Tool-Supported Optimization with the R/3 Analyzer."

- Where do you draw the line between Customizing and developing new software?

  SAP R/3 Customizing is discussed in Chapter 7, "R/3 Customizing." It helps you pick out the functions you will need and make them exactly fit your business. Try to find a way of using standard SAP business software before launching on new program development.

■ Can I afford a software development project?

   Perhaps a study using the SAP R/3 Project System is in order. Consult Chapter 16, "Understanding the PS-Project System Module."

■ How can I manage Business Process Reengineering if it includes developing new software?

   The ABAP/4 Development Workbench includes the ABAP/4 Development Organizer, which is a comprehensive supporting tool for this work.

■ I need to take a close look at how my company does business.

   Try the SAP Business Workflow Management tool, discussed in Chapter 30, "R/3 Business Workflow Management."

Chapter 29

The Business Engineer

The purpose of the SAP R/3 Business Engineer is to help you configure an implementation by selecting the parts you need and putting them all together quickly to yield a robust, flexible, and efficient business system.

This chapter will remind you that there are effective and easy-to-use tools and methods for building and updating a modern business system.

The Business Framework

The Business Engineer is a development from the R/3 Analyzer and R/3 Reference Model which give you a full toolkit to exploit the open Business Framework architecture.

The key addition to the functionality is the facility with which components and subsystems may be integrated with the core SAP R/3 system as they become available after SAP certification. It is not necessary to adhere to the formalities of the release cycle in which the entire system is converted to the updated software. Nor is it necessary to limit the system to applications supported by SAP.

This important contribution to flexibility and rapid implementation is made possible because of a wide range of robust messaging technologies which can bridge the communication and control gaps between systems and installations that might otherwise be incompatible. SAP ALE, Application Link Enabling, and SAP Business Workflow are examples. The widespread use of business objects comprising data and processing components is another reason why contemporary business systems can be quickly implemented in spite of their complexity.

For example, your company might wish to choose the following SAP applications to be preconfigured and customized by the Business Engineer and thus become components of your Business Framework:

- The Business Framework is the methodology of making all components fit seamlessly together. They will work the first time.

- The Business Engineer is for all SAP R/3 implementations.

- Network-enabled systems can be built from existing components.

- Productive SAP R/3 systems can be reconfigured and updated without disruption.

- Third-party systems can be integrated with SAP R/3.

- HR-Human Resources

- PDM-Product Data Management

- Treasury

- ATP, Available-to-Promise Server

- Reporting Server

Configured, Inspected, and Tested Before Installation

A particular advantage of the Business Engineer programming interface lies in the fact that R/3 processes can be used and tested before you install an R/3 System. Typical transaction data can be processed and displayed on screens that have been customized for your specific situation. You can make alterations before implementation. You can also use the same interface to make alterations to the processing and the reporting after the system has gone live.

Dynamic and Continuous Business Reengineering

By controlling your processing sequences with the SAP Business Workflow, perhaps via an intuitive graphical display, you can automate and timetable the execution of related activities across application boundaries, components, and organizational units.

Recommended for all R/3 Implementations

The Business Engineer has become the recommended mode of designing and building a focused implementation of the R/3 system. When the system is in productive operation, the same interface will handle system maintenance because it can select and de-select R/3 applications and modules and authorize settings and formats specific to the user; and all this at the graphical flow diagram level if required.

Architecture for the Internet in R/3 Releases 3.1 and 4.0

SAP R/3 has always been thought of as a layered system. Outside is the presentation and user interface; below this resides the application layer in which the processing takes place; and in the core is the database and its processors. The layered concept is implemented so as to allow as much processing power and data storage capacity to be assigned to each layer as the volume and type of traffic demands. New processors can be brought in as the load increases. This dynamic and largely automatic control allows the system to be scaled up to handle larger numbers of users and also to execute more complicated processing where this is required.

Thin Clients

If your processor does not have the code to do what you require, it can be made to download this code from a central repository. You may not be allowed to alter it, and when you next download it, there may have been some updates carried out centrally. This thin client working is standard in SAP installations.

If your processor is an NC, Network Computer, or perhaps a NetPC, Network Personal Computer, then you may be operating from a screen that is entirely driven by code which has come to you from afar. The Java language is designed to run on almost any kind of computing device. It builds a Java Virtual Machine that will then respond appropriately to Java Application Elements, "applets," which will present you with such items as display windows and active forms into which you are invited to enter data or choose an option.

The attraction of the thin client is the small bandwidth it needs in order to communicate with its host. An intranet within a company, or the Internet worldwide, could be the link, even if there has to be a tone-modulated stage using an analogue telephone line.

There are not enough high-performance workstations and advanced PC devices to provide terminals for all the people who would like to communicate over the Internet. Thin client technology enables them to use whatever computing devices can be made available. The user console may be just a television display and a set of response buttons.

Components for Internet and Intranet Use

There are two ways of developing your business system via a network. You could open links to a public or private network and then restrict certain operations to users who had been identified as authorized individuals. Sales orders might be acceptable from those with sufficient credit, and information inquiries might be limited to representatives of registered companies. The other way of developing your business is to initiate coded messages on a network that are understood only by their intended recipient. A command to a warehouse to dispatch an item would have to be coded. Several different types of components are needed to do business over the networks.

Browser

Netscape Navigator and Microsoft Internet Explorer are two browsers that can be used to present screens and transmit data to a user who is at the end of a low-bandwidth Internet channel. If you "Open a location," you will see a display that will be maintained by a distant computer which selects the display according to the details you entered when you specified the "location." If your terminal is connected to a computer that does not have the location you are seeking, then it will try another computer, and so on until the searching is fruitful, exhausted, or timed out.

The job of a browser is to put together the responses from the location so that the user is not aware of the complexity of the selection and delivery processes; although the delay in response may suggest that the mechanism is by no means straightforward.

Browsers are often given away free to those who rent a telephone line. Their operation is becoming familiar to an increasing number of people. They can be made to operate in just about any language. They can be mounted in very modest computing and display devices.

Web Server

A Web server is a computing resource assigned to the job of connecting Web clients, whether thin or thick, with the database or other service that has been requested. The server can be a standard software package such as the Microsoft Internet Information Server or the Netscape Enterprise Server.

Internet Transaction Server

The ITS (Internet Transaction Server) connects Internet Application Components and the Web server. It presents information in Web page format that can be accessed by employees, customers, and other users via a browser. The ITS manages network transactions and supports Java.

SAP Automation

SAP Automation is a programming interface. It allows Internet Application Components and other third-party application components to automate the interaction with R/3. It also integrates R/3 with new technologies such as COM/DCOM, OMG CORBA, and Java, as well as with external applications such as IVR (Interactive Voice Response) applications and forms-based interfaces.

A SAP Automation Integration Toolkit is discussed later as an aspect of the Business Engineer.

Internet Application Components

SAP IACs are easy-to-use software modules that customers can use to perform specific business tasks and operations across the Internet and intranets. SAP has available 25 IACs and 10 Employee Self Service Application Components for human resources.

Business Application Programming Interfaces

BAPIs are open object-oriented interfaces based on SAP business objects. Several hundred BAPIs have been defined across all R/3 business application areas. They integrate IACs and core R/3 system functions and reside in the application server layer. Both SAP and independent developers can use the BAPIs to build Internet and intranet solutions using R/3 and other business applications. BAPIs are Microsoft COM/DCOM-compliant and OMG CORBA-compatible.

Object-Oriented Information Engineering

OOIE, Object-Oriented Information Engineering, is a language for specifying object types, associations between object types, subtyping, and partitioning. This logically formal language extends the concept and usefulness of an EPC, Event-driven Process Chain, as the fundamental unit for designing business processes. OOIE adds to the EPC elements the concept of an Operation that is defined in terms of a request to achieve a certain goal. The operation is complete when all the state variables in it have been transformed to the values that will constitute a satisfactory result. "Find me a person who is available now to perform this task," could be regarded as a shorthand description of an object operation that could be used to yield a set of values in the form of a Human Resources data object holding a person's name, qualifications, and availability.

The trigger for an operation or set of operations is defined as a set of specific values in a particular data object. There are also control conditions that can apply logical operators to model processes of any complexity. IntelliCorp ModelStore Repository is a multiuser capability for the LiveModel SAP R/3 Edition that integrates a number of business modeling tools to support the OOIE discipline and, for example, allows a business process graphical diagram to be executed to test its validity.

The Concept of Network Computing

Network computing is a form of distributed computing where applications and data reside on a network and users can access resources anywhere on the network, not just on their own PC. The annual expense for a typical desktop computer running a standard set of business productivity applications is believed to be $8,000 to $12,000. Much of this is spent on support, training, and maintenance. Updating the software, for instance, entails reloading each PC.

A Net Presence Is Expected

Many businesses use, or plan to use, the World Wide Web for marketing and for sales transactions. The commercial success of SAP users over the Web depends on the development and implementation of SAP R/3 Internet and intranet solutions at customer sites. SAP is gathering customer input via the Internet through the use of an "electronic framework" form. This information will influence how the repository of BAPIs is extended. Customers can access the repository via the Internet to test their own applications with new BAPIs as they are released.

The Business Engineer Is Focused on Network Centered Computing

Effective network-centric applications are compact for quick delivery over a network. Small size makes it practical to maintain the applications centrally. Users work with a set of features that is no larger than they need. There are no superfluous options. Being modular, the network-centric applications can be downloaded only to the users that have need of them.

The applets can connect to each other and to legacy systems such as spreadsheets and corporate databases. The communication process need be no more difficult than using a Web browser, which will become a standard skill.

Customers, business partners, suppliers, and managers can all have controlled access to the same processes and information that is current. Their separate hardware and operating systems will all be able to run the Web browsers and such inclusions as the Java Virtual Machine. A business application written entirely in Java will work on any machine without editing.

Aspects of the Business Engineer

The function of the Business Engineer is to serve as a business system Implementation Assistant. You can see which elements of R/3 you will need, and the Implementation Management Guide will show you how to put them to work using your data and your way of doing business.

The graphical modeling displays can be used to control the Business Engineer, or you can work with tabular data if you prefer.

Tools to Update the Data Objects

Any editor can be used to insert your particular terminology and other information. You then reload the changed information to the R/3 Repository. Advanced assistants such as the ARIS Toolset, IntelliCorp's LiveModel for R/3, and Visio's Business Modeler can be used.

Configure to Order

The Business Engineer supports the SAP Configure-to-Order initiative and some automatic custom R/3 configurations. For example, R/3 can be customized on the basis of components and procedures, and specific user interfaces can be generated from standard settings, for example, to create transaction dialogs for a particular industry solution.

Continuous Customization

Interactive process optimization and the addition of new processes or components to live R/3 applications would be examples of continuous customization. The Business Engineer will keep track of the changes and allow testing and simulation before releasing any newly customized element.

Extending SAP Business Framework Architecture

The Business Engineer includes new release and system upgrades, and the IAC Internet Application Components.

Intranet Applications

When enterprise solutions are extended to a corporate intranet, you can expect to have a large number of users who may be unfamiliar with R/3. Help and training advice systems must be carefully tailored because traditional application training may not be cost-effective for such a group. Intuitive interaction and familiar browsers may allow data entry and maintenance to be reliably moved from the back office to the points at which the data originates.

Business-to-Business Applications

R/3 allows integrated business systems to cooperate across the Internet by using open standards for business transactions, such as the BAPI standard. Business components can interact with many different business systems. For example, fully electronic extended supply chain management may become feasible.

Consumer-to-Business Applications

Consumers anywhere in the world can use their standard Web browser to access authorized portions of the corporation's R/3 system to gain information and transact real-time business securely.

Employee Self-Service Applications

In an installation with an open framework extending right through a complex of business applications, you may well find that you can apply for jobs and get an answer without leaving your terminal. Similarly, you may be able to look at, but not alter, your remuneration package, or your leave entitlement. These examples illustrate the self-service Internet application components that are now available and that can make significant additions to the added value chains of your company.

SAP Automation Integration Toolkit

To facilitate the automation, not only of the office but also of the laboratory and their links to the production and storage facilities of a worldwide network of business partners, SAP R/3 is delivered with an Automation Integration Toolkit that includes the following packages:

- GUI, Graphical User Interface, Library of display and interaction functions that can be assembled to deliver a particular working environment that will integrate with SAP R/3
- GUI Component, which is a framework for building a user interface
- SAPGUI in Java to execute any SAP GUI Component at any terminal able to run a Java Virtual Machine
- SAP Business Objects Repository, which contains all the data objects used in SAP R/3 together with the associated processing components
- BAPI Component, which is a Business Application Programming Interface of which there are several hundred available so as to be able to link with and control most business systems
- RFC Library, which contains the Remote Function Calls needed by most business systems where a BAPI is not available or not necessary
- RFC Component, which is the SAP open programmable interface to enable remote function calls to external applications, tools, and to ABAP/4 programming language routines
- Transaction Component, which is a programmable interface to set up the control parameters for transaction processing
- SAP Assistant, which performs the functions of workflow manager and documentation assistant for the work of the Business Engineer

Unified Modeling Language Repositories

UML is an emerging standard for component-based software systems in which you have to specify your business processes in a particular formal language. This UML format can be interpreted by a range of high-level modeling tools and gives you a simulation of the process. You can also modify the model of your process and test it again. When the model is working perfectly, you can send it to whatever systems are supported by the particular modeling tool you are using.

A UML Repository is a storehouse of reusable software that can be set to work in a wide variety of system environments. One of the first UML-compliant repositories, the Microsoft Repository, was first populated via the UML facility in SAP R/3.

From Here...

- If I wanted a change from system design, and if I had made my career in accounting, which chapter should I read next?

  Chapter 12, "Understanding the FI-Financial Management Module," will be quite different from Business Engineering.

- Has SAP recognized that software development projects can be difficult to control?

  Chapter 16, "Understanding the PS-Project System Module," recognizes how difficult it can be to get something done when there are programmers about.

- If I were a simple manufacturer where should I look to see things that I deal with every working day?

  Chapter 17, "Understanding the PP-Production Planning and Control Module," is about factories and their problems.

- If SAP and the Internet are going to make a big difference to my company, which SAP programs are most likely to be involved?

  Chapter 20, "Understanding the SD-Sales and Distribution Module," is about an area which will probably embrace the network theme with enthusiasm.

Chapter 30

R/3 Business Workflow Management

The organization of work has a long history with two branches: The *craft* tradition, with the emphasis on one skilled person doing all the work; and the *work sharing* tradition, where several people share the work, each doing only part of the process and perhaps, as a consequence, not being fully aware of how his or her part fits in with the rest.

The SAP R/3 Business Workflow is both a concept and a cluster of program components that finds its place between the standard business software of SAP R/3 and the Enterprise Data Model upon which the customer application will depend.

The basis of the workflow concept will be introduced and developed to set the scene for the more technical matters of importance to the SAP implementers and the company that will benefit.

The Relation of Business Workflow to SAP R/3

SAP Business Workflow® is part of SAP R/3 Basis and is integrated in the SAP development environment as a function within the BPT-Business Process Technology component of the CA-Cross Application module. The SAP process model provides the basis for the methodology and graphical representation. The SAP R/3 Analyzer and the ABAP/4 Development Workbench can provide powerful supporting tools for establishing a Business Workflow Management system.

SAP Business Workflow® is closely integrated with the SAP R/3 HR-Human Resources Organization module. It is this close connection between SAP components that allows the organizational structure, the operational structure, and the workflow model to be related to each other without redundancy and without repeated entering of the significant data objects, such as job titles and responsibilities. If the jobs are to be associated with named individuals in the model, changes in these names and other particulars will be propagated automatically from the Human Resources components.

Target Areas for Business Workflow

All customers with SAP R/3, whether or not other SAP components have been installed, can use SAP Business Workflow. Examples follow of workflow models that can be customized and integrated as subworkflows in larger structures:

- Release of budgets
- Release of invoices
- Engineering Change Management
- Availability checks
- Project management
- System-controlled document management
- End-of-period settlement
- Processing of customer inquiries and orders that affect other departments
- Support for automatic escalation
- Purchase requisitions
- Purchase order releases
- Requests for leave or vacation
- Travel expense accounting
- Workflow management of applications developed by ABAP/4 Workbench

The Concept of Business Workflow Management

A workflow management system is intended to manage business processes automatically or semi-automatically by controlling the sequence of activities. It should ensure that the appropriate steps are carried out at the right moment by specific people or groups, or by particular data processing programs and the machinery they control.

The simplest workflow system is a sequence of operations carried out on a work item. The workflow begins when the worker takes up the work-piece, and each operation begins when the previous operation has been completed. The worker will take time off; there may be delays where some operations have to be allowed time, for the work-piece to cool off, for example; there may be delays awaiting a missing component or because the customer has to be asked for more information about his requirements. The workflow ends when the final inspection shows the job to be finished to the standard required.

Should the workflow include delivery and payment? And after-sales service?

Traditional legacy workflow management was the task of the supervisor. Spare sets of materials were kept ready so that no worker had idle time because there was nothing to do. Anyone slacking or going slow would be cautioned. Work study loomed large.

Task definition is a matter of dividing work into units that make sense. Here is a simple job with three tasks: Get the tools and materials ready, do the work, and check the work before passing it on.

You might prefer to look at work from back to front. The task is not finished until the work has been checked and found to be up to standard. It will not be up to standard unless you have done some work on it. And you can't do any work unless you have the materials and the tools.

There is another sort of task that does not have any elements that directly alter the work item. This might be an inspection task that effectively diverts some work items along one workflow path because they are up to standard, and sends other items along a different route as rejects that are to be scrapped or repaired. This task may add a lot of value to the business by making sure that bad products do not get offered for sale.

If a person is doing the inspection task, there is a clear relationship with the people who are upstream in the workflow, those who are responsible for making or changing the work items. Either the inspector or the creator of the work-piece may be a machine; both may be automated. If they are also linked by a feedback loop, the faults detected by the inspector can be used to alter the task carried out by the creator.

In this context, the historical approach to workflow management was considered to be a matter of dividing the jobs into tasks that could be done repetitively by workers who needed almost no training and very little inflow of information because each job item was the same. Managers had most of the information.

Skilled craftsmen demonstrated a different style of workflow, however. One of the signs of a high level of skill is the ability and habit of anticipating what should come next. The skilled person is using information to manage the details of the workflow. Waiting times are used to prepare for the future and to tidy up from the past. And the craftsperson is not above telling management to order fresh stocks and tools in anticipation.

It is obvious that people at work need certain information and are often able to provide information that can be used elsewhere for the benefit of the business. Workflow refers to the movement of work items through a series of operations that add value to these items. It also refers to the flows of information that must take place if this added value is to be optimized.

SAP Business Workflow® is a concept that permeates the SAP R/3 system and is devoted to developing and managing the flows of work and information that will make a business as effective and efficient as possible. The programs necessary to do this are an integral part of SAP R/3.

Because there may be a mix of people and automatic processes in the workflow, such a system can form bridges, not only between process chains from different SAP applications, but also between SAP processes and activities that are being carried out on other systems or by essentially manual procedures.

Automation of Information and Process Flows

The principle of information flow depends on data being collected directly or entered manually at one or more places and then being selectively distributed to wherever they could usefully take part in a decision process. By itself, data are not actually informative: you have to know what they mean. This usually boils down to knowing when this item of data could make a difference in how a task is being performed. Automation of information flows refers to the design and implementation of systems so that all the information required to make each decision in the best possible way is made available to the program or the person responsible for making it. The data has to be accurate and timely. It may have to be summarized or interpreted.

The automation of process flows refers to the methodology of using information about a process to adjust or initiate some control over this process. A thermostat senses temperature and switches a heater or cooler on or off to control the process of supplying energy. The thermostat is obeying rules about what information to use and what to do with this information.

The thermostat is an automated control system in which both the information flows and the process flow controls have been automated—even the decision-making has been automated.

A human operator standing by to react to a pointer on a dial is an example of a system that is only partially automated. The information flow to the dial has been automated, but the task of reacting to this information is left to the human operator. In some watch-keeping tasks, the operator has been given strict instructions about when to react; in others, the operator has to build up experience and take into account many other factors before deciding when and how to react.

The advantages of automating both information flows and process flows, if this is feasible, are that the system can be run according to decision rules that are applied continuously and reliably. If a fine adjustment has to be made, it can be put into effect immediately. The results of this adjustment will be available for monitoring through the automated information system. If the need for an adjustment is a complicated matter of weighing the pros and cons of changing things, then an automated information system will have access to a process-modeling facility on which to simulate the process and try out the effects of any adjustment that might be contemplated.

The adjustment may be a matter of small changes to the operating parameters, or the proposal may be to reroute part of the process or rebuild part of the workflow model. The SAP Workflow Management system facilitates both.

Active Linking of Work Steps

Waiting consumes time, one of the most costly business expenses. As soon as one task has been completed, the next one in the workflow should begin. Expensive processes, like talking to a medical consultant, may well work out cheaper in the long run if there is a queue of work items, or patients, in the waiting room. Since the medical consultant cannot say how long each consultation will take, it is customary to work with a pool of jobs from which work can be drawn. Partial automation in this field has enabled the doctor's receptionist to access the medical records and the patient information so that appointments may be arranged and the queuing in the waiting room made as discrete and efficient as possible. SAP IS-H, The SAP Industry Solution for Hospitals is an industry-specific application that is specifically directed at the processes and information flows of the hospital and medical arena.

Under the SAP Business Workflow regime, the users are actively informed about jobs that need to be carried out, and there is automatic execution of work steps and subprocesses wherever possible.

Significant Concepts and Design Decisions

SAP Business Workflow will control the flow of work through a network of SAP applications, key work stations, and external systems. It is applicable to companies of all sizes and industries.

SAP Business Workflow comprises a set of workflow definition tools with which to create a runtime business management system. These tools are included in SAP R/3, from Release 2.1.

An organization model must be specified so as to generate a workflow pattern exactly suited to the requirements of the customer. SAP R/3 has available a range of workflow templates that can be used like samples as the basis for a customized workflow.

SAP HR-Human Resources components are integrated with Workflow so that a person can be chosen for any task according to their skills, authorization, availability on site at the moment when the task is to be performed, and the role definition for it.

There will be a range of issues that have to be taken into account before beginning implementation or at an early stage. SAP Business Workflow provides tools and prompts, but the customer management team will have to arrive at suitable conclusions and decisions.

Task definitions must be established for each element of the business processes. In some cases, it may be decided that individuals should define their own tasks in the first instance; SAP Business Workflow allows this.

Workflow has to be specified as a set of linked processes that are either standard business processes or processes to be developed to meet the specification determined by SAP R/3 on the grounds that everything must integrate. The Reference Model of SAP R/3 must be used to select templates for the processes as the starting points for customizing.

Role definitions may be needed for responsibilities that may affect several tasks and for tasks that can be carried out by a range of personnel.

Object interfaces will be required where the attributes of an information object may be inspected or copied automatically.

Event interfaces must be defined where a sensing device, a data-link, or a person may change the information that is stored as part of an information object.

User interfaces to a work list client are usually terminals at which an end user or operator can see what work items remain on the work list and make a decision on which to tackle next. They provide a flexible means of presenting the activities of the SAP R/3 application and of influencing them.

Runtime systems are controlling programs through which SAP R/3 can direct a set of workflows and provide monitoring information about its progress. Automatic execution of work steps may be possible. Its scope and functions have to be established.

Deadline monitoring can be specified, with appropriate dunning.

Escalation procedures can be arranged to increase automatically the resources for work steps that have been revealed as critical by the on-line monitoring. Design decisions have to be made regarding their scope and supervision.

Workflow Definition Tools

Standard SAP R/3 business processes tasks may be used in establishing a workflow, or tasks and object types may be defined to suit the customer company. Specialized document types and documents that are not native to SAP R/3 may also be defined.

Task Types

SAP Business Workflow supports a range of task types:

- Standard tasks that are part of SAP R/3

- Customer-defined tasks created by calling object methods that ensure that the tasks so defined will be fully integrated with the rest of the SAP R/3 application

- Manual tasks that are at the discretion of the person assigned. These manual tasks need inputs and staffing, and create outputs. Therefore, they have to be defined in the task catalog of the customer's organization model so that they will be integrated with the rest of the SAP R/3 application.

Reference Models

SAP R/3 includes a Reference Model that shows how all the standard business processes fit together, with all the information flows and supporting services in place. In addition, the SAP R/3 Repository contains a very large library of successful work process models compiled in the SAP R/3 system. The SAP Business Navigator is able to present these models as seen from different points of view:

- Process view

- Function view

- Communication view

- Information flow view

- Organization view

The process view variants of these successful work process models are available in graphical form as event-driven process chains, which may be inspected in order to select a suitable reference model for a particular implementation of SAP R/3.

The SAP R/3 Analyzer is a stand-alone PC tool for establishing how the SAP R/3 models may be used in the elaboration of an enterprise model for a new implementation.

Workflow Templates

The following workflow templates are provided in SAP R/3:

- The Malfunction Report

- Preliminary Invoice Posting

- Budget Release Management

- Engineering Change Management

They are fully elaborated model examples that may be copied and subsequently modified to suit the customer.

Customizing

SAP R/3 Customizing is a module that offers default settings and recommendations to help custom-build a process to suit a customer's situation, especially when business process reengineering has been initiated. It will often be quicker to modify a reference model than to design the new system from scratch.

The SAP R/3 Customizing module includes a model company with project management and documentation for training and testing purposes.

Event-Driven Process Chains

The concept of workflow entails a sequence of steps that progress a work item through tasks performed on it which add value to it. Pointless work is activity that does not add value to the company. This flow of work items will usually pass via several people and processes; and some of these people may take on different roles according to the progress of a work item along the workflow.

A workflow definition may be like a simple chain which has a beginning and an end, and for which no variation is allowed or expected in the order in which the steps, the links of the chain, are traversed. If the flow is not a chain, it is vital to set out the conditions that have to be evaluated at each option point. What are the signs or symptoms that should cause the workflow to take a side turning? How will the program or the person know when to switch the process from one track to another?

One of the central ideas of SAP programming is to define business in terms of event-driven process chains (EPC), which are workflows, each attached inexorably to an event that constitutes the signal for it to begin. It is no use having a procedural chain of tasks if you do not know when to use it.

Whatever the shape or complexity of the workflow, there will be flows of information between some steps and events. The design team has to consider whether there are any other information flows that ought to be established. The team must also consider which information flows are not necessary and which should be formalized as essential requirements. Traditional information flows are not always a good guide as to which information pathways really add value to the business and which are just wasteful.

The starting point of a formal workflow definition in SAP R/3 must be a workflow task stored in the task catalog of the organization model being used as the reference model during implementation and being adjusted toward the model that will be used on startup.

Within the definition of this starting point task already stored in the task catalog, there must be a stored parameter value. If this value changes in a certain way, this will be the event which signals for the workflow to begin.

Under control of the SAP Graphical Workflow Editor, a workflow is defined by means of specific types of steps, as follows:

- Activity
- User Decision
- Wait
- Subworkflow

These workflow steps may be defined for concurrent execution or for serial execution under the runtime environment.

Conditions that control alternative branches in the workflow can be based on selected characteristics or attributes of the processed business objects, or on attributes of the workflow itself such as wait times or associated costs.

Conditions may be in logical or numerical form beginning with "If", or they may be "Case" conditions which are to be interpreted as reading "If this is a case of ..., then ....."

If a task can be performed by a program or a subworkflow of tasks that is already implemented and available for work at the moment when it is required, this task may be released for automatic performance, and no human intervention need be called for.

If there is no automatic procedure available for the task, for whatever reason, then the SAP Business Workflow will call on the HR-Human Resources application to supply the name of a person suitable for this responsibility, by virtue of their position or their experience. Anyone who is not at work at the time will not be assigned this task. If no one can be found, the task will be defaulted to the person responsible for this section of the workflow.

Static assignment refers to the process of deciding who should perform a task by reference to the task catalog in the organization model, where the person will have been defined by name, position, organization unit or as the responsible user. Dynamic assignment takes place at runtime by reference to a defined role which must be discharged at this point in the business process. For example, the task of inspection by a specialist may not be assigned to a named person until a specific work item is being processed, so that the nature of the work item may be used to select an appropriate specialist.

When a suitable person takes up the task, the Workflow object will supply a text for guidance—a definition of what will constitute a satisfactory termination of events for this task, and a reference to the object method that can be used to solicit on-line help or documentation that will show everything needed to perform and check this task.

Objects

An *object* in SAP R/3 is a named set of information items that are grouped together because it is convenient to move them about as a group. Some objects are defined so as to improve computer activities; some are defined because they make good business sense.

The information items belonging to an object may represent any of the following:

- Attributes of the object

- Methods that are operations performed on objects

- Events that are changes in the state of certain objects; in particular, changes in the value of one or more parameters held in specific data fields of an object

One of the guidelines for using object-oriented programming is to try to ensure that each item of information is held in only one place. For example, a customer object will have places to hold address and telephone number. If the number is changed, only one data location has to be altered. Every process or person who needs this number will look in the same place for it, so as soon as it is changed, all the users of it will be up to date.

SAP standard business processes are objects. All who use them find them in the same place, which is the SAP R/3 Reference Model. If they are altered, it will have been by the central in-house development team, and everyone will know as soon as they next use them. If an implementer customizes a standard process, it will be a copy under a new name that is altered, not the master.

The organization structure of a company is stored as an object. Each position contains a reference to the person currently filling it; a new face in that job will mean a new reference in the organization object. But the particulars of each employee are held in employee objects, not in the organization object. Master data is entered once only.

Object Methods

An object can perform one or more tasks by invoking what are called object methods. An example follows:

Object Export1 includes four items:

- Invoice document
- Order
- Material
- Archived document

This example object Export1 invokes three object methods concerned with processing the invoice in three steps:

- Export1: Create invoice document
- Export1: Edit invoice document
- Export1: Display invoice document

Each step of invoice processing for object Export1 entails a task recognized by SAP R/3 as a component of the organization model.

Each task will have been assigned to a role that could be performed by a person with suitable qualifications and experience—perhaps an export invoice clerk in this example.

Object Interface

The SAP system operates on units of information that are carried as computer documents to wherever they are needed. These units may be combined in various ways to form larger units.

When information is entered into SAP, it becomes a data object, and is passed about just like a tangible object.

An *object interface* is a device or a process running on a programmed device that is able to extract the information needed to build the data object required by the workflow at a particular stage.

This object interface may get the information it requires from a sensing device, such as a bar code reader, for example, or it may have to collect a great deal of information from many sources and carry out some data processing on this information before it can create the object that it requires. For example, there may be an object interface that has been given the job of finding out whether there are any bottlenecks in a production process. The required object is a parcel of information that specifies which processes are being held up, if any.

The object interface will usually be able to say one of two things: Yes, here is the information; No, the required information is not available.

Events

An *event* is a change of state in one or more attributes of an object. Therefore, the event belongs to and is a characteristic of an object.

An event will invoke a method, which is a procedure or process that has been specified and is awaiting only a signal to begin.

Events belonging to two or more objects may be linked. For instance, an event occurring in one SAP application may elicit a defined response in another, perhaps causing the transport of data from one application to the other.

An event may prompt a workflow to start.

A change of state in one object, an event, may be used to direct the flow of information or processing, not necessarily in the same workflow.

Events may also terminate or abort a task, even if they originate outside the workflow to which the task belongs.

Event Interface

A workflow is a combination of steps, events and conditions for making decisions. An *event interface* is a method of allowing events from other workflows to have some influence on how this process shall proceed. For example, there is usually an event interface between a production process and a financial control system. Lack of finance may well shut down the production process; early warning of it may effect just a prudent slowing down.

Workflow Manager Runtime Environment

Given that a workflow has been properly defined in terms of the tasks, roles, objects, and interfaces, there will often exist the possibility of setting up a runtime system that can control and progress work items through the steps of their appropriate workflow. If the decision is to install an automated runtime system when a workflow has been designed using the SAP R/3 tools, it will be possible to call on the Workflow Manager, which is a runtime environment, to progress the event-driven process chains that constitute the workflow.

For testing purposes, a model client company can be engaged and simulations of the workflow carried out.

The same runtime environment can be used to manage the workflow when the application runs with the customer company as client.

The Work Item Manager has the role of assigning work items to places defined in the organization model where they may be progressed to the next stage of the workflow. Items of a similar type will be sent to a Work List Client.

A Work List Client will receive work items from the Work Item Manager according to the range of work types for which it is suitable. The Work List Client may serve one or more terminals where people who are suitable for the role are likely to be working. The products of their work are returned to the Work List Client on their way to their next step in the workflow.

Role Definition

Role definition is a process of recording who is responsible for what. In particular, a role definition should specify what information and experience is to be brought to bear on a particular task. One type of role is the inspector who has to decide what happens next in a region of the workflow where there can be a choice.

A role definition may also include an obligation to ensure that the process has not come to a halt or changed its rate outside specified limits.

Dynamic role assignment can take place at runtime if the process is able to furnish the required information. For example, a role may be designated as "responsible for material." In this case, it may be necessary to know what material is identified on the invoice document before a suitable person can be selected to discharge this role.

Dynamic role assignment may also have to take place to provide stand-ins, deputies, or proxies in the event that the designated person or position holder is unavailable.

Runtime Information System

Retrieval of workflow information can be based on the volume or costs of work items, or on any other data available in the fields of the objects in the system. For example, it is possible to retrieve the number of times a function has been called in a period of time.

Full analysis facilities are accessible on-line during workflow management, and statistics can also be compiled for subsequent scrutiny.

Yields in processing industries and job times will be available; therefore, active escalation or deceleration of processes can be mandated under control of the Work Item Manager, which will call on SAP and OLE methods to manage the objects entailed in this work.

Several related workflows may have been defined through the Workflow Editor, in which case the Workflow Manager will be responsible for control and coordination.

The results from the Workflow Item Manager will be one or more work lists directed at the Work List Client which will service one or more users through a user interface. Dynamic allocation of staff to work items may be one of the responsibilities of the Work List Client. If two or more users have signed on with the same role, they will see identical work lists, but items cleared by one will be deleted from the lists of all the others.

Each user may customize his or her work list client interface to sort and display the work items in the most congenial manner. The interface will include an inbox to the SAPoffice component. The SAPoffice function is distributed in the CA-Cross Application module as a part of the CA-BPT Business Process Technology component.

The work list client may also have access to SAP e-mail, Internet, X.400, and SoftSwitch interfaces to non-SAP e-mail systems. Sources which use the EDI, Electronic Data Interchange, protocol may be accessed via the SAP ArchiveLink and SAP Intermediate Document interfaces. These routes allow images of original documents to be accessed if required.

Application Interfaces

Work lists can be exported completely out of the SAP R/3 system via the Microsoft MAPI, Messaging Application Programming Interface, if necessary. Workflow interfaces are available to allow the conduct of workflows on other SAP applications or on systems external to SAP.

Communications and the controlled exchange of data between a SAP R/3 system and other applications, including workflow systems, are matters which are in rapid evolution.

Linking Requirements

Event linking entails establishing relationships between events and therefore between the process chains that are driven by them. The following possibilities are examples of workflow connections that may have to be established in a specific workflow network:

- External systems may have to trigger SAP R/3 events or workflows.

- SAP R/3 events may have to elicit responses in external systems.

- Links between events must be established for generating and processing work items and workflows.

- Links between events must be established to work list clients which are managing the work lists of different user groups and their user interfaces.

SAP R/3 Standard Interfaces

SAP R/3 supports the following standard interfaces:

- OLE

- ODBC

- X.400

- EDI

- CPI-C

- TCP/IP

- ANSI-SQL

These standard interfaces are able to implement communications and the controlled exchange of data between R/3 and other applications, including workflow systems from other vendors. However, for the effective implementation of distributed application systems, an object-oriented approach with open integration between the modules is required. SAP R/3 Release 3.0 includes business API, Application Programming Interfaces, and workflow API to meet this requirement.

The concept of coupling is relevant. Tight coupling uses a central database to ensure guaranteed data consistency and business integration. Loose coupling allows master data to be held on more than one database. In this case, there has to be a particularly careful control of how applications exchange messages—whether synchronously or asynchronously.

Loose coupling has advantages: Each application is autonomous. For example, different releases of the SAP R/2 and R/3 systems may be in use in separate satellite systems without conflict. Also, one or more applications may be permitted temporary stand-alone operation. Another advantage of loose coupling is that SAP applications can easily communicate with third-party applications, and business processes can be integrated across multiple systems.

SAP Business Workflow is able to support such heterogeneous systems by use of its wide variety of messaging interfaces.

SAP R/3 Release 3.0 offers two types of interface:

- Open Integration Modules as Application Interfaces (Business APIs)

- Interfaces for SAP Business Workflow (Workflow APIs)

Business Application Interfaces (Business APIs)

SAP supports loose coupling using Open Integration Modules as application interfaces within the scope of Application Link Enabling (ALE). In particular, SAP has recognized a requirement for external systems to be able to invoke SAP R/3 applications. This has been implemented and will be followed by a facility to transmit consistent data objects.

Workflow Application Interfaces (Workflow APIs)

Pending the development of a standard for workflow interfaces, SAP has developed a number of interfaces for specific workflow systems. Their capabilities are likely to be shared with whatever standard is established.

From Here...

The SAP Business Workflow® is a set of work process definition tools and a suite of programs which can manage work processes in workflow sequences which may extend across departments and work centers, across SAP and non-SAP application modules. It is an integral part of the R/3 Basis module and relates to workflow functions in all the SAP R/3 applications.

- When should a new implementation start looking at workflow? Chapter 5, "The R/3 Reference Model," and Chapter 6, "Tool-Supported Optimization with the R/3 Analyzer," discuss the SAP method of looking at the workflows in your company and relating them to the standard business software available in the R/3 system and its applications.

- What is the relationship between SAP Business Workflow and the control of production? Chapter 17, "Understanding the PP-Production Planning and Control Module," shows how this module applies the workflow concept to a manufacturing process, whereas the SAP Business Workflow concept can be applied to all the work in your company, including the office tasks.

- How can I apply SAP Business Workflow to custom software development? Chapter 16, "Understanding the PS-Project System Module," concerns the management of any project. Chapter 28, "ABAP/4 Program Development with the R/3 Workbench," tackles the work of programming which can be subjected to the workflow procedures, like any other activity in your company.

VI

Maintaining

Part IX

Implementation Issues

France 117
Belgium 70
Italy 62
Spain 59
Denmark 56
Czech Republic 41
Sweden 39
Hungary 26

479
54
24
16
4

Japan 100
Australia 68
Singapore 32
Malaysia 22
Korea 10
Hong Kong 7
Thailand 7

South Africa 69
Saudi Arabia 9
Israel 3
Arabic Emirates 2
Namibia 2

Products
71%

teel,
l Engineering,
ormative

Food and Tobacco Industry

Office & EDP Equipment

8.0%

7.3%

6.6%

4.6%

Mining, Utilities, Transportation

 amercial
l Social
10.3%

4.5%

Trade, Retail and Wholesale

3.9%

Traffic and News
Communication

ics, Precision
anics, Optics
14.5%

3.8%

Metal Products and
Primary Metal

3.6%

Universities and
Technical Colleges

Chemical Industry,
Mineral Oil Production
18.2%

Others
(see chart below)
11.6%

2.9%

Wood, Paper and
Printing Industry

hers

dit Banks, Financial Services 1.9
arrying, Fine Ceramics, Glass 1.9
spitals 1.7
cellaneous 1.7
urance Companies 1.6
ding Trade, Construction 1.4
ther, Textile and Clothing Industry .9
de Associations and Federations .3
iculture, Forestry, Fishing .2

le product

evelop
lete and
stomized

Customized tools

Develop

eliver

High

Build large market
share as fast as
possible – at
reasonable cost

- Identify effective sales and marketing
  campaigns – quick feedback on results
- Build sales capacity quickly using
  standardized multimedia product
  presentations
- Erect entry barriers to keep out
  competition – customer database used
  for attractive after-sales service and
  support

Develop
for right
and at le

- Im
  be
  an
- Us
  exp

Reduce sales and
marketing costs while
maintaining market
share

- Service low value customers using low
  cost channels eg. telesales, direct mail
- Contact database to help retain key,
  high value, customers
- Link purchase patterns to SOP to
  prompt for automatic reordering

Reduce
key cus
for cros
opportu

- Sa
  pa
- Lo
  sy
  cu

Low
High

Rate of market growth

Relative market sha

High

Four Seasons

Seed

Agnos

ICL

British Rail

Customer Attractiveness

Chapter 31

Overview of SAP Implementations

If you are considering or actually implementing SAP, then you are joining an ever-increasing number of the world's largest and most respected companies. The rise of the R/3 system has been nothing less than sensational. Since its launch in December 1992, the number of R/3 installations has increased to over 5,000 in 1996 with in excess of 350,000 users.

SAP has some excellent tools that significantly improve implementation quality and speed. Systems implementations in general are rarely easy, but SAP offers among the best tools and support in the industry.

Companies implementing SAP have to be focused, and the whole project has to be broken down into small manageable chunks. There has to be a strong management team and strong support from the highest levels in the company.

Good preparation, planning, and control are vital. You will inevitably need external advice and support, and you should aim to get the very best.

Understanding the Scale of SAP Projects

One of the great difficulties of any computing project lies in quantifying the project's scale, and SAP is no different. However, in choosing to implement an SAP system, you are also choosing a ready-made and proven application that needs only to be configured to meet your business requirements.

This choice would appear to offer great advantages over building a custom application, and in most cases it does. You should be aware, however, that SAP might not meet all your business requirements, and for reasons of efficiency you might have to change your business practices to work within SAP's capabilities. In the relatively few instances in which SAP cannot meet your business requirements, you may be faced with changes to the core system. This can involve expensive development, and since SAP may not support this development, you may have problems when you need to upgrade.

In this chapter, you learn:

- To understand the scale of SAP Projects.

- To identify reasons why SAP should be implemented.

- How to create your own vision for the future.

- The steps needed to produce a discounted cash flow for SAP projects.

- An appreciation of the difficulties in quantifying the benefits and assessing the risks of an SAP implementation.

- The issues arising out of SAP project initiation.

It is difficult to know in advance whether SAP can meet all your business requirements, since the full business requirements frequently do not come to light until the project is well established. With the phenomenal growth of SAP, most of your business requirements have probably already been encountered by other users and accommodated in SAP. Your company's business requirements are likely to be similar to those of other companies in your industry, and you should be able to benefit from the fact that industry solutions have already been developed for major industries. However, you should also be prepared for finding business requirements that cannot be accommodated by the system.

Management quite rightly will want to know:

- How long will it take to implement SAP?

- What resources will they need, human and other?

- How much will it cost?

There are no easy answers to any of these questions, since there are so many variables to take into account. The best management can do is to consider every aspect very carefully, take professional advice from as many different sources as possible, and make a calculated guess. SAP themselves, or a reputable and experienced SAP implementation specialist company, may be able to give you a reasonable estimate; however, they don't know your business, and may be influenced by their desire to sell you their products or services.

If you intend to implement a number of the major modules, you should be prepared for a major project that is going to need lots of resources, careful planning, and quality management over a long period of time—anywhere from four months to a number of years. A decision to implement SAP should not be taken lightly. It is best to consider all the implications carefully before making any decisions.

Starting a SAP Project for the Right Reasons

SAP is causing so much excitement around the world that it is easy to get caught up in the tidal wave of enthusiasm, and rely too much on the confidence that so many of the world's major companies are using it. While I am not seriously suggesting a sheep syndrome, in which companies blindly jump into SAP because "everyone is doing it," I *am* saying that you should be choosing SAP for the right reasons. These may include any number of the following (or indeed other) reasons.

Business Process Reengineering. SAP and business process reengineering go hand-in-hand. In fact, the latest concept from SAP is that of using SAP as a means of "Continuous Business Engineering." You can use the flexibility of SAP to continually reengineer your business, rather than go through a single reengineering process. One can hardly argue with the sense of this concept.

Staff Reduction. Emotive as it may be, SAP is frequently seen as a means of reducing headcount by streamlining organizations and making systems more efficient. It is hardly the message that companies want their employees to hear when they need every employee's cooperation to enable implementation. A worried workforce is not good for business, and can cause all sorts of motivational problems. When you take employees out of their line jobs and put them into a project team, they will naturally question what they are going to do when the project is completed.

While you may well be able to achieve headcount reductions in line jobs after SAP implementations, you have to consider the personnel requirements to support the system after the implementation.

Those companies working hard at reducing their head count may well consider training key users well so they are able to support their organization, thus avoiding the need for specialist support teams.

Organizational Change. You need a very good knowledge of SAP and your own organization and business to be able to predict what future organization you are going to require post implementation. Frequently, the post implementation organization does not get properly considered until the project is reaching its advanced stages.

The organizational change is linked closely to the business process reengineering, which is to a great extent controlled by the nature of the system.

Integrated System/Module Software. A well-integrated system can be a great aid in helping the company run efficiently. One of SAP's greatest advantages is its full integration, yet surprisingly, some companies implement only one or a few modules.

While there is no doubt that the performance and functionality of the individual SAP modules rivals—and in most cases exceeds—that of other companies' stand-alone applications, SAP's integrated nature has to be one of the greatest reasons for choosing it. The benefits of the system handling complete processes seamlessly are difficult to ignore. You can forget problems of interfaces, system mismatches, duplicated data, and complex reporting problems.

The modular nature of the SAP software is a distinct advantage. You can purchase modules to meet your business requirements now, and add more modules to them whenever required.

Integration with Other Systems and Distribution Across Multiple Platforms. In large companies, a large number of different systems are inevitably used. SAP R/3 offers great flexibility in terms of hardware, operating systems, databases, and graphical user interfaces.

Client Server Technology is generally regarded as reliable, efficient, flexible, and cost effective. SAP offers the best advantages of both relational database and client server technologies.

Corporate Standard. Most major Corporations want to standardize their business operations to improve efficiency and increase their flexibility in responding to market conditions. Expectations of customer service levels are continually rising, competition is fierce, and managers are under pressure to deliver good results for shareholders.

IX

Implementation

The argument is compelling for doing away with a mish-mash of old systems that operate independently and require different skills and training requirements, and replacing them with a standard one that can be implemented worldwide. At a sweep, training and system support can be rationalized and more importantly management gains flexibility and access to information.

The issues of business globalization are at the forefront of board room strategy in most major corporations. As communications improve, and world trade increases, companies not only have to look to exploiting world markets but also to trading on a global level. Historically corporate affiliates worldwide have tended to operate independently, but nowadays companies need to operate more as one global entity. A single, fully integrated business system like SAP makes good business sense.

Capacity to Manage High Volumes of Processing. There can be nothing worse than investing huge sums of money in new systems and technologies only to find business growth and expansion stretching them to their limits in a short time. With SAP you can sleep at night with the reassurance that 120 of the world's top 500 companies use the systems. SAP's huge R&D effort and testing of existing SAP Systems in operation guarantees the ability of the systems to meet the large volumes of processing required by major corporations.

You should be aware however, that the software is only as good as the platform it is running on and the communications hardware.

New Startup Operations. SAP offers the opportunity for new businesses to get up and running within a very short period of time. The tools that the system offers are perfect for developing new organizations and efficiently engineering the business.

Reducing Processing Costs. Depending on the type of systems and hardware already being used, it may be possible to reduce processing costs with SAP. Research and analysis would be required on an individual basis to show the effect of an SAP implementation upon processing costs.

Real-Time Processing. Real-time processing is the technology of today, and is one of the key features of SAP. The combination of a fully integrated and real-time system can offer businesses a competitive edge, and contribute significantly to high efficiency and good customer service.

Standardizing Skill Requirements of Staff. The nature of the working world seems to be changing globally. An increasing number of companies are requiring a flexible workforce that can readily adapt to changing roles and circumstances. By adopting SAP systems and standardizing, companies can benefit from the resultant more standardized skill requirements. The great thing about working with SAP is that while the functions change throughout the system, the user interface is very similar across the modules. It is therefore much easier for users to gain skills on different parts of the system than it would be if each part were an independently purchased component.

Industry Standard Solutions. The old saying "Why reinvent the wheel?" applies to SAP's Industry Solutions, which are essentially modules configured and enhanced to meet the requirements of particular types of industries.

It is very much a question of buying a shoe that fits rather than buying a kit of parts that you need to put together and modify.

Fast Development with Good Prototyping. SAP offers fast development and good prototyping capability, which are good reasons to chose the system. The cost of any systems development is linked to the time that the development takes. Equally, the faster the system can be developed, the earlier the benefits can be realized.

Powerful Development Tools. SAP's development tools have made a significant impact on the speed and quality of SAP configuration. They have developed an impressive and comprehensive range of tools which have been designed to handle almost every aspect of development and implementation, bringing real cost and project quality benefits.

Multi-Language Capabilities. SAP's multi-language capability is awe-inspiring. The system can be run in 15 different languages, including Mandarin, and allows for the global adoption of SAP as a corporate standard.

Creating Your Own Vision for the Future

Whatever the reasons for choosing SAP, companies should develop their vision for the their future at an early stage. It is only by clearly knowing what you want to achieve that you can direct your project to take you to that future.

Two companies implementing exactly the same module may have very different objectives and may receive very different benefits. Companies need to make the system work for them to enable them to achieve their business goals.

Once you have defined your vision for the future, you must publicize it well internally so that all employees are aware of what they are working toward.

Creating a Cash Flow Forecast for SAP Systems

At some stage in the decision-making process, you must create a cash flow forecast to support the proposal. This task presents many challenges, because 70 percent of the figures in the forecast will probably be assumptions, with the remaining 30 percent representing reasonably accurate known costs.

In the most simple analysis, you have two areas to consider. The first is the software and hardware itself, and the second is the cost of installing, configuring, training, and implementing. It is the second area that presents the greatest difficulty since you will undoubtedly have to make some uncomfortable assumptions. So many different factors have an influence on the costs that it would be impractical to cover them all in this book. Systems projects in general are prone to budget and cost overruns, and even some of the most well-respected SAP implementers have had problems keeping cost and schedule under control.

Putting more effort and care into the planning and preparation before the project starts can lessen the risk and make the predictions more accurate. The success of the project lies as much in the approach taken by the company buying the system as it does in the skills of contracted implementers.

The Steps to Produce a Discounted Cash Flow

When you perform an evaluation of an SAP project using discounted cash flow techniques, there are six basic steps that need to be undertaken. They are:

1. **Determine the economic life of the SAP investment**.

   The economic life of the SAP system is the number of years that the system will continue to be in use—taking into account system upgrades and enhancements. It is likely to be around five to ten years.

2. **Identify the relevant cash flows.**

   The relevant cash flows should be those cash flows in and out of the business that occur only as a result of the decision to undertake the SAP project. As discussed above, it is important to ignore accounting adjustments for depreciation and central overheads, and to consider carefully the real cost of DP/IT department support rather than the costs generated by arbitrary cost allocations.

   Two conceptual decisions will affect the relevant cash flows: the treatment of tax and the treatment of inflation. Whatever the decision, it needs to be documented and applied consistently throughout the investment appraisal.

   Apart from the decision to include or exclude tax cash flows, only one other type of cash flow may be ignored—the payment or receipt of interest. In general, interest is taken care of in the discounting process, so to include it would give rise to double counting. The only exception might be those projects where a special financing deal has been set up to finance hardware or software.

3. **Establish the discount rate to be used.**

   The discount rate to be used should be the minimum rate of return required for a capital investment. Most companies use a version of their historical average cost of capital, adjusted to reflect forecast inflation. Some, as discussed above, adjust the discount rate to reflect any significant risks associated with the investment. If the relevant cash flows exclude the effects of inflation, the discount rate used should also be adjusted to exclude inflation. If the project is likely to be specifically funded by subsidized loans, grants, or even venture capital, the specific forecast funding costs can be used as the discount rate.

4. **Specify the compounding frequency.**

   The dates of the incoming and outgoing cash flows will determine when those cash flows are available to be reinvested—and so earn interest—to be financed—and so incur interest. Therefore, in theory, the cash flows should be dated as accurately as possible and the compounding time interval should be set to reflect the frequency with which the cash is financed or reinvested. In practice, most companies assume that the cash flows occur at the year-end, on the assumption that they are likely to be spread more or less evenly over the life of the investment.

5. Perform the net present value calculations.

The next step is to calculate the value (in today's currency) of each of the SAP investment's cash flows. The NPV (Net Present Value) of the investment is the sum of today's values. The easiest way to do the calculations is to use a spreadsheet.

6. Evaluate the investment NPV against the base case.

The NPV of a capital investment proposal indicates the net wealth to be earned, after financing costs, from adopting the proposal. The implication is that there are only two alternatives: continue operations as they are, or adopt the proposal. However, in many cases there are better competing alternatives or versions of the same proposal that can be compared and contrasted.

Although discounted cash flow is one of the best ways of evaluating the financial viability of an SAP project, it is important to remember that IT project financial appraisals often contain subjective elements. Assumptions about inflation, funding costs, markets, competition, and the softer costs and benefits mean that the output of the appraisal, an estimated NPV, (net present value) is only an estimate.

The decisions that managers make concerning the structure and strategy for their companies' information technology assets need to be tempered by many considerations that cannot be easily quantified and assimilated into a discounted cash flow model.

Difficulties of Quantifying Benefits and Assessing Risks

Most company directors have experienced the effort and pain involved in obtaining board-level approval for capital equipment purchases. Justifying investments in computer systems can be even more time-consuming and painful. One reason is that many of the benefits, in particular those relating to improved effectiveness, may be difficult both to identify upfront and to quantify. How, for example, can cost savings from new business processes be identified when the outcome of a SAP-centric process reengineering project is itself unknown?

Another reason why cost-justification can be so painful is that while the costs of the system are often borne by the Sales, Finance, or IT departments, some of the benefits, such as improved sales forecasting, may be companywide, spanning marketing, production, and even customer service.

Finally, cost-benefit analyses are often produced by accountants with little understanding of the marketing or sales functions. The accountants may be reluctant to include estimates of benefits produced on a "best guess" basis.

This section is designed to help companies to prepare better information on costs and benefits—both prior to the purchase decision and during SAP implementation. It starts by exploring the real reasons that underpin the cost-benefit analyses that companies undertake. It is all too easy for managers to be naïve in this complex and politically charged area! We then suggest how managers might change the focus and presentation of their cost-benefit analyses to better meet the real objectives of the exercise. We

IX

Implementation

explain the types of risks that a SAP project might involve and discuss some techniques for evaluating the likely impact of risk and uncertainty. We give advice on how to recognize the real costs and benefits and provide a brief checklist of possible costs and benefits associated with SAP. Finally, we set out the key steps involved in producing a discounted cash flow forecast for an SAP project.

Why Companies Really Undertake Cost-Benefit Appraisals. In theory, the aim of a cost-benefit evaluation is to make sure that scarce resources—such as cash—are channeled into the areas that will make the organization more profitable. Yet in practice, the reasons why managers in companies put considerable effort into cost-benefit appraisals are not as straightforward as they might seem.

In 1994, Hewson Consulting Group (HCG) conducted detailed research into how companies evaluate their investment in sales-driven and marketing-driven IT systems. The results are thought to be representative of most IT systems. They found that although 55 percent of systems appear to require a fully worked cost-benefit justification to obtain funds, the informal realities are quite different. In reality, this research showed that the numbers that companies produce on the benefits side are frequently there to make the official justification look good. Many managers have already made up their minds that the IT investment is worthwhile, and they need to invent the numbers to sell the idea to the board. In this case, the evaluation takes on a political role.

Other organizations undertake formal cost-benefit analyses because they believe that "whatever gets measured gets done." For these companies, the aim of the benefit appraisal is not to control the allocation of resources to different IT projects, but rather to help set targets to control the project itself and to drive through the realization of the planned benefits. Finally, some organizations will identify the system costs and benefits retrospectively, as part of a post-project appraisal aimed at improving their capital investment processes.

It seems obvious, therefore, to conclude that in the complex world of business decision-making, not all cost-benefit evaluation exercises are as they seem. The secret of success is to understand exactly why the cost-benefit evaluation exercise is really needed in your company. It may be:

- Economic—an objective assessment of the options open to the company undertaken to establish whether investment in SAP will add value to the organization and represents the best use of company resources

- Political—a sales exercise undertaken to convince the budget holders that the investment is worthwhile, using whatever means necessary

- Control—an exercise to identify, quantify, and communicate the target benefits and costs in order to drive through their realization

- Retrospective—a review of how the investment decision was made in order to learn from experience

Although this section concentrates on the first use of cost-benefit evaluations, which is to decide if an SAP project makes economic sense, Figure 31.1 outlines how the focus of the exercise might change if, for example, the evaluation was considered to be more political than economic.

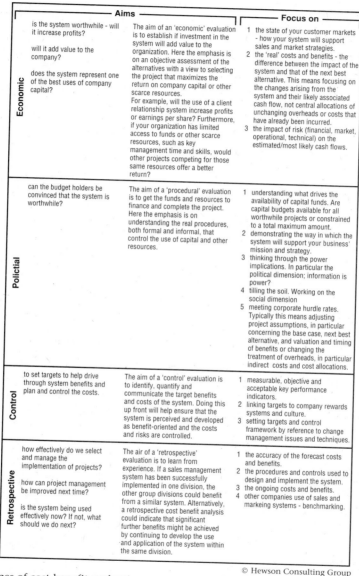

		Aims	Focus on
Economic	is the system worthwhile - will it increase profits? will it add value to the company? does the system represent one of the best uses of company capital?	The aim of an 'economic' evaluation is to establish if investment in the system will add value to the organization. Here the emphasis is on an objective assessment of the alternatives with a view to selecting the project that maximizes the return on company capital or other scarce resources. For example, will the use of a client relationship system increase profits or earnings per share? Furthermore, if your organization has limited access to funds or other scarce resources, such as key management time and skills, would other projects competing for those same resources offer a better return?	1 the state of your customer markets - how your system will support sales and market strategies. 2 the 'real' costs and benefits - the difference between the impact of the system and that of the next best alternative. This means focusing on the changes arising from the system and their likely associated cash flow, not central allocations of unchanging overheads or costs that have already been incurred. 3 the impact of risk (financial, market, operational, technical) on the estimated/most likely cash flows.
Politcial	can the budget holders be convinced that the system is worthwhile?	The aim of a 'procedural' evaluation is to get the funds and resources to finance and complete the project. Here the emphasis is on understanding the real procedures, both formal and informal, that control the use of capital and other resources.	1 understanding what drives the availability of capital funds. Are capital budgets available for all worthwhile projects or constrained to a total maximum amount. 2 demonstrating the way in which the system will support your business' mission and strategy. 3 thinking through the power implications. In particular the political dimension; information is power? 4 tilling the soil. Working on the social dimension 5 meeting corporate hurdle rates. Typically this means adjusting project assumptions, in particular concerning the base case, next best alternative, and valuation and timing of benefits or changing the treatment of overheads, in particular indirect costs and cost allocations.
Control	to set targets to help drive through system benefits and plan and control the costs.	The aim of a 'control' evaluation is to identify, quantify and communicate the target benefits and costs of the system. Doing this up front will help ensure that the system is perceived and developed as benefit-oriented and the costs and risks are controlled.	1 measurable, objective and acceptable key performance indicators. 2 linking targets to company rewards systems and culture. 3 setting targets and control framework by reference to change management issues and techniques.
Retrospective	how effectively do we select and manage the implementation of projects? how can project management be improved next time? is the system being used effectively now? If not, what should we do next?	The air of a 'retrospective' evaluation is to learn from experience. If a sales management system has been successfully implemented in one division, the other group divisions could benefit from a similar system. Alternatively, a retrospective cost benefit analysis could indicate that significant further benefits might be achieved by continuing to develop the use and application of the system within the same division.	1 the accuracy of the forecast costs and benefits. 2 the procedures and controls used to design and implement the system. 3 the ongoing costs and benefits. 4 other companies use of sales and markeing systems - benchmarking.

© Hewson Consulting Group

Fig. 31.1 Types of cost-benefit evaluations.

When to Do a Cost-Benefit Analysis. Most organizations analyze costs and benefits before making the decision to acquire a system. They generally incorporate some form of cost-benefit analysis into the organization's capital approval process. However, if your SAP investment is considered high-cost and high-risk, you should also review the costs and benefits at the end of each stage of the project, before proceeding to the next stage.

IX

Implementation

This will help ensure that, if market conditions change or the original estimates of costs and benefits were wrong, the project plan can be modified appropriately.

Linking Systems Objectives to Corporate Strategies. Much has been written about the potential mismatch between corporate business strategies and IT strategies. HCG's research indicates that managers feel that many sales and marketing systems do not fully support their business's sales and marketing objectives.

Now that the use of personal computers and open systems architecture has reduced the time it takes to get systems operational, in principle it is easier to link systems objectives to business strategies. This means that systems strategies can now follow, rather than precede, business strategies.

Your investment in SAP is likely to earn you money only if it enables you to achieve your business objectives more quickly, more cheaply, or at less risk. The first step in producing a cost-benefit evaluation is to set out clearly how SAP might best support your business strategies.

While it is relatively simple to demonstrate how SAP might help companies to reduce overhead costs, it is considerably harder to explore how SAP might help improve an organization's competitive position in terms of improved customer service and better product development. Yet many business practitioners have emphasized IT's importance in changing marketing processes and improving competitive position and customer management.

Frameworks to Identify IT Investments Supporting Business Strategies. SAP is such a vast system that you must consider it on a module-by-module basis. Depending upon how many of SAP's modules you are going to implement, you may find that SAP will be able to support many different business strategies across a wide cross-section of your company's operations. Because of the integrated nature of the system, it is frequently at the center of a company's entire business. Linking the system processes to your corporate strategies is a large undertaking. It is best achieved by creating frameworks to enable the analysis. It is well worth considering employing a suitable expert to help you do this.

For example, HCG uses three frameworks to attempt to identify sales- and marketing-based IT investments that best support business strategies. They are:

- Critical success factors
- Product market life-cycle analysis
- Customer needs and opportunities analysis

The first, critical success factor analysis, applies equally well to all potential IS projects, whether their focus is on cost reduction or some form of improved market positioning. The other two approaches, product market life-cycle analysis and customer needs and opportunities analysis, are an extension of the critical (or key) success factor method of aligning IT investment to business strategy. Effective business strategy must forge a strong link between looking outward to the market and looking inward to the firm's assets and capabilities. Looking outward to the market means paying attention to the complex requirements and dynamics of carefully delineated customer market segments.

Therefore, in addition to traditional CSF (Critical Success Factor) analysis, which has tended to be conducted on a top-down basis, organizations seeking to use IT to exploit an externally driven and market-focused business strategy need to use frameworks that help them develop bottom-up IS strategies through a detailed market analysis.

Critical Success Factors. Critical Success Factors (CSFs) are the limited number of areas in which results will ensure successful competitive performance for the organization—in simple terms, the few things an organization has to do well in order to survive. While an organization's business objectives state what needs to be achieved and by what deadline, the CSFs indicate how the objective will be achieved. For example, a business objective might be to increase market share by five percent over the next three years. The associated CSFs might be:

> *We must provide a more efficient distribution system.*
>
> *We must better identify high-volume customers.*
>
> *We must make it easier for customers to do business with us.*

Every CSF should be viewed as beginning with the words "We need..." or "We must..." Each CSF must be necessary to the goal and sufficient to achieve it. Typically, a business unit might have between five and fifteen business objectives and two to six critical success factors for each objective. Not all CSFs will be best met through an IT/IS project or solution, and some SAP projects may help an organization to achieve more than one CSF.

The advantage of using a CSF approach is that it can lead to a consensus view among managers as to where the greatest opportunities for IT investment lie—especially if done in a workshop setting. The disadvantage is that it can be too introspective and subjective and is too easily affected by strongly held views of vociferous individual managers.

Product Market Analyses. For product-focused companies with clearly articulated product market strategies, Figure 31.2 shows how the market objectives for SAP projects can be identified by reference to product portfolios and product life cycles. It illustrates some appropriate systems objectives for each stage of the product life cycle.

For products marked with ? in Figure 31.2, primary system objectives might be collection of information on potential products and markets to facilitate new product development. Organizations with many people and significant costs in this area might use groupware systems to enhance internal coordination between new product development (NPD), sales, and marketing, breaking down traditional functional barriers. The objectives would be reduced communications costs, enhanced likelihood of successful NPD, and a significantly quicker product development cycle.

IX

Implementation

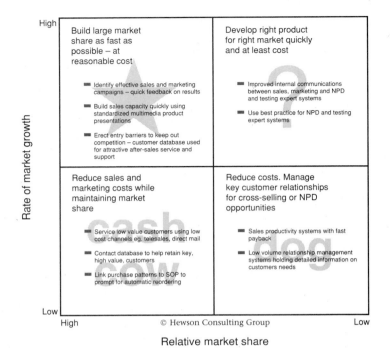

Fig. 31.2 Some typical system objectives determined by product life cycle status.

For products marked with * in Figure 31.2, a primary market objective might be to build market share as cheaply and quickly as possible. Systems might be used to get rapid feedback on the effectiveness of sales and marketing campaigns. Since it is often cheaper to build market share in growing markets, valid system objectives might be to obtain new customers, increase market share, improve decision-making about marketing campaign effectiveness, and understand the market. For example, a high-technology products company might use SAP order entry to record market segment information at the time of entry, such as how the products will be used, so that better information on the effectiveness of marketing strategies can be obtained.

Strategically inclined companies with aspirations to large market share use systems at this stage to build entry barriers through blocking distribution, creating significant product differentiation, locking new customers into long-term loyalty programs, or building switching costs.

Systems used to support "cash cow" products tend to have more defensive objectives. As the rate of market growth declines, building market share becomes more expensive. In addition, as competition intensifies, products become less differentiated and prices fall. You might also find that the market is flooded with too much product, as competitors have continued to plan for product expansion without sufficiently anticipating the slowdown in market growth.

Cash cow system objectives might include reducing costs, making better use of existing resources, increasing customer service (as a way of maintaining product differentiation for as long as possible), and customer retention. At this stage, a cash cow's market might be subsegmented into, for example, customers by future profit potential. Computer-aided techniques such as direct marketing can be used to service low-profit-potential customers more cost-effectively. Relationship management (or key account management) systems might be used to increase the quality of service provided to high-potential customers. Economies of scale might be achieved by using marketing databases to cross-sell.

More strategic uses of systems might be to build entry barriers to keep out new, low-cost competition and thereby maintain the status quo as long as possible.

For dogs in declining product markets, a company might wish to reduce sales and marketing costs, increase operating efficiencies, eliminate competitors, or even, if sufficiently committed to the market, put off new entrants. Frequently, companies with declining products—but high customer knowledge and loyalty—use relationship management systems to cross-sell new products to a loyal customer base and identify opportunities for new product development.

Customer Needs and Opportunities Analysis. Customer-focused companies will want to use a customer life-cycle analysis to review the link between their systems and sales and marketing strategies. This analysis classifies customers according to their business potential and the compatibility of their needs with an organization's product offerings. The goal is to identify key customers and then to analyze how well in relation to the competition your products and services meet their requirements. It is a variation of the directional policy matrix traditionally used for product markets, which seeks to establish and present, as the basis of future action, how well in comparison to the competition an organization's existing products and services fit customer requirements.

It is important to assess compatibility relative to the competition and from the customers' point of view. Customers are classified into "agnostics," "seeds," "allies," and "dogs" (see Figure 31.3). Customer strategies can be developed for each group, and sales and marketing systems' objectives can be focused more precisely on the areas of greatest profit potential.

Once you have fine-tuned your customer strategies, the next step is to ensure that the planned systems expenditure delivers benefits that closely support those strategies. For example, if you intend for your investment in SAP to support a customer retention strategy by improving customer service, you should justify it on the basis of a customer needs survey.

The critical areas for action revealed by customer needs surveys should be reflected in sales and marketing strategies and should be linked to sales and marketing system features. Figures 31.4 and 31.5 show an example of how you can relate customer needs to customer retention strategies and cascade them down to IS objectives. The systems implications for each objective can be made explicit at this stage.

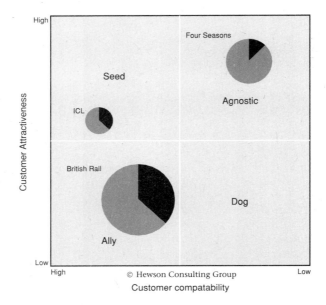

Fig. 31.3 Segmenting customers and developing customer strategies.

© Hewson Consulting Group

Fig. 31.4 Using a customer needs survey to make systems more customer-focused.

Using these formal techniques makes explicit the relationship between proposed sales and marketing systems and an organization's marketing and sales strategies. Unsupported assertions that "the system is essential to our strategies" typically indicate that benefits have not been properly thought through. Systems proposals that do not support sales and marketing strategies should be rejected, or the strategies themselves should be reexamined. Only after the system has been related to acceptable sales and marketing strategies should the most appropriate evaluation methods—financial or otherwise—be considered.

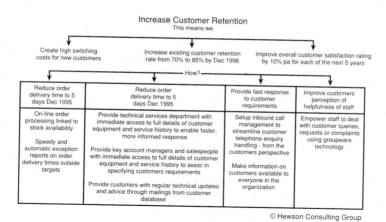

Fig. 31.5 An example of linking sales and marketing systems' features to strategies.

Assess the Impact of Risk. All large gains arise from a bet against poor odds.

Do they? HCG's research shows that the majority of respondents perceive the use of sales and marketing systems as low-risk. The riskiness of any system is important, because the amount of risk determines the likelihood that planned benefits will not be achieved or that the budgeted costs will be exceeded. In this sense, from a practical point of view, risk is the same as uncertainty.

Types of Risks. As an example, the types of risks that may affect sales and marketing systems fall into three categories: technical risk, user risk, and market risk. Each is briefly described below. The first two risks could be applied to any SAP module. There may be other risks pertaining to other SAP modules too, such as legislative requirements imposed by governments (for example, new taxes to be applied to particular types of goods).

1. **Technical risk.** Will the software, hardware, and communications actually work? This applies to any system, regardless of function.

   The effect of a system that works too slowly, crashes, or fails to accept or output information can seriously decrease user acceptance and enthusiasm. You can minimize technical risks by using proven combinations of software, hardware, and communications. This is particularly critical for systems using distributed databases, supporting remote users on a WAN, or requiring file transfers to and from portable computers. Technical risks can also be minimized, at a cost, by using pilot studies and extensive testing before the system is implemented.

   SAP software itself probably offers the lowest possible risk in terms of software performance. However, it will perform only as it has been configured to, and it depends on the proper functioning of its hardware platform and communications equipment.

IX

Implementation

2. **User risk.** Users take longer than planned to benefit from the system.

> How will users react to the system? Will they feel threatened, coerced, or resentful? How will the system change their existing status, job satisfaction, workflow, processes, or daily routine? Is their existing compensation package still appropriate? Therefore, how long is it likely to take users to learn how to use the system and to start to obtain the benefits?

> All of these risks are manageable providing that each is properly addressed.

3. **Market risk.** Customers or markets change, making the current sales and marketing strategies invalid.

> This is the risk that, having installed your sales and marketing system, something dramatic happens in the marketplace that invalidates your current strategy.

> For example, the success of a low-cost foreign competitor might make the market economically unfeasible to pursue, particularly if your costs are highly geared (high fixed cost, low avoidable cost). Other factors might include government legislation affecting permitted sales and distribution channels (important in the utilities, financial services, brewing/leisure, and pharmaceutical sectors in the UK), rapid changes in consumer preferences, technological advances or breakthroughs leading to product obsolescence, or industrywide decisions affecting many customers. (Consider the "Dash to Gas's" impact on the UK coal industry, or the impact of BMW's acquisition of Rover on the UK components industry.)

> The importance of assessing the likelihood of changes in your markets is key for major sales and marketing systems with long development time scales, large fixed costs, and long payback periods.

In my experience, project risks are the most likely type of risk to cause a project to fail. Let's start out by looking at steps that you can take to alleviate these risks.

Project Risks—(User and Market). The following list shows project risks and give advice to overcome them.

Lack of top management commitment:

> Provide full information on project costs and benefits, and ensure you get the buy-in of senior management.

Senior people do not understand the solution:

> Hold walk-throughs explaining the the way things will be when the new system is implemented.

Fear of cost levels:

> Do not consider the costs in isolation from the benefits.

Inadequate budget set:

> Use a conservative cost/benefit analysis to create the budget, while expecting to spend less.

Doubts as to whether benefits will be achieved:

> Produce a rigorous cost/benefit analysis and get buy-in from senior management who should take responsibility for the benefits to be realized.

Lack of interest by end users:

> Run a "sales campaign" for the systems.

Lack of commitment from first line management:

> Focus on distinct benefits for managers.

Lack of ability to define requirements:

> Use prototyping to obtain sufficient user involvement.

Inexperience in projects of this scale:

> Learn from other people's experience.

Poor use of systems in the field (and thus underachievement of benefit levels):

> Change business processes to make an element of system use mandatory.

System falls into disuse after initial euphoria:

> Plan for continual updating of systems, and budget for them.

Project fails due to inertia:

> Buy the right level of external assistance. Give someone experienced an incentive to make it work. Do not buy external assistance as a commodity.

Steps to Minimize General Technical Risks.

Use of new unproven technology:

> Buy external expertise.

Use of old technology (in packaged solution):

> Do not only go for solutions that have worked—they probably use old technology and are narrow in scope.

Inadequate current internal skill levels:

> Accept that it will always be impossible to keep up with all new advances, and effect a skills transfer program on the technology chosen.

Fear of technological cul-de-sac given the current pace of change:

> Appropriate technical architecture can "future proof" developments by making them reusable alongside later applications.

Current technical architecture is unable to support new developments:

> Develop new, flexible technical architecture using modern methodology.

IX

Implementation

Data architecture is unable to support distributed systems:

> Rigorous data analysis is the key to avoid integrity problems; you can buy experience by employing an experienced person or contracting another company to provide the expertise.

The human/computer interface is too complex:

> Prototype during development using a range of users, and test for usability.

Lack of experience in GUI systems design:

> Take the best ideas from the market.

Problems changing old mainframe systems:

> "Ring fence" old systems as far as possible, providing the flexibility to replace them later.

Inability to support applications after initial development (for example, package implementation, turnkey solution):

> Ensure that development is completed by mixed teams of in-house and external staff.

Difficulty supporting distributed users:

> Beginning early in the project, consider what might be an appropriate level of outsourcing or resource support

Late delivery of software:

> Set expectations carefully, and plan phased implementation, allowing applications slippage.

Hardware delivery problems:

> Plan a contingency for each item.

Impact on core product processing systems:

> "Ring fence" old systems with new and control interfaces. (For example, you might "drip feed" data into old systems.)

Implementing a number of partial solutions that do not work when integrated:

> Verify system/application design end-to-end.

Central system development too large:

> Phase functionality implementation with "quick wins," concentrating on areas of key business benefit.

Techniques for Evaluating Risks and Uncertainty. In cases where the intangible costs or benefits are significant but can only be quantified on a "best guess" basis, you can use one or several of the techniques below to try to get a better fix on the intangibles.

1. Analyze the costs and benefits twice—using the most optimistic/most pessimistic estimates in turn.

   The aim here is to identify how sensitive the cost-benefit analysis is to your assumptions on the monetary value of, for example, improved customer loyalty. You may find that the system can be cost-justified on both a best- and worst-case basis, a best-case basis only, or on neither a best- nor a worst-case basis.

2. Use probability theory to estimate the expected value of costs and benefits.

   If you are unsure about the extent of future costs and benefits but a number of possible outcomes are likely, you can use probability theory to calculate their value on a weighted average basis. A weighted average is best used in cases where there are a number of possible outcomes covering a continuum of benefits.

   Suppose you are unsure about the impact of the system on levels of sales and the sales mix. You can estimate the probability or likelihood of increased sales across various product lines or customer groups. You consider it highly probable that sales will increase by $15 million to $20 million, but the increase could actually be as great as $40 million. You set out the probabilities following:

   A. 40 percent chance of increased sales of $20 million

   B. 40 percent chance of increased sales of $15 million

   C. 10 percent chance of increased sales of $40 million

   D. 10 percent chance of increased sales of $7 million

   You then estimate the benefit that would be gained from each increased level of sales—in this case, the gross margin/contribution:

   A. Benefit $3,250,000

   B. Benefit $2,200,000

   C. Benefit $6,800,000

   D. Benefit $1,050,000

   The expected benefit is then calculated by multiplying the estimated benefit of each increase in sales by the estimated probability of the increase being achieved. The expected benefit is the sum of the benefit of each outcome times the probability that the outcome will occur. In this example, the expected value of the sales forecasts is $2,965,000.

Benefit of Outcome	Probability of Outcome	Expected Benefit
A. $3,250,000	40%	$1,300,000–40%×$3,250,000
B. $2,200,000	40%	$880,000–40%×$2,200,000
C. $6,800,000	10%	$680,000–10%×$6,800,000
D. $1,050,000	10%	$105,000–10%×$1,050,000
Total Expected Value of Benefit:		**$2,965,000**

You can expand the expected value technique to allow for multiple probabilistic conditions linking—for example, the probabilities of initial and repeat sales. You can also use it with decision trees to model the expected value of the likely outcomes of several alternative scenarios over the life of the system.

You would not use probability to calculate the weighted average of two very dissimilar outcomes, as the concept of a weighted average would be meaningless. For example, if you were to place a bet on the toss of a coin, a million dollars each way, the weighted average outcome for you would be zero—a 50 percent chance of winning $1,000,000 and a 50 percent chance of losing the same amount. In this case the fact that the bet is worth zero on a weighted average basis is clearly not very helpful. (Although it is a useful statistic to present to your boss if you were to lose!)

3. Identify the cost of achieving the intangible benefits.

This method works back from the known costs and benefits to identify the residual level of cost that cannot be justified by the quantified benefits. For example, if the total cost of the system (including cost of capital and inflation) is $1,250,000, but only $1,000,000 worth of other (hard) benefits can be identified, to break even the system would have to generate an extra profit of $250,000 through increased sales or cost reductions. As a matter of business judgment, does your organization consider that the extra cost of $250,000 can be justified by resultant (but as yet unknown) increased levels in sales or cost reductions? How much are you prepared to risk, and what does the $250,000 extra mean in terms of the extra turnover required? Is it a large or small increase on existing sales trends?

4. Use a high cost of capital to compensate for risk.

This is the least preferable method, although it is one often used by large corporations to set project hurdle rates of return and business unit ROI. The argument for the method is that the cost of capital for a project should take account of inflation and the risk premium required by investors. Therefore high-risk projects have higher costs of capital. However, HCG has two objections to its use: it assumes that all the project's cash flows are equally risky, and it does not encourage management to investigate in detail the particular risks of a project.

Identify the "Real" Costs and Benefits. The system's real costs and benefits are the difference between the impact of the system and that of the next best alternative. HCG always suggests that the systems investment should be compared to the next best alternative. Companies tend to evaluate systems investments using two scenarios—business with the system and business as it is now. They forget that the real decision is between the investment in SAP and the investment in the alternative system.

The choice of the base case or next best alternative is also important but difficult. To decide if the system is worthwhile and will add value to your company, you need to ask "add value in relation to what?" Other projects competing for resources may offer a better return. One of the best ways of getting board approval for a favored but not necessarily profitable project is to chose the "right" base case!

The real costs and benefits are the likely cash flows associated with the changes arising from the system. Notice that the emphasis is on cash—not profit. It is important to ignore accounting adjustments for depreciation and central overheads. Focus instead on how the system will change the cash going in and out of your organization. Carefully consider allocations of the costs of DP/IT department support. Do they have real cost implications? Consider also the cost of line management staff—particularly your sales and marketing staff's time. What does it cost in terms of lost business opportunities elsewhere? We find that the opportunity costs of redirecting productive or creative staff from their front-line tasks are, almost without exception, ignored by organizations.

Estimating the monetary value of costs and benefits has been described as more of an art than a science! For sales and marketing-focused implementations of SAP in particular, there are two reasons why costs and benefits are particularly difficult to estimate. The first is the extent and nature of the system's potential impact. Introducing a system may alter how you advertise, promote, or sell your products. The second reason why the costs and benefits of sales and marketing systems are particularly difficult to estimate is the intangible (or intermediate) nature of some of the benefits and the uncertainty as to the final outcome.

The checklist that follows includes some brief advisory notes on quantification.

Example of Costs for Marketing-Based System. Table 31.1 shows a checklist of costs and benefits.

Table 31.1   A Checklist of Costs and Benefits

Type	Comment
Hardware	Initial purchase cost plus maintenance
Software, networks, and communications	Initial purchase cost plus maintenance, support, upgrades, and organization specific work
Project management and use of IT or support departments	If you get charged for the use of, for example, your IT department, you may be inclined to include the charges as a consulting cost. If your organization does not have guidelines as to how you should treat the costs of other internal departments, you should consider the impact that your system will have on those departments and include only those costs that will be incurred by internal departments as a result of their contribution toward your proposed system.
Publicizing the system/training	Cost of training courses, lost time of staff, manuals, and so on
Data transfer to new system	Cost of transferring data on customers, prospects, and so on, to the new system
Productivity lag	Cost of the time spent by your staff being trained, understanding the system, changing the way they do things, and ascending the learning curve. The costs will be a mixture of reduced administrative efficiency (overtime payments) and possible reductions or delays in achieving forecast sales.
Revenues/Savings	Before you start to identify areas where savings can be made, it is necessary to estimate the change between how you do things now and how they are planned to be done in the future.

IX

Implementation

(continues)

Table 31.1 Continued

Type	Comment
Increased sales	There are two ways of calculating the benefit. If sales could be increased another way, through employing more salespeople or increased advertising, for example, the benefit is the costs saved by not increasing sales through the best viable alternative method. If there is no viable alternative, the benefit is the contribution the increased sales will make to your bottom line (normally sales revenues less direct costs).
Better sales mix	By better sales mix, we mean increasing the sales of higher-margin or key strategic products.
Better customer mix	By better customer mix, we mean selling to your most profitable or key strategic customers. This may mean customers who buy high-margin products with a high probability of repeat or additional sales.
Greater customer loyalty	The benefit, as with increased sales, can be calculated as the costs saved through not adopting the best viable alternative or the value of the sales contribution.
Direct response advertising	Cost savings will depend on the aims of the system. Is it to increase the number of leads for the same expenditure, to reduce expenditure to obtain the same number of leads, or to obtain better quality leads (in which case the costs savings will be later in the sales cycle)? If the reasons for advertising are mixed (for example, direct response plus market presence), reducing advertising expenditure may have a hidden cost.
People cost savings	People costs will be saved if either the activities that cause costs are reduced in number (for example, reducing the number of backorders) or the administration process is improved. For all people cost savings, you should include salaries, pension, N.I., bonus, car costs (but not necessarily gas/travel), recruitment and nonproductive time of new hires, training, travel and subsistence, and so on. However, for small or incremental headcount reductions it is generally inappropriate to also include savings in office overheads, payroll administration, and so on as none of these savings is likely in practice to occur! The same logic applies to salespeople's cost savings.
Staff motivation and loyalty	For all types of staff, increased motivation and loyalty should lead to reduced staff turnover. The benefits will be savings in recruitment and training costs and initial low productivity as new staff climb the learning curve. For administrative staff, increased motivation should, over time, contribute to efficiency gains. Even if you can not identify specific future headcount reductions resulting from efficiency improvements, it will generally be realistic to assume that if efficiency improves by, say 10 percent, over the life of the system, your headcount-related costs (see previous) will be reduced by an equivalent amount.
More accurate sales forecasting	The benefits will depend on the way you produce your goods and services. For some organizations, better sales forecasting will enable reductions in inventory (which provide savings on stock holding costs), production to be scheduled more efficiently (at lower unit cost), and the risk of stock obsolescence to be reduced.

Type	Comment
Reduced sales lead time	Reducing your sales lead time will tend to result in a one-off benefit of accelerating revenue collection.
Potential for cross-selling	As with increases in sales, there are two ways of calculating the benefit: the costs saved by not cross-selling using the best viable alternative method, or, if there is no viable alternative, the benefit of the contribution the increased sales will make to your bottom line (normally sales revenues less direct costs).
Ability to respond to competition or changes in the market place	Very difficult to quantify! The benefit will depend on the strength and style of your existing and future competition. In highly competitive and volatile markets, it is worth more to be able to notify customers of price and product changes and to be able to adapt your sales techniques quickly than it is in less competitive and volatile markets. The benefits can be assessed in a number of ways: the costs of the best viable alternative, the reduce identified risks, or the expected value of the cost of not being able to respond to market or competitive risk.

Project Initiation

There is often a blur between SAP being investigated and a SAP project being initiated. It is possible for a SAP project to be initiated and the conclusion be that it is not implemented, although I have never heard of this happening.

SAP project initiation is defined as the time at which there has been a formal management decision to start a project.

Who Should Initiate the Project?

The first question that arises is whether the SAP project should be initiated by Business or Systems people. SAP systems are used by the people running the business. It is therefore logical that these same people should initiate the project. Unfortunately, the people running the business are not always systems experts and are not necessarily aware of the benefits that SAP could bring to their business.

The key question, therefore, is "Who is going to initiate the project, and why?" It would be more obvious if existing systems didn't meet the business requirements, for it would naturally become an issue that needed to be resolved. However, in most companies where SAP has been implemented, there have been previous systems in place that were generally able to meet the existing business requirements. Why, therefore, should anyone consider implementing SAP?

The answer probably lies in strategy. Good managers are continually looking at ways to improve their company, and consider the short-, medium-, and long-term future of the business. Considerations of products, plants and equipment, markets, and sales will probably be higher on the manager's agenda than systems, which are often regarded as costly overheads.

There is no doubt that SAP can make an enormous contribution to the success of major companies, yet it is very difficult to actually quantify that contribution. Senior managers

IX

Implementation

who are ultimately going to have to make the decision to move to SAP are going to have to read SAP literature and articles in their management magazines or attend specialist conferences and seminars to understand what SAP could do for their company.

IT staff are much more likely to know about SAP, and to have a greater understanding of the technical and operating benefits, than the business people. The logical conclusion is that business managers and systems people should work together to initiate the project.

Difficulties Management Faces in Understanding the Issues

Managers face a very difficult task in understanding the important issues relating to the implementation of SAP, both in advance and during the project itself.

The demand on managers' time is the greatest limiting factor in their understanding of the issues that arise. They are paid to do the very demanding job of running the business, yet are faced with an additional workload that could arguably justify a full-time job in itself.

In this imperfect situation, managers are in a difficult position. They have a choice of either educating themselves in SAP so that they can understand most of the issues themselves, or paying someone to advise them. Most often, they choose the latter, but with this comes the risk of bearing the cost of bad advice. In addition, the advisors will probably not know as much about the individual business requirements as the managers themselves know.

My advice to managers is to have some training on SAP and use a variety of independent advisors to get as balanced a view as possible. You should be concerned if you are receiving conflicting advice, and you should avoid making any decisions until you fully understand the issues.

Impact of Project Development Policy

Many issues arise out of SAP project development and it is advisable to develop a formal policy to give everyone concerned guidance. The first issue is whether at the feasibility stage it should be secret or open.

SAP projects invariably start with some sort of feasibility assessment. The initial investigations into the possibilities of using SAP frequently form part of a wider strategy study. Because these types of studies frequently look at the possibility of radical changes, discussions often take place behind closed doors. These simple brainstorming exercises can easily lead to rumors of massive job cuts or reorganizations spreading through the company grapevine, which can be very damaging to staff morale.

When ideas that are considered by many to be negative are bounced around organizations, there is an understandable rallying call by the opposition, who use all the tools in their armory to defeat or knock new plans off course. Some of the many tactics used include lobbying senior management, trying to discredit plans, and talking about ruin and disaster. Management plans become twisted in the rumor mill and stories get changed in the telling, all of which is completely unproductive.

However, the case for secrecy in the feasibility stage has some advantages. You should consider using confidentiality agreements with project team members. The management team has a choice of either announcing that a feasibility study is going on, and stating when the results will be available, or keeping the whole thing completely hush-hush and announcing the plans when they are ready. Each choice has its own merits and disadvantages that have to be weighed by the executive management team.

The greatest danger is that a secret study becomes common knowledge, which leads to a feeling of conspiracy.

Early Consideration of Control and Security

Control and security are very important and should be considered from the very earliest stages of a project. It is well worth forming a special advisory team to investigate and advise you on the relevant issues. Such a team should include the internal audit manager, the system security manager, and representative line managers from the user community. It is well worth involving an SAP security and controls consultant to advise you from the earliest planning stages through to implementation and beyond.

There probably won't be any security or control issues that can't be resolved. However, the integrated nature of SAP can give rise to security problems if not properly addressed. There are many ways in which the overall system can be adequately controlled and security maintained. Job segregation, authorizations for particular system transactions, and control reports can all be used. Third-party access to the system must also be considered, for customers and suppliers.

Simply configuring the system properly can resolve many of the issues. In many cases the move to SAP involves going back to the drawing board to develop security and control policies and procedures. You will be most vulnerable to security breaches at the time of implementation, when there may be uncertainty, many temporary staff, and heavy workloads for everyone. Possible redundancies and uncertainties might make loyal employees unsettled and the remote chance of system sabotage or fraud should never be taken lightly. Those who work closely with the system will be well aware of any holes in security.

Project Methodology

In order to stand any chance of successfully implementing SAP on time, within budget, and to a good standard, you must adopt a formal project methodology.

You will receive useful guidance from SAP and their business partners, and you will find a plentiful supply of independent consultants with a wide variety of offerings. There is not one correct implementation method; you must judge each on its merits.

The project methodology can be split into two parts. The first area deals with the system configuration and implementation, and the second deals with every other aspect of the project and change.

The first area has been addressed so comprehensively by SAP that one needs look no further. The experience gained by over 4,500 SAP installations has been channeled into the development of specialist tools that provide an unbeatable framework to model business processes and configure the system. The SAP Procedure Model offers project and implementation management guidance. It provides a detailed guide of every stage of the project from the earliest planning stages through post-installation operation.

Procedure Model. The Procedure Model is now an integral component of R/3. It provides guidance on the entire implementation process, including organizational and concept design, detailed design and system setup, preparations needed for going live, and production operation. It covers the processes of:

Organization and Conceptual Design

- Project preparation
- Setting up system environments
- Training the project team
- Defining functions and processes
- Designing interfaces and enhancements
- Project management

Detailed Design and System Setup

- Conceptual design, including quality checks
- Establishing global settings
- Establishing company structures
- Establishing master data
- Establishing functions and processes
- Creating interfaces and enhancements
- Establishing reporting
- Establishing archiving management
- Establishing authorization management
- System testing
- Developing application systems

Preparations for Going Live

- Creating the "going live" plan
- Creating user documentation
- Setting up the production environment
- Training users

- Establishing system administration
- Transferring data to the production system
- Supporting quality systems

Production Operation

- Supporting production operation
- Maximizing production operation
- System maintenance and release upgrades

The Procedure Model uses:

- IMG—Implementation Guide

  Used for documenting the system settings during configuration

- SAPoffice

  Used for storing and editing text and graphical information created during the course of project work. It offers links to PC packages such as Microsoft Word, Excel, PowerPoint, Lotus Screen Cam.

- Business Navigator

  Used for displaying graphical models of business processes and functions

R/3 Business Engineering Workbench. Chapter 29 describes the R/3 Business Engineering Workbench, which has been designed to:

1. Reduce implementation times dramatically by focusing on the most essential elements.

2. Facilitate post-configuration and change management across releases throughout the entire life cycle of R/3.

3. Supply a complete business repository in the form of active business reference models, together with their configuration options.

4. Demonstrate how process-driven configuration can be used to control the customizing process.

Procuring SAP Services

The blistering speed of change within the technological arena implies that many critical decisions get made on obsolete data. (yesterday's facts). To be presumptuous in the IT environment today suggests ignorance. Never has information been so readily available to anybody interested in being at the cutting edge (real-time/online) of technology.

The problem should not be the "best fit" selection of hardware and software for a business, but rather the evolution of the selection.

IX

Implementation

Thus, a successful SAP implementation is not complete without an adequate technical SAP R/3 infrastructure. To create an alliance with the best supplier of computer services you need a plan, which will predict your long-term expenditure. This plan should look into the obvious topics of a Request For Quotation (RFQ) as shown in the following typical RFQ structure:

Risk reduction

Cost implication

Rental cost versus Purchasing

Installation cost

Service implication

Warranty versus Guarantee

Service Response times

Legal implication

Ownership of Customization

Non-Delivered Goods/Services

Technical implication

Technical system change

Backup procedures

Replacement Services

Supplier Profile

Organizational capabilities

Financial strength

Future growth Planning Purposes

Staffing Requirements

Training Requirements

Technical Support Structure

Software Patches

Hardware Fixes

Installation Plan

Servers and Software PC roll-out Plan

The mammoth sizing scoping and planning work for SAP in determining the options of various solutions must finally be crystallized, that is, find the hardware and software platform.

Project Managers have often utilized a tender process for various requests and find themselves comfortable with this inquiry tool. Past experience has shown that SAP R/3 platform tenders had left some questions open, particularly when you discuss the comparative analysis processes. As a tender strategist you can develop many methods to achieve structured responses. The Request For Quotation (RFQ) in Appendix D is an example that has been used very successfully by various management consultants and companies to provide a structured and reliable response from the service supplier.

What Type of Tenders Exist?

In many countries we have to take into consideration the legal implications of using words like Tender, Quotation, or Proposal. The tendering process is often a governmental request to get pricing of services or goods, whereby not only quantitative but also qualitative information is taken into account. The legal terms for each country are different but are mostly handled by a tender committee, which is governed by the tender board rules. A more commercial version is the Request For Proposal (RFP), whereby implicit in the statement is that we receive an offer of services or goods.

A much more deterministic approach would be the Request For Quotation (RFQ), whereby we, the requester, provide and define the boundaries of the expected solution. This approach seems to be more exacting, as we already know the product (SAP R/3.)

It is not sufficient to express the fact that you will be implementing SAP R/3, but rather to build a framework for the supplier with rules of how to deliver these services. The framework and the rules are the ABCs of a comprehensive RFQ. It will eliminate all vague expectations of the deliverables required by all parties involved.

In a complex systems plan there are some imperatives, correct mix of specialist resources and careful consideration of each of the tasks duration.

The RFQ Differentiater

The need for practical guidelines in a Request For Quotation (RFQ) is based on the required predictability of an implementation plan. Often companies provide the supplier with some questions, not knowing or aware of the fact that the supplier has only a vague understanding of the requests that are related to the product serviced by the supplier.

Tender responses often answer the possible fit of a client's profile rather than his or her actual needs. Thus, an unclear picture is painted that results in disputes and potential litigation.

How to Manage the Tendering Process?

Clarity of thought and professional help are the major success factors in this area. Like so many things in life, a little bit of effort up front pays huge dividends over time. Given that SAP implementations require considerable investment, there can be considerable cost implications when choosing a consulting partner.

Using the Request For Quotation example in Appendix D should be a starting point. ASAP World Consultancy are one of a relatively few companies that offer specialist consultancy services in this area. Their Procurement Consultancy Practice Manager said, "We believe that three areas of expertise are required: Legal, Accounting, and Implementation Knowledge. We provide a team bringing together the highest caliber people with these areas of expertise. Our service might be expensive, but it must surely be a wise investment." Unfortunately, it is difficult for companies to keep control of costs, differentiate between the many offerings of SAP consulting companies who are all trying very hard to differentiate themselves from each other.

Building a Project Team

Every project has a beginning, middle, and end. Therefore, a team that you bring together to pursue a project is "on board" for only a finite period of time. For many, their place on a project is a temporary position where they are on loan from their existing job, and they may still owe allegiance to another role and another taskmaster. As such, many team members have half of their thoughts still on the job they have come from and the other half on what will become of them when the project is over. This leaves the project manager with the challenge of enlisting the team members' best efforts in service of the project—a job that can be likened to herding cats.

Of all the skills a project manager must master, therefore, the ability to build a strong and cohesive team must be at the top of the list. But the pursuit of this grail has left many otherwise high flyers exhausted and confused on the wayside.

So what is it that makes a team? What are the basic ingredients of the recipe for teamwork? And in what order should they be added to the mix? There follows a list of ingredients that should be considered and added to the pot in sequential order.

1. Choosing a Project Manager

2. Determining the Requirements of a Project Manager

3. Determining the Requirements of a Project Advisor

4. Devising Roles of Project Team Members

5. Drawing up Project Team Organization Charts

6. Determining how Projects Fit Within the Traditional Organizational Structure

7. Determining how Projects Fit Within the New Organizational Structure

8. Recruiting/Assembling the Right Team

Choosing a Project Manager

This is step one, and the sooner in the planning process it is completed, the better. Few things are more motivating to a person than to have the opportunity to oversee and contribute to the plan that they are going to later be expected to carry out. Therefore, it's important to select the person for the job and brief them as early in the process as possible.

But where do you find the person with the "right stuff?" The project manager is the person who is responsible for a project being completed on time, within budget, and to the agreed upon specifications. It is a demanding task, and successful project managers have much to be proud of. In fact, anyone who shows the ability to successfully run a project is usually so highly thought of that they are soon promoted to a line management post worthy of their proven organizational skills. Unfortunately, the flip-side of the project manager's red carpet to corporate stardom is a dearth of experienced project managers ready and willing to take on the *next* project.

To compound the problem, the lifestyle of a project manager in these days of globalization is rarely conducive to a happy family life. Project managers are expected to spend many nights away from home, and at the very least will spend many a late evening at the office. This makes it difficult to find experienced people who are truly content to be at the beck and call of a project.

What should you do? Appoint an experienced hand despite his or her family commitments, or some young "flyer" whose enthusiasm and lack of family ties is in inverse proportion to work experience? The answer may lie somewhere between the two extremes. Combine the one's experience with the other's flexibility. Consider appointing youth to the role of project manager and experience to the role of resident advisor. If they can work hand-in-hand (and admittedly this is no small "if"), you may just have a recipe for success and a project management template that could have many applications within your organization.

The project manager's role is "hands on" irrespective of time or place, while the advisor's role can be mainly confined to being "in residence" and available during normal working hours. Moreover, world time differences are dissolved these days through voicemail and e-mail, and should provide no hindrance to the parties maintaining a valuable working relationship.

What Should You Require of a Project Manager? From the project manager you will want at least minimal competence and ability in several areas.

Corporate Standing. The project manager must command influence within the organization commensurate with the importance of the project entrusted to him or her. Project managers must draw on corporate resources and will often need to scavenge these resources with at least the connivance of those "in charge."

Interpersonal Skills. These are needed to recruit and lead a diverse group of people, many of whom are likely to be strangers to each other and to the project manager, irrespective of the time they have spent working in the same company! This person has the important job of enlisting hearts, heads, and hands 100 percent in service of the project.

Cultural Sensitivity. You will also expect someone who is at least aware of the importance of cultural differences, even if they need to brush up on the particular cultures they are likely to face in bringing a project to term.

IX

Implementation

Energy and Drive. Some people have the kind of life-force that others may call charisma. This quality is especially important in creating the kind of tight coalition of minds that project management requires.

Business Savvy. Project managers must be aware of the business case. They must know where the project fits into overall business strategy. The more comprehensive the implementation of SAP, the more the demands in this respect and the more senior this person will need to be.

Technical Know-How. To earn respect among the team and to competently assess the risk factors associated with the project, the project manager must be able to show a full grasp of the major issues, even though many details will be outside his/her experience.

Project Management. You will need someone who has worked in a project environment and who is aware of the phases that a project goes through, in particular the importance of controlling and reducing the time taken to navigate the critical path. Add to this an ability to keep costs under control.

What Should You Require of a Project Advisor? Your project advisor should fit with the dictionary definition of "don," in other words, a member of the "teaching staff," a person of rank, and someone who dominates (the root of the word "don") their subject. They are at the center of your organization's claim to be a "learning organization." They should exhibit the following qualities.

Project Management. This person will have a number of successful projects tucked under his or her belt.

Mentoring Skills. The advisor will also be a person of "character," someone who project managers will actively seek to consult with because of the way he/she is able to listen and offer advice.

Well Networked. Help that the advisor cannot give from his or her own experience can be sought from other experienced hands whom the advisor knows and to whom he/she can refer the project manager.

Devising Roles of Project Team Members

Team members should be enrolled as early in the project process as possible so that they have the opportunity to participate at an early stage in the planning phase. But the desire to populate the project must give way to the need to build the project team in the correct fashion. The flow chart on the left side of Figure 31.6 shows the traditional way that organizations and project teams tend to be constructed. That is, you look at who is available, invite them to join up, assign roles, and then turn to the task to see what exactly needs to be done and what skills will be demanded of those present.

A more appropriate way of approaching this aspect of team building is illustrated on the right side of Figure 31.6, where the structure of the project team is designed as an outcome of processes, roles, and skills. This methodology derives from the ideas developed by CSC Index, the management consultants that brought us process reengineering.

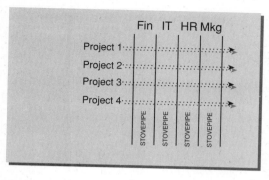

Fig. 31.6   The traditional approach versus process approach.

What the flow chart on the right of the chart achieves is a strong fit between the demands of the project and what the team members have to offer. This can only be motivating for the team members and good for the outcome of the project.

Drawing Up Project Team Organization Charts

As a result of planning roles (see previous section) you will develop a firm idea of who does what and how each team member interrelates to the others. In SAP projects, traditional hierarchical organigrams are an inappropriate structure for faithfully representing the flow of information and the direction of project reporting lines. Roles tend to be varied with people frequently reporting to different managers for different parts of their work.

What we need is a new way of thinking about and graphically displaying the interrelationships to help people change the way in which they view project management.

How Projects Fit Within Organizational Structures

In the past, project management in traditional stovepipe companies would cut across the pipes, drawing out their needs as and when required (see Figure 31.7).

Fig. 31.7   In a stovepipe structure power lies with the functions; projects are a side issue.

But this model leaves project managers without the most important traditional management tool: hierarchical position. Many projects owe their premature demise to the project manager's lack of corporate clout.

So what happens when you cannot base leadership on hierarchy? In a project team that cuts horizontally across departmental functions, there is no top and no bottom—the membership is organized in a circle, and the group's willingness to put the project manager at the center of it will determine the team's success. Such willingness can only come from respect and trust, and these two forces combine to glue the team together (see Figure 31.8).

How Do Projects Fit Within the New Organizational Structure?

The changing market and industry conditions is leading to a slow breakdown of the stovepipe model of organization.

Departmental empires are being toppled and are rising from the ashes in service to projects (see Figure 31.9).

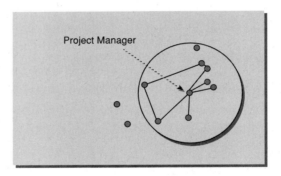

Fig. 31.8   In the absence of hierarchy, the team's willingness to put the project manager at the center is critical.

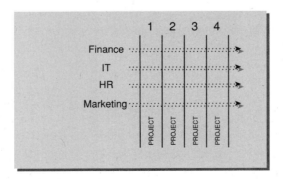

Fig. 31.9   Independent departments are being replaced with project-oriented teams.

As the departments rise from the ashes, they are unrecognizable in their new incarnation. Rather than being well-entrenched baronies, they are now loose affiliations and networks of people whose main allegiance is to a project but who have common (often professional) interests, be they in human resources, information systems, or safety at work.

Recruiting/Assembling the Right Team

Once you have determined the roles that need to be filled, by analyzing the tasks that need to be completed and the skills they demand (see "Devising Roles of Project Team Members" earlier in this chapter), you are ready to seek the right people for the job.

Each role demands a particular mix of attributes and competencies. If your HR department maintains a central register of employees that shows the package of competencies each one has, all you need to do is browse through and select the people you need. More likely, however, no such register exists in your company and you must rely on people's reputations within the organization to guide your choices.

In any event, resist the temptation to select only the people you "get on with." Such a narrow specification may exclude talented newcomers or forgotten old-timers who may have the exact skills you need. No matter who you end up bringing together, they will need some help finding the best ways to work together. This is true even if they have worked alongside each other before. (This is covered in the next section.)

The team you end up with may be full-time or part-time, begged or borrowed, but it is likely in any event that you will have a mixture of the following types of team players.

Employees. These are directly employed staff of your company, chosen above all for their technical and administrative skills.

Consultants. These are outside experts who can bring in technical skills and others you enlist to facilitate the management processes and teach interpersonal skills.

They may include:

- SAP Business Partners
- Independent SAP Contractors
- Documentation/Training Consultants
- Human Issues Consultants
- Internal & External Communications Consultants
- Specialist SAP Security Consultants
- Project Planning Consultants

Customers. "Customers" in this case means representatives of the people whom the project has been designed to serve. This may include a member of the senior management team if the project is internally focused, or an actual client of the company if the project is externally focused.

IX

Implementation

Building Team Relationships

If anyone knows about building relationships, it has got to be the military. In a profession where lives hang on teamwork, team spirit is a top priority. If someone is charged with watching your back, you want to be able to rely on them 100 percent.

Therefore, when not actively engaged on defending the realm, the military works on building team spirit. The result is a regimental pride that stays with its members forever. It is not achieved by accident. It is carefully crafted by the officers, people who know how to mold a disparate group into a team. The end result is a fitness for purpose and a readiness to go into action.

So much for the Army—what about "real life?" How do you build the kind of relationships that you can depend on in civilian life, relationships that work outside hierarchy that are strong enough to survive the rough and tumble of life outside the secure walls of the departmental edifices. How, in other words, do you ensure you have a real "relationship" and not just a "relationdinghy"!

This is the concern of every organization that has realized the importance of basing its future on trust and camaraderie rather than fear and autocracy. These are companies that are beginning to appreciate that if they want to emulate the military's exceptional teamwork, they have to put a similar emphasis on instilling the necessary behaviors, preferably before the rubber hits the ground and the team scatters in all directions in pursuit of their various tasks.

Here are some concrete steps that you can take to create strong teamwork:

1. Appoint team-building specialists to manage the process, emphasizing self-awareness and communication skills. If outdoor adventure training or yachting is part of the package—fine, but the kernel of this work should be to intensively investigate each team member's preferred way of operating. The team must learn what communication methods can overcome their stylistic differences and get everyone working well together.

2. Agree upon a strategy that covers not only team-building, but also team-maintaining during the term of the project. You may wish to schedule team maintenance interventions far ahead on the calendar, for otherwise such maintenance is likely to be overlooked in the heat of battle.

3. Brief the entire team, including consultants and customers, on the way in which teamwork is to be developed and maintained. Ensure that each participant has a personal reason for taking part, so that individual advantage is the basis for team advantage.

4. Assemble all team members at an off-site location (off-site because it minimizes distraction from the office). This kind of work typically takes a number of days, not necessarily all at once, but usually involves a night or two in residence at the conference site. Select a hotel that reflects the importance you feel should be given to the issue of teamwork.

Adopting Effective Working Practices

As a project manager, how do you go about instilling effective working practices in your team? This is especially important when members of your team are on board because of their proficiency in areas of which you have minimal knowledge. Indeed, some projects can involve a multitude of different skill sets.

And yet as project manager, you must guide the team in the right direction, and in doing so instill effective working practices. How can you do this? The answer is to shape the culture in which your team operates. The culture then helps to influence the behavior of the team.

Whereas management by objectives tells a manager what they ought to do, and the proper organization of their job enables them to do it, it is the culture of the organization that determines *whether* they will do it. It is the culture that motivates, that calls upon a person's reserves of dedication and effort, that decides whether they will give of their best or just do enough to get by.

In running a project, you have an opportunity to shape the kind of culture you need. Even though you must do so within the context of the larger organizational culture, your team will look to you to set the tone for this particular project. Your ability to do so, and do it well, will seriously affect your success at completing the project on time, within budget, and to specification.

Shaping culture entails a straightforward process of describing the behaviors you want and ensuring they are displayed. But why would anyone want to change their behavior and perhaps have to act "out of character" just because it suits your ideal of the perfect culture? The answer can only be that it is in their own best interests to do so. They must want to be involved for their own ends, whatever they may be. So your job as Project Manager is to find out your team members' agendas—*and to remain aware of them as they develop through the life of the project.* The extent to which the project acts as a vehicle for the team members' own aspirations will determine the degree of effort you can expect from them. In simple terms, you must put out the bait! Remember though, whereas all cats like fish, your team members will have multifarious reasons for enlisting on the project team.

So now you have a project to complete and a number of prospective team members. How can you set about shaping a culture appropriate to the demands of the project? Here is a step-by-step guide:

Meet all team members individually. Brief them on the purpose of the project. Explain the roles you have in mind for them. Ask them to tell you the reasons they might accept the role; for example, how will the project further their own ambitions?

Articulate the project purpose to the team as a whole. Underscore the aspects that are of particular importance to the client. These are likely to include cost, timeframe, and certain technical specifications. In some cases, where the final payback is likely to dwarf the development costs (such as is typical in the drug industry), cost of development may not be a critical issue—but time taken to bring the product to the market is. Be clear about what actually counts.

Take time out to begin the task of building strong teamwork. (See "Building Team Relationships" earlier in this chapter.)

Armed with the knowledge of each individual's aims, synthesize a vision for the project that encompasses their aspirations as well as those of your client. Your team can help you do this. "Synthesizing a vision" merely means describing, in as much detail as possible, what the project's outcome will look like, even what it will feel like! Add in the ramifications of completing it on time, within budget, ahead of the competition, or whatever else raises the energy level of those present.

Now that you know what you want to achieve, how do you want to achieve it? You don't have to have a detailed plan at this point, but what overall means are you prepared to use to achieve your ends? This is about the values you hold important, the standards you want to underpin the operations of the team. This is not a "would be nice if we had them" list, but rather a list of values which, if lived out, would definitely make a difference to the smooth running of the project and the achievement of your vision. Again use your team to distill the core values.

Next, begin the process of underpinning the values by translating them into specific behaviors that you deem important. For example, if "respect for others" is a value that should govern the way things are done, what specific behaviors will show such respect in the workplace? Some examples might be: (1) keep abreast of team members' ambitions; (2) ensure a balanced lifestyle for team members; and (3) start and end meetings on time.

Put in place support structures to ensure that the agreed behaviors are adhered to. The extent to which each behavior is already entrenched will determine what kind of support structure will be needed to encourage its adoption. Some examples of support structures for the behaviors listed above might be: (1) introduce a periodic career review; (2) lock the car park at 6 p.m., and (3) start promptly without waiting for latecomers. Of course, the team must agree upon such structures in order for them to be acceptable. And they need to be maintained only up to the point that the desired behavior becomes the norm. Remember in all of this that people in general want to do their best, and if you have selected your team well, this will particularly apply to them. The emphasis of the structures that you introduce is not so much to penalize unproductive behavior but to make it very plain to all what "best" means in the context of your project.

Ensure that everyone is properly briefed on their part in the project and invited to take on certain responsibilities by the person or people from whom they take instruction. The word "invited" is used deliberately. Peter Drucker, doyen of management gurus, would have us think of the people who work for us as "volunteers" and treat them as such. If it makes sense to do so within the command and control structures of companies, it must definitely make sense to do so when enrolling people on a project outside the system, given that they often have a "day job" to return to.

Use the tried and tested (and computerized) project management tools where appropriate, such as:

- ■ **PERT and Critical Path Management**: Used to focus attention on those activities that, if foreshortened, will advance completion of the project

- ■ **Gantt Chart**: Preferred by many because of its ease of use

Experienced project players may feel comfortable without these graphic aids. It really depends on the size of your project and the amount of resources you need to employ and keep tabs on. One advantage of using them is that they are said to steepen the "worry curve," and thereby minimize the risk of leaving too much to the end of the project.

Provide timely and crystal clear feedback to individuals on their performance and the contribution that their behavior makes to the project culture as a whole.

Keys to Success

Most people want to have a successful project and implementation, but in such a complex area with so many different aspects to consider it can be difficult to achieve.

When the complex details are removed there are a number of key areas that have a significant affect on the likely success of the project. If these areas are dealt with well, there is a good likelyhood that the project will be successful. We have identified these main areas as keys to succes which are listed below.

Know Your Business

To implement SAP, you need to know your business. While you might think this seems obvious, and it can appear to be one of the easiest tasks to perform, it is in fact extremely difficult when you start to look closely at this area.

If you are considering implementing SAP, your company is probably fairly large, with lots of employees, departments, plants, locations, processes, and procedures that all have to interact with each other. When you start an SAP project, the issue of knowing your business appears to be relatively straightforward. You have probably worked in your business for many years and have a very wide experience of your company's operations.

However, for the purposes of implementing SAP, your knowledge must be at a very low, basic level. You need to know the smallest details. You need to know absolutely everything that goes on: what every person does, every procedure, every policy, every detail on every subject you can possibly think about. You need to understand not only what is going on currently, but also what things are in the process of changing.

Few businesses remain static, and markets and business requirements invariably change. It is only by consulting everybody in the business—with no exceptions—that you can begin to really know your business at the lowest level. You must not only understand your business in its current form, but you must also be aware of the direction in which it is moving. An example of this might be the knowledge of some governmental legislative changes with which your company will have to comply at some known date in the future.

IX

Implementation

It is highly unlikely that any one person, or indeed group of people, will know your business well enough for the purposes of implementation. The detailed knowledge of your business that you need is held by every employee, every temporary worker, every contract staff member, and perhaps even by another company that you have contracted to handle a particular side of your business, such as transport. An analogy of a huge jig-saw puzzle can demonstrate the situation. There are tens of thousands of tiny pieces, and each holds unique information that is difficult to make sense of. Yet by bringing each of those tiny pieces together, you are able to see the whole picture. If even a few small pieces are missing, the image is spoiled.

At the start of the project, it is common for people to find it hard to look at a low enough level. The detail is everything. If the detail is ignored at the beginning of the project, the problems that will occur later on will multiply tenfold. If you don't really get to know your business early on in the project, there is every likelihood that your project will end up over budget and behind schedule.

However, the job of really getting to know your business is an awesome one. Be relentless in your search. Leave no stone unturned.

> **Tip**
>
> The following are practical ideas that can be used to get to know your business in the detail that is required for a SAP project.
>
> 1. Involve everyone, including:
>   - all employees
>   - temporary staff
>   - contractors
>   - third-party companies
>   - possibly even customers
> 2. Find an effective way of documenting the business.
> 3. Divide up the areas of business that are likely to be affected, and allocate responsibility to trusted personnel. When people know they are accountable, they are likely to take the task very seriously.

Know Your Existing Systems

There is an obvious link between knowing your systems and knowing your business. However, it will help you considerably if you catalog all your existing systems. Include mainframes, PCs, and all other platforms in use by any person in the company, whether they are employees, temporary staff, contractors, third-party companies, or even customers. You will need to gain a very thorough picture of your existing systems to enable you to move toward implementing SAP.

You will need to record the following information about each system:

1. System name
2. Description of its function
3. Person in charge of it
4. Platform
5. Interfaces
6. Comments

Know Your Organization

One major company moving into a massive office designed and built to its exact specifications was embarrassed to find that the building wasn't big enough to accommodate all the staff. The reason for the situation was that each department had many temporary staff, some who were administered by the HR Department and others who were administered independently. When the HR Department had been asked to provide details on the number of employees and temporary staff, they did so diligently, but they were simply not aware of all the other temporary staff being used.

When implementing SAP, information must be checked and double checked. Not only will you need to know your own organization well, but you will also need to know how it interrelates to the environment in which you operate. For example, you may well have temporary staff, contractors, customers, and suppliers involved in your business processes, all of whom may have an impact on your SAP development and planning.

By knowing your organization, you will be in a better position to develop your vision for the future and implement SAP in a way that will enable you to realize your vision.

You will need to record the following information about each person:

1. Job title
2. Job description
3. Location
4. Person currently filling the position
5. Department
6. Status: contractor/temporary/supplier/customer
7. Direct supervisor
8. Who reports to him/her

Know Your Objectives

It can be particularly hard to define objectives since there are invariably many of them. Defining clear objectives will help everybody: management, employees, and members of the project team. It is very easy as the project progresses for everybody to forget the objectives that were defined originally as the objective of simply implementing the system takes over and becomes the main objective. If throughout the duration of the project everyone stays focused on the objectives that have been defined, then you stand a much greater chance of achieving them.

> **Tip**
>
> A good tip is to write down the objectives and laminate them and distribute them to all employees in the company and members of the project team. They can pin them up all around the work area so that everyone is absolutely clear on the overall objectives.

System Testing Overview

System testing in an integral part of the system development process. You must carry out the testing on a function-by-function, process-by-process basis and then expand it to fully integrated tests. When you have successfully completed the fully integrated tests, you must then carry it out using as close to full live system volumes of processing as possible.

The testing is a vital part of the project development, and provides an excellent progress indicator. The tests must be well planned and executed, and you must accurately record the results.

Planning and preparing for the tests is a major task and comes at times of maximum workload and pressure for system developers. It is only by splitting the tasks into small, manageable chunks and allocating responsibility for each task to a particular individual that you can hope to complete the planning and tests themselves. During formal testing, system development invariably gets slowed down, as resources have to be allocated to the tests.

Testing is the greatest indicator of readiness to go live, yet it is a tremendously difficult thing to manage. You might consider bringing in specialist teams to help prepare and run the tests.

Functionality Testing

Functionality testing is a daily task of the system developers. They model, configure, and test as a routine. The difficulty is the dependency between different teams or different team members. These dependencies might be the shared use of master file information that needs to be set up or the reliance on others to process transactional data.

Even on the development systems, there has to be system control and authorization so that particular parts of the system are closed to all except those needing to work with them.

Integrated Testing

Integrated testing requires great cooperation between project team members, and confusion can arise if roles and responsibilities are not clearly defined and understood.

For example, the integrated testing of a number of processes across a number of SAP modules can involve many different teams. Financial modules rely on data from the sales module. Testing a customer placing a simple order can involve the processes of:

- Customer establishment
- Order placement, with credit checks at the time of placement
- Delivery note creation
- Picking list creation
- Shipment creation
- Delivery and goods issue creation
- Invoice and statement creation
- Accounts Receivable collection
- Financial postings
- Payment allocation

The correct entries have to be made in the general ledger, the warehouse management systems have to deal with the order, and the production systems need to make or replenish the stock. This may trigger the purchasing systems to order the materials to make the stock, and so on. At the end of these processes, the reporting has to be tested.

Integrated testing relies on the creation of clearly defined scenarios that have defined purposes. To make them work, responsibility for performing the test has to be allocated to teams or individuals.

It is equally important to review the results of the tests and to be able to take the appropriate action and retest the scenario.

Even in a company of modest size, the number of integrated test scenarios can run into thousands, becoming completely impractical and unmanageable. It is difficult to establish who should be driving the integrated tests. Each area of the project team will need to test its own area, and yet the system performance acceptability is best evaluated by the people who are having to use it.

Each area of the project should be able to define a series of tests that they need to carry out. If you were to look at each test, you would probably find that each team's requirements could be combined into a single scenario. Such analysis is immensely time-consuming, however, and it still leaves the problem of whose test it is and who is judging whether the test was a success. It could well be that six or eight different people are judging the success of a single scenario.

For tests to work, the system has to be set up, the environment has to be clean of rubbish data that could spoil the test, and there have to be strict controls on system activity. The testing of weekly or monthly reports and rebate schemes that apply in arrears, and so on, are more difficult to test because they rely on an interval of time that is difficult to recreate.

IX

Implementation

If you have documented your business requirements well, they can be used as a source for developing test scenarios.

Volume Testing

Volume tests are the same as integrated tests, but on a larger scale. The object is to simulate the system activity as if the system were live and the business were being run on it.

If integrated tests are hard, then it is not difficult to imagine the difficulties that can be encountered with volume testing. Undertaking volume testing requires, by its very nature, huge quantities of human resources. The question of where these resources come from is difficult to answer. There are probably not enough people on the project team, so you must involve users or others. Managed well, volume testing can function as a valuable part of the user training program, since it enables users to become familiar with the system.

The great difficulty, of course, is how companies manage to take users away from their jobs of running the business. Night sessions, weekend working, and cancelled holidays are all options. None of these are likely to be too good for morale, however, and everyone will probably be under immense pressure as it is. You could hire in a team of testers, but that comes at a heavy price, since the testers need some training to enable them to carry out the tests.

Evaluating Test Results

Testing is a waste of time unless the results are properly documented and evaluated. Every test that failed any aspect has to generate a task to put right the failure, and the fix itself has to be retested.

The difficulty with so much system development going on at the same time is that the testing process has to be continual. What worked today may not work tomorrow if someone has altered a setting.

There is a huge risk in going live without having completed successful volume integrated tests, as you discover that things don't work only when it really matters.

Small problems that can be overcome quickly are manageable, but as is often the case, some problems take time to fix, and if you can't service your customers or run your business, the cost can be massive. Disasters with SAP implementations may be very rare, but they have happened. You should take testing very seriously, and allocate sufficient resources.

Going Live

At the start of a project, the thought of going live seems a long way off, yet the time soon comes when the fruits of everyone's labor make it a possibility.

Before going live, you must ensure that you have, as a minimum, done *all* the following:

- Configured the system to meet your business requirements

- Thoroughly tested the system, not only function-by-function but in a fully integrated environment

- Trained all the users

- Put in place new internal organizations

- Installed and tested all the necessary hardware

- Printed new stationery if required

- Developed all interfaces with other systems

- Transferred master data and relevant transactional data from old systems, including customer master, material master, open orders, and accounts receivable and payable data

- Put in place a support structure for the new system

Even the smallest implementation requires a huge amount of effort and planning. The best way to plan an implementation is to create a critical path of tasks that need to be completed before you can go live. The critical path list needs to be developed by all the key team leaders and project managers together with the business managers. The best way of building up a critical path is to get everyone involved, including users, to create their own lists. If managers in each area combine the tasks that need to be achieved, then they can be further combined with those of other managers to produce a definitive plan.

It makes sense to dedicate somebody to the job of managing the planning. By using a Project Management System, project managers can know how the implementation is progressing and decide when it is realistic to go live.

Planning is more an art than a science, and you will need to get used to making assumptions and calculated guesses. It is easy to become a slave to the planning systems—you have to be careful that you don't spend half your time recording what everyone has done and inputting data to produce meaningless reports.

It is also easy for managers to feel out of control, and for good reason. It is very difficult to estimate how long a task is going to take when you haven't done it before and will probably never do it again. Even the most skilled and respected consultants can make mistakes when trying to estimate when companies will be ready to go live. You have to accept that in any systems implementation, most companies are embarking on a journey without knowing exactly when or where they will arrive.

By having direct control over as many factors as possible, you minimize the chance of the unknown throwing you violently off course. It is difficult to describe the pressures that senior managers are under to complete the project on time and within budget. The pressure to go live on time is immense, yet the consequences of trying to do so before you are ready can be catastrophic. The pressures are inevitably and quite rightly passed down the line, for it takes total commitment, superhuman effort, and gritty determination to implement on time. SAP implementations are no place for weak-minded or second rate people—the project team and users need to be hard-working, flexible, and determined.

If you are one of the senior managers making the go/no-go decision, you have my sympathy. If all your team leaders and users are confident that they are ready, you are a very lucky person, but in most cases the reality is that not all the items on your critical path are completed. You are now in a situation of compromise, and you start to ask the question: "What would happen if we were to go live without these particular tasks being completed?" If the answer is inconvenience or a little extra work internally, then you might be able to live with it, but if you can't invoice your customers or your warehouse management system doesn't work properly, then the situation is very different. More often than not, the issues are not black-and-white but shades of gray, making the decision all the more difficult.

If you are implementing a financial module, you might need to go live at a month-end or year-end. You might need to take the opportunity of a national holiday when the company isn't open for business or you may need the cooperation of your customers and suppliers, all of which require advance notice and planning. Whatever the issues, if you are responsible for making or recommending the decision to go live, you need to be well aware of all the factors that influence that decision.

Big Bang versus Phased Approach

Depending on how many modules are being implemented, there are two possible approaches to implementation: the Big Bang or the Phased Approach.

Big Bang. This approach takes courage. On a particular day you stop using your old systems and start using SAP.

The advantages are:

- Implementation is quicker, and therefore staff and expensive project costs can be released earlier to save money.

- New system benefits can be realized sooner.

- Duplication of file maintenance in new and old systems can be minimized.

- Fewer interfaces to old systems are required.

The disadvantages include:

- Risk of catastrophic disaster is greater than with phased implementation—if something goes wrong, it could affect your whole business.

- There is more preparation needed, and if you are not careful implementation can slip.

- All users need training at the same time, which puts a huge strain on the training organization.

- The support groups need to be larger to cope with problems after implementation.

Phased Approach. With this approach, you implement module-by-module over a period of time.

The advantages are:

- The risk factor is lower.

- Support teams have a more manageable workload.

- The workload of the project team is more manageable, as they are able to concentrate on a smaller area at a time rather than on everything all at once.

The disadvantages are:

- You will have far more interface issues. You will need to write and test interfaces to and from existing systems that will be required only until you replace them with other SAP modules.

- The project will last longer.

- The full benefits of using SAP will be gained later.

- It will cost considerably more than the Big Bang approach (even assuming it goes according to plan).

- Extended projects can be more mentally and physically wearing for users and project team members.

Disaster Recovery Plan

Most major companies have a disaster recovery plan that can be pulled into force if anything goes wrong with their computing systems. However, during times of change when workload is at its greatest, uncertainty is commonplace and companies are at their most vulnerable if something goes wrong.

It is easy to forget to update your disaster recovery plans before an implementation, but it is well worth the investment of bringing in additional help if necessary to create and rehearse a plan for your new systems before you go live.

Accounting Implications

Project managers should make sure they are aware of all the accounting implications at the beginning of the project. It is well worth ensuring that a senior manager from the accounting department is involved in the early stages of the project. Some issues to consider are as follows:

- The need to implement at month-end or year-end versus a quieter time of year

- Tax reporting periods and reconciliations

- Setting up the general ledger

- Managing open items from other systems when going live

- Transferring receivables and outstanding balances

- Establishing controls and audit procedures

Open Transactions in Old Systems

When going live, you have a choice of processing open transactions completely in an old system or transferring them to a new system. The decision as to how to manage each situation will depend on which modules are being implemented and what old systems are in place.

There can be a multitude of issues arising that all need to be addressed. For example, if orders are taken in an old system, should they be recreated in SAP? If they are, how do you prevent duplicating them? If they are not recreated in SAP, then how do you manage the picking lists, dispatch notes, goods issues, and receivables? If the transaction goes through outside of SAP, how do you get the inventory to balance and how do you cope with the impact on the production forecasting? There are lots of questions and no easy answers. The only way to deal with the issues of open transactions in old systems is to identify what they are and decide how each one is going to be administered.

If you close down for a few days, perhaps using a weekend and a national holiday, you might be able to clear all the outstanding orders in the old system and transfer just the financial balances.

Interfaces

Depending upon which SAP modules you are implementing, you will need to consider the question of interfaces at an early stage.

It is more than likely that you will need a number of interfaces both in and out of SAP. You will need to create specifications, write the appropriate codes, and test them. You will also need to schedule when the interface programs are going to run. You should consider the control and security implications of accessing and amending master files and transactional data in SAP.

Dual Maintenance of Data

As you get closer to implementation, you will need to build and maintain your master files. The prospect of maintaining old systems along with SAP doesn't sound like much trouble until you actually have to do it. Invariably users have this task, which provides a good opportunity for gaining system familiarity before going live. However, the timing is very important—if you do it too early, the workload for users can be immense, and if implementation is delayed, the dual maintenance can collapse and the whole process has to be started again nearer to the date of going live.

Working with SAP Systems After Implementation

When SAP has been successfully implemented, project team members feel relief, managers are able to sit back in their chairs again, and life for everyone can begin to return to normal. Going live might give everyone the feeling that it's all over, but there are normally a multitude of things that have to be dealt with, including:

■ Fixing system bugs in the configuration

- Supporting users with help desk and additional training
- Making system developments that are required but were not ready at time of going live
- Organizing the system operation
- Operating control and security procedures
- Correcting errors in transactional and master data
- Ensuring reporting functions are operating correctly

In many cases, you have to wait for the first of particular activities to take place before you can assess how each function works. Examples include Orders, Delivery Notes, Picking Lists, Shipments, Goods Issues, Invoices, Statements, Payments Allocations, Accounting Entries, Work Orders, Production Planning, and so on.

SAP as an integrated system deals with entire business processes, and it is not until these entire business processes are completed that you can assess whether the system is functioning properly. You might need to wait until your first month-end to establish whether the accounting functions are working as they should, or wait until orders have been processed to check your sales reporting. It can therefore be some time before you can be determine how successful the implementation was. In the same way that it is easy for runners to slow down as they near the finishing line, it is easy for project teams to slow down after implementation. But remember, "it isn't finished until it's finished."

Despite who officially owns the system before going live, it is the project team who feels most comfortable with it. However, upon going live, the emphasis shifts immediately to the users. The project team had the opportunity to build confidence with the system without the pressure of running the company on it. The users, even though they received some training, probably feel like they have been thrown in at the deep end of the pool and expected to swim.

There are always teething problems with a new system, usually minor issues, but an infrastructure must be in place to deal with them quickly and efficiently.

There is a natural settling down period immediately after going live, which should quickly give way to normal working.

Supporting the Systems and Users After Implementation

When SAP has been implemented the effective suppport of the system and users becomes essential. The use of the system is now an integral part of the organizations operation and any failure in the system or the way that it is operated becomes a failure in the organization itself.

Careful planning is needed to ensure that the necessary support is in place. In most cases the support structure that was in place during system development can be adapted. However, the number of users is likely to increase, and many problems will be urgent ones.

The system itself is likely to respond differently with the large volume of processing created by a live system. Interfaces that have worked in testing will have to work in the live environment, and there will be an inevitable settling down period where problems will arise and need to be resolved.

Most companies will develop their own support organization and procedures. An internal help desk is a necessity and provides both a focal contact point for users and also a central area where system performance can be monitored.

Follow-up system training for users should be considered as well as preparing training for new employees.

SAP Services

R/3 Services is the collective name for the comprehensive range of support services offered by SAP. They include the following:

- Problem Solving
- Remote Support
- Information
- Customer Support
- Product Design
- Certification

Problem Solving. There are three problem-solving services designed to resolve technical problems and questions that result from the everyday use of SAP.

First Level Service. This service is offered by one of two different mediums:

1. Telephone Support
2. The Online Service System (OSS)

Quick assistance is provided by experts who are able to help with all types of system problems. A 24-hour emergency service is available.

Error Notes Q&A Service. This support requires online connection to SAP, and enables access to the "Error Notes Database" through the OSS. This database holds information based on experience with SAP installations and stores notes to help resolve problems that other clients have encountered before you. The system offers a context-sensitive search facility to help you find information.

Online Correction Service. This facility will be available in future releases, and will enable SAP's consultants to assign available solutions to problems that have been submitted. Corrections will be continuously updated and maintained.

Remote Support. These services are designed to identify and prevent potential system errors and optimize system performance.

Early Watch Service. This service enables SAP experts to access SAP installations remotely and optimize system performance by identifying system problems and eliminating resource and system bottlenecks.

The online connection is regulated by the customer and the service is offered on a "by request" basis.

Remote Consulting Service. The Remote Consulting Service enables customers to make an appointment with a skilled SAP consultant to discuss problems, analyze solutions or discuss general issues.

This service uses video-supported communications, which reduces consultant travel time and expenses.

Information. SAP's Information Services enable customers to access information on a wide variety of subjects, including the R/3 product itself.

Info DB Service. Information is available online through the Online Service System (OSS). You can access information on a variety of different subjects, including training courses and SAP publications.

Hot News Service. The Hot News Service provides online information about the latest high-priority R/3 system information, including error alarm messages, release strategy information, system enhancement information, and service event schedules.

Information is transmitted electronically to customer mailboxes and the system is audited to ensure that customers receive the information sent.

CD-ROMs. SAP produces a number of different CD-ROMs that contain a wide range of R/3 system information.

Customer Support. SAP's Customer Support services are aimed at quick problem solving and up-to-date information transfer.

Customer Competence Centers (CCC). This service is available to large organizations that have purchased the R/3 system. It offers on-site support by providing the entire R/3 services within a customers' organization. Customers have direct access to SAP tools, information, and communications systems.

The CCC is run by the customer's own staff, who are given training and are certified at regular intervals.

Active Customer Relationship. SAP offers a central point of contact for customers and partners that provides "personal intensive support for customer concerns and integration of customer development requests and implementation of these requests in SAP and partners' services." (source: *SAP Services* brochure)

Product Design. SAP has long relied on customer feedback to develop its systems. They have developed a number of channels through which customers can influence future product design.

IX

Implementation

Customer Verification Shipment. Customers are encouraged to submit requests for new features and enhancements directly to SAP. If these requests are incorporated into the standard product, the customer has the option of testing the relevant systems. During this time, the customers receive intensive support and preferential query handling.

First Customer Shipment. This facility allows customers to test new releases in advance and to influence the development of future upgrades.

Development Request Service. SAP system development requests can be sent to SAP directly or through the Online Services System. On receipt, requests go to a product planning committee that considers them for inclusion in the standard product.

Certification. SAP's R/3 services are aimed at achieving high-quality standards by constant improvement to services. To ensure that their partners maintain these same standards, they have a certification scheme in place.

Audit Service. SAP's certification scheme integrates their partners into their own quality assurance procedures. This offers customers a guarantee of a high standard of service.

From Here...

In this chapter we have looked at the many different aspects of SAP implementations including the reasons why one might be considered, how management can learn to understand the complex issues, how to plan, budget, build a team and prepare for going live. We have also looked at system testing, and some of the fundamentals of successful implementations and how to support the system and users post implementation. We have considered project managment techniques and the importance of early consideration of security and control issues.

There is a lot to take in, which is why SAP implementations may appear so daunting and why so many external consultants become involved. If all the tasks or considerations are broken down into little pieces you will find that the whole is not as daunting as you may think. There is a worldwide drive to make SAP implementations quicker, cheaper, and easier, which is why SAP has developed tools to assist in the planning, developing, and implementing.

- Chapter 33, "SAP Control and Security"
- Chapter 34, "Managing Communications Internal and External"
- Chapter 35, "Training for SAP"

Chapter 32

Implementing SAP by Business Processes

Business systems have evolved to the point where they can closely model a business's internal processes. This means that companies can save significantly on internal administration costs by automating standard business procedures.

The role of the employee is moving away from basic business administrator to a more challenging operator role. In particular, new working practices concentrate on three areas:

- Setup and Configuration of Business Entities
- Management of Business Databases
- Exception Handling

SAP is a very advanced business systems package. It aims to maximize the automation of standard processes within a company. It allows a very high level of internal automation. This gives it a great advantage over its competitors. To achieve the maximum gains from these processes, users must learn to become computer confident and literate.

The radical changes that are taking place in the workplace with the arrival of more sophisticated business software require companies to make a significant investment in time and money.

This chapter describes philosophies that will provide the most cost-efficient method of implementing SAP while reengineering the business. It helps you plan the evolution of your company, using SAP implementation, through the use of two documents:

- The Business Process And Task Hierarchy
- The Job Profile Task Mapping

In this chapter, you learn:

- How to produce a coherent business process mapping for your company.

- How to link the set of business processes to the set of standard SAP processes.

- How to derive a job matrix from the mapping.

- How to adjust the business process definition according to changing company and project circumstances.

IX

Implementation

Optimization of the SAP Implementation

You will have gathered by now that SAP is not just another software package. There is no Plug-and-Play technology involved, so SAP cannot simply be left to the IT department to "get on with it." Implementing SAP involves most of the people in an organization, many of whom will have had only limited exposure to a computer.

Experience has shown that the best way to take a company through the specifics of SAP implementation is with a business process-oriented approach.

First of all, we need to look at some of the problems that would be encountered if SAP were implemented using a traditional business change management methodology.

The Traditional "As Is" and "To Be" Approaches

The traditional business change management scenario, shown in Figure 32.1, takes a three-stage approach to business change implementation:

1. Define where the company is at the moment ("as is").

2. Decide where the company will be in five years' time ("to be").

3. Decide how the company is going to get from where it is now to where it is going to be in five years' time.

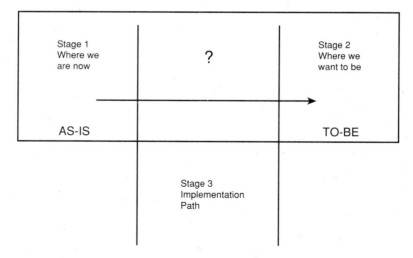

Fig. 32.1   The three phases of the traditional business change management approach.

There are a number of problems with this approach, some relating to SAP specifically:

■ Most companies (even those with ISO9OOO~1 accreditation) do not have a clear idea of all their internal business processes, and the idea of mapping them out can appear to be an expensive luxury.

- Many companies feel they cannot afford the expense of setting up working groups to debate the possible position of the company in years to come.

- SAP offers a particular philosophy about the way that businesses should be structured, and despite its flexibility, implementing SAP would necessarily force particular procedural changes. Consequently, any proposed business strategy that does not acknowledge the implementation of the SAP way of business is likely to require substantial revision.

A SAP-Oriented Approach

The success of SAP is due in part to the highly efficient business solution that it provides. If a company decides to "go with" SAP software, it must also accept that the millions of hours of development effort put into the system have come up with some pretty nifty solutions. In cases where a business and SAP disagree on the business approach to a particular problem, any business should seriously think about changing its approach to match that of SAP.

Provided that a company is prepared to do this, following SAP-oriented business methodology will:

- Maximize the benefit of the changes

- Minimize the cost

- Maximize the return of the whole exercise

There are 4 stages to the methodology I have outlined:

Stage 1

Map the company onto a business hierarchy. Include all functions of the company. The business hierarchy must match SAP business structures.

Stage 2

Identify where SAP business processes fit in at the bottom of the hierarchy, and include them in the mapping.

Stage 3

Divide all tasks at the bottom of the hierarchy into one of three types:

- Automated: Tasks that SAP will do

- Manual: Tasks that a person will do

- Transactions: Tasks that a person working on SAP will do

Stage 4

Define the extent and limits of all the tasks, including the frequency and resource usage.

Note

There are many possible variations on a SAP implementation methodology. What this one does is pick out the basic elements.

Let's look at what makes a successful IT project.

What Makes Successful Project Definition?

Experience has shown that the most successful SAP implementations have implemented using a map of business processes. This is a hierarchical picture of how the business is to be designed. At the top of the hierarchy is the company. At the bottom are the individual tasks performed by individuals on a minute-by-minute basis. This map explains what everyone in the company is doing and how each task fits into the overall corporate plan.

To maximize the efficiency gains achieved by implementing SAP, you must define—and more importantly, redefine—a company's business processes. The SAP system provides a reference model that you can use to aid this process. However, the most successful companies will be those that drive the business model development through their own experience. When an SAP project fails, it is generally because the scope of the project had not been fully mapped out beforehand.

Early Error-Checking Saves Money

The quality of the initial design work will have a significant effect on the cost of the implementation. Although it may seem an obvious point, many SAP projects are founded on a lack of initial design work, so the lesson obviously takes some time to absorb. For example, one client spent over $100,000 extra simply because the company had implemented an ill-thought out mechanism for recording sales cost (2 or 3 fields on the order entry screens).

The stages of a SAP project follow the pattern:

1. requirements

2. design

3. configuration

4. unit testing

5. acceptance testing

6. maintenance

The later in this process that an error is detected, the more costly it is to correct the error.

Errors detected at the maintenance stage are generally over 100 times more expensive to fix than those detected at the requirements stage.

Users First, Computer Scientists Second

When you implement SAP, you must get early involvement of the users. In the "old days," we just used to let the computer experts get on with it, and then there was this rather boring phase called "user acceptance" in which the users would see the system and say what they thought of it.

Those old methods worked for the smaller, less complicated systems of days gone by. Today, however, SAP has over a million lines of code, in addition to all those table settings, and so early involvement of the users is essential. The first part of the SAP implementation defines how exactly the users will use SAP.

Building the Function Hierarchy

When building the function hierarchy, use the functional (and modular) structure of SAP to map your business. You will find that this leads to a cleaner solution and more efficient results that using other analyses such as product-based structures.

Map Company onto Business Hierarchy

To build a model of the new business structure, you must assemble a hierarchical model of the business. The very act of putting this model together enables you and your company to assess the efficiency of your company's business processes. Ordinarily you do not have the time to assess the efficiency of the work you do, since you are too busy *doing* it!

Level 1—Top of Hierarchy. The top of the hierarchy, shown in Figure 32.2, is a single box, the company itself. This includes all activities that affect the balance sheet and profit and loss statement of a company.

ACME Corporation

Fig. 32.2   Top of the business process hierarchy.

Level 2—Division by Business Group or SAP Module. One of the key issues is how the SAP implementation must reflect the most efficient use of the system. To do this, a company must be prepared to adopt SAP's own business philosophy.

A common method of viewing a company is to divide the company into product groups, as this very often reflects the organization of a company. This is especially true when the company has been formed through mergers and takeovers of competing companies. This also reflects the "marketing department's view of the universe."

As an example, let us imagine a company with four basic product groups:

> Consumer Product Group 1
>
> Consumer Product Group 2
>
> Medical Products
>
> Industrial Products

This is illustrated in Figure 32.3.

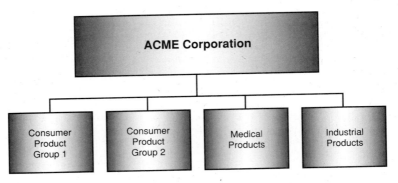

Fig. 32.3   The hierarchy by product group.

This way of viewing the company makes sense from a business point of view. It reflects the structure required to report on activities for the purposes of product costing and profitability analysis. However, it is not necessarily the best way of viewing the SAP implementation. Similar business functions are carried out for each of the products. You should instead consider planning by SAP module (see Figure 32.4).

Try to make as many similar cross-company business processes as possible. This is a new version of the old Adam Smith principle of *Specialization,* in which the efficiency gains in companies are made by breaking up tasks into their smallest parts and allocating individuals to those parts.

Level 3—Division by SAP Submodules. Within each of the SAP modules, split up the sections by those parts of the submodules that your company is planning to use.

> **Note**
>
> Although a company might think that it is implementing, for example, CO-Controlling, in reality the company is probably only going to be implementing part of that module. Therefore, it must be clear what component parts of each module are being used. In our example in this chapter, we will implement three parts of the FI-Finance module and two parts of the CO-Cost Center Accounting module (see Figure 32.5).

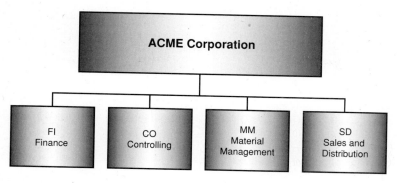

Fig. 32.4   The hierarchy by SAP module.

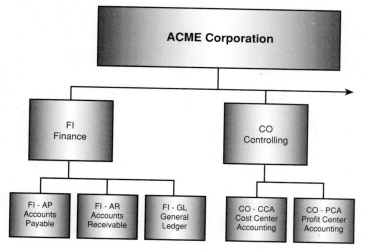

Fig. 32.5   The hierarchy down to SAP submodule.

Submodule as Core Business Unit

The submodules of the basic SAP modules represent a whole suite of functions around a single SAP business entity. Each submodule is based around an entity which mirrors a real world business concept.

Here are a few examples:

CO-CCA: Cost Center Accounting

In the case of Cost Center Accounting, the basic entity is the cost center. Cost centers are used to measure the costs incurred by individual departments.

MM: Materials Management

In the case of Materials Management, the basic entity is the material. The material represents a single product. Materials identify the nature and characteristics of the products held by a company.

This entity is reflected in SAP by the underlying database structure, so it is worthwhile using these entities, not only to form the basis of the task groups that the users will be given, but also to define the scope of the database administrators' work.

Note

If you are familiar with object-oriented programming, you will see similarities between Objects and the way that SAP models business entities.

Table 32.1 shows the core SAP business entities around which the SAP business systems operate. In larger projects, for each entity used, the definition of the characteristics (i.e. fields), can be a task assigned to a task force.

Table 32.1   Common SAP Business Entities

Submodule	Entity
FI-AP Accounts Payable	Vendor
FI-AR Accounts Receivable	Customer
FI-GL General Ledger	G/L Account
CO-CCA Cost Center Accounting	Cost Center
CO-PCA Profit Center Accounting	Profit Center
CO-OPA Order Process Accounting	Internal Order
MM-Material Management	Material
MM-Purchasing	Supplier
SD Sales and Distribution	Customer

Note

A key part of SAP approach to finance is the distinction SAP makes between financial and management accounting. Traditionally, many companies have a single set of financial accounts that covers both the requirements of a company to report on the balance sheet and profit and loss statement, and to provide internal management cost monitoring tools. The use of a set of controlling (CO) business entities distinct from finance (FI) entities gives added flexibility in financial reporting. This must be reflected in the breakdown in tasks on the business process hierarchy.

SAP Business Entities: Business Functions

Within each entity there are three basic business functions:

■ Entity Management

Entity management includes setting up new entities, changing the characteristics of the entities, and archiving the entities when they are no longer needed.

- Postings To the Entities

    Postings to the entity affect the values of the entity. In the Material Management modules, those values represent the quantities of stock held. In the Financial modules, Fl and CO, the values are the financial values of the postings.

- Reporting On the Entities

    This is the most important of all the functions—the capability to examine the first two functions' progress.

SAP Business Entities: Basic Model

The basic model that we must follow puts our tasks in a hierarchy as follows:

ENTITY

ENTITY MANAGEMENT

POSTINGS TO THE ENTITY

REPORTING ON THE ENTITY

An example of how this would apply to cost center accounting is shown in Table 32.2. How this fits into the hierarchy is shown in Figure 32.6.

Table 32.2	The Three Functions of Cost Center Accounting
Entity	**Function**
Cost Center Accounting	Cost Center Management
	Cost Center Postings
	Cost Center Reporting

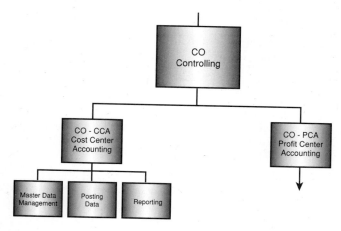

Fig. 32.6 Division of submodule by process types.

Table 32.3 Division of Functions into Task Groups	
Function	**Task Groups**
Entity Management	Create a Cost Center
	Display a Cost Center
	Change a Cost Center
	Cost Center Postings
	Maintain Cost Center Hierarchies
Postings to the Entity	Post Cost Adjustments
	Reallocate Costs Across Cost Centers
Reporting on the Entity	Display a list of the cost centers
	Display cost center master records
	Display costs per period
	Display costs per quarter
	Display plan vs. actual costs
	Display plan vs. forecast costs
	Display actual vs. forecast costs

Each of the tasks is represented by an SAP transaction.

Tasks and the SAP Transaction Concept

The tasks at the bottom of the hierarchy are individual units of work. These units are done either by a person or a computer, or in some cases by both.

Manual tasks are performed by humans. You must plan for them. Their development is outside the scope of this book.

Automated tasks are planned and programmed by system designers. Once in place, they require relatively little maintenance.

User Transactions are the key to the whole process. They require the coordination of both man and machine. User transactions form the bulk of the information traffic flowing into and out of your databases. Transactions enable you to set up SAP databases, examine them, and modify them. These user transactions are the basic units around which you must plan, design, and build your system.

SAP uses transactions as the basic system process. You access them through the menu structures, which try to model the hierarchical patterns into which business functions fit.

A transaction is a single business task carried out by a user. It consists of a set of screens that the user passes through in order to complete the task (see Figure 32.7).

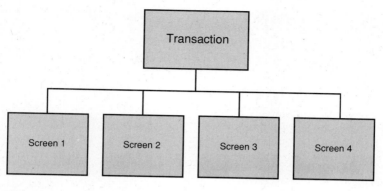

Fig. 32.7 Transactions are made up of a number of screens.

A screen contains a number of fields, as shown in Figure 34.8. A field relates to the contents of a part of a database.

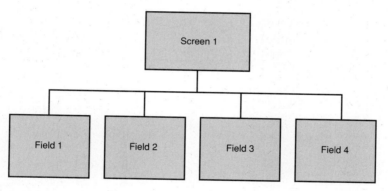

Fig. 32.8 Each screen has a number of fields.

In order to carry out a transaction, the user must access the correct menu item within the correct menu screen.

For example, the transaction Display Cost Center appears within the cost center accounting screen.

Note

Transactions have short-codes that enable a configurer or user to jump to a particular transaction from anywhere in the system. However, most people use the menu bars to navigate the system.

Building the Business Processes

Business processes are core concepts for implementing your SAP system. Figure 32.9 shows how a single business process is composed of a series of tasks which link together. The business process provides the context into which individual tasks fit.

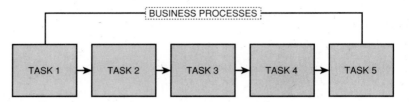

Fig. 32.9   The business process as a sequence of tasks.

A task may be carried out manually (such as filling out a form), or be a transaction carried out by the system.

Each task must have a named profile of the employee who will carry out the task, as shown in Figure 32.10.

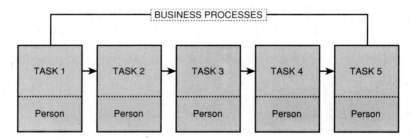

Fig. 32.10   Tasks must be linked to job profiles.

For example, setting up a new cost center is not something that happens in isolation from other events in business administration. Usually, there is a sign-off mechanism in which named individuals take responsibility for spending against the cost center. You must work these authorizations and forms into the system design before implementation activities take place.

We can take an example from the accounts payable function. Within the SAP accounts payable screens you will find a set of processes that you can use, no matter what business that you are involved in. That is because paying a vendor who has sold you a photocopier and paying a vendor who has sold you a machine tool are very similar processes.

Table 32.4 Steps of the FI-Accounts Payable Process	
Step	**Function**
Stage 1	Receive the invoice.
Stage 2	You enter the invoice into the SAP system ("receive invoice" function).
Stage 3	The invoice is matched with the purchase order.
Stage 4	The invoice is matched with the goods receipt note.
Stage 5	The invoice is cleared for payment.
Stage 6	A payment proposal is run.
Stage 7	The payment proposal is authorized.
Stage 8	The payment program runs.
Stage 9	Either a check is printed or an automatic bank transfer credit occurs.

Some of the processes are manual, and others are computer based. It is this flow of tasks that provides your company with the foundation for meeting International quality standards such as ISO9000~1.

Job Function Matrix

You will need to allocate the list of SAP tasks defined within the scope of the project to job profiles. This is necessary in order to meet the control criteria required in all companies and provide a framework for user training.

Controls are required to prevent corruption. For example: a single employee is not given access to all the features needed to create an order, dispatch the goods, and process an invoice, as this power would provide a very tempting opportunity for theft. For the same reason, warehouse employees are not usually given access to information about the value of the goods on invoices.

Having created our business process hierarchy, and grouped tasks into business processes, we can put together a matrix to meet the authorization and control requirements of your project.

The matrix should list job titles. For each job title, list the system tasks that will be carried out. One copy of this matrix should be passed in front of the accounting department for review from a controls perspective. The other can be used by the Basis team to set up user authorization profiles.

Table 32.5 **Example of a Task Listing**	
Job	**Task**
Accounts Payable Clerk	Enter the invoice.
	Match the invoice.
	Execute the check payment run.
	Execute the electronic payment run.
	Display a list of vendors.
Accounts Payable Manager	Display a list of venders.
	Display outstanding payments.
	Display payments made per month.
	Display payment per business area.

This mapping is then used:

- by the Training Department, to determine the contents of training courses that need to be given

- by the System Administrator, to set up the user profiles of the users

Issues Around Business Process Modeling

So far we have been dealing with a formal method for mapping business process requirements. Now we are going to look at some of the strategic and tactical issues that arise before, during, and after the business process definition that may affect the optimal approach.

What Portion of the Company Is Moving to SAP?

If 100 percent of the business is moving to SAP, then the business process modeling includes all parts of the company. This simplifies the whole process, as it means that no time need be spent on defining project limits.

If less than 100 percent of the business is being transferred to SAP (for example: you are implementing for a division of the company) then you need an extra step. Make some clear statement on the scope of the implementation. Make sure that all relevant managers have seen, digested, and approved of the scope of the document. You can use the business process hierarchy to clearly define the required processes.

Contracts with Outside Agencies

A common area of dispute between companies and outside IT consultants is the scope of work that is covered by the implementation. The business hierarchy can be used to precisely define the limits and extent of the contracted work.

Internal Contracts

Even for internal budget allocation, politics raises its ugly head. Within a company the scope of a project must be clearly defined too. Internal political processes will result in ambitious managers under-quoting estimates for total project costs, often when the scope of the whole project is not yet clearly defined. The business process hierarchy can be used to precisely define the limit and extent of the implementation.

The Inclusion of System Maintenance Functions

The maintenance of SAP brings with it a number of maintenance functions that must be factored in as business processes. These processes fall into four categories:

- Hardware Maintenance

  The provision and support of all required pieces of hardware, including printers, cables, portable PCs

- Help Desk

  Any unexpected problems that users have

- Database Archiving

  The removal and storage of database records no longer required for immediate on-line processing. Over time, SAP databases will grow beyond the size necessary to run the business, so archiving will save disk space and improve system processing times.

- User Authorization Management

  The set up and maintenance of user-specific authorization profiles that dictate what specified users can do on the system. Security profiles must be set, managed, and set up to enable all users to carry out the system tasks necessary to do their jobs.

Iterative Development of Business Processes

As your SAP system development continues, you may find it necessary to adjust this hierarchy. For example, as the Accounts Payable function develops, you might decide to include electronic banking alongside your manual check clearing and distribution. In that case you must add an additional business process to the part of the hierarchy that includes the payment methods:

Business Process	Description
Before:	
Vendor payment	Payment of a vendor by check
	Payment of a vendor by cash
After:	
Vendor payment	Payment of a vendor by check
	Payment of a vendor by cash
	Payment of a vendor by electronic banking

Addition to the hierarchy will mean additional project costs. Consequently, you must build a contingency into the project resources upfront for additional business processes being added. Some of the new business processes will be the result of additional requirements that your business will have to meet. Others may be due to improvements in technology.

Reduction of Project Costs

One of the most common ways to reduce project cost is to reduce the number of business processes covered. In the previous example, the scope of the original project was extended to include electronic banking. Where unforeseen circumstances lead to delays in reaching target dates, or a reduction in budget enforced upon a project, cutting out single business processes is often a much more efficient way forward than delaying the whole project. So, in our example, waiting until after the live date to install the electronic banking part of accounts payable would mean that all other parts of the project could progress on time.

Keep It Simple

SAP is a complex package, and the greatest efficiency improvements will be made where the defined processes are simplest.

It is likely that there are business process variations within your company that are not easily reproducible on the SAP systems. Before deciding to automate these functions a cost benefit analysis of the effect of implementing the variations would be worthwhile.

The benefit is the extra functionality that the system provides: this can be calculated in terms of the number of hours work saved per year in having the extra processes automated.

From user managers you can establish estimates for time saved due to the extra functionality on a weekly or monthly basis. You can then convert this into a yearly figure.

The cost is the implementation, training and change management cost associated with the additional functionality. This too can be calculated in number of work hours required to implement it. Note that a hidden cost of adding complexity to the system is that it tends to increase the overall cost of maintaining it, since "bugs" are harder to track down.

The following is an example of a Cost Benefit Analysis (adding extra order types to handle a specialist product):

      Estimated Number of hours work saved per week   2 Hours

therefore,

      Estimated Number of hours work saved per year   104 Hours

Number of hours work to add the changes:

Design	24
Changes	24
Testing	40
Training	44
Total Cost	132 Hours

If the SAP system will be in use for a year or less, then the changes are not worthwhile. If the changes will be operating for more than two years, then it may be worth considering adding them in.

Developing Nonstandard SAP Functions

SAP provides a full set of development tools for clients to use to develop their own transactions, screens, and even databases.

Though these tools are available, the following points should be borne in mind before deciding to develop nonstandard SAP functions:

1. The high cost of the license fees that SAP users pay reflects the amount of development work that has gone into the package over the last 20 years.

2. Any problem that you have come across has almost certainly already occurred with some other client, somewhere else.

3. Where a number of SAP clients have come up with a business requirement, SAP has incorporated the requirement into the basic system.

4. Your company is unlikely to have many unique processes.

In general, try to avoid modification of the basic package as much as possible.

From Here...

In this chapter, we have covered the principles of producing a business hierarchy that can be used to define the scope of an SAP implementation.

This hierarchy will help your company:

- Define the extent and limits of the SAP implementation.

- Provide a model for implementing business processes in accordance with International ISO9000~1 standards.

- Provide the basis for defining new job profiles.

- Provide the starting point for designing the security profiles required for the maintenance of the system.

IX

Implementation

Related Chapters:

- For information on developing controls and user authorizations see Chapter 33, "SAP Control and Security."

- For information on the management of project information see Chapter 34, "Managing Communications Internal and External."

- For information on training see Chapter 35, "Training for SAP."

Chapter 33

SAP Control and Security

Where SAP is implemented as an integrated application, as it is most commonly seen, there are some considerable risks involved. Apart from the exposure of holding all of an organization's key business data and processing most of its transactions within one application, SAP typically replaces a host of legacy systems where cross-application security and data integrity are not a significant issue. A user in the accounts payable function will have access to the accounts payable system and nothing more. With SAP we face a situation where a user will have access to SAP—the functions he can perform and the mitigating controls must be defined during system configuration and implementation. In addition, the broad and detailed functionality offered by SAP means that the operation of such control and security mechanisms is very complex and requires dedicated expert resources.

Controls and Security usually appear on a project plan, somewhere. However, in priority terms they are generally fairly low, and in the pressure of meeting an impending implementation deadline, are often pushed aside. This can lead to major problems post implementation, although the costs of any associated losses are difficult to quantify as a lack of control, as well as making them easier to occur, can mean they go undetected as well.

This section aims to give an overview of the key functionality in these areas and to propose some ways in which the control issue in general may be addressed during the implementation and use of an SAP system. It is, however, worth noting at this early stage that controls are not owned by the project, by an IT security function, or by internal or external audit, but should be regarded as an integral part of each and every business process, and as such should be accepted, both in terms of the cost of operating controls as well as any residual risks, by the business owner.

The SAP Control Environment

As with any implementation issue, it is useful to work within a framework to address control issues so that they may be considered in a structured fashion.

In this chapter, you learn:

- How, based on a standard "controls template," the SAP Controls Environment is characterized.

- How the critical area of access control, SAP's "Authorization Concept" is managed.

- How change control is operated in SAP through its Correction and Transport System.

- How SAP updates its database and how this can go wrong.

IX

Implementation

The model used here is fairly standard and could be applied to the implementation of any application system. Controls are essentially viewed in the following categories:

Access Security Controls	The technical controls within an application that allow functions (business and technical) to be restricted to appropriate personnel. Controls in the various operating system and database technologies that can be used by the system are not covered in detail here.
System Integrity Controls	The technical mechanisms within a system that allow for the management of change control within its internal framework.
Processing Controls	The technical controls within a system that allow for data integrity, both within the application and with regard to data interfaced from other systems.
Application Controls	Controls required by the business and which form an integral step in each business process. These are discussed only in general terms—the requirements in this area will vary greatly between installations and are implemented through the normal business process mapping and system customization processes.
Data Entry Controls	Controls that ensure the integrity of data at the point of user interface—they could be in the form of error/warning messaging, validation against master- or table-held data, and so on.
Detect/Compensating Controls	"Backstop controls"—those which can be relied on as a last resort should controls in any of the other categories failed. These are typically in the form of automatically generated reports that require post-facto user validation/approval.

SAP is, like any system, stronger in some of these areas than in others. As an overview, the system could be characterized within this framework as follows:

Access Security Controls	Despite some identified weaknesses, this is generally a strong area of functionality in SAP. However, it is extremely complex to understand and implement correctly.
System Integrity Controls	SAP R/3 has developed an integral change management system whereby any program or table changes can be amended and recorded in a development environment and then promoted to a productive environment. There are, however, some significant weaknesses with this system.
Processing Controls	Being an integrated system, SAP should have fewer data integrity problems than the architecture typically represented by legacy system environments with multiple interfaces which require control. However, the promotion of programs, tables and other data dictionary objects between systems is critical, and the setup of SAP's systems to achieve this is, again, very complex.
Application Controls	SAP offers, through the customization of internal tables, the opportunity to implement a whole range of application controls. Once implemented, such controls are reliable, although they may not always be flexible

enough to meet the requirements of individual users. Extra development or reliance on post-facto control is often necessary in this area.

Data Entry Controls

Generally, because SAP is an integrated application, controls here are very powerful—master files can be looked up across modules to select the appropriate record and data entry is checked real-time against information held elsewhere in the system. The ability of users to override key fields defaulted into transactions from other parts of the system should, however, be noted as a key weakness.

Detect/Compensating Controls

This is probably the weakest area of SAP. Very few usable post-facto reports are delivered as standard, and those that are there are notoriously hard to find. If control reporting is required, you are generally on your own, and reports will have to be coded prior to implementation.

Access Control

As discussed in the previous section, SAP Security, or the "Authorization Concept" as it is termed by SAP, is a relatively strong area of control functionality and due to the integrated nature of SAP it's implementation is critical to the success of an SAP project. This section provides a general overview of SAP functionality in this area together with an explanation of some important weaknesses to bear in mind whilst implementing the system.

General Security Guidelines

In general terms there is essentially nothing special about the management of access security in a SAP environment. Various frameworks are available for the evaluation of information systems security, for example, the following system:

- Security policy
- Security organization
- Assets classification and control
- Personnel security
- Physical and environmental security
- Computer and network management
- System access control
- System development and maintenance
- Business continuity planning
- Compliance

Examples of documents containing guidance of this nature are the "Orange Books" published by the U.S. Department of Defense and "A Code of Practice for Information Security Management" published by the U.K. Department of Trade and Industry.

There is, as yet, no computer security certification generally available. In the U.K. there is a standard, BS7799, which is currently under review by the DTI but is generally thought to be some way from formal endorsement. Again, it can serve as a useful guideline.

Operating System, Database, and Network Security

Unlike some platforms and applications, the greatest degree of functional control in SAP is exercised from within the application itself. If managed properly, there should be few concerns and a minimum of administration required in the operating system and database environments. The benchmark SAP architecture of a UNIX operating system and ORACLE database requires only a handful of users. Apart from the SAP application itself (which needs to be established as a user in both UNIX and ORACLE) and system administrators there should be few if any other users. There is certainly no need to establish SAP users in these environments in order for them to be able to access the application.

This scenario does, of course, assume that there are no applications other than SAP R/3 running in the environment. If, for example, other UNIX-based applications are running on the same server as SAP R/3 there are likely to be other control considerations to be accounted for.

The area of network security is one, however, which requires careful consideration. For a start, each SAP user has to be established as a user on the network. Also, network security in a client-server environment should be viewed as very much an emerging and unproven technology. There is not the degree of comfort that we can draw, for example, from years of working with products such as RACF and ACF2 in a mainframe environment.

Just one word of caution in this area: It is possible to drop from SAP into UNIX and to execute certain, limited commands. This can be done through the use of the ABAP SAPMSOS0 or transaction.

Overview of SAP Authorization Concept

The authorization concept in SAP R/3 is predicated upon the logical relationship between a user ID and the range of system authorizations with which it can be associated (see Figure 33.1). The user ID provides a gateway through which a user can enter the system; once log-on has been achieved, the authorizations determine which system resources can be accessed by the user ID.

The architecture of the authorization system is based around the utilization of several individual but related logical components, as follows:

- Profiles
- Objects
- Fields
- Authorizations

Within the system, the user ID refers exclusively to *profiles* when defining access privileges, rather than to individual authorization values. Every profile grants a set of specific system access authorities to a user, and a virtually unlimited number of profiles can be assigned to a user ID. Composite profiles can be defined, consisting of several concatenated single profiles.

An *object* is a logical entity used to group together one or more related *fields* that require authority checking within the system. Objects themselves contain no values; instead, it is the fields that contain values for authority checking, and it is the combination of field values for an object that constitutes an *authorization*. Therefore, a profile references any number of authorizations that in themselves define the system resources that can be accessed.

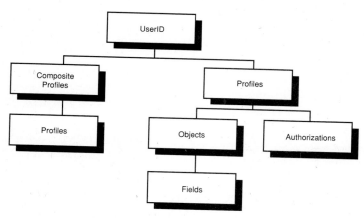

Fig. 33.1   SAP R/3 authorization entity relationship.

Every object and profile must be uniquely named. Authorizations, however, can be identically named, but must hold different values for their constituent object fields. This is because they are linked to an object name, and are therefore both physically and logically separate from each other.

Authorization Objects

All objects are defined in table TOBJ. This table lists the object name, together with the individual field names associated with the object. Table TOBJT provides a separate list of objects, each accompanied by a textual description.

Objects can be grouped generically into object classes via transaction SU21. Classes provide a means of readily identifying functionally related groups of authorization objects (for example, Basis Administration, Financial Accounting, and so on).

Since the values of an object field may contain multiple (or a range of) values, it is often convenient to define a field group for an object. A field group contains the relevant values required for an authorization, and can be shared across objects. Field groups are defined in the following:

T055	Field group fields
T055G	Field groups
T055T	Field group descriptions

An authorization object may consist of single or multiple fields. In the case of two-field objects, commonly one field describes the field value (for example, company code), and the other, the type of activity that can be performed on it (for example, add or change). This is most typical in objects associated with FI-Financial Accounting Module. Fields are defined in the internal table AUTH.

The types of activities available are recorded as two-digit numeric values and are defined in the following:

TACT	Activity codes
TACTT	Activity codes descriptions
TACTZ	Valid activity codes for each authorization object

Only activity codes defined within these tables can be used for assigning as values for authorization object fields.

Authorization checking is performed when a user requests access to system resources. This is performed by a dedicated subroutine called AUTHORITY-CHECK. This routine interrogates the system and returns a message indicating whether a user has the required authorization values for the relevant object in his or her profile. An error message will result if insufficient authority exists.

This routine can be called directly from coding embedded within user-developed ABAP programs using the AUTHORIZATION-CHECK statement. In these cases the object name and all fields of the object (together with submitted values) must be coded, otherwise the authorization check will fail. If the AUTHORIZATION-CHECK statement is not coded within ABAP programs, the relevant authorization checks will not be performed.

As explained above, each SAP transaction will, during processing, check online the values assigned to a specified authorization object in the user's master record, or rather, the profiles assigned to it. The authorization objects checked during transaction processing are hard-coded into the ABAP code for that transaction and are not easily accessible. This presents a problem when establishing user profiles—it may be known which transactions need to be accessed, but the authorization objects that need to be granted in order for them to be successfully executed are difficult to derive.

SAP has provided what can only be described as a partial solution to this problem in the Trace Function. Executed via transaction SE30 "ABAP/IV Run-Time Analysis," this allows a trace to be started, a transaction to be processed and then a button selected that will display, in theory, all the authorization objects accessed through the execution of the transaction. For example, if the trace were run against transaction FB01 (post document) it may be expected to show authorizations covering general ledger account authorization, company code authorization, and so on.

Use of the trace function has a few drawbacks, though, as follows:

- It is very time-consuming—to perform it for each transaction required in a large implementation would be very resource-intensive.

- It is not comprehensive—there are some authorizations that simply are not picked up and displayed in the trace function.

- There are so many options within some transactions and so many data fields that it is almost impossible to ensure that every potential authorization check is invoked.

One large accounting firm has even gone to the lengths of rewriting the SE30 trace function in-house, so as to ensure that a greater number of authorization objects are picked up. There is, however, some light at the end of the tunnel. The SAP profile generator functionality promised as a part of a future release of Version 3.0 of SAP R/3 will provide a direct link between transactions and the authorization objects checked by them.

Another feature provided by SAP is within transaction SU53 which provides details of a transaction which has not been executed due to authorization check failure and displays the authorization objects missing from a user's profile. In order for this transaction to work, system parameter "Auth/check value write on" must be set to a value greater than one.

User Profiles

Most SAP implementation projects will develop user profiles specific to the job functions performed by individuals within the organization. For example, an accounts payable clerk will need access to certain authorization objects, and so a profile containing the objects with the appropriate values assigned to them will be created. This is often done using the Trace Function, described previously.

SAP as delivered, however, contains several hundred "standard" profiles, and some projects pressed for time may be tempted to use these rather than go through the pain of defining their own. It is generally advisable to develop site-specific user profiles as these are more likely to match the business requirements of a particular SAP implementation.

Some of the more sensitive standard profiles delivered with the system are within the Basis (BC) area, particularly for use by security officers in assigning user authorizations. They range in the level of system access they provide but generally they are powerful, particularly with respect to those that offer blanket access to related authorization objects (see Table 33.1). Use of these profiles is optional, but due to their sensitivity it is advised that they be reviewed prior to implementation to ensure that only authorized users have them assigned.

Table 33.1   Basis System Standard Profiles

Profile Name	Description
S_ABAP_ALL	All ABAP/IV authorizations
S_ADMI_ALL	All system administrative functions

(continues)

IX

Implementation

Table 33.1 Continued	
Profile Name	**Description**
S_BDC_ALL	All batch input activities
S_BTCH_ALL	All batch processing authorizations
S_DDIC_ALL	DDIC: All authorizations
S_DDIC_SU	Data Dictionary: All authorizations
S_NUMBER	Number range maintenance: All authorizations
S_SCD0_ALL	Change documents: All authorizations
S_SCRP_ALL	All SAPscript texts, styles, layout sets maintenance
S_SPOOL ALL	All spool authorizations
S_SYST_ALL	All system authorizations
S_TABU_ALL	Standard table maintenance: All authorizations
S_TSKH_ALL	All system administrative authorizations
S_USER_ALL	User maintenance: All authorizations
SAP_ALL	See Section 30.3.12
SAP_ANWEND	All SAP R/3 (excluding system) application authorizations
SAP_NEW	See Section 30.3.12
Z_ANWEND	All user authorizations (excluding BC system)

SAP has advised that if use of standard basis or application system profiles is intended, they should ideally be copied and renamed. This would prevent problems in conversion during future upgrades of the SAP R/3 system.

Profiles and authorizations exist in both maintenance and active versions. This configuration provides a means of amending profile and authorization data without impacting the online usage of user IDs that reference the profiles and authorizations. All changes are performed on maintenance versions. A separate step is required to activate any changes; when this is done, the existing active version is supplanted by the maintenance version as the new active version. This also offers the advantage of segregating the maintenance and activation functions between different security officers, if required.

Security officers are able to grant access to functional authorizations for which they themselves do not have access e.g. a security officer can grant a user access to create a customer without requiring those authorizations himself. This feature of SAP R/3 means that security officer activities can be restricted through profiles to only the system resources they need to perform security activities. Profiles are altered and activated using transaction SU02 and authorizations, using transaction SU03.

Password and User ID Parameters

Each user in SAP R/3 must enter a unique user ID and password when logging on to the system. The user ID is assigned by a system administrator using transaction SU0 and belongs to a single user for the duration of his or her required system access. This transaction is used for assigning profiles to the user ID and also for defining basic user-ID-specific parameters. Note that although SU01 offers the facility to add or delete profiles from user IDs on an individual basis, transaction SU10 can be used to achieve the same end for a specified range of users.

Each user must be assigned to a user type. This indicates the type of processing that the user ID can perform. Table 34.2 shows the available choices for user type.

Table 33.2 User Types	
Online	normal dialogue user
BDC	batch input session user
Batch	batch job processing user
CPIC	CPIC (external system) user IDs

Batch and CPIC user IDs cannot be used for online system logon, and are excluded from regular password change requirements. No feature exists in the SAP R/3 system to allow a user read-only access.

A user can optionally be assigned to a user group, which provides a means of functionally and logically grouping user IDs. This facility can be used to limit the user IDs that can be updated by system administrators. Those user IDs not assigned to a user group are available for update by all system administrators. The user group can be entered in free textual format; no edit checking of the entered user group occurs. Typing errors can therefore result in the mismatch of values for user group on the user's record and the related authorization.

A user ID can optionally have a validity period defined, outside of which the user ID cannot be used. Similarly, a user ID can be locked or unlocked, which determines whether it can be used for logging on to the system.

User IDs can be deleted individually using SU01. Alternatively, transaction SU12 can be used to delete all users defined in the system. This transaction is very powerful, and should be used with extreme caution, as it does not offer the ability to exclude user IDs from the mass-deletion process. SAP recommends that defunct user IDs be blocked rather than deleted from the system, in order to preserve an audit trail, although this approach could potentially impact efficient user ID administration.

The system administrator assigns an initial password to a user ID, which the system requires to be altered at the logon screen when the user ID is used for the first time. A user can change his or her own password on the initial screen during any subsequent logon. A system administrator with access to transaction SU01 can alter the password of any user at any time.

A number of rules govern the format of passwords; these are described below.

Passwords must not:

- Be less than three characters

- Begin with "!" or "?"

- Begin with any sequence of three characters contained in the user ID

IX

Implementation

- Begin with three identical characters

- Be any of the previous five passwords used

- Be "pass" or "SAP*"

- Include spaces as the first 3 characters

Additional organization-specific password checks can be coded for user ID logon processing. This is achieved through modification of the standard ABAP program SAPMS01R. Any edit checks added to this program are automatically executed during logon for every user ID. Since this program is delivered only once (at the initial installation of SAP R/3 in an organization), this program will not require repetitive modification during subsequent system version upgrades. From Version 3.0 onwards custom password checks are added to table USR40 rather than through using SAPMS01R.

Global system parameters can be set by system technical administrators that affect the logon validation procedure for all users. These parameters are described in Table 33.3.

Table 33.3   System Parameters for Configuring User Logon

Parameter Name	Description
Login/min_password_lng	Minimum password length. The default is three, and can be altered to four to eight characters
Login/password_expiration_time	Number of days after which a password must be changed
Login/fails_to_session_end	Number of unsuccessful logon attempts before the system ends the logon procedure
Login/fails_to_user_lock	Number of unsuccessful logon attempts before the system locks the user
Auth/check_value_write_on	Capture the last security check failure
Rdisp/gui_auto_logout	SAPGUI timeout

These parameters can be viewed via transaction TU02. Access to view these parameters is controlled through the setting of user authorizations for object S_TOOLS_EX. They cannot be set using SAP transactions. Instead, they can be amended via either of the two following methods:

- Run SAP-supplied ABAP RSPROFIL, which gives the option of viewing or amending system profile data

- Set manually within the UNIX operating system, in the UNIX file <systemid><instance>

- In Versions 3.0 onward the menu path Tools->Administration->Computing Centre->Management System and the Configuration->Profile Maintenance can be used to set these parameters

Note that Version 3.0 of SAP R/3 offers an additional parameter that allows blocking of user IDs that have been inactive in the system for a specified number of days.

Segregating User, Profile, and Authorization Maintenance

SAP R/3 offers the facility to divide responsibility for maintenance of user IDs, profiles and authorizations. Additionally, responsibility for maintaining and activating profiles and authorizations can be segregated.

The advantages of segregating such access are:

■ By dividing the authority of security officers, a situation is prevented whereby a single security officer can create a user, define profiles and authorizations, and then activate them without any independent review. Since profiles and authorizations can be shared by many users, any changes to them should be reviewed before activation.

■ Administration workload can be divided by cost center, department or any other relevant criteria.

■ Administration of users can be moved into the line where more timely information regarding the status of employees is likely to reside.

Note that SAP technical consultants have indicated that dividing maintenance responsibility in this way may not be suitable for small or medium-sized installations where only a moderate number of users is involved, since by its nature it requires multiple security officers to administer, thereby involving a potentially unacceptable cost overhead. For other than large installations it may be more effective only to partially implement the concept (for example, splitting update from activation administration, but allowing a single security officer to define user IDs, profiles, and authorizations). Alternatively, since user IDs can be assigned predefined profiles, it may be advantageous to rely on the business line functions to create users as required, and restrict security officer activities to profile/authorization maintenance (which requires activation). This decision is at the discretion of the individual organization.

Three objects are used to define security officer authorizations (see Tables 33.4, 33.5, and 33.6). Note that all activity codes are numeric, and permissible values are defined in tables TACT and TACTT. Activity codes are not limited to user master objects and are used extensively in other SAP R/3 authorizations.

Object S_USER_GRP determines which user groups can be administered and, consequently, all users who are assigned to those groups. Individual user IDs cannot be specified. If a user is not assigned to a user group, he or she is unprotected from update by any user who has the SU01 transaction.

Table 33.4 User Master Maintenance for User Groups

Object Name:	S_USER_GRP
Field Names:	
ACTIV_AUTH	Comment: Activity
XUCLASS	Comment: User groups that can be accessed

IX

Implementation

Object S_USER_PRO determines which authorization profiles can be administered. Specific or generic profile names can be entered, as profiles are not assigned to groups.

Table 33.5 User Master Maintenance for Authorization Profiles	
Object Name:	**S_USER_PRO**
Field Name:	
ACTIV_AUTH	Comment: Activity
XUPROFNAME	Comment: Profile names that be accessed

Object S_USER_AUT determines the authorizations that can be administered. Specific or generic authorization names can be entered. Additionally, it is possible to limit access to authorizations relating to a limited number of authorization objects.

Table 33.6 User Master Maintenance for Authorizations	
Object Name:	**S_USER_AUT**
Field Name:	
ACTIV_AUTH	Comment: Activity
XUAUTH	Comment: Authorization name that can be accessed
XUOBJECT	Comment: Object names for which authorizations can be accessed

Table 33.7 shows an example of the settings of security officer authorization objects.

Table 33.7 Security Officer Authorization Objects with Examples		
Object/Fields	**Values**	**Comment**
S_USER_GRP:		
ACTIV_AUTH	2 - 3	Change and display
XUCLASS	TECH	All users assigned to class "TECH"
S_USER_PRO:		
ACTIV_AUTH	7	Activate
XUPROFNAME "S_TABU"	S_TABU*	All profiles with name commencing
S_USER_AUT:		
ACTIV_AUTH	*	All activities
XUAUTH	*	All authorizations
XUOBJECT	V_VER*	All objects with name commencing "V_VER"

Transaction Access

Access to most resources in the SAP R/3 system is achieved through running dedicated transactions. As discussed in the introduction, these can be initiated through keying of the transaction code or selection of the appropriate menu options, which in themselves initiate the relevant transaction. The controls on access are identical and independent of the means used to initiate the transaction.

Each transaction code consists of a four-digit identifier and must be defined in the following:

TSTC   Transaction codes

TSTCT   Transaction code descriptions

Update access to table TSTC is controlled via authorization settings for object S_ADMI_FCD or (in 3.0 and later) S_DEVELOP). Update can be achieved through the menu path tools->case->transactions.

Two different levels of user transaction access authorization checking are available:

1. Transaction Entry

This type of authorization checking involves establishing whether the user has the necessary authority to execute the transaction, and is performed when the user keys the actual transaction code. This is achieved through use of the Transaction Check Object.

The check object is a normal authorization object residing in table TOBJ that is intended for providing checks on user transaction access authorization. Each check object and its fields (usually an activity code and a second authorization qualifier such as company code) is also defined in table TSTCA. The values for activity code listed in table TSTCA (effectively the required authorization for the transaction) must be matched by the authorizations contained in the user profile. This check is undertaken automatically by the system when the transaction code is keyed. If the check object authorization in the user profile does not match that in table TSTCA, the user is denied access to the transaction. Transaction SE93 also offers the facility to view the check object associated with a transaction.

Use of check objects for transactions is not mandatory; where no check object exists for a transaction, no authorization check at transaction entry is performed.

2. Internal Checks

These are performed while the transaction is running. They are application-specific and involve checking a user's authority to access the various system resources referenced by the transaction. The resources are protected by authorization objects; therefore, each object referenced within the transaction is checked against the user's authorizations for the object in his or her profile.

The check is performed through the Authority-Check statement in ABAP coding. An error message is displayed if a violation is encountered, and this prevents further processing of the transaction.

Transactions can be globally blocked from use via transaction SM01. If a transaction is blocked, it cannot be accessed by any user, and consequently the system does not carry out any of the authorization checking described previously. Access to SM01 is protected by a check object, S_TSKH_ADM, supplied by SAP.

IX

Implementation

Table Access

Tables can be designated for online maintenance by setting an indicator using transaction SE11 in the data dictionary. If this indicator is set, the table contents can be updated using transactions SM30 and SM31, subject to user authorization settings. Transaction SM31 is the standard table maintenance interface, and SM30 is the enhanced table maintenance interface, also known as VIEW, which offers more sophisticated editing facilities and is intended to replace SM31 altogether in later releases of SAP R/3. There is no system facility to prevent online update of table data on a global or individual table basis.

Tables can be assigned to classes in order to assist in access protection. Table TDDAT defines the link between tables and their authorization classes. The SAP R/3 system is delivered with all tables assigned to an authorization class, and SAP recommends that these tables not be moved from the delivered program class. If these tables are moved to other classes, this should be documented so that equivalent changes can be made should a migration take place.

Object S_TABU_DIS is used for controlling table access authorization (see Table 33.8). This object comprises two fields: an activity code, and the table classes for which access is authorized. Access cannot be restricted on the basis of table name.

For those tables that are client-independent (that is, available across more than one client in an installation) an additional object, S_TABU_CLI, is employed. This supplements the authority checking already offered by S_TABU_DIS, and is required due to the sensitivity of client-independent tables.

Table 33.8   Table Maintenance Authorization Objects

Object Name:	S_TABU_DIS
Field Name:	
DICBERCLS	Comment: Table classes for which a user access is authorized
ACTVT	Comment: Activity code
Object Name:	**S_TABU_CLI**
Field Name:	
CLIIDMAINT	Comment: Access indicator

ABAP Program Access

Three objects are available for controlling access to ABAP programs. These objects control program execution, program editing, and program debugging access, respectively. Table 33.9 outlines the structure of the first two objects.

Table 33.9   ABAP Authorization Objects with Examples

Object/Fields	Values	Comment
S_PROGRAM:		
P_GROUP	Any	Program group (for example, TEST)
P_ACTION	SUBMIT	Execute program
EDIT		Maintain program attributes and texts
VARIANT		Start and maintain variants
BTCSUBMIT		Submit programs for background execution
S_EDITOR:		
P_GROUP	Any	Program group (for example, TEST)
EDT_ACTION	SHOW	Display program source
EDIT		Amend program source

Programs can be assigned to *authorization groups* for access protection. In order to obtain access to an ABAP program, the user's profile settings must match the program group to which the ABAP belongs. Those ABAPs not assigned to a group are available to all users. There is no edit checking against tables of the entry of program authorization group data, thereby increasing the possibility of error and gaps in program authorization protection.

Note that ABAP programs are not assigned to authorization groups at time of system installation. Programs are, however, assigned to functional *classes* through entries in the following:

TRCL   Program classes

TRCLT   Program class descriptions

Although program classes offer no access protection (as opposed to authorization groups), they do provide a means of functionally identifying programs.

System Administration Functions

The authorization object S_ADMI_FCD is used to provide access control over a number of diverse sensitive system functions. One of these objects is ABAP/IV debugging. Table 33.10 displays all possible values for this object and, where possible, groups together those values that are functionally similar.

Table 33.10   System Authorization Functions Object and Possible Values

Object/Field	Values	Comment
S_ADMI_FCD:		
S_ADMI_FCD	TRAC	ABAP/IV trace authorization
	STOP	ABAP/IV program debugging mode
	REPL	Altering values in debugging mode

(continues)

Object/Field	Values	Comment
Table 33.10 Continued		
S_ADMI_FCD:		
	KERN	Examining the system kernel from within the ABAP/IV debugger
	CUAD	SE41 GUI interface maintenance
	DDIC	Data dictionary maintenance
	TCOD	Transaction code maintenance
	SE01	Transport system transaction SE01
	EVNT	Maintaining system event IDs
	SPAD	Cross-client spool administration
	SPAR	Client-specific spool administration
	SPTD	Cross-client TemSe administration
	SPTR	Client-specific TemSe administration
	SP01	Cross-user spool transaction handling
	FONT	SAPscript font maintenance
	STOM	Changing system TRACE switches
	STOR	Evaluating traces
	SM21	Evaluating system logs
	UNIX	Issue UNIX commands via SM52

Most of the available settings of S_ADMI_FCD are extremely sensitive, and consequently their allocation to any other than a highly restricted number of users will constitute a control risk. For example, having "UNIX" in a user authorization for this object will allow the user to issue any of the UNIX operating system commands from within the SAP application. Also, users with both "STOP" and "REPL" will be able to run ABAP programs on a line-by-line basis and change the values of program variables while doing so.

Note that transaction SM52 may not be available in some installations. However, the SAP-supplied ABAP program SAPMSOS0 will generally be available, and this offers the ability to issue UNIX commands independent of SM52. This program should therefore be controlled through user settings of the authorization object S_PROGRAM.

The SAP Super User

A default super user, SAP*, is supplied in the form of a user master record with every SAP R/3 installation. This user ID has special properties, including unlimited access privileges that can be used for the purpose of defining access privileges for all other system users.

The SAP* user ID is also programmed into the system, so that if the SAP* user master record is deleted, the system-programmed SAP* user ID automatically replaces it as the super user. This ensures that a SAP* user ID exists in the system as the super user at all times. It is at the discretion of the installation as to whether they create a user master record version for this id or leave the system version of SAP* in the system . However, since the system version of SAP* has unlimited authorizations and also an unchangeable password, "PASS," it is highly recommended that a SAP* user ID be created using SU01, so that normal user ID authorization and password checks can be instituted.

The SAP* user ID can be additionally protected by hiding its global authorizations in another, secret, user ID, and giving the visible SAP* user ID read-only access. This would provide some protection from unauthorized use of SAP* by someone with some SAP knowledge who might hack into the system and attempt to use SAP*.

SAP supplies a special user group SUPER and a number of profiles for use with the SAP* super user ID. Use of the SUPER user group ensures that the SAP* user ID cannot be deleted by any other user.

Special profiles are also available for assigning to the SAP* user ID (see Tables 33.11 and 33.12). Note that as from Version 2.1D the standard profiles illustrated in Table 33.11 are no longer supported, and are intended for replacement by those described in Table 33.12.

Table 33.11	SAP Super User Profiles (Pre-Version 2.1D)
S_USER_ALL	Provides unlimited access to maintain users, profiles and authorizations
SAP_ALL	Provides unlimited access to maintain all SAP R/3 system authorizations, with following exceptions: 1. maintenance of users in user group SUPER 2. maintenance of profiles and authorizations with names beginning S_USER
SAP_NEW	Provides unlimited access to all authorizations added with new releases of SAP R/3

User IDs with SAP_ALL cannot access user IDs within user group SUPER, thereby preventing modification of the SAP* user ID. Additionally, the settings of profile SAP_ALL prevent the allocation of the powerful privileges associated with profile S_USER_ALL.

Table 33.12	SAP Standard and Super User Profiles (Version 2.1D Onward)
S_A.SYSTEM	Unlimited access to all users, profiles and authorizations (as offered by S_USER_ALL)
S_A.ADMIN	Authorizations for SAP system administration. This includes all authorizations except for: 1. maintenance of users in user group SUPER 2. maintenance of profiles and authorizations with names beginning "S_A."
S_A.CUSTOMIZ	Authorizations for use in the SAP Customizing system
S_A.DEVELOP	Authorizations for use in the SAP Development environment (excludes any user or profile authorizations)
S_A.USER	Basis system authorizations for end-users (e.g., S_PROGRAM, S_BDC_MONI etc)

S_A.SYSTEM and S_A.ADMIN operate similarly to the profiles S_USER_ALL and SAP_ALL.

IX

Implementation

Other Key Authorization Objects

Some other key authorization areas/objects which are not covered in detail above, but still require careful attention and implementation are described below.

Batch Input Authorization. A single object is available for use in controlling access to batch input sessions, S_BDC_MONI. Table 33.13 shows the fields and range of valid values for this object.

When a session is generated, a user ID and client number must be associated with it. When the session is processed in the background by the system batch input utility, ABAP RSBDCSUB, the profile settings of this user ID are used for authorization checking. If the session is released interactively (that is, manually by a user), the profile settings of the online user are used for authorization checking. There are no special authorizations required to submit a batch session—it is only the management (for example, release, deletion, or change) of sessions to which authorization objects are applied.

Each batch session writes entries to a log when it runs. This log contains details of error messages generated and also general summary statistics, and can be interrogated online to check on the status of batch sessions.

Table 33.13 Batch Input Session Authorization Object		
Object/Fields	**Values**	**Comment**
S_BDC_MONI:		
BDCGROUPID	Any	Name of batch sessions for which a user is authorized (for example, "FRED")
BDCAKTI	ABTC	Submit sessions for execution
	AONL	Run sessions in interactive mode
	ANAL	Analyze sessions, log and queue
	FREE	Release sessions
	LOCK	Lock/unlock sessions
	DELE	Delete sessions

Number Range Authorization. Authority to maintain number ranges is controlled via authorizations for the object S_NUMBER (see Table 33.14). This object in itself defines the activities that can be performed on number range objects.

Number range objects are used to define number range data within the system. These objects contain number range numbers, type, and other reference data specific to each business entity in the system that requires numbering. A uniquely named number range object exists for each entity requiring numbering; for example, objects KREDITOR and DEBITOR are, respectively, the number range objects associated with the vendor and customer number ranges.

Number ranges can be internally or externally assigned, depending on the configuration of the installation. Multiple number ranges can exist for the same number range object. Tables TNRO and TNROT define number range objects and number range object descriptions, respectively.

Number ranges can be maintained via transaction SNRO or directly from within an application.

Table 33.14 Number Range Authorizations

Object/Fields	Values	Comment
S_NUMBER:		
NROBJ	Any	Number range object name (for example, "KREDITOR" for vendors)
ACTVT	02	Change number range intervals
	03	Display number range intervals
	11	Change the last-used number in a number range interval
	13	Initialize the last-used number when transporting ranges between clients
	17	Maintain number range objects (pre 3.0c only)

Change Document Authorization. Access to change documents is achieved through authorizations relating to the object S_SCD0. Table 33.15 describes valid authorization values for this object.

Table 33.15 Change Document Authorization Object

Object	Field	Value	Description
S_SCD0	ACTVT	02	Maintain and display change documents
		06	Delete change documents
		08	Display change documents
		12	Maintain change document objects

Segregation of Duties. In an integrated system, segregation of duties between related business functions, as represented by SAP transactions, is critical. To use a classic example, the procurement cycle from requisition through to vendor payment is all contained within the one application. The risks of broad access are obvious—if a user were able to create a fictitious vendor, generate purchase orders, receive goods, and generate payment, the risks of fraud would be significant.

In order for this type of risk to be mitigated, it is necessary to identify these incompatible functions, or "conflicts," and attempt to ensure that user profiles are established accordingly. A useful approach in doing this is to follow the following steps:

- Group SAP transactions identified as required by the business into generic areas— for example, vendor master maintenance, goods receipt, general ledger postings, and so on.

- Put these transactions into a matrix, as shown in Table 33.16.

- Identify conflicts appropriately.

IX

Implementation

An example showing a subset of the complete matrix that covers the procurement area is given here:

Table 33.16 Segregation of Duties Matrix										
	01	02	03	04	05	06	07	08	09	10
01 Maintain Vendor					X	X				X
02 Vendor Evaluation			X		X					X
03 Requisitioning			X		X	X				
04 Request for Quotation			X							
05 Purchase Orders	X	X	X				X	X	X	X
06 Agreements/ Info. Records	X						X			
07 Materials						X	X		X	X
08 Goods Receipt					X		X		X	X
09 Material Movements					X		X	X		
10 Invoice Posting		X	X			X			X	

Such a matrix would be used as a tool during the implementation of SAP—all user profiles developed would be validated against it prior to activation. Some large SAP users have taken the route of developing tables and ABAP reports within SAP to automate this process.

Reporting Tools

Generally speaking, the amount of information about access security available within SAP R/3 is very limited. Simple basic query tools are not provided—for example, a report of which users have access to a given authorization is not available. A SAP information system is provided from within the user administration menus, which provide a few standard queries, such as:

1. Lists of authorizations, profiles, users, and objects in the system.

2. Values assigned to a given profile or a given user.

3. Change documents for authorizations, profiles, and users.

In addition, a number of potentially useful ABAP reports are available, and these are listed in Table 33.17.

Table 33.17	**Standard Reports for Use in Control and Audit**
RSAVGL00	Table comparison across clients
RSDECOMP	Comparing tables across two systems
RSDELSAP	Delete SAP* from client 066 (EarlyWatch client)
RSKEYS00	Tables comparison: system versus sequential file
RSTABL00	As for RSKEYS00
RSSTAT92	Table changes for a selected month
RSSTAT95	Table access statistics
RSPARAM	Display system parameter settings
RSUSER01	Test SAP_ALL
RSUSR000	List all active users

However, it is anticipated that each organization would need to construct their own dedicated reports in order to be able to perform effective audits and control reviews. It is important to set aside time and resource for this during the development and implementation phases of a SAP project.

Access Control in SAP R/2

In SAP R/2 (Version 5.0 and later) access security is essentially handled, internally to SAP at least, in the same way as SAP R/3. The concepts of user master records, profiles (composite and simple), and authorization objects are still valid. As in SAP R/3, an authorization object contains fields to which values are assigned—in SAP R/2 this entity is known as a *Value Set,* whereas in SAP R/3 it is known as an *Authorization.* An example is given in Table 33.18.

Table 33.18	**SAP R/2 Authorization Objects and Value Sets**		
Object:	BUK	Transactions authorized in a company code	
Fields:	BUK	Company Code	
	TCD	Transaction Code	
Value Set:	BUK01		
		Fields:	Values:
		BUK	01
		TCD	TS01

In the above example, a user who had a profile containing the value set BUK01 would be able to execute transaction TS01 in Company 01.

Another key difference between SAP R/2 and SAP R/3 is in the transactions used to manage access security. A list of key transactions is given in Table 33.19.

Table 33.19	**SAP R/2 Access Security Transactions**
TMU1	Specify user authorizations
TMU2	Maintain authorization profiles
TMU3	Maintain value sets

(continues)

Table 33.19 Continued	
TMU4	Display user master and authorization information
TMU5	Maintain user parameters
TMU6	Activate profiles
TMU7	Activate value sets
USER	A menu of the above transactions

These transactions should be split between user administrators, authorization administrators, and activation administrators, to avoid segregation of duties problems in the access security administration area.

A list of the some of the more critical authorization objects provided to control access to ABAP programs and tables in SAP R/2 is provided in Table 33.20.

Table 33.20 SAP R/2 Critical Authorization Objects	
Object	**Description**
PROGRAM	Execution of ABAP programs, maintaining variants, attributes and texts
SAP-SQL	Execute programs that contain SQL instructions
EDITOR	Execute programs that do not contain SQL instructions
DBS	Access logical databases
RSTABLE	Modify and display table contents, table headers

As in SAP R/3, there are few useful standard reports in SAP R/2. Most audit and control type reports will have to be developed in-house either during implementation or subsequent to that. A list of potentially useful reports is given in Table 33.21.

Table 33.21 Potentially Useful SAP R/2 Reports	
RSBLOG00	Reports the contents of the SAP System log (TRAC file). Must be run in batch mode
RSSLOG00	Reports the contents of the SAP System log. The online version of RSBLOG00
RSCLOG00	Reports the contents of the SAP system log, showing additional error references
RSAQUSGR	Creates a list of all users, including the user groups to which each user is assigned
RSTAPROT	Reports table changes made online
RSACDI00	Reports table updates that are made both online and in batch. Must be run in batch mode

System Integrity Controls (Correction and Transport System)

The key mechanism for maintaining effective change control within SAP is the correction and transport system (CTS). This section is devoted to an explanation of the key features and control implications of the associated mechanisms.

Overview

The correction and transport system is used to migrate different elements from one SAP R/3 system to another. The CTS can apply corrections to more than one client at a time. The following elements can be migrated:

- ABAP programs

- SAP table structures (and other data dictionary objects)

- SAP table entries

- Data elements

- Domains

In order to process a change in one of these objects to a target system, the following procedure must be followed:

- A correction is set up for each change required. This can be automatically requested for some appropriate objects (for example, ABAP programs) or may have to be set up manually as the object is changed in the source environment.

- A correction must then be released to a Transport Request. A number of corrections can be included in a transport request.

- The transport request is released. It is thereby automatically copied to a UNIX file.

- An import is initiated from UNIX to import the request and update the target system.

Each of these steps is described in more detail in the sections below.

The Correction System

The correction system ensures that formal development work on objects is registered and documented, and that parallel, uncoordinated changes to objects are not possible, even in different SAP systems. A log of all corrections to ABAP programs and tables is also maintained in SAP.

Creations of or modifications to objects can be carried out only when a correction is opened. Corrections can be opened whilst editing an object (for example, in transaction SE38 for an ABAP program) or directly through the correction system (transaction SE01) prior to editing or creating an object. Opening a correction in advance allows all objects to be maintained to be locked from maintenance by other users. Corrections can also be linked together. Multiple environment objects can be linked to the same correction.

Corrections can be opened only in the system where the original copy of an object is located.

The original location of an object can be defined as one of two systems:

- The system in which the object was created (usually the development system)

- The system "SAP" for objects delivered by SAP

IX

Implementation

A correction name is assigned when an ABAP program is created or changed. The format is shown in Table 33.22.

Table 33.22	Correction Format	
Correction	C11K9000115	
Where	C11	System Name
	K	Transport Request Type
	9000115	Number

The sequential correction number is automatically generated by SAP—but it can be changed (to allow a previous correction to be worked with), and so the correction sequence may not be complete. It is preferable to keep the number of corrections in each Transport Request as low as possible—in case it is decided not to process a correction through to Production.

Once an item is included in a correction list, the details can be reviewed using TOOLS -> CASE -> MAINTENANCE -> CORRECTIONS (which is the SE01 "Transport and Correction System"). The Editor Button can be used to see entries and tables.

The PROTECT button within the transaction prevents users putting items in your correction, but does not stop users changing the base table or data. It is best, therefore, to transport corrections as soon as possible after they are set up.

Transport Requests

The transport system is used for moving objects from a development SAP system to a production system or, in fact, between any systems. The transport system can be used to:

- Overwrite components and data in a target system
- Delete and replace objects
- Insert objects without overwriting existing ones
- Delete objects

CTS mechanism operates with reference to a number of systems, shown in Table 33.23.

Table 33.23	CTS System Definitions
Integration System	The "original" system, where software is delivered from SAP, and where development work is carried out
Consolidation System	The primary production system, and target of all integration system releases
Recipient System(s)	Additional production systems. Releases to the consolidation system are automatically forwarded to the recipient systems
Development System(s)	Optional. These can be used to develop objects separately from the integration system (e.g., third-party development). Originals are still located in the integration system

Transports must be done through opening a transport request. Objects in corrections are then assigned to the transport request. All transport requests are logged. TRs are applied chronologically and replace the existing object in the target client. This applies to both client-dependent and client-independent data and tables. The default is to import the TR into the same client number the TR is being exported from—though this default can be overwritten.

The number of TRs should be minimized, to minimize administration effort. The TR releaser has to be the owner (that is, the raiser) of the TR. However, the TR owner can be changed to another user—by someone other than the TR owner—via the CHANGE USER NAME option in the EDIT menu option in SE01. This is sometimes needed for operational flexibility by programmers. This can also be done for corrections in the same way.

Procedures should require sign-off on all TRs being migrated into the production system, to verify that they are satisfied this is a valid update.

A copy should always be transported—that is, Transportation Code "K" should normally be used. If Code "C" is used, SAP will think the original now resides in the Target system, not the Source system—this can cause problems with upgrades and so on. Transportation Code "C" is not applicable for tables, but is for ABAPs.

Information relating to the success of an export can be derived from transaction SE01 by selecting menu option UTILITIES —> TRANSPORT UTILITIES. A multilevel system log can be displayed that provides information regarding both imports (in the consolidation system) and exports (in the integration system). An Exit Code of 0 indicates a successful result.

It is possible to get a list of TRs released from the Source system and a list of those imported into the Target system—but not a list of those TRs released but not yet imported. Either a manual comparison and list can be kept, or an ABAP can be written perform this comparison.

Repairs

Urgent corrections to objects are sometimes required in a non-original system, where time or other factors precludes creation of a correction and execution of a transport. These can be done by means of a "repair." Any objects altered via a repair cannot be altered via a normal correction until the repair has been closed. Repairs must be used for any objects where the original system is defined as "SAP" (that is, SAP-delivered). Repairs cannot be added to transport requests and moved between systems.

System-Wide Parameters

Certain system parameters are maintained in the following tables that define the migration path between SAP environments. In the examples shown in Table 33.24, it is assumed that a three-tier (production, preproduction, development) architecture is implemented.

IX

Implementation

Table 33.24	**Key CTS Tables**
TSYST	Defines the system names in SAP in relation to the operating system and the Oracle database names. The system names are denoted by a three-character name, and "SAP" always appears as one of these—this is to enable the identification of the receipt of corrections from SAP Waldorf.
TASYS	Defines the relation between the consolidation system and one or more recipient systems to which transports can be "auto-forwarded". The system "SAP" again appears in this table
TDEVC	Lists all the development classes of development objects within the system. Related objects can be grouped together in these classes. For all standard classes (for example, those assigned to delivered SAP objects) this will read "SAP" for both. For development classes assigned to user developed objects this defines the preproduction and development systems.
TADIR	Defines the available development environment objects in a system. The level of development allowed in each environment is also defined in a system parameter contained in this table—Program ID HEAD, Object Type SYST. The field "Can be edited" can be set to:

A	Any change allowed
R	Urgent repairs allowed
_	No changes allowed

During a development phase this can be set to R but in a productive system should always be set to "_." "A" should never be used

Development Classes

Development classes are defined for each object in table TADIR. These must be assigned to ABAP programs upon creation as a part of the object attributes. The development class is used to group together interdependent objects logically. All delivered SAP objects are predefined in development classes and all user-defined development classes should be prefixed "Z."

ABAP Programs

When an ABAP program is changed, it is not necessary to identify included modules, CUA definition, screens, texts, or documentation together with the source code.

When an ABAP in a development system is being changed using transaction SE38, a correction is requested. The details of a new or existing correction must then be entered. A numeric version number of each ABAP program is assigned automatically by the system. The correction can then be released and assigned to a Transport Request from the same screen.

SAP Tables

The use of CTS in the maintenance of SAP tables is rather patchy, certainly in versions before Version 3.0. Tables can be maintained through the Customization process or through using transaction SM31 to update the transaction directly.

If a table is being maintained through the customization process, there is generally an option available to assign the changes to the table contents made to a correction. This is usually under the menu option "TABLE VIEW—> TRANSPORT" although it is sometimes hidden under another option. Using this sets up a correction which can then be released and assigned to a transport request in the normal manner.

For tables that are not maintained through the customization process, transaction SM31 must be used. For some tables that are predefined to the CT system, a correction will automatically be generated, the details of which will have to be completed before the maintenance can take place. For other tables, a correction must be set up directly within transaction SE01 and the table arguments to be transported defined manually in a correction.

There is no simple means of establishing which tables:

- Are updated only through the customization process
- Have been predefined to the CTS

In both of these cases only the table data which has been changed will be included in the correction.

Generally, tables are not assigned a development class, and therefore the target system needs to be defined when the correction is set up. This is defaulted from parameters contained in files in the UNIX directories shown in Table 33.25.

Table 33.25 CTS UNIX Directories	
/usr/sap/trans/log	**logs**
/usr/sap/trans/buffer	information on which transports are to be imported
/usr/sap/trans/cofiles	information on transport requests
/usr/sap/trans/sapnames	information for users on transport request status
/usr/sap/trans/tmp	temporary data

Tables can be set with a flag "Table Maintenance Allowed" which is set using transaction SE11. This means that online maintenance using transaction SM31 can be disallowed, so that only updates by TRs are allowed.

The table entries at the time the transport takes place are transported—not those at the time the correction is set up. It is possible to change a table that has been set up to be transported if the particular table is not locked. This is common to many SAP tables.

Authorizations

UNIX security over the transport request file in SAP is a critical issue and must be addressed.

Within SAP R/3 it is important to ensure that check objects are assigned to the CTS transactions. This may not be a major concern, as all these transactions do is to copy data out into the UNIX area—and they do not actually import them into any client; that is, no updates are performed. However, since the command to import the transport request into the target client is done via UNIX, this will be done by technical support staff—who will likely not know the contents of the transport request and so may just import any and all TRs they are asked to import.

Accordingly, even if SAP does not consider there is a need to put an authorization check on the CTS process, such authorization access should at least be in place over the release

IX

Implementation

of transport requests—this would prevent unauthorized users from releasing (potentially dangerous or fraudulent) TRs to be imported in the next import due.

Transaction SE01 "Transport and Correction System" is protected by the check object S_ADMI_FCD with a value of SE01. However, an unprotected transaction STAR is also provided in the system.

Processing Controls

Some key processing or technical controls are subsequently discussed, the correct and controlled implementation of which are essential to data integrity within an SAP system.

Dialogue and Update Tasks

A key element of SAP R/3 processing is the way in which database update tasks are performed. There are essentially two steps to a SAP transaction: The *dialogue* task and the *update* tasks.

The dialogue task involves user terminal input being accepted by the SAP front-end software through a series of SAPGUI display screens. Following this, conversion to SAP's proprietary format takes place, and resultant processing requests are placed in an SAP request queue. These conversion and enqueue processes are performed by the SAP Dispatcher.

A log of all updates waiting to be passed on to the database is maintained in a file VBLOG. Cases can occur where a dialogue task has been completed—that is, as far as the user is concerned his/her transaction has been posted—but the update task fails, and therefore the database is not been updated with the relevant information. Such cases have serious implications for system database integrity. The record on VBLOG is set with an error flag and remains (successful updates are deleted from VBLOG). It is also possible to configure the system so that an *express mail message* is sent to a nominated database administrator should this occur.

Managing Batch Sessions

Batch (BTC) sessions can be created in SAP to do the following:

- Use a validation step in interfacing data from an external system
- Pass data from one part of a SAP system to another

Effective batch session management is critical to ensure that data is passed on to its target on a timely basis. The way BTC sessions are managed in SAP typically means that they have to be manually released, so that data update can be performed. There are a number of inherent risks associated with this process, as follows:

- Access security must be effectively established so as to allow only authorized users to manage, release, and delete batch sessions. Authorization objects are provided for this purpose.
- Should a batch session fail to be released successfully (through a processing error) the data within the session can be manually amended from within the batch

session maintenance transactions. Unfortunately, there is an audit trail of any changes to data made in this manner, but there is nothing that can be done about this.

■ Should batch sessions not be cleared on a timely basis, this can lead to confusion for users, such as releasing the wrong batch session, or can lead to errors in the original batch session should related records have been changed or deleted from the database in the interim.

Unfortunately, but not surprisingly, there is a lack of helpful reporting tools within SAP in this area. It is therefore likely that some custom ABAP reports may have to be developed in this area, to list aged BTC sessions, for example.

Interface Controls

Automated interfaces into and out of SAP are typically managed using BTC sessions. The following control guidelines should be used when dealing with inbound and outbound interfaces:

■ Control reports should be automatically produced from both the source/receiving system and SAP to show the following for records input, accepted, and rejected:

  Record count

  Total number of customers/vendors processed (where applicable)

  Total value Cr (where applicable)

  Total value Dr (where applicable)

  Total amount (where applicable)

  Total volume (where applicable)

■ Control reports should also list all input parameters entered when an ABAP report is run.

■ Controls should be established over transactions in error which can be held in suspense files so that they are non-amendable prior to reinput.

■ For certain interfaces it should be possible to run a non-updating version of an interface program prior to a live run, so that inputs can be checked before transactions are actually created.

■ All interface files produced by either SAP or an external system should be uniquely identifiable by the use of interface type, creation date, creation time, and run number, so as to ensure that files are not confused or processed twice.

■ All interface programs should be thoroughly tested, documented, and subjected to user acceptance prior to implementation.

■ Users must be assigned responsibility for each interface and must be trained in the methods of controlling the interface.

IX

Implementation

For certain interfaces it may be desirable to load data direct from a PC environment (for example, Excel spreadsheet) into SAP. This is a particularly common case where the upload of journal voucher information into the SAP FI-Financial Accounting Module General Ledger is required. In this case, the spreadsheet is being used merely to perform a complex calculation to arrive at the value of a journal or series of journals that would otherwise be input manually into SAP. It is not data from a controlled application and therefore need not be subject to all the above controls. However, it should be subject to the same controls as if it were input manually—for example, online validation, postfacto reporting, supervisory review, and so on.

Application Controls

Application controls are, by definition determined by the requirements of the business, and thus cannot be discussed in as specific terms as we can, for example, talk about access security functionality. The functionality available to build application controls is discussed in detail in the relevant chapters of this publication, however, there are a few general points to be made in this area.

Application controls in SAP are typically table-driven and are established through the Customization process during implementation. These type of controls are generally rather rigid—once they have been implemented, it is difficult to switch them on and off dynamically. A couple of the more critical areas of application are discussed below by way of example: Value based limit of authority controls in the procurement cycle, and online customer credit checking in the sales cycle.

Limits of Authority

SAP-provided functionality over the release of purchase requisitions relies on the definition of the following:

- Release Strategy—defines the process of approval of purchase requisitions, based on their total value and the level(s) and order in which they must be approved online within the organization. Release values are determined at a line item level, and up to eight release points can be defined for each release strategy.

- Release Condition—determines which release strategy is applied to a requisition, and depends on the account type, material group, plant, and value.

- Release Indicator—indicates the status of a requisition and determines, for example, whether the item can be ordered and whether the quantity or delivery date can be changed.

All of these parameters are defined in tables during the Customization process and must be established and agreed with management prior to their implementation.

Online Credit Checking

SAP provides sales functionality centered around the use of sales order types. The type of credit check performed can be defined relative to specific order types—for example an intercompany sales order can be processed with no credit check, whereas a standard order could be defined as having a credit check which would, should it fail do one of the following:

- Display a warning message

- Prevent the order from being posted

- Accept the order but block it from delivery

In addition, it is possible to define the values taken into account when the credit check is performed—that is, whether the following sales are included:

- Ordered but undelivered

- Delivered but uninvoiced

- Invoiced but unpaid

Each order type would have to be configured for these and a host of other parameters. This would be undertaken preimplementation during the Customization process.

Data Entry Controls

Data entry into SAP is critical. One of the system's most appealing selling points is that data need be entered into the system only once. The downside of this is that should data be entered inaccurately, this will have serious ramifications throughout the system in terms of processing, particularly in the case of master file data that is referred to on numerous occasions throughout transaction input.

There are a number of important features in SAP that assist in the accurate entry of data into the system, as follows:

- Matchcodes—used to look up relevant data (generally master files) when entering a transaction. For example, when entering a sales order, matchcodes are used to select the correct customer record and material. This can be done without knowing the record number and without leaving the transaction. A customer could be identified through knowing the postal code and a material through knowing the product name it represents. Using matchcodes therefore assists in the accurate cross-referencing of other system data when processing a transaction.

- Data Tables—used within the system to hold commonly accessed data elements and prevent the need for them to be entered continuously. For example, bookkeeping exchange rates are held in a table in SAP and automatically defaulted into the relevant fields when processing foreign currency general ledger postings, sales orders, purchasing transactions, and so on.

There is however a significant area of exposure in the override of defaulted data entered into SAP. For example, when a sales order is raised, certain data can be defaulted in to the document, as follows:

- Delivery address (from the customer master)

- Terms of delivery (from the customer master)

- Sales tax rates (from a combination of customer master and tables)

- Payment terms (from a combination of customer master and tables)

- Exchange rates (from data tables)

- Sales prices (from the pricing file)

Depending on the way the system is configured, any or all of these fields may be changed, or overridden, by the user entering the sales order into SAP. An implementation team configuring the system faces the paradox of wanting to maintain flexibility by allowing the user to change defaulted data, while needing to retain a degree of functional control.

During the system design phase, it is therefore critical correctly to configure the complex tables that lie behind the control of dynpro field selection. All of this work should of course be discussed with the relevant functional system owner to determine the degree of freedom that will be allowed and the degree of control to be foregone.

Compensating Controls

The problems associated with inflexible application controls and the potential ability to amend and override previously validated data means that, in an environment where tight supervisory control has been the norm, there may be some problems in managing expectations about the effectiveness and nature of the control environment following the implementation of SAP. Although many companies are moving away from the traditional hierarchical organization and direct supervisor-subordinate reporting relationships towards flatter organizations and more empowered cultures, they may feel unwilling to sacrifice controls they have always viewed as sacred.

The implementation of such controls is likely to rely heavily on the use of system-generated post-facto control reports. Such reports could be broadly divided into a number of categories, examples of which are listed below:

Master Data Creation/Change Authorization Reports

Customer master creations/changes

Vendor master creations/changes

Material master creations/changes

GL account master creations/changes

Master Data Validation Reports

Potential duplicate vendors

Customers also established as vendors

Customers with unlimited credit

Transaction Default Override Reports

> Critical fields overwritten on sales orders/invoices
>
> Critical fields overwritten on purchase orders
>
> Critical fields overwritten on GL posting documents

Authorization Reports

> Purchase orders in excess of commitment authority
>
> Sales orders blocked, having failed credit check

Backlog Monitoring

> Customers orders unfulfilled
>
> Purchase orders not printed/issued
>
> Quality inspection stock levels

Account Reconciliation

> Accounts payable to general ledger reconciliation
>
> Accounts receivable to general ledger reconciliation
>
> General ledger postings (can be restricted by certain value and account parameters, for example, postings with a P&L impact only)

It will not come as any surprise that SAP delivers very little in this area by way of standard reports. A significant amount of specification, programming, and testing is required. It is not uncommon to see in excess of a hundred post-facto control reports developed in some large SAP implementations, especially with a more traditional culture and control environment.

When coding control reports it is important to ensure that the following is borne in mind:

1. Reports should always have pages numbered.

2. The message "End of Report" should always appear on the last page.

3. Report distribution should be automated wherever possible. This may involve setting up an internal table of users listing supervisor/department relationships. Page breaks should be inserted before each new user is listed.

4. All reports should list:

> user ID and name
>
> user department
>
> time/date stamp
>
> before and after images, where appropriate

IX

Implementation

It is also important that retention periods for control reports are agreed in advance with both internal and external auditors as well as any relevant tax or other government authorities.

In a SAP implementation project where controls have been specified at a level that requires the development of a large number of post-facto control reports, it is always a struggle to get the user community to accept them. SAP is often replacing legacy systems where controls have been developed within the system and a minimum of reports is necessary. To face the arduous task of reviewing what might seem like mountains of paper will not be popular. It is therefore important to ensure that these are kept to a minimum and, where they are required, full endorsement from owners is gained and the business risks associated with not using the reports explained.

Addressing Control Issues During a SAP Implementation

Most organizations have enough to think about during an SAP implementation project without having to worry about the control issue. However, if not addressed at this stage serious problems are inevitable later on and it is almost impossible to "retrofit" controls into an SAP environment. This section provides a few key pointers for project managers, controllers and internal audit managers which they should consider before embarking on such a project.

Using Dedicated Controls Resources

Control issues do not generally come at the top—or even close to it—of a SAP implementation project's list of priorities. Basic business processes may still need to be designed, tested, and implemented, users trained, and data converted. Even if controls are considered important at the outset, they are often pushed back in the implementation schedule or not addressed at all. This can have disastrous results following implementation—attempting to retrofit controls is almost impossible in some areas of SAP and, moreover, any exposures to the business are quantifiable during this period.

It is for these reasons that it is strongly recommended that dedicated controls specialists be used on any SAP implementation project. Such individuals may be taken from a number of areas, as follows, to ensure the right people with relevant expertise are used:

> **Internal Audit**—a common source of controls staff on SAP projects. Using these staff has the advantage that any specialist controls knowledge is retained within the organization and, assuming a reporting line to audit is maintained, they retain independence from the project and their diversion to noncontrol-related activities can, it is hoped, be prevented. The main disadvantage of using internal audit staff

is that there is a very steep and expensive learning curve in getting up to speed on SAP, and that a staff of at least three is required to become sufficiently expert in the control environment of the various modules. Assigning one individual from audit to work part-time on a SAP project, as often happens, is fairly worthless in terms of performing detailed control evaluation of the system.

Project Team Members—can be assigned to address control issues during implementation. Although this has the advantage of keeping the work within the project, it invariably results in the individuals concerned being taken off controls work and assigned to tasks perceived at the time as more pressing. Very rarely is this strategy successful.

External Consultants—now available who are able to provide specialist advice in the area of security and controls. The most common place to look for such advice is from the Big Six accounting companies. The quality of service and depth of specialist knowledge is currently variable within such organizations but is improving. In addition, there is a number of individual experts in the field who are available to provide advice in this area. As with all stages of an SAP implementation, the use of consultants has to be carefully managed. Terms of reference have to be tightly defined and the expertise of the consultants proposed fully vetted.

Control Issues

Addressing control issues on a SAP project should be viewed in the context of two major phases, as follows:

1. System Development and Configuration

The main tasks of the controls advisor in the development phase of a SAP implementation are:

- To review the functionality of each business process to determine whether there are any associated SAP weaknesses. This can only be done through detailed review of all dynpros and related master file information, and review of all customized table entries behind each transaction. This is a very lengthy process and requires a considerable degree of expertise to perform.

- To develop potential solutions to the control weaknesses identified. These commonly come in the form of: Changes to table settings through the Customization process or the development of post-facto control reports.

  It is generally best to avoid any source code changes unless a control issue is very high-profile and there is no other acceptable solution.

- To meet and agree controls with functional owners of the system.

IX

Implementation

2. System Implementation

During the system implementation phase of the project, a number of important control issues should be addressed, as follows:

Access security

Data conversion

Automated interfaces

Change control

The development of procedures and implementation of control reports

Access Security. The key tasks involved in a preimplementation review of access security are detailed below.

With regard to the establishment of users, it is essential to ensure the following:

- All access privileges are consistent with individuals' job responsibilities.

- Transaction access is reviewed for adequate segregation of duties.

- Transaction access is also reviewed for particularly sensitive transactions and access to these is kept to an absolute minimum.

- Third-party access is controlled in accordance with the company guidelines.

- All relevant details are completed on the user master (for example, some fields such as department can be used for the sorting of reports).

- Appropriate naming conventions are used for all users and authorizations.

In addition, procedures should be developed to ensure the following:

- User IDs that have not been recently used are identified and suspended.

- Users who leave the company or are transferred are able to be identified, and access deleted and recreated as appropriate.

- Each change to a user ID is supported by a formally documented and authorized change request.

- Ownership of system transactions/authorizations is established, and all requests for access to those transactions are approved by the owners.

The broad access generally given to support and development users must also be properly controlled. This access should be subject to review and approval prior to implementation. It is quite common to agree a period of grace (say 30 days) during which team members continue to have broad access for immediate support requirements.

Data Conversion. Data conversion controls should be established to encompass the following:

- Conversion planning and the identification of dependencies
- A data clean-up exercise prior to conversion, to ensure that all data to be converted is accurate, valid, and current
- Procedures for the reconciliation and validation of all data
- Procedures for the parallel maintenance of master files
- Ownership of converted SAP files to enable user acceptance and sign-off procedures to be established
- That the involvement of noncompany (that is, contract) personnel is kept to a minimum and all data input by temporary staff is subject to extra validation

Automated conversions require specific extra considerations to be taken into account to ensure adequate control, as follows:

- Control reports should be automatically produced from the input, interim, and final files.
- Control reports should include both record counts and control totals on key fields.
- Listings of records not transferred to SAP due to error should be automatically produced (including record counts and control totals) and procedures developed for error handling.
- Records in error in batch sessions should be amended with care.
- SAP tables may need to be set up to be referenced during the automated conversion. Conversion procedure should include the maintenance of these.
- All conversion programs should be fully tested with user involvement and the test results documented.

Manual conversions also require some specific controls to ensure accuracy and completeness, as follows:

- Input forms should be developed to collate data in a form suitable for entry to SAP.
- If any fields have been changed or not included in previous files, they should be suitably approved and verified online to input forms.

Automated Interfaces. A checklist of key interface controls is provided. It is important that for each interface identified, adequate control mechanisms are in place prior to implementation, as well as properly documented procedures for use in the operation of the interfaces.

Change Control. The correct establishment and implementation of change control is critical to the integrity of any SAP system. Not only must the relevant tables be customized and access to critical transactions be restricted and segregated, but procedures for the operation of change requests should also be developed, documented, and circulated to all development staff.

IX

Implementation

Procedures and Control Reports. A list of all post-facto control reports developed to compensate for weaknesses in the SAP system should be used as the basis for inclusion in local procedures. Each report should be reviewed by users and relevant implementation team members to determine the following:

- Whether the report is applicable to the particular business unit in question
- Whether the report is in a format and sort sequence that meets user requirements
- Whether the report will be run online or in batch
- The frequency and scheduling of the report in batch
- The recipient(s) of the report. The recipient must be independent of the activity being reported.

The method of report distribution is also a critical area, the most efficient and secure method of distribution being to ensure that reports automatically reach the intended recipient.

In many cases, the control reports will be required prior to the official implementation date. Maintenance of converted data and input of transactions prior to implementation—for example, customer orders—will require review of the control reports.

Business procedures should be developed to cover all areas in which the system operates. Existing company policy/procedure guides should be used as the basis for developing new SAP-relevant procedures. From a control point of view, particular attention should be paid to ensure the following:

- Manual procedures compensate for all control weaknesses of SAP
- All control weaknesses arising as a result of noncore or nonstandard functionality are addressed
- Procedures are included for the use of all control reports
- Procedures for the authorized update of all user tables are included
- Procedures for the update and addition of master records and the relevant approval are included

Auditing SAP

Following the implementation of SAP a serious challenge is faced by the organizations auditors, both internal and external, in how to modify and develop their audit approach and to ensure their staff have the right skills and tools to do this work. This section provides some useful tips on how to go about addressing this challenge.

Developing SAP Skills in the Audit Function

The best way of developing SAP skills within the audit function is to involve audit staff in the development and implementation phases of the project. A rough estimate of the learning curve associated with SAP in this area is that it can take 12 to 18 months of full-time effort for an experienced system auditor to become fully conversant with the control functionality of one module of SAP. If a system-based audit approach where SAP is intensively evaluated and interrogated is to be used, this level of expertise will be necessary.

It is recognized, however, that for some organizations this is an expensive luxury and not a practical route to auditing SAP. Alternative audit approaches are discussed below.

More recently a number of training courses have been developed, largely by the Big Six accounting firms, specifically addressing audit and control issues. These tend to focus mainly on the technical areas of control within SAP—access security and change control feature prominently. They generally avoid looking at application controls within the modules in any great detail, apart perhaps from a cursory review of the FI-Financial Accounting Module.

SAP itself currently offers very little in the way of training for auditors. Some of the technical courses on access security and the correction and transport system are worth attending, but again, there is very little available in the area of application control. SAP is rumored to be developing a SAP Audit training course, but what this covers and when it might be available is unclear.

Audit Approaches

Depending on the size of the organization and prevalence of SAP within it, several of audit approaches are possible, as follows:

1. Dedicated SAP Controls Group—"The Rolls Royce approach"

    Some large companies have established groups of dedicated SAP experts within their audit function. Such groups are responsible both for providing controls advice to any SAP implementation project and for developing and maintaining any tools for use in auditing the system postimplementation. Such a group can also be given the responsibility for actually performing audits of the system, although it may be desirable for reasons of independence to keep this separate—it is perhaps difficult to rely on the objectivity of an auditor reviewing a SAP system which he/she has helped design and implement.

2. Dedicated SAP Expert Auditors

    Smaller companies are likely to assign responsibility for SAP review, project involvement and audit to certain EDP auditors in the audit function, often to be performed in tandem with other responsibilities. This approach obviously does not provide for the same level of SAP expertise, but is quite common in smaller organizations. SAP audit tools are likely to be developed on an ongoing basis during audits and not maintained in the interim.

3. Auditing around the System

    If a system-based audit approach is not used, a more traditional approach of validating the input and output of a computer system can be used. This approach does

IX

Implementation

not rely at all on any understanding of how the application functions, rather reviewing it as a "black box," and relying on statistically generated samples of what are viewed as key documents. This approach is not really to be recommended unless SAP represents a small part of an organization's business or an audit department is very small.

4. Outsourcing Review of SAP

The outsourcing of internal audit is a growth area, and as most big accounting firms are large enough to have developed at least some SAP expertise, this is an option. However, unless the whole internal audit function is outsourced, this can provide some communication problems.

Documenting Control Concerns

A key part of any SAP audit approach is how to document control features identified during evaluation of the application. Suggested audit steps could also be provided where specific weaknesses have been documented. A possible approach to documentation could be based on control objectives which some organizations have already documented—for example:

- Control objective

- SAP-related strength

- SAP-related weakness

- Associated audit step

The audit step could be running a computer audit program, verifying that a control report is produced and reviewed or performing a test of a manual procedure in cases where the control objective is not addressed by SAP functionality.

Audit Software

Developing Computer Assisted Audit Techniques (CAATs) is an important part of developing a SAP audit approach. Any computer audit programs developed can do the following:

- Test users' access to key system resources.

- Read data files and report exceptions.

- Review system settings (that is; customized table entries).

- Look at other system-held information.

There are several choices available in the use of software, as follows:

1. ABAP

ABAP (or ABAP/IV) is SAP's proprietary programming language and has been used to write the majority of the program code making up the SAP application modules. ABAP programming is undertaken from within the SAP application using standard menu/transaction options. There are a number of important advantages and disadvantages associated with using ABAP.

Advantages

- ABAP is fully integrated with the SAP application. Programs can be run from alternate sessions within SAP, toggling, for example, between a display transaction and report output.

- ABAP programs can be started by any user with basic SAP navigational skills. There is no need to become familiar with an external query package.

- As ABAP is a part of the SAP application, it will always read the most up to date data—it runs directly against the same Oracle (or other database) tables as the application.

- ABAP takes advantage of the links between SAP data elements and Oracle table and field names. Therefore the SAP data dictionary can be used to ensure that the correct field descriptor, for example, is output on reports.

- A wide range of selection options can be specified in the report screen which will enable a user to reduce the quantity data read by the program.

- There are options available to download ABAP output to Excel spreadsheets if required.

- Certain SAP elements (for example, user master and security information) is held in SAP pool tables and can only be read using the ABAP language (this problem may be lessened in Version 3.0 which uses fewer pool tables).

- There are several of standard SAP ABAPs delivered with the application which, although they are not audit-specific, can be amended to serve as audit tools.

Disadvantages

- ABAP is not a true fourth-generation language. Programmers require a high level of training to become expert and can demand high renumeration. Current demand for ABAP programmers is high, and continuity of staff is a problem.

- ABAP does not provide flexible options to manipulate data on screen. Once the program output has been produced, this can only be done using a download option.

- Changes to reports will require a change in a development environment and promotion to production. This may prove to be a time-consuming process.

2. Downloading Data

It is possible to write a single ABAP program that will download data to a flat file external to SAP. This can then be interrogated using any number of data query/analysis packages. Again, the advantages and disadvantages of such an approach are detailed next:

Advantages

- The cost of employing expensive ABAP programmers is avoided—only the download ABAP need be written.

- Audit queries can be written by audit staff.

- Programs are easily amended and flexible.

- Programs are highly transportable.

Disadvantages

- Data downloaded is not always reviewed on a timely basis—it soon becomes out of date.

- Through not using an integrated solution, users have to learn to use two systems—they are likely to still have to log on to SAP to execute display transactions and so on.

- It is not possible to run a query that interrogates data and tables concurrently.

- It is not possible to download certain information—for example, user master records and authorizations.

3. Alternative Software

There are several packages available that are capable of directly interrogating SAP R/3 data, for example as held within the Oracle database. These allow direct and real-time access to the data, but there is a problem in this area: The SAP data are held in Oracle tables, and the names of these tables and of the fields within them are not represented by business-relevant text. Therefore it is extremely difficult to construct a query using one of these packages, as it is not possible to determine the data being analyzed. The link between SAP field names and their equivalent in the Oracle database is held within the SAP data dictionary, but it is not easily accessible. There are some software companies who are looking at establishing files that provide this mapping within their own package, but as yet these are very much in the formative stage.

Audit User Groups

An excellent means of sharing information, exchanging ideas, and jointly developing control and audit relevant information is through the user group network. Audit specific groups have been established and are very active in the U.K., U.S., and Benelux countries. Active participation by all audit departments in organizations where SAP has been implemented is to be encouraged.

From Here...

- For more information on R/3 customization, see Chapter 7, "R/3 Customizing."

- For more information on managing workflow, see Chapter 30, "R/3 Business Workflow Management."

Chapter 34

Managing Communications Internal and External

The formation of project teams frequently takes people away from their normal jobs, leaving a workload that needs to be covered by others. SAP projects are typified by the bringing together of business and IT staff from the company with a whole variety of external staff brought in to support the project. The working environment is probably new, and many people do not know each other, let alone their positions and indeed what is expected of them. The business personnel probably do not know too much about SAP, and the systems personnel probably do not know too much about the business. For the project to succeed, there has to be a huge volume of knowledge transfer and tremendous cooperation between team members and users. Effective communication is therefore vital and needs to be addressed before the project even begins.

Time is the most valuable asset on a SAP project. The second the project starts, the costs start rising—with senior consultants costing upwards of $2,000 dollars a day, you cannot afford to waste time, yet it is a remarkably easy thing for all of us to do. Unnecessary meetings, meetings with no framework, and floods of e-mail are the worst culprits. Information overload is as serious a problem as lack of information.

Overview of SAP Project Communications Issues

If you want your project to be a success, you must take the issue of communications seriously. Ideally, project management should seek some professional help from communications consultants to plan and monitor an effective communications policy.

In this chapter, you will be examining the following questions:

- what you need to communicate
- to whom

In this chapter, you learn:

- What the communications issues are on SAP implementations.

- The importance of effective communication.

- How to develop a SAP project communications strategy.

- How to manage internal and external communications.

- How to effectively manage meetings.

- How groupware can be used in SAP implementations.

IX

Implementation

- how

- when (timing and timescales)

You will be establishing for yourself how to (a) answer these questions, and (b) deploy your answers in formulating your communications strategy.

You will be reviewing your organization's existing methods of communication and looking at how best to transmit the message of your organization's renewed dynamism once SAP has been implemented.

Undertaking a SAP project in a large company is a significant task that may well affect every person in the organization.

The following need to be considered and communicated to those who need to know:

- The implications of SAP implementation

- The progress of SAP implementation

- The benefits of the SAP System—for example, the streamlining of business processes and resultant ease of operation

- The training requirements, which are a necessary corollary of the successful implementation of SAP, and details of the relevant course or courses

Do not leave these matters to the corporate grapevine—it is vital that the facts about SAP are not left to the often-fertile imaginations of employees, especially those likely to react adversely to the perceived effects of technological advance and change. Do remember that corporate grapevines can operate at extraordinary speed. You need to avoid and, at best, preempt this.

Remember, as with project management, the timing of communications—as much as their clarity—is of the essence. You will need, also, to identify and focus on your audiences.

Subsequently, you will need to advise your customers about your organization's adoption of the SAP system. It is important to relay this information positively. After all, SAP will make an enormous and quantifiable difference to your service levels and, as a direct consequence, to your level of client satisfaction. Your organization's resultant increase in skills base, efficiency, and speed of response are good news; it is worth putting in some effort to get the message across.

And, of course, you will need to provide for the transmission of your messages to a wider external audience—the trade and national/international press, your shareholders (if any), and your suppliers.

The Importance of Effective Communication in SAP Projects

Good communications are not simply important, they are essential—they can improve working conditions and relationships within an organization, and promote confidence, growth, and success both internally and externally. Good communications enhance such areas as productivity, innovation, harmonious teamwork, good media relations, and optimum shareholder relations.

Good communications should form part of an organization's strategy, and be adhered to at all corporate levels.

Nobody likes to think he or she is a poor communicator, but however high your rating may be, there is always room for improvement. The same, of course, applies to organizations and corporate entities. The acid test of communication is always the vital, tripartite question: Has the message been (a) understood, (b) registered, and (c) accepted?

A great deal of research has been carried out on basic communication during the past ten years. The results may give you pause for thought. Consider the following:

- Of oral instructions given, only about 50 percent were received and retained (see Figure 34.1).

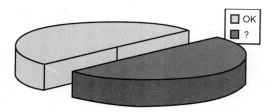

Fig. 34.1 This figure shows that only 50 percent of oral instructions given are received and retained.

- Retention of information delivered at a lecture series drops from an upper limit of only 52 percent down to an unsatisfactory 25 percent.

- Of information passed from boss to subordinate on a one-to-one basis, only between 20 percent and 60 percent is absorbed.

Think about the matter in more depth and you will find plenty of useful examples from your experience. You may find the following familiar:

- As the recipient of information, you can edit out unwelcome news, remembering only the positive elements.

- Everyone switches off if given too much information at once.

- We all tend to restrict information-sharing by, for example, passing it on to a small, selected audience or even restricting it to an individual.

- The fewer links in the chain of communication, the easier it is to convey the message.

- Information conveyed orally is better understood and accepted if accompanied by open questions, including hostile ones.

Of course, entire chapters could be devoted to the ramifications of each of the above examples. They are all fruitful and useful points for discussion, especially within the context of brainstorming sessions (these are one of the most useful management tools prior to determining strategy, as their informal context enables all imaginable points arising from a set of issues to be raised and dealt with creatively before practical testing).

Developing a SAP Project Communications Strategy

Before you formulate your communications strategy, look at how your organization currently conducts communications. Are there any channels that are already working well? This means, in effect, that messages are conveyed with clarity and rapidity, the channel operates as a two-way conveyor of information, and the efficacy of the process can be measured. If you already have efficient systems in place, you may simply need to update and upgrade them.

First Steps: The Communications Audit. Whatever the state of your organization's existing communications, your first step should be to conduct a communications audit. This will be a combination of desk research (involving, for example, a review of your corporate identity and information and support literature, together with press coverage files) and active research, which means surveying the attitudes of receivers of corporate messages transmitted internally and externally.

An audit may appear to be tedious and time-wasting. After all, you know all about your communications—but experience demonstrates that it is more likely that you only think you do.

It is surprising how frequently communications, both external and internal (and especially the latter), are ignored. Managers often assume the channels are open and operating, without necessarily paying attention to whether or not messages are properly conveyed. Deficient communications can mean reduced efficiency and morale and, ultimately, their necessary corollary of reduced productivity and sales.

In any case, an audit will save you a great deal of time when you reach the stage of determining your communications strategy. Indeed, you will find that many of the elements of your strategy will have been identified for you by the audit results.

If your budget allows you to commission independent communications consultants to conduct the audit on your behalf, this is advisable. You will achieve a truly independent perspective on your existing communications channels and effectiveness, plus the bonus of expert recommendations.

If you are operating under budgetary constraints, it is still possible for you to effect an efficient audit for yourself. Remember, it must be as comprehensive, as thorough, and as objective as possible.

You can employ a number of research techniques. Typically, these will include questionnaires (including a feedback section and allowing for anonymity), group discussions, and in-depth interviews. Always run a pilot study first; it is essential to keep you on track in your lines of questioning and may reveal areas of concern to your audiences which you had overlooked.

Whichever option you choose, you will almost certainly find that your respondents will readily make suggestions for improvements. In many cases, such suggestions will be especially valid because of their source: people who are actually carrying out or overseeing a process or those on the receiving end can normally be relied upon to produce good ideas for its improvement. This is as true of communications as it is of any other industrial and commercial practice.

Once you have completed your audit, you will find the results are an invaluable aid to formulating your strategy. The extent and nature of your strategy will be governed in other respects by two main factors—the size of your communications budget, and the availability of trained staff to drive the strategy through the organization.

Ideally, your trained staff should be in a position to train others, as communications is an all-embracing corporate discipline. Communications involves *everybody* in your organization; it is not the sole preserve of one department or senior manager. For example, consider the fact that the receptionist is often a client's first contact within an organization. This person can deal with a client in such a way as to facilitate or lose a sales/promotional opportunity.

Determining Strategy. When you are formulating your communications strategy, you will need to ask such questions as:

- With the help of SAP, where will the organization be in X years' time?

- How do you propose using SAP to get there?

- What external factors will affect corporate development? What systems, for example, do your competitors have in place and will SAP offer quicker deliveries, fewer errors, or better customer service? Positive benefits must be transmitted to employees and customers—both present and potential.

- How will the SAP system itself help streamline and speed up communications channels?

Once these questions have been satisfactorily answered, you will need to define your objectives.

Define Objectives. What are the principal aims of your strategy? What do you need them to achieve for your organization? Agree on the answers to these questions, and then go on to identify your target audiences.

Identify Your Audiences. With whom should you be communicating? Segment your audience, which may break down as follows:

- Employees

- Shareholders

■ Customers

■ Suppliers

■ Media

■ Project team

■ External contractors and consultants

Try to be as specific as possible in defining the different groups your strategy must reach, as this will help you to agree on your priorities.

Agree on Priorities. Which of your objectives are the most important or urgent? Agree on these, so that resources can be allocated accordingly. You will probably find that there is insufficient funding to allow you to do everything at once. You will also need to set targets.

Set Targets. You will need to monitor the implementation of your strategy at various key points. If you have set targets at this stage, the procedure will be easier; it will also help you to decide later on whether or not to continue with certain activities, depending on their success rate. To do this, you will need to draw up a timescale.

Draw Up a Timescale. At the risk of stating the obvious, this must be realistic. The resources available to you should give you an indication of timescales. Remember, though, to build some slack into your timescales: Allow extra time for interruption by urgent tasks, for example, and for surprise developments (they do happen—see the later section on "Contingencies"). It helps to map the timescale on a chart, which leads to your next task.

Plan Your Communications Campaign. You must be meticulous about this, but do not forget that all-important element of creativity—good ideas; when realized, they often produce remarkably good results.

Be alert to opportunities; you will need to respond to them—and quickly. A couple of examples:

■ A well-known journalist wants to do a story about the effects on your organization of SAP implementation. You should have all the information he or she needs at hand, and a representative of your organization adept at explaining SAP should be available to offer a detailed briefing and, time permitting, a tour of the premises.

■ A member of staff suggests a further application for your SAP system, which looks likely to enhance productivity. If you think this is the case, act on it—and make sure that the activity, its originator, and its results are publicized within the organization (and externally, if appropriate). A reward to the originator of the concept is good practice, too, as it serves to encourage further constructive suggestions from within your organization. You may even consider setting up a reward system.

But whatever you do, allow for contingencies.

Contingencies. As stated previously, you should always be prepared for the unexpected when planning and budgeting.

Some communications projects may cost more if they are well-received. For example, that notional journalist previously cited could turn out to have colleagues in the same or other media, domestically or overseas, who require similar services from you. Or demand for a brochure could exceed the specifications of your print run.

Allowing for contingencies will also enable you to measure your results.

Measure Results. Once your strategy has been in place for around six months, further research will be necessary. This is to make sure that you can monitor changes in knowledge, perception, and attitudes. The results will give you a clear indication of what your strategy has achieved and what, if necessary, you need to do in order to enhance your continuing communications program.

Remember, your communications program is not just a one-off. You must keep the momentum going (see Figure 34.2).

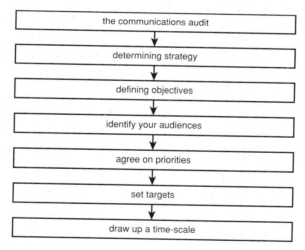

Fig. 34.2 Communications strategy: A flow chart.

The Elements of Communications

Some of these have already been touched upon in the previous sections. The bases are, of course, good written and oral skills. And it cannot be overemphasized how important these are. You may need to look at the possibility of further in-house training in, for example, presentation skills, as these are crucial to the success of communication.

The essential style of your organization may have changed as a result of SAP, together with a number of practices. You may need to have your logo redesigned to symbolize these changes, and overhaul your corporate identity accordingly. This is often the case at time of major change. Always examine these elements in detail before launching your program—you may need to obtain further budget allocation for design work.

As you will almost certainly now be engaged in raising your profile in the marketplace, you must make sure that the image you convey is right for your organization. The image of your organization conveyed by your corporate identity must reflect your positioning in the marketplace, as well as the style and nature of your organization.

As for addressing your external and internal audiences, you will find that the nature of your audience will determine the mode of communication. Once you have identified your audiences, you will have a clear idea of the medium to use for addressing them. If not, you will need to seek expert advice from a communications consulting firm or PR agency.

You will address your audiences in a number of ways. Your message may be transmitted via press releases together with a conference, via CD-ROM, or by means of a series of lectures given to relevant staff followed by an informal question-and-answer session.

If you have a corporate newsletter or paper, then you will need to ensure that a series of features on your system migration to SAP gives positive and interesting information.

If you do not have such internal publications (which may also be released to external audiences, such as trade press and shareholders), then you should consider using the medium of a dedicated SAP newsletter to keep everyone concerned fully informed of progress. You can produce it quickly and cheaply in-house, using your DTP facilities. This is also a useful medium for relaying information about the effects of SAP implementation and about training for its use.

Given the nature of SAP and its extensive applications throughout all the activities of your organization, you should consider setting up an internal library of self-training, desk- and computer-based training (CBT) materials. All employees at all levels within your organization would have access to these materials, promoting a sense of ownership and self-determination from an early stage. Here, too, employee access to information on CD-ROM can be very helpful indeed.

You will find that external and internal (in-house) communications will go hand in hand to a great extent. Make sure, though, that employees are aware of external promotional initiatives before these happen.

Now you know what you want to say and to whom. The next question is, of course, how.

Conducting a Presentation on the SAP Audience. Whatever your audience, whether internal (employees) or external (the press, customers, or shareholders), there are several points you should consider before opting for an open address.

The manner of a speaker is very important. First, you will be more effective if you seem to be an expert on your subject. Secondly, you must appear well-intentioned towards your audience.

These factors apply whether you are seeking to convey information, change attitudes, or influence behavior. While they may strike you as self-evident, it is surprising how often they are ignored. Many a crucial presentation has been ruined because the speaker is inaudible, boring, unconvincing, nervous, cannot handle an audience, or merely presents good material badly (with delivery militating against content).

You should have a friendly, agreeable, and lively manner and should seek to make the presentation interesting and enjoyable throughout. Your aim is to convey confidence and enthusiasm, and you should therefore be in constant contact with and control of your audience.

If you have any doubts on these scores, seek help. It may be that you need to take on further training. But whatever you decide, it is always a good idea to rehearse a presentation in front of a colleague or group of colleagues you know will give you constructive criticism and sound advice.

If it is possible, inspect the venue beforehand. Everyone should be able to see and hear you—and your visual aids. Make sure the room is arranged appropriately, and will comfortably accommodate the expected attendees.

Oral presentations can vary enormously. However, for the purposes of presenting information about your SAP system, the following guidelines will prove useful:

1. Opening

   This is when you make contact with the audience, securing their attention. In doing so, you should make sure you put them at ease and ensure receptivity by mentioning your links to them or related self-presenting, and explaining what you are going to talk about and why.

   Remember, what you are going to talk about is important and interesting; SAP is going to help your organization solve important problems. These thoughts will help you focus on arousing and maintaining interest from your audience.

2. Positive statements and arguments

   Make these sound, with supporting evidence, good illustrations, and clear visual aids.

   Structure your arguments. Make sure the materials you use in support are inherently interesting. When you are explaining unfamiliar ideas or procedures, try using striking examples. These will help change audience attitudes.

3. Drawing conclusions

   You must not overlook this, otherwise your presentation will be left hanging in the air and will not be fully received by your audience.

IX

Implementation

4. Dealing with discussions

You will have indicated in advance that the floor will be open for discussion.

You should take audience contributions seriously and sympathetically—make an effort to understand the points of view put forward. You should not only deal with the points raised, but also try to work out the best solutions, preferably enlisting the assistance of the audience as this promotes both understanding and acceptance.

You must avoid any form of confrontation with the audience or individual members. Remember, your aim is to inform, persuade, and motivate.

5. Dealing with objections

Always deal with these honestly, addressing the objector directly but keeping an eye on the rest of the audience so that your answers apply to all those present. Use examples to illustrate your themes, and make sure that your replies are full and factual.

An exercise which will prove useful in the event is to try and anticipate objections in advance, and consider how you will address them. Remember, the better you know or have researched your audience, the better position you will be in to deal with any of their objections—if, that is, there are any.

At all times you must retain your audience's interest. Here are a few tips to help you do so:

Speak clearly! This often means loudly and distinctly. Try projecting your voice to all corners of the room, while keeping the quality of your voice—timber and pitch—under control. Unless you are an experienced speaker, you may need help with this.

You must avoid the major pitfalls of public speaking. These are:

- sounding nervous

- acting superior

- being boring

You should be able to vary the tone and pitch of your voice to make your delivery more interesting.

Using visual aids:

Visual aids should be of high quality. Try to avoid cramming too much information onto them; your audience is unlikely to be able to (a) decipher it all, and (b) take it in. One to three points may be covered in a single slide, for example, depending on the amount of information you need to convey. Remember, the visual aids act as a summary and focus; you will be outlining in more detail the statements, proposals, or arguments.

You should make sure visual aids are:

- Legible
- Comprehensible
- In color

External and internal promotion—some further thoughts on seminars/lectures and conferences:

Seminars, lectures, and conferences for teams, groups, and departments are also important. Make sure that whoever addresses these audiences can do so clearly, confidently, and positively.

The speakers(s) must:

- Inform
- Build loyalty
- Motivate the audience

Other factors:

Always bear in mind that the audience may be resistant.

Bear in mind, too, that the audience will definitely be collectively asking itself the questions:

"What's in it for me?"

"How will this affect my job?"

You must make sure these questions are anticipated and answered as fully as possible—evasion does not work. However complex or antagonistic a question, always answer it. Evade a question, and your audience will lose faith in you, just as most of us do when watching a politician deliver a series of nonanswers to an interviewer on our television screens. Be calm, be honest, and be positive.

Things to avoid in this context may seem obvious, but are always worth stating. They are:

- Do not patronize your audience.
- Do not treat an audience as a homogeneous mass; they are individuals.
- Do not be impersonal—if you know the names of questioners, address them by name when replying.
- Do not be irrelevant.

Use humor by all means, and always match the style of humor to the type of audience.

IX

Implementation

Always stress that the successful implementation of SAP is dependent upon teamwork and relationship building—and these involve everybody. The key phrases here are "How we are going to succeed together" and "How this will benefit you." And these gain force if you look at your audience when you express them.

Lastly, keep an eye on the clock; try not to overrun your scheduled time.

Internal Promotion: Meetings. We all know that a major part of business is conducted at meetings. We all know, too, that not everybody enjoys meetings, whether they are chairing or participating. This is normally because meetings can frequently prove unproductive at best, and counterproductive at worst.

How can you avoid these outcomes?

Before the meeting you should:

- Start by considering your approach. What do you need to achieve? How much progress can you hope for? What decisions do you want to see made, and what actions do you want agreed?

- You usually have a major advantage because you will already know the other attendees—and their concerns and attitudes. Try, therefore, to anticipate any opposition to your plans. And develop arguments to deal with this effectively.

- Rehearse your arguments as if you were going to present them on a stage. Break them down into key points, and know them so well you are able to present them in any verbal form.

- Be ready to negotiate—and to listen. With each of your arguments there should be one key point upon which you are prepared to compromise, within reason.

- Discuss proposals with team members and other allies to elicit their views and support.

- Make contact with your potential opponents: be friendly, and try to find some common ground.

At the meeting you should:

- Arrive on time—make sure you do not miss anything (or put yourself in the position of being discounted due to an absence, however brief).

- Greet everyone. Try to create an informal and cooperative atmosphere. People who are relaxed are more receptive.

- Make sure everybody can hear you, and that you have captured their attention.

- If your proposal is complex, say it twice using different phraseology—for example, to simplify, "the SAP system will save us xxx dollars on distribution channels. In other words we'll save x percent of our operating budget."

- Keep it short. When you have finished making a point, especially a complicated one, there will probably be a few seconds' silence. Do not be tempted to fill it; your colleagues are engaged in absorbing what you have just said. Remember that extra words can dilute the force of an argument—and even fuel opposition.

- Concentrate on contributing to the important issues of the meeting. But do not feel you have to participate in every discussion; some of these may be trivial, and if so, your joining puts you at risk of being perceived as petty and tiresome.

- Always deal with objections competently. Consider them carefully, and address objectors in a friendly fashion. Look your critic in the eye as you respond, and make your points brief and hard-hitting while keeping your voice friendly.

The Use of Structured Meetings. The notice in Figure 34.3 was pinned to a notice board of a SAP project, bringing a few smiles to the faces of stressed project team members. The sad fact was that it seemed to apply perfectly to a great many of the meetings.

Fig. 34.3   A notice which appeared on the notice board of a SAP project.

It is inevitable that meetings are a major part of SAP projects, and used well they contribute enormously to a projects' overall success. By following a structured approach, as follows, it is possible to greatly enhance their efficiency:

1. Ensure ownership of the meeting.

   Whoever arranges the meeting should take ownership of it.

2. Create an agenda.

   The meeting's owner should issue a written agenda that clearly defines:

   - Where the meeting is to be held
   - When the meeting starts and how long it will take
   - Who is attending the meeting
   - The purpose of the meeting
   - What is expected of those attending
   - The expected outcome of the meeting

3. Use a facilitator.

   A facilitator is an independent person who is not the owner. His or her purpose is to control the meeting and ensure that it meets its objectives and does not get sidetracked and that the points raised and issues are captured.

   Typically, a facilitator will introduce the meeting and ask all those attending what they would like to achieve by the end of the meeting. He or she will then write up on flip charts what everyone wants to achieve. As the meeting progresses they will capture on paper the issues as they arise; toward the end of the meeting they will establish how the meeting has met the expectations of the members and will pull together next steps with details of who should do what and by when.

4. Issue minutes.

   The meeting's owner then issues minutes, which summarize the results of the meeting and list who should do what and by when.

By controlling meetings in this way, everyone's intentions are focused on what the meeting is trying to achieve. Issues raised in the meeting are not lost, and a clear way forward is identified, with individuals knowing exactly what they have to do and by when.

Internal Promotion: Training. You will save time and effort if your internal communications program is drawn up in tandem with a training program. You will need to communicate closely with trainers on materials, actions, and progress.

First, you will need to plan your program with care to ensure that (a) nobody is excluded and (b) priority groups are established before implementing the program.

Aspects you will need to cover include career progression and the overall market perspective. Your organization has become more dynamic because of your adoption of SAP; this overall effect will demonstrate itself, but it will need to be promoted.

Always ensure that your trainees can comment on their training, once completed. There may have been gaps; there may be areas which need further expansion or illumination; all these will need to be amended as the program progresses.

Remember:

- Plan
- Implement
- Monitor
- Measure
- Proceed on the basis of your findings

You and your organization will not be standing still. With the SAP system, you will always be going forward.

Internal Communications: User Groups. Once training is completed, user groups are a useful channel for quality initiatives, internal promotion, and further training (often of the self-determined variety).

Encourage teams to set up such groups wherever possible. You should make sure that these groups are not operating in a vacuum. Informal liaisons between different teams can iron out problems of comprehension, speed up adoption of new procedures, and reinforce a sense of involvement in SAP throughout the organization. Such lines of communication also facilitate quality control.

Set up a series of reporting lines which are efficient and easy to use. For example, e-mail and groupware can be effectively exploited to these ends. Trainers and IT management should be actively examining the application of SAP to the communications arena.

External and Internal Promotion: Publications. Again, a dedicated newsletter can be useful. Always invite questions, comments, and contributions from your audience(s). Much of this feedback will prove helpful in, for example, identifying areas where further communication is required or where training must be focused.

Articles must be factual, but they must not be dry—you want people to read them, after all. If you have access to professional corporate writers, then you are best advised to use them.

External Communications: Advertising. You will not need to be told that advertising is expensive. Before instructing an agency, try to see how much precampaign work you can do in-house. Study your competitors; look at the trade/business and national press, and advertising in other media. Determine what resources you need to devote to advertising your new message or messages.

Try to decide which media are most suitable for your organization. It may be that exploiting a combination of trade press and billboards may be a winner for you. Of course, your agency will be able to advise you well on this. But, as ever, the more informed you are at the beginning, the more quickly you will achieve the desired results.

IX

Implementation

External Communications: PR and Media Relations. If you do not have in-house professionals, then it is time to consult the experts. Remember, they are not cheap, but they can save your organization money; for example, editorial coverage can raise your organization's profile more precisely and more cheaply than advertising. Public relations is one of the most cost-effective promotional media.

You should maintain a close working relationship with your consultants—you will need to know what they are doing for you and what the results are likely to be. You should be in a position to monitor the results; even though the consultants will be doing this, too, it is always worthwhile to double-check.

After all, the results your consultants achieve are usually measurable. These may be in increased trade and/or national/international press coverage, increased sales, and an encouragingly favorable shift in customer attitudes. Always ensure that any results are measured according to the correct criteria for the action involved.

And do not forget to publicize encouraging results throughout the organization and its relationship network (where appropriate). You may do this via correspondence circulation, noticeboards, or your newsletter or publications—even a combination of all three.

Targeting a Large Audience. The conference is your optimum method for reaching a large audience in the shortest possible time. If you lack in-house resources to plan and organize such events, then you will have to look further afield.

Many PR agencies are expert in conference planning and organization. There are also specialist conference organizers. In a busy organizational environment, subcontracting such services can make sense; it saves your organization time and resources, and a really well-run conference is enormously valuable.

The experts in this field have a track record in ensuring that conference delegates are amused as well as informed—and the increased motivation this gives to a salesforce, for example, will literally pay dividends.

Again, do your homework before selecting your consulting firm. Know your own messages and the audiences you wish to reach. Speak to several different agencies, taking care to ensure that the ones you interview are (a) experts in your own field, and (b) entirely sympathetic to your organization's activities and aims.

Remember, the most successful conferences are those that are based upon a strong overall theme to which the attendees can relate. The most common thematic examples in the industrial and commercial conference world are drawn from either sports or war. But the field is wide open, and you will be able to devise your own suitable concept. You are free to exercise your imagination, but bear in mind that what you are doing is:

- Informing
- Promoting loyalty
- Motivating by means of enthusiasm

External and Internal Communications: Writing Skills. Many academics, teachers, and authors are of the opinion that someone who cannot express his or her beliefs, thoughts, or feelings clearly in writing is not capable of cogent thought. While this opinion may seem rather too damning, it does have a great deal of validity in the corporate environment.

How many times have you wasted precious time working out what that memo-writer really means in paragraph 3—only to find he or she has repeated the same ideas in paragraph 12 (clouded, if possible, by even greater opacity)?

Examples of bad writing in business and professional life, if systematically collected, would fill another book. Perhaps they already have! However, the rules for good writing—that is, clarity of expression—are very straightforward and easy to adhere to.

One of the most helpful guides to good writing is contained within George Orwell's essay "Politics and the English Language." Before you start writing, you should, says Orwell, ask yourself four primary questions. These are:

> What am I trying to say?
>
> What words will express it?
>
> What image or idiom will make it clearer?
>
> Is this image fresh enough to have an effect?

While writing and editing, you should also pose the following two questions:

> Could I put it more succinctly?
>
> Have I said anything that is unavoidably ugly?

I have summarized most of Orwell's essential rules that apply in this context as follows:

1. Never use a metaphor, simile, or other figure of speech that you are used to seeing in print.

2. Never use a long word where a short one will do.

3. If it is possible to cut out a word, always cut it out.

4. Never use the passive voice where you can use the active.

Remember, today's popular catchphrase dates rapidly; a metaphor that is overused loses its force. Do not use such terms: They will make you sound lazy and unoriginal—which you are not.

Try replacing "with regard to" by "on;" "in respect of" by "about." Your sentences will be shorter and sharper. Keep your writing "voice" active: It will sound more immediate (and closer to your speaking voice).

IX

Implementation

A useful rule for paragraphs is to cover one point per paragraph. Long paragraphs have a tendency to weary the eye of the reader, whose attention you really need to attract. Further, long paragraphs containing several, tangled arguments tend to reduce both the effectiveness and the lucidity of those arguments.

A note about jargon—as you know, jargon can save time and effort. But when using jargon, beware. Unless you are addressing fellow specialists, remember to think about your audience; they may not have a clue what you are talking about when you use strictly technical terms. Do not employ jargon or technical language unless you are sure it will be fully understood or you have sufficient space in your document to enable you to explain your terminology. If you take this course, the same rules apply: Keep your explanations brief and make them as clear as possible.

If you follow these rules, you will find it easier to organize your writing. There will be the additional benefit of producing written work that is fresh, attractive, and concise. It is therefore far more likely to be read.

External and Internal Communications: Body Language. Whatever message you are putting across in person, it can be contradicted by your body language. It is no good to stand on a platform and declaim boldly a brave, new message if your posture is hunched and defensive.

Body language need not be the preserve of social anthropologists and zoologists. Anybody can learn about body language. You already possess the principal qualifications for engaging upon such a study: your eyes, and your powers of observation and recall. Watch groups at work and at play. Who is dominating? How? Who is resistant? How can you tell?

It is surprising how illuminating this unspoken language can be. Observe for yourself, and adopt practices that suit you and your style and with which you feel comfortable. If you feel you need further help, there are plenty of publications on the subject, which are widely available—in your public library, for example.

The Use of Groupware in SAP Implementations

If groupware is not already in use by your company, it should be seriously considered for your SAP project and implementation.

Irrespective of the brand of software you choose, groupware offers a tremendous tool to manage communications. The ability to look into anyone's diary and schedule a meeting, book a meeting room, and issue agendas and minutes is invaluable. You can raise issues, get people's comments, and come to speedy resolutions with the greatest efficiency.

Conclusions

We are all potentially better communicators than we think. With a little effort, we can achieve great results.

Effective communications will not only boost productivity and morale within a company; they will also increase sales and goodwill.

Good communications make life more pleasant for everybody. Use your communications channels and techniques regularly and well—if everybody relevant is in the know about developments, they are not only more comfortable with your organization, but also in a better position to act positively.

Ensure that your communications are regularly monitored to measure their effectiveness. For most elements of your communications program, a six-month review will serve you well.

Your organization's communications are part of its wider corporate identity. You must ensure that your corporate image and your organization's aims and activities are clearly reflected in any communications exercise.

You have taken the decision to opt for SAP. This is good news for your organization, but good news ceases to be good news if it is not broadcast. Even though SAP's new tools and experienced team members enable easier implementations, all projects rely heavily on effective communication.

From Here...

In this chapter we have looked at the importance of effective communications in SAP projects. We have identified how to approach the effective management of communications by developing a strategy.

We have looked at different communications media and offered practical advice on how to use them effectively.

- Chapter 31, "Overview of SAP Implementations"
- Chapter 36, "The Human Issues of SAP Implementation"
- Chapter 43, "Managing the Change in Organization and Job Functions"

IX

Implementation

Chapter 35

Training for SAP

The delivery of training is usually subject to severe time restraints. Frequently, large numbers of personnel need to be trained within a short period of time. Training schedules need to be flexible, to allow for the real world of people not being available, courses being missed, holidays, and the system not being available.

Training material has to be relevant to the users and well written to ensure that it is easily understood. There are normally tight time constraints on the preparation of material. Whether training material is computer-based or documentation written for guides or courses, it should be created with care.

You need to create a training environment within the SAP system to use for training without disturbing the development or production system and also create a physical training area with training rooms, computer terminals, and other equipment.

Before training starts, there should have been a program of education and communication to gain commitment to the introduction of SAP and an understanding of the real issues. This is particularly important if the project involves significant business process reengineering.

Having spent hours working on your training schedule, you will want to monitor each individual's attendance and keep a record of non-attendance and adjust the plan accordingly.

Whatever the methods of training or the organization or facilities that are in place, the most important thing is the effectiveness of the training given. An important aspect of the training process is to monitor effectiveness at every stage. If what you have planned and prepared is not effective, you need to change it quickly.

The training requirement carries on well beyond implementation. People not on the original training such as new recruits and users will require training in the future and will need to learn about changes to the system. A long-term training strategy needs to be created to deal with all future training requirements.

In this chapter, you learn:

- How to train a project team.
- How to define training requirements.
- How to identify suitable training methods.
- How to develop a training team.
- How to prepare a training plan.
- How to prepare a training schedule.
- How to prepare training material.
- How to create the right training environment.
- How to control the training program.

IX

Implementation

This chapter deals with the training of the people who will be using SAP to perform their jobs—in other words, end-user training. However, before launching into this topic, we shall briefly consider the options for training your project team members.

We shall then look in more detail at the "life-cycle" of an end-user training program, starting by identifying the needs of the users. Our focus in this chapter will be on the functional or process-related tasks with which specific individuals or groups must be familiar in order to use SAP to do their jobs in the most effective way possible. However, please read Chapter 34, "Managing Communications Internal and External," as introducing SAP can have a significant impact on an organization and job functions. If there is no project-wide communications program, then the task of communicating the impact of SAP's implementation to a particular user or group can default to the trainer. The section in this chapter "Communication, Education, and Training" explores this topic in greater detail.

Having identified the end-user training requirements, the chapter goes on to consider the various delivery methods available and how to assess them, how to build your training team, and how to plan and schedule your training within the overall project plan. We shall consider various approaches to providing training documentation and managing the training environment throughout the implementation.

Finally, this chapter will help you assess the effectiveness of your training and develop a long-term training strategy.

Project Team Training

More and more commercial companies will be offering SAP project team training in the future as the SAP market continues to grow, but currently the most reliable training is offered by SAP itself. SAP offers approximately 400 courses, although availability varies around the world. In the UK, SAP has a brand new training center at Heathrow. Details of companies offering SAP training can be found in Appendix F, "Companies Providing SAP Services." Project teams will need to be trained in the project methods that are being used, project policies and procedures, and many other things.

Defining Training Requirements

It is a lot easier to define who needs training in what skills if you have already defined the organization's business processes in an earlier phase of the project. In Chapter 31, "Overview of SAP Implementations," we have looked at the importance of knowing your business and knowing your organization. Since this amounts to a prerequisite to a successful SAP implementation, let's assume that this has been done. Your first step, therefore, is to match particular business processes to particular job functions—it is normally preferable to use job titles rather than named individuals—and to establish which modules and transactions each job needs to perform each process.

In addition, you will need to make sure that nothing has been overlooked. When a process is initiated in one department and then passed to another for completion or authorization, it can fall between the cracks. Neither department considers the process its responsibility and, therefore, neither department manager identifies it as a process. For example, let's say that sales users make a contract with an overseas customer. The business requires that cover is taken by Treasury to safeguard against fluctuations in exchange rates. This means that an exchange rate is fixed by a bank for transactions that will take place in the future. A mechanism is needed in the system to create a system message advising the Finance department that a new sales contract number has been created. It is only by this electronic system message that Finance knows to set up a new currency contract correctly in SAP. Until this is done, the Sales department will not be able to place orders against its sales contract.

Given the integrated nature of SAP, it is obviously very important to pick these things up. Two approaches to gathering all the information you require:

- Interviews with Key Users: Conduct structured interviews with key users and senior management who have a special interest in SAP's successful implementation.

- Questionnaires: Design a questionnaire for key users to complete to capture their thoughts on training requirements. Interviews can form a useful backup on completion.

Once you have gathered the data, enter it into some form of matrix, the details of which will obviously differ according to your organization's own particular requirements. However, it should show the relationship between business processes and functional work groups (for example, Accounts Receivable, Warehouse X, Retail Sales). You should now be able, with some confidence, to answer the question: "Who needs training on what aspects of SAP's functionality, so that SAP's introduction into our organization will be as efficient and effective as possible?" However, do not expect this first pass to be your last—you will need to be flexible to accommodate changes as the implementation progresses.

You will also need to address other questions, such as:

- What training methods will be most effective?

- What resources will we require to develop and deliver the training?

- Where should users receive their training (centrally or at local sites)?

- At what stage before "going live" should the users be trained?

These questions will be considered in further sections of this chapter.

Identifying Suitable Training Methods

You should carefully consider the method of delivering your training, as your decision will have a huge impact on the project budget. In this respect there is nothing unique about an SAP implementation; the same options are open to you as with the implementation of any other computer system:

- Traditional classroom training, in which one trainer trains a homogenous group of users in a room set up for the purpose

- Individual coaching, where the user is trained one-on-one either at his or her workplace or in the classroom

- Computer-based training packages

The method or combination of methods that you use will depend on your own organization's particular circumstances, your budget, and to some extent on your personal preferences.

Classroom Training

You may or may not already have a training room set up. If not, there will be a cost involved in setting one up. The number of users you train at any one time will depend on a number of factors—how many PCs are there in your training room? How many people can the trainer "control?" How many people can be pulled away from their jobs at a time? Obviously, the more you can process at a time, the cheaper your training will become, but experience shows that a group of more than about 8 to 10 people is difficult to handle.

Individual Coaching

Unless you have a very small implementation, this method is unlikely to be cost-effective. However, coaching may be necessary to scoop up any individuals who have missed the main training program or who may have fallen behind and not learned enough in their classroom training.

CBT

There are a number of computer-based packages on the market. Some require skilled programmers to tailor them, while others are less complex and can be used by an ordinary trainer! However, there are certain advantages and disadvantages shared across the board:

Advantages:

- Trainees can train themselves at a time suitable to the individual and acceptable to the business.

- Other than explaining how to load the package and get started, trainers do not play much of a role. This reduces ongoing costs greatly.

- Any decent package includes a feature that monitors the trainees' progress, preventing trainees from going on to the next step if they have failed to grasp the principles of the current stage.

- Most packages have a function that records trainees' scores. You can use these scores to identify people needing extra help, so a human trainer can provide extra coaching.

- Training is consistent for each individual across the business.

- Training is available to new people coming in after implementation and for refresher courses.

Disadvantages:

- The upfront purchase cost can be significant.

- A large development effort may be required, depending on the package and the complexity of your implementation. One supplier quoted a ratio of 150 development hours to one hour's training.

- Lack of human contact means that questions may go unanswered and business issues unresolved.

- A CBT package is less "fun" than a warm, friendly human trainer.

Developing the Training Team

Having chosen your method of training, you can now go on to build the team that will develop and deliver the training.

The makeup of this team will vary depending on the method you chose. For example, if you chose the CBT route, you will need a large number of developers and very few deliverers. If you chose mainly classroom training, you may wish to have the people who develop the training materials deliver the training, or you may have a centralized development team that sends out the material for delivery by local trainers.

A further consideration is what type of people you want on the team: Do you want users co-opted on to the project team, IS people from the project team, or external consultants? Obviously, there are no hard and fast rules here but some points for you to consider:

Using Users

The advantages of using key business users include:

- They know how the business operates.

- They know their audience.

- They are cheaper than external consultants.

- They will be an immediately accessible source of help for other users after SAP has been implemented.

- The skills that they will have to develop will be kept in-house.

However:

- There is a significant learning curve required to learn SAP, expensive in both time and money if they are sent on SAP's own courses, for example.

IX

Implementation

- They will need training skills training and possibly some training on managing change if the implementation is to result in a major change of business practice.

- There must be total commitment from management to release the users on to the project or users will be impossibly stretched between its demands and the demands of their "real" jobs.

- In order to retain their skills in-house, users and their managers should consider and make explicit plans for career progression post-implementation.

Using IS Team Members

The advantages of using your own IS people as developers and deliverers of training include:

- They are already familiar with SAP.

- They are already familiar with the business's use (or planned use) of SAP.

- It is cheaper than using external consultants.

- The skills they develop when learning the skills themselves prior to training will be useful to them personally in their future careers within the company.

- Making this choice leaves the users free to run the business.

However:

- The people chosen as trainers will need to acquire training skills.

- Their time must be carefully managed and you must get a commitment from the Project Manager not to pull them off training development when problems arise in other IS areas.

- Training IS people in SAP gives them a highly marketable skill. To avoid having your IS people lured away into the SAP contract market, give serious consideration to their career progression after the implementation.

Using External Consultants

The advantage of using external consultants is that they already have the SAP skills and the training skills to develop and deliver your SAP training. (If a consultant doesn't already have these skills, why use him?) However, there are a number of considerations:

- They are expensive.

- They will not know your business, and so will need to spend some time with your key users to understand it before they can start to be productive.

- Users may be distrustful of outsiders telling them how to do their jobs.

- Some external consultants have ideas that may not suit the project.

Whatever approach you choose, remember that to gain the most benefit from your training program, you should identify and begin to involve the trainer(s) from a very early stage of the project. It is unrealistic to wheel someone in the last few weeks before going live and expect them to deliver effective training.

Preparing the Training Plan

You should incorporate training in the project plan and budget from the inception of the project. Costs that some companies overlook include the "hidden" costs of releasing personnel for training—documentation costs, overtime, and the cost of finding someone to cover the users' jobs while they are at the training.

A key decision is when to start. Starting early minimizes the overall project elapsed time (by overlapping development of training environment and materials with system testing) but may well generate substantial rework as system changes are made. It also complicates the coordination of system build and training activities for individual project team members.

Starting later reduces the need to rework the material, but unless resources are available for very intensive course development and delivery, you may need to extend overall project timescales to allow for training time. As a rough guideline, you should not release parts of the system into training development until they are at least 80 percent correct and complete. You can build decisions on the readiness of particular modules of functionality for training development into QA points—for example, at the end of build work, before system testing starts.

Given the dependency of the progress of systems build work and testing on the development of training materials there should be open communication between the project manager and the training manager throughout the project's life. You can't develop training material when the system is being built because you don't know how it is going to work. Training development and delivery should be formally linked via precedence relationships in the project plan to agreed project milestones. For example, you could specify that training is not to start until system testing is completed. Therefore, if project milestones move, the impact on training schedules is apparent immediately.

You should also draw up a full training plan using the same planning tool and standards as the overall project plan. You must identify your own specific task lists, including:

- Course specification and design
- Quality assurance
- Creation of a training environment populated with valid data
- Production of training materials and user documentation (if a distinction is being made between these)
- Delivery (including delivery scheduling)

Preparing the Training Schedule

In the earlier section "Defining Training Requirements," you learned an approach to analyzing training needs and answering the question "Who needs training in what?"

Now that you have identified your training course requirements, you need to specify the contents of each course and design it.

Once you have gone through that process, you should be able to make an estimate of how long each course will take to deliver. You can then do the simple calculation of dividing the number of users who need to go on each course by the number of individuals you have decided is optimal and then multiplying that result by the number of days of the course's duration. This gives you the number of training days you need to schedule.

This makes it sound simple, but scheduling can become extremely complicated. The business will impose limitations on your plans, so that you will need to work around:

- Business needs—for example, customer orders still need to be met during the training period
- Particularly busy periods for certain departments—for example, period ends for Accounting
- Holidays, vacations, and planned shutdowns
- Shift patterns
- Sickness

There are some specialist software tools on the market that can help you schedule, but you will need to remain flexible. Not allowing people to be ill when they should be attending a SAP training course unfortunately does not work. You may also find it helpful to have a local site contact to advise you on the best times to schedule courses. Personnel departments may take on this role and may also help in monitoring attendance and following up on non-attendance.

Preparing the Training Material

The physical appearance of the training documentation will vary from organization to organization. If you have chosen the CBT route, paper-based documentation may consist only of a guide to getting started on the package and maybe some quick reference help cards. Others will choose classroom training backed up by screen illustrations and explanation. Still others may want to draw a distinction between Training Materials and User Guides.

As a general rule, users tend NOT to reach for their training documentation when they have a problem. They usually ask a colleague. If your training budget is tight, keeping your training documentation short and simple could help to keep your costs down.

In an ideal world, the development team should generate some training documentation. At the very least, they should supply a series of flow diagrams or "route maps" that break down each business process into a series of steps and link each step to an individual transaction in SAP. Some system development approaches could provide even more material—for example, detailed business cases developed for acceptance testing could be recycled as training aids.

You can choose your training materials from the following list, putting greatest emphasis on the areas most important to your organization:

- Business processes and flow diagrams describing them
- Screen illustrations with text descriptions of key fields
- Introduction to basics of SAP (matchcodes, icons, and so on)
- Trainer demonstrations
- Trainee exercises and case histories
- Help (quick reference) cards

Other considerations include:

- Do you want to differentiate between business training (explanations of how SAP will affect procedures, responsibilities, organizational structures, and so on) and system training (hands-on operation of SAP)?
- Whatever form of documentation you use, spend some time deciding on standards so that it is consistent.
- It will take longer than you think for the documenter(s) to produce the materials!
- Don't forget to factor the lead-times required from external service suppliers such as printers, reproduction shops, laminators, and so on into your schedule.
- You may need to follow BS5750/ISO9000 procedures.

Note

There are many programs that enable you to capture screen illustrations. Lotus Screencam, for example, offers two very useful features. It captures still screens for inclusion in paper documentation, in file formats that you can import into nearly any word processor. It is also capable of recording a mini-video by capturing each key stroke in a process. With this feature, you can "film" any SAP process and then play it back as often as required.

Screencam is not a CBT program and its capabilities are too limited for you to consider using it to generate full-scale CBT instruction packages. However, its recording feature can be invaluable for passing along information from highly skilled developers to documenters who have very little knowledge of SAP. For example, the IS team can use Screencam to capture each process once it has been QA'd and pass it on to the documentation development team in this format. The documenter playing it back can see the process flow without needing to know how to use SAP.

Whatever form your training materials take, do not assume that they will remain static (see the section "Developing a Long-Term Training Strategy" later in this chapter) and build in a system of maintaining version numbers before you start.

Creating the Right Training Environment

"The right training environment" consists of two factors: The technical and the human. Let's look at these individually.

SAP Training Environment

You need to set up a separate training client or systems environment that represents the latest development work and that can be refreshed on a regular basis. It needs to be populated with sufficient data to make the training demonstrations and exercises realistic, including tables, master data, and documents. I recommend that you agree upon a procedure for updating and controlling the system with the system manager as early in the project as you can.

Physical Training Environment

Although you are running an in-house training program, it will be more effective if you treat the trainees as if they were volunteers attending an external course. The training room should be made as comfortable as your budget allows, with sufficient (and sufficiently comfortable) chairs and tables to make the experience an enjoyable one. Some organizations prefer to have two trainees to each PC, so that they can work together and learn from each other. Having more than two trainees per PC is not a practical option.

If you are setting up a room from scratch, remember to specify plenty of power connection points and communications connection points for the computer terminals. Also pay attention to the lighting, being careful to avoid direct sunlight on monitors and to exclude natural daylight altogether if using liquid crystal display tablets (LCD).

There are, broadly speaking, two methods of presenting trainer demonstrations to a large audience. The first is something that projects the image from the trainer's screen onto a large screen that can be seen by all. Examples include LCDs and BARCO projectors. The second is a mechanism that allows the trainer to control all the trainees' screens by switching them so that they see what is on his or her screen. This is commonly referred to as "slaving," and once under the "master's" control, trainees' keyboards become inoperable, thus removing the temptation for them to "explore" rather than working on the topic currently under discussion. In the UK, Ascot Systems supplies such a mechanism called the "Coursemaster."

Communication, Education, and Training

These are three different activities, all of which have their places within the life cycle of a project. Before training starts, there should have been a program of education and communication to gain commitment to the introduction of SAP and an understanding of the real issues. This is particularly important if the project involves significant business process reengineering.

You will need different approaches to communicate the impact that SAP will (or may) have to different management levels. Here are two approaches that have been successful in helping to gain commitment from the most senior people in the organization at the inception of the project:

- Illustrate how SAP will support your industry's accepted "Best Practices." There are a number of courses run that cover best practice (entirely independent of SAP). If you can find one appropriate to your board members, you can follow it up with an in-house presentation and discussion of how SAP will support them.

- Bring in a business "guru" to facilitate a discussion about the impact/benefits of introducing a fully integrated system.

To educate both senior and middle management, SAP runs a course that provides an overview of the business process flow (CAINT) and highlights the practical benefits of using a fully integrated system.

Once all the major decisions have been made, you must make all employees aware of what the impact will be. It is best to plan an ongoing communications program to ensure that employees have a chance to ask all the questions they want and receive answers to those questions as the project progresses. Tried and tested approaches include:

- In-house overviews emphasizing the need for change

- Roadshows/demonstrations of SAP functionality specific to the jobs of particular groups/departments

- Regular newsletters

- Online bulletins

Without effective education and communication, effective training is impossible. Instead of having a receptive audience willing to learn the functionality of SAP and knowing why they have to learn it, the trainer may be faced with a group of employees apprehensive about their futures and resistant to learning.

Controlling the Training Program

Having spent hours working on your training schedule, you will want to monitor each individual's attendance and keep a record of non-attendance. Another benefit of a successful education and communication program is that everyone will be aware of the importance of showing up for training when scheduled and managers will think twice before pulling people out of training for business "emergencies." However, there will be times when the business must take priority or when people are too ill to attend—or even when the trainer is too ill to attend. Therefore, it is important to keep records regarding who receives training so that additional training can be run if necessary.

Quality control is also an issue. You should define a post-course questionnaire to get as objective as possible feedback after each course. If there is consistent criticism of a particular aspect, this can be put right at an early stage of the program. Other considerations:

- Although in an ideal world, training should take place after testing has been completed, "bugs" and other problems may well manifest themselves during training. You should devise a formal method of capturing these and feeding them back to the development team before training starts.

- If there is an area that users consistently find difficult to master, you should plan to spend more time on that skill in class or develop a "help card" or similar tool to distribute.

- Experience shows that in order for people to refer to their manuals when they are using the system in a live environment, they need to have worked with them on the training course. Therefore, your training should include manual use.

Analyzing the Effectiveness of Your Training

Asking trainees to complete questionnaires after each course can provide some quality control feedback about the delivery method efficiency and the content of the course. However, the effectiveness of training—that is, how well it is preparing the trainee to do his job using SAP—is hard to gauge before going live. The trainers have a useful role here in feeding back their observations of skill acquisition during the courses themselves.

Analyzing calls to the help-desk in the first few weeks of implementation is one way of monitoring the effectiveness of training. Better still is one-to-one discussion with end users and their managers to get their feedback. This information is useful for:

- Establishing whether extra workshops/training sessions are required.

- Improving training for further phases of the project (if applicable).

- Improving training for new users.

Developing a Long-Term Training Strategy

In the euphoria of having successfully implemented SAP in your organization, you should not forget to put a long-term SAP training strategy in place. There are two main areas to look at:

- People not on the original training program who will require training in the future

- Changes to the system that need to be relayed to all users

Newcomers joining the company will obviously require training and the most appropriate way to cover this may be to build it into the standard induction program. Promotions and internal movement of staff may result in existing employees also requiring training. In addition, employees who originally thought they did not need to know about SAP may change their minds some time after implementation. This may be through a gap in the training needs analysis or through the individual feeling it would be "nice to know." Your response to the latter requests will doubtless depend on the training resources you have available.

System changes may occur as a result of bug-fixing or from requested and approved enhancements. You will need to communicate with the system maintenance team to pick up any changes and, having documented them, you will need to relay them to your users. You may choose to do this by distributing updates periodically, but to ensure they do not simply get shoved in a drawer you could run workshops to back up the updating procedure. Ideally, you should appoint a full-time training maintenance person, although your resources may not be sufficient to allow this.

From Here...

In this chapter we have looked at all aspects of training from developing a training team to training project team members and then users. We have looked at the importance of defining training requirements, identifying suitable training methods, and conducting the training. We have seen the importance of the training plan and the monitoring of the training schedule.

The infrastructure has to be created to deliver the training from training environments in the system to physical training requirements of workstations and work space for training team members. The training has to be controlled and evaluated and changes made if necessary. Finally, implementation of a long-term training strategy is needed to deal with new recruits and system changes, and so on.

Training is a vitally important area of a SAP project which has a great significance on the project's overall success.

- Chapter 31, "Overview of SAP Implementations"
- Chapter 34, "Managing Communications Internal and External"
- Chapter 36, "The Human Issues of SAP Implementation"
- Appendix F, "Companies Providing SAP Services"

Chapter 36

The Human Issues of SAP Implementation

Behind the amazing feats of reengineering with SAP or any other similar program lies many a tale of human insecurity as the world goes topsy-turvy and of management resistance as the carpet starts to move under their feet.

Indeed, James Champy, co-author of *Reengineering the Corporation* and chairman of CSC Index, the management consultancy that pioneered the development and practice of reengineering, emphasizes in his follow-up book, *Reengineering Management*, that "the only way we're going to deliver on the full promise of reengineering is to start reengineering management—by reengineering ourselves."

This then is the final hurdle, the need to reassess how we as human beings operate as individuals and in groups and evolve our learning and our behaviors if we are to willingly and whole-heartedly embrace the kind of change that SAP and its associated reengineering initiatives will bring in their wake.

The Effects of Major Change in an Organization

This section puts forward ideas which you can draw on to help your colleagues move through change successfully—even with alacrity! It offers you some guidance on how to build and maintain dedication of your colleagues through the process of rapid change and how best to provide them the required support.

IS—Today's Number One Change Agent

"Change is the only constant," said Heraclitus some 2,500 years ago, and the intervening years have not proven otherwise. Perhaps one of the most important recent changes as far as industry goes is a loss of confidence among workers in their job security. Undoubtedly one of the major contributing factors to this loss is the automation of processes. And the main contributor to automation has been the computerization of tasks hitherto performed manually.

In this chapter, you learn:

- How to lead your organization through the process of implementation.

- How to lay the foundation for cooperation and teamwork between members of the implementation task force.

IX

Implementation

Computers, or rather the applications that run on computers, have therefore been a double-edged sword. For it is the software programs that are bringing changes in the way we all work, especially those programs, like SAP, which automate every fundamental process within a company. Indeed, SAP throws the past out the window. The implementation of SAP effectively forces a company to consider every aspect of its operation.

Today, organizations are striving to be customer-focused machines and the implementation of new SAP systems is an important aid to effecting the necessary changes. But organizations are also repositories of people's hopes and aspirations and the stage on which they play out the major part of their lives. Changing a company's systems is akin to changing the plot and shifting the scenery and props of the play while it is in progress. It takes a dedicated actor to be able to give a good performance despite the changes. And it takes dedicated, well-guided and well-supported people in a company to thrive through the distractions that any radical system changes will entail.

But shouldn't people be used to change by now? What else can they expect? Well, the sobering reality is that the evolution of mankind is a slow process and the human continuum leads us to expect at a fundamental level that tomorrow will be the same as today.

Viewed against this backdrop, the implementation of SAP can be a potentially threatening event to some. People lose touch with the familiar, their usual work patterns, their colleagues or an area of work in which they feel proficient. In times of flux, people look for security. And security usually comes from the familiar. Centuries ago they found it among their own families and communities. As industrial growth led to the breakup of traditional communities, people transferred their handholds of security to their position in life, their job and their status within their company. Now it seems that the security of employment and status we have come to expect from the large companies (think of banks in particular) was only a passing phenomenon. There is no longer automatic security in employment.

This raises the question as to the role of management in all this change, and in particular the responsibilities that the project management team have when, through implementing SAP, they may seem to be the cause of it all!

Management's Role in Change

Management's role in change? Simple. Create the highest rate of change that the organization and the people in it can stand. Then manage the transition.

This begs at least two questions. First, change in what? And, second, how much change can your organization and people stand? The answer to the first question is a strategic issue which only experts within your field of business can respond to. The answer to the second is open to response from any human being, since we are all experienced at living through change.

Given this, you could do worse than ask your colleagues what helps them through change in general, and what in particular will help them through the process of change that implementing SAP entails. To find out their views, consider one-to-one interviews, group dialogues, surveys, or a combination of these methods.

The answers you will get—and there is no mystery to this since we all respond in a similar way—will include some of those listed below. But do not be seduced into relying on this list to the exclusion of finding out what is true for your colleagues, for you will note that the first item on the list is also probably first in importance when it comes to help in riding the waves of change:

Consultation. You should ask the people affected by the changes for their views on the change process and get them to suggest ways in which change can be absorbed by the organization. Act on these suggestions—even if only to say why a suggestion will not be taken up. You will have much more success in getting your changes implemented if you work on getting everyone to understand the changes and let them feel a part of the change process.

Communication. People will begin grieving in anticipation of loss well before it happens—if in fact it does ever happen. This is purely a function of the human mind's tendency to throw up worst-case scenarios so that we are ready to survive them. The trouble is, we start taking evasive action in anticipation of a threat, and acting as if the threat were real. At this point the rumor machine gets to work and begins the same irrational pattern of fear that, in 1945, caused thousands of Japanese civilians to throw themselves off the cliffs of "Suicide Island" in fear of the approaching (yet benign) U.S. Army, causing otherwise sane employees to ascribe agendas and motives to the perpetrators of change that are pure fiction. The human mind likes to know what is happening and more than likely will create meaning even if there is no basis for it. The antidote to this is to communicate, communicate, and communicate.

Job Security. People will be worried about their job tenure, about their future with the company, and about maintaining their lifestyle. The only honest response may be that employment can no longer be guaranteed and that the best the company can do is to boost each person's "employability," i.e., to ensure they have skills which will be sought after in tomorrow's job market—especially the company's internal job market. Companies which pride themselves on their loyalty to their staff might balk at the notion of offering "employability," with its connotation seemingly of preparing staff for redundancy. But it is important to note that equipping employees so that they can "surf the job market" is, especially in larger companies, a good way to add the value to your staff that your company could use at some later date—and it is the accepted tool of succession planners. But if "employability" is not the word for you, choose another.

Change Management. There will be a natural concern among some as to how they will cope with the new world, with new systems, with new people in their lives and with new, unfamiliar tasks. Those to whom such scenarios present little threat are those who have retained the ability to learn, the ability to create relationships and to maintain a forward-looking attitude. But for every "around the world adventurer" who positively seeks out such experiences there are ten others for whom routine is the lynchpin of their lives. It is the latter group who may need some hand-holding. And experience has shown that if their confidence in relationships to others can be boosted, their ability and willingness to learn and accept change follows closely behind (see the later section "Maintaining Sound Relationships").

IX

Implementation

As an individual moves through change, the responses that have helped with the change process are logged, stored in the person's memory, and are ready to be used again. In the same way, an organization can learn from experience and capture those change reflexes that have helped and those that haven't. Commonly the human resource function will take it upon itself to store this information, and it remains for the organization to draw upon this fount of knowledge whenever change is in the offing—which, in Heraclitus's book, is all the time. In fact, the ability to successfully operate such a system lies at the heart of a company's claim to call itself a "learning organization." Consequently, it is incumbent on those leading change to ensure that the company's data bank is updated for the benefit of those who follow in their footsteps.

Barriers to Change—How to Overcome Them

The biggest barrier to change is not lack of money nor lack of ideas nor lack of market imperatives, but is most commonly the attitude that: "If the system isn't broke, don't fix it."

Paradoxically, by this same token the companies that are probably most at risk from change are those which are currently most successful in terms of the bottom line. They are bringing in returns now for their stockholders so there is every reason to maintain things as they are. Eventually, the "way things are done around here" becomes a creed and then simply the "way," as in the "IBM Way" or the "HP Way." IBM followed their own sweet "way" throughout the 1980s and far beyond its shelf life. The HP Way continues to bring success at the time of this writing. How is your company's "way" doing?

If you want to change your company's way of doing things, and the fact that you are reading this book suggests you are serious, then I hope there are signs that your "way" is flawed, that the system is broken. For if not, you have a major challenge, somewhat akin to those streetside doomsday soothsayers who receive no more than the lift of a wry eyebrow. Remember, by the time the car manufacturer Rover was taken in hand in the mid 1980s, they had little reason to cling to historical ways of doing things. They were fed up with the tales of woe. They were open to change. This is not the case with most companies.

So what messsage can you put on your "sandwich board" that is going to make a difference? Some ideas follow.

Case for Action. Come up with the secular version of "Ye shall all burn in hell!" In fact, people commonly talk about going around and lighting fires to encourage action, so the analogy is not so far-fetched. Your job is to stir up a bit of divine discomfort. How you do this will depend on the particular set of circumstances that you find yourself in. Use your team to help brainstorm ways of doing this. But be sure that if you are "setting fires," that you have the metaphorical equivalent of those fire escape signs of green men running posted on every wall. In other words, avoid panic. Engender purposeful activity by pointing the way to safety. Do this by offering up images of a more attractive future. If the word "vision" fits, use it. It is a term that most people seem to understand. If you choose to use this tactic, however, remember that you need to consider the personality of the individuals you are dealing with—some people will not react well (or will react in almost the opposite of your desire) to this type of tactic.

Vision. At the same time you are building a case for action, rehearse some future scenarios with your team. Enlist outside expertise in the form of "futurists," people who make a point of anticipating the future and among whom you may find some expertise specific to your industry. The best kind of vision is expressed in positive terms and does not exist by reference to the past.

Leverage. To change anything, it helps to know a bit about the system. An organization is a machine, and just as every mechanical engineer will rely on a knowledge of the system to tweak at just the right place, so you need to discover the points of leverage within your company where the application of pressure will create the maximum effect. Knowing the system entails knowing whom to show your sandwich board to and knowing their agenda. How will your plans help them achieve their own? The synchronicity you create between your goals and those of the "movers and shakers" (e.g., the department "barons") will determine the success you enjoy.

Managing Issues of Morale

Will the implementation of SAP mean downsizing, rightsizing or just a plain old rationalization? If so, it is said that those made redundant are the "survivors" and those people who escape the cull are the "victims." The rationale is that depending on the way you have seen your colleagues treated, you are likely to fear for your own job once you have witnessed a few lay-offs. Morale can take a beating in such circumstances, and if it does it can take a long time to restore that confidence.

When morale has taken a beating in history, lessons have been learned in how to restore it, and, rather than reinvent the wheel, it pays to learn the lesson that worked so well last time.

In 1943, General William Slim took command of the Fourteenth Army. The all-conquering Japanese had driven it out of Burma, and it now sat in India, licking its wounds.

Slim identified his main problem: To restore the Fourteenth Army's morale. But how was it to be done? In *Defeat into Victory*, he recollected how he thought through the problem:

"So when I took command, I sat quietly down to work out this business of morale. I came to certain conclusions, based not on any theory that I had studied, but on some experience and a good deal of hard thinking. It was on these conclusions that I set out consciously to raise the fighting spirit of my army.

"Morale is a state of mind. It is that intangible force which will move a whole group of men to give their last ounce to achieve something, without counting the cost to themselves; that makes them feel they are greater than themselves. If they are to feel that, their morale must, if it is to endure—and the essence of morale is that it should endure—have certain foundations.

"These foundations are spiritual, intellectual, and material, and that is the order of their importance. Spiritual first, because only spiritual foundations can stand real strain. Next intellectual, because men are swayed by reason as well as feeling. Material last—important but last—because the highest kinds of morale are often met when material conditions are lowest."

This example applies well to the change you are about to make in your corporate workplace. Although each worker's life is not at stake, major changes in the workplace can often be interpreted very personally. Some workers will interpret the changes as destroying their place in the corporation—or at least everything they have worked for in the past. Overcoming these preconceived notions is one of your biggest challenges.

I remember sitting in my office and tabulating these foundations of morale something like this:

Spiritual. Set a great and noble object as the reason for your changes.

The achievement of this object must be vital.

In order to energize your employees, your method of achievement must be active and aggressive, not merely passive, defensive, or reactionary.

You need to make sure each person feels that what he is and what he does matters directly toward the attainment of the object.

Intellectual. The objective you are aiming at must be something that everyone believes can be obtained. It is impossible to build and sustain high morale for reaching an unobtainable goal.

You must also show the employees that the restructured organization is an efficient one—and will be able to achieve the object in the best way possible.

The employees must have confidence in their leaders and know that whatever dangers and hardships they are called upon to suffer will be respected and appreciated. Most employees will feel that they have quite a bit at stake in the current organization, so changes in that system are important.

Material. As already stated, each employee is sacrificing a lot that was at stake in the previous system; they must feel that they will get a fair deal from the leadership and the new system so that they will not be worse off than they were before.

You must convince the employees that they will be given all of the materials they need to meet the objective—including the best working conditions possible.

"It was one thing," Slim continues, "thus neatly to marshal my principles but quite another to develop them, apply them, and get them recognized by the whole army. We, my commanders and I, talked to units, to collections of officers, to headquarters, to little groups of men, to individual soldiers casually met as we moved around.

"In my experience it is not so much asking men to fight or work with inadequate or obsolete equipment that lowers morale but the belief that those responsible are accepting such a state of affairs. If men realize that everyone above them and behind them is flat out to get the things required for them, they will do wonders."

Whatever the details of one's morale-boosting efforts, it seems that General Slim's integrated three-part approach is a sound template for commercial application—and indeed such an approach is being "rediscovered" and used in earnest in industry today by leading corporate development strategists.

Demands on Management Time

Once a change program gets under way, its demands on the finite resource of management attention begins to be felt and something has got to give. Without exception, the extra workload and stress involved takes its toll on family life. And unless your company had the foresight to hire no one but recent college graduates, you and your colleagues have by now got families who are at risk of paying part of the price of your company's new obsession.

So what to do? Some suggestions:

For Ambitious Careerists. Take a word of advice from a man who rose from merchant seaman to chairman of British Airways: "If there is a job to be done, you must get on and do it. If that means setting aside personal things, so be it" (Colin Marshall, April 1996).

For the Rest of Us. Our "personal things" are likely to include our friends, our spouses, and our children. Accept the inevitable and negotiate with them. Trade some lost evenings for a weekend of your undivided attention at Disney World, or a Sunday picnic at a favorite location, a wild meal at Planet Hollywood, or a dinner for two at a romantic restaurant. Providing all concerned feel they are not getting the worst of the deal, peace and harmony will reign. By the way, brush up your negotiating skills.

As for ensuring people have a balanced life, well, this relies on management's sensitivity in the way they delegate, or rather negotiate, tasks and the readiness of people to say "no" in the face of an unreasonable workload. Both behaviors will be a function of your company's culture and your culture will be a function either of historical accident or, if you are fortunate, of conscious and calculated activity.

Introducing New Ways of Operating

Why the need to operate in new ways? The answer must lie in the changing complexion of competition in the marketplace. For instance, any manufacturer who is not facing the future head-on and actively considering the Far East as a source of competition or as a place to site its manufacturing operations must at least be nervously looking over its shoulder in that direction. Changes are upon us of such magnitude that if we do not continuously seek new ways of operating then we will be consigned to the margins of the world markets.

The implementation of SAP certainly entails operating in a new way. The systems you have are deeply embedded in your current way of doing business. So to change one entails changing the other, and before you know it you are reengineering the business from the ground up. If this is the direction that your project takes, then you must pause for thought. The clean slate approach of business process reengineering is an attractive proposition, for it has promised steep changes in business performance (see *Reengineering the Corporation* by Mike Hammer and James Champy), and yet, by its practitioners' own admission, fewer than 30 percent of projects achieve the results they were intended to.

IX

Implementation

The reason put forward is that business processes can only be successfully reengineered in tandem with the reengineering of management processes (*Reengineering Management* by James Champy). But that is still not the end of the story. For the master key to finding truly new ways of operating would seem to lie outside the realm of processes altogether, and instead has its roots in the way people think and behave in groups—or, in the terminology of today, in the "operating state" of the group.

The "operating state" of an organization refers to its members' state of collective consciousness, their combined self-awareness, and by extension, their ability to intitiate change from within. There are degrees of consciousness. Sleep is one level of consciousness. Being awake is another level. Beyond this there is the possibility of being awake to the extent to which one's surroundings are a reflection of oneself. Then beyond this lies mastery of those skills needed to change one's surroundings through personal and organizational transformation. An organization's operating state refers to its ranking in this hierarchy of consciousness.

The condition of an organization's operating state matters because it determines how smart it will be in shaping its future. And the good news is that an organization's operating state can be coached upward if its leaders and other moving spirits within the organization are willing themselves to acquire the "smart skills" needed. ("Smart skill" is a service mark of Harley Young.)

Such skills include:

- Conflict resolution
- Living in the question
- Listening for another's reality
- Transforming experience
- Straight talk
- "Save-as" thinking
- Context reframing

Managing Project Team and Staff Motivation

The ability to sustain motivation is the fundamental skill of any successful project manager and the degree of team and staff motivation you enjoy will, to a large extent, determine whether your implementation plan is completed on time, within budget, and to specification. This section is concerned with various complimentary ways in which you can ensure your team remains motivated throughout. The most important thing to realize, though, strange as it may seem, is that it is not up to you to motivate your team. But if you have done your job of recruiting people to the team well, you will have taken on motivated people, i.e., people who *given the chance* will do whatever they do to the best of their ability. (In fact, the idea that they need motivating is likely to seem patronizing to them.)

Your task (and it's a demanding one) is to give them the chance to provide the conditions within which they are able to exercise their skills. To do this you must minimize those things that tend to demotivate, deflate morale, and get in the way of getting the job done. Your job is to remove obstructions from the path. And the notes that follow give some guidance in how to do this.

Maintaining Sound Relationships

The bedrock of success in any group endeavor is the creation and maintenance of sound (i.e., open and respectful) relationships. The following notes provide a reminder of how to promote openness and respect.

While the section "Building Team Relationships" (in Chapter 31, "Overview of SAP Implementations) relates the first steps in building sound relationships, this section is concerned with the attributes of sound relationships in business. In successful relationships each party has to be at least:

- **Authentic**. "Be yourself" is an overworked yet still valid entreaty. But it is easy to act natural when you are at ease; the difficulty is to be authentic when under pressure. And this is particularly difficult for those in management who equate being a manager to being something different than who they really are. People who display leadership qualities are those who are at ease with themselves.

- **Flexible**. The opposite of "flexible" in this context is "wooden," a word used to describe the kind of behavior that seems incapable of responding to events. It is important to be flexible or appropriate in one's style if rapport is to be built with others. This does not mean being inauthentic; it simply involves showing the facets of your character. So you would respond differently to a judge in court than to a child at playschool. Both responses are equally authentic, and both are appropriate to the situation. As project manager you may need to show different facets of your management style in response to your different team members.

- **Attentive**. There is a story, passed down to us by Hsun Tzu (500 BC), that chronicles the lives of some successful leaders, including a successful Chinese general. This warlord walked alongside his men, shared their living conditions, and knew their day-to-day concerns. The story tells of a mother bemoaning the fact that this down-to-Earth leader had sucked poison from the leg of her son, who was one of his soldiers. Her cause for complaint was that the general had performed the same act of kindness several years earlier for her husband, who had then never left the general's side, eventually dying in battle.

Strong stuff, and yet Hsun Tzu's writings are to be found on the bookshelves amongst the more familiar guides to management. Translate this into the modern idiom and you will find yourself making time to be with your team members individually. Perhaps you will come in especially early knowing someone is in the office with whom you feel out of touch, perhaps you will use the pub as a forum for refreshing relationships—there are many ways of showing the attention that people warm to.

In every encounter it will be your ability to listen to your team member's story, to acknowledge it sincerely, and to respond as if it were true (for to them it *is* true) that will make for a sound relationship.

- **Trustworthy.** The creation of "trust" derives from the willingness to speak the "truth." The words have the same etymology. The "truth" in this connection is not some objective body of knowledge that has to be learned. Rather, it refers to "what is so" for you, your truth. A person can always speak his truth, providing he is aware of it. So the ability to be true depends on a degree of self-awareness, and the courage to speak it.

  In the workplace, this translates to your readiness to say how you feel about something, to declare what you think about some issue and to go to the source of the problem if something is troubling you (the alternatives are to remain tight-lipped, to gossip, or to play politics).

  Trustworthiness is frequently put to the test in business when two or more people make an agreement. The most common agreement made is to meet on a certain date at a certain time. Someone who is habitually late may lose the trust of the others, his word will not be considered law, and this may have repercussions in how he is treated in general in the business.

- **Trusting.** This is the other side of the coin to being trustworthy. It demands an optimistic outlook, and a willingness to be vulnerable to the extent that you are placing something of consequence in the hands of another. Sometimes you will be let down. More often you will be rewarded by the extra effort that people make to show that your trust has not been misplaced.

Establishing Strong Leadership

Given the basic operating principles of openness and respect, the foundation of strong leadership then rests on the ability to provide a clear brief at the outset and clear feedback during the course of the project.

Preparation for Briefing the Team Members. Prepare the following information which you will need at your fingertips when briefing the team members:

- Roles and areas of responsibility

- The minimum that each will be held accountable for

- Command and communication lines relevant to them

- The facilities and resources available to do the job

- The information and reports that you require

- A schedule of individual progress meetings, training sessions, and project appraisal meetings

Briefing the Team Members. The context you set at the briefing meeting will color the relationship you have with your team members for the duration of your project. For this reason it is vital to remember that all contexts work by common agreement. The degree to which contexts are set, understood, respected, and used will be the key to your success. With respect to each person reporting in to you:

1. Confirm purpose and length of meeting. Set the context for inviting this person in particular to take on this particular task, showing that you know how it would fit in with his career plan.

2. Explain your role and your relationship with the person for the duration of the task. Outline in general terms how you operate, your values, what you consider is negotiable and what is not.

3. Explain your immediate goal relating to this brief and how it fits within the overall company objectives.

4. Explain the person's role, responsibilities, and reporting and communication lines.

5. Clarify the minimum performance level (what they are accountable for). This should be measurable, and the more specific you are in terms of quantity and quality, the easier it will be for the person to understand and ultimately produce what is required.

6. List the resources and facilities available (e.g. people, support, offices, equipment).

7. Create a context for involvement and feedback.

8. Invite the person to take it on. Be prepared to negotiate. Treat your colleagues as if they are volunteers, for we all perform better when we act out of choice.

9. Arrange for the person to formulate a goal plan and to meet again with you to go through the goal plan, to agree to the nature and date of any reports you require, and to agree to the dates of checkpoints and progress meetings.

Offering Feedback. Feedback is traditionally saved up until the next scheduled performance review meeting, but this is a most unsatisfactory state of affairs and it is important to note that an appraisal system should not be used as a substitute for giving immediate feedback. Appraisal systems are a fall-back position, a long stop to ensure that feedback is given at some time, even if it is six months too late!

Besides, working in a project team probably places you outside the official performance appraisal system. Well, that's no loss, provided that when something needs saying within a relationship, you follow one of the two checklists described next.

The guidelines are very similar whether someone's impact on you is welcome or unwelcome. This is because the purpose in both cases is identical: to encourage what you feel is positive and productive behavior in this person and to keep your relationships fresh, alive and vibrant!

It is important to let your *current* thoughts and feelings resulting from the person's behavior be your fuel when responding. If it is appropriate to respond at the moment of impact, express *those* thoughts and feelings. If it is not till later that you are able to speak your mind, express your thoughts and feelings as they are at that *later* moment. Don't try to recapture or fake the initial thoughts and feelings; they will probably have changed. Talk about them, if at all, as thoughts and feelings that you *had*.

Checklist for Welcome Behavior. Get in touch with how you feel now about this person's actions. Take no more than 30 seconds to:

1. Set a context for what you are about to say—include your own thoughts and feelings.

2. Praise the behavior, not the person, using clear, concise and specific ideas.

3. Now let them know how you feel about it.

4. Next reinforce the positive action—"Thank You" often is enough.

5. Use physical contact (if appropriate) at any point to consolidate the relationship.

Checklist for Unwelcome Behavior. Get in touch with how you feel now in relationship to this person's actions. Take no more than 40 seconds to:

1. Set a context—include both thoughts and feelings.

2. Tell them, with clear, specific, and concise ideas, what you think about the behavior, not the person.

3. Let them know how you feel about it. (Be real and let them have all your feelings straight, so you can let them off the hook!)

4. Breathe and pause—to let them appreciate the impact it had on you, and for you to let go of that feeling.

5. Now reinforce positive behavior. Describe something they do or could do well. (Make it real and don't patronize them.)

6. Ask a question to check their understanding of your point. This is not to invite a "reasonable" reply or excuse.

7. Use physical contact (if appropriate) toward the end to consolidate the relationship.

Synthesizing a Desirable Future

People look for inspiration in their lives. In the Middle Ages it was provided by the Church, which was then the dominant institution strongly influencing the way people ran their lives. Later it was also provided by the military, which had grown steadily in influence (so the first son would join the army, the second the Church) and many companies were run (and still are) on military "orders are not to be questioned" lines.

Today, inspiration comes as well from our place of work. To many people, a career is the most important driving force and the organizations to which we belong provide the vehicle for our aspirations.

Within this context, the implementation of SAP can be seen in two ways:

- To the project team charged with carrying it out, the implementation of SAP is a venture which will occupy their best efforts for quite some time. Team members will invest part of their dreams in what they do and therefore the project must be a worthy repository of their dreams. The project manager's role is to "synthesize" these dreams (i.e., weave them into a shared vision of the future) and articulate this vision in a way that is meaningful to the whole team.

- To the other employees who do not have a direct part in implementing SAP, it is likely to represent a threat to their chosen vehicle and as such may be resisted, if not consciously then certainly unconsciously. By way of forestalling such resistance, you must ensure that they too are able to appreciate the future that is being created. Success in this will entail taking the kind of action that has been covered earlier in "The Effects of Major Change in an Organization," in Chapter 32.

Getting Stakeholder Support

Anyone who has a vested interest in the SAP project can be termed a "stakeholder." So this will particularly include:

- Senior management

- Other employees

- Employees' families

- The local community

- Suppliers

- Customers

- Shareholders

Senior Management. One of the project manager's prime tasks (see "What You Should Require of a Project Manager?" in Chapter 31, "Overview of SAP Implementations") is to be familiar with the business case for implementing SAP. In the nature of things, especially in the fast-moving world of business, what yesterday seemed important today does not seem as urgent as the content of the last phone call.

Thus to maintain support for the SAP project, it is important at every opportunity to reiterate the business case to senior management and to stay alert to anything that may affect it and respond appropriately.

Other Employees. See the section "The Effects of Major Change in an Organization" in Chapter 31, "Overview of SAP Implementations." Of course, it helps to have a mandate from employees to bring about necessary change. Mandates can be created through carrying out surveys of staff, customers, and suppliers, providing that such surveys are used as the basis for benchmarking the company against the competition or against the

IX

Implementation

company's own aspirations. The results can then be used to reveal a performance gap to which the implementation of SAP may prove to be part of the solution.

In seeking backing for the project, pay particular attention to those people whose "empires" will be affected by the implementation of SAP. These may include:

- Department heads
- IT personnel
- Secretarial & Administration

Employees' Families. Employee families are a much underrated constituency and one which deserves due attention. In as much as a person's job impacts on his lifestyle, the family bears the brunt of any changes. As always the simple device of letting people know what is going on may elicit the understanding needed when it most counts. How you manage this communication depends very much on the relationship that exists between the company and employees' families.

The Local Community. How does your company impact the local community? How will the project you have in mind affect this impact? How can you ensure that the perception the community has of your company is a positive one? These are questions that need to be considered.

Suppliers. How will your plans impact on your suppliers? To serve you well they need to plan so that the earlier you are able to bring them into the loop the better.

Customers. Customers are the arbiters of your success. Naturally, they need to be involved at every stage and even included as part of the project team (see "Recruiting/ Assembling the Right Team" in Chapter 31, "Overview of SAP Implementations"). This is the group which is most free to vote with its feet, so leave no stone unturned in canvassing their views. Methods to employ include:

- Survey questionnaires
- Group dialogues
- One-to-one interviews

Shareholders. The shareholders are left till last because if you do right by the preceding groups, your success will be ensured and this group will be in clover.

Maintaining Robust Communication

In today's globalizing companies, the job of keeping people informed and including them in the decision-making process, where necessary, is becoming increasingly fraught with difficulty. It is more than likely that you will have to rely on electronic communication as much as, if not more than, face-to-face communication. You may be accustomed to the new forms of communication, but others within your team may not be and will probably welcome some guidance in how to cope with the following:

- E-mail—Have a clear protocol as to who should have copies of e-mail. Attach a status coding to each e-mail so that the recipient is able to prioritize messages and therefore manage his time well. Use e-mail in preference to fax because it is usually easier to handle at the other end—but check preferences first.

- Voice mail—Institute a similar protocol for voice mail. Keep messages short. Respond immediately even if only to say that the message is being considered and you will get back by a certain date.

- Telephone and videophone conferencing—Already well in use, especially among larger companies, conferencing is acquiring a protocol along the following lines.

Preparing the Call. The chairperson, normally the person who calls the meeting, needs to be familiar with the correct procedures. The chairperson should:

- Communicate the objectives of the conference. Ensure the purpose of the conference is known to and agreed to by all prospective participants.

- Establish the duration of the call, stipulating start and end times.

- Where appropriate, circulate an agenda in advance and let individuals know if any preparation is called for.

Starting the Call. The chairperson should:

- Take a roll-call. Clarify at the beginning of the call who is in attendance, who is acting as chairperson.

- Ensure everyone's presence is acknowledged and that (for teleconferencing) each person says something to begin with so that voices can be recognized.

- Ensure that people who haven't met or spoken to each other before are formally introduced to each other and get a chance to say a few words to each other.

- Reestablish call parameters. Remind everyone of the purpose of the call and its duration.

- Remind participants of the appropriate ways of doing things, e.g., to get everyone else's attention when they want to speak.

- Acknowledge the fact that people may accidentally cut across each other.

- Check the level of preparation. Check that everyone has a copy of the agenda or, if the conference is less formal, that everyone is clear about the objectives which need to be reached.

During the Call. All participants should:

- Ensure full participation. Draw out all pertinent facts and opinions. Respond to sighs or hesitations or any other subtle suggestions that somebody may have something else to say. This will help ensure that the more reserved participants do get to fully contribute and that the medium is not "squashing" the message.

IX

Implementation

- Sustain interest. If there's a time delay, such as if you can't find the piece of paper you want to refer to, or anything else goes wrong or isn't going according to plan, make sure you let the others know what's happening; i.e., as a general rule, always explicitly acknowledge the obvious.

- Acknowledge audibly. If statements are met only by silence as people quietly nod or shake their heads, speakers may succumb to the urge to repeat themselves until they are convinced that the point has been taken onboard.

- Encourage dialogue. It can be helped along by the speaker seeking a direct response to the points being made via the use of an open question immediately afterward, i.e., "I think we ought to do this, this, and this, what are your thoughts?", or even more direct, the speaker may request a response from a particular person, i.e., "Jill, what do you think?"

- Stay on course. If a point is raised that takes the conversation onto a different tangent from the agenda at hand, intervene; acknowledge the point being discussed and ask whether it should be discussed in another forum or if the existing agenda should be altered. Don't let themes carry on and either run out of time or get other agenda points squashed.

The chairperson should:

- Watch the clock. Alert the others to the amount of time remaining to ensure that the call doesn't run over and everyone gets their point of view across. If it appears as though the agenda isn't going to be completed then signal your concern as far in advance as possible.

Addendum for Video Conferences Only. Chairperson should:

- Check visibility. Ensure at the beginning of the call that everyone can be seen and that if necessary you ask that the lighting be altered if it will help people's faces to be seen more clearly. It's a good idea to ensure that the remote camera is focused on the face of the person speaking.

- Check audibility. Get both/all sides to check the sound levels for each individual at the beginning of the call so people are aware in advance as to whether the microphone needs to be moved or not.

Some Tips on Motivation

There is no shortage of research into the roots of motivation. The difficulty is to extract something that makes absolute sense and is immediately transferable to the workplace. Of all the ideas that have passed over my desk in the last decade, there are just a few that stand out, and these I relate here.

The Hawthorne Findings. Once upon a time long ago some tests were done in a factory in the USA. The management wanted to know how light levels affected productivity. So they began some scientific tests. First they raised the light level: production went up.

Then they lowered the light level: production went up again. Then they lowered the light level still more: once more production went up. Baffled they quizzed the employees about the effect of light levels on their work. The response? "To heck with the light, we just like the attention!"

Maslow & Herzberg—Hygiene Factors versus Motivational Factors. Maslow told us there is a hierarchy of needs. It is only when we have got our basic needs for air, water, food and shelter handled that we turn our attention to higher needs such as the need for community, self-expression and self-actualization. Nowadays, however, this message seems to be forgotten by managers as well as employees as each side searches for the grail: an amount of money destined to bestow ultimate happiness.

If only they had heeded Herzberg. This behavioral scientist proposed a simple model of human motivation that is particularly pertinent to these days of disposable income. It points out that whereas food is important to life, there comes a time when increases in quantity bring diminishing returns. He distinguishes, for example, the ability to satisfy one's hunger (a "hygiene factor") from the ability to realize an important goal (a "motivational factor"). Figure 36.1 presents the full range of factors.

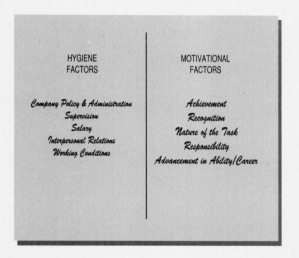

Fig. 36.1 The hygiene factors can demotivate but not motivate; the motivational factors can motivate but not demotivate.

Of course it is obvious to us that too much food loses its appeal after the second helping—but too much money? Too many holidays? Too large a car? Well, that depends.

The chart suggests, and many would concur, that the factors on the left have only the potential to demotivate by their absence, but not to motivate by their presence, while the factors on the right have the potential to motivate by their presence and a questionable ability to demotivate by their absence.

Managing Stress of Project Team and Users

In the early 1990s a survey was carried out by the National Association for Mental Health (Mind) of 109 British companies. It revealed that directors and managers believe stress at work, heightened by the recession and fear of redundancy, causes them more perturbation than any personal difficulties. In January 1992, a leading Japanese newspaper conducted a poll and found that one in every two Japanese admitted to fears of becoming a victim of *karoshi*, i.e. death from stress or overwork. In Britain 40 percent of absenteeism is attributed to stress-related illnesses by the Health and Safety Commission. And who knows how much "presenteeism" (i.e., unproductive busy-ness) is also due to stress. So what exactly is stress?

Stress—What Is It?

What actually happens within a person's body to cause stress? Stress is produced in response to a person's environment. When a stimulus from your environment registers on your eyes or ears, it travels to your thalamus and then to both your hippocampus and your auditory and visual cortices, where you attach meaning to the stimuli. If the stimulus is threatening, your brain tells your adrenal glands to produce epinephrine and norepinephrine (otherwise known as "noradrenaline") which gear up the body for an emergency. But because this is apt to be a long-winded process (since it involves thought) evolution has equipped us with a short circuit that cuts out your frontal lobes. This mechanism is designed to have us react first then ask questions later. So if you hear a low growl behind you, your involuntary reflex actions would be to prick up the hairs on the back of your neck, quicken your heart rate, and prepare for flight, or in fact flee. All this happens in a second before your conscious mind has time to interrupt with the realization that it was merely a noise from the central heating.

Our emotional mind is the first to react and thus determines our response. What happens under stress is that the pattern of thought into which the sufferer has slipped triggers the same flight mechanism every time the thought surfaces. The body can only take so much of this, and soon begins to creak at the seams, giving rise to the symptoms described below.

Recognizing the Symptoms of Stress

"I feel a sort of general nervousness, with a feeling that if anybody said or did something to upset me, I would be likely to erupt like a seething volcano. I have a couldn't-care-less attitude toward what other people think of me and a deep desire to be left alone. My self-confidence has been shattered, and I no longer feel capable of handling anything that is thrown at me. I have lost interest and enthusiasm. I feel disillusion, resentment and despair. A great lethargy and depression, like a dark cloud, hangs over my head, I feel squeezed dry." (From *Management Week*, 27 November 1991, "Highly Stressed and Underperforming")

Desperate enough, you would think, but this litany of angst taken verbatim from a manager is just part of the whole story, namely the internalized feelings or *psychological* symptoms. Another part is made up of the *physiological* symptoms. Stress suppresses the immune system by way of diverting resources to the (supposed) emergency at hand. The result: insomnia, aches and pains including migraine and arthritis, hair loss, weight loss or gain, shortness of breath including asthma, irritable bowel syndrome, peptic ulcers, heart disease, cold sores, and lingering colds and flu. And finally there are the *social* symptoms. Victims become silent, cynical, and fractious—at home as well as at work. They are unable to enjoy others' success and may become increasingly dependent on alcohol or drugs. And as if this was not enough, sufferers become accident-prone!

For a fuller list of the symptoms that can be caused by stress I refer you to *Emotional Intelligence* by Daniel Goleman, who emphasizes that the research does not suggest that everyone who suffers stress goes on to develop a disease.

The only conclusion that follows from this is that stress is severely toxic. The challenge is to recognize the earliest symptoms of stress before they multiply and cause irreversible damage. There is *theoretically* a simple way of doing so, and that is to be alert for any feelings of hostility toward anyone within the working environment. If these feelings are not caught early and dealt with then it is likely that they will gradually mutate into feelings of agitation, then despair, and finally numbness, i.e., it is possible that the sufferer will, in the end, claim to be indifferent to the object of his initial hostility. From there the route to acquiring the full range of symptoms can be short.

The word "theoretically" in the paragraph above should be taken under advisement. Many people, and this includes senior managers, successful or otherwise, have difficulty recognizing what they are feeling. Even feelings of hostility may go unnoticed or unremarked. The solution in this event is to provide education in emotional literacy, which is covered later, in the section "Management's Role in Alleviating Stress."

Assuming, for the moment, an ability to recognize and articulate one's feelings, the primary contributors to a stress-free working life are the ability and willingness to:

Accept responsibility for generating a particular feeling or set of feelings (i.e., it is not someone's behavior that makes you feel a certain way, rather it is just the way you have learned to react in response to this kind of behavior).

Reexamine the thoughts that led to the feeling. So if the thought was "So-and-so is ignoring me," recognize that your conclusion is no more than the result of your interpretation of someone's behavior. Consider alternative interpretations such as "So-and-so is very self-preoccupied. Perhaps he is under pressure and needs some help. What can I do to help?"

Should efforts to reinterpret the situation fail, then check out your reality, your perception of what is really going on with the person in question. As soon as possible seek out the object of your hostility (agitation, despair, etc.) and follow the guidelines set out earlier in "Offering Feedback." You will note that this skill is included under the head of "Establishing Strong Leadership." This doesn't mean you have to be the person's "leader" to apply this skill; it simply means that within this relationship you will be taking the lead and showing leadership qualities.

IX

Implementation

Is There a Right Amount of Stress?

No. Not if stress is taken to derive from an inability to cope with one's environment. But what about the gap between one's goals and the current reality? Surely this creates stress? Yes, perhaps it does, but if it does, it is to be redressed and not accepted as a condition of being in management.

Peter Senge in his best-selling book *The Fifth Discipline* sums up the difference between destructive stress and what he calls "creative tension," or the force that brings vision and reality together through the natural tendency of tension to seek resolution. "The principle of creative tension," he writes, "is the central principle of personal mastery…Yet, it is widely misunderstood. For example, the very term "tension" suggests anxiety or stress. But creative tension doesn't feel any particular way. It is the force that comes into play at the moment when we acknowledge a vision that is at odds with reality." How do you tell the difference between stress and creative tension? The former produces negative thoughts and feelings. The latter produces a rush of positive energy.

Management's Role in Alleviating Stress

There may not be a right amount of stress, but there is a right amount of creative tension. In General Slim's words (see above "Managing Issues of Morale") any person who takes on a goal "must be convinced that the object can be obtained; that it is not out of reach." Naturally management has an important role to play in this.

So there is a balancing trick involved. We each have a certain tolerance for taking on challenges. There are goals that we are confident about achieving and we talk of these as being within our "comfort zone." Then there are goals which go beyond what we have achieved to date. These lie within our "stretch zone." Finally there are goals that are way in excess of what we consider reasonable and here we enter our "panic zone!" Providing that goals do not enter this final domain and that appropriate support is given for activities within the stretch zone, stress should not be a problem. An athlete's training regime will, for instance, depend on staying within the stretch zone, and consistently expanding the zone into new territory.

What can management do to alleviate stress? There are a number of "tools" at their disposal.

Appraisal. It is important for a manager to consider each individual on his team individually and how that individual will react to the overall objective and to his personal goals in particular. Research shows that a person's proneness to stress is programmed into his brain. Some people (approximately a fifth of the population) have a neurochemistry that is far more sensitive than the average. As such they are more prone to stress. Look out for the symptoms of stress (see the earlier section "Recognizing the Symptoms of Stress") and catch them early, if not pre-empt them, by getting to know your people well and fine-tuning your expectations to their individual abilities and aspirations.

Know the part that you have in contributing to a stressful situation by providing the opportunity for at least two-way feedback, if not 360 degree feedback.

Empowerment. Studies of the British Civil Service have shown that the prevalence of stress within the lower ranks far exceeds that in the higher ranks. Part of the difference is attributed to the fact that those in the higher ranks have more control over their destiny and those below suffer from a lack of autonomy (recall the behavior of rats earlier in the sections "Management's Role in Change" and "Consultation"). Empowerment is a management tool that can be used by managers to devolve authority and by their reports to take on that authority.

Relationships. Maverick troubleshooters still, it seems, have their place. Brought in to rapidly strip out layers of management, they are "uncluttered" by relationships with their victims and can perform their duty to the shareholders with a clear conscience. But once the organization has to be rebuilt, it is time for the kind of management that is able to coax the best out of people, that sets store on creating a strong matrix of relationships throughout the organization and takes the necessary steps to build them. See the section "Building Team Relationships" in Chapter 31, "Overview of SAP Implementations," for guidance.

Environment. There is an argument about how much of behavior is determined by genes and how much by environment. But everyone is agreed on one thing: the environment has a part to play. From the ages of approximately 18 to 65, one half of our waking life is spent within the work environment. The quality of our surroundings is determined by what is called the "social architecture," an area of science concerned with the effect that buildings and infrastructure have on people. Factors to consider include:

Location. Is it at a site remote from town center amenities? Is there adequate transport to the amenities?

Outlook. Is the area where the offices are situated uplifting to the human spirit or a cause for alarm? What alternatives are there?

Layout. Are people kept apart or thrown together by the way the office is laid out? Are there common areas where people can congregate?

Facilities. Are the basic requirements a person needs near to hand: Work station, catering, drink machines, rest rooms, stationery, library, communications, car parking, child care, airport, and so on?

Lighting. Natural daylight provides the best possible kind of light. Are you making the best of what's available?

Noise. Machinery, lighting, water pipes, and air conditioning all conspire to produce a background drone that can induce a dream-like state of unreality. What can be done to stop it?

Consider soundproofing and separating people from the things that cause noise. In the final analysis, should you move locations to a better-designed building?

Air. Are you getting enough fresh air or is it endlessly recirculated?

IX

Implementation

How to Cope with High Pressure

Of all the factors that serve to help people cope with high pressure, quantity and quality of relationships must top the list.

By way of creating strong relationships and following through with the right actions, you would do well to ensure that you and your colleagues:

- Create a context for times of high pressure.

- Balance home and work life.

- Learn to say "No."

- Delegate work that helps others enter their own stretch zone.

- Break down goals into achievable chunks.

- Learn to act on hostility before it declines into the lower energy emotions such as nervousness, despair, and apathy.

- Learn how to give feedback and receive it.

Personal Coaching and Other Remedies

There is a true story of a managing director who, while showing a prospective client around the offices, entered the marketing director's office only to find the blinds shut, the room in semi-darkness and the silhouette of someone lying flat out on the desk apparently asleep. Quickly withdrawing, the embarrassed MD blustered some excuse to his guest and moved on hurriedly. Later he reproached the marketing director for his behavior, to which the reply was: "My title is Creative Marketing Director. I think best with my eyes closed and my feet up. This is what you pay me for!"

Every manager needs some time for thinking, time that is undisturbed, and, usually, our body clocks will tell us exactly when the best time is. For some it will be the period as we sink into sleep, for others it will be the state of semi-sleep we enter before fully waking up, for the man in the story it was the top end of the day. The ability to recognize the need for reflection, and to then reflect, is key to remaining beyond the grip of stress.

Other sources of assistance are:

Counseling—One-to-One. There is a growing tendency among high flyers to seek out opportunities for personal coaching, tailored to their specific areas for improvement. Of those candidates who are encouraged by their manager or the human resource department to undertake personal counseling, by far the largest group comprises people who are either stressed themselves or are causing stress among their colleagues.

Assertion Training. If steam builds up in a relationship and threatens to come to a head, there are ways that the relationship can be managed through to a point of satisfaction with the help of an experienced facilitator or qualified psychotherapist using techniques borrowed from and initially proven in prisons, where tensions often need to be defused.

Hospitals. There are institutions that offer a wide range of services including anxiety management, treatment for depression, relaxation therapy, assertiveness training, and psychotherapy. Some also run alcohol treatment programs. Patients learn how to cope with their responses and reactions to external events by participating in various group and individual therapies.

Transcendental Meditation. Transcendental meditation involves practicing some mental exercises twice a day for 20 minutes (e.g., yoga and the Alexander Technique). The effect is to alleviate the symptoms of stress and one research study has shown heart disease and diseases of the nervous system were reduced by 87 percent and tumors by 55 percent. Proof of the pudding may lie in the fact that U.S. medical insurance companies offer a discount on premiums to patients who meditate, because their health record is 50 percent better.

Religion. For many this is the first recourse if the going gets tough. If a person has a spiritual belief, there is much that his religion can do help him through difficulties. Religious officials have more experience than most in counseling people through the depths of feeling, especially bereavement, and they can be a constant and reliable source of support.

From Here...

This chapter sheds some light on the human cost of bringing about major change within an organization. It alerts managers to the impact that SAP implementation may have on employees. It describes the types of issues of which the manager must be aware in dealing with those affected. And it shows how to maintain morale despite the concerns that a change of systems can bring.

- For more information on the impact of SAP implementation, see Chapter 31, "Overview of SAP Implementations."

- For more information on managing the communication lines between employees and managers throughout the change, see Chapter 34, "Managing Communications Internal and External."

IX

Implementation

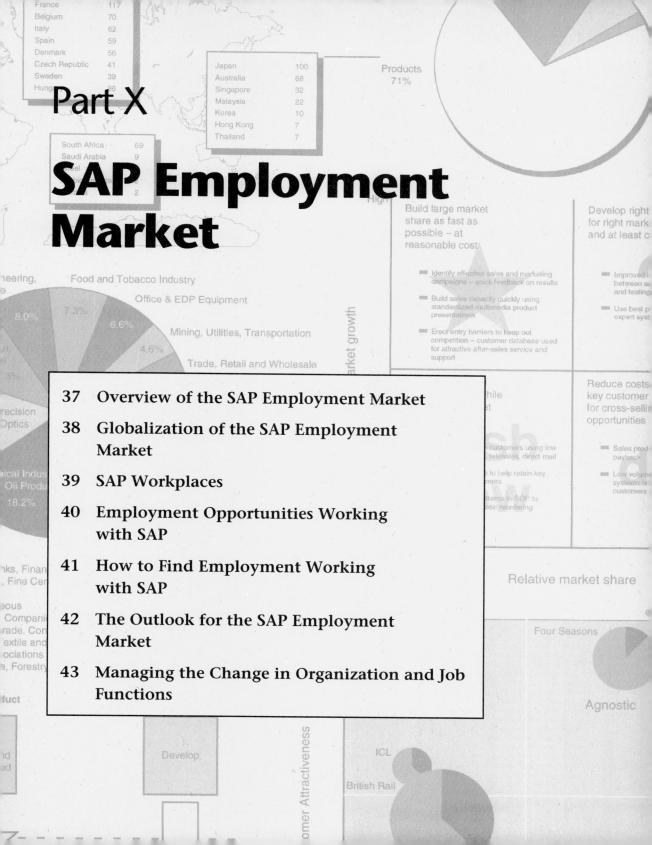

Part X

SAP Employment Market

Netherlands	130
France	117
Belgium	70
Italy	62
Spain	59
Denmark	56
Czech Republic	41
Sweden	39
Hungary	26

	479
	54
	24
	16
	14

Japan	100
Australia	68
Singapore	32
Malaysia	22
Korea	10
Hong Kong	7
Thailand	7

South Africa	69
Saudi Arabia	9
Israel	3
Arabic Emirates	2
Nambia	2

Products
71%

High

Build large market share as fast as possible – at reasonable cost

- Identify effective sales and marketing campaigns – quick feedback on results
- Build sales capacity quickly using standardized multimedia product presentations
- Erect entry barriers to keep out competition – customer database used for attractive after-sales service and support

Devel
for rig
and a

Reduce sales and marketing costs while maintaining market share

- Service low value customers using low cost channels eg. telesales, direct mail
- Contact database to help retain key high value customers
- Link purchase patterns to SOP to prompt for automatic reordering

Redu
key cu
for cr
oppor

Low

High

Rate of market growth

Relative market s

Steel,
al Engineering,
tomotive

Food and Tobacco Industry

Office & EDP Equipment

8.0%

7.3%

6.6%

Mining, Utilities, Transportation

4.6%

ommercial,
nd Social
10.3%

Trade, Retail and Wholesale

3.9%

Traffic and News Communication

onics, Precision
anics, Optics
14.5%

3.8%

Metal Products and Primary Metal

3.6%

Universities and Technical Colleges

Chemical Industry,
Mineral Oil Production
18.2%

Others
(see chart below)
11.6%

2.9%

Wood, Paper and Printing Industry

thers
redit Banks, Financial Services	1.9
uarrying, Fine Ceramics, Glass	1.9
ospitals	1.7
iscellaneous	1.7
surance Companies	1.6
uilding Trade, Construction	1.4
eather, Textile and Clothing Industry	.9
ade Associations and Federations	.3
griculture, Forestry, Fishing	.2

ble product

Develop
nplete and
ustomized

Customized tools

Develop

High

Four Seasons

Seed

Agno

ICL

British Rail

er Attractiveness

Chapter 37

Overview of the SAP Employment Market

This chapter will give you a broad picture of the main characteristics of the SAP employment market, the most important trends in it, and some forecasts of growth.

SAP has been a hugely successful phenomenon, and the SAP world has unique and attractive characteristics as a generator of employment. It is also one that needs careful study if you want to get the best out of it, or to decide whether it's the right workplace for you. The earlier part of the book tells you about the product and how to implement it, but that's only half the story. If you're reading this book with a view to create or develop a career in SAP, then you need to know your way around the diverse environment that is the SAP world.

Main Features of the SAP Employment Market

To understand the SAP employment market, you need to know how SAP finds its way from factory to user, because this is central to the whole success of SAP, and also to the nature of the employment market it generates.

SAP is brought to the user by an extended "virtual organization" of SAP AG and its subsidiaries, its network of business partners, and the users' own IT departments. Partnering to market software is not unique to SAP, but SAP has been particularly successful at it, and partners have integrated their activities more than is usual in IT distribution channels, without sacrificing their business independence.

The virtual organization has wider purposes than simply selling SAP products. It is also driven by the partners' need to sell services (as well as products sometimes). At base, it delivers solutions to the problems of business process re-engineering, and the software suite that SAP produces is only one component of this. The people who identify the problems, propose solutions, and

In this chapter, you learn:

■ To understand the key features of the SAP employment market.

You can gain a broad understanding of what the SAP world exists to do, the sort of organizations that play a part, and the employment opportunities they create.

■ What the main trends are that will impact SAP employment over the next few years.

You can get a quick insight into the major influences and initiatives that will drive change in SAP employment.

use the SAP software to implement them are also part of the salable product. They have to work in close concert in teams that span more than one employer, and this dictates the need for many of the qualities demanded of the ideal SAP person.

The nature of the SAP user base also places special demands on SAP practitioners. Some 25 percent of the world's largest corporations use SAP (as of mid-1996), and they usually do so across multiple operations and multinationally. The SAP employment market is founded on these "blue chip" companies, and the equally prestigious management consultancies who service them. This, together with the nature of the SAP product, creates a market for the highflying type of individual who is comfortable talking about big issues with big clients. It also means that systems are large and complex, and that project timescales are long.

SAP's big company orientation has also had the felicitous (from the employee point of view) effect of keeping salaries for SAP-skilled people at or near the top of the IT league.

A person with suitable IT skills and experience of installing packaged software, or of business systems analysis, can expect to gain a premium of 25 percent or more by getting one year's SAP experience onto his or her résumé. People with senior project management experience may gain more than this, provided they can handle the cultural, logistical, and technical complexities of large multinational projects.

The SAP world offers more than just high salaries (and indeed it is highly suspicious of anyone who appears too interested in just the money). As IT becomes a more and more pivotal part of companies' operations, and a company's systems infrastructure is recognized as one of its most important assets, the route to the boardroom opens up for IT professionals, especially those who think strategically about its application to the company's business. No one is better placed to exploit this route to the top than experienced SAP consultants.

If travel is one of your career objectives, then SAP will provide you with lots of opportunities to pursue it. Since many of the employers are multinational, and the systems are rolled out across many subsidiaries, you can build up a lot of air miles in the right position. You may find that to get the option of travel, you have to accept the obligation of it, however, and most people who think constant business travel is lots of fun haven't done too much of it.

In contrast, the majority of people who have actually lived abroad for any length of time wouldn't swap the experience. You can really experience a country only by living in it, and the expatriate life has many merits. SAP, with its lengthy contracts and enough skills shortfall to fuel international recruitment, offers the chance to get to know many fascinating parts of the world. But not all parts of the world are equally enjoyable, and if you want to travel, make sure you want the lifestyle you are taking on, and not just the money.

The high salaries in the SAP world are not totally due to SAP's big company background. The laws of supply and demand also prevail, and demand outstrips supply in the SAP employment market. But if you are looking to cross-train into SAP, be aware of the true nature of the supply and demand imbalance. There is a shortage of fully trained and competent SAP consultants, but no shortage of applicants to train in it.

Even for experienced SAP people, the demand is only for the best. The SAP world is a competitive one, in which your performance is visible, and merit will prevail. It is stimulating (unless you're bored by business systems). It is nonhierarchic, and you won't be deterred by authority from taking the initiative. But it is also demanding—of your technical skills, your commitment, and your personality.

As you will have gathered from the earlier chapters (if you didn't know already), the heart of the SAP product is a set of high-level building blocks and the means of configuring them to re-engineer business processes. It is not a set of tools that you use after you have decided exactly what you want from the system, and then say, "Okay, now program that for me." The configuration process is inseparable from the whole process of defining strategies, analyzing business needs, and considering such issues as legacy systems and user interfacing. A pragmatic path has to be sought that optimizes the synergy between the users' needs and the functionality of SAP.

Most of the roles in the SAP world carry in their title the word "consultant," and whatever the area of specialty, in the traditional management consultancy skills.

These are not what many people imagine them to be. They are not mostly about "being consulted," or cogitating and pontificating from your superior knowledge and thought processes. The first skill in management consultancy is the ability to sell yourself. People use management consultants to keep in step with the latest mainstream thinking—as a knowledge conduit and as an insurance policy. They can get these benefits only from someone they trust and to whom they will listen.

This makes very little room for the pure technician, and it doesn't suit everybody. Many people in IT (almost all of them, to some extent) are fascinated by technology. You need to be fascinated by business and by people as well if you are to succeed in the SAP world.

If you're reading this as an aspiring entrant to the SAP world, you should be prepared to put some serious effort into it, and possibly lay a deeper plan than simply applying for SAP positions. SAP has lots of areas where requirements for other skills overlap or sit alongside the need for SAP skills. If you are skilled in UNIX-based networks, for example, you will have a much better chance of acceptance into a SAP user (present or prospective) who needs those skills if you don't emphasise your ambitions to cross-train into SAP when applying for a job. Be prepared to deliver productivity in your present area of expertise at first. Once you establish yourself as a valued employee, your prospects of getting cross-training are several hundred percent better than they are as an outside applicant.

Trends in the SAP Employment Market

Some major trends will impact the SAP market over the next few years:

■ The SAP market is still a young one, but as it matures, the number of installed systems increases relative to the number of new ones being sold, with a resultant change in the mix of implementation and support staff.

■ SAP is actively seeking to market into much smaller companies than have been its target in the past. It is also engaging more heavily in vertical marketing.

■ The range of platform and complementary product technology that sells along with SAP is increasing all the time, and opening ever more bridges into SAP for people with skills in these areas.

■ SAP has a large focus on making its development workbench tools easier to use. It expects this to help balance the supply and demand equation in SAP employment. It also changes the skills requirement for configurers.

Chapter 42, "The Outlook for the SAP Employment Market," explores some of these trends, and their effect on the employment picture.

There are two other trends worth noting here:

■ There is an increase in international recruitment, as the emerging markets seek to recruit the experienced people from the more established ones. This mostly means heavy recruitment from Europe for the Americas and Asian regions.

■ More employers are becoming aware that they will have to provide training in SAP, and that they can end up with better people as a result, because in the long term, a person's underlying attributes are more important than an extra year's SAP experience. Just in the period of producing this book, we have seen a modest but discernible increase in the number of employers opening the doors to SAP entrants of the right caliber.

Growth in the SAP Employment Market

SAP revenue growth, which is public information, forms the underpinning for employment growth. SAP was formed in 1972 when the five founders—Dietmar Hopp, Hans-Werner Hector, Hasso Plattner, Klaus Tschira, and Klaus Wellenreuther—acquired the rights to a financial accounting package. Wellenreuther had developed this package originally (while an IBM employee) for Naturin, an IBM customer.

The founders, with their infant company, set about the design and implementation of a real-time finance system, based largely on Wellenreuther's experience in the application.

ICI became the first customer for this system, and as well as buying the package, they commissioned a bespoke materials management system. This provided cash flow for the development of the FI system, as well as the nucleus of the MM standard package. The further development of MM was financed from sales of the FI package, and the show was on the road.

MM and FI formed the first modules of what was then called System R. Only after the successor versions R/2 and R/3 were introduced was System R renamed to R/1.

As a mainframe product, SAP R/2 was very successful in Germany, and made some inroads elsewhere, but it really took off in 1992 with the launch of R/3 as a UNIX client/server-based system. This was exactly the right time for such a product, and its combination of business process module orientation and client/server architecture was just what the large consultancies needed to implement the vision and change what they sell.

Since then, it has grown to be the world's fourth-largest software company, and a huge success on the stock market. By the end of 1995, there were approximately 20,000 SAP consultants employed by SAP and its business partners combined.

Chapter 42, "The Outlook for the SAP Employment Market," contains some forecasts from around the industry of the growth that can be expected in the future.

The company is currently achieving around 40 percent growth. In the last full year for which figures are available, Europe achieved 19 percent, and that market is several years more mature than the rest of the world. The Americas achieved 82 percent, and the Asia Pacific Region 68 percent.

The effect that this has on employment growth is to some extent mitigated by the better development tools that SAP is producing, but the market will expand to accommodate their extra throughput while it remains resource-constrained. It should also be remembered that employment growth is partly a function of the installed base, which will continue to expand long after SAP sales performance has levelled off (as long as sales don't fall to zero).

Forecasts for the increase in SAP employment over next year range from 20 percent as an overall figure, to over 100 percent from individual partners.

A view based on considering everything in this book would suggest that the number of SAP consultants worldwide will grow by at least 40 percent per year for the first couple of years from the end of 1995. How accurate this proves, you'll be able to watch for yourself, as SAP regularly publishes the figures.

People often pose the question for SAP employment as for many industry stars before it—when will the bubble burst? The answer is that it won't, because there is no bubble to burst. SAP is based solidly on the superiority of real-time processes in business, and SAP employment is based on understanding these processes.

The client/server platform, although it has been instrumental in SAP's phenomenal recent growth, is not crucial to its future. Indeed it is arguable that provided SAP saw a successor to client/server systems coming, it would profit hugely from it. Change is SAP's business.

Any real threat in the foreseeable future has to come from some competitor doing what SAP does but better. In the long term, it would have to be something that makes SAP's concept of real-time processing for the back office obsolete.

This would have to be a fairly drastic change in the whole concept of business, backed up by some superior technology. If micromachines are forecast (as they are) to circumvent the long-intractable problems of turbulence on the airplane wing among a host of other problems, by approaching it in a totally different way, then why shouldn't the whole concept of business be changed with similar radicalism? Well, probably more for reasons of sociology, economics, and vested interest than anything technical.

All this says is that we're well into the realms of futurology before we can see a point for SAP careers to be under threat.

From Here...

In this chapter, you have learned about the main features of the SAP employment market, and gained an overview of important trends and forecasts that may affect future prospects.

The following chapters will explore the SAP employment market in a little more depth. They will also point you to ways in which you can expand your knowledge beyond the contents of this book, and you will also find the appendixes contain useful practical details that you will want to know when developing career options in SAP:

- In Chapter 39, "SAP Workplaces," you can learn more about how the SAP world is structured, and how to find your way around it. You can gain a better understanding of the roles that the different types of employers play in the overall process of delivering SAP systems.

- Chapter 40, "Employment Opportunities Working with SAP," describes some of the functions you can fill, the skills they require, and the job titles that they carry in the SAP world. You can learn how to map your own skills to the needs of SAP employers.

- In Chapter 41, "How to Find Employment Working with SAP," you can find some useful advice on getting into SAP, whether or not you have a special skill to offer; Appendix C, "Sample SAP-Related Job Descriptions," contains some example job descriptions that do not require previous SAP experience.

- In Chapter 42, "The Outlook for the SAP Employment Market," you can learn in more depth about the outlook for the future in SAP employment, and where the new jobs will arise. You can also learn to evaluate how the major trends will change the nature of SAP jobs and how they will affect supply and demand.

- In Appendix A, "SAP Offices Around the World," Appendix B, "SAP Business Partners," and Appendix H, "Complementary Solutions," you will find many useful contact addresses. These provide start points from which you can network out along lines dictated by your own special areas of interest.

Chapter 38

Globalization of the SAP Employment Market

SAP has developed as a very international employment opportunity. This chapter will provide a brief guide to the global distribution of SAP, its internationalist culture, and travel opportunities.

SAP Worldwide Presence

SAP has offices and partners in 53 countries around the world. The over 4,000 installations it had as of May 1995 were distributed as shown in Figure 38.1.

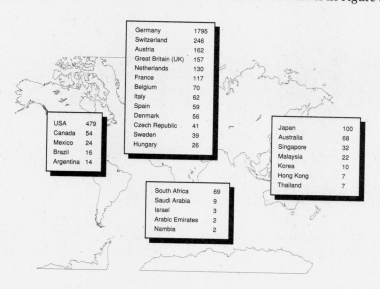

Germany	1795
Switzerland	246
Austria	162
Great Britain (UK)	157
Netherlands	130
France	117
Belgium	70
Italy	62
Spain	59
Denmark	56
Czech Republic	41
Sweden	39
Hungary	26

USA	479
Canada	54
Mexico	24
Brazil	16
Argentina	14

Japan	100
Australia	68
Singapore	32
Malaysia	22
Korea	10
Hong Kong	7
Thailand	7

South Africa	69
Saudi Arabia	9
Israel	3
Arabic Emirates	2
Namibia	2

Fig. 38.1   In May 1995, SAP installations worldwide numbered over 4,000, and were distributed as shown here.

Since those figures were compiled, SAP has experienced growth in excess of 50 percent, and in percentile terms, the Asian and American installations have grown fastest. This is part of an underlying, and perfectly normal

In this chapter, you learn:

- How SAP installations are distributed worldwide, and which are the growth regions for SAP employment.

- How the SAP Internationalist Culture has developed, and where it is going.

  SAP is becoming ever more international, and you can cultivate globetrotting opportunities if you want to. But consider the pros and cons first.

pattern—where there is more untapped potential, expansion is fastest. In Europe those countries with less penetration have grown fastest, although Germany still managed not far short of 20 percent.

If you look at the figures with even a rudimentary knowledge of geography (or the aid of an atlas) and of world economic trends, it is not difficult to see where the growth areas are going to be. All around the Pacific rim SAP will be growing fast for the next few years. The USA is the prime engine for this, and is recruiting SAP expertise as fast as it can. But also the "tiger economies" of Southeast Asia are taking-off economically, led by the tiny but flourishing state of Singapore. At over ten SAP installations per million of population, Singapore challenges the Germanic countries for worldwide leadership in SAP usage.

Singapore, which leads Southeast Asia, has built its success on the wholehearted and planned acceptance of high technology. Like Hong Kong, it has strong ethnic and linguistic links with China, and can be the catalyst that opens the emerging new style economy of China to SAP. Many other (and much larger) parts of Southeast Asia have high-growth economies and are developing their business culture around the English language.

Other areas where modern business economies are likely to develop fast are the former communist countries of Europe and the improving economies of South America.

SAP can be expected to flourish in these sorts of situations, because it is an agent of change, but more importantly, it is the agent of change of choice for multinational corporations. These multinationals are the main transferors of business practice to modernizing economies. Global economic trends, notably the internationalization of business, has increased their influence enormously, and where they go, SAP goes.

In these emerging SAP markets, all sorts of infrastructure employment opportunities will open, in marketing, training, administration, and so on, within partners, service providers, and SAP subsidiaries themselves. But the largest and most critical requirement will be for the skilled SAP consultants and project managers that form the bulk of the SAP employment market anywhere.

Internationalist Culture

The globetrotting aspects of SAP employment have actually been less prevalent than you might expect, given its internationalism, but they are nonetheless exciting, and are increasing. Apart from the routine "short stay" business travel that is involved in working for international organizations, there are more substantial overseas relocation opportunities.

The internationalist culture that is growing around SAP has strong foundations:

The large management consultancies that are partners with SAP have a long history of operating internationally, and have propagated the SAP message worldwide.

Similarly, the SAP platform and technology partners are some of the largest in the world, and very international in outlook.

The partnership approach that SAP has adopted has allowed it to expand worldwide very rapidly without prohibitive investment demands.

The SAP culture of open communication and the transfer of knowledge and skills is highly palatable to operations thousands of miles from the home base.

SAP has adopted English as its first language from its early days, despite its German origins, and English is the global language of commerce.

International demand for SAP systems and the level of experience needed to implement them have meant that new markets have had to obtain this experience from more established markets, thus encouraging globalization of employment.

Building on these foundations, SAP has pursued an ethos which allows each SAP subsidiary to develop its own culture—at Walldorf, for example there is a "techno-academic" almost campus-style culture, while Philadelphia prefers a more typical modern U.S. business culture.

The common denominator, to which all subsidiaries work, is to keep its structure non-hierarchic, nonbureaucratic and very partner-oriented, and to espouse "virtuality" in building its operations. By virtuality, SAP means that functional teams and organizations can be formed by people and resources working in partnerships, and not necessarily employed or owned by the same company.

SAP is extending the internationalism of its operations wherever it is practicable, not just in the appointment of partners and development of marketing subsidiaries, but also in the siting of strategic resources. While at present 95 percent of product development is done in Germany, this is changing. The U.S.A. is performing product development now, as is the UK, to a smaller extent, and some localized language versions of the product will be produced together with local partners. ICOEs (Industry Centers of Expertise) are also strategic resources and these are sited in far-flung locations. Worldwide special interest groups are encouraged, and are not necessarily headquartered in Germany.

SAP has emphasized this trend by the recent restructuring of its alliance program management, which is absolutely critical to its partner-based marketing strategy. This will now be coordinated worldwide by SAP's global partner management group in the U.S.A.

One of the group's first moves, aimed at generating add-on business for partners, was to propose a focus on rolling out existing SAP systems internationally. There are many clients with large potential for this activity.

Independently of SAP's own efforts, the recruitment industry is advertising very much on an international basis. In Europe, SAP ranks among the highest IT specialties in terms of the ratio of international appointments to local ones. This trend can be expected to continue, and as the U.S.A. gets its SAP numbers up, it can expect also a significant "brain drain" to the smaller SAP markets.

For the time being however, the U.S.A. movement is mostly inward. The large U.S. consulting companies are offering high inducements to take people to the U.S.A., as well as to the Eastern Pacific. Contractors and employees moving to the U.S.A. can get good relocation perks as well as high earnings.

More of the international vacancies advertised are for consultants, module configurers, and project leaders than for ABAP programmers, although ABAP does feature to some extent.

Good SAP consultants gain a reputation internationally and can ply their skills in most parts of the world. Those who relocate regularly for the duration of projects can find themselves in a "global village" culture like those that arise in the oil industry, diplomacy, international banking, and other international activities.

If you are looking to join this community, and have the skills to offer to it, you should consider your options carefully and plan to locate where you really want to go. Not all the locations you can end up in are exotic and many are not suitable for taking families. On the other hand, expatriate life can enrich your life enormously. The keys to success are to evaluate carefully the location and the culture (you don't have to go anywhere just for the money in SAP, and the location is probably the most important part of your employment decision), make sure you have the full support of any partner you're taking, and expect it to be different from home. Expatriates who spend a lot of time whining about things the location lacks that they're used to at home are not usually happy or popular.

Those who take the trouble to adapt to "culture shock" and value what other societies can offer are usually very happy, and only compromise their popularity when they get home by overdosing their friends with enthusiastic travelers' tales.

From Here...

In this chapter, you have been introduced to the internationalist aspects of the SAP employment world. You have learned something about SAP global penetration and potential for growth in broad geographic terms.

If you want to look more specifically at any region of special interest to you, you will find that SAP regularly publishes international lists of reference installations, partners, and subsidiaries. You can get these by contacting your nearest SAP subsidiary. (See Appendix A for addresses.) Meanwhile, there are some other parts of this book that will be useful:

- Chapter 40, "Employment Opportunities Working with SAP," includes a section on levels of pay working in SAP, with some examples of salaries advertised for positions around the world. The lack of variation by geography (relative to general wage scales in the countries concerned), and the fact that they all appeared in Europe, indicates the internationality of the SAP workplace.

- Appendix A, "SAP Offices Around the World," and Appendix B, "SAP Business Partners," contain contact addresses for all the countries where SAP operates.

Chapter 39

SAP Workplaces

If you are seeking to work with SAP, or are already doing so but looking for change, this chapter will help you decide how and where your own skills are most marketable. You need to know where the niches exist if you are to find the best one for you.

This chapter provides a guide to the sorts of organizations that employ people with SAP and associated skills. It also describes what these organizations do and how they interrelate in the processes of producing, marketing, and delivering SAP systems.

This chapter starts with an overview of the whole structure—how SAP and its partner companies are held together in a working organization to produce and deliver SAP end systems to users. Then it looks at each of the components—SAP the corporation, the different types of partners that get involved in marketing and implementing SAP systems, and of course the users themselves. Each of these "links in the chain" has its own place in the overall process, which is useful background information when assessing that part of the chain as a potential source of employment.

An Overview of the SAP Working World Structure

SAP could never have reached its market position by simply selling the SAP software as a package and providing just routine technical support. The real salable product is an amalgam of the SAP core product and the consultancy and implementation services that together deliver the benefits of SAP systems to users.

Had SAP tried to provide all these essential value-added services itself it would have been unable to progress beyond the status of a consultant/implementer —with a very good systems-implementation technology, but nonetheless constrained by people resources from achieving the kind of growth that we have seen.

In this chapter, you learn:

- How the SAP extended organization works to deliver its products to the customer.

- What the role is of SAP itself, and how it is structured.

- What the different types of business partners do.

- How SAP certifies complementary products suppliers.

- The roles that anciliary suppliers play

- Who uses SAP.

It was when management consultancies found a strong affinity with the product—saw it as a massive step forward in enabling technology for the vision and change management that is their prime offering—that the product really took off, and burgeoned internationally. The marketing resources that these consultancies have, especially their access to top management in major end user companies, were huge levers on the marketplace, and their position, at base, as suppliers of high order people skills, meant that what was to SAP a potential problem, was to them an opportunity—and vice versa. So a large industry has grown up around marketing and implementing SAP systems, without SAP having to face the investment and growing pains of trying to control it all directly.

SAP people like to refer to the whole infrastructure that creates, markets, and delivers SAP systems to users as the "virtual organization," and this is a quite apt description.

It involves many and various activities, and in the SAP world the people who carry these out may be employed (or contracted) by SAP AG and its subsidiaries, partners of various types, and the end users themselves. They often need to work in "virtual teams" that cross employer boundaries.

Many subsidiary virtual organizations form and reform, often at the project level, including some end user personnel who are seconded into the SAP world only for the project duration—they will return to mainline business management roles after completion.

SAP software is realized on many platforms—database systems as well as OS and hardware platforms—by vendors with whom SAP has partnership agreements. It also extends its capability by providing links with complementary software products, in some cases together with partners. All this means that "ownership" of the virtual organization is further extended.

In this situation, cooperation, rather than hierarchy or proprietorship, rules. Cohesion is achieved through influence, quality control, shared aspirations, communication, and so on, rather than by command. This non-hierarchic, project-orientated approach is popular in many consultancy environments, and it suits the SAP world very well.

The organization as a whole exists to market solutions built from these component products and services:

- The SAP software
- Platform hardware and software
- Complementary products
- Consultancy and implementation services

These are brought together into working SAP solutions at the individual customer level. They can also be combined at levels that mediate between their individual "factories" and the individual customer. For example, at the industry sector level a partner will create a value-added offering to target a vertical market sector.

The main lines show the flow in terms of product delivery. What motivates the parties is the common interest in delivering a product together, but the glue that holds the virtual organization together is more than that. The "binding agents" include:

- Business management
- Quality control
- Information flow
- Concerted marketing effort

SAP does not own the virtual organization in the way a single company owns its organization—nobody owns it in that sense—but SAP leads it, and has the central role in cultivating these binding agents. (Partners of course lead other "virtual organizations," which they drive, and in which SAP is only one contributor, but they are not our topic.) SAP does this in four ways, which will be outlined in the following sections:

- Business management
- Quality control
- Information flow
- Concerted marketing effort

Business Management

Business management is the main difference between the virtual organization and a "real" organization (i.e., one owned by a single company). Within its owned organization a company can command policies, actions, and priorities not only through its statutory rights to do so, but also through financial controls—it holds all the purse strings. SAP has no such control over its virtual organization, so its business management outside its own company walls is exerted by negotiation and contractual arrangements. This is no different from any other company that has marketing partners, but because the partners' value-added services are such a large and integral part of most SAP sales, the SAP partner program and the agreements it incorporates are absolutely central to its operation. The essentials of the different partner agreements are discussed later in this chapter.

Quality Control

Quality control, extending beyond the core product to all the value-added elements, is a major feature for many multi-owned virtual organizations, from IT marketing partner operations to franchised hotel and fast food outlets, and it is also important for SAP. The main planks in SAP's direct quality controls over the extended operation are:

- The partner accreditation process, which accepts only partners who can meet and commit to maintaining SAP's quality standards.

- Customer satisfaction programs. End user satisfaction is regularly monitored, and partners' performance in this respect is visible.

- The complementary solutions certification program, which is designed to ensure that third party solutions interface properly with SAP.

- SAP consultant accreditation. This is a program which SAP is rolling out worldwide, to accredit individual consultants within partner organizations.

Depending on your definition, you might include quality improvement within the term "quality control." Here SAP's main policy is to seek improvement by encouraging the best practice and knowledge transfer, by providing conduits for open interchange of information, and also by providing a good example. SAP is unusual in its openness, and this has placed it in good stead.

Information Flow

SAP has been quick to espouse the "information superhighway," and delivers its "SAP Infoline" service via the World Wide Web, Compuserve, Lotus Notes, and The Microsoft Network. As well as disseminating SAP news and information, the Infoline encourages discussion forums, provides a common medium for any participant in the SAP world to promote itself and share knowledge, and acts as a directory of sources of further information. You can learn a lot more about all these services yourself if you have access to e-mail, by using the Internet e-mail address **infoline@sap-ag.de**. Alternatively you can access the SAP Web page at its URL—**www.sap.com**.

A growing range of "knowledgeware" and general information in multimedia format augments this online information.

For SAP users, The Online Service System (OSS) goes further. SAP introduced it into its R/3 Service System in 1994, and accepted the ten thousandth user of OSS in 1995. OSS provides SAP users with a problem management system with interactive facilities that assist in the whole area of support, commercial facilities (such as course registrations, ordering of documentation), and information.

SAP also engages fully in the "traditional" marketing communications activities. For example, it produces a very informative house magazine, which is recommended reading for anyone seeking to keep informed about the SAP world (SAP "INFO," around 60 pages, published quarterly and available from your nearest SAP subsidiary, which you will find listed in Appendix A, "SAP Offices Around the World"). SAP also participaties in a full international program of events, seminars, conferences, and so on, and channels information through its marketing organization, focused in various ways—by product types, business sectors, and so on.

Good communications are crucial to the SAP operation, and none of the above activities would unify the virtual organization as well as they do without the interpersonal communications skills that the SAP world consistently seeks in its recruits.

Concerted Marketing Effort

From SAP's own point of view, of course, the development of the extended virtual organization is in itself a major marketing effort, but SAP also has to lead the efforts to market the combined output of that organization.

SAP's primary role in this is to provide a broad framework of general marketing directions backed up by investment in strategic marketing resources and image creation. Partners add a lot of input to this process. SAP is not the font of all wisdom, and partner initiatives, stemming from their own experience, often determine strategic directions. SAP is the unifier and a major source, but not the sole source, of marketing creativity.

The drive toward industry-specific, or vertical marketing solutions, and the push into the volume market for mid-sized and smaller companies are examples of major directional thrusts, each of which has many subsidiary threads.

The partner organizations take their cue from these general directions, and build their own focuses to ride with the main thrusts and complement them.

While SAP still handles some end users itself, partners provide the majority of the sales (as opposed to marketing) effort. SAP sales involve high-level decisions, and consultants are well-equipped to influence these. As a SAP alliance manager put it, "Senior executives don't buy products, they buy solutions."

We have been talking basically about achieving marketing cohesion, and one factor that you should not ignore is the importance of the general spirit of cooperation that exists among SAP and its partners. The conduit provided by regular human contact and co-operation at project level is a major factor in creating a cohesive marketing force from the virtual organization.

The structure of the SAP working world, then, is a non-hierarchic, virtual organization. People working in it need to be self-reliant types. It's been said that your boss can be defined as the person who approves your holidays and your salary raises, but in many environments he or she also manages the projects you are working on from month to month. This is not true in much of the SAP virtual organization. Projects are often long and require a lot of commitment, and your project responsibilities are what you have to answer to.

The traditional boss is also a person you can use as a single source "supplier" to get things done or approved. In the virtual organization there is often no one you can use as a one-stop shop in this way. You are expected to use initiative and find the people who can help you get the job done. That's one of the reasons why good communication skills are so highly valued. It's also one of the reasons that people with the right attributes find the SAP world so satisfying.

SAP—The Company

SAP's corporate structure is less important than how well it manages the aforementioned activities, because its policy is not to over-manage the subsidiaries, but rather to put in place the standards and strategic policies, and then give the subsidiaries substantial autonomy to run the business within them.

The broad structure is as shown in Figure 39.1. The individual subsidiary shown is that of the UK, which is a good example, as it is neither in the very top or the bottom rank in importance, penetration, or potential. Structures vary from country to country, but most of the functions shown will appear in one guise or another in most subsidiaries.

Bear in mind that the subsidiaries handle some direct end user accounts as well as support partner activities. The consulting groups have a major role in this, though they also combine in "virtual teams" with partner consultants. The motivation behind direct sales is to meet customer preference for this, where it exists, and to keep in touch with the battlefront. SAP charges for its consultancy services, but the objective of the SAP consulting group is not to generate revenue from consulting, but rather to maximize product sales.

It is worth expanding a little on one or two of the roles within the consulting group:

- **Project advisors** act as customer service managers, but at the project rather than the account level.

- **Product managers** are experts in particular modules. They "champion" these modules internally, and act as a conduit between SAP Headquarters at Walldorf and the client on anything related to those modules.

- **Application consultants** are the largest group, accounting for some 40 percent of a subsidiaries headcount. The applications they specialize in are "horizontal" ones—i.e., not so much industry-specific as function-specific, and they perform configurations to ensure that the required functionality is built in to end user systems.

- **Basis consultants** deal with the underlying systems components and tools. They are concerned with such things as datacoms, operating systems, databases, and ABAP programming.

If you are looking for employment opportunities in an SAP subsidiary, you will find in Appendix D several example role descriptions for the sorts of positions subsidiaries have, and these will give a good picture of the attributes required.

Essentially, SAP needs its own people to have all the SAP consultant skills in sufficient quantity to set the standards that it promotes among the partners. This applies both to technical expertise as well as interpersonal skills. In the early days SAP consultants came out of the development team, and SAP will rarely employ anyone in a consulting role unless that person has good SAP experience. The ideal is that SAP people should be able to solve problems that have escalated from partner and end user consultants. They should also be able to pass on their skills, so training capability is desired.

The area where SAP has found it beneficial to engage people from outside the SAP world is in marketing roles, where SAP has learned from the recruits as well as taught them.

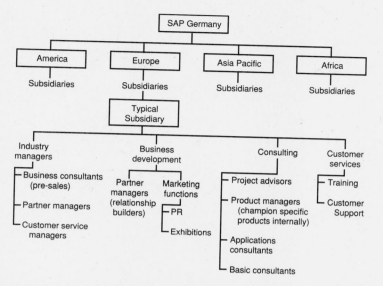

Fig. 39.1 The structure of a typical SAP subsidiary shows the roles it carries out and how people are organized to fulfill them.

SAP Business Partners

SAP has employed the partner program in the context of a global strategy (which has succeeded) aimed at making SAP the global market leader for standard applications. This has involved accreting a tremendous range of capability, quickly.

The program is founded on the philosophy that strategic alliances are a better way to develop and acquire new strengths than going it alone or buying up other companies. When individual companies bring their particular abilities into a partnership alliance, they get faster exploitation of the synergies without becoming wrapped up in the mechanics (or financial implications) of mergers, takeovers, and large scale management change.

SAP believes that this approach can give a company a competitive edge, but an essential precondition for success is, as expressed in its partner handbook, "the planned creation and development of a superior ability to cooperate in terms of a cooperative and dependable approach on the part of employees and an organizational structure that encourages cooperation."

The philosophy further says that to make this work, everyone involved must constantly seek ways to cooperate and think in terms of the collective benefits, rather than narrow partisan advantages. They must constantly strive to develop a mutual understanding of each other's situations and aims.

If this sounds like a string of platitudes, don't be misled. It is a very real policy that works. SAP must be at least a contender for the title "Most Effective Marketer through Partnerships in the IT World." While a lot of that success is due to having a product that partners want, SAP's approach to the partner relationship has also been crucial, and its consistent pursuit of cooperation and communication at the individual employee level is the cornerstone of that.

The partner program is organized, in broad terms, as shown in Figure 39.2. The relationship management aspects are handled via an alliance manager structure, headed in the USA by global alliance management, which manages the alliances with partners who have Global Logo status, as well as directs the activities of the SAP regional and national alliance managers, who have direct "line responsibility" to the subsidiaries or regions where they are employed.

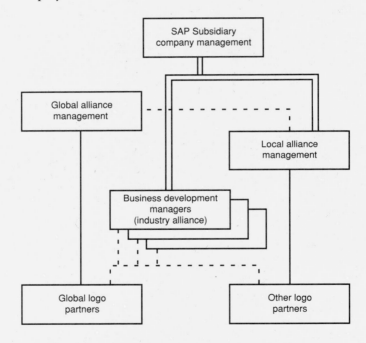

Fig. 39.2   Global alliance management works through locally employed alliance management groups, but directly manages the "Global Logo" partners.

The relationship management aspects are substantial. Partner companies usually restructure their own organizations to best realize cooperative potential, and the contractual rights and obligations are intended to secure commitment to clear strategic goals understood by both parties, as well as operational ones, such as customer satisfaction.

As well as the alliance managers, partners have direct access to the industry-aligned business development managers, who are their first port of call to keep coordinated with, and informed on, the activities of other partners and SAP itself within given industry groupings. This is being instituted worldwide at the time of this writing, in line with the increasing verticalization of SAP's marketing.

The partner program has worked well so far for the partners and SAP alike. The partners have given SAP a better understanding of the "corporate change" market, market penetration and leverage, and extended resources. SAP has given consultants an enabling technology. Consultants sell "vision," and SAP is the enabling technology for realizing that vision, which is why the synergy between SAP and consultancy organizations is so strong. As SAP goes from strength to strength, and more end users become aware of its potential, it positively creates a demand for change (and therefore consultants) as well as helping to realize that change.

This provides the classic "win/win" scenario. SAP executives like to extend this, and talk of a "win/win/win" philosophy. In other words, an arrangement has to benefit the customer, as well as SAP and the partner.

The main partner types in the SAP world are platform partners, technology partners, consulting partners, systems resellers, and complementary products partners.

Platform Partners

Platform partner relationships are in place with the major hardware vendors who implement some form of UNIX operating system, and some Windows NT specialists. AT&T, Bull Information Systems, Compaq, Data General, Digital Equipment Corporation, Hewlett Packard, IBM, Sequent, Siemens Nixdorf Information Systems, and SUN are all SAP hardware platform partners.

The main requisite for platform partners is to obtain platform certification by SAP (or iXOS on SAP's behalf in the case of NT systems), but in fact the level of cooperation runs far deeper than that.

SAP sets up joint R/3 competence centers with its platform partners, either in Walldorf or appropriate subsidiaries, and these, apart from migrating R/3 to the vendors' platforms, provide a nerve center for cooperation across a wide spectrum of activity—marketing strategies, sales team activities, events, and mutual training among them.

Some of the platform partners are also consulting, implementation, technology, and/or complementary products partners. IBM, for example, has accreditation in all categories.

Part of the attraction to SAP in forming these relationships is the access it gives SAP to the far larger national and international sales, distribution, and support networks that these hardware vendors have, compared to SAP. This may be an attraction to employees also. Something like 20 percent of SAP vacancies in some recruitment outfits emanate from hardware vendors.

If you are a SAP consultant seeking a change of environment, this is a fruitful area to consider. Virtually any of the whole range of SAP skills may find a home. If you are seeking to gain your first experience in SAP and finding it difficult, you may find a platform supplier will open the door, if you have experience that it wants in a technology other than SAP. The best route is to first get the platform partner to employ you, then wait until you are entrenched and valued before seeking to divert yourself into its SAP activities.

Technology Partners

Technology partners are mainly the big database players, together with a few hardware vendors. Partners include Apple Computer Inc., Hewlett Packard, IBM, Informix, Intel, iXOS Software, Microsoft, Oracle, Platinum Technology, Siemens Nixdorf Information Systems, and Software AG.

Each technology partner agreement is based on an individual contract, and the focus is to exchange knowledge and engage in common activities to optimize the use of SAP and the partners' products together. These agreements secure essential technological underpinnings, such as databases and systems tools.

SAP-based activities in technology partners are more specialized and less wide-ranging than they are in platform partners.

They are nonetheless quite committed. Microsoft has had a strategic cooperation agreement with SAP since 1993. Windows NT is a strategic product for SAP and it has signed an agreement with Microsoft to jointly develop Internet strategy. Oracle has been involved since the development of R/3 in 1987, and claims that SAP implementations are based up to 75 percent upon Oracle. iXOS, as well as concerning itself with its imaging and archiving software, provides SAP with systems testing services, notably for the certification of Windows NT platforms.

As an employment prospect for the experienced SAP consultant with technical leanings who is ideally skilled in some other area of relevance, you might find a high premium on your ability to bring SAP into the particular fold of a technology partner, while for the would-be SAP entrant, the story is much the same as it is with platform partners. You will need to have something to offer that meets a partner requirement, and use that as your ticket.

Consulting Partners

Consulting partners are also known as logo partners, and there are three levels, which are outlined in the following sections:

- Global logo partners
- Regional logo partners
- National logo partners

Global Logo Partners. A global logo partner operates in the same way in all SAP geographical regions, and maintains a consistent infrastructure for the support of globally active R/3 customers. The partner must qualify for regional logo partner status in at least two SAP regions, and the global partnership is managed by SAP global alliance management, based in the USA.

Each global partner is entitled to use the logo "R/3 International Consulting Partner/ Global."

Global logo partners include the major management consulting firms Andersen Consulting, Coopers & Lybrand, Ernst & Young, ICS (Deloitte & Touche Consulting Group), KPMG, and Price Waterhouse, as well as such hardware vendors as Digital Equipment, Hewlett Packard, IBM, and IT specialists CSC, EDS, and Origin.

Regional Logo Partners. A regional logo partner operates mainly in one SAP geographic region, and maintains a regional infrastructure that corresponds with its SAP activities. The partner must qualify for national partner status in a certain number of countries, which varies by region—for example two countries in the Americas region, four countries in Asia, and so on. The partnership is managed by alliance management at the regional level.

Each regional partner is entitled to use the logo "R/3 International Consulting Partner/ Europe" (or /Asia, /Americas, /Africa as appropriate).

National Logo Partners. A national logo partner operates mainly in one country, and has to meet the requirements of that country's SAP national cooperation agreement, which would typically include a satisfactory business plan, a minimum number of R/3 consultants, and a regular audit. The partnership is managed by the local SAP subsidiary, normally via the national alliance manager.

Each national partner is entitled to use the logo "R/3 Consulting Partner/France" (with the SAP national affiliation on the end).

The logo partners are a prime source of employment opportunity, for those with the right skills and qualifications. Broadly speaking there are two opportunity areas.

First, your career as a management consultant is more important than the SAP involvement. The large consultancies especially like to recruit and develop people with longer-term aims. This is discussed more in Chapter 41, "How to Find Employment Working with SAP," where the general message is to think management consultancy, not SAP, when approaching the global logo partners. Some of the national and regional logo partners are entirely dedicated to SAP, so you need to find out how much of a SAP specialist a partner is, and how much a management consultant, before deciding how promising they are for you, and what your best line of attack is.

Most of the logo partners have SAP training and induction programs, and this trend is growing, so the route is good for new SAP entrants with good management consultant attributes, especially if these are backed up by some sort of IT expertise.

The second opportunity area with logo partners is for people with SAP skills to develop and widen their horizons. All of the logo partners will be interested in SAP experience.

A particular area as of mid-1996, and likely to continue for some time, is the drive by some global partners to recruit internationally to service the big SAP growth in the USA and the Pacific Rim. The urgency of this is overriding the general recruitment priorities described earlier, and they are usually looking for specific SAP skills to fill an immediate need. If you have these skills, they can provide the entry into an environment which can lead to broader opportunities.

If you are reading this outside the USA and want to work there, here is a generalized profile for SAP people recruited overseas into the USA for a "big six" consultancy. It's not "written in stone," and other international recruiters will vary a little, but it provides a rough scoresheet to help you to assess your prospects.

- **Age**—28 to 35 is best. The large consultancies find it easier to induct younger people into their culture. Even within this range, nearing the top end you will be required to have more experience, particularly in project or module leadership. Above the range you will have to be exceptional, and there is a near disbarment for persons past their 40s.

- **Marital Status**—Single people are generally preferred due to their greater flexibility when it comes to travel. If you are married, or have other familial attachments, consider and be prepared to explain to the employer how they will deal with travel, any U.S. work interests, and so on.

- **SAP Experience**—The consultancy for whom this profile was prepared asked for a minimum two years of hands-on implementation experience, and experience in configuring SAP in a relevant area. (Sales order management and distribution, financial, and/or manufacturing were the relevant areas to this consultancy's immediate needs.)

  You will need a sound understanding of the tables and transactions in your area of expertise, and a working knowledge of SAP module integration and the typical issues involved in interfacing with other systems.

  R/3 experience is highly desirable. People who have functioned in an SAP consulting role are preferable, because they understand the professional services role better. Working in a project rather than a transaction environment is preferred. People with SAP experience only from a user perspective normally lack the ability to configure the system, and would have to provide evidence that they can do so.

- **SAP Training**—You should have undertaken at least four SAP courses in your area of implementation experience.

- **Intelligence**—People of high intelligence (which as a rule of thumb can be taken as meaning an IQ within the top 10 percent of the population) are required. This is considered likely to make you quickly learn the client's situation, be analytical, take broad perspectives but also delve into detail, think on a conceptual level but understand the practical implications, have a questioning mind, and always be looking to do things better.

- **Interpersonal**—You should be a good listener, like to work with others, be able to build good relationships, be empathetic, and function well as part of a team.

- **Communication**—English language skills are essential. Candidates must be able to understand and speak English well in a work environment. Equally important is that they can communicate ideas clearly and succinctly.

- **Motivation**—People who are enthusiastic, who take charge, have direction, plan and control their actions to meet deadlines, and in general are very results-oriented have a good opportunity.

The international recruitment drive is not only aimed at senior SAP consultants and project managers, but also targets people with more specific skills, such as applications engineers and module configurers.

Some logo partners are more specifically oriented towards IT and less toward general management consultancy. Indeed, as mentioned earlier, some are exclusively devoted to SAP.

These more "IT-based" partners, while still requiring the right personality type and the ability to deal with senior management concerns, tend to focus a little more on the traditional IT system house virtues. This extract from a job requirements statement is a good example. (The full version is in Appendix C, "Sample SAP-Related Job Descriptions.")

Candidates should have:

> Worked in pre/post sales support
>
> Implemented several large IT projects in commercial organizations
>
> Worked in consultancy or with a specialist software house
>
> Ideally trained in R/3, have R/2 experience, and/or have comparable product experience
>
> Extensive knowledge of the appropriate application area (in the case from which this example was extracted, appropriate areas were financial accounting systems, logistics/material management, and/or manufacturing)
>
> Overall experience of large commercial implementations which would be expected to extend over five years

Implementation Partners

These are sometimes referred to as another case of consulting partners, and the cooperation agreement for implementation partners is regarded as the first step to becoming a logo partner.

The relationship does not include the intensive support and cooperation that logo partners enjoy, but allows a consultancy firm to gain access to the SAP marketplace and the SAP provided infrastructure (demonstration system, documentation, training facilities, and so on). The qualification process for a partner is less onerous, but the partner must maintain appropriate capability—for example, dedicated SAP consultants and demonstration capability.

You will find much the same employment opportunities in implementation partners as in logo partners, and some of them have put a lot of creativity into developing their SAP business.

R/3 System Resellers

System resellers engage in the promotion and sale of R/3 itself. They must develop value-added software themselves, and have a product of their own which might be complementary to SAP R/3 or be replaceable by it. They also must have sales, consulting, training, and support resources in place before being accepted as an R/3 system reseller.

At mid-1996, resellers were still restricted to a few companies, mostly operating in Germany and the immediate environs. By late 1996, a global strategy was starting to emerge, in countries like those within the UK, where a number of resellers have been appointed, with special skills in promising areas, notably manufacturing.

This development is worth watching as it advances globally, because it will open all kinds of new employment opportunities.

Complementary Product Suppliers

The design of the SAP R/3 system—its inherent modularity, and its position as the world's leading client/server product—makes it an attractive vehicle for many third-party software developers.

SAP has encouraged this by the interface technologies it has used in R/3: Application Link Enabling (ALE), Object Linking and Embedding (OLE), Remote Function Calls (RFCs), and Open Database Connectivity.

SAP certifies third-party products for connection to its various R/3 interfaces, and these are categorized as follows (the SAP interfaces are in parentheses):

> Archive Software/Imaging Software (SAP ArchiveLink *R*)
>
> Computer-aided Design (CAD)
>
> EDI Subsystems (WF-EDI)
>
> Plant Data Collection (PP-PDC)
>
> Product Data Management (CAD)
>
> Process Control Systems (PI-PCS)
>
> Machine Data Collection (PP-PDC)
>
> Laboratory Information Management Systems (QM-IDI)

Third party solution providers with products in these categories that are either certified or awaiting certification are listed in Appendix H, "Complementary Solutions."

These are mostly in Germany, in line with SAP's history, but some are in the USA and the UK, and more are expected to come from these countries and elsewhere, in line with its present and future.

As well as certified solutions, there are a number of complementary solutions that are not subject to certification. These are primarily used in conjunction with communications services. Both R/2 and R/3 systems allow access to these services directly from within the SAP system, and add-on product suppliers have developed in the following areas:

Electronic Mail

Fax, Telex, Teletext

Sending and Receiving EDI Documents

Telephony

Again, you can find addresses for product suppliers in these categories in Appendix H, "Complementary Solutions."

As a source of employment, the complementary solutions providers as a group offer a tremendously wide scope, although individually they are often highly specialized. They offer a "bridging opportunity" for SAP-experienced people seeking to divert from the mainstream SAP world and advance up to another area of specialty, and also for SAP entrants to go the other way, using another skill to move into SAP.

Those people more interested in technicalities than using interpersonal and business skills will have a better chance of progression in a complementary solutions niche than in most places in the SAP world.

Ancillary Service Providers

Ancillary service providers are independent companies that provide support services to the SAP market that contribute to the "SAP Virtual World." Details of companies offering ancillary services can be seen in Appendix C.

Employment Agencies/Recruitment Consultants

People are the most valuable resources in the SAP working world. It is therefore not surprising that there has been explosive growth in the number of firms specializing in recruiting contract and permanent SAP workers.

Documentation Specialists

Because each system is independently configured, there is a need to develop company-specific training and user documentation.

When the project teams have disbanded, the documentation produced offers a lasting record of what has been done and how the system should be used.

As most companies implementing SAP will be operating a quality management program, there is frequently a need to update procedures, guidelines, roles, and responsibilities. There are also disaster recovery plans and other kinds of system documentation that need to be produced.

Human Issues Consultants

SAP is inextricably linked with BPR and change. There are many human issues which need to be addressed from structuring the right project team to dealing with change, uncertainty, and stress. Human issues consultancy is a field of activity which is evolving as a specialist area within the management change activity. Human issues consultants help to identify potential problem areas related to psychological responses to change, and propose strategies for avoiding them. They also troubleshoot and offer counselling and reconciliation services when problems have arisen. The objective is to retain morale and team spirit through potentially testing times.

Good human issues consultants will be worth their fees many times over.

Security and Control Consultants

SAP security and control is a specialist area that requires specialist knowledge. Any software system has its own characteristics from the perspectives of data and systems security, and SAP security and control consultants need to know SAP well from these standpoints, as well as being expert in the general field of security and control. They also have to understand any special security and control considerations of the particular platform and complementary technologies that an individual client may be using.

Internal and External Communications Consultants

Communications form a vital element in the running of an SAP project and managing the change in an organization.

Training Providers

Training is needed for project team members, management, and users alike. Some is available off the shelf from SAP itself and other companies, but there is always a requirement for company-specific training.

Company-specific training for users is normally required over a very short period of time, when sufficient system development has been completed and before the going live date.

Project Planning Consultants

SAP projects require the highest level of project management skills. The planning and control role is often best delegated to a well-focused professional team who can work with SAP's "Project System" as well as other project-management tools.

System Testing Consultants

Integrated and volume testing are the greatest indicators of project progress and readiness to go live. They create, however, a logistical nightmare, both in planning and execution.

There are companies which specialize in planning test programs and arranging the resourcing.

Career Management Specialists

This is a new service that is being pioneered by Rivermead Associates in the UK. (You can reach this service by e-mail at **rivermead@globalnet.co.uk**.) It is a career management service acting as an agent for SAP consultants wishing to operate as a business in consortium with others. It claims this will maximize consultants' earnings and options while providing a secure career path.

SAP Users

You can consider the end users as part of the SAP virtual organization because of the way that they merge into virtual teams with SAP's and the partners' people.

End users employ a range of skills that extend further down the scales into support roles and business analysis roles. They also make more use of ABAP programmers than other parts of the SAP world, because ABAP is mainly used to make minor systems adjustments, rather than in the main installation phase of a project. They also employ or contract higher level SAP skills—from senior SAP consultants to configurers. This varies from user to user, some passing almost total responsibility to their SAP partner/installer, and others choosing to resource their own team, recruiting individual employees or contractors themselves.

There is usually a strong input, often including the project manager, from end users' own business management and IT teams. People seconded across to the SAP project are intended to return to the mainstream after it is completed, and usually find they have enhanced their career prospects because of their experience in the SAP world.

Some (usually from an IT background) don't return to their employer's mainstream, but instead divert to a SAP career—consultants and SAP itself recruit many of their people from end users. End user management finds this easier to bear when the defector goes to SAP itself or the installing partner, because at least the person's knowledge is not totally lost. Cases have been known where employers have deliberately encouraged SAP to recruit key people, as the lesser of two evils, knowing of the impending possibility of those people being recruited to work halfway across the globe.

If you are a systems person and your company is looking at installing SAP, you are in the right place at the right time.

If you have key project management or configuring skills in SAP, you can command a premium, in terms of cash or career progression, with installing end users.

If short-term cash is your goal, then contracting is probably the best answer, whether you organize it yourself or go through an agency. Employers can pay contractors what it's worth to the project, which they can't do with employees without upsetting corporate payscales. Because SAP contracts can be so long, contractors have the chance to get the best of both worlds—getting paid for taking the free-lance contractor's risk without actually taking much of it.

If you are more interested in building a career in management, you'll find it better to commit yourself to an employer. Not only will this give you the chance to use the project to lever yourself up the particular employer's management ladder, but it will also look much better on your résumé for future purposes.

Profile of the User Population—Who Uses SAP

SAP's customers include many of the world's largest "blue chip" organizations, among whom it is the predominant standard application software. It has now started to make inroads into mid-sized companies (roughly speaking, those with less than $100 million turnover).

From its origins in the chemical industry, it has spread over a vast range of industry, as Figure 39.3 illustrates.

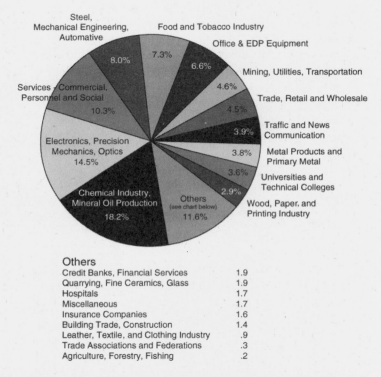

Others

Credit Banks, Financial Services	1.9
Quarrying, Fine Ceramics, Glass	1.9
Hospitals	1.7
Miscellaneous	1.7
Insurance Companies	1.6
Building Trade, Construction	1.4
Leather, Textile, and Clothing Industry	.9
Trade Associations and Federations	.3
Agriculture, Forestry, Fishing	.2

Fig. 39.3 The distribution of SAP installations by industry in mid-1995 still bears some evidence of SAP's origins in the chemical industry, but a strong presence in a wide range of industries has developed.

The figure shows the distribution of installations across industry sectors as of May 1995, based upon SAP's published list of reference installations (after excluding partners and consultancies). Installations were spread across 53 countries all around the world.

SAP has enjoyed massive growth since May 1995, so the overall volume will have increased significantly, but the distribution by industry will not have changed so much, and studying it will give you a good insight into the industries where SAP employment is to be found.

Emerging User Marketplace—The Next Generation of Users

The two main market thrusts which will affect the customer base are:

- The drive into middle sized and smaller companies
- Vertical marketing initiatives

These are discussed further in Chapter 42, "The Outlook for the SAP Employment Market," but it's worth mentioning here that SAP has currently earmarked banking, hospitals, oil industry, retail, public sector, publishers, and utilities for special attention. These are mostly areas where SAP already has a good foothold, and they are fairly broad areas.

Partners are picking up on the vertical market thrust and looking for niches in more specific areas, such as the beverage industry, estate administration, laboratory systems, and so on.

The next generation of users can be expected to be smaller, and more specialized, and they will not expect to bear the extended installation times and costs that the giants have. You can also expect them to be engaging in intercompany systems access with the larger companies in their own vertical supply chain, many of which will already be using SAP. It may well be that this development, which combines elements of both the mid-sized company and vertical marketing drives, will be a dominating feature of systems fashion in the next few years, and will have a profound effect on the pattern of employment in SAP.

From Here...

In this chapter you have learned about the way the SAP world is structured, and what the various players in it do. You have also learned broadly what that structure means for it as an employment market, and gained an insight into where particular kinds of employment exist.

- In case you haven't already read Chapter 38, "Globalization of the SAP Employment Market," you can learn a bit more there about the geographic disposition of SAP employment, and the prospects for international travel that it offers.

- In Chapter 40, "Employment Opportunities Working with SAP," you can learn how to map your own skills to the needs of SAP employers. This chapter will give you some more detail about some of the functions you can fill, the skills they require, and the job titles that they carry in the SAP world.

- In Chapter 41, "How to Find Employment Working with SAP," you can gain some useful advice on the actual process of finding employment in SAP, which will be particularly useful if you haven't worked with SAP before. Appendix C, "Sample SAP-Related Job Descriptions," contains some example job descriptions which do not require previous SAP experience.

- In Chapter 42, "The Outlook for the SAP Employment Market," you can learn in more depth about the outlook for the future in SAP employment, and where the new jobs will arise. You can also learn to evaluate how the major trends will change the nature of SAP jobs and how they will affect supply and demand.

- In Appendix A, "SAP Offices Around the World," Appendix B, "SAP Business Partners," and Appendix H, "Complementary Solutions," you will find contact addresses for many organizations. These are classified (by partner type and so on) so that you can see where they fit into the structure you have learned in this chapter.

- Appendix C, "Sample SAP-Related Job Descriptions," provides some real-life examples of job descriptions.

Chapter 40

Employment Opportunities Working with SAP

Chapter 39, "SAP Workplaces," looked at how the SAP world is structured, and some of the general prerequisites for entering different parts of it.

This chapter will help you match your skills and aspirations to the activities and roles that exist within the SAP structure. It will then give you some guidance on what it takes to succeed in SAP terms, and what you can expect to earn by doing so.

Table 40.1 lays out the essential functions that have to take place in bringing SAP systems to the customer, and some of the special skills that are brought to bear on them. It uses a generalized set of function and skill descriptions that will be understood by everyone. This is so that you can map into it, on one hand the skills that you have (or would like to develop), and on the other the various job titles and activity descriptions used by potential employers. In other words, it serves as a common language interface.

In this chapter, you learn:

- The essential functions that the SAP world carries out, and the skills it needs to do so.

- How to classify your own skills and recognize their usefulness to the SAP world.

- To familiarize with the language of the marketplace and recognize how service-providing partners describe what they do.

- What some frequently used job titles mean.

- What it takes to succeed in the SAP world.

- The levels of pay you can expect working in SAP.

Table 40.1   Special Skills and Experiences Required for Each SAP Function (Scale: Blank=Not Required, 1=Beginning, 2=Intermediate, 3=Advanced)

Function	Vertical Business Sector Knowledge	Business Function Knowledge	Special Knowledge of the Technology	Systems Analysis Skills	Program-ming Skills
Developing the SAP Core Product	2	3	2	2	3
Extending Platforms and Interfaced Technologies			3	1	3
Extending the SAP Product with Solutions	3	2	1	3	3

(continues)

Function	Vertical Business Sector Knowledge	Business Function Knowledge	Special Knowledge of the Technology	Systems Analysis Skills	Program-ming Skills
Management Consulting	3	3	1	2	
Project Management	1	3	1	2	
Business Analysis	2	3	2	3	1
Fitting Business Needs with SAP	2	3	1	3	1
Modeling, Configuring, and Testing	2	3	2	1	1
ABAP Modifications	1	3	3	2	3
Installing "The User" (Documentation, Support, and Testing)	2	2	2	3	
Ongoing Technical Support		2	3	1	2
Systems Administration and Management	2	2	2	2	1

Table 40.1   Continued

The functions and the skills mapped out in Table 40.1 are worth a little closer examination.

Functions—In Producing, Selling, Implementing, and Using SAP

Developing the SAP core product is the prime job of the development group at Walldorf, together with the smaller development group in the USA and other outposts. The core product includes the modules programmed in ABAP using the development workbench and the workbench itself. Some localized foreign language versions are being developed with "country partners," for example in Korea.

Extending Platforms and Interfaced Technology

SAP developers work together with platform partners to port SAP onto new platforms and thereby add value in the shape of special platform benefits. Complementary solution providers create interfaces to SAP, which SAP tests and certifies thus extending the SAP capability to embrace the special benefits of each complementary solution.

Extending the SAP Product with Solutions

SAP produces some vertical market modules, such as Industry Solutions—Oil and R/3 Retail, as part of its development activities. In addition, some consultancy partners are adding value in the shape of vertical market solutions. This whole vertical market product activity is a growth area. Complementary solutions providers are not usually vertical market solutions, but more technical ones, such as data storage or data communications systems. A company has to have a marketable solution in place before it will interest SAP, so to the complementary solution partner it is more a case of adding SAP to the solution, rather than the solution to SAP, but it extends SAP's capability nonetheless.

Management Consultancy

SAP partners, especially the larger logo partners, are heavily centered on management consultancy. Their contribution in strategic vision, change management, and BPR is a significant part of the virtual organization's overall business. SAP subsidiaries also perform management consultancy for their direct accounts, and the Walldorf development team gets involved in this with German customers.

Project Management

Project management may be provided by all levels in the SAP supply chain, from SAP itself through all partner types to the end-user. End-users may choose to appoint their own project manager, and resource the project without handing over implementation responsibility to a partner.

Business Analysis

When we refer to business analysis here, what we mean is analysis of business needs at the individual project or client level. (Elsewhere in the book you will see mentioned a marketing role of "business analyst," which is not quite the same thing. As a marketing role it is concerned with analyzing the needs of a whole marketplace.) All consultants, employed anywhere from Walldorf through the whole subsidiary, partner, and end-user chain, need to have some business analysis skills, and each project requires them in a pertinent industry.

Fitting Business Needs with SAP

This is an activity that demands a combination of SAP knowledge and business knowledge. It fits the business needs (identified by management consultancy and business analysis) with the configurability of SAP, to arrive at an optimum solution. The optimum solution is one that gets as close as possible to the ideal working system for the user, without imposing excessive or avoidable demands for customization of SAP modules.

Modeling, Configuring, and Testing

Configuring is the really crucial skill that can only be acquired with SAP training and experience. It is right on the critical path for SAP's business development. SAP is putting considerable investment into providing tools to lighten the task, but the complex nature of the product suite means that skilled configurers will always be in demand.

ABAP Modifications

ABAP programmers are often employed by end-users directly. They are usually engaged in making minor modifications after implementation. (The majority of implementations are done without ABAP programming upfront.) Less usually, a substantial module modification will be specified at implementation time, occasioning an ABAP design effort. Some partners do employ ABAP programmers, and supply their services to clients for all purposes; this is also a fruitful area for contracting houses.

"Installing the User"—Documentation, Training, and Support

Hardware and software do not make a working business system by themselves. The people who use the system, provide input, and operate it are important components, as are the surrounding manual systems that they use. Helping to train and support the users is often part and parcel of a systems analyst's work, but special roles may be created to handle these tasks in some companies.

Ongoing Technical Support

First level technical support is usually provided by the implementing partner to the end-user, who in turn receives second level support from SAP. SAP provides first level support to its direct end-user customers.

The SAP Walldorf development team gets involved in support, providing guidance on maintenance levels, release procedures, and so on, and the support activity overlaps with marketing to some extent in the SAP subsidiaries.

Systems Administration and Management

End-users normally keep responsibility for ongoing systems administration and management, and involve their mainstream management in the function (although they can also outsource the function from partners). From the users a so-called "super-user" will often emerge, who understands how SAP "thinks" and knows how to get the best out of it, and ensure that it meshes with the surrounding procedures and objectives. This person can be very useful in making systems run smoothly, and may progress into SAP consultancy.

Apart from the general capability to carry out the preceding functions, some special skills are required, which cut across the functional lines.

In Table 40.1, these are grouped into broad skill types and cross-referenced to the main functions, according to what level each skill is required to carry out the function well. They are worth exploring a little further.

Skills Required to Perform Functions

Vertical business sector knowledge is needed at all levels, to a greater or lesser extent. SAP has developed by gaining practical field experience, taking it back up the supply chain, incorporating it into the product at "factory level" where possible, and distributing it with the product back down the supply chain. This practical field experience includes vertical market experience.

Business Function Knowledge (Module Application Knowledge)

Again the need for this arises at all levels. The product is based around a defined set of business functions and the modules aligned with them. The remarks made on vertical business sector knowledge apply equally here.

Special Knowledge of Other Technology

Apart from the platform technology development arena, a need for knowledge of particular technologies can arise at the individual project level, because of the variety of platform systems and interfaced systems that users may have. Where such a need does arise, both end-users and partners will seek to recruit special technical skills. The job specifications in Appendix C, "Sample SAP-Related Job Descriptions," show examples of this.

Systems Analysis Skills

These are the essential skills that interface on one hand, user management—its operational objectives, constraints, and priorities with—and on the other hand, SAP and the implementation process. They are valuable in virtually all functional stages, but especially from the stage where SAP implementation is agreed upon.

Programming Skills

As with many other 4GLs, the ABAP programming and the analysis/design skills often reside in the same people. Where this is not the case, then the analyst needs an appreciation of programming and vice versa. But practical programming skills are only a strict necessity when the systems analysis yields a requirement for ABAP programming.

There are many specialities within each of the preceding skill types—as many as there are permutations of vertical markets, business functions, other technologies, and areas of systems and programming experience.

How SAP Partners Describe Their Services

Similarly, the function titles in Table 40.1 are boiled down from the kaleidoscopic variety of descriptions the SAP world uses to describe its activities.

That boiling down makes analysis manageable, but robs the descriptions of their variety and "color." You can only get that by looking at examples. The list that follows shows a (far from exhaustive) sample of ways that partners describe the SAP-related services they perform. Each partner will include anything from 6 to 20 or more of these in its brochure. Looking at them all together, and mixing the superficial descriptions with the more detailed ones, gives a clearer picture of the activity spectrum, and what the descriptions mean, though the sample does not aspire to be a glossary.

Remember that service suppliers in the real world are more concerned with differentiating themselves, and suggesting special benefits of their particular offerings, than they are with fitting neatly into your paradigm.

Even if you can't really classify all of the real-life descriptions, you'll find that just being aware of them helps when reading literature produced by SAP employers. You will be more comfortable with the terminology and better placed to probe confidently.

- ABAP programming from customer specifications or as part of project
- Act as either project manager or prime contractor
- Activity plans with date and effort control mechanisms
- Assessment of migration impact
- Assume full responsibility for R/3 projects and the integration of complementary products and services into a complete customer specific solution
- Basis consulting
- BPR consulting
  - Define specific improvement objectives
  - Redesign business operations in ways to help achieve the objectives
  - Define the new business processes to support the new operations
  - Manage the implementation of the solution and drive this through into SAP implementation
- BPR consulting
  - Business Change Management Consulting
  - Assess degree of change requirement
  - Design framework for change
  - Identify components of change program
  - Develop detailed plans for change
  - Drive through into changes/enhancement requirements of the SAP systems
- Business operations analysis
- Business Reengineering
- Business Workgroup Performance Consulting
  - Align workgroup process with business improvement objectives
  - Define operation of workgroups to enable objectives to be met
  - Assess information required, expertise of workgroup members, training, and tools needed
  - Plan and manage the improvements
  - Software and technical training

- start-up support
- maintenance, fine tuning
- development of additional applications
- help desk, FM services

■ Change management

■ Client specific module expansion/modification

■ Concurrent Transformation (concurrently reengineer your processes with SAP R/3 installation)

■ Configuration design

■ Configuration management

■ Contingency planning and disaster recovery

■ Conversions

■ Customization

■ Database workshops

■ Data migration and coexistence management

■ Data transfer or supply of interfaces to link up with remote systems

■ Data Warehouse consulting

■ Database design and programming

■ Design and establish new IT infrastructure

■ Design of framework for change

■ Develop individual applications with R/3

■ Development of common standards and architecture for SAP projects

■ Development of industry templates, prepackaged configurations, and tools

■ EDI integration services

■ Estimation of implementation effort

■ Evaluation consulting

■ Hardware and Network configuration, design, implementation, and management

■ Hardware services

■ Implementation

■ Industry solutions

- Integration Advocacy programs
- Integration of R/3 business processes
- Integration with legacy systems
- Logical and physical Database design
- Long term support provision
- Management of backups, recovery, scheduling, and output for R/3 systems
- Migration change control
- Monitor production environment
- Monitor R/3 project status
- Needs analysis
- Network integration services
- Network security administration
- Optimize balance between Business/organization needs and R/3 functionality
- OPMS (Online Project Management System)
- Optimize systems availability
- Performance analysis
- Performance optimization
- Planning, management, and implementation of migration tools
- Private lessons onsite or remote
- Process alignment
- Process improvement to an optimum
- Produce conversion and interface link programs for legacy systems
- Production handover and training
- Project management
- Provide integrated performance support software environment
- Release upgrades
- Remote development facility linked to SAP R/3 Workbench
- Remote R/3 preventative maintenance and diagnosis
- SAP concepts Education Workshop
- Service level agreements

- Software and technology selection
- Structured methodology
- Submit back-up/recovery concepts
- System and Network management
- Systems cloning (for example, split R/3 for demerging companies)
- System configuration checking
- Systems Integration
- Systems performance monitoring, control, and improvement
- Technology consultancy
- Training on EDI integration within SAP R/3
- Transfer of procedure models into prototypes
- Tuning guidance and implementation
- Tuning of individual ABAP programs
- Tuning of R/3 systems
- User and technical support and help desk
- Win NT Services

To add further variety some partners develop applications, development tools, or market platform and complementary products. Such partners have their own special product focuses, which are not reflected in the previous "function-based" descriptions.

Both your employment prospects and your understanding of them will increase the more you get familiar with the terminology that potential employers use.

To assess where the employment opportunities lie from your own perspective, you need to profile your experience in terms of the functions you can handle and the special skills you have (in terms of specific vertical markets, business processes, and so on, not just the general skill types), and investigate where the employment market is generating jobs with a good match.

You don't, of course, need to seek a perfect match. You will probably want to extend your capabilities to some extent when making a job change, but you need to have as many of the requirements already as the employer can reasonably hope to get. Your best opportunities to develop often come not when you're changing employers, but rather through moving across your employer's spectrum of activities.

When pursuing a career in SAP, as in many other fields, remember you have to constantly negotiate an unwritten compromise between your desire to develop yourself (a desire shared to some extent by your employer) and your employer's need to get productivity by reusing your existing skills (a need shared to some extent by you). How well you fare in this negotiation will in large part determine the return you get on your efforts over your career. Good negotiation happens when both parties get a fair deal. If you keep your eye on the "ball" of your own advancement and also address your employer's needs fairly, you will build a solid career and a good reputation.

Job Titles in the SAP World

The job title consultant appears in a lot of SAP world jobs, and different employers have different terminology. A cross section of full role descriptions is shown in Appendix C, "Sample SAP-Related Job Descriptions," showing the requirements of applicants as well as the roles they are expected to carry out.

Appendix C includes a number of examples of positions that occur in the SAP development group and in SAP subsidiaries. These are worth reading if you aspire to the development, marketing, or special consulting roles that are particular to SAP itself.

But SAP itself is not where the bulk of employment opportunities lie, so we will concentrate here on job titles that occur more widely.

You will often see the title "SAP consultant." This catch-all title means a lot of different things, and you have to look at the details to see what the job entails. It usually means that SAP expertise (of whatever kind) is the prime requirement and is more important than industry or other ancillary knowledge.

Here are some examples of more specific job titles that occur in the SAP world, in recent advertisements and job descriptions, and what some of them mean (or at least have meant in example cases).

ABAP Programmers

In end-users, the ABAP programming role involves mainly modifying systems that have been configured from SAP modules. Only occasionally will a fairly major functional addition be programmed. ABAP is a high level 4GL, and so there is not always a division of labor between programmer and analyst (Though some companies still preserve the traditional programmer/analyst split, the trend with modern development tools is away from that distinction). In SAP itself, of course, the development team uses ABAP for major module development tasks, and so do some developmental partners.

ABAP openings are very often associated with specific SAP modules, so knowledge of that particular module, or the application for which it is designed, is pertinent.

ABAP Designers

Those more significant developments that take place in ABAP, whether in end-users or elsewhere, have to be designed to integrate with the rest of the system, as well as to provide the required functionality. ABAP designers are expected to have knowledge of ABAP programming, and engage in systems analysis and design at a little more detailed level than SAP configurers, because although ABAP is a high level "language," it is still a lower level "language" than module configuration.

ABAP Developers

This title often appears in advertisements, and depending on the advertiser, it can mean programmers or designers or programmer/designers. The demarcation lines are not always clear, and agencies who advertise usually have several positions to fill anyway. By using this "catch-all" title they can attract candidates for a number of them.

Application Engineer

Partner employers have used this title to describe people who take their brief from the business requirements as defined by the R/3 implementation analysis, and use R/3 configuration tools to meet these requirements. They may then follow through to provide remote and onsite support to completed implementations.

BASIS Consultant

This title is often suffixed with a vertical market specialty in advertisements—for example, "BASIS consultant—correction and transport," and sometimes with a functional specialty, for example, "BASIS consultant—security/support," or a platform technology skill, for example, "BASIS consultant—HP-UX support," or "BASIS consultant—Oracle."

BASIS consultants engage in "deep configuration" and have to understand the R/3 architecture and supporting BASIS technology.

Business Analyst

Typically, a business analyst has to define the needs of the business and understand its processes, interfacing management and user needs to the SAP capability. Depending on the other strengths in the employer's team, the business analyst may need a technical background (not always just in SAP but sometimes in relevant technologies such as Oracle, Networking, UNIX, and so on).

Commercial Analyst

This is synonymous with the term "Systems Analyst" (described later), but particular to "commercial" systems. A commercial system can be any system that is concerned with transacting business. The term excludes systems for such purposes as technical design, process control, or scientific analysis. Depending on the organization, commercial systems may include financial systems.

Financial Analyst

This is synonymous with the term "Systems Analyst" (described later), but particular to financial systems. Financial systems, depending on the organization, may include anything from investment management down through financial planning and accounting systems, and even billing, payment, and collection systems in some companies' terminology.

Industry Module Consultant

This title will include the particular industry module when it is advertised—for example, "IS-OIL consultant," or "R/3 Retail consultant." A module consultant configures the particular module and also needs the business and industry knowledge to discuss its benefits and limitations at the senior management level. In addition, he or she needs sufficient technical knowledge of the module, and of the integration issues surrounding it, to resolve problems.

Integration Managers

This title often implies duties very similar to those described later for "Module Configurers." It does not always imply any extra responsibility for interfacing with other technology.

Junior Module Consultant

Occasionally, the term "junior" will appear in a title. This offers you the opportunity to get into that area to expand your general experience and possibly to gain your first SAP experience after training.

MIS Manager (Management Information Systems Manager)

This position is of strategic importance to some end-users, and often reports directly to the managing director. The role includes responsibility for strategy, budgets, vendor negotiations, resource allocation, project prioritization, performance and security issues, SLAs (service level agreements), and the corporate interface. It's mentioned here because SAP experience is considered increasingly important in the role.

Module Configurers

Although, as the title suggests, configuring SAP is an essential function, this is never done in isolation from the exploration of needs, and the role overlaps with business and systems analyst roles. As a typical example, one employer specifies module configurer responsibilities as: "Working closely with clients to assess their requirements in finance, materials management, sales and distribution, production planning, and human resources."

Project Leader

Often an end-user will employ a project leader as the steward of its interests, employing someone, usually from its existing staff, with more knowledge of the user's business than of SAP. Such a project leader would need to develop SAP knowledge, but would have more experienced SAP consultants available in the team.

Project Manager

The scope of a project manager depends entirely on the project, but many SAP projects are large and wide-ranging. (See also "Senior Consultant/Analyst." Senior Consultants are often *de facto* project managers.) The different "project leader" role described in the preceding section can also be designated project manager by some end-users.

R/3 Business Consultant

This title in consulting partnerships has been used to describe a consulting role with a high pre-sales content in promoting R/3 (in one example specifically alongside Siemens Nixdorf's LIVE approach, but other consulting partnerships would have other value-added focuses). The job includes the typical pre- and post-sales support activities of an IT consulting partnership or specialist software house, and experience in these activities is as important as SAP knowledge.

SAP Analyst/Business Analyst

These titles have been used to describe a role that involves having capability as a "Business Analyst," but with a greater orientation towards SAP. The person would be championing the use of SAP, advising on its functionality and configuration, and solving integration problems.

Senior Consultant/Analyst

How senior is "senior" depends a lot on the employer, and sometimes its pay scale policies (it has to call you senior to justify what it has to pay in the SAP market). But usually it will imply responsibility for coordinating SAP introduction across a wider range of functional areas and geographical locations, including other SAP consultant activities, and for integrating these into a cohesive strategy. A senior consultant in the SAP world is often in effect a project director.

Systems Analyst

This title can stand alone or be incorporated into titles such as "Commercial Analyst" or "Financial Analyst," which specify the business process areas in which the analyst will work.

Systems analysts can expect to define processes and requirements, engage in detailed design, configure SAP systems, and follow through to perform documentation and user training. Some degree of project management is involved, as is planning and implementing systems cutover. Expertise in appropriate business areas is valued, sometimes to the extent that it will override lack of SAP experience, and provide an entry into SAP.

Technology Manager

This title designates the person responsible for international rollout of network technology, including R/3 systems. He or she manages the technical, installation, and testing aspects and interfaces with the application design team.

In addition to the preceding and their derivations, you will also see advertised titles including the sort of special activities that are self-explanatory, such as security, auditing, and testing, which are performed around SAP systems.

The SAP world is unusual in the width of applications and ancillary technology knowledge that it embraces. This is because of its nature as a standard applications suite built on core business processes, plus the way that a wide range of platform and technology partners have espoused it.

This chapter can only give you a feel for its richly varied employment openings, especially the ones that crop up in this book, and you can enhance that by looking at the job specification examples in Appendix C.

Again, if and when you start looking at the SAP job market in earnest, you can expect to come across lots more job titles not covered here. But don't be fazed by that. They will boil down to something not too different from the titles we have covered here.

What It Takes to Succeed—The Personal Attributes

Success is many things to many people. It's not anyone's place to tell you what you should want out of life, so we'll limit ourselves to addressing success within the limited definition of achieving a "goal" position—a point where you have maximum career options.

The goal position is to achieve the status of "Senior Consultant/Analyst" described earlier, with an international reputation for managing large and complex projects.

We're not saying that this should represent your life's ambitions, but only that from there you're on your own. Options are open from there to climb on up the management ladder, go it alone, or simply enjoy a comfortable lifestyle.

You are in a position which many people would consider as having achieved success. Senior positions are now in your range, in consulting partnerships, large end-user organizations, or SAP itself. Beyond this point you are dependent on your management skills. SAP experience will have helped you up the ladder, but it won't by itself take you much further. You may, like many before you have done, choose to operate your own consulting partnership or "take the money" and go for the top priced contracts that are available to you.

Before reaching that goal there is a key "switchpoint" on your progression, and it occurs when you have gained solid experience as an SAP consultant, and are beginning to aspire to gaining "senior consultant" experience. The switchpoint is a good time to consider widening your experience by moving across into another employer type—from end-user to partner or SAP, or vice versa, or between SAP and partner.

To reach the goal, you obviously must have the basic qualifications to get started (see Chapter 41 "How to Find Employment Working with SAP"), and develop the skills to do the job along the way. But given these basics, excellence in certain personal attributes show up time and time again as being what sets the high achievers apart in the SAP world. They are:

- **Self starter attributes**—Initiative, enthusiasm, and the ability to organize yourself, plan and achieve your own goals, be proactive, and find better ways of doing things. This may seem paradoxical given the emphasis on teamwork, but it's not. A good team member is someone the other members can rely on.

- **Intellectual ability**—A high level of intelligence is indispensable to really succeed in the SAP world. The abilities to think broadly and conceptually while handling details well and to merge an analytical approach with pragmatic realism require high intelligence as a prerequisite.

- **Ability to work under pressure**—Deadlines are important in the SAP world, and delays are very expensive.

- **Interpersonal communications attributes**—The ability and inclination to communicate openly and honestly, and a generosity in sharing information and transferring knowledge, as well as the ability to communicate and make good relationships at all levels, be empathetic, be a good listener, and adopt team-building attitudes.

- **Credibility**—Communicating in a friendly way is not enough by itself when large investments hang on your advice. You must also cultivate credibility. In part, this arises naturally from your work record, and also some people have a natural *gravitas* that inspires confidence. But good preparation and care with the acquisition and preparation of facts will help you make the most of what you have with the hand you have been dealt.

- **Commitment**—Requirements for motivation, flexibility, and a willingness to travel are likely to place demands on your commitment if you want to excel.

- **Leadership skills**—The ability to motivate others and get the best out of them. If you have the qualities mentioned so far, then you are well on the way.

- **Enterprise-wide business understanding**—Knowing the logistics and culture of enterprise-wide software solutions, how and where integration and standardization should prevail over local priorities and vice versa, and the ability to coordinate projects across a very wide range of activity and cultures.

- **Vertical business sector understanding**—An in-depth knowledge of business issues in one or more vertical markets will help bring you a breadth of vision and increase your credibility and value.

These qualities create the team-building, wide-visioned manager around whom successful project teams are created, and who are in such high demand in the SAP world.

Although this section is not about specific SAP skills development, one point is worth mentioning. As you are making your way in the SAP world, you will have consistently wider options if you have the ability to configure SAP and understand its architecture thoroughly. You should take the opportunity to acquire this knowledge as early as possible.

Some of the preceding attributes you can cultivate, others are not so amenable. You either have them ingrained from your infancy (and in part, some would say, your genes) or you don't. Take a realistic view of how far you have these attributes, and how far you can, or want to, change yourself to gain them. Then set your career goals accordingly. Don't be seduced by financial prospects into taking a route that's unsuitable for you.

Having said that, the financial rewards throughout the SAP world are good.

Levels of Pay Working with SAP

SAP is in the premium-bearing band of IT employment. Comparing SAP positions with the general run of non-SAP ones (of similar seniority and skills requirement) shows that SAP confers a premium of the order of 25 percent. People skilled in its closest competitors such as Oracle and Peoplesoft also command premiums, as do some other software specialty areas that are in demand. But as of mid-1996 SAP heads the league.

The positions where SAP people enjoy the greatest salary premiums are at the top end. Those people with the capability to manage large multifaceted projects with several major projects in their resumé are most in demand, and least likely to have their premiums eroded by the improved systems development tools that SAP is turning out.

Configuration skills are also much sought now, but the general view in the recruitment and contracting market is that, while the jobs will last, the really heavy premiums for this skill will not. It is more possible to balance supply and demand in configuration by training and productivity tools than it is at a more senior level. Configuration skills will still remain highly valued, though, and in demand.

If your primary interest is in fast earnings then, provided you are highly competent (whether or not you have yet reached "top end" status) you will do best by "contracting," either via a contracting agency or directly onto a project team. At the time of this writing senior consultants who are able to place themselves directly can get rates as high as $8,000 (U.S.) per week, while those who go through an agency can command a salary in excess of $5,000 (U.S.) a week.

This is around twice the rate for permanent employees of a similar caliber (taking into account employee fringe benefits), and represents the reward a contractor gets for taking risks. However, as SAP projects are so long, and the demand is so high, the risks are minimal, and contracting is the way to the highest earnings in the shortest term.

Long-term earnings are a different matter. Contracting is not the best way to climb the management ladder in a large company. Played for the long term, SAP offers a route into positions of strategic importance that can lead to the boardroom, where salaries, executive perks and share option schemes may yield the sort of serious money that makes even SAP contracting rates look puny. To equal that by taking the contracting route means investing your extra early earnings wisely. If you are career planning for maximum overall financial benefit, you have some interesting comparative arithmetic to do.

Meanwhile, back to the present. Table 40.3 shows some examples of permanent positions being advertised internationally in mid-1996 (with all salaries translated to US dollars). These were all advertised in the European computer press.

Table 40.3 Job Positions and Annual Salaries

US$	Location Specified	Position
150,000	USA	Senior Consultant MM,SD
150,000	Texas, USA	Project Manager
140,000	USA	Project Manager
125,000	City of London, UK	Senior Implementation Manager
110,000	Singapore	Senior Consultant FI,CO
60,000 to 150,000	Europe	Implementation specialists, Module Consultants, BASIS consultants and ABAP analyst/programmers
to 110,000 95,000	Australia/USA Sydney, Australia	R/3 Module Consultants

US$	Location Specified	Position
45,000 to 110,000	UK	SAP BPR Consultants
to 70,000	Australia	Module Consultants
to 85,000	USA	Implementation Consultants
75,000	Europe	Project Manager
75,000	UK	SAP Business Analysts
to 70,000	UK	ABAP Developers
70,000	USA	R/3 Module Configurer
70,000	Germany	BASIS Consultant
70,000	Saudi	BASIS Consultant
62,000	London, UK	ABAP Programmer
60,000	Germany	Project Manager
60,000	South East Asia	Project Manager

These absolute figures will raise a smile, no doubt, in a few years, as the value of money changes. That's an occupational hazard of quoting the price of anything in a book, but for the time being they give a fair picture of where SAP salaries sit.

From Here...

In this chapter, you have learned a way of looking at and classifying the SAP employment market, and what it does that will help you match your skills and interests to it. You have also learned to expect and cope with some widely varying terminology from the marketplace.

- If you haven't yet read Chapter 39, "SAP Workplaces," you can learn more there about how the SAP world is structured, and the roles that the different types of employers play in the overall process of delivering and supporting SAP systems. These roles embrace the functions you have learned to recognize in this chapter.

- In Chapter 41, "How to Find Employment Working with SAP," you can get some practical advice on how to set about the actual process of getting into SAP, and Appendix C, "Sample SAP-Related Job Descriptions," contains some example job descriptions, which do not require previous SAP experience.

- In Chapter 42, "The Outlook for the SAP Employment Market," you can look at the outlook for the future in SAP employment, and see how the emphasis on different skills and functions might change. You can also learn to evaluate how the major trends affect supply and demand, and consider what effect that will have on levels of pay.

- In Appendix A, "SAP Offices Around the World," Appendix B, "SAP Business Partners," and Appendix H, "Complementary Solutions," you will find many useful contact addresses. You can obtain literature and advice from most of these sources that will help you develop your fluency in the language of the marketplace.

■ Appendix C, "Sample SAP-Related Job Descriptions," provides some real life examples of job descriptions, which will fill out the understanding you have gained from this chapter.

Chapter 41

How to Find Employment Working with SAP

This chapter is aimed first and foremost at those seeking to break into SAP. If you already have SAP experience, you will know that you have lots of employment options. You are on the right side of a supply-and-demand imbalance, and your main concern will be to make the best choices, from the many open to you, in order to direct your career towards achieving whatever your life goals are. This chapter may help in that process by widening your choices, and perhaps suggesting some new avenues through which to exploit your advantage. It is potentially useful reading.

If, however, you are on the outside looking in, then options are not so plentiful, supply and demand does not work in your favor, and this chapter is not merely useful but essential reading.

In mid 1996, recruiters in the SAP industry are forecasting growth of between 50 percent and 100 percent in the number of people working in SAP, either for SAP itself or with partners. And such people presently number close to 20,000. That is without counting end-user employees. The shortfall in SAP-skilled people is a prime topic anywhere SAP is discussed.

It can be frustrating to hear all this talk of shortfall, and then when you offer your services to help meet it, you find only closed doors. Why does this happen, and how can you get around it?

Well, there's bad news and good news. Let's get the bad news out of the way first.

Whereas for experienced SAP people there are more openings than qualified applicants, it is the other way around for new entrants to SAP. Supply and demand is against you.

In this chapter, you learn:

- Why it is worth persevering if you want to break into SAP.

- How to assess yourself and your prospects for working in SAP.

- How to prepare yourself to gain a foothold in SAP.

- How to locate the sources of job opportunities.

- What to read next.

A typical recruitment agency dealing in SAP jobs internationally, reports that at least 50 percent of the "overtures" it receives for SAP employment are people who are seeking to get their first SAP experience. This is true whether they are responding to advertised vacancies or making unsolicited inquiries. In contrast, less than 10 percent of the vacancies advertised are for new entrants to SAP. This is about par for the SAP recruitment world.

SAP itself receives thousands of unsolicited resumes. In Germany, as well as in the subsidiaries, these may outnumber vacancies by a factor of 20 to 1.

All this really means is that if you don't have SAP experience, the employers won't come looking for you, because they do not need to, and they can afford to be selective when you go looking for them. It does not represent an insurmountable barrier, provided you have some useful expertise outside of SAP (more of that later).

Console yourself, also, with the thought that the apparent "closed shop" that thwarts the inexperienced has always existed somewhere in computing (and indeed very many other careers). SAP is just today's prime example.

Also, isn't the fact that it's a privileged club at least part of your reason for wanting to join it? Certainly it's the reason why the salary levels are so good, and Groucho Marx had a point in his oft-quoted assertion that "I wouldn't want to join any club that would have someone like me as a member."

So, on to the good news: However they do it, and wherever the new people come from, the fact is that the industry as a whole must train and accept in excess of 10,000 people per year worldwide as SAP consultants. No amount of movement by existing SAP people between employers can obscure that. In the USA alone, an estimated 2,000 new SAP consultants are coming on-stream per year.

Given some of the developments in the marketplace, these figures may turn out to be gross underestimates.

The supply-and-demand situation looks likely to remain as it is for some years yet, with high premiums being paid to very experienced SAP people. At the same time, SAP is pressing on with lots of developments (discussed in Chapter 37, "Overview of the SAP Employment Market," and Chapter 40, "Employment Opportunities Working with SAP"). Many of these are designed to make installing SAP easier and, to some extent, reduce the need for manpower, but new departures always offer opportunities to the newcomer, because the "sitting tenants" have less advantage—"everybody's a trainee."

The move into the market for smaller companies is proceeding apace, and these companies may provide a good route into SAP. The smaller companies simply cannot afford the huge budgets that the giants are spending on business systems reengineering, so they will have to accept less experienced people. SAP is moving toward more "load and go" type systems for this marketplace, and these should place less of a premium on experience.

Although SAP experience is considered vital, there are many other skills involved in realizing SAP systems—that is in the nature of the product. Knowledge of special application areas, business processes, platforms, and complementary technology all need to be welded to SAP skills in some part of the SAP activity spectrum. This provides a lot of potential entry tickets. If you have some of these skills, you have something to bring to the party, and the right employer could consider it worth developing your SAP skills to complete the set.

Despite the premium being placed on experience, it is interesting that recruitment specialists, partners, and end-users alike express the view that SAP knowledge is not the most important predeterminant of success in implementing SAP projects. Some measure of it, of course, is essential, but the emphasis placed on other qualities, skills, and experience offers you, the novice, the chance to be a special candidate. Previous SAP experience is not everything.

In summary, if you have something to contribute, don't be deterred by the SAP experience barrier. As an absolute fact, thousands of people are going to break through it in the next year. Some of them will do it by chance—by being in the right place at the right time. This chapter can help you to do it by design.

Although there is competition for the openings, many of your competitors will take a passive approach—looking at advertisements, perhaps mailing their resumes to agencies or known employers. Few will mount a pro-active, planned and concerted campaign, and if you do so, you will have put yourself into a select group already.

The fact that it might take application and persistence to break into SAP is not a reason to give up. There is only one reason for giving up, and that is because a rational assessment leads you to believe you would not succeed and be happy at it, once inside. This is not the same thing as being deterred by the difficulty of getting there.

Self-Assessment—Know Your Realistic Options

The first year of SAP experience will transform your prospects in the SAP world enormously, but what are your realistic options for getting that experience?

The answer to that will depend on a matching process between you, the individual, and the requirements of the various roles that can provide an entry.

Roles and Requirements

Let's consider the various roles in which it is possible to spend that vital first year. Those that exist in any real quantity fall into four main categories, or at least they do for present purposes. These are:

- Management consultants
- Analysts/implementers

- Project managers
- ABAP programmers/developers

Other categories, such as trainers and salespeople, are on the borders of SAP specialization. A trainer might want to move into training in SAP, and it's not unheard of for trainers to move across into support and consultancy in most software environments, so there is no reason to suppose it won't happen in SAP. However, for the most part, trainers are not assumed to be seeking an entry into a career based on their SAP skills.

Similarly, sales and marketing people do not rely primarily on their technical skills, and, in any case, the role of the pure salesperson is not central to the consultancy centered process that sells SAP installations. So while there are important sales and marketing roles, notably in SAP subsidiaries and headquarters, these are rather special cases.

SAP acknowledges, however, that it has learned to be more commercial and sales-oriented by importing experienced marketers from backgrounds in major systems, large scale software, and consultancy. If you are in this category, there will be opportunities around SAP, and some example of marketing job description are included in Appendix C, "Sample SAP-Related Job Descriptions."

Greater opportunities could arise in the traditional sales executive role as penetration of smaller companies proceeds. It is arguable that the whole process will have to become a bit less wed to management consultancy, and more like a typical solution sale, if SAP is to realize its full potential with smaller companies.

That said, neither training nor sales and marketing roles are considered as a major category.

Specialist documenters also fall into the "special case" group, although one company at least—Documentation Associates—has built a large business out of documenting SAP based systems, and there are specialists opportunities for individual documenters at SAP headquarters for programmers, business analyst/implementers, project managers, technology. Another outfit—Documentation Consultants (UK) Ltd.—is currently building its team and looking for top-class documenters. Both of these are listed in Appendix F, "Companies Providing SAP Services."

Reiterating, the four main categories we'll be looking at are management consultants, analyst/implementers, project managers, and ABAP programmers/developers.

For any of these roles you will need to have something of an outgoing confident personality, and be good at teamwork and at organizing yourself to meet goals and deadlines. A glance through the example job/role descriptions in Appendix C, "Sample SAP-Related Job Descriptions," will show how regularly such qualities are demanded, in one guise or another. Some of the roles described demand a lot more of these attributes than others, but all require a fair amount.

The nature of the SAP product means that it reaches out, communicates, and integrates, and the SAP world expects its people to do the same.

There is very limited scope for the backroom computer whiz who likes to withdraw into machines and technology. The SAP core product development team is the place which could most easily tolerate lack of personal communications skills in order to gain brilliance in software design. The recent advertisements on the Internet for developers in SAP's development team in Walldorf, Germany, place at least as much emphasis on technical skill as on personality, though they do stress the need to work cooperatively, and the general culture is one of easy communication. The difference, at least in some of the roles, is that you would be less required to communicate with business management than in most other places in the SAP world. The core product development activity is tiny, though, compared to the vast opportunities out in the field, consulting on, designing, and implementing SAP systems.

Among end-users there are some who need ABAP programmers simply to be good programmers, because these employers maintain the old distinction between analysts and programmers. But even there, if your aim is to progress from ABAP programming up any of the worthwhile career paths to which it could lead, you're going to need the typical SAP personality traits.

So if you lean toward the reclusive rather than the outgoing, then however brilliant your technical ability, you might be better to apply it in some area other than SAP.

On the other hand, if you like personal responsibility, teamwork, and partnership better than hierarchical command structures, you are likely to fit in well and be happy working with SAP.

The second prerequisite quality is a minimum level of intelligence, providing the ability to think logically, analytically, and constructively. In this regard it is little different from working with other software, although SAP probably places a higher premium on the ability to take a broader perspective—to marshal high-level options, and puts less value on brilliant invention, relative to many other software environments.

Given these two things—the right personality type and the right intellect—you have the ability to perform well in the SAP world, provided you can acquire the necessary training and experience.

To get that training and experience, you will almost certainly have to have some other advantages going for you. Some of these you either have or don't have, and if you don't, there's not much you can do about it. Others you can cultivate, if you really want to.

So much for the common prerequisites. What specific ones do you need in each category?

Management Consultants. The large management consulting firms provide a major entry path to SAP for those who can meet their demanding standards.

All of them have a large commitment to developing people, in SAP as well as in other areas, but Andersen Consulting is the first (and by mid-1996 the only one) of these to have acquired the license to deliver SAP accreditation, so their view is worth exploring.

Andersen policy is not to recruit in response to specific project demands. Rather it has a supply side and a demand side, and the supply side tries to forecast and foresee demand, and develop capability to meet it. This is on a more strategic basis than simply meeting the needs of the moment. Andersen wants people it recruits to have a career potential that goes well beyond the lifespan of the current SAP dominance.

The central message is that meeting the "Andersen profile" is much more important than SAP experience.

In the words of a senior manager "People get too hung up on the dearth of SAP skills. The success of projects has a lot less to do with SAP skills than with project management skills. The most important skills are in handling big projects with complex structures, across multifarious cultures."

Andersen takes people in at all ages from early twenties up. Basically, there are two types of intake:

- The fresh graduate (including those with minimal experience)
- The experienced manager/consultant

There has been a shift in recent times toward the older, more experienced, recruit.

As a fresh graduate, you will need:

A good degree (3.5 or higher, in U.S. terms), ideally with postgraduate qualifications. The subjects studied are not very important.

The right personality type. An executive directly concerned with recruitment summed this up in these terms:

- Self confident
- Professional
- Comfortable dealing with directors
- Has drive/motivation—is a self starter

You will need to pass muster on all of these fronts. A combination of intellect and personality is required. A brilliant first-class degree holder would not be hired without the right personal attributes.

As an experienced manager/consultant you will need:

A similar education to the fresh graduate, though there is less emphasis on this, the more advanced in your career you are.

The same personality type as for the fresh graduate, though there is more focus on relevance of skills and experience. "Cultural fit" is important, and you are most likely to have that fit if you have worked in another consulting firm or in management with a large "blue chip" organization.

Most important are very good skills in some of these:

- Business skills
- Industry skills
- Project/change/strategic management
- Appropriate technology

The majority of experienced people taken are in their thirties, but can be up to any age, provided they have commensurate experience. The older you are, the better experience you need.

If you are recruited as an experienced person, you have to be ready to be put out in front of clients and be useful to them very quickly.

The first year induction process into the SAP team is to take a SAP course, and then work on a project either uncharged or at reduced rate (to the client). You would be in a team with experienced people and be expected to pick things up quickly.

Andersen uses modern information tools to harness and disseminate experience. Lotus Notes, discussion databases, and expert networks are all used extensively.

Most of the foregoing holds good for all the leading management consulting firms, and for lesser management consulting firms unless they are totally focused on SAP.

These consulting firms represent a prime opportunity area to top class entrants to SAP looking for a career rather than to make "a quick buck" out of SAP, and their stated policy is not to evaluate purely on SAP experience.

Whether they can avoid having to chase ready-made SAP skills from time to time is another matter. Price Waterhouse, for example, has been mounting a massive campaign to recruit SAP expertise from around the world for the USA, and many consultants find themselves obliged to fill gaps by using contractors. The general recruitment policy, nonetheless, provides a very good pathway into SAP.

Business Analysts/Implementers. This is a very large employment area in SAP. Opportunities exist with the implementation partners, contractors, and end-users. Each of them would much prefer people experienced in SAP, but supply and demand dictates that some of them have to accept the training responsibility sometimes, or leave jobs unfilled. For the partners and contractors, an unfilled post means loss of profit, and for the end-user worse—loss of development and gain of pain.

SAP itself, in its subsidiaries (from where the SAP product is sold and supported), is not an employer of new entrant SAP people. It has to have top quality people to fulfill its role there. It is a great starting point for information (more of that later), but if you want to start out in SAP with the producer itself, then check out how you match the requirements of the development team, as described under "ABAP programmers/developers" later in this chapter.

A contracting agency will be more likely to help you break into SAP if you already have a good working relationship with it. Contracting houses are geared to delivering people who are the finished article, immediately useable—that's why their clients use them, so developing people is a minority activity. Because of the extreme shortage of SAP people, however, some of them have helped convert their existing contractors to SAP, and may even help convert new applicants—but you will have to offer some other immediately usable skill. The skills in demand can easily be assessed by looking at advertisements by contracting houses in the computer press. A good background in client/server systems, UNIX and 4GLs (fourth generation language) are often cited as key requirements. You should be prepared to accept a reduced rate while you learn SAP and find an agency you can do a deal with.

The end-user route has the problem that most large SAP users have staff of their own that they can retrain. This problem is exacerbated by the fact that business reengineering with SAP is likely to cost jobs in the user organization. To overcome this, you need to find the opportunity to match some special requirement that can't be filled from inside.

End-users will, from time to time, find a particular skill is so important to them that they will provide SAP training in order to get it. Sometimes the skill can be application- or industry-related, and sometimes it is in some other technology—specific OS, database, or platform experience. The examples shown later related to ABAP programmers are just as pertinent to analysts/implementers.

To break into SAP as an analyst/implementer there is a general specification that you will need to meet. It is not hugely different from one employer type to another. It is described by different employers in different ways, and each has its own emphasis, but if you have the underlying personal qualities described earlier, and score well against the following requirements, then you'll be a good candidate:

- Experience in installing package based solutions in a large commercial organization. This is a different process from designing systems from scratch.

- Demonstrable ability to think in depth about systems—their effect on the organization, and how they are integrated.

- Good analytical skills—the typical systems/business analyst skill set.

- Experience in client server systems (although there is still a lot of activity in R/2 systems, R/3 is where the growth is).

In addition, you will have a great advantage if you have a more specific hook on which to hang your application. This could be either one or both of the following:

- In-depth knowledge and working experience of a particular business application or process in which SAP may be applied.

- In depth knowledge and working experience of a complementary technology—platform OS, database, interfacing technology, and so on.

These will have to match the specific needs of the particular employer. It is quite possible that you are interested in broadening your experience, but if you want to make the change to SAP, you'll find it much easier if you play to your strengths in other respects for the time being.

It is obvious from the preceding that this type of role in SAP is not the best place to cut your teeth in computer systems. If you need to do that, and you don't qualify for the graduate entry points in development or management consultancy, the only way to do it with SAP is to get into a company which is using SAP, in a user role.

There are cases of people who have started off on the shop floor in quality control, or in fairly routine clerical positions, who have become what one employer describes as "superusers"—people who understand how the system "thinks," and find their way around problems with it. From there they have obtained SAP training and gone on to a wider career as SAP consultants.

To be honest, though, they have usually "been in the right place at the right time." Could this be achieved by design? It might be possible to engineer the situation if you are willing to do a lot of research and have lots of determination.

Project Managers. "Project manager" is a term meant to include all very senior versions of analysts/implementers.

The "real diamonds" as one employer describes them, are people with good SAP experience, and the ability to manage projects with a wide sweep, appreciating all the strategic possibilities and implications, and how business processes integrate to form the organization. These projects amount to reengineering the business, and the description "project manager" might not do them justice.

These are the people who are attracting the large salaries, or fees, as the case may be, whether they are called senior consultants, project managers, or whatever.

They probably have in their background most of the characteristics of the analyst/implementer, but have progressed beyond that level and have the full project management skill set.

The actual SAP experience is not necessarily the most differentiating asset these people have. In other words, they are probably more different from an average SAP consultant than they are from an excellent non-SAP consultant/manager.

If you have demonstrated all the other assets described, except for SAP experience, then you will find a move into SAP could be highly profitable. To get the first years experience, you may have to take a drop in position, but probably not in earnings, and the rewards after the first year in SAP would be substantial.

All the employer options discussed above for analyst/implementer are available to you, and similar considerations on the value of "relevant though non-SAP" experience apply.

Options described for "management consultants" may also be available to you, depending on meeting the educational requirements.

ABAP Programmers/Developers. At the peak of the pyramid for ABAP programmers/developers is SAP's own development team. This is mainly based in Germany, at Walldorf, near Heidelberg, but development activity is increasing in the USA, and a small amount is carried out in the UK. German language is not a prerequisite, but English is, and being multilingual will score points.

The development team provides the best opportunities for ambitious programmers/developers to get SAP experience, and also its activity areas and skill requirements provide a template for what to expect in the other parts of the SAP world.

The best way to keep in touch with this is via the Internet. SAP publishes a number of job opportunities there.

A cross section of examples from early 1996 is included in Appendix C, "Sample SAP-Related Job Descriptions." Reading them will give you valuable insight into what they are looking for, and how you might fit, but they are only a current cross section. If you're looking seriously in that direction, watch that Internet space regularly.

Development is done using ABAP/4, and development tools such as active Data Dictionary, Screen Painter, and Dialog Manager.

Education is important, and good degrees are valued, but they are not always absolutely essential. Here is a sample of stipulations for different development jobs:

First class degree in computer science or business/economic studies with computing

A good university degree in Medicine/business with computing, computer science mathematics, business/economics or natural science

A university degree

Information technology with business management, preferably a university or higher technical college degree

No education specified (for senior professionals in retail systems development)

SAP needs to bring in expertise from many different business areas, and very good experience in those areas can overcome shortcomings in formal education. The scope of SAP is vast and expanding. Applications and industry solutions currently enjoying attention are:

- Human resources
- Payroll administration
- Retail systems
- Oil industry

- Medical records
- Retail systems

The utilities industry is forecast to be a major growth area.

Your own industry and application area, even if not among those mentioned, may very well be on the agenda in other months.

Technical backgrounds which appear as requirements or "desirable extras" for SAP developers are equally varied. The sample which follows is culled from just the current batch of vacancies.

"Programming skills, experience of PC applications"

"Basic professional experience in similar application area"

"C, 4GL programming, databases, PC software products"

"Database administration, preferably Oracle, system administration in UNIX"

"IBM 370 architecture, MVS, CICS, and VSAM in IBM 370 Assembler programming"

"Hands-on programming in C"

"In-depth technical knowledge of different UNIX systems (BSD and System V)"

"Excellent knowledge of the UNIX environment"

"Excellent knowledge of TCP/IP-based network programming"

"Experience of designing complex distributed software applications in C"

"Experience in development of error-tolerant software"

"Knowledge of current databases (for example, Oracle, Informix, Microsoft SQL Server)"

"Knowledge of Windows, Windows NT, Windows 95"

"Knowledge of C, C++, and particularly Visual Basic"

"Experience in Windows 6/32 bit environments as well as OLE2 Automation and OCX"

Any of the examples in Appendix C might ask for one or more of the previous experience sets.

Outside SAP itself, the complementary, or "interfaced" skills requirement is just as varied. There are numerous modules in SAP, and its range will be apparent from other parts of this book. Provided you have some area of expertise, it's just a question of finding where your expertise is most needed. For ABAP programmers, the bulk of opportunities lie with contracting agencies and end-users, so that is the place to look, even though both groups pose problems for the inexperienced.

Contractors' attitudes to ABAP learners is much the same as it is to the inexperienced SAP analyst/implementer.

End-users are important employers of ABAP programmers, because ABAP is mainly used for relatively minor modifications to systems that have been configured with very little use of ABAP, and this tends to be the sort of work that goes on long after the project is "completed," as the system is "tweaked" to match user needs.

For the same reason, ABAP programming does not figure largely in the priorities of the partners who undertake implementations, so the partners are not an opportunity area for the ABAP entrant.

Preparation to Gain a Foothold

Having decided that SAP might provide the right workplace for you, the next step is to prepare yourself to maximize your chances in the process of finding the opening. Get the product right before you try to sell it, if you like to think of the exercise in marketing terms.

The main ways open to you to do this are training courses, self development, and interview preparation.

SAP Training—Is It Worth Getting First and How?

Some people in the industry express the view that training without experience is worthless, and certainly not worth buying with your own money.

A more measured view, and one shared by many employers of SAP skilled people, can be summed up as this:

> "A training course will only be an advantage if all other things are equal"—in other words, when recruiting people without previous SAP experience, their general potential will be more important than whether or not they have taken a course, but in a tie-breaker situation, the course could make the difference."

A course will rarely get you considered alongside experienced people for a position where experience is asked for, though some cultural differences exist from country to country. The highly "qualification-oriented" view in much of mainland Europe means your SAP education carries greater weight there, and this is probably true in much of Asia, while in the United States and most of the English-speaking world, experience is valued more highly.

Wherever in the world you are looking for work, your course will be an asset of sorts, but in most situations, you should approach the task of obtaining SAP employment as suggested for inexperienced people, regarding your SAP education as an advantage up that pathway, rather than as a ticket to the routes available to those with SAP experience.

You may, of course, have already taken a course, but if not, is it worth buying your own course?

The idea of buying your own course has become more acceptable. SAP has recently started an accreditation process which will maintain quality as more organizations acquire the ability to deliver SAP courses. These organizations and their courses are a far cry from some of the computer training courses which gave self-funded computer education a bad name in earlier times. You will be required to demonstrate prerequisite qualities before being accepted on them. To date, most of the people using them have been practicing computer consultants and contractors adding SAP to their capabilities.

But how valuable is having a course anyway, without the experience? One point about having an employer pay for your course is that you can be pretty sure he has plans to use your knowledge on a project.

The answer to this depends where you are coming from, and where you are looking for the opening.

If you are in the "graduate entry" class, there is not much point in buying an SAP course, since the major consulting firms are more interested in your wider career potential than your usefulness in SAP, while SAP itself in recruiting graduates for its development team is looking for raw potential and excellence in computer science. Graduates from German universities are likely to have had some SAP education, as it happens, but SAP recruits from outside Germany as well.

For the "man in the street" class (someone with little IT experience, and not qualified for the graduate entry route) there are two major problems.

Firstly, you may not meet the prerequisites for the courses, or you could find difficulties in keeping up, because you don't have prior knowledge that the course assumes.

Secondly, your path into SAP will be more tenuous, quite probably involving a spell as a user, so there is a greater risk that you will gain little return on your investment in a course.

If you are absolutely sure that you have the basic attributes, coupled with the desire to break into SAP and a dogged determination to do so, and if you can easily afford the course, then consider buying one, but don't do so hoping it will provide an automatic entry.

Along with the graduate entry class, the group of recruits the SAP world will most readily accept without SAP experience are those who match the specifications described earlier for analysts/implementers, project managers, and ABAP programmers. If you fall into one of these groups, then a course could be a good investment for you.

Anyone can buy a place on a standard SAP course from SAP itself, and third parties are offering intensive courses for much less cost. Some sources are shown in Appendix F, "Companies Providing SAP Services."

The best advice is to make sure that buying a course is part of a clear plan of how to market yourself, rather than a hopeful leap before looking. Also, the workings of the accreditation program should be watched with interest. What effect it has on the salability of non-accreditation-bearing training, and what accreditation is available to the private course purchaser could be crucial.

Self-Development

You have taken at least one self-development step by reading this book. How far can you usefully go under your own steam?

As far as SAP skill experience is concerned, it is, like any technical subject, much easier to acquire by attending a course, and at some time or another you will need to do so. But if your strategy does not include buying a course, then your aim has to be to get an employer to provide one. If you do so, of course, you'll have killed two birds with one stone, because you will also be assured of the work experience to follow it.

However, it is possible to learn a great deal about SAP without going on a course. SAP, as a company, is very open with information.

You can't create experience out of thin air, but if you can't be experienced in an area, next best is to be well informed. Talking to people in SAP who come from a similar background to your own will help you build a special insight, but the main message is simply to start building your own knowledge base. Remember that any outstanding student gains most of his knowledge by self-organized reading, not by sitting in the classroom.

Think about the wider issues of corporate integration, and absorb the approach to it that SAP offers. Many recruiters say the real key skill is that ability to see the big picture. They say that it tends to dawn on SAP people after they've implemented one or two modules. You can develop that way of thinking about business processes by conscious application. There's nowhere anyone can go to really acquire the mind-set that's any better than your self-training plan.

If you do this, then even if you never get involved with SAP, you'll still have gained knowledge that will stand you in good stead for your career in business and information technology.

But it may very well help you to get involved, because it will show that you have potential to develop, and that will help justify the employer going to the trouble of training you.

Finally, don't forget the underlying attributes. Since the SAP world places a high premium on interpersonal communication and self-organizing skills, isn't it worth giving some thought to how you might develop these?

Personal presentation skills will most directly help you get the job, as well as help you do it. It is one area where you get the chance to give your prospective employer a sample of "the product." You don't have to tell them, you can show them.

Communicating well is something which some people do more naturally than others—that is undeniable. But at whatever level you start, it is possible to learn and improve. Trained salespeople and other professional communicators of all sorts know this.

Not everyone thinks that these personal communications qualities are vital in life, and throughout history, some people without them have been happy and successful and have enriched the world. In the SAP world, though, they are important, and if you are not totally happy with your endowment of them, then consider what you can do about it.

Preparation for Interview

Whichever route you take to finding work in SAP, at some stage or another you are likely to be attending interviews. As a newcomer to SAP, you are in a highly competitive contest, and when the employer does the post-interview evaluation, the decision will often be more finely balanced than most interviewees ever realize. Even if you are an experienced SAP professional with lots of options, the job you most want is likely to be the one you have to stretch for. In all cases, the edge you can get from good preparation is worth having.

There are more books on the subject of how to perform well at interviews than there are about SAP, and they can teach you, or at the very least remind you, of some basics that will increase your chances. These represent a whole body of useful knowledge which is ignored by a large percentage of interviewees.

The point here is not to offer our own alternative to these, but to suggest, at risk of being obvious, that you read at least one, especially if you haven't been on the interview round recently. An hour or two browsing in your local library or bookstore is guaranteed to prompt some useful thoughts. You could dismiss 90 percent of what you read as banal or inappropriate and still get very good value out of the exercise from the remaining 10 percent.

There are a couple of points worth making directly here, though. Surprising though it is, many candidates show up at interviews with very little knowledge of the company they are looking to join. This gives an immediate advantage to anyone who has taken the trouble to do a little research. The more you can bone up on the company and its operations, the better, for a number of reasons.

An attribute probably overvalued by most interviewers is the ability to come up with good reasons for why you want to join the company. This ability might really prove no more than that you know how to prepare for interviews, but it leaves a strong impression on the interviewer. The research you do for this question might also help you really decide if you do indeed want to join that company.

If you are offering experience in a business process, industry application, or technology area, it will help your case if you have considered in advance how your experience might "map" across to the activities of the potential employer, especially those where SAP is being applied.

Any common ground that you can find between you and the employer, however irrel-evant to the job, tends to "flag you up" in the interviewers mind. You have a much bet-ter chance of finding such common ground if you've thought about it in advance.

The knowledge you have gained will enable you to ask informed questions, engage in intelligent discussion, and generally help make the interview flow. You, of course, won't need to be told not to use your knowledge to cut off, contradict, or otherwise embarrass the interviewer, or to unload your knowledge and tell the company how to run its busi-ness.

Many companies inviting you to an interview will send you out some sort of informa-tion pack, and the main message is to study it thoroughly. But if you are taking the ini-tiative, and not applying for advertised positions, you may have to ask for a pack, or indeed you may have gotten it already, as part of your "market research."

One source of information on the company's broad objectives and direction that you should always try to get is the annual report. This is usually available on request, along with an information pack from a press officer, corporate communications officer, or similar person.

You will not normally have to be very original to get the information you need, but if you have to be, it is effort well spent.

Sources of Job Opportunities

Where to look for the most open doors, or at least the less closed ones, is a question that you will want to answer, if you are seeking the quickest way into SAP.

Proceeding from the obvious to the not-so-obvious, let's look at a number of sources, from the point-of-view of the new entrant to SAP.

Advertised Vacancies

We pointed out earlier in the chapter that less than 10 percent of advertised SAP vacan-cies were open to people without previous SAP experience. This, of course, is much better than zero, so it is worth keeping watch for them.

A perusal of such previous advertisements gives some picture of what to expect:

> They are usually for people with good computer experience—in UNIX and C-based systems. Advertisers regard experience in installing package-based systems involv-ing process change as a good advantage, as they also regard experience in the client's particular industry. Beyond that, experience in the particular hardware or OS are plus points, and, of course, advertisers often seek the more general systems analysis, implementation, and project management skills.

The clients are usually end-users, some of whom are willing to provide training in return for the large savings they can make in salary. Sometimes they have corporate pay scales that prevent them from paying more for experience, even if they would like to, say to their agencies, while others may be driven by the sheer unavailability of SAP-experienced people.

Leaving aside the major management consultancies, the partner consulting firms also intake and advertise for a small proportion of their SAP consultants as new entrants to SAP. They are driven by the need to build their organizations. There are perceived to be a lot of large SAP contracts awaiting fulfillment, held up by the lack of resources to fulfill them within consulting partners.

The major management consultancies will rarely advertise for new entrants to SAP; neither will SAP themselves or contracting houses.

Details with brief job requirements for some advertised positions not requiring prior SAP experience are included in Appendix C, "Sample SAP-Related Job Descriptions."

If you have taken a SAP course, you may have some success in applying for jobs where minimal experience (say six months) is required. Certainly some people with one year's experience are going for, and getting, jobs where the advertiser stipulated two years, and with six months they are picking up those where one year is stipulated, so perhaps the syndrome might work back as far as the newly trained person getting a job advertised for someone with six months experience.

Recruitment Agencies—Can They Help Proactively?

You can look at recruitment services as being broadly in two categories, though there is a fair degree of overlap.

The project-based agency works closely with a client brief and mounts a campaign to solve a client recruitment requirement—usually with high-profile advertising. This type of agency usually offers executive search—so called "headhunting" services.

The database oriented agency keeps large lists of candidates, and frequently circulates known recruiters with details of candidates on file. They are a "matching" service, essentially.

In neither case are they really geared to doing a hard sell to help you into new areas. The database agencies will put out your resume where they think there is a chance, but it will sit with a lot of others from inexperienced people.

Some of the more project-oriented agencies, when asked how to get SAP training, will advise applicants to talk to SAP, or approach end-users directly, and try to find those who would rather train than pay large premiums.

You have to accept, as a would-be entrant into a lucrative field, that you've got a little self-marketing job to do. The recruitment industry is paid by the employers, not by you, and its job is to meet their objectives. So the agencies are not geared to doing a big selling job on your behalf. You are, or should be.

Contracting Houses

Contracting houses are only really interested in selling the finished article, although, as discussed earlier, extreme supply and demand situations can cause them to be more developmental. Realistically, you'll have to work on building some confidence in your capability before a contracting agency is likely to help you develop into a new area as sought after as SAP. Provided you can do that, you could certainly help your case by thinking about the agency's problem, which is how to make sure it gets a return on its effort, and coming up with some concessions that might solve it. In other words, talk sensible business and there might be a deal to be done.

An interesting new development, not quite describable as a contracting house, is detailed in Appendix F, "Companies Providing SAP Services." This outfit—Rivermead Associates— aims to provide career management and marketing services to potential high earners in software and consulting and has targeted the SAP world for early attention. It claims to have novel approaches to the vital first-year conundrum.

Self-Marketing

If you really want to take control of your own destiny, then the way forward is to devise and carry out your own marketing plan. You are a good product, in which you are an expert, so why not?

There are lots of ways of conducting a marketing campaign, and one of these—a "scatter-gun" approach, mailing out the same message to lots of people—is most used by job-seekers. It is easy to produce vast quantities of resume copies, and you only feel the pain of rejection at a distance. Unfortunately, it is the wrong technique for the purpose. Mailshots can be very effective for selling lots of similar articles to lots of similar buyers, but is that the kind of marketing we are engaged in?

Other kinds of marketing are more suitable to the "big game hunter"—someone who is trying to make only a small number of big and important sales. You are the ultimate big game hunter. You only need to make one sale in your whole campaign.

The technique recommended here is one which has had proven success in that sort of marketing campaign.

```
Start at those points where information is easiest to get, and from there
build as big a "database" of prospects as possible. SAP itself is a useful
starting point, because the company is very open with its information. You
will not find it difficult to compile a list of all the SAP users in your
locale. Other useful start points are employment agencies and contractors.
This book provides you with lots of partner names. Don't forget to "network
out" as you go along. In other words, ask any contact for other contacts.
```

Their purpose at this stage is to provide as many names as possible of companies involved with SAP in your area of interest. You are looking for market information, not direct openings. If you approach the exercise in research mode, you will gain far more from it.

Having widened out the "prospect base," you now want to narrow it down, by eliminating all but the most promising cases for you.

Before you start, devise a simple questionnaire that will remind you what information you are seeking from each group. This should include information that will identify characteristics that match well with your USPs (unique selling points), as well as information which will subsequently help you prepare a sales call, including the name of the decision-maker on SAP recruitment.

Do as much of this narrowing as possible by desk research and telephone contact with people other than those who will ultimately make the hiring decision. The decision-makers should only be approached when you are a little better armed.

When you have narrowed the target group down to prime prospects only, you can prepare your sales effort for each prospective employer individually, with a resume that highlights experience relevant to that employer and a prepared approach.

At this stage you are ready to contact the decision-makers in your target group. If you can, you want to talk to the "problem holder" rather than personnel managers. Telephone each of them, seeking an appointment to discuss how you might be able to help him or her.

This is a plan that a professional salesperson might use to address the task, and there's no reason why you shouldn't be equally professional. A properly conducted, research-based self-marketing campaign will not only give you the best chance of finding the right opening, but will also make you much more knowledgeable about the SAP world. This will increase your credibility and broaden your options throughout your career in SAP.

From Here...

In this chapter, you have learned how to assess your suitability for the various work opportunities in the SAP world, and how you might prepare yourself to take advantage of them.

You have also acquired some ideas on how to locate SAP jobs, and how to set about undertaking a self-marketing plan.

You will find these other parts of the book useful in preparing for and carrying out your search for SAP employment:

- In Chapter 40, "Employment Opportunities Working with SAP," you can learn more about the way the whole SAP world is structured, so you can approach your job search with a better appreciation of the environment in which your prospective employers operate.

- In Chapter 42, "The Outlook for the SAP Employment Market," you can learn more about the outlook for the future in SAP employment, and where the new jobs will arise. You can also learn what major factors impact supply and demand in SAP employment, and how they will change the nature of SAP jobs.

- In Appendix A, "SAP Offices Around the World," Appendix B, "SAP Business Partners," Appendix F, "Companies Providing SAP Services," and Appendix H, "Complementary Solutions," you will find many useful contact addresses. These provide starting points from which you can network out along lines dictated by your own areas of special interest.

Chapter 42

The Outlook for the SAP Employment Market

This chapter is designed to help you look ahead in the SAP employment market and to provide some ideas on what to watch for in forming your own view of the future of SAP.

Most independent forecasters paint a rosy picture for SAP in the foreseeable future, and these are echoed in the forecasts made by various parts of the SAP "virtual organization"—that is, SAP itself and its partners, some of which are drawn on here.

Although you might argue that the "SAP-interested" sources drawn on are not entirely unbiased, they are in fact among the most reliable.

Why? Because they incorporate independent research, often from several research outfits, together with their own unique, internal insights, before they make their forecasts, and because they have to stake cash, effort, and "opportunity cost" on being right. Their money is where their judgment is.

Nonetheless, you will want to form your own view, which is ultimately the one you have to back with your own time and effort. Also you may want to focus on your own special areas of interest within the overall SAP employment scene.

To do each of these things, you need to look at the factors that will drive or hold back growth—both the underlying factors, and the initiatives under way or planned. These will dictate not only the amount of growth in SAP employment, but also the directions that growth will take.

The second part of this chapter discusses some of these factors—but first, some forecasts from the SAP world.

Growth Forecasts and Indicators

The SAP group is enjoying revenue growth of 40 percent per year based on the latest published figures at the time of writing (mid-1996), which compare first quarter 1996 with first quarter 1995.

In this chapter, you learn:

- To estimate the growth in SAP employment.

- What the main factors are that will affect supply and demand in SAP employment and how they will affect your prospects.

- How the maturation of the SAP market will change the mix of skills required.

If you look at the geographical disposition of this growth, there is every reason to suppose that it can continue fairly close to this for several years. Those parts of the world where SAP is growing fastest—the Americas, which saw growth of 82 percent and the Asia Pacific region, which achieved 68 percent—have a huge untapped potential.

Europe grew at a relatively modest 19 percent, but that is good going for a market so well penetrated already.

Consider the actual values achieved—Europe DM 380 million, Americas DM 233 million and Asia Pacific DM 64 million. If the much younger American and Asian markets continue to grow at the present rate, together they will soon outstrip Europe and will have a greater influence on the overall growth rate. Figure 42.1 illustrates the effect, though it is not a forecast as such.

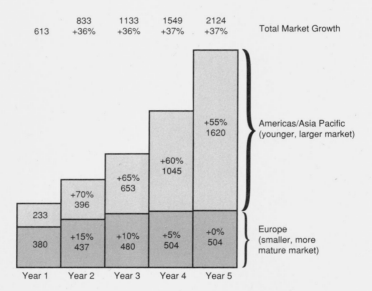

Fig. 42.1   The younger and potentially bigger SAP markets overtake the more mature ones, while still young, thus lowering the average age and raising the average growth rate of the total worldwide market.

Remember we are looking at growth in sales here. If you want to look at growth in installed base, you have a different, though no less promising progression.

SAP's revenue growth, of course, is not exactly mirrored by growth in SAP employment, and indeed SAP is at great pains to contain the need for SAP skills and prevent it from growing as fast as the product revenues. SAP is having some success in this, with the introduction of various productivity aids, but nonetheless revenue growth is obviously a vital underpinning for employment growth.

Indications from various SAP statistics are that a 40 percent growth in revenues has incurred about 30 percent growth in SAP's own head count, and SAP believes that it can improve revenue per employee further with the improved development tools it is rolling out. It also believes these tools will help partners meet the resource gap without massive expansion in employment. SAP sources forecast that the total number of SAP consultants required (in the "virtual organization" of SAP and partners combined) will increase by about 20 percent over 12 months.

Partners, in the main, make higher forecasts for SAP employment growth—or at least, each intends itself to grow faster than that.

Partners' forecasts more directly address personnel growth, because consulting is a large part (in some cases all) of the salable product of most partners, whereas to SAP the software sale is the goal. Although SAP charges for its consulting, it is not pursued for profit but, rather, to enable sales of software.

The following are some indications and forecasts from a short cross-section of partners large and small:

■ Figure 42.2 charts the actual (up to 1995) and forecast (beyond 1995) growth of SAP-skilled employees at Intelligroup Inc., the New Jersey-based SAP implementation partner. These are shown together with non-SAP employees. The growth in 1996 was forecast at 80 percent, dropping only slightly to 70 percent for 1997.

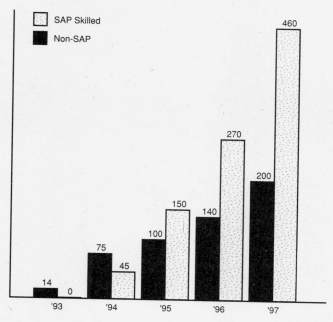

Fig. 42.2 Intelligroup, a SAP implementation partner, forecasts imminent growth in SAP-skilled employment will far exceed that in other areas.

■ iXOS, the German technology partner, now also operating in Prague and in Belmont, California, has grown from 30 employees in 1990 to 130 in 1995, and is forecasting a growth of 23 percent to 160 employees in 1996.

■ Clarkston-Potomac, one of the smaller U.S. implementation partners, more than doubled its complement of SAP consultants in 1995 and plans to double again in 1996, from just over 50 to over 100.

■ Atlanta-based Bureau Van Dijk has grown from 50 SAP specialists in 1990 to 170 in 1995, and expects to grow by 47 percent to 250 in 1996. The company became a U.S. national implementation partner in 1995.

■ Siemens Nixdorf was reported in the December issue of "SAP Info" to have designated R/3 a separate business division in its own right, with over 750 employees. It expects to recruit 600 to 1,000 new consultants in the next two years—which is growth compounding at between 34 percent and 53 percent. All Siemens Nixdorf consultants in the division will be required to earn SAP certification.

■ IBM, at year-end 1995, claimed over 2,100 SAP consultants worldwide and planned to increase that by 2,000, or just over 95 percent, by the end of 1996.

A look at some of the activities that IBM has under way lends credence to its forecast (and indirectly to the general partner forecasts). At the end of 1995, IBM had over 20 joint development projects with SAP.

These include the following:

■ Industry solutions, such as Finance Advisor, I/S Retail, Factory Automation, and Electronic Commerce

■ Across varied platforms—RISC System/6000 and SP, AS/400, PC Server/NT, MVS Open Edition (R/3) and MVS Sysplex (R/2)

■ Service and support offerings such as integrated SAP/IBM support, migration (R/2 to R/3), outsourcing, business recovery services, IBM Global Network, and added-value tools and templates

■ Technology implementation projects, including HAC MP (high availability), MQ Series (message queuing), ADSM (storage management), DB/2, Print Services Facility/6000, Systemview (Netview for AIX), Lotus SmartSuite Integration, and Lotus Notes Integration

IBM has declared its SAP consulting and services primary growth areas to be the following:

■ Roll out AS/400-based offerings to medium and small customers

■ Expand outsourcing options for new and existing SAP clients

■ Lead the development of SAP education and training offerings

■ Provide migration support for SAP R/2 customers through IBM's extensive R/2 to R/3 Migration Factory (platform independent)

■ Capitalize on IBM's industry alignment and expand into global industry-focused SAP practices

- Leverage IBM's Complementary Software products
- Business recovery services

The other partners in or near the IBM league, such as Siemens Nixdorf, Digital, and Hewlett Packard, have comparable commitments in scale with their size.

The large consulting partners continue to build SAP expertise at an undiminished rate, while many of the smaller, more SAP-specialized consulting firms have quite specific plans and programs for the growth they anticipate.

In the U.K., for example, one of the "Big Six" accounting companies, Andersen Consulting, plans to train 24 new SAP consultants every three weeks, while Surrey-based SAP implementation specialist Diagonal has invested heavily in developing its own SAP R/3 training schedule and, perhaps more importantly, its consultant development and SAP skills transfer methodology.

These are no more than a small sample, and most other partners could justify a mention if space allowed. You can keep up to date with partner activities very easily by accessing the Internet or asking your local SAP office for details of relevant publications.

The point here is to show that there is some substance to the thought that the SAP partners are backing their forecasts with commitment and planned activity.

We have not forgotten, by the way, that end users are also employers of SAP skills and their employees are not considered in any of the above forecasts, but it is reasonable to assume that their growth will run alongside the growth in partner staff.

In summary, there is some divergence between the SAP view and the partners' on the quantification of growth. It is not our function here to adjudicate. It is possible to argue that the partners have their ears closer to the ground. Some perceive that there is a large raft of big SAP projects waiting to be had and held up only by the lack of resources, that is, SAP-skilled people. In other words, whoever can put the team together can get the business. The view of some recruitment specialists, though, is that some big potential projects are being "double-counted"(or more than double) in these perceptions, because several partners are forecasting to win the same business.

Also it is possible to argue that SAP is more aware than the partners of the impact of its productivity tools.

What is agreed all 'round is that growth will continue, and it seems likely that supply and demand will continue to favor the SAP-skilled employee, while SAP's efforts and those of its partners will prevent the balance from getting totally out of hand.

Factors in the Supply and Demand Equations

As we have said, it is a good idea to consider the underlying factors that will impact on supply and demand before arriving at a personal view of long-term SAP employment prospects.

To do this really means taking a view on the whole SAP marketing strategy and the market influences with which it has to live. In the case of SAP, this is a very wide set of considerations, and it would be presumptuous to pronounce the "final word" on them in one small chapter here.

We can, though, look at some of the marketing considerations and the most vital planks in SAP's strategy from the standpoint of their effect on employment.

The main features we will look at are the following:

- Market maturation—Markets are said to mature as they approach saturation—the point at which almost everybody who needs the product has bought it, roughly speaking. Although the SAP marketplace is a long way from being mature, it is, like anything else, maturing all the time. The ratio of installed base to new installation potential increases with each sale that is made.

- The volume market in mid- and small-sized companies—SAP has built its success mainly by selling to large and ultra-large companies. It now has definite strategies to increase its penetration of mid-sized companies and possibly smaller than mid-sized.

- Vertical marketing moves—A strong current thrust in SAP is toward industry-specific marketing and product development. This offers new and different ways of adding value to the product.

- Expansion in the range of platforms and interfaced technology—The range of platforms on which SAP can be installed is increasing all the time, giving new options for both downsizing and upsizing. The range of other software products with which SAP will work and communicate is also expanding.

- New productivity tools for designers and implementers—SAP has a number of developments that are designed to make installing SAP systems more efficient. These tools form a central part of its strategy for balancing supply and demand in the SAP skills market by keeping demand from getting out of hand.

- Training initiatives—The other side of the supply and demand equation, of course, is supply, and the key SAP strategy for this is to improve it by developing training capacity, both internally and via partners.

- Underlying market trends—Finally, SAP, like every other company, is dependent on the infrastructure that the wider world provides. The SAP success phenomenon has arisen in large part through being the right product for its time. Will times change, and if they do, how well-placed is SAP to adapt?

Each of these factors has an effect on the people requirement, both in terms of the overall quantity and the mix of skills required.

They are worth looking at in a little more detail, as follows.

Market Maturation

There is a lot of steam left in the SAP boiler, evidenced by the forecasts from the SAP world and supported by judgment based on the underlying factors. Forecasts and judgments alike indicate that the market for SAP will be buoyant for several years to come. SAP skills will continue to be in demand to create brand-new SAP installations.

We will be discussing here what happens as the market matures, but nothing we say should be taken to indicate that maturation is imminent. The growth in new installations is forecast to proceed for years to come.

The demand from established users will eventually overtake that from new installers, though, as the market proceeds towards maturity. As market penetration proceeds, and the percentile growth in new users slows down, so the ratio of existing to new customers will increase.

Figure 42.3 illustrates this graphically.

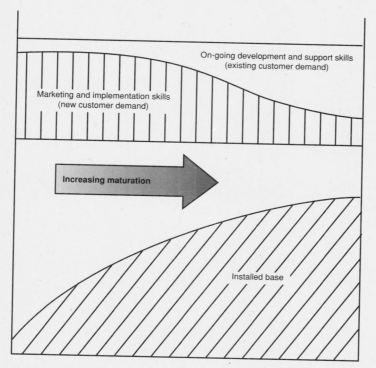

Fig. 42.3   As market penetration proceeds, so employment in existing SAP installations increases relative to employment in installing new SAP sites.

SAP users continue to need SAP skills long after the initial implementation. That ongoing need generates employment not only with the end users themselves, but also within partners and SAP itself.

SAP is expecting partners will generate business from existing customers in the following areas:

- Providing increased functionality:
  - Installing additional modules
  - Adding functionality within modules
  - Extending systems to include supplier and customer database interchange and interaction

- Extending the geographic reach of systems:
  - Roll-out into other countries
  - Roll-out through other divisions

- Incorporating new technology:
  - As new technologies assume importance, SAP systems need to be adapted to work with them.
  - Migration projects—at present this means migrations from SAP R/2 to SAP R/3.

The "secondary development" areas listed preceding are of most interest to the partners as a source of business from existing customers. Secondary developments of this sort will still require many of the skills used in initial systems implementation, although some of the activities place less emphasis (than do new implementations) on the wider skills of business process reengineering.

Each of these opportunity areas will demand a slightly different mix of skills, and there is clear potential for new specialization in the whole spectrum of "add-on" activities.

Unlike the partners, SAP itself does not always see special requirements as opportunity areas pure and simple. The company is finding that large customers are looking to SAP to provide more functionality and relieve the pressure on their own IT departments, and this places demands on SAP that can sometimes run counter to the needs of the mass market that it wants to address. Large customers will continue to demand the functionality, though, and this will sustain the need for SAP skills as the market matures.

In both the partners and SAP itself, ongoing systems support roles will grow in number relative to developmental ones as the market matures, and will offer opportunities across a wide range of specialization. These support roles may diminish in status and benefits, however, as the trend towards remote and automated support continues.

End users, of course, are where the demand for ongoing SAP-skilled employment originates, and they will meet some of it by employing people directly. End users most frequently undertake with their own staff the following post-initial-implementation functions:

- User support (as opposed to specialized system support)
- Minor systems modifications, often carried out with ABAP/4
- Systems administration

Up to now, recruitment companies have reported slightly less demand for ABAP programmers than for SAP systems people, but the mix is likely to change as the market matures. ABAP programmers are likely to be needed for longer, as ABAP is mainly used for small-scale changes, which continue to take place long after implementation.

What we have been discussing is essentially the market for SAP R/3, and it is still quite a young market. No one is anywhere near forecasting what its successor might be, but it is hard to think there will not be one when the SAP R/3 market matures. It is equally hard to believe that SAP R/3 skills will not be valuable in whatever migration process might take place then, just as SAP R/2 skills are valuable in a market dominated by SAP R/3.

Sooner or later, of course, even the most dominant of software products may be overtaken by a competitor development, but the people who work with such overtaken products do not become immediately obsolete. Rather, they move gradually to being more of a niche resource, or they cross-train into some successor technology.

The SAP product, interfacing as it does with so many other technologies, is always likely to provide an escape route if you see yourself primarily as a "systems technologist," even when the product passes its peak.

If you are, or become, one of the large body of SAP consultants who are essentially management, business process, or systems consultants to whom SAP is simply a tool, you have developed skills that you can apply with or without SAP. It may be that SAP skills are what allowed you to progress and acquire those other skills, but you are not dependent on them, and certainly the large management consulting-based partners will seek to develop you as a more versatile resource than just a SAP specialist. You would be more at risk from any diminishment in the whole management and computer consulting industry (unlikely though that may be) than from the demise of SAP as the industry darling.

The Volume Market in Mid- and Smaller-Sized Companies

SAP has established some penetration in Germany and neighboring countries among what Germans refer to as the "Mittelstand." It refers to a stratum of small- and medium-sized businesses—component and subassembly suppliers, flooring and ceiling specialists, garden furniture and tools manufacturers, and a host of others, mainly in manufacturing, owner-managed, and fairly specialized and skills-based.

The Mittelstand is particularly strong in Germany because of Germany's localized banking support and other infrastructure factors, but it has its equivalents in mid-sized businesses around the world.

To appreciate the potential in this industry stratum, and the likely success of SAP's strategies, it is worth taking a brief look at the story so far.

The potential market worldwide among such companies is huge, and SAP's initial idea for addressing it was to develop a version of SAP that would be tailored specially for this marketplace.

Its early experiments in the U.S. were designed to establish the market requirements for this version, but yielded instead a rethink of that whole approach.

The exercise reminded SAP that mid-sized companies are not really very different from large companies. They often need more functionality, rather than less, in each business process they operate. Being more specialized, they usually have fewer of these business processes, but it is not always easy to say which ones will not be used, and they will vary from industry to industry and, indeed, from company to company.

The upshot of this is that SAP has decided it is not a practical proposition to write a special SAP version for smaller businesses. What a smaller company needs is the full-specification SAP with the ability to bypass the processes it does not use.

There is no major cost problem in delivering the whole system. From a pricing strategy point of view, the "per-seat" pricing policy that SAP adopts makes for a natural adjustment to the price, which runs roughly alongside the client's size and consequent ability to pay, without offending larger users. From a practical point of view, it actually costs SAP less to deliver the whole thing than to cut down the functionality. Also there is very little additional "platform space" (increase in computing and storage resources) involved, because inactive SAP modules do not carry much of a penalty.

The real problem is to save the user from grinding through myriad irrelevant options. That is the key to ease of use, and SAP has gone for "down-configuration" as its strategy for achieving it.

How well this works will be a major determinant of its success with the mid-sized and smaller companies, and SAP has developed a concept for its realization, which it calls "configure to order" (in line with the "assemble to order" concept), within an overall strategy, which it calls "Delta Customizing." You can learn more about the assistance this provides configurers later in this chapter, in the section on "New Productivity Tools for Designers and Implementers."

Other moves—toward more vertical marketing and platform downsizing—will have important enabling roles in penetrating the mid-sized companies. They too are described later in this chapter.

The SAP attention to the mid-sized company marketplace has stimulated activity from the partners. For example Clarkson-Potomac have announced their intention to create a strong presence in the middle market. The company claims to have been working closely with SAP to prepare for this, and has plans to add value in the area of easy configuration tools.

IBM, as mentioned earlier, sees one of its primary growth areas for SAP as being to roll out AS/400-based offerings to medium and small-sized customers.

The smaller, more SAP specialized partners look likely to be better able to exploit the middle market than will the large "Big Six" type of operations, with their background in accountancy and management consulting. This is because the sales and installation process seems likely to become more like a typical software solution sale than it has been in selling to the large companies. New partner types are emerging, sometimes as distinct "middle-market divisions" within existing partner types.

The mix of skills and the total number of person-days required "per seat" to sell, design, and implement systems are going to change when each system contains fewer seats. Figure 42.4 shows the sort of effect to be expected.

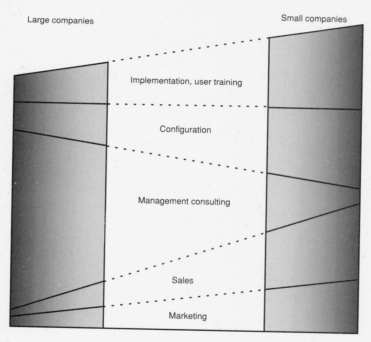

Large companies   Small companies

Implementation, user training

Configuration

Management consulting

Sales

Marketing

Fig. 42.4   As each system contains less seats, the profile of the installation and support effort changes.

If this market continues to expand as expected, look for emerging employment opportunities not only in specialized "configure to order" skills, but also in those sales roles traditionally associated with computer solutions and so far largely absent from the SAP world.

Vertical Marketing Moves

SAP has built a successful product by pinning down key business processes and providing for them with real-time interaction between configurable modules that encapsulate "best practice."

These modules have always been to some extent aligned with industries—or at least industry groups. The original SAP product sprang from the needs of "supply chain driven" organizations, such as the chemicals producers, and from the essential processes involved in meeting those demands.

This is not the same thing as producing a vertical market package. Off-the-shelf vertical market packages are largely the preserve of smaller specialist software houses. There are many thousands of these packages, most of which sell in only small numbers. Your author worked on a planned directory of vertical market packages in the eighties that was abandoned because the number of packages was so vast that it was impossible to describe their features in enough detail to be useful.

SAP is not in the business of producing that kind of product, but it is moving more towards vertical marketing of the SAP product, where its architecture of configurabilty layered on top of well-engineered central processes is a great asset. Any industrial category big enough to be worth addressing will have a lot of divergences within it.

Underlying Vertical Marketing Considerations. In the IT world, vertical markets are often defined in terms of shared functionality and therefore shared systems characteristics—for example, all wholesalers or all manufacturers can be looked at as one, to some extent. But there are other issues to consider as a vertical marketer: as well as producing for the market, you want to have convenient ways of reaching it. Manufacturers, wholesalers, and retailers of food, for example, have very disparate systems, but they have a common interest in the food business and share some media readership, event attendance, and so on.

It is becoming more and more important to look at verticalization in this way rather than by systems characteristics, for the following reason.

In the next decade, it is most likely that we shall see a big increase in intercompany systems access, fueled in part by the Internet and intranet developments, and also by the expanding range of tools for linking applications. To persist with the food industry example, the whole process of getting food from farmer to consumer can be viewed as one supply chain, with participants along the route linked into each other's systems.

Some parts of industry, of course, have long provided shared systems between supplier and supplied on a committed basis, but the developments anticipated will advance the options and allow more free-ranging links to be formed. SAP the product provides a very good platform for building the systems that will facilitate this, and SAP the company is already promoting intercompany systems linking.

All of this means that broadly based "industry skilling" is the key to successful vertical marketing in the SAP world. This requires elements of expertise in the marketplace combined with understanding of the business processes, across several types of operation. It has to be married to the ability to configure and modify SAP modules to produce "industry solutions," modifiable at individual customer level.

All of these skills will only rarely be found in the same person, but partner organizations will be building teams to incorporate them all. SAP itself will be a part of this, with its industry-skilled people involved in the kind of "virtual teams" that are central to the SAP partnership philosophy.

SAP Vertical Marketing Initiatives. SAP's industry focused activity has the following two main threads:

- The partner program has been reorganized along industry-specific lines. In the SAP world the partners are the most significant sales resource, so this is a highly significant move. The organization is described more fully in Chapter 38, "SAP Workplaces," but the key point here is that the pivotal interface between partners and SAP marketing resources becomes the business development manager (BDM), and BDMs are dedicated to particular industry groups. This means that the main marketing delineation for the "virtual organization"—the communications channels that extend through SAP resources and into partner's resources—is vertical.

- Both SAP and the partners are developing more industry-specific solutions.

SAP has currently earmarked a number of sectors for SAP product development attention, including the following:

- Banks—risk management, statutory reporting, controlling
- Hospitals—patient administration and accounting, hospital control systems
- Insurance companies—securities, loans, and real estate
- Oil industry—exploration, transport, distribution
- Public sector—financial budget planning and management
- Publishers—subscription management, advertising management
- Retail—product structure, distribution logistics, point of sales systems
- Utilities—device management, house connections, meter readings processing, billing

This list is expanding all the time, and other sectors are being singled out for marketing attention, often at individual SAP subsidiary—that is, country—level. At subsidiary level, it is likely to prove more flexible for the SAP marketing team to promote "vertical value-added" product development via the partners.

Partners are already promoting solutions in categories such as the following:

- Airports
- Automobile industry and suppliers

- Banking and insurance
- Beverage industry
- Construction industry
- Energy supply
- Estate administration
- Export, shipping, and customs handling
- Financial services
- Hospital systems
- Laboratory and analytical systems
- Media management
- Mining industry
- Plant construction
- Production process data capture
- Transportation industry
- Warehousing, transportation, and storage

Verticality and Smaller Business Penetration. The term "vertical market" has become almost synonymous with industry-specific marketing. It was originally coined to describe markets that are, well, vertical. That is to say that you can move up and down the company size strata, and customers of all sizes can be fitted into the same category.

This feature applies to a greater or lesser extent in many of the SAP industry targets, and vertical focus will provide direction in the efforts to market to smaller companies. It is a way of relating SAP's experience in giant corporations to its target audience of smaller companies. Smaller companies specially value specific industry knowledge and experience.

Once a partner has used this vertical market knowledge to penetrate the smaller company strata, "horizontal" marketing direction can be used to spread into other industry areas in that strata. Figure 42.5 illustrates this graphically.

Because SAP has organized itself further toward industry-specific marketing, it is possible to forecast a massive proliferation of "virtual teams" marketing and delivering to vertical markets.

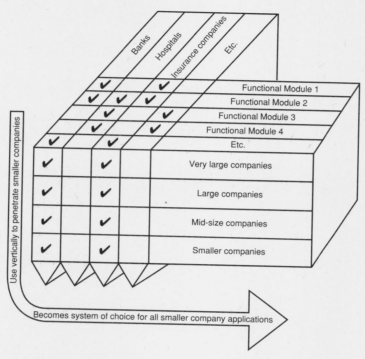

Fig. 42.5 Vertical marketing provides a route into smaller companies for a supplier such as SAP with its track record in larger ones.

The SAP product has brought real-time processing to the back office, and it is hard to think of any industry where companies cannot benefit from the extra efficiency and responsiveness this can bring. But they have to be shown how SAP can do this for them, and they are most likely to be convinced by vertical marketing.

Partners will seek to gain an edge by differentiating themselves and exploiting any specific industrial expertise they have, new partners will enter the SAP arena specifically to exploit some vertical market strength, and SAP will reach out into ever more industries.

Expansion in the Range of Platforms and Interfaced Technology

Of all the factors that make an IT product successful, perhaps the most important historically has been to catch the right technology tide. SAP itself is an instance of that with SAP R/3, which was ideally positioned for the growth in client/server systems.

Today there are many strands of technology seeking to prosper in the client/server environment, and SAP needs to ensure that it "covers any moves" that technology fashion takes. It is very well placed to do this, because its now-massive R&D capability coupled with its capability to build partnership relationships means that it is able to cover virtually all likely moves.

This capability to build partnerships is greatly assisted by the nature of the product, which provides a fount of applications solutions. Technology providers recognize that applications software is a key requirement to drive and facilitate sales of their products. Hence the major technology players need SAP just as much as SAP needs them.

The following sections give a few examples of the technologies that are currently extending the SAP marketplace and a little insight into SAP strategy, so that you can take your own view on their likely success and the impact on employment prospects.

Windows NT as a Platform. The most strategic direction that SAP has taken since the introduction of SAP R/3 is its adoption of Windows NT as a platform. The first SAP system on Windows NT went live at the Swiss company, Bally, in August 1994, and by October 1995 around 650 such installations were in place.

The company now sees itself as having evolved from a mainframe-focused company to one whose primary focus is on PC networks. Windows NT is a central feature in this change of focus. A few of the reasons for this are as follows:

- Windows is the industry standard GUI. The vast majority of SAP R/3 users are familiar with it from their desktop systems and have developed Windows skills. With the server operating under Windows NT these skills are exploited, and systems consistency produces efficiency in many areas.

- The consistency of the Windows user interface reduces training costs.

- SAP R/3 users on Windows NT have experienced substantial savings in cost of ownership per seat, compared with those running on UNIX servers.

- Windows NT provides an operating environment rich in the sort of services needed to build distributed and integrated computing environments.

- SAP regards Microsoft's OLE (Object Linking and Embedding) as a key technology, which allows customers to leverage their investment in desktop applications, such as Microsoft Office, when using SAP R/3.

- Windows NT is the fastest growing operating system for the midrange and above server environment.

Joint developments between SAP and Microsoft continue unabated. For example Microsoft's SQL Server 6.0 has recently been implemented primarily to target mid-sized installations running in homogeneous client/server environments.

You can expect to see a continued expansion in the number of hardware platforms running SAP R/3 on Windows NT. iXOS Software GmbH has set up a SAP R/3 NTC competence center for SAP to run a certification program specially for Windows NT platforms. Products from companies such as AT&T, Compaq, Data General, Hewlett Packard, IBM, Sequent, Siemens Nixdorf, and Zenith have already received this certification.

Windows NT client/server systems will often be wedded to other (notably UNIX-based) technology. Data General, which is both a SAP platform partner and a Microsoft solutions partner, was the first to combine a Windows NT-based operating environment with the choice of a Windows NT or UNIX database. This extended the benefits of Windows NT into enterprises with very large databases and user counts.

Data General's AViiON range can support both Windows NT operating systems, and SAP R/3 can run under Windows NT while supporting databases on either Windows NT or DG/UX.

Major Platforms and Technology. The Windows NT thrust is additional to, rather than instead of, expansion in the UNIX world and beyond.

Release 3.0 of SAP R/3 is compatible with most of the leading hardware and operating systems, including Digital Alpha AXD and UNIX, IBM AS/400 and AIX, SNI SINIX, and SUN Solaris. It is also compatible with the leading database platforms, such as Informix, Oracle and Adabas.

Its list of platform and technology partners alone assures it of a foothold in any major technology directions. These partners include the following:

- Apple
- AT&T
- Compaq
- Data General
- Digital Equipment
- Hewlett Packard
- Hitachi
- IBM
- INFORMIX
- Intel
- iXOS Software
- Microsoft
- Oracle
- Platinum Technology
- Siemens Nixdorf

Recent moves with IBM provide ample evidence that SAP intends to continue extending its capability with large systems: It has taken steps into the fast-growing world of scaleable parallel computing with the announcement that SAP will now operate on IBM's RS/6000 POWERParallel System (SP), using Oracle's parallel database, ORACLE 7 parallel server.

Also IBM would reportedly like to see SAP R/3 running on its mainframe platforms, and is looking at the possibilities of using the mainframe as a database server and possibly an applications server.

Complementary Technology. Less central to SAP's existence, but very important in its expanding influence and applicability, are the many third-party solutions that interface with SAP.

Numbers of products are certified or awaiting certification under SAP's Complementary Software Program, in the following categories:

- Archive software/imaging software
- Computer aided design (CAD)
- EDI subsystems
- Laboratory information management systems
- Plant data collection/machine data collection
- Process control systems
- Product data management

In addition, several categories of communications services are encouraged, though not certified.

Complementary solution providers are listed in Appendix H, "Complementary Solutions," together with their solutions. The complementary software program is expected to result in many more solutions being added over the next few years.

The technologies that develop around SAP not only will influence SAP's continuing success, but will also extend the width of skills that are involved in the SAP world. A glance at the small sample of job specifications in Appendix C, "Sample SAP-Related Job Descriptions," illustrates how different technology skills are welcomed into the SAP camp.

Opportunities to use experience in complementary and platform technology alongside SAP skills (or as a ticket to get an opening into SAP) exist at all levels—not just with SAP itself and the technology and platform partners, but also with the other partners and end users who are implementing systems that combine SAP with these technologies.

New Productivity Tools for Designers and Implementers

Independent industry analysts' ratings of SAP for ease of implementation and flexibility are in sharp contrast to their rating of its product generally. Its ability to deliver and support a full range of modern client/server applications, for example, puts SAP well ahead of the field, while it has been rated near the bottom of the league for ease of implementation.

This means that there is a lot of room for improvement here, which SAP has already started, with the release of SAP R/3 3.0, and plans to continue. Ease of implementation will be a focus for its advertising as it seeks to redress this perceived weakness, and the words are being backed up by action. SAP spends around one million dollars per day on R&D, and a substantial part of this is going into productivity tools for systems designers and implementers.

No one is yet putting firm figures on the impact this will have on SAP employment, but it is a central part of SAP's strategy and will certainly have some effect in mitigating demand.

Bear in mind, though, that in many installations much of the project time attributed to SAP implementation and customizing is in fact spent on redefining customer requirements, which are often ill-documented and unclear. The consulting business time that goes into this area will not be impacted much by improved implementation tools.

Some of the initiatives taken by SAP to ease implementation will affect employment qualitatively as well as quantitatively. Skills in using the new tools will become important, and some configuration skills will become, while not exactly redundant, at least at less of a premium.

It is worth understanding the following main areas of focus in recent improvements:

The ABAP/4 Development Workbench has been given significant productivity improvements:

- Simplified database analyses
- Simplified dictionary maintenance
- Integration of the data-modeller
- Repository information system—a central storage system for all development objects that describe the application
- Open repository interface
- Enhancements to the SAPGUI
- Computer aided test tools (CATT).

SAP R/3 Customizing Tools have been considerably enhanced:

- A new procedure model is aimed at providing transparent management of the implementation process.
- IMG (the implementation guide), an interactive procedural model based on SAP R/3 implementation experience, will now provide project-specific views. You can determine the relevant functions from your business processes, and make the necessary settings guided by your own specific IMG with graphics support. The settings are automatically recorded ready to simplify production start-up.
- ALE (applications link enabling) functions are embedded in the customizing facilities, making design, implementation, and maintenance of distributed applications simpler.

- Scenarios can be modeled with a methods-based procedure that maintains consistency and traps errors while obviating the need to perform myriad actions. The scenarios are transferred to implementations in the constituent systems.

The Business Engineering Workshop now enables SAP R/3 to be a true "configure to order" application suite:

- It includes a business process repository (which acts as a master blueprint for SAP R/3 system capabilities), graphical process models, and scenario-testing customizing tools.

- Once complete, the customer's unique, "living" business process model can be stored within the business engineering workshop and used to engineer ongoing changes.

The most important overall thrust is toward the concept that SAP calls Delta Customizing.

In this, all models—data, business, and process models alike—will be shipped along with the SAP system, and SAP wants implementations to be based increasingly on these models.

Figure 42.6 illustrates the process graphically.

Delta Customizing is a stripping-down process that can leave as little as a few percent of the shipped system operative. Ideally the system will guide the user through this, providing instructions each time he or she wants to activate a function.

Dr. Hasso Plattner, SAP-AG Vice Chairman, has characterized the ideal as being able to run a complete SAP R/3 system on a laptop and configure it in an airplane on his way to see a customer—and being able to add any function he had forgotten in a few minutes in the customer's office.

This ability to customize the system by "computer aided downsizing" is expected to reduce consulting time significantly, because of the reduced need to pore over irrelevant documentation: you look only at the bits the system tells you to.

The Delta Customizing concept is not directed only at mid-sized and smaller customers, but it has particular relevance for them.

SAP is working on a model designed to speed up implementation at these smaller customer sites. This model involves mapping out procedures for the first three weeks of implementation. SAP marries this approach to a sales concept tailored to the special needs of this marketplace. Paul Wahl, Head of Marketing at SAP AG, has said that the aim is to achieve more fast implementations and fewer customer-driven ones.

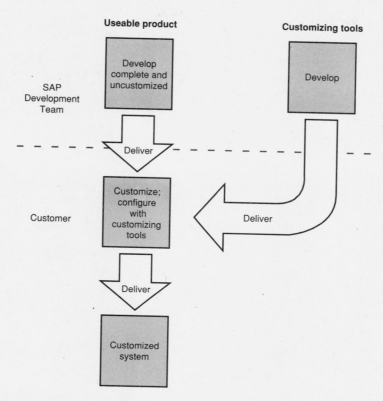

Fig. 42.6   In Delta Customizing, the whole SAP product is shipped, together with the tools that enable the customer to down-configure it.

This lighter process will modify the increased demand for SAP employment as SAP surges in the mid-sized and smaller market (discussed earlier in this chapter). Remember, though, this is largely a new market anyway, and additional to growth in SAP's traditional large company marketplace, so we're talking about holding down the increase in demand, rather than reducing it.

SAP's own efforts to improve implementation tools are not the only ones being made. Partners are always seeking to gain an edge by their ability to implement efficiently and many of them have developed their own productivity tools, which are expected to yield reduced implementation times in the future.

Overall, increased productivity will certainly play a part in keeping demand within suppliable limits. It will also have an effect on the mix of skills required. One feature of this is that it will swing demand more and more toward "personal interfacing" and business skills, and away from "lower-level" SAP skills. As tools become more user-friendly and powerful, the ability to work the tool becomes less of a factor compared to the knowledge of what you are trying to do with it.

Training Initiatives

SAP has learned from its market research (and from the partners themselves) that its partners have been "resource-constrained" in meeting the market demand for its products. The partners also required more business process orientation and enhanced skills in the area of module integration.

SAP is trying to solve this with a worldwide training approach that is business process-oriented and hands-on, and an early example of this is provided by the Consultant Academy operated by SAP in the UK.

Academy courses are designed specifically to meet the needs of consultants working in SAP itself and in the partner organizations. The academy opened in September 1995 and had processed 120 consultants by the end of that year; in 1996 its target is 500 consultants.

The academy teaches the major building blocks and is much more process-oriented than the standard courses. It seeks to show consultants how to find their way around SAP—to teach them what they need to know and where to find what they do not know.

The three-week introductory course does not assume any previous SAP knowledge but requires a good background in business processes and IT. It is not suitable for new graduates with little or no business knowledge.

All SAP's own UK consultants and product managers will attend and most are expected to teach at the academy, the principle being that "it takes a consultant to teach a consultant."

Participants are expected to carry on after the introductory course to take standard courses. These are more concerned with functional detail and less with cross-module integration than are the academy courses.

The academy approach is well targeted and should help to induct into SAP more of those broad-reaching consultants with good understanding of business processes that the SAP "virtual organization" needs.

If you meet that specification and want to use this route to induct into SAP, you will have to get into a partner organization first, because, outside SAP employees, the scheme is open only to partners.

The initiatives that SAP is taking are not limited to classroom training; SAP has a number of other strategies, as follows:

- An accreditation program, not dependent upon attendance at SAP's own courses but based upon the ability to satisfy examination requirements, will enable SAP to exert quality control while allowing partners to expand their training activities.

- Knowledgeware, in the form of digestible chunks of information on CD-ROMs or other suitable media, will be increasingly produced as a cost-efficient way of reducing classroom time.

- Night schools for ABAP programming and links with universities are other ways in which at least some SAP subsidiaries will be seeking to boost training throughput.

Perhaps the most important of these will be the accreditation program, which sends a signal to partners that they can engage much more heavily in training. SAP is giving positive encouragement to partners to do this, and there are signs from all around the partner spectrum that the challenge is being accepted.

IBM has declared one of its primary growth areas as leading the development of SAP education and training offerings.

Andersen Consulting was the first and, at time of writing, the only partner to have acquired the right to deliver SAP's standard courses, but a growing number of other consultants are now looking to develop and train SAP skills. They are producing rational programs to induct people carefully into SAP, and that involves having the right framework to introduce them into projects with customer concurrence.

The overall drive to produce more SAP people will go a long way to satisfying demand for people with "some SAP skill," but the senior people, around whom you can build a team and provide a framework for inducting "SAP apprentices," will still command a premium that the training efforts will not affect for several years—until the new intake become senior figures themselves.

Underlying Market Trends

If it is true that "no man is an island," it is even more true that no company is, and SAP's prospects depend upon how well it is adapted to its environment. You could divide the main underlying conditions that define SAP's wider environment into three main areas: technology, corporate practice, and socioeconomics. Trends in these areas are very much interwoven and interdependent, but the division provides a convenient way of looking at things.

Technology trends have been touched upon earlier in the chapter. Client/server systems growth has provided the main technology groundswell that SAP has exploited with SAP R/3. All forecasts are that the client/server market will continue to grow, and the convenient vehicle it provides for many of the other technology trends mean it is very hard to see it failing to do so.

The other key trends are concerned with applications connectivity. The Internet will provide an increasing impetus to this, as will the many connectivity tools that are constantly being developed. SAP has a good foothold in this area, provided by the strategic relationships it has built with partners and complementary solution providers in the connectivity arena. SAP the product, of course, is well placed to benefit from and contribute to the trend.

SAP is already taking some very positive steps in Internet use, developing information and support systems for access by the World Wide Web, CompuServe, and the Microsoft Network, as well as facilities within SAP R/3 to allow the development of intranet and intercompany systems directly from within SAP R/3 applications.

CPU and storage technology developments, unless of a profoundly revolutionary architecture, will not affect SAP's progress, as they provide a lower-level platform that will find a place however they are configured into broader systems' architectures.

It is hard, all in all, to see any serious threat from changes in underlying technology for the near- and medium-term future. The eventual threat to SAP is likely to come from directly competitive technology. SAP found a "better way to build mousetraps" and the world beat a path to its door (well, nearly). Until someone finds a better way yet, SAP will predominate.

But changes in the underlying technology will offer new options, and it is when these occur that a competitor will have the best chance of creating an alternative to SAP that will oust it as the foremost applications solution. So it is worth keeping an eye on base technology developments, but not too anxiously.

Corporate practice has become much more internationalized, and multinational corporations have been very important to SAP's growth. All the signs are that this trend to multinationalism will continue, and it favors SAP and its partners. Many international corporations, while extending geographically, want to reduce the diversity of their applications and espouse open systems. They also need their suppliers to have a global outlook, and most SAP partners are geared to service this need in one way or another. Not only will this trend help enhance the SAP employment outlook in general, but it will also maintain and extend the opportunities for travel and emigration in the SAP world.

Running almost parallel with SAP's history, socioeconomic conditions in much of the developed world have become more monetarist at the same time as unfettered free-marketism has been espoused. The effect of both together has been to cause companies to seek efficiency by reductionist means—such as the oft-heard retreat into "core business" and the ploughing of investment into takeovers and mergers rather than organic development. This has caused a shedding of labor, which in theory should be available for use in new enterprises.

The investment community, however, in a monetarist world, has found the opportunity to take up this spare labor and invest in it less attractive than the activity of stripping down businesses to shed it. Hence much of the business process reengineering that SAP has been used to effect has been concerned with reductionism.

It is not our brief here to pass judgment on the economic value or social ethics of these forces, but only to say that the fashion (which is prevalent mainly where Western-style mobile capital controls events) will pass eventually, and to look at the effect of that on the outlook for SAP.

There is no reason to think that any reversal of the trend will disadvantage SAP. SAP is an agent of change in business processes. It happens that the business changes during its lifetime have been reductionist in the main and arguably short-termist (ironically, given its German origins; Germany has a far more long-termist investment structure than most in the West), but SAP is equally well-equipped to help business creation, when that once again becomes the prevalent driver of change.

Summary of SAP Employment Outlook

SAP, and especially SAP R/3, is a product still on the rise, and employment prospects surrounding it look undiminished for a number of years to come.

These pages should have conveyed some idea of the rich tapestry of activities into which SAP is woven, and only if you are bored by business and business technology should you fail to be excited by the opportunities it offers.

Certainly very few people are bored by the prospect of high earnings, and the tales of huge contract fees and salaries for SAP consultants could very well be one of the reasons for your having read this book. Supply and demand will continue to favor the employee in the SAP world, although strenuous and promising efforts are being made to prevent staff shortages from hindering SAP's growth.

But high short-term earnings should not be the overriding consideration. The SAP world is wary of consultants out to make a quick buck, and is seeking to encourage people who have a genuine interest in what the product can do for business and an empathy with the SAP way of working. Many recruitment and contracting professionals forecast that the SAP jobs boom will last longer than the very high salaries.

SAP projects tend to be long, and this can provide security and job satisfaction, as well as lucrative assignments for contractors—but it cuts both ways, and locking yourself into a project for a number of years does not suit everyone.

If you are the sort of person the SAP world needs, then SAP will continue to provide a secure source of employment for many years and a first-rate platform for building a career in business and information management.

From Here...

In this chapter you have learned what growth to expect in SAP employment, the main changes in it that current initiatives might bring about, and the underlying trends that affect it.

You have also learned about some key SAP strategies, and why they are important to anyone working in the SAP world.

You will find these other parts of the book useful in furthering your understanding of topics raised in this chapter:

- If, as many people do, you have started by reading the last chapter first, and want to learn more about the employment market, read Chapter 37, "Overview of the SAP Employment Market," and the earlier chapters in Part X, "SAP Employment Market," next. You can learn lots more about the way the whole SAP world is structured, what jobs exist in it, and how to set about securing them.

- In Appendix H, "Complementary Solutions," you will find examples of the complementary solutions that are expanding the width of skills required in the SAP world.

Chapter 43

Managing the Change in Organization and Job Functions

The business world is changing, and at a far faster rate than ever before. Organizational structures and methods, many of them dating back to the First World War and beyond, have now been outgrown. More often than not, organizations are finding themselves obliged to alter direction, style, operations and policies, usually in reaction to changes happening around them. In this respect, it is unusual for organizations to anticipate and preempt change.

New information technology is designed to help organizations cope with these structural and cultural changes. SAP is designed for this purpose. But for the new technology to reach optimum levels of effectiveness, the people using it have to change. The main emphasis in today's employment markets is on employability. In effect, this means that employees and job candidates must possess a number of relevant competencies and up-to-date skills. Whether people within organizations are to adapt to change by attitudinal shifts or by redirected training (or, more commonly, by combining the two), the complex question of how to best manage people within a changing organization must first be addressed.

Change, by its very nature, has an inherent tendency to destabilize that which it affects. This destabilizing quality is especially evident to most of us when the affected entity is socio-economic. Whether the entity is an organization, a social structure or a personal relationship, even beneficial change can often be devastating to the old attitudes, forms and norms of behavior.

For this reason, while change is often welcomed verbally when proposed within an organization, the underlying unspoken reaction to its imminent arrival is more often one of alarm and mistrust.

Inside an organization, alarm and distrust can wreak havoc. The fact that these emotions are normally entertained out of all proportion to the object of alarm and distrust is rendered irrelevant. They cause far too much counterproductive damage, especially given their effect's necessary corollary: They tend to extend their effect to external factors, so external relations and operations are also adversely affected as a consequence.

In this chapter, you learn:

- The importance of change to a business.

- What changes an SAP implementation might bring to your organization.

- How to avoid the pitfalls in managing change.

- How to prepare for change in your organization.

The primary task of a change manager is to face up to and seek to calm these fears. It is clear from this that change must always be handled with sensitivity in order to secure its acceptance.

Change must be effectively—and positively—communicated. It must be communicated with great clarity. Its benefits must be outlined with enthusiasm; potential problems or obstacles in the way of its successful progress must be identified, and solutions devised.

Major organizational change, which is just what you and your colleagues are undergoing as a result of installing SAP, is often mishandled. The consequence is decreased morale and efficiency leading to decreased performance and results. In this chapter, you will be exploring means to avoid these pitfalls.

Introduction to Managing Change

As you have seen indicated previously, most change is reactive. That is, the organization has to change for identifiable commercial, social, or legislative reasons, although, of course, change may be forced upon an organization by external forces.

Whatever the reasons for change, a guidance program must always be drawn up by management. The program should encourage those involved to take a proactive stance, thereby increasing its chances of success by means of ownership and opportunities for active contribution to the various processes entailed. Thus the reasons for change should always be communicated, and comprehensively so.

In the case of SAP implementation, many of the resultant changes will be immediately self-evident prior to implementation. SAP will provide solutions to questions raised across the entire spectrum of an organization's business needs. Restructuring your organization around information provision by means of new systems will affect all facets of your business. There will probably be an emphasis on aspects.

Management information and control systems that will, typically, be changed by SAP implementation include:

- Marketing and sales control—control of the processes whereby orders are obtained from customers, and linked to requisitions

- Operations control—covering control of product and service outputs, quality and reliability, flexibility and responsiveness, timely delivery, facility capacity use, manpower efficiencies, and materials usage efficiencies

- Control of materials—procurement and availability

- Manpower control

- Facility control and maintenance

- Cost and revenue control—your budget

- Control of debtors and creditors

- Control of capital expenditure and financing

You can expect an increased focus on the activity of specialists. General managerial, administrative, and support functions will probably be reduced once you have introduced the SAP system. However, while the various administrative functions of the SAP system will deliver consistent quality, the completely successful deployment of these functions will depend entirely on detailed, accurately drawn objectives. The applied systems you will be using are reliably excellent; but they need to be amply and expertly employed to ensure that they achieve excellence in practice.

The organizational change involved here, then, is all-embracing. However, it is important that the change program be flexible, as should the attitudes of those driving it, in order to account for any additional developments. There will be unpredictable events and results, which will often present themselves as opportunities for fine-tuning your change program or even for introducing further, innovative progress. Be prepared for the unexpected.

Elements of Change: The SAP Program

The immediate issues raised during your implementation of SAP will cover such areas as:

- Amendments to job descriptions
- Amendments to working practices
- Amendments to corporate organization charts
- Reorganization of office layouts
- Relocation of staff (if necessary)

With all of the preceding, as much openness and honesty as possible will pay dividends in terms of morale and acceptance.

Use these tasks as opportunities to "flatten out" the hierarchy and speed efficiency in communications and performance. The sooner everybody concerned understands his or her new role and is accustomed to a new theoretical or physical working environment, the better.

Operating teams are perfectly capable of writing their own job descriptions in close consultation with line management. Also, change teams, acting in collaboration with existing operating teams, can help to make the necessary amendments to their stated functions.

From the previous list, it is obvious that a number of different departments will be actively liaising at the program planning stage. These will, of course, include the personnel or human resources department. You should make full use of the personnel management function to ensure that the following conditions and practices are well established:

- You have an organizational structure that supports corporate and local strategies and gives a necessary focus (reinforcing the mission and related goals).
- Departments have a clear idea of their accountabilities (where there is no overlap in results). If this is the case, the accountabilities will be shared.

- Opinion surveys are carried out, and results are circulated to those concerned, leading to an action plan. This should be done, ideally, on an annual basis and in every division and department.

- Organizational change is professionally managed, with a documented communication plan, full information describing the change(s) and answers to likely questions provided, where appropriate.

- Organizational charts are both freely available and regularly updated.

To summarize: The overall program, its nature and steps, must be made crystal clear to all concerned. The communication of the program, the reasons for it and its proposed methodology, must be clearly communicated: the keywords here are, as ever, clarity and timeliness.

But before the change program is introduced, you should ensure that you have prepared the way for its acceptance.

Preparing the Way for Change in Your Organization

Most organizations are internally focused, many of them to a degree that allows for complacency. When changes occur in their markets, such factors as increased or new sources of competition, for example, can appear suddenly, finding an organization unprepared and inducing, sometimes, a state of panic.

Clearly, such a state must be avoided. But how? Many successful organizations have a readiness for change incorporated into their everyday operations. These organizations have built into their overall strategy an element of advantageous impatience. This means that they do not devote resources to resolving outdated issues or to solving outdated problems. Instead, these successful organizations devote their prime intellectual resources, together with the necessary budgetary flexibility, to researching developments and seeking business opportunities. You will certainly find, using the SAP system, that you will have more time to reflect on and devote to these considerations.

In many of the previously mentioned cases of successful organization change, that same successful embracing of change is initiated by two factors: the organization's vision and its mission.

Perhaps your organization already has a vision and a mission statement. Installation of the SAP system may render them obsolete. Whether you have a corporate vision and mission or not, you will find it useful to investigate the possibility of devising ones which will assist you in managing change.

Your Organization: Its Vision. The vision of an organization originates at the top, or at least, very close to the top. It is a matter of shared values and rests on considerable leadership qualities. It may exist independently of radical strategic redirection. Whatever its status, the vision must describe the desired future state of an organization. It is a goal or series of goals that the organization must seek to achieve. Whether these goals are attained or not, the essential vision must not be lost or obscured. And of course, your organization's vision should be deployed in order to promote change.

Developing a vision allows you to think freely and without constraint. This is important, as you will need to look forward rather than being bound by the dictates of past conditions. Current limitations to your organization's freedom of action should not prevent you from envisaging any new strategic direction.

Remember: Developing a vision for an organization means that you are not planning ahead, you are imagining ahead. You are thinking about what it is possible to achieve or what it is possible to become. And if your organization's vision is wrong, change it accordingly.

You will find that the vision is fragile and tentative in the early stages. Thus you and your colleagues will need to alter it, test it, and support your findings with data, if your vision is to become robust enough to withstand close and critical scrutiny. After all, the vision must be accepted throughout the organization.

For a vision to be effective, that is, accepted and adopted, it is vital that senior management demonstrates complete commitment to it, and does so convincingly.

Once your vision is formulated correctly, you will be ready to present and promote it. Before you do so, prepare the ground as follows:

- Encourage the formation of discussion groups, or forums, in which possible alternative developments are discussed at all levels within your organization. This will encourage staff to become accustomed to challenging current assumptions and methods. In order to do so, you must demonstrate that senior management is wholeheartedly committed to your new purpose.

- Arrange informal meetings with staff where you can introduce the new thinking.

When you are ready to launch your vision, you will need to present it so as to achieve the following:

- It must be inspirational, motivating everybody to participate positively in your organization's new direction.

- It must, therefore, give staff a sense of purpose and direction, and demonstrate commitment from the top.

- It must be credible and feasible; far reaching for the unattainable will demoralize your staff.

- It should give some indication of how the vision will be realized in practical terms.

It goes without saying (or should) that the successful launch of your vision will demand a high standard of presentation skills (refer to Chapter 34, "Managing Communications Internal and External," for some useful advice on this topic). Remember, you are effectively selling a concept that will take your organization forward in line with the increased technical and informational powers provided by SAP.

Your Organization: Its Mission. First, ask yourself the most basic questions. These may be "What business are we in?" and "What business should we be in, in X years' time?"

They may focus on how your company operates, and how it should be operating, given the implementation of the SAP program. Remember, you will need to project into the future, and it must be both a desired and a feasible future.

Given that the primary responsibility of senior management is for performance and results, senior management should be posing themselves such questions as:

"What do we need to do to produce/improve upon results?"

You should not ignore the possibility that your organization may be doing a number of things correctly. In which case, you should also explore the question:

"Is there anywhere within our organization where we are doing X already?"

It may be that your mission is to practice what your organization is already preaching—perhaps, so far, unheard or unexecuted.

If not, then senior management will need to ask the following questions of line management and employees:

"What do we do that helps you produce the results that we all agree are our aims?" and "What do we do that hampers your producing these desired results?"

These questions should be answered as a primary task before formulating either mission statement or consequent strategy.

Your mission statement is your means of defining your organization's commercial rationale and identifying its markets and goals. You will need to ensure that your organization's mission serves as a focus of corporate cohesion, the values expressed are to be shared in pursuit of a common purpose.

These values might include such active qualities as a stronger emphasis on service and customer care. Whatever your organization's set of values, care must be taken that the mission incorporates these values.

Remember, you need everybody in the organization to adhere to certain standards and work to a common purpose.

Strategy goes hand in hand with your organization's mission. It is all very well to have a purpose, but you must have some idea of how that purpose will be achieved. Your strategy might identify new markets and how your organization will seek to establish a competitive edge in those markets.

Your mission must openly contain a message that challenges your staff. This may appear to be blindingly obvious, but it is surprising how often managers fail in this vital respect. Your organization has good team members, and you want to keep them. Remember, people want to work for a dynamic, thriving organization, nobody wants to work for an ostrich.

Remember, too, "purpose" and "strategy" are worthless words unless you put them into action.

Finally, your mission statement will only fulfill its purpose of creating a coherent and cohesive sense of corporate direction if you have identified the appropriate means and methods and requisite performance standards. These, once identified, must be clearly communicated to your audience at the launch of your mission.

Further, mission-related change needs to be reinforced by actions aimed at bringing about change in operating behavior. Here, you will find that training focused on changing or adapting attitudes, beliefs and behavior (as opposed to being solely focused on imparting information) is very effective.

One of your objectives is to help your organization become one that constantly learns, and hence constantly makes progress in line with social, economic, and market developments.

Change is more easily accepted when it is incorporated into an organizational structure based on updating and improving existing skills and acquiring new ones. In a plethora of systems and procedures designed to move products and services, it is easy to forget that the main resource of any business consists of its people.

But first of all, you will need to design your plan of campaign.

Planning Your Change Management

Once you have clearly communicated the reasons for change, you must devote time and resources to ensuring that all stages of your change strategy implementation are agreed and communicated.

Before the new strategy can be implemented, you will need to agree and plan the following:

- The program for change

- The identification of change agents, for example, in the case of drawing up new job descriptions, personnel management, line managers and their teams

- Informing and consulting with those involved about the change process, shared ownership and an atmosphere of active collaboration should be established

- Identifiying those who are unlikely to agree with the change program and persuading them of the benefits

Finally, if you need to set up a program of downsizing, adopt the following tactics:

- Proceed with great care, but announce your final plan openly.

- Wherever possible, seek voluntary layoffs, notably from among members of dissenting groups.

- Ensure that outplacement consultancy services are available, check these out first; use your networks to identify consultancies that will provide the quality service your organization gives, in this as in all other areas. These will serve to reduce stress among candidates for laying off and, as a result, among their colleagues.

■ If valuable personnel are lost to your organization because of insufficient work for them to do, take steps to remain in touch with these people. Such people often become consultants, and their services may well be called upon by your organization in the future. New consultants often find, upon leaving employment, that their first customer is their last (most recent) employer.

Remember, layoffs hurt but they are rarely fatal. Most laid-off employees find work within six months of "Downsizing Day," and most of the rest succeed in finding employment during the course of the year following "D-Day."

Of course, significant and increasing numbers of laid-off employees opt for setting up independently of an employer. This may mean setting up a consultancy practice, a small business, or a franchise.

If your valued and now lost employees choose to take this route, it is always best practice to remain on good terms with them. As previously indicated, it is surprising how many newly established small businesses and consultancies find that their first project is commissioned by their previous employer. Such relationships can be both highly cost- and time-saving, with obvious beneficial shortcuts (based on an established mutual understanding).

You must also bear in mind at this stage that it is always a mistake to try and change everything at once. Given the destabilizing effect of change we noted at the beginning of this chapter, you will be aware that everybody needs some element of stability, however vestigial that may be.

Change is best implemented in stages, progressively. So before you begin your implementation program, remember the following:

■ Try to produce steady change.

■ Management must avoid getting out of phase with the rest of the organization.

■ Do not throw out perfectly good elements of your old systems, which have historically encouraged success: Wait until these have been superseded.

■ Avoid experimentation, especially when perceived as a fashionable, "academic" solution: Opt for the practical and feasible procedure every time.

You will find that the implementation program itself is best broken down logically in discrete components. These are as follows:

1. Agree to the timescale(s).

2. Agree to the overall goals.

3. Agree to the strategy.

4. Agree to the interventions to be used.

5. Watch, observe, and record the change process.

6. Evaluate the findings.

7. Take corrective action.

8. Identify and deal with any obstacles.

9. Publish the success.

These nine components are described in detail in the sections that follow.

Agree to the Timescale. The change implementation program must have a definite starting point. The program is the responsibility of line managers; it must always be perceived as being owned by management, consultants are best deployed in planning and training for change, or in assisting with corporate communications and internal and external monitoring.

You will find that the shorter the agreed timescale for change in your organization, the more likely it is that the change will be contained and controlled. This means that the results will necessarily have a greater degree of predictability.

Conversely, the longer the agreed timescale, the less predictable will be the results. However, you should bear in mind that a longer time frame, with less predictability, will allow for increased opportunism.

You should, of course, agree to the timescale that suits your business: its size, scope, and current conditions. The SAP system will assist you in determining the amount of time needed for streamlining business reengineering, for example.

Agree to the Overall Goals. The goals must be agreed in advance and made public throughout the organization. These goals must be both understood by all and achievable. See the earlier sections on vision and mission: The goals have already been devised. The two will act as mutual reinforcement. Certain therapeutic regimes that include more than one drug are said to be more powerful in their effects than a single drug used alone; the same is true of vision plus mission plus stated goals. When they are acting together, the combination is more effective than any one of them acting alone.

Your goals will be both qualitative and quantitative. To take an example, when formulating a marketing strategy you will be seeking to answer the following goal-related questions, among others:

Qualitative:

- Positioning—how to achieve a stronger position in the marketplace and among competitors

- Differentiation—how your organization differs from others offering similar products or services

- Segmentation—how to acquire increased knowledge of the demographics and qualitative characteristics of your market segments

- Cultural—how to improve the sense of identity, quality and common purpose

- Stylistic—how to achieve an improved image for your organization that impacts positively on its culture

- Functional—what purpose or purposes your organization fulfills beyond its own needs

Quantitative:

- Budget adequacy as well as constraints

- Costing methods and cost characteristics

- Price strategy

- Market share

- Growth rate

All the preceding commercial elements will be familiar to you. They are not limited to a strategy confined to marketing; they apply to the majority of corporate strategies.

The marketing strategy analogy holds good. Just consider how increasing segmentation in the market is a feature of the contemporary business world. The spread of increasingly demanding customers and increasingly sophisticated consumers serves to produce this effect, together with an increasing overlap between the various segments, and with the products and services devised to meet their demands. SAP is designed to help you meet these and other functional demands and their allied activities.

Agree to the Strategy. The strategy of implementation now asks the question "How are we going to produce/improve upon results?" You will need to consider this, and may find the following list of prompting questions useful (you will probably be able to add to this list):

- Is the implementation plan going to be initiated entirely from the top, from senior management, or will it be generated via consultative processes from the lower levels within your organization? Or will it be a mixture of both top-down and bottom-up? (Whichever option you select, make sure that it is one that suits the style and culture of your organization.)

- How do we consult with individuals, teams, departments, and so on?

- What are we offering our staff and when do we need to know their responses?

- Will the change be made by division, by department, or at some other level?

- What degree of responsibility are we going to allow departmental managers in the decisions to be made?

- What methods of communication are we going to use to inform staff of what is happening? (Refer to Chapter 34, "Managing Communications Internal and External," for some further tips on internal communications best practice.)

- What external assistance will we be likely to require, and when?

- What training strategies are we going to use?

- How do we measure success?

- What is this going to cost, and who is going to monitor the budget? (You must devise a way of drawing up a budget which takes into account the unpredictable, however anomalous this may seem. Change contingent upon SAP implementation is cost-effective within a given term, but the implementation of a change program should not itself be a matter for cost-cutting exercises.)

Agree to the Interventions to Be Used. You will need to use some forms of intervention to coach and motivate those concerned, and drive the change through your organization. These processes must be understood by everybody concerned. You should also take care to avoid expressing these methods in terms that allow your audience to perceive them as manipulative.

Examples of intervention procedures could be as follows:

- Further training

- Time off for hours worked, where goals have been achieved

- Recognition events (informal celebratory gatherings)

- In-house promotion of information about the change program via, for example, dedicated newsletters or open access to change program rationale and process on CD-ROM

Watch, Observe, and Record the Change Process. You will find that follow-up and reinforcement are necessary to keep your change program on track. At all stages you must be aware of levels of:

- Understanding

- Acceptance

- Progress

And, of course, you must be able to monitor performance in terms of results.

Change agents in the front line must feel part of the change process in order for them to:

- Feel in control of their element or elements of the program

- Maximize their contributions

Your change program should be flexible enough to allow for amendments by those driving it. Where possible, the work teams themselves should also observe and record the change process as it relates to them. These results should be fed back to senior management.

> **Note**
>
> Remember, no plan is going to be 100 percent accurate and successful. Just try to aim at a target as close as possible to that figure, and give yourself and your team or teams a suitably metaphorical pat on the back if you attain a 70 percent to 90 percent success rate. After all, you will be performing a delicate balancing act in managing change, balancing the demands of entrepreneurial and developmental opportunism with those of planning and control. It is not easy.

Evaluate the Findings. You will need to determine:

- What has been done

- What effect this is having on the organization and the business

You may find the following evaluation methods useful:

- Local meetings and site/division visits, held by senior management

- Discussion groups and invitations to analysts to review the organization and business postchange will provide helpful feedback

- Customer visits and seminars to monitor external effects

- Brainstorming sessions among teams involved

- You may also find that some people need to air complaints (which is often a function of human nature rather than poor change management). If this is the case, then make time to allow people to complain. Do not let complaints fester, deal with them as quickly and as constructively as possible.

- Surveys by means of, for example, questionnaires (which may be transmitted via e-mail).

You will, of course, use these findings to adjust your change program accordingly. Be prepared to change the change program. Remember, you have designed it to be as flexible as possible, as you will be aware that change itself is not always entirely predictable.

However beneficial and positive your organizational change is, you should bear in mind that change is frequently perceived as, at best, unwelcome and unsettling, and at worst, a threat to the security, stability and livelihood of those on the receiving end.

This constituent of change, allied with your preparedness to cope with unexpected developments, means you are likely to discover at times a need for the subject of the next section.

Take Corrective Action. As you will have seen in the previous list, your change program feedback will often lead to further corrective action. You must ensure that such action is immediate and effective. You should also ensure that it is properly publicized, you must give explanations of why an action was necessary.

Where possible, you should give feedback to corrective action teams, made up of those people doing the job where the problems are arising.

> **Note**
>
> Remember, timing is important, and speed of response is of the essence, but make sure you get your facts right.

When corrective action has been taken, it may be necessary to rework the evaluation of findings to determine what effect the action has had.

> **Note**
>
> Do not be too quick to take corrective action. You should first ensure that the stated problem has not been exaggerated and is not the result of a lack of training or understanding. Do not allow yourself to be panicked into a firefighting mode, as panic spreads faster through an organization than good news does, and the deleterious effects on morale are obvious. Poor morale always acts as a brake on the successful implementation of a change program.

Identify and Deal with the Obstacles. Any obstacles (and you will be living in a perfect corporate world if there are none) must be identified. These obstacles are often in the form of one or more of the following:

- Lack of commitment from senior management (which you should have obviated by means of vision and mission formulation and acceptance)

- Lack of involved responsibility, people waiting for somebody else to make decisions and make things happen

- Out-of-date working methods (that, for example, do not take into account the versatility and comprehensive nature of the SAP system)

- An inadequately trained workforce, unaware of the issues involved in the change program. Further training needs may be identified, and meeting them will prove invaluable in the medium- to long-term.

The communications strategy contained within your change program should enable you to cope successfully with the majority of these problems. Remember, regarding these obstacles as opportunities for further, tangible (and measurable) change will help you greatly when you are incorporating them into the main body of your change program.

Publicize the Success. Your change program will not be just a matter of gaining commitment, promoting development, and overcoming obstacles. You will have successes to enjoy, as well. These successes must be publicized, making their celebration as visible and enjoyable as possible.

After all, you are promoting confidence and enthusiasm. You are also ensuring that the continuance of your change program is facilitated and its future success has a firm foundation.

You will know what to publicize. This may include such successes as the following:

- Meeting a key date ahead of or on the date designated by the time plan
- Implementing a change within budget
- The establishment of a successful new working method
- Achieving cost savings
- Receiving customer praise
- Good, positive press coverage
- Increase in customer base
- New product or service launch
- Corrective action team results

You will certainly find that all of the preceding, and more, will be possible with SAP. However, you will also be wondering how best to communicate your successes. You may do so via the following methods:

- Dedicated newsletters (produced in-house, exploiting your DTP package to save costs)
- Articles in corporate publications
- Group meetings
- Two-way communication channels, inviting feedback and suggestions (a success may provide opportunities for further successes)
- Notice boards

Your celebration of success (congratulations, by the way) should never ignore the possibility of eliciting useful feedback. As previously suggested, opportunities can lead to further opportunities. You should be alert to this possibility, and ensure that everybody knows your program aims to build on success.

You will find, if you have not discovered this already, that publicizing success helps to maintain impetus and morale. So remember to keep everybody informed. And remember to celebrate each and every one of your successes in a style that is appropriate to your organization.

Change is never easy, but when the correct balance between planning and control and openness to unforeseen opportunities is achieved, change is highly stimulating to growth and development. It is also a means of maintaining a sense of belonging and of involvement among those engaged with implementing change and meeting its challenges. And that, of course, means everybody in your organization everywhere.

Beneficial organic change will affect those within and without the bounds of your organization. Your customers and suppliers, too, will benefit, as will your shareholders and, in fact, all those with a stake in your organization.

Be sure to check their opinions in order to keep up the momentum of change and ensure that your direction is the right one for your organization.

Finally, a checklist of principal operative words and phrases:

- Agreed-upon aims
- Build on existing strengths
- Collaboration
- Commitment
- Common cause
- Communication
- Consultation
- Control
- Corrective action
- Flexibility
- High standards
- Openness to opportunity
- Readiness to act
- Speed of response

From Here...

In this chapter, we have covered the issues of change that have to be dealt with when implementing an SAP system. In many cases, the main reason for implementing SAP is to facilitate change, to make organizations more efficient, responsive, and profitable. Even though the process of change has become commonplace in the business world, it is frequently poorly managed resulting in the failure to maximize the potential benefits.

By recognizing the need for change and the practical processes necessary to successfully achieve it, you will be well placed to manage this important area of the SAP implementation process.

- Chapter 31, "Overview of SAP Implementations"
- Chapter 34, "Managing Communications Internal and External"
- Chapter 36, "The Human Issues of SAP Implementation"

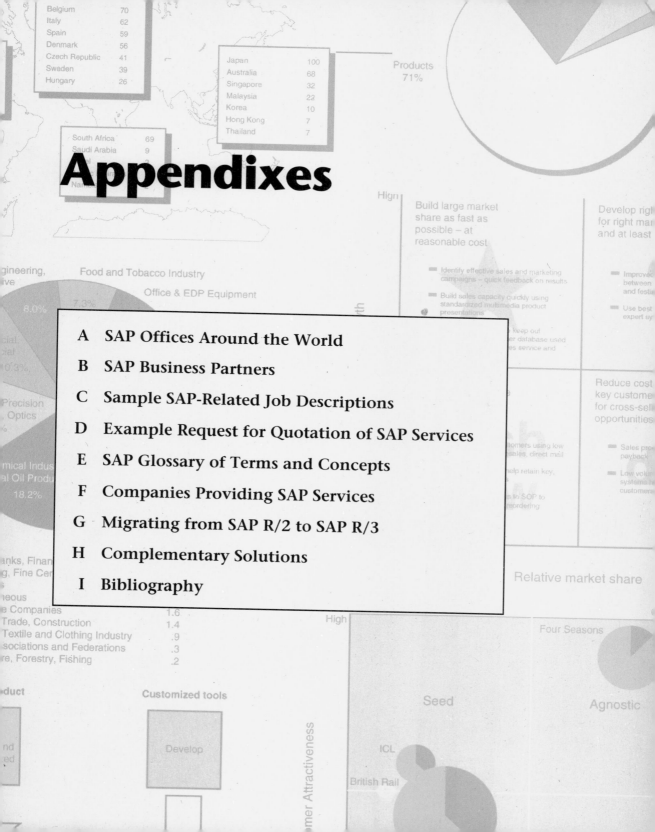

Appendixes

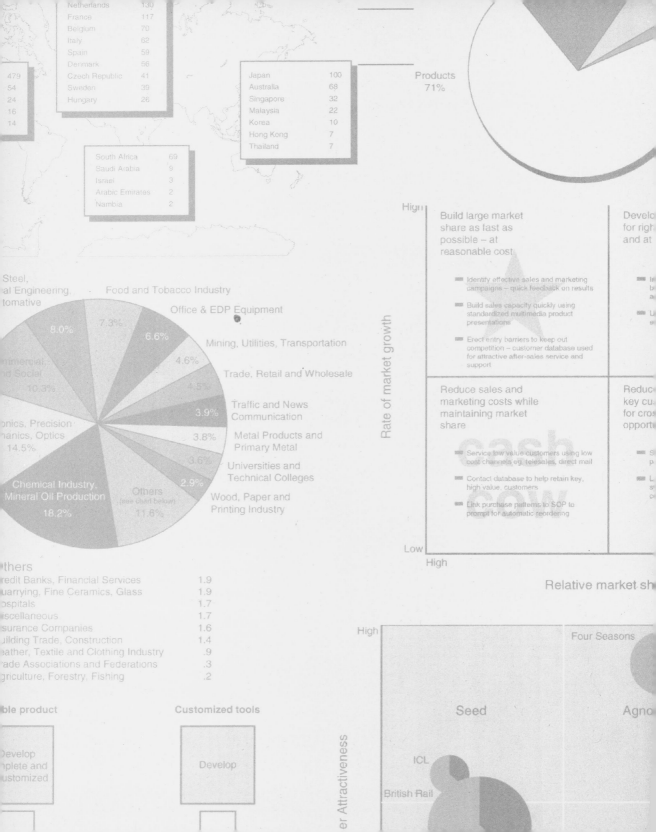

Appendix A

SAP Offices Around the World

This appendix lists SAP's offices around the world. They can deal with product sales or other inquiries.

SAP Americas

Corporate Headquarters
SAP America, Inc.
701 Lee Road, Suite 200
Wayne, PA 19087
Tel +1 (610) 725-4500
Fax +1 (610) 725-4555

Argentina
SAP Argentina
Torre Bouchard
Bouchard 547, 12° piso 1106 Buenos Aires
Tel +54 (1) 317-1700
Fax + 54 (1) 317-1701

Brazil
SAP Brazil Comércio e Representacoes Ltd.
Rua Guararapes 2064 - 11° andar
Brooklin, Sao Paulo,
C.E.P. 04561 - 004
Tel +55 (11) 505-5757
Fax +55 (11) 505-2307

Canada
SAP Canada, Inc.
4120 Yonge Street,
Suite 600
North York, Ontario M2P 2B8
Tel +1 (416) 229-0574
Fax +1 (416) 229-0575

Branch Offices
Calgary
Western Regional Office
400 3rd Avenue, S.W.
Suite 1515, Canterra Tower
Calgary, Alberta T2P 4H2
Tel +1 (403) 269-5222
Fax +1 (403) 234-8082

Montreal
380 Rue St. Antoine
Bureau 7300
Montreal, Quebec H2Y 3X7
Tel +1 (514) 350-7300
Fax +1 (514) 350-7500

Ottawa
155 Queen Street,
Suite 900
Ottawa, Ontario K1P6L1
Tel +1 (613) 786-3270
Fax +1 (613) 786-3271

Vancouver
1300-666 Burrard Street
Vancouver,
British Columbia V6C3J8
Tel +1 (604) 681-3809
Fax +1 (604) 688-0739

Mexico
SAP Mexico
Edificio Plaza Reforma Santa Fé
Prol Paseo de la Reforma No 600-200
Col. Pena Blance Sta. Fé
01210 Mexico, D.F.
Tel +52 (5) 257-7500
Fax +52 (5) 257-7501

USA
SAP America Inc.
Corporate Headquarters
701 Lee Road,
Suite 200
Wayne, PA 19087
Tel +1 (610) 725-4500
Fax +1 (610) 725-4555

Branch Offices
Atlanta
Six Concourse Parkway
Suite 1200
Atlanta, GA 30328
Tel +1 (770) 353-2900
Fax +1 (770) 353-2950

Bellevue
800 Bellevue Way, N.E.
4th Floor
Bellevue, WA 98004
Tel +1 (206) 462-6395
Fax +1 (206) 462-2082

Boston
Bay Colony Corporate Center
1000 Winter Street
Suite 4400
Waltham, MA 02154
Tel +1 (617) 672-6500
Fax +1 (617) 672-6501

Chicago
5 Westbrook Corporate Center
10th Floor
West Chester, IL 60154
Tel +1 (708) 947-3400
Fax +1 (708) 947-3404

Cincinnati
312 Walnut Street
24th Floor
Cincinnati, OH 45202
Tel +1 (513) 977-5400
Fax +1 (513) 977-5401

Cleveland
Society Center
127 Public Square
Suite 5000
Cleveland, OH 44114
Tel +1 (216) 615-3000
Fax +1 (216) 615-3001

Denver

4600 South Ulster Street
Suite 700
Denver, CO 80237
Tel +1 (303) 740-6696
Fax +1 (303) 740-6612

Foster City

950 Tower Lane
12th Floor
Foster City
California 94404-2127
Tel +1 (415) 637-1655
Fax +1 (415) 637-9592

Houston

200 City West Blvd.
Suite 1600
Houston, TX 77042
Tel +1 (713) 917-5200
Fax +1 (713) 917-5201

Irvine

18101 Von Karman Ave.
Suite 900
Irvine, CA 92715
Tel +1 (714) 622-2200
Fax +1 (714) 622-2201

Irving

600 East Las Colinas Blvd.
Suite 2000
Irving, TX 75039
Tel +1 (214) 868-2000
Fax +1 (214) 868-2001

Lester

Northeast Regional Office
International Court One
100 Stevens Drive
2nd Floor
Lester, PA 19113
Tel +1 (610) 595-4900
Fax +1 (610) 521-6290

Minneapolis

3530 Dain Bosworth Plaza
60 S. 6th Street
Minneapolis, MN 55402
Tel +1 (612) 359-5000
Fax +1 (612) 359-5001

Parsippany

Morris Corporate Center
300 Interplace Parkway, Atrium A
4th Floor
Parsippany, NJ 07054
Tel +1 (201) 331-6000
Fax +1 (201) 331-6001

Philadelphia District Office

100 Stevens Drive
Suite 350
Philadelphia, PA 19113
Tel +1 (610) 595-4900
Fax +1 (610) 521-6290

Pittsburgh

301 Grant Street
One Oxford Street
Suite 1500
Pittsburgh, PA 15219
Tel +1 (412) 255-3795
Fax +1 (412) 255-3797

St. Louis

City Place One, Suite 430
1 City Place
St. Louis, MO 63141
Tel +1 (314) 213-7500
Fax +1 (314) 213-7501

Appendixes

SAP Europe

SAP Aktiengesellschaft
P.O. Box 1461, D-69185 Walldorf
Neurottstrasse 16, D-69190 Walldorf
Tel +49 (180) 534-3424
Telex 466 004 sap d
Fax +49 (180) 534-3420

Austria
SAP Ges.m.b.H.
Austria
Stadlauer Strasse 54
1221 Vienna
Tel +43 (1) 220-5511
Fax +43 (1) 220-5511-222

Branch Offices
Linz
Langgasse 11
4020 Linz
Tel +43 (732) 600460-0
Fax +43 (732) 600460-11

Salzburg-Wals
Loiger Strasse 220
5071 Salzburg-Wals
Tel +43 (662) 853687
Fax +43 (662) 853687-22

Belgium
N.V. SAP Belgium SA
2, Bld. de la Woluwedal
1150 Brussels
Tel +32 (2) 778-0511
Fax +32 (2) 772-5051

Czech Republic
SAP CR s.r.o.
Nové Butovice
Za mototechnou 971
15500 Praha 5
Tel +42 (2) 65197-01
Fax +42 (2) 65198-43

Denmark
SAP Danmark A/S
Ringager 4B
2605 Brøndby/Copenhagen
Tel +45 (43) 43-3900
Fax +45 (43) 43-1688

France
SAP France SA
"Les Olympiades"
10/12 Avenue des Olympiades
94132 Fontenay-sous-Bois
Tel +33 (1) 49 74 45 45
Fax +33 (1) 48 75 20 96

Germany
SAP Aktiengesellschaft
P.O. Box 1461, D-69185 Walldorf
Neurottstrasse 16, D-69190 Walldorf
Tel +49 (180) 534-3424
Telex 466 004 sap d
Fax +49 (180) 534-3420

Branch Offices
Berlin
P.O. Box 510547
13365 Berlin
or
Waldstrasse 86-90
13403 Berlin
Tel +49 (30) 41092-0
Fax +49 (30) 41092-111

Düsseldorf
P.O. Box 3227
40849 Ratingen
or
Berliner Strasse 91
40880 Ratingen
Tel +49 (2102) 4802-0
Fax +49 (2102) 4802-11

Hamburg
Hans-Henny-Jahnn-Weg 35
22085 Hamburg
Tel +49 (40) 22707-0
Fax +49 (40) 22707-101

Munich
Max-von-Eyth-Strasse 3
85737 Ismaning
Tel +49 (89) 960907-0
Fax +49 (89) 960907-33

Great Britain
SAP (U.K.) Limited
7, New Square
Bedfont Lakes, Feltham
Middlesex, TW14 8HA
Tel +44 (181) 893-2893
Fax +44 (181) 844-1200

Greece
SA Hellas S.A.*
103 Kallirois Street
11741 Athens
Tel +30 (1) 924-0242
Fax +30 (1) 924-0350
* Through Partners

Hungary
DYNASOFT Kft*
Bartfai u. 54
1115 Budapest
Tel +36 (1) 2034272
Fax +36 (1) 2034273
* Through Partners

Italy
SAP Italy SpA
Centro Direzionale Colleoni
Viale Colleoni 17
Palazzo Orione 3
20041 Agrate Brianza/Milano
Tel +39 (39) 68 791
Fax +39 (39) 60 91 005

Branch Offices
Rome
Via Bianchini 51
00150 Rome
Tel +39 (6) 51956-22
Fax +39 (6) 51956-27

Netherlands
SAP Nederland B.V.
Bruistensingel 400
5232 AG's-Hertogenbosch
P.O. Box 3292
5203 DG's-Hertogenbosch
Tel +31 (73) 645 7500
Fax +31 (73) 641 9130

Norway
Branch Office
of SAP Danmark A/SSAP Norge
Postboks 58, Fjodveien 1
1322 Høvik
Tel +47 (67) 53-1570
Fax +47 (67) 53-5117

Poland
SAP Polska Sp. z.o.o.
ul. Migdalowa 4
02-760 Warsaw
Tel +48 (22) 645-1101
Fax. +48 (22) 645-1112

Portugal
Branch Office
of SAP Espana y Portugal, S.A.Lisboa
Av. Liberdade 245-9° C
1250 Lisboa 2
Tel +351 (1) 312-9000
Fax +351 (1) 312-9015

Russian Federation
SAP CONSULT C.I.S.
Simonowskij wal 26-A
109088 Moscow
Russian Federation
Tel +7 (095) 275-0189
Fax +7 (095) 275-6181

Branch Office
Moscow
Simonowskij wal 26-A
109088 Moscow
Tel +7 (95) 275-0454
Fax +7 (95) 275-6181

Appendixes

Slowakia
Branch Office
of SAP CR s.r.o Bratislava
Kutlikova 17
P.O. Box 229
8500 Bratislava 5
Tel +42 (7) 834-663 or -673 or -650
Fax +42 (7) 830-792

Spain
SAP Espana y Portugal, S.A.
Torre Mapfre
Carrer de la Marina 16-18, 11 B/C
08005 Barcelona
Tel +34 (3) 483-3500
Fax. +34 (3) 483-3501

Branch Office
Madrid
Edificio Torre Picasso
Pza. Pablo Ruiz Picasso, S/N 4D
28020 Madrid
Tel +34 (1) 456-7200
Fax +34 (1) 456-7201

Sweden
SAP Svenska AB
Box 12297
Gustavslundsvägen 151
10227 Stockholm
Tel +46 (8) 80 96 80
Fax +46 (8) 26 22 78

Switzerland
SAP (Switzerland) AG
Leugenestrasse 6
P.O. Box 130
2500 Biel 6
Tel +41 (32) 427-111
Fax +41 (32) 427-211

Branch Offices
Zürich
SAP (Schweiz) AG
Schulungszentrum (Zürich)
Eichwatt 3
8105 Regensdorf

Tel +41 (1) 8711-511
Fax +41 (1) 8410-708

Lausanne
SAP (Suisse) SA
WTCL
Avenue Gratta-Paille 2
Case postale 469
1000 Lausanne 30 Grey
Tel +41 (21) 641-5555
Fax +41 (21) 641-5550

Turkey
SAP Istanbul*
Fahtettin Kerim Goekay Cad.22
Altunizade/Istanbul
Tel +90 (216) 3918462
Fax. +90 (216) 3335389
* Through Partners

SAP Africa and Middle East

Israel
Advanced Technology Ltd.*
Atidim
Neve Sharet
P.O. Box 58180
Tel-Aviv 61581
Tel +972 (3) 5483-530
Fax +972 (3) 5483-653
* Through Partners

Saudi Arabia
SAP Arabia/Saudi Arabia*
Jamjoom Center
P.O. Box 4836
Jeddah 21412
Tel +966 (2) 660-8211
Fax +966 (2) 660-7757
* Through Partners

South Africa
SAP SA (Pty) Ltd.
Dunkeld Crescent North
Cnr. Albury & Jan Smuts Ave.
Dunkeld West 2196

or
P.O. Box 254
Randburg 2125
Tel +27 (11) 2 69-48 00
Fax +27 (11) 8 80-65 35

Branch Offices
Cape Town
Metropolitan Life Building
25th Floor
7 Coen Steytler Avenue
P.O. Box 4716
8000 Cape Town
Tel +27 (21) 418-2860-7
Fax +27 (21) 419-9583

Durban
4th Floor
Morningside Chambers
510, Windermere Road
Durban-4001
Tel +27 (31) 231-157
Fax +27 (31) 231-157

United Arabian Emirates
SAP Arabia/Gulf Region*
P.O. Box 33188
Dubai U.A.E.
Tel +971 (4) 31-0777
Fax +971 (4) 31-0410
* Through Partners

SAP Asia Pacific Rim

China
SAP/China
99 Shuang Quing Lu
Hai Dian District,
Beijing, China
Post Code: 100084
Tel +86 (10) 262-3388
Fax +86 (10) 261-0214

Hong Kong
SAP Hong Kong
Suite 1111 - 1114,
11/F, Cityplaza 4
12 Taikoo Wan Road
Taikoo Shing
Hong Kong
Tel +85 (2) 2539-1800
Fax +85 (2) 2539-1818

Japan
SAP Japan Co. Ltd.
Loop-x 17 fl, 9-15,
9-15 Kaigan, 3-chome, Minato-Ku,
Tokyo 108
Tel +81 (3) 5440-2001
Fax +81 (3) 5440-2021

Branch Offices
Tokyo
Gotenyama Mori Bldg.
4-7-35 Kita-Shinagawa, Shinagawa-ku
Tokyo 140
Tel +81 (3) 5423-9300
Fax +81 (3) 5423-9399

Korea
SAP Korea
23/F SsangYong Tower
23-2 Yoido-dong, Youngdeungpo-ku
Seoul 150-010l
Tel +82 (2) 3771-1800
Fax. +82 (2) 3771-1818

Malaysia
SAP Data Processing (Malaysia) Sdn Bnd
Letter Box 14
14/Floor Bangunan Arab-Malaysian
55 Jalan Raja Chulan
50200 Kuala Lumpur
Tel +60 (3) 201-3233
Fax +60 (3) 201- 2688

Appendixes

Philippines
SAP Philippines
32/F Citibank Tower
Citibank Plaza
8741 Paseo de Roxas
1200 Makati City
Metro Manila
Tel +63 (2) 848-0181
Fax +63 (2) 848-0168

Singapore
SAP Asia Pte Ltd.
750A Chai Chee Road
7th Floor
Chai Chee Industrial Park
Singapore 469001
Tel +65 446 1800
Fax +65 249 1818

Thailand
SAP Thailand Limited
22nd Floor
Liberty Square Building
287 Silom Road, Bangrak
Bangkok 10500
Tel +66 (2) 631-1800
Fax +66 (2) 631-1819

SAP Australia and New Zealand

Australia
SAP Australia Pty. Ltd.
Northside Gardens
Level 1,
168 Walker Street
North Sydney NSW 2060
Tel +61 (2) 9935-4500
Fax +61 (2) 9935-4644

Branch Offices
Adelaide
Level 24
State Bank Building
91 King William Street
Adelaide, SA5000

Tel +61 (8) 233-5814
Fax +61 (8) 233-5834

Brisbane
Level 21
Gold AMP Building
10 Eagle Street
Brisbane, QLD 4000
Tel +61 (7) 232-0326
Fax +61 (7) 323-0331

Melbourne
Level 3
Digital Building
564 St. Kilda Road
Melbourne, VIC 3004
Tel +61 (3) 9207-4100
Fax +61 (3) 9207-4244

New Zealand
SAP New Zealand Limited
Level 20 ASB Bank Center
135 Albert Street
Auckland
Tel +64 (9) 357-5050
Fax +64 (9) 358-7340

Branch Offices
Wellington
Level 5
Castrol House
36 Customhouse Quay
Wellington
Tel +64 (4) 499-9866
Fax +64 (4) 499-8035

Appendix B

SAP Business Partners

SAP Business Partners are a very important part of the SAP world, and in Chapter 38 you can learn more about what the different types of partners do, and the partner certification process.

Underneath the name of each partner listed here, you will see one or more of the following legends:

- Business Development
- Complementary Product
- HR Consulting
- Independent Vendor
- Implementation
- Logo
- Platform
- Systemhouse
- Technology

This denotes what type of partnership agreement the partner has.

Partners may have more than one partnership agreement type; for example, both may be a logo and a platform partner—and each known partnership is shown.

In this appendix, partners are listed alphabetically within countries. Where the partner requests that contacts about SAP from a country be made to another country, or to an e-mail address, the SAP contact points out that the partner requests are shown.

If you are using the list to locate a supplier of SAP-related services, you will find that the contact points take you to the right part of the organization (for example, the global IBM number is the SAP information desk, not just IBM in general).

If you are using the list as a source of SAP employment, then you should use the contact points here to direct you to the most suitable person for your purpose. Chapter 41, "How to Find Employment Working with SAP," contains some helpful advice. The list is not exhaustive. If you are a SAP partner, and want to be included in the next edition, please e-mail information about your company to: **info@asap.consultancy.co.uk.**

Ernst & Young
Logo
Diego Scanappieco
Maipu 942 - Ground Floor
1340 Buenos Aires
Argentina
+54-1-313-5327
+54-1-313-2176

IBM Corp.
Logo
IBM SAP Consulting Hotline
ibmsap@vnet.ibm.com
http://www.csc.ibm.com/
sap/Argentina
800-IBM-0222-USA-;
610-892-3009
please phone or e-mail

IBM Corp.
Platform
Technology
IBM SAP Competency
Centers
ibmsap@
vnet.ibm.com
http://
www.csc.ibm.com/
sap/Argentina
800-IBM-0222-USA-;
610-892-3009
please phone or e-mail

KPMG
Logo
Fernando Dolto
Av. Leandro n. Alem 1050,
5th Floor
1001 Buenos Aires
Argentina
+54-1-313-9633

ORIGIN INTERNATIONAL
Logo
Vedia 3892
1430 Buenos Aires
Argentina
+54-1-5452862
+54-1-5452927

A.T. KEARNEY
Logo
Mr. Tony White
Level 10, 124 Walker St
North Sydney 2060
Australia
+61-612-993 54376
+61-612-993 54395

ANDERSEN CONSULTING
Logo
Mr. Mark Dowling
141 Walker Street
North Sydney NSW
Australia
+61-2-9922 6708
+61-2-9922 2065

AT&T GIS AUSTRALIA
PTY LTD
Platform
Mr. Graham Brown
8-20 Napier Street
North Sydney
NSW 2060
Australia
+61-2-9964-8
+61-2-9964-8372

Ernst & Young
Logo
Terry Young
The Ernst & Young
Building
321 Kent Street
Sydney
NSW 2000
Australia
+61-2-248-555
+61-2-262-6565

Hewlett-Packard
Logo
Implementation
Platform
Technology
SAP-HP Competence Center
Level 2, 186 Walker Street
North Sydney
NSW 2060
Australia
+61-2-9935-4069
+61-2-9935-4610

KPMG
Logo
John Hunt
The KPMG Centre
45 Clarence Street
Sydney
NSW 2000
Australia
+61-2-335-7000

Ernst & Young
Logo
Joannes Heiling
Teinfaltstrasse 4
1010 Vienna
Austria
+43-1-535-4414
+43-1-535-4004

IBM Corp.
Logo
IBM SAP Consulting Hotline
ibmsap@vnet.ibm.com
http://www.csc.ibm.com/
sap/Australia
800-IBM-0222-USA-;
610-892-3009
please phone or e-mail

Oracle Deutschland GmbH
Technology
Nick Evered
Level 12, 1 Pacific Highway
North Sydney 2060
Australia
+61-2-9900-1000
+61-2-9900-1915

Hewlett-Packard
Logo
Implementation
Platform
Technology
SAP-HP Competence Center
Lieblgasse 1
1222 Vienna
Austria
+43-1-250006750 ext.6900
+43-1-25000272

IBM Corp.
Platform
Technology
IBM SAP Competency
Centers
ibmsap@
vnet.ibm.com
http://
www.csc.ibm.com/
sap/Australia
800-IBM-0222-USA-;
610-892-3009
please phone or e-mail

ORIGIN
INTERNATIONAL
Logo
P.O.Box 6373
North Sydney
NSW 2060
Australia
+61-2-99661811
+61-2-99661844

IBM Corp.
Logo
IBM SAP Consulting
Hotline
ibmsap@
vnet.ibm.com
http://
www.csc.ibm.com/
sap/Austria
800-IBM-0222-USA
610-892-3009
please phone or e-mail

IBM Corp.
Platform
Technology
IBM SAP Competency
Centers
ibmsap@vnet.ibm.com
http://
www.csc.ibm.com/
sap/Austria
800-IBM-0222-USA-;
610-892-3009
please phone or e-mail

KPMG
Logo
KPMG Austria
Grosse Mohrengasse 1
1020 Vienna
Austria
+43-1-2166-8700

LMS Umweltsysteme
Independent Vendor
DIpl.-Ing. Dr. Hans Kerzl
Franz-Josef-Strasse 6
8700 Leoben
Austria
+43-842-46 6 77
+43-3842-46 6 77-9

ORIGIN INTERNATIONAL
Logo
Triersterstrasse 66
1101 Vienna
Austria
+43-60101
+43-60235568

Siemens AG Osterreich
Independent Vendor
Hr. Dr. Leyrer
Gudrunstrasse
1100 Wien
Austria
+43-1-1707 46320
+43-1-1707 56668

TOPCALL International
Ges.m.b.H
Independent Vendor
Fred Zimmer
Zetschegasse
1232 Wien
Austria
+43-1-661 330
+43-1-661 3321

ACEC-OSI
HR-Consulting
Gilbert WAUTHIER
Rue Vital FRANCOISSE 205
Marcinelle 6001
Belgium
+33-71-4462-01
+33-71-4462-62

CALLATAY & WOUTERS
Implementation
P de Wouters
Rue Pire De Deken, 14
1040 Brussels
Belgium
+32-2-736-10-07
+32-2-736-67-02

Dialogic Telecom
Europe/Gammalink
Independent Vendor
Mr. Thierry Delire
Airway Park
Lozenberg 23
1932 St Stevens Wolwe
Belgium
+32-2-712-43-11
+32-2-712 43 00

Elsag Bailey Process
Automation
Complementary Product
Flavio TOLFO
Elektronikalaan 12-14
Wilrijk 2610
Belgium
+32-3-828-05-1
+32-3-830-21-65

Ernst & Young
Logo
Jef Galein
Avenue Marcel Thiry 204
1200 Brussels
Belgium
+32-2-774-91-11
+32-2-774-90-90

Expert Finance
Consultancy
Implementation
Axel de Ville/Petra Tiels
Rue Charles
Legrellestraat 17
Brussels 1040
Belgium
+32-2-732-7670
+32-2-732-64-50

IBM Corp.
Logo
IBM SAP Consulting Hotline
ibmsap@vnet.ibm.com
http://
www.csc.ibm.com/
sap/Belgium
800-IBM-0222-USA-;
610-892-3009
please phone or e-mail

ORIGIN INTERNATIONAL
Logo
Mr. J.J.M. van den Buys
Anspachlaan 1 (B17)
1000, Brussels
Belgium
+32-2-229-2600
+32-2-229 2849

IBM Corp.
Platform
Technology
IBM SAP Competency Centers
ibmsap@vnet.ibm.com
http://www.csc.ibm.com/
sap/Belgium
800-IBM-0222-USA-;
610-892-3009
please phone or e-mail

Soft Guide n.v.
HR-Consulting
Dullaert Guy
Desguinlei 50
2018 Antwerp
Belgium
+32-3-248-7374
+32-3-248-73-83

KPMG
Logo
Joseph de Gheldere
Rue Neerveld 101-103
1200 Brussels
Belgium
+32-2-773-4777

Ernst & Young
Logo
Klaus Werner
Av.Presidente
J Kubitschek 1830
Torre1-Fl.5-8
04543-900 Sao Paulo
Brazil
+55-11-821-5360
+55-11-829-6296

IBM Corp.
Logo
IBM SAP Consulting Hotline
ibmsap@vnet.ibm.com
http://
www.csc.ibm.com/
sap/Brazil
800-IBM-0222-USA-;
610-892-3009
please phone or e-mail

ORIGIN INTERNATIONAL
Logo
Av. das Nacoes
Unidas,11.633.17
04578-901 Sao Paulo-SP
Brazil
+55-11-5055066
+55-11-5055067

IBM Corp.
Platform
Technology
IBM SAP Competency Centers
ibmsap@vnet.ibm.com
http://www.csc.ibm.com/
sap/Brazil
800-IBM-0222-USA-;
610-892-3009
please phone or e-mail

Cognos Incorporated
Independent Vendor
Stephanie Gillard
3755 Riverside Drive
Box 9707
Ottawa
Ontario K1G 4K9
Canada
+1-613-738-1440 ext-3146
+1-613-738-9203

KPMG
Logo
Carlos E. Cardoso
Caixa Posta 22273
(Post Box)
01498-970 Sao Paulo, SP
Brazil
+55-11-897-1515-1500

Coopers & Lybrand
Consulting
Logo
Mr. Jeremy Hacking
145 King Street West
Toronto
Ontario M5H 1V8
Canada
+1-416-941-8267
+1-416-941-8421

Crystal A Seagate Company
Implementation
Philipp Kaszuba
1095 West Pender Street,
4th Floor
Vancouver
British Columbia
Canada
+1-604-893-6382
+1-604-681-2934

Ernst & Young
Logo
Louis Lamoureux
222 Bay Street
Toronto
Ontario M5K 1J7
Canada
+1-416-943-3574
+1-416-864-1174

Hewlett-Packard
Logo
Implementation
Platform
Technology
SAP-HP Competence
Center
4120 Yonge Street
North York
Ontario M2P 2B8
Canada
+1-416-229-9767
+1-416-229-0181

IBM Corp.
Logo
IBM SAP Consulting Hotline
ibmsap@vnet.ibm.com
http://
www.csc.ibm.com/
sap/Canada
800-IBM-0222-USA-;
610-892-3009
please phone or e-mail

IBM Corp.
Platform
Technology
IBM SAP Competency Centers
ibmsap@vnet.ibm.com
http://www.csc.ibm.com/
sap/Canada
800-IBM-0222-USA-;
610-892-3009
please phone or e-mail

KPMG
Logo
Stephen Goodman
Suite 212
Yonge Corp. Centre
120 Yonge Street
North York
Ontario M2P 2B8
Canada
+1-416-250-2585

OmniLogic Systems Group
Logo
Michael Alkier
Suite 210
4120 Yonge Street
North York
Ontario M2P 2B8
Canada
+1-416-226-6664
+1-416-226-1305

ORIGIN INTERNATIONAL
Logo
5500 Explorer Drive
Suite 200
Mississauga
Ontario L4W 5C7
Canada
+1-905-602-5222
+1-905-602-5225

RSI Realtime Consulting
Implementation
Helmut Mayer
4120 Yonge Street
Suite 205
North York
Ontario M2P 2B8
Canada
+1-416-226-4505
+1-416-226-4866

SHL Systemhouse Inc.
Logo
Jeffrey Dale
501-50 O'Connor Street
Ottawa K1P 6L2
Canada
+1-613-236-9734
+1-613-236-8984

Sierra Systems
Consultants Inc.
Implementation
Don Stuckert
1400-1177 West Hastings
Street
Vancouver
BC V6E 2K3
Canada
+1-604-688-1371
+1-604-688-6482

Ernst & Young
Logo
David Faille
Casillas 50080 and 2186
Santiago
Chile
+56-2-638-2364
+56-2-638-3622

IBM Corp.
Logo
IBM SAP Consulting Hotline
ibmsap@vnet.ibm.com
http://
www.csc.ibm.com/
sap/Chile
800-IBM-0222-USA-;
610-892-3009
please phone or e-mail

IBM Corp.
Platform
Technology
IBM SAP Competency Centers
ibmsap@vnet.ibm.com
http://www.csc.ibm.com/
sap/Chile
800-IBM-0222-USA-;
610-892-3009
please phone or e-mail

KPMG
Logo
Robert Robinson
Chile
+44-171832-8553

COMSOFT CR s.r.o.
Logo
Implementation
Herr Kindermann
K Hajum 948
15500 Praha 5
Czech Republic
+42-02-651-6895
+42-02-651-7120

Ernst & Young
Logo
John Glover
P.O.Box 136
Rienca 1
81499 Bratislava
Czech Republic
+42-7-533-0-793
+42-901-700-258

Globe Data s.r.o. (Ltd.)
Implementation
Mary Huang
Vinohradsk 93
120 00 Praha 2
Czech Republic
+42-2-6273728, 6272762
+42-2-6273758

IBM Corp.
Logo
IBM SAP Consulting Hotline
ibmsap@vnet.ibm.com
http://
www.csc.ibm.com/
sap/Czech Republic
800-IBM-0222-USA-;
610-892-3009
please phone or e-mail

IBM Corp.
Platform
Technology
IBM SAP Competency Centers
ibmsap@vnet.ibm.com
http://www.csc.ibm.com/
sap/Czech Republic
800-IBM-0222-USA-;
610-892-3009
please phone or e-mail

INIT s.r.o.
R/3 Systemhouse
Ing. Jiri Krupicka,
Dr. Josef
Prause
Sadov 5
702 00 Ostrava 1
Czech Republic
+42 69 622 7001
+42 69 622 7001

Appendixes

KPMG
Logo
Graham Jones
Jana Masaryka 12
PO Box 107
12000 Praha 2
Czech Republic
+42-2-6190-194

IBM Corp.
Logo
IBM SAP Consulting Hotline
ibmsap@vnet.ibm.com
http://
www.csc.ibm.com/
sap/Denmark
800-IBM-0222-USA-;
610-892-3009
please phone or e-mail

ORIGIN INTERNATIONAL
Logo
Prags Boulevard 80
2300 Copenhagen
Denmark
+45-32-882219
+45-32-883909

IBM Corp.
Logo
IBM SAP Consulting Hotline
ibmsap@vnet.ibm.com
http://
www.csc.ibm.com/
sap/Finland
800-IBM-0222-USA-;
610-892-3009
please phone or e-mail

PC-DIR, spol.s.r.o.
R/3 Systemhouse
Matej Peterka
Hlinky 142c
Bmo, 657 53
Czech Republic
+42-5-43321315
+42-5-43211283

IBM Corp.
Platform
Technology
IBM SAP Competency Centers
ibmsap@vnet.ibm.com
http://www.csc.ibm.com/
sap/Denmark
800-IBM-0222-USA-;
610-892-3009
please phone or e-mail

Carelcomp Industria Oy
Implementation
Kim Lindgren
It„tuulenkuja 11A
02100 Espoo
Finland
+358-0-3486 4101
+358-0-3486 4040

KPMG
Logo
Robert Robinson
Finland
+44-171832-8553

Ernst & Young
Logo
Finn Pedersen
Tagensvej 86
2200 Copenhagen N
Denmark
+45-35-82-4848
+45-35-82-4760

KPMG
Logo
Stig Due
Borups Alle 177
Postboks 250
2000 Frederiksberg
Denmark
+45-3818-3818

IBM Corp.
Platform
Technology
IBM SAP Competency
Centers
ibmsap@
vnet.ibm.com
http://
www.csc.ibm.com/
sap/Finland
800-IBM-0222-USA-;
610-892-3009
please phone or e-mail

Business Objects
Independent Vendor
Eric Faurisson
5 rue Chantecoq
92 808 Puteaux cedex
France
+33-1-4125-2121
+33-1-4125-2120

ELSOP France
Logo
Paul Miliopoulos
77-79 Bd. J.B.Oudry
94000 Creteil
France
+33-1-4980-5683
+33-1-4956-0548

IBM Corp.
Logo
IBM SAP Consulting Hotline
ibmsap@vnet.ibm.com
http://www.csc.ibm.com/
sap/France
800-IBM-0222-USA-;
610-892-3009
please phone or e-mail

IBM Corp.
Platform
Technology
IBM SAP Competency
Centers
ibmsap@
vnet.ibm.com
http://
www.csc.ibm.com/
sap/France
800-IBM-0222-USA-;
610-892-3009
please phone or e-mail

KPMG
Logo
Joel Templier
Tour Flat
Codex 16
92084 Paris
La Defense
France
+33-1-4796-2000

ORIGIN INTERNATIONAL
Logo
48, Avenue des Champs
Pierreux
92000 Naterre
France
+33-1-4614-1800
+33-1-4614-1818

SOURCE
INFORMATIQUE
Implementation
22 Rue de L'Arcade
75008 Paris
France
+33-47-4206-00
+33-47-4269-47

A.I.S. GmbH
Independent Vendor
Herr Siegfried Mack
Universitätsstrasse 140
44799 Bochum
Germany
+49-234-9709-0
+49-0-234-9709-520

Actis in Berlin GmbH
Complementary Product
Jansen-Denninghaus, Udo
Kurfürstendamm 65
10707 Berlin
Germany
+49-30-88 444-0
+49-30-88 444-100

ADA Das Systemhaus
Implementation
Dipl.-Kfm.Wolfgang
Strasser
Ringstr 38-44
50996 Köln
Germany
+49-221-935503-0
+49-221-935503-11

Addison-Wesley Verlag
Independent Vendor
Ralf Kaulisch
Wachsbleiche 7-12
53111 Bonn
Germany
+49-228-98515-0
+49-228-98515-99

Agens Consulting GmbH3
Implementation
Herr Thomas Klein
Buchenweg 11-13
25479 Ellerau
Germany
+49-4106 7777 0
+49-4106 7777 333

Amdahl Deutschland
GmbH
Implementation
Herr Schultze-Bohl
Otto-Vogler-Strasse 7c
65843 Sulzbach
Germany
+49-6196-5843
+49-6196-584584

Appendixes

ANDERSEN CONSULTING
Logo
Mr. Martin Erb
Otto Volgen Strasse 15
65483 Sulzbach
Frankfurt
Germany
+49-6196-5760
+49-6196-57610

ASET GmbH
Independent Vendor
Horst Blumenstein
Sodener Strasse 41 a
65779 Kelkheim
Germany
+49-6195-99 45 00
+49-6195-99 45 01

B/1/C GmbH
Logo
Helmut Tiemann
Portastrasse 29
32545 Bad Oeynhausen
Germany
+49-5731-3063-13
+49-5731-3063-25

CAE Electronics GmbH
Independent Vendor
Manfred Hoffman
Steinfurt 11
52222 Stolberg
Germany
+49-2402-106-0
+49-2402-106-498

ANTARIS
Informationssysteme GmbH
Implementation
H Robert Münchmeier
Moosbürger Strasse 20
92637 Weiden
Germany
+49-961-416 0 216
+49-961-89 401

ATTRIBUT SOFTWARE GmbH
& Co.TRADING KG
Independent Vendor
Gerhard Sass
Lindenstrasse 11
22941 Bargteheide
Germany
+49-4532-2702-0
+49-4532-2702-10

C & S Consulting &
Solutions GmbH
R/3 Systemhouse
Herren Raiss, Rathgeber,
Albrecht
Schönscheidtstrasse 28
45307 Essen
Germany
+49-201-1721100
+49-201-1721177

Camos Software und
Beratung GmbH
Independent Vendor
Michael Hellenkremer
Am Wallgraben 100
70565 Stuttgart
Germany
+49-711-78066-0
+49-711-78066-60

AsCon Software
GmbH
Implementation
Herr Roland Fierle
Richard-Reitzner-Allee 8
85540 Haar
Germany
+49-89-46265-0
+49-89-46265-199

B+B
Unternehmensberatung
GmbH & Co. KG
Implementation
Herr Felix Burger
Bruchstrasse 79
67098 Bad Dürkheim
Germany
+49-6322-9445-0
+49-6322-1244

CAE Electronics GmbH
Independent Vendor
Manfred Hoffmann
Steinfurt 11
52222 Stolberg
Germany
+49-2402-106-0
+49-2402-106-498

CAS Computer
Anwendungsberatung
Implementation
Dr. Peter Schulz
Lembergerstrasse 14
66954 Pirmasens
Germany
+49-6331-7270
+49-6331-727272

CAS Comuter
Anwendungsberatung
Implementation
Dr. Peter Schulz
Lembergerstrasse 14
66954 Pirmasens
Germany
+49-6331-7270
+49-6331-727272

CE Computer Equipment
GmbH
Complementary Product
Jürgen Brintrup
Herforder Strasse 155a
33609 Bielefeld
Germany
+49-521-9318-01
+49-521-9318-111

CMG Computer
Management Group
Implementation
Bernd Rehbein
Kölner Strasse 10
65760 Eschborn
Frankfurt
Germany
+49-6196-963 600
+49-6196-963 702

Cognos Incorporated
Independent Vendor
Uwe Weimer
Lyoner Strasse 40
60528 Frankfurt
Main
Germany
+49-69-665-600
+49-69-666-1061

Com-EM-Tex
Independent Vendor
Fr.Domdey-Utpadel
Hohenwarter Str.1
80686 München
Germany
+49 89 54 61 30-0
+49 89 54 61 30-22

Command
Computer-Anwend.-
Beratungs-GmbH
R/3 Systemhouse
Antje Nielsen
Eisenstock 17
76275 Ettlingen
Germany
+49-7243-590230
+49-7243-590235

COMSOFT GmbH
Logo
Implementation
Herr Will
Zufuhrstrasse 12
90443 Nürnberg
Germany
+49-911-9263-0
+49-911-9263-200

Condat GmbH
Implementation
Ulla Möller
Alt-Moabit 91 d
10559 Berlin
Germany
+49-30-39094-105
+49-30-39094-300

ConnectIT Computer
Consult GmbH
Independent Vendor
Ulrich Tolkmitt
Weihauss Strasse 22
50939 Köln
Germany
+49-221-944092-0
+49-221-944092-99

COPA GmbH
R/3 Systemhouse
Herr Olaf Dahmen
Mottkestrasse 8
46483 Wesel
Germany
+49-281-154-0
+49-281-154-99

CTH Consult TEAM
Hamburg GmbH
Implementation
Peter H. Thiesen
Osterbekstrasse 90 c
22083 Hamburg
Germany
+49-40-27 83 70-0
+49-40-27 83 70-30

D&B Information
Solutions
GmbH
Independent Vendor
Hahnstrasse 31-35
60528 Frankfurt
Germany
+49-69-66 303-0
+49-69-66 303-215

Daimler-Benz Aerospace
Complementary Product
Heinz Grote
Mainzer Strasse 36-52
53179 Bonn
Germany
+49-228-8554-119
+49-228-8554-237

Digital Equipment GmbH
Platform
SAP Expertise Center
Max Planck Strasse 8
69190 Walldorf
Germany
+49-6226-34 45 45
+49-6227-34 45 99

Ernst & Young
Logo
Peter Kroll
Lübeckerstrasse 1
22087 Hamburg
Germany
+49-40-254-49102
+49-40-254-4911

F&F Computer
Anwendungen
GmbH
Implementation
Rainer Fritzen
Redesheimer Strasse 4
80686 München
Germany
+49-89-576017
+49-89-5706043

Debis Systemhaus
Division Industrie
GmbH
Logo
Herr Reck
Lademannbogen 21/23
22413 Hamburg
Germany
+49-40-53951331
+49-40-53951610

DMC GmbH
Implementation
Herr Angelo Zenz
Wamslerstrasse 5
81829 München
Germany
+49-89-42774-100
+49-89-42774-199

ESOFT Informatik GmbH
Implementation
Steffen Elbel
Am Muehlbuck 22
91639 Wolframs-Eschenbach
Germany
+49-9875-9701-0
+49-9875-9701-50

FIS Informationssys. u.
Consulting
GmbH
Implementation
Herr Lang
Bodelschwinghstrasse 3
97421 Schweinfurt
Germany
+49-9721-78 75-11
+49-9721-78 75-10

DETEC Decision
Technology
Software GmbH
Independent Vendor
Johannes Thurner
Industriestrasse 9
82110 Germering
Germany
+49-89-8943400
+49-89-8401664

EIGNER + PARTNER
Complementary Product
Heinrich Windhorst
Ruschgraben 133
76139 Karlsruhe
Germany
+49-721-62 91 0
+49-721-62 91 88

EXTRA Softwaresysteme
Independent Vendor
Hajo Meissner
Postfach 5726
65732 Eschborn
Germany
+49-180-53-1234 1
+49-6173-320615

GAMBIT
Consulting GmbH
Implementation
Herr Mehling
Kaiserstrasse
53840 Troisdorf
Germany
+49-2241-88450
+49-2241-884599

GARANT Treuhand-GmbH
Implementation
Dipl.-Kfm.Heiner Gehlmann
Am Hintergraben 37
64404 Bickenbach a.d.B.
Germany
+49-6257 63696
+49-6257 3538

GE Information Services
Independent Vendor
Dr. Alfred Werner
Bavariaring 8
80336 München
Germany
+49-89-53988-331
+49-89-53988-340

Gelma
Industrieelektronik
GmbH
Complementary Product
Heinz Grote
Mainzer Strasse 36-52
53179 Bonn
Germany
+49-228-8554-119
+49-228-8554-237

Ges.1.Mathematik u.
INFORMATIK mbH
Business Development
W Schauerte-L ke
Buchkremerstr.6
52062 Aachen
Germany
+49-241-47072-0
+49-241-33682

GPS mbH
Independent Vendor
Frau Grabisch
Kaiserstrasse 100
52134 Herzogenrath
Germany
+49-2407-5069
+49-2407-2778

Hewlett-Packard
Logo
Implementation
Platform
Technology
SAP-HP Competence
Center
Max Planck Strasse 8
69190 Walldorf
Germany
+49-6227-3659
+49-6227-3360

IBM Corp.
Logo
IBM SAP Consulting Hotline
ibmsap@vnet.ibm.com
http://
www.csc.ibm.com/
sap/Germany
800-IBM-0222-USA-;
610-892-3009
please phone or e-mail

IBM Corp.
Platform
Technology
IBM SAP Competency Centers
ibmsap@vnet.ibm.com
http://www.csc.ibm.com/
sap/Germany
800-IBM-0222-USA-;
610-892-3009
please phone or e-mail

IBS Dr.-Ing. Schröder
GmbH
Implementation
Independent Vendor
Dr.-Ing. Klaus Jürgen
Schröder
Rathausstrasse 69
56203 Hehr
Grenzhausen
Germany
+49-2624 91800
+49-2624 918010

Appendixes

ICM
Unternehmensberatung
GmbH
Implementation
Friedrich Boesl
Carl-Zeiss-Ring 4
85737 Ismaning b.
München
Germany
+49-89-996559 0
+49-89 9965599 33

IDS Prof.Scheer GmbH
Logo
Implementation
Stefan Eichacker
Attenkesseler Strasse 17
66015 Saarbrücken
Germany
+49-681-99 21-724
+49-681-99 21-701

INCA GmbH
Complementary Product
Anton Engl
Marsstrasse 7
85609 Aschheim
Germany
+49-89-909-9680
+49-89-909-9660

INFOMATEC GmbH
Implementation
Höfele Alexander
Steinerne Furt 76
86167 Augsburg
Germany
+49-821-270 90 00
+49-821-270 90 05

INFORMIX Software GmbH
Technology
SAP Informix Competence
Center(Intl)
Max-Planck Strasse 8
69190 Walldorf
Germany
+49-6227-34-5827
+49-6227-34-5842

Infosoft
Computersysteme
GmbH
Implementation
Herr Kappus
Maria Trost 25
56070 Koblenz
Germany
+49-261-80700-0
+49-261-80700-239

Inside
Unternehmensberatung
GmbH
Implementation
Herr Jürgen Schulz
Marschweg 22
26122 Oldenburg
Germany
+49-441-955 96-0
+49-441-955 96-40

INTERFLEX DATENSYSTEME
GMBH
Complementary Product
L. Zeitler
Zettachring 16
70567 Stuttgart
Germany
+49-711-1322-0
+49-711-1322-111

ISGUS J.Schlenker-
Grusen
GmbH
Complementary Product
Frau Waldmöller
Oberdorfstrasse 18-22
78054 Villingen-
Schwenningen
Germany
+49-7720-393-180
+49-7720-393-184

ISO GmbH
Implementation
Michael Brux/
Wolfram Weber
Eichendorffstrasse 29
90491 Nürnberg
Germany
+49-911-995 94-0
+49-911-59 57 94

IXOS Software
Technology
Katia Follner
Bretonischer Ring 12
85630 Grasbrunn
Germany
+49-89-46005-0
+49-89-46005-199

Kaba Benzing GmbH
Complementary Product
Wolfgang Blender
Albertistrasse 3
78056 Villingen-
Schwenningen
Germany
+49-7720-603-0
+49-7720-603 102

Ketteler & Partner GmbH
Implementation
Herr Christoph B Pap
Clarholzer Strasse 3
33428 Harsewinkel
Germany
+49-5247-2085
+49-0-5247-1324

Lion
Logo
Juergen Breithaupt
Deutz-Mülheimer-
Strasse 111
51063 Köln
Germany
+49-221-808-4219
+49-221-808-5201

Microsoft GmbH
Technology
Patrick Schellscheidt
Edisonstrasse 1
85716 Unterschleissheim
Germany
+49-89-3176-3759
+49-89-3176-3710

Oracle Deutschland GmbH
Technology
Fritz Düsterhaus
Hanauerstrasse 87
80993 München
Germany
+49-89-149770
+49-14977-150

Kiefer & Veittinger GmbH
Independent Vendor
Herr Sehringer
Willy-Brandt-Platz 3
68161 Mannheim
Germany
+49-621-1255-0
+49-621-1255-170

MCA GmbH
Independent Vendor
Michael Knauff
Postfach 1406
52138 Würselen
Germany
+49-2405-6004-55
+49-2405-6004-75

MLC Systeme GmbH
Independent Vendor
Herr Schwan
Am Br ll 19
40878 Ratingen
Germany
+49-2102-8506-0
+49-2102-8506-30

ORBIS GmbH
Logo
Implementation
Herr Kurt Puderbach
Brühl 66
04109 Leipzig
Germany
+49-341-21 88 632
+49-341-21 88 599

KPMG
Logo
Paul Scott
Olof-Palme-Strasse 31
60439 Frankfurt
Main
Germany
+49-69-9587-1323
+49-9587-1341

Micronet GmbH
Implementation
Herr Lutz
Schnetzenhauser
Strasse 2
88048 Friedrichshafen
Germany
+49-7541-9500-0
+49-7541-9500-95

MPDV Mikrolab GmbH
Complementary Product
Herr Deisenroth
Atte Neckarelzer
Strasse 23
74821 Mosbach
Germany
+49-62 61-9 20 90
+49-62 61-181 39

ORBIS GmbH
Logo
Implementation
Herr Markus Backec
Attenkesseler Strasse 17
66115 Saarbrücken
Germany
+49-681-9762-320
+49-681-9762-324

ORDO
Unternehmensberatung
GmbH
Logo
Herr Dipl. Kfm. Wolfgang
Kasprowicz
Remerallee 32
53909 Zülpich
Germany
+49-2252-9411-0
+49-2252-9411-94

Organisation Management
Consulting
Implementation
Schanzenstrasse 34
40549 Düsseldorf
Germany
+49-211-557 07 57
+49-211-558 16 24

ORIGIN
INTERNATIONAL
Logo
Frau Ritter
Billstrasse 80
20529 Hamburg
Germany
+49-40-7886360
+49-40-7886535

P.M. Belz
Unternehmensgruppe
AEB/AFI
Independent Vendor
Marcus Hellmann
Julius-Hölder-Strasse 39
70597 Stuttgart
Germany
+49-711-72842-0
+49-711-722-2384

PCS Systemtechnik GmbH
Complementary Product
Wilhelm F. Jambor
Pfälzer-Wald-Strasse 36
81539 München
Germany
+49-89-6 80 04-4 43
+49-89-6 80 04-5 55

Phinware Beratung und
Software GmbH
Independent Vendor
Herr Dipl.-Ing.
Martin Fromm
Leopoldstrasse 16
40211 Düsseldorf
Germany
+49-211-16686-0
+49-211-16686-66

Pioneer
Produkt-Entwicklung
GmbH
Implementation
Ernst R Kochne
Fasanenstrasse 108
82008 Unterhaching
Germany
+49-89-611 13 65
+49-89-611 15 12

PLATINUM Technology
Complementary Product
Ellen Hommrich
Emanuel-Leutze-Strasse 4
40547 Düsseldorf
Germany
+49-211-5306-0
+49-211-5306-100

Realtime Consultancy
GmbH
Implementation
Herr Frank Lemm
Bahnhofstrasse 35
40764 Langenfeld
Germany
+49-2173-91 66-0
+49-2173-91 66-33

S+P Software Support GmbH
Implementation
Herr Brunner
Hapstrasse 10
67489 Kirrweiler
Germany
+49-6321-95001
+49-6321-58695

SAG Systemhaus GmbH
Logo
Implementation
Herbert Gilbert
Alsfelder Strasse 15-17
64289 Darmstadt
Germany
+49-6151-92-3214
+49-6151-92-3264

Siemens AG
Complementary Product
Herr Lahm, ANL A334
Siemensallee
76181 Karlsruhe
Germany
+49-721-595-4465
+49-721-595-2806

Siemens Nixdorf
Office Solutions
Independent Vendor
Werner Radermacher
Sietec EC Bln
Nonnendammallee 101
13629 Berlin
Germany
+49-30 386 26849
+49-30 386 27402

Siemens Nixdorf
Informationssysteme AG
Independent Vendor
Platform
Technology
Dietrich Christine
Otto-Hahn-Ring 6
81739 München
Germany
+49-89-636-43582
+49-89-636-44224

Siemens Nixdorf
Informationssysteme AG
Independent Vendor
Platform
Technology
Herr Knauer
Otto-Hahn-Ring 6
81730 München
Germany
+49-89-636-42953
+49-89-636-41717

Siemens Nixdorf
Informationssysteme AG
Independent Vendor
Platform
Technology
Herr Wetzig
Heinz Nixdorf Ring 1
33106 Paderborn
Germany
+49-5251-815714
+49-5251-815702

Siemens Nixdorf
Informationssysteme AG
Independent Vendor
Platform
Technology
Mr. Wolfgang Sitte
Otto-Hahn-Ring 6
81730 München
Germany
+49-89-636-46286
+49-89-636-53958

Siemens Nixdorf
Informationssysteme AG
Independent Vendor
Platform
Technology
Ulrich Becker
Heinz Nixdorf Ring 1
33106 Paderborn
Germany
+49-5251-8 25183
+49-5251-8 29960

SLIGOS Industrie
R/3 Systemhouse
Horst Heckel
Rober-Bosch-Strasse 5
63303
Dreieich-Sprendlingen
Germany
+49-6103-9334-22
+49-6103-9334-50

Softlab GmbH
Implementation
Mr. Klaus Wandel
Zamdorfer Strasse 120
81677 Munich
Germany
+49-89-9936-0
+49-89-937529

SPO CONSULTING
GROUP
Implementation
Herr Jung
Finkenwiesen 3
55442
Germany
+49-6724-9 55 20
+49-6724-9 22

Strässle Informations-
systeme GmbH
Independent Vendor
Richard Spengler
Vor dem Lauch 14
70567 Stuttgart
Germany
+49-711-7256-319
+49-711-7256-340

Tds tele-daten-service
gmbh
R/3 Systemhouse
Reiner Knapp
Titotstrasse 7-9
74072 Heilbronn
Germany
+49-7131-62 35-0
+49-7131-62 35-1 15

Titze Datentechnik
GmbH
Complementary Product
Herr Jürgen Weinhardt
Dieselstrasse 10
71272 Renningen
Germany
+49-7159-92-36-0
+49-7159-92 36-60

TOPAS EDV-
BERATUNG GmbH
Logo
Anja Brockhaus
Martin-Schmeisser-Weg 16
44227 Dortmund
Germany
+49-231-97-97-0
+49-231-97-97-50

ZEDA GmbH & Co.
Implementation
Herr Gerd Döring
Am Diek 52
42270 Wuppertal
Germany
+49-202-564-4626
+49-202-564-4610

Dimiourgiki-C.M.S.
Independent Vendor
Dimitrios Vrontos
21 Dodekanisou
Thessaloniki 546 26
Greece
+30-31-541248
+30-31-532514

IBM Corp.
Logo
IBM SAP Consulting Hotline
ibmsap@vnet.ibm.com
http://
www.csc.ibm.com/
sap/Greece
800-IBM-0222-USA-;
610-892-3009
please phone or e-mail

Transport-Inform.u.
Logistik-Consulting
Independent Vendor
Martin Rühl
Bahnhofstrasse 36
65185 Wiesbaden
Germany
+49-611-1734-61
+49-611-1734-68

Zentrum für Logistik GmbH
(ZLU)
Implementation
Dipl.-Ing. Martin Coenders
Gustav-Meyer-Allee 25
13355 Berlin
Germany
+49-30-464-002-0
+49-30-464 002-11

ELSOP Hellas
Logo
Paul Miliopoulos
36 Messogion Avenue
11527 Athens
Greece
+30-1-74-80810
+30-1-77-10809

IBM Corp.
Platform
Technology
IBM SAP Competency Centers
ibmsap@vnet.ibm.com
http://www.csc.ibm.com/
sap/Greece
800-IBM-0222-USA-;
610-892-3009
please phone or e-mail

UBIS GmbH
Independent Vendor
Dr. Michael Klotz
Alt-Moabit 98
10559 Berlin
Germany
+49-30-399 29-600
+49-30-399 29-900

ZUENDEL & PARTNER
Systems
Consultants GmbH
Logo
Frau Elke Matuscheck
Dülkener Strasse 5
41334 Nettetal
Germany
+49-2153-7376-0
+49-2153-7376-16

Ernst & Young
Logo
Kosmas Michail
3 llission Street
11528 Athens
Greece
+30-1-7759-780-4
+30-1-7710-293

KPMG
Logo
Virgil Touineas
15 Messoghion Avenue
Ambelokipi
11526 Athens
Greece
+30-1-77-52001

Unisoft S.A.
Logo
Mr. Vas Ioannou
Sygrou Avenue, 294
Kallithea
Athens 176 73
Greece
+30-9571081-2, 9574390-1
+30-9571080

KPMG
Logo
Robert Robinson
Hong Kong
+44-171832-8553

IBM Corp.
Platform
Technology
IBM SAP Competency
Centers
ibmsap@vnet.ibm.com
http://
www.csc.ibm.com/
sap/Hungary
800-IBM-0222-USA-;
610-892-3009E
please phone or e-mail

IBM Corp.
Logo
IBM SAP Consulting Hotline
ibmsap@vnet.ibm.com
http://www.csc.ibm.com/
sap/Hong Kong
800-IBM-0222-USA-;
610-892-3009
please phone or e-mail

ORIGIN INTERNATIONAL
Logo
5th Floor,
Chung Nam Building
1 Lockhart Road
Wanchai
Hong Kong
+852-25286222
+852-28655289

KPMG
Logo
Janos Tomka
XII Maros Utca 19-21
1122 Budapest
Hungary
+36-1-202-2299

IBM Corp.
Platform
Technology
IBM SAP Competency
Centers
ibmsap@
vnet.ibm.com
http://
www.csc.ibm.com/
sap/Hong Kong
800-IBM-0222-USA-;
610-892-3009
please phone or e-mail

IBM Corp.
Logo
IBM SAP Consulting
Hotline
ibmsap@
vnet.ibm.com
http://
www.csc.ibm.com/
sap/Hungary
800-IBM-0222-USA-;
610-892-3009
please phone or e-mail

IBM Corp.
Logo
IBM SAP Consulting
Hotline
ibmsap@
vnet.ibm.com
http://
www.csc.ibm.com/
sap/India
800-IBM-0222-USA-;
610-892-3009
please phone or e-mail

Appendixes

IBM Corp.
Platform
Technology
IBM SAP Competency
Centers
ibmsap@vnet.ibm.com
http://
www.csc.ibm.com/
sap/India
800-IBM-0222-USA-;
610-892-3009
please phone or e-mail

KPMG
Logo
Ashwin Parekh
The Metropolitan
West Wing, Fl.3
Bandra-K. (E-B)
Bombay 40051
India
+91-22-645-6032

ORIGIN
INTERNATIONAL
Logo
SDF-1,
Units 126/127 SEEPZ
Andheri (East)
Bombay 400 096
India
+91-22-8382900
+91-22-8364744

ANDERSEN CONSULTING
Logo
Mr. David Busham
Jalan Jend
Sudirman Kav 21
Jakarta 12910
Indonesia
+62-21-520 8199
+62-21-570 4347

IBM Corp.
Platform
Technology
IBM SAP Competency Centers
ibmsap@vnet.ibm.com
http://www.csc.ibm.com/
sap/Indonesia
800-IBM-0222-USA-;
610-892-3009
please phone or e-mail

IBM Corp.
Logo
IBM SAP Consulting
Hotline
ibmsap@
vnet.ibm.com
http://
www.csc.ibm.com/
sap/Indonesia
800-IBM-0222-USA-;
610-892-3009
please phone or e-mail

KPMG
Logo
Robert Robinson
Indonesia
+44-171832-8553

IBM Corp.
Logo
IBM SAP Consulting Hotline
ibmsap@vnet.ibm.com
http://www.csc.ibm.com/
sap/Ireland
800-IBM-0222-USA-;
610-892-3009
please phone or e-mail

IBM Corp.
Platform
Technology
IBM SAP Competency
Centers
ibmsap@
vnet.ibm.com
http://
www.csc.ibm.com/
sap/Ireland
800-IBM-0222-USA-;
610-892-3009
please phone or e-mail

KPMG
Logo
Nial O'Reilly
Russel Court
Stockes Place
St. Stephen's Green
Dublin 2
Ireland
+353-1-708-1828

DMW Ltd
Independent Vendor
Mr. Eligur Zion
87 Ben Gurion Blvd.
Tel-Aviv
Israel
+972-3-5240254
+972-2-5271481

IBM Corp.
Logo
IBM SAP Consulting
Hotline
ibmsap@
vnet.ibm.com
http://
www.csc.ibm.com/
sap/Israel
800-IBM-0222-USA-;
610-892-3009
please phone or e-mail

IBM Corp.
Platform
Technology
IBM SAP Competency
Centers
ibmsap@vnet.ibm.com
http://
www.csc.ibm.com/
sap/Israel
800-IBM-0222-USA-;
610-892-3009
please phone or e-mail

KPMG
Logo
Robert Robinson
Israel
+44-171832-8553

EniData SpA
Logo
Ing.Salvatore Tarantini
Via Medici del Vascello,
26
Milano 1-20138
Italy
+39-2-520-29352
+39-2-520-25175

Ernst & Young
Logo
Mario Tana
Via Romagnosi 18/A
00196 Rome
Italy
+39-6-36-2101
+39-6-36-210263

Hewlett-Packard
Logo
Implementation
Platform
Technology
SAP-HP Competence Center
Via Nuova Rivivoltana, 93
20090 Limito
Italy
+39-2-921-244-59
+39-2-753-0645

IBM Corp.
Logo
IBM SAP Consulting
Hotline
ibmsap@
vnet.ibm.com
http://
www.csc.ibm.com/
sap/Italy
800-IBM-0222-USA-;
610-892-3009
please phone or e-mail

IBM Corp.
Platform
Technology
IBM SAP Competency
Centers
ibmsap@vnet.ibm.com
http://
www.csc.ibm.com/
sap/Italy
800-IBM-0222-USA-;
610-892-3009
please phone or e-mail

Intema S.p.A.
Logo
A. De Luca
V. le Castello della
Magliana 75
Rome 00153
Italy
+39-6-655931

KPMG
Logo
Armando Greco
Via Vittor Pisani 25
20124 Milan
Italy
+39-2-67631
+39-6-65593310

ORIGIN INTERNATIONAL
Logo
Via Gasparotto, 1
20124 Milan
Italy
+39-2-667221
+39-2-66722895

SAN GIORGIO SYSTEM
TECHNOLOGY
Logo
Ing. R. Volontieri
Via C. Colombo 49
20090 Trezzano s/naviglio
(Ml)
Italy
+39-484341
+39-48434240

ANDERSEN
CONSULTING
Logo
Mr. Takashi Shimodoi
Daini Bldg 7-1-16
Akasaka
Minato-ku
Tokyo 107
Japan
+81-3-3470 9241
+81-3-3423 2544

Chuo Coopers & Lybrand
Consulting Ltd
Logo
Mr. Tetsuo Karasama
3-2-5 Kasumibaseki
Chiyoda-Ku
Tokyo 100
Japan
+81-3-3502 3701
+81-3-3502 3788

Hewlett-Packard
Logo
Implementation
Platform
Technology
SAP-HP Competence Center
-chome Sinagawa-Ku4
Kitashinagawa
Tokyo 140
Japan
+81-3-5423-9556
+81-3-5423-9550

Hitachi Ltd. System
SAI1-WS
Logo
Shunichi Harada
890 Kashimada
Saiwai-Ku
Kawasaki-Shi
Kanagawa-Ken F2 1
Japan
+81-44-549-1263
+81-44-549-11176

IBM Corp.
Logo
IBM SAP Consulting Hotline
ibmsap@vnet.ibm.com
http://
www.csc.ibm.com/
sap/Japan
800-IBM-0222-USA-;
610-892-3009
please phone or e-mail

NEC Software Ltd
Logo
Mr. Hiromi Kamiya
1-18-6 Shinkiba Koutou-ku
Tokyo
Japan
+81-3-5569 3145
+81-3-5569 3282

SUMISHO COMPUTER
SYSTEMS CORPORATION
Implementation
Mr. Ryohei Joki
10-14, 2-Chome
Ryogoku 130
Japan
+81-3-5624-1794
+81-3-5624-1795

IBM Corp.
Logo
IBM SAP Consulting Hotline
ibmsap@vnet.ibm.com
http://
www.csc.ibm.com/
sap/Korea
800-IBM-0222-USA-;
610-892-3009
please phone or e-mail

IBM Corp.
Platform
Technology
IBM SAP Competency Centers
ibmsap@vnet.ibm.com
http://www.csc.ibm.com/
sap/Japan
800-IBM-0222-USA-;
610-892-3009
please phone or e-mail

Price Waterhouse
Consultants Co.Ltd.
Logo
Mr. Ken Kramme/Mr. Ken Mori
Yebisu Grarden Place
Tower 14F
20-3, Ebisu 4-Chome
Shibuya-ku
Tokyo 1505
Japan
+81-3-5424 8400
+91-3-5424 8422

TOKYO ENGINEERING
CORPORATION
Logo
Mr. Ryusuke Nakamura
3-2-5 Kasumi Gaseri
Chiyodaku
Tokyo 100
Japan
+81-3-3592 7443
+81-3-3592 7407

IBM Corp.
Platform
Technology
IBM SAP Competency Centers
ibmsap@vnet.ibm.com
http://www.csc.ibm.com/
sap/Korea
800-IBM-0222-USA-;
610-892-3009
please phone or e-mail

KPMG
Logo
Paul Scott
Olof-Palmer Strasse 31
60439 Frankfurt
(Germany)
Japan

Software AG of Far East
Inc.
Implementation
Mr. Yoshiki Suga
Shiniuku L Tower
1-6-1 Nishi-Shinjuku
Shinjuku-ku
Tokyo 160
Japan
+81-3-3340 2471
+81-3-3340 2470

ANDERSEN
CONSULTING
Logo
Mr. Keith Newton
Suite 300, 17-3
Yoidodong
Yeoungdeungpo-ku
Seoul 150-010
Korea
+82-2-786 2000
+82-2-769 1900

KPMG
Logo
Robert Robinson
Korea
+44-171832-8553

Appendixes

IBM Corp.
Logo
IBM SAP Consulting Hotline
ibmsap@vnet.ibm.com
http://
www.csc.ibm.com/
sap/Luxembourg
800-IBM-0222-USA-;
610-892-3009
please phone or e-mail

IBM Corp.
Platform
Technology
IBM SAP Competency Centers
ibmsap@vnet.ibm.com
http://www.csc.ibm.com/
sap/Luxembourg
800-IBM-0222-USA-;
610-892-3009
please phone or e-mail

KPMG
Logo
Colin Holland
121 Avenue
de la Faiencerie
1511 Luxembourg
Luxembourg
+352-46-7838-2

ORIGIN INTERNATIONAL
Logo
204, Route d/Arlon
8010 Strassen
Luxembourg
+352-313637
+352-313883

Physical Distribution
Systems Ltd
Independent Vendor
5, Rue Guillaume Kroll
1882
Luxembourg
+352-48 07 15
+352-49 00 83

ANDERSEN
CONSULTING
Logo
Mr. Sadeesh Raghavan
Flr.26, Menara Tun Razak
Jalan raja Laut
50350 Kuala Lumpur
Malaysia
+60-3-293 5133
+60-3-293 5360

DFI Consulting Sdn Bhd
Implementation
Berend Adrian
Suite 8-12B-3
8 Jalan Raja Chulan
Kuala Lumpur 50200
Malaysia
+60-3 201 2968
+60-3 201 2969

IBM Corp.
Logo
IBM SAP Consulting Hotline
ibmsap@vnet.ibm.com
http://www.csc.ibm.com/
sap/Malaysia
800-IBM-0222-USA-;
610-892-3009
please phone or e-mail

IBM Corp.
Platform
Technology
IBM SAP Competency
Centers
ibmsap@
vnet.ibm.com
http://
www.csc.ibm.com/
sap/Malaysia
800-IBM-0222-USA-;
610-892-3009
please phone or e-mail

KPMG
Logo
Sharudin Sulaiman
Komplek pejabat Damansara
Jalan Dungun (Bl.B)
50490 Kuala Lumpur
Malaysia
+60-3-255-7177

ORIGIN INTERNATIONAL
Logo
76 Jalan Universiti
46200 Petaling Jaya
Selangor Darul Ehsan
Malaysia
+60-3-7505330
+60-3-7581586

Hewlett-Packard
Logo
Implementation
Platform
Technology
SAP-HP Competence
Center
Col.Lomas Santa Fe
Prol Reforma 600,
3rd Floor
012120 Mexico
Mexico
+52-5-257-7580
+52-5-257-7585

IBM Corp.
Logo
IBM SAP Consulting Hotline
ibmsap@vnet.ibm.com
http://
www.csc.ibm.com/
sap/Mexico
800-IBM-0222-USA-;
610-892-3009
please phone or e-mail

IBM Corp.
Platform
Technology
IBM SAP Competency Centers
ibmsap@vnet.ibm.com
http://www.csc.ibm.com/
sap/Mexico
800-IBM-0222-USA-;
610-892-3009
please phone or e-mail

KPMG
Logo
Olivia Sadati
Bosque De Duranznos
no.55
2o.piso
Bosq.d.l.Lomas
Mexico D.F.C.P.11700
Mexico
+52-5-726-4343

ORIGIN INTERNATIONAL
Logo
Presidente Masarik no. 101
Col. Polanco, 11570, D.F.
Mexico
+52-5-2547800
+52-5-2031164

IBM Corp.
Logo
IBM SAP Consulting Hotline
ibmsap@vnet.ibm.com
http://www.csc.ibm.com/
sap/Middle East
800-IBM-0222-USA-;
610-892-3009
please phone or e-mail
Analoog Data BV

IBM Corp.
Platform
Technology
IBM SAP Competency
Centers
ibmsap@
vnet.ibm.com
http://
www.csc.ibm.com/
sap/Middle East
800-IBM-0222-USA-;
610-892-3009
please phone or e-mail

KPMG
Logo
Robert Robinson
Middle East
+44-171832-8553

Independent Vendor
Mr. J L Boerema
v.d. Feltzpark 3
9401 HM Assen
Netherlands
+31-592-314 282
+31-592-316-344

Ernst & Young
Logo
Dennis Muntslag
Varrolaan 100
3584 B.W. Utrecht
Netherlands
+31-20-588-588
+31-30-588-100

IBM Corp.
Logo
IBM SAP Consulting Hotline
ibmsap@vnet.ibm.com
http://
www.csc.ibm.com/
sap/Netherlands
800-IBM-0222-USA-;
610-892-3009
please phone or e-mail

IBM Corp.
Platform
Technology
IBM SAP Competency Centers
ibmsap@vnet.ibm.com
http://www.csc.ibm.com/
sap/Netherlands
800-IBM-0222-USA-;
610-892-3009
please phone or e-mail

KPMG
Logo
Robert Robinson
Netherlands
+44-171832-8553

Magnus Align Consulting
Logo
Ir.W.Hulshof,
Ir.K.J.Hoogsteen
Gooimeer 5-39
1411 DD/Netherlands
Netherlands
+31-35-6950690
+31-0-35-6950932

ORIGIN INTERNATIONAL
Logo
P.O. Box 42611
3006 DC Rotterdam
Netherlands
+31-10-2122888
+31-10-4520382

Roadshow
Independent Vendor
Richard Dobber
Villawal 1
3432 NX Nieuwegein
Netherlands
+31-3060-53444
+31-3060-52922

IBM Corp.
Logo
IBM SAP Consulting Hotline
ibmsap@vnet.ibm.com
http://
www.csc.ibm.com/
sap/New Zealand
800-IBM-0222-USA-;
610-892-3009
please phone or e-mail

IBM Corp.
Platform
Technology
IBM SAP Competency Centers
ibmsap@vnet.ibm.com
http://www.csc.ibm.com/
sap/New Zealand
800-IBM-0222-USA-;
610-892-3009
please phone or e-mail

KPMG
Logo
Robert Robinson
New Zealand
+44-171832-8553

Ernst & Young
Logo
Ellen Maurstad
Tullins gate 2
P.O.Box 6834
St.Olvas plass
0130 Oslo
Norway
+47-22-03-6000
+47-22-03-6380

IBM Corp.
Logo
IBM SAP Consulting Hotline
ibmsap@vnet.ibm.com
http://www.csc.ibm.com/
sap/Norway
800-IBM-0222-USA-;
610-892-3009
please phone or e-mail

IBM Corp
Platform
Technology
IBM SAP Competency
Centers
ibmsap@
vnet.ibm.com
http://
www.csc.ibm.com/
sap/Norway
800-IBM-0222-USA-;
610-892-3009
please phone or e-mail

KPMG
Logo
Robert Robinson
Norway
+44-171832-8553

IBM Corp.
Logo
IBM SAP Consulting Hotline
ibmsap@vnet.ibm.com
http://www.csc.ibm.com/
sap/Philippines
800-IBM-0222-USA-;
610-892-3009
please phone or e-mail

IBM Corp.
Platform
Technology
IBM SAP Competency
Centers
ibmsap@
vnet.ibm.com
http://
www.csc.ibm.com/
sap/Philippines
800-IBM-0222-USA-;
610-892-3009
please phone or e-mail

KPMG
Logo
Robert Robinson
Philippines
+44-171832-8553

ORIGIN INTERNATIONAL
Logo
34-C Rufino Pacific Tower
Ayala Avenue
Makati
Metro Manila
Philippines
+63-2-8111160
+63-2-8111160

Business Consulting
Center.
Sp.z.o.o
Independent Vendor
Mr. Dominik Tulczynski
ul.Niedzialkowskiego 1
61-578 Poznan
Poland
+48-61-337 511 ext.320
+48-61-337 623

Appendixes

IBM Corp.
Logo
IBM SAP Consulting Hotline
ibmsap@vnet.ibm.com
http://
www.csc.ibm.com/
sap/Poland
800-IBM-0222-USA-;
610-892-3009
please phone or e-mail

EDINFOR, S.A.
Logo
Eng.Silva Santos
Av.Casal Ribeiro, nø50-4ø
Lisboa 1000
Portugal
+351-1-353-1101
 -350 34 67
+351-1-847 82 71

IBM Corp.
Platform
Technology
IBM SAP Competency
Centers
ibmsap@vnet.ibm.com
http://
www.csc.ibm.com/
sap/Portugal
800-IBM-0222-USA-;
610-892-3009
please phone or e-mail

IBM Corp.
Platform
Technology
IBM SAP Competency Centers
ibmsap@vnet.ibm.com
http://www.csc.ibm.com/
sap/Poland
800-IBM-0222-USA-;
610-892-3009
please phone or e-mail

Ernst & Young
Logo
Jose Lucas
Edifico Republic
Av. da Republica, 90
1600 Lisbon
Portugal
+351-1-791-2000
+351-1-795-7588

KPMG
Logo
Robert Robinson
Portugal
+44-171832-8553

KPMG
Logo
Robert Robinson
Poland
+44-171832-8553

IBM Corp.
Logo
IBM SAP Consulting
Hotline
ibmsap@
vnet.ibm.com
http://
www.csc.ibm.com/
sap/Portugal
800-IBM-0222-USA-;
610-892-3009
please phone or e-mail

ORIGIN
INTERNATIONAL
Logo
Rua Soeiro Pereira Gomes
Lote 1, 11 D
Lisbon
Portugal
+351-1-795-7766
+351-1-795-7768

IBM Corp.
Platform
Technology
IBM SAP Competency
Centers
ibmsap@vnet.ibm.com
http://
www.csc.ibm.com/
sap/PR China
800-IBM-0222-USA-;
610-892-3009
please phone or e-mail

IBM Corp.
Logo
IBM SAP Consulting Hotline
ibmsap@vnet.ibm.com
http://www.csc.ibm.com/
sap/PR China
800-IBM-0222-USA-;
610-892-3009
please phone or e-mail

KPMG
Logo
Robert Robinson
PR China
+44-171832-8553

ORIGIN INTERNATIONAL
Logo
6th Floor, EBT Building
No. 2
889 Yishan Road
Shanghai 200233
Hungiao District
PR China
+86-21-4850067
+86-21-4851014

Ernst & Young
Logo
Dima Vologzhanin
Podsonsensky Pereulok 20
103062 Moscow
Russia
+7-502-220-4664
+7-502-220-4682

IBM Corp.
Logo
IBM SAP Consulting
Hotline
ibmsap@
vnet.ibm.com
http://
www.csc.ibm.com/
sap/Russia
800-IBM-0222-USA-;
610-892-3009
please phone or e-mail

IBM Corp.
Platform
Technology
IBM SAP Competency
Centers
ibmsap@vnet.ibm.com
http://
www.csc.ibm.com/
sap/Russia
800-IBM-0222-USA-;
610-892-3009
please phone or e-mail

ICT Company, Moscow
Implementation
Antipov Konstantin
9B Rogozhsky s/str
Moscow, 109147
Russia
+7-095-9119300,01,02
+7-095-9119300,01,02

KPMG
Logo
Robert Robinson
Russia
+44-171832-8553

MENATEP-RCB
Implementation
Mr. Kiselev
Goncharnaya 3, Block 1
Moscow 109240
Russia
+7-095-9153922
+7-095-9153922

Ernst & Young
Logo
Anis Sadek
Abanumay Commercial Cen.
Salah Eddin Alayobi St.
Riyadh
Malaz
Saudi Arabia
+966-1-477-6272
+966-1-477-6352

IBM Corp.
Logo
IBM SAP Consulting
Hotline
**ibmsap@
vnet.ibm.com
http://
www.csc.ibm.com/
sap/Saudi Arabia**
800-IBM-0222-USA-;
610-892-3009
please phone or e-mail

IBM Corp.
Platform
Technology
IBM SAP Competency
Centers
**ibmsap@vnet.ibm.com
http://
www.csc.ibm.com/
sap/Saudi Arabia**
800-IBM-0222-USA-;
610-892-3009
please phone or e-mail

KPMG
Logo
Robert Robinson
Saudi Arabia
+44-171832-8553

ANDERSEN
CONSULTING
Logo
Mr. Peter Goh
152 Beach Road #19-00
Gateway East
Singapore 0718
Singapore
+65-291-9611
+65-291-7177

Ernst & Young
Logo
Winnie Cheong
36 Robinson Road
#17-00 City House
Singapore 905257
Singapore
+65-220-1135
+65-225-0465

Hewlett-Packard
Logo
Implementation
Platform
Technology
SAP-HP Competence Center
750 A Chai Chee Road
7th Fl. Chai Chee I.P.
Singapore 469001
Singapore
+65-249-1352
+65-249-1308

IBM Corp.
Logo
IBM SAP Consulting
Hotline
**ibmsap@
vnet.ibm.com
http://
www.csc.ibm.com/
sap/Singapore**
800-IBM-0222-USA-;
610-892-3009
please phone or e-mail

IBM Corp.
Platform
Technology
IBM SAP Competency
Centers
ibmsap@vnet.ibm.com
http://
www.csc.ibm.com/
sap/Singapore
800-IBM-0222-USA-;
610-892-3009
please phone or e-mail

KPMG
Logo
Robert Robinson
Singapore
+44-171832-8553

ORIGIN
INTERNATIONAL
Logo
No. 6 Shenton Way
#12-11 DBS Tower 2
Singapore 0106
Singapore
+65-2256760
+65-2254064

COMSOFT Slovakia s.r.o.
Logo
Herr Kindermann
Kudlikoya 17
85102 Bratislava
Slovakia
+42-07-582-1110
+42-02-582-1098

Data-consulting
software sro
Implementation
Dr. Zorkovsky Belo
A.Rudnaya 21
010 01 Zilina
Slovakia
+421-42-89-41683
+421-42-89-34728

IBM Corp.
Logo
IBM SAP Consulting
Hotline
ibmsap@
vnet.ibm.com
http://
www.csc.ibm.com/
sap/Slovakia
800-IBM-0222-USA-;
610-892-3009
please phone or e-mail

IBM Corp.
Platform
Technology
IBM SAP Competency
Centers
ibmsap@vnet.ibm.com
http://
www.csc.ibm.com/
sap/Slovakia
800-IBM-0222-USA-;
610-892-3009
please phone or e-mail

K+K kancel rskatechnika
Implementation
Jan Sledek
Bratislavsk 31
Zilina 01001
Slovakia
+42-89-623395

KPMG
Logo
Robert Robinson
Slovakia
+44-171832-85553
+42-89-646987

Combined Design Engineers
(Pty) Ltd
Independent Vendor
Mr. Paolo Masselli
(Director)
P O Box 2680
Rivonia 2128
South Africa
+27-83-255 5572 -
cellular-
+27-949-303 953 264

Ernst & Young
Logo
Hans Visser
4 Pritchard Street
Johannesburg
South Africa
+27-11-498-1695
+27-11-498-1464

Hewlett-Packard
Logo
Implementation
Platform
Technology
SAP-HO Competence
Center
Jan Smuth Avenue
Hyde Park 2196
Johannesburg
South Africa
+27-11-447-4673
+27-11-447-4674

IBM Corp.
Logo
IBM SAP Consulting Hotline
ibmsap@vnet.ibm.com
http://
www.csc.ibm.com/
sap/South Africa
800-IBM-0222-USA-;
610-892-3009
please phone or e-mail

IBM Corp.
Platform
Technology
IBM SAP Competency Centers
ibmsap@vnet.ibm.com
http://www.csc.ibm.
com/sap/South Africa
800-IBM-0222-USA-;
610-892-3009
please phone or e-mail

KPMG
Logo
Robert Robinson
South Africa
+44-171832-8553

Ernst & Young
Logo
Mike McKay
Torre Picasso
Plaza Pablo Ruiz Picasso
28020 Madrid
Spain
+34-1-572-7204
+34-1-572-7450

IBM Corp.
Logo
IBM SAP Consulting Hotline
ibmsap@vnet.ibm.com
http://www.csc.ibm.
com/sap/Spain
800-IBM-0222-USA-;
610-892-3009
please phone or e-mail

IBM Corp.
Platform
Technology
IBM SAP Competency
Centers
ibmsap@
vnet.ibm.com
http://
www.csc.ibm.com/
sap/Spain
800-IBM-0222-USA-;
610-892-3009
please phone or e-mail

KPMG
Logo
Robert Robinson
Spain
+44-171832-8553

OFFILOG
Logo
Mr. Augest Keller
Via Augusta 125,1.1.
08006 Barcelona
Spain
+34-3-414-7274
+34-3-414-722

ORIGIN
INTERNATIONAL
Logo
Gran Via de les Corts
Catalanes, 184, 7 5aBIS
08004 Barcelona
Spain
+34-3-332-0112
+34-3-296-8595

Ernst & Young
Logo
Per Bragee
Adolf Fredriks Kyrkogata 2
Box 3143
10362 Stockholm
Sweden
+46-8-613-9717
+46-8-10-7002

IBM Corp.
Logo
IBM SAP Consulting Hotline
ibmsap@vnet.ibm.com
http://www.csc.ibm.
com/sap/Sweden
800-IBM-0222-USA-;
610-892-3009
please phone or e-mail

IBM Corp.
Platform
Technology
IBM SAP Competency
Centers
ibm.com
ibmsap@vnet.
http://www.csc.
ibm.com/sap/Sweden
800-IBM-0222-USA-;
610-892-3009
please phone or e-mail

KPMG
Logo
Robert Robinson
Sweden
+44-171832-8553

ORIGIN INTERNATIONAL
Logo
Kottbygatan 7
Akalla
16485 Stockholm
Sweden
+46-8-6322700
+46-8-6322765

Ernst & Young
Logo
Carlo Imboden
Belpstrasse 23
P.O.Box 5032
3001 Berne
Switzerland
+41-31-320-6752
+41-31-320-6829

FIDES Informatik
Implementation
Dr. Hans-Ulrich Koller
Innere
Margarethenstrasse 5
4002 Basel
Switzerland
+41-61 286 93 70
+41-61 286 94 04

Georg Fischer Logimatik AG
Logo
Hans Peter Josf
Ebnatstrasse 91
8201 Schaffhausen
Switzerland
+41 52 631 38 52
+41 52 631 28 35

IBM Corp.
Logo
IBM SAP Consulting
Hotline
ibmsap@vnet.
ibm.com
http://www.csc.
ibm.com/sap/
Switzerland
800-IBM-0222-USA-;
610-892-3009
please phone or e-mail

Appendixes

IBM Corp.
Platform
Technology
IBM SAP Competency
Centers
ibmsap@vnet.ibm.com
http://www.csc.ibm.
com/sap/Switzerland
800-IBM-0222-USA-;
610-892-3009
please phone or e-mail

Information Management
Gesellschaft AG
Logo
Marcel Eichenberger
Splügenstrasse 9
9008 St. Gallen
Switzerland
+41-75 237 18 18
+41-75 237 18 37

IPM Informatik Projekt
Management AG
Implementation
Herr A.Guillebeau
Schützenstrasse 5a
9500 Wil
Switzerland
+41-71-910 06 65 ab
31-03-1996
+41-71-910 06 66 ab
31-03-1996

KPMG
Logo
Robert Robinson
Switzerland
+44-171832-8553

MC CONLOG
Logo
Herr Werner Glauser
Industriestrasse 42
8117 Föllanden (ZH)
Switzerland
+41-1-825 63 32
+41-1-825 63 40

ORIGIN
INTERNATIONAL
Logo
Zugerstrasse 6
6330 Cham
Switzerland
+41-42-380833
+41-42-380835

SDC Consulting AG
Implementation
Daniel Hladky
St Jakobs-Strasse 110
4132 Muttenz
Switzerland
+41-061 466 77 00
+41-061 466 77 10

SLI Consulting AG
Logo
Christian Schuler
Zürcherstrasse 300
8500 Frauenfeld
Switzerland
+41-54 728 06 28
+41-54 728 06 20

IBM Corp.
Logo
IBM SAP Consulting
Hotline
ibmsap@vnet.
ibm.com
http://www.csc.ibm.
com/sap/Taiwan
800-IBM-0222-USA-;
610-892-3009
please phone or e-mail

IBM Corp.
Platform
Technology
IBM SAP Competency
Centers
ibmsap@vnet.ibm.com
http://www.csc.ibm.com/
sap/
800-IBM-0222-USA-;
610-892-3009
please phone or e-mail

KPMG
Logo
Robert Robinson
Taiwan
+44 171832-8553

ORIGIN
INTERNATIONAL
Logo
133, Min Sheng E. Road
Room B, 12th Floor
Taipei, Section 3
Taiwan
+886-2-7187007
+886-2-7197244

Hewlett-Packard
Logo
Implementation
Platform
Technology
SAP-HO Competence Center
Denizcilik Is Merkezi
A Blok Kat 81190
Turkey
+90-216-333-5333
+90-212-224-5939

IBM Corp.
Logo
IBM SAP Consulting Hotline
ibmsap@vnet.ibm.com
http://www.csc.ibm.com/
sap/Turkey
800-IBM-0222-USA-;
610-892-3009
please phone or e-mail

IBM Corp
Platform
Technology
IBM SAP Competency
Centers
ibmsap@vnet.
ibm.com
http://
www.csc.ibm.com/
sap/Turkey
800-IBM-0222-USA-;
610-892-3009
please phone or e-mail

ANDERSEN CONSULTING
Logo
Mr. Patrick J Mullany
2 Arundel Street
London WC2R 3LT
UK
+44-171-438-5390
+44-171-304-8030

Axon Solutions Ltd
Logo
Mark Hunter
Sinclair House
The Avenue
West Ealing
London W1R 8NT
UK
+44-181-758-7536
+44-181-758-7505

Druid
Logo
Rachael Blondeau
Abbeyfield House
Gogmore Lane
Chertsey
Surrey KT16 9AP
UK
+44-1932-571212
+44-1932-571552

Ernst & Young
Logo
Hannah Godman
Becket House
1 Lambeth Palace Road
London SE1 7EU
UK
+44-171-931-5186
+44-171-931-3302

Fisions Labsystems
Independent Vendor
Mr. John Gabathuler
No. 1 St Georges Court
Hannover Business Park
Altrincham
Cheshire WA14 5TP
UK
+44-161-942 3000
+44-161-942 3006

Hewlett-Packard
Logo
Implementation
Platform
Technology
SAP-HP Competence
Center
Cain Road
Bracknell
Berks RG12 1HN
UK
+44-1344-36-5053
+44-1344-36-2187

121 Consulting Limited
Logo
Two Duke Street
Sutton Coldfield
West Midlands B72 IRJ
UK
+44-121-717-2121
+44-121-717-2100

Compaq Computer Ltd
Platform
Hotham House
1 Heron Square
Richmond
Surrey TW9 IEJ
+44-181-332-300
+44-181-332-1962

Coopers & Lybrand
Logo
1 Embankment Place
London WC2N 6NN
UK
+44-171-213-8486
+44-171-213-2485

Appendixes

Diagonal Computer
Services Ltd
Logo
Wey Court
Farnham
Surrey GU9 7PT
UK
+44-1252-736-666
+44-1252-736-667

Digital Equipment Co Ltd
Logo
Platform
Digital Park
Imperial Way
Reading
Berkshire RG2 0TE
UK
+44-1734-868711
+44-1734-867969

Hoskyns UK SAP Centre
Logo
Hoskyns South Bank
95 Wandsworth Road
London SW8 2HG
UK
+44-171-917-4914
+44-171-917-4666

Microsoft Ltd
Technology
Microsoft Place
Winnersh
Wokingham
Berkshire RG11 5TP
UK
+44-1734-270001
+44-1734-270002

"Plaut (UK) Limited
Logo
Status Park 4
3 Nobel Drive
Hayes
Middx. UB3 5EY
UK
+44-181-384-1046
+44-181-384-1047

Sun Microsystems LTD
Platform
Sun House
31-41 Pembroke Broadway
Surrey GU15 3XD
UK
+44-1276-62111
+44-1276-692241

Touche Ross Management
Consultants
Logo
Friary Court
65 Crutched Friars
London EC3N 2NP
UK
+44-171-936-3000
+44-171-480-6958

IBM Corp.
Logo
IBM SAP Consulting Hotline
ibmsap@vnet.ibm.com
http://www.csc.ibm.
com/sap/UK
800-IBM-0222-USA-;
610-892-3009
please phone or e-mail

IBM Corp.
Platform
Technology
IBM SAP Competency
Centers
ibmsap@vnet.ibm.com
http://www.csc.ibm.
com/sap/UK
800-IBM-0222-USA-;
610-892-3009
please phone or e-mail

ICI SYSTEMS
Logo
Tim Wilkins
PO Box 13, The Heath
Runcorn
Cheshire WA7 4QF
UK
+44-1928-513201
+44-1928-513338

KPMG
Logo
David Boyd
8 Salisbury Square
PO Box 695
London EC4Y 8BB
UK
+44-171-311-8483

MORSE GROUP LTD
Logo
Mr. Laurence Menear
Brentside Exec Centre
Great Western Road
Brentford
Middlesex TW8 9HE
UK
+44-181-380 8000
+44-181-560 7700

ORIGIN
INTERNATIONAL
Logo
21 The Science Park
Milton Road
Cambridge CB4 4FH
UK
+44-1223-425110
+44-1223-425075

ANDERSEN CONSULTING
Logo
Mr. Jeffrey A Hicks
1717 East Ninth Street
Cleveland
Ohio
USA
+1-216-771-2195
+1-216-781-3683

ARIS Corporation
Implementation
Andrew Simcock
6720 Fort Dent Way
Suite 150
Seattle
WA 98188-2555
USA
+1-206-433-2081
+1-206-433-1183

AVP Systems
Complementary Product
Dan Cronin
27 Congress Street
Salem, MA 01970
USA
+1-508-741-0101,
ext-107
+1-508-741-0222

PERWILL BUSINESS
SOLUTIONS LTD
Independent Vendor
Mr. Bill Pugsley
13A Market Square
Alton GU34 1UR
UK
+44-1420 545000
+44-1420-545001

Apple Computer, Inc.
Technology
Patrica Dickens
1 Infinite Loop
Cupertino
CA 95014-2084
USA
+1-408-974-5510
+1-408-974-8181

AT&T Global
Information Solutions
Platform
AT&T R/3 Competence
Centres
USA
+1-316-634-3138
+1-316-634-3131

BSG Alliance/IT, Inc.
Implementation
Bill Boschma, Director
SAP Services
Eleven Greenway Plaza
Suite 800
Houston
Texas 77046-1102
USA
+1-713-965-9000
+1-713-993-9249

The SQL Group
Implementation
Patrick Tobin
1 Nine Elms Lane
London SW8 5NQ
UK
+44-171-887 0700
+44-171-887 0707

Applied Integration
Services, Inc.
Implementation
Grace Braese
USA
+1-513-831-2020
+1-513-248-5563

AutoTester Inc.
Independent Vendor
Tom Kanuch
8150 N. Central Expressway
Suite 1300
Dallas
Texas 75206
USA
+1-214-368-1196
+1-214-750-9668

BUREAU VAN DIJK
COMPUTER SERVICES
Implementation
Luc De Groof
Five Concourse Pkwy
Suite 2875
Atlanta
GA 30328
USA
+1-770-395-2833
+1-770-395-2836

Appendixes

Cap Gemini Sogeti
Logo
Bob Howerter
5847 San Felipe,
Suite 990
Houston
Texas 77057
USA
+1-713-307-7900
+1-713-307-7901

CISCORP
Implementation
Linda Behling
Penn Center West 11
Suite 430
Pittsburgh
PA 15276
USA
+1-412-787-9600
ext- 105
+1-412-787-3070

Computer Aid, Inc.
Implementation
Tim Campbell
901 Market Street
Suite 1200
Wilmington
DE 19801
USA
+1-302-594-3097
+1-302-888-5443

Coopers & Lybrand
L.L.P.
Logo
Herbert B Vinnicombe
2400 Eleven Penn Center
Philadelphia
PA 19103
USA
+1-215-963-8530
+1-215-963-8824

Chaptec Group Inc.
Implementation
Roger S Webb
5525 N. MacArthur Blvd
Suite 280
Irving
Texas 75038
USA
+1-214-751-1310
+1-214-550-1620

Clarkston-Potomac
Group Inc.
Implementation
Tom Finegan
100 Europa Drive
Suite 555
Chapel Hill
NC 27514
USA
+1-919-932-1089
+1-919-933-6521

Computer Communications
Specialists
Implementation
Bill Hutchison
6529 Jimmy Carter Blvd.
Atlanta
GA 30071
USA
+1-770-441-3114
+1-770-263-0487

Data General Corporation
Platform
Jose Leruth
3400 Computer Drive
Westboro
MA 01580
USA
+1-508-898-6664
+1-508-898-4063

CIMMETRY SYSTEMS INC
Independent Vendor
678 Mass. Ave; Suite 501
Cambridge
MA 02139
USA
+1-514-735-3219
+1-514-735-6440

Compaq Computer
Corporation
Platform
USA
+1-800-345-1518

Computer Sciences
Corporation
Logo
Stephen C Sperry
200 Park Avenue
32nd Floor
New York
NY 10166
USA
+1-212-251-6076
+1-212-251-6066

DDS, Inc.
Logo
Terri Gaddis
80 S. 8th Street
Suite 4400
Minneapolis
MN 55402
USA
+1-612-332-5200
+1-612-332-4539

Deloitte & Touche
Consulting
Group/ICS
Logo
Dawn De Santis
Chadds Ford Business
Campus
Chadds Ford
PA 19317
USA
+1-610-558-3900
+1-610-558-7200

Deno Morris Group
Implementation
Nicholas Mastrandrea
2391 Anthony Avenue
Clearwater
FL 34619
USA
+1-908-274-2639
+1-908-438-0388

Decision Consultants Inc.
Implementation
Bob Hanson
13535 Feather Sound Drive
Suite 220
Clearwater, FL 34622
USA
+1-813-573-2626

Documentation Associates
Independent Vendor
Joan Oelze
14400 Northwest Freeway
Suite 200
Houston
Texas 77092
USA
+1-213-682-3393
+1-213-682-3396

EDS/ATKearney
Logo
Ron Crumpler
5400 Legacy Drive
(MS)A1-6A-11
Plano, TX 75024
USA
+1-800-724-3316
+1-214-604-6861

Ernst & Young
Logo
Jane Vaughan
600 Peachtree Street
Suite 2800
Atlanta
Georgia 30308-2215
USA
+1-404-817-5530
+1-404-817-4324

FileNet Corporation
Complementary Product
Michael Stiles
3565 Harbor Blvd
Costa Mesa
California 92626-1420
USA
+1-714-966-3000
+1-714-966-3490

Gammalink Division of
DIALOGIC
Independent Vendor
Sales Department
1314 Chesapeake Terrace
Sunnyvale
CA 94089
USA
+1-800-755-4444
+1-908-744-1900

Gelco Information Network
Independent Vendor
Mr. Regan Hutton
10700 Prairie Lakes Drive
Eden Prairie
MN 55344-3886
USA
+1-612-947-1500
+1-612-947-1525

Harbinger Enterprise
Solutions
Complementary Product
Mr. Douglas Stewart
2425 North Central
Expressway
Richardson
TX 75080
USA
+1-214-479-1260
+1-214-479-9779

Appendixes

Hewlett-Packard
Logo
Implementation
Platform
Technology
SAP-HP Competence Center
100 Stevens Drive,
Suite 245
Philadelphia
PA 19113
USA
+1-610-595-4040
+1-610-595-4041

IBM Corp.
Logo
IBM SAP Consulting Hotline
ibmsap@vnet.ibm.com
http://www.csc.ibm.com/
sap/USA
800-IBM-0222-USA-;
610-892-3009
please phone or e-mail

IBM Corp.
Platform
Technology
IBM SAP Competency
Centers
ibmsap@vnet.
ibm.com
http://www.csc.ibm.
com/sap/USA
800-IBM-0222-USA-;
610-892-3009
please phone or e-mail *

IBS Consulting
Services Ltd
Implementation
Independent Vendor
Kimberley Nicholas
Marketing Mgr
The Coach House
145 Church Lane East
GU11 3ST
USA
+1-252-341-515
+1-252-345-003

IDS Prof. Scheer Inc.
Logo
Implementation
D Pezzetti
100 Dickinson Drive
Bldg.2,Suite 30
Chadds Ford
PA 19317
USA
+1-610-558-7600

INCODE Corporation
Complementary Product
250 Exchange Place
Herndon
VA 22070
USA
+1-703-709-7667
+1-703-709-0195

Information Builders
Independent Vendor
Kevin Mergruen
1250 Broadway
New York
NY 10001
USA
+1-212-736-4433
+1-212-629-8819

Integraph Computer Systems
Implementation
289 Dunlop Blvd.
Huntsville
AL 35894
USA
+1-800-763-0242
+1-205-730-6188

Integraph Corporation
Complementary Product
Implementation
Mr. Brimmer Sherman
289 Dunlop Blvd.
Huntsville
Alabama 35894-0001
USA
+1-205-730-1230
+1-205-730-1263

Intel Corporation
Technology
Steve Levich
(SAP Program Manager)
2111 NE 25th Ave.
MS:JF3-133
Hillsboro
OR 97124
USA
+1-503-264-7623
+1-503-264-5889

KPMG
Logo
Robert Robinson
USA
+44-171832-8553

ORIGIN INTERNATIONAL
Logo
430 Mountain Avenue
Mountain Heights Center
Murray Hill
NJ 07974-2732
USA
+1-908-508-1700
+1-908-508-0882

RSA COMPANIES
Independent Vendor
Mr. Jacob Joseph
7400 East Orchard Road
Englewood
CO 80111
USA
+1-303-741-3105
+1-303-741-3105

Intelligroup, Inc.
Implementation
Raj Koneru
5 Lincoln Highway
Edison, NJ 08820
USA
+1-908-603-8909
+1-908-603-8819

Multimedia Professionals,
Inc.
Independent Vendor
Stephen Borman
PO Box 223081
Chantilly
VA 22022
USA
+1-800-621-1369

Platinum Technology Inc.
Technology
Sales Information Hotline
1855 Meyers RO
Oakbrook Terrace
IL 60181
USA
+1-800-442-6861;
1-708-620 5000-8777
+1-708-691-0708

SCS America, Software
Consultancy
Service
Implementation
Dan Arra
1730 S Amphlett Blvd
San Mateo
CA 94403
USA
+1-415-286-4420
+1-415-286-4421

IXOS Software
Technology
Brent M Jackson
1070 Sixth Avenue,
Suite 200
Belmont
CA 94002
USA
+1-415-610-8240
+1-415-802-9570

Novell, Inc.
Implementation
Brent Garlick
mailstop: ORMB 313
1555 North Technology
Way
Orem
Utah 84057
USA
+1-801-228-7267

Proactive Systems Inc.
Independent Vendor
Bob Kaehler
4 Main Street
San Francisco
CA 94022
USA
+1-415-949-9100
+1-415-959-9111

Seltmann, Cobb &
Bryant, Inc.
Implementation
Steven Horward
1365 West Brierbrook
Road
Memphis
TN 38138
USA
+1-800-221-1640
+1-901-758-0515

Software Consulting
Partners Inc.
Implementation
Ulrich Neubert
200 East State Street,
Suite 105
Media
PA 19063
USA
+1-610-892-7100
+1-610-892-7105

Sterling Software
Complementary Product
Interchange Software
Division Sales
4600 Lakehurst Ct.
Dublin
OH 43017
USA
+1-614-793-7000
+1-614-793-7221

TALX Corporation
Complementary Product
Carey Albritton
1850 Borman Court
St Louis
MO 63146
USA
+1-314-434-0046
+1-314-434-9205

SPO America, Inc.
Implementation
Michael Adolphs
8 Woodstock Drive
Framingham
MA 01701
USA
+1-508-877-7100
+1-508-877-7110

Syntra Ltd
Independent Vendor
Mr. Pano Anthos,
Managing Director
505 Eighth Avenue
Floor No 15
New York
NY 10018
USA
+1-212-714-0440
+1-212-967-4623

Technology Solutions
Company
Implementation
Mr. Ard Geller
205 North Michigan Ave;
Suite 1500
Chicago
IL 60601
USA
+1-312-819-2250
+1-312-819-2299

St Paul Software
Complementary Product
Dee Thibodeau
1450 Energy Park Drive
St Paul
MN 55108
USA
+1-612-603-4400
+1-612-603-4403

SYSTEMS AMERICA INC
Independent Vendor
Mr. Adesh Kumar
3521 Silverside Road,
Suite 212
Wilmington
DE 19810
USA
+1-302-478-2990
+1-302-478-2995

Tivoli Systems Inc.
Independent Vendor
Sales
9442 Capital of Texas
Highway North
Austin
TX 78759
USA
+1-512-794-9070
+1-512-794-0623

Trinary Systems, Inc.
Implementation
Executive Assistant
38345 W. Ten Mile Road
Suite 330
Farmington Hills
Ml 48335
USA
+1-800-377-9120
-edi@trinary.com
+1-810-442-9125

TSI International
Independent Vendor
45 Danbury Road
Wilton
CT 06897
USA
+1-203-761-8600
+1-203-762-9677

Vertex Inc.
Independent Vendor
Paul W Beirnes
1041 Old Cassatt Road
Berwyn
PA 19312
USA
+1-800-355-3500
+1-610-640-2761

Whittman-Hart L.P.
Implementation
Glenn O. Gumley
6400 S. Fiddlers Green
Circle
Suite 200
Englewood
CO 80111
USA
+1-303-889-0572
+1-303-773-1404

Ernst & Young
Logo
Hector Crespo
Av. Principal El Bosque
Caracas
1050-A
Venezuela
+58-2-731-0133
+58-2-731-1670

IBM Corp.
Logo
IBM SAP Consulting
Hotline
**ibmsap@vnet.
ibm.com
http://www.csc.ibm.
com/sap/Venezuela**
800-IBM-0222-USA-;
610-892-3009
please phone or e-mail

IBM Corp.
Platform
Technology
IBM SAP Competency
Centers
**ibmsap@vnet.ibm.com
http://www.csc.ibm.com/
sap/Venezuela**
800-IBM-0222-USA-;
610-892-3009
please phone or e-mail

KPMG
Logo
Robert Robinson
Venezuela
+44-171832-8553

121 Consulting
Limited
Logo
Two Duke Street
Sutton Coldfield
West Midlands B72 IRJ UK
+44-121-717-2121
+44-121-717-2100

Compaq Computer Ltd
Platform
Hotham House
1 Heron Square
Richmond
Surrey TW9 IEJ UK
+44-181-332-300
+44-181-332-1962

Coopers & Lybrand
Logo
1 Embankment Place
London WC2n 6NN UK
+44-171-213-8486
+44-171-213-2485

Appendixes

Diagonal Computer
Services Ltd
Logo
Wey Court
Farnham
Surrey GU9 7PT UK
+44-1252-736-666
+44-1252-736-667

Digital Equipment Co Ltd
Logo
Platform
Digital Park
Imperial Way
Reading
Berkshire RG2 0TE UK
+44-1734-868711
+44-1734-867969

Hoskyns UK SAP
Centre
Logo
Hoskyns South Bank
95 Wandsworth Road
London SW8 2HG UK
+44-171-917-4914
+44-171-917-4666

Microsoft Ltd
Technology
Microsoft Place
Winnersh
Wokingham
Berkshire RG11 5TP UK
+44-1734-270001
+44-1734-270002

Plaut (UK) Limited
Logo
Status Park 4
3 Nobel Drive
Hayes
Middx. UB3 5EY UK
+44-181-384-1046
+44-181-384-1047

Sun Microsystems Ltd
Platform
Sun Hourse
31-41 Pembroke Broadway
Camberley
Surrey GU15 3XD UK
+44-1276-62111
+44-1726-692241

Touche Ross Management
Consultants
Logo
Friary Court
65 Crutched Friars
London EC3N 2NP UK
+44-171-936-3000
+44-171-480-6958

Appendix C

Sample SAP-Related Job Descriptions

These examples are real-life examples of descriptions published inside companies or prepared for recruitment companies. In some cases, where the employer wishes to preserve anonymity, examples have been edited slightly, but only enough to satisfy employers' wishes; the substance is unaltered.

Description of Jobs Carried Out in SAP Subsidiaries

Although the structure of jobs in SAP subsidiaries and SAP partners is changing and differs according to the history and work areas of the company, there are certain key positions that will be recognised, even if the have a "local" title.

Account Executive (Customer Support Manager)

Scope:

- Responsible for the measurement of customer satisfaction by being the principal point of contact throughout the time that the organization remains a customer.

- Develops ongoing business within the account by proactively anticipating customer needs and applying SAP solutions to meet these needs.

- Maintains multiple customer relationships simultaneously within one or several vertical market sectors.

Experience:

- Experience of implementing enterprise-wide software solutions.

- Fundamental understanding of business issues within appropriate market sectors.

- Track record of empathizing with customer to achieve results and the management of long-term customer relationships.

The descriptions are grouped as follows:

- Jobs carried out in SAP subsidiaries.

- Examples of SAP-related jobs advertised on the Internet, which include several in the SAP development team.

- Job descriptions from SAP business partners.

- Job descriptions of positions with end-users.

Functional Knowledge:

- An expert in relationship building.
- Proficiently applies a logical methodology to servicing a customer's requirements.
- Liaisons between partners and SAP to ensure customer satisfaction.
- Monitors customer satisfaction on a regular basis.

Product Knowledge:

- A high-level understanding of the functionality of the product suite.
- An understanding of the integration and implementation issues involved.

Industry Knowledge:

- An understanding of current and future business issues within one or more vertical markets.
- Credibility within the vertical market as an expert.

Business Vertical or Technological Knowledge:

- A broad, high-level understanding of all applications in the current product suite.
- A high-level understanding of the business issues within the application areas.

Assignment Management:

- Plans, schedules, and manages to achieve the measurement of customer satisfaction.
- Liaisons internally to inform the appropriate bodies on the state of customer satisfaction within their accounts.
- Maintains and develops contacts with key influencers and decision-makers.

Leadership/Teamwork:

- Assumes overall responsibility for customer.
- Acts as a role model and mentor.
- Influences the direction and effectiveness of the organization in achieving the highest levels of customer service.
- Conducts timely and effective administrative duties associated with a key role within the organization.
- Develops and maintains good working relationships within SAP and with partners.

Communication:

- Able to communicate at all levels within a customer organization/SAP and with partners.

- Skilled at both written and oral communication.
- Open, honest, and credible.

Training:

- Acts as an internal educator for business issues relating to customers and vertical markets.

Business Development:

- Quickly establishes good relationships with customers, based on credibility.
- Identifies, qualifies, and develops opportunities for further business within account.
- Ensures he or she knows, understands, and can actively promote new product developments.
- Maintains a complete and concise record of SAP and customer relationships.
- Understands and actively sells SAP UK and SAP AG Services, SAP Partner philosophy, and SAP Implementation strategy.

Alliance Partner Manager
Scope:

- Leads, develops, and manages partner relationships to ensure company and customer satisfaction and to generate revenue targets.

Experience:

- Experience at building and developing client/partner relationships.
- Experienced in developing informal networks.
- Experience of developing third-party relationships to achieve customer satisfaction and revenue targets.

Functional Knowledge:

- Recognized as a central point of contact for issues relating to partner management.
- Assists in the implementation of "Partner Academy" initiative and ancillary partner training.
- Champions the partners internally within the organizations, particularly with the vertical market teams.

Product Knowledge:

- A high level of understanding of the functionality of the product suite.
- An understanding of the integration and implementation issues related to the product suite.

Industry Knowledge:

- An understanding of current and future business issues within the IT market.

Business Vertical or Technological Knowledge:

- A high-level understanding of all the applications in the current product suite.
- A high-level understanding of business issues related to the application area.

Assignment Management:

- Plans, schedules, and manages to achieve customer and partner satisfaction.
- Internal liaison to champion appropriate partners.
- Maintains and develops contact with key influencers and decision-makers.
- Maintains timely and critical partner information to position partners within SAP and customers' organizations.

Leadership/Teamwork:

- Assumes responsibility for the partners.
- Acts as a role model and mentor.
- Influences the climate of the organization in terms of new incentives relating to partner management.
- Performs administrative duties associated with the role.
- Develops and maintains good working relationships with appropriate internal agencies.

Communication:

- Able to communicate at all levels with a partner organization.
- Skilled at both written and oral communication.
- Helps internal organization to be informed of developments with the partner community.

Training:

- Acts as mentor.

Business Development:

- Positions SAP with the partner community to achieve maximum advantage.
- Generates a positive image for the product suite.
- Coordinates SAP's Sales and Marketing function, developing partner relationships in specific vertical account sections.

Business Consultant

Scope:

- Presents a business-focused SAP solution to prospective customers by using in-depth knowledge of one or more vertical markets, and is instrumental within the industry team in facilitating the sale.

- To be seen both internally and externally as a vertical market center of exchange.

Experience:

- Competent at providing an integrated system solution within a business context.

- Experience in the ways of doing business within the appropriate vertical.

Functional Knowledge:

- Capable of proficiently demonstrating the SAP business solution to provide a formal response to the prospective customer's business needs.

- Understands and contributes to relevant aspects of the sales cycle.

- Understands customer motives and buying criteria.

Product Knowledge:

- Knowledge of one area of the product suite.

- A broad knowledge of all other areas.

- An in-depth understanding of implementation issues.

Industry Knowledge:

- An in-depth understanding of all the business aspects pertaining to a vertical market.

- The ability to apply this knowledge in other areas.

- To be seen as an industry "guru."

- Keeps abreast of competitor activity within vertical market.

Business Vertical or Technical Knowledge:

- A broad knowledge of all application areas within the product suite.

Assignment Management:

- As part of an industry team, employs flexible and adaptable strategies in providing business solutions.

- Understands the sales cycle as a broad framework within which to work.

- Works quickly to establish the customer's business needs.

- Can work on multiple assignments.

Leadership/Teamwork:

- Acts as a role model and mentor.
- Influences other areas of the organization.
- Conducts administrative duties associated with a leadership role.
- Develops and maintains strong working relationships with the leadership team.
- Transfers business knowledge to others.

Communication:

- Effectively communicates with prospects at all levels both orally and in writing.
- Effectively communicates with team members and other units within SAP.
- Actively supports the maintenance and/or development of prospect/customer relationships.
- Provides feedback to other parts of the SAP organization.

Training:

- Acts as a mentor and coach for other employees within their market sector.

Business Development:

- Quickly establishes good relationships with prospects based on credibility.
- Takes a pivotal role in bringing a prospect to a close.
- Is viewed as a specialist by the customer within the appropriate market sector.

Consultant

Scope:

- Leads consulting assignments to support customers in the implementation of a SAP solution to satisfy a business need.

Experience:

- Evidence of having the ability to implement a standard application software-based, business-oriented solution within a project environment.

Functional Knowledge:

- Ability to apply a logical methodology for the collection and analysis of business and/or technical issues.
- Leads and/or advises on the processes needed to implement solutions.
- Ability to gain customer's agreement on outcomes and deliver results.

Product Knowledge:

- Requires in-depth knowledge of at least one area of the product suite.

- Has broad knowledge of other areas.
- Has an understanding of the integration issues related to the product's implementation.
- Can align product's functionality with complex business needs.

Industry Knowledge:

- Requires knowledge of one or more business sectors.
- Able to align business issues within a sector to the product's functionality.

Business Vertical or Technological Knowledge:

- Has either an in-depth knowledge of one or more specific applications areas or a broad knowledge of technology.

Assignment Management:

- Leads, plans, schedules, and manages assignments, using established processes.
- Establishes requirements for assignments.
- Can work on multiple assignments.

Leadership/Teamwork:

- Makes decisions with minimal direction.
- Acts as a mentor.
- Transfers industry product and technical knowledge to others.
- Develops a working relationship with multiple levels within SAP.

Communication:

- Effectively communicates with consulting team members and other units within SAP.
- Effectively communicates with customers at multiple levels.
- Supports the maintenance and/or development of customer relationships.
- Develops and assists in making customer presentations.

Training:

- Participates in the development and teaching of product-related training course.

Business Development:

- Assists in scoping assignments.
- Identifies opportunities for additional business.
- Participates in the sale of consulting services to potential customers.

Industry Manager (Sales)

Scope:

- To achieve the sales and support revenue target for the industry sector.

- To achieve customer satisfaction and referenceability by working as a team player.

Experience:

- A track record of selling integrated software solutions.

- A broad knowledge of IT-related business issues within nominated industry sector.

Functional Knowledge:

- A fundamental knowledge of the sales cycle.

- An understanding of buying motives at high level within customer organization.

Product Knowledge:

- Must have a broad, high-level overview and understanding of the business impact of the product's functionality.

- An understanding of related implementation issues.

Industry Knowledge:

- An in-depth knowledge of business issues relating to one or more vertical markets.

Business Vertical or Technological:

- A broad, high-level overview of all the applications within the Knowledge product suite.

Assignment Management:

- Leads, plans, schedules, and manages prospects and internal staff to convert prospects to customers.

- Has a flexible approach to each customer's issues.

Leadership/Teamwork:

- Sets the lead in getting maximum utilization from the team to obtain commitment to the plan and achieve results.

- Conducts administrative duties relating to role.

Communication:

- Develops and cultivates prospect relationships at all levels.

- Effectively communicates with prospects at all levels both orally and in writing.

- Effectively communicates with team members and other units within SAP.

- Provides feedback to other parts of the SAP organization.

Training:

- Acts as a mentor and coach.

Business Development:

- Quickly establishes good relationships with prospects based on personal credibility.
- Responsible for closing sales.

Instructor
Scope:

- Responsible for maintaining the quality of training systems and documentation and for giving courses in one or more application areas.

Experience:

- Experience of consistent high performance as a dedicated software systems trainer.
- Experience of training and/or implementing some or all aspects of the product suite.

Functional Knowledge:

- Capable of proficiently training in one or more aspects of the product suite.
- Capable of developing course material to meet new and existing functionality.
- Capable of taking a consultancy role on certain product implementations.

Product Knowledge:

- Requires an in-depth knowledge of one of the product suites.
- Has a broad knowledge in other areas.
- Has an understanding of the integration issues related to the product's implementation.

Industry Knowledge:

- Has a broad, high-level understanding of the business issues within the markets in which we operate.

Business Vertical or Technological Knowledge:

- Has either an in-depth knowledge of one or more specific applications areas or a broad knowledge of technology.

Assignment Management:

- Plans, schedules, and manages issues as they arrive, to achieve customer satisfaction.
- Can multitask.

Leadership/Teamwork:

- Makes sure that decisions are made by using the best information available to the team.
- Networks within the training team and with other areas of the organization.

Communication:

- Effectively communicates with customers, team members, and other areas of the organization.
- Has highly developed presentation skills.
- Supports the maintenance and/or development of customer relationships.
- Liaison with SAP AG trainers/course developers.

Training:

- Acts as a center of excellence for training issues.
- Delivers training courses to achieve customer satisfaction.
- High standard of training delivery based on own credibility.

Business Development:

- Quickly establishes good rapport with customers.
- Is instrumental in achieving add-on business by ensuring customer satisfaction.
- Understands the services of other SAP departments and actively sells them.
- Understands and actively sells the SAP Partner philosophy.
- Understands and actively sells SAP Implementation approach.
- Sells training services.

Product Manager

Scope:

- Is seen as a product center of excellence.
- Is the single point of contact for all issues related to a specific area of the product suite.
- Leads multiple and/or complex assignments to support customers in the implementation of a SAP solution to satisfy a business need.

Experience:

- Extensive reputation for product knowledge.
- Has proven ability to implement standard application software based on business solutions within complex project environments.

Functional Knowledge:

- Proficiently applies a logical methodology for the collection and analysis of issues related to the product suite.

- Leads and/or advises on the development of programs that implement solutions.

- Has ability to gain others' agreement on outcomes and deliver results.

Product Knowledge:

- Is recognized as a center of expertise for one area of the product suite.

- Has an in-depth knowledge of other areas that directly impact product expertise.

- Has an in-depth understanding of the integration issues related to the product's implementation.

- Can align product's functionality with complex business needs.

- Able to facilitate communication between business and technical experts.

Industry Knowledge:

- Requires knowledge of one or more business sectors.

- Able to align business issues within a sector to the product's functionality.

Business Vertical or Technological Knowledge:

- Has either an in-depth knowledge of one or more specific applications area or a broad knowledge of more technical issues.

Assignment Management:

- Leads, plans, schedules, and manages multiple and/or complex assignments, using established processes.

- Establishes requirements for assignments.

- Internal liaison to champion the product.

Leadership/Teamwork:

- Acts as a role model and mentor.

- Influences the strategic direction of the group.

- Conducts administrative duties associated with a leadership role.

- Develops and maintains a strong working relationship with the leadership and development teams.

Communication:

- Develops and cultivates customer relationships at senior and executive levels.

- Effectively communicates with consulting team members and other units within SAP and facilitates information flow from SAP AG.

- Supports the maintenance and/or development of customer relationships.
- Develops and assists in making customer presentations.

Training:

- Participates in the development and teaching of product-related training courses.

Business Development:

- Assists in scoping assignments.
- Identifies opportunities for additional business.
- Participates in the sale of consulting services to potential customers.
- Liaison with research and development teams to make sure that they are aware of how the products could better suit the requirements of potential customers.

Remote Consultant

Scope:

- To provide first-line applications support to customers in specified application areas.

Experience:

- Evidence of having the ability to provide applications support to customers within a remote services environment.

Functional Knowledge:

- Proficiently applies a logical methodology to the collection, analysis, and solution of customer problems and support issues.
- A fundamental commitment to customer satisfaction.

Product Knowledge:

- Requires an in-depth knowledge of at least one area of the product suite.
- Has broad knowledge of other areas.
- Has an understanding of the integration issues related to the product's implementation.

Industry Knowledge:

- A broad, high-level understanding of the business issues within the markets in which we operate.

Business Vertical or Technological Knowledge:

- Has an in-depth knowledge either of one or more specific applications or of one or more technology (BASIS) areas.

Assignment Management:

- Plans, schedules, and manages issues as they arrive, in order to achieve a satisfied customer.

- Can work on multiple issues.

Leadership/Teamwork:

- Makes decisions with minimal direction.

- Networks both within the Remote Consulting team and with other areas of the SAP organization.

Communication:

- Effectively communicates with customers, team members, and other areas of the SAP organization.

- Supports the maintenance and/or development of customer relationships.

Training:

- Acts as a coach to customers within a specialized area of expertise.

- Is responsible for keeping their knowledge up-to-date and relevant.

Business Development:

- Quickly establishes credibility with the customer.

- Is instrumental in achieving add-on business by ensuring customer satisfaction.

Senior Consultant

Scope:

- Leads multiple and/or complex assignments to support customers in the implementation of a SAP solution to satisfy a business need.

Experience:

- Has proven ability to implement standard application software-based business solution within complex project environments.

- Extensive reputation for product knowledge.

Functional Knowledge:

- Proven ability to apply logical methodology for the collection and analysis of issues related to the product suite.

- Leads and/or advises on the processes needed to implement solutions.

- Ability to gain others' agreement on outcomes and deliver results.

- Leads a team to deliver results.

Product Knowledge:

- Has an in-depth knowledge of multiple areas within the product suite.
- Has an in-depth understanding of the integration issues related to the products' implementation.
- Can align product's functionality with complex business needs.
- Able to facilitate communication between business and technical experts.

Industry Knowledge:

- Requires knowledge of one or more business sectors.
- Able to align business issues within a sector to the product's functionality.

Business Vertical or Technological Knowledge:

- Has an in-depth knowledge of one or more specific applications areas and a broad knowledge of more technical issues.

Assignment Management:

- Leads, plans, schedules, and manages multiple and/or complex assignments using established processes.
- Establishes requirements for assignments.

Leadership/Teamwork:

- Acts as a role model and mentor.
- Influences the strategic direction of the group.
- Conducts administrative duties associated with a leadership role.
- Develops and maintains strong working relationships with the leadership and development teams.

Communication:

- Develops and cultivates customer relationships at senior and executive levels.
- Effectively communicates with consulting team members and other units within SAP.
- Supports the maintenance and/or development of customer relationships.
- Develops and assists in making customer presentations.

Training:

- Participates in the development and teaching of product-related training courses.

Business Development:

- Assists in scoping assignments.

- Identifies opportunities for additional business.

- Participates in the sale of consulting services to potential customers.

Senior Remote Consultant

Scope:

- To provide first-line applications support to customers in specified application areas.

Experience:

- Evidence of having the ability to provide applications support to customers within a remote services environment.

Functional Knowledge:

- Proficiently applies a logical methodology to the collection, analysis, and solution of customer problems and support issues.

- A fundamental commitment to customer satisfaction.

Product Knowledge:

- Is an expert in one area of the product suite to the highest level.

- Has broad knowledge in other areas.

- Has an understanding of the integration issues related to the product's implementation.

Industry Knowledge:

- Has a broad, high-level understanding of the business issues within the markets in which we operate.

Business Vertical or Technological Knowledge:

- Has an in-depth knowledge either of one or more specific applications or of one or more technology (Basis) areas.

Assignment Management:

- Plans, schedules, and manages issues as they arrive, in order to achieve a satisfied customer.

- Can work on multiple issues.

Appendixes

Leadership/Teamwork:

- Makes sure that decisions are made by using the best information available to the team.

- Networks both within the Remote Consulting team and with other areas of the SAP organization.

Communication:

- Effectively communicates with customers, team members, and other areas of the SAP organization.

- Supports the maintenance and/or development of customer relationships.

Training:

- Acts as a coach to customers within a specialized area of expertise.

- Is responsible for keeping knowledge up-to-date and relevant.

- Is responsible to mentor and nurture new staff.

Business Development:

- Quickly establishes credibility with the customer.

- Is instrumental in achieving add-on business by ensuring customer satisfaction.

Sample SAP-Related Job Descriptions Advertised on the Internet

Advertisements for jobs tend to carry titles designed to attract suitable applicants. The title may not be the most apt name for what the position entails.

SAP Development Team

A team engaged in developing standard business process software may be part of the SAP corporation; or it may be located in one of the partner organizations which can provide particular industrial or commercial expertise. In either case, the software will have to receive SAP Certification after formal testing before it can be released for use in a SAP R/3 implementation. Both types of development team will therefore be working towards the same standards.

SAP R/3 Installation Tools Developer. The Software Logistics Department develops tools and technologies for managing the SAP R/3 system internally (source code control and transport systems) and implementing the system at the customer site (installation, upgrade).

The R3INST tool is currently being used to support the installation of distributed SAP R/3 system configurations on eight different UNIX platforms in conjunction with four different relational database systems and on Windows NT with three different relational database systems.

Our small development team is seeking a new member, whose main area of responsibility will be maintaining and enhancing the R3INST tool. Our requirements:

- In-depth technical knowledge of different UNIX systems (BSD and System V).

- Hands-on programming experience in C.

- Knowledge of database systems would be an asset.

- Good command of English.

- Ability to work in a team, communication skills.

- Commitment and flexibility.

Senior SAP R/3 Software Developer to Enhance the Error Tolerance of SAP's R/3 BASIS Software. Your duties will include:

- Highly responsible tasks in the design and implementation of SAP R/3 BASIS software.

- Analyzing the error-tolerance of SAP R/3 BASIS software and developing a concept to increase SAP R/3 System availability.

You will have:

- Experience in designing complex distributed software applications in C.

- Excellent knowledge of the UNIX environment.

- Excellent knowledge of TCP/IP-based network programming.

- A university degree.

- At least three years of relevant work experience.

- Experience in the development of error-tolerant software would be an advantage.

- Preferably some knowledge of current databases (for example, Oracle, Informix, Microsoft SQL Server).

- A good knowledge of English.

SAP R/3 Software Developer. Your duties will include:

- Cooperation in the design and implementation of SAP R/3 BASIS software.

- Providing support in analyzing the error-tolerance of SAP R/3 BASIS software and developing a concept to increase SAP R/3 System availability.

You will have:

- Experience in designing complex distributed software applications in C.

- Excellent knowledge of TCP/IP-based network programming.

- A university degree.

- Experience in the development of error-tolerant software would be an advantage.

Appendixes

- Knowledge of current databases (for example, Oracle, Informix, Microsoft SQL Server) would be an advantage.
- A good knowledge of English.

ISS Internal Service Systems. Your duties will include:

- Developing in the internal information systems area.

We expect:

- Knowledge of Windows, Windows NT, Windows 95.
- General experience with PCs.
- Knowledge of the programming languages C, C++, and particularly of Visual Basic.
- Experience in working in Windows 6/32-bit environments as well as in OLE 2 Automation and OCX.
- General understanding of relational databases.
- Flexibility, motivation, and the ability to cope with stress.
- Creativity.
- A sound knowledge of written and spoken English.
- Communication and teamwork skills.

We offer:

- A challenging, rewarding position in a leading-edge company at a time of global expansion.
- A pleasant working environment in a young team.
- Personal and professional development in our ongoing internal training program.
- An excellent compensation package.

Software Developers: HR-Human Resource Systems—International Developments. Our Software Developers are based at our Development Center in Walldorf, near Heidelberg, Germany.

They work with our own development tools, such as ABAP/4 (4th generation programming language), Active Data Dictionary, Screen Painter, and Dialog Manager.

Your tasks:

- As a member of an international team, you will develop and enhance the national versions of our HR products for the European market.
- Coordinating the international functionality of our HR module and communicating with our international subsidiaries and customers is an important aspect of the work.

We require:

- A first-class university degree, preferably in computer sciences or business studies/ economics with computing.

- Excellent programming skills.

- Knowledge of German is not essential.

- Fluent English essential, knowledge of other languages would be an advantage.

- A strong interest in the practical application of business concepts.

- Capability for interdisciplinary and intercultural work and above-average motivation and commitment.

- Willingness to work abroad.

We offer:

- Ongoing challenges in one of the world's leading technology enterprises that is continuously expanding.

- Stimulating working atmosphere in a young team.

- A program of continuous personal development and subject-related training.

- Generous benefits.

Software Developers: HR-Human Resource Systems—Personnel Administration and Payroll. Our Software Developers are based at our Development Center in Walldorf, near Heidelberg, Germany.

They work with our own development tools, such as ABAP/4 (4th generation programming language), Active Data Dictionary, Screen Painter, and Dialog Manager.

Your responsibilities:

- You will work in an international team on important and challenging tasks in the areas of Personnel Administration and Payroll.

- You and your colleagues will create HR-oriented concepts in coordination with our international subsidiaries and customers and implement these with state-of-the-art software technology.

We expect:

- An excellent university or higher college degree, preferably in the areas of information management, economic science, mathematics, or physics.

- Very good programming knowledge.

- Fluent English knowledge, other languages are advantageous.

- A keen interest in the productive implementation of business concepts.

- The ability to work in an interdisciplinary and multicultural team and to offer above-average commitment.

We offer:

- Ongoing challenges in one of the world's leading technology enterprises that is continuously expanding.

- Stimulating working atmosphere in a young team.

- A program of continuous personal development and subject-related training.

- Generous benefits.

Product Developers: Patient Management/Accounting (IS-H) Module. The IS-H module has been on the market for two years and constitutes the core of our SAP R/3 Hospital Information System, which has been installed at more than 80 hospitals in Germany, Austria, and the Netherlands.

Our current development focus is on meeting and keeping up-to-date with our German customers' requirements, in accordance with German health care legislation, and on the continuing internationalization of this product.

We require:

- A good university degree in medicine/business with computing, computer science, mathematics, business/economics, or natural sciences.

- A keen interest in translating hospital-specific requirements into an IT solution.

- Programming skills, experience in PC applications.

- A sound knowledge of English and German.

- Basic professional experience in a similar area, if possible.

- The successful candidate will have the ability to work in a team and in a variety of disciplines, above-average commitment and motivation, excellent communications skills, and a strong commitment to customer satisfaction.

We offer:

- Ongoing challenges in one of the world's leading technology enterprises that is continuously expanding.

- Stimulating working atmosphere as part of a young team.

- A program of continuous personal development and subject-related training.

- A broad range of benefits.

Software Developer: SAP R/3 IS-Oil. Job description:

- Development of business application software using the SAP Development Workbench for the SAP R/3 IS-Oil industry solution in cooperation with international oil companies.

- Performance of tasks in the following software development phases: concept, design, implementation, quality assurance, and software maintenance.

- Use of methods for object-oriented analysis of business processes in the oil industry supply chain.

- Implementation of functions in SAP R/2 technology.

- Use of SAP tools and methods for software quality assurance.

Requirements:

- Training/Education:

  Information technology with business management, preferably a university or higher technical college degree.

- Practical experience:

  4GL programming, databases, PC software products, teamwork.

- Additional knowledge:

  Knowledge of English.

  Experience in customer relations.

- Personal qualities:

  Reliable, able to work under pressure, analytical approach.

Development of SAP R/3 IS-Oil. Your duties will include:

- Handling of software logistics for the decentralized IS-Oil development.

- Coordination of the operation of SAP R/3 development systems with the computer center and the database group.

- Installation of SAP R/3 maintenance levels in IS-Oil development.

- Managing projects for software assembly and delivery.

- Coordination of cooperation with the Software Factory.

- Technical creation of maintenance levels, advance corrections, and releases.

- Take on the remote support and HelpDesk of customers who are installing IS-Oil or maintenance levels.

We expect:

- Database administration, preferably ORACLE, system administration in UNIX environments, C programming.
- Ideally SAP R/3 system administration, service experience, problem analysis.
- English language ability.
- Experience in customer relations.

Software Developer: SAP R/2 IS-Oil. Job description:

- Development and maintenance of business application software for the SAP R/2 IS-Oil industry solution in cooperation with international oil companies.
- Performance of activities in the following software development phases: concept, design, implementation, quality assurance, and software maintenance.
- Design of software functions for the supply chain.
- Implementation of functions in SAP R/2 technology.
- Use of SAP tools and methods for software quality assurance.

Requirements:

- Training:

   Information technology with business management, preferably a university or higher technical college degree.

- Practical experience:

   4GL programming, databases, PC software products, teamwork.

   Preferably experience with SAP R/2 Basis and RM or RV.

- Additional knowledge:

   Knowledge of English.

   Experience in customer relations.

- Personal qualities:

   Reliable, able to work under pressure, analytical approach.

- Willingness to work in the mainframe environment.

Development: SAP R/2 IS-Oil. Your duties will include:

- Handling of software logistics for the decentralized IS-Oil development.
- Coordination of the operation of SAP R/2 development systems with the computer center and the database group.
- Installation of SAP R/2 maintenance levels in IS-Oil development.

- Managing projects for software assembly and delivery.
- Coordination of cooperation with SAP R/2 Services.
- Technical creation of maintenance levels, advance corrections, and releases.
- Taking on the remote support and HelpDesk of customers who are installing IS-Oil or maintenance levels.

We expect:

- IBM 370 architecture, MVS, CICS, and VSAM in IBM 370 Assembler programming.
- Ideally, SAP R/2 system administration, service experience, problem analysis.
- English language ability.
- Experience in customer relations.

SAP R/3 Retail. SAP is currently developing SAP R/3 Retail, an industry solution within SAP R/3, tailored to the requirements of the retail sector. The project comprises a number of sections such as Application Development, Documentation, Sales, Consultancy, and Implementation. SAP R/3 Retail has met with tremendous response from the market, because it offers a full-fledged business solution for all the different retail formats and gives retailers unprecedented global networking ability supported by a powerful central information system. Each installation requires innovative, proactive thinking and provides enormous scope for direct personal involvement.

Duties Profile 1: Senior professionals with specific skills in the development of retail systems and in other project areas to actively support our development team. Familiarity with topics such as ECR, EDI, EPOS, store management, merchandise planning, and retail information systems. Successful candidates will have proven track records as consultants to the major players in the retail sector and have the ability to communicate at senior management and departmental management level.

- High degree of flexibility.
- Profound understanding of international relations.
- Willingness to travel.
- Knowledge of foreign languages.

Duties Profile 2: Top retail graduates from international business schools and universities. Familiarity with topics such as ECR, EDI, EPOS, store management, merchandise planning, and retail information systems. Detailed knowledge in specific areas of the retail trade would be welcome.

- High degree of flexibility.
- Profound understanding of international relations.
- Willingness to travel.
- Knowledge of foreign languages.

Appendixes

Documentation Developer. Your responsibilities:

- Create excellent documentation on the BASIS system software of SAP's R/3 client/server system, in written and in multimedia form.

Priorities:

- User-friendly documentation for end-users.
- Real-world documentation of system administration and system programming tasks.

Our requirements:

- You must have the ability to present complex information clearly and concisely.
- You must be a self-starter with a commitment to quality and innovation in the presentation of information.

The following qualifications are helpful:

- Experience in documentation development in technical areas such as programming and system or database management.
- Experience or education in programming, in information management, or in the management and operation of modern information systems.
- Experience with multimedia.
- Experience with authoring tools.

Documentation Developer—Banking Sector. Your duties will include:

- You will create user documentation for application software in the banking sector in cooperation with the development team.
- You will participate in creating a process-oriented online help system.

We expect:

- You have practical experience in creating documentation or in basic programming, as well as knowledge of business administration.
- You have a basic knowledge of data processing.
- You have knowledge of the banking sector; previous bank employment experience is desirable.
- You are able to turn complicated information into clear and understandable information for the end user.
- You have experience in WinWord, Excel, and PowerPoint.
- You have good written and spoken English.

Logo Partner

The term "Logo Partner" has tended to be used for associated companies who have been given permission to use their SAP connection as a selling point and therefore as a reference when recruiting.

SAP Consultant with "Big Six" Management Consultancy. Position is based in U.S., but consultants must be prepared to travel extensively.

Experience:

■ Candidates should have a minimum two years' experience of implementing SAP systems, and SAP R/3 experience is highly desirable.

Experience should include one or more of the following areas:

■ Financial applications.

■ Distribution and sales order management.

■ Manufacturing.

Candidates should have in their area of proficiency:

■ A good understanding of business processes.

■ Experience of configuring SAP to meet corporate needs.

■ A good understanding of the transactions and tables.

■ A sound working knowledge of issues regarding SAP module integration and interfacing with other systems is also required.

It is advantageous if:

■ Experience has been gained in a consulting role, within a project environment.

■ The candidate has a good background in technology.

SAP Training:

■ A minimum of four SAP courses should have been taken.

Personal attributes:

■ Highly intelligent—in the top 10% of the population. Candidates should have good analytical capability, be able to think broadly and conceptually, but also handle detail well, and understand practical considerations.

■ Good interpersonal skills—people who work well with others, are empathetic, and build good relationships.

■ A questioning mind, with the desire to do things better.

Appendixes

- Enthusiasm and ability to plan and control actions to achieve results, meet deadlines, and provide direction.

- The ability to communicate ideas and facts clearly and succinctly in the English language.

Jobs with SAP Business Partners

The following is a job with Consultancy Partners.

SAP R/3 Business Consultant. Duties and Responsibilities:

- The business consultant has a presales role, and works closely with the SAP R/3 sales team promoting our approach to implementation with a strong emphasis on implementation analysis. The business consultant must be capable of presenting and demonstrating both the specific implementation philosophy and SAP R/3 functionality. He/she would then take responsibility for conducting the implementation analysis—evaluating the technical configuration aspects and the economics of the SAP R/3 project.

Ideal experience:

- Worked in pre/postsales support.

- Implemented several large IT projects in commercial organizations.

- Worked in consultancy or with a specialist software house.

- Ideally have trained in SAP R/3, have SAP R/2 experience, and/or have comparable product experience.

- Have extensive knowledge of financial accounting systems, logistics/material management, and/or manufacturing.

- The overall experience of large commercial implementations would be expected to extend over five years.

Personal attributes:

- Able to present an experienced professional image to prospects and customers.

- Able to discuss intelligently and provide consultancy on all aspects of corporate business with senior managers in large companies.

- Highly developed presentation skills, and experience in using them in a presales environment.

- Self-starter.

Implementation Partner

The following is a job with an Implementation Partner.

Application Engineers. Duties and Responsibilities:

- Use the SAP R/3 configuration tools to meet the requirements as defined and interpreted by the SAP R/3 implementation analysis, and follow through to provide both remote and on-site support to completed implementations.

Experience required in:

- Business analysis in an IT environment.
- Implementing large projects in commercial organizations, preferably in finance, materials management, sales and distribution, or production.
- Either working in an IT supplier/software house environment, or in a large commercial organization's IT department.
- Overall experience in analyzing requirements and implementing IT-based business solutions in large commercial organizations should extend to 10 years.

Personal Attributes:

- The personality type required is able to interface at senior levels in the organization, and be a dynamic self-starter.

Module Configurers for International Projects. Duties and Responsibilities:

- Working closely with clients to assess their requirements in finance, materials management, sales and distribution, production planning, and human resources.

Requirements:

- Minimum one year's experience with SAP.
- Good degree.
- Excellent interpersonal and presentation skills.

Job Description of Jobs with End-Users

The following is a job with an end-user.

Commercial Analyst

(Position not requiring previous SAP experience)

Reports to: MIS Manager.

Responsible for:

- All aspects of commercial systems development based on SAP software modules.

Specific responsibilities:

- Acquire SAP skills by attending formal courses and by working with a team of SAP consultants.
- Communicate with all levels of management and staff.
- Establish and manage project plans and budgets.
- Define the scope and requirements of new developments.
- Carry out detailed system design and write specifications.
- Configure SAP and document the configuration.
- Train users at all levels.
- Test new developments.
- Plan and implement the cut-over to new systems.

Experience:

- Sound experience in commercial business systems in appropriate areas (logistics, sales, and marketing).
- IT background.

Key skills/attributes:

- Proactive, self-motivated with the ability to motivate others.
- Outgoing personality with well-developed communications skills.
- Potential to assume a management role as the MIS department expands.

Financial Analyst
(Position not requiring previous SAP experience)

Reports to: European MIS Manager.

Responsible for:

- All aspects of financial systems development based on SAP software modules.

Specific responsibilities:

- Acquire SAP skills by attending formal courses and by working with a team of SAP consultants.
- Communicate with all levels of management and staff.
- Establish and manage project plans and budgets.
- Define the scope and requirements of new developments.
- Carry out detailed system design and write specifications.

- Configure SAP and document the configuration.
- Train users at all levels.
- Test new developments.
- Plan and implement the cut-over to new systems.

Experience:

- Sound experience of financial business systems in appropriate areas.
- IT background.

Key skills/attributes:

- Proactive and self-motivated, with the ability to motivate others.
- Outgoing personality with well-developed communications skills.
- Potential to assume a management role as the MIS department expands.

Systems Analyst

(Position does not require previous SAP experience)

The opportunity:

- The position offers the satisfaction of solving problems, taking projects from early investigation of user needs right through to implementation. It also offers the opportunity to develop new skills working with modern IT tools.

  Systems analysts can readily transfer to other business functions for career development.

Responsibilities:

- Develop personal SAP knowledge and skills through formal courses and informal induction and training.
- Help user departments to assess business needs.
- Develop SAP-based business systems designs for new applications, and act as liaison to user departments and IT functions throughout their implementation.
- Conduct feasibility studies into new applications.
- Provide support and training to users of existing SAP and legacy systems. Resolve problems and develop systems enhancements.

Background required:

- A wide variety of backgrounds can provide the business experience required, including finance, manufacturing, and marketing.

Attributes required:

- An analytical approach to problem-solving, coupled with the ability to conceptualize systems.
- The ability to relate to the needs and problems of users.
- Awareness of business issues.

Project Leader
(Position does not require previous SAP experience)

The opportunity:

- The position offers the opportunity to develop systems awareness, as well as team-working, leadership, and project management skills.

  Project leaders can subsequently pursue careers in information systems or return to mainstream positions within their functional area.

Responsibilities:

- Analyze business processes and procedures with a view to computerizing them.
- Develop personal SAP knowledge and skills through formal courses and informal induction and training.
- Provide a link between user and IT personnel, translating user requirements into logical, well-defined steps.
- Develop, implement, and test systems to meet changing business requirements.

Background required:

- It is likely, though not absolutely required, that project leaders will be recruited internally, and will have a good understanding of the user department to which the project pertains.

Attributes required:

- An analytical approach to problem-solving, coupled with the ability to conceptualize systems.
- The ability to apply patience and logical thought to complex problems.
- Awareness of business issues concerning the specific area of business to which the project pertains.

SAP Business Analyst
Responsibilities:

- Support an international SAP R/3 implementation and roll-out.
- Provide business analysis consultancy.

- Identify and champion appropriate use of SAP R/3 to meet changing business requirements.

- Provide consultancy on SAP functionality and configuration.

- Identify, specify, and design interface solutions between SAP R/3 and legacy systems, providing business analysis in this area.

- Specify and apply suitable testing and quality monitoring procedures, and assume responsibility for the quality of developed solutions.

- Maintain quality and efficiency by applying prescribed policies and standards.

Requirements:

Education and experience required:

- Degree level or equivalent in computer science or a business systems-related subject.

- At least three years' experience in systems development using structured methods and CASE tools.

- At least two years' systems experience in a "supply chain" or manufacturing environment.

- At least two years' hands-on experience with SAP (R/3 or R/2).

Other requirements:

- Good communication and interpersonal skills.

- Good organizational skills, with the determination and dedication to meet objectives and get the job done.

- A customer-focused, service attitude.

SAP Analyst

Prime Responsibilities:

- Analyze business requirements for an information system, and produce an agreed upon and documented set of user requirements from it.

- Determine level of fit of SAP with the above needs, configure the SAP system to fulfill them, and make alternative recommendations where appropriate.

- Produce system documentation, and assist in the production of user documentation.

- Provide training and support for users of the system, and for other SAP-based systems.

Requirements:

- Educated to degree level or equivalent.

- A minimum of two years' experience in an IT environment.

- Working knowledge of SAP.

- Good interpersonal and communications skills, preferably gained within an IT context, and involving contact with all personnel levels.

- An appreciation of the relevant business processes, and experience in them would be an advantage.

MIS Manager

Reports to: Managing Director

Responsible for:

- Overall UK and European IT strategy and budgets.

  All accounting and logistics systems are to be upgraded using SAP R/3. Sales force automation is to be undertaken, and Windows technology to be introduced.

Specific Responsibilities:

- Vendor negotiations, resource allocation, project prioritization, performance and security issues, SLAs (service level agreements), and the corporate interface.

Experience:

- Appropriate management experience, preferably involving a SAP project.

Key skills/attributes:

- Financial, budgetary, and management skills, and ability to communicate plans and objectives at board level.

Appendix D

Example Request for Quotation of SAP Services

DREAMCAR OF SOUTH AFRICA
REQUEST FOR QUOTATION
FOR THE PROVISION OF A
COMPUTING INFRASTRUCTURE TO SUPPORT SAP R/3

Table of Contents

Section 1 - Summary of Quotation

Section 2 - Supplier Profile

>   Organization
>
>   Experience
>
>   Reference Sites

Section 3 - Hardware

>   Hardware Components
>
>   Environment Requirements
>
>   Hardware Sizing
>
>   Upgradability
>
>   Back-up facilities
>
>   Fault Tolerance and Resilience

Section 4 - System Software

>   Software Description
>
>   Software History
>
>   Software Licenses

Section 5 - Hardware Warranty, Maintenance, and Support

Section 6 - Software Maintenance and Support

Section 7 - Implementation Plans

>   Implementation
>
>   Project Organization
>
>   Project Staffing
>
>   Training
>
>   Documentation

Section 8 - Summary of Costs

>   Capital Costs
>
>   Continuing Costs

Part C - Technical Requirements Specification

>   Introduction
>
>   Key User and Business Volumes
>
>   High Level Design

Timing Requirements

Technical Requirements

Supplier and Support Requirements

Benchmarking and Acceptance Tests

Structure of Request for Quotation

This Request for Quotation (RFQ) is structured in three parts.

Part A - The Quotation Process

The introduction and purpose of this document, confidentiality, and the offer conditions

The selection process including the quotation return date, the contact persons, and the selection criteria

An introduction to the company, including an overview of the current technology

The scope of this RFQ

An outline of the required structure and format of your offer response

Part B - The Quotation Contents

Detail of the required structure and format of your offer response (that is, the questions that you, the supplier, are requested to answer)

Part C - Technical Requirement Specifications

An introduction into the technical requirements

Key users and business volumes

Benchmarking procedures and acceptance tests

All supplier response documentation packs must be compiled in the required format and sequence for ease of reference and analysis

Part A - The Quotation Process

Introduction - Purpose of Document

100   This document is a formal Request for Quotation (RFQ) for the supply and installation of a new computer (server) environment to support the SAP R/3 package at Dreamcar of South Africa (DCSA).

101   This RFQ describes the system for which hardware, system software, and other services are required and sets out the details to be included in your quotation. The technical requirements and reply format of this RFQ are not open to negotiations, but the final extent and content of the contractual arrangements between the selected supplier and DCSA will be negotiated.

Confidentiality

102 This RFQ, its technical requirements, and any related documents, information, and discussions are to remain strictly confidential and must not be communicated to anyone not directly involved in the preparation of your quotation.

103 No information may be provided to any third party or publicized unless specifically authorized by DCSA.

Conditions of Request for Quotation

104 In issuing the RFQ, there is no implied obligation on DCSA to procure any of the systems being proposed.

105 Any statement made by a supplier in its quotation concerning equipment, software, performance, and costs will be considered to form part of any contract that may be entered into in the event that DCSA enters into such contract with such supplier.

106 Suppliers should respond on the basis of being appointed to design, purchase, deliver, implement, and commission the specified configuration. Any limitations of responsibility that suppliers want to negotiate should be clearly stated.

107 Suppliers should respond on the basis that this will be a fixed-price contract. Prices should be given for all the hardware, software, consultancy, ancillary items, and continuing support necessary to meet DCSA requirements. Suppliers should state the length of time for which the prices quoted will remain valid.

108 This RFQ is issued on the understanding that suppliers will not levy a charge for the quotation preparation, or for arranging and conducting reference site visits and benchmark demonstrations and other related activities.

109 No additional charges or levies will be entertained unless by prior negotiation and written authorization from DCSA.

110 Suppliers must be prepared to:

- Answer any questions relating to their quotation and provide additional information as requested
- Make a formal presentation of their quotation
- Give a benchmark demonstration of their proposed solution
- Nominate relevant reference sites for DCSA staff to contact or to visit

111 The issues relating to a breach of the contractual obligations on the part of the supplier will be discussed, negotiated, and finalized at the time DCSA enters into an agreement with the preferred supplier. These issues will cover the following:

- Technical faults in the delivered system
- Inability to meet preagreed deadlines

- Inability to rectify system hardware and software errors

- The supplier will be appointed on DCSA's standard terms and conditions applicable to the goods and services purchased and/or manufactured and installed

- A performance guarantee equal to the contract sum will be required

112   Should the supplier not conform to these requests, Dreamcar of South Africa will not accept the participation of your company in the quoting process.

Quotation Return Date

200   Three copies of your quotation should be delivered by hand or by courier to DCSA by not later than 10 A.M. on ....1996. Your quotation will not be assessed if it is delivered after this date and time.

The copies of the quotation must be addressed to:

Mr. John Wilkinson
Purchasing Officer
Purchasing Department
Dreamcar of South Africa
Golden Road
Johannesburg

Please note that telefaxed documentations are not accepted.

Contact Persons

201   Any technical queries relating to this RFQ should be addressed to any of the following DCSA officials.

Name	Telephone Number	Telefax Number
Peter Mall	011 112-5558	011 134-5421
Gavin Rink	011 112-4728	011 345-5421

202   Any commercial queries relating to this RFQ should be addressed to any of the following DCSA officials.

Name	Telephone Number	Telefax Number
Mike Brent	011 456-5036	011 345-5521

Selection Criteria

203   The following criteria will be used to evaluate a supplier's response and it is advisable that these issues receive due attention during the process of quotation preparation. These criteria, if specifically addressed by a supplier, should appear in the relevant sections of the quotation format in Part B:

- The closeness of fit of the proposed solution to the technical specification

- The reliability and performance of the hardware and software as demonstrated by a proven track record at other customer sites

- The field upgradability and scalability of proposed hardware (including CPU, disk storage, memory)

- The experience, track record, and organizational characteristics of the supplier's own organization

- The support capability of the supplier's organization (including, for example, installation assistance, technical support, user training, and continuing hardware and software maintenance)

- The cost of equipment, implementation, installation, and continuing support

- The time scales required for the complete installation

- The financial stability of the supplier

- Level of confidence in the supplier's quotation (e.g., depth of understanding shown, quality of staff, and abilities)

- Strategic positioning and strength of the supplier in the server/mid-range computing market

- Successfully completed site(s)

Business and Information Technology Overview

Company Background

300   Dreamcar of South Africa, a wholly owned subsidiary of Dreamcar AG, is predominantly a motor vehicle manufacturer, producing some 70,000 passenger and light commercial vehicles for the local market.

301   It is managed by an executive committee consisting of six directors and a chairman of the board. Reporting to them is a team of approximately 100 managers. The company employs about 6,600 people in one main production plant in Johannesburg and a number of supporting plants in the Johannesburg and Johannesburg districts. There is also a Parts and Accessories warehouse located in Germiston.

302   Dreamcar of South Africa supports approximately 200 franchise dealerships throughout South Africa, Botswana, Swaziland, and Namibia. This support structure comprises regional offices in Johannesburg, Cape Town, Durban, and Bloemfontein.

303   Dreamcar of South Africa intends to replace its predominantly legacy systems as part of its IT modernization strategy. The international VW-Group is currently considering the adoption of SAP as the preferred application systems package with a view to standardizing the process throughout all subsidiaries.

304   Thus, in line with VW international policy, DCSA is compelled to adopt SAP R/3 for the administrative sector and will therefore implement the Finance, Human

Resources, and Purchasing (Non-Production) in the immediate future. In the medium- to long-term, the scope of the project will extend to Sales and Distribution, Materials Management, and Production Planning.

Technical Overview

305   Dreamcar of South Africa is currently running its systems on a combination of processing platforms:

- IBM 3090 running MVS
- HITACHI 7/90 running VM
- IBM RS/6000's running AIX v4—Catia and Racking Store
- PCs (386-Pentium) running SCO UNIX—Racking Store, Vehicle Tracking
- PCs (286-386) running DOS—Companywide
- PCs (486-Pentium) running DOS and Windows 3.11—Companywide
- File servers running Novell—Companywide

306   DCSA have recognized that there are significant opportunities to reduce the technical complexity of the current technology architecture. Most of the platforms are located in Johannesburg, with a few file servers and PCs distributed nationwide. All of the technical support staff is located in Johannesburg. DCSA relies mainly on in-house support structures.

307   The Local Area Network (LAN) comprises a fiber-optic backbone, connecting a variation of thick, UTP, and predominantly thin cable. We run at 10 Mbps throughout the LAN and will soon be upgrading the backbone to 100 Mbps. We use the IPX/SPX and TCP/IP protocols, with the intention of using only TCP/IP in the future. Currently we are using Novell file servers and these will be replaced with Windows NT. This project will begin in the next few months.

RFQ Scope

401   The scope of this RFQ covers the detailed technical design, a proven benchmark test from your Competency Center, and the delivery and installation of the processing platforms, complete with associated software and network connections that will support the SAP R/3 application system implementation. This project will be completed when the processing platforms have been successfully commissioned, linked to the network, and the DCSA staff has been trained to a competent level. In delivering this package, you should take into account the following major assumptions:

- SAP R/3 is the application package of choice
- Oracle or DB2 is the relational database management system
- Both the Data Center and the Disaster Recovery site will be situated at Dreamcar of South Africa's Main Plant in Johannesburg

Appendixes

- UNIX or Windows NT is the operating system

- Standard network protocol is TCP/IP

- The processing platform and any associated software must successfully integrate to the current LAN

- The technical configuration must be demonstrated and support the performance requirements

- Conform to the high-level design, which is defined in detail in Part C

402   The installation of all of the users' PCs, together with the SAP "Presentation Layer," will be the responsibility of the supplier. DCSA will be responsible for the procurement of the PCs and will ensure that all software will be preloaded.

Form of Response

500   A supplier who intends to prepare and submit a quotation in terms of this RFQ is required to first complete and return to DCSA the Intention to Quote Form no later than one week before the due date of the RFQ. This form, duly completed and signed, may be forwarded by hand or fax or prepaid mail to the street, fax, or mail addresses furnished on the form. The onus is on the sender to ensure that this Intention to Quote Form is duly received by DCSA. Noncompliance with this requirement will lead to the exclusion by DCSA of a quotation submitted by such supplier.

501   The supplier should then respond to the RFQ in the following structure and format as more fully outlined under Part B:

General
Section 1 - Summary of Quotation
Section 2 - Supplier Profile

Hardware & System Infrastructure
Section 3 - Hardware
Section 4 - System Software

Maintenance and Support
Section 5 - Hardware Warranty, Maintenance and Support
Section 6 - Software Maintenance and Support

Implementation
Section 7 - Implementation Plans

Finance
Section 8 - Summary of Costs

502   Appendixes to be provided by a supplier include:

Appendix I	Quotation Overview
Appendix II	Supplier's Profile
Appendix III	Hardware Quotation
Appendix IV	Sizing Rationale
Appendix V	Hardware and Software Maintenance Contracts
Appendix VI	Implementation Plan
Appendix VII	Curricula Vitae of Team Members
Appendix VIII	Supplier's Annual Report
Appendix IX	Summary of Costs
Appendix X	Details of partnerships or associations formed for the purposes of this RFQ

503   Part B of this RFQ describes the structure, format, and content of the Suppliers quotation, using the structure described as "Form of Response." More-detailed information will be referenced in Part C of this document. Each question posed in the RFQ should be answered in full—an incomplete response to any question will imply a negative answer from the supplier.

Part B - Quotation Contents

Table of Contents

Section 1 - Summary of Quotation

Please provide as part of Appendix I a summary of your quotation, including:

101   A high-level diagram and description of your proposed solution.

102   A high-level implementation plan.

Appendixes

103   The main advantages and special features of your proposed solution.

104   A summary of the costs in the following format, including any assumptions on exchange rates:

CAPITAL COSTS

Hardware	XXX XXX.XX
Software	XXX XXX.XX
Implementation	XXX XXX.XX
Training	XXX XXX.XX
Total (Capital)	XXX XXX.XX

CONTINUING COSTS

Software	XXX XXX.XX
License Fees	XXX XXX.XX
Support	XXX XXX.XX
Total (Continuing)	XXX XXX.XX

105   A brief statement of your capabilities and the main reasons why you believe that DCSA should accept your quotation.

106   A statement accepting the terms and conditions detailed in this Request for Quotation.

Section 2 - Supplier Profile

Organization

Please provide as part of Appendix II the following information.

201   Background information on your organization:

- Your company's legal status, the name of the holding company (if a subsidiary), international offices, alliances

- The date your company or office was established in South Africa

- The number and locations of your sites/offices

- The total number of staff employed worldwide by your company currently and for the last two years

- A copy of your latest annual report (this to be included as Appendix VIII).

202   What are the main business activities of your company? Please provide a breakdown of the extent of revenue from each of these activities.

203   Please give an indication of your company's likely future growth and business direction.

204   Please give the total number of staff employed currently and for each of the last two years, in South Africa, and neighboring countries, stating for each location:

- Total number of staff

- Sales staff

- Administration staff

- Development staff

- Implementation staff

- Support staff for the proposed software and hardware

- Management staff

- Other (please specify)

205   Please explain the business and legal relationships between all the suppliers in your quotation (e.g., between yourselves and any subcontractors).

206   Please provide details of any past and pending legal actions or claims against your company.

Experience

207   Please outline your company's experience in:

- Proposed hardware and operating system software

- Target application environment (SAP R/3)

208   What are the total number of staff members currently working on the technical configuration and what are their roles (technical, support)?

209   What is the average length of experience of the installation and support staff on the proposed technical configuration?

Reference Sites

210   Please provide details of appropriate reference sites for the proposed system (in South Africa and abroad). For each, please detail:

- The name, address, and telephone number of the company

- The name and title of a contact

- The scope and length of involvement with the reference site.

Section 3 - Hardware

Hardware Components

300   In Appendix III, please provide:

- A detailed design of the proposed hardware configuration

- A detailed list of all system components including:

    Memory

    Storage devices

    Workstations

    Printers

- For each component, please specify:

    Original manufacturer and model number

    Rated speeds, capacity and modes of operation

    Number of components proposed

    Lead-time for delivery

    Cost of the component

    Any plans to extend the range of components with target availability dates

    Warranty periods (where applicable)

- Details on any limitations on the hardware used (e.g., connectivity protocols, maximum number of lines, maximum number and types of workstations)

Environment Requirements

301   Also include in Appendix III full details of the recommended environmental conditions for the hardware, to include:

- Air conditioning

- Floor space requirements

- Cabling requirements

- Main stabilizers

- Ancillary equipment

Hardware Sizing

302   Please detail in Appendix IV the rationale used for your hardware sizing exercise.

Upgradability

303   Please supply details of the hardware upgrade path for the proposed configuration.

Back-Up Facilities

304   Describe any back-up facilities available in the event of a disaster at the primary site including:

- Availability of back-up equipment

- Availability of alternative sites

- Details of any disaster recovery plans available with yourselves, the supplier, or any third party

- Costs for the recovery services

Fault Tolerance and Resilience

305   In connection with fault tolerance and resilience, please outline:

- All hardware modules that are fault-tolerant

- All hardware components that are hot-swappable

- Describe the software (if any) that supports the fault-tolerant hardware

- Whether full "English" error condition messages are produced on a console

- Describe the resilience features of all your proposed hardware components

306   What facilities exist for regenerating the system in the event of a system failure. Please specify the following:

- Minimum time to restart system

- Procedures for warm and cold start

- Procedures for reloading data

Section 4 - System Software

400   Please provide for each system proposed, full details of all system software. The system software described should comply with all technical requirements as described in Part C. The system software must include:

- Operating system

- Ancillary utilities to support SAP R/3 environment. These utilities must cater to the following functions:

    Access protection

    Data integrity

    Backup and recovery of data

    Performance monitoring

Software Description

401   For *each* of the preceding specified software please provide:

- An outline description of the software

- Main function supported by the software

- Any proposed customization required to meet DCSA's needs.

Software History
- Original date and authorship
- Place of origin of the software
- Brief supplier profile (for any third-party software)
- Date and version number of the last major rewrite or revision
- Major developments planned for the next 12 months including a description of the additional features and the planned release date

Software Licenses
- Terms of the software license and such license period
- License fees and charges in the stated currency
- Software warranties specific to South Africa

Section 5 - Hardware Warranty, Maintenance, and Support

500   Describe the legal relationship between yourselves and any third party made responsible for maintenance and support and your interpretation of the legal relationship between DCSA and these parties.

501   Please provide full details of the hardware warranties provided.

502   Please specify the cost and types of hardware maintenance that are available:

- Preventative
- Fix on failure
- Repair on site
- Replace with new

503   Please provide as Appendix V a standard copy of your proposed hardware maintenance contract.

501   What are the standard hours of service for onsite support?

505   With the location of the data center being in Johannesburg, what are the guarantees and average response times to hardware failure:

- During standard hours?
- Outside standard hours?

506   What are the procedures for hardware fault reporting?

507   Where is the support center located?

508   What help desk facilities are provided?

509   Please specify the number and experience of support staff.

510   How is the maintenance charge calculated?

511   Indicate your anticipated time during which these maintenance charges would remain fixed.

512   Indicate an estimated annual increase that could potentially be submitted for consideration.

513   In your experience, please specify the number and caliber of DCSA staff required to manage the proposed hardware and software. Briefly describe each position.

514   Please describe any services you have to offer in the form of facilities management including:

- Location
- Service description
- Cost
- Loan system facilities in the event of malfunctioning equipment

515   For each component in your proposed solution, please specify:

- Spare parts that will be held in Johannesburg
- Spare parts not held in Johannesburg and their guaranteed delivery time
- The expected MTBF (Mean Time Between Failures) giving the source of your data

516   Please calculate the expected MTBF for the total system solution, providing the method used for calculation.

Section 6 - Software Maintenance and Support

Your responses to this section should be included as Appendix V.

600   Describe the legal relationship between yourselves and any third party made responsible for system software, maintenance, and support and your interpretation of the legal relationship between DCSA and these parties.

601   Please provide (as part of Appendix V) a standard copy of your proposed software maintenance contract. Please note that the terms, conditions and time frames of software maintenance and support will be negotiated at the time DCSA enters into an agreement with the preferred supplier.

602   What are the standard hours of service for software support?

603   What is the procedure for fault reporting?

604   Given that Johannesburg is the location, what are the guaranteed and average response times to software failure on the central development system:

■ During standard hours?

■ Outside standard hours?

605   Where is the support center located?

606   What help desk facilities are provided?

607   Please specify the number and experience of support staff.

608   Describe your policy for the maintenance and support of your proposed software and system software upgrades.

609   How is the maintenance charge calculated, if any?

610   Indicate your anticipated time during which these maintenance charges would remain fixed.

611   Indicate an estimated annual increase that could potentially be submitted for consideration.

Section 7 - Implementation Plans

Your responses to this section should be included as Appendix VI.

Implementation

700   Please confirm that you will take total responsibility for the implementation of the proposed solution.

701   Please provide a detailed implementation plan specifying the following activities:

■ System installation and customization

■ Site preparation

■ Training

■ Delivery of equipment

■ User procedures

■ System data preparation/initialization

■ Acceptance testing

702   For each of the preceding activities , please show:

■ The key tasks to be undertaken

■ Total-man-day effort

Total-man-day effort by type (e.g., project manager, analyst, programmer, and so on) for:

Supplier staff

DCSA staff

Elapsed time

All major dependencies between activities

703 Please outline any dependencies on third-party suppliers (e.g., for equipment, supplies, and key dates for delivery).

704 Please indicate any external events that could cause delay.

705 Please specify the level of contingency you have assumed in your plans.

706 Please confirm that the implementation cost is included in the contract price. If not, please specify the additional cost (travel and accommodation expenses).

Project Organization

707 Describe reporting procedures you will adopt to report to DCSA.

708 Provide details on the timing and frequency of meetings.

709 Describe any project planning and control methodologies/tools you intend to use.

710 Please specify the configuration control and quality control procedures that will be used during the project.

Project Staffing

711 Outline the proposed team structure, including client staff.

712 Outline the project responsibilities of all team members.

713 Where will the project team be located?

714 What will the availability of team members be during the assignment, expressed as number of days per week throughout the course of the project?

715 What are your standard charge rates for different grades?

716 What are the project charge rates for all team members?

717 Please provide as part of Appendix VII curricula vitae of key team members.

Training

718 Please describe the training courses that would be appropriate to DCSA. For each course, please specify:

- The level of staff at which the course is aimed (i.e., operator, technician, and so on).

- The course format (i.e., workshop, presentation).

- The numbers permitted on the course.

719   Where is training provided (i.e., onsite, offsite venue)?

720   How much of this training is included in the contract price and what is additional?

721   What training literature will be made available to DCSA? What is included in the contract price and what is additional?

Documentation

722   Please describe what documentation (i.e., user, operational, technical, etc.) will be made available to DCSA. For each type, please specify:

- Format

- Scope and content

- What is included in fixed price and what is additional

- Media

- Which recognized standards the document conforms to, and for which regulatory authority

- Cost, if appropriate

Section 8 - Summary of Costs

Your responses to this section should be included as part of Appendix IX.

800   Please specify costs as detailed in the following, indicating percentage in foreign currency where applicable and exchange rate assumption.

801   Please state the period for which this quotation and the costs quoted are valid.

802   The summary of costs must be presented in the format as shown at the end of this section.

Capital Costs

803   For the proposed hardware configuration, please provide summary information for each of the following capital costs:

- Each item of equipment for the central hardware (e.g., processor, disk storage, tapes, and so on) and the total cost for all central site equipment

- Each item of communications and network equipment, and the total cost for the entire communications configuration (LAN card and so on)

- Each peripheral item (console, workstations, printers) and the total cost for all peripheral items regarding servers

- Any other hardware costs not itemized previously (e.g., any extra charges for delivery, shipping, transport, insurance, warranty, installation, commissioning)

- Summary of total cost

You *must* list these costs in the format shown in the example at the end of this section.

804   Please state your policy on when hardware costs are payable to you.

805   Please provide details for each of the following software capital costs:

- Operating system software licenses

- Each item of customization showing the cost and effort required (if any)

- Ancillary software licenses

- The charge for all documentation

- Any other software capital costs payable but not itemized previously

- Summary of total cost

You *must* list these costs in the example format shown at the end of this section.

806   Please state your policy on when the software license costs are payable to you.

807   Please outline the installation costs of your proposed system. Please outline for each of the following categories the costs, type of staff proposed, and number of days required for:

- Assistance with testing

- Training

- Site planning

- Project management

Continuing Costs

808   Please provide details for each of the following hardware continuing costs:

- Summary total cost

- Each item of equipment for the central hardware

- Each item of communications and network equipment

- The total continuing costs for peripheral devices (consoles, printers, and so on)

- Any other hardware maintenance costs not included in the preceding

You *must* list these costs in the format shown in the example for continuing costs at the end of this section.

809   Please state clearly the warranty and the basis of this warranty available on each item of hardware in the proposed system. (e.g., carry-in, parts only, labor and parts, fix onsite, and so on)

810   For all continuing hardware maintenance costs, please indicate your proposed due dates for payment.

811   Please provide details for each of the following software continuing costs:

- Systems software (operating system)

- Ancillary software

- Operating licenses (e.g., if there are remote site copies of software)

- Any other continuing software costs not included previously.

You *must* list these costs in the format shown in the example for continuing costs at the end of this section.

811   Please state clearly the warranty and the basis of this warranty available on all software in the proposed system.

812   For all continuing software maintenance costs, please indicate your proposed due dates for payment.

813   Please ensure that all costs are quoted on a uniform basis throughout your offer response (for example, monthly or annually).

814   Example for capital cost.

CAPITAL COSTS		Costs	Costs	Costs
HARDWARE	Central Hardware		xxx xxx.xx	
	Item 1 (DB Server)	xxx xxx.xx		
	Item 2 (App Server)	xxx xxx.xx		
	Item 3	xxx xxx.xx		
	Communications/Networks		xxx xxx.xx	
	Item 1 (modem)	xxx xxx.xx		
	Item 2 (LAN Card)	xxx xxx.xx		
	Item 3	xxx xxx.xx		
	Peripheral Items		xxx xxx.xx	
	Item 1 (laser printer)	xxx xxx.xx		
	Item 2	xxx xxx.xx		

CAPITAL COSTS		Costs	Costs	Costs
	Delivery/installation and other		xxx xxx.xx	
	Item 1	xxx xxx.xx		
	Item 2	xxx xxx.xx		
	TOTAL		(Hardware)	xxx xxx.xx
SOFTWARE	Operating System Software		xxx xxx.xx	
	Package 1	xxx xxx.xx		
	Package 2	xxx xxx.xx		
	Ancillary Software		xxx xxx.xx	
	Package 1	xxx xxx.xx		
	Package 2	xxx xxx.xx		
	Documentation		xxx xxx.xx	
	Item 1	xxx xxx.xx		
	Item 2	xxx xxx.xx		
	Other		xxx xxx.xx	
	Item 1	xxx xxx.xx		
	Item 2	xxx xxx.xx		
	TOTAL		(Software)	xxx xxx.xx
INSTALLATION	Acceptance Testing	xxx xxx.xx		
	Training	xxx xxx.xx		
	Cabling installation	xxx xxx.xx		
	Site Planning	xxx xxx.xx		
	Project Management	xxx xxx.xx		
	Travel and Accommodation	xxx xxx.xx		
	Other	xxx xxx.xx		
	TOTAL		(Installation)	xxx xxx.xx
	TOTAL CAPITAL			xxx xxx.xx
CONTINUING COSTS				
HARDWARE	Central Hardware		xxx xxx.xx	
	Item 1 (DB Server)	xxx xxx.xx		
	Item 2 (App Server)	xxx xxx.xx		
	Item 3	xxx.xxx.xx		

(continues)

(continued)

CAPITAL COSTS		Costs	Costs	Costs
	Communications/Networks		xxx xxx.xx	
	Item 1 (modem)	xxx xxx.xx		
	Item 2 (LAN Card)	xxx xxx.xx		
	Item 3	xxx xxx.xx		
	Peripheral Items		xxx xxx.xx	
	Item 1 (laser printer)	xxx xxx.xx		
	Item 2	xxx xxx.xx		
	Other		xxx xxx.xx	
	Item 1	xxx xxx.xx		
	Item 2	xxx xxx.xx		
	TOTAL		(Hardware)	xxx xxx.xx
SOFTWARE	Operating System Software		xxx xxx.xx	
	Package 1	xxx xxx.xx		
	Package 2	xxx xxx.xx		
	Ancillary Software		xxx xxx.xx	
	Package 1	xxx xxx.xx		
	Package 2	xxx xxx.xx		
	Other		xxx xxx.xx	
	Item 1	xxx xxx.xx		
	Item 2	xxx xxx.xx		
	TOTAL		(Software)	xxx xxx.xx
	TOTAL CONTINUING COSTS			xxx xxx.xx

Part C - Technical Requirements Specification

Introduction

100   Part C of this RFQ specifies the technical requirements that must be satisfied by your proposed solution. Key transaction figures are provided to enable you to

size your solution. Also contained is a high-level configuration to guide your detailed design. The viability of the design must be proven by your conformance to the benchmarking procedures, as defined in Part C.

Key User and Business Volumes

200   Appendix B contains the current key transaction volumes for each SAP module. The table contains an average month's transactions. These transactions are taken from the existing systems and reflect the current business operation. It is estimated that the business transactions will grow at an annual rate of approximately 10 percent.

More importantly, it is expected that demand for SAP services will expand well beyond the Finance and Human Resource areas to Material Management, and Sales and Distribution. While you are not expected to size your solution for these additional components, your solution should have sufficient inherent scalability to grow significantly beyond the proposed installation.

201   Appendix B shows the current number of users by business units. These are total users, not concurrent users. For the purposes of memory sizing, you should treat these as concurrently logged-in users but not necessarily active users. These figures should be used as a guide for your design.

202   The system must store up to two years of history except for the HR module where 10 years history is required.

High-Level Design

300   This design has three key features, described in the following, to provide high availability, disaster recovery, and commonality of disk systems.

301   The technical architecture will be a three-tier client server distributed system. It will have a main "productive" data server with a "backup" data server that will also serve as the development system. A third machine will be configured as a "Central" SAP R/3 system, and it will be used as a test system. It will reside in the "main" computer center.

302   DCSA has two computer rooms, separated by 500 meters. It is intended that the data server reside in the newer, "main" computer center and the backup/development system reside in the "old" computer center. The disc system must also be partitioned between the two computer centers. The objectives are twofold:

- Allow quick restart in the event of computer failure.

- Allow processing to carry on in the alternative site should one of the sites be destroyed by a disaster.

303   Both computer centers are powered by UPS systems.

304   The system will be connected to the SAP Early Watch service.

305   DCSA supports three different types of computing platform, each with its own disk storage systems (file servers, mid-range computers, and IBM mainframe computers). It is intended to replace the three disparate disk systems with a single, uniform system. The chosen disk system must be capable of supporting all three platforms and be fault-tolerant.

306   While the immediate goal of the disk subsystem is to support SAP R/3, it will in the future be expanded to support the file servers and the IBM host mainframes.

307   Please produce a detailed design and associated costing for your proposed system setup. Identify any operating assumptions in your response.

308   In the design, provide a detailed response to the benchmarking procedures of the proposed system.

Timing Requirements

400   The following timing requirements are essential for a successful implementation of the SAP R/3 product at Dreamcar of South Africa:

■ A Development/Training environment by September 1, 1997

■ A Production and Test environment by December 1, 1997

Technical Requirements

500   All requirements to be satisfied by the system are listed in Appendix D. The requirements are shown as a set of tables.

501   List in a table format, as shown in Appendix D, all proposed components and indicate on the right side the degree to which the components satisfy the requirements.

502   Following are the priority ratings for the requirements:

■ E—Essential requirements that must be satisfied

■ R—Requirements that should be satisfied, exceptional conditions may warrant exclusion

■ D—Desirable requirements, the obligation to satisfy them is optional

503   You, the supplier, should indicate your proposed component's ability to satisfy each requirement as follows:

■ F—System will fully satisfy the requirement

■ P—System will partially satisfy the requirement

■ X—System will not satisfy the component

504   You should also indicate the level of customization you will need to do to enable your system to satisfy each requirement.

■ N—No customization required

■ C—Some customization required

■ MC—Major customization required

505   You are reminded that completion of the table in this document represents merely a summary of your response to the technical requirements. Please ensure that you have specified your proposed solution in detail as requested in Part B of this RFQ.

Supplier and Support Requirements

600   All of the supplier profile and support requirements are listed in Appendix F. The requirements are shown as a set of tables.

601   List in a table format, as shown in Appendix F, the degree to which your company will satisfy the requirements.

602   Following are the priority ratings for the requirements:

■ E—Essential requirements that must be satisfied

■ R—Requirements that should be satisfied, exceptional conditions may warrant exclusion

■ D—Desirable requirements, the obligation to satisfy them is optional

603   You, the supplier, should indicate your ability to satisfy each as follows:

■ F—Supplier can satisfy the requirements completely

■ P—Supplier can satisfy the requirement

■ X—Supplier cannot satisfy the requirement

604   You should also indicate the degree to which your organization would need to change (locally, nationally, and internationally) to satisfy each requirement.

■ N—No changes required

■ C—Some changes required

■ MC—Major changes required

605   You are reminded that completion of the table in this document represents merely a summary of your response to the technical requirements. Please ensure that you have specified your proposed solution in detail as requested in Part B of this RFQ.

Benchmarking and Acceptance Tests

700   Please submit details of any previous benchmarks performed by using the same or similar configuration of SAP R/3, your hardware, and operating system.

701   Please submit for each machine in your configuration the following benchmark data:

- TPC-A

- TPC-C

- TPC-D

702   Please submit the following data for your proposed configuration:

- SAP's throughput

- Number of benchmark SD users at 60 percent processor utilization.

703   Submit in detail your calculations and rationale for arriving at your proposed sizing configuration.

704   Before your quotation can be accepted, you will be required to formally demonstrate the capabilities of your proposed solution. This demonstration may be conducted at any one of your competency centers.

705   Please confirm your willingness to formally demonstrate the capabilities of your configuration once your solution has been short-listed.

(Note: Copyright of this section remains with Dr. Max Nyiri.)

Appendix E

SAP Glossary of Terms and Concepts

Terms Used in Implementing a SAP R/3 System

ABAP/4 Advanced Business Application Programming/4 is a fourth-generation language in which SAP R/3 application software is written. It has been developed by SAP.

ABAP/4 Data Dictionary Store of metadata which contains descriptions of tables, data elements, domains, and views.

ABAP/4 Native SQL A method for accessing a specific database by using its proprietary commands to implement the Structured Query Language.

ABAP/4 Open SQL A portable method for accessing all supported databases by the Structured Query Language commands.

ABAP/4 Query User tool for generating special report programs without requiring any knowledge of ABAP/4.

ABAP/4 Repository Store for all objects managed by the ABAP/4 Development Workbench.

ABAP/4 Repository Information System Navigation aid for the ABAP/4 Repository.

ABAP/4 Workbench Development environment which contains all the necessary tools for creating and maintaining business applications within the R/3 System.

ABAP/4 Workbench Organizer Software development project management tool, which is an integral component of the ABAP/4 Development Workbench.

ABC Analysis Analysis of, for example, materials, may be conducted according to several criteria, e.g., importance or consumption value:

- Important part or a material with high consumption value

- Less important part or material with medium consumption value

- Relatively unimportant part or material with low consumption value

Account Assignment Element   Work breakdown structure element to which actual or commitment postings can be made.

Active SAP R/3 Repository   The directory currently in operational use that contains descriptions of all the application data of an enterprise and their interrelationships, including how they are used in programs and screen forms. During ABAP/4 program development, a separate development repository directory is maintained for versions of the program components undergoing development or modification.

Activity (Controlling)   Internal or external; physical measure of the activity output of a cost center according to activity type.

Activity (Project System)   An activity is an instruction to perform a task within a network in a set period of time. Work, general costs, or external processing can be associated with it.

Activity Input   Transaction to plan the secondary cost quantities on a receiver cost center that uses activity from a sender cost center.

Activity Logs   Records of all activities in the SAP R/3 system for each transaction and for each user.

Activity Type   Classification of an activity and the data structure, for example, as follows:

- Number of units produced

- Hours

- Machine times

- Production times

Actual Costs   All the costs accruing to an object in a period.

ALE Application Link Enabling   SAP method for using documents to carry messages that control distributed applications while maintaining integration and consistency of business data and processes across many systems.

Allocation Group   Defines which orders within one controlling area are to be settled together, as follows:

- By settlement timing—monthly, weekly, and so on

- By order types—repair, capital spending, and so on

- By settlement receivers—cost center, GL account

Allocation Receiver   Object to which the costs of a cost center or order are allocated.

API Application Programming Interface   Interface to support communication between applications of different systems.

ASCII   American Standard Code for Information Interchange.

Asynchronous Database Updating   A method of updating a database separately from the management of the dialog part of the transaction.

Background Process   Non-interactive execution of programs, sometimes using pre-pared file data to replicate the user dialog so as to utilize the same standard functions.

Backward Scheduling   Scheduling a network where the latest start and finish dates for the activities are calculated backwards from the basic finish date.

Billing Element   In a work breakdown structure, a data object to which you can post invoices and revenues.

Budget   Prescribed and binding approved version of the cost plan for a project or other task over a given period.

Business Segment   Intersection of criteria to suit the relevant operating concern, for example, as follows:

- Country, U.S.
- Industry, farming
- Product range, animal feeds
- Customer group, wholesale

Business Segment Criterion   Chosen from SAP proposal list or existing tables, or created manually. Comprises a field name and a field value.

Business Segment Value Field   Holds a number, a code, or a string.

Business Transaction   A recorded data processing step representing a movement of value in a business system, such as cost planning, invoice posting, movement of goods, for example.

Calculated Costs   An order's progress towards completion represented in value terms. There are two methods for determining the calculated costs: calculation on a revenue base and calculation using quantity produced as a base. If, for an order, planned revenue is more than planned costs, there are two corresponding methods for calculating the (interim) profit realization.

Calculated Revenue   The revenue that corresponds to the actual costs incurred for an order, determined from results analysis as:

- Actual costs * planned revenue / planned costs

Capacity (Cost Accounting)   Output of a cost center and activity that is technically possible during a specific period. Differentiated by category and arranged hierarchically.

Capacity (Production Planning)   Ability of a work center to perform a specific task.

Capacities are differentiated according to capacity category. Arranged hierarchically under a work center.

Capacity Planning   Includes the following:

- Long-term rough-cut capacity planning (RCCP)
- Medium-term planning
- Short-term detailed planning (CRP)

Capitalized Costs   Difference between the actual costs and the calculated costs of an order, calculated by results analysis. With deficit orders, this figure is reduced to allow for the loss realized.

Capitalized Profit   Calculated in results analysis by subtracting the capitalized costs from the value of the inventory from which revenue can be generated.

Cardinality   The number of lines in a dependent table to which the table under consideration, in principle, can or must relate.

A line in a table may be related to another dependent line in a cardinality of one-to-one correspondence. The relationship may be one-to-many if there can be several dependent lines for any referenced line.

CCMS   Computing Center Management System.

CIM   Computer Integrated Manufacturing.

Classification   When an object is assigned to a class, values for the object are assigned to characteristics belonging to the class.

Client   The highest level in SAP R/3. The data of one client may not be accessed by another client. There are often a training client and a testing client, in addition to the client code that represents your group or corporate identity and under which the SAP system runs normal business. Some data is managed at the client level, because everyone in the corporate group of companies will want to refer to exactly the same information and be certain that it has been maintained as up-to-date and correct. Vendor addresses would be an example of data managed at the client level.

Client Caches   Work areas set up in the database application servers for data frequently accessed by the client's applications.

Company Code   A unit within a client that maintains accounting balances independently and creates the legally required balance sheet and the profit and loss statement.

Compiler   A tool that translates source code statements written in a general programming language into statements written in a machine-oriented programming language.

Contingency Order   A results analysis object on which the costs of complaints are collected. Reserves are created by results analysis for the expected cost of complaints, and are drawn from as costs are incurred.

Control Indicator   Determines, in cost accounting, which application components are active, how certain data is stored, what types of validation are to take place.

Control Key   Determines how an activity or activity element is to be processed in such operations as orders, costings, capacity planning.

Controlling Area   Area within an organization that shares a cost accounting configuration: normally the same as company code. For cross-company cost accounting, one controlling area may be assigned to multiple (more than one) company codes of one organization.

Controlling Area Currency   Default currency in cost accounting objects, cost centers, orders, and so on.

Controlling Functions   Financial Controlling, investment controlling, cost and profitability controlling.

Controlling Tasks   Planning, monitoring, reporting, advising, informing.

Conversion   Translation from one data format to another; for example, from decimal to binary code.

Cost Center   Place in which costs are incurred. A unit within a company distinguished by area of responsibility, location, or accounting method.

Cost Component   A group of cost origins.

Cost Component Layout (Product Cost Accounting and Cost Center Accounting)   A technical term. Controls how results of a product cost estimate are saved. Assigns cost elements to cost components and determines the following:

- How the costs for raw materials, finished, and semi-finished products are rolled up in a multilevel assembly structure

- Which portion of the costs is treated as fixed costs

- Which costs are treated as the cost of goods manufactured

- Which are sales and administration costs

- Which are the cost of goods sold

Cost Element   Mandatory criterion for classifying costs arising in a company code, as follows, to:

- Direct cost elements for goods and services procured externally

- Indirect (internal activity) cost elements

Direct cost elements are maintained in the General Ledger master records. Indirect cost elements have no counterpart in the financial accounts and are maintained exclusively in cost accounting.

Cost Element Group   A technical term for a conjunction of cost elements used to select records and to define lines and columns in reports. They can be used for planning purposes.

Cost Element Planning   Planning primary and secondary costs on a cost center, order, or project.

Cost Element Type   Classification of cost elements by uses or origin; for example, material cost element; settlement cost elements for orders, cost elements for internal cost allocations.

Cost Object   An account assignment term for individual cost objects to which actual data, i.e., costs, budgets, sales revenues, can be assigned. It can consist of individual products, such as product groups, or local situations based on classification criteria, such as shop floor areas.

Cost Object Hierarchy   Structure of cost objects as nodes to which actual data can be assigned.

Cost Origin   A logical category to which costs may be assigned.

Activity types and cost elements are cost origins.

Cost Planning   Planning the costs to be incurred during a transaction.

Cost Planning Type   A technical term that indicates the purpose of a cost planning method. For example:

- Rough planning: estimating costs to be incurred for an order or for an element in a work breakdown structure

- Cost element planning

- Unit costing

Cost-Of-Sales Accounting   Form of results analysis. Sales deductions and unit costs are assigned to the sales transaction.

Costing   Calculating total production costs of individual product units, which may be a piece, a batch, a lot, or an order, for example. Costing may also take place on the provision of services.

Costing Type   Technical term used to control unit costing and product costing. The costing type determines the following:

- For which reference object a costing may be used

- Which costing object will be updated

- How the key of the costing file is made up

- Which costing application can use this costing type

Costing Variant   Technical term to determine criteria for a cost estimate. Comprises mainly the following:

- Costing type

- Valuation variant

- Organizational level

- Quantity structure determination, which will include the date control parameter

Costing Version   Technical term that determines the quantity structure when cost estimates are created. When production alternatives exit, there can be more than one product cost estimate for a material. Cost estimates with different production alternatives are given different version numbers.

CPI-C   Common Programming Interface-Communications. A set of standardized definitions for communications between programs.

Customizing   SAP tool, provided as part of the SAP R/3 system, comprising two components: implementation guides, and customizing menus and the associated functions. It does not change the program coding. This tool provides support for all the activities necessary for the following:

- Initial configuration of the SAP system before going into production

- Adjustment of the system during production

- Implementation of additional SAP applications

Data Element of a Field   A description of the contents of a record or field in terms of their business significance.

Database Interface   A work area to receive data from ABAP/4 Data Dictionary tables and from which any data that is changed may be passed to the database.

DBMS   Database Management System, which is a software system used to set up and maintain a database. It will include SQL facilities.

DDL   Data Definition Language, which is used to define database objects under the DBMS.

Delta Management   System of transferring only data that has changed when using Remote Function Call (RFC).

Dialog Module   A group of dialog steps in a program.

Direct Cost   Costs that are directly and fully identifiable with a reference object according to the costs-by-cause principle.

Distribution (Controlling) A business transaction used to allocate primary costs. The original cost element is retained on the receiver cost center. Information on the sender and the receiver is documented in the cost accounting document.

Distribution Key Contains rules on how the costs are to be distributed. It is used for the following:

- Planning to spread costs over the planning period

- Assessment

- Distribution of direct costs in order to divide the costs of a sender cost center among the receivers

DLL Dynamic Link Library, which is integral to the functioning of the Windows architecture at runtime.

DMS Document Management System.

Domain A description of the technical attributes of a table field, such as the type, format, length, and value range. Several fields with the same technical attributes can refer to the same domain.

Dynpro A dynamic program that controls the screen and its associated validation and processing logic to control exactly one dialog step.

EBCDIC Extended Binary-Coded Decimal Interchange Code.

EDI Electronic data interchange is a standardized scheme for exchanging business data between different systems via defined business documents such as invoices and orders.

Enqueue Service A SAP R/3 system mechanism for the management of locks on business objects throughout client/server environments.

Entity An entity is the smallest possible collection of data that makes sense from a business point of view and that is represented in the SAP R/3 system.

Entity Relationship Model Entities may be linked by logical relationships that have business significance. Entities and their interrelations can be used to build static models of the enterprise, which, in turn, are portrayed in the respective computer application with its tables.

Environment Analyzer A help program that generates a list of the development objects that belong together and the boundaries between development classes.

EPC Event Driven Process Chain. A process chain describes the chronological and logical relationship of functions of the R/3 System and business system statuses which initialize the functions or are generated as a result of function execution.

Equivalence Number A specification of how any given value is to be distributed to the different receiving objects.

Event (Reference Model) An event is a status that has business relevance. It can trigger a SAP system function, or it can be the result of such a function.

Event (Workflow Management) An event is a collection of attributes of objects, which describes the change in the state of an object.

External Activities Non-stock components and/or activities in a production order that are produced or performed outside the company.

Float Period of time that allows you to start a network or activity at a later date without incurring a delay in scheduling.

Follow-up Costs Incurred after the actual manufacturing process has been completed. For example, costs of rework and warranties.

Foreign Key A foreign key defines a relationship between two tables by assigning fields of one table (the foreign key table) to the primary key fields of another table (the check table).

Forward Scheduling Way of scheduling a network, starting from the basic start date and adding durations to determine the earliest start and finish dates for successive activities.

Free Float Time that an activity can be shifted into the future without affecting the earliest start date of the following activity or the end date of the project. Must not be less than zero or greater than the total float.

Function Module A program module that has a clearly defined interface and can be used in several programs. The function module library manages all function modules and provides search facilities in the development environment.

Function-Oriented Cost Accounting Assigning costs to a business function for the purpose of analysis.

General Costs Activity General costs incurred during the lifetime of a project are planned via this type of activity in a network. Examples of such planned costs are insurance, travel, consulting fees, royalties.

GUI Graphical User Interface. The SAPGUI is designed to give the user an ergonomic and attractive means of controlling and using business software.

Hypertext Online documentation that is set up like a network with active references pointing to additional text and graphics.

IDOC Intermediate document. The SAP R/3 system EDI interface and the ALE program link enabling both use standardized intermediate documents to communicate.

IMG Implementation Guide, a component of the SAP R/3 system that provides detailed steps for configuring and setting the applications.

Imputed Costs Do not represent operational expenditure or correspond to expenditures in either content or timing. For example: depreciation, interest.

Indirect Costs   Costs for which one single receiving object cannot be directly and fully identified according to the cost-by-cause-principle; for example:

- Indirect expenses, such as building insurance
- Indirect labor cost, such as supervisor wages
- Indirect materials cost, such as coolant cleaning materials

Initial Cost Split   Cost component split for raw materials procurement showing such details as the following:

- Purchase price
- Freight charges
- Insurance contributions
- Administration costs

Inventory from which Revenue Can Be Generated   The revenue expected in view of the costs which have already been incurred can be divided into capitalized costs and capitalized profits. It is calculated as Calculated Revenue minus Actual Revenue. Results analysis calculates the inventory for profit orders.

Job Order Cost Accounting   Instrument for the detailed planning and controlling of costs. Serves for the following:

- Collecting
- Analyzing
- Allocating the costs incurred for the internal production of non-capitalized goods

Joint Products   Made in the same manufacturing process.

Kerberos   A technique for checking user authorizations across open distributed systems.

Library Network   Generic network structure which can be used by many projects. Used in project system for repetitive processes or for process planning.

Line Item   Display of posting according to activity and document number.

Logical Database   A set of predefined paths for accessing the tables in a specific database system. Once defined and coded, they can be used by any report program.

Logical System   A system on which applications integrated on a common data basis run. In SAP terms, this is a client in a database.

Loop   Circular path through activities and their relationships.

Lot-Size Variance   Variances between the fixed planned costs and the fixed allocated actual costs that occur because part of the total cost for an order or a cost object does not change with output quantity changes. For example, setup costs that do not change no matter how often the operation is carried out.

LU6.2   IBM networking protocol used by the SAP R/3 system to communicate with mainframe computers.

LUW   Logical Unit of Work: an elementary processing step that is part of a SAP transaction. A logical unit of work is either executed entirely, or not at all. In particular, database access is always accomplished by separate LUWs, each of which is terminated when the database is updated or when the COMMIT WORK command is entered.

Make-To-Order Production   Type of production in which a product is generally manufactured only once, and to a customer order.

MAPI   Messaging Application Programming Interface, which is part of the WOSA, Microsoft Windows Open Service Architecture.

Master Data   Data relating to individual objects, remains unchanged for a long time.

Matchcode   An index key code attached to the original data that can be used to perform quick interactive searches for this data.

Material Requirements Planning   Generic term for activities involved in creating a production schedule or procurement plan for the materials in a plant, company, or company group.

Material Type   An indicator that subdivides materials into groups, such as raw materials, semi-finished materials, operating supplies, and that also determines the user screen sequence, the numbering in the material master records, the type of inventory management, and the account determination.

Measuring Point   Physical and/or logical place at which a status is described; for example:

- temperature inside a reactor
- speed of revolution of a wind wheel

Menu Painter   A SAP R/3 system tool for developing standardized menus, function keys, and pushbuttons in accord with the SAP Style Guide.

Metadata   Information about data structures used in a program. Examples of metadata are table and field definitions, domains, and descriptions of relationships between tables.

Mode   A user interface window in which an activity can be conducted in parallel with other open modes.

Modified Standard Cost Estimate   A costing type; uses the quantity structure that has changed during the planning period to calculate the cost of goods manufactured for a product.

Moving Average Price   Value of the material divided by the quantity in stock. Changes automatically after each goods movement or invoice entry.

Network   In SAP R/3, activity-on-node structure containing instructions on how to carry out activities in a specific way, in a specific order, and in a specific time period. Made from activities and relationships.

Network Type   Distinguishes networks by their usage. The network type controls the following:

- Costing variants for plan, target, actual costs
- Order type
- Number ranges
- Open items
- Status profile
- Authorizations

Object Currency   The currency of the controlling area is the default currency of a cost accounting object, such as cost center, order, and so on.

Object Overview   Customized list of data and line display layout; for example, routings, inspection plans, maintenance tasks, networks.

ODBC   Open Data Base Connectivity, which is a Microsoft standard based on SQL Access Group definitions for table-oriented data access.

OLE   Object Linking and Embedding, which is a Microsoft technology to enable the connection and incorporation of objects across many programs or files.

Open Item   Contractual or scheduled commitment that is not yet reflected in financial accounting, but will lead to actual expenditures in the future. Open item management provides for early recording and analyzing for cost and financial effects.

Operating Concern   An organizational unit to which one or more controlling areas and company codes can be assigned. Certain criteria and value fields are valid for a specific operating concern. The criteria define business segments, and the value fields are then updated for these objects.

Operating Level   The planned and/or actual performance of a cost center for a period; for example, output quantity, production time, machine hours.

Operating Rate   Ratio of actual and planned operating level. Measures the effective utilization of a cost center or activity.

Operating Resources   Personnel and material necessary to carry out a project.

> Can be used once or many times. Defined in value or quantity units. Planned for a period or a point in time. Includes, for example, materials, machines, labor, tools, jigs, fixtures, external services, work centers.

Operational Area   A technical term used to signify a logical subdivision of a company for accounting or operational reasons and therefore indicated in the EDM-Enterprise Data Model. An operation area is an organizational unit within logistics that subdivides a maintenance site plant according to the responsibility for maintenance.

Operations Layout   List, sorted by operations, of costing results from product costing and final costing.

Order   Instrument for planning and controlling costs. It describes the work to be done in a company in terms of which task is to be carried out and when, what is needed to carry out this task, how the costs are to be settled.

Order Category   The SAP application to which the order belongs; SD, for example.

Order Group   Technical term for grouping orders into hierarchies. Use to create reports on several orders, to combine orders, and to create order hierarchy.

Order Hierarchy   Grouping of orders for processing at the same time as in order planning and order reporting.

Order Phase   System control instrument for the order master data. Allows and prohibits operations on orders depending on the phase or stage: opened, released, completed, or closed.

Order/Project Results Analysis   Periodic valuation of long-term orders and projects. The o/p results analysis evaluates the ratio between costs and a measure of an order's progress towards completion, such as revenue or the quantity produced. The results analysis data include the following:

- Cost of sales
- Capitalized costs or work in progress
- Capitalized profits
- Reserves for unrealized costs
- Reserves for the cost of complaints and commissions
- Reserves for imminent loss

Order Settlement   Complete or partial crediting of an order. The costs that have accrued to an order are debited to one or more receivers belonging to financial or cost accounting.

Order Status Instrument to control whether an order may be planned or posted to. Reflects the operational progress, the order phase. Determines the following:

- Whether planning documents are created during cost element planning
- The transactions allowed at the moment (phase) such as planning, posting actual costs, and so on
- When an order may be flagged for deletion

Order Summarization Allows you to summarize data by putting orders into hierarchies. Also allows you to analyze the order costs at a higher level.

Order Type Differentiates orders according to their purpose: repair, maintenance, marketing, capital expenditure, for example.

Overall Network Network resulting from the relationships between all the existing networks.

Overhead Total cost of indirect expenses, indirect labor, indirect materials (indirect costs). Allocated to cost objects by means of overhead rates.

Overhead Cost Management The entirety of cost accounting activities for planning and controlling the indirect costs, as follows:

- Responsibility-oriented overhead cost management by cost centers
- Decision-oriented overhead cost management by action-oriented objects, which are orders and projects

Overhead Costing Most common method in product cost accounting. Method as follows:

- Assign the direct costs to the cost object.
- Apply the indirect (overhead) costs to the cost object in proportion to the direct costs, expressed as a percentage rate.

Overhead Group Key that groups materials to which the same overheads are applied.

PA Settlement Structure To settle costs incurred on a sender to various business segments depending on the cost element. The profitability analysis settlement structure is a combination of assignments of cost element groups to profitability segments.

Period Accounting One basis for profitability analysis. Costs are identified in the period in which they occur, irrespective of the period in which the corresponding revenue occurs.

Plan Version   Control parameters for comparative analyses in planning in cost accounting. The plan version determines, as follows, whether:

- Planning changes are documented.

- A beginning balance is to be generated.

- The planning data of another version can be copied or referenced.

Planned Activity   The planned cost center activity required to meet the demand, measured in the corresponding physical or technical units.

Planned Delivery Time   Number of days required to procure the material via external procurement.

Planning   Assigning estimates of the costs of all activities that will be required to carry out the business of an organizational unit over the planning period.

Planning Document   Line item for documenting planning changes.

Planning Element   Work breakdown structure (WBS) element on which cost planning can be carried out.

Pooled Table   A database table that is used to store control data, such as program parameters, or temporary data. Several pooled tables can be combined to form a table pool, which corresponds to a physical table on the database.

Price Difference Account   To record price differences for materials managed under standard prices, or differences between purchase order and billing prices.

Price Variance   Occurs if planned costs are evaluated in one way and the actual costs in another. The planned standard rates for activities might change in the meantime, for example. Can also be the result of exchange rate fluctuations.

Primary Cost Planning   By values and as quantities.

Primary Costs   Incurred due to the consumption of goods and services that are supplied to the company from outside. Costs for input factors and resources procured externally; for example, as follows:

- Bought-in parts

- Raw materials

- Supplies

- Services

Process Manufacturing   A production type; continuous manufacturing process from raw materials to finished product.

Product Costing   Tool for planning costs and setting prices. It calculates the cost of goods manufactured and the cost of goods sold for each product unit using the data in the PP-Production Planning module.

Product costing based on bills of material and routings is used for the following:

- Calculating production costs of an assembly with alternatives for

  - Showing the costs of semi-finished products

  - Detailed estimate of the cost components down to their lowest production level

Production Costs, Total   The costs of finished products bought for resale, or the costs of goods manufactured, plus sales overhead, special direct costs of sales, administration overhead.

Production Cycle   A manufacturing process in which the output of the final manufacturing level (or part of it) becomes input for lower manufacturing levels of the same process (recycle).

Production Order   For the production department to produce a material. It contains operations, material components, production resources and tools, costing data.

Production Resources and Tools (PRT)   Needed for carrying out operations at work centers. Assigned to activities for whose execution they are necessary.

Stored as various master data, as follows:

- Material master

- Equipment master

- Document master

Include the following:

- Job instructions

- Tools

- Test equipment

- Numerically controlled programs

- Drawings

- Machinery and fixtures

Profit Center   Area of responsibility for which an independent operating profit is calculated. Responsible for its own profitability. Separate divisional result is calculated.

Profit Order   Order whose planned revenue is greater than the planned costs. Results analysis uses the profit percentage rate of a profit order to calculate the inventory from which revenue can be generated, and to calculate the cost of sales.

Profit Percentage Rate   Planned revenue divided by planned costs of an order.

Profitability Analysis   In SAP R/3, by cost-of-sales approach or period accounting.

Project Definition   Framework laid down for all the objects created within a project. The data, such as dates and organizational data, are binding for the entire project.

Project Management   An organizational structure created just for the life of the project, to be responsible for planning, controlling, and monitoring of the project.

Project Structure   All significant relationships between the elements in a project.

Project Type   Capital spending or customer project, for example.

Q-API   Queue Application Program Interface, which supports asynchronous communication between applications of different systems by using managed queues or waiting lines.

Quantity Structure   The quantity-related basis for calculating costs. The bill of material and the routing form the quantity structure for product costing and the preliminary costing of a production order.

Quantity Variance   Difference between the target costs and the actual costs, which results from the difference between the planned and actual quantities of goods or activity used.

For example:

- More raw materials from stock for a production order

- Fewer activities from a cost center than were planned for

Rate of Capacity Utilization   Ratio of output to capacity. Fixed costs can be divided into used capacity costs and idle time costs.

Realized Loss   Usage of reserves for imminent loss by results analysis. Loss can be realized when actual costs are incurred and/or when revenue is received. Results analysis realizes loss as the difference either between the actual costs and the calculated revenue, or between the calculated costs and the actual revenue, as follows:

- Actual costs minus calculated revenue

- Calculated costs minus actual revenue

Reference Date   Using the reference dates and the offsets, the start and finish dates of the suboperation or the production resource/tool usage are determined.

A time within an activity; for example, the start date. Reference dates are used to determine the start and finish dates of suboperations as well as usage dates for production resources/tools.

You can enter time intervals for reference dates.

Relationship (Project System)   Link between start and finish points of two activities in a network or library network. In SAP R/3, the relationship types are the following:

- SS   start-start
- FF   finish-finish
- SF   start-finish
- FS   finish-start

Repetitive Manufacturing   A production type. Many similar products are manufactured together or one after another. In SAP R/3, bills of materials and routings are created for each product.

Reserves for Costs of Complaints and Sales Deductions   Inventory cannot be created for certain costs, for example, costs arising under warranties or because of sales deductions. For such costs, results analysis creates reserves equal to the planned costs. These reserves are then used when (and if) actual costs are incurred.

Reserves for Imminent Loss   Results analysis creates reserves equal to the planned loss. These reserves are reduced as (and if) this loss is realized.

Reserves for Unrealized Costs   Calculated in results analysis by subtracting the actual costs from the cost of sales.

Resource-Usage Variance   Occurs if the used resource is different from the planned one; for example, the actual raw material used is different from the planned raw material.

Results Analysis   Periodic valuation of long-term orders. Results Analysis compares the calculated costs and the actual cost of an order as it progresses towards completion. It calculates either inventory (if actual costs are greater than calculated costs) or reserves (if actual costs are less than calculated costs).

The data calculated during results analysis is stored in the form of:

- Cost of sales
- Capitalized costs
- Capitalized profit
- Reserves for unrealized costs

- Reserves for costs of complaints and commissions

- Reserves for imminent loss

Results Analysis Account   General Ledger account that records the figures calculated during results analysis.

Results Analysis Data

- Work in progress and capitalized costs

- Reserves

- Cost of sales

Results Analysis Key   Determines for results analysis:

- Whether revenue-based, quantity-based, or manual

- Basis on which it is carried out (planned or actual results)

- How profits are to be realized

- Whether to split inventory, reserves, and cost of sales

Results Analysis Version   Describes the business purpose for which results analysis was carried out.

Determines, for example:

- Whether in accordance with German and American law

- For financial accounting purposes

- For profitability analysis

- To which results analysis accounts to post the results

- How the life cycle of an object is to be broken down into open and closed periods

Revenue   The operational output valued at market price in the corresponding currency and sales quantity unit.

Quantity * Revenue = Sales.

RFC   Remote Function Call, which is a protocol, written in ABAP/4, for accessing function modules in other computers. RFC-SDK is a kit for integrating PC applications so that they can access SAP R/3 functions.

RPC   Remote Procedure Call, a protocol for accessing procedures residing in other computers from C programming environments. Corresponds to RFC.

Scheduling, Network   Determines earliest and latest start dates for activities and calculates the required capacity, as well as floats.

Screen Painter   An ABAP/4 Development Workbench tool that can be used to create, modify, display, and delete dynpros.

Secondary Cost Element   Cost centers require services from other cost centers to produce activity of their own. These are secondary costs. Planned assessment is used to plan the secondary cost quantities. Activity input is used to plan the secondary cost values.

Settlement Parameters   Control data required for order settlement as follows:

- Allocation group
- Settlement cost element
- Settlement receiver

Simultaneous Costing   Process that displays the actual costs incurred to date for such things as an order. The process describes all costings of an order in the SAP system, including order settlement. These costings come in the form of preliminary costings and actual costings. The values can then be analyzed in final analysis.

Spooling   Buffered relaying of information to output media, across multiple computers, if necessary.

SQL   Structured Query Language, defined by ANSI, American National Standards Institute, as a fourth-generation language for defining and manipulating data.

Standard Cost Estimate   Calculates the standard price for semi-finished and finished products. Relevant to the valuation of materials with standard price control. Usually created once for all products at the beginning of the fiscal year or a new season. The most important type of costing in product costing. The basis for profit planning or variance-oriented product cost controlling.

Standard Hierarchy   Tree structure for classifying all data objects of one type. For example, the cost centers belonging to a company from a cost accounting point of view will be represented by a standard hierarchy copied from the R/3 Reference Model and customized.

Standard Price   Constant price with which a material is evaluated, without taking into account goods movements and invoices.

For semi-finished and finished products calculated in product costing.

Style Guide   A collection of the SAP design standards for uniform design and consistent operation routines for SAP applications.

Summarization Object   An object containing data calculated during order summarization, project summarization, or the summarization of a cost object hierarchy. A summarization object can, for example, contain the costs incurred for all the orders of a specific order type and a specific responsible cost center.

Surcharge Supplement, usually as percentage, which is used to apply overhead in absorption costing.

Target Costs Calculated using the planned costs, along with the following:

■ The planned activities divided by the actual activities (for cost centers)

■ The planned quantities divided by the actual quantities of goods manufactured (for orders)

Task List Type Distinguishes task lists according to their functionality. In production planning task lists, for example, a distinction is drawn between routings and reference operation sets.

TCP/IP Transmission Control Protocol/Internet Protocol, the standard network protocol for open systems.

Time Interval Period of time between at least two activities linked in a relationship. The relationship type determines how start and finish times are used in the calculation.

Total Float Time that an activity can be shifted out into the future starting from its earliest dates without affecting the latest dates of its successors or the latest finish date of the network.

Transaction The series of related work steps required to perform a specific task on a business data processing system. One or more screens may be required. From the point of view of the user, it represents a self-contained unit. In terms of dialog programming, it is a complex object which consists of a module pool, screens, and so on, and is called with a transaction code.

Transaction Currency Currency in which the actual business transaction was carried out.

Unit Costing Method of costing where bills of material and routings are not used. Used to determine planned costs for assemblies or to support detailed planning of cost accounting objects such as cost centers or orders.

Usage Variance Difference between planned and actual costs caused by higher usage of material, time and so on.

User-Defined Field Types A classification code which is used to interpret the meaning of a user-defined field. For example, a user may designate a specific field as one of the following types:

■ General field of 20 characters to be used for codes or text

■ Quantity fields with a unit

■ Value fields with a unit

■ Date fields

■ Check boxes

User-Defined Fields Entry fields that can be freely defined for an activity or a work breakdown structure element (Project System) or an operation (Production Planning).

User Exit An interface provided by a SAP R/3 application that allows the user company to insert into a standard R/3 component a call to an additional ABAP/4 program that will be integrated with the rest of the application.

Valuation Date Date on which materials and internal and external activities are evaluated in a costing.

Valuation Variant Determines how the resources used, the external activities, and the overheads are to be valued in a costing (i.e., at what prices).

Variance Category Distinguishes variances according to their causes.

- Input: price and usage variances

- Yield: scrap, mix variances, labor efficiency variances, schedule variances

- Allocation: fixed cost variances, over-absorption variances, under-absorption variances

Variance Key Technical term; it controls how variances are calculated. Assigning a variance key to an object determines, for example, whether variances are calculated for the object by period or for the life of the object, which may be a cost center, an order, or a cost object identifier (ID).

Variance Version Technical term, specifies the basis for the calculation of variances as follows:

- How the target costs are calculated

- Which actual data is compared with the target costs

- Which variance categories are calculated

View A relational method used to generate a cross-section of data stored in a database. A virtual table defined in the ABAP/4 Dictionary can define a view by specifying how and what will be selected from whichever tables are targeted.

Volume Variance Cost difference between the fixed costs estimated for the products based on standard capacity and the allocated fixed costs that are either too low or too high due to operating either below or above capacity.

WBS Work Breakdown Structure.

WBS Element A concrete task or a partial task that can be subdivided.

Work Breakdown Structure A model of a project. Represents in a hierarchy the actions and activities to be carried out on a project. Can be displayed according to phase, function, object.

Work in Progress   Unfinished products, the costs of which are calculated by subtracting the costs of the order that have already been settled from the actual costs incurred for the order or by evaluating the yield confirmed to date.

Work Order   Generic term for the following order types:

- Production order

- Process order

- Maintenance order

- Inspection order

- Network

Work Process   A SAP R/3 system task that can be assigned independently to, for instance, a dedicated application server. For example, dialog processing, updating a database from change documents, background processing, spooling, lock management.

Workflow Management   Tool for automatic transaction processing used in a specific business environment.

Appendix F

Companies Providing SAP Services

This appendix lists companies who offer SAP-related services and are not listed under the SAP Business Partner appendix. If you would like your company included in future editions, please e-mail information about your company to ASAP World Consultancy: **sales@asap-consultancy.co.uk**.

SAP Recruitment Consulting
ASAP World
  Consultancy
ASAP House
PO Box 4463
Henley on Thames
Oxfordshire
RG9 6YN
England
Tel: +44 (0)1491 414411
Fax: +44 (0)1491
  414411
New York - USA -Virtual
  Office
Tel / Fax: (212) 253-
  4180
E-mail: **sales@asap-consultancy.co.uk**
Web: **http://
  www.asap-
  consultancy
  .co.uk/index.htm**

Allen Davis and
  Associates
Jon Reed, SAP
Recruiting Director
P.O. Box 2007
Amherst, MA 01004
USA
Tel: (413) 253-0600
x125
Web: **http://www.
softwarejobs.com**

Austen Consultancy
  Limited
Mr. George Glallant
Austen House
Fleet
Hampshire
England
GU13 9PE
Tel: 01252 816634
Fax: 01; 2 811075
E-mail: **austen@pncl
.co.uk**

Chase Management
  Systems Limited
Business & Technology
  Centre
Crewe
Cheshire
England
CW2 5PR
Tel: 01270 886182
Fax: 01270 886142
E-mail: **chase@
chaseman.
demon.co.uk**

Computer Futures
2 Foubert's Place
London
England
W1V 2AD
Tel: 0171 446 6666
Fax: 0171 446 0095
E-mail: **contract@
compfutures.co.uk**

Computer People
  Ireland
Mr. Grainne Martin
Carmichael House
Dublin 2
Ireland
Tel: 00353 1 6614998
Fax: 00353 1 6762664

Computer Power Group
Mr. Alistair Lee
Nordic House
Purley
Surrey
England
CR8 2AD
Tel: 0181 6601177
Fax: 0181 668 0721
E-mail:
**computer.power@
cpg-uk.demon.co.uk**

Computing Resource
  Centre Limited
Ms. Shirley MacGowan
West Lodge
London
England
W3 9SH
Tel: 0181 896 3110
Fax: 0181 896 2912

Cray Systems
127 Fleet Road
Fleet
Hampshire
England
GU13 8PD
Tel: 01252 775200
Fax: 01252 775299
E-mail:
swc@fleet.craysys.co.uk

DART Resourcing
MDA House
Slough
Berkshire
England
SL1 1RH
Tel: 01753 575577
Fax: 01753 534610

DPP Belgium
Mr. Mark Montgomery
Bessenveldstraat 251831
Diegem
Belgium
Tel: 00 322 716 4834
Fax: 00 322 716 4735
E-mail:
markfoxwell@dpp.be

DPP International Ltd
Mr. Tom Bannister
34 The Quadrant
Richmond
Surrey
England
TW9 1BR
Tel: 0181 332 2555
Fax: 0181 940 9864
E-mail: **dpp@dpp.co.uk**

Elan Computing Ltd
3rd Floor
Merrion Centre
Leeds
England
LS2 8LY
Tel: 0113 245 5322
Fax: 0113 244 6076
E-mail:
**info@elanleed.demon
.co.uk**

Eurocity
Ms. Sue Cameron
15 Spechtenstraat
3098 Everberg
Belgium
Tel: 323 759-2378
Fax: 323 759-6222
E-mail: **100305.1401@
compuserve
.com**

Eurolink
Blenheim House
Brighton
England
BN1 1NH
Tel: 01273 202316
Fax: 01273 723078
E-mail: **eurolink@fastnet
.co.uk**

Eurosoft
Services Limited
Midland Drive
Sutton Coldfield
England
B72 1TX
Tel: 0121 354 9911
Fax: 0121 354 1565

Executive Recruitment
  Services
Ms. Christine Trybus
Boundary Way
Hemel Hempstead
Hertfordshire
England
HP2 7RX
Tel: 01442 231691
Fax: 01442 230063
E-mail:
**executive@dial.pipex
.com**

Formula Systems
7a Milburn Road
Bournmouth
England
BH4 9HJ
Tel: 01202 752660
Fax: 01202 752665
E-mail:
**contracts@formula.demon
.co.uk**

Gatton Computastaff
Gatton Place
Redhill
Surrey
England
RH1 1TA
Tel: 01737 774100
Fax: 01737 772949#
E-mail:
**gatton@cix.compulink
.co.uk**

Hands-On Consultancy BV
7a Royal Terrace
Edinburgh
Scotland
EH7 5AB
Tel: 0131 478 0859
Fax: 0131 478 0860

Hays ASAP Worldwide
PO Box 4463
Henley on Thames
Oxfordshire
England
RG9 6YN
Tel: +44 (0) 118 931 1015
Fax: +44 (0) 118 975 2002
E-mail: **sales@hays--
asap.co.uk**
Web: **http://www.hays-
asap.co.uk.**

Input
Lindum House
Sleaford
Lincs
England
NG34 7BX
Tel: 01529 414077
Fax: 01529 395511

IT Link Limited
17 St Mary's Road
London
England
W5 5RA
Tel: 0181 567 7121
Fax: 0181 840 3667
E-mail: **itl-info@itlink
.co.uk**

Kenda System Limited
Gebouw Rivierstaete
Postbus 74700
1070 DJ Amsterdam
The Netherlands
Tel: 0171 816 6560

Kingfisher Consultancy
Mr. Steve Bennett
PO Box 2556
22 Bromsgrove Road
Redditch
Worcestershire
England
B97 4AA
Tel: 01527 595700
Fax: 01525 595720

M3 Group PLC
20 The Drive
Sevenoaks
Kent TN13 3AE
ALISTAIR LEE
Tel: 01732 452530
E-mail:
M3@dial.pipex.com
Web: **http://
www.m3group.com**

Marshall-Wilkins
Roger Wilkins
or David Lloyd
Suite 2, The Centre
Colchester Business Park
Colchester
Essex CO4 4YQ
England
Tel: +44 (0) 1206 845 666
Fax: +44 (0) 1206 845 941
E-mail: **marshal@
wilkins.win-uk.net**

Mortimer & Spinks
22 Great Marlborough Street
London
England
W1V 3HL
Tel: 0171 734 3499
Fax: 0171 734 3306

Olympian Consultancy
14-16 King Street
East Grinstead
West Sussex
England
RH19 3DJ
Tel: 01342 314000
Fax: 01342 314200
E-mail: **100442.1376@
compuserve.com**

Progressive Computer
Recruitment, Ltd.
Ms. Elaine Platt
Europa House
London
England
SW15 6TQ
Tel: 0181 9571700
Fax: 0181 7809844
E-mail: **contract@
progcr.demon.co.uk**

James Rushmore Limited
32a Westminster Palace
Gardens
Artillery Row
London
England SW1P 1RR
Tel: 44 0171 222 4900
Fax: 44 0171 222 4330
E-mail:
rellis@rushmore.co.uk
E-mail:
jdavies@rushmore.co.uk

Roche Consulting PLC
Mr. Andrew Montgomery
22 Godstone Road
Kenley
Surrey
England
CR8 5JE
Tel: +44 (0)181 763 1501
Fax: +44 (0)181 668 7280
E-mail:
mail@roche.co.uk

Software Personnel plc
  FREEPOST University of
  Warwick Science Park
Coventry
England
CV4 7BR
Tel: 01203 690966
Fax: 01203 690772
E-mail: **contracts@
softwarepsnl.co.uk**

SPAN Consultancy
Sheridan House
Winchester
Hampshire
England
SO23 8RY
Tel: 01962 844080
Fax: 01962 842370
E-mail: **100634.426@
Compuserve.com**

Square One Resources,
Ltd.
Mr. Martin Rush
154 Bishopsgate
London
England
EC2M 4LN
Tel: 0171 4260110
Fax: 0171 4260111
E-mail: **101551.2156@
compuserve.com**

Strand Computer
Systems, Ltd.
Ms. Claire Hayward
Wey Court
Franham
Surrey
England
GU9 7PT
Tel: 01252 721 222
Fax: 01252 733 825

UPP Business Systems
One TransAm Plaza Drive
Oakbrook Terrace, IL
60181
USA
Tel: 708 932-4300
Fax: 708 932-7652
E-mail: **upp@
vpnet.chi.il.us**

Votive Systems Limited
256 Odessa Road
London
England
E7 9DZ
Tel: 0181 221 0777
Fax: 0181 221 0888
E-mail:
**Votive_Systems@
msn.com**

**SAP Implementation
Consulting**
ASAP World Consultancy
ASAP House
PO Box 4463
Henley on Thames
Oxfordshire
RG9 6YN
England
Tel: +44 (0)1491 414411
Fax: +44 (0)1491 414411

New York- USA-Virtual
  Office
Tel / Fax: (212) 253-4180
E-mail: **sales@asap-
consultancy.co.uk**
Web: **http://www.asap-
consultancy.co.uk/
index.htm**

McHugh Hill Associates, Ltd.
70 Netheravon Road
London
W4 2NB
Tel/Fax:
+44 (0)181 994 3565

Realtime USA, LLC
1350 Deming Way, Suite 440
Middletown, WI 53562 USA
Tel: 608 827-0300
Fax: 608 827-0301
Web: **http://
www.realtimeusa.com**

Realtime Partner UK Limited
Alte Bahnhofstrasse 3
D-53173 Bonn
Germany
Tel: 49 0228/93560-0
Fax: 49 0228/9356099
Web: **http://
www.realtime-uk.de**

Realtime RT Limited
7 Rivertree, Walnut Tree
Close Guildford
Surrey
England
GU1 4UX
Tel: 44 01483 563 673
Fax: 44 01483 567 729
Web: **http://
www.realtime-rt.co.uk**

The McConnell Blair Group
14 Beaver Dam Rd.
Newtown, CT 06470 USA
Tel: 01 203-270-9488
Fax: 01 203-270-9484
E-mail:
mcbgroup@aol.com

SAP Documentation Consulting

ASAP World Consultancy
ASAP House
PO Box 4463
Henley on Thames
Oxfordshire
RG9 6YN
England
(Services also available in
Australia and S.E. Asia)
Tel: +44 (0)1491 414411
Fax: +44 (0)1491 414411

New York-USA -Virtual
Office
Tel / Fax: (212) 253-4180
E-mail: **sales@asap-
consultancy.co.uk**
Web: **http://www.asap-
consultancy.co.uk/
index.htm**

Documentation
Consultants (UK)
Limited
C/O
ASAP World Consultancy
PO Box 4463
Henley on Thames
Oxfordshire
RG9 6YN
England
Tel: +44 (0)1491 414411
Fax: +44 (0)1491 414411

New York-USA-Virtual
Office
Tel / Fax: (212) 253-4180
E-mail: **sales@asap-
consultancy.co.uk**

SAP Training

ASAP World Consultancy
ASAP House
PO Box 4463
Henley on Thames
Oxfordshire
RG9 6YN
England
Tel: +44 (0)1491 414411
Fax: +44 (0)1491 414411

New York-USA -Virtual
Office
Tel / Fax: (212) 253-4180
E-mail: **sales@asap-
consultancy.co.uk**
Web: **http://
www.asap-
consultancy.co.uk/
index.htm**

SAP Access and Security Consulting

ASAP World Consultancy
ASAP House
PO Box 4463
Henley on Thames
Oxfordshire
RG9 6YN
England
Tel: +44 (0)1491 414411
Fax: +44 (0)1491 414411

New York-USA -Virtual Office
Tel / Fax: (212) 253-4180
E-mail: **sales@asap-
consultancy.co.uk**
Web: **http://www.asap-
consultancy.co.uk/
index.htm**

SAP Project Internal & External Commun- ications Consulting

ASAP World Consultancy
ASAP House
PO Box 4463
Henley on Thames
Oxfordshire
RG9 6YN
England
Tel: +44 (0)1491 414411
Fax: +44 (0)1491 414411

New York-USA-Virtual
Office
Tel / Fax: (212) 253-4180
E-mail: **sales@asap-
consultancy.co.uk**
Web: **http://www.asap-
consultancy.co.uk/
index.htm**

SAP System Testing, Consulting, and Resourcing

ASJ? World Consultancy
ASAP House
PO Box 4463
Henley on Thames
Oxfordshire
RG9 6YN
England
Tel: +44 (0)1491 414411
Fax: +44 (0)1491 414411

New York-USA -Virtual
  Office
Tel / Fax: (212) 253-4180
E-mail: **sales@asap-consultancy.co.uk**
Web: **http://www.asap-consultancy.co.uk index.htm**

SAP Human Issues Consulting

ASAP World Consultancy
ASAP House
PO Box 4463
Henley on Thames
Oxfordshire
RG9 6YN
England
Tel: +44 (0)1491 414411
Fax: +44 (0)1491 414411
New York-USA -Virtual
  Office
Tel / Fax: (212) 253-4180
E-mail: **sales@asap-consultancy.co.uk**
Web: **http://www .asap-consultancy .co.uk/index.htm**

Hambleden Consulting
Hambleden
Henley on Thames
Oxfordshire
RG9 6SH
Tel: +44 (0) 1491 414 020
Fax: +44 (0) 1491 414 020
E-mail: **hambleden@ dial.pipex.com**
Web: **http:// dialspace. dial.pipex.com/ hambleden/**

Harley Young
The Hangar
Highlands Farm
Highlands Lane
Henley on Thames
Oxfordshire
RG9 4PR
England
Tel: 01491 410995
Fax: 01491 577683
E-mail: **harley.young@ dial.pipex.com**

SAP Resource Planning Consulting

ASAP World Consultancy
ASAP House
PO Box 4463
Henley on Thames
Oxfordshire
RG9 6YN
England
Tel: +44 (0)1491 414411
Fax: +44 (0)1491 414411

New York-USA -Virtual
  Office
Tel / Fax: (212) 253-4180
E-mail: **sales@asap-consultancy.co.uk**
Web: **http://www.asap-consultancy.co.uk/ index.htm**

Rivermead Associates
13 Boulters Gardens
Maidenhead
Berkshire
England
SL6 8TR
Tel: +44 (0) 1628 31151
Fax: +44 (0) 1628 25630
E-mail: **rivermead@ globalnet.co.uk**

Business Process Reengineering and Change Management Consulting

ASAP World Consultancy
ASAP House
PO Box 4463
Henley on Thames
Oxfordshire
RG9 6YN
England
Tel: +44 (0)1491 414411
Fax: +44 (0)1491 414411

New York-USA -Virtual Office
Tel / Fax: (212) 253-4180
E-mail: **sales@asap-consultancy.co.uk**
Web: **http://www.asap-consultancy.co.uk/ index.htm**

Hewson Consulting Group
Witan Court
317 Upper Fourth Street
Central Milton Keynes
MK9 1ES
Tel: 01908 677840
Fax: 01908 677850

Hardware and Installation Consulting
ASAP World Consultancy
ASAP House
PO Box 4463
Henley on Thames
Oxfordshire
RG9 6YN
England
Tel: +44 (0)1491 414411
Fax: +44 (0)1491 414411

New York-USA -Virtual
  Office
Tel / Fax: (212) 253-4180
E-mail: **sales@asap-consultancy.co.uk**
Web: **http://www.asap-consultancy.co.uk/index.htm**

Virtual Office Communication Facilities for SAP Consultants and Companies
JFAX Communications, Inc.
244 Madison Avenue
Suite 191
New York, NY 10016
Tel: (212) 431-3833
E-mail: **hq@jfax.net**

SAP Career and Business Development Services
ASAP World Consultancy
ASAP House
PO Box 4463
Henley on Thames
Oxfordshire
England
RG9 6YN
Tel: +44 (0)1491 414411
Fax: +44 (0)1491 414411

New York, USA—
Virtual Office
Tel/Fax: (212) 253-4180
E-mail: **sales@asap-consultancy.co.uk**
Web: **http://www.asap-consultancy.co.uk/index.htm**

Rivermead Associates
13 Boulters Gardens
Maidenhead
Berkshire
England
SL6 8TR
Tel: +44 (0)1628 31151
Fax: +44 (0)1628 25630
E-mail: **rivermead@globalnet.co.uk**

SAP Acquisitions, Mergers, and Joint Ventures
ASAP World Consultancy
ASAP House
PO Box 4463
Henley on Thames
Oxfordshire
England
RG9 6YN
Tel: +44 (0)1491 414411
Fax: +44 (0)1491 414411

New York, USA—Virtual
Office
Tel/Fax: (212) 253-4180
E-mail: **sales@asap-consultancy.co.uk**
Web: **http://www.asap-consultancy.co.uk/index.htm**

Rivermead Associates
13 Boulters Gardens
Maidenhead
Berkshire
England
SL6 8TR
Tel: +44 (0)1628 31151
Fax: +44 (0)1628 25630
E-mail:
rivermead@globalnet.co.uk

Appendixes

SAP Procurement Consultancy
ASAP World Consultancy
ASAP House
PO Box 4463
Henley on Thames
Oxfordshire
England
RG9 6YN
Tel: +44 (0)1491 414411
Fax: +44 (0)1491 414411
New York, USA—Virtual Office
Tel/Fax: (212) 253-4180
E-mail: **sales@ asap-consultancy.co.uk**
Web: **http://www. asapconsultancy.co.uk/ index.htm**

SAP Career and Business Development Services
Rivermead Associates
13 Boulters Gardens
Maidenhead
Berkshire
SL6 8TR
England
Tel: 01628 31151
Fax: 01628 25630
E-mail: **rivermead@ globalnet.co.uk**

Migrating from SAP R/2 to SAP R/3

R/2 and R/3 systems can link together in many ways to suit the needs of your company and your progress in the evolution of your computer support installation. Chapter 6, "Tool-Supported Optimization with the R/3 Analyzer," discusses the improvement of your business computing facilities by developing new programs. Some of these programs may be directed at forging automatic links with systems, such as databases, that your company has been using for some time and that probably contain valuable data and perhaps specific procedures unique to your particular business.

This chapter concentrates on the situations where some of your existing installations are SAP systems that are going to be improved, either by being moved to a different hardware configuration, referred to as "migration," or by acquiring new releases of the SAP software.

The third possibility is to have a SAP system operating in the position of a satellite system that communicates with the central host system whenever this is necessary. The satellite system will usually be able to continue functioning on its own in between the occasions when it links up to the central or "hub" system. This arrangement is discussed in Chapter 3, "System Architecture and Distributed Applications."

Relationships Between R2 and R3

A stand-alone mainframe system will use a release of the R/2 system. Client/server installations will use the R/3 for best results. Systems using R/2 may be linked to R/3 systems on a permanent basis, or the linkage may be used as a transition stage in the process of migrating completely to an R/3 installation.

SAP Release and Migration Tools

It is the policy of SAP to provide tools to support each update of your system, whether it be a full migration to a different host or an update occasioned by the purchase of a new release of existing software.

The release and migration tools, although different in scope, provide the same basic support to the user organization:

- Information on the new functions and facilities available when the update is completed

- Update to the R/2 or R/3 Reference Model, which includes the additional functions

- Support for using the updated reference model to design any modification to your business procedures, which will be required in order to make best use of the new functions

- Support for establishing trials where necessary of the new functions

The main modules of R/2 Release 5.0 are as follows:

- Logistics

  - RM-MAT Materials Management

  - RM-PPS Production Planning and Control

  - RM-INST Plant Maintenance

  - RM-QSS Quality Assurance

  - RV Sales and Distribution

- Accounting

  - RF Financial Accounting

  - RA Assets Accounting

  - RK Cost Accounting

- Human Resources

- Basis

The SAP R/2 system is a highly developed mainframe system that has been enhanced to include the following types of functionality:

- Seamless transfer to new hardware concepts

- Integration with workstations and PC terminals

- Support for the CUA user interface, which allows a choice of graphical or character-based presentation screens

- Flexible classification of objects in the SAP R/2 system such as routings, materials, documents, vendors, and items of equipment through the SAP R/2 Classification System, which supports the manipulation of classes of data objects

- Extensive additions to the Logistics, FI-Accounting, and HR-Human Resources application areas

- Provision for satellites to the R/2 system as of R/2 Release 5.0E

Migrating Data and Functions from SAP R/2 to SAP R/3

The SAP modules of standard business software are designed to accommodate the widest possible variety of user organizations and an extensive range of hardware and software systems. For example, the SAP R/2 system was developed in the context of mainframe architectures, which were integrated with server systems for specific purposes such as database management. This could be said to be a relatively homogeneous environment.

By contrast, the thrust of SAP R/3 system design and development has been towards heterogeneous architectures comprising multiple layers of client/server configurations that could take advantage of the rapid but uneven developments by the vendors of low-cost equipment and operating systems for tasks such as user interface and database management. With the improvement of communications facilities, the development of worldwide business systems has progressed considerably.

Many companies will want to take advantage of their archived business information and the most recent transaction data when they install new equipment or software components, and when a complete business process reengineering project is being conducted.

The objective is to transfer data and perhaps customized business functions to the new SAP R/3 system installation or application module.

Migration Data Objects

The SAP R/3 system is focused on the handling of structured data objects that may be of any complexity and yet be accessed as single entities. It is by such techniques that the SAP R/3 system generates both its power and its flexibility without excessive annexation of computing resources. The SAP R/2 system does not manipulate data objects in the same manner. It relies on access to fields and tables of fields.

The migration process has to allow the information in the SAP R/2 tables to be rebuilt into the structures of the SAP R/3 system. In effect, what is migrated is a collection of migration objects that make sense in the business context and are named accordingly. They have to be unloaded from the SAP R/2 database, transferred to the SAP R/3 database, and made available to the SAP R/3 system as a whole.

Special Migration Functions

The data in the SAP R/2 system is exported as DDIC, Database Decimal Interchange Code structures that contain the data objects in EBCDIC, Extended Binary-Coded Decimal Interchange Code format, which has to be converted to ASCII. The programs to create the export structures are automatically generated in the SAP R/2 system in real time. Similarly, the SAP R/3 system generates import programs to receive and integrate the structures and their data objects. All the customers' conversion rules and their program logic are integrated into the import programs.

Linked System Windows

The CUA graphical interface is available in both the SAP R/2 and the SAP R/3 systems. Separate windows at the user interface can independently display the progress of functions in both systems and from any integrated PC systems that may be running. The following products are included in the list of front-end systems that can be used to display essentially the same screens and conduct the relevant dialog activities:

- Windows
- SF/Motif
- Presentation Manager

Varieties of Migration Strategy

Although the "Big Bang" creation of a totally new business process support system is a feasible project, it is by no means the only option. There are many ways in which coexistence between some or all of the legacy system hardware and software components can be brokered. They range from the evolution of peripheral SAP R/3 system functionality to a complete redesign and fresh implementation of what must be regarded as a new business entity.

SAP R/3 System Satellites

The increasing range of independent systems that can be managed by program-to-program communications allows the use of specialized and optimized systems for the business functions that might otherwise co-opt excessive amounts of shared computer resources. The same style of configuration can be adopted to effect a flexible migration strategy between the various SAP R/2 and SAP R/3 system possibilities.

The satellite systems can, for example, serve the purpose of introducing new SAP applications, hosted from the start by a SAP R/3 system, on which experience can be gained on the route to a future total SAP R/3 system solution.

The following functional areas have been successfully supported by SAP R/3 system satellites to a central SAP R/2 system host:

- Application-neutral servers, which perform particular functions such as optical archiving of mass data and documents
- Consolidation of financial statements from corporate cost centers
- Cash and capital fund management through the treasury workstation
- Executive information system services
- Time management of decentralized personnel
- Decentralized production control and quality assurance
- Managing dispersed warehouses
- Decentralized shipping control
- Industry solutions, which entail specialized satellites in, for example, banks, hospitals, and insurance companies

Key Date Total Migration

Upon a planned key date, your entire business operation can be migrated to the SAP R/3 system environment, perhaps leaving a few independent database servers, running now as satellites.

One Company Code Structure at a Time

It may be the case that your corporation has acquired a number of subsidiaries that are not all at the same stage in the evolution of their data processing facilities. The SAP systems can support the integration of heterogeneous systems in which each company code is supported by a different computer configuration. Each of these may choose to migrate to an integrated SAP R/3 system at different times.

The functions of legal consolidation and enterprise management in general can continue without interruption as the waves of migration occur.

Full SAP R/3 Business Process Reengineering with Minor Migrations

You may decide that your business deserves a thoroughgoing overhaul in terms of its data processing and, hence, management functions. Tools to support this are described in Chapter 6, "Tool-Supported Optimization with the R/3 Analyzer."

There may be some important data that should be migrated to the SAP R/3 environment when the design of the new system has been established.

Application Link Enabling with R/3 System Logistics Modules

An important type of satellite constellation can be seen in connection with applications in the Logistics group. The following systems can be controlled and accessed using the Application Link Enabling (ALE) technology:

- DASS manufacturing control station
- DASS-QSS quality control station
- DISS maintenance control station
- Decentralized LVS inventory management system
- Cross-platform CAD interactive interface

Coexistence and Linkage Scenarios

The trend for coexistence is supported by a wide range of linkage programs that use the standard business functions together with specialized ABAP/4 program elements to effect whatever links are required to make possible continuous business development without loss of effectiveness as new technology is introduced.

Wherever possible, these linkage scenarios are executed in the SAP R/3 system environment, where they can be automatically integrated and where they will benefit from enhancements to this system.

Special Migration Provisions

Although migrating data may be required, there are some circumstances where the migration of functionality is not necessary.

Superior SAP R/3 Modules

In most cases, it is not usual for migration to be effected for the logic of SAP R/2 systems for which there are fully developed SAP R/3 applications. The following are examples:

- RV-Pricing
- RM-Plant Maintenance
- RM-Production Orders
- RK-Orders/Projects/Profit Analysis
- RP-Human Resources Management

Specialized System Enhancements

Full migration is not indicated if your system has already been extensively specialized by a standard modification package. The following are examples:

- IS-OIL, Industry Solution for the petroleum industry
- RIVA
- RV-CPG, Sales and Distribution central processing
- RV-Export
- RV-Transport
- RV-Steel Trading

Migration Alternatives for SAP R/2 Prior to Release 5.0

There are a number of options available if software releases 4.3 and 4.4 require migration, as follows:

- Upgrade the SAP R/2 system to Release 5.0 and apply the standard package for migration from Release 5.0 to the SAP R/3 system.
- Commission a specific enhancement to the standard migration package to take account of your SAP R/2 system Release 4.3 and 4.4 modules.
- Redesign your system in SAP R/3. Historical data and document data will not be transferred, but minor amounts of master data can be migrated in batch mode.

Customer-Specific ABAP/4 Program Migration

The standard migration package will not carry out conversion of customer-developed ABAP/4 programs, because changes in the logical database and the field names will not necessarily be correctly migrated.

Many SAP R/2 reports developed specifically for customer installations are not necessary under the SAP R/3 system, because of the highly flexible reporting systems built in. It is not normal to have them transferred.

The standard migration package includes migration programs, planning advice, and a handbook to highlight the differences between SAP R/2 and SAP R/3; in particular, the organizational structure changes, which make for better mapping of your company onto the SAP R/3 Enterprise Data Models.

Migration Project Steps

The data migration element of a SAP R/3 system implementation is best effected under the control of a project plan. The following steps are indicated:

- Arrange for the personnel to become familiar with the SAP R/3 system.
- Define the data migration strategy.
- Establish a formal SAP R/3 system implementation project with the data migration phase included.
- Rework the functions and processes that exist in the SAP R/2 system so that they will take advantage of the enhancements of the SAP R/3 system.
- Completely customize the target SAP R/3 system prototype.
- Install the mechanisms by which high-speed file transfer can occur between the SAP R/2 system mainframe and the SAP R/3 system—File Transfer Protocol (FTP), for instance.
- Carry out data migration tests and verify the transfers.
- Conduct large-scale volume tests for data conversion.
- Plan and optimize the schedule for closing the production system and transferring the data.
- Run the SAP R/3 system live in the productive situation.

The task force needed to carry out such a migration project will depend on the complexity and extent of the changes envisioned. In most instances where a substantial SAP system is already in operation, the enhancements to the system will be related to existing components and the pilot project team will want to refer to the relevant reference model to see just how far the new requirements can be met by using the existing software installation.

Three key experts are needed: a specialist in the business requirement; a specialist in the existing software installation and its development potential; and a specialist who can see how the system can be best developed by installing and configuring the products available, whether they be SAP or from other suppliers.

Appendixes

A pilot scheme may include several independent modules that are under separate development teams although working under a strict management regime so that nugatory work is avoided.

Many organizations will want to minimize downtime on their productive capacities. Their choice will therefore incline toward the establishment of a satellite configuration for the new module which can coexist with the established arrangements until the case for full integration has been demonstrated.

Complementary Solutions

SAP has encouraged third-party software developers to interface with SAP and thus extend the functionality of the R/3 suite. The technologies it has used in R/3 have helped make this possible—technologies such as Application Link Enabling (ALE), Object Linking and Embedding (OLE), Remote Function Calls (RFCs), and Open Database Connectivity. You can get a fuller appreciation of the place that complementary solutions providers occupy in the SAP world in Chapter 44, "The Outlook for the SAP Employment Market." These companies are of special interest to people seeking to "bridge" into SAP work on the strength of a particular technology expertise.

SAP operates a certification program to ensure that complementary products interface properly with SAP, though it does not evaluate other aspects of complementary solution software. All the products listed here are either certified by SAP or awaiting certification. The list is growing all the time. The complementary solutions are grouped according to their classification by SAP. SAP classifies them into groups according to function, and to the SAP R/3 interfaces for which SAP certifies their connection. The interface for which each group is shown in parentheses alongside the group classification—for example, "Computer-Aided Design (CAD)" and Product Data Management (PDM)—are both functional groups that connect to SAP R/3 via the CAD interface.

Vendor details are shown for each product named within each group. A contact name (or names) is given in most cases. This a general contact point for the product (not specifically for recruitment). Some of the vendors are partners, and will also be listed as such in Appendix B, while others are listed only here.

Computer-Aided Design (CAD)

Vendor	Siemens
Address	Otto-Hahn-Ring 6, D-81739 München, Germany
Phone	+49 89 636 46 789
Fax	+49 89 636 49625
Contact	Mr. Gerhard Wetzel
Product	Sigraph Design
Remarks	Certified Interface: Sigraph-Ratio V1.0.

EDI SUBSYSTEMS (WF-EDI)

Vendor	ACTIS Angewandte Computertechnik für Informationssysteme in Berlin GmbH
Address	Kurfürstendamm 65, D-10707 Berlin, Germany
Phone	+49 30 88444 0
Fax	+49 30 88444 100
Contact	Mr. Arp
Product	EDI Manager Version 1.0
Remarks	EDI subsystem certified for SAP R/3 2.1 and 2.2; Standard: EDIFACT 91.1

Vendor	GEIS—GE Information Services
Address	Robert-Bosch-Strasse 6, D-50354 Huerth (Efferen), Germany
Phone	+49 2233 609 1
Fax	+49 2233 609 286
Contact	Mr. Paul O. Olson, Mr. Wolfhard Kleinemeyer
Product	EDI Transit Version 2.10.06
Remarks	EDI subsystem certified for SAP R/3 2.1 and 2.2; Standard: EDIFACT 91/1

Vendor	Harbinger Corp.
Address	Harbinger Enterprise Solutions Division, P.O. Box 831119, 2425 North Central Expressway, Richardson, TX 75080, U.S.
Phone	+1 214 479 1260
Fax	+1 214 479 9779
Contact	Mr. Douglas J. Stewart
Product	Intouch
Remarks	EDI subsytem certified for SAP R/3 2.1 and 2.2; Standard: ANSI X12 3/20

Vendor	LION EDInet Gesellschaft für Kommunkation mbH
Address	Teletower, Deutz-Müulheimer-Str.111, D-51063 Köln, Germany
Phone	+49 221 935500 - 16 or -0
Fax	+49 221 935500 - 11
Contact	Mr. Jürgen Otto
Product	Tiger

Remarks	EDI subsytem certified for SAP R/3 2.1 and 2.2; Standard: EDIFACT 91.3
Vendor	Perwill EDI, Inc. German Distributor: Tangram Unternehmensdienste GmbH
Address	7550 Lucerne Drive 307, Middleburg Heights, OH 44130, U.S.
Phone	+1 216 891 0096, +49 7034 9244 0
Fax	+1 216 891 0299
Contact	Mr. Jan Pallenik, President Tangram: Mr. Klaus Bröhl
Product	Perwell EDI Version 420
Remarks	EDI subsystem certified for SAP R/3 2.1 and 2.2; Standard: EDIFACT 92.1
Vendor	Seeburger Unternehmensberatung GmbH
Address	Hermann-Beuttenmüller-Strasse 6, D-75015 Bretten, Germany
Phone	+49 7252 9358 0
Fax	+49 7252 9358 33
Contact	Mr. Hartmann
Remarks	EDI subsystem certified for SAP R/3 2.1 and 2.2; Standard: ANSI X12 3/20
Vendor	Siemens Nixdorf Informations Syteme AG
Address	Otto-Hahn-Ring 6, D-81739 München, Germany
Phone	+49 89 636 45672
Fax	+49 89 636 40935
Contact	Mr. Thomas Meyer, D122
Product	SNI SEDI Server
Remarks	EDI subsystem certified for SAP R/3 2.1 and 2.2; Standard: EDIFACT 91.1
Vendor	Sterling Software Group
Address	4600 Lakehurst Court, P.O. Box 7160, Dublin, OH 43017, U.S.
Phone	+1 614 793 5971, +1 614 793 7268
Fax	+1 614 793 7221
Contact	Mr. Todd Coombs (Alliance Marketing), Mr. Jim Aten (Director of Product Management)
Product	Sterling Basic for Unix 1.1
Remarks	EDI subsystem certified for SAP R/3 2.1 and 2.2; Standard: ANSI X12 3/20
E-mail	**todd_combs@dublin.sterling.com** or **jim_aten@dublin.sterling.com**
Vendor	St. Paul Software Incorporated
Address	754 Transfer Road, St. Paul, MN 55114, U.S.
Phone	+1 612 641 0963
Fax	+1 612 641 0609

Appendixes

Contact	Mr. Tom Boutin, Mr. Gary Anderson (President)
Product	spEDI tran Rel. 3.0, Rel.2.X
Remarks	EDI subsystem certified for SAP R/3 2.1 and 2.2; Standard: ANSI X12 3/20
Vendor	Trinary Systems, Inc.
Address	38345 West Ten Mile Road, Suite 330, Farmington Hills, MI 48335, U.S.
Phone	+1 810 442 8540 (extension -133)
Fax	+1 810 442 9125
Contact	Ms. Lydia Maes
Product	EDI Windows 4.1
Remarks	EDI subsystem certified SAP R/3 2.1 and 2.2; Standard: ANSI X12 3/20

Plant Data Collection (PP-PDC)

Vendor	A & B Systems GmbH
Address	Sebaldstrasse 23, D-73525 Schwäbisch Gmünd, Germany
Phone	+49 7171 39024
Fax	+49 7171 38726
Contact	Mr. Aigner
Product	FIT
Remarks	Certified for: SAP R/3 Release 1.1., Attendance Time Recording not certified; Operating system: UNIX
Vendor	DASA Deutsche Aerospace GmbH
Address	Mainzer Strasse 36-52, D-53179 Bonn, Germany
Phone	+49 288 8554 119
Fax	+49 228 8554 237
Contact	Mr. Gruban, Mr. Grote
Product	BESSY
Remarks	Certified for: SAP R/3 Release 2.0, 2.1, 2.2; Attendance Time Recording only; Operating system: Windows NT
Vendor	EIPC Data
Address	17 Kingfisher Court, Hambridge Road, Newbury, Berkshire RG14 5SJ, U.K.
Phone	+44 1 635 521 140
Fax	+44 1 635 521 486
Contact	Mr. Paul Bennett
Product	Data Collection Manager
Remarks	Certified for: SAP R/3 Release 1.1; Operating system: VMS
Vendor	GFOS GmbH
Address	Cathostrasse 5, D-45356 Essen, Germany
Phone	+49 201 660001
Fax	+49 201 619317

Contact	Ms. Cassens
Product	X/TIME
Remarks	Certified for: SAP R/3 Release 2.0, 2.1, 2.2

Vendor	Hengstler GmbH
Address	Uhlandstrasse 49, D-78550, Aldingen, Germany
Phone	+49 7424 89-314
Fax	+49 7424 89-565
Contact	Mr. Böhret
Product	VARIDAT
Remarks	Certified for: SAP R/3 Release 2.0, 2.1, 2.2; Attendance Time Recording only; Operating system: UNIX

Vendor	IBM Deutschland
Address	Pascalstrasse 100, D-70569 Stuttgart, Germany
Phone	+49 711 785 0 +49 711 785 4968, +49 711 785 4976
Fax	+49 711 785 4991
Contact	Mr. Steudle, Mr. Minniti
Product	DASSCO
Remarks	Certified for: SAP R/3 Release 2.0, 2.1, 2.2; Operating system: OS/2

Vendor	INCA Systeme GmbH
Address	Marsstrasse 7, D-85609 Ascheim, Germany
Phone	+49 89 9099 960
Fax	+49 89 9099 9660
Contact	Mr. Engel
Product	INCA-Z
Remarks	Certified for: SAP R/3 Release 1.1; Operating system: UNIX

Vendor	Interflex Datensysteme
Address	Greschbachstrasse 3a, D-76229 Karlsruhe, Germany
Phone	+49 721 9630 0, +49 711 1322 106
Fax	+49 721 9630 222
Contact	Mr. Sigmund, Mr. Dreu
Product	System 4000
Remarks	Certified for: SAP R/3 Release 1.1 to 2.2, Attendance Time Recording only; Operating systems: UNIX, VMS

Vendor	INSO Informationsverabeitung und Software-Entwicklung
Address	Tullastrasse 25-29, D-76131 Karlsruhe, Germany
Phone	+49 721 96 20 201
Fax	+49 721 96 20 222
Contact	Dr. Herrmann, Mr. Roth (Sales)
Product	CIPDIALOG 3.07
Remarks	Certified for: SAP R/3 Release 2.0, 2.1, 2.2

Appendixes

Vendor	ISGUS J Schlenker-Grusen GmbH
Address	Oberdorfstrasse 18-22, D-78025 Villingen-Schwenningen, Germany
Phone	+49 7720 393 222
Fax	+49 7720 393 184
Contact	Mr. Jürgensen
Product	SAP-Talk
Remarks	Certified for: SAP R/3 Release 2.0, 2.1, 2.2; Attendance Time Recording only; Operating system: DOS

Vendor	Kaba Benzing GmbH
Address	Hans-Böckler-Strasse 11,D-63263 Neu-Isenburg, Germany
Phone	+49 6102 7168 0
Fax	+49 6102 7168 30
Contact	Mr. Kopp
Product	B-Comm für SAP R/3
Remarks	Certified for SAP R/3 Release 1.1 to 2.2; Operating system: UNIX

Vendor	Miditec Automatisierungstechnik GmbH
Address	Bürgermeister-Smidt-Strasse 24-28, D-28195 Bremen, Germany
Phone	+49 421/17581 0
Fax	+49 421/17581 30
Contact	Mr. Niendorf
Product	MTZ 2500
Remarks	Certified for: SAP R/3 Release 2.0, 2.1, 2.2; Attendance Time Recording only; Operating system: AIX

Vendor	MPDV Mikrolab GmbH
Address	Alte Neckarelzer Strasse 22,D-74821 Mosbach, Germany
Phone	+49 6202 94450
Fax	+49 6202 13791
Contact	Mr. Deisenroth
Product	HYDRA
Remarks	Certified for: SAP R/3 Release 2.0, 2.1, 2.2; Attendance Time Recording only; Operating system: AIX

Vendor	PCS Systemtechnik GmbH
Address	Pfälzer-Wald-Strasse 36, D-81539 München, Germany
Phone	+49 89 68004 0, +49 89 68004 289
Fax	+49 89 68004 312
Contact	Mr. Gruber
Product	DEXICON
Remarks	Certified for: SAP R/3 Release 1.1; Operating system: VMS

Vendor	Robert Bosch GmbH
Address	Geschäftsbereich Industrieausrüstung, Berlinstrasse 25, D-64711 Erbach, Germany
Phone	+49 6062 78108
Fax	+49 6062 78553

Contact	Mr. Mangold
Remarks	Certified for: SAP R/3 Release 1.1; Operating system: VMS

Vendor	Siemens AG
Address	ANL A334, D-76181 Karlsruhe, Germany
Phone	+49 721 595 4465
Fax	+49 721 595 6055
Contact	Mr. Lahm
Product	SIPORT OS
Remarks	Certified for: SAP R/3 Release 2.0, 2.1, 2.2; Attendance Time Recording only; Operating system: EXOS

Vendor	Siemens AG
Address	AUT 411, Gleiwitzerstrasse 555, D-90475 Nürnberg, Germany
Phone	+49 911 895 2674
Fax	+49 911 895 4948
Contact	Mr. Raimund Spengler
Product	Sicalis PDA
Remarks	Certified for: SAP R/3 Release 2.0, 2.1, 2.2; Operating system: UNIX

Vendor	Dr. Städtler GmbH Unternehmensberatung
Address	Pillenreuther Strasse 165, D-90459 Nürnberg, Germany
Phone	+49 911 450090
Fax	+49 911 4500959
Contact	Dr. Dobler
Product	BDE-Manager
Remarks	Certified for: SAP R/3 Release 2.0, 2.1, 2.2; Attendance Time Recording only; Operating system: UNIX

Vendor	Strässle Informationssysteme GmbH
Address	Vor dem Lauch 14, D-70567 Stuttgart, Germany
Phone	+49 711 7256 319
Fax	+49 711 7256 302
Contact	Mr. Spengler
Product	IBIX 2000
Remarks	Certified for: SAP R/3 Release 1.1 to 2.2; Attendance Time Recording only; Operating system: OS/2

Vendor	Titze Datentechnik GmbH
Address	Dielstrasse 10, D-71272 Renningen, Germany
Phone	+49 7159 923 60
Fax	+49 7159 923 660
Contact	Mr. Weinhardt
Product	PIDS/2
Remarks	Certified for: SAP R/3 Release 2.0, 2.1, 2.2; Operating system: OS/2

Appendixes

Product Data Management (PDM)

Vendor	Eigner+Partner GmbH
Address	Ruschgraben 133, D-76139 Karlsruhe, Germany
Phone	+49 721 629 0
Fax	+49 721 6291 88
Contact	Mr. Dahley
Product	CADIM/EDB
Remarks	Certified Interface: CADIM/EDB 2.0

Vendor	Hewlett-Packard GmbH
Address	Herrenberger Strasse 130, D-71034 Böblingen,Germany
Phone	+49 7031 14 3428
Fax	+49 7031 14 2246
Contact	Mr. Michael Frey
Product	Workmanager
Remarks	Certified Interface: HP/SAP Communication-Software Rev. 1.0.

Vendor	Sherpa Corp.
Address	611 River Oaks Parkway, San Jose, CA 95134, U.S.
	Carl-Zeiss-Ring 19-21, D-85737 Ismaning, Germany
Phone	U.S.: +1 408-433-0455
	Germany: +49 89 99684 0
Fax	U.S.: +1 408 943 6622
	Germany: +49 89 99684 185
Contact	Mr. John Lipp (U.S.)
	Mr. Jürgen Marialke (Germany)
Product	PIMS
Remarks	Certified Interface: Sherpa PIMS 2.0 for SAP System

Archive Software/Imaging Software (SAP ArchiveLink)

Vendor	AIS GmbH
Address	Universitätsstrasse 140, Postfach 10 01 29, D-44799 Bochum, Germany
Phone	+49 234 9709 0
Fax	+49 234 9709 520
Contact	Mr. R. David, Mr. Neugebauer
Product	Mega Media SAP/Link V1.1

Vendor	Computer Equipment
Address	Postfach 100841, Herforder Strasse 155a, D-33508 Bielefeld, Germany
Phone	+49 521 9318 298
Fax	+49 521 9318 111
Contact	Mr. Udo Bergmann
Product	CE Archiv/2

Vendor	DDV AG
Address	Edisonstrasse 60, D-90431 Nürnberg, Germany
Phone	+49 911 9617 611
Fax	+49 911 9617 630
Contact	Mr. Peter Listl
Product	DDV Image, DDV Archive Rel.3.2

Vendor	Digital Equipment
Address	Max-Planck-Strasse 8, D-69190 Walldorf, Germany
Phone	+49 6227 34 4521 (DEC CC)
Fax	+49 6227 34 4599 (DEC CC)
Phone	+49 6204 708 141 (Imaging Systems Appn Center)
Fax	+49 6204 79611 (Imaging Systems Appn Center)
Contact	Digital SAP Competence Center
Product	Digital SAP R/3 Archive

Vendor	FileNet
Address	Dietrich-Bonhoeffer-Strasse 4, D61350 Bad Hamburg, Germany
	3565 Harbor Blvd., Costa Mesa, CA 92626-1420, USA
Phone	+49 6172 963 123, +1 714 966 3400
Fax	+49 6172 963 478
Contact	Mr. Jürgen Rentergent, Ms. Reckert, Mr. Michael Stiles
Product	FileNet Document Warehouse

Vendor	Hewlett-Packard
Address	Hewlett-Packard GmbH, Herrenberger Strasse 130, D-71034 Böblingen, Germany
Phone	+49 7031 14 3428
Fax	+49 7031 14 2246
Contact	Herr Michael Frey
Product	iXOS Archive 1.2

Vendor	Infosoft Computer Systeme GmbH
Address	Maria-Trost-Strasse 25, D-56070 Koblenz, Germany
Phone	+49 261 80700 205
Fax	+49 261 80700 253
Contact	Mr. Kappus
Product	eASys

Vendor	MBG
Address	IBM Deutschland GmbH, Geschäftssegment Image, Uberseering 24, D-22297 Hamburg, Germany
Phone	IBM: +49 40 63 890: MBG: +49 211 99414 0
Fax	+49 211 376020 (MBG)
Contact	Mr. Puschendorf (IBM), Mr. Knut Voortman (MBG), Mr. Voss (MBG)
Product	Interface to SAP ArchiveLink (MBG); Image Plus Visual Info (IBM)
Remarks	IBM can be contacted for the product connected to the interface of MBG.

Appendixes

Vendor   SER Reinhardt GmbH
Address   Schloss Hagerhof, Menzenberg 13, D-53604 Bad Honnef,
            Germany Im Wiesengrund 13, D-53577 Neustadt/Wied, Germany
Phone   +49 2224 71771, + 49 2683 300 70
Fax   +49 2224 72060
Contact   Mr. Freisberg (sales), Mr. Reinhardt
Product   ITA

Vendor   Siemens Nixdorf Informations Syteme AG
Address   Otto-Hahn-Ring 6, D-81739 München, Germany
Phone   +49 89 636 45672
Fax   +49 89 636 40935
Contact   Mr. Thomas Meyer, D122
Product   SNI SEDI Server

Vendor   iXos Software
Address   52 Egbert Ave., Morristown, NJ 07960
Phone   +1 201 984 5889
Fax   +49 89 636 40935
Contact   Mr. Bill Ash
Product   Archive Link, Internet Transaction Server

Process Control Systems (PI-PCS)

Vendor   Digital Equipment (DEC England)
Address   2 Celvin Close, Birchwood Science Park,
            North Risley, Warrington WAB 7PB, U.K.
Phone   +44 925842670
Fax   +44 925841010
Contact   Mr. Chris Brookes
Product   PDAS

Vendor   Elsag Bailey
Address   12-14 Elektronikalaan, B-2610 Wilrijk, Belgium
Phone   +32-3 828 05 11
Fax   +32-3 827 87 28
Contact   Mr. Flavio Tolfo, Vice President Chemicals
Product   DCI—System SIX (Release 4.1)

Vendor   Foxboro Deutschland GmbH
Address   Heerdter Lohweg 53-55, D-40549 Düsseldorf, Germany
Phone   +49 211 5966 0
Fax   +49 211 5966 167
Contact   Mr. Wallraf
Product   I/A

Vendor   HERMOS GmbH
Address   Bürgermeister-Neff-Str.4, D-68519 Viernheim, Germany
Phone   +49 6204 9692 0
Fax   +49 6204 9692 11
Contact   Mr. Uwe Koppert
Product   PROLINE

Vendor   iCD GmbH
Address   Robert Perthel Strasse 23, 50739 Köln, Germany
Phone   +49 221 91740 80 (iCD)
            +49 201 7297 242 (IBM)
Fax   +49 221 91740 890 (iCD)
            +49 201 7297 242 (IBM)
Contact   Mr. Bernd Winker (iCD)
            Mr. Hans-Peter Klur (IBM)
Product   Labs/Q
Remarks   Cooperation between iCD and IBM

Vendor   Incode
Address   250 Exchange Place, Herndorn, VA 22070, U.S.
Phone   +1 703 709 7667
Contact   Mr. Curtis Crina
Product   POMS 2.2

Vendor   Propack Data, Soft und Hardware Entwicklung GmbH
Address   Vincent-Priessnitz-Strasse 1, D-76131 Karlsruhe, Germany
Phone   +49 721 607055
Fax   +49 721 606946
Contact   Mr. Karl Linder
Product   PMS

Laboratory Information Management Systems (QM-IDI)

Vendor   Fisons Instruments Labsystems
Address   Hanover Business Park, 1 St. George's
            Court, Altrincham, Cheshire WA14 5TP, U.K.
Phone   +44 161 927 7323
Fax   +44 161 927 7126
Contact   Mr. John Gabathuler
Product   SampleManager SAP-Link

Vendor   iCD GmbH
Address   Robert Perthel Strasse 23, 50739 Köln, Germany
Phone   +49 221 91740 80 (iCD)
Fax   +49 201 7297 635 (IBM)
Contact   Mr. Bernd Winker (iCD)
            Mr. Hans-Peter Klur (IBM)

Product	Labs/Q
Remarks	Cooperation between iCD and IBM

Vendor	IBS GmbH
Address	Rathausstrasse 69, D-56203 Höhr- Grenzhausen, Germany
Phone	+49 2624 91800
Fax	+49 2624 918010
Contact	Mr. Torsten Schulz
Product	CAQ=QSYS

Vendor	Hewlett-Packard
Address	Analytical Products Group Europe, Hewlett-Packard-Strasse 8, D-76337 Waldbronn, Germany
Phone	+49 7243 602 156 (main office)
	+49 6241 93 50 43(Mr. Gross)
Fax	+49 7243 602 155 (main office)
	+49 6241 93 50 44 (Mr. Gross)
Contact	Mr. Dieter Gross
Product	HP Chem LMS

Vendor	Perkin Elmer Nelson Division
Address	3833 North First Street, San Jose, CA 95134-1701, U.S.
Phone	+1 408 577-2200 (front desk)
	+1 408 577-2305 (Mr. Ziabattoni)
Fax	+1 408 894 9307
Contact	Mr. Lou Ziabattoni
Product	SQL LIMS Release 3.0

Appendix I

Bibliography

Books

Curran, Tom, and Peter Zencke.

"Business Process Reengineering—Trend, Reality, or Vision." In SAP AG (ed.), *SAPinfo—Business Reengineering*. Walldorf 1995.

Fritz, Franz-Josef.

"Workflow Implementation Based on the R/3 Reference Model." In SAP AG (ed.), *SAPinfo—Business Reengineering*. Walldorf 1995.

Hammer, M., and James Champy.

Reengineering the Corporation. New York 1993.

Huck, V., H.P. Müller, and H.J. Uhink.

"Costs Slashed by Business Process Reengineering." In SAP AG (ed.), *SAPinfo—Business Reengineering*. Walldorf 1995.

Keller, G., and S. Meinhardt.

"'SAP R/3 Analyzer'—A Computer-Assisted Consultancy Tool for Introducing SAP." In SAP AG (ed.), *SAP Information*, Issue 38/39. Walldorf 1993.

Keller, G., and S. Meinhardt.

"'SAP R/3 Analyzer'—Business Process Reengineering Based on the R/3 Reference Model." In SAP AG (ed.), *SAP Information*. Walldorf 1994.

Keller, G.

"Transparent Design of Business Process with 'Event-Controlled Process Chains' (EPC)." In SAP AG (ed.), *SAPinfo—Business Reengineering*. Walldorf 1994.

Keller, G.

"A Strategic Challenge." In SAP AG (ed.), *SAPinfo—Business Reengineering*. Walldorf 1995.

Meinhardt, S.

"Process-Oriented Implementation of R/3." In SAP AG (ed.), *SAPinfo—Business Reengineering*. Walldorf 1995.

Meinhardt, S.

"Interesting Ways to Optimize Business Processes." In SAP AG (ed.), *SAPinfo—Business Reengineering*. Walldorf 1994.

Popp, Karl.

"Business Process Reengineering with the R/3 Reference Model." In SAP AG (ed.), *SAPinfo—Business Engineering*. Walldorf 1995.

Teufel, T., and F. Ertl.

"Process-Oriented Implementation with R/3 Analyzer." In SAP AG (ed.), *SAPinfo—Business Reengineering*. Walldorf 1995.

Tschira, K., and P. Zencke.

"Business Process Optimization with the SAP R/3 System." In SAP AG (ed.), *SAPinfo—Business Reengineering*. Walldorf 1994.

Coleman, Daniel.

Emotional Intelligence. Bloomsbury.

Hammer, Michael, and James Champy.

Reengineering the Corporation. Nicholas Brealey.

Champy, James.

Reengineering Management. Harper Collins.

Gray, John.

Men Are From Mars, Women Are From Venus. Thorsons.

Herzberg, F., et al.

The Motivation to Work. John Wiley & Sons.

Hewson, Wendy.

The Impact of Computerised Sales and Marketing Systems in the U.K. Hewson Consulting Group 1994.

Ernst & Young.

A 1990 U.K. study by Ernst & Young reported that only two out of the 86 organizations surveyed had IT and business strategies aligned.

Strassmann, Paul.

The Business Value of Computers. The Information Economics Press.

Strassmann, Paul.

The Impact of Sales and Marketing Systems in the U.K.

Ernst & Young.

Audit Control and Security Features of SAP R/3.

Department of Trade and Industry (U.K.).

A Code of Practice For Information Security Management.

Davis, Alan M.

Software Requirements—Objects, Functions, and States. PTR Prentice Hall 1993.

CD-ROM
R/3 System Online Documentation (CD-ROM)

SAP Training Course Material
SAP Training Material Courses:

CA010 SAP Authorization Concept

BC010 SAP Architecture

BC110 R/3 Correction and Transport System

Index

executing
  payment proposals,
    Accounts Payable module,
    245
  projects, 351-353
**Executive Information System
  (SAP-EIS), 323-324**
  CO-CCA Cost Center
    Accounting, 326
  CO-OPA Order and Project
    Accounting, 326-327
  CO-PA Profitability Analysis,
    331
  CO-PC Product Cost
    Accounting, 328-331
  FIS-Financial Information
    System, 324
  HRIS-Human Resources
    Information System, 325
  LO-LIS Logistics Information
    System, 324
**existing systems, integrating
  R/3, 613-614**
**expense postings,
  intercompany accounting
  (FI-Financial Accounting
  module), 209-210**
**exploding bills of materials
  (BOMs), MM-Materials
  Management module,
  540-541**
**explosion numbers (bills of
  material), 363**
**export data records (SD-FT
  Foreign Trade module), 169**
**Extended Binary-Coded
  Decimal Interchange Code
  (EBCDIC), 1086**
**Extended General Ledger
  module, 217-225**
  assessment, 220-221
  data transfer, 219-220
  distribution, 221
  functions, 219
  integrating with other SAP
    components, 218
  planning, 218-219, 222-226
  reports, 223-225
  sets, 221-222
  target values, 222

extended memory, 56
external
  account classes, General
    Ledger module, 204
  activities, 1087
  communications
    advertising, 811-812
    body language, 814-815
    public relations, 812
    publications, 811
    target audience, 812-813
    writing skills, 813-814
  postings, order settlement,
    300

F

failures in business, 155
fast entries
  screens, HR-Human
    Resources modules, 485
  trip data, PA-TRV Travel
    Expenses component, 523
**FI-AA Asset Accounting
  module, integration with
  Order and Project
  Accounting module, 303**
**FI-AP Accounts Payable
  module, 198, 238-248**
  alternative payment
    recipients, 242, 247
  automatic payments,
    244-245
  business functions, 238-239
  cash discounts, 245-246
  clearing Contra accounts,
    247
  credit and debit memos, 248
  down payment requests, 244
  EDI (Electronic Data
    Exchange), 242
  GAAP compliance, 239
  head office-branch accounts,
    241-242
  intercompany payments,
    247
  invoices, 242
  manual invoice entry, 243
  master records, 240-241
  net vendor invoices, 244

  one-time accounts, 241
  payment methods, 246-247
  recurring entries, 243
  reverse documents, 248
  special transactions, 243-244
  transactions, 242
**FI-AR Accounts Receivable
  module, 198, 225-238, 477**
  alternative payers, 228
  audit trails, 237-238
  automatic clearing, 233
  bank fees, 232
  bills of exchange
    discount ledger, 236
    receivable, 235-236
  cash receipts, 230
  country-specific payment
    procedures, 233
  currencies, 229-230
    exchange differences, 232
  down payments, 232, 235
  dunning letters, 233-234
  guarantees, 237
  head office-branch accounts,
    227-228
  master data records, 226-227
  one-time accounts, 227
  open items, 232-233
    searching for, 230-231
  partial payments, 231-232
  recurring entries, 229
  reports, 237
  security deposits, 236-237
  special transactions, 229,
    234-236
  transactions, 228-229
  vendor open items, 232
**FI-CM Cash Management
  module, 248-253**
  annual cash plan, 251-252
  automatic bank account
    clearing, 251
  electronic banking, 250-251,
    253
  forecasting, 251
  objects, 249-250
  transactions, 250
**FI-FA Financial Assets
  Management module,
  256-264**

W-X-Y-Z

ASAP Worldwide
Enterprise Applications Resourcing & Recruitment

The company established in July 1997 has ambitious plans to become the world's largest global recruitment company specialising entirely in "the placement of permanent, temporary and contract staff who will be engaged in the implementation, support, training and documentation of systems known as enterprise applications". These include: SAP, BAAN, Peoplesoft, Oracle Applications, System Software Associations, Computer Associates, JD Edwards, Markam, JBA etc.

The company benefits from:

- Detailed knowledge of the market, its requirements and dynamics.

- Use of one of the world's most advanced recruitment systems.

- Access to large databases of candidates.

- A global approach to the staffing problems of a global market.

- Unique and innovative solutions for solving the staffing problems of a high growth market.

- A commitment to offer clients and candidates a professional, efficient and high quality service that is second to none.

- A commitment to the continual development of the services that we offer.

- Reciprocal partnership arrangements with other recruitment companies worldwide.

A S A P
WORLDWIDE™

ASAP WORLD CONSULTANCY
SAP specialists – author of this book – (Established 1996)

ASAP World Consultancy is a high quality international consultancy specialising in SAP and other Enterprise Applications including, Peoplesoft, Baan, Oracle Applications, J D Edwards etc., which operates worldwide from its UK Headquarters. The ASAP group comprises of a number of focused divisions and companies.

ASAP For Companies Implementing SAP

SAP Documentation Consultancy & Authorship • SAP Training • SAP Access and Security Consultancy • SAP Recruitment - Permanent and Contract • SAP Internal & External Communications Consultancy • SAP System Testing Consultancy & Resourcing • SAP Human Issues Consultancy • SAP Resource Planning Consultancy • Business Process Re-engineering and Change Management Consultancy • Hardware and Installation Consultancy • SAP Implementation Consultancy • Introductory SAP Courses: USA, UK & Singapore & Other Countries • SAP Skills Transfer to Your Employees • Consultancy for the procurement of SAP systems and services.

ASAP For SAP Business Partners and Other Consultancies

We can work on a subcontract basis for local SAP partners and other consultancy firms. We can also work with and alongside other consultancies. We engage in SAP market research, acquisitions and joint ventures and the development of complementary solutions.

Why Use ASAP World Consultancy?

The most important ingredient of your SAP project are the people who implement, support and operate it. We are fully committed to providing the best people and applying the best techniques and methodologies. ASAP World Consultancy has a career development strategy that enables us to;

- Recruit the best quality SAP project managers and experienced SAP consultants.
- Recruit and select for SAP training the brightest potential and the best experience in your industry and in the complementary technologies that are involved in your SAP realisation.
- Help you to make the best use of internal recruitment and cross-training your own staff in SAP, with full consideration of the economic and human issues involved.
- Transfer skills locally and internationally

We deliver people as teams or individuals, and offer highly cost effective solutions, whether your need is management consultancy, a full project management service, a particular project service, or an individual with specific skills. Having authored the world,s biggest and most recognised independent SAP book, we have a team of leading SAP communicators, and offer special capability in systems documentation services, with top quality standards of presentation and accuracy.

Are you interested in joining the ASAP Group?

Services to companies looking for staff

Permanent, Contract & Temporary Recruitment

ASAP Worldwide has a deep understanding of the enterprise application resourcing market, its requirements and dynamics. Whether your requirement is for a single individual or a team of hundreds, we offer the best practices and standards of service you would expect from one of the world's most professional recruitment companies to solve your staffing requirements.

In such a high growth market where the right people are at a premium, it takes a very different approach to find and place candidates. We offer a unique range of services to companies of all sizes and in all sectors worldwide. We leave no stone unturned in our search for candidates and we have unique techniques for selecting the very best candidates to offer you. We offer originality and innovation that make us stand out from the crowd.

Service to people looking for work

We believe that there is far more to our work than simply trying to fill job vacancies. We believe that we are providing a service of equal value to both employers and candidates looking for work. We are genuinely interested in your personal and career development and we undertake to try our very best to find you the work that best meets your requirements. Because of the size of our network, we are able to offer a truly global service, so whatever part of the world you would like to work in, whatever the type of employer and whatever the type of work you would like, we believe that we are better placed to give you what you want.

Send us a copy of your C.V./resumé and receive a free copy of our "Career Development Programme" booklet, designed to help you advance your SAP career.

How to contact us:

ASAP Worldwide
PO Box 4463 Henley on Thames
Oxfordshire RG9 6YN UK
Tel: +44 (0)1491 414411
Fax: +44 (0)1491 414412

ASAP Worldwide - 24 Hour - Virtual Office - New York, USA
Voice Mail: (212) 253 4180 Fax: (212) 253 4180

E-Mail: enquiry@asap-consultancy.co.uk

Web site: http://www.asap-consultancy.co.uk

A S A P
WORLDWIDE™

Why Join the ASAP team?

We are a fast growing dynamic group of companies operating globally in an exciting new virtual environment. We have the simple aim to be the best at what we do. We therefore look to recruit the best people on either contract or permanent basis

If you are any of the following, we would like to hear from you.

1. Highly Skilled and Experienced SAP Consultant.

You will have been working with SAP systems for many years and will be a project manager or consultant of standing in the industry. If you are willing to assist in the training and development and perhaps recruitment of your team, then we will be able to offer you exceptional financial rewards and the opportunity of developing the career of your choice.

2. Skilled in Another Area and Looking to Cross Train

You may be a computer expert or a business person with expertise in a particular area, perhaps, logistics, finance, distribution or H.R. etc., and/or with a particular industry knowledge. If you are committed to working with SAP systems in the long term, we will be able to offer you SAP cross training and vital experience. You must have a proven track record in your field and must be prepared to defer financial advancement whilst training and gaining experience. If you have the commitment and the skill you will in time be able to receive from us the high financial rewards and career development choice above.

3. A Person who has worked in a functional job
for an End User Company and who has been involved in all aspects of an SAP project from initial scoping to implementation and post implementation support.

You will have an excellent understanding of the industry or business function you are in. You are likely to have a good degree, ambition, drive, flexibility and the potential to become a top SAP consultant. You will thrive on the prospect of travel and living and working in other countries, jetting off around the world at short notice and working as part of a highly motivated and productive team. You must be committed to a long term career working with SAP. We will be able to offer you an interesting and rewarding career, giving you training and experience in a number of different roles. If you can prove yourself, you can expect rapid career development, with excellent financial rewards. Your only limit is your ability and your aspirations.

How To Contact Us

ASAP World Consultancy, ASAP House, PO Box 4463,
Henley on Thames, Oxfordshire RG9 6YN, UK
Tel:+44 (0)1491 414411   Fax: +44 (0)1491 414411

ASAP - 24 Hour - Virtual Office - New York, USA
Voice Mail: (212) 253 4180 Fax: (212) 253 4180

E-Mail: info@asap-consultancy.co.uk

Web site: http://www.asap-consultancy.co.uk/index.htm

A S A P
WORLD CONSULTANCY ™

Check out Que® Books on the World Wide Web
http://www.quecorp.com

As the biggest software release in computer history, Windows 95 continues to redefine the computer industry. Click here for the latest info on our Windows 95 books

Make computing quick and easy with these products designed exclusively for new and casual users

Examine the latest releases in word processing, spreadsheets, operating systems, and suites

The Internet, The World Wide Web, CompuServe®, America Online®, Prodigy® —it's a world of ever-changing information. Don't get left behind!

Find out about new additions to our site, new bestsellers and hot topics

In-depth information on high-end topics: find the best reference books for databases, programming, networking, and client/server technologies

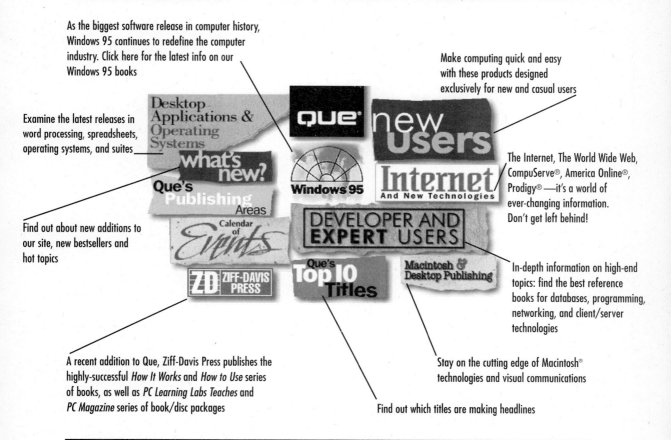

A recent addition to Que, Ziff-Davis Press publishes the highly-successful *How It Works* and *How to Use* series of books, as well as *PC Learning Labs Teaches* and *PC Magazine* series of book/disc packages

Stay on the cutting edge of Macintosh® technologies and visual communications

Find out which titles are making headlines

With 6 separate publishing groups, Que develops products for many specific market segments and areas of computer technology. Explore our Web Site and you'll find information on best-selling titles, newly published titles, upcoming products, authors, and much more.

- Stay informed on the latest industry trends and products available
- Visit our online bookstore for the latest information and editions
- Download software from Que's library of the best shareware and freeware

MACMILLAN COMPUTER PUBLISHING USA

A VIACOM COMPANY

Technical ---- Support:

If you need assistance with the information in this book or with a CD/Disk accompanying the book, please access the Knowledge Base on our Web site at **http://www.superlibrary.com/general/support**. Our most Frequently Asked Questions are answered there. If you do not find the answer to your questions on our Web site, you may contact Macmillan Technical Support **(317) 581-3833** or e-mail us at **support@mcp.com**.

Complete and Return this Card
for a *FREE* Computer Book Catalog

Thank you for purchasing this book! You have purchased a superior computer book written expressly for your needs. To continue to provide the kind of up-to-date, pertinent coverage you've come to expect from us, we need to hear from you. Please take a minute to complete and return this self-addressed, postage-paid form. In return, we'll send you a free catalog of all our computer books on topics ranging from word processing to programming and the internet.

Mr. ☐   Mrs. ☐   Ms. ☐   Dr. ☐

Name (first) [＿＿＿＿＿＿＿＿＿＿＿] (M.I.) [＿] (last) [＿＿＿＿＿＿＿＿＿＿＿]

Address [＿＿＿＿＿＿＿＿＿＿＿＿＿＿＿＿＿＿＿＿＿＿＿＿]

[＿＿＿＿＿＿＿＿＿＿＿＿＿＿＿＿＿＿＿＿＿＿＿＿]

City [＿＿＿＿＿＿＿＿＿＿＿] State [＿＿] Zip [＿＿＿＿＿ ＿＿＿]

Phone [＿＿＿] [＿＿＿＿] [＿＿＿＿] Fax [＿＿＿] [＿＿＿＿] [＿＿＿＿]

Company Name [＿＿＿＿＿＿＿＿＿＿＿＿＿＿＿＿＿＿＿＿＿＿＿＿]

E-mail address [＿＿＿＿＿＿＿＿＿＿＿＿＿＿＿＿＿＿＿＿＿＿＿＿]

1. Please check at least (3) influencing factors for purchasing this book.

Front or back cover information on book .... ☐
Special approach to the content .... ☐
Completeness of content .... ☐
Author's reputation .... ☐
Publisher's reputation .... ☐
Book cover design or layout .... ☐
Index or table of contents of book .... ☐
Price of book .... ☐
Special effects, graphics, illustrations .... ☐
Other (Please specify): _____ ☐

2. How did you first learn about this book?

Saw in Macmillan Computer Publishing catalog .... ☐
Recommended by store personnel .... ☐
Saw the book on bookshelf at store .... ☐
Recommended by a friend .... ☐
Received advertisement in the mail .... ☐
Saw an advertisement in: _____ ☐
Read book review in: _____ ☐
Other (Please specify): _____ ☐

3. How many computer books have you purchased in the last six months?

This book only .... ☐   3 to 5 books .... ☐
2 books .... ☐   More than 5 .... ☐

4. Where did you purchase this book?

Bookstore .... ☐
Computer Store .... ☐
Consumer Electronics Store .... ☐
Department Store .... ☐
Office Club .... ☐
Warehouse Club .... ☐
Mail Order .... ☐
Direct from Publisher .... ☐
Internet site .... ☐
Other (Please specify): _____ ☐

5. How long have you been using a computer?

☐ Less than 6 months   ☐ 6 months to a year
☐ 1 to 3 years   ☐ More than 3 years

6. What is your level of experience with personal computers and with the subject of this book?

	With PCs	With subject of book
New	☐	☐
Casual	☐	☐
Accomplished	☐	☐
Expert	☐	☐

Source Code ISBN: 0-7897-1351-9

7. Which of the following best describes your job title?

Administrative Assistant .... ☐
Coordinator .... ☐
Manager/Supervisor .... ☐
Director .... ☐
Vice President .... ☐
President/CEO/COO .... ☐
Lawyer/Doctor/Medical Professional .... ☐
Teacher/Educator/Trainer .... ☐
Engineer/Technician .... ☐
Consultant .... ☐
Not employed/Student/Retired .... ☐
Other (Please specify): _____ ☐

8. Which of the following best describes the area of the company your job title falls under?

Accounting .... ☐
Engineering .... ☐
Manufacturing .... ☐
Operations .... ☐
Marketing .... ☐
Sales .... ☐
Other (Please specify): _____ ☐

9. What is your age?

Under 20 .... ☐
21-29 .... ☐
30-39 .... ☐
40-49 .... ☐
50-59 .... ☐
60-over .... ☐

10. Are you:

Male .... ☐
Female .... ☐

11. Which computer publications do you read regularly? (Please list)

_____
_____
_____
_____
_____
_____
_____
_____
_____

Comments: _____
_____
_____

Fold here and scotch-tape to mail.